THE OXFORD ENCYCLOPEDIA

OF THE

Modern Islamic World

THE OXFORD ENCYCLOPEDIA OF THE Modern Islamic World

John L. Esposito
EDITOR IN CHIEF

VOLUME 2

New York Oxford
OXFORD UNIVERSITY PRESS
1995

Oxford University Press

Oxford New York
Athens Auckland Bangkok Bombay
Calcutta Cape Town Dar es Salaam Delhi
Florence Hong Kong Istanbul Karachi
Kuala Lumpur Madras Madrid Melbourne
Mexico City Nairobi Paris Singapore
Taipei Tokyo Toronto

and associated companies in
Berlin Ibadan

Published by Oxford University Press, Inc.,
200 Madison Avenue, New York, NY 10016

Library of Congress Cataloging-in-Publication Data

The Oxford encyclopedia of the modern Islamic world
John L. Esposito, editor in chief
p. cm.
Includes bibliographic references and index.
1. Islamic countries—Encyclopedias. 2. Islam—Encyclopedias.
I. Esposito, John L.
DS35.53.095 1995 909'.097671'003—dc20 94-30758 CIP
ISBN 0-19-506613-8 (set)
ISBN 0-19-509613-4 (vol. 2)

Grateful acknowledgment is made to grantors of permission to use the following illustrations in this volume. Gardens and Landscaping, *article on* Traditional Forms: *figure 1, courtesy of D. Fairchild Ruggles; figure 2, courtesy of Board of Trustees of the Victoria and Albert Museum.* Gardens and Landscaping, *article on* Contemporary Forms: *figure 1, photograph by Isabel Cutler; figure 2, photograph by Klaus Klein; figures 3-4, photographs by Walter B. Denny.* Iconography: *figure 1, courtesy of* Aramco World, *by permission of Kamal Boullata; figure 2, photograph by Nik Wheeler, courtesy of* Aramco World.

Printing (last digit): 9 8 7 6 5 4 3 2 1

Printed in the United States of America
on acid-free paper

F

CONTINUED

FAQĪH. The verb *faqiha* denotes in nontechnical contexts a correct understanding of matters that are not readily grasped. The fifth form of the verb, *tafaqqaha,* occurring in the Qur'ān (9.122), refers to the close study and understanding of a specific issue. In the technical legal usage of the eighth century, *faqīh* (pl., *fuqahā'*) signified an expert in *fiqh,* the specialized knowledge of law. When legal theory *(uṣūl al-fiqh)* emerged toward the beginning of the tenth century, the term *faqīh* came to refer to a legist who can reason and meditate on a particular case of substantive law on the basis of textual evidence specifically relevant to that case. In contradistinction to the *faqīh,* a legist who specializes in the study of the sources and methodological foundations of the law and who treats of positive law only as a means for constructing a legal theory is known as an *uṣūlī,* a legal theoretician. Thus by the beginning of the tenth century at the latest, the technical term *faqīh* came to refer exclusively to a specialist in case law, the so-called "branches" *(furūʿ)* of the law. In pedagogical technical terminology, a *mutafaqqih* is a student of positive law, and *tafaqqaha ʿalā* is the verb connoting the activity of studying under an authority on substantive law.

The *fuqahā'* constituted a major segment of the religious elite of Islam, the *ʿulamā',* who were considered the guardians of the community and its religion. Socially they were the pillars of their communities, and legally they functioned as judges and jurisconsults (*muftī*s). As judges, they acted as trustees of the properties of orphans, as supervisors of charitable trusts, and as marriage guardians for women who had no male relative to function in this capacity. As jurisconsults, they issued opinions (*fatwā*s) on legal questions addressed to them by members of the community.

On the practical level, the *fuqahā'* derived their authority from the very functions they fulfilled in Muslim society; but on the theoretical level, they were deemed—and reckoned themselves—to continue the works of the prophets. As such, they were thought to be the custodians of the *sharīʿah,* the means to salvation in the hereafter, and thus to be the keepers of religion. The legitimation of their authority is explicitly attested in the oft-quoted prophetic tradition, "The *ʿulamā'* are the heirs of the prophets."

As a result of the massive twentieth-century reforms in the legal systems of Muslim countries, the institution of the *fuqahā'* has steadily been on the decline. They have substantially lost not only their influence as a religious elite, but also their functions as jurists, judges, legal guardians, and, to a lesser degree, as jurisconsults. The introduction of European codes and Western-style courts has made it necessary to phase out the functionaries of the traditional system. They have been largely replaced by modern lawyers, jurists, and judges. Their function is now limited to a narrowly defined jurisdiction in family law, and even this is not without the encroachment of state secular legislation.

[*See also* ʿUlamā'; Uṣūl al-Fiqh.]

BIBLIOGRAPHY

Schacht, Joseph. *An Introduction to Islamic Law.* Oxford, 1979.

Tyan, Émile. "Judicial Organization." In *Law in the Middle East,* edited by Majid Khadduri and Herbert J. Liebesny, pp. 236–278. Washington, D.C., 1955. Concise statement on the religious character of the *fuqahā'* and their functions as judges, jurisconsults, guardians, etc.

WAEL B. HALLAQ

FARḌ AL-ʿAYN. Almost all religio-legal obligations in *sharīʿah* (the divine law) are *farḍ al-ʿayn* (obligations on the individual), that is, they must be discharged personally by the individual; they cannot be performed vicariously.

The term *farḍ al-ʿayn* is more common among the non-Ḥanafī schools of law. For the Ḥanafīyah, *farḍ* is ordinarily an epistemological term signifying obligations of unambiguous certainty. In this, they are distinguished from the category of *wājib,* which for the Ḥanafī means an obligation of probable certainty, that is, one based on a probable reading of the Qur'ān, or a *ḥadīth* that is probably reliably translated.

For the non-Ḥanafīyah, however, there is no term that refers to epistemically certain or probable obligations. Obligations in general are referred to using the term *wājib*. An obligatory act is that for the doing of which there is reward, and for the neglect of which there is punishment, or, primarily in Muʿtazilī and Ithnā ʿAsharī and Zaydī Shīʿī circles, that for the doing of which there is praise and for the neglect of which there is blame.

Comparative ethicists have remarked that the Muslim categories of moral-legal assessment *(ḥukm;* pl., *aḥkām)* are not simply binary compliance/noncompliance categories. Obligatory *(wājib),* proscribed *(maḥẓūr)* and neutral/permitted *(mubāḥ)* are central categories of assessment in Muslim law. But equally important are the categories of supererogation, *mandūb* ("recommended") and *makrūh* ("reprehensible"). These latter two are defined in terms of incitement, but not sanction, that is, *mandūb* is that for the doing of which there is reward, but for the neglect of which there is no punishment; *makrūh* is that for the avoidance of which there is reward, but for the doing of it there is no punishment. Consequently there is no domain of behavior bereft of moral assessment, particularly since for most jurists even the neutral category was described as "permitted," a positive assessment rather than truly "neutral," a category of moral indifference. The five categories express the totalism of *sharīʿah* theory in its power to assign value to all acts whatsoever.

In the modern period *farḍ al-ʿayn* and its complement *farḍ al-kifāyah* have been the object of some discussion by those seeking to reinterpret Islamic, particularly social, doctrines. The question of whether "reproaching the unjust ruler," or more generally the obligation to "commend the good and forbid the reprehensible" ("al-amr bi-al-maʿrūf wa-al-nahy ʿan al-munkar") is an obligation on each individual, or is devolved on a sufficiency within the community has received attention, particularly among Shīʿī scholars. Some, such as Aḥmad Tayyibī Shabistarī, have in effect argued that "commending the good" is an obligation on all Muslims who can meet the necessary preconditions, and if they cannot meet the preconditions, they are obliged to strive to remedy their situation so as to be competent to undertake the commending and forbidding (Enayat, 1982, pp. 179–180).

[*See also* Farḍ al-Kifāyah.]

BIBLIOGRAPHY

Enayat, Hamid. *Modern Islamic Political Thought.* Austin, 1982.

Faruki, Kemal A. "Al-aḥkām al-khamsah: The Five Values." *Islamic Studies* 5 (1966): 43–98.

Reinhart, A. Kevin. "Islamic Law as Islamic Ethics." *Journal of Religious Ethics* 11.2 (1983): 186–203.

A. KEVIN REINHART

FARḌ AL-KIFĀYAH. In Muslim legal doctrine the *farḍ al-kifāyah* (lit., "duty of the sufficiency") defines a communal responsibility. According to this doctrine, within a community of Muslims, if some religious obligation belonging to the category of *farḍ al-kifāyah* is not fulfilled, the whole have collectively sinned. If a sufficient number of the community undertake the duty, however, the responsibility on the community is discharged; for example, it is necessary that at least one Muslim recite the funeral prayers. If no one does, the entire community is at fault. If, however, someone performs the service, the obligation is lifted from the entire community. If a foundling is neglected, the entire community is at fault; if someone cares for it, the penalty is not applied to the community. The remarkable feature of this doctrine is that for this set of obligations a Muslim may have his or her duty discharged by someone else; likewise, for someone's neglect, another Muslim can be punished.

Although it is tempting to describe the *farḍ al-kifāyah* as a collective duty, it is one which can in some cases be discharged by a single individual. It is more accurate to say that *farḍ al-kifāyah* can be an occasion for collective transgression if it is not sufficiently discharged.

The doctrine of *farḍ al-kifāyah* is an old one, though the terminology is post-Qur'ānic. It is plausible to suppose that it is implicit in the Qur'ānic assumption that some, but not all, will "struggle in the way of God." In any case, by the time of al-Shāfiʿī (d. 820) the doctrine is taken for granted—returning a greeting, prayer for the dead, and the obligations of *jihād* are all assumed to be obligations of the sufficiency (*Risālah,* section 971). In a foreshadowing of the importance that *farḍ al-kifāyah* is to have, al-Shāfiʿī extends the scope of the doctrine to argue that there are two sorts of knowledge and hence two sorts of obligations: those incumbent on scholars and those incumbent on the generality of Muslims.

Farḍ al-kifāyah was one of the major vehicles used by jurists to talk about society in the aggregate, as a collective entity. It is not too much to suggest that *farḍ al-kifāyah/farḍ al-ʿayn* take the places in moral discourse of the concepts of public and private spheres. By the eleventh century CE, the sources' lists of *farḍ al-kifāyah*s are a virtual compendium of the religious and moral obligations that glued Islamic society together, including: undertaking proofs and demonstrations to know what God has established and what attributes must be ascribed to him; the study of the sciences of the *sharʿ*, that is, Qur'ānic commentary, *ḥadīth,* and the law; the quest for the legal position on novel cases *(ijtihād);* serving as judge; issuing legal opinions; competence in medicine; the ability to determine the direction of prayer; preparation of the dead; returning a greeting; bearing witness; calling to prayer; the practice of crafts and industries; buying and selling; warehousing; writing biographical dictionaries; rescuing a foundling; undertaking *jihād;* and commanding the good and forbidding the reprehensible.

In recent Muslim literature, there is some evidence of a reconsideration of this doctrine as a way to discuss social responsibility. Sayyid Quṭb, for example, in his *Social Justice in Islam* (1987) contrasts social concern *(al-takafful al-ijtimāʿī)* and public concern *(takafful ʿāmm),* which "makes everyone in a locality directly responsible for those who suffer from hunger" (p. 62; 70) Ayatollah Ruhollah Khomeini, in his *Tawẕīḥ al-masā'il* (1983) says that commanding the good and forbidding the reprehensible is a *farḍ al-kifāyah (wājib kifā'ī)* unless accomplishing this requires the whole of those morally responsible to act (p. 573 ff.; questions 2786 ff.). In this instance, it becomes an obligation to act together. *Farḍ al-kifāyah* may prove an important concept in the restatement of values that in the 1990s is so prominent in the Muslim world.

[*See also* Farḍ al-ʿAyn.]

BIBLIOGRAPHY

Khomeini, Ruhollah al-Musavi. *Risālah-i Tawẕīḥ al-Masā'il.* Tehran, 1983. Translated by J. Borujerdi as *A Clarification of Questions: An Unabridged Translation of Resaleh Towzih al-Masael.* Boulder, 1984.

Quṭb, Sayyid. *Al-ʿadālah al-ijtimāʿīyah fī al-Islām.* Cairo and Beirut, 1987. Translated into English by John B. Hardie as *Social Justice in Islam.* Washington, D.C., 1953.

A. KEVIN REINHART

FĀRŪQĪ, ISMĀʿĪL RĀJĪ AL- (1921–1986), Islamic scholar and activist. Born in Jaffa, Palestine, Fārūqī received an education that made him trilingual (Arabic, French, and English) and provided him with multicultural intellectual sources that informed his life and thought. He studied at the mosque school, attended a French Catholic school, College des Freres (St. Joseph) in Palestine, and earned a bachelor's degree at the American University of Beirut (1941). Having become governor of Galilee in 1945, Fārūqī was forced to emigrate from Palestine after the creation of the state of Israel in 1948; he then earned masters degrees at Indiana and Harvard Universities and a doctorate in philosophy from Indiana University (1952).

Both a poor job market and an inner drive brought Fārūqī back to the Arab world, where, from 1954 to 1958, he studied Islam at Cairo's al-Azhar University. He subsequently studied and conducted research at major centers of learning in the Muslim world and the West as Visiting Professor of Islamic Studies at the Institute of Islamic Studies and a Fellow at the Faculty of Divinity, McGill University (1959–1961), where he studied Christianity and Judaism; Professor of Islamic Studies at the Central Institute of Islamic Research in Karachi, Pakistan (1961–1963); and Visiting Professor of History of Religions at the University of Chicago (1963–1964).

Ismāʿīl al-Fārūqī taught in the Department of Religion at Syracuse University (1964–1968) and then became Professor of Islamic Studies and of History of Religions at Temple University (1968–1986). During a professional life that spanned almost thirty years, he wrote, edited, or translated twenty-five books, published more than a hundred articles, was a visiting professor at more than twenty-three universities in Africa, Europe, the Middle East, South and Southeast Asia, and served on the editorial boards of seven major journals.

For Fārūqī, Arabism and Islam were intertwined. His Arab-Muslim identity was at the center of the man and the scholar. His life and writing reveal two phases or stages. In the first, epitomized in his book *On Arabism: Urubah and Religion,* Arabism was the dominant theme of his discourse. In the second, Islam occupied center stage, as he increasingly assumed the role of an Islamic activist leader as well as of an academic. His later work and writing focused on a comprehensive vision of Islam and its relationship to all aspects of life and culture.

Living and working in the West, Fārūqī presented Islam in Western categories to engage his audience as well as to make Islam more comprehensible and respected. Like the founders of Islamic modernism in the late nineteenth and early twentieth centuries, he often presented Islam as the religion par excellence of reason, science, and progress with a strong emphasis on action and the work ethic.

If during the 1950s and 1960s Fārūqī sounded like an Arab heir to Islamic modernism and Western empiricism, by the late 1960s and early 1970s he progressively assumed the role of an Islamic scholar-activist. This shift in orientation was evident in the recasting of his framework: Islam replaced Arabism as his primary reference point. Islam had always had an important place in Fārūqī's writing, but it now became the organizing principle. Islam was presented as an all-encompassing ideology, the primary identity of a worldwide community *(ummah)* of believers and the guiding principle for society and culture. Like Muḥammad ibn ʿAbd al-Wahhāb and Muḥammad ʿAbduh, Fārūqī grounded his interpretation of Islam in the doctrine of *tawḥīd* (the oneness of God), combining the classical affirmation of the centrality of God's oneness (monotheism) with a modernist interpretation *(ijtihād)* and application of Islam to modern life. In *Tawḥīd: Its Implications for Thought and Life,* he presented *tawḥīd* as the essence of religious experience, the quintessence of Islam, and the principle of history, knowledge, ethics, aesthetics, the *ummah* (Muslim community), the family, and the political, social, economic, and world orders.

This holistic, activist Islamic worldview was embodied in this new phase in his life and career as he continued to write extensively, to lecture and consult with Islamic movements and national governments, and to organize Muslims in America. During the 1970s he established Islamic studies programs, recruited and trained Muslim students, organized Muslim professionals, established and chaired the Islamic Studies Steering Committee of the American Academy of Religion (1976–1982), and was an active participant in international ecumenical meetings where he was a major force in Islam's dialogue with other world religions. Fārūqī was a founder or leader of many organizations, including the Muslim Student Association and a host of associations of Muslim professionals, such as the Association of Muslim Social Scientists; he served as Chairman of the Board of Trustees of the North American Islamic Trust; he established and was first president of the American Islamic College in Chicago; and in 1981 he created the International Institute for Islamic Thought in Virginia.

At the heart of Fārūqī's vision was the islamization of knowledge. He regarded the political, economic, and religiocultural malaise of the Islamic community as primarily a product of the bifurcated state of education in the Muslim world with a resultant loss of identity and lack of vision. Fārūqī believed that the cure was twofold: the compulsory study of Islamic civilization and the islamization of modern knowledge.

Ismāʿīl al-Fārūqī's life ended tragically in 1986 when he and his wife, Lois Lamyā' al-Fārūqī, also an Islamic scholar, were murdered by an intruder in their home.

[*See also* Education, *article on* Islamization of Knowledge.]

BIBLIOGRAPHY

Works by Ismāʿīl Rājī al-Fārūqī

On Arabism. 4 vols. Amsterdam, 1962.

Christian Ethics. Montreal, 1967.

"Islam and Christianity: Diatribe or Dialogue?" *Journal of Ecumenical Studies* 5.1 (1968): 45–77.

"Islam and Christianity: Problems and Perspectives." In *The Word in the Third World,* edited by James P. Cotter, pp. 159–181. Washington, D.C., 1968.

Historical Atlas of the Religions of the World. New York, 1974.

"Islamizing the Social Sciences." *Studies in Islam* 16.2 (April 1979): 108–121.

Islam and Culture. Kuala Lumpur, 1980.

"The Role of Islam in Global Interreligious Dependence." In *Towards a Global Congress of the World's Religions,* edited by Warren Lewis, pp. 19–38. Barrytown, N.Y., 1980.

Essays in Islamic and Comparative Studies. Washington, D.C., 1982. Collection of essays edited by al-Fārūqī.

Islamic Thought and Culture. Washington, D.C., 1982. Collection of essays edited by al-Fārūqī.

Islamization of Knowledge. Islamabad, 1982.

Trialogue of the Abrahamic Faiths: Papers Presented to the Islamic Studies Group of the American Academy of Religion. 2d ed. Herndon, Va., 1986. Collection of essays edited by al-Fārūqī.

Tawḥīd: Its Implications for Thought and Life. 2d ed. Herndon, Va., 1982.

Other Sources

Esposito, John L. "Ismail R. al-Faruqi: Muslim Scholar-Activist." In *The Muslims of America,* edited by Yvonne Yazbeck Haddad, pp. 65–79. New York and Oxford, 1991.

Ibn ʿAbd al-Wahhāb, Muḥammad. *Sources of Islamic Thought: Three Epistles on Tawḥīd.* Translated and edited by Ismāʿīl Rājī al-Fārūqī. Indianapolis, 1980.

Quraishi, M. Tariq. *Ismail R. al-Farūqi: An Enduring Legacy.* Plainfield, Ind., 1986.

JOHN L. ESPOSITO

FĀSĪ, MUḤAMMAD ʿALLĀL AL- (1906–1973), Moroccan intellectual, historian, legal scholar, teacher, poet, and political leader, a founder of the Istiqlāl Party. Son of the *muftī* of Fez, al-Fāsī was born into a prominent religious and literary family claiming descent from Arabia through Andalusian Spain. He studied Islamic law at al-Qarawīyīn University. In the late 1920s al-Fāsī criticized the French Protectorate from a perspective of Islamic modernism and reform. In 1927 he was a founder of the Moroccan Action Committee, a loose coalition of intellectuals in Fez and Rabat. In 1930 the Committee criticized the French authorities for the Berber Decree, which they saw as an attempt to divide Arabs and Berbers.

Al-Fāsī received his diploma in Islamic law in 1930, remaining at al-Qarawīyīn to teach Islamic history. In 1934 al-Fāsī and his activist compatriots publicly issued a Moroccan Reform Plan. When there were no reforms, despite the coming to power of the Popular Front in France in 1936, they turned to organizing public protests, and al-Fāsī and others were arrested. Under al-Fāsī's presidency the group split over tactical questions in 1937, with al-Fāsī remaining as the leader of its largest contingent. His group was banned in March 1937 but reorganized as the National Reform Party. Following new demonstrations, al-Fāsī and other leaders of the party were arrested.

Al-Fāsī was exiled by the French to Gabon until 1946, although he remained a continuing influence on Morocco. The National Reform Party was reorganized as the Istiqlāl (Independence) Party in 1943. In January 1944 the Istiqlāl issued a manifesto for Moroccan independence under the sultan. Al-Fāsī returned from Gabon as head of the Istiqlāl Party in 1946; in April 1947 the sultan gave a speech that reflected the growing influence of al-Fāsī and the Istiqlāl.

Al-Fāsī again fled Morocco in May 1947, this time to Cairo, where he remained in exile until Moroccan independence in 1956. From Cairo he traveled and lectured in the Middle East, South Asia, Europe, and North America. His most important writings date from this period, including *The Independence Movements in Arab North Africa* (1947), *Self-Criticism* (1951), and two collections—*From the Occident to the Orient* (1956) and *The Call of Cairo* (1959).

The independence movement grew steadily during al-Fāsī's exile. Upon Morocco's independence in 1956 al-Fāsī returned as president for life of the Istiqlāl and professor of law at the new University of Rabat. He joined the government only in June 1961, after the death of King Muḥammad V and the accession of King Ḥasan II. He resigned as Minister of Islamic Affairs in January 1963 because of policy differences with the king. The Istiqlāl became the major opposition party under the leadership of al-Fāsī, who wrote and taught until his death in 1973.

Al-Fāsī was above all an Islamic modernist and reformer, advocating Islamic renewal, a return to original sources, Arabic language reform, and avoidance of imitating the West. He was an early critic of the protectorate and an early advocate of Moroccan independence. As a nationalist al-Fāsī claimed that Morocco includes the Western Sahara, Mauritania, and territories that had been included in western and southern Algeria by the French. Al-Fāsī consistently supported the ʿAlawī monarchy and sought to influence successive monarchs, but he was also a constitutionalist who did not hesitate to criticize royal policies when he felt they compromised Moroccan independence or social justice.

[*See also* Istiqlāl; Morocco.]

BIBLIOGRAPHY

Cohen, Amnon. "'ʿAllāl al-Fāsī: His Ideas and His Contributions towards Morocco's Independence." *Asian and African Studies* 3 (1967): 121–164.

Fāsī, ʿAllāl al-. *The Independence Movements in Arab North Africa* (1947). Translated by Hazem Zaki Nuseibeh. Washington, D.C., 1954.

Fāsī, ʿAllāl al-. "Mission of the Islamic ʿUlema." Translated from Arabic by Hassan Abdin Mohammed. In *Man, State, and Society in the Contemporary Maghrib*, edited by I. William Zartman, pp. 151–158. New York, 1973. Short speech by al-Fāsī delivered in 1959 to a conference of Islamic clergy.

Gaudio, Attilio. *Allal El Fassi, ou, l'histoire de l'Istiqlal*. Paris, 1972. Laudatory biography with a short preface by Jacques Berque and a useful 122-page appendix of statements, letters, articles, and interviews of al-Fāsī, in French translation.

Gellner, Ernest. "The Struggle for Morocco's Past." In *Man, State, and Society in the Contemporary Maghrib*, edited by I. William Zartman, pp. 37–49. New York, 1973.

LAURENCE O. MICHALAK

FASTING. *See* Ṣawm.

FATHY, HASSAN (1900–1989), more properly Ḥasan Fatḥī, Egyptian architect, teacher, philosopher, and reformer. Born in Alexandria, Hassan Fathy pursued a prolific architectural career for more than a half century as a lonely reformer whose success was only evident toward the end of his life and after it. His reformist agenda was systematically opposed to official architectural discourse in Egypt. Early in his career he defied his own French Beaux-Arts education in a series of modernist designs reflecting affinities with contemporary European avant-garde trends, sharply contrasting with the so-called Islamic Style (an orientalization of Beaux-Arts rules applied in Cairo during the 1920s). After nearly ten years of experimentation, however, Fathy became an adamant foe of the International Style, which subsequently dominated architectural practice in Egypt. Fathy deplored the attempt of its adherents to alter what they saw as the decadent status quo of Muslim societies by enforcing universalizing modern technology and standardized architectural expression.

No viable reform, Fathy maintained, can result from forcing on the public an alien elitist taste and arbitrary innovations that disregard the local traditions and environment of a country like Egypt, the majority of whose population were poor peasants. To achieve an authentic and affordable architecture, Fathy advocated the regeneration and esthetic adaptation of indigenous building technologies and their associated traditional myths and rituals. This vision was partly inspired by his observing the impoverishment as well as the untapped traditional resources of villagers during visits to his father's agricultural estates and Upper Egypt.

Fathy thus synthesized his formal language by borrowing from the rural mud architecture of Upper Egypt and the urban vernacular and high architecture of medieval Cairo, fusing rural folk practice with the monumental urban tradition. He applied sun-dried mud brick both as a harmonizing formal medium for his synthetic forms and as the structural core of an inexpensive vaulting technique transmitted to him by Nubian craftsmen, repeating this architectural syntax tirelessly throughout the rest of his career.

In 1945–1948 a government commission to design an entire town, New Gourna, to relocate villagers near Luxor in Upper Egypt, provided Fathy with an exceptional opportunity to implement his vision on a full urban scale. This experience was, however, marred by bureaucratic obstacles, which Fathy documented in his 1968 *Architecture for the Poor,* and was tragic in its consequences. The incomplete design met the resistance of the villagers, who were alienated not only by government coercion but also, ironically, by what they perceived as Fathy's parochialism. The villagers would not tolerate visual/spatial segregation from their few precious animals, so they rejected the split-level arrangement of the basic house unit Fathy had designed out of concern for improving their hygiene. Ominous to them, too, were Fathy's abrupt transpositions of symbolic forms like domes—which villagers traditionally associate with burial places—to crown living spaces. Fathy's frustration was compounded by the failure of the design to appeal to the internationally oriented architectural establishment in Egypt, who have continued until today to perceive Fathy as a naive reactionary.

After five years of self-imposed exile and practice in Greece (1957–1962), Fathy's career was marked by a significant shift in social emphasis. Although he never relinquished the cause of sheltering the poor, Fathy's clientele gradually shifted to be almost exclusively the upper-class elite. These patrons appreciated the romantic as well as environmental qualities of his style and hence its capacity to represent both their sophisticated taste and their cultural authenticity. The suburban villas Fathy designed for them during the 1970s and 1980s on the road to the Saqarra pyramids near Cairo and elsewhere in the Arab world represent fine, picturesque examples of his later work, in which he also applied more durable and expensive materials such as stone.

Fathy was internationally recognized late in his life after the English and French publication of his *Architecture for the Poor* in 1973, a time of considerable disenchantment in the Western world with the failure of International Modernism to communicate shared meanings. Fathy consequently received numerous honors and was invited in 1980 to transpose his utopia to the United States by designing Dar al-Islam, a settlement for converted Muslims in Abiquiu, New Mexico. Simultaneously, some of his disciples successfully marketed his design formula to Saudi royal patrons for rebuilding a series of important historic mosques. Driven by the concern to reinforce its own legitimacy, the Saudi monarchy apparently hoped that monumentalization of the traditional imagery of Fathy's style would engage increasing pro-Islamic sentiments more successfully than the previously adopted, abstract International style. Indeed, the current influence of Fathy's message and forms on many young Arab architects seeking authentic cultural expression cannot be underestimated. Fathy's reform thus seems to have gone full circle, from representing an oppositional marginal culture, via the bourgeois elite, to an official state style. To what extent this transformation is a triumph for Fathy's thought is open to debate.

[*See also* Architecture, *article on* Contemporary Forms.]

BIBLIOGRAPHY

Works by Hassan Fathy

Gourna: A Tale of Two Villages. Cairo, 1969.

The Arab House in the Urban Setting: Past, Present, and Future. London, 1972.

Architecture for the Poor: An Experiment in Rural Egypt. Chicago, 1973.

"Constancy, Transposition, and Change in the Arab City." In *From Madina to Metropolis,* edited by L. Carl Brown. Princeton, 1973.

Natural Energy and Vernacular Architecture: Principles and Examples with Reference to Hot Arid Climates. Chicago, 1986.

Other Sources

DePopolo, Margaret, and Reinhard Goethert. *Hassan Fathy, Architect: An Exhibition of Selected Projects.* Cambridge, Mass., 1981.

Holod, Renata, and Darl Rastorfer. "Hassan Fathy, Chairman's Award." In *Architecture and Community Building in the Islamic World Today,* pp. 235–245. New York, 1983.

Richards, J. M., et al. *Hassan Fathy.* Singapore, 1985.

Steele, James. *Hassan Fathy.* London, 1988.

Steele, James, comp. *The Hassan Fathy Collection.* Geneva, 1989.

YASIR M. SAKR

FĀṬIMID DYNASTY. The institutional embodiment of the Ismāʿilīyah, a Shīʿī sect that arose from the disputed succession to Jaʿfar al-Ṣādiq (c.700–756), the sixth imam of mainstream Shiism (the Imāmīyah), was called the Fāṭimid dynasty. Al-Ṣādiq's son and designated successor, Ismāʿīl, had predeceased him, and some Shīʿīs took Ismāʿīl's son, Muḥammad, as the imam, rather than Ismāʿīl's brother, Mūsā al-Kāẓim, who was accepted by the majority. By the end of the ninth century, Muḥammad ibn Ismāʿīl's messianic role as the Mahdi was no longer recognized by many Ismāʿīlīyah, leading to an internal split. Direct spiritual leadership (and ʿAlid descent through Ismāʿīl) was now claimed by a certain ʿAbd Allāh (also known as ʿUbaid Allāh), who, with other members of his family, had been living in Salamīyah, an Ismāʿīlī center in Syria. His actual descent is a matter of dispute, especially as the predominantly Sunnī sources have energetically vilified him and his successors.

The Ismāʿīlī movement—which held to a revolutionary messianism, claimed access to esoteric truths, and developed an elaborate Gnostic cosmology, later adding elements of Neoplatonism—was spread by a network of secret cells. As an offshoot of a "mission" in Yemen, a *dāʿī* (agent) called Abū ʿAbd Allāh al-Shīʿī began a propaganda campaign among the Kutāma Berbers in 893. Operating from the Kabyle Mountains in what is modern Algeria, and capitalizing on Berber hostility to the Aghlabid governors, who ruled in Qayrawān and Raqqāda (in what is modern Tunisia) as representatives of ʿAbbāsid Sunnism, the new movement achieved great success, and the Ismāʿīlīyah defeated the Aghlabids in 909.

ʿAbd Allāh had left Salamīyah and, after some perilous adventures, arrived to take over the active leadership of the Ismāʿīlīyah in North Africa, adopting the messianic title of the Mahdi. Despite the subsequent execution of Abū ʿAbd Allāh and Berber revolts, especially that of the Khārijite Abū Yazīd (943–947), a Fāṭimid state (so named because of claimed descent from Fāṭimah, the Prophet's daughter and ʿAlī's wife) was established with loyal Berber support and elements of the former Aghlabid army and bureaucracy. A new capital, al-Mahdīyah, was founded in 920.

The logic of militant Ismāʿīlī Shiism, with its claim to universal power and authority in Islam, led to attempts at eastward anti-ʿAbbāsid expansion. The extensive Fāṭimid possessions in North Africa, however, were consigned to vassals and in due course lost. A series of expeditions against Egypt ended with its conquest in 969 by Jawhar, the general of the Fāṭimid caliph, al-Muʿizz (d. 975). A new residential and administrative complex was founded, north of previous centers, named al-Qāhirah (Cairo), to which al-Muʿizz moved in 973. Naval and military power, the splendor of the court, and Egypt's artistic productions and burgeoning international trade projected the Fāṭimid regime as an equal of the Byzantine and ʿAbbāsid empires. Politically and militarily, however, its efforts to advance through Syria were checked by a resurgence of Byzantine power in the second half of the tenth century and by the new Türkmen and Seljuk incursions in the eleventh century.

Internally, the dogmas of Ismāʿīlīyah made but little headway among the population at large. It was confined to the court and the state apparatus. Alexandria in particular remained a bastion of opposition as a strong center of Mālikī Sunnī law and belief. Cairo, however, functioned as the center of an extensive network of propaganda cells that reached as far as the Indus Valley and attempted to destabilize other Islamic regimes to bring on the triumph of Ismāʿīlīyah. The religious center of this movement was the mosque of al-Azhar, founded in 970.

The solidity of the Fāṭimid regime was tested by the eccentric reign of al-Ḥākim (r. 996–1021), and later, in the eleventh century, there were economic troubles exacerbated by insufficient Nile floods, famines and plagues, and growing bedouin depredations. There were also conflicts within the army, for the palace was increasingly unable to control the various contingents of Berbers, Arabs, Sudanese, Armenians, and Turks. The 1070s began a period of domination of the state by military men. The Armenian Badr al-Jamālī (d. 1094) was the first of the "viziers of the sword." The ideology of the Fāṭimids became increasingly irrelevant, and when the vizier al-Afḍal (d. 1121) ousted Nizār, the designated successor of al-Mustanṣir (r. 1036–1094), the Ismāʿīlīyah of Iran threw off their allegiance.

The internal weakness of Egypt encouraged the Crusaders to intervene, which led to a protracted contest for control of the country between the Kingdom of Jerusalem and Nūr al-Dīn (r. 1144–1174) of Aleppo and Damascus. Saladin emerged as the new power in Egypt, initially as lieutenant for Nūr al-Dīn, and the Fāṭimid caliphate was abolished in 1171.

[*See also* ʿAbbāsid Caliphate; Egypt; Ismāʿīlīyah.]

BIBLIOGRAPHY

Canard, Marius. "Fāṭimids." In *Encyclopaedia of Islam.*, new ed., vol. 2, pp. 850–862. Leiden, 1960–. Good introductory study.

Kennedy, Hugh. *The Prophet and the Age of the Caliphate: The Islamic Near East from the Sixth to the Eleventh Century*. London and New York, 1986. See pages 315–345.

Lewis, Bernard. "Egypt and Syria to the End of the Fāṭimid Caliphate." In *The Cambridge History of Islam*, vol. 1, *The Central Islamic Lands*, edited by P. M. Holt et al., pp. 184–201. Cambridge, 1970.

O'Leary, De Lacy. *A Short History of the Fatimid Khalifate*. London, 1923. Rather old-fashioned, but one of the rare monographs devoted to the subject.

Stern, S. M. *Studies in Early Ismāʿīlism*. Jerusalem, 1983. Collection of Stern's important and wide-ranging published articles, with notes on unpublished material.

D. S. RICHARDS

FATWĀ.

[*To describe the role of* fatwā *as an instrument of religious law, this entry comprises three articles:*

Concepts of Fatwā
Process and Function
Modern Usage

The first article provides a general overview, with attention to variations in meaning of the term: the second describes how fatwās *are generated and produced; and the third considers the history of use and the political utility of* fatwās *in the nineteenth and twentieth centuries. For related discussions, see* Ijtihād; Law; Muftī; ʿUlamāʾ.]

Concepts of Fatwā

An overview of the history of *fatwā* suggests three different concepts associated with the term: management of information about the religion of Islam in general, providing consultation to courts of law, and interpretation of Islamic law. The first concept, which has been central through history, has reappeared more prominently in modern times, as is evident from the contents as well as from the definitions given in modern collections of *fatwā*s. For instance, *Fatāwā Dār al-ʿUlūm Deoband* (Deoband, 1962) defines *fatwā* as "an issue arising about law and religion, explained in answer to questions received about it" by the *muftī*s of Deoband, a reformist school of religious learning established in 1867. The continuity of tradition in these modern developments cannot properly be appreciated without a look at the semantic growth of the concept in early Islam.

Literally, *fatwā* is derived from the root *fata*, which includes in its semantic field the meanings "youth, newness, clarification, explanation." These connotations have survived in its various definitions. Its development as a technical term originated from the Qur'ān, where the word is used in two verbal forms meaning "asking for a definitive answer" and "giving a definitive answer" (4.127, 176).

The concept of *fatwā* in early Islam developed in the framework of a question-and-answer process of communicating information about Islam. Its subject was *ʿilm* (knowledge) without further specification. Later, when *ʿilm* was identified with *ḥadīth*, *fatwā* came to be associated with *ra'y* (opinion) and *fiqh* (jurisprudence or law). The technical usage of the term was further refined when, after the compilation of legal literature by the different schools, the term *fatwā* was used for cases not covered in the *fiqh* (law) books.

The contrastive method of defining *fatwā*, as employed in the Islamic literature, in fact reflects the varying emphases in the concepts of *fatwā*. From the perspective of the scope of subjects covered, *fatwā* is contrasted with *mutūn* (textbooks of Islamic law); *fatwā* covers a wider scope, including matters of legal theory, theology, philosophy, and creeds, which are not included in *fiqh* books. Thus the concept of *fatwā* retains a broader concern about religion and society than is reflected in the formal Islamic law defined by the schools. From the perspective of judicial authority, jurisdiction, and enforceability, *fatwā* is contrasted with *qaḍā* or court judgment. The jurisdiction of *fatwā* is wider than *qaḍā;* matters such as *ʿibādāt* (religious duties or obligations) are excluded from the jurisdiction of the courts, even though they are essential parts of Islamic law and appear very prominently in *fiqh* books and *fatwā*s. Note, however, that *qaḍā* is binding and enforceable, but *fatwā* is not. The concept of *fatwā* can therefore be seen as an indirect instrument for defining the formal concept of law as applied in courts. From the perspective of moral and religious obligation, *fatwā* is contrasted with *taqwā* or piety. For instance, a *fatwā* may allow choice between a lenient *(rukhṣah)* and a severe *(ʿazīmah)* view about the permissibility of a certain matter, or it may resort to legal devices *(ḥīlah)* to circumvent the strict implications of a law, but *taqwā* may not approve of such strategies. This last contrast is often referred to in literary and Ṣūfī writings.

Fatwā functioned independent of the judicial system, although in some systems *muftī*s were attached officially to the courts. Thus in Andalusian courts *muftī*s sat as *mushāwar* (jurisconsults), and in early British Indian courts they sat as *mawlawī*s (men of learning). The jurists compiled volumes of *fatwās* stating, for the benefit of the judges, the consensual and authoritative views and doctrines of a particulate school.

The position of *muftī*s in a Muslim political system was defined depending on the role and place of *fiqh* in the society. In Andalusia the jurists were indeed powerful; they were part of the Shūrā (council) of the amirs and caliphs. In the Ottoman and Mughal political systems the chief *muftī* was designated as *shaykh al-Islām. Muftī*s were also appointed to various other positions including market inspectors, guardians of public morals, and advisors to governments on religious affairs.

Under colonial rule the *madrasah*s took over the role of *mufti*s as religious guides. The *madrasah*s established the institution of *dār al-iftā*, a place to issue *fatwā*s. The print and electronic media in the nineteenth and twentieth centuries reinforced the role and impact of *fatwā*s. *Muftī*s were faced with day-to-day changes in society in the fields of economics, politics, science, and technology. Not only did the scope of *fatwā* widen, but because of its instant availability to a wider public, its language, presentation, and style also changed.

The ideological authority of the *fatwā* is invariably explained by saying that a *muftī* is the deputy and successor to the Prophet, the lawgiver. Legally, the authority of the mufti is derived from the doctrine of *taqlīd* (adherence to tradition), which demands consulting the learned, often those of a particular school of law, and following their opinions. Since a *muftī* has to cite authorities for his opinion, his authority is moral and institutional, not personal. For this reason the qualifications of a *muftī* and the rules for issuing a *fatwā* have been developed in considerable detail. A *mustaftī* (inquirer) should accept and obey the opinion of the *muftī* when he is satisfied that he is competent and that his opinion is based on earlier authorities. Theoretically, a *muftī* must be a *mujtahid* (an interpreter of law qualified to exercise legal reasoning independently of schools of law) yet a *muqallid* (an adherent to a school) is also allowed to issue a *fatwā*, as long as he mentions the source of his citation.

Modern scholars usually define *fatwā* as a formal legal opinion given by an expert on Islamic law. Émile Tyan (1960, p. 219) argues that this institutional came into being because no legislative power existed in Islam. He sees the role of the *muftī* in the Muslim political system in the perspective of *shūrā* (consultation) and legislation.

Muslim states, especially in the modern period, have tried to control *fatwā* by instituting organizations that provide consultation to the state and issue *fatwā*s, such as the Council of Islamic Ideology in Pakistan or the Hay'ah Kibār al-ʿUlamā' in Saudi Arabia. Their role is advisory, and they are part of the religious, not justice, ministries. In order to appreciate current trends and developments, *fatwā* today should be seen as a function of management and the communication of information.

[*See also* Law, *article on* Legal Thought and Jurisprudence; *and* Muftī.]

BIBLIOGRAPHY

Hunter, W. W. *The Indian Musalmans.* London, 1871. Provides excellent insight into the colonial perception of the role of *fatwā* in a Muslim society in the early nineteenth century, especially its use by the British and Muslims during the 1857 uprising in India against the British.

Qaraḍāwī, Yūsuf al-. *Al-fatwā bayna al-inḍibāṭ wa-al-tasayyub.* Cairo, 1988. Modern restatement of traditional discussions about the rules and etiquette of writing a *fatwā*. The author provides a comprehensive summary of the legal theory of *fatwā* and a good introduction to some problems in its modern practice.

Qāsimī, Muḥammad Jamāl al-Dīn al-. *Al-fatwā fi-al-Islām.* Beirut, 1986. Excellent summary of the *adab al-muftī* literature dealing with the rules and regulations of writing a *fatwā* and qualifications of a *muftī*.

Schacht, Joseph. *An Introduction to Islamic Law.* Oxford, 1964. Concise introduction to the nature of the institution of *fatwā* (see pp. 73–75).

Tyan, Émile. "Fatwā." In *Encyclopaedia of Islam,* new ed., vol. 2, p. 866. Leiden, 1960–. Short discussion of the concept and history of the subject, particularly with reference to modern developments.

Tyan, Émile. *Histoire de l'organisation judiciare en pays d'Islam.* 2d ed. Leiden, 1960. Excellent review of the history of the institution, and of the discussion of the qualifications, method, and technique of *fatwā* in the Islamic literature (see pp. 219–230).

MUHAMMAD KHALID MASUD

Process and Function

Issued by a *muftī* and taking the form of an answer to a question, a *fatwā* is a considered opinion embodying an interpretation of the *sharīʿah.* A key legal-religious institution, the giving of *fatwās* has flourished across time and place in Muslim societies from early in the Islamic era to the present day, contributing fundamentally to the continuing dynamism of the law and to the regulation of local practices. As a category of legal specialization, however, the issuing of *fatwās* is less familiar than judging. *Fatwās* are similar to the opinions of Roman jurisconsults and to the responsa of Jewish scholars. Compared with the court judgments of their colleagues, the Muslim *qāḍīs*, *fatwās* have a distinct type of authority. In terms of technical status, judgments are "creative" or performative acts while *fatwās* are "informational" or communicative ones; judgments thus are binding and enforceable while *muftīs*' opinions are advisory. But in the absence of a conception of precedent formation in connection with *sharīʿah* court rulings, the authority of judgments tended to remain narrowly specific, pertaining only to particular cases; that of *fatwās*, by contrast, was general, potentially extending to all similar configurations of fact. Judgments were entered into court registers but were not otherwise reported or published, while *fatwās* by noted *muftīs* were apt to be collected, circulated, and cited.

Judges always were public figures, appointed and salaried by the state; *muftīs*, however, were likely to be private scholars, although in a number of historical settings, such as the Ottoman Empire, *muftīs* also served as public officials. In the practical world of *sharīʿah* application, especially before the rise of nation-state legal institutions, the work of *muftīs* complemented that of the court judges, and in many instances there were formal ties between *muftīs* and courts. The two roles were always distinct, however. Where judges heard opposed claims and evidence from pairs of adversaries and then handed down a ruling, the interpretive interchange that resulted in the delivery of a *fatwā* was of a different character. *Muftīs* responded to individual questioners, who typically posed their questions voluntarily. Unlike court judges, who were investigators of evidential fact, *muftīs* took the configurations of fact presented in questions as given. Both judges and *muftīs* are *sharīʿah* interpreters, but their interpretive acts have differing points of departure. While a judge's interpretive work is directed to understanding evidential forms such as testimony, acknowledgment, and oath, that of the *muftī* seeks out indications in the textual sources of the law, including the Qur'ān and the *sunnah*.

Muftīs were identified with specific interpretive communities, such as the various schools (*madhhabs*) of legal thought that subdivide both the Sunnī and Shīʿī traditions, and sometimes also with the programs of particular instructional institutions, such as that at Deoband in India or al-Azhar University in Cairo. Especially in the twentieth century, however, many *muftīs* began to assert their intellectual independence from all such interpretive traditions. Earlier, as is discussed in special treatises concerned with the muftiship (the *adab al-muftī* literature), levels of competence among *muftīs* were specified; the highest was the "absolute" or "independent" interpreter. As a matter of principle, such *muftīs* did not follow the opinions of other jurists or the positions of the schools, but directly interpreted the law through their personal analyses of its basic sources, the Qur'ān and the *sunnah* of the Prophet. Below this highest category were "non-independent" or "affiliated" *muftīs* of several levels, all technically classified as *muqallids*, followers to some degree of established doctrine. *Fatwās* of the highest caliber contain explicit exercises of *ijtihād,* or formal, reasoned interpretation, but even the most unpretentious opinion, which simply states the law in connection with an uncomplicated matter, is an interpretive act.

In theory, *fatwās* could be delivered orally, but aside from the existence of an office established for this specific purpose within the Ottoman *fatwā* administration, it is uncertain how frequently this occurred. Among written *fatwās*, many—perhaps the great majority—were considered routine and as a consequence were dispersed directly to questioners, in some cases without leaving a documentary trace. For the Ottoman Empire and certain of the schools in India, for example, massive collections of such ordinary *fatwās* exist in archives. The early nineteenth-century Yemeni jurist al-Shawkānī distinguished between his unrecorded "shorter" *fatwās*, which "could never be counted," and his major *fatwās*, which were collected and preserved in book form. At the turn of the twentieth century Muḥammad ʿAbduh, the grand *muftī* of Egypt, in addition to his official opinions on matters of state, also issued numerous ordinary *fatwās* to private individuals. The thousands of *fatwās* delivered over several decades by a mid-twentieth-century *muftī* in provincial Yemen, however, were neither collected nor preserved, even as copies, but were written directly on slips of paper containing the original queries, which were returned and carried away by the questioners.

Varying widely in scope, *fatwās* have comprised both the single-word responses ("yes," "no," "permitted," etc.) characteristic of some official Ottoman *muftīs* and also virtual treatises approaching book length. Questioners have ranged up and down the social hierarchies, including both men and women of every status, from the ordinary populace to members of the elite, scholars, court judges, and even heads of state. The *muftīs* themselves have included modest, local-level scholars who occasionally and informally replied to queries arising in their districts and, at the other extreme, the greatest legal minds of an era or powerful state officials at the apex of *fatwā*-issuing bureaucracies. *Fatwās* tend to differ in content according to the level of the *muftī* and the status of the questioner addressed. In general, responses to the untutored are likely to be nontechnical, whereas those issued to scholars typically contain precise citations of sources and indicate the methods of reasoning employed.

The relationship between a *muftī* and an ordinary questioner was predicated on a differentiation of roles. Before the rise of modern school curricula and universal education, *sharīʿah* knowledge was the centerpiece of advanced instruction in societies characterized by patterns of restricted literacy. As a consequence, a limited group of scholarly interpreters controlled an essential body of cultural capital, which included not only the many specific details concerning ritual provisions fundamental for the religious life, but also the precise rules of a wide variety of contracts, transactions, and dispositions that structured legal-economic relations. In such social settings it was considered incumbent on those who had acquired knowledge to communicate it, either through teaching or through acting as a *muftī*. Reciprocally, it was incumbent on the untutored to ask such knowledgeable individuals whenever the need to know a *sharīʿah* principle arose. Ideally, *muftīs* were meant to be exemplary moral individuals whose intellectual achievements were matched by appropriate personal decorum. In accord with the social honor vested in them, *muftīs* were approached with respect and deference.

Although the *muftī* of a given locale was typically a well-known figure, some questioners had to make inquiries or travel to find a suitable scholar. Others had to choose among several available *muftīs*. The *adab al-muftī* treatises suggest that a questioner should seek out public information about a *muftī*'s scholarly reputation, but it is acknowledged that such information would be difficult for an uneducated individual to evaluate. The basic recommendation is that the questioner follow the advice of a single just person or trust his or her own sense of the potential *muftī*'s piety. In some settings, questioners dissatisfied with a first *muftī*'s response could seek out a second for another *fatwā*, which they hoped would contain a different view. In other settings, opponents in a dispute approached different *muftīs* to obtain competing *fatwās* to buttress their respective positions.

The interpretive exchange opened with the posing of the question. In their widely varying patterns and concerns, questions provide rich information about the concrete affairs of specific Muslim societies. Questions are of great significance to the interpretive process because they define the terms of the *muftī*'s engagement with the problem under consideration. At the same time, questions frequently were carefully constructed to highlight certain facts or to elicit a particular response. Since *muftīs* are not examiners of the facts, these are taken as they are provided in the questions. Whereas judges are permitted to act on the basis of their own knowledge about cases, *muftīs* are not, unless this information is provided in questions. For these reasons, the opinion to be contained in the *fatwā* is constrained at the outset by the formulation of the question. In addition, in the Ottoman Empire, questions were rewritten by functionaries to facilitate brief answers from the *muftīs*. In theory, questions posed to *muftīs* should pertain to actual events and should not be hypothetical or imaginary. In formulation, however, questions characteristically are presented in generic terms, leaving out details such as place names and using conventional substitutes for actual personal names (e.g., "Zayd" and "ʿAmr" in Ottoman *fatwās*) or simply "a man" or "a woman." This standard feature in the design of questions underscores the directionality of the *muftī*'s attention, which led away from consideration of the contextual circumstances of a case and toward an assessment of an assumed set of facts in terms of the law.

Muftīs responded to questions received according to their understanding of the contents. Such comprehension frequently depended on the *muftī*'s grasp of both local custom and colloquial expression. In most *fatwā* collections, the incidence of poorly formulated, ambiguous, or otherwise deficient queries has been masked by editorial redrafting of questions or by their omission altogether. According to the theory of the treatises, and also in Ottoman practice, when a question remained unclear, *muftīs* could include explicit caveats in their responses, stating that the value of the answer depended on the information made available in the question. *Muftīs* typically would handle questions touching on the full gamut of *sharīʿah* subject matter, including areas such as contracts and punishments, which usually were also within the jurisdictions of the courts, and areas such as ritual issues, which generally were not. In some historical settings, *muftīs* addressed issues well beyond these strictly legal topics, although some of the early theorists argued that *muftīs* should not respond to questions in certain fields, such as Qur'ānic exegesis or theology. Beyond their responses in matters covered by the *sharīʿah,* Ottoman *muftīs* commonly issued *fatwās* on issues regulated by secular state law. In the early decades of the twentieth century, responding in print to letters his journal received from around the world, Muḥammad Rashīd Riḍā gave *fatwās* on an extremely wide variety of legal, social, and political topics that confronted the Muslims of the day.

While sharing a common identity—as answers to questions—*fatwās* nevertheless took many regional forms depending on local legal cultures and their usages. *Fatwās* from different regions thus vary widely in language, conventional formulas, and rhetorical style. The theoretical treatises suggest proper wording for openings and closings and special terms of address; they also discuss *Allāhu aʿlam,* "God knows best," and other related expressions, one of which appears at the end of most *fatwās*. The treatises also consider the physical organization of *fatwā* texts and recommend against such practices as the leaving of blank spaces or the use of more than one sheet of paper, so as to guard against additions or alterations. Unlike the question, which could be in the hand of the questioner or a secretary, the *fatwā* itself generally had to be written in the authoritative script of the *muftī*. Before actually delivering the *fatwā,* a *muftī* ideally would consult with scholarly colleagues present at the session about his finding. If upon receipt the questioner failed to understand the *fatwā,* he could turn to the *muftī* or individuals in the sitting room for assistance. In some places, further questions could be posed to explore implications or alternatives. If the response of a private *muftī* proved unacceptable, the questioner was free to consult a different *muftī* for another opinion.

Muftīs often were powerful figures. Some "*muftīs*," such as the mid-twentieth-century Lebanese *muftī* of the republic, were actually important political leaders. Others, such as the grand *muftīs* appointed in various states over the past century, have wielded considerable political influence through their official *fatwās*. The heads of the great *fatwā*-issuing bureaucracies, such as the Ottoman *shaykh al-Islām,* were among the highest-ranking state officials. [*See* Shaykh al-Islām.] For the scholarly, another form of influence was measured in reputational terms and expressed in estimations of juristic preeminence, which entailed leadership in such activities as writing, instruction, and *fatwā*-giving, and also control of certain tax and endowment revenues. In both political and scholarly communities, doctrinal struggles between opposed states or competing instructional centers have been played out in "*fatwā* wars." Although the theory of private *fatwā*-giving held that *fatwās* should be given for free, gifts and various forms of pious support were common. Official *muftīs*, however, were salaried or received set fees from their questioners, and many grew wealthy in their positions. In historical contexts where there were formal requirements to obtain *fatwās* as part of the litigation process, *muftīs* issued opinions that had direct bearing on court outcomes; in other contexts, approaching a *muftī* amounted to a cheaper, less conflictual, and more efficient alternative means of dispute resolution.

The overall significance of the *fatwā* is twofold. *Fatwās* by leading jurists articulated formal, legal-religious views of important doctrinal questions, societal issues, and political events. At this level, *muftīs* employed their creative interpretations of the *sharīʿah* to grapple with the major continuities and changes in Muslim life. The impact of such interpretations, however, depended on the overall place of the *sharīʿah* in their respective societies. On the other hand, the mass of unremarkable *fatwās* issued by *muftīs* official and unofficial, and of diverse schools and statures, has assisted Muslims from all walks of life in efforts to arrange their affairs in accord with the design of the *sharīʿah.*

[*See also* Ijtihād; Law, *article on* Legal Thought and Jurisprudence; Muftī.]

BIBLIOGRAPHY

Heyd, Uriel. "Some Aspects of the Ottoman Fetva." *Bulletin of the School of Oriental and African Studies* 32(1969): 35–55. The best examination of the textual features of a *fatwā*-issuing institution.

Ibn Khaldūn. *The Muqaddimah: An Introduction to History*. 3 vols. Translated by Franz Rosenthal. New York, 1958. Contains an institutional view of official *muftīs*, appointed by the imam.

Masud, Muhammad Khalid. "*Adab al-Mufti:* The Muslim Understanding of Values, Characteristics, and Role of a Mufti." In *Moral Conduct and Authority: The Place of Adab in South Asian Islam*, edited by Barbara D. Metcalf, pp. 124–150. Berkeley, 1984. Survey of theoretical manuals concerned with the muftiship.

Messick, Brinkley. *The Calligraphic State: Textual Domination and History in a Muslim Society*. Berkeley, 1993. An anthropological and textual study of *muftīs* in Yemen (see pp. 135–151).

Nawawī, Abū Zakariyā Yaḥyā al-. *Adab al-fatwā wa-al-muftī wa-al-mustaftī*. Damascus, 1988. Typical "*adab al-muftī*" treatise concerned with the muftiship, by a thirteenth-century author.

Qarāfī, Aḥmad ibn Idrīs al-. *Al-Iḥkām fī tamyīz al-fatāwā ʿan al-aḥkām wa-taṣarrufāt al-qāḍī wa-al-imām*. Cairo, 1989. Comparative analysis of the judge and the *muftī* by a thirteenth-century jurist.

Weber, Max. *Economy and Society*. 2 vols. Berkeley, 1978. Compares *muftīs* with Roman jurisconsults (see pp. 798–799, 812–821).

Weiss, Bernard G. *The Search for God's Law: Islamic Jurisprudence in the Writings of Sayf al-Dīn al-Āmidī*. Salt Lake City, 1992. On the theory of the interpretive interchange see pp. 717–728.

BRINKLEY MESSICK

Modern Usage

Fatwā emerged as an informal institution long before the formal establishment of the public office of the *muftī*, and its social and political potentials are discernible in the early theoretical discussions of *iftāʾ* (the act of issuing *fatwās*). The subject of *fatwā* is usually treated in works on the principles of jurisprudence *(uṣūl al-fiqh)* following the section on *ijtihād*. Whereas *ijtihād* refers to the scholarly, intellectual effort of seeking an opinion regarding applied law, *fatwā* refers to the social role of a *mujtahid* as a consultant in matters of law, contrasted with the well-defined role of a *qāḍī* (judge). A *fatwā* is defined as an unbinding legal opinion issued in response to the question of a *mustaftī*. Thus a *muftī* is inherently biased, because he responds to a question presented by only one party to a dispute. Conceding this bias, *uṣūl* works distinguish between the unbinding opinion of a *muftī* and the binding ruling of a judge. Furthermore, it is up to a judge to verify whether a *fatwā* is applicable in a specific case. These differentiations conceptually situate the institution of *fatwā* in an intermediary plane between the theory of law as articulated by *mujtahids* and the practice of law as exercised by judges. As such, a *muftī* contributes both to the ongoing development of the legal doctrine of a school of law and to its practical application.

Before the eleventh century CE a *muftī* was simply someone who issued *fatwās*, knowledge and recognition by the scholarly community were the only prerequisites for a *muftī*. Beginning in the eleventh century a public office of *muftī* was affixed to the private vocation of *iftāʾ*. In eleventh-century Khurasan, the *shaykh al-Islām* of a city was the official head of its local *ʿulamāʾ*, and functioned as its chief *muftī*. Under the Mamlūks, one *muftī* of each school was appointed as part of the appeal courts of provincial capitals. The Ottomans appointed a *muftī* in each city, integrated *muftīs* into the bureaucratic system, and organized *iftāʾ* as a routinized state procedure. Under Sultan Murad II (r. 1421–1444, 1446–1451), the once honorific title *shaykh al-Islām* was transformed into the official title of the chief *muftī* of the empire. By the time of Sülayman Kanuni (r. 1520–1566) the office had developed from a part-time occupation into a fully formalized one; Sülayman appointed the *muftī* of Istanbul to the office of *shaykh al-Islām* and made him the head of the religious establishment of the whole empire. The Ottomans thus gave *fatwā* political sanction it had lacked earlier. The *shaykh al-Islām* was appointed and dismissed only by the sultan; the sultan in turn was confirmed or deposed by the shaykh's *fatwā*. The *shaykh al-Islām*, however, still depended on the secular authority and the *qāḍīs* to execute his judgments.

The ambiguity in the actual power of the Ottoman *shaykh al-Islām* gave rise to several theories on the origins of this office. One theory proposes that the office arose in imitation of the Patriarch of Constantinople, but this fails to account for the pre-Ottoman history of the office of the *muftī* in general and of the title *shaykh al-Islām* in particular. A more pertinent question is whether the office was founded to give religious legitimacy to secular authorities, or whether it was founded to coopt the religious institutions in an attempt to bring them under the control of the state. It is probable that the office was initially founded to confer Islamic legitimacy on the state and in recognition of Islam as the main source of social and political cohesion; however, as the Ottomans developed a secure tradition of ruling, the office was formalized and absorbed into the state bureaucracy, and the *shaykh al-Islām* was in effect demoted from a theoretical equal to a definite subordinate of the sultan. [*See* Shaykh al-Islām.]

Parallels to the office of *shaykh al-Islām* existed outside the Ottoman Empire, although usually under different titles. In Mughal India, the *ṣadr al-ṣudūr* was the head of the religious corporation, whereas the *shaykh al-Islām* looked after the affairs of the Ṣūfīs. In Ṣafavid Iran, the *shaykh al-Islām* was neither the grand *muftī* nor the head of the religious hierarchy. These functions were reserved for the *ṣadr,* who controlled the religious institutions on behalf of the state and who was in charge of the officially sponsored spread of Shiism. The *ṣadr* was appointed by the state, and was charged with appointing *qāḍī*s, supervising *waqf*s, and functioning as the official head of the *ʿulamāʾ* class. In addition to the *ṣadr, shaykh*s *al-Islām* were appointed by the state in the capital and several other provincial cities and towns. These *shaykh*s *al-Islām* functioned as the chief religious officials in their areas, and were under the general supervision of the *ṣadr.* They were also in charge of supervising the local *qāḍī*s. The organization of the religious establishment under the Ṣafavids presupposed the religious authority of the rulers as the descendants of the hidden imam (thus the title "shadows of God"). In time, this authority was challenged, and the role of representing the hidden imam was reclaimed by the *mujtahid*s. These were independent scholars who filled no office, were not appointed by the state, and were not on its payroll. During the eighteenth century, a theological controversy between two Shīʿī schools, the Uṣūlīs and the Akhbārīs, was resolved in favor of the former. According to the Uṣūlīs, Muslims were under the obligation to choose and follow a living *mujtahid* known as a *marjaʿ al-taqlīd*. Under the Qājārs, the body of *mujtahid*s further articulated the claim of collective deputyship of the imam. On account of his knowledge and piety, a *mujtahid* or a *marjaʿ* had the authority to interpret and explain the law to ordinary Muslims. Thus both the Sunnī *muftī* and the Shīʿī *mujtahid* shared the function of interpreting the law. There are, however, some important differences between the two offices. Whereas the *fatwā* of a Sunnī *muftī* was not binding, that of a Shīʿī *mujtahid* was. Moreover, with the passage of time, the Ottoman office of the *muftī* was successfully coopted into the state bureaucracy, while the Shīʿī *mujtahid*s gradually gained a greater measure of independence from the ideological and physical control of the state. [*See* Ṣadr; Marjaʿ al-Taqlīd.]

As a result of a gradual bureaucratization of religious institutions in the Islamic world in general, and of the office of the *muftī* in particular, the class of *ʿulamāʾ* came to enjoy greater social prestige, higher and steadier incomes, and improved promotional opportunities. Official *muftī*s, however, had no monopoly over issuing *fatwā*s, and private *muftī*s did not require government approval to engage in *iftāʾ*. Recognition of the semiprivate nature of the institution of *iftāʾ* was even reflected in the official appointment of *muftī*s. In the Ottoman Empire, for example, a *muftī*'s appointment was theoretically for life, and in any case was for a long duration; in contrast, the appointments of judges were for one-year terms. Moreover, while a judge was a Ḥanafī Ottoman trained in the schools of Istanbul, *muftī*s often belonged to the local non-Ḥanafī elites of the cities and towns in which they served. These local *muftī*s had better knowledge of the conditions and customs of their cities and were often chosen by the local elites and simply confirmed in office by the central authorities in Istanbul.

Owing to its dual private and public traits, the institution of *fatwā* evinces a multitude of social manifestations. A formal *fatwā* in response to a formal inquiry may serve as a technical tool in the legal proceedings of a court, or as a scholarly endeavor through which a standard legal doctrine is expanded, modified, or developed. Alternatively, a *fatwā* may be issued at a scholar's own initiative in the form of a treatise, proclamation, or lesson. In any of these forms a *muftī,* scholar, teacher, or preacher may give what amounts to a minor or a major *fatwā*. A minor *fatwā* usually involves one or more of the following: the practical application of the law; an explanation of the law in complicated cases or to people who have no direct access to its technical formulations; instructions on correct social behavior or lawful religious beliefs and practices; or suggestions for settling disputes without further recourse to courts. Such *fatwā*s contributed to social stability by both providing formal administrative organization and informal networks for running the affairs of society.

A major *fatwā,* by contrast, involves a significant statement on public law and policy and may often lead to the expansion of the corpus of law. In the Ottoman Empire, for example, declarations of war and peace, as well as administrative and fiscal measures and reforms, were sanctioned by the *fatwā*s of the *shaykh al-Islām.* Not only were *fatwā*s used to justify extra-*sharīʿah* laws (for example, Ottoman taxation and criminal laws) issued by the secular authorities, but the authority of the sultan was itself legitimized or denied on the basis of such *fatwā*s; for example, Sultan Murad V was deposed by an 1876 *fatwā* on grounds of insanity. *Fatwā*s were also used to legitimize new social and economic practices. In the Ottoman Empire, for example, a *fatwā* issued in 1727 authorized the printing of nonreligious books; vaccination was declared legitimate in an 1845 *fatwā;* and several *fatwā*s were used to legitimize low-rate interest, selling on credit, and the practice of establishing cash *waqf. Muftī*s also played a role in curbing the powers of judges and other secular functionaries. By giving voice to the complaints of the people and by providing authoritative articulations of their legal rights, *fatwā*s often permitted individuals or groups to seek redress and justice in courts.

Parties to social and religious conflicts also solicited *fatwā*s in support of their contentions. In the Ottoman Empire, for example, leaders and members of puritanical movements often approached *muftī*s for *fatwā*s condemning Ṣūfī practices. Most of the responses, however, were intentionally moderate. Thus in a famous *fatwā* the great Ottoman *shaykh al-Islām* Ebüssu'ûd Mehmet Efendi (Ar., Abū al-Suʿūd Afandī; 1545–1574) censored Ṣūfī excesses as well as the extreme intolerance of their critics; in the same *fatwā* he confirmed the legitimacy of Ṣūfī music and rhythmic dancing, which were the intended targets of the solicitors of the *fatwā*.

Major transformations engulfed the Muslim world during the nineteenth and twentieth centuries. The decline in the centralized power of the Ottoman state and the corresponding increase in European domination over Muslim territory changed the sociopolitical significance of the institution of *fatwā*. The practical pertinence of formal *fatwā*s diminished owing to the seizure of executive and judicial powers first by European colonial administrations and later by the nation-states that inherited the colonial legacies. During this period, however, *fatwā*s became tools for mobilizing the population in both active and passive anticolonial resistance and in the struggle for national independence. Anticolonial *fatwā*s focused on defining Islamic territory *(dār al-Islām)* and the territory of war or unbelief *(dār al-ḥarb, dār al-kufr)*, and on the related question of whether it was obligatory for Muslims to wage war against or emigrate from *dār al-ḥarb*.

The nineteenth century abounds with examples of such *fatwā*s. In 1804 ʿUthmān ibn Fūdī (Usuman Dan Fodio, d. 1817) declared *jihād* in West Africa (present-day northern Nigeria). Ibn Fūdī justified his declaration of war by arguing that the land was ruled by unbelievers, making it *dār al-ḥarb*; he added that it was obligatory for Muslims to emigrate from lands ruled by unbelievers and to participate in the war against them. A year before, the Indian scholar Shāh ʿAbd al-ʿAzīz (d. 1824), the son of the celebrated Indian scholar Shāh Walī Allāh (d. 1762), declared that India under British rule had become *dār al-ḥarb*; his *fatwā* was also justified on the grounds that India was ruled by the laws of non-Muslims. Following his lead, the Mujāhidīn movement under Sayyid Aḥmad Barelwī (d. 1831) declared most of India a land of unbelief and enjoined Muslims to emigrate to northern India and join the *jihād* against the Sikhs of the northwestern frontier. A similar logic was also employed during the 1857 mutiny, when a *fatwā* was issued by the *ʿulamā'* of Delhi justifying *jihād* against British rule. Nonetheless, designating a territory as a land of unbelief did not always lead to the radical reactions of emigration and *jihād*. The Farā'iẕī (Ar., Farā'iḍī) movement of mid-nineteenth-century Bengal, for example, considered India *dār al-kufr*; rather than declaring *jihād,* however, it resorted to the symbolic posture of suspending public rituals (such as the Friday congregational prayers) which presuppose an Islamic political order.

The unrealistic demands of the radical choices of emigration and *jihād* were soon widely recognized. For example, in 1870, the *ʿulamā'* of northern India issued *fatwā*s stating that the Muslims of India were not obliged to rebel against the British nor to emigrate from their homes. A similar tension is discernible in the Algerian anti-French rebellion led by ʿAbd al-Qādir al-Jazā'irī (d. 1883). During the period of his leadership (1832–1847), ʿAbd al-Qādir solicited several *fatwā*s from Mālikī and Ḥanafī scholars residing in Algeria and elsewhere regarding the following questions: the obligation to emigrate from the French-controlled parts of Algeria and to join the *jihād* against the French; legitimate penalties against Muslims who stay under French rule and those who refuse to take part in the *jihād* against them; and legitimate punitive measures against collaborators and against the Moroccan sultan who, under French pressure, turned against ʿAbd al-Qādir. Although all responses were sympathetic to the Algerian struggle, they differed on the criteria for designating a land as enemy territory. The variance reflected the difference between the Mālikī school, for which the status of the land followed the status of the ruler, and the Shāfiʿī and later Ḥanafī schools, for which the main criterion is the ability of individuals to practice Islam. Following the arrest of ʿAbd al-Qādir the active resistance against the French subsided, but many Algerians continued to emigrate to other Muslim countries. To appease the Muslims of Algeria and stop them from leaving the country, French authorities obtained *fatwās* from Shāfiʿī and Ḥanafī Meccan *muftīs*; these stated that Muslims under the rule of unbelievers were not obliged either to fight or to emigrate, as long as they were free to practice Islam without danger to their lives and wellbeing. [*See the biography of* ʿ*Abd al-Qādir.*]

As organized parties started to play a larger role in national politics, pamphlets and declarations often substituted for *fatwās*. In 1937, for example, the Muslim Brotherhood of Egypt published a pamphlet declaring that *jihād* for Palestine became an individual obligation for every Muslim; in 1938 similar statements were issued in Syria and Iraq. The political utility of *fatwās*, however, was not restricted to the declaration of war. On numerous occasions, *fatwās* served as instrumental modes of intervention in the political process. For example, in 1904, the *ʿulamā'* of Fez issued a *fatwā* demanding the dismissal of European (especially French) experts hired by the state. In 1907, the *ʿulamā'* of Marrakesh issued a *fatwā* deposing the sultan of Morocco for failing to defend the state against French aggression. In both cases the demands were heeded. Equally effective was an 1891 *fatwā* by the Iranian *mujtahid* Mīrzā Ḥasan Shīrāzī, who prohibited smoking as long as the British tobacco monopoly continued. In the twentieth century several other *fatwās* were issued calling on Muslims to boycott un-Islamic pursuits; for example, a 1933 *fatwā* by the *ʿulamā'* of Iraq called for boycotting Zionist products. Another famous example is the 1971 proclamation by Ayatollah Khomeini regarding the celebration of the 2,500th anniversary of monarchy in Iran. In this proclamation Khomeini called for boycotting the celebration and stated that "anyone who organizes or participates in these festivals is a traitor to Islam and the Iranian nation." In addition to his call for passive resistance and for rebellion, Khomeini used proclamations and *fatwās* to introduce and legitimize institutions such as the Council for the Islamic Revolution and the parliament of the Islamic Republic of Iran. His most-publicized *fatwā*, however, was issued on 14 February 1989 regarding the book *The Satanic Verses*. In this *fatwā* Khomeini called for the execution of author Salman Rushdie for blasphemy, apostasy, and scornful attack on Islam. The book was banned in most Muslim countries and was condemned by many religious scholars, including those of al-Azhar University in Cairo; the latter, however, added that Rushdie himself could not be condemned to death before having a trial and an opportunity to repent.

The social impact of a *fatwā* depends on the level of a self-imposed commitment by people who are able to abide by the prescriptions of the *fatwā*. This impact is also a function of the credibility and reputation of the *muftī*, the constraints for social and political action, and the responses of the authorities. Historically, *fatwās* have functioned as instruments for the regulation and reconstitution of society. Today, the institution of *fatwā* remains a viable tool through which a society can adjust itself to internal and external social, political, and economic change.

[*See also* Ijtihād; Muftī; Rushdie Affair.]

BIBLIOGRAPHY

Ahmad, Aziz. "The Role of the Ulema in Indo-Muslim History." *Studia Islamica* 31 (1970): 2–13.

Antoun, Richard. *Muslim Preacher in the Modern World: A Jordanian Case Study in Comparative Perspective*. Princeton, 1989. Close examination of the role of preachers in contemporary Muslim society.

Berkes, Niyazi. *The Development of Secularism in Turkey*. Montreal, 1964. Contains useful information on the role of the religious institution in the development of secularism.

Bulliet, Richard W. "The Shaikh al-Islām and the Evolution of Islamic Society." *Studia Islamica* 35 (1972): 53–67. Summary of the earliest uses of the term *shaykh al-Islām*, beginning with eleventh-century Khurasan.

Çağatay, Neş'et. "Ribā and Interest Concept and Banking in the Ottoman Empire." *Studia Islamica* 32 (1970): 53–68. Lists some *fatwās* and court rulings legalizing interest at low rates and the establishment of cash *waqf*.

Gibb, H. A. R., and Harold Bowen. *Islamic Society and the West*. Vol. 1, part II. London, 1950. See especially pages 70–164. Contains a detailed description of the organization of the *ʿulamā'* class in the Ottoman Empire, and on the position of Shaykh al-Islām within the religious and administrative hierarchy.

Hallaq, Wael B. "From Fatwās to Furū': Growth and Change in Islamic Substantive Law." *Islamic Law and Society*, Special Sample Issue (1993): 1–33. Makes a strong case for the responsibility of the *muftī* in the development of legal doctrine.

Heyd, Uriel. "Some Aspects of the Ottoman Fetva." *Bulletin of the School of Oriental and African Studies* 32 (1969): 35–55. Classical study of *fatwās* in the Ottoman Empire.

Inalçik, Halil. *The Ottoman Empire: The Classical Age, 1300–1600*. London, 1973. The best social history of the Ottoman Empire for the period 1300–1600, with sections on the structure of Ottoman religious and bureaucratic hierarchies.

Jennings, R. C. "Kadi, Court, and Legal Procedure in Seventeenth-Century Ottoman Kayseri." *Studia Islamica* 48 (1978): 133–172, and 50 (1979): 151–184. Contains detailed description of *fatwās* and their role in court proceedings and in the social life of an Ottoman city.

Keddie, Nikkie R., ed. *Scholars, Saints, and Sufis*. Berkeley, 1972.

Contains several useful articles on the social and political role of the *ʿulamāʾ* in various periods and regions. See, in particular, the articles by Richard L. Chambers, "The Ottoman Ulema and the Tanzimat"; Aziz Ahmad, "Activism of the Ulama in Pakistan"; Edmund Burke, III, "The Moroccan Ulama, 1860–1912"; and Hamid Algar, "The Oppositional Role of the Ulama in Twentieth-Century Iran."

Khomeini, Ruhollah al-Musavi. *Islam and Revolution: Writings and Declarations of Imam Khomeini.* Translated and annotated by Hamid Algar. Berkeley, 1981.

Lambton, Ann K. S. "The Tobacco Regie: Prelude to Revolution." *Studia Islamica* 22 (1965): 119–157, and 23 (1965): 71–90. Contains a detailed account of the 1891 *fatwā* outlawing smoking as long as the British tobacco monopoly remained.

Lambton, Ann K. S. "A Nineteenth-Century View of Jihād." *Studia Islamica* 32 (1970): 181–192. Brief exposition of conceptual developments in Shīʿī political theory and the resulting change in the Shīʿī concept of *jihād.*

Lambton, Ann K. S. *Theory and Practice in Medieval Persian Government.* London, 1980. The second and third chapters in this book, entitled "*Quis custodiet custodes:* Some Reflections on the Persian Theory of Government," are especially useful on the structure of Shīʿī religious hierarchy in Ṣafavid Iran.

Peters, Rudolph. *Islam and Colonialism: The Doctrine of Jihad in Modern History.* The Hague, 1979. Extremely useful reference work containing accounts of the major *fatwās* used for active or passive resistance in the nineteenth- and twentieth-century Sunnī world.

Rāzī, Fakhr al-Dīn al-. *Al-Maḥṣūl fī ʿIlm al-Uṣūl.* Edited by T. J. F. al-ʿAlwānī. 2d ed. Beirut, 1992. Volume 2, part 3 contains a classical theoretical discussion of *ijtihād* (pp. 7–92) and *fatwā, muftī,* and *mustaftī* (pp. 93–128).

Repp, R. C. *The Müfti of Istanbul: A Study in the Development of the Ottoman Learned Hierarchy.* London, 1986. Includes a summary and discussion of theories on the rise of the office of Shaykh al-Islām.

Walsh, J. R. "Fatwā." In *Encyclopaedia of Islam,* new ed., vol. 3, pp. 866–867. Leiden, 1960–.

Zilfi, Madeline C. *The Politics of Piety: The Ottoman Ulema in the Postclassical Age, 1600–1800.* Minneapolis, 1988.

AHMAD S. DALLAL

FÉDÉRATION NATIONALE DES MUSULMANS DE FRANCE. Founded on 30 November 1985 "to act officially for the Muslims in France and to protect them," the Fédération Nationale des Musulmans de France (FNMF) is governed by the Law on Associations of 1901. It shares its registered office in Paris with the French branch of the Muslim World League (Rābiṭat al-ʿĀlam al-Islāmī).

The federation was started by a French convert to Islam, Daniel Youssof Leclerc, who is president of Taybat (Ar., *ṭayyibāt;* "excellent things"), a group committed to a more rigorous standard for the production and sale of *ḥalāl* meat than that practiced by the Paris mosque. The mosque has traditionally been led by an Algerian imam, who alone has had the authority to control the slaughtering of animals. Taybat has contested this particular authority and, in general, the leadership of Algeria over Muslims in France.

The initial political purpose of the federation was, therefore, to free the Muslim community of the influence of Algeria. But its main object is to coordinate the actions of the approximately one hundred Muslim associations that originally comprised the FNMF, to assure their defense if necessary, and to facilitate the practice of the faith in a non-Muslim country. It seeks a friendly relationship with French society and hopes to instill a better knowledge of Islam. It wishes to implement the Islamic standard of living in every domain of life and the application of the *sharīʿah* (the divine law), although this may run counter to the laicist or secular orientation of French public life (including schools), as instituted in the relevant law of December 1905. Nevertheless, the FNMF does not demand the opening of specifically Muslim schools and universities or the practice of polygamy.

The federation's council consists of fifteen members and seven deputies (five members are chosen from old French Muslim families). All members are chosen by the associations which comprise the FNMF. Since 1985, there have been fifty ethnically distinct members of various political opinions within the council. The FNMF's first president was a Frenchman, Jacques Yacoub Roty, whose family had been converted to Islam by René Guénon. However, Roty left the federation in 1986 in order to found his own association, Vivre L'Islam en Occident (To Live Islam in the West). Daniel Youssof Leclerc was chosen president in December 1986 and remains a member of the constituent council of the Muslim World League.

It is noteworthy that the rector of the Muslim Institute of the Mosque of Paris since 1985, Shaykh Haddām Tidjānī—a member of the High State Committee that has ruled Algeria since January 1992—is a member of FNMF's administrative council. He is also a member of the Conseil Religieux de l'Islam en France (CORIF), created by the French government in 1990 to serve as the representative of French Muslims to the government and probably to break the monopoly of the Algerian leadership over French Muslims—a target that FNMF has clearly not achieved. Taybat is an active opponent to CORIF, which it considers as "collaborationist."

The present president of FNMF is a Turk, Mustafa Dogan, who is also a member of CORIF. The deputy president is Mohamed El Naceur Latreche, an Algerian who hails from the Muslim community of Strasbourg.

The federation raises its funds from its member associations, but it does not interfere with their programs or in their management. The assistance of the Muslim World League has been very important to the FNMF since its foundation.

[*See also* France.]

BIBLIOGRAPHY

Bulletin d'Information. Periodical publication of the Federation.

L'Index. Free newspaper, published monthly by Taybat.

Kepel, Gilles. *Les banlieues de l'Islam*. Paris, 1987. Empirically based study of Muslims in France and their many organizations.

Krieger-Krynicki, Annie. *Les musulmans en France*. Paris, 1985. Study of the social composition of revivalist Islam in France.

ANNIE KRIEGER-KRYNICKI

FEDERATION OF ISLAMIC ASSOCIATIONS. Formed through the efforts of first-generation American-born Muslims, mostly of Syrian and Lebanese origin, the Federation of Islamic Associations was created as a corporate body to help maintain ties between scattered Muslim communities. Abdullah Igram of Cedar Rapids, Iowa, a World War II veteran, was instrumental in bringing together Muslims from the United States and Canada. His efforts led to the incorporation of the International Muslim Society (IMS) in 1952. The goals of the IMS were to help coordinate efforts to keep the faith of Islam, to preserve Muslim culture, to expound Islamic teachings, and to propagate true information about the faith. During its third annual meeting, held in Chicago in 1954, the members adopted a new name: the Federation of Islamic Associations of Canada and the United States (FIA).

During that same year Igram made a personal request to President Dwight Eisenhower to grant Muslims in the American armed services the right to identify their religion on their name tags. This was perceived by members of the community as official recognition of their American identity. The FIA concentrated on holding annual meetings and conventions, which were attended mainly by persons of Arab background (with a few Muslims from Eastern Europe and Turkey). The organization also provided the opportunity for young people to meet potential marriage partners from within a common religious and cultural heritage. The recollections of participants in these conventions from the 1950s and 1960s are of pleasant social events in which camaraderie and informal interaction, even some forms of folk dancing, were encouraged.

The FIA has been hampered by lack of funds or trained indigenous leadership. Its assimilationist tendencies have been condemned by more conservative Muslims. In 1970, the FIA published a book that included selected readings from the Qur'ān as well as a directory of Muslims in the United States. Efforts by the FIA leadership to compile a census of American Muslims have fared no better than those of any other group attempting such a task. They also tried unsuccessfully to create a standardized curriculum of Sunday school materials to be used by the various centers. The FIA is aware of the hostile media treatment of Arabs and Muslims in the United States and has concentrated its efforts on combating such misinformation.

At the peak of its popularity, the FIA listed some fifty mosques and organizations as its members. In recent years the membership has dramatically declined owing to disagreement with the leadership over policies. The current leader, Nihad Hamid, has been accused of receiving funding from Iraq as well as Saudi Arabia. The *Muslim Star*, the official organ of the FIA, has provided extensive coverage about the "bloody" nature of the regime of Ayatollah Ruhollah Khomeini in Iran, as well as justification of the Iraqi position in the Iran-Iraq War. Its public attacks on fellow Muslim organizations, such as that launched against the Muslim World League, have left it with decreasing grassroots support. By 1994, *Muslim Star* had ceased publication. FIA members had taken Nihad Hamid to court in order to regain possession of the headquarters but the court ruled in his favor. An alternate coalition of mosques has been formed; they continue their annual conventions but have dissociated themselves from the FIA.

[*See also* Islamic Society of North America; United States of America.]

BIBLIOGRAPHY

Haddad, Yvonne Yazbeck, ed. *The Muslims of America*. New York and Oxford, 1991.

Haddad, Yvonne Yazbeck, and Adair Lummis. *Islamic Values in the United States*. New York and Oxford, 1987.

YVONNE YAZBECK HADDAD

FEMINISM. This article examines the feminism, or more precisely feminisms, Muslim women have created as independent agents to redefine their own lives as women, countering patriarchal hegemony and striving for more egalitarian gender arrangements in families, communities, and nations in the modern era. In the second half of the nineteenth century some Muslim women began to articulate an awareness of the unequal construction of gender and the domination of males over females. Elaborations of this understanding and the innovative forms of activism to which it gave rise constitute Muslim women's feminism. Women of the middle and upper classes have produced diverse feminist discourses and movements in varying communities at different historical moments. A broad definition of Muslim women's feminism includes women's awareness of constraints placed upon them because of gender, women's rejection of these disabilities, and their efforts to construct a more equitable gender system involving new or improved roles for women and more optimal relations between the sexes. Muslim feminists have insisted on the equality of women and men as citizens in the public sphere and have accepted complementarity of roles in the family sphere. Muslim women's feminisms have been articulated in the discourses of their national, secular, and religious cultures. Forms of feminist thinking have emerged in Muslim societies undergoing modernization, urban expansion, modern state formation, colonization and imperialization, national independence movements, wars and aggression, and democratization. Highly visible, independent organized feminist movements have surfaced in some countries only after national independence or the consolidation of modern nation-states permitting free expression. Muslim women have sometimes been able to sustain camouflaged forms of feminist activism under repressive regimes and hostile societal environments.

Feminist discourses whose central concern is women engage or intersect with other discourses concerned with the nation, Islam, or democracy. Muslim women's feminisms have contested various patriarchal systems, redeploying the language of the very orders they aim to unsettle. Thus during nationalist movements or at moments of liberal nation-building, some feminists tried to reconfigure patriarchal nationalist ideology into a more gender-egalitarian nationalist ideology. Feminisms in Muslim societies, whether articulated in liberal nationalist terms or socialist terms, have affirmed Islam. Male-controlled, patriarchal Islamic fundamentalist movements have not accorded ideological or activist space for women's feminism. Some Muslim feminists using *ijtihād* (individual inquiry into scriptures), however, have articulated an egalitarian Islam.

There have been three major modes of feminist expression. The first is individual writings such as poems, short stories, novels, autobiography, journalistic articles, essays, and scholarly works which express forms of gender consciousness, disseminate feminist ideas, generate debate, and consolidate women's networks. The second is "everyday activism," which includes individual innovations in daily life, creating social service associations, and pathbreaking in education, and pioneering in the modern professions. The third is organized movement activism, which is highly visible and more directly confrontational. Some Muslim women have been guided by their feminist ideas in their daily lives but have eschewed organized political activism and public identity as feminists. Others have found it crucial to declare a public feminist identity and to engage in movement feminism. Some women have combined feminist writing with forms of activism, while others have preferred to focus more exclusively on contributing to the development of feminist theory and analysis or spreading feminist awareness through literary works.

Early individual expressions of Muslim feminist consciousness and thought from the late nineteenth to mid-twentieth centuries confronted middle- and upper-class women's domestic seclusion and veiling, articulated calls for female literacy and education, and sought to absolve Islam from women's oppression. ʿĀ'ishah Taymūrīyah, an Egyptian poet and writer, and Zaynab Fawwāz, a Lebanese essayist, broke through their domestic isolation by communicating with other secluded women. The Indian Rokeya Sakhawat Hossain attacked the system of female domestic cloistering in a tale inverting gender seclusion; her countrywomen Naẓar Sajjād Ḥaydar, through short stories, novels, and articles, also confronted women's confinement. Several women produced memoirs of their lives during this period, recording the unfolding of gender consciousness and what were then bold innovations serving as inspiration to other women; they include Raden Adjeng Kartini of Java, Emilie Ruete of Zanzibar, Tāj al-Salṭanah of Iran, and Hudā Shaʿrāwī and Nabawīyah Mūsā of Egypt. Fatme Âliye of Turkey and the Egyptian Malak Ḥifnī Nāṣif, known as Bāḥithat al-Bādiyah, published feminist essays advocating new forms of education and work for women.

In the second half of the twentieth century, when upper- and middle-class women had gained fuller access to public life and integration into society, feminists wrote about gender roles and relations in both the family and society, about sexual abuse and exploitation, misogyny and patriarchy, and women's combined gender and class oppression linked with imperialist oppression. The Egyptian physician and socialist feminist Nawāl al-Saʿdāwī has written essays and articles on social, economic, sexual, and psychological issues, and as a novelist has reached out to wide audiences, treating issues in the context of everyday life. The Moroccan scholar Fatima Mernissi has published sociological and historical works, and with the Pakistani Riffat Hassan has produced works of religious interpretation. The Algerian Assia Djebar, in novels and essays, has exposed women's oppression and the obstruction of feminism under patriarchal nationalism. Women have continued to convey complex feelings about body and soul through poetry, exemplified by the works of Furūgh Farrukhzād of Iran, Hudā Naʿmānī of Lebanon, and Fawzīyah Abū Khālid of Saudi Arabia; the Lebanese authors Ghādah Sammān and Ḥanān al-Shaykh have explored sexual and social issues in short stories and novels. Continuing to record personal memoirs—and creating a new genre of prison memoirs—women such as the Egyptians Nawāl al-Saʿdāwī, Laṭīfah al-Zayyāt, and Injī Aflāṭūn have exposed the oppressive workings of family, society, and state on women. Such writers and their works have provoked debate but not consensus about feminism and women's lives.

There have been a wide range of feminist organizations and movements in Muslim countries, which have arisen under diverse state systems and societal conditions. Several trends can be discerned in twentieth-century feminist movements; these include attempts to construct modern women citizens, moves to reform family law, respecting women's bodies, and confronting issues related to women's dress and mobility.

Muslim feminists have undertaken diverse forms of collective action to help construct the modern woman citizen. In Egypt this was done by the Egyptian Feminist Union formed under the leadership of Hudā Shaʿrāwī in 1923. Following the nationalist struggle, in which women participated, the new state conferred political rights upon male citizens only. The EFU mounted a well-organized, highly visible, independent feminist movement calling for educational, professional, and political rights for women, rights to health care for all citizens, reforms in family law, and an end to state-regulated prostitution. In 1948 Durrīyah Shafīq founded the Daughter of the Nile (Bint al-Nīl) Association, which led a militant suffragist campaign and a countrywide effort for female literacy. Both organizations were shut down by the state in the mid-1950s after women had been granted the right to vote, ending three decades of independent feminist activism.

As the new state of Turkey was being consolidated, feminists tried unsuccessfully to organize a political party in 1923; the following year they were permitted to form the Turkish Women's Federation under the presidency of Latife Bekir. Women who found it difficult to organize independently of the state under Mustafa Kemal Atatürk were nonetheless granted many rights by the government. The state led the way in an unveiling campaign and in 1926 enacted the Civil Code, a totally secular code of law regulating the family. Although women thus gained certain rights in marriage and divorce, the man was officially pronounced the head of the family, and women were required to take their husband's name at marriage. The state granted women the right to vote in 1934, but shortly afterward the Turkish Women's Federation was forced to dissolve.

In Iran during the 1905–1911 Constitutionalist movement, women organized many small feminist groups and journals. These included the Patriotic Women's League founded in Tehran in 1910, the Association of Revolutionary Women established in Shiraz in 1927 by Zandukht Shīrāzī, and the Isfahan Women's Association founded by Sediqeh Dovlatabady in 1918. These scattered and often loosely organized groups supported women's education and were attentive to health issues; some favored unveiling and women's political rights. With the consolidation of the power of Reza Shah in the early 1930s, Iranian women, like Turkish women, lost the ability to conduct an independent feminist movement. The state outlawed the veil in 1936 and promulgated a liberal family law as part of a drive to modernize and to contain religious forces. Women were granted the vote in 1963. Following 1979 and the advent of the Islamic Republic in Iran, public feminist activism ended.

In the early 1960s, after Kuwait became fully independent and was granted a constitution, women were deprived of their full political rights by an electoral law. Feminists mounted public protests, burning their *ʿabā-*

*yah*s (concealing garments). Women formed a number of associations, including the Women's Social and Cultural Society and the Young Woman's Club, to campaign for political rights. Following the occupation of Kuwait by Iraq at the beginning of the 1990s, when women formed the backbone of civil resistance, feminists renewed their suffrage demands with greater urgency and enhanced claims on the nation. They have defended their cause in the media and through public protest, but they have been unable to organize a broad-based feminist movement under a united leadership in a country where the ruler and most political parties affirm the principle of women's political rights but stop short of implementing it. Kuwait and several other countries in the Arabian Peninsula are the last Muslim countries to withhold full political rights for women.

It has been within the sphere of the family that Muslim feminists have met with the least success. Although they have won certain changes in repressive family laws, in many countries reactionary regimes mobilizing a highly patriarchal form of Islam have rescinded liberal laws. Egyptian feminists, who began agitating for family law reform in the 1920s, saw only minor changes until a 1979 revision that the state revoked in 1985 but reinstated in modified form after an intensive and united feminist campaign. The most liberal family laws in Muslim countries—such as the 1926 secular Civil Code in Turkey, the 1956 Tunisian family law, and the Iranian Family Protection Acts of 1967 and 1975 (rescinded after 1979)—did not result from feminist agitation but were issued from above to serve the regimes' larger political objectives. In Algeria in 1981, feminists mobilized a broad base of women in protest against a draft family law, meeting with temporary success; three years later, however, the government promulgated the first code of family law since independence, based on a conservative reading of the *sharīʿah*. The Algerian feminist activist Marieme Helie-Lucas and the Lebanese feminist lawyer Azizah al-Hibri have exposed the divergent manifestations of patriarchy in family laws in Muslim countries through comparative examination, demonstrating the different modes of control over women.

In the past three decades feminists have also addressed issues relating to women's bodies, which include physical and psychological health, beating, sexual assault, and prostitution. In Egypt in the 1970s, the feminist physician Nawāl al-Saʿdāwī wrote about female psychological trauma relating to obsession with female virginity, the physical and psychological dangers of clitoridectomy, and the problem of incest. The Egyptian Feminist Union had earlier fought the legal regulation of prostitution by the state; al-Saʿdāwī documented its destructive effects on prostitutes themselves in a fictional rendering of a real-life tragedy. In Turkey in the 1980s a new generation of feminists organized around personal everyday problems such as wife-beating and public sexual harrassment. In 1987 women marched in Ankara and Istanbul to protest the battering of women in the home. Women held public discussions on the issue and set up groups such as the Association of Women against Discrimination in Istanbul and the Women's Solidarity Association in Ankara to organize against public sexual harassment of women, state-sanctioned attestation of virginity for female state bureaucrats, and domestic violence against women; in 1990 feminists opened the Purple Roof Women's Shelter Waqf. They also published a booklet containing testimonies of battered women. Meanwhile, in Malaysia feminists also spoke out against domestic violence; a group calling itself Sisters in Islam, formed in 1991 to explore Islamic teaching on women, published a booklet condemning wife-beating by using Qur'ānic arguments. Malaysian Muslim women joined forces with women of other religions in 1985 to found the All Women's Action Society in Kuala Lumpar and Selangor, and a publication called *Waves*, to speak out against physical and sexual abuse of women and more generally to confront "structures and systems" oppressive to women. In Pakistan feminists also confronted issues relating to violations of the female body when they created the Women's Action Forum to protest the implementation of the Hudood Ordinance of 1979; this law, imposed by a right-wing military regime, called for severe "Islamic" punishments for criminal offenses in a manner discriminatory to women—for example, blurring the distinction between adultery and rape and excluding a woman's evidence in assigning maximum punishment. Feminists mobilized in cases of poor women who acknowledged rape and then were accused and convicted of adultery, while the rapists were exonerated for lack of acceptable evidence (the testimony of four Muslim male witnesses).

Dress, in particular covering of the face or hair (both of which have been referred to as veiling), has been a perennial feminist issue. In Egypt, where turn-of-the-century feminists discovered that covering the face was not required by Islam, Muslim women decided for themselves when to unveil. In Lebanon Naẓīrah Zayn al-Dīn published a treatise in 1928 condemning face-veiling as un-Islamic. In Turkey in the 1920s and 1930s and in Iran in the 1930s, the state through different means imposed unveiling the face. In various Muslim countries and communities in recent decades Islamist movements have been encouraging reveiling (mainly of the hair rather than the face) and promoting a retreat of women back to the home, but feminists have stood their ground. In Iran women have been unable to oppose the veiling imposed by the Islamic Republic. In Saudi Arabia the state and religious authorities have continued to enforce face veiling, except for women in rural areas. Here, where women are also forbidden to drive cars, several feminists staged a driving protest in 1990 on the eve of the Gulf War, when Western troops, some of them female, came to defend their country. The state and Islamic authorities, including the *muṭawwa'* or "morals police," arrested these protestors and imposed severe punishments, including firing women from their jobs. Saudi Arabia is the only Muslim country where women are prohibited from driving cars.

Muslim women have also formed wider regional and international feminist alliances. One example of regional organizing is the Arab Feminist Union, founded by Muslims and Christians in 1945 as countries of the Arab East were achieving freedom from colonial rule and forming independent nation-states. They adopted a broad feminist agenda drawn up at a conference in Cairo the previous year. The Arab Feminist Union, which acquired a semiofficial character, has expanded over the years to include women from more than twenty countries.

A group of women formed an international network to advance the causes of women who live under Islamic laws and "laws of custom" in Muslim communities throughout the world. The International Solidarity Network of Women Living under Muslim Laws (WLML) grew out of an action committee formed in 1984, founded explicitly as a network to facilitate contacts among women and the flow of information. The information gathered by the WLML reveals the diverse and sometimes contradictory ways Islamic law is interpreted and codified in modern statutory family law codes and the varying ways in which interpretations of the *sharīʿah* have influenced customary law and everyday behavior; this information is disseminated in the network's *Dossier* and information packages. The network is also actively engaged in defending women against human-rights abuses and protecting women's endangered rights, supporting the freedoms not only of Muslim women but of all women through circulating news of abuses and encouraging women's protests to official bodies. The network also holds workshops, conferences, and exchanges.

Another way in which Muslim feminists have transcended the barriers erected by nation-states and nation-based feminisms is by articulating a Muslim liberation theology. Muslim feminists have historically located their movements within the context of Islam, applied Islamic modernist arguments to revise family law and end veiling and domestic confinement, and evoked Islam to legitimize calls for education and work rights for women, educing the examples of women in early Islam to authenticate these rights; however, the majority of women have historically been deprived of literacy and education, and most are still forbidden formal training in such religious subjects as theology and jurisprudence necessary to become religious scholars or jurists. Only recently have Muslim women begun systematic investigation using *ijtihād* to expose the flaws in patriarchal interpretations of Islam detrimental to women. The scholars Riffat Hassan of Pakistan and Fatima Mernissi of Morocco undertook an examination of the Qur'ān and *ḥadīth*, entering an interpretive arena Muslim men had monopolized. Riffat, through careful interpretation of Qur'ānic verses, demonstrates the absolute equality between women and men, exposing the androcentric readings that have created a patriarchal construction of Islam. Mernissi's historical and methodological investigation of *ḥadīth* has exposed misogynist *ḥadīth*s and demonstrated the historical operation of patriarchy. Insights of liberation theology were transmitted at an international Qur'ānic interpretation meeting held by WLML in Karachi in 1990. The Malaysian Sisters in Islam published a booklet intended for popular distribution, explaining Qur'ānic pronouncements of gender equality in Islam and stating, "Our research has shown that oppressive interpretations of the Qur'ān are influenced mostly by cultural practices and values which regard women as inferior and subordinate to men." Liberation theology struggles for a postpatriarchal Islam. Patriarchal readings of the Qur'ān and *ḥadīth* which have informed the *sharīʿah* have had the most direct and pervasive effects on women through codes of family law based on the *sharīʿah*.

Muslim feminists, whether in secular discourse accommodating Islam, or increasingly, in religious discourse, strive for nonsexist and postpatriarchal societies in which women will enjoy their rights in the family and in society and will have the opportunity to realize their full potential. Muslim women's feminisms call for implementation of democracy, respect for human rights, and a nonpatriarchal Islamic state and society.

[*See also* Family Law; Women and Islam; Women and Social Reform; Women's Action Forum; Women's Movements; *and the biographies of Mernissi, Mūsā, Nāṣif, Shafīq, and Shaʿrāwī.*]

BIBLIOGRAPHY

Arat, Yesim. "Women's Movement of the 1980s in Turkey: Radical Outcome of Liberal Kemalism?" Revised edition of an article in *Toplum ve Bilim,* Istanbul (Spring 1991).

Asian Women's Resource Centre. "Muslim Women's Voices: Some Current Trends in Malaysia." Kuala Lumpur, 1990.

Badran, Margot. *Feminists, Islam, and Nation: Gender and the Making of Modern Egypt.* Princeton, 1995.

Badran, Margot, and Miriam Cooke. *Opening the Gates: A Century of Arab Feminist Writing.* Bloomington, 1990.

Naṣīf, Malak Ḥifnī (Bāḥithat al-Bādiyah). *Al-nisāʾīyāt.* Cairo, 1909.

Hassan, Riffat. "Muslim Women and Post-Patriarchal Islam." In *After Patriarchy: Feminist Transformations of the World Religions,* edited by Paula M. Cooey, William R. Eakin, and Jay B. McDaniel, pp. 39–64. Maryknoll, N.Y., 1991.

Hibri, Azizah al-, ed. *Women and Islam.* New York, 1982.

Hibri, Azizah al-. "Muslim Laws In Muslim Countries: A Comparative Study of Certain Egyptian, Syrian, Moroccan, and Tunisian Marriage Laws." *International Review of Comparative Public Policy* 4 (1992): 227–244.

Hossain, Rokeya Sakhawat. *Sultana's Dream.* Calcutta, 1905.

Kandiyoti, Deniz. *Women, Islam and the State.* London and Philadelphia, 1990.

Lateef, Shahida. *Muslim Women in India: Political and Private Realities, 1890–1980s.* New Delhi, 1990.

Mernissi, Fatima. *Beyond the Veil: Male-Female Dynamics in Modern Muslim Society.* Bloomington, 1987.

Mernissi, Fatima. *Women and Islam: An Historical and Theological Enquiry.* Oxford, 1991.

Moghadam, Valentine, ed. *Identity Politics and Women: Cultural Reassertions and Feminisms in International Perspective.* Boulder, 1994.

Mumtaz, Khawar, and Farida Shaheed. *Women of Pakistan: One Step Forward, One Step Back?* Lahore, 1987.

Mūsā, Nabawīyah. *Al-marʾah wa-al-ʿamal.* Alexandria, 1920.

Saʿdānī, Nūrīyah al-. *Al-masīrah al-tārīkhhīyah lil-ḥuqūq al-siyāsīyah lil-marʾah al-Kuwaytīyah.* Kuwait, 1982.

Saʿdāwī, Nawāl al-. *Al-marʾah wa-al-jins.* Cairo, 1971.

Saʿdāwī, Nawāl al-. *The Hidden Face of Eve.* London, 1979.

Sanasarian, Eliz. *The Women's Rights Movement in Iran.* New York, 1982.

Sirman, Nükhet. "Feminism in Turkey: A Short History." *New Perspectives on Turkey* 3 (Fall 1989): 1–34.

Women Living under Muslim Laws. *Dossiers,* Grabels, France, 1986–.

MARGOT BADRAN

FEZ. The city of Fez in northern Morocco is the most prominent legacy of the Islamic Idrīsid Dynasty (788–974 CE). The first capital and Islamic spiritual center of Morocco, it was founded in 789 by Idrīs ibn ʿAbd Allāh, a descendant of the prophet Muḥammad, who had fled to Morocco to escape persecution by the ʿAbbāsids. However, it was his son, Idrīs II, who actually began the development of the city in 809. The city received its Arab character from waves of immigrants from Córdoba in 818 and from Kairouan (Qayrawān, in present-day Tunisia) between 824 and 826, who settled on either side of the city's river. As the city grew, important new mosques, the Qarawīyīn and Andalus, were built in 859 and 862 respectively. These mosques, especially Qarawīyīn Mosque and University, helped give Fez its stature as a prominent Islamic center of learning that rivaled al-Azhar University in Cairo. Although Fez fell to the Almoravids in 1075 and then to the Almohads in 1145, it continued to prosper. The Almoravid leader Yūsuf ibn Tāshfīn unified the city within one wall; this, along with its importance for two great dynasties, gave Fez commercial, administrative, and religious roles. The city was once more captured in 1248 and became the capital of the Marīnid dynasty. For three centuries Fez experienced its golden age as the political, religious, intellectual, and economic leader of Morocco.

The importance of Fez as a Moroccan city declined under the Saʿadians (1517–1666), who chose Marrakesh as their capital. Under the ʿAlawids Fez fared better, and its political status was rejuvenated in the period before the French Protectorate was imposed on Morocco in 1912. From the death of Sultan Sulaymān in 1824 until 1912, the prominent religious families of Fez, as descendants of the Prophet and keepers of Morocco's Islamic traditions, legitimized the actions of the rulers of Morocco. Under ʿAbd al-ʿAzīz Fez once more became the capital of Morocco; under his successor ʿAbd al-Ḥafīẓ the city was occupied by French forces in 1911.

Although Fez suffered politically under French rule and economically through French-imposed modernization, protest against the French first manifested itself along religious lines. As the traditional religious center and former capital of Morocco, Fez was the place where the religious protest of the Salafīyah movement and Moroccan nationalist agitation converged. Many important demonstrations took place there, and its leaders played an important role in the Moroccan independence movement. Indeed, the leadership of the Istiqlāl party is said to be predominantly composed of the political elite from Fez.

Currently Fez's importance as a primary national city has diminished, although it remains the capital of a province. Its role as an administrative center has been supplanted by Rabat, and Casablanca has superseded it as the nation's commercial center. Nevertheless, the leading families of Fez make up a fair portion of the Moroccan political elite, and the city itself remains an important national historical and religious center.

[*See also* ʿAlawid Dynasty; Idrīsid Dynasty; Istiqlāl; *and* Morocco.]

BIBLIOGRAPHY

Abun-Nasr, Jamil M. *A History of the Maghrib in the Islamic Period.* Cambridge and New York, 1987.

Burckhardt, Titus. *Fez, City of Islam,* translated by William Stoddart. Cambridge, 1992.

Le Tourneau, Roger. *Fez in the Age of the Marinides.* Translated by Besse Alberta Clement. Norman, Okla., 1961.

Waterbury, John. *The Commander of the Faithful.* New York, 1970. Study of the Moroccan political elite.

ELIZABETH HIEL

FIDĀ'ĪYĀN-I ISLĀM. The religio-political organization known as the Fidā'īyān-i Islām (Devotees of Islam) was created in 1945 in Tehran by Sayyid Mujtabā Navvāb Ṣafavī. Born in 1923, Navvāb claimed descent from the Prophet on his father's side, and on his mother's side, from the Ṣafavid dynasty (1501–1722).

Training to become a cleric, Navvāb attended the Shīʿī theological school of Najaf in Iraq, where he came across the anticlerical writings of Aḥmad Kasravī. Finding Kasravī's works heretical, Navvāb made an unsuccessful attempt on Kasravī's life, then in March 1946 two of Navvāb's followers murdered Kasravī. [*See the biography of Kasravi.*]

Taking advantage of the publicity surrounding Kasravī's murder, Navvāb formed an alliance with the powerful political cleric Ayatollah Abū al-Qāsim Kāshānī (Abol-Qāsem Kāshāni). This union signaled a new activist phase in the life of Fidā'īyān-i Islām. In May 1948, the Fidā'īyān held a public demonstration of several thousand people in Tehran supporting the Palestinian Arabs and denouncing the Zionists. The following February, an assassin attempted to kill Shah Muhammad Reza Pahlavi. Although not charged directly, the Fidā'īyān were suspected of collusion, and their patron, Kāshānī, was exiled abroad for his alleged involvement in the plot.

At Kāshānī's behest, the Fidā'īyān intensified their public agitation. In November 1949, the Fidā'iyān assassinated an avowed enemy, the former prime minister and the sitting minister of court, ʿAbd al-Ḥusayn Hazhīr. Martial law was declared in Tehran, and after a short trial, the convicted murderer was hanged. This execution increased public tension, particularly in the holy city of Qom. Finally, as agitation intensified, the government permitted Kāshānī's return.

The Fidā'īyān soon found themselves involved in the public debate on oil nationalization. Prime Minister Ḥusayn ʿAlī Razmārā, who was negotiating with the British for a new oil agreement, was assassinated in March 1951 by a close follower of Navvāb. Although Kāshānī was implicated in Razmārā's assassination, no action was taken against him, and the assassin spent only a few months in jail.

Less than two weeks after Razmārā's death, the dean of the School of Law at Tehran University, ʿAbd al-Ḥamīd Zanganah, was assassinated. The atmosphere of terror associated with the Fidā'īyān clearly contributed to this new act.

After the National Front government of Dr. Muḥammad Muṣaddiq (Mohammad Mossadegh) came to power, the Fidā'īyān's relationship with Kāshānī ruptured. Left without a prominent protector, Navvāb and most of the Fidā'īyān's top leadership were jailed by the government. In February 1952 the Fidā'īyān attempted to assassinate Dr. Ḥusayn Fāṭimī, a prominent National Front Majlis ("parliament") deputy. Navvāb was kept in jail, then released in early 1953.

The coup of August 1953 returned the shah to the throne and ushered in a new phase for the Fidā'īyān. At first quiescent, the Fidā'īyān attempted to assassinate Prime Minister Ḥusayn ʿAlā in November 1955 on the eve of his departure for Iraq to formally sign Iran's participation in the pro-Western Baghdad Pact. Although injured, the prime minister proceeded to Baghdad as scheduled.

The government swiftly arrested the Fidā'īyān leaders, including their former associate, Kāshānī. Most of those arrested were soon released, but Navvāb and three of his closest allies were sentenced to death and executed in January 1956. Even though the trials and executions ended the Fidā'īyān as an organization, some of their followers continued to operate clandestinely.

The Fidā'īyān's name was associated indirectly with a

group known as Ḥizb-i Milal-i Islāmī (Islamic Nations Party), which succeeded in assassinating Prime Minister Ḥasan ʿAlī Manṣūr in January 1965. Some members of this group had been members of the Fidā'īyān. After the success of the Islamic Revolution in 1979, the Fidā'īyān reemerged under the self-proclaimed leadership of the cleric Ṣādiq Khalkhālī. But because many of the Fidā'īyān goals were already enshrined in the new regime's programs, they soon disappeared from the political arena.

The actual size of the Fidā'īyān membership is in dispute. At its height, the organization probably had somewhere between thirty thousand and forty thousand members and a much larger number of sympathizers. The membership was concentrated in a few major cities, particularly Tehran, Mashhad, and Qom. The Fidā'īyān attracted young semiliterate and illiterate Muslims on the fringes of urban society. Most were youths between the ages of fifteen and twenty-five who held low-status occupations in or around the bazaar. Navvāb remained the acknowledged leader of the group, although his lieutenants, the Vāḥidī brothers, continued to play a key role in the organization.

The Fidā'īyān's strength was based on their critical alliance with the clergy and their acts of terror. They also established contacts with Muslims in other countries. Navvāb traveled to Egypt, saw leaders of the Muslim Brotherhood, and made contacts with coreligionists in Jordan, Iraq, and probably Turkey. Yet none of these were ties of long-range significance.

The Fidā'īyān's finances were secured through influential sympathizers in the bazaar merchant community and among certain clerical elements. They disseminated their messages through several publications, including newspapers, regular broadsheets, and leaflets. Their major book of ideology, *Rāhnamāh-yi ḥaqā'iq* (The Guide to Truth), published in 1950, includes their most complete statement and blueprint for a new Shīʿī Islamic order.

Highly puritanical in scope, *Rāhnamāh-yi ḥaqā'iq* pronounced the Fidā'īyān's ultimate goal to create a new order based on *sharīʿah* (Islamic law). It envisaged a state in which religion and politics were necessary parts of the same system and a society in which the divine laws and injunctions provided the moral and legal basis for all acts. In such a system parliament would not legislate; it would be merely a consultative assembly ensuring that all existing and future regulations were in accordance with Shīʿī Islamic precepts. Monarchy was not necessarily unacceptable if the monarch obeyed Islamic precepts. The clerics in the Fidā'īyān state would be entrusted with a multiplicity of functions, ranging from administering to the masses' religious needs, to serving as judges of the Islamic courts, to implementing an Islamic educational system. The clerics would ensure that ethics and morality would be observed and gender separation in the public sphere, including schools, would be strictly observed. As judges of the Islamic courts, the clerics would supervise a strict penal code that included cutting off a thief's hand and public whipping of an adulterer.

The Fidā'īyān perceived women as second-class citizens, confined to the home. They viewed the idea of women's rights as detrimental to the moral fabric of the social order and endorsed the Shīʿī concept of temporary marriage as a remedy for prostitution. The Fidā'īyān were also minimally tolerant of certain religious minorities, such as Christians, Jews, and Zoroastrians, who were given limited protected rights. The Bahā'īs had no place in the Fidā'īyān system.

The Fidā'īyān considered the accumulation of wealth a legitimate economic activity and encouraged commerce as long as Islamic antiusury norms were maintained. They combined encouragement of business with a strong sense of social welfare and general charity toward the poor.

The importance of the Fidā'īyān in Iranian and Islamic history lies in their forceful articulation of certain rigid principles of religion for the social order. However, their willingness to legitimize violence on the basis of religious dogma and their daring acts of violence made their impact far greater than their organizational strength or numbers justify.

[*See also* Iran *and the biography of Kāshāni.*]

BIBLIOGRAPHY

Enayat, Hamid. *Modern Islamic Political Thought*. Austin, 1982. Useful overview of modern movements in the Islamic world, with some attention to the Shīʿī areas.

Ferdows, Amir K. "Khomeini and Fadayan's Society and Politics." *International Journal of Middle East Studies* 15 (May 1983): 241–257. Interesting comparison of the Fidā'īyān ideology and its relevance to the Islamic Republic of Iran as envisaged by Ayatollah Khomeini.

Fidā'īyān-i Islam. *Rāhnamāh-yi ḥaqā'iq* (The Guide to Truth). Tehran, 1329/1950. The Fidā'īyān's major statement of ideology and their blueprint for a new Shīʿī-Islamic order.

Kazemi, Farhad. "The Fada'iyan-e Islam: Fanaticism, Politics, and Terror." In *From Nationalism to Revolutionary Islam*, edited by Said Amir Arjomand, pp. 158–176. London, 1984. Comprehensive overview of the Fidā'īyān's history, organization, political involvement, social base, and ideology.

Kazemi, Farhad. "State and Society in the Ideology of the Devotees of Islam." *State, Culture, and Society* 1 (Spring 1985): 118–135. Analysis of the Fidā'īyān's major book of ideology, *The Guide to Truth.*

Rahnema, Ali, and Farhad Nomani. *The Secular Miracle: Religion, Politics, and Economic Policy in Iran.* London, 1990. Interesting analysis of interactions between religion, politics, and economic policy in Shīʿī Iran with special attention to four subsystemic roots of the Islamic Republic, including the Fidā'īyān's.

Richard, Yann. "L'organisation des Feda'iyan-e Eslam, Mouvement Intégriste Musulman en Iran, 1945–1956." In *Radicalismes Islamiques,* vol. 1, *Iran, Liban, Turquie,* edited by Olivier Carré and Paul Dumont, pp. 23–82. Paris, 1985. Account of the Fidā'īyān's rise, history, ideology, and relevance to the Islamic Republic of Iran.

FARHAD KAZEMI

FILM. *See* Cinema.

FIS. *See* Islamic Salvation Front.

FITNAH. The Arabic root *f-t-n* means "burn." It is used also of melting gold or silver with fire, to try them. Hence it is both a burning and a trial, or a temptation, and by extension a seduction or a charming—an enchantment. Thus in the Qur'ān (20.40) it is said that God *tested* Moses; in surah 9.126, the faithful are *tested* by being called out to war with infidels; the Helltree Zaqqūm is a *punishment* for evildoers (37.62f.); it occurs to David that he is being *tried* by God and he begs for pardon (38.24); the faithful pray not to be made a *lure* for tyrants to oppress (10.85); the goods and children of the faithful are a *temptation* to forsake righteousness (8.28); the Muslims are ordered to fight those who fight them, if necessary even in the Holy Mosque, and to expel them, for their *persecution* is worse than killing (2.191); the *oppression* of the idolators is a worse fault than killing in the sacred month (2.217); if the hypocrites had gone out with the Muslims, they would have stirred up *sedition* (9.47); God tries every soul with good and evil as an *ordeal* (21.35); God allows Satan to cast his own verses into the revelations of the prophets as a *temptation* for those in whose hearts is sickness (22.53).

Hence *fitnah* is generally negative, but it can have positive aspects. A girl child today may be named "Fātin," or "Fitnah," in the hope that she will be not a seductress, but charming or alluring. However, some modern feminists desire to see in the name "Fitnah" for a beautiful woman evidence of a negative view toward women generally among Muslims. There is also a *ḥadīth* to the effect that the greatest *fitnah* for men is women, and the *ḥadīth* is sometimes explained by reference to the story of Adam and Eve.

In early Islam, the term is particularly used for trials and temptations to which the Muslim community is exposed. The "Great *Fitnah*" is the division that occurred from the murder of ʿUthmān, through the Battle of the Camel and the schisms that led to the formation of the Khawārij and the Shīʿīs and the seizure of power by Muʿāwiyah, founder of the Umayyad dynasty. Here *fitnah* is civil strife, war, division, and those situations that tempt Muslims to depart from the straight path of unity and right action.

The connotations of *fitnat* in Persian are fully as negative as in Arabic. The Steingass *Persian-English Dictionary* gives as possible meanings "temptation, sedition, insurrection, discord, riot, war, anarchy, trial, affliction, calamity, malignity, impiety, crime, sin, error, madness, wealth, wife, and children."

Where *fitnah* in modern political terminology has negative insinuations, *thawrah:* "revolution," may have quite positive implications, just as it might in English.

The major *ḥadīth* collections, such as Bukhārī and Muslim, have sections on *fitan,* trials of the community, represented as foretold by the Prophet and leading up to the signs that will usher in the return of Jesus, the end of the world, the resurrection, and the final judgment. The term later came to be applied to any group departure from the collectivity, as well as to religious uprisings like those of the ʿAlid family in the Hejaz in 762 CE, in which it was easy for people to be confused as to which course to follow. It was also to be applied to religious disturbances such as the riots between the Ashʿarīs and the Ḥanbalīs in Baghdad in the tenth century CE. The disorders that brought the collapse of the Umayyad caliphate in Andalusia and the rise of the factional kings in the early eleventh century were also called the *fitnah* in that part of the Muslim world.

Again, *fitnah* is generally a negative term, and the *ʿulamā'* warn against it. Ḥasan of Basra is quoted as saying that anyone who instigates *fitnah* is an innovator in religion, who according to the *ḥadīth* will go to hellfire. Here, apparently, civil strife and rebellion against the authorities are intended; Ḥasan was known to consider that the actions of tyrants were a trial to be patiently endured rather than opposed by arms.

The Arab lexicons give *fitnah* as a synonym for "error," "crime"; Satan is *al-fātin, al-fattān,* because he leads people into error, while an assayer who melts gold and silver is also *fattān*. One who is *maftūn* is afflicted with madness or demonic possession. Thus the learned shaykh Ibn Hurmuz of Medina stated as his defense, when apprehended in the ʿAlid rebellion against the ʿAbbāsids in 762 CE, that he had been carried away by a general *fitnah,* and he was forgiven. The term is also used for the inquisition in the grave by Munkar and Nakīr, and the trials of the dead in their graves.

The *kalām* treatises usually discuss *fitnah* in connection with the imamate or caliphate. When there is no clear imam, there will be *fitnah;* an imam is necessary to prevent schism in the community. There is discussion as to whether an imam should be appointed during a time of *fitnah:* not if it will make things worse, but certainly if it will help bring *fitnah* to an end, since nothing is worse than *fitnah*. Even tyranny is greatly preferable. Ibn Jamāʿah of Cairo (d. 1333) states that if a king gains power by usurpation or force in a Muslim country, the caliph should then recognize him and delegate the affairs of that place to him, to avoid *fitnah* and guarantee Muslim unity.

The appearance of a claim to be the Mahdi was seen as a clear invitation to *fitnah,* and so medieval monarchs were instructed to see it as their duty to punish condignly such claimants. The pious sultan Fīrūz Shāh of Delhi (d. 1388) proudly records that he executed a man who claimed to be the Mahdi but only imprisoned a man who claimed to be God. Ibn Khaldūn (d. 1406) regards the whole Mahdi idea as an occasion for *fitnah* and argues that it has no real basis in Islam, since all of the *ḥadīth*s it rests on are spurious. This helps explain why in modern times claimants to be the Mahdi have been ruthlessly punished. In the early 1860s, one Aḥmad al-Ṭayyib, who had been acclaimed as the Mahdi in Upper Egypt, was massacred with his followers by government troops, even though they had not made an uprising. This attitude has continued in modern times, even when it meant using armed force in the Holy Mosque at Mecca (on the basis of the Qur'ān, surah 2.191) in 1979. The very appearance of a Mahdi brings *fitnah,* and this may be reckoned one of the signs of the Hour.

In some of the *fiqh* books, selling weapons at a time of *fitnah* to a person known to be engaged in it is a reprovable practice, because it will lead to sin. If it is not known that the person is so engaged, then there is no harm in it.

A curious example of use of the term occurred in sixteenth-century Syria when a Shāfiʿī *qāḍī* accused the new Ottoman regime of provoking a *fitnah* in Islam by imposing a marriage fee, a practice unknown under the previous Mamlūk regime. He seems to have meant that it was a scandalous and innovative practice.

The quotation from the Qur'ān (2.191, 217), "*Fitnah* is worse than killing," could be used to justify putting down peasant revolts and urban unrest by often harsh methods. For example, in 1605 the heterodox shaykh Yaḥyā ibn ʿĪsā al-Karakī was judged worthy of execution by the *ʿulamā'* of Damascus, who justified this to the Ottoman authorities on the grounds that he had a following among the rural immigrants to the city of the Maydān quarter and might cause a *fitnah*.

The term could on occasion be applied to situations outside the Muslim community. The first Muslims to write about the French Revolution of 1789 identified it as a *fitnah* and clearly took a quite negative view of it.

The 1860 civil war in Lebanon and the ensuing massacre of Christians in Damascus was also characterized by contemporaries as a *fitnah*. In more recent times, the abolition of the caliphate by the Turkish Republic was widely termed *fitnah* by those who wanted the caliphate maintained or restored.

Fitnah in a social sense is thus seen almost always as highly undesirable, a temptation to the Muslims to forsake the service of God, and "worse than killing." As a term of opprobrium, it can conveniently be used to characterize the actions of opponents, as it often is in modern journalism and polemical literature. The uprising of the supporters of the Muslim Brotherhood in Hamah, Syria, decisively put down by armed government forces in 1982, was called a *fitnah* by their opponents. Attacks on Christians by Islamists in Upper Egypt are called *fitnah,* and the word is occasionally used to describe the activities of Islamists in North Africa. Anything that might polarize or divide society may be called *fitnah;* on the other hand, attempts by governments to put an end to potentially destabilizing activities by Islamic religious groups may in turn be labeled *fitnah* by adherents of those groups.

In political discourse, *fitnah* is today a value-laden term that can be used to discredit opponents. Frequently the division of the original community at the end of the period of the Rightly Guided Caliphs is evoked as a fearful and deterrent example.

BIBLIOGRAPHY

ʿAqīqī, Anṭūn Ẓāhir. *Thawrah wa Fitnah fī Lubnān.* Translated by Malcolm H. Kerr as *Lebanon in the Last Years of Feudalism, 1840–1868.* Beirut, 1959.

Berque, Jacques. *The Arabs: Their History and Future.* London, 1964.

Fīrūz Shāh Tughluq. *Futūḥāt-i Fīrūz Shāhī.* Aligarh, 1954. Partial translation in H. M. Elliot and John Dowson, *History of India, as Told by Its Own Historians: The Muhammadan Period,* vol. 2, pp. 378–379. London, 1877; reprint, New York, 1966.

Gardet, Louis. "Fitna." In *Encyclopaedia of Islam,* new ed., vol. 2, pp. 930–931. Leiden, 1960–.

Ibn Manẓūr. *Lisān al-ʿArab,* "f-t-n."

Jurjānī, ʿAlī ibn Muḥammad. *Sharḥ al-Mawāqif,* vol. 8, pp. 344f. Cairo, 1907.

Laoust, Henri. *La profession de foi d'Ibn Batta.* Damascus, 1958.

Marghinānī, Burhān al-Dīn al-*Al-Hidāyah,* vol. 4, p. 90. Beirut, n.d. Translated by Charles Hamilton as *The Hedàya, or Guide.* 2d ed. London, 1870.

Mernissi, Fatima. *Beyond the Veil: Male-Female Dynamics in Modern Muslim Society.* Rev. ed. Bloomington, 1987.

Muḥibbī, Muḥammad Amīn al-*Khulāṣat al-Athar fī Aʿyān al-Qarn al-Ḥādī ʿAshar,* vol. 4, pp. 478–480. Cairo, 1869.

Williams, John Alden. "The Expected Deliverer." Chapter 4 of *Themes of Islamic Civilization.* Berkeley, 1971.

JOHN ALDEN WILLIAMS

FOUNDATION FOR THE DISINHERITED.

See Bunyād.

FRANCE. Owing to the forty years of Muslim domination of the southern part of the country during the eighth century, France came into contact with Islam at a relatively early date. Other attempts at penetration continued into the tenth century but were not successful. Throughout the Middle Ages and in spite of the prevailing spirit of the Crusades, Muslims left their mark in several regions of France; this was especially true of the merchant class. At the beginning of the seventeenth century, a group of Spanish Muslims deported from Spain settled permanently beyond the Pyrenees.

The Muslim presence in France became significant in modern times with the colonization of North Africa beginning in 1830. Peddlers called *turcos* came from Algeria after 1850, but it was not until the turn of the century that the first Algerian and later Moroccan immigrants arrived to work on the docks of Marseilles, in the construction of the Paris Metro, and in the mines of northern France. During World War I the migration of more than 132,000 North Africans to take the place of the French as farmhands and in weapons factories was encouraged. More than 15,000 others were called to arms.

Although a great number of those Muslims were repatriated after the war, from the early twenties until the depression of the 1930s waves of laborers returned to France; World War II played a similar role in the transfer of male North Africans, as well as Senegalese, to France. Although a severe shortage of manpower encouraged immigration to France following the war, the 1960s, and especially Algerian independence in 1962, marked the beginning of a flood of Muslim workers from Algeria, Morocco, and later Tunisia. In an attempt to counter its economic problems, in July 1974 the French government interrupted this migration of the labor force. At the same time, it initiated a policy of family reunification, allowing women to join their husbands, which led to the gradual stabilization of the immigrants in their new society.

Meanwhile, the Muslim community in France began to diversify with the arrival of Turks, Africans (primarily from Senegal, Mali, Mauritania), Middle Easterners (from Egypt, Syria, Iraq, Lebanon), and Western and Central Asians (Iran, Afghanistan, Pakistan). Besides workers, increasing numbers of students, professionals, and businesspersons arrived, including many North Africans. Through this process Islam gradually became the second most important religion in France.

General Data. Attempting to quantify the Muslims in France is a delicate task. In fact, the available data only approximate their numbers, because all censuses since 1968 exclude information on religious affiliation. Therefore, only by assuming that certain categories of residents are probably Muslim can an evaluation proceed. Four groups of people are concerned:

1. Foreigners originating from Muslim or predominantly Muslim countries. For example, the 1990 census reported 614,207 Algerians, 575,652 Moroccans, 206,336 Tunisians, and 197,712 Turks.

2. Algerian nationals of Muslim faith, long misnamed *harkis* or French Muslims. Having sided with France during its war with Algeria, they opted for French citizenship and had to leave their country on its independence. According to official evaluations, this includes nearly 500,000 people, a distinct group whose uneasiness seems particularly striking. Not only do they

see themselves as exiles from their former country, but they are also perceived by Algerians in a historical perspective as traitors for their procolonialist views. Nonetheless, their assimilation into French society has not been as successful as they would have hoped. In addition to this group of Algerian nationals, we also find some Muslims of Indian origin repatriated from Indochina.

3. The "newly French," those who were able to attain citizenship by birthright or through naturalization. Their status as citizens permits them an active role in French society. Of all the Muslim groups, it will be their opinion that will count the most in the debate over Islam in France.

4. French converts to Islam, who often play the role of mediator between the Muslim community and the rest of society.

Today, it is generally accepted that the number of Muslims of French nationality is equivalent to the number of foreign-born Muslims, permitting a rough estimate of nearly four million Muslims in France. This figure represents more than 7 percent of the total population. Thus France appears to be the European country with the greatest percentage of Muslims, as well as the greatest number.

The Islam practiced in France is predominantly North African and is therefore Sunnī, even though there is an intermixing of the various cultures from the whole Islamic world. Certain local characteristics occur; one of the most marked is the concentration of Turks in Alsace, a frontier region where migrants coming from the south intersect with those coming from the east. As a result, in this region the North African Islamic practices predominant in France come into contact with those of a more Middle Eastern nature, which are predominant in Germany.

Muslim settlement has not been homogeneous throughout the French mainland. As they are for the most part blue-collar workers, they tend to settle the major industrial centers, principally around Paris but also in the south of France, in the Rhone valley, as well as in the east and north. Despite the emergence of an elite group, Muslims as a whole are still more often unskilled or semi-skilled workers and, when not affected by the rising unemployment, are usually resigned to the lowest-paying jobs. As a consequence of the family reunification policy, French Muslims are a young population—those under thirty are the vast majority. Men outnumber women, although the percentage of the latter is continually increasing. According to the last reliable source—the census of 1990 concerning foreign nationals—statistics indicate 60 percent men to 40 percent women. This varies by community, with percentages larger for women of more recently emigrated populations, such as the Turks.

However, these general statistics do not precisely represent these four million Muslims, as they do not constitute one homogeneous community. In effect, national, ethnic, and community divisions are still very pronounced. Individuals are also divided by generation, rural or urban roots, and familial or social boundaries. But it can be said overall that belonging to the Islamic community, as passed down from one generation to the next, is seldom contested. Despite occasional exceptions precipitated by the confrontation with change that result in a falling away from daily practice, Muslims continue to adhere, at least emotionally, to the religion of their parents. Their sense of belonging is marked especially in their celebration of the two ʿĪds, the celebrations during the evenings of the month of Ramaḍān, as well as the practice of circumcision and funerals.

In spite of the existence of a "silent" Islam associated with the private sphere, which is probably the most widespread form in France, the past fifteen years have witnessed a shift that reflects an ever more public expression of the adherence to the faith.

The Emergence of a Visible Islam. Previously, Islam in France was basically linked to the workplace—factories and boarding houses—and appeared to have a transient position in society. Since 1974 when the family reunification policy was put into effect, resulting in the progressive stabilization of migrant workers and their families, Islam has become noticeably more visible in housing projects, schools, and the urban setting in general. For many migrant workers, the presence of spouses and children has pushed the idea of returning to their homeland further and further into the future. But the rhythm of daily life has become laborious and filled with conflict in a host society that does not always offer the warmest of welcomes and whose norms and values often remain abstruse for this transplanted population. The affirmation of Muslim religious identity as a means of cultural identity is one possible response to this growing uneasiness.

The first of these affirmations came at the end of the 1970s with the opening of places of worship in residence halls (*sonacotra*) and on company grounds, such as in the factories of Renault Billancourt. During the autoworkers' strike of 1982–1983, Islam continued to be a factor. During the mediation process, the public became sharply aware of the religious singularity of the Muslim immigrants. At the same time, Muslims took interest in social undertakings at various levels. Many *ḥalāl* groceries and butcher shops were opened, while the number of prayer halls increased considerably. By 1989, the last official inquiry counted 1,035 of the latter (parliamentary document, National Assembly no. 1348) whereas there were only 255 in 1983 (*Journal officiel*, January 9, 1984). Women wearing the *ḥijāb* were increasingly seen with their heads covered on the city streets. From a private and individual religion, Islam moved toward being a public and collective one.

Organization. The French Muslims took full advantage of the law adopted 3 October 1981, which allowed foreigners the right of assembly. In effect, based on the strict separation of church and state practiced in France since 1905, the regulation of religious communities is a matter of individual right. No religion is officially recognized, but the government guarantees freedom of religion as long as this does not infringe on public security or the rights of another religion. The only exceptions to this principle occur in three eastern departments of France, Bas-Rhin, Haut-Rhin, and Moselle, whose local civil codes have remained unchanged since the time of the German occupation. These ordinances concerning religion are based on a nineteenth-century agreement that grants the Catholic, Lutheran, and Reformed churches and Jews the right to public worship. Muslims who have settled in that region, constituting more than 8 percent of the population, are conscious of their exclusion from this legal validation.

The Muslims of France have made good use of their right to assemble, for in 1992, ten years after the application of the 1981 law, Muslim associations numbered around 1,300 in all of France.

These associations can be classed into two types: religious and cultural. The religious ones are characterized by a specific religious aim. They generally own their own buildings, sometimes purchased with donated funds. They attempt also to compensate for the deficiencies of their host society with religious teaching. Activities of the religious associations' social networks are held around the prayer room. Mutual aid and assistance based on solidarity between "brothers of faith" are one of their main features. By encompassing ever-increasing aspects of life, as Islam claims to pertain to all facets of life, and by giving value to their connection with faith, these associations play an undeniable role in the affirmation of religious identity. At the same time, they exert a certain social control in the attempt to impose an Islamic standard.

The forcefulness of the call for the recognition of Islam differs depending on whether one belongs to the more or less radical trend. Those who rally around a slightly "adapted" Islam integrate themselves without major difficulties into the secularity of French society and contrast sharply with others taking up a more militant viewpoint of a radical and pure Islam. The positions of these latter associations can vary greatly, ranging from the pietism of Foi et Pratique (Jamāʿat al-Tablīgh) to the political movements inspired by the ideology of the Muslim Brotherhood and Ṣūfī groups of North Africans, black Africans, and Turks.

Besides the purely religious-oriented associations, there are others for whom religion is not the central theme. These social clubs, often national in scope and always relating to the culture of the homeland, display a less ostentatious adherence to their faith. In much the same way that these traditional cultural associations have emerged, the new generation that is native to France is forming their own associations, such as France Plus, Génération Égalité, and Génération Beur. The predominant aim of these young people, whose secular physical appearance seemingly contradicts their affiliation with Islam, is sure footing on the sociopolitical field, where they have taken up the cry against a country that still considers them second-class citizens.

Structure. Faced with so many trends and organizations, attempts at coordination and federation have occurred on a national level. The Paris Mosque, often a focus of the discussions on Islam in France, has initiated some of those debates. The statutes of this prestigious institution, which was inaugurated in 1926 during the French occupation of Algeria to honor Muslims who fought on the side of France, have been widely discussed. In fact, despite its attachment to the French Ministry of the Interior, the Algerian government continues to exert control on the activities of the Paris Mosque. This foreign interference is contested by most of the other French organizations. Its most recent director, nominated in April 1992, was the first French citizen to hold such a post. This fact, among others, has helped relieve the enormous tension that existed in the past few years between the Paris Mosque and the FNMF (National Federation of the Muslims of France), which were competing for sole representation of the

Muslim community. The current cross-dialogue seems to be leading to negotiations between the Paris Mosque and other Islamic associations. However, the struggle to be the dominating power continues, focusing on three major groups: the Paris Mosque, the FNMF, and the UIOF (Union of Islamic Organizations of France). The second comprises many associations in eastern France that stem from the UIF (Islamic Union of France), which in turn unifies the associations close to the Turkish Necmettin Erbakan's Millî Görüş. The third has seen major expansion since the opening of its theological institute in Nièvre. The UIOF in itself controversial for having accepted funding from Saudi Arabia. Meanwhile, the repatriated Muslims have also begun to organize.

The visibility of Islam and the proliferation of organizations has placed the second most important religion in France in the center of the discussion on immigration. The French authorities have been alarmed by foreign interference in the affairs of French Islam. Certain countries have intervened in the recruitment of imams, for example. Algeria, in the search for an imam, is ideologically close to the Paris Mosque. Other countries, such as Morocco and Turkey, intervene through diplomatic delegations that counsel those associations unified under the "official" Islam. Still others, such as Saudi Arabia, Libya, and Iran, play a less-defined role through contacts with the major French organizations mentioned above, as well as the AEIF (Islamic Students Association).

Moreover, certain problems related to the structure of Muslim daily life seem difficult to resolve. A few of the numerous examples: the selection of the official to assure the proper slaughter of meat by one of the above organizations who must also obtain the approval of the French government in order to work in the slaughterhouse; the coordination of the dates of the beginning and end of the month of Ramaḍān; the creation of a "Muslim section" in the cemeteries where the orientation toward Mecca is respected; and the inadequate numbers of Muslim leaders to offer spiritual guidance in hospitals, prisons, and the armed forces. The idea of private Muslim schools is regularly debated. Lengthy negotiations on the founding of an official Muslim Institute of Theology, which was to have produced the religious leaders of France, never materialized. In January 1992, the UOIF inaugurated its own school of theology that was not, however, supported by all Muslim associations. For that reason, the FNMF and the Paris Mosque each created its own institute at the end of 1993.

In the 1990s a "*ḥalāl* businesses" sector has emerged parallel to the mainstream economy, establishing itself in the food, clothing, and cultural industries, for example the press, although this is less developed than in some neighboring countries. Also popular are religious objects and travel agencies that offer pilgrimages to Mecca and voyages to home countries. These businesses also comprise their own import-export networks covering several European countries.

It is clear that there are indications of an established and stable Islamic community. However, despite its presence, Islam still remains an intangible concept to many. It is this difficulty with definition and the lack of an official interlocutor that led the Minister of the Interior to create the Council for the Reflection on Islam in France (CORIF) on 6 November 1989. This advisory council is composed of fifteen members who represent themselves rather than an association and are charged to lead the study of the problems concerning the Muslim community and to attempt to organize the representation of Muslims in France. However, the legitimacy of the CORIF is sometimes contested, as it is not accepted unanimously by all the associations in France. But the French government has the habit of consulting such advisory boards, as it also created the High Council on Integration and the National Council on Immigrant Populations.

Christian churches have also favored closer relations between Christians and Muslims. France was the first European country where an Office for Relations with Islam was created by the Catholic church in 1973 and where a Churches-Islam Commission was formed a few years later by the Protestant churches.

In general, the authorities would prefer to have better control over this dynamic Islamic community but are unsure of how to undertake the task. Local governments are trying to stop the expansionist wave of a religion frightening to them by refusing construction authorizations. Certain incidents occurring within French society, such as the terrorist attacks in Paris in 1986, the "headscarf affair"—a debate over the permissibility of religious clothing in public schools—in the autumn of 1989, and the provocative book by Jean-Claude Barreau, *De l'islam en général et de la laïcité en particulier* in 1991, compounded by international political affairs, have served to harden public opinion against this community.

It is important to note that Islam continues to be linked with the colonial past in the minds of the French and the Muslims, which exacerbates the passions of both parties. This vibrant second religion in France is constantly reviving the debate on secularity. This debate could lead to the challenge of the principle of secularity in the French government itself.

[*See also* Avrupa Millî Görüş Teşkilati; Conseil Nationale des Français Musulmans; Fédération Nationale des Musulmans de France; Groupement Islamique en France; *and* Union des Organisations Islamiques de France.]

BIBLIOGRAPHY

The Muslims of France have inspired a prolific literature that varies in quality. Nevertheless, studies on Islam as a religion are still rare. Rather, researchers have been interested in Islam as a sociological phenomenon. The works listed below discuss the topic from diverse perspectives.

Boyer, Alain. *L'institut musulman de la mosquée de Paris*. Paris, 1992. Historical overview of the Paris mosque.

Cahiers d'Études sur la Méditerranée Orientale et le Monde Turco-Iranien 13 (1992). Special issue: "L'immigration turque en France et en Allemagne." The first collection of essays on Turkish immigration in France.

Etienne, Bruno. *La France et l'Islam*. Paris, 1989. Original and personal reflection on Islam in France.

Etienne, Bruno, ed. *L'Islam en France*. Paris, 1991. Probably the best collection of essays from varied viewpoints.

Kepel, Gilles. *Les banlieues de l'Islam*. Paris, 1987. The best study to date of the emergence of Islam in France.

Krieger-Krynicki, Annie. *Les musulmans en France*. Paris, 1985. The first book on the subject.

Lacoste-Dujardin, Camille. *Yasmina et les autres de Nanterre et d'ailleurs*. Paris, 1992. Interesting study of the daughters of Muslim immigrants from an anthropological perspective.

Projet 231 (1992). Special issue: "Musulmans en terre d'Europe." The most recent collection of essays on the subject.

Roux, Michel. *Les harkis, ou, Les oubliés de l'histoire*. Paris, 1991. Interesting study of Algerian nationals who became French citizens.

Wihtol de Wenden, Catherine. *Citoyenneté, nationalité et immigration*. Paris, 1987. Overview presenting a clear discussion of citizenship and secularity from a distinctly French viewpoint.

NADINE B. WEIBEL

Translated from French by Kirstin Calamoneri

FRONT ISLAMIQUE DU SALUT. *See* Islamic Salvation Front.

FULĀNĪ DYNASTY. *See* Sokoto Caliphate.

FUNDAMENTALISM. The activist affirmation of a particular faith that defines that faith in an absolutist and literalist manner is termed fundamentalism. It involves the effort to purify or reform the beliefs and practices of adherents in accord with the self-defined fundamentals of the faith. Fundamentalist interpretation entails a self-conscious effort to avoid compromise, adaptation, or critical reinterpretation of the basic texts and sources of belief. Fundamentalism is a distinctive way of defining and implementing a particular worldview, and fundamentalisms are most frequently presented as styles of religious experience within broader religious traditions.

Originally, fundamentalism was the name applied to a specific Christian experience that emerged as a response to the development of Christian "modernism" in the nineteenth century. While modernism elicited reaction in many areas, it was most vehement in the United States. Between 1909 and 1915 a group of American theologians wrote and published a series of booklets called *The Fundamentals: A Testimony to the Truth*, in which they defined what they believed to be the absolutely fundamental doctrines of Christianity. The core of these doctrines was the literal inerrancy of the Bible in all its statements and affirmations. During the debates of the 1920s, the supporters of this position came to be called Fundamentalists.

For many years the term "fundamentalism" was applied almost exclusively to this particular Christian tradition. By the 1970s, as scholars and the general public became increasingly aware of the resurgence of religion in many different societies, the term began to be applied to movements of religious revival in a wide variety of contexts. People spoke of Hindu and Jewish fundamentalism and, in the context of the ideological debates of the 1990s, it was even possible for a major scholar such as Ernest Gellner to speak of "Enlightenment Secular Fundamentalism" when describing the position that both rejected relativism and denied the possibility of revelation (*Postmodernism, Reason and Religion*, London, 1992). When applied to non-Christians, the term most denoted individuals and movements in the Islamic resurgence of the final quarter of the twentieth century. By the 1990s the phrase "Muslim fundamentalism" (or "Islamic fundamentalism") was widely used in both scholarly and journalistic literature.

The application of the term "fundamentalism" to Muslims is controversial. Much of the debate starts from the pejorative implications of the term, even when used to describe Christians. It is said by some that the term has connotations of ignorance and backwardness and thus is insulting to movements of legitimate Islamic revival. Others have argued that there is no exactly cognate term in Arabic or other major languages of Muslims, and that this indicates that there is no cognate phenomenon in Muslim societies to which the term might apply.

Despite this, there is general recognition that activist movements of Muslim revival are increasingly important and reference must be made to them. Among the many terms used for this purpose are Islamism, integrism, neo-normative Islam, neo-traditional Islam, Islamic revivalism, and Islamic nativism. However, "fundamentalism" remains the most commonly utilized identification of the various revivalist impulses among Muslims. More technically accurate terms and neologisms have not gained wide acceptance.

The description and analysis of Islamic fundamentalism in the modern era gives rise to many debates. Among the most important of these is whether Islamic fundamentalism is a distinctively modern phenomenon. Such scholars as Fazlur Rahman, R. Hrair Dekmejian, and John O. Voll argue that throughout Islamic history it is possible to see activist movements advocating a return to the pristine fundamentals of the faith. From this perspective, the Ḥanbalī tradition, especially as defined by Ibn Taymīyah in the fourteenth century, and reformers in South Asia such as Aḥmad Sirhindī (d. 1625), and possibly even early Islamic radicals like the Khārijī sect, represent premodern expressions of a fundamentalist style of Islamic affirmation. In this view, the fundamentalist movements of the eighteenth century in many parts of the Islamic world, most notably the Wahhābī movement in the Arabian Peninsula and *jihād* efforts organized by Ṣūfī *ṭarīqahs* in Southeast Asia, West Africa, and elsewhere provide an important foundation for Islamic fundamentalism in the modern era.

In contrast, the scholars Martin Marty and R. Scott Appleby (who direct the Fundamentalism Project of the American Academy of Arts and Sciences), as well as Bruce Lawrence, argue that fundamentalisms are distinctively the products of the modern era, even though they may have some historical antecedents. In this view, the conditions of modernity are unique, and fundamentalisms are distinctive responses to the religious challenges of modernity. The major examples of Islamic fundamentalist movements are, from this perspective, not the traditionalist movements or nativist revolts of the nineteenth century nor the puritanical holy warriors of premodern times. They are those movements—for example, the Muslim Brotherhood in Egypt, that developed in the twentieth century and became most visible in the Islamic resurgence of the last quarter of that century.

Among Muslims there is also a broad spectrum both in the use of the term "fundamentalism" and in evaluation of the phenomenon. In the nineteenth century most Muslims were aware of the power of Western societies and the relative weakness of Muslim communities. One of the major themes of Muslim history in the modern era is the interaction of Muslims with the West and the efforts to revive and/or reform the world of Islam. The first modern response was to adapt to the new world conditions and utilize Western models in reforming Muslim societies. By the second half of the twentieth century, it became clear that the results of these reform programs were not satisfactory, and new, more revolutionary efforts were undertaken. Among these efforts are the major Islamic fundamentalist movements, which adopt positions rejecting the simple copying of Western methods and affirming the comprehensive and effective nature of the Islamic message.

In the 1970s most Muslim analysts rejected the term "fundamentalism" as an identifying label for the movements of Islamic affirmation. By the 1990s, however, Muslim critics of fundamentalism began to use the term in political and scholarly debates, and some supporters also accepted the term, recognizing its wide use and visibility. Writers in Arabic by the 1980s began to use the term *uṣulīyah,* an Arabic neologism that is a direct translation of "fundamentalism" based on *uṣūl,* the Arabic word for "fundamentals." In this way, "fundamentalism" became a part of the vocabulary of the Islamic resurgence itself as well as of the study of that resurgence.

[*See also* Muslim Brotherhood; Revival and Renewal; Salafīyah; Shīʿī Islam, *article on* Modern Shīʿī Thought; Sunnī Islam, *article on* Modern Sunnī Thought; Wahhābīyah; *and the biographies of Ibn Taymīyah, Rahman, and Sirhindī.*]

BIBLIOGRAPHY

Akhtar, Karm B., and Ahmad H. Sakr. *Islamic Fundamentalism.* Cedar Rapids, Iowa, 1982. Analysis by two American Muslims showing that, in contrast to Christian fundamentalism, Muslim fundamentalism is beneficial to humanity.

Choueiri, Youssef M. *Islamic Fundamentalism.* Boston, 1990. Historical account by a Lebanese scholar who presents Islamic fundamentalism as a contemporary right-wing radicalism working to establish a totalitarian state.

Dekmejian, R. Hrair. *Islam in Revolution: Fundamentalism in the Arab World.* Syracuse, N.Y., 1985. Systematic analysis of fundamentalist movements that notes continuities with premodern movements.

Esposito, John L. *The Islamic Threat: Myth or Reality?* New York, 1992. Clear delineation of the political issues involved in Western perceptions of Islamic fundamentalism.

Lawrence, Bruce B. *Defenders of God: The Fundamentalist Revolt against the Modern Age.* New York, 1989. Analysis of fundamentalisms in many different religious traditions, viewing them as distinctively modern phenomena.

Marty, Martin E., and R. Scott Appleby, eds. *Fundamentalisms Observed.* Chicago, 1991. The first volume of studies from the AAAS Fundamentalism Project, which includes discussions of many different fundamentalisms as well as comparative, methodological essays by Marty and Appleby.

Marty, Martin E., and R. Scott Appleby. *The Glory and the Power: The Fundamentalist Challenge to the Modern World.* Boston, 1992. Companion volume to Public Broadcasting System documentaries on fundamentalisms, with an important presentation of fundamentalism in Egypt and clear theoretical discussions of fundamentalisms as modern phenomena.

Mohaddessin, Mohammad. *Islamic Fundamentalism: The New Global Threat.* Washington, D.C., 1993. Forceful attack on contemporary Islamic fundamentalist movements by a leader in the Iranian opposition movement in exile.

Nasr, Seyyed Hossein. *Traditional Islam in the Modern World.* London and New York, 1987. Sympathetic presentation of traditional Islam by an influential Iranian scholar, distinguishing among modernist, traditional, and fundamentalist forms of Islam.

Rahman, Fazlur. "Revival and Reform in Islam." In *The Cambridge History of Islam,* edited by P. M. Holt et al., vol. 2, pp. 632–656. Cambridge, 1970. Important analysis of the historical tradition of revivalism in Islam by an influential Islamic modernist scholar.

Voll, John Obert. *Islam, Continuity, and Change in the Modern World.* Boulder, 1982. 2d ed. Syracuse, N.Y., 1994. Broad survey of Islamic movements in the modern world that defines fundamentalism in terms of continuity and as a style of Islamic experience.

JOHN O. VOLL

FUNERARY RITES. [*To articulate religious values and traditions reflected in funerary rites in modern Islamic societies, this entry comprises two articles:* Legal Foundations *and* Modern Practice.]

Legal Foundations

The Qur'ānic kerygma is grounded in the fact of human mortality, and death is referred to euphemistically as "the certainty" *(al-yaqīn).* Natural death is part of the order of things, while unnatural death evokes particular responses. Suicide is a terrible sin: "One who kills himself by means of something will be tormented with it at the resurrection" (Ṣaḥīḥ Muslim, *Kitāb al-īmān*). Martyrdom and its equivalents (such as death in childbirth, from the plague, by burning, falling from a building, at sea, or in a foreign land, can call for funeral rituals different from those given to those dead by natural causes (*Kanz al-ʿummāl,* 4.415, *fī al-shahādah al-ḥukmīyah*).

The treatment of the dead is a major subject of legal thought, and every legal work has an extensive chapter on funerary rituals, located in the section on prayer in a subsection on the funerary prayer. Islamic legists have three concerns in their work on funerary rites: to present the death as instructive of the fate that awaits all, to treat the dead in an appropriate manner, and to suppress what are perceived as non-Islamic customs that obscure the message of death.

The dying are enjoined to be aware of their death, to repent, and if possible to perform ritual ablutions. Making a will determining the disposition of up to one-third of one's property is encouraged. It is desirable to repeat the *shahādah* to the dying one, and for him or her to repeat it without being prompted. The responsibilities of preparing the body for funerary washing, of performing the washing, and of leading the funerary prayer devolve upon the members of the family roughly according to age, with males preferred over females. The responsible party *(walī)* undertakes to close the eyes, secure the jaw, and flex the joints to insure mobility for washing. Washing is then performed, ideally while the deceased remains covered: the washing is repeated at least three times, during which all filth is removed. It is advised to seal the body's orifices with cotton. The body is then enshrouded with clean, undyed cloth, covering at least the torso of a man and the whole of a woman's body. Use of perfumed unguents is commended as part of the shrouding process.

There are two cases in which the status of the Muslim at death interferes with the normal funerary practices: when the person died in *iḥrām* (ritual purity) status during the pilgrimage, or when the person is martyred in the course of *jihād.* In the former case the rules of *iḥrām* apply, and a man's shroud man must have no sewn seams; a woman's face may not be covered. In the case of martyrdom or its equivalents, there is no cleansing of the body, and it is buried as it fell.

The funeral prayer must be said by at least one male, if one is available; in default of men, women may perform this act. The body is oriented in the mosque, as throughout the washing and burial, facing Mecca; that is, at least the axis of the body is aligned with the *qiblah,* feet foremost, and ideally the body is on its right side facing the *qiblah.* The imam leads the prayer while standing by the head of a man or by the torso of a woman.

Burial itself is in a grave deep enough to conceal odor and prevent abuse of the body by animals. Within the grave a niche is dug on the *qiblah* side of grave, or else a smaller trench is dug in the floor of the grave. Into this the body is placed without a coffin, lying on its right side, facing the *qiblah.* The cheek is bared and placed on a stone. The niche or trench is then sealed with bricks or stones, and earth is replaced in the grave and mounded slightly above ground level. These burial stipulations reflect the belief that the individual is questioned by two angels at death, and those who answer unsatisfactorily are chastised by the pressure of earth upon their bodies until the last judgment.

Religious reformers from the Prophet's time onward have sought to eliminate "innovations" in the form of intrusions of local custom on funerary practices. Particular points of friction have included the lamentations of women at the burial, inclusion of food or bedding with the burial, the visiting of graves, and the erection of elaborate structures over graves. The Wahhābīs of Arabia outraged many Muslims at the time of their conquest of the peninsula in 1804–1806 and again in 1924, when they destroyed the shrines of notable Muslims throughout Arabia.

[*See also* Rites of Passage.]

BIBLIOGRAPHY

Granqvist, Hilma. *Muslim Death and Burial: Arab Customs and Traditions Studied in a Village in Jordan.* Helsinki, 1965.

Muttaqī, ʿAlī ibn ʿAbd al-Malik al-. *Kanz al-ʿummāl fī sunan al-aqwāl wa-al-afʿāl.* 5th ed. Edited by Bakrī Ḥayyānī and Ṣafwat al-Saqqā. Beirut, 1985.

O'Shaughnessy, Thomas. *Muhammad's Thoughts on Death: A Thematic Study of the Qur'anic Data.* Leiden, 1969. Despite the unfortunate title and the assumptions behind it, this is a sensitive study of the Qur'ānic discourse on death that informs later Muslim speculation on the subject.

A. Kevin Reinhart

Modern Practice

The Qur'ān contains much about human death and its religio-moral meanings but nothing about funeral rites. There is much information in the *ḥadīth,* but precise regulation must be sought in the books of *fiqh.* Significant variations—mostly folk customs—occur regionally, but modern reformist influences have produced a widespread preference for canonical funerary rites. Muslims have widely shared customs concerning proper Islamic attitudes, procedures, and rites connected with anticipating death, preparing the body for burial, and committing it to the grave.

Muslims believe that death should be contemplated throughout life and viewed not as its conclusion but as the most critical stage in the progress of the soul. At the onset of death, a Qur'ānic surah, preferably *Yā Sīn* (surah 36), should be recited. Relatives and companions should be present to pray for the dying person and provide solace. The first Shahādah (creed) should be recited in the dying one's ear in the hope that he or she will remember it and other fundamentals of Islam when interrogated in the grave by the angels Munkar and Nakīr.

Muslims are required to bury their dead as soon as possible, ideally before nightfall on the day of death. Notice of death should be prompt. When the body has become cool, its eyes and mouth are closed, its limbs straightened, and the body covered by a sheet. If possible, the dying one should lie on the right side, facing Mecca. A close relative of the same sex, a spouse, or a professional washer of the dead gives the body a complete washing in a ritually regulated way, usually three times, while preserving the utmost modesty and decorum. Cloth is placed in the orifices and scent is applied to the limbs, extremities, and body cavities. [*See* Purification.]

There are variations, but simplicity is preferred in the final winding of the corpse. This normally requires three pieces of cloth for males and five for females, with each sex completely enclosed by the final, tightly tied covering. Although a simple coffin may be used, it is not required. A Muslim martyr, however, is promptly buried in the clothes worn at death, without washing or further ceremony beyond the funeral *ṣalāt* and burial.

The funeral service *(ṣalāt al-janāzah)* may be held in any clean, dignified place indoors or outside, but normally not in a mosque. The brief, four-part service is performed with the congregation standing throughout.

The body is then committed to the grave, which should be deep enough to be safe from animals and sufficiently filled in to prevent unpleasant odors from escaping. It is preferred that the body be laid on its right side, facing Mecca, in a niche *(laḥd)* hollowed out of the grave wall. The head rests on a support and the grave clothes are loosened. The person who places the body in its final position should pronounce the Shahādah in the deceased's ear. Then the grave is filled in, with each member of the party casting some soil into it. Someone pronounces a final benediction containing a summary of Islam's key beliefs. Shīʿīs also list the twelve holy imams.

A simple headstone may mark the grave, but anything more elaborate is to be avoided. Loud lamentation, particularly by paid mourners, is forbidden and thought to increase the deceased's suffering in the grave during the interrogation. Visiting the grave and offering prayers for the deceased are meritorious acts, but mourning should be limited to three days (four months and ten days for a widow), according to *fiqh*. However, in many Muslim societies (for example, Malaysia) mourning is observed also on the third, seventh, fourteenth, fortieth, and hundredth days after death. Qur'ānic recitation is a major part of such observances. [*See* Qur'ānic Recitation.]

In addition to the basic core of Islamic funerary practices summarized here there are many regional and folk practices. Among these are cow sacrifice (southern Philippines); feasts (various places); placing food offerings under the bed of the deceased daily during the first forty days after death (Java); including grave goods like rosaries of unbaked Karbala clay and seals inscribed with the names of Muḥammad, Fāṭimah, ʿAlī, Ḥasan, and Ḥusayn (Shīʿīs); wrapping the body with a cloth inscribed with Qur'ānic quotations (traditional Iran); depositing an arrangement of pebbles over the grave (Sudan); placing betel-nut scissors between the stomach and chest of the newly deceased in order to prevent demons and ghosts from stepping on the body (Malaysia); high-pitched wailing by women mourners (Egyptian bedouin); close relatives walking under the litter three times before it is borne away to the cemetery (Java); baking special pastry as a sacrifice for the dead (Lebanon); and having an open casket viewing of the corpse's cosmetically enhanced face (United States).

Muslims today as always are deeply concerned about conducting their lives in obedience to God, knowing that the present life is merely a stage on the way to the afterlife. In Western countries too Muslims are taking pains to ensure that their funerary duties and customs are properly preserved. One finds mortuaries in mosques, which have become (for example, in America) the principal places for the funeral service—a distinct departure from traditional practice. Muslim communities in the West are also acquiring tracts for cemeteries, strong evidence of a successful establishment of the *ummah* in new lands.

[*See also* Rites of Passage.]

BIBLIOGRAPHY

Algar, Hamid. "Burial: In Islam." In *Encyclopaedia Iranica*, vol. 4, pp. 563–565. London and New York, 1987–. With special reference to Shiism.

Ali, Maulana Muhammad. *A Manual of Hadith*. New York, 1988 (original publication date unknown). Contains Arabic text with facing English translations. See chapter 15, "Burial Service."

Bowen, John R. "Death and the History of Islam in Highland Aceh." *Indonesia* 38 (October 1984): 21–38. Highly perceptive, field-based treatment of traditional Gayo death rites and the challenge of modern *fiqh*-based reformism, which the author argues has undermined the "life-giving" benefits of traditional customs in favor of seeing death as a passage to final judgment.

Donaldson, Bess Allen. *The Wild Rue: A Study of Muhammadan Magic and Folklore in Iran*. London, 1938. Contains absorbing detail, for instance, on the terror and pain believed to be experienced by the deceased in the grave. See chapter 7, "Death, Burial, and Resurrection."

Jazīrī, ʿAbd al-Raḥmān al-. *Al-Fiqh ʿalā al-madhāhib al-arbaʿah* (Islamic Jurisprudence According to the Four [Sunnī] Schools). Cairo, 1984. Funeral rites are treated on pages 386–425, with clear expositions of the variations among the schools of law.

Khaṭīb al-Tibrīzī, Muḥammad al-. *Mishkāt al-Maṣābīḥ*. 4 vols. Translated by James Robson. Lahore, 1964–1966. Extensive collection of *ḥadīths*, from the widely used medieval anthology, *Maṣābīḥ al-sunnah*, compiled by al-Baghawī and further arranged by al-Khaṭīb al-Tibrīzī. Highly recommended. See Book 5, "Funerals" (vol. 1, pp. 320–370).

Khomeini, Ruhollah al-Musavi. *A Clarification of Questions*. Translated by J. Borujerdi. Boulder, 1984. Detailed guidance on funerary matters from a Twelver Shīʿī perspective (see pp. 70–89).

Koentjaraningrat. *Javanese Culture*. Singapore and New York, 1989. Anthropological study, with mortuary rites treated on pages 361–365 and *passim*.

Kutty, Ahmad. *Islamic Funeral Rites and Practices*. Toronto, 1991. Simplified yet comprehensive guidance for Muslims in North America.

Lutfiyya, Abdulla M. *Baytīn, a Jordanian Village: A Study of Social Institutions and Social Change in a Folk Community*. The Hague, 1966. Death and burial are treated on pages 62–67.

Massé, Henri. *Persian Beliefs and Customs* (1938). New Haven, 1954. Absorbing travelers' accounts of traditional funeral customs (see pp. 80–107).

Mohtar bin Md. Dom, Haji. *Traditions and Taboos*. Kuala Lumpur, 1979. Covers Malaysian customs. See chapter 6, "Funerals."

Nadel, S. F. *Nupe Religion: Traditional Beliefs and the Influence of Islam in a West African Chiefdom* (1954). New York, 1970. Compares and contrasts traditional African and Islamic beliefs and practices in a time of change.

Rauf, M. A. *Islam: Creed and Worship*. Washington, D.C., 1974.

Clear, detailed, learned description of funeral prayers, the washing of the corpse, and burial, with recommended prayers in romanized Arabic and English translation.

Smith, Jane I., and Yvonne Yazbeck Haddad. *The Islamic Understanding of Death and Resurrection*. Albany, N.Y., 1981. Highly sophisticated survey of traditional and contemporary ideas concerning death and the afterlife, based on classical sources as well as interviews with leading Muslim scholars of today.

Waṣfī, ʿĀṭif Amīn. *An Islamic-Lebanese Community in U.S.A.: A Study in Cultural Anthropology*. Beirut, 1971. Funerals are discussed on pages 82–85.

FREDERICK MATHEWSON DENNY

FUNJ SULTANATE. In about 1500, after several turbulent centuries of transition in Nubia, a new Islamic government reunited much of the northern Nile-valley Sudan in the area bounded by Egypt, Ethiopia, the Red Sea, Darfur, and the vast swamps of the White Nile. Within this precapitalist agrarian polity, an ethnically heterogeneous class of subjects, through an ingeniously structured system of payments in labor and in kind, supported a hereditary ruling elite known as the Funj. The Funj monarch ruled from an elaborate central court through a hierarchy of subordinate governors over the eight central provinces and tributary princedoms such as Fāzūghlī and Taqalī, and beneath these, the numerous lesser lords of districts and tribes. The Funj government, though Islamic by faith and (for administrative purposes) Arabic by speech, also drew heavily upon older Sudanic traditions of statecraft; notably, the geographical and historical coherence of the Funj elite depended on the institution of matrilineal kinship inherited from the states of medieval Christian Nubia.

During the latter half of the seventeenth century, a series of strong sultans brought the originally mobile royal court to rest on the Blue Nile at Sinnār, henceforth the eponymous capital of the realm. They also opened the country to unprecedented commercial relations with neighboring lands via royally sponsored caravans; by 1700 Sinnār had become a large and cosmopolitan city. Exposure to imported commercial capitalist principles from the Islamic heartlands stimulated the appearance of an indigenous middle class within the Funj kingdom during the eighteenth century; about twenty new towns arose, and the money economy interposed itself into many social and political relationships. Meanwhile, increasing contact with the cultural usages of the Islamic heartlands also challenged the sultanate's corporate, communal vision of Islam, according to which all loyal subjects of the king were Muslims by definition, despite folkways that were often heterodox. During the eighteenth century, middle-class religious sophisticates imported standard legal handbooks from the Islamic heartlands. They wielded the principles found therein as a weapon of social criticism against the tolerant Funj version of a medieval synthesis that had accommodated universal faith to particularistic culture. Henceforth, communal loyalty to the Muslim king was no longer a substitute for conformity to the stipulations of religious law.

Middle-class partisans of the intrusive fundamentalist Islamic culture began to identify themselves as "Arabs" and undertook to seize power. The old matrilineal dynasty was overthrown in 1719, and in 1762 a clique of middle-class warlords known as the Hamaj imposed one of their own as ruling *wazīr* (vizier). Yet no new order was achieved; rather, the collapse of Funj kinship discipline precipitated civil war at all levels of government. In 1820–1821 the remnants of the kingdom fell to Muḥammad ʿAlī, Ottoman viceroy of Egypt, with little resistance.

BIBLIOGRAPHY

James, Wendy. "The Funj Mystique: Approaches to a Problem of Sudan History." In *Text and Context: the Social Anthropology of Tradition*, edited by R. K. Jain, pp. 95–133. Philadelphia, 1977. Perceptive critique of the diverse and sometimes misleading uses of the term "Funj" by scholars.

O'Fahey, R. S., and Jay Spaulding. *Kingdoms of the Sudan*. London, 1974. Survey of the history of the kingdom.

Spaulding, Jay. *The Heroic Age in Sinnār*. East Lansing, Mich., 1985. Examines the decline and fall of the kingdom during the eighteenth and early nineteenth centuries.

Spaulding, Jay, and Muḥammad Ibrāhīm Abū Salīm. *Public Documents from Sinnār*. East Lansing, Mich., 1989. Surviving government records of the kingdom, in Arabic with an English translation and notes.

JAY SPAULDING

FUTŪWAH. Based on the word *fata* ("youth") as representing an ideal of manhood and chivalry, *futūwah* is linked to the idealized figure of ʿAlī ibn Abī Ṭālib, the prophet Muḥammad's cousin and the first youth to convert to Islam. Historically, *futūwah* has been associated with popular forms of revivalist Islam, Ṣūfī orders, craft guilds, and elite chivalric orders. As an idea, *futūwah* probably has pre-Islamic roots in the Middle East, which explains the diversity of forms in which *futūwah* groups have appeared in different locations at different times, notwithstanding basic similarities among them. Thus in Seljuk Anatolia, *akhī* brotherhood associations extended hospitality and protection to travelers; in medieval ʿAbbāsid Baghdad, however, *futūwah* groups appeared as *ʿayyārūn,* described sometimes as "Robin Hood" operations, and other times as criminals and social riffraff who were feared by the wealthier classes. Historical conditions in medieval Baghdad illustrate the close link between socioeconomic conditions and the particular shape in which *futūwah* groups appear. Central authority was quite lax in the ʿAbbāsid empire from the tenth to twelfth centuries, and poverty and social strife were prevalent. Brotherhood associations among the poorer urban elements of society came in answer to a power vacuum and the lack of real legitimacy for the Būyids and other military usurpers of the caliph's authority. The same type of phenomenon appeared in late eighteenth-century Egypt, when Mamlūk factions fought over control of central authority, and *futūwah* groups representing the different *ḥāras* (quarters) of Cairo formed vigilante brotherhoods that filled a security vacuum and provided the *ḥāras* with protection.

It was natural that there was a connection between a particular guild corporation and the *futūwahs* of a *ḥāra* dominated by that guild, and also that there was an affiliation to the predominant Ṣūfī order of the quarter. For example, Cairo's Ḥusaynīyah quarter had one of the more formidable *futūwah* groups. Like other "guild-quarters," the Ḥusaynīyah, where butchers usually lived, was dominated by the butchers' guild, and most were affiliated to the Bayūmīyah Ṣūfī order, also associated with butchers.

The connection among craft-guilds, Ṣūfī orders, and *futūwah* is more a function of the historical situation than a constant relationship. Thus there are cases where a caliph became a member or even founder of a *futūwah* group, for example the thirteenth-century chivalric brotherhood organized by the caliph al-Nāṣir. *Futūwah* brotherhoods are also credited with creating dynastic states; for example, the Ṣaffārid state of Iran said to have begun as a *futūwah* brotherhood.

Futūwah groups have also often acted as thugs, as gangs, and as extortionists. Thus the *ʿayyārūn* in Baghdad often forced their "protection" on the wealthier members of their community, established their authority over the local markets, and exacted tribute from merchants and inhabitants of their quarters. Groups like the *ḥarāfīsh* in twentieth-century Egypt acted in the same way and had the same type of *ʿaṣabīyah* (esprit de corps), which kept their brotherhoods closely associated. The *ḥarāfīsh,* however, are not really recognized as *futūwah* because of the general acceptance that such orders ceased to exist with the establishment of modern nation-states.

There is a case for historical continuity to be made in regard to the similarities between premodern *futūwah* groups and contemporary radical Islamic cells. Both phenomena represented elements of popular political resistance, opposition to state authority, and class struggle; they required absolute loyalty from their members, whether or not they administered an oath and held a ceremony of induction; and they demanded obedience to a recognized leader, *amīr,* or *qā'id.* Their heroes were Muslim "activists" like the prophet Muḥammad, ʿAlī, Abū Muslim al-Khurāsānī or, for modern groups, "martyrs" like Ḥasan al-Bannā'. Both groups espoused a purist and righteous Islamic ideology that justified whatever actions were deemed necessary for the good of the group. These actions could include robbing non-Muslims, punishing "bad" Muslims, assassinating enemies, or exacting tribute from merchants, craftsmen, and inhabitants of the quarters and towns they dominated. Both modern and premodern groups have been known to work closely with the police of *shurṭah,* sometimes cooperating with them and working against them at other times, depending on whether their interests coincided. The contemporary reappearance of traditional indigenous forms of social alliances as preferable methods of class struggle partially explains the lack of a viable activist labor movement in Islamic countries. Islamic brotherhoods join together diverse elements of the public, including students, skilled labor, semiskilled labor, professionals, and often police and army officers. In the final analysis, notwithstanding their outward shape, ceremonies, or names, modern Muslim brotherhoods, like their medieval and premodern precedents, draw their members from popular and impoverished social elements; and their associations, however different they may be, represent a historically recurrent form of resistance to the official power of the state.

[*See also* ʿAṣabīyah; Guilds.]

BIBLIOGRAPHY

Raymond, André. *Artisans et commerçants au Caire au XVIIIe siècle.* Vol. 1. Damascus, 1973.

Staffa, Susan Jane. *Conquest and Fusion: The Social Evolution of Cairo, 642–1850.* Leiden, 1977.

Taeschner, Fr. "Futuwwa." In *Encyclopaedia of Islam*, new ed., vol. 2, pp. 961–969. Leiden, 1960–.

AMIRA EL AZHARY SONBOL

FYZEE, ASAF ALI ASGHAR (1899–1981), Indian educator, public official, and internationally known writer on Islamic law. Fyzee was born at Matheran near Bombay on 10 April 1899 into a Sulaimānī Bohora family. The Bohoras are mainly concentrated in western India and are descendants of Hindu converts and Yemeni Arabs. They supported al-Mustaʿlī's (r. 1094–1101) claim to succeed his father al-Mustanṣir as the Fāṭimid caliph.

Fyzee was educated at St. Xavier's College, Bombay (B.A. and LL.B.) and St. John's College, Cambridge, where he received a double first in Oriental languages (1925) and was subsequently called to the bar. He married the writer Sultana Asaf Fyzee, daughter of Kazi Kabiruddin and an active supporter of the Muslim Ladies Club.

For nearly a decade from 1938 Fyzee was the principal of Government College, Bombay, and Perry Professor of Jurisprudence. From 1947 to 1949 he served as a member of the Bombay Public Service Commission and in 1949 was appointed as Indian ambassador to Egypt and minister plenipotentiary to Syria, Lebanon, and Jordan. From 1952 to 1957 he served as a member of the Union Public Service Commission. Subsequently he held visiting professorships at McGill University and the University of California at Los Angeles. He also served as the vice-chancellor of Jammu and Kashmir University.

Fyzee received honors both at home and abroad. He was made an honorary member of the Arabic Academy in both Cairo and Damascus. He served as president of Anjuman Taraqqī-i Urdu and as honorary secretary of the Islamic Research Association. In 1962 he received the award of Padma Bhushan from the Indian government.

Fyzee's fame rests primarily on his numerous writings on Islamic law. His most famous work, *Outlines of Muhammadan Law,* is characterized by a modernistic and radical approach to the subject but is also sensitive to Muslim sentiments, a balance that others who tried to emulate him found difficult to maintain. He argued that in order to understand the system of Islamic jurisprudence, one ought to be familiar with the historical and cultural background of the law. By the time the second edition of his book was published, Joseph Schacht's *Origins of Muhammadan Jurisprudence* (Oxford, 1950) had already appeared. Fyzee was impressed by Schacht's thesis and, in a revised introduction to the *Outlines,* suggested that the views of Goldziher, Bergstraser, and Schacht seemed to have superseded earlier positions such as those of Abdul Rahim, a judge of the Madras High Court, who in 1907 gave the Tagore Lectures at Calcutta University which were later published as *The Principles of Mohammedan Jurisprudence* (London, 1911). Islamic law, Fyzee suggested, is the result of a continuous process of development over fourteen centuries and should not be seen as a systematic code. Fyzee agreed in part with Schacht's thesis that pre-Islamic customs and elements of Roman law influenced the development of Islamic jurisprudence, but he accepted Schacht's arguments only with some reservations. Fyzee was aware of the inappropriateness of the term "Muhammadan" law and apologized for using it, arguing that for him it denoted those aspects of Islamic law that were applicable in Indian courts.

Like the famous poet-philosopher Muhammad Iqbal, Fyzee called for a reinterpretation of law *(ijtihād)* that would bring the law into conformity with the perceived needs and realities of modern existence. Given such apparent similarity of views, it is important to remember that whereas Iqbal's call for reinterpretation was based essentially within a traditional Islamic paradigm, Fyzee's desire was in part a concession to modern demands. Impressed by the Turkish Revolution and the experiments at codification of law in various Middle Eastern countries, Fyzee veered dangerously close to suggesting a uniform civil code for India. Only his caution as a public figure and as a scholar sensitive to his subject kept him from openly advocating it.

Fyzee is an outstanding example of that generation of Indian Muslim scholars who on one hand were struggling to distance themselves from an earlier apologetic trend of writing and on the other felt a powerful pull toward the Western tradition of critical scholarship—to the extent that, ironically, they often adopted the conclusions of these modern researchers uncritically.

As a brief systematic textbook, the *Outlines of Muhammadan Law* is a valuable introduction to Islamic personal law as practiced in India, and it continues to have much utility. However, despite the author's sincere understanding of the subject, some of its assumptions about Islamic jurisprudence are questionable and its perspective at times too reliant on the Western scholarship of Fyzee's contemporaries.

BIBLIOGRAPHY

Works by Fyzee

Introduction to Muhammadan Law. Oxford, 1931.
Ismaili Law of Wills. Oxford, 1933.
Islamic Culture. Bombay, 1944.
Outlines of Muhammadan Law. Oxford, 1949.
A Modern Approach to Islam. Bombay, 1963.
Mohammadan Law in India. N.p., 1963.
Cases in the Muhammadan Law of India and Pakistan. Oxford, 1965.
The Importance of Mohammadan Law in the Modern World. N.p., 1965.
Improvement of Mohammadan Law in the Modern World. Ahmadabad, 1965.
Introducing the Middle East. Mysore, c.1967.
Compendium of Fatimid Law. Simla, 1969.
The Reform of Muslim Personal Law in India. Bombay, c.1971.
The Middle East. Patna, 1985.

Other Sources

Muslims in India: A Biographical Dictionary, vol. 1. Lahore, 1985.

FARHAN AHMAD NIZAMI

G

GAMBIA. The history of Islam in the present Republic of the Gambia goes back to the days of the medieval empires of Ghana and Mali. When the Ghana empire ruled the Sahel, Muslim traders and their African counterparts had some contact with peoples who are now the inhabitants of the Gambia. Composed largely of ethnic groups belonging to the Mande-Wolfulbe cultures, the present-day Gambia is home to descendants of Mande-speaking groups who emigrated from Mali at the height of its power in the fourteenth century. They came directly into northern Gambia or indirectly by way of Kaabu in southern Senegal and northwestern Guinea Bissau. Their northern Mande-speaking cousins, the Serahuli and the Jahanke, who ruled ancient Ghana one thousand years ago, entered the Gambia during the Malian era. Wolof elements of the population came from the northern bank of the Gambia River, where they and their Serere cousins had settled in the kingdoms of Saloum and Sin. The Fulbe portion of the Gambia's population came from either the Fula Toro region of modern-day Senegal or from the Futa Jalon area of modern Guinea, where their ancestors had emigrated in the early eighteenth century.

Islam did not become a major force in the Senegambia until the nineteenth century, when a number of Muslim scholars decided to embark on a preaching *jihād*. These men of faith tried to set up Islamic states in the heart of the Senegambian region. Feeling threatened by the dominant non-Islamic cultures and determined to maintain their Islamic identity, these Muslim leaders began to strengthen and create more of the Muslim towns and villages known as Morokundas to Western travelers. These settlements were founded by itinerant Muslim scholars and their students and by Muslim merchants.

During the nineteenth century Muslims found themselves facing two forces whose interests clashed with their own. They had to contend with the non-Islamic status quo, and they also had to face the challenges posed by the rising power of European trading groups along the African coast. By the end of the century Gambian Muslims found themselves under the growing power of the British Empire. Their leaders were either defeated in battle or coopted into the new order. As a result, Islam at the beginning of the twentieth century was not a state religion but the religion of individual believers who had affiliations with Ṣūfī orders such as the Qādirīyah, Tijānīyah, or Murīdīyah.

Islam grew from a minority religion in the nineteenth century into a modern majority religion largely because of the favorable socioeconomic conditions created by colonial rule. This increase in the number of believers was the unintended result of particular policies and activities by the colonial rulers. By building roads to previously inaccessible areas of the country and opening the hinterland of the Gambia River, the British enabled Muslim leaders and traders to link up with one another and to expand their horizons. By the time the decolonization process came to an end, Muslims constituted more than 90 percent of the population. Mosques were built throughout the country, along with hundreds of Qur'ānic schools. The British acknowledged the centrality of Islam in Gambian life by making room for some elements of the *sharīʿah* in the legal system of colonial Gambia. *Qāḍīs* were appointed in the Muslim courts, and a Muhammadan School was built in Banjul for Muslim children who wanted to combine their Islamic education with Western subjects.

Islam in postcolonial Gambia is not radically different from what it was during the colonial period; however, four important developments within the larger Muslim community are now noteworthy. First, the Islamic community has become more diverse and tolerant. This is evidenced by the acceptance of the Aḥmadīyah movement, an organization that is often opposed or suppressed in the Muslim countries of the Middle East and South Asia. A second development is the emergence of a new group of young Muslim intellectuals who are disenchanted with traditional Ṣūfī ideas about Islam. Generally known to the French-speaking Africans as the Arabisants, these graduates of Arab universities have set up new Muslim organizations that are engaged in both *daʿwah* (mission) and development-oriented activities. Today they share the limelight with both older and more recently organized national Muslim groups such as the Gambia Muslim Association, the Gambia Islamic Union, and the Supreme Islamic Council. Within the same domain of operation are smaller groups known as *dayirahs*. These local Ṣūfī organizations are designed to bring the faithful together to celebrate the praises of God in the mosques and beyond.

The third development is the greater accessibility of Islamic literature in English. This has resulted in the intellectual revival of Islamic consciousness among a sizable number of Gambian youths whose previous knowledge of their faith was limited. The new access to Islamic literature can be traced to the activities of international Muslim organizations that are competing with both the Aḥmadī missionaries in Africa and their Christian counterparts from the West. The fourth development that resulted in the renewal of Islam in postcolonial Gambia was the brief period of Afro-Arab cooperation in the 1970s. This opened the Gambia to countries such as Libya and Saudi Arabia, and *daʿwah* groups from these countries played an important part in the dissemination of Islamic literature there.

In conclusion, three points are to be emphasized. The first is the historical fact that Gambia became a Muslim state largely because of the efforts of the Muslim *jihād* leaders of the nineteenth century, and also because of the state of peace brought about by the British colonial power. Second, it should be noted that the Muslim sense of tolerance in the country is largely the work of the present leadership, who have decided to build on the colonial legacy of religious pluralism. Finally, Islam in the Gambia is no longer isolated from the mainstream of Islam in the Middle East because the revolution in world communications has created a permanent bridge between Gambians and other Muslims. This bridge of cooperation and understanding is used not only during the *ḥajj* but throughout the year.

BIBLIOGRAPHY

Anderson, J. N. D. *Islamic Law in Africa*. London, 1954.

Archer, Francis Bisset. *The Gambia Colony and Protectorate*. London, 1967.

Gailey, Harry A. *A History of the Gambia*. New York, 1965.

Gray, J. M. *A History of the Gambia*. Cambridge, 1940.

Nyang, Sulayman S. "A Contribution to the Study of Islam in the Gambia." *Pakistan Historical Journal* (April 1977): 125–138.

Nyang, Sulayman S. "Saudi Arabian Foreign Policy towards Africa." *Horn of Africa* 5.2 (1982): 3–17.

Quinn, Charlotte A. "Traditionalism, Islam, and European Expansion: The Gambia, 1850–1890." Ph.D. diss., University of California, Los Angeles, 1967.

Reeve, H. F. *The Gambia: Its History, Ancient, Mediaeval, and Modern*. London, 1912.

SULAYMAN S. NYANG

GAMES AND SPORT. Islam recognizes that human beings need to eat, drink, relax, and enjoy themselves. Hanẓalah, a companion and scribe of the Prophet, said "there is a time for this and a time for that." Muslims enjoy humor, laughter, play, and sport. Various activities can relax their bodies and minds. The mind gets tired and so does the body, so there is no harm in Muslims relaxing the mind and refreshing the body with permissible sport or play. This should not, however, be at the expense of religious obligations.

Sources of the Islamic faith are the Qur'ān, regarded as the uncreated, eternal Word of God, and tradition (*ḥadīth*) regarding the sayings and the deeds of the Prophet, who is a model for the community. Islam is a way of life, a revolutionary religion that provides guidance for individuals and nations. It is a message of peace and prosperity, as well as health and happiness. Acquiring knowledge and skill is compulsory for every Muslim, boy or girl, man or woman. Muslims are to refrain from all sorts of undesirable activities and to value personal health and cleanliness, which are fundamental principles useful for everyone.

Islam has five pillars. One is to pray five times a day. Before one can pray, one must wash so one is clean and ready to pray. Prayer is an excellent activity for maintaining flexibility. It includes bending at the hip, stretching, and moving the head forward to touch the floor. Flexibility is one of the health-related fitness objectives. Since prayer is done five times a day, it is an excellent exercise of the body.

Afyular Rahman, the author of *Role of Muslim Women in Society* (London, 1986), says, "Allah has created human beings with needs and desires, so that they need to eat and drink, they also need to relax, and to enjoy themselves." Relaxing of the body and mind can be attained by means of play, leisure, recreation, games, and sports. There are many kinds of games and sports that the Prophet recommended to the Muslims for enjoyment and recreation, such as foot racing, wrestling, archery, spear play, horseback riding, tumbling, backgammon, and playing chess. The *ḥadīth*s say, "Teach your sons the art of archery, swimming, and riding." At the time of the Prophet, these activities were for survival and warfare. These sports are still very popular activities today.

Support for participation in games and sport is found in *ḥadīth*s, which report that the Prophet encouraged people to race on foot; Muḥammad even raced with his wife ʿĀ'ishah. The Prophet wrestled and encouraged archery. However he warned archers against using chickens for target practice, since human beings have no right to have fun and sport at the expense of living creatures.

Moreover, traditions tell us that the Prophet let ʿĀ'ishah watch a performance of spear play in the mosque, a form of amusement and recreation. The mosque is not only used for worship but also as a social and cultural center. Hunting and horseback riding is another activity encouraged by Islam as a sport, an exercise, and a means of livelihood. It was said, "Teach your children swimming and archery and tell them to jump on the horse's back" (al-Qaraḍāwī, 1980, p. 296).

Islam provides a standard for a person's life called *ḥalāl*, which means "acceptable," "allowed," or "permitted." *Ḥalāl* regulates all human affairs of Muslims. It emphasizes food, eating, and one's physical as well as spiritual health. In Islam education includes knowledge and training; therefore, the Muslims must educate themselves and their families about that which is good for them (*ḥalāl*) and which is bad for them (*ḥaram*). Islam has prohibited certain things pertaining to food, drinking, recreation, and sex. The Qur'ān has laid down a guide for life, and the individual has to know in play, games, leisure, recreation, and sport if something is *ḥalāl* or *ḥaram*.

European colonial presence influenced the implementation of physical training. Physical training emphasized formal mass calisthenics, gymnastics, and military drills. Sports were not a part of the school day but a voluntary activity after school hours. French and English models of physical education were used in schools. The elementary physical education programs stressed a wide program of activities, including indigenous games, rhythms, lead-up games, and self-testing, aquatic, and fitness type activities. The secondary schools had a limited program of physical activities. Most countries have a system of examination. Physical education is not included as one of the required examination subjects. Because of this, students, parents, and teachers gave little importance to classes in physical education. In the past ten to twenty years, fitness and game skills have been introduced into the program with physical training nearly eliminated. Stress has been placed on a balanced program of indigenous activities, individual and team sports, aquatics, and gymnastics.

In many Muslim countries, British influences decreased after independence. Yet European and American methods have been introduced. Broad and varied programs of physical education are replacing the more limited programs of years ago.

Religion can play an important role in attitudes toward physical education. The Muslim people can be more content to stress arts and music in a passive manner than to promote healthy exercise. The climate and geographic location of many parts of the Muslim world is not conductive to an all-year outdoor program because of heat and humidity. Therefore, the physical activities causing perspiration and fatigue are looked down on, and more favorable activities are encouraged.

Physical education programs can be found at the primary, intermediate, high school, and university levels. The sports club level identifies potential talent and administers athletic preparation and training. In some countries, funding, organization, and administration of sports clubs come from the central government. Sports federations and other major organizations, such as the National Olympic Committee, might also be organized under an established ministry. Sport federations are charged with the responsibility of developing their particular sports (basketball, soccer [football], volleyball, handball, gymnastics, swimming, judo, tennis, fencing, and others), including preparation of national teams for international competition. For many years, Muslim countries have participated in the Olympic games, and many of them have excelled individually in sports such as weight lifting and track and field. The sport movement in Muslim countries has also flourished through the development of private sport clubs.

In the promotion of sports for men and women at the university level, one finds that at least thirteen Islamic countries have training institutes of physical education and sports for women. These institutes are in such countries as Algeria, Egypt, Iraq, Iran, Morocco, Syria, Tunisia, and Turkey (Safeir, 1985). They are mainly for the training of teachers of physical education.

The five new independent Muslim states of the former

Soviet Union emphasize the role of games, recreation, and sports as part of their culture and their way of life. They encourage participation in exercise and physical activity. The Islamic Centers in North America emphasize the concept of Muslim youth camps.

Non-Arab Muslim countries as well as the Arab states have established a parallel to the world Olympics whereby the Muslim countries can compete in world sports events. These countries participate in the World Health Organization, whose aims are to aid the attainment of the highest possible level of health. Another support of these games is the United Nations Educational, Scientific, and Cultural Organization, whose aim is to promote collaboration among the nations through education, science, and culture in order to further justice, rule of law, and human rights and freedom without distinction of race, sex, language, or religion.

Women are sure to be spectators of sports on television in the privacy of their own homes. One can receive the happenings of the world in minutes, and sports contests make up a large share of television coverage. It would be impossible for women to escape such events as the Olympic Games, the World Cup playoffs, and the Pan-Asian games. The increased changes in the status of Muslim women are owing to the growth of the feminist movement, the spread of education, and the increased participation of women in the labor force. These changes will result in more participation of women in sports at the local level and perhaps even at the regional level for the skilled individual. The reasons women have not been active sports participants in the past are traditional restrictions, culture, education, and restrictions owing to religion. The educational system was separate for boys and girls; physical education, sports, and youth programs may not have been a part of the educational system. In just the past few decades, physical education has become compulsory for girls. The participation of Muslim women has been low in highly competitive sports. The participation of Islamic countries at the Olympic level is also low compared to world participation. Leila Safeir, a sociologist, wrote that women athletes from Algeria, Libya, and Syria participated in the 1980 Olympic games and that Egypt in 1984 sent the first six female athletes to the Olympic games (Safeir, 1985). One can see that Islamic countries send few women to the world games but send more female participants to games at the regional level, such as the African, Asian, Arab, or Mediterranean games. When women do participate at the regional and national level, they wear sport dresses and appear in public places where there is extensive media coverage.

In recent years women have had more opportunities to participate in leisure and recreational activities through the educational system and in private sports clubs as facilities become increasingly available to them. Research and the media have increased the awareness that there are important health benefits to exercise and recreational activities. As the knowledge and material available on the benefits for a more healthy lifestyle increase, the more women will participate in physical activities. Once again, there are differences from country to country and from the rural areas to the urban areas because of the differences in educational systems, structure of sports, and available facilities.

Islam is based on respect for the body and soul that involves both the physical and spiritual aspects of humankind. Physical activity is for the strengthening of the body and knowledge for the soul. Anyone with a healthy body is able to meet everyday tasks and have enough energy for recreation and sport and to meet emergencies. Each country and its organizations has had to adjust its program to meet the needs and the understanding of its own tradition, culture, and religion. This might be tribal, regional, national, or even worldwide. The Qur'ān has laid down the groundwork and the philosophy of sound moral conduct for the guidance of games and sport.

BIBLIOGRAPHY

ʿAbd al-ʿAṭī, Ḥammūdah. *Islam in Focus*. Indianapolis, 1975.

Denffer, Ahmad von. *Islam for Children*. Leicester, 1990.

Du Toit, Stephanus F. "Physical Education in South Africa." In *Physical Education around the World*, edited by William Johnson, pp. 58–62. Indianapolis, 1966.

Hanafy, Earleen Helgelien, and March L. Krotee. "A Model for International Education Comparison: Middle East Perspective." In *Comparative Physical Education and Sport*, vol. 3, edited by March L. Krotee and Eloise M. Jaeger, pp. 253–266. Champaign, Ill., 1986.

Hussaini, Mohammad Mazhar. *My Little Book of Halal and Haram*. Chicago, 1988. Written for Muslim children with standards of *ḥalāl*.

Johnson, William. "Physical Education in Pakistan." In *Physical Education around the World*, edited by William Johnson, 43–50. Indianapolis, 1966.

Mawdūdī, Sayyid Abū al-Aʿlā. *Towards Understanding Islam*. Translated and edited by Khurshid Ahmad. Cedar Rapids, Iowa, 1980.

Qaraḍāwī, Yūsuf al-. *The Lawful and the Prohibited in Islam (Al-Ḥalāl wa-al-Ḥarām fī al-Islām)*. Indianapolis, n.d. (1980?).

Qaraḍāwī, Yūsuf al-. *Islamic Education and Hassan al Banna*. Translated by Shakil Ahmed. Beirut, 1984.

Rahman, Afzalur. *Role of Muslim Women in Society*. London, 1986.
Rauf, Abdur. *Hadith for Children*. Chicago, 1980.
Rauf, Abdur. *Qur'an for Children*. Chicago, 1980.
Rosendich, T. J. "Sports in Society: The Persian Gulf Countries." *Journal of the International Council for Health, Physical Education, and Recreation* 27.3 (1991): 26–30.
Safeir, L. "The Status of Muslim Women in Sport: Conflict between Cultural Traditions." *International Review for the Sociology of Sport* 20.4 (1985): 283–306.
Van Dalen, Deobold B., and Bruce L. Bennett. *A World History of Physical Education*. 2d ed. Englewood Cliffs, N.J., 1971.

EARLEEN HELGELIEN HANAFY

GARDENS AND LANDSCAPING. [*This entry comprises two articles. The first considers the history and development of traditional forms of the Islamic garden and assesses the current state of scholarly understanding; the second focuses specifically on contemporary gardens and landscaping practices in the arid climate of the Middle East and North Africa.*]

Traditional Forms

Islamic gardens from India to Morocco have fascinated architects, historians, and travelers since the fifteenth century CE and have been the subject of exuberant descriptions and representations. Today, unfortunately, few of the flowers and planting arrangements in the palace courtyards, tomb gardens, and pleasure retreats are historically accurate, yet a sense of the original often lingers in the layout of stone walkways leading to ornamental pools and fountains, overlooked by charming airy pavilions. One of the most striking elements of the Islamic garden is the use of pools of water as reflective elements mirroring adjacent pavilions, the water's placid horizontal surface enlivened by occasional fountain jets spurting vertically. The water is often conducted from one pool to another in small channels running alongside of paved walkways, the path of the water and pedestrian together delineating the garden's geometrical plan.

Despite the universal appeal of Islamic gardens, their documentation has leaned more toward the descriptive than the analytical, with the result that fundamental issues of garden typology and meaning have not been satisfactorily explained. For example, there is an ongoing debate among twentieth-century scholars regarding the origins of the Islamic garden. Its primary focus—the cross-axial plan exemplified by the fourteenth-century Court of the Lions of the Alhambra Palace in Granada and the linear plan exemplified by the Alhambra's Court of the Myrtles (figure 1)—are generally traced to Persian or Roman antecedents. Many scholars reject the idea of

FIGURE 1. *Plan of the Alhambra.* Granada, eleventh to fourteenth century. L = Court of the Lions; M = Court of the Myrtles.

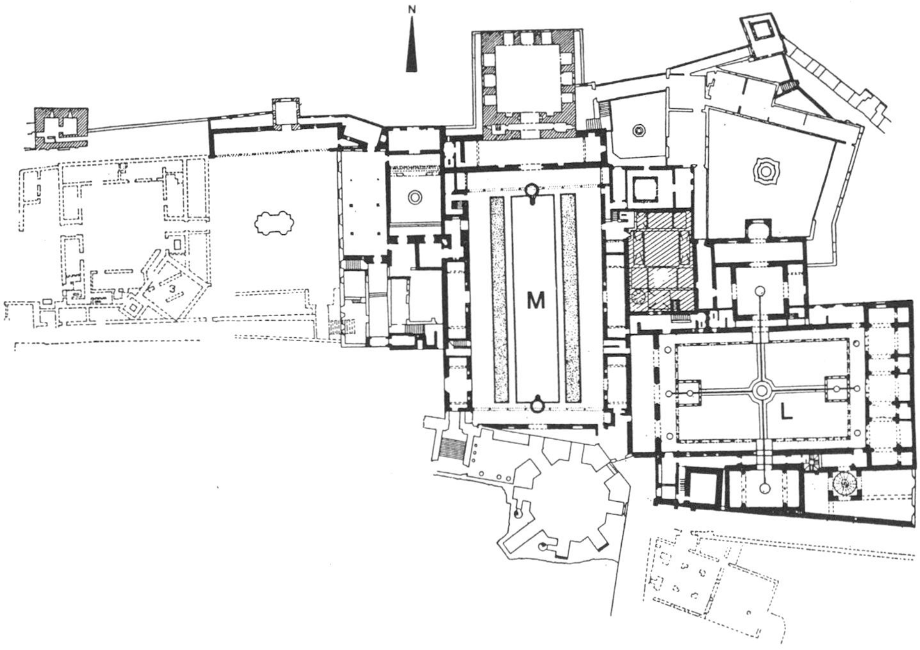

Eastern influence and propose a strictly Roman legacy of peristyle courtyards and impluvia, as found at Conimbriga in Portugal (see Alvas de Araujo, 1975, pp. 155–160). Perhaps the divide is caused by the failure to recognize that Islamic culture rests equally on the two foundations, and that the contribution of Persian culture is stronger in the East while Roman influence is more powerful in the Mediterranean.

The question of the origins and development of the Islamic garden is complicated by certain modern historiographic factors. First, the sources of information exist in languages as diverse as Arabic, Turkish, Persian, French, German, and Spanish, making most readers dependent upon translations by Orientalist scholars. In many cases, key sources have been translated poorly or not at all. Second, until recently the excavations of historic sites have focused exclusively on architectural remains, ignoring altogether opportunities for the excavation of gardens. However, current research may be bringing us closer to understanding the origins and the development of Islamic garden typology.

Several scholars have identified the existence of two types of gardens, linear and cross-axial. Georges Marçais (1960) writes that landscape gardening began in Iran before the advent of Islam. It consisted of two types: the courtyard garden and esplanade within an architectural framework, as depicted in Persian miniatures and garden carpets; and the larger suburban park *(ḥayr)*, associated with palaces such as the ninth-century Jawsaq al-Khāqānī at Samarra (Iraq) where it was a royal game preserve. In contrast, James Dickie, while also identifying two formal plans, traces both to Roman urban and rural garden types. He regards the cross-axial plan as belonging to the *villa rustica* and the linear as belonging to the enclosed courtyards of the *domus urbana* (1981, pp. 127–149). Unfortunately there has been little agreement among scholars as to the degree to which the two types developed independently or in relation to each other; however, new evidence suggests that the two gardens may have arisen from different contexts.

David Stronach (1994) has identified at Cyrus the Great's palace at Pasargadae what appears to be the earliest datable cross-axial garden. On the basis of excavated evidence from Pasargadae, it is now possible to trace the origins of the quadripartite Persian garden plan to the sixth century BCE. Additionally, Tilo Ulbert, working at the Byzantine-Islamic city of Rusafa in Syria, has excavated the earliest surviving dated Islamic garden with a cross-axial plan. It consists of an irregular enclosure fed by a seasonal stream and walled with mud brick. In the center was a square pavilion raised on a plinth with axial walkways leading in the four cardinal directions.

Among the many excavated and studied Roman gardens one garden is known to have had a true (as opposed to an implied) cross-axial plan, leading to the tentative conclusion that the linear axis may have predominated in Roman Mediterranean context whereas the cross-axial form (in Persian, *chahar bagh*) was a Mesopotamian contribution (see Ruggles, 1993). Ultimately both forms proliferated in the Islamic world: the cross-axial type can be found abundantly in Morocco and the West; the linear type is found in the terraced gardens of Kashmir. Moreover, both forms are used today by contemporary landscape designers throughout the Islamic world.

Descriptions of gardens abound in historical sources. Early ones are often found in the writings of Arabic geographers such as Ibn Ḥawqal (second half of the tenth century), who traveled to Sicily, Spain, North Africa, Egypt, Iraq, Iran, and Transoxiana. He is a particularly accurate source, having based his work on direct observation, whereas many other geographers relied on hearsay. Such texts tend to be brief and nonspecific; they often mention the existence of gardens and occasionally state who owned them and their source of water, but rarely do they offer much information as to their appearance.

Poetic panegyrics can be useful as well, although they are prone to exaggeration. Such an example is al-Shaqundī's poem boasting of the wonders of Spain. Of Malaga he wrote, "its environs are so covered with vines and orchards as to make it almost impossible for the traveller to discover a piece of ground which is not cultivated" (see Gayangos, vol. 1, p. 49). Also valuable are chronicles and dynastic histories eulogizing the accomplishments of a royal house, such as Yaʿqūbī's ninth-century history of the ʿAbbāsids with its description of the founding of Samarra and its landscape of orchards and gardens. Likewise, the *Baburnamah* recorded Babur's patronage and planting of gardens in sixteenth-century Central Asia at the stations where his army camped on their way into India. Babur is particularly important as it was he who brought the Persian garden form to India, and yet with the exception of a lotus-shaped pool in one garden and the debated layout of another, nothing remains from this important formative phase from which the great Mughal garden tradition emerged.

Travel writers (like geographers) are particularly useful because they describe gardens for an audience that has not seen them and does not fully understand their context. Thus in the account of Timur's gardens of Samarkand, the ambassador Ruy Gonzalez de Clavijo describes a geometrical layout on sloping terrain with a central axial canal, pools, trees, a central pavilion, and an entrance portal. Similarly, there are several descriptions of the gardens of Isfahan recorded by foreign visitors such as John Chardin, Jean-Baptiste Tavernier, and Engelbert Kaempfer. The last is noteworthy for having made the inclusion of an engraved plan of the palace quarter with its extensive gardens.

Despite the abundance of written texts, few historic gardens have been studied or excavated to discover their material remains. Unusual is M. T. Shepard Parpagliolo's study (1972) of a sixteenth-century garden in Afghanistan; this is a preliminary survey prior to an excavation that never occurred, combining historical descriptions with observations at the site. Also notable is Henri Seyrig's discussion (1931) of a garden attached to the Umayyad agricultural estate Qasr al-Hayr. In Morocco, a twelfth-century garden was excavated by Jacques Meunié and Henri Terrasse (1952). In Spain, renowned for palace gardens, studies have been made of Murcia Castillego, the Seville Alcazar, Madinat al-Zahra', and the Alhambra (see especially Torres Balbás, 1958, pp. 171–192, and a recent reappraisal of the sequence of excavations in the Islamic western Mediterranean by Ruggles, 1993). However, generally in these excavations it is the architecture of the garden that has been examined—pavements, water channels, and pavilions—rather than botanical remains. Gardens are indicated on plans as empty spaces; this is visually misleading, yet to fill the spaces with imagined vegetation would be equally misleading because we have very little idea of the contents and organization of gardens. Thus, without seed flotation, pollen analysis, and simple digging to unearth buried tools and ceramic containers, an important aspect of garden history may be overlooked.

FIGURE 2. *Babur Directing the Building of the Bagh-i Vafā.* Persian miniature, from a manuscript of the *Baburnamah*, Victoria and Albert Museum, London.

Occasionally manuscript illustrations may yield reliable factual information on the floral content of gardens. A particularly useful case is a sixteenth-century manuscript of the *Baburnamah* showing the architect holding a grid plan as he directs workers laying out the Bāgh-i Vafā garden (figure 2). This is the only garden plan known to survive. For the purpose of showing the garden in its entirety, the convention was adopted of representing it as a tiny plot of land, accuracy of scale being sacrificed for the sake of including detail. The garden consisted of a walled enclosure with fruit trees and a raised bed divided into symmetrical quadrants, the cross-axial plan defined by raised walkways lined with water channels. The techniques of mensuration, leveling, spading, and design—and even the patron, Babur—are all depicted. Also valuable are the agricultural manuals, botanical manuals, and almanacs that exist for the medieval and later periods. Daniel Varisco (1989) has worked on Yemen (1989, pp. 150–154), Jürgen Jakobi (1992) has worked on Iran, and Lucie Bolens (1981) has published extensively on the botanicals of medieval Islamic Spain. For a study of the economics of agriculture, plant migration, and the impact of the introduction of new plant types, based largely on his reading of these manuals, Andrew Watson (1983) is a useful source. John Harvey's studies in *Garden History* of plant lists inform us as to the contents of the gardens but not their organization. A notable exception is a manuscript by Ibn Luyūn that gives instructions for the optimal placement of the house, arbor, pavilion, vines, and other features in a Andalusian garden (Dickie, 1981).

In addition to studies of treatises and agricultural practice, there are a few rare studies of gardens within the conceptual framework of human geography. James Wescoat (1990), for example, looks at Mughal gardens within a larger landscape context, seeing them as the combined product of a Pan-Islamic typology and regional hydraulic, climatic, and social requirements.

Unfortunately, the abundance of informative texts notwithstanding, without more excavation of specific sites and examination of landscapes in their entirety, interpretive studies of garden iconography and meaning will continue to make assertions for which there is little confirming evidence. One such assertion is the widespread notion that all Islamic gardens have a paradisiac dimension. While paradise is specifically invoked in the building inscriptions of later gardens such as the Taj Mahal in Agra, where the choice of Qur'ānic verses is insistently eschatological, in fact, the paradisiac theme may not have been explicitly incorporated into garden design and meaning until the eleventh century. At this time the Islamic world underwent a number of changes—architecturally in the proliferation of mausoleums as a new form of architectural patronage (particularly in Egypt, Iran, and Central Asia) and politically in the fall of the Umayyad caliphate of Spain, the rise of new dynasties throughout the Islamic world, and the presence of ever increasing numbers of Turks throughout central and eastern Islam.

Without a detailed understanding of the botanical character of historic gardens, it is difficult to make accurate restorations; thus bougainvillea, a New World vine, anachronistically adorns Spanish Islamic gardens today. Despite the difficulties, however, garden designers of the twentieth century often draw on past forms in an attempt to reassert a self-conscious Islamicism, in some cases in defiance of international modernism (regarded as antithetical to the expression of national identity), or in other cases in an attempt to blend nationalism (often confused with "tradition") with modernity by realizing in new materials designs using a historically based vocabulary of fountains, ornamental water chutes *(chadar)*, pools, and paved walkways.

[*See also* Architecture, *article on* Traditional Forms; Urban Planning.]

BIBLIOGRAPHY

Alvas de Araujo, I. "On the Origins of Patios and Gardens of the Islamic Period in Spain and Portugal." In *Les Jardins de l'Islam*, pp. 155–160. Paris, 1975.

Beveridge, Annette S. *The Babur-nama in English*. London, 1922.

Bolens, Lucie. *Agronomes andalous du moyen âge*. Geneva and Paris, 1981.

Dickie, James. "The Alhambra: Some Reflections." In *Studia Arabica et Islamica: Festschrift for Ihsan 'Abbas on His Sixtieth Birthday*, edited by Wadād al-Qāḍī, pp. 127–149. Beirut, 1981.

Dickie, James. "The Islamic Garden in Spain." In *The Islamic Garden*, edited by Elisabeth MacDougall and Richard Ettinghausen, pp. 87–105. Washington, D.C., 1976.

Environmental Design: Journal of the Islamic Environmental Design Research Centre. Rome, 1985–. Issues published annually.

Gayangos y Arce, Pascual de. *The History of the Mohammedan Dynasties of Spain*. 2 vols. London, 1840.

Gonzalez de Clavijo, Ruy. *Narrative of the Embassy of Ruy Gonzalez de Clavijo to the Court of Timour at Samarkand, A.D. 1403–1406*. Translated by C. R. Markham. London, 1870.

Habib, Irfan. *The Agrarian System of Mughal India, 1556–1707*. Bombay and New York, 1963. Important study of agricultural history.

Jakobi, Jürgen. "Agriculture between Literary Tradition and First-hand Experience: *The Irshad al-zira'a* of Qasim b. Yusuf Abu Nasri Haravi." In *Timurid Art and Culture*, edited by Lisa Golombek and Maria Subtelny, pp. 201–208. New York, 1992.

MacDougall, Elisabeth, and Richard Ettinghausen, eds. *The Islamic Garden*. Washington, D.C., 1976.

Marçais, Georges. "Būstān. I. Gardens in Islam." In *Encyclopaedia of Islam*, new ed., vol. 1, pp. 1345–1347. Leiden, 1960–.

Meunié, Jacques, et al. *Recherches archéologiques à Marrakech*. Paris, 1952. See pages 27–30.

Moynihan, Elizabeth B. *Paradise as a Garden: In Persia and Mughal India*. New York, 1979.

Reifenburg, A. *The Struggle between the Desert and the Sown: The Rise and Fall of Agriculture in the Levant*. Jerusalem, 1955. Important contribution to agricultural history.

Ruggles, D. Fairchild. "Il giardini con pianta a croce nel Mediterraneo islamico e illoro significato." In *Il giardino islamico*, edited by Attilio Petruccioli. Milan, 1994.

Seyrig, Henri. "Les jardins de Kasr el-Heir." *Syria* 12 (1931): 316–318.

Shepard Parpagliolo, Maria Theresa. *Kabul, the Bagh-i Babur: A Project and a Research into the Possibilities of a Complete Restoration*. Rome, 1972.

Smart, Ellen. "Graphic Evidence for Mughal Architectural Plans." *Art and Archaeology Research Papers* 6 (1974): 22–23.

Stronach, David. "Parterres and Stone Watercourses at Pasargadae: Notes on the Achaemenid Contribution to Garden Design." *Journal of Garden History* 14 (1994): 3–12.

Titley, Norah, and Frances Wood. *Oriental Gardens*. San Francisco, 1992.

Torres Balbás, Leopoldo. "Patios de Crucero." *Al-Andalus* 23 (1958): 171–192.

Varisco, Daniel. "Medieval Agricultural Texts from Rasulid Yemen." *Manuscripts of the Middle East* 4 (1989): 150–154.

Watson, Andrew M. *Agricultural Innovation in the Early Islamic World.* Cambridge, 1983.
Wescoat, James. "Gardens of Invention and Exile." *Journal of Garden History* 10 (1990): 106–116. Examines gardens as units within the larger system of hydraulics and spatial organization.
Wilbur, Donald. *Persian Gardens and Garden Pavilions* (1962). 2d ed. Washington, D.C., 1979.

D. FAIRCHILD RUGGLES

Contemporary Forms

Contemporary landscape design in the Middle East and North Africa is a little-documented subject. In contrast to the dynamic architectural inventiveness of the region, there has been little of an innovative nature either in design or in the use of plant materials, despite the strong historical traditions of garden design in the Islamic world. Nevertheless, several projects of note can be cited, and important trends can be identified that help situate gardens and landscaping in the context of the environmental, social, and cultural context of the region. Two critical areas of environmental pressure in the region—the degradation of urban environments and the declining availability and quality of freshwater resources—intensify the importance of gardens and green space to the inhabitants of the Middle East and North Africa.

Since the 1960s the cities in the Middle East and North Africa have seen the most radical transformation ever experienced in their millennia of urban development. Urban populations have quadrupled from about 32 million people to about 130 million in one generation. Today the region's cities house more than 50 percent of the total population and are continuing to grow at explosive rates of 4 to 6 percent a year. As the urban sprawl and population have increased, especially in the megacities of Cairo, Tehran, and Istanbul, the area reserved for gardens and parks has contracted. Many Middle Eastern cities, for example Algiers and Tunis, have almost negligible green space per inhabitant. World standards for green space in urban situations recommend five acres per 1,000 people; in 1983 Alexandria, Egypt offered only one-third acre per 1,000 inhabitants, down from three-quarters twenty-five years earlier. Moreover, massive air pollution problems in the megacities, as well as in secondary cities such as Sfax and Oran, argue for the planting of city trees and the creation of new parks to help the cities and their inhabitants breathe. The urban land-use policies of most of the region have failed to provide for adequate access to parks and gardens for city dwellers.

Even more threatening to health and human welfare in the region is the crisis of water supply. Water has always been a limited resource in much of the Middle East and North Africa. Nevertheless, only thirty years ago, renewable freshwater resources were estimated at 3,000 cubic meters per person per year, or about three times the conventional definition of water scarcity of 1,000 cubic meters. Rapid population growth, inefficient use of water for irrigation, and new industrial requirements have created a situation in which, in 1990, only seven countries in the region had a per-capita supply exceeding 1,000 cubic meters; by 2025 water availability for the region as a whole is expected to drop to less than 700 cubic meters per person per year. The implications for continued existence of gardens and parks is obvious, as nearly all vegetation in the arid countries demands irrigation. As the water crisis becomes more acute, landscape designers will need to develop strategies to reduce water consumption or rely on water reuse.

Perhaps the most outstanding example of recent landscape design in the Middle East is the Diplomatic Quarter in Riyadh, Saudi Arabia, completed in the late 1980s. It has the distinction of being the only landscape project to be given the Aga Khan Award for Architecture. The project transformed a featureless expanse of the bare and rocky Saudi desert into a large urban parkland. Almost 75,000 cubic meters of rock and earth were excavated and nearly half of that volume of rocks and boulders and a further 35,000 cubic meters of topsoil were put in place to create the Diplomatic Quarter landscape. The scheme consists of extensive gardens around the 12-kilometer (7.2 mile) circumference of the Diplomatic Quarter, adjacent access gardens, and the neighborhood's residential intensive gardens. A thorough knowledge of the Riyadh ecosystem, including its limestone geology, drainage patterns, and climatic conditions, informed the choices of the landscape designers. The patterns of social and recreational use were also analyzed, and the scheme encourages both vigorous and contemplative activities. The cliff edges of the Wadi Hanifah became a dominant motif in the general landscape design. The extensive areas of the project, the transition between the found landscape of the wadi, escarpment, and desert and the new city, were developed with native plants and locally found construction materials. The intensive landscape areas are an expression of the idea of the Islamic garden, a refuge of aromatic greenery. In the neighborhood centers of the Diplomatic Quarter, near mosques and shopping centers, they offer verdant islands. Among the design features are shaded walkways and screened seating areas, often within garden pavilions. Fountains and water channels create an atmosphere of repose. The landscape team used an extensive palette of native plants in the project. Plants and seeds were collected in the desert and a specially built greenhouse was established. More than fifty herbaceous plants were used, ranging from well-known varieties such as aloe *(Aloe vera)* and sagebrush *(Artemisia judaica)* to rare species such as Egyptian broomrape *(Orobanche aegyptiaca)*. Among the trees were five types of acacia as well as jujubes *(Ziziphus spina-christi)*, athel tree *(Tamarix aphylla)*, and a relative of the flame tree. Wild fig trees proved very successful. (See figures 1 and 2.)

Saudi Arabia has also built a much-admired system of local, regional, and national parks in recent decades. Unfortunately, other countries in the region have devoted little attention to park planning, with the exceptions of Jordan and Cyprus.

FIGURE 1. *Diplomatic Quarter, Riyadh.* Neighborhood garden on the city limits overlooking Wadi Hanifah.

Several landscape projects were proposed for the 1992 Aga Khan Architecture Award. A Cultural Park for Children in Cairo, the result of a national design competition, is built on the site of an existing green space in the densely inhabited historic urban center. Its facilities include an open-air theater, children's museum, and structures for the use of the local community. Also in Egypt is the Alexandria International Garden, which is significant because it is built on the site of the former municipal refuse dump. Planned as an active space, with sport fields, playgrounds, and an open air theater, it is a step in meeting the severe shortage of open space in Alexandria. Moreover, it transforms an environmental health hazard into a recreational and green space. The landscaping of the Gold Horn in Istanbul is another project submitted to the Aga Khan Award Committee (see figure 3). After the Golden Horn was cleared of polluting industries and an improved infrastructure for sewerage and industrial waste provided, landscaping was carried out. Green areas were planted and promenades and playgrounds built. It should also be noted that historic buildings were razed indiscriminately and an appropriate archaeological survey was not undertaken before park construction took place. Although the hazardous health conditions and general deterioration characteristic of the Golden Horn have been arrested, a recent site visit indicates that the parks have not been adequately maintained. Each of the above projects serves an important social need, but none are outstanding in their use of plant materials, design concept, or execution.

Luxury hotels in the region are also the focus of landscape design. Well-designed gardens, particularly from the point of view of planting, are the Palais Jamai in Fez (see figure 4) and the Sheraton (formerly Hilton) Hotel in Rabat, Morocco. The Rabat garden is planted with a profusion of flowering plants and shrubs, mixed with various kinds of cactus. The Cirgan Palace Hotel in Istanbul is provided with an elaborate waterfront esplanade and fountains.

Another project of importance is the Paphos Archaeological Site Improvement (Cyprus), financed by the World Bank. The landscape architect in charge has designed a system of raised walkways and landscape treatment for a major archaeological site in which the site's conservation, presentation, and interpretation are enhanced. This project represents one of the first landscape plans for an archaeological zone that takes into account conservation needs and the inherent landscape

FIGURE 2. *Diplomatic Quarter, Riyadh.* Pedestrian zone.

FIGURE 3. *Park at Azap Kapı, Golden Horn, Istanbul.*

FIGURE 4. *Gardens of the Palais Jamai, Fez.*

potential of the site. The rich botany of the site, with numerous endemic plants, has become a focus of the visitor's experience of the site.

An area of some activity has been the restoration of historic gardens. Key examples are the gardens at Topkapı in Istanbul and the courtyard garden in Marrakesh in Morocco undertaken by the Aga Khan Trust for Culture. One can also point to the restoration of historic gardens carried out by the Turkish Touring Association at Yildiz Park in Istanbul. Much of this work, however, has been done without the benefit of detailed examination of the historical record or archaeological investigations that would permit a more reliable view of the historic appearance of the gardens and the plant materials that were used.

Landscape architecture as a professional degree is not offered in university curricula in the region. Therefore, most projects are undertaken by foreign-trained professionals (educated usually in Germany, France, Britain, the United States, or Canada) or by expatriates. Establishment of a university-level course in landscape architecture would be an important step in strengthening local capacity and furthering appreciation of landscape design.

BIBLIOGRAPHY

Aga Khan Award for Architecture. *Place of Public Gardening in Islam.* Proceedings of Seminar Five in the series Architectural Transformation in the Islamic World, held in Amman, Jordan, 4–7 May 1980.

Aga Khan Award for Architecture. 1992.

Cochrane, T., and J. Brown, eds. *Landscape Design for the Middle East.* London, 1978.

Klein, K., and June Taboroff. "Landscape Art in the OQ." *Aramco World* 1992.

Landscape Design, no. 114 (May 1976). Special issue on Middle Eastern landscape design.

Mimar 8. Gardens and Landscapes, 1981.

World Bank country and urban sector studies. Washington, various dates.

JUNE TABOROFF

GASPRINSKII, ISMAIL BEY (1851–1914), Crimean Tatar reformer, educator, and publicist, regarded as an architect of modernism among Muslim Turkic subjects of the Russian Empire. Born in a small Crimean village to a family that had served in the Russian military for two generations, Ismail Bey was schooled first in a local *maktab* and then in Russian military academies before spending nearly three years abroad, principally in France and the Ottoman Empire. Upon his return to Crimea he taught Russian briefly in the Zincirli *madrasah* and served a four-year term as mayor of Bakhchisarai from 1878 to 1882. In that period he published a defining essay, *Russkoe musul'manstvo,* which challenged his community and its Russian leaders to awaken to a new age; he also received permission to produce a newspaper, *Perevodchik/Tercüman* (The Interpreter) that would appear in both Russian and Turkic. With the first issue, dated 10 April 1883, Gasprinskii launched one of the most important ethnic periodicals in Russian history and firmly committed himself to a life of public service dedicated to the modernization of Turkic society and the Islamic way, both within Russia and abroad.

For the next thirty years Gasprinskii endeavored to persuade his brethren to reassess their intellectual assumptions and sociocultural practices so as to overcome those conditions, derived largely from the influence of a misdirected religious orthodoxy, that he believed condemned Muslims to cultural inferiority under modern Western technological, military, political, and intellectual hegemony. The declining fortunes of Muslims everywhere, along with his own cosmopolitan experiences, impelled Ismail Bey to advocate a message that change was not only possible and good, but was also absolutely necessary for cultural survival. He further argued that progress could be ensured only by educating children in modern schools teaching a modern curriculum by modern methods (*uṣūl al-jadīd*), by encouraging social and economic cooperation, and by developing a willingness to borrow from other cultures (especially Europe) whatever might prove useful and beneficial. *Perevodchik/Tercüman,* countless pamphlets, and (after 1905) other periodical publications (*Alem-i nisvan, Alem-i sibyan, Al-nahḍah,* and *Kha! Kha! Kha!*), became the vehicles by which Gasprinskii spread his ideas and inspired the movement known as Jadīdism (modernism).

For Gasprinskii, creation of a new society able to compete effectively meant generating "new people." Education, of course, stood at the center of his project, for it was expected to reorient the way the younger generation thought and behaved. Islam would remain in the curriculum for moral guidance, but it would cease to dominate, replaced in that role by the sciences, mathematics, foreign languages, philosophy, and a range of practical subjects. The "new man" would be complemented by the "new woman," still expected to shoulder the major responsibility for nurturing society but given more autonomy and broader opportunities to participate in public affairs. Mobilization of the talents, resources, and energies of the largest possible number of people permeated Gasprinski's writings, leading him to call for the development of a common Turkic literary language, the establishment of mutual-aid societies, and cooperation with the Russian government and people. By the second decade of the twentieth century, Gasprinskii's influence, intellectually moderate and consummately practical, was felt throughout Turkic Russia, as well as in Turkey, Egypt, and even Muslim India.

[*See also* Jadīdism.]

BIBLIOGRAPHY

Gasprinskii, Ismail Bey. "Russo-Oriental Relations: Thoughts, Notes, and Desires." Translated by Edward J. Lazzerini. In *Tatars of the Crimea: Their Struggle for Survival,* edited by Edward Allworth, pp. 202–216. Durham, N.C., 1988. Translation of his *Russko-vostochnoe soglashenie* (1896).

Lazzerini, Edward J. "Ismail Bey Gasprinskii, the Discourse of Modernism, and the Russians." In *Tatars of the Crimea: Their Struggle for Survival,* edited by Edward Allworth, pp. 149–169. Durham, N.C., 1988.

Lazzerini, Edward J. "Ismail Bey Gasprinskii's *Perevodchik/Tercüman:* A Clarion of Modernism." In *Central Asian Monuments,* edited by Hasan B. Paksoy, pp. 143–156. Istanbul, 1992.

EDWARD J. LAZZERINI

GAZA. *See* West Bank and Gaza.

GEOMANCY. The term *geomancy* comes from medieval Latin *geomantia,* first used in Spain in the twelfth century as a translation of the Arabic *ʿilm al-raml* ("the science of sand"), the most common name for this type of divination. The practice is to be distinguished from a Chinese form of prognostication based on landforms, also called "geomancy" in English, that is entirely unrelated to the Islamic art. The origin of the practice is a matter of speculation, but it appears to have been well established in North Africa, Egypt, and Syria by the twelfth century. The majority of existing treatises on the subject are from the fourteenth century, but many were still being written in the nineteenth and twentieth centuries.

The divination is accomplished by forming and then interpreting a design, called a geomantic tableau, consisting of sixteen positions, each of which is occupied by a geomantic figure. The figures occupying the first four positions are determined by marking sixteen horizontal lines of dots on a piece of paper or a dust board. Each row of dots is examined to determine if it is odd or even and is then represented by one or two dots accordingly.

Each figure is then formed of a vertical column of four marks, each of which is either one or two dots. The first four figures, generated by lines made while the questioner concentrates on the question, are placed side by side in a row from right to left. From these four figures the remaining twelve positions in the tableau are produced according to set procedures. Various interpretive methods are advocated by geomancers for reading the tableau, often depending on the nature of the question asked. The course and seriousness of illness, the outcome of pregnancy, the location of lost or buried objects, and the fate of distant relatives are among the most popular questions addressed to geomancers.

Virtually no scholarly attention has been given to modern geomantic practices, except for those found in Africa. African geomancy has been the subject of several anthropological studies, most notably the form called *gara* practiced in Chad, the Yoruba practice of *ifa*, and the Madagascar form called *sikidy*. These practices are simplified but clearly derivative versions of classical Islamic geomancy.

In Egypt the medieval geomantic practices continue with little alteration. In the nineteenth and early twentieth centuries there were several printings of an Arabic manual using the name of the great thirteenth-century master of the art, al-Zanātī, as well as printings of essays on *raml* appended to a magical treatise by al-Būnī (thirteenth century) and to a popular medical manual by Dā'ūd al-Anṭākī (d. 1599). Treatises by early twentieth-century geomancers such as ʿAlī Ṣāliḥ al-Asyūṭī and ʿAbd al-Fattāḥ al-Sayyid al-Ṭūkhī are still available in Cairo bookshops. Nearly all large collections of Islamic manuscripts include Arabic geomantic manuals by seventeenth- and eighteenth-century Syrian or Yemeni authors as well as nineteenth-century Egyptian and North African geomancers, while numerous Turkish treatises written in the nineteenth century still await examination.

In Iran the term *raml* is applied to two types of divination. One type, frequently described by travelers such as E. G. Browne (*A Year Amongst the Persians*, London, 1893, reprinted 1984, p. 58), employed the throwing of brass dice that were strung together in groups of four. Although these are commonly referred to as geomantic dice, they are not marked so as to produce a geomantic figure, and thus the divination is a form of lot-casting or sortilège rather than true geomancy. *Raml* is also used for the classical form of geomancy, and in modern Persian writings the art often attains an astounding degree of complexity, with successive tableaux generated from previous ones. A large number of lithographed Persian texts published in India in the nineteenth century—notably by Raushan ʿAlī Faiẕābādī (Lucknow, 1881), Khudā-Bakhsh of Gujarat (Meerut, 1881), and Nūr Muḥammad Rammāl (Lucknow, 1891)—drew upon the Persian geomantic manual written before 1768 by ʿAbd al-Ghanī Shīrwānī that was lithographed in Lucknow a number of times between 1877 and 1895. Shīrwānī's treatise in turn incorporated many of the techniques described by the astrologer Hidāyat Allāh Shīrāzī, who acknowledged more than fifty sources used in his geomantic tract dedicated in 1592 to the Mughal emperor Akbar I.

In nearly all Islamic lands, geomancy and related methods of divination are still practiced. The popular forms vary from the simple casting of favorable or unfavorable geomantic figures to the complex interpretation of tableaux employing a large number of procedures.

[*See also* Astrology; Divination; Numerology.]

BIBLIOGRAPHY

Bascom, William R. *Ifa Divination: Communication between Gods and Men in West Africa*. Bloomington, 1969. Definitive study of the Yoruba form of geomancy *(ifa)* practiced in Dahomey and Nigeria. Includes an extensive bibliography.

Jaulin, Robert. *La géomancie: Analyse formelle*. Paris, 1966. Anthropological and structuralist analysis of Islamic geomancy extrapolated from his study of practices in Chad. Robert Ferry contributed sections on the mathematical significance of the system.

Peek, Philip M., ed. *African Divination Systems: Ways of Knowing*. Bloomington, 1991. Contains a chapter by Pierre Vérin and Narivelo Rajaonarimanana on *sikidy* geomancy that includes a good bibliography ("Divination in Madagascar: The Antemoro Case and the Diffusion of Divination," pp. 53–68), and a chapter by Susan Reynolds Whyte on a popular form of geomancy introduced in 1902 into Eastern Uganda ("Knowledge and Power in Nyole Divination," pp. 153–172).

Savage-Smith, Emilie, and Marion B. Smith. *Islamic Geomancy and a Thirteenth-Century Divination Device*. Malibu, 1980. The most comprehensive guide to the origin and practice of Islamic geomancy, with a bibliography of historical studies on the subject published prior to 1980.

Skinner, Stephen. *Terrestrial Astrology: Divination by Geomancy*. London, 1980. Written by an advocate of the art, the study is marred by a lack of knowledge of Arabic and insufficient acquaintance with original sources. Includes chapters on Islamic origins, with examples drawn from a modern Sudanese village, and on the Yoruba practice of *ifa* and on *sikidy* used in Madagascar.

Smith, Marion B. "The Nature of Islamic Geomancy with a Critique of a Structuralist's Approach." *Studia Islamica* 49 (1979): 5–38. Important critique of the structuralist analysis of Islamic geomancy made by Jaulin. Includes a guide to earlier anthropological as well as historical studies.

There are no European-language translations of any Arabic, Persian, or Turkish geomantic treatises. Some modern manuals have been printed, but are not readily available in even the largest libraries. The following are two of the more recent Arabic books:

Asyūṭī, ʿAlī Ṣāliḥ al-Falakī. *Kitāb ʿĀlam al-arwāḥ*. Cairo, about 1970.
Ṭūkhī, ʿAbd al-Fattāḥ al-Sayyid. *Manbaʿ uṣūl al-raml . . . al-musammā al-Durrah al-bahīyah fī al-ʿulūm al-ramlīyah*. Cairo, 1956.

EMILIE SAVAGE-SMITH

GERMANY. The knowledge of the Islamic Orient accumulated by envoys, pilgrims, and prisoners during the Middle Ages in German-speaking countries (e.g., contacts between the Carolingian court and the caliphate of Baghdad, during the Crusades and the Ottoman conquest of large parts of southeastern Europe) was important but did not result in a systematic academic reception. In this sense the sixteenth and part of the seventeenth centuries belong to the "prehistory" of Arabic and Islamic studies. In contrast to Paris or Leiden, German universities were for a longer period unsuccessful in creating permanent teaching positions for the contemporary languages of the Orient. Nevertheless, Arabic was taught at Faculties of Divinity as well as in some *Gymnasiums* and *Lateinschulen*. After the foundation of the Universities of Halle (1694) and Göttingen (1738), Oriental languages were part of the curriculum of the Faculty of Philosophy, although the first scholars in this field were primarily engaged in theological questions, for example Johann David Michaelis (1717–1791) and Johann Gottfried Eichhorn (1752–1827). The Collegium Orientale Theologicum founded in Halle in 1702 by August Hermann Francke (1663–1727) combined biblical philology with missionary zeal. The almost exclusive use of Latin by German scholars (until the middle of the nineteenth century) did not facilitate a broader reception of Eastern languages and cultures.

Modern German Scholarly Interest in the Islamic Orient. In western Europe, the age of the French Revolution witnessed a vivid interest in the contemporary Orient. The works of William Jones (1746–1794), Friedrich von Diez (1751–1817), Prussian *chargé d'affaires* in Constantinople, and Joseph von Hammer-Pürgstall (1774–1856) explain the extraordinarily broad influence on some Arab, Persian, and Ottoman authors on Johann Wolfgang Goethe and his contemporaries von (*West-östlicher Diwan*, 1819). The ingenious translations of Friedrich Rückert (1788–1866), including the Qur'ān and Ḥarīrī's *Maqāmāt* cannot be overestimated. Around 1800 a limited number of periodicals devoted to the Islamic East appeared (such as *Asiatisches Magazin* in Weimar, 1802, and Leipzig, 1806–1810; and *Fundgruben des Orients/Mines d'Orient* in Vienna, 1809–1818). The first form of institutionalization was the foundation of the German Oriental Society (Deutsche Morgenländische Gesellschaft) and the publication of an annual (ZDMG [1845, 1847]). In Leipzig, Heinrich Leberecht Fleischer (1801–1888), a student of Silvestre de Sacy, was the most influential German Arabist of the century with a large number of students from many countries. Besides extensive work on the texts and manuscripts, many German scholars concentrated on the life of Muḥammad, the history of the Qur'ān (e.g. Theodor Nöldeke [1836–1930], *Geschichte des Koran*, 1860, and the early centuries of the caliphate (Gustav Weil [1808–1889], *Geschichte der Chalifen*, 1846–1851, Julius Wellhausen [1844–1918], *Das arabische Reich und sein Sturz*, 1902). Important monographs were devoted to Persian and Turkish subjects.

After the proclamation of the Second German Empire (1871) the need for trained civil servants, officers, missionaries, and businessmen became more apparent. The Seminar für Orientalische Sprachen (S.O.S.) was created in the German capital in 1887 to cover these requirements (it is now affiliated with the University of Bonn). Academic teaching was still characterized by the close integration of Arab and Persian studies in their "mother philologies"—Semitic or Indo-European Studies. The first professorship devoted exclusively to Turkish was created for Karl Foy at the S.O.S. *Der Islam* (Berlin 1910–) and *Die Welt des Islams* (Leiden 1913–; and until 1923 the organ of the Deutsche Gesellschaft für Islamkunde) started to appear in these years. Important contributions to Islamic studies were done by learned "men on the spot," such as the consuls Johann Gottfried Wetzstein (1815–1905) and Johann Heinrich Mordtmann (1852–1932).

Against the philological mainstream some scholars advocated an integrated research of the contemporary Orient disregarded convential borderlines between disciplines. Carl Heinrich Becker (1876–1933) who occupied between 1908 and 1913 a chair of history and culture of the Orient at the new *Kolonialinstitut* in Hamburg, and Martin Hartmann (1851–1918) in Berlin were the most prominent representatives of a sort of *Islamkunde* (Islamic Studies) embedded in sociological and historical studies. Concurrently area studies *(Auslandskunde)* in the service of national political and economical interests were born. *Auslandskunde* reappeared in the 1960s under the label of *Regionalforschung* (regional studies) but did not lead to the development of larger departments or institutes.

World War I saw an unprecedented instrumentalization of the Oriental disciplines in the service of political aims. An important number of Orientalists served in Ottoman uniforms (e.g., Gotthelf Bergsträsser, Franz Babinger, Helmut Ritter). This generation occupied academic positions until the next postwar period. National Socialism compelled many scholars to leave the country and created a serious discontinuity in many branches of *Islamwissenschaft,* in which Germany had taken a leading position. Prominent emigrants to the United States, Britain, and Turkey were Ettinghausen, Herzfeld, Kahle, Rosenthal, Schacht, Süssheim, and Walzer.

The recovery of Islamic studies after 1945 was slow. Only a limited number of newly created universities showed interest in non-European studies (e.g., Bochum, Bayreuth, Bamberg). There are successful interdisciplinary research and publication projects such as *Verzeichnis der Orientalischen Handschriften in Deutschland* or *Tübinger Atlas des Vorderen Orients.* With the foundation of a research institute and library in Beirut and Istanbul, the German Oriental Society has become a significant platform of scholarly communication.

German Political Interest in the Islamic World. Prussia delegated in 1756 an extraordinary envoy to Istanbul, who, in 1761, concluded a treaty of friendship and trade with the Ottoman Empire. Two years later, the Turkish ambassador Ahmed Rismi Efendi traveled to Vienna and Berlin. The year 1790 marked the formation of a Prussian-Ottoman alliance. During the nineteenth century a network of consular missions of Prussia and other German principalities emerged in the provinces of the Ottoman Empire. After the proclamation of the Second Empire, Germany endeavored to diminish British influence by close cooperation with the Ottoman Empire. Respecting its territorial integrity Germany considered the Turkish realm a marketing area and source for raw materials. Important landmarks were the foundation of the Société du Chemin de Fer d'Anatolie (1889) and a growing military involvement after 1882. During his first voyage to the Orient Wilhelm II declared himself protector of 300 million Muslims. In 1903 Germany finally received the concession for the Baghdad railway. The Berlin-Baghdad "axis" was supposed to counterbalance the Gibraltar-Cairo-Calcutta connection and was the most severe test of German-British relations. The German assistance to the regimes of Abdülhamid II (r. 1876–1908) and the Young Turks presupposed "a political indifference toward the sufferings of the Christian peoples of the Turkish Empire" (Naumann, 1899). The appointment of Otto Liman von Sanders as chief of the German military mission in Constantinople in October 1913 was widely understood as a strengthening of the German position in the Near and Middle East. Generally, considerations of political prestige were stronger than economic reasons, as in the Morocco crises of 1907–1911. At the outbreak of World War I Germany occupied second place to France as creditor of the Ottomans (20.1 to 50 percent). In contrast to the Turkish and Moroccan engagement, German politics were more reserved toward Egypt and Iran.

During the World War I the Nachrichtenstelle für den Orient was charged with the support of mutineers in the British and French colonies. German war propaganda was mainly influenced by Pan-Islamic motives. At the same time, German and Austrian advisers and teachers occupied many positions in the Ottoman administrative and educational apparatus.

Prominent Germanophiles among Turkish and Arab intellectuals were Mehmed Âkif [Ersoy] (1873–1936), Aḥmad Shawqī (1868–1932), and Sāṭiʿ al-Ḥuṣrī (1882–1968). As in prewar times, Turkish authors were fascinated by the formation of the German state, and Arab nationalists, such as the Baʿth, saw it as a model for nation-building [*See the biographies of Ersoy and Ḥuṣrī.*]

Islam in Germany and German Muslims. The earliest Muslim presence in German-speaking countries is connected with Ottoman prisoners of war after the imperial *reconquista* of the Balkans. Some of them converted to Christianity. Until the mass immigration of "guest workers" (*Gastarbeiter*) in the 1960s as a consequence of the German-Turkish treaties of 1961 and 1964, Muslims did not represent an important demographic factor. Larger cities such as Berlin (whose first mosque in the quarter of Wilmersdorf completed in 1927), had a heterogeneous colony of diplomats, students, and merchants. In May 1958 refugees from the Soviet Union and Yugoslavia formed a Religöse Verwaltung der Muslemflüchtlinge in der Bundesrepublik Deutschland und Berlin. The administration edited a journal in German, *Al-muhâdschirûn.*

The organized immigration of Turkish and Yugoslav (and to a limited degree Moroccan and Tunisian) guest workers found its end with the "recruitment stop" of November 1973. Even though a small percentage of the workers returned to their countries of origin, the phenomenon of "chain migration" (mainly of separated families) and the important number of Turkish, Lebanese, Syrian, and Iranian citizens demanding political asylum (in accordance with Article 16 of the German Constitution) have steadily increased the Muslim population of Germany. The Turks concentrate in big cities and industrial agglomerations, but are more or less present in the whole country except the former East German states. Although the number of places of worship of the different ethnic groups and schools is high (roughly 1,000–1,200), most mosques are provisionally accommodated. The inauguration of the Faith Camii in Neo-Ottoman style in the southwestern town of Pforzheim in 1992 was generally interpreted as a breakthrough to normality.

There are no reliable figures on German converts to Islam by conviction or marriage. After their first meeting in Aachen 1976, conferences of German-speaking Muslims assembled 500 persons or more. Recent estimates count 8,000 converts, 30,000 Muslims by marriage (mostly German wives of Turkish immigrants), and a total of 100,000 German citizens confessing Islam (*Der Spiegel*, no. 14 [1992]). Striking is the almost complete absence of prominent converts (but note the high-ranking diplomat Murad Hofmann, born in 1931, and his book *Der Islam als Alternative*, Munich, 1992).

The Turkish minority, which in 1989 constituted some 1.6 million individuals, is composed of Sunnī and heterodox (Alevi; Ar., ʿAlawī) members, but this cannot be determined exactly. The Alevi/Bektaşi (Ar., Bektāshī) groups have started a religious-based organization, and there are have been attempts to recreate the traditional prayer ceremony, the Cem, attracting Alevis of different regional and ethnic origins.

The federal structure of the German political system in combination with the unsolved problem of the Muslim community as a "recognized public body" renders the solution of questions of education and cultus difficult. Most states lack Muslim groups of a multiethnic/multinational representation that can serve as viable negotiator with German authorities (the Berlin Islamföderation being an exception). After many setbacks in the 1970s there has been a tendency to consolidate existing Muslim networks in uniform and effective federations. A common feature of these federations is that their central administrations are concentrated in Cologne. They coordinate activities in neighboring countries (particularly France and the Benelux countries), and some of them are on good working terms with international Islamic organizations.

Another distinctive feature of Muslims in the German diaspora is a continued process of fission since 1970s. The first generation of immigrants who shared the hope of a quick return to their home countries had no desire to contribute to the institutionalization of Islam. Later, groups such as the Süleymanlı brotherhood (founded by Süleyman Hilmi Tunahan [d. 1959]) were extremely active in the gaining control of "neutral" mosques (directed by a registered Verein according to the law of associations) under the name of Islamic Cultural Centers (İslam Kültür Merkezleri Birliği/İKM). In 1992 there were approximately 200 centers under the umbrella of the İKM and their members rose from 12,000 in 1981 to 20,000. [*See* Islamic Cultural Centers.]

The Presidency of Religious Affairs (Diyanet İşleri Başkanlığı [DİB]) in Turkey, anxious not to lose influence among the Turkish minorities abroad, controls a growing number of communities by means of its own federation (Diyanet İşleri Türk İslam Birliği). On the occasion of the great religious festivals, the Directorate of Religious Services Abroad (Dış Hizmetleri Müdürlüğü) sends abroad a number of high-ranking servants as preachers. The Organization of the National Vision (Avrupa Milli Görüş Teşkilatı [AMGT]) seems to be by far the largest and most influential federation to be formed since 1977. AMGT is the international organization of the Turkish Millî Refâh Partisi (National Welfare Party), the successor since 1982 of Necmettin Erbakan's Millî Selamet Partisi (National Salvation Party). The organization had at least 20,000 members in Germany in 1992. [*See* Avrupa Millî Görüş Teşkilatı; Refâh Partisi; *and the biography of Erbakan*.]

Cemalettin Kaplan, a former adherent of AMGT organized in 1985 the radical İslam Cemiyetleri ve Cemaatları Birliği [İCCB]. Composed of roughly 5,000 members in 1992, it sympathizes with the Iranian concept of an Islamic Republic. In March 1993 Kaplan declared himself caliph of the Muslims. The hermetic Nurcu movement, with so-called *madrasahs* as meeting places, is omnipresent. The first nucleus of this expanding organization was created in Berlin in 1967. [*See* Nurculuk.]

With regard to transnational connections, among the above-mentioned groups only the DİB officials are connected with the consular service of the Turkish Republic. It is known that the Muslim World League supported individual *imām-hatip*s during the 1980s. The Süleymanlı are a modern branch of the Naqshbandīyah Ṣūfī order. A strictly hierarchically organized inner group is distinguished from an outer group of mere sympathizers. The organization exists in the conditions of *dār al-ḥarb* (the non-Muslim realm in Islamic jurisprudence) and is thus prepared to make compromises in questions of everyday life. The National Vision has a developed political program in Turkey and offers itself as the Islamic alternative to the established parties, whereas Kaplan's group (İCCB) rejects all forms of cooperation with a secular system. Among the federations, the National Vision has a clear proximity to the Muslim Brotherhood.

Even though there is no sign of the formation of a supraethnic Islamic community in Germany, many common traits on the local level exist. After most Muslims in Germany abandoned the option of returning to Turkey, kindergartens, social clubs, youth and women's associations, *ḥalāl* businesses, Islamic colleges for girls, Qur'ān courses, and religiously oriented summer camps have flourished. The relatively high standard of living makes the Muslims in Germany a favorite clientele for international Islamic banking and insurance organizations.

Migrant Islam in Germany has anticipated many trends of the new Islamic pluralism in Turkey after the 1980s. The future will show if it contributes to the formation of a "parallel society" sharing many of the mores of the larger German society or to the emergence of a German Islam with particular institutions and values.

BIBLIOGRAPHY

Abdullah, Muhammad S. *Geschichte des Islams in Deutschland*. Graz, 1981. Written for a broad public, without references and unreliable, but still the only book claiming to describe the history of Islam in Germany.

Antes, Peter, and Klaus Kreiser. *Muslims in Germany—German Muslims? Questions of Identity*. Birmingham, 1985. General overview.

Binswanger, Karl, and Fethi Sipahioğlu. *Türkisch-islamische Vereine als Faktor deutsch-türkischer Koexistenz*. Benediktbeuren, 1988. Important study of Turkish Muslim organizations in Germany, based on official sources.

Bobzin, Hartmut. "Geschichte der Arabischen Philologie in Europa bis zum Ausgang des achtzehnten Jahrhunderts." In *Grundriß der Arabischen Philologie*, edited by Wolfdietrich Fischer, vol. 3, pp. 155–187. Wiesbaden, 1992. Many references to sources and research literature.

Denffer, Ahmad von, ed. *Islam hier und heute: Beiträge vom 1.–12. Treffen Deutschsprachiger Muslime, 1976–1981*. Cologne, 1401/1981.

Gerholm, Tomas, and Yngve Georg Lithman, eds. *The New Islamic Presence in Western Europe*. London and New York, 1988. Important articles on many neglected aspects of European and especially German Islam.

Kreiser, Klaus, et al., eds. *Germano-Turcica: Zur Geschichte des Türkisch-Lernens in den Deutschsprachigen Ländern*. Bamberg, 1987. On the history of German interest in Turkish civilization.

Lähnemann, Johannes, ed. *Kulturbegegnung in Schule und Studium: Türken—Deutsche, Muslime—Christen, ein Symposium*. Hamburg, 1983. Other volumes of the "Nürnberger Forum," with many contributions on Islamic-Christian relations in Germany, appeared in 1986 and 1989.

Marré, Heiner, and Johannes Stüting, eds. *Der Islam in der Bundesrepublik Deutschland*. Aschendorff, 1986. Mainly on legal aspects of the Islamic community in Germany.

Nielsen, Jørgen S. *Muslims in Western Europe*. Edinburgh, 1992. Includes a chapter on the situation in the former West Germany (pp. 13–38).

Nirumand, Bahman, ed. *Im Namen Allahs: Islamische Gruppen und der Fundamentalismus in der Bundesrepublik Deutschland*. Cologne, 1990. Well-informed collection of articles from an agnostic viewpoint.

Schiffauer, Werner. *Die Migranten aus Subay: Türken in Deutschland, eine Ethnographie*. Stuttgart, 1991. Excellent, theoretically demanding monograph on a group of Turkish immigrants.

Wild, Stephan A. "National Socialism in the Arab Near East between 1933 and 1939." *Die Welt des Islam* 25 (1985): 126–173.

KLAUS KREISER

GHANA. The first Muslims to enter the area of modern Ghana were Dyula (Wangara) traders from the metropolitan districts of Mali. Attracted into the Voltaic region in the late fourteenth century by the gold trade from the Akan forest, these merchants established themselves in the numerous trading colonies that developed on the routes leading to the greater markets of the western Sudan. Their major settlement in the Voltaic region was Bighu. Leading Muslim families of Wa to the northwest also claim Dyula origins. In the fifteenth century Muslim kola traders from the Hausa states also arrived in the northeastern section of Ghana. With the expansion of the trade in the eighteenth century and the conclusion of the Fulani *jihād* of the early nineteenth century, Hausa immigration into Ghana increased. Contacts with Hausa traders contributed to the growth of Yendi and Salaga as important markets. The Qādirīyah order had been introduced into the region by the second decade of the nineteenth century.

For most of the nineteenth century the Muslim and non-Muslim communities accommodated each other. Farther south in the Asante capital of Kumasi, for example, Muslims even served in the king's council. By the mid-nineteenth century a more permanent Islamic service group, the Asante Nkramo, had been created as part of Asante institutions. The apparent rejection of *jihād* as an instrument of change by most Muslims in Ghana, is attributed by recent scholarship to these Muslims' acceptance of the Dyula-Suwarian teaching that true conversion occurred in God's own time.

Limited cases of militant Muslim activity occurred in the final decades of the nineteenth century. These included the extension of the *jihād* activities of Muhmud Karantao of Wahabu in Burkina Faso to parts of northern Ghana. Wa and western Gonja came briefly under the control of Samori Ture's Mande empire. In the central districts of northern Ghana, Zabarima and the locally recruited forces of Alfa Kazare and Babatu attempted to lay the foundation of an Islamic state. These activities were ended, however, when the French and British brought the areas under their respective colonial control. The ubiquitous presence of Muslims in twentieth-century Ghana, therefore, is the result of extensive migration rather than of mass conversion.

In the first post-independence census, conducted in 1960, Muslims accounted for 12 percent of the national population of 6.5 million; this rose to 15 percent in the estimated 1990 population of 15 million. Compared to the Christian share of 40 percent in 1960 and an estimated 60 percent in 1990, the relative growth of the Muslim community was minimal. At a seminar organized by the Center for the Distribution of Islamic Books in April 1989, Ghana's traditional Islamic education, which emphasized basic reading of the Qur'ān, was described as the leading cause of "illiteracy and ignorance," thus rendering the religion less attractive to potential converts. A central government effort to improve Islamic education had begun two years earlier in April 1987, when an Islamic Education Unit was created within the education ministry and charged with the responsibility of enforcing stricter educational standards in the nation's orthodox Islamic schools.

The Aḥmadīyah movement has been active in Ghana since the 1885 conversion of Benjamin Sam and Mahdi Appah on the Fante coast. Since 1921 Aḥmadī missionaries operating from their headquarters at Saltpond have managed to establish important centers at Kumasi and Wa. Unlike the orthodox Sunnī Muslim community, the Aḥmadīs invested in Western-style schools as a means of spreading their influence. The Ghana Aḥmadīyah Movement runs one missionary training college at Saltpond, seven secondary schools, and about one hundred Western-style elementary schools. Their few mission hospitals are also well staffed. [*See* Aḥmadīyah.]

Historical research into the nature of Muslim organizations in Ghana is limited. It is, however, evident that both the Qādirīyah brotherhood, introduced in the early nineteenth century by Hausa intermediaries, and the Tijānīyah order have followers here. Introduced from the Senegambia region in the second half of the nineteenth century, Tijanīyah teaching continues to spread from Meccan contacts. Although their numerical strength is difficult to estimate, the Tijanīs are a vocal group. In Kumasi mosque affairs, for example, they appear to counter the influence of the clerical establishment. [*See* Qādirīyah; Tijānīyah.]

Since Ghana's post-independence constitutions prohibited political parties founded on religious lines, the only Muslim political party in the nation's history was the Muslim Association Party, which was disbanded in 1957. The remaining Muslim associations in the country include the Ghana Muslim Mission, the Supreme Council for Islamic Affairs, and the Ghana Muslim Students Association. The umbrella organization is the Muslim Representative Council, which oversees matters affecting social, economic, and religious interests, such as arranging for pilgrimages to Mecca.

BIBLIOGRAPHY

Fisher, Humphrey J. *Aḥmadiyyah: A Study in Contemporary Islām on the West African Coast*. London, 1963. Excellent introduction to scholarly analysis of the Aḥmadīyah movement. The chapter on Ghana covers only the rise of the sect in the country.

Kramer, Robert S. "Social and Political Dynamics in the Kumasi Zongo." Paper presented at the thirty-fifth Annual Conference of the African Studies Association, Seattle, 1992. The most recent discussion of Zongo politics in Kumasi.

Levtzion, Nehemia. *Muslims and Chiefs in West Africa*. Oxford, 1968. Remains the best overview of the spread of Islam in Ghana from early times to the nineteenth century.

Owusu-Ansah, David. *Islamic Talismanic Tradition in Nineteenth-Century Asante*. Lewiston, N.Y., 1991. Offers an interesting discussion on the use of Islamic charms in non-Muslim Asante, an example of what some scholars have referred to as the accommodative nature of Islam in sub-Saharan Africa.

Schildkrout, Enid. *Islam and Politics in Kumasi: An Analysis of Disputes over the Kumasi Central Mosque*. New York, 1974.

Schildkrout, Enid. *People of the Zongo: The Transformation of Ethnic Identities in Ghana*. Cambridge, 1978. Pioneering work on the internal politics of Muslim communities in non-Muslim Asante.

Silvermann, Raymond, and David Owusu-Ansah. "The Presence of Islam among the Akan of Ghana: A Bibliographic Essay." *History in Africa* 16 (1989): 325–339. Important historiographical essay on Ghana.

Wilks, Ivor. *Wa and the Wala: Islam and Polity in Northwestern Ghana*. Cambridge, 1989. Study of an important Muslim community in Ghana; documents the place of Islam in those northern Ghanaian societies in which an Islamic superstructure was imposed on traditional substructures.

Wilks, Ivor, Nehemia Levtzion, and Bruce M. Haight. *Chronicles from Gonja: A Tradition of West African Muslim Historiography.* Cambridge, 1986. Excellent analysis of the place of Muslims in the important nothern state of Gonja.

DAVID OWUSU-ANSAH

GHANNŪSHĪ, RĀSHID AL- (b. 1941), Islamic thinker, activist, and political leader in Tunisia. Born to a peasant family in Tunisia, Rāshid al-Ghannūshī (often spelled Ghannoushi in Western literature) is the head of the Ḥizb al-Nahḍah (Renaissance Party; formerly called Ḥarakat al-Ittijāh al-Islāmī, or Islamic Tendency Movement) and its chief theoretician. Ghannūshī grew up in a religious household and received his early education in the traditional Zaytūnah schools. In 1968 he received a degree in philosophy from the University of Damascus, Syria. After a year in France, Ghannūshī returned to Tunisia to become a secondary-school philosophy teacher, and to establish—along with a group of young Tunisians increasingly at odds with the secular policies of Habib Bourguiba's regime—an organized Islamic movement. In 1981 he was sentenced to eleven years' imprisonment for operating an unauthorized association; he was released in 1984. In 1987, he received a life term of forced labor but was discharged in 1988. In the early 1990s Ghannūshī was living in Europe as a political exile.

Ghannūshī's thought reflects a masterly understanding of western and Islamic philosophies and a genuine concern for reconciling the basic tenets of Islam with modernity and progress. Ghannūshī maintains nontraditional views on several issues. He evaluates the West within the philosophical dimension of East-West dialogue. Unlike Sayyid Quṭb of Egypt's Muslim Brotherhood, he perceives the West as an ideological counterweight to Islamic doctrines: the West is considered neither superior nor inferior to Islam. Ghannūshī sees coexistence and cooperation as the basis for the relationship between the two. What sets the two worlds apart, however, is the difference in their perception of the fundamental concepts, or "effective ideas," that move their cultures: the value and place of humanity in the universe. Islam replaces the Western "man-god" formula with an Islamic one, "man the vicegerent of God on earth"; Islam posits God as the ultimate value in the universe; it acknowledges the material and spiritual essences of humanity and attempts to reconcile them; and it directs human activities according to the divine regulations and concise values embodied in the *sharīʿah.*

Ghannūshī acknowledges that the system of democracy was a direct consequence of a particular Western experience. He perceives democracy as a method of government and as a philosophy. In his view, the Muslims' problem is not with democratic institutions themselves, but with the secular and nationalistic values behind democracy. Islamic democracy is distinguished from other systems by its moral content as derived from the *sharīʿah.*

Ghannūshī makes an important intellectual contribution by linking westernization with dictatorship. He believes two common characteristics dominate the political systems of the Arab and larger Muslim world—westernization and dictatorship by ruling elites. Because of its alienation from the masses, the westernized elite resorts to violent and repressive means to impose its foreign-inspired models and perpetuate its rule.

Ghannūshī advocates an equal role for women in society and their right to education, work, choice of home and marriage, ownership of property, and political participation. He considers the veil a matter of personal choice that is not to be imposed by the state.

Because he takes a gradualist stance in advocating social and political change, Ghannūshī seeks to inspire a more vital cultural model. He relies on orthodox ideas while in fact reinterpreting them to accommodate the modern issues of his society. His ideas, though sometimes controversial, are paid much attention by Muslim activists and intellectuals. Ghannūshī's intellectual contributions and political activism have gained him prominence within the contemporary Islamic movement.

[*See also* Ḥizb al-Nahḍah; Tunisia.]

BIBLIOGRAPHY

Ghannūshī, Rāshid al-. *Maqālāt* (Essays). Paris, 1984. Collection of articles written by Ghannūshī from 1973 to 1982.

Ghannūshī, Rāshid al-. *Fī al-Mabādiʾ al-Asāsīyah lil-Dīmuqrāṭīyah wa-Uṣūl al-Ḥukm al-Islāmī* (The Principles of Democracy and the Fundamentals of Islamic Government). N.p., 1990. Comparison between Islamic and Western perspectives on the principles of democracy and government.

Ghannūshī, Rāshid al-. "We don't Have a Religious Problem" (interview with Wendy Kirstianasen). *Middle East* 203 (September 1991): 19–20.

Ghannūshī, Rāshid al-. *Ṭarīqunā ilá al-Ḥaḍārah* (Our Path to Civilization). Tunis, n.d. Insightful interpretation of the causes of the decline of the Muslim nation and ways to its recovery.

Ghannūshī, Rāshid al-, and Ḥamīdah al-Nayfar. *Mā Huwa al-Gharb?* (What Is the West?). Tunis, n.d. Critical overview of the West and its basic philosophical values.

Ghannūshī, Rāshid al-, and Ḥasan al-Turābī. *Al-Ḥarakah al-Islāmīyah wa-al-Taḥdīth* (The Islamic Movement and Modernization). N.p., n.d. Important analysis of contemporary Islamic movements and the strategy of Islamic activism.

Shahin, Emad Eldin. "The Restitution of Islam: A Comparative Study of the Contemporary Islamic Movements in Tunisia and Morocco." Ph.D. diss., Johns Hopkins University, 1989. Study of the evolution, composition, and dynamics of the Islamic Tendency Movement in Tunisia and an analysis of Ghannūshī's thought.

EMAD ELDIN SHAHIN

GHAYBAH. The Arabic word *ghaybah* literally means absence, but in the theological constructs of the Twelvers (Ithnā ʿAsharīyah, a Shīʿī sect) it designates the "occultation" of the twelfth imam, Muḥammad, son of al-Ḥasan ibn ʿAlī al-ʿAskarī (d. 874). He has gone into hiding, but he remains present in the community, and will return as an eschatological figure *(al-mahdī, al-qā'im)*. He will come with the sword, he will fill the earth with justice, and his reign will usher in the last days and the Resurrection.

The idea that a particular leader has not died and is but temporarily absent is perhaps universal. It had arisen among Shīʿī groups already at the death of ʿAlī, the first imam (d. 661), and emerged again upon the deaths of various later imams. The enduring success of the Twelvers' formulation is probably owing to the prior existence of traditions (both Sunnī and Shīʿī) which, drawing on ancient numerological preferences, mentioned twelve just rulers or leaders. Transforming the historical facts and integrating them into a mythic/theological structure was a process occupying generations of thinkers, who elaborated it in heresiographical works and in special studies of the Ghaybah. The standard version accounts for the disappearance of the last Imam by reference to excessive persecution.

The Twelvers believed the Ghaybah to have two stages. During the Lesser Occultation, the Imam continued to communicate with his community through four successive appointed agents, the last of whom died in 944 [*see* Wakālah al-Khāṣṣah, al-]. During the Greater Occultation, which continues to the present, there is no special agent, although the Imāmī jurists *(fuqahā'*; sg., *faqīh)* are recognized in a general sense as agents of the Absent Imam [*see* Wakālah al-ʿĀmmah, al-]. The doctrine of the Ghaybah enabled the Imāmīs to create a hermeneutical structure mirroring that already created by the Sunnīs. As the source of authority was absent, his authority resided now in literary texts. The first of these was the Qur'ān, the result of God's revelation to the Prophet. The second and much larger corpus was *ḥadīth,* as transmitted from the sinless imams. Thereafter, real practical authority depended on interpretation (hermeneutics), the monopoly of the learned classes, the *ʿulamā'* and the *fuqahā'*. It is probable that these classes had achieved rudimentary existence prior to the Ghaybah and so facilitated the emergence of the doctrine.

Imāmī Shīʿī political theory is conditioned by the doctrine of the Ghaybah. Since the imam was the only rightful leader of the community and administrator of the *sharīʿah,* those who actually ruled during the Ghaybah were perceived to be usurpers and, in some sense, illegitimate. In time the theory emerged that the only rightful agent of the imam, the only one to administer the *sharīʿah* in his absence, was the fully qualified *faqīh.* The ramifications of this theory secured to the jurists an independent income (since they, in the place of the imam, administered the tax known as *khums*) and prompted them to significant political activity. This was particularly noticeable in the late Qājār period in Iran, and more recently in the Islamic Revolution of 1979 in Iran.

[*See also* Imam; Ithnā ʿAsharīyah; Mahdi; Shīʿī Islam, *historical overview article.*]

BIBLIOGRAPHY

Sachedina, A. A. *Islamic Messianism: The Idea of the Mahdi in Twelver Shīʿism.* Albany, N.Y., 1981.

Sachedina, A. A. *The Just Ruler in Shīʿite Islam: The Comprehensive Authority of the Jurist in Imamite Jurisprudence.* New York, 1988.

NORMAN CALDER

GHAZĀLĪ, ABŪ ḤĀMID AL- (1058–1111), or Abū Ḥāmid al-Ghazzālī, medieval Muslim theologian, jurist, and mystic. Few individuals in the intellectual history of Islam have exerted influence as powerful and varied as did Abū Ḥāmid al-Ghazālī. When he died at the age of fifty-two, he had attempted, with an exceptionally perspicacious mind and a powerful pen, a grand synthesis of the Islamic sciences that has ever since evoked the wonder and admiration of scholars, both Muslim and non-Muslim.

Born in 1058 in Tus in the province of Khurasan in Iran, al-Ghazālī studied mysticism, theology, and law with a number of teachers, including the famous Ashʿarī theologian Abū al-Maʿālī al-Juwaynī. He gained distinction in the court of the Seljuk vizier Niẓām al-Mulk, and at the age of thirty-four he was appointed professor at the Niẓāmīyah college at Baghdad. After teaching there for several years, al-Ghazālī suffered a crisis of confidence. Losing faith in the efficacy and purpose of the learning he had acquired and was now disseminating, he searched for the truth and certitude that alone could set his moral doubt at rest. He left his position at the Niẓāmīyah, withdrew from practical life, and spent eleven years in travel, meditation, and reflection. When he returned he had found the object of his search—in Sufism. This was to be a watershed in his personal life and in the intellectual history of Islam. After a brief career at the Niẓāmīyah of Nishapur, he spent the last five years of his life in his native town teaching and writing.

The details of al-Ghazālī's quest for knowledge that would give certitude are found in his autobiography, *Al-munqidh min al-ḍalāl* (Deliverer from Error). Al-Ghazālī tells us that, of the four groups of people who claimed to be in possession of the truth, he found that the theologians were engaged in pointless hairsplitting; the philosophers, who followed the Greek tradition, spun insubstantial metaphysical cobwebs; while the esotericists (the Ismāʿīlī *taʿlīmī*s who believed that only a perfect imam could provide true and authoritative knowledge) could in practice offer nothing better than cheap, diluted Pythagoreanism. It was only the fourth group, the Ṣūfīs, who walked the right path, because they combined knowledge with action, had sincerity of purpose, and actually experienced the serenity and contentment that comes from direct illumination of the heart by God.

Al-Ghazālī's critique of the philosophers, the esotericists, and the theologians constituted the critical aspect of his work, but there was a constructive aspect to it also; in fact the two aspects are closely linked. In a sense the principal motif of all al-Ghazālī's work is spiritualization of religious thought and practice: form must be imbued with spirit, and law and ritual with ethical vision. Taking salvation in the hereafter as the final goal, and therefore the ultimate point of reference, he set out to identify and analyze the aids and impediments to that goal. This resulted in his best-known work, *Iḥyā' ʿulūm al-dīn,* an attempt to integrate the major disciplines of Islamic religion—theology and law, ethics and mysticism. Here as in other works al-Ghazālī seeks to demystify Islam. He maintains, for example, that in order to be a Muslim it is sufficient to hold the beliefs that have been laid down by God and his Prophet in the Qur'ān and *sunnah,* and that knowledge of the complex arguments advanced by the theologians is not a requisite of faith. In law, similarly, casuistry is condemnable, for by retaining the form at the expense of the spirit, it defeats the very purpose of the law. In ethics he offers a detailed discussion of a series of vices and virtues, calling love of the world the root of all evil and love of God the highest good. The essence of religion is experience, not mere profession, and the Ṣūfīs are the ones who are able to experience the realities that theologians only talk about. The *Iḥyā'* is thus not only a theoretical statement, it is also a practical guide, and it is this union of theory and practice, of form and spirit, that gives it its special place in Islamic literature.

Al-Ghazālī was concerned not only with reviving the Islamic disciplines but also with reforming society in a practical way. In his works he offers candid assessments of the roles of different groups in society. He comes down hard on the generality of Muslim scholars, who, he believes, are chiefly to blame for the social and moral decadence of Muslim society. Worldliness has turned them away from their primary function of guiding the rulers and the commoners, and they are busy ingratiating themselves with the powerful and influential. They are moreover involved in petty disputes and have shut their eyes to the real and pressing problems facing society. The rulers are autocratic and misuse the public treasury. Al-Ghazālī wrote letters to several sultans and viziers reminding them of their duties in this world and of accountability in the next. He also criticized the rich for their callousness and the poor for their superstitions and non-Islamic practices.

Al-Ghazālī's method is no less important than the substance of his work; the former, in fact, has a direct bearing on the character of the latter. His method may be described as critical-analytical. Al-Ghazālī holds that everything is worthy of study and subject to scrutiny; analysis reveals the strengths and weaknesses of a view or thought-system; and the truth, once discovered, deserves to be accepted on its own terms. This approach leads him to conclude that theology, though it serves its avowed purpose well, fails to yield absolute certainty, and further that the philosophers' views were not only incompatible with Islam but also lacked internal consistency. His critique of philosophy illustrates his method best. Al-Ghazālī did not make a blanket criticism of philosophy. Dividing this discipline into six areas—mathematics, logic, physics, metaphysics, politics, and ethics—he found nothing wrong with the first three and was willing to consider the philosophers' contributions in the last two. It was in metaphysics, he maintained, that the philosophers had committed major errors, and this was due to their claim to competence in an area where they had nothing to go on. The philosophers failed to follow the rules of demonstrative reasoning because they had no data and no evidence to support their wild speculations concerning such matters as the origin and structure of the universe. Al-Ghazālī thus parts company not only with the Muslim philosophers but also with those of the orthodoxy who were not content with anything less than a total rejection of the Greek tradition.

His vast learning, his systematic thought, his lucid style, and above all his utter sincerity and objectivity ensured al-Ghazālī an exceptionally wide audience within his lifetime, and his works in various fields have continued to exercise a powerful influence on Muslim thought ever since. Today he is one of the writers who have received the most attention from Western as well as Muslim scholars—and for good reason. His work, in both substance and method, has a distinctly "modern" temper, and thus has great appeal for a modern audience. It offers on the one hand criticism of blind acceptance of authority *(taqlīd),* insistence on a thorough study of a discipline with a view to discovering its fundamental principles, and objectivity of approach; and on the other, it focuses on the essentials of religion as distinguished from historical accretions of secondary importance, an attempt to arrive at an integrated understanding of religion, a willingness to entertain doubt and put it in perspective, and a concern with the moral well-being of the ordinary believer.

[*See also* Philosophy; Sufism, *article on* Ṣūfī Thought and Practice; Theology.]

BIBLIOGRAPHY

The *Iḥyā' ʿulūm al-dīn*

The complete Arabic text of the *Iḥyā'* is available in a five-volume edition (Beirut, 1991). A good English translation of the full work does not exist yet, though many of its forty books have been individually translated.

Other Works by al-Ghazālī

ON THEOLOGY. *Al-iqtiṣād fi al-iʿtiqād* (Cairo, 1971); and *Iljām al-ʿawāmm ʿan ilm al-kalām,* edited by Muḥammad al-Baghdādī (Beirut, 1975). ON PHILOSOPHY. *Maqāsid al-falsafah,* edited by Sulaymān Dunyā (Cairo, 1967); and *Tahāfut al-falāsifah,* edited by Sulaymān Dunyā, 2d rev. ed. (Cairo, [1955]), available in English translation by Sabih Ahmad Kamali (Lahore, 1963). ON LOGIC. *Miʿyār al-ʿilm fi al-manṭiq,* edited by Aḥmad Shams al-Dīn (Beirut, 1990); and *Kitāb miḥakk al-naẓar fi al-manṭiq* (Beirut, 1966). ON MYSTICISM. *Mishkāt al-anwār,* edited by Badīʿ al-Laḥḥām (Beirut, 1990), available in English translation by William H. T. Gairdner (Lahore, 1952). ON LAW. *Al-mustaṣfā min ʿilm al-uṣūl* (Cairo, 1937). ON THE QUR'ĀN. *Jawāhir al-Qur'ān* (Beirut, 1985), translated by Muhammad A. Quasem as *The Jewels of the Qur'ān* (London, 1983). REFUTATION OF THE BĀṬINĪYAH. *Faḍā'iḥ al-Bāṭinīyah,* edited by ʿAbd al-Raḥmān Badawī (Cairo, 1964), selections translated into German by Ignácz Goldziher as *Streitschrift des Gazali gegen die Batinijja-Sekte* (Leiden, 1916); and *The Just Balance (al-Qisṭāṣ al-Mustaqīm),* translated by D. P. Brewster (Lahore, 1978). RESPONSE TO CRITICS. *Fayṣal al-tafriqah bayna al-Islām wa-al-zandaqah* (Cairo, 1961). AUTOBIOGRAPHY. *Al-munqidh min al-ḍalāl wa-al-mūṣil ilā Dhī al-ʿizzah wa-al-jalāl,* edited by Jamīl Ṣalība and Kāmil ʿAyyād ([Damascus], 1981), translated by W. Montgomery Watt in *The Faith and Practice of al-Ghazali* (London, 1953).

Works on al-Ghazālī

Badawī, ʿAbd al-Raḥmān. *Mu'allafāt al-Ghazālī.* Cairo, 1961. Excellent and thorough bibliographical study of al-Ghazālī's works, by a major Arab scholar. Also available in French *(L'oeuvre d'al-Ghazzali).*

Nadvī, Abulḥasan ʿAlī. *Rijāl al-fikr wa-al-daʿwah fī al-Islām.* Kuwait, 1397/1977.

Ormsby, Eric L. *Theodicy in Islamic Thought: The Dispute over al-Ghazali's "Best of All Possible Worlds."* Princeton, 1984.

Sharif, M. M., ed. *A History of Muslim Philosophy.* Vol. 1. Wiesbaden, 1963. See M. Saeed Sheikh, "Metaphysics" and "Mysticism" (pp. 581–624), and Abdul Khaliq, "Ethics" (pp. 624–637).

Smith, Margaret. *Al-Ghazālī, the Mystic.* London, 1944.

Umaruddin, M. *The Ethical Philosophy of al-Ghazzali.* 4 parts. Aligarh, 1949–1951.

MUSTANSIR MIR

GHAZĀLĪ, MUḤAMMAD AL- (b. 1917), Egyptian religious scholar and former leading member of al-Ikhwān al-Muslimūn (Muslim Brotherhood). Born in Buhayra Province, he graduated from al-Azhar in 1941 and has occupied influential positions in his own country and in other Arab states. In Egypt, he was director of the Mosques Department, director general of Islamic Call *(daʿwah),* and under secretary of the Ministry of Awqāf. He has also taught at the Universities of al-Azhar (Egypt), King ʿAbd al-ʿAzīz and Umm al-Qūrā (Saudi Arabia), and Qatar and was the academic director of Amīr ʿAbd al-Qādir's Islamic University in Algeria.

Al-Ghazālī was dismissed from his position in the *hay'ah ta' sīsīyah* (constituent body) of the Ikhwān in December 1953, reportedly after attempting, with two other prominent members, to unseat the organization's leader, Ḥasan al-Ḥudaybī (with the approval, some Muslim Brothers suspected, of Gamal Abdel Nasser and the Free Officers). Many feel that he still remains an Ikhwānī in all but name, and he certainly favors the formation of an Islamic party in Egypt today.

Active in publishing, al-Ghazālī has written approximately forty titles including such important works as *Moral Character of the Muslim, Islam and Economic Affairs, Islam and Political Despotism, A Constitution for Cultural Unity,* and *Prejudice and Tolerance in Christianity and Islam.* He has established a reputation for being a reasonable, well-balanced, and independent scholar. He is a rigorous jurist, although by no means a traditionalist, and his positions on various issues are taken seriously by the mainstream of the Islamic movement.

Substantively, al-Ghazālī submits the important thesis that contemporary Muslims have paid excessively detailed jurisprudential attention to matters of cleanliness, prayers, pilgrimage, and rituals while lagging far behind the West with regard to matters of government, the economy, and finance.

Al-Ghazālī is strongly supportive of an extensively defined concept of *shūrā* (political consultation), and he is regarded as somewhat modernist in social and technological matters, condemning the austere, simplistic orientation of what he terms *al-fiqh al-badawī* ("nomadic jurisprudence"), and he does not preclude the experience of other (non-Muslim) societies as a source of inspiration for Muslim societies. For example, he cites both historical Islamic as well as contemporary non-Islamic examples to support the case that a woman may legitimately assume any high post in society.

Methodologically, al-Ghazālī's main, and rather daring, contribution has been his attempt to reduce what he regards as an excessive reliance on the *ḥadīth* in contemporary jurisprudence. He admits only the *ḥadīth*s that have a Qur'ānic credibility and excludes *aḥādīth al-āḥād* ("single sayings"), if they appear odd or ill reasoned. He maintains that "a little reading of the blessed Qur'ān and a lot of reading of the *aḥādīth* does not give an accurate picture of Islam." In his view, it is this lopsided methodology in approaching Islam that partly explains what he regards as the "infantile" attitude of militant Islamists; they are obsessed with power but poorly trained.

Al-Ghazālī's strict scrutiny of the *ḥadīth* thus enables him to criticize simultaneously both the Muslim social reactionaries, who use *ḥadīth*s on the flimsiest grounds to justify such practices as beating and sodomizing wives, and the Islamist political radicals, who have used similar *ḥadīth*s to justify forcing their own views and authority on society at large.

[*See also* Egypt; Fundamentalism; Modernism; Muslim Brotherhood, *article on* Muslim Brotherhood in Egypt.]

BIBLIOGRAPHY

Ghazālī, Muḥammad al-. *Humūn dāʿiyah.* Cairo, 1983. Useful collection illustrating al-Ghazālī's position on several religious and social issues.

Ghazālī, Muḥammad al-. *Al-sunnah al-nabawīyah bayna ahl al-fiqh wa-ahl al-ḥadīth.* Cairo, 1991. Tenth edition in two years of a book in which al-Ghazālī illustrates how his methodology of jurisprudence may be applied to the analysis of various religious and social issues.

Ḥasanah, ʿUmar. *Fiqhh al-daʿwah.* Qatar, 1988. Contains an interview in which al-Ghazālī clarifies his views on several contemporary issues. See chapter 7, "Ḥiwār maʿa al-Shaykh Muḥammad al-Ghazālī."

NAZIH N. AYUBI

GHAZĀLĪ, ZAYNAB AL- (b. 1917), prominent writer and teacher of the Muslim Brotherhood, founder of the Muslim Women's Association (1936–1964). The daughter of an al-Azhar-educated independent religious teacher and cotton merchant, she was privately tutored in Islamic studies in the home in addition to attending public school through the secondary level, and she obtained certificates in *ḥadīth,* preaching, and Qur'ānic exegesis. Her father encouraged her to become an Islamic leader, citing the example of Nusaybah bint Kaʿb al-Māzinīyah, a woman who fought alongside the Prophet in the Battle of Uḥud. Although for a short time she joined Hudā Shaʿrāwī's Egyptian Feminist Union, she came to see this as a mistaken path for women, believing that women's rights were guaranteed in Islam. [*See the biography of Shaʿrāwī.*] At the age of eighteen she founded the Jamāʿat al-Sayyidāt al-Muslimāt (Muslim Women's Association), which, she claims, had a membership of three million throughout the country by the time it was dissolved by government order in 1964. Her weekly lectures to women at the Ibn Ṭulūn Mosque drew a crowd of three thousand, which grew to five thousand during the holy months of the year (interview with the author, 13 September 1988). Besides offering lessons for women, the association published a magazine, maintained an orphanage, offered assistance to poor families, and mediated family disputes. The association also took a political stance, demanding that Egypt be ruled by the Qur'ān.

The similar goals of the Muslim Brotherhood were noted by its founder, Ḥasan al-Bannā', who requested that al-Ghazālī's association merge with the Muslim Sisters, the women's branch of his organization. She refused until 1949, shortly before al-Bannā's assassination, when, sensing that it was critical for all Muslims to unite behind al-Bannā's leadership, she gave him her oath of allegiance and offered him her association. He accepted her oath and said that the Muslim Women's Association could remain independent. [*See the biography of al-Bannā'.*] During the 1950s the Muslim Women's Association cooperated with the Muslim Sisters to provide for families who had lost wealth and family members as a result of Nasser's crackdown on the Muslim Brotherhood.

Al-Ghazālī was instrumental in regrouping the Muslim Brotherhood in the early 1960s. Imprisoned for her activities in 1965, she was sentenced to twenty-five years of hard labor but was released under Anwar el-Sadat's presidency in 1971. She describes her prison experiences, which included suffering many heinous forms of torture, in a book entitled *Ayyām min ḥayātī* (Days from My Life; Cairo and Beirut, 1977). She depicts herself as enduring torture with strength beyond that of most men, and she attests to both miracles and visions that strengthened her and enabled her to survive. She sees herself as the object of President Gamal Abdel Nasser's personal hatred, for she and her colleague ʿAbd al-Fattāḥ Ismāʿīl "robbed" him of the generation that had been raised on his propaganda (p. 185). She believes that the superpowers were involved in singling her out to Nasser as a threat, and indeed she affirms that Islam's mission means the annihilation of the power of the United States and the Soviet Union (p. 185). Nonetheless, she denies that the Muslim Brotherhood intended to assassinate Nasser, for "killing the unjust ruler does not do away with the problem" of a society that needs to be entirely reeducated in Islamic values. In her book she condemns tactics of murder, torture, and terrorism and denies that the Muslim Brotherhood wanted to usurp power (p. 144). Later, however, she justified the threat of violence against unbelievers in order to bring them forcibly "from darkness to light," comparing such tactics to snatching poison from the hands of a child (interview with the author, June 1981). She defined the Muslim Brotherhood as the association of all Muslims and said that Muslims who did not belong to it were deficient, although she did not go so far as to call them unbelievers. At that time she supported the Iranian Revolution, but in a later interview (13 September 1988) she said that both the Shiism of the regime and the tactics of violence against its citizens had led her to conclude that it was not really an Islamic state.

The Muslim Women's Association was taken from al-Ghazālī's hands in 1965 and merged with a rival association of the same name founded by a former member of her group. The rival group was a religious voluntary association. Such associations, which number in the thousands, have played a major role in the religious life of women in Egypt in this century, offering lessons in the Qur'ān and Islamic law, classes in sewing and other crafts, and pre-schools for children, among other social services.

After her release from prison, al-Ghazālī resumed teaching and writing, first for the revived Muslim Brotherhood's monthly magazine, *Al-daʿwah,* banned by Sadat in September 1981, and then for another Islamist publication, *Liwā' al-islām.* She describes herself as a "mother" to the Muslim Sisters, as well as to the young men she helped organize in the early 1960s. She was editor of a women's and children's section in *Al-daʿwah,* in which she encouraged women to become educated, but to be obedient to their husbands and stay at home while raising their children. She blamed many of the ills of society on the absence of mothers from the home. This conservative stance appears to be contradicted by the historical figures she used as models of womanhood in short vignettes in that same section, courageous women warriors from the early period of Islam, including members of the extremist Khārijī sect, which was virtually obliterated in warfare with the larger Muslim community.

Al-Ghazālī's own example as an activist in the public sphere who divorced her first husband for interfering with her Islamic activities and threatened her second husband with the same also appears to contradict her own advice. When asked about this discrepancy, she said that her case was special, because God had given her the "blessing"—although not viewed as such by most people—of not having conceived any children (interview with the author, 13 September 1988). This gave her a great deal of freedom. Her husband was also quite wealthy, so she had servants to do her housework. She further regarded it as a boon that her husband was a polygamist, for whenever he went to see one of his other wives, "it was like a vacation" for her. She insists, nonetheless, that she has remained obedient to her husband. She believes that Islam allows women to be active in all aspects of public life, as long as it does not interfere with their first and most sacred duty: to be a wife and mother. Her second husband died while she was in prison (having divorced her under threat of imprisonment himself). Having fulfilled her duty of marriage, she feels free to devote all of her energies to the Islamic cause. Although the Islamic movement throughout the Muslim world today has attracted large numbers of young women, especially since the 1970s, Zaynab al-Ghazālī stands out thus far as the only woman to distinguish herself as one of its major leaders.

[*See also* Egypt; Muslim Brotherhood, *article on* Muslim Brotherhood in Egypt; *and* Women's Movements.]

BIBLIOGRAPHY

Works by Zaynab al-Ghazālī

Ayyām min ḥayātī (Days from My Life). Cairo and Beirut, 1977. Al-Ghazālī's prison memoirs, reprinted in at least eight editions. A detailed review of this book by Valerie Hoffman-Ladd may be found in the newsletter of the Association of Middle East Women's Studies, no. 5 (October 1987).

Naḥwa baʿth jadīd (Toward a New Renaissance). Cairo, 1987.

Works on Zaynab al-Ghazālī

Hoffman, Valerie J. "An Islamic Activist: Zaynab al-Ghazālī." In *Women and the Family in the Middle East: New Voices of Change*, edited by Elizabeth W. Fernea, pp. 233–254. Austin, 1985. Includes portions of the author's June 1981 interview with al-Ghazālī, and a translation of chapter 2 of *Ayyām min ḥayātī*, which contains the story of how she became involved with the Muslim Brotherhood and helped organize the brotherhood's activities in the early 1960s.

Hoffman-Ladd, Valerie J. "Polemics on the Modesty and Segregation of Women in Contemporary Egypt." *International Journal of Middle East Studies* 19 (1987): 23–50. Includes al-Ghazālī's perspectives on women's social roles.

Sullivan, Earl T. *Women in Egyptian Public Life*. Syracuse, N.Y., 1986. Discusses Zaynab al-Ghazālī on pages 115–117.

Zuhur, Sherifa. *Revealing Reveiling: Islamist Gender Ideology in Contemporary Egypt*. Albany, N.Y., 1992. Chapter 5, "Construction of the Virtuous Woman," includes Zaynab al-Ghazālī's perspectives, with portions of an interview conducted by Zuhur.

VALERIE J. HOFFMAN-LADD

GHAZW. From an Arabic word that means "to want," *ghazw* came to denote expeditionary raids by bedouin tribes against a rival tribe. A corrupted version of the word found its way into French *(rezzou)* and English *(razzia)*. Originally, *ghazw* referred to the classical form of nomadic attacks against another tribe for the attaintment of booty. In pre-Islamic times (and afterward) *ghazw* was conducted according to a strict form of tribal etiquette and protocol. Nomadic raids were not always accompanied with bloodshed, because every tribe had to rely on this practice for its livelihood. It was a measure of protection against the harsh and unpredictable changes in climate. Camels were the most common desirable booty. The major *ghazw* occurrence was usually preceded by miniraids to warn the rival tribe of an incoming *ghazw*. Most *ghazw* were successful, because the element of surprise was absent to avoid violent confrontations.

The word (or its variants, like *maghāzī* or *ghazawāt*) was later used to denote the series of military campaigns that helped in the expansion of the Islamic empire. Muslim apologists wish to dissociate the military campaigns by early Muslims from the classical nomadic raids, although it is clear that early Muslims were motivated at least partly by the promise of booty and plunder. Islamic historiography downplayed the classical *ghazw* element from what was portrayed as pure *jihād* (war against nonbelievers).

Ghazw should be distinguished from other forms of nomadic warfare, like those motivated by acquisition of additional territory or by blood feuds. It is limited in duration and purpose. Ibn Mandhūr in *Lisān al-ʿArab* traces the origin of the word to a word that means to seek and want. Later military campaigns by Islamic armies for the defense and expansion of the state gave a new meaning to the word. It then denoted marching toward an enemy and fighting it.

Associated with the practice of *ghazw* is the elaborate system of distribution of the spoils *(ghanā'im* or *anfāl)* gained from a battle. The prophet Muḥammad did not deprive his troops of the spoils, as they were to receive four-fifths of the entire booty, with the remainder belonging to God (Qur'ān 8.41). In Muḥammad's lifetime, the latter portion went to him. After Muḥammad's death, there was no consensus among scholars of jurisprudence on the exact interpretation of the cited Qur'ānic verse. They could not agree on whether the imam should receive the one-fifth of the spoils that belonged to God.

Ghazw was such an integral part of the nomadic lifestyle that it was detailed and celebrated in poetry and prose. The decline of the nomadic lifestyle and the rise of the modern state that monopolized the use of force in society almost ended this practice.

In modern linguistic usage, the word is used to denote what the English words "raid," "invasion," and "aggression" mean. In some contemporary usages, the Israeli invasion of Lebanon in 1982 is referred as *ghazw Lub-*

nān (invasion of Lebanon). Sometimes *ghazw* is used to refer to any hostile movement. There have been many books written in the second half of the twentieth century with titles like *Al-ghazw al-fikrī* (cultural [or thought-related] invasion) in reference to the Western influence on Arabic thought, which is deemed to be harmful by most Islamic fundamentalist thinkers and writers.

[*See also* Jihād.]

BIBLIOGRAPHY

ʿAsali, Bassam al-. *Al-Madhab al-ʿAskarī al-Islāmī* (The Islamic Military Doctrine). Beirut, 1993.

Balādhurī. *Futūḥ al-Buldān* (Conquest of Countries). 3 vols. in 1. Al-Qahirah, 1956.

Dickson, H. R. P. *The Arab of the Desert*. London, 1949. Description of the life styles of nomads, including the customs of *ghazw*.

Donner, Fred McGraw. *The Early Islamic Conquests*. Princeton, 1981. Useful description of early Muslim military/political campaigns, drawing on Islamic sources.

Musil, Alois. *The Manners and Customs of the Rwala Bedouins*. New York, 1928. Description of the social and military customs of a classic bedouin group.

Wāqidī, Muḥammad ibn ʿUmar al-. *Kitāb al-Maghāzī lil-Wāqidī*. Edited by Marsden Jones. London, 1966. Classic Arabic source on the subject from which all other sources derive.

AsʿAD AbuKhalil

GIRŪGĀN. *See* Hostages.

GÖKALP, MEHMET ZİYA (c. 1875–1924), Turkish social scientist, writer, and nationalist. Born in Diyarbakır to a family of mixed Turkish and Kurdish origins, Mehmet Ziya attended the Imperial Veterinary School (1896) at Istanbul, where he joined the revolutionary Committee of Union and Progress (CUP). He was dismissed from the school, arrested, and jailed when his affiliation with the CUP was discovered by the secret police in 1897. After his release from prison, he returned to his native city and married his cousin Cevriye in 1898; they had three daughters who survived him and a son who died at an early age. Gökalp devoted his time in Diyarbakır mostly to ethnographic research among Kurdish and Turkoman tribes and to the study of Durkheimian sociology. Following the Young Turk revolution of July 1908, he founded a local branch of the CUP. He was a delegate to the important CUP Congress of Thessaloniki in 1909 where he was elected a member of the Central Committee, a position he held until the party dissolved in November 1918. Gökalp's brilliant career as a nationalist thinker started in Thessaloniki, with the nationalist literary journal *Genç kalemler* (1911), where he used the pseudonym "Gök Alp" for the first time. When the Balkan War (1912–1913) broke out, he established himself in Istanbul, and continued to publish in various journals, notably *Türk yurdu* (1912–1914), *Halka doğru* (1913–1914), *İslam mecmuası* (1914–1915), and *Yeni mecmua* (1917–1918). In 1915, he became a professor of sociology at Istanbul University. As a member of the Central Committee of the CUP, he was arrested and tried after World War I as a war criminal and deported to Malta by the British (1919). After his release he lived for a short period in Diyarbakır where he published the journal *Küçük mecmua* (1922–1923). Although he was elected deputy for Diyarbakır in 1923 on a Kemalist slate, he remained quite isolated in the capital city owing to his record as a notable CUP member and an admirer of Enver Pasha. He soon moved to Istanbul because of poor health and died there on 25 October 1924.

As a thinker, sociologist, poet, and politician, Ziya Gökalp has been one of the most influential minds in twentieth-century Turkish political and intellectual history. He is the theoretician par excellence of Turkish nationalism as a ground for synthesis of secularist westernization and Islamic reform movements. He never published a major work to express methodically his idea of nationalism. Even his *Principles of Turkism* (1923), which can be considered his final word on the subject, is a collection of essays on nationalism previously published in journals and newspapers. Yet, despite the tentative character of some of his ideas and his occasional modification of them, a highly articulate understanding of nationalism emerges in the numerous essays he published over a period of fifteen years.

Like almost all his contemporaries, Gökalp was obsessed with the predicament of the Ottoman state, and his initial quest for a solution to keep that polity viable can be considered an expression of Social Darwinism. What made him move away from his predecessors and contemporaries, however, was his conversion to French sociological thought through the works of Emile Durkheim and his subsequent reflection on the structure of Europe. This led him to make a distinction between culture, which remained national, and civilization, which was shared internationally. European society was divided into nation-states despite centuries of identification with the same religion and a few multiethnic polities. Since that history could not obliterate the differences of language and customs, nationality was the most essential characteristic of human societies. Hence, Gökalp believed that Western civilization represented the sum total of Western nation-states who shared a material and political civilization. According to Gökalp, this civilization cannot be related to Christianity for two reasons. First, despite the fact that religions are shared internationally, they exercise their appeal on individuals through a national language and a series of rituals that differ from one nation to another and are thus "nationalized." Second, Western civilization was based on a suprareligious political organization and had already incorporated non-Christians such as Jews and Japanese. Gökalp contends that not only would the reorganization of the Ottoman Turkish polity along nationalistic lines invigorate that polity, but it would also pave the way for the Ottoman Turks to join Western civilization. In other words, unearthing the national genius was synonymous with westernization. In accordance with this thought, he vehemently insisted that Turkish nationalism would be a source of strength for the Ottoman Empire and contended, somewhat later, that the empire should be reorganized as a confederation of Turks and Arabs.

To join Western civilization meant for Gökalp both political action and social engineering. Political action consisted of secularization *(muasırlaşmak)* of all aspects of social life, to the point of confining religion to the strictest individual sphere. As an influential member both of the Central Committee of the CUP and of the parliamentary commission that drafted the Turkish constitution, he was the mastermind in the secularization process at two important turning points, in 1917 and in 1923–1924. His insistence on placing the *evkaf* (Ar., *awqāf;* sg., *waqf*) schools under the jurisdiction of the Ministry of Education and the *şeriat* (Ar., *sharīʿah)* courts under the jurisdiction of the Ministry of Justice in 1917 can be considered as the first steps, respectively, toward the Law on the Unification of Education passed in 1924 and the Civil Code adopted in 1926. In perfect harmony with positivistic determinism, yet another fashion of his age, Gökalp thought that social engineering too was necessary, for Turkish society had developed structural shortcomings for historical reasons. Composed almost exclusively of bureaucrats and agriculturalists, this society lacked the entrepreneurial class that had the most crucial role in the social division of labor in modern nation-states. Thus, Gökalp was also the initiator of the mobilization for "national(ist) economy" *(millî iktisat),* which consisted of a propaganda campaign aimed at developing the moneymaking instinct of the Turks and a series of legal measures, the most significant of which was protectionism.

Ziya Gökalp's name has been associated with Pan-Turanism and protofascistic solidarism. It is true that during the period between 1912 and the end of World War I, Gökalp leaned toward Pan-Turanism under the influence of Russian émigrés and particularly of the Azeri publicist Hüseyinzade Ali, active in Istanbul. This leaning also partly explains his sympathy for Enver Pasha, the champion of Pan-Turanism among the CUP leadership, to whom he dedicated his collected poems, *Kızıl elma,* published shortly after the Ottoman Empire entered World War I. This romantic weakness of Gökalp survives also in his *Principles of Turkism,* though in the form of a mild utopianism. In the final analysis, his Pan-Turanism can be considered as a symptom of an age when the boundaries of a self-contained nation-state still appeared too modest to Turkish imperial hangover. His solidarism is less evident. There are sections in his *Principles of Turkism* that contradict each other, some thoroughly liberal and other solidaristic professions of faith. This is a result of the effect of the World War and the Bolshevik Revolution on Gökalp. The scramble for mandates in the Middle East and the social upheavals in Europe in the aftermath of the war were rationalized by Gökalp as the outcome of capitalistic greed. In 1923 he still thought of the entrepreneurial class as essential in the social division of labor, but he also advocated that the individual ventures be monitored by the state for the general good of the society.

Obsessed as he was with the nation-state, Gökalp neglected the study of the Ottoman Empire, a polity he discarded as a cosmopolitan, hybrid oddity. It is this weakness in historical outlook that led him to equate secularization exclusively with westernization; he ignored, for instance, the secular *kanun* tradition that constituted one of the pillars of the Ottoman Empire. This is yet another characteristic typical of the generation who founded the Turkish Republic, for which Ziya Gökalp was undoubtedly a spiritual father.

[*See also* Nation; Ottoman Empire; Pan-Turanism; Young Turks; *and the biographies of Atatürk and Enver Pasha.*]

BIBLIOGRAPHY

No complete, reliable edition of Gökalp's works is available in Turkish. Consult the following primary sources and discussions of his work:

Gökalp, Ziya. *Turkish Nationalism and Western Civilization: Selected Essays of Ziya Gökalp*. Translated and edited by Niyazi Berkes. London and New York, 1959.

Gökalp, Ziya. *The Principles of Turkism*. Translated and annotated by Robert Devereux. Leiden, 1968.

Heyd, Uriel. *Foundations of Turkish Nationalism: The Life and Teachings of Ziya Gökalp*. London, 1950.

Parla, Taha. *The Social and Political Thought of Ziya Gökalp, 1876–1924*.) Leiden, 1985.

CEMAL KAFADAR and AHMET KUYAŞ

GOVERNMENT. *See* Ḥukūmah.

GREAT BRITAIN. Once the source of a great Christian out-migration to the colonies of the British Empire, the British Isles have in return become the home of significant numbers of Muslim immigrants from the former colonies. In 1991 there were between 1.25 and 1.5 million British residents of Muslim background.

History. Apart from a few individuals, Muslims only begin to settle in Britain to any significant extent as a result of British colonial expansion in India. During the late eighteenth and early nineteenth centuries seamen recruited by the East India Company often found themselves laid off when their ships docked in London. However, it was only when ships started recruiting in Aden after the opening of the Suez Canal in 1869 that such settlements of seamen led to the founding of small Muslim communities in port cities such as Cardiff, South Shields (near Newcastle), London, and Liverpool. As colonial activities expanded, so did the sources of such seamen, and Liverpool witnessed the growth of West African settlement. At the same time, British overseas merchants and colonial civil servants established links with local elites. As a result there grew up a cosmopolitan expatriate colonial community in London, many of whom were Muslim.

The first Muslim institutions to appear were ʿAlawī *zāwiyah*s serving the Yemenis and Somalis recruited in Aden. In 1889 members of the London Muslim elite founded a mosque in the southwestern suburb of Woking; two years later, a row of houses in Liverpool was converted into a mosque with associated activities. In both initiatives British converts to Islam played a prominent role. The Liverpool mosque ceased to exist at the beginning of World War I when its founder, ʿAbdallāh (Henry William) Quilliam had to withdraw from public life because of his association with the Ottoman government. The Woking mosque continued to be active into the interwar years, when the Qur'ānic translators Marmaduke Pickthall and ʿAbdullāh Yūsuf ʿAlī were closely associated with it. For a time it was linked with the Lahori branch of the Aḥmadīyah movement, but as Indian Sunnī opposition to the Aḥmadīs grew, that link was finally severed in 1935.

During the 1930s plans had been developed to establish a central mosque in London, encouraged by the establishment of one in Paris in 1926. For a time this had the support of the *nizam* of Hyderabad, and it received a further boost when King George VI in 1944 donated a plot of land in Regent's Park in recognition of the Egyptian government's donation of land in Cairo for a new Anglican cathedral. The economic effects of the war and then of the conflicts around Indian and Pakistani independence, not to mention uncertainties in the Middle East, combined to delay the completion of the project until the 1970s. Only in 1977 was the present Central Mosque and Islamic Cultural Centre finally opened. But by this time the nature of the Muslim community in Britain had undergone drastic changes.

As British industry grew in the two decades after World War II, it soon started recruiting workers from colonial and former colonial territories—first from the Caribbean, then from India, and by the late 1950s from Pakistan, mainly from the western sector but later also from the eastern sector that would become Bangladesh in 1971. Immigrants from both parts of Pakistan were almost all Muslims, and so were a substantial minority of those from India and small numbers from the Caribbean. In addition, other Muslims came from Cyprus, Morocco, and parts of sub-Saharan Africa, especially from Kenya and Uganda when those countries introduced a policy of "africanization" in the late 1960s and early 1970s.

Immigrants of Muslim background from the Indian subcontinent came from very limited areas. Villagers from Pakistan originated primarily from parts of the Punjab and the region of Mirpur in Pakistani-held Kashmir, and those from Bangladesh were mostly from the Sylhet region in the north. From India, the Muslims were mainly Gujarati traders.

Britain was the first major western European country to move toward a cessation of labor immigration, with the Commonwealth Immigration Act of 1962. The intention of the Act was to stop the influx of unskilled labor, but within two years its effect was extended to include semiskilled labor and most professionally trained people. However, the Act did not prevent family reunion. The first consequence of the Act was major immigration especially of Pakistanis in the eighteen months before it was adopted and implemented. Second, the character of the flow of immigration changed to consist predominantly of wives, fiancées, and children of men already in Britain. Several subsequent acts have been passed further restricting immigration. As elsewhere in western Europe, the major inward movement of people since the mid-1970s has consisted of refugees rather than economic migrants. This has included significant numbers of people of Muslim background from the Middle East, especially Lebanon, Palestine, Iraq, and Iran. In addition, the country has always welcomed people of personal wealth, and London has thus acquired substantial communities from the Arab Gulf States and Saudi Arabia.

Demographics. These developments are reflected in the figures available from the decennial censuses, which record place of birth. The first recording of Pakistanis in the census showed approximately 5,000 in 1951, rising to under 25,000 in 1961. Ten years later the figure (now for Pakistan and Bangladesh together) had risen to 170,000, and by 1991 it was 636,000. The 1991 census produced the following figures relating to country of birth: Bangladeshis, 160,000; Pakistanis, 476,000; Indians, 134,000; Malaysians, 43,000; Arabs, 134,000; Turks, 26,000; Turkish Cypriots, 45,000; and sub-Saharan Africans, 115,000, for a total of 1,133,000. Corrections suggest that the total 1991 population of Muslim background was between 1.25 and 1.5 million.

The Muslim immigrants from Pakistan came primarily for work, and their geographical distribution reflects this. They were employed mainly in the older industries—iron and steel foundries and textiles—and in semiskilled service industries such as public transport. The Bangladeshis were the latest group to arrive, by which time the old industries were in increasingly sharp decline, so a much higher proportion settled in London. The 1991 census figures illustrate this with reference to selected areas: in Greater London, 89,000 Pakistanis and 87,000 Bangladeshis; in the West Midlands, 89,000 and 18,000 respectively; in West Yorkshire, 86,000 and 6,000; in Manchester, 50,000 and 13,000; and in Glasgow and environs 22,000 Pakistanis and no Bangladeshis.

Another consequence of the process of immigration and settlement is that the Muslim population is much younger than the national average. This can be illustrated again with reference to the 1991 census for that part of the population which originated in Pakistan, as shown in Table 1.

The 1962 immigration act triggered the major change from a Muslim population consisting mainly of migrant laborers to an immigrant settler community composed of a mixture of ethnic minorities (British conversion to Islam has been very small, probably not more than 5,000 in total up to the present). The establishment of families brought with it a variety of practical concerns which involved aspects of life and culture deeply imbued with Islamic elements. This particularly was the case with women and childbirth and with children and school.

Institutions. The activation of Islam as a result of family settlement after 1962 is shown most clearly in the figures for annual registrations of mosques. In 1963 thirteen mosques were registered with the Registrar-General, a department of government for England and Wales. The number rose steadily, to 49 in 1970, 99 in 1975, 193 in 1980, 314 in 1985, and 452 in 1990. The majority of these mosques are properties bought and converted from other use. Some were formerly domestic dwellings; others were small factories or warehouses, or occasionally cinemas.

During the first period of settlement, the emphasis in the development of Muslim institutions in Britain was on the establishment of facilities for worship and for passing on Islamic teaching and practice to the next generation. This work tended to concentrate around the mosques, and local planning authorities have learned to expect that permission to establish a place of worship will also usually have to include permission to use the facilities for educational purposes, a separate category in planning law.

The organizations which have set up these facilities and the related activities, such as providing personnel

TABLE 1. *Ages of Pakistani and White Populations*

AGES	PAKISTANIS	WHITES
0–4	13.13%	6.36%
5–15	29.52	12.97
16–24	17.47	12.55
25–44	25.79	29.01
45–64	12.35	22.32
65+	1.73	16.8

and publications, have come from a variety of backgrounds. Usually the initiative has arisen within a local community, but as its resources were limited, it was often necessary to find sponsors. It was at this point that a number of organizations from the countries of origin entered the scene.

The most successful formal network is rooted in the Jamāʿat-i Islāmī of Pakistan and includes the UK Islamic Mission, which runs a series of mosques with education and community work; the Muslim Educational Trust, which provides peripatetic teachers to take classes in state schools outside formal teaching hours; the fortnightly newsmagazine *Impact International;* and the Islamic Foundation, a center for research, training, and publishing. The Islamic Council of Europe, established in 1973, sponsored conferences on the future of the Muslim economic order and the status of Muslim minorities. In 1982 it was renamed the Islamic Council, producing the "Universal Islamic Declaration" and the "Universal Islamic Declaration of Human Rights."

Although successful, this network is not the largest. The Deobandī and Barelwī movements have also spread to Britain, where they often find themselves continuing the rivalry started at home. The Deobandī network is more integrated than that of the Barelwīs, with two seminaries in the north of England providing a growing number of imams and teachers for Deobandī mosques. The Tablīghī Jamāʿat is also active in Britain. The Barelwī network is fragmented among various prominent *pirs* and their lieutenants. Overlapping with the Barelwīs are a number of Ṣūfī orders, with branches of the Naqshbandīs and Chishtīs especially prominent. For a long time the Ṣūfīs were hardly noticeable, as they functioned in informal personal networks; in recent years, however, some Ṣūfī groups have taken on more recognizably British organizational structures, often because this made it easier to get access to local sources of influence and financial subsidies. Among the Muslims from the Indian subcontinent there is a small following of the Ahl i-Ḥadīth movement, especially in the English Midlands. [*See* Deobandīs; Barelwīs; Tablīghī Jamāʿat.]

There have long been attempts to form national umbrella organizations. The first was the Union of Muslim Organisations (1970) which, although it did not achieve its aim, still exists. Since then several other attempts have been made, some sponsored by the Saudi-based Muslim World League and one by the Libya-based Islamic Call Society. The Muslim Institute, founded in 1972 by the journalist Kalim Siddiqui, probably with Saudi assistance, for most of the 1980s was linked with Iran. In 1991 it set up the so-called Muslim Parliament, which has been greeted with skepticism by most of the British Muslim community.

In addition to these locally based institutions, the World Ahl al-Bayt Islamic League (WABIL) is an international Shīʿī organization with headquarters in London and affiliates in various countries. Currently its secretary-general is Ḥujjat al-Islām Sayyid Muḥammad al-Mūsāwi, a Lebanese Shīʿī *ʿālim.* Its activities include the performance and registration of marriages and divorces; the distribution of authoritative opinions by senior officials (*marjaʿ al-taqlīd*); announcement of the start and end of the lunar month, important for observation of Ramaḍān; the provision of teachers and religious leaders to Shīʿī communities requiring them; the coordination of the programs of its various branches; assistance to Shīʿī victims of natural disasters, largely through the distribution of *zākat;* the provision of aid to students for study in *madrasahs* in Qom, Najaf, and elsewhere; and the countering of hostile prejudices and propaganda among both non-Muslims and Sunnī Muslims.

Another Shīʿī organization with a base in London is the Al-Khoei Benevolent Foundation, established around the followers of the leading ayatollah, Imām Abū al-Qāsim al-Khū'ī, whose family was imprisoned and then executed by the Iraqi regime during the 1980s. Since the Gulf War, the Foundation has been taking an increasing interest in the Muslim community in Britain. [*See* Al-Khoei Benevolent Foundation.]

As Muslim organizations have begun to take a more active part in the wider society, many have also begun to establish various forms of cooperation with other religious groups, especially the churches at both local and national levels. Muslim organizations played a prominent part in the founding in 1987 of a national Interfaith Network, and both during the Rushdie affair and later during the 1990–1991 Gulf crisis and war there was active consultation between Muslim organizations and churches locally and nationally.

Political and Social Programs. During the 1980s many local Muslim organizations were beginning to feel more self-confident and learning how to function with more success in local politics. They have thus begun to integrate into local political life, often quite successfully. Coming together around educational issues, the Muslim Liaison Committee in Birmingham linked some sixty local Muslim groups and was able to negotiate with the city's education authority to produce guidelines for schools on how to treat Muslim children. Since then they have conducted several further successful negotiations with other parts of the city government and have also agreed on a common dating and advance notice of ʿĪd al-Fiṭr. In Bradford, Muslims cooperated in the mid-1980s in a campaign to change many aspects of local educational policy. Out of this local cooperation arose the first public initiative in the long-running campaign against Salman Rushdie's *Satanic Verses*. [*See* Rushdie Affair.] In many cities Muslims have been elected to the city council, although there is not yet a Muslim member of Parliament.

A concern for educational issues has been one of the main characteristics of many of these organizations. For almost two decades there have been sporadic campaigns for Muslim schools to be established with public money, just as there are publicly funded Roman Catholic, Anglican, and Jewish schools. So far such campaigns have not been successful, and the only Muslim schools remain about thirty private institutions of varying size. As British government structures have become more centralized since 1979, so central government has increasingly become the target of these campaigns. Following the Rushdie affair, central government has also begun to respond more openly and, at least on the surface, more positively. Thus government supported the establishment at a Birmingham teacher-training college of a program for training Muslim teachers for religious education in the state system. Likewise, the Department of the Environment (responsible for local government) has set up an Inner Cities Religious Council.

As young Muslims born in Britain have grown up, they have begun to loosen their links with the countries and cultures of their parents. In the last few years many, especially the better-educated, have begun to move into the management of existing Muslim organizations. Others have established their own youth organizations. In the universities, they are gradually becoming an important force in Islamic student societies previously dominated by foreign students. A number of English-language Muslim weekly newspapers have been started by such groups. This change of generation is also beginning to lead to a change in the Muslim community's reference points in the Islamic world. While the immigrant generation continue to look back to the regions and cultures from which they came, other perspectives are beginning to be voiced by the young. There is clear evidence of the development of a British Muslim lifestyle in which the cultural traditions of the northern Indian subcontinent are being laid aside. The younger Muslims are much more actively concerned with events in Bosnia and Palestine than with developments in their parents' regions of origin. Although a few appear to be attracted by radical groups such as Ḥizb al-Tahīr, the great majority are developing a mode of participation which includes local and national activity within Britain as well as a concern for wider issues of the Muslim world community.

[*See also* Islamic Foundation; United Kingdom Islamic Mission.]

BIBLIOGRAPHY

Anwar, Muhammad. "Muslims in Britain. 1991 Census and Other Statistical Sources." *CSIC Papers: Europe* 9 (September 1993).

British Muslims: Monthly Survey. Birmingham, February 1993–. Monthly record of events affecting Muslims in Britain, published by the Centre for the Study of Islam and Christian-Muslim Relations (CSIC), Selly Oak Colleges, Birmingham.

Lewis, Philip. *Islamic Britain: Religion, Politics and Identity among British Muslims*. London, 1994.

Modood, Tariq. "Muslims, Race and Equality in Britain: Some Post-Rushdie Affair Reflections." *CSIC Papers: Europe* 1 (June 1990). Observations on what racial equality and pluralism mean in post-*Satanic Verses* Britain.

Nielsen, Jørgen S. *Muslims in Western Europe*. Edinburgh, 1992. Places development of Muslim communities and institutions in Britain in larger comparative context.

Siddique, Mohammed. *Moral Spotlight on Bradford*. Bradford, 1993. Critical Muslim analysis of social and political life of a Yorkshire city.

Jørgen S. Nielsen

GROUPEMENT ISLAMIQUE EN FRANCE.

In the 1980s Islam came to the center of political debates in France and in Europe generally. Many organizations were established by Muslim intellectuals or students of Arab origin in order to awaken Islamic feelings among adults and ensure the religious education of children. In some neighborhoods where North African immigrant families are concentrated, housing projects or residences for immigrants have come to be used for collective prayers or Qurʾānic classes. On a national level, federations of Islamic groups such as the Association des Etudiants Islamiques en France (AEIF, Association of Islamic Students in France) were already emerging in the early 1960s. This organization's aim was to bring together Muslim students of different nationalities, although most of its membership consisted of Maghribis living in France.

In 1979 a student of Tunisian origin broke from the AEIF and formed his own group, the Groupement Islamique en France (GIF), in Valenciennes in the north of France. Its goal was to expand Islamic preaching to immigrant workers influenced by the Tablīghī Jamāʿat, a transnational organization of South Asian origin (Kepel, 1987). Intellectually influenced by Islamist currents in the Middle East, such as that of the Egyptian Muslim Brotherhood, which are more politically engaged than the Tablīghī Jamāʿat, the aim of the GIF is, as Kepel puts it, "a theoretical and practical reeducation by sermons, conferences and social structure that will give a foretaste of what Islamic life will be like under the *sharīʿah*." The organization's headquarters moved to Paris in 1981.

The GIF is officially subsidized by donations from members. The publication and distribution of an Islamic calendar and such activities as annual congresses on Islam in France, conferences and discussions, an Islamic book exhibit, and the pilgrimage to Mecca are also sources of income. Besides purely Islamic ventures, the leaders and members engage in many cultural and social activities. For example, sports have become a major interest; also, in order to create and reinforce solidarity among Muslim workers, members are encouraged to make regular visits to those who are in hospitals and prisons.

In 1986 the GIF became a member association of the Union des Organisations Islamiques de France (UOIF), created in 1983. This umbrella organization joins forty to fifty member associations of Maghribi origin. They share the ideology of Islamic assertiveness and a commitment to islamization, in contrast to the Fédération Nationale des Musulmans de France (FNMF). This latter group works for a French Islam. Its leaders emphasize their Islamic identity, but argue the compatibility of Islam with French republican values and negotiate with public authorities for a better integration of Muslims into French society. Both the UOIF and the FNMF are members of CORIF (Conseil Religieux de l'Islam en France), a state organization created in 1990 by Minister of Internal Affairs Pierre Joxe to serve as official representative and intermediary of Muslims in France.

[*See also* Fédération Nationale des Musulmans de France; France; *and* Union des Organisations Islamiques de France.]

BIBLIOGRAPHY

Diop, M., and Riva Kastoryano. "Le mouvement associatif islamique en Ile de France." *Revue Européenne des Migrations Internationales* 7.3 (1991): 91–119.

Kepel, Gilles. *Les banlieues de l'Islam*. Paris, 1987.

Leveau, Rémy, and Gilles Kepel, eds. *Les musulmans dans la société française*. Paris, 1988.

RIVA KASTORYANO

GUARDIANSHIP. The term *walāyah* (guardianship) literally means having "contiguity to something." The root is frequently found in Islamic religious thought: *walīs* are "protégés" of God, or saints; the *walī* is the guardian of a minor or the member of a family deputed to act on his or her behalf; a tribal client is a *mawlā;* and *walī* is also a straightforward political term, usually translated as "governor" or "regent."

The term is particularly important in Twelver Shīʿī political theory, where it signifies the legitimacy of ʿAlī's claim, together with that of his successor imams, to lead the Islamic community. When the Prophet at Ghadīr Khumm held ʿAlī's hand aloft and said, "he who is my *mawlā,* is now ʿAlī's *mawlā,*" he was, according to the Shīʿah, declaring that the authority over the community, in matters temporal and religious, belonged to ʿAlī. The legitimacy of the claim of *walāyah* is distinguished from a claim based solely on *salṭanah* (force).

The notion of *walāyah* is justified from the Qur'ān, where it is declared that "God is your *walī,* and His Apostle, and those who are faithful" (surah 5.55). The Prophet's guardianship is by delegation from God, and he in turn delegated his authority to the house of ʿAlī. "Those who are faithful," are understood then to be the imams.

Throughout the first half of Islamic history, Shīʿī claimants invoked the concept of *walāyah* as part of their claim to replace whatever dynasty they opposed. This was particularly true with the ideological claims of the Fāṭimid-Ismāʿīlī imams in Cairo who opposed the Sunnī claims of the ʿAbbāsids. The great Fāṭimid jurist, al-Qāḍī Nuʿmān, wrote extensively on *walāyah* in his magnum opus, the *Daʿā'im al-Islām*. There he used historical and exegetical evidence to argue that Islamic political history had been awry from the time of the Prophet's death. Only now was a rightful claimant once more in a position to join *salṭanah* with *walāyah,* and lead the Muslim community.

The concept of *walāyah* has recently attracted considerable attention because it has been deployed by Imam Khomeini to justify the hierocratic state structure evoked in the Constitution of the Islamic Republic of Iran. According to this theory, the imams deputed jurists and judges to act on their behalf even during their lifetimes. That guardianship does not end with the occultation of the Twelfth Imam, but rather requires an enhanced role for the scholars who were his heirs. Accordingly, Khomeini and his followers have argued that the guardianship of the jurist is "general" in its scope, and not restricted; that it applies to all phases of the law, and that such efficacy must be realized with power as well. Accordingly the foremost jurist is to be regarded as the *walī al-amr* ("guardian of command") with temporal authority over the state.

[*See also* Mawlā; Sainthood.]

BIBLIOGRAPHY

Corbin, Henry. "Sur la notion de '*walāyat*' en Islam Shīʿite." In *Normes et valeurs dans l'Islam contemporain*, edited by Jean-Paul Charnay, pp. 38–47. Paris, 1966.

Nanji, Azim A. "An Ismāʿīlī Theory of *walāyah* in the *Daʿā'im al-Islām* of Qāḍī al-Nuʿmān." In *Essays on Islamic Civilization: Presented to Niyazi Berkes*, edited by Donald P. Little, vol. 1, pp. 260–273. Leiden, 1976.

Sachedina, A. A. *The Just Ruler (al-Sulṭan al-ʿĀdil) in Shīʿite Islam: The Comprehensive Authority of the Jurist in Imamite Jurisprudence.* New York, 1988.

A. Kevin Reinhart

GUILDS once played a decisive role in the life of Arab cities in various ways: economically, they controlled production and trade; socially, they provided a framework for the active population (which is to say, most of the population, with the exception of the ruling class, usually dominated by foreigners); and finally, in the absence of specialized urban agencies, guilds were one of the entities that permitted cities to function.

Given the aforementioned factors, it is all the more striking that there is no Arabic equivalent of the word *guild: ḥirfah* and *ṣinf* actually mean "trade," and the term *ṭā'ifah* (pl., *ṭawā'if*), often used to refer to guilds, denotes in a larger sense a community or any kind of group (particularly religious or national groups). The surprising lack of an exact equivalent for "guild" might be the result of the belated appearance of guilds in the Arab world. Louis Massignon's theories on the Muslim—more specifically, Ismāʿīlī origins—of guilds in the ninth century (1920), to which Bernard Lewis in his article entitled "The Islamic Guilds" (1937) gave a classic formulation, have been criticized by Claude Cahen and Samuel Stern in *The Islamic City* (1970). They suggest that true guilds only came into existence during the Ottoman period. In Anatolian Turkey, professional organizations with strongly religious overtones appeared in the fourteenth century and included *akhī* ("brothers") and *fityān* ("young people") described in detail by Ibn Baṭṭūṭah (*Voyages*, vol. 2, pp. 260–65); their activities presaged the corporate rituals of the *futūwah*. This revisionist view might be too extreme, however. There are a number of accounts attesting to the existence of professional groups *(jamāʿa)* headed by shaykhs and controlled by market provosts *(muḥtasib)* well before the Ottoman conquest. These guilds were particularly active in Andalusia where the *ḥisbah* (enforcement of public morals) was very well organized. Indeed, Andalusians who emigrated to North Africa in the sixteenth century are credited with organizing guilds in Tunisia.

From the sixteenth to the nineteenth century, guilds were organized around trade and commerce as well as the artisanal activities: urban markets, including those operated by major spice and fabric merchants *(tujjār)* were part of the system. Even less-respectable trades had their guilds: thieves apparently had one.

Naturally, the number of guilds in different cities varied according to the local economy and the number of trades. Istanbul allegedly had 1,109 guilds, according to somewhat implausible estimates provided by the seventeenth-century Turkish voyager Evliya Çelebi (Mantran, 1962). More realistic figures indicate an estimated 250 in Cairo, 160 in Aleppo, 80 in Tunis, and 60 in Algiers. The number could vary: neighborhood guilds were created as the city and number of markets grew (8 brokers' guilds or *dallālīn* in Cairo); technical guilds reflected the division of labor (5 dyers' guilds were organized according to colors and materials used). New guilds were created whenever a new activity or product appeared (8 tobacconists' and pipe makers' guilds, also in Cairo), an indication that the system was not as rigid as some have claimed.

In general, guilds were geographically determined as trades were grouped in clearly delineated zones (neighborhoods, streets) inside the city. A guild thus corresponded not only to a trade but also to a specific urban zone.

It is clear that guilds were hierarchically structured, although more precise details with regard to particular aspects are lacking. The hierarchy of ranks is known—

apprentice *(mubtadi'*; Tk., *çırak)*, journeyman *(sani*ᶜ; Tk., *kalfa*), and master *(muᶜallim*; Tk., *usta)*—but information regarding specific criteria for rising up the ranks is scant. For instance, very little information is available with respect to tests or the creation of a masterpiece, which would entitle a member to practice his profession.

Guilds were headed by a shaykh (Near East) or *amīn* (Maghrib) chosen by guild members and confirmed by local or central authorities (as evidenced by nomination devices in Istanbul). It seems that the authorities intervened in particular when problems arose with the nomination of a shaykh or *amīn* by his peers. Accession to the title of shaykh most likely depended on the candidate's professional and moral qualities, as well as his renown and familial prestige. It was not uncommon for the title to be handed down in a family, much like the common practice of a son inheriting his father's trade. The shaykh or *amīn*'s various assistants included the *naqīb* and *katkhudā*. The oldest and most respected masters *(ikhtiyārīyah)* formed an elite from whom the shaykh often sought counsel and support.

In several cities, urban guilds came under the jurisdiction of a *shaykh al-mashā'ikh*, as in Damascus (Qoudsî, 1885; Rafeq, 1991) or of an *amīn al-umanā'* in Algiers (Touati, 1987), although this role might have been more ceremonial than professional or administrative.

In Tunis, the Andalusians who dominated the *shawwāshī* (hat makers') guild succeeded in controlling the entire guild system. The *amīn* of the *shawwāshī* was also the *amīn al-tujjār* (leader of the traders) and the president of the trade court (whose ten members included eight Andalusians).

Religious rituals within guilds are characteristic of the eastern regions of the Arab and Muslim world. Although work in the guilds took place in a deeply religious atmosphere (Touati, 1987), guilds in the Maghrib do not appear to have adopted these religious rituals per se. The existence of a corporative ritual (*futūwah*, a term originally denoting "chivalry" but which came to refer more narrowly to life within trades and neighborhoods; see Cahen, 1970) has been documented for both Damascus (Qoudsî, 1885) and Cairo (Baer, 1964; Raymond, 1974): it possibly originated in Anatolian Turkey (see Ibn Baṭṭūtah). The *futūwah* manuals provide an image of rituals similar to those described in Evliya Çelebi's *Seyahatname* around the mid-seventeenth century; the same rituals have been found in Central Asia (Gavrilov, 1928).

The guilds mentioned (only seventy-five) are linked to the Prophet through their patron saints *(pīr)*: ᶜAlī is initiated by Muḥammad during the *shadd* (binding) ceremony. ᶜAlī in turn initiates seventeen *pīrs*, and then Salmān al-Fārisī (the Prophet's companion and patron of barbers) swears in the patrons of other noneconomic guilds (muezzins, standard bearers) and nontraditional guilds (coffee is mentioned but not tobacco), thereby indicating that rituals developed at a later time. The *futūwah* books describe the transmission of *futūwah* from Adam to Muḥammad, ᶜAlī, and the *pīrs*, as well as the initiation rites of shaykhs, which consisted of a series of questions and answers reflecting a concern solely for religious and moral edification. The crucial role played by ᶜAlī and the Shīᶜī nature of this ritual are especially noteworthy (thus explaining Massignon's theory of the origins of guilds).

The *shadd* ritual (which consisted of tying a varying number of knots according to the initiate's rank) and related ceremonies are documented in sources other than the *futūwah* manuals. A meeting was called by the guild's shaykh (through the *naqīb*), during which the initiate received a belt knotted in three to seven places; this was followed by a meal *(walīmah)* shared by a given number of master craftsmen. At least a few of the guilds held celebrations to honor their patron or a particularly revered saint.

In Cairo, guilds actively participated in the *ruᶜyah* (moon-gazing) ceremony, which took place on the eve of Ramaḍān at a gathering of the *muḥtasib* and afforded an opportunity for a review or parade of the principal trades. This tradition, with major changes, continued in the form of a cavalcade in Cairo up until the 1950s. Guilds participated in many collective celebrations and displayed signs, banners, musical instruments, and decorated floats.

The quite varied roles that guilds played in Arab cities are well known and will therefore be briefly summarized. Their participation in the economic domain included regulating the production of goods, maintaining a professional code of ethics, overseeing prices, particularly during times of crisis, maintaining good relations among members, and supplying labor. Guilds determined entrance requirements for joining trades by means of the *gedik* (professional license); this effective *numerus clausus* favored the practice of inheriting trades. Although guilds probably contributed to the technical stagnation which characterized Arab countries during this period, the creation of guilds based on new products (coffee, tobacco) indicates a certain capacity for the system's growth. Their administrative role was no less important: they provided a link between tradesmen and authorities whose job of administrating the working urban population was thus greatly facilitated. For instance, taxes were levied on the basis of lists drawn up by the shaykhs of members under their control. Guilds assisted in the management of the city in their own economic areas and no doubt in the maintenance of order as well. Hence, they represented an indispensable urban mechanism in a city that lacked a real administrative structure. By organizing the working population according to professions, guilds contributed in an efficient manner to social equilibrium.

The nineteenth century witnessed the gradual decline of guilds and their eventual disappearance. This occurred rather slowly, however. Even in countries affected by the sudden modernization of their institutions and economies—for example, Egypt (beginning in 1805 under Muḥammad ʿAlī)—guilds did not completely lose ground until the 1870s. In preparing Cairo for its transformation into a modern city, ʿAlī Pāshā Mubārak relied on construction guilds to provide a framework for the urban development project financed by Khedive Ismāʿīl in 1868.

Generally speaking, traditional guilds disappeared as a result of economic, social, political, and administrative changes in countries undergoing internal and external transformations and not because of administrative decisions.

Economic changes in Arab countries from the nineteenth century onward (already apparent in the mid-eighteenth century) had the most significant impact. Formerly prosperous artisanal trades were hit hard by vigorous European penetration that eventually led to their ruin. It was the case for the textile trade, which had flourished in the eighteenth century but could no longer compete with European products: in Damascus, foreign-made fabrics and European fashions became the norm (Rafeq, 1991). Local copper and wood craftsmen who produced everyday utensils were hurt by the introduction of modern European goods. Traditional trade based on caravans to transport goods also fell victim to the new means of transportation introduced by Europe. Modern techniques and the introduction of machinery had similar effects on local craftsmanship. Muḥammad ʿAlī's efforts to industrialize Egypt almost certainly contributed to the decline of local, traditional products. New production techniques in imitation of Europe's naturally developed outside the traditional guild system.

As a consequence of the mass urbanization that affected Arab countries beginning in 1850, cities saw an influx of rural inhabitants who did not belong to guilds and were therefore not subject to the strict entrance requirements set by guilds to practice a trade. Thus, an increasing percentage of the working population was not under the guilds' control. In 1927, only 10 percent of Damascus's working population belonged to traditional guilds (Louis Massignon, "Structure du travail à Damas en 1927," *Cahiers internationaux de sociologie* 15 [1953]: 34–52).

The profound political changes that occurred in Arab countries had equally negative consequences for guilds. The reforms adopted by some countries (Egypt under Muḥammad ʿAlī and, later, Tunisia), intended to modernize administrations, resulted in guilds gradually becoming useless where administrative tasks were concerned: this was particularly true for the levying of taxes, which was handed over to specialized agencies.

In even more extreme fashion, colonization (Algeria in 1830, Tunisia in 1881, and Egypt in 1882) imposed not only new political and administrative structures but also an economic system whose growth was hindered by guilds. Europeans took over the principal commercial sectors and industrial production and thus competed with indigenous craftsmen; the latter, limited to providing traditional goods seen as "old-fashioned," found themselves unable to compete. In Tunisia, shashiya making, which had employed 20,000 workers in the early nineteenth century, employed no more than 6,000 or 7,000 around 1850 and 1,000 around 1934 (Pennec, 1964).

Guilds thus gradually broke up and were limited to a small number of traditional crafts; there was no need for formally dissolving them. In Cairo, the decline of guilds accelerated around 1890 when free enterprise was established (Baer, 1964) and, in particular, when shaykhs no longer were responsible for supplying labor. Until very recently, a few guilds continued to exist but were largely considered obsolete and a mere curiosity. In 1947, *Images*, a Cairo newspaper, published an interview with Shaykh Muḥammad Sharkas describing the copper makers' guild he had headed. But guilds had then ceased to exist for a long time. It cannot be said with certainty that the gradual decline of guilds coincided with the appearance of modern trade unions.

When the origins of trade unions in Hama, Syria, were investigated (Gaulmier, 1932), for example, the two phenomena appeared to be totally unrelated.

[*See also* Bazaar; Futūwah.]

BIBLIOGRAPHY

Baer, Gabriel. *Egyptian Guilds in Modern Times*. Jerusalem, 1964.

Baer, Gabriel. "The Organization of Labour." In *Handbuch der Orientalistik*, vol. 6, pp. 31–52. Leiden, 1977.

Cahen, Claude. "Y a-t-il eu des corporations professionnelles dans le monde musulman classique?" In *The Islamic City*, edited by Albert Hourani and S. M. Stern, pp. 51–63. Oxford, 1970.

Gaulmier, Jean. "Notes sur le mouvement syndicaliste à Hama." *Revue des Études Islamiques* 6.2 (1932): 95–125.

Gavrilov, Michel. "Les corps de métiers en Asie Centrale et leurs statuts *(rissala)*." *Revue des Études Islamiques* 2.2 (1928): 209–230.

Gibb, H. A. R., and Harold Bowen. *Islamic Society and the West*. 2 vols. London, 1950–1957. See pages 281–295.

Lewis, Bernard. "The Islamic Guilds." *Economic History Review* 8 (1937): 20–37.

Mantran, Robert. *Istanbul dans la seconde moitié du XVIIe siècle*. Paris, 1962. See pages 349–393.

Massignon, Louis. "Les corps de métier et la cité islamique." *Revue Internationale de Sociologie* 28 (1920): 473–489.

Massignon, Louis. "Enquête sur les corporations musulmanes d'artisans et de commerçants au Maroc." *Revue du Monde Musulman* 58 (1924).

Pennec, Pierre. *Les transformations des corps de métiers de Tunis sous l'influence d'une économie externe de type capitaliste*. Tunis, 1964.

Qoudsî, Elia. "Notice sur les corporations de Damas." In *Actes du sixième congrès international des Orientalistes*, vol. 2, pp. 7–34. Leiden, 1885.

Rafeq, Abdul-Karim. "Craft Organization, Work Ethics, and the Strains of Change in Ottoman Syria." *Journal of the American Oriental Society* 111 (1991): 495–511.

Raymond, André. *Artisans et commerçants au Caire au XVIIIe siècle*. 2 vols. Damascus, 1974. See pages 503–585.

Raymond, André. *Grandes villes arabes à l'époque ottomane*. Paris, 1985. See pages 129–133.

Stern, Samuel M. "The Constitution of the Islamic City." In *The Islamic City*, edited by Albert Hourani and S. M. Stern, pp. 25–50. Oxford, 1970.

Toledano, Ehud R. *State and Society in Mid-Nineteenth-Century Egypt*. Cambridge, 1990. See pages 206–213 and 227–230.

Touati, Houari. "Les corporations des métiers à Alger à l'époque ottomane." *Revue d'Histoire Maghrébine* 47–48 (1987): 267–292.

André Raymond

Translated from French by Monique Fecteau

GUINEA. Estimates of the size of Guinea's Muslim community range from 80 to 92 percent of the country's approximately 7.5 million residents. According to the latest survey of religious affiliation (1945), the Peul population is the most heavily islamized (98 percent); the Malinke and Sousou are also strongly Islamic (with regional variations of 39 to 85 percent). Among forest populations such as the Guerze, Toma, Kissi, and Mano who have traditionally resisted Muslim teachings, Islamic influence is increasing.

Most Guinean Muslims follow the Sunnī faith and Mālikī law. The majority also claim allegiance to one of two Ṣūfī brotherhoods. In the eighteenth century al-Ḥājj Solimou Toure introduced the Qādirīyah to the Malinke population living in northern Guinea. In the mid-nineteenth century al-Ḥājj ʿUmar Tal's Toucoulor and Peul followers joined the Tijānīyah. In the 1960s, according to government figures, 75 percent of Guinea's marabouts (holy men) were Tijānī and 13 percent were Qādirī. Each brotherhood is headed by a caliph general. [*See* Tijānīyah; Qādirīyah; *and the biography of* ʿ*Umar Tal.*]

Islam was introduced into the region in the eleventh century by Muslim Sarakole merchants from Ghana seeking kola nuts to trade. Significant islamization began after Sundiata Keita (r. 1230–1255) incorporated northern Guinea into the Mali empire. Muslim merchants and scholars became indispensable to Malinke rulers in the Guinea region, who adopted Islam and encouraged its expansion among their immediate followers. By the mid-fifteenth century, however, these small states had begun to shrug off Mali's authority. Over the next two centuries, despite the missionary efforts of Malinke marabouts living in Kankan, Islam virtually disappeared from upper Guinea.

During the seventeenth century Muslim Peul from the Niger state of Macina launched a *jihād* against indigenous traditionalists living on the Futa Jalon plateau in central Guinea and established an Islamic state there. The state was divided into nine provinces whose chiefs elected an *almamy* with overall political and religious authority, an officer chosen in rotation from two founding families for a two-year term of office. Over time, a highly stratified society emerged on the Futa in which Muslim nobles, freemen (generally herders and clerics), and artisans enjoyed rights and privileges denied serfs, who were forbidden to read the Qur'ān. Despite frequent successional disputes, the state survived until the colonial era.

During the nineteenth century Islam played a significant role in resistance to the European penetration of

Guinea. Regional Muslim political leaders, including al-Ḥājj ʿUmar and Samory Touré, raised large forces in the region and declared *jihād*s to reform and enlarge the Muslim community and stem the tide of European expansion from the coast. From 1850 to 1864, ʿUmar extended his authority over northern Guinea and much of the present republic of Mali. From 1870 to 1898 Samory Touré, a Malinke trader who had converted to Islam, proselytized many living in upper Guinea and the forest areas. Although the French defeated the jihadists and established a colony in Guinea (1891), their hold on the region was fragile. They attempted to win the support of the Muslim community through special favors, particularly in the Futa Jalon. Freeing serfs in the Futa disrupted its economy, however, and undermined the position of the Muslim leadership there.

Guinea became an independent republic in 1958 under the leadership of Sékou Touré, who although a nominal Muslim was heavily influenced by Marxist attitudes toward religion. At first Touré attempted to neutralize Muslim institutions that might challenge his ruling party by reducing Islamic leaders' traditional sources of wealth and prestige. In 1961 he closed the Qur'ānic schools that had supported the Muslim clerical class. In the Futa he encouraged low-caste populations to take over valuable farming lands held by the Muslim nobility. In the 1970s, however, as Touré's popularity waned, he turned to the Muslim community hoping to enhance his government's legitimacy and its credibility with countries in the Middle East. In 1977 he created the National Islamic Council to encourage islamization, with structures paralleling those of the ruling party down to the village level. With the support of Saudi Arabia, the government built Conakry's Fayṣal Mosque, said to be the largest mosque in sub-Saharan Africa.

Since President Touré's death in 1984, cooperation between the Muslim community and the government has continued. The Islamic Council (now the National Muslim League) functions at the district and local level and is responsible for Islamic education and administration of the *ḥajj*. For the majority of Muslims, Guinea's mosques continue to be a source of spiritual and social support. However, as increasing numbers of Guineans study in North Africa and the Middle East, the younger generation, in touch with trends in world Islam, sometimes clashes with the established leadership of the Muslim community.

BIBLIOGRAPHY

Levtzion, Nehemia. *Ancient Ghana and Mali*. London, 1973. Innovative study of Islam in the early states of the western Sudan.

Lewis, I. M., ed. *Islam in Tropical Africa*. London, 1966. Places Guinea's experience in its African context.

Marty, Paul. *L'Islam en Guinée*. Paris, 1921. Islam during Guinea's colonial period.

Person, Yves. *Samori: Une révolution Dyula*. 3 vols. Nimes, 1968–1975. Exhaustive study of the jihādist.

Touré, Ahmed Sékou. *La révolution guinéenne et le progrès social*. Conakry, 1967.

Trimingham, J. Spencer. *A History of Islam in West Africa*. Oxford, 1962. Trailblazing study of West Africa's Islamic community.

Willis, John R., ed. *Studies in West African Islamic History: The Cultivators of Islam*. London, 1979. Thoughtful essays on the impact of the nineteenth-century *jihād*s in West Africa.

CHARLOTTE A. QUINN

GULF STATES. Bahrain, Kuwait, Qatar, and the United Arab Emirates stand at the intersection of several major currents in contemporary Islamic affairs. The 1978–1979 revolution in Iran inspired the sizable Shīʿī communities of Bahrain and Kuwait to become much more active in their respective political arenas; this event, however, provoked little if any sympathy among the Shīʿah of the United Arab Emirates, while the predominantly Muwaḥḥidīn population of Qatar remained heavily influenced by the religious establishment in neighboring Saudi Arabia. All four societies have exhibited pronounced tensions between moderate Islamist reformers on one hand and Islamist radicals who advocate more fundamental change in the existing order on the other. Moreover, the rulers of all four continue to manipulate Islamic doctrine and symbolism in ways designed to enhance the legitimacy of their respective regimes.

Bahrain. The heterogeneous population of Bahrain has been ruled since the late eighteenth century by preeminent shaykhs of the Khalīfah clan, in alliance with a collection of prominent, rich merchant families, whose younger members now occupy many of the senior positions in the central administration. The Āl Khalīfah follow the Sunnī branch of Islam and adhere to the Mālikī school of Islamic jurisprudence, which favors relatively strict interpretations of the Qur'ān and the traditions of the Prophet (*ḥadīth*), but which also tolerates considerable flexibility in applying the law for the benefit of the community as a whole. The commercial elite consists of both Sunnīs following the Shāfiʿī school, most of whom immigrated to Bahrain from the southern coast of Iran during the late nineteenth century, and rationalist, accommodationist (Uṣūlī) Twelver Shīʿīs who continue to enjoy close ties to the predominant Shīʿī centers of Iran and southern Iraq. There are also small but significant pockets of Sunnīs who adhere to the more literalist Ḥanbalī school of legal interpretation, and of Shīʿīs who accept the tenets of the more ecstatic Akhbārī school, which adopts a strict constructionist view of the Qur'ān and the received traditions of the twelve original imams. It is estimated that Shīʿīs make up almost seventy percent of the country's general population, a substantially higher proportion than that reported following the 1941 census, the last one that registered the local inhabitants' religious affiliations.

Widespread discontent within the Bahraini Shīʿah precipitated a wave of riots on the islands in 1923. In the wake of this episode, British agents deposed the country's ruler and inaugurated a series of fundamental reforms in the local administration. Sunnī notables opposed to overt British interference in the islands' internal affairs responded by organizing the Bahrain National Congress to demand the restoration of the old ruler and the creation of an advisory council to assist him in governing the country. Shīʿīs for the most part remained aloof from this early liberal national movement, but they did petition the ruler in 1934 to promulgate a basic law and to institute proportional representation on municipal and educational councils. Sunnī reformers demanded the creation of an assembly *(majlis)* and an end to administrative inefficiency in late 1938. When students and oilworkers threatened to call a general strike in support of the *majlis* movement, the regime's British protectors arrested a number of leading reformers and deported them to India.

Violence between Sunnīs and Shīʿīs erupted again in late 1952 over the sectarian composition of the Manama municipal council. Over the next two years, as workers in the petroleum sector struck repeatedly to protest the local oil company's policy of employing large numbers of expatriate laborers, liberal nationalist activists worked to channel popular discontent against the British administration and away from sectarian issues. This effort succeeded in generating virtually universal support for a Higher Executive Committee composed of four Sunnīs and four Shīʿīs. It also precipitated the formation of a number of grassroots organizations, such as the Shīʿī Jaʿfari League in Jidd Hafs, whose members voiced demands for more radical changes in Bahrain's political and social institutions. At the end of 1956 moderate reformers, fearful of losing control over the nationalist movement to representatives of more militant groups, abandoned their own platform and acquiesced in the government's suppression of the radicals.

Smoldering unrest among the country's Shīʿah resurfaced in the wake of the 1978–1979 revolution in Iran. Reformist associations such as the Sunnī Society for Social Reform and the Shīʿī Party of the Call to Islam steadily lost ground throughout the 1980s to more radical groups like the Sunnī Islamic Action Organization and the Shīʿī Islamic Front for the Liberation of Bahrain. In mid-December 1981, the authorities announced that they had broken up a clandestine network of saboteurs affiliated with the Islamic Front; those arrested were handed lengthy prison sentences the following March by a tribunal presided over by one of the senior shaykhs of the Āl Khalīfah. Sporadic arrests of members of militant Islamist cells occurred throughout the rest of the decade, but the evident efficiency of the state security services in rounding up dissidents, combined with the ruling family's comparative magnanimity in dealing with those arrested, largely stifled political activities on the part of both radicals and moderates within the country's variegated Islamist movement. The thirty-member advisory council appointed by the ruler in January 1993 included prominent representatives from both the Sunnī and the Shīʿī communities.

Kuwait. Since the early eighteenth century Kuwait has been ruled by preeminent shaykhs of the Ṣabāḥ clan, in alliance with prominent members of the indigenous commercial elite, whose sons now occupy many of the senior positions in the central administration. The Āl Ṣabāḥ follow the Sunnī branch of Islam and adhere to the Mālikī school of Islamic jurisprudence. The rich merchant community consists primarily of Twelver Shīʿīs from both southern Iraq and Iran, along with a smaller number of Sunnīs following the Shāfiʿī school who migrated to the country from southern Iran around 1900. In addition, Shīʿī tribespeople based in southern Iraq and in the eastern province of Saudi Arabia regularly traverse the country's northern and western borders, while significant numbers of poorer Twelver Shīʿīs entered the country during the years after World War II to work in the petroleum and construction industries. It is estimated that Shīʿīs make up a quarter of the indigenous population.

Sectarian conflict played little part in the merchant-led reform movements of 1921 and 1938, although members of the elected council *(majlis)* that arose out of the latter accused the ruler's Shīʿī chief adviser of mobilizing his coreligionists against the Sunnī-dominated *majlis*. Expatriate teachers founded a local branch of the Muslim Brotherhood (Ikhwān al-Muslimūn) in 1951, which later evolved into the moderate Social Reform Society. Popularly elected representatives to the National Assembly mandated by the 1962 constitution soon coalesced into two broad informal blocs: one comprised supporters of the Āl Ṣabāḥ, including settled bedouin, prominent Shīʿīs, and moderate Sunnī Islamists, while the other was made up of liberal nationalists. Rising tension between the elected assembly members and the appointed cabinet convinced the prime minister, Shaykh Jābir al-Aḥmad, to tender the government's resignation in August 1976, an act that entailed the immediate suspension of the parliament.

Disadvantaged Shīʿīs staged a series of demonstrations in the capital city in early 1979; the authorities responded by deporting the country's most influential Shīʿī notable, Ḥujjat al-Islām Sayyid ʿAbbās Muhrī, and prohibiting the display of posters depicting the new Iranian leader Ayatollah Ruhollah Khomeini. Demonstrations erupted again at the end of the year in response to the seizure of the Grand Mosque in Mecca by Sunnī militants who advocated an Islamic revolution in Saudi Arabia. Shortly thereafter, a group of Shīʿī intellectuals publicly accused the government of removing Shīʿī officers from command positions in the armed forces and police. These events prompted a severe backlash against the indigenous Shīʿah: in October 1983, for example, militant Sunnīs attacked workers building a Shīʿī mosque in the capital and looted the construction site. In an attempt to appease Islamists in both camps, the authorities imposed severe restrictions on the sale of alcoholic beverages and placed increasingly strict limits on the public activities of women, particularly at the university, during the mid-1980s. Nevertheless, Islamist militants carried out sporadic attacks on foreign diplomatic and economic installations in Kuwait throughout the decade.

In February 1985, candidates who espoused an overtly religious platform suffered significant losses in popular elections to the National Assembly, which had been reinstituted four years earlier. Members of moderate Sunnī organizations suffered as a result of the publication of a Saudi scholar's ruling *(fatwā)* concerning the evils of both coeducation and western music. Only one prominent Shīʿī representative was elected to the fifty-member parliament that year. Growing disaffection within the Shīʿah set the stage for a suicide attack on the ruler's motorcade at the end of May; a month later, a bomb went off at a café in Kuwait City that was attached to a meeting house sponsored by the ruling family for older citizens. These events contributed to the second dissolution of the National Assembly in July 1986, as well as to the promulgation of stricter state controls on the indigenous Shīʿah.

Militant Kuwaiti Shīʿīs responded to the regime's stepped-up campaign of intimidation and surveillance by launching a wave of attacks on government installations. In January 1987, radical activists belonging to the clandestine Revolutionary Organization-Forces of the Prophet Muḥammad were arrested and charged with planting explosive devices at three major state-owned oil facilities in an effort to disrupt the summit meeting of the Organization of the Islamic Conference. Moderate Shīʿī notables reacted to the arrests by taking out full-page advertisements in local newspapers denouncing the organization's actions and reaffirming their loyalty to the regime.

Prominent members of both communities joined in agitating for the restoration of the National Assembly at the end of 1989. Professional associations, university students, and trade unionists petitioned the ruler in February 1990 to authorize new parliamentary elections, while a group of twenty-eight former assembly delegates presented their demands directly to the prime minister at the beginning of March. These actions convinced the cabinet in late April to approve the formation of a seventy-five-member National Council charged with assessing the past and future role of the parliament in the emirate's affairs. Twenty members of the old National Assembly won seats on the new council in the elections of June 1990, but this body's deliberations were interrupted by Iraq's invasion of Kuwait two months later.

During the months of the Iraqi occupation, neighborhood committees and soirees *(dīwānīyat)* provided the primary locus of popular resistance on the part of Kuwaiti citizens unable to escape the country. Two Sunnī organizations, the Social Reform Society and the Heritage Revival Society, used their influence within the directorates of the state-affiliated food cooperatives to coordinate the distribution of foodstuffs, medicine, and fuel throughout the country. The hasty evacuation of

Kuwait by the Iraqi armed forces in March 1991 provided local vigilantes with arms, which they soon turned on suspected collaborators. Forces loyal to the Āl Ṣabāḥ moved to disarm these individuals with the assistance of United States military police as soon as they regained control of the emirate. In addition, the authorities immediately declared a state of martial law.

Elections for a reorganized National Assembly took place in early October 1992. Islamist candidates—both Sunnī and Shīʿī—won eighteen seats, giving critics of the Āl Ṣabāḥ a total of thirty-one delegates in the fifty-member parliament. The Islamists quickly coalesced into two distinct blocs, an avowedly reformist Islamic Constitutional Movement and a comparatively conservative Islamic Popular Alliance. Both blocs advocated amending the 1962 constitution to make *sharīʿah* the basis of Kuwaiti law.

Qatar. Since the late nineteenth century Qatar has been ruled by the senior shaykhs of the Thānī clan, in conjunction with a comparatively small number of indigenous rich merchants and a corps of religious notables. Virtually the entire population adheres to the literalist Ḥanbalī school of Sunnī Islam, and more precisely to the interpretation of Islam formulated by the eighteenth-century reformer Muḥammad ibn ʿAbd al-Wahhāb. Consequently, the country's Muwaḥḥidi religious notables exercise considerable influence over judicial and educational affairs, while advising the ruler on the legality of governmental decrees according to a strict reading of the Qur'ān and the *ḥadīth*. A growing minority of the commercial oligarchy consists of recent Shīʿī immigrants from southern Iran, although there is also a small number of Sunnīs who arrived in the country from the southern coast of Iran at the turn of the twentieth century. Unofficial estimates put the proportion of Shīʿīs in the indigenous population at around sixteen percent, making Qatar the most homogeneous of the Arab Gulf emirates in ethnic/sectarian terms.

Given the homogeneity of the country and the size of the ruling family, actions undertaken by Qatar's liberal nationalist opposition have for the most part been indistinguishable from challenges to the status quo on the part of dissident Āl Thānī shaykhs. The National Unity Front formed during the early 1960s, for instance, included both oilworkers and younger members of the Āl Thānī. More recently, in January 1992, representatives of fifty prominent Qatari families, both Sunnī and Shīʿī, petitioned the ruler to set up an elected national council as a means of increasing popular participation in policy-making. This demand was sidestepped by the authorities, who subsequently harrassed the signatories.

United Arab Emirates. The government of the United Arab Emirates is conducted by an alliance of the ruling families of the seven smaller Arab Gulf states lying along the former Trucial Coast (Abu Dhabi, Dubai, Sharjah, Ras al-Khaimah, Ajman, Umm al-Qaiwain, and Fujairah), in conjunction with prominent members of the indigenous commercial elite, who occupy many of the senior positions in the federal administration formed in 1971 as well as in the bureaucracies of the individual emirates. The different ruling families share an adherence to both Sunnī Islam and the Mālikī school of legal interpretation, while the federation's rich merchants are divided along sectarian lines in a number of ways: in Dubai, the most influential families are Sunnī immigrants from southern Iran, although there is also a significant community of Twelver Shīʿīs; in Sharjah, Shīʿīs from South Asia predominate; Abu Dhabi's much smaller rich merchant elite consists primarily of Sunnīs having close ties to the tribes of eastern Arabia, although there is a growing cluster of Twelver Shīʿīs within the emirate as well. For the federation as a whole, Shīʿīs are estimated to account for almost twenty percent of the indigenous population.

Sectarian conflict played virtually no part in the 1938 reform movement in Dubai, and opposition to the emirate's ruling family throughout the 1950s emanated from younger professionals sympathetic to the secular ideals of Arab nationalism, rather than from Shīʿī or Sunnī Islamists. The Iranian revolution elicited little sympathy and no political activity on the part of the federation's resident Shīʿah. The few challenges the rulers faced during the 1980s arose either from the sporadic activities of clandestine radical nationalist groups, or out of persistent internecine feuding among members of the emirates' respective ruling families, particularly among senior shaykhs of the Āl Qāsimī of Sharjah.

BIBLIOGRAPHY

Abdullah, Muhammad Morsy. *The United Arab Emirates*. London, 1978. Particularly good on the 1938 reform movement in Dubai.

Cole, Juan R. I. "Rival Empires of Trade and Imami Shiʿism in Eastern Arabia, 1300–1800." *International Journal of Middle East Studies* 19.2 (May 1987): 177–204. Thought-provoking deep background.

Cottrell, Alvin J., et al., eds. *The Persian Gulf States: A General Survey*. Baltimore, 1980. Collection of essays on virtually all aspects of the Gulf states' history, culture, geography, and politics, with extensive bibliographies.

Crystal, Jill. *Oil and Politics in the Gulf: Rulers and Merchants in Kuwait and Qatar*. Cambridge, 1990. Conceptually and empirically sophisticated study of ruling family–merchant relations both before and after oil, with extensive references.

Lawson, Fred H. *Bahrain: The Modernization of Autocracy*. Boulder, 1989. Comprehensive survey of Bahrain's political and economic history in modern times, with an extensive bibliographic essay.

Lawson, Fred H. *Opposition Movements and U.S. Policy toward the Arab Gulf States*. New York, 1992. Update on recent challenges to the Gulf regimes.

Nakhleh, Emile. *Bahrain*. Lexington, Mass., 1976. Exhaustive study of political attitudes, parties, and voting on the islands after the 1950s.

Naqeeb, Khaldoun Hasan al-. *Society and State in the Gulf and Arab Peninsula*. Stimulating revisionist account of societal transformation in the Gulf states from the 1700s to the present, with extensive references.

Peck, Malcolm C. *The United Arab Emirates: A Venture in Unity*. Boulder, 1986. Concise overview of political and economic history of the federation.

Peterson, J. E. *The Arab Gulf States: Steps toward Political Participation*. New York, 1988. Definitive treatment of national assemblies and reform movements in contemporary Bahrain, Kuwait, Qatar, and the United Arab Emirates.

Said [Zahlan], Rosemarie J. "The 1938 Reform Movement in Dubai." *Al-abhath* 23 (December 1970): 247–318. Classic narrative of events, including relevant documents.

Zahlan, Rosemarie Said. *The Making of the Modern Gulf States*. London, 1989. Brief introduction to the ruling families and political histories of Bahrain, Kuwait, Qatar, and the United Arab Emirates.

FRED H. LAWSON

H

HABOUS. *See* Waqf.

ḤAḌĀRAH. The classical Arabic word *ḥaḍārah,* which connotes a sedentary lifestyle in either city or countryside, is used as a technical term for "civilization" in modern Middle Eastern societies. It is used in the sense of "sedentary life" by Ibn Manẓūr (d. AH 711/1312 CE) in his *Lisān al-ᶜArab* and by Ibn Khaldūn (d. 808/1406) in his *Muqaddimah. Ḥaḍārah* is synonymous with *ᶜumrān* ("civilization") in *Al-muqaddimah li-Kitāb al-ᶜibar;* it is comparable to *madanīyah* in Muḥammad ᶜAbduh's (d. 1905) *Risālat al-tawḥīd* (Epistle on Monotheism), and identical with the usage of the Arabic term *tamaddun* ("civilization") in the title of Jurjī Zaydān's (d. 1914) *Tārīkh al-tamaddun al-Islāmī* (History of Islamic Civilization). In South Arabian usage, according to R. B. Serjeant, *ḥaḍar* are the artisans, laborers, and merchants of the towns and villages, as opposed to tribesmen who bear arms.

In Ibn Khaldūn's usage, the term *ḥaḍārah* and *badāwah* (nomadism) are contrasted as distinct lifestyles, often hostile to each other. The nomadic hordes constitute a closely knit society led by a chief *(shaykh)* who unites the clans of the tribe on the basis of *ᶜaṣabīyah* (esprit de corps, solidarity), which issues from kinship. In his analysis of North African history, Ibn Khaldūn formulates the theory of *ᶜaṣabīyah* as a cohesive force that transforms a tribe into a political power founding a dynasty or state *(dawlah).* Thus *ᶜaṣabīyah* leads to the formation of an institution that in its turn contributes to the development of *ḥaḍārah.*

During the course of the twentieth century *ḥaḍārah* as a term has acquired various shades of meaning. For instance, Adam Metz's *Die Renaissance des Islams* was translated into Arabic under the title *Al-ḥaḍārah al-Islāmīyah fī al-qarn al-rābiᶜ al-hijrī* (Islamic Civilization during the Fourth Century Hijrah), where *ḥaḍārah* is used in the sense of "renaissance"; similarly, V. V. Barthold's treatise *Mussulman Culture* was translated into Arabic by Hamzah Ṭāhir as *Al-ḥaḍārah al-Islāmīyah,* thus identifying *ḥaḍārah* with culture. A survey of half a dozen Arabic books on *ḥaḍārah* reveals the following common topics: the rise and fall of states, the founding of capitals and garrison towns *(amṣār),* the aesthetic values of art and architecture, economic life, the development of education and science, and spirituality. Islamic scholarship recognizes religion as the foundation and creative force in the civilization of the *ummah* (community). Modernist Arab scholars—such as Ṭāhā Ḥusayn (d. 1973) in his discussion of the future of culture in Egypt—view freedom *(ḥurrīyah)* and independence *(istiqlāl)* as desirable values but not as the goals of civilization. The future *ḥaḍārah,* Ḥusayn argues, should be based on science *(ᶜilm)* and Arab culture *(thaqāfah)* in order to create a civilization matching the glorious past.

[*See also* ᶜAṣabīyah.]

BIBLIOGRAPHY

Beg, M. A. J. *Islamic and Western Concepts of Civilization.* 3d ed. Kuala Lumpur, 1982.

Bustānī, Buṭrus al-, ed. *Dā'irat al-maᶜārif,* vol. 7, pp. 96–97. Beirut, 1883.

Ibn Khaldūn. *The Muqaddimah: An Introduction to History.* 3 vols. Translated by Franz Rosenthal. New York, 1958.

Ibn Manẓūr, Muḥammad ibn Mukarram. *Lisān al-ᶜArab.* 15 vols. Beirut, 1955–1956. See volume 7, pages 196–202.

Von Grunebaum, G. E. "Islam: Essays in the Nature and Growth of a Cultural Tradition." *American Anthropologist,* Memoir 81 (1955).

M. A. J. BEG

ḤADĪTH. In Islam *ḥadīth* is the term applied to specific reports of the prophet Muḥammad's words and deeds as well as those of many of the early Muslims; the word is used both in a collective and in a singular sense. After the Prophet's death, his companions collected reports of what he had said and done, and they recounted the reports among themselves in order that the living memory of Muḥammad's example might influence the community of believers. As preserved for subsequent generations these reports, or *ḥadīth,* take the form of usually short, unconnected pieces, each of which is preceded by a list of its authoritative transmitters. Although the reports were originally transmitted orally, some transmitters began early to record them in writing. The compilers were careful not to tamper with the texts as they received them from recognized specialists in *ḥadīth* transmission, and the collections reflect their spoken origins. The language is direct, conversational, active, often repetitive, with a characteristic use of formulaic expression. The *ḥadīth* literature is one of the best examples of Arabic prose from the period of the beginnings of Islam.

After two centuries of collecting, transmitting, and teaching *ḥadīth,* during which the quest for reports became one of the most respected occupations of the Muslim community, scholars intensified the work of codifying the bulk of the material. The ninth century CE produced six massive collections, which have won almost universal acceptance by the Sunnī community as the most authoritative. They are commonly known by the names of their compilers: al-Bukhārī (d. 870); Muslim ibn al-Ḥajjāj (d. 875); Abū Dā'ūd al-Sijistānī (d. 888); Ibn Mājah al-Qazwīnī (d. 887); Abū ʿĪsā al-Tirmidhī (d. 892); and Abū ʿAbd al-Raḥmān al-Nasā'ī (d. 915). Two other collections as well have always enjoyed great favor with the Sunnīs, namely those of Mālik ibn Anas (d. 795) and Aḥmad ibn Ḥanbal (d. 855). These are only the most important examples of the large number of collections that appeared during this period and later, which classified thousands of reports according to the transmission of different authorities.

The Shīʿīs use the above collections, but they are selective in their recognition of the companions as valid authorities. In addition, they consider *ḥadīth* from the imams as fully authoritative. From the standpoint of their particular beliefs, the Shīʿīs revere four books as particularly significant, the collections by Muḥammad ibn Yaʿqūb al-Kulaynī (d. 940), Muḥammad ibn Bābūyah al-Qummī (d. 991) and Muḥammad al-Ṭūsī (d. 1068) who compiled two collections.

Science of *Ḥadīth* Criticism. By the time these collections had been completed a science of *ḥadīth* criticism had developed, the purpose of which was to determine the authenticity of *ḥadīth* attributed to the Prophet and to his companions and to preserve the corpus from alteration or falsification. The scholars verified each report with a chain of authorities (sg., *isnād*), going back, insofar as it was possible, to the Prophet himself. In order to decide on the degree of authenticity of a text, traditionists examined the chains of transmission from three points of view: that of the number of transmitters (sg., *rāwī*), ranging from a great many persons, representing all generations up to the classical compilers, narrating a single report, so that its authenticity was absolutely assured (a *mutawātir ḥadīth*), to a limited number of narrators, and even to a single chain *(āḥād ḥadīth);* that of the credibility of the transmitters, which consideration gave rise to an extensive biographical investigation in which the individual narrators were judged according to their personal qualities and professional achievements (*ʿilm al-rijāl,* science of the sources of information); that of the continuity of the chains, ranging from an uninterrupted *isnād* (*musnad,* supported) going back to the Prophet, to chains presenting various kinds of lacunae.

The nature of the *ḥadīth* text *(matn)* constituted another criterion for testing the authenticity of the material. Scholars suspected reports that were illogical, exaggerated or of a fantastic or repulsive character, or that contradicted the Qur'ān. They called attention to a common practice of fabricating *ḥadīth (waḍʿ)* carried out by those who propagated false teachings, but also by teachers of the truth who sought by inventing *ḥadīth* to expose heresy. Still others spread false *ḥadīth* for personal advantage or to express zealous piety. A voluminous literature emerged because of concern for the *matn*: works dealing with the historical context of *ḥadīth,* lexicographical studies of difficult words, the study of texts which were abrogated by other *ḥadīth,* the explanation of apparent contradictions found in authentic *ḥadīth,* and the so-called "divine *ḥadīth*" *(ḥadīth qudsī),* a category of material in which the Prophet assumed the role of transmitter and reported sayings of God himself. *Matn* criticism also included discussion by scholars of the comparative value of reporting *ḥadīth* word for word as opposed to transmitting reports by their meaning only. Both of these tendencies are seen in the collections, and, as a result, many variant readings of texts exist. Although the authority of *ḥadīth* in the community is very great, its inspiration is considered to be of a lower degree than that of the Qur'ān, which is believed to be the very word of God.

Muslims use three terms of a general nature to assess the relative validity of *ḥadīth* texts: *ṣaḥīḥ* ("sound"), the most acceptable; *ḥasan* ("good"), somewhat below the first in excellence; and *ḍaʿīf* ("weak"). Scholars usually apply these terms in a relative way, depending upon the type of criteria that are used to judge the *ḥadīth.*

Another aspect of *ḥadīth* science is the technique of transmission. With the passage of time the number of transmitters increased enormously. Measures of control emerged to ensure that *ḥadīth* were properly passed on from teacher to students or from scholar to scholar. The manuals describe eight ways whereby people could become accredited transmitters of the *ḥadīth* material that they learned. These mechanisms of control are applied in cases ranging from a most direct and personal exchange between teacher and student to the situation of a scholar who might discover a previously unknown or neglected written collection by a respected authority, and be authorized to transmit it.

Throughout the history of Islam the Qur'ān and the *ḥadīth* have functioned together to shape the life of the community worldwide. *Ḥadīth* provide the basic sources for the biography *(sīrah)* of the prophet Muḥammad, filling in details regarding events mentioned briefly in the Qur'ān and providing a wealth of information on the personality, the family, and the career of the Prophet. Also Muḥammad's example in word and deed, as recorded in the *ḥadīth,* helps Muslims to interpret the Qur'ān by pointing out the circumstances in which portions of the Book were revealed, by giving the meanings of obscure verses and words, and by recounting incidents in which the Qur'ānic texts were applied to situations in life.

As the record of the *sunnah,* or example of the Prophet, the *ḥadīth* literature is one of the sources of Islamic law *(sharīʿah).* How legal thinking evolved in the community is a complex question, but it is clear that by the early ninth century CE *ḥadīth* were officially accepted as a basic source of law. Many of the collections of *ḥadīth* are arranged according to the subject matter of jurisprudence *(fiqh),* thus showing that these compilations early became the tools of the legal profession.

To return to the first function of *ḥadīth,* that of preserving the record of the Prophet's biography, this element is of greater scope than a merely formal *sīrah.* The vast number of supplicatory prayers, exhortations, theological statements, practical counsels, words of encouragement and comfort, warnings, and predictions contained in the *ḥadīth* have always served to direct the piety of Muslims, to provide an overall framework for reflection and practice, all the more significant because by it the Qur'ān is, so to speak, embodied and exemplified in the flesh of the Prophet and his companions.

Ḥadīth have continued their multiple functions in the Muslim community through the centuries, and no one today doubts that they retain their place of supreme importance in the religious consciousness of Muslims. The formal study of *ḥadīth* has continued, too, although, after the period of the classical collections and the codification of rules for judging authenticity and for transmission of reports, the style of research naturally changed. Scholars examined the "Six Books" from every angle, wrote commentaries on them, gathered selected material from them for smaller, more accessible collections, and wrote treatises on all aspects of the science of *ḥadīth.*

As study of the written collections became more formalized, the place of teaching changed from private homes and mosques to schools dedicated to learning and transmitting the material. Muslim historians describe a certain decline in devotion to *ḥadīth* research beginning around the twelfth century. It was then that institutes began to be founded called *dūr al-ḥadīth* (sg., *dār;* "houses of *ḥadīth*"); the first was in Damascus, then spreading to many Muslim lands. Until recent centuries, they kept alive a concern for *ḥadīth* scholarship. In the mid-twentieth century Morocco established a modern Dār al-Ḥadīth in Rabat for graduate study in connection with the university and for research and publication. The modern universities in Muslim countries may include courses on *ḥadīth* in their departments of *sharīʿah,* in some of which the methods of the social sciences are beginning to be applied to the study of the literature. Venerable institutions such as Dār al-ʿUlūm in Deoband, India, and al-Azhar in Cairo are centers for *ḥadīth* studies.

Modern Approaches. In the Arab world, as well as in India and Pakistan, the editing and publishing of ancient manuscripts have been marked features of the present scene. Scholars such as Nabia Abbott and M. M. Azami have opened new perspectives by their investigation of recently discovered material, but, in general, Muslims of today have not gone beyond the treatises and commentaries of *ḥadīth* scholars from former centuries. A few books are being published on rhetoric in the *ḥadīth,* continuing an interest that goes back to much earlier times. Ṣubḥī al-Ṣāliḥ (*ʿUlūm al-ḥadīth wa-muṣṭalaḥuh;* Beirut, 1959) and Nūr al-Dīn ʿIṭr (*Manhaj al-naqd fī ʿulūm al-ḥadīth;* Beirut, 1972) are representatives of a number of writers who have composed thoughtful modern restatements of the ancient manuals of *ḥadīth* science. They do not propose any radically new course for research, but their works show some sensitivity to modern problems. By far the most serious issue with regard to *ḥadīth* themselves is the attack on their authenticity. The attack has been made from two main quarters and from two different motivations.

From one side, the Orientalists, headed by Ignácz Goldziher and Joseph Schacht, called into question the attribution of *ḥadīth* to the Prophet and the reliability of the chains of transmission. They did so in the interest of scientific historical research. Muslims have almost unanimously rejected the orientalists' critique, but only a few have gone beyond negative counterattacks. Fuat Sezgin (*Buhârî'nin kaynakları: hakkında araştırmalar;* Istanbul, 1956) has done original work on the written sources of al-Bukhārī, in partial refutation of the orientalists' positions. The critics have pointed out that Muslim *ḥadīth* scholars through the centuries dwelt almost exclusively upon the evaluation of the *isnād* ("chain of authorities") to the neglect of the *matn* ("text"). Nūr al-Dīn ʿIṭr takes this criticism seriously in the work cited above, and he proposes a new enterprise of research in which equal attention is given to *matn* and *isnād*. He points out that the canons of *matn* criticism have always existed. Modern research in the direction that he suggests would involve simply the reestablishment of the equilibrium needed in an integral program.

From another side, some Muslim reformers have called *ḥadīth* into question as a part of their struggle to overcome *taqlīd* (slavish conformity to ways of the past) and to promote the use of reason. Sayyid Aḥmad Khān (d. 1898) in India, Muḥammad ʿAbduh (d. 1905), Muḥammad Rashīd Riḍā (1935) in Egypt, and others wrote with varying degrees of forcefulness to decry the way traditional Muslim thinking had refused to apply a rigorous critique to the *ḥadīth* literature. Their writings influenced others, and one, Maḥmūd Abū Rayyah, published a highly critical book in 1958 (*Aḍwāʾ ʿalā al-sunnah al-muḥammadīyah,* Cairo) that provoked much discussion in the Middle East. G. H. A. Juynboll has written a useful account (*The Authenticity of the Tradition Literature: Discussions in Modern Egypt;* Leiden, 1969) of the course of these and other exchanges among the intellectual elite. However sharp the attacks may have been there was no basic opposition to *ḥadīth*. Critics only wanted Muslims to be more discerning in their acceptance of material attributed to the Prophet. As yet, however, no comprehensive program has emerged for a revival in *ḥadīth* study along the lines proposed by the reformers.

In the 1990s Islamic political and ideological movements are in the ascendancy. The theoreticians of these parties use *ḥadīth* to support their arguments without taking the time to discuss the problem of how to approach the literature. Among the masses, attachment to the *ḥadīth* constitutes a veritable ethos, and popular leaders depend on carefully chosen *ḥadīth* texts to give prophetic authority to their directives.

A few voices give promise of new directions in *ḥadīth* research. They represent no movement, no school of thought, but their views are respected by many. Fazlur Rahman (d. 1988), a Pakistani who spent many years at the University of Chicago, points out the crucial fact that *ḥadīth* provide the only access Muslims have to Muḥammad and the Qurʾān. To facilitate this access for the present generation, Fazlur Rahman feels that scholars should study, using modern techniques, the connections between Muḥammad and the early Muslim community, between the evolution of thought and practice and the growth of *ḥadīth* (see his *Islam;* 2d ed., Chicago and London, 1979, pp. 66, 67). [*See the biography of Rahman.*]

The Algerian philosopher Mohammed Arkoun, of Paris, describes *ḥadīth* as a "cultural expansion" of the phenomenon of Holy Scripture (Qurʾān); as such it is far more than an intellectual achievement. To understand it adequately requires an integrated approach taking into account both the rational development of the community and its creative imagination (see his "The Notion of Revelation: From Ahl al-Kitāb to the Societies of the Book," *Die Welt des Islams* 28 [1988]: 75–76). [*See the biography of Arkoun.*]

Modern technology has facilitated the cataloging and publication of manuscripts that have lain unused for centuries. Also Muslims are using the computer to gain better physical access to the thousands of reports that make up *ḥadīth* collections. One of the most concrete results of several recent international conferences on *ḥadīth* and *sīrah* has been to put in motion a project to computerize *ḥadīth*. In 1991 M. M. al-Azami reported ("A Note on Work in Progress on Computerization of Ḥadīth," *Journal of Islamic Studies*, 2.1 [Jan. 1991]: 86–91) that prototype CD-ROM discs were produced in 1990 containing the material of seven collections of *ḥadīth* and translations of selected texts in ten languages, 75,000 *ḥadīth* in all.

[*See also* Law; Muḥammad.]

BIBLIOGRAPHY

Collections of *Ḥadīth*

Abū Dā'ūd Sulayman ibn al-Ashʿath al-Sijistānī. *Sunan Abū Dawūd.* 3 vols. Translated by Ahmad Hasan. Lahore, 1984. English rendering of one of the "Six Books" of *ḥadīth.* Only the first guarantor of each chain of authorities is given. Contains many explanatory notes by the translator.

Bukhārī, Muḥammad ibn Ismāʿīl al-. *The Translation of the Meanings of Sahih al-Bukhari.* 9 vols. 4th ed. Translated by Muhammad Muhsin Khan. Chicago, 1979. Generally considered by Muslims to be the most authoritative collection. The complete Arabic text is included in columns parallel to the English translation. Only the first guarantor of each chain is given in the translation. Contains a few explanatory notes.

Mālik ibn Anas. *Al-Muwaṭṭa'.* Translated by ʿĀ'isha ʿAbdarrahman at-Tarjumana and Yaʿqub Johnson. Norwich, 1982. Excellent translation of one of the most important early collections. Especially significant for the development of Islamic law. Includes a glossary and a good index.

Muslim ibn Ḥajjāj al-Qushayrī. *Ṣaḥīḥ Muslim: Being Traditions of the Sayings and Doings of the Prophet Muḥammad as Narrated by His Companions and Compiled under the Title Al-Jāmiʿ-uṣ-Ṣaḥīḥ by Imām Muslim.* 20 fasc. Translated by ʿAbdul Hamid Siddiqi. Lahore, 1971–1975. Extensive notes by the translator accompany this rendering of the second most authoritative work of the "Six Books." Only the first guarantor of each text is mentioned.

Nawawī, Yaḥyā ibn Sharaf al-. *Gardens of the Righteous: Riyadh as-Salihin of Imam Nawawi.* Translated by Muḥammad Ẓafrullah Khan. London, 1980. Topically arranged collection by one of the greatest scholars of *ḥadīth* (thirteenth century CE). Contains selections from the canonical collections.

Ṭabāṭabā'ī, Muḥammad Ḥusayn. *A Shiʿite Anthology.* Translated with explanatory notes by William C. Chittick. Albany, N.Y., and London, 1981. One of the few collections available in English of sayings from the imams of Shīʿī Islam. Good notes and references by the translator.

Books about *Ḥadīth*

Abbott, Nabia. *Studies in Arabic Literary Papyri,* vol. 2, *Qur'ānic Commentary and Tradition.* Chicago, 1967. Working with previously unpublished material and examining the literature on *ḥadīth* science, the author breaks new ground by showing the importance of early written collections of *ḥadīth.*

Azami, Muhammad Mustafa. *Studies in Ḥadīth Methodology and Literature.* Indianapolis, 1977. Concise and clearly written introduction to the field of *ḥadīth.*

Azami, Muhammad Mustafa. *Studies in Early Ḥadīth Literature, with a Critical Edition of Some Early Texts.* Indianapolis, 1978. Another original investigation into early *ḥadīth* collections.

Goldziher, Ignácz. *Muslim Studies (Muhammedanische Studien),* vol. 2. Edited by S. M. Stern. Translated by C. R. Barber and S. M. Stern. Chicago and New York, 1971. Probably the most important modern book on *ḥadīth* written by a non-Muslim. Investigates the entire field with remarkable erudition. A basic reference, although Muslims often regard it as excessively negative in its assessment of the nature of *ḥadīth.*

Graham, William A. *Divine Word and Prophetic Word in Early Islam: A Reconsideration of the Sources, with Special Reference to the Divine Saying, or, Ḥadīth Qudsī.* The Hague and Paris, 1977. Discussion of the early Muslim understanding of divine revelation and how the *ḥadīth qudsī* fits into the picture. Outstanding description and analysis of this particular kind of *ḥadīth.*

Guillaume, Alfred. *The Traditions of Islam: An Introduction to the Study of the Hadith Literature* (1924). Reprint, Salem, N.H., 1980. Quite old, but still the most accessible general introduction to the field.

Schacht, Joseph. *The Origins of Muhammadan Jurisprudence.* Oxford, 1950. Second only in importance to the work of Goldziher (mentioned above) as to its influence on modern thought regarding the *ḥadīth.* Deals with legal material and reaches negative conclusions as to the authenticity of the chains of transmission supporting legal *ḥadīth.*

Siddiqi, Muhammad Z. *Ḥadīth Literature: Its Origin, Development, Special Features, and Criticism.* Calcutta, 1961. Reliable and clear survey by an Indian scholar. A mine of quickly accessible details, but somewhat difficult to obtain.

Speight, R. Marston. "The Function of *Ḥadīth* as Commentary of the Qur'ān, as Seen in the Six Authoritative Collections." In *Approaches to the History of the Interpretation of the Qur'ān,* edited by Andrew Rippin. Oxford, 1988. Description, with examples, of how each of the "Six Books" presents material on the Qur'ān.

Wensinck, A. J. *A Handbook of Early Muhammadan Tradition, Alphabetically Arranged.* Leiden, 1960. Topical index covering eight collections of *ḥadīth.* Includes a list of book (section) titles in each of the eight collections.

R. MARSTON SPEIGHT

HAGIOGRAPHY. *See* Biography and Hagiography.

ḤĀ'IRĪ YAZDĪ, ʿABD AL-KARĪM (1859–1936), the most prominent teacher among the *ʿulamā'* (community of religious scholars) in the city of Qom from 1921 to 1936. He received religious training in Iraq from Mīrzā Ḥasan Shīrāzī (d. 1896), Muḥammad al-Fishārakī al-Iṣfahānī (d. 1899), and Mullā Muḥammad Kāẓim Khurāsānī (d. 1911). He persisted throughout his life in maintaining a position of strict noninvolvement in political matters. Between 1900 and 1913 he moved between the western Iranian town of Arak, where he had established a center of learning, and Iraq in order to avoid being involved in political matters, such as the Persian Constitutional Revolution of 1905–1909 and the anti-British movement in Iraq. From Karbala, Iraq, he moved to Arak in 1913, and then to Qom in 1920. There, he founded a seminary called the Hawẓah-yi ʿIlmiyah, which became the premier institution of religious education in Iran (Tihrani, vol. 3, pp. 1158–1167; Hairi, p. 136).

Ḥā'irī maintained his policy of strict nonintervention in political affairs throughout his stay in Qom and until the end of his life in 1936. This is clear from his silence during the British expulsion of Shīʿī leaders from Iraq in 1923 and the insurrection by some Isfahan clergy in Iran in 1924 (over opium production) and in the case of the exiling of Ayatollah Muḥammad Taqī Bāfqī (owing to his criticism of the behavior of ladies of the royal court in the Qom shrine) in 1928. Apart from his wish not to invite military intervention by Reza Khan Pahlavi, which might hurt the Hawẕah-yi ʿIlmīyah, there was also the fact that he considered these activities as political (Tihrani, vol. 1, p. 249; vol. 3, pp. 1158–1167; Hairi, pp. 135–136). This position of political noninterference over the years was a cause of wonderment to many, but, according to one of his sons, was rooted in his natural disposition (Hairi, p. 136). During his stay in Qom, he became involved with political issues only twice, and even then only momentarily and against his better judgment. It was Ḥā'irī, together with Muḥammad Ḥusayn Nā'īnī (d. 1936) and Abū al-Ḥasan Iṣfahānī (d. 1945), who convinced Reza Khan in 1924 to drop the idea of making Iran a republic (Hairi, pp. 142–143). In 1932 Ḥā'irī sent a strongly worded message to Reza Shah in which he said that, although up to then he had not interfered in any political matters, certain new policies (the Dress Law of 1928 and the general curtailment of the *ʿulamā*'s social standing) were contrary to Shīʿī law and that he was duty-bound to inform the shah that his actions were intolerable (Razi, pp. 35–36).

Ḥā'irī did not press this and other issues and, out of concern for the long-term well-being of Islam and the clerical community, he did not exhort other *ʿulamā'* or his followers to openly revolt against the government. He once publicly stated, "It is due to this security [brought by Reza Shah] that I can fulfill my duties to Islam and teach in this city," and he exhorted all Iranians to follow their progressive monarch (Faghfoory). Ḥā'irī's most famous student was Ayatollah Ruhollah Khomeini (d. 1989), who clearly disagreed with his teacher on the role of the *marjaʿ al-taqlīd*, the most distinguished rank among the religious leaders. Ḥā'irī advanced the notion that a Shīʿī could follow more than one *marjaʿ al-taqlīd* on different aspects of Islamic law, a position later supported by Ayatollah Murtaẕā Muṭahharī (d. 1979), who was one of Khomeini's most famous students and who believed that Islamic jurisprudence had grown too complex to be mastered by one individual in all its aspects (Muṭahharī, vol. 1, p. 218).

[*See also* Constitutional Revolution; Qom; *and the biographies of Nā'īnī and Pahlavi.*]

BIBLIOGRAPHY

Āghā Buzurg al-Ṭihrānī, Muḥammad Muḥsin. *Ṭabaqāt Aʿlām al-Shīʿah* (The Shīʿī Clergy). 3 vols. Najaf, 1954–1962. Standard source for the biographies of modern Shīʿī clergy.

Faghfoory, Mohammad H. "Modernization and Professionalism of the *ʿUlamā'* in Iran, 1925–1941." *Journal of Iranian Studies* 26.3–4 (Summer–Fall 1993). Discusses trends in the religious institution during the rule of Reza Shah.

Fischer, Michael M. J. *Iran: From Religious Dispute to Revolution.* Cambridge, Mass., 1980. Study of cultural idioms, religious discourse, and the Iranian clergy, particularly in Qom, in the Pahlavi period.

Hairi, Abdul-Hadi. *Shīʿism and Constitutionalism.* Leiden, 1977. Investigates the role of the clergy in the early twentieth century, with a focus on the Constitutional Revolution and the early Reza Shah period.

Muṭahharī, Murtaẕā. "Aṣl-i Ijtihād dar Islām" (The Basis of *Ijtihād* in Islam). In *Guftār-i Māh.* 3 vols. Tehran, 1959–1961. Argues that *fiqh* has become too complex to be mastered by any one religious leader.

Raẕī, Zangīpūrī Muḥammad. *Āsār-i Ḥujjah va Tārīkh va Dā'irah-yi Maʿārif-i Ḥawẕah-yi ʿIlmīyah-yi Qumm* (The Works of Proof and the History and Cycle of Learning of the Qom Seminary). Qom, 1959. History of Qom's seminary, with a focus on personalties.

WILLEM FLOOR

ḤAJJ. Unique among the world's great pilgrimages, the *ḥajj* is in many ways also the most important. Even compared to the ancient and highly developed international pilgrimage systems of Christianity and Hinduism, the *ḥajj* is remarkable in its doctrinal centrality, its geographic focus, and its historical continuity. The size and global coverage of the *ḥajj* are unparalleled. It regularly attracts one million overseas pilgrims from virtually every nation—about 50 percent of them from the Arab world, 35 percent from Asia, 10 percent from sub-Saharan Africa, and 5 percent from Europe and the Western Hemisphere. These are joined in Mecca by another one million local pilgrims, mostly foreigners working in Saudi Arabia. The combined contingents form the largest and most culturally diverse assembly of humanity to gather in one place at one time.

The *ḥajj* is the annual pilgrimage to Mecca during the second week of Dhū al-Ḥijjah, the final month of the Islamic lunar calendar. All adult Muslims are required to perform the *ḥajj* at least once in their lifetimes provided they possess adequate resources and their absence from home will not create unreasonable hardships for their families. No other pious journey may be equated with or substituted for the *ḥajj;* this includes visits to the tombs of saints (*ziyārahs*), to Muḥammad's tomb in Medina, or to Mecca itself at other times of the year (*ʿumrah*). Nor can the *ḥajj* be replaced by a spiritual "inner pilgrimage" through meditation or mystical enlightenment.

The *ḥajj* includes an intricate series of highly symbolic and emotional rituals performed in unison by all pilgrims. The sequence of rites observed today was determined by Muḥammad shortly before his death and is regarded as a ritual reenactment of critical, faith-testing events in the lives of Abraham, the ancient founder of monotheism, his wife Hajar, and their son Ismāʿīl. When Muslim pilgrims replicate Muḥammad's movements, they recall not the pagan ceremonies of pre-Islamic Mecca (some of which were also known as *ḥajj*), but the much older models of the earlier prophets.

Before the *ḥajj* begins, all male pilgrims don a special garb (*iḥrām*) consisting merely of two white sheets or towels covering the upper and lower parts of the body. Female pilgrims have greater freedom of dress as long as they remain modest and tasteful. The primitiveness and uniformity of the *iḥrām* symbolizes the radical equality and humility of all believers before God regardless of worldly differences in race, nationality, class, age, gender, or culture. The *iḥrām* is a metaphor for how people will appear when they emerge from the grave on Judgment Day to confront their creator. Many pilgrims retain their *iḥrām* for years after the *ḥajj* and use it as a burial shroud.

The initial rite of the *ḥajj,* the *ṭawāf,* is performed at least twice—immediately upon arriving in Mecca and just before departing after the completion of all other rites. The *ṭawāf* is a sevenfold circumambulation of the Kaʿbah, the cube-shaped "House of God" first built by Abraham and Ismāʿīl and the spiritual center of the world which all Muslims face during prayer. The Kaʿbah is often called an earthly counterpart to God's throne in heaven, and the *ṭawāf* is described as a human imitation of the angels' circling his throne in adoration. During the *ṭawāf* many pilgrims approach the corner of the Kaʿbah that holds the Black Stone, a mysterious "heavenly rock" resembling a meteorite whose origins and alleged powers are widely disputed. Most pilgrims merely salute the Black Stone from a short distance as a gesture of their renewed covenant with God. Others struggle to touch or kiss the Black Stone, believing that it physically absorbs sin.

The *ṭawāf* is followed immediately by the *saʿy,* in which the pilgrim runs back and forth seven times between two small hills close to the Kaʿbah. This recalls Hajar's frantic search for water after Abraham was forced to abandon her and Ismāʿīl in the desert. After the exertion of the *ṭawāf* and *saʿy* most pilgrims wash and relax at the nearby well of Zamzam, which appeared miraculously to rescue Hajar and her son from death. Pilgrims drink Zamzam water throughout their stay in Mecca and frequently take home small flasks as souvenirs for friends and relatives who are unable to make the *ḥajj* themselves.

The climax of the *ḥajj* is the massive procession to the plain of Arafat just outside Mecca on the ninth day of Dhū al-Ḥijjah. Two million pilgrims from more than one hundred countries gather in tents that cover the valley and surrounding mountains as far as the eye can see. From just after noon until shortly after sunset they are absorbed in continuous prayer and conversation. Many believe that at this spot and time God's spirit descends closest to earth, making it easier for human prayers to attract his attention.

Some of the most devout pilgrims scale the sides of the Mount of Mercy where Muḥammad delivered a famous sermon during his "farewell pilgrimage"; however, the vast majority remain in tents sheltered from the dangerous midday sun. The encamped congregation at Arafat is a beehive of activity, constantly exchanging news and ideas about the condition of Islam in every corner of the world. Each camp combines the air of a religious retreat, a country picnic, and a town meeting.

Promptly after sunset, two million people and a hundred thousand vehicles break camp and rush out of the valley, creating the world's largest traffic jam (*nafrah*). They inch their way through the narrow mountain pass of Muzdalifa, where they spend the night in the open under the starry desert sky. The complete lack of accommodations at Muzdalifa makes this one of the most ascetic phases of the *ḥajj,* and for many Muzdalifa is the most inspiring and calming part of the pilgrimage. On the tenth day of Dhū al-Ḥijjah, at sunrise, pilgrims continue on to the adjacent valley of Mina, where another colossal tent city is erected between Arafat and Mecca.

Mina is the site of two ritual dramas poignantly replicating Abraham's crisis in fulfilling God's command to sacrifice his son Ismāʿīl. Pilgrims reenact Abraham's rejection of Satan's temptation to disobey the divine order by hurling seven pebbles at a tall stone pillar (*jamarah*) representing the devil. The massive crush of humanity and flying stones about the pillar create the most frenzied and cathartic moments of the *ḥajj*, as well as some of the most perilous. Afterward, each pilgrim offers an animal sacrifice *(qurbān)* commemorating the sheep that God ultimately accepted from Abraham in place of his son. Muslims all over the world participate vicariously in this phase of the *ḥajj* by simultaneously making their own sacrifices at home on ʿĪd al-Aḍḥā, Islam's most important holiday. [*See* ʿĪd al-Aḍḥā.]

During the next two or three days, until the twelfth or thirteenth day of Dhū al-Ḥijjah, pilgrims constantly shuttle back and forth between Mina and Mecca via clogged highways and wide pedestrian tunnels cut through the mountains. Following a slightly more flexible schedule, they perform at least six more stonings in Mina and at least one more *ṭawāf* and *saʿy* in Mecca. In the final few days of the ceremonies male pilgrims wear the *iḥrām* garb less frequently. Instead, they wear various combinations of their regular national costumes and local Arabian dress, signifying their gradual return to the profane world and their closer identification with Muḥammad and his companions.

A properly performed *ḥajj* creates spiritually reborn pilgrims absolved from all previous sins. At this point, elderly and infirm pilgrims sometimes express a readiness for death, particularly in Mecca, believing their purified souls will enter paradise immediately. However, a *ḥajj* is only valid if God accepts it, and his judgment cannot be known with certainty by the pilgrim or anyone else. The hallmark of a valid pilgrimage is not performing each ritual with precision, but undertaking the entire journey with the sincere intention *(nīyah)* of coming closer to God. If a pilgrim's intentions are spiritually sound, then all but the most flagrant breaches of ritual formality can be corrected by sacrificing additional animals in Mecca or by special acts of charity and fasting after returning home.

The *ḥajj* is unique in its symbolic richness as well as its far-reaching political ramifications. The extraordinary interplay of symbolism, ritual, and power links pilgrims with one another and with Muslims around the world in a feeling of common destiny extending from the time of creation until Judgment Day. The dream of preserving and harnessing the unifying power of the *ḥajj* has long fascinated and frightened elites in the Muslim world and beyond. The struggle to control the organization and interpretation of the pilgrimage has persisted throughout Islamic history and has become a major religio-political conflict in the twentieth century. Since World War II, newly independent states throughout the Muslim world have adopted elaborate programs to manipulate the *ḥajj* for political and economic gain. However, controlling the *ḥajj* is far more difficult than the technocrats imagine; its pluralistic symbolism and multifunctional ritual defy the modern state's penchant for standardization and regimentation.

The symbolic structure of the *ḥajj* contains numerous layers open to alternative interpretations. At each phase of the rites the pilgrim reenacts dramatic events associated with multiple, often overlapping characters. Any analysis of this symbolism soon becomes an investigation of archetypes derived not only from the Qur'ān and *sunnah* but also from local legend and oral tradition. In many accounts Muḥammad's association with shrines and sites is preceded not only by Abraham and his family (a pre-Islamic layer), but also by Noah and Adam (a prehistoric layer) and by Gabriel and other angels (a preterrestrial layer).

Interpretation of this sacred symbolism has always been pluralistic and controversial. Orientalists such as von Grunebaum have claimed that the rites have no meaning and that pilgrims perform the *ḥajj* with no comprehension of their actions beyond blind obedience. In contrast, some esoteric writers see every place and persona as a profusion of signs pointing toward a unique truth for each pilgrim and each pilgrimage. Many pilgrims, literate or not, carry government-approved guide books that reveal the "secrets" or hidden meanings of the *ḥajj* as though there were a single, standard message that could be decoded once and for all.

Muslim commentators generally acknowledge that the *ḥajj* contains many mysteries that no human intellect grasps fully. However, they then proceed to interpret these latent themes in ways that reflect conventional differences among *ʿulamā'*, Ṣūfīs, Shīʿīs, modernists, and fundamentalists. For many of these writers, the symbolism of the *ḥajj* serves as a metalanguage inviting critical and creative thought, open to periodic reinterpretation and congenial to wide variations in culture, nationality, and politics. Even the government of Saudi Arabia, which tries to set the limits of respectable discourse and conduct during the *ḥajj*, recognizes that such disagreements are inevitable and perhaps desirable.

The ritual functions of the pilgrimage are just as diverse as its symbolic structure. Anthropologists who specialize in the study of ritual commonly distinguish between rites of passage, rites of renewal, rites of reversal, and rites of affliction. Although these concepts generally describe discrete phenomena, each is appropriate in highlighting a different facet of the *ḥajj*.

Pilgrimage frequently coincides with major turning points in the life cycle such as adulthood, marriage, career change, retirement, illness, and death. It may also serve as a flexible and repeatable initiation for people of any age, including new converts to Islam or those seeking spiritual rejuvenation after a personal crisis or loss. Viewed as a rite of passage, the *ḥajj* appears capable of helping individuals adapt in various cultures and social structures with generally conservative, system-supporting implications.

On the collective level, the *ḥajj* celebrates the reunion and renewal of the *ummah,* the worldwide community of Muslims. Indeed, the pilgrimage is the symbolic rebirth of the *ummah* every year. It is the most powerful reminder of Islam's ideals of unity across cultures and its continuity over time. Pilgrims retrace the footsteps of the founders of monotheism and Islam. They discuss and debate the role of the *ummah* country by country, in the international system and in the course of world history. Afterward, they return home with a stronger sense of the transcendent, charismatic quality of the community—a sentiment shared and reaffirmed by neighbors and countrymen unable to perform the pilgrimage themselves.

By symbolically negating all status and hierarchy, the *ḥajj* devalues the status quo in all its forms. It is true that the reversal of roles is only temporary and fictional. In fact, throughout their stay in the holy land pilgrims enjoy vastly different accommodations and comforts depending on their nationality and class. Nevertheless, repeated stress on the ultimate irrelevance of all distinctions among believers challenges the legitimacy of economic and political inequalities both nationally and internationally. As with other rites of status reversal, the *ḥajj* has mixed implications for authority. It can produce either catharsis and acquiescence or empowerment and protest. Controversies over control of the *ḥajj* reflect recurrent struggles between elites who favor these opposing goals.

During the past two decades, controversy has centered on Saudi Arabia's attempts to use the pilgrimage as a rite of reconciliation versus Iran's desire to turn it into a platform for revolution. King Fayṣal (r. 1964–1975) frequently told pilgrims that the *ḥajj* should serve not only to heal their spiritual ailments but also to mend the political splits in the *ummah* as a whole so that it could become a more effective force in world affairs. He portrayed the *ḥajj* as a period of reflection and self-criticism that should be institutionalized in a permanent international forum. Fayṣal lobbied Muslim heads of state attending the pilgrimage to found the Organization of the Islamic Conference (OIC) as a Muslim counterpart to the United Nations.

During the 1980s, when Iran's revolutionary government disrupted the *ḥajj* and demanded its removal from Saudi supervision, the OIC provided decisive support for Fayṣal's successors. More than forty member-states of the OIC not only reaffirmed Saudi protection of the holy cities but also endorsed an unprecedented quota system limiting the number of pilgrims in each nation's delegation. In an effort to further centralize *ḥajj* management, many Muslim technocrats have urged the OIC to establish an international agency to coordinate the burgeoning government bureaucracies that currently regulate all aspects of the pilgrimage in their respective countries. [*See* Organization of the Islamic Conference.]

These proposals simultaneously reflect and aggravate the growing politicization of the *ḥajj* at both national and international levels. Entrenched elites manipulate the pilgrimage at their own peril. Government sponsorship and control frequently swell into a virtual state monopoly over a lucrative *ḥajj* enterprise. Such monopolies commonly breed favoritism, resentment, and heightened conflict between parties, regions, classes, and ethnic groups. This sort of pilgrimage policy not only threatens to undermine the political elites who wield it, but it also ultimately contradicts the ideals of the *ḥajj*.

[*See also* Mecca; Pillars of Islam.]

BIBLIOGRAPHY

Aḥsan, ʿAbdullāh al-. *The Organization of the Islamic Conference.* Herndon, Va., 1988. Overview of the OIC's origin, structure, and activities.

Birks, J. S. *Across the Savannas to Mecca: The Overland Pilgrimage Route from West Africa.* Totowa, N.J., 1978. Detailed study of pilgrimage routes before the dominance of air travel.

Campo, Juan Eduardo. *The Other Sides of Paradise: Explorations into the Religious Meanings of Domestic Space in Islam.* Columbia, S.C., 1990. Contains an excellent chapter on pilgrimage art in Egyptian villages.

Chélini, Jean, and Henry Brauthomme. *Histoire des pèlerinages non-*

chrétiens. Paris, 1987. Comprehensive survey and comparison of non-Christian pilgrimages.

Eickelman, Dale F., and J. P. Piscatori, eds. *Muslim Travellers: Pilgrimage, Migration, and the Religious Imagination*. Berkeley, 1990. Contains good chapters on the *ḥajj* from Malaysia and India.

Eliade, Mircea. *The Myth of the Eternal Return, or, Cosmos and History*. Princeton, 1954. Classic analysis of universal themes in religious myth.

Firestone, Reuven. *Journeys in Holy Lands: The Evolution of the Abraham-Ishmael Legends in Islamic Exegesis*. Albany, N.Y., 1990. Careful comparison of Islamic and pre-Islamic legend concerning Abraham and Mecca.

Fischer, Michael M. J., and Mehdi Abedi. *Debating Muslims: Cultural Dialogues in Postmodernity and Tradition*. Madison, Wis., 1990. Contains a chapter on radical Iranian views of the pilgrimage.

Kamal, Ahmad. *The Sacred Journey*. New York, 1961. Useful guide to *ḥajj* rituals that provides many widely accepted interpretations.

Kramer, Martin. "Khomeini's Messengers: The Disputed Pilgrimage of Islam." In *Religious Radicalism and Politics in the Middle East*, edited by Emmanuel Sivan and Menachem Friedman, pp. 177–227. Albany, N.Y., 1990. Good overview of the clashes between Iran and Saudi Arabia during the 1980s.

Long, David E. *The Hajj Today: A Survey of the Contemporary Makkah Pilgrimage*. Washington, D.C., 1979. Still useful study of Saudi *ḥajj* administration.

Matheson, Virginia, and A. C. Milner. *Perceptions of the Haj: Five Malay Texts*. Singapore, 1984. Various written accounts of Malay pilgrims from different historical eras.

McDonnell, Mary Byrne. "The Conduct of the Hajj from Malaysia and its Socio-Economic Impact on Malay Society: A Descriptive and Analytical Study, 1860–1981." Ph.D. diss., Columbia University, 1986. Excellent study of a leading example of modern *ḥajj* management.

Naqar, ʿUmar ʿAbd al-Razzāq. *The Pilgrimage Tradition in West Africa: An Historical Study with Special Reference to the Nineteenth Century*. Khartoum, 1972. Describes the many functions of the *ḥajj* in African society.

Partin, Harry B. "The Muslim Pilgrimage: Journey to the Center." Ph.D. diss., University of Chicago, 1967. Contrasts pre-Islamic and Islamic versions of the *ḥajj*.

Sharīʿatī, ʿAlī. *Hajj*. Bedford, Ohio, 1977. The most influential example of revolutionary Shīʿī interpretations of *ḥajj* symbolism.

Snouck Hurgronje, Christiaan. "Notes sur le mouvement du pèlerinage de la Mecque aux Indes Neerlandaises." *Revue du Monde Musulman* 5 (1911): 397–413. Classic colonialist view of how pilgrimage should be controlled.

Snouck Hurgronje, Christiaan. "La pèlerinage a la Mekke." In his *Selected Works*, edited by G.-H. Bousquet and Joseph Schacht. Leiden, 1957. Emphasizes the political context in which Muḥammad formulated the *ḥajj*.

Turner, Victor. *The Ritual Process: Structure and Anti-Structure*. Ithaca, N.Y., 1969. Major theoretical discussion of ritual, emphasizing its relations with authority.

Turner, Victor, and Edith Turner. *Image and Pilgrimage in Christian Culture: Anthropological Perspectives*. New York, 1978. The best study of pilgrimage within a social science framework.

Von Grunebaum, G. E. *Muhammadan Festivals*. New York, 1951. Compares the *ḥajj* with other Islamic rituals.

ROBERT BIANCHI

ḤAKĪM, MUḤSIN AL- (1889–1970), most widely followed Shīʿī *mujtahid* (interpreter of Islamic law) of the 1960s. Sayyid al-Ḥakīm was born in Najaf, Iraq, into the religiously prominent Ṭabāṭabāʾī family of Iraq, Iran, Lebanon, and Pakistan. He was trained in Islamic law and theology in Najaf, studying with Ayatollah Muḥammad Kāẓim Yazdī, Ayatollah Muḥammad Ḥusayn Nāʾīnī, and others. Recognized as the leading teacher at the seminaries in Najaf, he became Shiism's chief authority when Ayatollah Moḥammad Ḥosayn Borujerdi of Qom died in 1962. With the tithes of the faithful, forwarded to him by his clerical representatives around the Shīʿī world, Ayatollah al-Ḥakīm administered the *ḥawzah* (theological center) of Najaf and provided for the financial needs of educational centers in Iraq and other countries. His hallmark was giving mosques and Islamic centers gifts of books and libraries.

Ayatollah al-Ḥakīm was moderate in his theology. His initiatives were educational, and in his later years, political, as he led Shīʿī clerics in an offensive against communism. His relations with Iraq's Hashemite government (1923–1958) were amiable, but Iraq's subsequent governments he deemed to be religiously illegitimate. He sought to meet the challenge of secularism through a series of steps aimed at educating Muslims to the need for Islamic standards in government and society and through cooperation with practicing Sunnī Muslims. Among his initiatives were the sponsorship of Jamāʿat al-ʿUlamāʾ (Society of Religious Scholars) and endorsement of Ḥizb al-Daʿwah (Party of the Call [to Islam]), clandestine groups that strove to educate Shīʿīs to the need for government that meets minimum Islamic requirements. To this end, he dispatched politically activist clerics to Lebanon and elsewhere and sanctioned political assertiveness by Shīʿīs, a major change from traditional Shīʿī quietism and a major contributor to subsequent political ferment in such countries as Iraq.

Ayatollah al-Ḥakīm opposed the Iraqi Government of ʿAbd al-Karīm Qāsim (1958–1963) because it was secular and because its land reform involved confiscation of private property, considered to be protected by Islamic law. Alarmed by the appeal of "atheistic" communism to Muslims, he issued a *fatwā* (religious proclamation) in 1960 forbidding Shīʿīs to have any connection with the Communist Party. He lent his name to a joint Shīʿī-Sunnī political party during the brief period in 1960 when the Iraqi government allowed organized opposition. He also led the Shīʿī clergy in opposition to the Iraqi governments of ʿAbd al-Salām ʿĀrif and ʿAbd al-Raḥmān ʿĀrif (1963–1968), judging them to be sectarian, as well as secular and socialistic.

During the last two years of his life, Ayatollah al-Ḥakīm was tormented by Iraq's Baʿthist Government. In 1969, when he declined to side with the government in its quarrel with the shah of Iran, he was placed under house arrest. His son Mahdī was sentenced to death and funds belonging to the *ḥawzah* were confiscated by the government. Ayatollah al-Ḥakīm responded with a *fatwā* forbidding practicing Shīʿīs from membership in the Baʿth party.

Ayatollah al-Ḥakīm fathered ten sons, many of whom, along with their sons, were executed by the Baʿth government of Saddam Hussein during the 1980s.

[*See also* Iraq.]

BIBLIOGRAPHY

Husain, Sayyed Murtaza. *Hayat-e-Hakeem: The Life of Syed Mohsin al-Hakeem*. Karachi, 1973. The only book-length biography of Ayatollah al-Ḥakīm.

Khaṭīb ibn al-Najaf, al-. *Tārīkh al-Ḥarakah al-Islamīyah al-Muʿ āṣirah fī al-ʿIrāq* (History of the Contemporary Islamic Movement in Iraq). Beirut, 1982. Insider's account of the Iraqi Shīʿī clergy's attempts to counter secularism and unbelief.

Momen, Moojan. *An Introduction to Shiʿi Islam*. New Haven, 1985. Excellent depiction of Shiism and its prominent leaders.

JOYCE N. WILEY

ḤĀKIMĪYAH. *See* Islamic State.

ḤALĀL, The Qur'ānic term *ḥalāl* denotes that which is lawful or allowed. The word can refer generally in Muslim practice to that which is proper and therefore permitted for use; more specifically, in Muslim legal discourse it has come to be applied to rules pertaining to the consumption of food and drink, and related issues, where it is contrasted with the notion of *ḥarām*, the forbidden.

The Qur'ān addresses *ḥalāl* in a larger context in which developing Muslim practice and conduct are defined and elaborated in relation to existing pre-Islamic practices. It permits Muslims to eat the food of the "people of the book" *(ahl al-kitāb)*, and to marry women from among them. It also emphasizes that the good things of the world are part of God's bounty to humanity, made available for their sustenance and daily use, and that this part of existence is no longer subject to arbitrary custom and interpretation along various religious, social, or ethnic lines.

Ḥalāl food includes the meat of permitted animals that have been ritually slaughtered, hunted game over which the name and praise of God have been pronounced, and fish and marine life. In cases of extreme necessity in which survival is at stake, consumption of prohibited categories of food and drink—such as pork, blood, alcoholic drinks, scavenger animals, carrion, and improperly sacrificed meat—is permitted.

With the development of jurisprudence among Muslims, issues pertaining to proper action were classified within a fivefold regulatory scheme of actions *(al-aḥkām al-khamsah): wājib/farḍ*, obligatory or required acts; *mandūb*, recommended acts; *mubāḥ*, indifferent acts, whose performance merited neither reward nor punishment; *makrūh*, reprehensible acts; and *ḥarām*, totally prohibited acts. The rules of *ḥalāl* and *ḥarām* were thus integrated into a larger moral framework that lent itself to legal as well as ethical definition and elaboration.

Historical developments and influences affecting the Muslim world in the nineteenth and twentieth centuries have led to discussions of the relevance of such traditional codes of conduct and purity to the modern technologies of production, distribution, and consumption of food resources. The impact of these global changes has been felt both in Muslim societies and in those in which Muslims live as minorities. Muslim scholars and jurists have by no means been of one opinion in these matters, but they have sought guidance based on established Muslim ethical and legal principles. They have emphasized the rational basis of the Qur'ānic prescriptions and suggested their importance for hygienic and environmental reasons.

The concept of *ḥalāl* in Islam today, as is the case with comparable ideas in other religious traditions such as Judaism, may also be regarded as part of an integral code of ethics and purity. Its perspectives on rules of permissibility, cleanliness, and purification relating to food and drink, the body and its functions, rites of passage, rituals of pilgrimage and prayer, and sacred space and times enable Muslims to frame their behavior in ethical terms that are in accord with their understanding of Islam as a complete moral code displaying reverence for life in all its forms.

[*See also* Dietary Rules; Ḥarām; Purification.]

BIBLIOGRAPHY

Faruki, Kemal A. "Legal Implications for Today of *Al-Aḥkām al-Khamsa* (The Five Values)." In *Ethics in Islam,* edited by Richard G. Hovannisian, pp. 65–72. Malibu, 1985. Modern Muslim scholar of Islamic jurisprudence argues for integrating the legal and ethical foundations of these established values into contemporary Muslim life.

Firmage, Edwin B., et al., eds. *Religion and Law: Biblical-Judaic and Islamic Perspectives.* Winona Lake, Ind., 1990. Useful collection of papers on the relationship of religion and law in Islam and Judaism, incorporating discussion of ritual.

Qaraḍāwī, Yūsuf al-. *The Lawful and the Prohibited in Islam.* Indianapolis, 1980. This English-language version presents a useful survey by a scholar of al-Azhar University, combining traditional sources and relating them to a wide spectrum of contemporary issues.

Azim A. Nanji

ḤAMĀS. The organization Ḥarakat al-Muqāwamah al-Islāmīyah (Movement of Islamic Resistance), the most important Palestinian Islamist organization in the occupied West Bank and Gaza Strip, is known by its acronym Ḥamās. A non-Qur'ānic word, Ḥamās also means "zeal." It was established in December 1987, at the very beginning of the Palestinian uprising *(intifāḍah),* as the organizational expression of Muslim Brotherhood participation in the anti-Israeli resistance after two decades of Islamic political quietism. Its armed wing is called ʿIzz al-Dīn al-Qassām Forces, a reference to the *shaykh* killed by the British at the beginning of the great Palestinian revolt in 1936.

Until the *intifāḍah,* Islam rarely constituted the primary justification for the liberation struggle of the Palestinians; rather, this was maintained in the name of Arab or Palestinian nationalism. "Official" Islam, an integral part of Jordanian authority in the West Bank or an autonomous force in Gaza, was content to preside solely in religious matters. At the end of the 1970s, however, a new type of Islamic activism appeared. Claiming the authority of the Muslim Brotherhood and linked with its Egyptian and Jordanian branches, this movement had as its primary preoccupation the reislamization of society. This quest was characterized by vigorous preaching in the mosques and also by attacks on unveiled women and the destruction of bars and cinemas. Some of these new Islamists had a strongly anti-Israeli discourse—Israel is believed to constitute the spearhead of Western aggression against Islam, so the liberation of Palestine is fundamentally a religious question; their practice, however, was politically restrained. The Muslim Brothers refrained from confronting the occupying power and confined their political activities to the struggle against the Palestinian Communist Party. At this time Fatah, the main wing of the Palestinian Liberation Organization (PLO), and Jordan were happy to encourage the Islamist attacks on the left, and Israel had an interest in encouraging any division among the Palestinians. Although this political behavior cost the Muslim Brothers political legitimacy in the view of many Palestinians, they managed to establish a large social welfare network in the Gaza Strip under the charismatic coordination of Shaykh Aḥmad Yāsīn, a handicapped schoolmaster. They also infiltrated the majority of mosques in Gaza and came to control the Islamic University. In the West Bank, however, the Muslim Brothers failed to establish a network or to find a charismatic leader; their only strongholds were in the universities.

With the appearance at the beginning of the 1980s of Islamic Jihād cells—rivaling the Muslim Brotherhood in Islamic activism but fundamentally different in political behavior—Islam became truly integral to the politics of the occupied territories. Under the leadership of Shaykh ʿAbd al-ʿAzīz ʿAwdah, a lecturer at the Islamic University in Gaza, and Dr. Fatḥī Shiqāqī, a physician from Rafiah on the Egyptian border, various small groups made *jihād* against Israel in all its forms, including armed struggle, the central religious duty. In doing so, they claimed the authority of Sayyid Quṭb, the Egyptian Muslim Brotherhood leader executed in 1966, of some Egyptian Islamic Jihād members, and of intellectuals of the Islamic revolution in Iran. Their activists came either from the ranks of the Muslim Brothers, whose political conduct they criticized, or from the religious wing of Fatah. In 1986–1987 they engaged in a series of anti-Israeli guerrilla operations; although maintaining a very small membership, they thus played an important role in inciting the *intifāḍah.* In the process, Islam regained political legitimacy among the Palestinians for the first time since the 1930s.

Almost spontaneous at the beginning, the uprising very quickly became organized through local and regional committees. Within this mobilization of the entire Palestinian society, Ḥamās was created in Gaza at the initiative of Dr. ʿAbd al-ʿAzīz al-Rantīsī, a physician working at the Islamic University, and of Shaykh Yāsīn. This new organization initially attracted Muslim Brothers only on an individual basis; in February 1988, however, the brotherhood formally adopted Ḥamās as its "strong arm." In its covenant *(mīthāq)* published in August 1988, Ḥamās explains its anti-Israeli engagement in terms of *jihād,* now an individual religious duty, and claims continuity with the *jihād* of the Muslim Brothers since the 1930s. Israel, the state of the Jews who want the destruction of Islam, cannot legitimately exist, and the military option as embodied in holy *jihād* is the only one available for the liberation of Palestine. Ḥamās presents its relationship with the PLO as that of a relative: "Can a Muslim abandon his relatives and friends? Our homeland is one, our disaster is one, our fate is one." In spite of this, the seeds of tension with the nationalists remain: for Ḥamās, "Palestine is on Islamic *waqf* (pious endowment) until the end of time. Neither it nor any part of it may be given up." Furthermore, "the Islamicity of Palestine is a part of our religion and whoever gives up on his religion is lost." In the name of religion, therefore, Ḥamās rejects the political program adopted by the PLO when creating the Palestinian state in November 1988; the PLO had recognized the legitimacy of the Israeli state's existence and demanded the holding of an international conference under United Nations auspices for the creation of an independent Palestinian state alongside Israel.

In 1993, more than five years after its foundation, Ḥamās could boast an important following, estimated at 30 to 40 percent of the population. This was due in part to growing frustration and despair and to the political legitimacy it had gained by its anti-Israeli commitment, but also to its capacity to mobilize at the same time the most traditional sectors of the society. In spite of sporadic tensions, general violent confrontation between Ḥamās and Fatah was avoided. Ḥamās has denounced the 13 September 1993 breakthrough in which the Israelis and the PLO agreed to limited Palestinian autonomy in Jericho and the Gaza Strip, and it has continued to target both Israelis and Palestinian "collaborators." The movement is banned by Israel, and its founder Shaykh Yāsīn and hundreds of its followers are in jail.

[*See also* Arab-Israeli Conflict; Muslim Brotherhood, *overview article;* Organization of the Islamic Jihād; Palestine Liberation Organization; *and* West Bank and Gaza.]

BIBLIOGRAPHY

Abu Amr, Ziad. *Islamic Fundamentalism in the West Bank and Gaza: Muslim Brotherhood and Islamic Jihad.* Bloomington, 1994.

Ibn Yūsuf, Aḥmad. *Aḥmad Yāsīn, al-ẓāhirah al-muʿjizah wa-ustūrat al-taḥaddī* (Aḥmad Yāsīn, Miraculous Phenomenon and Myth of Challenge). Amman, 1990.

Johnson, Nels. *Islam and the Politics of Meaning in Palestinian Nationalism.* London, 1982.

Legrain, Jean François. *Les voix du soulèvement palestinien, 1987–1988.* Cairo, 1991. Systematic compilation of leaflets published by the United National Leadership of the Uprising and the Movement of Islamic Resistance, and French translation in cooperation with Pierre Chenard.

Legrain, Jean-François. "Palestinian Islamisms: Patriotism as a Condition of Their Expansion." In *Accounting for Fundamentalisms: The Dynamic Character of Movements,* edited by Martin E. Marty and R. Scott Appleby. Chicago, 1993.

Rashad, Ahmad. *Hamas: Palestinian Politics with an Islamic Hue.* Annandale, Va., 1993.

Sahliyeh, Emile F. *In Search of Leadership: West Bank Politics since 1967.* Washington, D.C., 1988.

Schiff, Zeev, and Ehud Yaari. *Intifada: The Palestinian Uprising—Israel's Third Front.* Translated by Ina Friedman. New York, 1990.

Shadid, Mohammed. "The Muslim Brotherhood Movement in the West Bank and Gaza." *Third World Quarterly* 10.2 (April 1988): 658–682.

JEAN-FRANÇOIS LEGRAIN

HAMDARD FOUNDATION. The name *Hamdard* or "companion in pain" was given by Ḥakīm ʿAbdulmajīd to the herb shop he established in Delhi in 1906. The Greco-Arab system of treating illness with herbs was an established practice among Muslims and was used at Hamdard. When ʿAbdulmajīd died in 1922, his work was continued by his family. Shortly before the partition of India in 1947 Hamdard was given the status of an Islamic *waqf* (an irrevocable charitable trust) by the family.

When Pakistan came into being on 14 August 1947, the younger son, Ḥakīm Muḥammad Saʿīd, migrated and settled in Karachi, where he opened the Hamdard clinic in a small room in 1948. The work expanded rapidly and attracted many physicians, both male and female. By 1953 Hamdard Pakistan had become a full-fledged pharmaceutical industry. In the same year Ḥakīm Muḥammad Saʿīd made it a *waqf* with a board of trustees, constituting the Hamdard Foundation of Pakistan. Hamdard clinics are now established in other major cities and towns of Pakistan. Treatment is inexpensive, and free for the poor. Under Saʿīd's leadership the Hamdard Foundation has expanded; it currently holds assets worth several billion rupees and employs a staff of several thousand.

The Hamdard Foundation derives its inspiration from Islam as expressed in the Qurʾān and exemplified by the life of the prophet Muḥammad. Islam is interpreted as an eternal code of life based on love, equality, and respect for all human beings that urges believers to avoid extremes, practice temperance, spend generously on charity, avoid amassing wealth, seek knowledge, and promote health. The Hamdard Foundation bases its practice on eastern medical philosophies. It declares as its primary mission the worldwide propagation of the scientific nature of eastern medicine, including the Arab, Indian, and Chinese systems, and its development in the light of modern research. In this connection the foundation sponsors lectures, scientific conferences, the creation of international networks of scholars, and the publication of journals and pamphlets. The Hamdard Foundation also publishes scholarly books, academic journals, children's magazines, and story books.

International recognition of and support for various Hamdard initiatives in the field of medicine, culture, and education have been growing, with the United Nations Education, Scientific, and Cultural Organization and the World Health Organization among its supporters. In 1983 Hamdard laid the foundation stone of a new city called Madīnat al-Ḥikmat ("city of knowledge") about 27 kilometers from Karachi. This visionary project aims at the development of a self-contained residential educational complex for men, women, and children. It will promote learning in every branch of knowledge. In 1991 a charter was granted by the government of Pakistan to establish Hamdard University. The Bayt al-Ḥikmat Library contains more than half a million books in addition to specialized journals, newspapers, and magazines, with the capacity to house three million volumes.

BIBLIOGRAPHY

D'Silva, Lily Anne, and Masood Ahmad Barakatee. *Hakim Mohammad Said: Profile of a Humanitarian*. Karachi 1989. Good sketch of the multifarious activities of the founder of the Hamdard Foundation of Pakistan.

Madinat al-Hikmat, City of Education, Science, and Culture: The Vision and Reality. Karachi 1990. Useful presentation, with pictures, graphs and tables, of the Hamdard Project to build a new city of learning outside Karachi.

Ishtiaq Ahmed

HAMKA (1908–1981), acronym of Haji Abdul Malik Karim Amrullah, Indonesian religious scholar and the most prolific of modern Indonesian Islamic writers. Hamka was born in the small village of Sungai Batang in the Minangkabau region of West Sumatra on 17 February 1908. His mother came from the *adat* aristocracy, and his father, Syekh Dr. Abdulkarim Amrullah, a member of a long-established *ʿulamā'* family, was a pioneer in the modernist reform movement. Although his father was the leading teacher of a traditional religious school that soon became a radical reformist school, the famous Sumatra Thawalib, the young Malik was enrolled in the Diniyah School, the first religious school to use the modern system of education, established by Zainuddin Labay el-Junusyah. Malik was not successful there and transfered in 1922 to Parabek (Bukittinggi), a school run by another modernist *ʿālim,* Syekh Ibrahim Musa. Instead of studying the *kitāb*s (Islamic commentaries), he preferred Minangkabau traditional literature. It was only after he suffered a serious case of smallpox in 1923 that he began in earnest the career of a talented autodidact.

In 1924 Malik went to Java to visit his older sister, whose husband A. R. Sutan Mansyur was the chairman of the local branch of the Muhammadiyah. The visit gave him a chance to attend public courses presented by important Muslim leaders. At the end of 1925 he entered the world of journalism by sending articles to the daily *Hindia Baru* (The New Indies), edited by Haji Agus Salim, an Islamic political leader. On his return to Padang Panjang Malik established the first Muhammadiyah journal, *Chatibul ummah.* He soon traveled to Medan and to Mecca in 1927. The short but intense exposure to the Arab world not only immensely improved his linguistic ability but also introduced him to the treasures of Arabic literature.

On his return to Padang Panjang he began his career as a writer and adopted the nom de plume of Hamka. His first book, a Minangkabau novel titled *Si Sabariah* (A Girl Named Sabariah), was published in 1925. He regularly sent articles to local journals and published booklets on Minangkabau *adat* and Islamic history. His activities in the Muhammadiyah organization brought him to Makasar (1932–1934), where he published two journals, novels, and a book on Islamic history. In 1936 he received an offer to become the editor in chief of a new Islamic journal in Medan, *Pedoman Masyarakat* (Social Compass). Under his editorship the journal became one of the most successful in the history of Islamic journalism in Indonesia. The sojourn in Medan (1936–1945) constituted the most productive years of Hamka's life. During this period he published most of his novels, notably *Dibawah lindungan Ka'bah* (Under the Shadow of the Ka'bah, 1936) and *Tenggelamnya kapal van der Wijck* (The Sinking of the *van der Wijck,* 1937), as well as his noted books on Islamic ethics and mysticism, including *Tasauf Modern* (Modern Mysticism, 1939), *Lembaga budi* (The Realm of Morality, 1939), and *Falsafah hidup* (The Philosophy of Life, 1940).

At the same time Hamka was a leading figure in the revolutionary struggle for national independence in West Sumatra from 1945 to 1949. In 1950 he moved to Jakarta. Appointed as a high official of the Department of Religious Affairs, Hamka spent most his time teaching, writing, and editing and publishing the journal *Panji Masyarakat* (The Banner of the Society). In 1950 he published a widely acclaimed biography of his father, *Ayahku* (My Father), which also gives a historical account of Islamic movements in Sumatra, in addition to his four-volume memoir *Kenang-kenangan hidup* and the first volume of the projected four-volume *Sedjarah umat Islam* (History of the Islamic World). In 1955 Hamka was elected a member of the Constituent Assembly, representing the Islamic modernist political party, the Masjumi. His political career ended with the dissolution of the Assembly by President Sukarno. [*See* Masjumi.] In 1960 he was elected as "great imam" of al-Azhar Mosque. Falsely accused of involvement in the attempted murder of the president, he was detained in 1964. He spent twenty months in the hospital, where he completed the drafts of his thirty-volume *Tafsir al-Azhar*.

After the fall of Sukarno Hamka was released and resumed his position as the great imam of al-Azhar Mosque with its prestigious elementary and secondary school. As the most sought-after *mubaligh* (public speaker) and a popular broadcast personality with books published in Malaysia, Singapore, and Indonesia, he was undoubtedly the most famous religious scholar in the Malay-speaking world. In 1975 he accepted the post of chairman of the new government-sponsored Indonesian Council of Ulama and was reelected in 1980 but resigned owing to a political conflict with the minister of religion. His position, however, had popular support, and congratulatory letters flooded his house. A few months after the last volume of *Tafsir al-Azhar* was published, Hamka died on 21 July 1981, leaving ten children.

Hamka wrote more than one hundred books, including fiction, politics, Minangkabau *adat,* history and biography, Islamic doctrine, ethics, mysticism, and *tafsīr*. About twenty of these have enjoyed several reprintings and are still in print. Several collections of his writings have also been published posthumously. He received honorary degrees from al-Azhar University in Cairo (1958) and the University Kebangsaan in Kuala Lumpur (1974). The daily *Berita Buana'* named him "Man of the Year" in 1980. He was also the "spiritual father" of most newly converted Chinese.

A keen student of history, Hamka not only made the long-forgotten past alive but also never failed to find the moral messages that history held for the present. His literary works show his concern for the little people and the human sufferings in his transitional society. His writings on Minangkabau reflect the attitude of a modernist *'ālim* toward his beloved matrilineal society. He offered an influential interpretation of the Indonesian national ideology, the Pancasila, by making its first principle the recognition of the oneness of God *(tawḥīd)*. Since his major concern was the maintenance of *īmān* (faith) and *'aqīdah* (creed) in changing times, it is understandable that in his *Tafsir* he often deviates from the traditional Asyhariate school of theology, which is still the foundation of Islamic orthodoxy in Indonesia.

[*See also* Malay and Indonesian Literature; Indonesia.]

BIBLIOGRAPHY

Hamka. *Kenang-kenangan hidup*. 4 vols. Jakarta, 1950. Autobiography, from childhood to 1950. Volume 2 contains Hamka's views on art and literature. The complete set has been reprinted in Kuala Lumpur and Jakarta.

Kenang-kenangan 70 Tahun Buya Hamka. Jakarta, 1978. Festschrift for Hamka on his seventieth birthday, including many recollections of colleagues, friends, and students.

Moussay, Gérard. "Une grand figure de l'Islam indonesien: Buya Hamka." *Archipel* (Paris) 32 (1986): 87–112. Balanced and accurate short biography of Hamka, written by a Catholic priest who has lived for many years in the Minangkabau region.

Teeuw, Andries. *Indonesian Literature*. Vol. 1. The Hague, 1969. Contains a section on Hamka's place in the literary history of modern Indonesia.

Yusuf, M. Yunan. "Corak Pemikiran Kalam *Tafsir al-Azhar:* Sebuah telaah tentang pemikiran Hamka dalam teologi Islam." Ph.D. diss., IAIN Syarif Hidatullah, Jakarta, 1989. Thesis on Hamka's theological thought as reflected in his *Tafsir al-Azhar*.

TAUFIK ABDULLAH

ḤANAFĪ. *See* Law, *article on* Legal Thought and Jurisprudence.

ḤANAFĪ, ḤASAN (often spelled Hassan Hanafi in Western-language writings, b. 1935), Egyptian reformist thinker and professor of philosophy. Born of Berber and bedouin Egyptian ancestry, Ḥanafī earned a bachelor's degree in philosophy at the University of Cairo in 1956 and a doctorat d'état at the Sorbonne in 1966. He taught Arabic at the École des Langues Orientales to supplement a fellowship while he was a graduate student in Paris (1956–1966). On his return to Egypt, he taught medieval Christian thought and then Islamic philosophy at the University of Cairo, where he continues to be a member of its department of philosophy. As a visiting professor, he also taught at universities in Belgium (1970), the United States (1971–1975), Kuwait (1979), Morocco (1982–1984), Japan (1984–1985), and the United Arab Emirates (1985), and he was academic consultant at the United Nations University in Tokyo (1985–1987).

As a student at Khalīl Āghā Secondary School in Cairo (1948–1952), Ḥanafī was introduced to the thought and activities of the Society of the Muslim Brothers. In the summer of 1952 he formally joined the Muslim Brothers and, as a University of Cairo student (1952–1956), fully participated in their movement until they were banned. His studies and travels overseas broadened his intellectual horizons and helped to deepen his conviction that Islam has a leading role in world culture as a unique program for humanity. A staunch supporter of the populist ideals of the Egyptian Revolution of 1952 (frustrated, in his opinion, by President Anwar el-Sadat, 1970–1981), he believes in a fusion of these ideals within a revitalized, reinterpreted Islam in order to form what he calls "the Islamic Left" and bring about national unity in Egypt, social and economic justice for the downtrodden masses, a democratic state free from Western domination and Zionist influence, the unification of the Arab world, and the restoration of Islam to a central position in world culture.

Ḥanafī's major intellectual contribution is a lifetime project he calls *Al-turāth wa-al-tajdīd* (Heritage and Renewal). Apart from his journalistic articles in Arabic—written originally for the general public and later collected in *Qaḍāyā muʿāṣirah* (Contemporary Issues, 2 vols., Cairo, 1976–1977), *Dirāsāt Islāmīyah* (Islamic Studies, Cairo, 1981), *Dirāsāt falsafīyah* (Philosophical Studies, Cairo, 1988), and *Al-dīn wa al-thawrah fī miṣr: 1952–1981* (Religion and Revolution in Egypt: 1952–1981, 8 vols., Cairo, 1989)—Ḥanafī is engaged in producing a multivolume scholarly study. It reconstructs the Islamic heritage in a new historicist and critical interpretation; it reassesses Western culture within a decentering and downsizing critical approach; and it builds a new hermeneutic of religious culture on a global scale in which Islam is the ideological foundation of a modern humanity liberated from alienation and provided with a comprehensive program of positive action leading to happiness, peace, prosperity, and justice for all.

Ḥanafī divides his project into three "fronts," each of which has a theoretical introduction and is planned to be completed in several books. The fronts are the following: "Our Attitude to the Old Heritage" in seven multivolume books; "Our Attitude to the Western Heritage," originally planned to be in five books but later reduced to three; and "Our Attitude to Reality" in three books.

Of these planned works, only some have been published. *Al-turāth wa-al-tajdīd: Mawqifunā min al-turāth al-qadīm* (Heritage and Renewal: Our Attitude to the Old Heritage, Cairo, 1980) introduces the project and offers a conspectus of its content and direction. *Min al-ʿaqīdah ilā al-thawrah: Muḥāwalah li-iʿādat binā' ʿilm uṣūl al-dīn* (From Doctrine to Revolution: An Attempt to Rebuild the Science of Religious Fundamentals, 5 vols., Cairo, 1988) is the first book of the first front. It is an attempt to reconstruct past Islamic theology, showing on the one hand its rational relation to divine revelation in the Qur'ān and on the other its circumstantial relation to the historical conditions to which its development succumbed as it tried over the years to consolidate Islamic dogma and to defend its world view against internal sectarian dissension and other religions. Ḥanafī argues that human beings and history are at the center of Islamic religious consciousness, and so he integrates the needs of modern Muslims into the Islamic theology he reconstructs, thus creating a liberation theology intended to serve as a revolutionary ideology enabling Muslims to face modern challenges and fight poverty, underdevelopment, coercion, westernization, and alienation.

His most recent work is a hefty tome entitled *Muqaddimah fī ʿilm al-istighrāb* (Introduction to the Science of Occidentalism, Cairo, 1991), which he offers as a theoretical introduction to the second front of the project and as a temporary substitute for the three books on the Western heritage, while he continues writing the planned volumes of the first front. In addition to creating the discipline of Occidentalism opposed to Orientalism, its purpose is to stem westernization among Muslims and to offer a critical reconstruction of Western culture showing its limitations, its provincialism, and its conditioning by its own circumstances. Ḥanafī sees the Western heritage as a historical product in which divine revelation is no longer central, unlike the Islamic heritage that is strongly based on divine revelation recorded in the Qur'ān, from which all aspects of Islamic civilization and history flow. He argues against the claim of Western culture to universality and makes great efforts to reduce it to what he believes to be its natural size within world culture. His analysis of Western consciousness from its beginnings to modern times leads to the conclusion that it is in crisis today and overcome by self-doubt and nihilism, while Islamic consciousness is on the rise to take its rightful place of world leadership, if properly oriented.

Despite Ḥanafī's genuine interest in the Muslim masses, he has never gathered a popular following, and his influence has been limited to academics, students, and other intellectuals. The significance of his thought lies in the fact that he has forcefully articulated the modern Muslim need for self-assertion. For him, Muslims are not mere objects of study or manipulation by others; they are subjects in their own right. Islam, as he has reinterpreted it, is a viable way of life that can and should have a leading role in the world.

BIBLIOGRAPHY

Ḥanafī's works not mentioned above include the following: *Les méthodes d'exégèse: Essai sur la science des fondements de la compréhension, ʿilm uṣūl al-fiqh* (Cairo, 1965); *Religious Dialogue and Revolution: Essays on Judaism, Christianity, and Islam* (Cairo, 1977); *L'exégèse de la phénoménologie: L'état actuel de la méthode phénoménologique et son application au phénomène religieux* (Cairo, 1980); and *La phénoménologie de l'exégèse: Essai d'une hermeneutique existentielle à partir du Nouveau Testament* (Cairo, 1988). The 1965, 1980, and 1988 publications represent his triple doctoral dissertations at the Sorbonne.

Ḥanafī edited a journal entitled *Al-Yasār al-Islāmī: Kitābāt fī al-Nahḍah al-Islāmīyah* (Cairo), no. 1 (1981), which discontinued publication thereafter. He was also editor and/or translator of the following: Muḥammad ibn ʿAlī Baṣrī, *Al-Muʿtamad fī Uṣūl al-Fiqh*, 2 vols. (Damascus, 1964–1965); *Namādhij min al-Falsafah al-Masīḥīyah* (Alexandria, 1968); *Spinoza: Risālah fī al-Lāhūt wa al-Siyāsah* (Cairo, 1973); *Lessing: Tarbiyat al-Jins al-Basharī wa-Aʿmāl Ukhrā* (Cairo, 1977); *Jean-Paul Sartre: Taʿālī al-Anā Mawjūd* (Cairo, 1978); Ruhollah al-Musavi Khomeini, *Al-Ḥukūmah al-Islāmīyah* (Cairo, 1979), and *Jihād al-Nafs, aw, al-Jihād al-Akbar* (Cairo, 1980).

Sources on Ḥanafī and his work include Issa J. Boullata, *Trends and Issues in Contemporary Arab Thought*, pp. 40–45 (Albany, N.Y., 1990), and Marc Chartier, "La rencontre Orient-Occident dans la pensée de trois philosophes égyptiens contemporains: Ḥasan Ḥanafī, Fu'ād Zakariyyā, Zakī Naǧīb Maḥmūd," *Oriente Moderno* 53.7–8 (July–August 1973): 603–642.

ISSA J. BOULLATA

ḤANBALĪ. *See* Law, *article on* Legal Thought and Jurisprudence.

ḤAQQ. *See* Ethics.

ḤARAKĀT AL-TAWḤĪD AL-ISLĀMĪ. A militant Sunnī movement, the Ḥarakāt al-Tawḥīd al-Islāmī (Islamic Unification Movement) emerged out of the political turmoil of the 1980s in the northern Lebanese port city of Tripoli. Tawḥīd, the term by which the movement was popularly known, was formed from a coalition of Islamic and Arab nationalist groups, which included Jund Allāh, the Muslim Youth (Pro-Fatah), Popular Resistance, and the Lebanese Arab Movement. It came to power in the context of the Lebanese civil war in Tripoli through armed insurrection in October 1983 and October 1985.

Tawḥīd was part of a broader current of radical Islamic movements to emerge in the early 1980s in Lebanon. As Imam Awada (1988) notes, the post-1982 period, the year of Israel's invasion of Lebanon, saw at least eight radical Islamic groups form in Lebanon. All shared a radical rejection of Lebanese confessional politics and supported the idea of creating an Islamic state. Although these movements drew on the Sunnī and Shīʿī radicalism of the period, the political climate created by the Israeli invasion was an important factor in mobilizing both popular local and international support for these movements.

Civil war and the collapse of the Lebanese state strongly influenced the character of Tawḥīd's organization, as they had affected the secular Lebanese parties that preceded it in Tripoli. Although politically, militarily, communally, and geographically restricted, Tawḥīd was unique because it was a religious movement in the predominantly Sunnī city of Tripoli, projecting a radical Islamic image and explicitly linking itself with the Islamic militancy of the Iranian revolution.

The movement was organized into five districts, each controlled by an "emir." These districts coincided with the traditional administrative and clientalist arrangements of the city quarters. Islamic ideology provided the basis for unity, but administrative responsibilities were shared between the different founding groups, each controlling separate districts.

The movement's leader, Shaykh Sayyid Shaʿbān, promoted the movement as an ecumenical one for both

Lebanese Sunnī and Shīʿī Muslims. The tangible expression of this ecumenism was his membership in the small Lebanese Association of Muslim ʿUlamā' (Tajammu')—an organization in which the Sunnī *ʿulamā'* have accepted the *ʿulamā'* as the "heirs of the Prophet" and Ayatollah Khomeini as the leading religious figure of this generation. As Emmanuel Sivan (1989) points out, Shaykh Shaʿbān's ecumenical orientation and support for Khomeini's leadership of Islamic radicalism was tempered by historical theological differences between Sunnism and Shiism. These included the issue of the recognition by Sunnī orthodoxy of all of the Rightly Guided Caliphs and the six Sunnī codices of *ḥadīth*s as the basis for interpreting the Qur'ān. Shaykh Shaʿbān was also critical of the Iranian rather than Muslim character of Khomeini's regime in Iran. He once suggested that the reestablishment of the caliphate in Mecca was a better strategy to achieve Muslim unity.

Tawḥīd was a millenarian movement whose project was to bring Islamic order to the anarchy of Tripoli and to work toward the formation of an Islamic state. It was not, however, a broadly populist movement but an expression of the new coalition of local and international forces that controlled northern Lebanon. It was a politico-military group with an Islamic platform, which achieved power through arms by replacing a secular coalition of Lebanese nationalists and communists. It borrowed heavily from the revolutionary symbols of the Iranian revolution, including the turbaned, bearded, and armed clergy and the veil. Some Tawḥīd clerics even took to riding around Tripoli on horseback as a symbol of their return to the cultural origins of Islam in the first community *(ummah).*

Tawḥīd's ascent to power in Tripoli and its confinement to the city limits were reflections of the urban concentration of the Sunnī population in Lebanon and the political eclipse of the Sunnīs as the most powerful Muslim sect during the course of the civil war. Its most influential political links were not with other Lebanese Sunnī communities but with the Shīʿīs, especially the radical Shaykh Muḥammad Ḥusayn Faḍlāllah and Ḥizbullāh, as was borne out in the final siege of Tripoli when pro-Iranian radicals in West Beirut kidnapped Soviet diplomats in an effort to halt the Syrian bombardment by political pressure.

The involvement of Sunnī clerics in Tawḥīd represented a radical departure from the traditionally conservative politics of the Lebanese Sunnī religious establishment. Michael Humphrey (1989) observed that the Tawḥīd shaykhs were drawn from a stratum of local community shaykhs who only recently had been incorporated in the Lebanese Sunnī religious establishment through the policy of increased bureaucratization and religious education. This connection made them more dependent economically on the state and exposed them to more militant Islamic thought and politics.

Of particular significance were their links with radical Egyptian al-Azhar shaykhs, which they first established either as theological students in al-Azhar University or as labor migrants in the Arab world. Fuad Khuri (1990) points out that there were two predominant al-Azhar networks in northern Lebanon. At least one Egyptian al-Azhar shaykh from these networks was directly involved in the initial organization of the movement in Tripoli. The politicization of the Sunnī clerics through their international links occurred with the decline of the Sunnī religious establishment on the collapse of state authority. This paralleled a similar process in secular politics whereby international patronage had been substituted for state patronage.

The Islamic program Tawḥīd sought to implement was limited and piecemeal. The sale of alcohol was banned, and some shops were destroyed by over-enthusiastic militiamen. The veil became more common, and a religious tax was imposed on wealthier businessmen to help fund welfare services to the poor. In practice, however, the Tawḥīd shaykhs preached individual Islamic moral rectitude as the basis for social transformation and the ultimate realization of an Islamic state.

The military defeat of Tawḥīd on 6 October 1985 reflected the limited popular base of its support in Tripoli and, perhaps more critically, the change in Syrian attitudes to independent militia rule in Lebanon. Shaykh Shaʿbān survived the military defeat, but several of the leading shaykhs and many militiamen did not. The movement was all but destroyed. Shaykh Shaʿbān still lives in Tripoli, but his activities have been restricted to social welfare.

[*See also* Ḥizbullāh, *article on* Ḥizbullāh in Lebanon; Lebanon; *and the biography of Faḍlallāh.*]

BIBLIOGRAPHY

Awada, Hassam. "Le Liban et le flux islamiste." *Social Compass* 35.4 (1988): 645–673. Good study of Lebanese Islamic movements in a Pan-Islamic context.

Humphrey, Michael. *Islam: Sect and State*. Oxford, 1989. A sociological analysis of the Tawḥīd movement and its sociopolitical background.

Khuri, Fuad. *Imams and Emirs: State, Religion, and Sect in Islam.* London, 1990. Excellent sociological differentiation of religious forms and society.

Sivan, Emmanuel. "Sunni Radicalism in the Middle East and the Iranian Revolution." *International Journal of Middle East Studies* 21 (1989): 1–30. Good comparative summary of Sunnī and Shīʿī radicalism and their common ground.

MICHAEL HUMPHREY

ḤARĀM. The root *ḥ-r-m* is among the most important Arabic roots in the vocabulary of Islamic practice. The root meaning is something like "forbidden" or "taboo" and evokes constraint, and often heightened sanctity as well. In legal thought an act deemed *ḥarām* is one forbidden. Usually the term is coterminous with "proscribed" *(maḥẓūr),* but it is sometimes used to denote the negative side of the legal scale of value, incorporating both the proscribed and the "reprehensible" *(makrūh).*

The most important ritual usage of the term is to refer to the area around the three holy cities of Islam—Mecca, Medina, and Jerusalem. Within the precincts of these cities, which are defined with considerable precision (Mecca having the largest *ḥarām,* Jerusalem the smallest), certain restrictions apply that both reflect and define their sanctity. Hunting is forbidden, as is uprooting any tree or harvesting grain. Violence toward humans is proscribed, except for what is absolutely necessary to maintain order. Some have argued that even carrying weapons in the area was proscribed. Likewise, entry into the two Arabian *ḥarams* is proscribed for non-Muslims. The sanctity of the place is protected, and it protects those who flee to it; even the grossest tyrants cannot be killed within its precincts.

The root also yields the word *iḥrām,* the state of ritual purity of one going on the greater or lesser pilgrimage. While in this state, the pilgrim wears a particular sort of garment and is enjoined from cutting hair or nails, wearing perfume, or having sexual intercourse.

The best known usage of the root is in the words pertaining to restrictions on women's access. The root is used to describe those family members who may associate across genders without restriction; these are called *maḥram* and define the degrees of relation within which marriage is unacceptable: parents, siblings, foster-siblings, and the like. Because they are forbidden to marry, they are permitted to associate. Finally, *ḥarīm* (harem) refers to the part of the house in which women are protected from encounters with non-*maḥram* males. In this section of the house are not just wives, but also daughters, sisters, and mothers; by extension *ḥarīm* can euphemistically refer to the family in general, in greetings and inquiries as to health.

[*See also* Purification; Seclusion.]

BIBLIOGRAPHY

Lewis, James R. "Some Aspects of Sacred Space and Time in Islam." *Studies in Islam* 19 (1982): 167–178.

Von Grunebaum, G. E. "Islam: Experience of the Holy and Concept of Man." In *Islam and Medieval Hellenism: Social and Cultural Perspectives,* pp. 1–39. London, 1976.

Zarkashī, Muḥammad ibn ʿAbd Allāh al-. *Iʿlām al-sājid bi-aḥkām al-masājid.* Edited by Abū al-Wafā Muṣṭafā al-Marāghī. Cairo, 1964.

A. KEVIN REINHART

ḤARB. *See* Dār al-Ḥarb.

HATT-I HÜMAYUN OF GÜLHANE. *See* Tanzimat.

HEALTH CARE. Healing traditions of the Islamic world exhibit broad historical and sociocultural variation. Although a certain complex of therapeutic conventions is generally associated with Islamic societies, it represents but one expression of a dialectic of unity and diversity. Specific health practices are not distributed uniformly throughout Muslim communities. Neither are such elements of healing culture unique to these communities, reflecting the distribution of pre-Islamic therapeutic traditions over vast civilizational areas, and the protracted encounter between islamized peoples and non-Muslims.

Although the link between Arabic-Islamic and Greco-Roman medicine has been privileged in Eurocentric scholarship, cross-cultural appropriations and influences far exceed the bounds established by traditional historiography. Contemporary research has highlighted the diversity of health and medical traditions, suggesting that the conventional understanding of Islamic medicine be expanded beyond its common referents of Greco-Islamic and Prophetic healing to more accurately reflect the therapeutic heterogeneity of Islam. For instance, medieval Arabic-Islamic medicine was also informed by African and Asian literate medical traditions—including ancient Egyptian, Indian, Persian, and Syriac—as well as pre-Islamic popular health practices and local modes of organizing health maintenance in islamized communities. Prophetic medicine, which in many respects resembles pre-Islamic bedouin healing traditions, attends to hygienic and dietary concerns, as well as psychosocial distress, including forms in which the spirit world, the evil eye, and sorcery are implicated. The *barakah* (blessing) of the Qur'ān, its learned "carriers," and holy descendants of the Prophet, are central to this tradition. And in Islamic humoralism, nature, with its four elements, and the human body, with its four humors, are focal in definitions of health-sickness and derivative healing regimens. Humoral conceptions of balance (health) and imbalance (sickness) involve notions of hot and cold and the interaction of natural elements with the four humors of the body (blood, phlegm, bile, and black bile). As with the integrative character of Islamic culture in general, pre-Islamic and Islamic health care practices and institutions have been adapted to different social and ecological conditions.

While religious teachings enjoin Muslims to protect and restore their health, there is no specification as to type of treatment. In fact, as noted by the fourteenth-century social historian Ibn Khaldūn, Muslims are not obligated to follow the medical prescriptions handed down even in authentic traditions attributed to the Prophet. Among Indian Muslims, for example, reliance on the healing power of the Qur'ān does not preclude resort to Āyurveda. Similarly, Arab Muslims are known to visit Christian places of worship in pursuit of restoration of health. And as recently as the middle of the twentieth century, some urban Egyptian families engaged Jewish religious specialists for the circumcision of their sons.

Elements of ancient and medieval healing traditions are but partial constituents of the Islamic world's medical pluralism. Health care practices also reflect changes in political economies over the course of modern history. Thus, while Ṣūfī holistic healing in the Arab world exemplifies the general association between healing and religion, its significance in addressing psychosocial problems from the sixteenth to the nineteenth century is related to modern global developments. It has been suggested that these regimens acquired particular significance in relation to the pressures of market forces linked to Western encroachment. Those segments of the population adversely affected by the new market relations found refuge in Ṣūfī forms of socially grounded healing. On the other hand, ruling-class authorization of positivist biomedicine was consistent with the support of nineteenth-century periphery capitalism.

Today, the health policies of the Islamic world's nation-states, like those of international health organizations, are based on the premises of pathology-focused biomedicine. The principles of this cosmopolitan healing tradition, rather than Islamic medical texts of the past or their popularized forms of the present, inform state regulation of health throughout the Islamic world. Although connected to ancestral Islamic empirical/literate traditions (such as those elaborated by al-Rāzī, Ibn Sīnā, Ibn Rushd, Ibn Maymūn [Maimonides], and Ibn al-Nafīs), modern biomedical traditions originate in a fundamentally different global system, with its particular state institutions, regulatory mechanisms, and local modes of organization. In this regard, the "Islamic Clinics" established in recent years represent a cultural veneer overlaying the basic conceptual framework of cosmopolitan medicine.

Tradition, Continuity, and Context. Coexisting with different forms of officially sanctioned, clinic-centered health care are numerous other healing practices utilized by members of Islamic communities around the world. These include household-based herbal medicine and dietary regimens for the maintenance or restoration of the body's vitality. Also prevalent in Islamic communities are notions of the unity of soma and psyche, the ideal of exercising moderation in food, drink, and sex, reliance on the healing power of *barakah*, associated with Qur'ānic texts and recitations, as well as visits to the shrines of holy persons. In addition, the protection or restoration of health may involve the use of amulets against the evil eye, and a variety of hygienic practices, ranging from male circumcision to the differentiation of the use of the right and left hands for the handling of food as opposed to "polluting" substances such as feces and urine. Spiritual healers, including those who possess Qur'ānic knowledge, are also frequented for diagnosis of possession illness and pacification of the spirits believed to cause it, as well as the healing of sorcery-induced afflictions.

The health regimens of contemporary Islamic communities share certain structural features and specific practices with past cultures, including Mesopotamian, Egyptian, Phoenician, and medieval Islamic. Parallels include the dual role of central authorities in keeping order and regulating health, biological inheritance of the healing power of *barakah*, the close relationship between religion, magic, and medicine, the use of amulets against the evil eye, music therapy, exorcism of spirits, and the practice of cupping, bloodletting, and cauterization.

Beyond recognizing general similarities between health care practices of today's Islamic world and historical therapeutic traditions, it is important to recognize that contemporary forms are not simply straightforward reproductions of past regimens. Among other examples of local particularity is the case of the Malay Peninsula, where treatment of the majority of illnesses entails restoration of the body's humoral balance. Although many of the precepts of medieval Islamic theory were incorporated into Malay medicine, historically informed ethnographic analysis reveals that pre-Islamic aboriginal ideas continue to be operative. Furthermore, some radical alterations have affected the received theories of Islamic humoralism. Other examples of local specificity are disclosed by comparing the ways in which the risks to health of emotional distress are managed in different Muslim communities.

Working in Islamic communities in Iran, Turkey, Malay, Yemen, Egypt, and Morocco, some researchers suggest that formulations of Greco-Islamic medicine, notably those pertaining to reproductive health, and notions of health as a manifestation of humoral balance, continue to be significant as a basis of dietary regimens and the differentiation of states of compromised health among members of these communities. Addressing this issue on the basis of their experiences in some of the same Islamic societies, namely Yemen and Egypt, in addition to Islamic communities of Nigeria, other researchers report lesser evidence of the classical humoral theories than suggested by European-language literature. For example, in rural Egypt, where therapeutic measures similar to those of medieval Islamic medicine are practiced, their utilization is distanced from the coherent logical framework of classical humoralism. Bloodletting, for instance, is not linked to the elaborate medieval humoral model of balance (health) and imbalance (sickness). In other African societies, Prophetic components of Islamic medicine, rather than humoral concepts, have taken root as significant elements of medical pluralism. Among the Muslim Hausa of northern Nigeria, as elsewhere in the Islamic world, hygienic and dietary practices, as well as the use of Qur'ānic charms associated with this therapeutic tradition, coexist with pre-Islamic practices of the pacification of spirits that are believed to precipitate illness. The possession cults of Ṣūfī orders are also found throughout Islamic communities on the continent and beyond, including Morocco, Tunisia, Egypt, Senegal, Mali, Sudan, and Iran.

Biomedicine and the Colonial Legacy. Within the framework of nineteenth-century global political and economic relations, biomedicine gained prestige and legitimation through the patronage of indigenous rulers and the policies of colonial administrators. For example, Iran witnessed the decline of the indigenous decentralized *bazaar* system of healing in favor of the centralized biomedical form sanctioned by the shah. Competing for political influence and economic gain in the Iranian court, European powers were well served by the healing skills of their physicians. Mechanisms for regulating public health, namely quarantines and sanitary councils, were also deployed in the economic contests between European rivals.

In the colonized Muslim world, the primary concern of colonial administrators was the protection of their own subjects, military and civilian. For many nineteenth-century colonial administrators and medical personnel, the dangers of disease were taken for granted as part of a hostile, "tropical" environment. Although European healing during the early nineteenth century was no more effective than Greco-Islamic medicine, it was nevertheless asserted that only through European knowledge and intervention would it be possible to bring under control the diseases of the empire's colonies. Supported by political and military power, European medicine was considered a form of progress toward a more "civilized" social and environmental order.

During the imperial age, "disease" constituted a central element of the conceptualization of the "tropical" colonized world, which was constructed as the antithesis of sanitary Europe. As Franz Fanon described for Muslim Algeria, this discourse of empire served as a rationale for "racialism and humiliation." In Algiers and other North African cities of the nineteenth century, residential areas were segregated by the French. Under these conditions, the visit of the European doctor, often a military man, was by no means welcomed by the indigenous Muslim population. While some of the foreign doctors were considered skillful healers at whose hands relief from pain could be obtained, others were regarded with suspicion. Judged to be spies, some European physicians were murdered.

Propelled by "curative confidence," biomedicine eclipsed earlier literate Islamic medical traditions. Simultaneously, it served as a mechanism of social control in colonized Islamic societies, but not without historically specific variations in local articulations, resistance, or acceptance.

In Egypt, biomedicine took root prior to the British occupation of 1882, coinciding with the nineteenth-century rationalization of the economy during the reign of Muḥammad ʿAlī (1805–1848). With the aim of creating a powerful army and a large productive labor force of men and women, the state's public health program was designed to combat epidemics and reduce infant mortality. State-sponsored health care providers included women health officers. Countrywide vaccination campaigns involving trained local paramedics eliminated smallpox by mid-century.

But the establishment of biomedical health care in nineteenth-century Egypt was hardly a case of "modernity" landing on the virgin soil of "tradition." Ibn Sīnā's work had remained influential in Europe up to the sixteenth century. Thereafter Muslim scholars in Turkey and elsewhere followed its elaboration in Europe, in addition to other developments in positivist medicine. The philosophical legitimation of Muḥammad ʿAlī's reform policies derived from the Islamic tradition of *kalām,* wherein logic, argumentation, medicine, and the natural sciences were significant. Thus, local therapeutic traditions converged with Europe's developing scientific trends. By the latter part of the nineteenth century, professional medical practitioners, by now committed to biomedicine's normalizing knowledge of desocialized disease, came to regard psychosocially oriented healing regimens beyond their domain as "quackery."

With the British occupation of 1882, and consistent with the colonial extractive strategies in the Egyptian "cotton farm," hydraulics and agricultural modernization were given priority, to the detriment of public health and medical education. Colonial authorities privatized medical education and promoted this relationship in health care. With the Arabic language declared unfit for "scientific" study, the anglicization of curricula extended to medical education. Under pressure from nationalist forces, and with the failure of British physicians to "spread the light of Western science throughout the country" (as the British consul general, Lord Cromer, put it), the 1920s and 1930s witnessed the revival of some older public health strategies of the Muḥammad ʿAlī era, albeit in greatly compromised form. For instance, the former era's state-sponsored training of female medical officers in preventive health care, surgery, obstetrics, and gynecology was replaced by the Florence Nightingale model of hospital-based nursing.

In other parts of the Muslim world the ascendancy of biomedicine came about differently than in Egypt, where European doctors had been invited by Muḥammad ʿAlī for the express purpose of training Egyptians within the framework of an integrated state-centered development scheme. In Tunis the nineteenth-century colonial government severely undermined the role of indigenous doctors by restricting licensing to Europeans. Within a decade of the French occupation of 1881, indigenous doctors were reduced to the status of *médecin tolére,* and their practice was soon rendered less than legal.

Medical Pluralism in Nation-States. Beyond its political and economic instrumentality, cosmopolitan health care introduced in Islamic societies during the colonial era was very limited; most of the population continued to rely primarily on traditional forms of healing. Aside from variation in the extent of state commitment to provide public health care, skewed distribution of cosmopolitan medical services generally continued in the postindependence period.

Presently, the authoritative role of global biomedicine in regulating social life in Islamic nation-states underscores the conviction that societal homogeneity is a function, not of Islamic legal traditions, but of mechanisms of control perfected by modern nation-states. While officials of these states may continue to honor their Arabic-Islamic literate medical heritage, they are committed to cosmopolitan medicine as the foundation of medical education, research, and public health programs. Western professional accreditation remains a mark of distinction among physicians in Muslim countries. Similarly, among patients the resort to modern medicine is a symbol of social privilege.

In spite of the limitations surrounding access to cosmopolitan health services, legal sanction of healing remains limited to professional practitioners and, with the exception of midwives, does not extend to traditional healers. The 1983 National (Sudanese) Council for Research Act represents a rare form of official support for researchers "to evaluate TM (Traditional Medicine) in the light of modern science so as to maximize useful and effective practices and discourage the harmful." Although not legally sanctioned, traditional healing continues to be tolerated by the authorities. In some cases it may be the only accessible form of health care. In others, it is preferred over biomedical care. For although biomedicine has gained popularity and prestige throughout the Islamic world, its utility in addressing culturally meaningful, socially defined afflictions remains limited.

Prevention is central to popular health care in Islamic societies. The "word of God," either written or oral, is deemed effective in warding off evil, including sickness precipitated by the covetous gaze of the evil eye or spirit intrusion. Preventive health care is primarily household-centered, with women shouldering major responsibility for the execution of preventive regimens and home remedies. Assistance during birth is also part of women's responsibilities, whether as midwives or simply experienced elders.

Traditional healers, found throughout the Islamic world, include practitioners of natural medicine. Their practice is informed by certain variants of Islamic humoralism, knowledge of bonesetting, and herbal medicine. Spiritual healers, on the other hand, diagnose and treat sickness of supernatural etiology, including sorcery-induced afflictions and spirit possession. The literate among them rely on their knowledge of the Qur'ān to gain access to the supernatural realm. Paramedical variants of health care are also significant to the socially disadvantaged sectors of Muslim societies. As in the case of pharmacists, paramedics provide advice on medication and administer injections.

Transcending the medical model of health care, some health activists in different parts of the Muslim world have emphasized sociopolitical conceptions of health. Reminiscent of al-Suyūṭī's medieval treatise on the medicine of the Prophet, which recognizes deprivation as a cause of poor health, activists have stressed the relationship between health and, for instance, military occupation, or the distribution of health resources, including adequate nutrition, housing, and water supply. Feminists, in particular, have called attention to the impact of gender differentiation on health maintenance, and have defined the practice of genital surgery as both a human rights and health issue. Although state-sponsored and international health programs often give priority to the regulation of Muslim women's fertility, public policy affecting women's lives and health does not reflect an awareness of the ways in which compromised health is socially produced. As official pledges of "Health for All" gave way to selective maternal and child health programs during the eighties, women were burdened with still additional responsibilities for their family's health. Meanwhile, their own health continues to suffer as a result of laboring in the household, field, or factory, and associated exposure to smoke, pesticides, and industrial contaminants, respectively, in addition to malnutrition and infectious diseases, among other physical and mental afflictions.

Political Islam and Health Care. While Islamic teachings do not instruct Muslims to adopt specific forms of healing, the banner of Islam has served to lend legitimacy to one healing tradition or another. This was the case in nineteenth-century northern Nigeria, where health and healing were integral to the Fulānī *jihād*. Under the leadership of Usuman dan Fodio, and later his successor as sultan of Sokoto, Muhammad Bello, the rural Hausa Qur'ānic scholars known as *malamai* gained great authority. As a concerted effort was made to crush the power of the practitioners of pre-Islamic healing, Prophetic medicine, legitimated by political authority, gained prominence.

During the twentieth century, the relation between political and medical authority has not been lost to state managers. The religiously sanctioned provision of charitable health care has also been part of reformist Islamist agendas. In Egypt during the 1940s, the Muslim Brothers organized teams of physicians and students who engaged in public health education among the poor, particularly in rural areas. While physicians from among the Muslim Brothers operated charitable clinics, the brothers saw in Islamic teachings a more fundamental solution to health problems. Having defined poverty as a primary cause of compromised health, they advocated Islamic regulation of wealth distribution.

Although sharing other Muslims' belief in the holiness of the Qur'ān and the wisdom of Prophetic traditions, the Muslim Brothers' health programs were clearly informed by biomedical logic. Today a similar scientific orientation is manifest in the practice of Muslim African-American physicians. In the Nation of Islam's Abundant Life Clinic in Washington, D.C., AIDS patients are treated with Immuviron, a derivative of the drug Kemron.

The commitment to biomedicine is also evident in the Islamic Clinics established in some parts of the Muslim world, notably Jordan, Sudan, and Egypt, over the past decade. Although very little published material is available on the operation of these clinics, they are generally considered to be an expression of the rise of political Islam. For Sudan, anthropologist Ellen Gruenbaum (1989) notes that the establishment of private clinics by the National Islamic Front coincides with the coming to power in June 1989 of a new regime that implemented the Front's policies. Through the Front, the clinics are financed by Islamic banks established with Saudi capital.

For Egypt, Islamic Clinics include numerous one- or two-room clinics established by religious voluntary associations and attached to modest mosques, as well as some major health care centers such as the Muṣṭafā Maḥmūd Islamic Clinic. These health care facilities are dependent on financial contributions from nongovernmental sources. In addition to local charitable contributions, Gulf petro-wealth has served indirectly to support their low-priced medical services. In some cases, the Islamist private commercial and financial sectors contribute financially to Islamic Clinics, as well as the Physicians' Syndicate, a stronghold of political Islam.

The "Islamic Alternative" in health care is presented by its advocates as a private initiative to address unmet health care needs at a time when state support of public health is less than adequate. Far from representing an alternative health care strategy that challenges state authority, the charitable health services offered by Islamist groups help maintain an indispensable component of the social welfare package. This in turn helps such groups gain legitimacy in, and affirm the legitimacy of, the established social order. Cognizant of the political value of such a reciprocal relationship, the Egyptian state has financed Islamic social service centers, including clinics, thus reinforcing the appearance of state commitment to Islamic tradition. But, as in other clinics, the health care provided by service centers remains distanced from the tenets of medieval Arabic-Islamic medicine. In fact, it does not even resemble such exceptional attempts as those undertaken by Essedik Jeddi's team to integrate Arabic-Islamic healing into the biomedical psychiatric work conducted at Al-Rāzī University in Tunis during the 1970s.

As is the case of professional medical practitioners throughout the Islamic world, those working in Islamic Clinics are trained in biomedicine and committed to its practice. While the patrons of the clinics may be gratified by their proximity to a place of worship, they expect high-technology medical care, not Islamic medicine, whether in its Prophetic or humoral form. For their part, physicians serving in these clinics take pride in their access to the "most advanced" medical technology imported from the West.

Supporters of Islamic Clinics sometimes present them as an embodiment of the Prophet's *ḥadīth* describing science as a method blending theology and medicine ("the science of religion [theology] and the science of the body [medicine]"). Beyond such rationalizations, it is important to note the historical context of the establishment of these clinics, namely the development of a petro-economy in the Gulf and the regional development of political Islam, catalyzed by the Islamic Revolution in Iran.

As Gulf petro-wealth and Islamic political agendas left their mark on intellectual developments in the Muslim world, this extended to medical and health care. Professional and academic associations, such as the Kuwait Islamic Organization for Medical Sciences and the College of Medical Sciences at King Faisal University, launched various publications devoted to the relationship between Islam and medicine. The "authentication" of cosmopolitan medicine has been the subject of numerous international conferences held in different Islamic countries. Participants, including Muslim physicians and clerics, have attempted to define an Islamic perspective on a wide range of health issues, from preventive care, birth spacing, prenatal care, and breastfeeding, to the treatment of emotional disorders. Conferees have also addressed the religious/ethical implications of a variety of modern medical practices and biomedically defined altered states of health, including the implantation of body parts, artificial insemination, and AIDS.

International conferences in which scientific, including medical, phenomena are addressed in relation to Qur'ānic knowledge have drawn criticism from some Muslim intellectuals. For example, Munawar Ahmad Anees has attached the designation "scientific fundamentalism" to the current trend of "islamization of knowledge." Similarly, Pervez Hoodbhoy, in a book introduced by the Muslim physicist and Nobel laureate, Mohammed Abdus Salam, suggests that today's so-called Islamic science, which seeks to capitalize on the science practiced by the early Muslims, betrays a fundamental misunderstanding of the scientific achievements of Islam's golden age. Highlighting the works of the Muslim physicians al-Rāzī (865–925), Ibn Rushd (1126–1198), and Ibn Sīnā (980–1037), Hoodbhoy argues that these scholars, while deeply committed Muslims, practiced science of an essentially secular kind.

[*See also* Family Planning; Medicine; Science.]

BIBLIOGRAPHY

Earley, Evelyn. "The Baladi Curative System of Cairo, Egypt." *Culture, Medicine, and Psychiatry* 12 (1988): 65–83.

Fanon, Franz. *Studies in a Dying Colonialism*. New York, 1965. Clas-

sic work on colonialism that includes insightful discussions of the politics of health in colonized North Africa.
Feierman, Steven, and John M. Janzen, eds. *The Social Basis of Health and Healing in Africa*. Berkeley, 1992. Excellent volume on African healing as a socially and historically constituted complex of traditions. Includes essential readings by Ismail H. Abdalla on the history of Islamic medicine in northern Nigeria, Bernard Greenwood on Moroccan therapeutics, and Murray Last on healing knowledge in Hausaland.
Gallagher, Nancy E. *Medicine and Power in Tunisia, 1780–1900*. Cambridge, 1983.
Gallagher, Nancy E. *Egypt's Other Wars: Epidemics and the Politics of Public Health*. Syracuse, N.Y., 1990.
Gran, Peter. *Islamic Roots of Capitalism: Egypt, 1760–1840*. Austin, 1979. Focused on Egypt during the eighteenth and nineteenth centuries, this study of intellectual developments, including medical concerns, provides a refreshing alternative to modernization theorists' tradition-modernity dualism.
Gran, Peter. "Medical Pluralism in Arab and Egyptian History: An Overview of Class Structures and Philosophies of the Main Phases." *Social Science and Medicine*. 13B (1979): 339–348.
Greyhton, M. L. "Communication between Peasant and Doctor in Tunisia." *Social Science and Medicine* 11 (1977): 319–325.
Gruenbaum, Ellen. "Changes in the Health of Women in Rural Sudan." Paper presented at the Annual Meeting of the American Anthropological Association, 1989.
Hoodbhoy, Pervez. *Islam and Science: Religious Orthodoxy and the Battle for Rationality*. London, 1991.
Kuhnke, LaVerne. "The 'Doctress' on a Donkey: Women Health Officers in Nineteenth-Century Egypt." *Clio Medica* 19 (1974): 193–205.
Kuhnke, LaVerne. *Lives at Risk: Public Health in Nineteenth-Century Egypt*. Berkeley, 1990.
Leslie, Charles, and Allan Young, eds. *Paths to Asian Medical Knowledge*. Berkeley, 1992. Informative volume on Asian medicine that includes contributions on Islamic humoral traditions in a chapter co-authored by Byron Good and Mary-Jo DelVecchio Good, and in another by Carol Laderman. Together these two chapters bring into focus the central elements of the debate on Islamic medicine as a living tradition.
Lewis, I. M., Ahmed El Safi, and Sayyid Hurreiz, eds. *Women's Medicine: The Zar-Bori Cult in Africa and Beyond*. Edinburgh, 1991.
MERIP Report 161 (1989). Special issue of the journal entitled "Health and Politics," with articles on medical education, health under military occupation, medical technology, women and medicine, and occupational health.
Morsy, Soheir A. "Islamic Clinics in Egypt: The Cultural Elaboration of Biomedical Hegemony." *Medical Anthropology Quarterly* 2.4 (1978): 355–369.
Morsy, Soheir A. *Gender, Sickness, and Healing in Rural Egypt: Ethnography in Historical Context*. Boulder, 1993.
Munawar Ahmad Anees. "Islam and Scientific Fundamentalism." *New Perspectives Quarterly* 158 (Summer 1993): 61–63.
Myntti, Cynthia. "The Social, Economic, and Cultural Context of Women's Health and Fertility in Rural North Yemen." In *Micro-Approaches to Demographic Research*, edited by John C. Caldwell et al., pp. 165–169. London, 1988.
Paul, Jim. "Medicine and Imperialism." In *The Cultural Crisis of Modern Medicine*, edited by John Ehrenreich, pp. 271–286. New York, 1978. Critical commentary on colonial medicine in Morocco.
Rahman, Fazlur. *Health and Medicine in the Islamic Tradition*. New York, 1987.
Sonbol, Amira El Azhary. *The Creation of a Medical Profession in Egypt, 1800–1922*. Syracuse, N.Y., 1991.
Wikan, Unni. "Bereavement and Loss in Two Muslim Communities: Egypt and Bali Compared." *Social Science and Medicine* 27.5 (1988): 451–460.

Soheir A. Morsy

HEKMATYAR, GULBUDDIN (b. 1947?), leader of Ḥizb-i Islāmī Afghānistān, one of the major Islamic political parties in Afghanistan. Hekmatyar is a Pushtun from a branch of the Kharoti tribe that resettled in the northern province of Kunduz. While a student in the College of Engineering at Kabul University in the late 1960s, Hekmatyar became one of the founders of the Organization of Muslim Youth (Sāzmān-i Javānān-i Musulmān). Inspired by the writings of Sayyid Quṭb and other Islamic political theorists to whom they were introduced by professors at the university, Hekmatyar and the other members of the Muslim Youth were actively involved in campus politics, particularly in response to the increasing activism of Marxist political parties that were also seeking members from the student population.

In 1972 Hekmatyar was arrested and imprisoned for his involvement in a campus demonstration in which a leftist student was killed. Released at the end of his sentence in 1973, Hekmatyar and other leaders of the Muslim Youth went into exile in Peshawar, Pakistan, where they began planning the violent overthrow of the government of President Muḥammad Dā'ūd. In 1975 Hekmatyar became the secretary *(munshī)* and head of military operations for the party. In this capacity, he was one of the principal proponents and organizers of a controversial plan to stage a coup d'état with sympathetic members of the military while simultaneously mounting rural insurrections in a number of provincial centers. The plan, which was carried out in July 1975, collapsed when the expected surge of popular support failed to materialize, and most of the top leaders of the Muslim Youth were captured and executed, either by the Dā'ūd government or later after the Marxist takeover in 1978. Following the failure of this operation, Hekmatyar became the dominant figure in the Organization of Muslim Youth, which was reconstituted as Ḥizb-i Islāmī Afghānistān in this same period.

As leader of Ḥizb-i Islāmī during the thirteen-year guerrilla war against the Marxist government in Afghanistan (1978–1992), Hekmatyar proved to be a controversial figure. He was respected for his organizational skills and energy and held in some awe for his oratorical powers and charismatic presence, but he has nevertheless inspired much hostility. Ruthless in his suppression of dissidents within the party and as energetic in fighting rival parties as in attacking enemy forces, Hekmatyar has frequently been accused of undermining the unity of resistance efforts in his search for power. Although he is recognized personally as one of the least corrupt of the major party leaders and one of the most successful at gaining international diplomatic and financial support for the resistance, he is also resented by many traditional Afghans for interjecting a divisive brand of revolutionary Islamic ideology into the *jihād*.

After the overthrow of the Marxists in April 1992, Hekmatyar stayed on the fringes of the coalition government that was established in Kabul from among the former resistance parties. He accused the new regime of opportunistically conspiring with Marxists and former militia leaders and of playing on Pushtun fear of Persian and Uzbek dominance in the new government. He set up a base of operations in Logar Province south of Kabul, where he sometimes shelled the capital and sometimes negotiated with the coalition leaders. In March 1993, an accord negotiated in Islamabad made him prime minister, but as his main rival, Aḥmad Shāh Mas'ūd, was made defense minister, the shelling did not stop and Hekmatyar's national authority was only nominal.

[*See also* Afghanistan; Ḥizb-i Islāmī Afghānistān.]

BIBLIOGRAPHY

Edwards, David B. "Summoning Muslims: Print, Politics, and Religious Ideology in Afghanistan." *Journal of Asian Studies* 52.3 (1993): 609–628.

Naby, Eden. "The Changing Role of Islam as a Unifying Force in Afghanistan." In *The State, Religion, and Ethnic Politics: Afghanistan, Iran, and Pakistan*, edited by Ali Banuazizi and Myron Weiner, pp. 124–154. Syracuse, N.Y., 1986.

Roy, Olivier. *Islam and Resistance in Afghanistan*. Cambridge, 1986.

Shahrani, M. Nazif, and Robert Canfield, eds. *Revolutions and Rebellions in Afghanistan: Anthropological Perspectives*. Berkeley, 1984.

DAVID B. EDWARDS

ḤIJĀB. The English term "veil" is commonly used to refer to Middle Eastern women's traditional head, face or body covers, but in fact it has no single equivalent in Arabic. Instead, different terms refer to diverse articles of women's clothing that vary according to region and era. Some of these Arabic terms are *burquʿ*, *ʿabāyah*, *ṭarḥah*, *burnus*, *jilbāb*, and *milāyah*. Overgarments such as the *ʿabāyah* of Arabia and the *burnus* of the Maghrib tend to be very similar for both sexes.

Origins. Islam did not introduce veiling or seclusion to the Arab region, nor are these institutions indigenous to Arabs. Strict seclusion enforced by eunuchs and the veiling of women were fully in place in Byzantine society. Some evidence indicates that in the southwestern Arab region, only two clans (the Banū Ismāʿīl and Banū Qaḥṭān) may have practiced some form of female veiling in pre-Islamic times. No seclusion or veiling existed in ancient Egypt either, although according to one reference some women may have been using a head veil in public in the later period, during the reign of Ramses III (20th dynasty).

Long before Islam, veiling and seclusion appear to have existed in the Hellenistic-Byzantine area and among the Sassanians of Persia. In ancient Mesopotamia, the veil for women was regarded as a sign of respectability and high status; decent married women wore the veil to distinguish themselves from women slaves and unchaste women—indeed, the latter were forbidden to cover head or hair. In Assyrian law, harlots and slaves were forbidden to veil, and those caught illegally veiling were liable to severe penalties. Thus veiling was not simply to mark aristocracy but to distinguish "respectable" women from disreputable ones.

Successive invasions brought into contact the Greek, Persian, and Mesopotamian empires and the Semitic peoples of the regions. The practices of veiling and seclusion of women appear subsequently to have become established in Judaic and Christian systems. Gradually these spread to Arabs of the urban upper classes and eventually to the general urban public.

At the time of the birth of Christianity Jewish women were veiling the head and face. Biblical evidence of veiling can be found in *Genesis* 24.65, "And Rebekah lifted up her eyes and when she saw Isaac . . . she took her veil and covered herself"; in *Isaiah* 3.23, "In that day the Lord will take away the finery of the anklets . . . the headdresses . . . and the veils"; and in 1 *Corinthians* 11.3–7, "Any woman who prays with her head unveiled dishonors her head—it is the same as if her head were shaven. For if a woman will not veil herself, then she should cut off her hair, but if it is disgraceful for a woman to be shorn or shaven, let her wear a veil. For a man ought not to cover his head, since he is the image and glory of God; but woman is the glory of man."

In medieval Egypt, public segregation of the sexes existed among Jewish Egyptians; women and men entered their temples from separate doors. Evidence suggests also that Jewish women of that period veiled their faces.

Veiling of Arab Muslim urban women became more pervasive under Turkish rule as a marker of rank and exclusive lifestyle. By the nineteenth century, upper-class urban Muslim and Christian women in Egypt wore the *ḥabarah,* which consisted of a long skirt, a head cover, and a *burquʿ,* a long rectangular cloth of white transparent muslin placed below the eyes, covering the lower nose and the mouth and falling to the chest. In mourning, a black muslin veil known as the *bisha* was substituted. Perhaps related to the origins of the practice among Jews and Christians, the word *ḥabarah* itself derives from early Christian and Judaic religious vocabulary.

Ḥijāb is not a recent term, but it was revived in the 1970s. It had been part of the Arabian Arabic vocabulary of early Islam. *Ḍarb* (adopting) *al-ḥijāb* was the phrase used in Arabia in discourse about the seclusion of the wives of the Prophet. When the veil became the center of feminist/nationalist discourse in Egypt during British colonial occupation, *ḥijāb* was the term used. The phrase used for the removal of urban women's face/head cover was *rafʿ* (lifting) *al-ḥijāb* (not *al-ḥabarah*).

Qur'ānic References. The Qur'ān has a number of references to *ḥijāb,* none of which concern women's clothing. At the time of its founding, as Islam gradually established itself in the Medina community, "seclusion" for Muḥammad's wives was introduced in a Qur'ānic verse: 'O ye who believe, enter not the dwellings of the Prophet, unless invited. . . . And when you ask of his wives anything, ask from behind *ḥijāb.* That is purer for your hearts and for their hearts" (33.53).

This refers not to women's clothing, but rather to a partition or curtain. Other references further stress the separating aspect of *ḥijāb.* For example, *al-ḥijāb* is mentioned in nongendered contexts separating deity from mortals (42.51), wrongdoers from the righteous (7.46, 41.5), believers from unbelievers (17.45), and light from darkness and day from night (38.32). With regard to the sexes, one verse tells men and women to be modest, and women to cover their bosoms and hide their ornaments: "Tell the believing men to lower their gaze and be modest. That is purer for them. And tell the believing women to lower their gaze and be modest, and display of their adornment only that which is apparent, and to draw their *khimār* over their bosoms, and not to reveal their adornment save to their own husbands" (24.30–31). Another verse states, "O Prophet, tell thy wives and thy daughters, and the women of the believers to draw their *jilbāb* close round them . . . so that they may be recognized and not molested" (33.59).

These verses refer not to *ḥijāb* but to *khimār* (head cover) and *jilbāb* (body dress or cloak), and the focus of both verses is modesty and special status. The desirability of modesty is further stressed by referring to the contrasting concept *tabarruj* (immodesty): "O ye wives of the Prophet! Ye are not like any other women. If ye keep your duty, then be not soft of speech, lest he in whose heart is a disease aspire, but utter customary speech. And stay in your houses. Bedizen not yourselves with the bedizenment of the Time of Ignorance" (33.32–33).

In none of these verses is the word *ḥijāb* used. The three terms *khimār, jilbāb,* and *tabarruj* were used to stress the special status of the Prophet's wives. *Al-tabbaruj* (immodest display of a woman's body combined with flirtatious mannerisms) was used to describe women's public manners in the pre-Islamic "days of ignorance." The phrase stands in contrast with *al-tahhajub* (modesty in dress and manners), a term that derives from the same root as *ḥijāb.*

Meaning. *Ḥijāb* is derived from the root *ḥ-j-b;* its verbal form *ḥajaba* translates as "to veil, to seclude, to screen, to conceal, to form a separation, to mask." *Ḥijāb* translates as "cover, wrap, curtain, veil, screen, partition." The same word refers to amulets carried on one's person (particularly as a child) to protect against harm. Another derivative, *ḥājib,* means eyebrow (protector of the eye) and is also the name used during the caliphate periods for the official who screened applicants who wished audience with the caliph.

Evidence from its usage in the Qur'ān and from early Islamic feminist discourse, as well as anthropological analysis, supports the notion of *ḥijāb* in Islam as referring to a sacred divide or separation between two worlds or two spaces: deity and mortals, men and women, good and evil, light and dark, believers and nonbelievers, or aristocracy and commoners. The phrase *min warā' al-ḥijāb* ("from behind the *ḥijāb*") emphasizes the element of separation/partition.

The connection among clothing, modesty, and morality in Islam can be found in the Qur'ānic imagery of creation. Here clothing acquires meaning beyond the familiar: "Satan tempted them, so that he might reveal to them their private parts that had been hidden from each other" (7.20); and "We have sent down to you clothing in order to cover the private parts of your body and serve as protection and decoration; and the best of all garments is the garment of piety" (7.26). In another context, "they [women] are a garment to you and you are a garment to them" (2.187), an interdependent mutuality of the sexes is expressed. By using the imagery of clothing, Islamic creation focuses on gender relations rather than on irreversible sin and conceptually links clothing with morality, privacy, sexuality, and modesty.

The European term "veil" (and its correlate seclusion), therefore, fail to capture these nuances and oversimplify a complex phenomenon. Furthermore, "veil" as commonly used gives the illusion of having a single referent, whereas it ambiguously refers at various times to a face cover for women, a transparent head cover, or an elaborate headdress. Limiting its reference obscures historical developments, cultural differentiations of social context, class, or special rank, and sociopolitical articulations. In Western feminist discourse "veil" is politically charged with connotations of the inferior "other," implying and assuming a subordination and inferiority of the Muslim woman. In fact, in the Middle East the veil was historically worn to distinguish women of high status; it was in the Hellenic, Judaic, and Christian systems to which the West traces its roots that veiling was associated with seclusion in the sense of the subordination of women.

Contemporary Issues. The Qur'ānic terms *ḥijāb, khimār, jilbāb,* and *tabbaruj* reappeared in the mid-1970s as part of an emergent Islamic consciousness and movement that spread all over the Islamic East. It was distinguished by the voluntary and active participation of young Muslim college women and men. Women's visible presence became marked when they began to don a distinctive but uniform dress, unavailable commercially, which they called *al-zī al-Islāmī* ("Islamic dress").

A *muḥajjabah* (woman wearing *ḥijāb*) wore *al-jilbāb*—an unfitted, long-sleeved, ankle-length gown in austere solid colors and thick opaque fabric—and *al-khimār,* a head cover resembling a nun's wimple that covers the hair, low to the forehead, comes under the chin to conceal the neck, and falls down over the chest and back. Whereas the nun's wimple is an aspect of her seclusion and a sign of her state of celibacy and asexuality, the Muslim woman wears *al-khimār* in order to desexualize public social space when she is part of it. Modesty extends beyond her clothing to her subdued, serious behavior and austere manner, and is an ideal applied to both sexes. A *munaqqabah* (woman wearing the *niqāb,* or face veil) more conservatively adds *al-niqāb,* which covers the entire face except for eye slits; at the most extreme, she would also wear gloves and socks to cover her hands and feet.

This Islamic dress was introduced by college women in the movement and was not imposed by al-Azhar University, where prescribed Islamic behavior often originates. By dressing this way in public these young women translated their vision of Islamic ideas into live contemporary models. Encoded in the dress style is a new public modesty that reaffirms an Islamic identity and morality as it rejects Western materialism, commercialism, and values. The vision behind the Islamic dress is rooted in these women's understanding of early Islam and the Qur'ān. Clearly, the movement was not simply about a dress code. It was, like early Islam, against *al-tabarruj* and for modesty in behavior, voice, body movement, and choices, now symbolizing a new identity distancing itself from Western values. In the 1980s the movement shifted from establishing an Islamic identity and morality to asserting Islamic nationalism, engaging in participatory politics, and resisting authoritarian regimes and Western dominance. Embedded in today's *ḥijāb* is imagery that combines notions of modesty, morality, identity, and resistance. Fighting it are women (and men) who oppose absence of choice, as in Iran. Resistance through *al-ḥijāb* or against it, whether it means attire or behavior, has generated dynamic discourse around gender, Islamic ideals, Arab society, and women's status and liberation.

[*See also* Dress; Modesty; Seclusion.]

BIBLIOGRAPHY

Ahmed, Leila. *Women and Gender in Islam.* New Haven, 1992. Good overview of literature on gender in the Middle East from ancient to modern times, hampered somewhat by superficial usage of archaeological findings and anthropological insights (not based on original field research), but a useful resource nonetheless for its extensive historical documentation on gender. The textual survey is framed from the perspective of feminist gender studies (misogyny, patriarchy, androcentrism), but is itself a critique of feminism.

Amīn, Qāsim. *Al-aʿmāl al-Kāmilah li-Qāsim Amīn.* Edited by Muḥammad ʿImārah. Beirut, 1976. This book divides into two parts, the first being the author's analysis and commentary on Amīn's reformist thought on women's issues, with a focus on the *ḥijāb.* The second part is a reprinting of Amīn's two original books on women's issues, *Taḥrir al-mar'ah* (1899) and *Al-mar'ah al-jadīdah* (1900), considered among the first classic Arab feminist works.

El Guindi, Fadwa. "Veiling Infitah with Muslim Ethic: Egypt's Contemporary Islamic Movement." *Social Problems* 28.4 (1981): 465–485. The first original field study on the subject using anthropological analysis, which has become a classic reference. There is still very little work on the subject based on systematic field research.

Goitein, S. D. *A Mediterranean Society: The Jewish Communities of the Arab World as Portrayed in the Documents of the Cairo Geniza*, vol. 3, *The Family*. Berkeley, 1978. Good source on Jewish life and detailed aspects of society in medieval Egypt.

Luṭfī, Hūdā. "Al-Ṣakhawī's Kitab al-Nisa'." *Muslim World* 71.2 (1981): 104–124. Informative discussion of al-Ṣakhawī's volume on women and a good source for the social and economic history of fifteenth-century Muslim women.

Mawdūdī, Sayyid Abū al-Aʿlā. *Purdah and the Status of Woman in Islam*. Lahore, 1972. Widely read source on the subject for believers in the Islamic movement, providing a nonorthodox interpretation of the Qur'ān on gender issues.

Pomeroy, Sarah B. *Goddesses, Whores, Wives, and Slaves: Women in Classical Antiquity*. New York, 1975. Provides historical information on the classical period of Greece and Mediterranean culture, useful for a comparison with Islamic societies.

Tabari, Azar, and Nahid Yeganeh. *In the Shadow of Islam: The Women's Movement in Iran*. London, 1982. Interesting collection of articles divided into analyses of the social origins of various currents among Iranian women and the relevance of Islam to the problem of women's oppression, and translations of original documents by Islamic Shīʿī male ideologues of the Islamic Revolution of Iran. Good source of critical feminist thinking about women's status under the Iranian Islamic regime.

Zuhur, Sherifa. *Revealing Reveiling: Islamist Gender Ideology in Contemporary Egypt*. Albany, N.Y., 1992. Field study of Egyptian Muslim women and ideologues in the contemporary Islamic movement, useful more for its original data than its conclusions or conceptualization.

FADWA EL GUINDI

HIJRAH. The Qur'ān identifies the use of the term *hijrah* (to migrate, abandon, or withdraw; exodus) in reference to the acts of migration of prophets, such as Abraham, Moses, Lot, and others (surahs 19.48–49, 60.4, and 11.69–83). In Islam, *the* Hijrah refers to the migration/exodus of Muḥammad and the *muhājirūn* (his companions) from Mecca to the city of Yathrib. Muḥammad departed from Mecca on Thursday, 1 Rabīʿ al-Awwal/13 September 622, arriving at Yathrib, actually Qubā', on Monday, 12 Rabīʿ al-Awwal/24 September 622.

The commemoration of the Hijrah was instituted in 637 by the second caliph, ʿUmar ibn al-Khaṭṭāb (r. 634–644), as the first year of the new Islamo-Arabic calendar. It is often treated as a motif in political, cultural, literary, and aesthetic expressions in the Islamic world.

Religiously, the Hijrah connotes a journey of religious intent. It is undertaken to inaugurate a new era—a symbolic refusal to lose hope in the face of persecution. The moral of Hijrah is that religious persecution is a violation of religious freedom, thus withdrawal from an oppressive to a more conducive environment is a suitable option. Hijrah is undertaken by Muslims individually or as a group in response to a threat to survival and social security (Qur'ān 2.218, 4.97). Hijrah is a testimony of devotion to Islam, indicating a willingness to endure all suffering caused by the movement to another locale for the sake of protecting one's life and faith (Qur'ān 3.195, 4.100, 9.20, 16.41, 22.58, and 29.56).

The Hijrah has been interpreted by Muslims in a variety of ways over the past fifteen centuries. It has been given different shades of meaning and imbued with symbolism to religiously validate various experiential dimensions of Islam.

In the Muslim political discourse of the eighteenth, nineteenth, and twentieth centuries, the paradigm of Hijrah has been employed by different Muslim politicoreligious movements: it was used by Shehu Usuman dan Fodio (1754–1817) of Nigeria to oppose religious syncretism in African Islam; by the Muslim Brotherhoods of North and West Africa to confront colonial rule; to justify the Muslim migrations of 1783–1914 from Russia and the Balkan states; and by the Khilāfat movement (1920) to legitimize its call to Indian Muslims to migrate from British India to Afghanistan. During the 1910s and 1920s, Hijrah was employed as a politicotheological construct by the new tribal state of Saudi Arabia to settle bedouin tribes in order to accomplish the goals of territorial expansion and consolidation of power. [*See the biography of Dan Fodio and* Khilāfat Movement.]

In the post–World War II era of Muslim nation-states, Muslim immigrants from India in the newly created state of Pakistan were called *muhājir*. Lately, because of ethnic tensions in Pakistan, the term *muhājir* has acquired a class distinction.

Since the 1940s, Hijrah has been ideologized by such neofundamentalist thinkers as Sayyid Abū al-Aʿlā Mawdūdī (1903–1979) of the Jamāʿ at-i Islāmī of Pakistan and Sayyid Quṭb (1906–1966) of the Muslim Brotherhood (al-Ikhwān al-Muslimūn) in Egypt. Both described Hijrah as withdrawal from the new Jāhilīyah, which they identified as the policies of secularism, capitalism, socialism, and modernization/westernization of the Muslim nation-states. [*See the biographies of Mawdūdī and Quṭb.*]

In the late 1970s and the 1980s, the Egyptian extremist group Jamāᶜ at al-Muslimīn (Community of Believers), popularly known as al-Takfīr wa al-Hijrah, founded by Shukrī Muṣṭafā (1942–1978), stretched the concept of the new Jāhilīyah further. In this group's view, Arab socialists, such as Gamal Abdel Nasser (1918–1970) and his successor Anwar el-Sadat (1918–1981), represent modern pharaohs who are to be opposed for introducing non-Islamic political, legal, and socioeconomic institutions. For Muṣṭafā and his followers, postcolonial Egypt represents evil, hence the obligation to withdraw from it. Emulating Muḥammad's Hijrah, Muṣṭafā declared Egyptian society to be non-Islamic and established an isolated commune called Jamâᶜ at al-Muslimīn at Mansura. It was to be the center of preparations for the overthrow of the Egyptian sociopolitical order. Thus, the Jamâᶜ at al-Muslimīn called for an internalization of the attitude of Hijrah as separation from an urban economic setting with the politicoreligious aim of seizing power. [*See* Takfīr wa al-Hijrah, al-; *and the biography of Muṣṭafā.*]

In Malaysia, the puritanical group Dar ul Arqam withdrew to an isolated commune as an expression of ethnic religiosity. [*See* Dar ul Arqam.]

Hence, in the modern, postcolonial period, the concept of Hijrah has acquired an intra-Muslim political signification leading to the emergence of different interpretations and the establishment of *hujar* (settlements) relevant to diverse Muslim geopolitical areas. As a political process, Hijrah contains a residue of the medieval Muslim political classification of the world into Dār al-Islām, Dār al-Ḥarb, and Dār al-Hijrah and its definition of *jīhad* (war against nonbelievers) as response to domestic and international pressures of the postcolonial era. It also contains intra-Muslim polemics concerning the nineteenth-century Islamic modernist movement.

In modern Ṣūfī literature, Muḥammad's Hijrah is considered an important stage in the inner spiritual journey of returning to Allāh. Enduring the physical hardships of Hijrah is viewed as a process of self-purification for love of Allāh.

More recently, in an age of Western dominance in areas of knowledge, technology, and material life, Muslim travel to the West for the purposes of acquiring an education, seeking economic betterment, and even political asylum is not unusual. This phenomenon of immigration to the West has added a new dimension to the discourse about Hijrah. It has stimulated reflections about the Muslim encounter with the non-Muslim West and also regarding the reception of Islam among Western citizens, such as the African-American Muslims, for whom Islam is the vehicle of a symbolic journey to Africa, and European converts to Islam, for whom Islam is a path of withdrawal from the excesses of Western materialism. Such Hijrah-related discussion has been the subject of various studies and novels about Muslim religious experience in recent times and has been featured in the writings of Muhammad Iqbal, Muḥammad Marmaduke Pickthall, Muḥammad Asad, Malcolm X, al-Ṭayyib Ṣāliḥ, Gai (Ḥasan) Eaton, Salman Rushdie, and others.

In 1982, the Muslim world celebrated the beginning of the fifteenth century of Hijrah.

BIBLIOGRAPHY

Ahmad, Aziz. *Islamic Modernism in India and Pakistan, 1857–1964*. London, 1967. Important reference work about the interactions between Islam and modernity in the Indian subcontinent.

Asad, Muhammad. *The Road to Mecca*. Gibraltar, 1980. Account of a European's journey to Islam.

Bukhārī, Muḥammad ibn Ismāᶜīl al-. *Ṣaḥīḥ al-Bukhārī*. Vol. 5. Translated by Muhammad Asad. Gibraltar, 1980. Chapter 51, section 21 of this volume contains *ḥadīths* relating to the Hijrah.

Eickelman, Dale F., and J. P. Piscatori, eds. *Muslim Travellers*. Berkeley, 1990. Comprehensive collection of essays on the theme of Hijrah and journey in the Muslim perspective.

Haddad, Yvonne Y. *Islamic Values in the United States*. New York, 1987. Excellent case study about the religious experience of immigrant Muslims in North America.

"Hegira, Year 1400." Special issue of *Cultures* (UNESCO) 8 (1980). Collection of extensive articles about the Hijrah.

Kepel, Gilles. *The Prophet and Pharaoh*. London, 1985. Detailed study of Muslim extremism in Egypt.

Malcolm X. *The Autobiography of Malcolm X* (1965). New York, 1992. Narrative of an African American's journey to Africa through Islam.

Martin, B. G. *Muslim Brotherhoods in Nineteenth-Century Africa*. Cambridge. 1976. Classic study of the confrontation between the African Ṣūfī brotherhoods and colonialism.

Mawdūdī, Sayyid Abū al-Aᶜlā. *Islam aur jāhilīyat*. Translated into English as *Islam and Ignorance*. Lahore, 1976. Pakistani thinker's perspective on Islam in modern times.

Newby, Gordon D. *The Making of the Last Prophet*. Columbia, S.C., 1989. Competent attempt by a historian to reconstruct an early biography of Muḥammad.

Quṭb, Sayyid. *Maᶜālim fī al-ṭarīq*. Translated into English as *Milestones*. Kuwait, 1978. Important attempt to construct an ideological vision of Islam by an Egyptian activist.

Imtiyaz Yusuf

ḤILF. *See* Covenants.

ḤILLĪ, ʿALLĀMAH IBN AL-MUṬAHHAR AL- (1250–1325), scholar and jurist of the Imāmī (or Ithnā ʿAsharī) Shīʿīs. Ḥasan ibn Yūsuf ibn al-Muṭahhar al-Ḥillī, known as ʿAllāmah ("most learned"), was born in Hilla in Iraq. His lifetime saw the Mongol capture of Baghdad (1258) and the foundation of the Il-khānid dynasty. The Mongols, contrary to their reputation, permitted, even encouraged, intellectual activity; Hülegü, for example, founded the observatory and informal academy at Maragha in 1259. ʿAllāmah benefited from this freedom. He probably studied at Maragha with Naṣīr al-Dīn al-Ṭūsī (d. 1274), but primarily found his teachers and colleagues in Baghdad, where also he became involved with the Il-khānid court during the reign of Öljeitü (r. 1304–1316). His education covered the usual curriculum, in its Shīʿī version, but included significant input from Sunnī thinkers.

ʿAllāmah's writings included works on grammar, logic, *ḥadīth, tafsīr* (Qur'ānic commentary), and biography, but his constructive achievement was in the areas of jurisprudence, theology, and polemics. His polemical works (defending the existence, necessity, and historical evolution of the imamate and exemplified in the *Minhāj al-karāmah*) are probably associated with his time at the court of Öljeitü, whose religious vacillation encouraged sectarian debate. In the field of theology *(kalām)*, ʿAllāmah was one of the most distinguished thinkers in the later Muʿtazilī tradition, which had been accepted into Imāmī Shīʿīsm in the Buyid period (945–1055). The *Kashf al-Murād*, ʿAllāmah's commentary on al-Ṭūsī's credal statement, the *Tajrīd al-iʿtiqād*, is a representative work. Its technical scholasticism remained a part of the tradition, but was not a key to its significant development; the great achievement of later Shīʿī theology is associated with Mullā Ṣadrā al-Shīrāzī (d. 1641), who drew rather on the philosophical tradition of Ibn Sīnā (d. 1037) and on the illuminationist theories of Suhrawardī (d. 1190). [*See also* Philosophy.]

In the field of jurisprudence, ʿAllāmah produced works of positive law *(furūʿ)* and of hermeneutical theory *(uṣūl)*. In the former area, he continued the work of his teacher Jaʿfar ibn al-Ḥasan al-Muḥaqqiq al-Ḥillī (d. 1277). This work was a reformulation of the tradition established by Muḥammad ibn al-Ḥasan al-Ṭūsī, Shaykh al-Ṭā'ifah (d. 1068), and reconciled some of the damaging disputes that had emerged in the intervening centuries. ʿAllāmah refined and expanded the Shīʿī corpus of *furūʿ al-figh,* notably exploring the range of dispute within the tradition in his *Mukhtalaf al-Shīʿah*. He perceived that justification and reconciliation within the tradition required a theoretical foundation achievable only within the discipline of *uṣūl*. His great achievement there, and of his scholarship as a whole, was to integrate the theory of *ijtihād* into the structures of Imāmī Shīʿī jurisprudence. ʿAllāmah perceived that *ijtihād* and its implications (previously rejected by the Shīʿīs) were not irreconcilable with the reality of interpretative development within Shiism. The theory of *ijtihād* explained dispute, permitted creative interpretation within the tradition, and justified the authority of the jurists. All subsequent Shīʿī thinking in this area can be seen as either a development of or a reaction to ʿAllāmah's ideas.

Reaction to this thinking is associated with Muḥammad Amīn al-Astarābādī (d. 1627), who fought against ʿAllāmah's innovations and inspired the Akhbārī movement, which was opposed by the Uṣūlī movement. The Akhbārī-Uṣūlī controversy may reflect literalist and rationalist tensions of earlier periods, but it was articulated solely in relation to aspects of the theory of *ijtihād*. It dominated juristic thinking throughout the seventeenth and eighteenth centuries, and was finally resolved in favour of the Uṣūlīs, whose thinking prevailed in the nineteenth and twentieth centuries.

[*See also* Akhbārīyah; Ijtihād; Ithnā ʿAsharīyah; *and* Uṣūlīyah.]

BIBLIOGRAPHY

Calder, Norman. "Doubt and Prerogative: The Emergence of an Imāmī Shīʿī Theory of *ijtihād*." *Studia Islamica* 70 (1989): 57–78.

Schmidtke, Sabine. *The Theology of al-ʿAllāma al-Ḥillī (d. 726/1325)*. Berlin, 1991.

NORMAN CALDER

ḤISBAH. The word *ḥisbah* literally means "sum" or "reward." Technically, however, it connotes the state institution to promote what is proper and forbid what is improper *(al-amr bi-al-maʿrūf wa-al-nahy ʿan al-munkar)*. Although the Qur'ān visualizes every Muslim in roles that lead to the propagation of good and the suppression of evil (surah 3.110), the state is empowered to institute arrangements to oversee the implementation of this injunction (surah 3.104). The function of *ḥisbah*, therefore, consists in maintaining public law and order and supervising the behavior of buyers and sellers in the market with a view to ensure right conduct. The Prophet took care to institutionalize the perpetuation of this code by enjoining on everyone to engage in *amr bil maʿrūf wa nahi ʿanil munkar*. In this regard, the Prophet has been termed the first *muḥtasib* (person responsible for the maintenance of the institution of *ḥisbah),* although subsequently others were appointed (Saʿīd ibn al-ʿĀṣ in Mecca and ʿUmar ibn al-Khaṭṭāb in Medina). The functions of the *muḥtasib* cover the rights of God and the people (duties regarding prayers, mosque maintenance, community matters, market dealings, etc). As stated by Ibn Taymīyah, the qualities of a *muḥtasib* of leading importance were knowledge, kindness, and patience. A separate department of *ḥisbah,* with a full-time *muḥtasib,* was first introduced by the ʿAbbāsid caliph Abū Jaʿfar al-Manṣūr in AH 157/773 CE. Although the institution of *ḥisbah* remained in practice during the early period of Islamic history, with the advent of Western colonialism, the *ḥisbah* disintegrated into a number of secular departments, either discarding its religious content as irrelevant or relegating it to secondary positions.

[*See also* Muḥtasib.]

BIBLIOGRAPHY

Ibn Murshid, ʿAbd al-ʿAzīz ibn Muḥammad. *Niẓām al-ḥisbah fī al-Islām: dirāsah muqāranah*. Riyadh, 1973.

Ibn Taymīyah. *Al-ḥisbah fī al-Islām*. Translated by Muhtar Holland as *Public Duties in Islam: The Institution of the Ḥisbah*. Leicester, 1982.

ABDUL RAHMAN I. DOI

HISTORIOGRAPHY. The modern-day historians of the Islamic world, particularly those of the Middle East and South Asia, are the heirs of a powerful and sophisticated tradition of historical writing, and they appeal to (or feel the burden of) this tradition on many levels. Historical writing was one of the earliest and most highly developed literary genres in every region and language of the Islamic world. The characteristic formal structures, subject matter, and explanatory paradigms of this literature took shape between the early eighth and eleventh centuries, and persisted—with much flexibility and elaboration but little change at a deep level—down to the early nineteenth century. By the 1840s, however, the forms and perspectives of traditional historiography, rich and varied as they were, no longer seemed adequate in face of the radical challenges posed by Europe to every aspect of life in the Islamic world. By the beginning of the twentieth century, a few historians were beginning to model their work (with mixed but not inconsiderable success) on European approaches and research methods. The 1910s and 1920s witnessed the founding of universities on the European model, and as an inevitable consequence, a growing professionalization of history. That movement has continued down to the present, so that now (as in Europe and America) the writing of history has become largely an academic enterprise, with all the gains and losses that this implies.

In a brief article we cannot follow the evolution of historiography throughout the entire Islamic world. We will therefore focus only on three areas: the central and eastern Arab lands (with an emphasis on trends in Egypt), Turkey, and Iran. Historiography in India and Pakistan on the one side, and North Africa on the other, has not developed in isolation from the Middle East; on the contrary, the parallels and mutual influences have been close and profound. But historical writing in these countries has followed a distinctive path, shaped by a far tighter (even suffocating) colonial domination, and marked by a clear preference for English and French (rather than Arabic or Urdu) among the leading modern historians.

Nineteenth Century. The challenge of Europe was of course felt most immediately in political and economic life, but that in itself might have compelled few changes in historical vision; Muslim intellectuals had faced many equally acute crises on this plane over the centuries, and the deeply rooted but still flexible conceptual tools and cultural resources of their societies had permitted them to address these quite effectively. The European cultural challenge cut deeper, however. Felt only by a tiny minority as late as the mid-nineteenth century, it had become inescapable to almost everyone (at least in the major urban centers) by the beginning of the twentieth. Not only did it threaten the political independence and economic autonomy of Muslim societies; it assailed the very foundations of Muslim identity.

The rapid intellectual readjustments of the late nineteenth century (down to World War I) of course affected historical writing, although the works produced in this genre do not reach the level of the political and cultural essays of Rifāʿah Rāfiʿ al-Ṭahṭāwī (1801–1873), Namık Kemal (1840–1888), Jamāl al-Dīn al-Afghānī (1839–1897), or Muḥammad ʿAbduh (1849–1905). This is probably due in large part to the fact that history continued to be (as it always had been in Muslim countries) the work of amateurs, and moreover was seldom attempted by the leading intellectuals of the age. As one might expect, the shift toward new forms and approaches began in Cairo and Istanbul, the two largest cities in the region, the seats of the most ambitiously reformist regimes, and the places most directly and profoundly exposed to Western pressures.

Cairo was the first and most important center of a changing historiography. It had in fact produced the last great work in a traditional mold, the *ʿAjāʾib al-āthār* of ʿAbd al-Raḥmān al-Jabartī (1753–1826). Al-Jabartī witnessed the catastrophic self-destruction of the Mamlūk regime in the late eighteenth century, the shock of the French occupation in 1798–1801, and the tumultuous changes forced on the country by Muḥammad ʿAlī (r. 1805–1848). He was an acute observer, but he regarded none of this as progress, and he was content to work within the chronicle/biographical dictionary framework bequeathed to him by the great Egyptian historians of the fourteenth and fifteenth centuries.

Muḥammad ʿAlī, illiterate soldier that he was, had more than a little to do with the rise of an altered historical consciousness. Quite apart from his military, administrative, and economic initiatives, so disruptive of deep-rooted institutions and habits of thought, he took the risk of sending student missions to study in France, thereby exposing at least a few of his subjects to the thought and culture of contemporary Europe. No less important was his founding of the Translation Bureau (under the directorship of al-Ṭahṭāwī), which rendered many works of medicine, engineering, geography, and even history into Turkish and Arabic. To be sure, the few historical works chosen for translation (e.g., Montesquieu's *Considérations sur les causes de la grandeur des Romains et de leur décadence,* or Voltaire's lives of Charles XII and Peter the Great) represented the Enlightenment, not the new scientific history of Ranke or the romantic nationalism of Michelet; even so, they suggested radically new ways of imagining and representing the past.

The first major history in Arabic to reflect new possibilities and tensions was *Al-khiṭaṭ al-tawfīqīyah al-jadīdah* (20 vols., Cairo, 1886–1888) by ʿAlī Mubārak (1824–1893), the engineer who oversaw Khedive Ismāʿīl's ambitious revamping of Cairo in the 1860s and early 1870s. Modeled to some degree on the classic work by Taqī al-Dīn al-Maqrīzī (d. 1442), it is a remarkably rich miscellany of historical-biographical information, geographical description, and administrative data. Conceptually and structurally conservative (like al-Maqrīzī's work, it is organized by toponym), its contents nevertheless reflect many aspects of the new order. A hybrid work of this kind could not generate many successors, although the *Taqwīm al-Nīl* (6 vols., Cairo, 1916–1936) of Amīn Sāmī (c. 1860–1941) comes closest in spirit and content. Like al-Ṭahṭāwī and ʿAlī Mubārak, Sāmī spent his life in loyal service to the regime, chiefly as an educator; he was director of the government teachers' college, Dār al-ʿUlūm, under Tawfīq and ʿAbbās II, and was appointed to the Senate by King Fuʾād.

In Egypt the political and ideological crisis of the ʿUrābī period proved in the long run to be a turning point, but for a time one sees only limited results—owing in large part to the stifling of political life under Lord Cromer until almost the turn of the century. An exception to this generalization would be Salīm al-Naqqāsh's passionate, richly detailed, but still little-studied history of the ʿUrābī Revolt, *Miṣr lil-Miṣrīyīn* (6 vols., Alexandria, 1884), based heavily on government documents and trial proceedings. By the end of the century we can perceive a marked shift from neotraditional to contemporary European models of historiography. Of the new historians by far the most successful and widely read was the staggeringly prolific Syrian immigrant Jirjī Zaydān (1861–1914). He edited several journals and wrote in many genres; among his works the most significant in the present context is his *Tārīkh al-tamaddun al-Islāmī* (5 vols., Cairo, 1902–1906). This is less an original work of scholarship than a popular synthesis derived in large part from European Orientalist scholarship; even so, it is a very competent job and earned an English translation of one volume (*Umayyads and Abbasids,* London, 1907) by the formidable David Margoliouth. Zaydān's was thus the first Arabic work in "modern" style to address medieval Islamic history. It was widely read but not much emulated, perhaps because as a Christian committed to a westernizing approach, Zaydān could not address adequately the deeper issues raised by his subject for modern Muslims. Nor could he really share the aspirations and frustrations of Egyptian nationalist writers. He was in fact offered the position in Islamic history at the new Egyptian University in 1910, but outrage in politically engaged circles compelled the offer to be withdrawn.

Istanbul was the home of a rather different historiographic evolution. It was still the capital of a vast empire, ruled by an autocrat who increasingly defined his role in terms of the Islamic caliphate. Moreover, its historians continued to be, as for centuries past, part of the scribal-bureaucratic elite whose careers and personal identities were closely linked to the fortunes of the Ottoman state. A strongly conservative trend is thus no surprise in the two leading historians of the mid/late-nineteenth century—Ahmed Cevdet Pasha (1822–1895) and Ahmed Lutfî Efendi (1816–1907), both of whom were official court historians *(vakanüvis),* the last men to hold that post under the Ottoman sultans. Both recognized the changes going on all around them, but Lutfî resisted them, while Cevdet Pasha exhibited a more realistic mentality. Lutfî, for example, drew heavily on the official gazette for his information on the Tanzimat decades—a method that ensured a narrow, superficial, and highly laudatory account of this critical period (*Tarihi Lutfî,* 8 vols., Istanbul, 1873–1910; the final volumes remain unpublished). Cevdet Pasha, in contrast, had a strong grasp of law and administrative institutions and was deeply concerned with the processes governing the decline and fall of states. He was several times Minister of Justice and of Education and occasionally acted as a provincial governor (usually in Syria). He was the editor in chief of the *Mecelle* (the *sharīʿah*-based code of civil law issued between 1870 and 1877) as well as a translator of Ibn Khaldūn. Although his chronicle of the crucial half-century between 1774 and 1826 (*Tarihi vekayii devleti âliye,* 12 vols., Istanbul, 1885–1892), composed over a period of some thirty years, is traditionally constructed, it makes considerable use of European as well as Ottoman documents. Apart from Cevdet and Lutfî, we should mention the several historical works of the leading Young Ottoman intellectual Namık Kemal, a far more progressive spirit than his two older contemporaries. But his historical writings (many either never published or quickly suppressed) were hastily written inspirational and patriotic exercises and had almost no impact on the development of modern Turkish historiography. [*See the biography of Kemal.*]

The old mold was broken first by the Young Turk seizure of power in 1908, and then, decisively, by the Kemalist revolution. Whatever his defects as a thinker and politician, Ziya Gökalp (1875–1924) brought contemporary European sociology and history into the mainstream of Turkish intellectual life, where it found a ready reception. After World War I, Atatürk's generation would create modern Turkish historical writing. [*See the biography of Gökalp.*]

Nineteenth-century Iran did not witness the deep intellectual transformations of Cairo and Istanbul; the country's poverty and isolation, not to mention the political ineptitude of the Qājār court, left its historians working in a traditional framework (albeit enormously sophisticated) until the turn of the century. The Constitutional Revolution (1905–1911) was the culmination of a long process, and it would be misleading to attribute the later explosion in Persian intellectual life solely to this cataclysmic event. Yet the Revolution did crystallize the new currents of thought in the country, still ill-formed and shallow-rooted before 1905. It also created a powerful myth of promise, betrayal, and struggle for redemption—a myth that continues even now to shape many realms of Iranian life.

Interwar Period, 1919–1945. World War I was the turning point in almost every aspect of Middle Eastern life; indeed, this titanic event really laid down the agenda for the entire twentieth century within the region. It created vast new hopes and possibilities, and of course even more bitter disappointments and insoluble problems. It is no surprise that it ushered in a new era of historical writing marked by several characteristics: growing, if far from complete, professionalization (with several scholars getting doctorates in Europe, especially from Paris), institutionalized within the new universities of Cairo, Istanbul, and Tehran; a much closer approximation in form and methodology to the kinds of historical writing practiced in Europe; and a definition of persistent subject-matter areas, somewhat different for each of the linguistic/cultural realms. One apparently odd product of the period was a marked bilingualism among the new generation of historians, who often wrote in French or English for European audiences, and in Arabic, Persian, or Turkish for their own countrymen; in the latter works the cultural agendas and conflicts of their native countries came to the fore. This phenomenon continues strongly in the present.

It would be incorrect to assume that all traces of traditional literary-historical culture disappeared during these two decades. On the contrary, some of the most significant and useful historical compositions adhere to long-established genres. Thus *Osmanlı devrinde son sadrazamlar* (Istanbul, 1940–1949) is an invaluable biographical compilation on the last thirty-seven Ottoman grand viziers by İbnülemin Mahmut Kemal İnal (1870–1957), himself a senior bureaucrat in the empire's final decades and a scholar steeped in all aspects of Ottoman literary culture. Another writer, Muḥammad Kurd ʿAlī

(1876–1953), the founder of the Arab Academy of Damascus and a prolific journalist and littérateur, composed a monumental history of Syria, *Khiṭaṭ al-Shām* (6 vols., Damascus, 1925–1929). Although Kurd ʿAlī was well acquainted with the critical methods of Western Orientalism, this is the last great work of historical topography, a Syrian tradition going back to Ibn ʿAsākir (d. 1176) that flourished at least until the eighteenth century.

Works of more "modern" style tended to reflect in quite direct ways the central contemporary political-cultural debates of the countries in which they were written. This was true not only of works on recent history, but of those dealing with the more remote past. Indeed, the segments of the past chosen for discussion provide an excellent index of these debates. In Egypt, attention was focused equally on the nineteenth century (especially Muḥammad ʿAlī, Ismāʿīl, and the ʿUrābī Revolt) and on the beginnings of Islamic history. On the nineteenth century, the key works were probably those written by ʿAbd al-Raḥmān al-Rāfiʿī (1889–1966), Muḥammad Ṣabrī (1894–1978), and Shafīq Ghurbāl (1894–1961). Al-Rāfiʿī, an ardent partisan of the old National Party founded by Muṣṭafā Kāmil at the turn of the century and deeply immersed in Egypt's political struggles, was self-taught as a historian and wrote exclusively in Arabic. Ṣabrī and Ghurbāl were professional academics; both took doctorates from the Sorbonne, held chairs at Cairo University, and published much of their major work in French or English.

In regard to early Islamic history, Ṭāhā Ḥusayn's *Fī al-shiʿr al-jāhilī* (Cairo, 1926), Muḥammad Ḥusayn Haykal's *Ḥayāt Muḥammad* (Cairo, 1934), and Aḥmad Amīn's three books on early Islamic history (*Fajr al-Islām, Ḍuḥā al-Islām,* and *Ẓuhr al-Islām*, Cairo, 1928–1953) are landmarks in their various ways. Ṭāhā Ḥusayn had taken a Sorbonne doctorate with a thesis on Ibn Khaldūn; his attack on the authenticity of pre-Islamic Arabic poetry was an effort (almost disastrous for him and Cairo University) to apply European textual criticism to a culturally sanctified body of literature. The works of Haykal and Amīn, in contrast, were attempts to synthesize Islamic piety and "scientific" historical method. However one judges Haykal's use of modern critical methods, his biography of the Prophet was a literary *tour de force*, a superbly integrated portrait infused with a distinctively twentieth-century sensibility. Aḥmad Amīn's studies, though less accessible, have commanded broad respect since their first publication. Although he was a graduate of the School for Qāḍīs and was largely self-taught as a historian, his European colleagues at Cairo University formally recommended him for a professorial chair on the strength of his publications.

In Turkey scholars followed Atatürk's lead by turning their backs on the recently-extinguished Ottoman Empire in favor of an older, more "authentic" Turkish history, in particular Central Asia and the Seljuks. Here the leading figures were two exact contemporaries. Zeki Velidi Togan (1890–1970) was an emigré from Russian Turkestan and devoted his life to the history and literature (both medieval and modern) of the Turkic peoples of Central Asia. Mehmet Fuat Köprülü (1890–1966), a descendant of a famous seventeenth-century vizierial family, was essentially an autodidact, but he became the most influential scholar of his generation in Turkish literature and the history of the Seljuks of Anatolia. He published mostly in Turkish, but his 1935 lectures in Paris, *Les origines de l'Empire Ottoman,* marked a turning point in the study of that controversial subject.

In Iran work was inevitably affected by the neo-Achaemenidism and anti-clericalism of the Reza Shah regime; the historiography of this era, though by no means always royalist in tendency, was deeply nationalist and often anti-clerical. These trends are perhaps most tellingly summed up in the writings of Aḥmad Kasravī (1890–1946). Born in Tabriz, politically the most progressive and cosmopolitan city in Iran at the turn of the century, and trained as a cleric, he abandoned that path by the age of twenty. In the early years of the Reza Shah era he served as a judge and lawyer and then taught history at the University of Tehran, but in 1934 he left these official careers for one as a journalist and cultural critic. His vitriolic attacks on Shiism and Iranian cultural traditions earned him both a devoted following and deadly hostility; his assassination by the Fidāʾīyān-i Islām was almost predictable. He was, when he set his mind to it, a talented historian. An early work, *Shahriyārān-i gumnām* (Forgotten Rulers, 3 vols., Tehran, 1928–1930), deals with the pre-Seljuk dynasties of his native province and is still regularly cited. His most important work, however, was on the Constitutional Revolution (*Tārīkh-i mashrūṭah-i Īrān*, 3 vols., Tehran, 1940–1943), in which he had participated as a youth and in which his native city of Tabriz had played a critical part. [*See the biography of Kasravi.*]

The leading historians of this period did not simply toe the official line. On the contrary, many of them were opponents of the new governments and often in trouble with them. Nor is their work merely a coded statement of their own ideological predilections, for the work of every writer mentioned above has proved of enduring value. Al-Rāfiʿī's books, for example, have been regularly reprinted down to the present. But it remains the case that all these works were shaped in the context of the political struggles of their day, including the struggles for cultural identity as Egyptian, Turk, Iranian, or Muslim.

Cold War and Middle Eastern Nationalisms, 1945–1970. World War II marked another watershed as the domination of the region by Great Britain and France collapsed, to be replaced by a bipolar world of American-Soviet rivalry. At least until the early 1970s, and in some arenas until the present, intellectuals in the Arab lands and Iran tended to interpret their past within a single broad framework, as a struggle against foreign domination—by England and France in the modern period, of course, but often by fellow Muslims (Mamlūk amirs, Arab invaders, and so on) in the medieval past. In the revolutionary age beginning in the mid-1950s, it was inevitable that many would also begin to look seriously at Marxism as an intellectual tradition, and thus to link issues of internal class struggle with long-established concerns about imperialism.

Turkish intellectual life moved along a somewhat different path. There the Atatürk revolution had successfully forestalled direct foreign domination. Likewise, while the Atatürk regime's étatist and autarchist policies may well have limited Turkey's economic growth, they also reduced concern over covert foreign influence, at least until the late 1960s, when a rise in anti-Americanism was provoked in part by the repeated crises over Cyprus. Marxist interpretations did, however, speak to the pervasive poverty of the Turkish countryside and the frustrations of an emerging working class in the major cities.

The inevitable engagement of historians in the political struggles of the postwar years did not prevent the increasing professionalization of historical writing. The process was rooted in the rapid growth of higher education in Middle Eastern countries: a flood of new students into the universities required more professors, and professors had to have advanced research degrees. Down to the early 1970s credible Ph.D.s could only be obtained abroad, preferably in Paris or London (the old imperial capitals, ironically), but many students found themselves in newer and less prestigious institutions in the north of England or the American Middle West. The bilingual nature of historical research among Middle Eastern scholars continued and even increased; many of the major French and English monographs published during these years had begun life as doctoral theses at the Sorbonne or the University of London.

Again, it would be extremely misleading to interpret scholarly production simply as a reflection of ideology and political conflict. If a test for the "pure scholarship" of a work is its usability by scholars of disparate political-ideological commitments, then much produced in this era must rank very high indeed. To take only the most eminent names, it is hard to imagine modern Ottoman studies without Halil İnalcık, or early Islamic history without ʿAbd al-ʿAzīz al-Dūrī. [*See the biography of Dūrī.*] The study of Seljuk history became a favored preserve of Turkish scholarship, and the collective contribution of Osman Turan, Mehmet Köymen, and İbrahim Kafesoğlu probably outranks work on this subject done anywhere else in the world. In spite of political controls placed on Egyptian scholars under the Nasser regime, the students of Muḥammad Anīs at Cairo University initiated a major body of scholarship on the social and economic history of nineteenth- and twentieth-century Egypt. For an earlier but hardly less-contested era, that of the Crusaders, Ayyūbids, and Mamlūks, Saʿīd ʿAbd al-Fattāḥ ʿĀshūr and his many students produced (and continue to do so) a major corpus of texts and studies still too little consulted among Western scholars. Even so, the free play of historical research was undeniably constrained by political pressures that far exceeded the partisanship of the previous era, notably the internal security apparatus of Nasser's Egypt and Muhammad Reza Shah's Iran, the unpredictable violence of political life in Syria and Iraq, the intermittent military interventions in Turkey, and the taboos inspired by the Arab-Israeli conflict.

Since 1970. Several of the underlying trends established during the 1950s and 1960s have continued apace, in particular the burgeoning of universities and research institutes throughout the Middle East. In spite of chronic underfunding and a strong emphasis on scientific-technical training, this trend has led to an expansion of academic history. Particularly important, especially for the Ottoman period in Turkey and the Arab lands, has been a great improvement in the organization of archives and documentation centers of all kinds. (Unfortunately, Iran seems not to have benefited from such a process under either the shah or the Islamic

Republic.) Another trend, already discernible before 1970 but much stronger since, has been the growing number of historians from the Middle East who hold permanent academic appointments in Europe and the United States. Admittedly, most of these completed their graduate studies in Western universities, but even so they bring a perspective rooted in the cultures and historical experience of the Middle East.

The political climate in which historians must try to work has been variable. Egypt has witnessed an unsteady but substantial liberalization; in contrast, Syria and Iraq have moved from instability to tightly regimented dictatorships. Turkey has experienced a cycle of almost chaotic openness, severe military censorship, and, since the mid-1980s, a gradual easing; however, it remains illegal to criticize Atatürk, which inevitably constrains work on the crucial quarter-century from 1914 to 1938. In Iran, the Islamic Revolution has opened up certain possibilities for research while closing others; historians of a secularist orientation have obviously had to choose their topics and their words with great tact. In general, the Islamic movement everywhere has increasingly affected historical inquiry and writing, as it has intellectual life in general. For example, a trend seen in the Arab world during the early 1970s—a radical critique of the nature of early Islamic society and even of the soundness of the sources—has been silenced or at least driven underground. There has been no real progress in Arabic-language works on the life of Muḥammad since Haykal's famous biography was published more than sixty years ago.

In spite of such official and cultural pressures, however, many periods and topics seem to be politically and religiously neutral, in the sense that historians are relatively free to construct their accounts of them in accordance with their own purposes and outlooks rather than externally-dictated agendas. The middle periods of Islamic history (c. 900–1500) have long fallen in this category, with the partial exception of the Crusades and the figure of Saladin, and we can now add the early ʿAbbāsids and the Ottoman era, no longer a useful target for Arab nationalist polemics. The social and economic history of the late eighteenth and nineteenth centuries in particular has attracted a great deal of first-rate work during the past two decades. In premodern times, the early ʿAbbāsids, the Seljuks, and the Mamlūks have continued to be the subject of valuable and sometimes ground-breaking studies. To name individual scholars for the last two decades seems invidious, since there are now so many historians at work, and it is hardly possible as yet to identify those whose contributions will prove seminal or enduring. What can be said is that there now exists, in all the major countries of the Middle East, a substantial corps of professional academic historians writing chiefly in the languages of the area. In this respect, the history of the region is increasingly in the hands of its own scholars—the natural state of things, we might suppose, but one that was hardly the case for most of the nineteenth and twentieth centuries.

BIBLIOGRAPHY

The reader may consult the new edition of the *Encyclopaedia of Islam* for useful, sometimes essential entries, on many key figures. See the following entries: Aḥmad Amīn; Aḥmad Djewdet Pasha; ʿAlī Mubārak; al-Djabartī (ʿAbd al-Raḥmān); Gökalp (Ziya); İnal (Ibn al-Amīn); Kasrawī Tabrīzī (Aḥmad); Kemāl (Nāmiḳ); Köprülü (Mehmed Fuad); Kurd ʿAlī (Muḥammad); and Luṭfī Efendi (Aḥmad). Other important sources are listed below.

Afshari, M. Reza. "The Historians of the Constitutional Movement and the Making of the Iranian Populist Tradition." *International Journal of Middle East Studies* 25.3 (1993): 477–494. A sophisticated ideological analysis of modern Iranian historiography.

Amanat, Abbas. "The Study of History in Post-Revolutionary Iran: Nostalgia, or Historical Awareness?" *Iranian Studies* 22. 4 (1989): 3–18. Astute and well-documented critique.

Crabbs, Jack A., Jr. *The Writing of History in Nineteenth-Century Egypt: A Study in National Transformation*. Detroit, 1984. Careful and extremely useful study, although the author's knowledge of premodern historiography is a bit superficial.

Delanoue, Gilbert. *Moralistes et politiques musulmans dans l'Égypte du xixe siècle, 1798–1882*. 2 vols. Cairo, 1982. Indispensable for nineteenth-century intellectual life, with extended treatments of the careers and writings of al-Jabartī, al-Ṭahṭāwī, and ʿAlī Mubārak.

Ende, Werner. *Arabische Nation und Islamische Geschichte: Die Umayyaden im Urteil arabischer Autoren des 20. Jahrhunderts*. Beirut, 1977. Classic discussion of how twentieth-century ideological conflicts have shaped the debate over the significance of the Umayyad dynasty in Islamic and Arab history.

Hourani, Albert. *Arabic Thought in the Liberal Age, 1798–1939*. London, 1962. Contains only occasional remarks on historians per se, but irreplaceable for its account of modernizing social and political thought among modern Arab intellectuals.

Humphreys, R. Stephen. *Islamic History: A Framework for Inquiry*. Rev. ed. Princeton, 1991. Recent overview of premodern Islamic historiography, from its origins down to (but not including) the Ottoman and Ṣafavid periods, with an extensive bibliography. See as well "Historiography, Islamic," in *Dictionary of the Middle Ages*, vol. 6, pp. 249–255 (New York, 1982–).

Kuran, Ercüment. "Ottoman Historiography of the Tanzimat Period." In *Historians of the Middle East*, edited by Bernard Lewis and P. M. Holt, pp. 422–429. London, 1962. Terse but useful overview.

Leiser, Gary, trans. and ed. *A History of the Seljuks: İbrahim Kafesoğlu's Interpretation and the Resulting Controversy*. Carbondale, Ill.,

1988. Translation of a significant piece of modern Turkish scholarship, framed by a review of the bitter academic and political quarrel connected with its writing.

Lewis, Bernard, and P. M. Holt, eds. *Historians of the Middle East.* London, 1962. Obsolete but still valuable collection of essays on many aspects of Islamic historiography, both medieval and modern.

Mardin, Şerif. *The Genesis of Young Ottoman Thought: A Study in the Modernization of Turkish Political Ideas.* Princeton, 1962. Still the best account of Ottomanism and early constitutionalism in the mid-nineteenth-century Ottoman Empire.

Philipp, Thomas, *Ǧurǧī Zaydān: His Life and Thought.* Beirut and Wiesbaden, 1979. The best study of a writer who is important both for his own literary achievement and for the broader intellectual trends which he symbolizes.

Rafeq, Abdul-Karim. "Ottoman Historical Research in Syria since 1946." *Asian Research Trends: A Humanities and Social Sciences Review,* no. 2 (1992): 45–78. Careful survey that throws much light on ideological and methodological shifts among historians in Syria, Jordan, and Lebanon.

Reid, Donald Malcolm. *Cairo University and the Making of Modern Egypt.* Cambridge, 1990. Invaluable for understanding the institutional milieu in which the most important body of twentieth-century Arabic historiography has been produced.

Shayyāl, Jamāl al-Dīn al-. *A History of Egyptian Historiography in the Nineteenth Century.* Alexandria, 1962. Distinguished Egyptian historian's interpretation of the work of his immediate intellectual ancestors. See as well "Historiography in Egypt in the Nineteenth Century," in *Historians of the Middle East,* edited by Bernard Lewis and P. M. Holt, pp. 403–421 (London, 1962).

Sivan, Emmanuel. "Modern Arabic Historiography of the Crusades." *Asian and African Studies* 8.2 (1972): 109–149. Perceptive if somewhat chilly critique of Arabic historical writing since 1952. See as well "Arab Revisionist Historians," *Asian and African Studies* 12.3 (1978): 283–311.

Smith, Charles D. *Islam and the Search for Social Order in Modern Egypt: A Biography of Muhammad Husayn Haykal.* Albany, N.Y., 1983. Essential for understanding the political and intellectual climate of the interwar period in Egypt.

Strohmeier, Martin. *Seldschukische Geschichte und türkische Geschichtswissenschaft: Die Seldschuken im Urteil moderner türkischer Historiker.* Berlin, 1984. Fundamental for the evolution of Turkish historiography since World War I.

Wessels, Antonie. *A Modern Arabic Biography of Muḥammad: A Critical Study of Muḥammad Ḥusayn Haykal's Ḥayāt Muḥammad.* Leiden, 1972. Very useful introduction to the problems presented by this crucial work.

R. STEPHEN HUMPHREYS

ḤIZB. Occuring twice in the Qur'ān with positive connotations in the compound term *ḥizaballāh* (party of God), the term *ḥizb* denotes factions or factionalism in the Qur'ān, referring to a state of affairs that should be avoided. In modern usage, *ḥizb* refers to a political party in a clearly defined manner. This usage is the result of an attempt to find an Arabic word for a European phenomenon. In 1906, Faraḥ Anṭūn (1874–1922), the Lebanese intellectual who spent most of his life in Egypt and the United States, defined the term in his journal, *Al-jāmiʿah,* as an organized group that is at loggerheads with other organized groups because of differences in views and interests. Soon after, in 1907, two parties were formed in Egypt: the Ummah party (Ḥizb al-Ummah) and the National party (Ḥizb al-Waṭanī). These were primarily secular nationalist parties, although the latter had a tinge of Pan-Islamism.

There has been a reluctance to accept the concept of political parties in Islamic countries because of the divisiveness which it implies. The first organized group with a clear Islamic ideology—and regarded as the mother of almost all major Islamic organizations—established in Ismāʿīlīyah in 1928, was called by its founder, Ḥasan al-Bannā' (1906–1949), the Society of Muslim Brothers (Jamʿīyat al-Ikhwān al-Muslimūn) rather than *ḥizb* or political party. Most offshoots of the Egyptian Muslim Brothers in other Islamic countries also avoided the use of the term *ḥizb*. In Sudan and Syria the groups have called themselves the Muslim Brothers. In Lebanon a similar organization was named al-Jamāʿah al-Islāmīyah (The Islamic Group). In Tunisia the equivalent of the Muslim Brothers called themselves Ḥarakat al-Ittijāh al-Islāmī (Islamic Tendency Movement), and later the name was changed to Nahḍah (Renaissance). In Algeria the major organization is called Jabhat al-Inqādh al-Islāmī (Islamic Salvation Front). The recent offshoots of the Jamīʿah al-Islāmīyah in the Gaza Strip are Ḥamās, the Arabic acronym of Ḥarakat al-Muqāwamah al-Islāmīyah (Islamic Resistance Movement) and the Jihād al-Islāmī (Islamic Holy War), and they keep the same tradition by not using the term *ḥizb*. Similarly, in Pakistạn the leading Islamic organization is called Jamāʿat-i Islāmī (Islamic Assembly).

There has been an increase in the use of the term *ḥizb* in Islamic organizations. For instance, Ḥizb al-Taḥrīr al-Islāmī (Islamic Liberation Party) in Jordan, the Islamic organization Refâh Partisi (Welfare Party) in Turkey, the Sunnī Pashtun-based Ḥizb-i Islāmī (the Islamic Party) in Afghanistan, and Ḥizbullāh (Party of God), the Shīʿī militant organization in Lebanon, formed under the influence of the ruling Iranian clergymen. Furthermore, Islamic organizations have been pushed willy-nilly to partake in parliamentary elections. Some elections were free, as in Pakistan in 1993, in which the Jamāʿat-i Islāmī participated and accepted the results, and as in the free elections of 1993 in Jordan, where Jabhat al-Amal al-Islāmī (Islamic Action Front) participated. Other elections were basically not free, as in Egypt in 1984 and 1987, where the Muslim Brothers participated, and in Lebanon in 1992, where both the Sunnī Islamic Group and the Shīʿī Ḥizbullāh participated.

Although the Islamic political organizations have come a long way from Ḥasan al-Bannā's condemnation of *al-ḥizbīyah* (party politics), a strong ambivalence toward elections and competitive party politics still exists. Perhaps there is a greater acceptance of competition if parties or groups have a particular Islamic ideology, as has been the case in Iran since the revolution of 1979. The most prominent ideologue of Ḥizbullāh in Lebanon, Shaykh Muḥammad Ḥusayn Faḍlallāh, shows this intolerance toward non-Muslim and secular political parties, which by their nature do not subscribe to his Islamic ideology, by depicting them as the "parties of unbelief and atheism" ("aḥzāb al-kufr wa-lā-ilḥād").

Another reason why political parties in the Islamic countries were not particularly interested in competitive party politics is that most of them had come into being during the struggle for independence from colonial rule. It is not surprising that they tended to concentrate on the unity of the nation rather than on competition among various political organizations. For instance, the mass-based Wafd, which came to being in 1919, was not regarded by its leader Saʿd Zaghlūl (1857–1927) as a *ḥizb*. The name used by Zaghlūl and later by his successor Muṣṭafā Al-Naḥḥās (1879–1965) was the Egyptian Wafd (al-Wafd al-Miṣrī). This emphasis on the anticolonial struggle made the leaders of these movements shy away from the use of the term *ḥizb*, because it might have implied that the national movement was not all-inclusive in its support. Political organizations formed under the rule of Gamal Abdel Nasser (1918–1970) were called, for instance, al-Ittiḥād al-Qawmī (National Union), and al-Ittiḥād al-Ishtirākī al-ʿArabī (Arab Socialist Union), rather than political parties.

The role of predominantly non-Islamic and secular parties in Islamic countries was a manifestation of socioeconomic forces, and ethnic and sectarian interests have been very extensive indeed. There was a proliferation of political parties in an open and mostly free political system in Egypt from 1923 to 1952 and in Lebanon from 1943 to 1975. In Turkey, Sudan, and Pakistan, whenever the military is not in power, political parties have played a major role. The future role of political parties in the Islamic countries will undoubtedly be one of paramount importance, as attested by greater political awareness throughout the Islamic world. These developments show clearly that political parties have become an integral part of the political life of Muslims, whether the parties are in power, in opposition in democratic or quasi-democratic polities, in opposition in exile, or as underground parties trying to topple dictators.

[*Most of the political parties named above are the subject of independent entries.*]

BIBLIOGRAPHY

Deeb, Marius K. *Party Politics in Egypt: The Wafd and Its Rivals, 1919–1939*. London, 1979.

Deeb, Marius K. "Continuity in Modern Egyptian History: The Wafd and the Muslim Brothers." In *Problems of the Middle East in Historical Perspective: Essays in Honour of Albert Hourani*, edited by John P. Spagnolo, pp. 49–61. Reading, 1992.

Faḍlallāh, Muḥammad Ḥusayn. *Al-Islām wa-manṭiq al-qūwah*. 2d ed. Beirut, 1981.

Ḥamrūsh, Aḥmad. *Qiṣṣat Thawrat 23 Yūliyū*, vol. 4, *Shuhūd Thawrat Yūliyū*. Beirut, 1977.

Mitchell, Richard P. *The Society of the Muslim Brothers*. London, 1969.

MARIUS K. DEEB

ḤIZB AL-DAʿWAH AL-ISLĀMĪYAH.

One of the three most important activist Shīʿī organizations in opposition to Saddam Hussein's Baʿth regime in Iraq, and the oldest among them, is the Ḥizb al-Daʿwah al-Islāmīyah (Islamic Call Party). The others are the Supreme Council of the Islamic Revolution in Iraq, founded in Iran in November 1982, and the Organization of Islamic Action, founded in Karbala in the 1960s.

Political History and Program. The party (known in short form simply as the Daʿwah) was established in October 1957 in Najaf by the young and ingenious Shīʿī religious authority, Muḥammad Bāqir al-Ṣadr (born in 1933 in Kazimayn, Baghdad, and executed by the Baʿth in April 1980). Cofounders were a group of junior Shīʿī clergy, some of whom achieved great prominence in later years (chiefly Muḥammad Bāqir and Mahdī, the two sons of Iraq's then chief *mujtahid* Muḥsin al-Ḥakīm, as well as two lay intellectuals). The decision to found a political party (which al-Ṣadr, using a Qur'ānic expression, dubbed Ḥizb Allāh, "Party of God"), whose sole purpose would be to call the people of Iraq back to Islam, was the result of the young clergy's realization that Islam and, in particular, Shīʿī Islam in Iraq was on the decline. Owing to a number of political, social, and economic developments under the monarchy, the number of students of religion in the two holy cities of Najaf and Karbala had declined steeply and many young Shīʿīs were estranged from religion and, markedly so, from the religious establishment. Under the republican regime of ʿAbd al-Karīm Qāsim, (14 July 1958–8 February 1963), followed by the short-lived Baʿth regime of 1963 and that of the ʿArif brothers, ʿAbd al-Salām and ʿAbd al-Raḥmān (18 November 1963–17 July 1968), relations between the Shīʿī establishment of the holy cities and the government were tense, but both sides refrained from drastic action. The regimes tolerated de facto Shīʿī autonomy in the religious educational institutions *(al-ḥawzāt al-ʿilmīyah)* of Najaf and Karbala, and the latter, for their part, kept their protest against the secularizing Sunnī ruling elites within strict limits. These circumstances permitted the Daʿwah to operate almost without restriction, not only in Najaf but also in Baghdad. (Indeed, the main opposition to its activity came, in those days, from the more conservative circles within the religious university of Najaf, who regarded activity along modern party lines as deviation from tradition. As a result, so as not to compromise his position as a *mujtahid,* Ṣadr was eventually forced to sever his organizational ties with the party.) The Daʿwah's main activity in Baghdad was aimed to win over young lay Shīʿī intellectuals (a few Sunnīs joined the party as well, but they were a small minority), and thus it concentrated its main effort among the students of Baghdad University and young professionals, as well as among high school students. Almost all the recruiting activity within these circles was conducted by lay university students and graduates.

At the same time, the party tried to expand its influence among the Shīʿī poor in the al-Thawrah slum (later Saddam City) on the outskirts of Baghdad, but this was done, mainly, through party members who were junior clergy. Until the Baʿth came to power (and, indeed, even two or three years afterward) this activity was carried out almost openly, with little or no official interference. It involved public prayers, gatherings to celebrate Islamic festivals, Islamic placards, and, for the hard core of activists, classes led by al-Ṣadr and others in Qur'ān interpretation and some advanced Islamic studies. Beginning in the late 1960s, the Daʿwah expanded its activities to other parts of the Shīʿī world, notably to Lebanon. According to an interview with a senior member in the 1960s, to disguise its activity somewhat, the Daʿwah also called itself the Fatimid Party (al-Ḥizb al-Fāṭimī) after Fāṭimah al-Zahrā', ʿAlī's wife and the Prophet's daughter.

In the second half of 1969, the Baʿth regime, when trying to eliminate the Shīʿī educational autonomy, cracked down in an unprecedented way on the *ḥawzāt* of Najaf and Karbala. This marked the beginning of a rapid deterioration of relations between the two establishments. The Daʿwah's activities, too, were severely restricted, and, eventually, it was forced to go underground. This, as well as its own theory of action that dictated a leap into political activity after a few years of purely educational work, drove the party to become progressively more militant. In 1970, the party's first member was martyred, and in 1974 the regime executed five more senior members. As reported by its own sources, in February 1977 the party was deeply involved in organizing the vast antigovernment demonstrations that occurred during a mass pilgrimage to Karbala to commemorate the anniversary of the fortieth day after the martyrdom of Imam Ḥusayn. But the Daʿwah's main political and guerrilla thrust occurred soon thereafter under the influence of Ayatollah Ruhollah Khomeini's February 1979 takeover in Iran. The party then engaged in organizing mass Shīʿī anti-Baʿth demonstrations and armed attacks against Baʿth party and internal security centers, all in an attempt to topple the regime and replace it with an Iranian-style Islamic republic. As a result of the regime's crackdown, hundreds of party members (including al-Ṣadr who, by then, no longer belonged officially to the party, but who remained its intellectual mentor) were executed, a few thousand members and supporters were arrested, and most other members fled the country.

Throughout the Iraq-Iran War (1980–1988) the Daʿwah's activity was fourfold: it acted inside Iraq, sporadically hitting at Baʿth targets; it had a small, regular unit that fought on Iran's side against Iraq; it carried out terrorist activities against pro-Iraqi regimes in the Middle East, chiefly in Kuwait, and against Western targets; and it endeavored to incorporate new members and supporters from among the Iraqi Shīʿī expatriates in the West and in Iran. At the end of the war, in order to improve its image in the West, the party stopped all armed activities outside of Iraq. During the Kuwait crisis (August 1990–March 1991) and following it, the party initiated a number of overtures toward Western governments, notably the United States and Britain, as well as toward anti-Baʿthist, pro-Western Arab regimes such as Saudi Arabia, with which they were at loggerheads during the Iraq-Iran War. Another aspect of their growing pragmatism was a claim, voiced by some of the party's spokesmen (but clearly not by all), to be in favor of Western-style liberal parliamentary democracy. As those spokesmen put it, if the majority in post-Saddam Iraq were to reject their notion of an Islamic republic, the party would accept the majority verdict. It then would continue its educational work designed to persuade the people of the need for such an Islamic rule. It is far too early to judge whether this claim to democracy represents a genuine change of heart.

In the era after the Iraq-Iran war some differences within the party between those whose main activity was in Iran and those who lived and worked in the West have been exposed. One major difference concerned the degree to which the party ought to be independent of Iranian dictates, now that the interest of the Iraqi opposition in continuing the struggle and that of the Iranian state in increasing stability were incompatible. Another difference, albeit a less important one, was over the degree of clarity with which the party should express its commitment to democracy. Those members operating in Iran (led by the party's spokesman Shaykh Muḥammad Mahdī al-Āṣafī) have been rather vague about democracy and have been receptive to Iranian policy dictates, whereas some party members who live in the West have inclined toward more independence and democracy. During the Kuwait crisis, the party suffered from at least one split. The new group, calling itself the Cadres of the Iraqi Islamic Daʿwah Party (Kawādir Ḥizb al-Daʿwah al-Islāmīyah al-ʿIrāqī), emphasizes its Iraqi identity and "the independence of the Islamic Iraqi decision-making" of Iranian policy. In addition, it claims that, for more than a decade, the Daʿwah has failed to provide a plan of action, and that an urgent need for such a plan exists. It is typical, however, of this closely knit and highly ideological movement that the two factions restrain their argument and refrain from the acrimonious accusations so widespread in political disputes in the Middle East.

The contribution of Daʿwah activists to the anti-Baʿthist Shīʿī *intifāḍah* or uprising of March 1991 is unclear. According to party members' reports, they were active in encouraging the masses to revolt, but it is clear that most of the uprising was spontaneous. Moreover, there is little doubt that a rival Shīʿī opposition organization, the Tehran-based Supreme Council of the Islamic Revolution in Iraq, was more prominent, sending into Iraq many hundreds of its Iran-based membership. Whatever the case, the regime's crackdown that followed weakened the party organization inside Iraq: members who exposed themselves during the revolt were later jailed or executed.

Organization. Owing to the requirements of its underground activity, the precise organizational structure of the party is a well-guarded secret. However, its general outlines may still be delineated. At the top of what is described as "a pyramidal structure" stands a collective body of around ten. Its first name was Majlis al-Fuqahā' (Council of Jurists); in later years it also included a few laymen, though they are still a small minority. In its contemporary incarnation it is reported as being called al-Qiyādah al-ʿĀmmah (General Leadership). One level lower is the Council of Leadership (Majlis al-Qiyādah) that consists of a few scores of activists. Its more contemporary name is either the General Congress (al-Mu'tamar al-ʿĀmm), or the Political Bureau (al-Maktab al-Siyāsī). This body, which consists mostly of lay intellectuals who represent their respective territorial branches, directs the day-to-day activity of the party branches. Under it one finds an unknown number of lower levels, ending with the basic unit, the Family (al-Usrah) or the Ring (al-Ḥalaqah). Inside Iraq, to minimize the danger of exposure, an ordinary member knows only other members of his own basic unit, and only vertical contacts between units are maintained. This structure is strongly influenced by the organizational structures of the Communist and Baʿth parties. Al-Ṣadr was the first to acknowledge that any organizational form was legitimate if it could spread "the call" more efficiently, and as long as it was not forbidden by the *sharīʿah*. "The Prophet," he explained, "had he lived in our age, would have used . . . the modern and suitable means of communications and spreading of the message." In Europe, where there is no danger of suppression, the lowest echelon is the local branch, apparently combining all party members in a town.

Ecumenism versus Particularism. On the face of it, the position of the Daʿwah publications is ecumenical. The party calls for the establishment of a full-fledged Islamic regime in Iraq that would apply the rules of the *sharīʿah* to every walk of life, regardless of differences between Sunnī and Shīʿī Islam (and, indeed, the differences between them in terms of substantive law are very small). A more careful reading, however, reveals strong Shīʿī undertones; for example, there are occasional inferences that once Saddam Hussein and his Baʿth regime are toppled, Shiism would become the dominant power in Iraq's political life. Shīʿī youth are called upon to be ready to sacrifice themselves, as did Imam Ḥusayn and most other Shīʿī imams. Although such appeals make it difficult for Sunnīs to join the movement, this has not prevented the Daʿwah from establishing cordial relations with the main (Sunnī) Kurdish opposition organizations. Unsurprisingly, however, the party has somewhat uneasy relations with the other main Shīʿī opposition groups, for they are all competing for the allegiance of the Iraqi Shīʿī expatriates in Iran and Europe.

The party's ideas were first expressed by al-Ṣadr in a magazine, *Al-aḍwā'* (The Lights), issued by an activist group of *ʿulamā'* in Najaf in the early 1960s. The party's own first magazine was called *Ṣawt al-daʿwah* (Voice of the Daʿwah), and it, too, came out in Najaf in the mid- and late 1960s. During most of the 1980s and the early 1990s, its main publications have been a weekly issued in Tehran, *Al-jihād*, and another issued in London, *Ṣawt al-ʿIrāq* (Voice of Iraq). The cadres issue a weekly magazine called *Fajr al-ʿIrāq* (Iraq's Dawn).

[*See also* Iraq; Shīʿī Islam, *article on* Modern Shīʿī Thought; *and the biography of Ṣadr.*]

BIBLIOGRAPHY

Baram, Amatzia. "Two Roads to Revolutionary Shiʿi Fundamentalism Iraq: Hizb al-Daʿwa al-Islamiyya and the Supreme Council of the Islamic Revolution of Iraq." In *Accounting for Fundamentalisms: The Dynamic Character of Movements*, edited by Martin E. Marty and R. Scott Appleby, pp. 531–586. Chicago, 1994.

AMATZIA BARAM

ḤIZB AL-NAHḌAH. Formerly called al-Ittijāh al-Islāmī (Mouvement de la Tendance Islamique, abbreviated MTI), the political movement that in 1988 adopted the name Ḥizb al-Nahḍah (Renaissance Party) is the principal representative of Islamist thought and political expression in contemporary Tunisia. The movement's relations with the government have from the outset been contentious, but it has survived successive waves of repression. It is thought to have the diffuse support of as much as one-third of the Tunisian population.

The contemporary Islamist movement traces its roots to the Qur'ānic Preservation Society (QPS), a cultural association founded in 1970 in reaction to modernist reforms promulgated in the 1960s, and to the Pakistan-based Daʿwah (The Call), which spread across the Maghrib in the early 1970s "calling" Muslims to return to the faith. Out of this group emerged a nexus of activists who were satisfied with neither the cultural critique of the QPS nor the more personal approach of the Daʿwah, but who focused rather on the role of Islam in society and openly preached reform *(tajdīd)*. As these sentiments sorted themselves out in the 1970s, young men with beards and women in the chador-like *ḥijāb* (veil) became a common sight in Tunis and other cities. By 1979 one group identifying itself as "progressive Islamists" and concentrating on the renewal of Islamic thought *(ijtihād)* had split off to pursue essentially intellectual matters. The energies of those who sought political action coalesced around Rashid Ghannoushi (Rāshid al-Ghannūshī) and Abdelfatah Mourou. Ghannoushi had recently returned from Syria, and Mourou, a jurist, had been studying at the Zaytunāh Mosque in Tunis. At a press conference in 1981 they announced the formation of the MTI, which officially called for the reconstruction of economic life on a more equitable basis, the end of single-party politics, and a return to the "fundamental principles of Islam" through a purging of what was viewed as well-entrenched "social decadence." Further, MTI representatives announced that they were seeking recognition as a political party according to guidelines established by the government in the preceding autumn. That request was denied, and less than two months later most of the MTI's leaders were imprisoned.

Despite this repression—or perhaps because of it—the MTI survived and even gained strength in the early 1980s. The MTI found allies in other Tunisian opposition forces, including the Movement of Democratic Socialists and the new Tunisian League of Human Rights, and its discourse took on egalitarian and republican overtones. Under pressure, the Tunisian government released MTI leaders in 1984, but its basic stance remained unchanged. The MTI's second bid for legal recognition was rejected in 1985, and, in a symbolic gesture, the government outlawed the *ḥijāb*. As the MTI's condemnatory rhetoric once again gathered steam, in spring 1987 the government intensified its efforts to eradicate the movement, arresting more than three thousand of its alleged supporters. The party's leaders were tried en masse before the State Security Court in August for ill-defined capital crimes, and several were sentenced to death in absentia.

The specter of politically motivated executions and uncontrollable social response created a backdrop for the coup instigated by Prime Minister Zine el Abidine Ben Ali a few months later. Islamists were the primary beneficiaries of the liberalizing policies introduced by the new regime. Prisons were emptied, a multiparty system was embraced, and the franchise was restored to those who had previously been imprisoned. The atmosphere of détente raised hopes among Islamists that they would be allowed to participate in the political system; to comply with new rules prohibiting parties from capitalizing on religious sentiments, the MTI changed its name.

The renamed Ḥizb al-Nahḍah reached a turning point in relations with the new regime in April 1989. Without legal recognition, Islamists were prevented from participating openly in Tunisia's first contested legislative elections, but the independent slates they fielded nevertheless garnered 14 percent of the popular vote (30 percent in certain Tunis suburbs) and sent shock waves through the government. Al-Nahḍah's pending request for recognition was denied, educational reforms aimed at curtailing Islamist influence were implemented, and the movement's leaders were taken in for questioning. Tensions were exacerbated by the Gulf War, which fanned flames of anti-Western sentiment. The death of one Islamist student, shot by government militia during a demonstration, sparked protests that inspired a new wave of arrests and further restrictions. An assault by Islamists on an office of the ruling Democratic Constitutional Rally (RCD) in February 1991, which killed one guard and injured another, heightened the political confrontation. Al-Nahḍah's formal responsibility for that attack was never made clear, but together with the discovery in subsequent months of two alleged plots to overthrow the government, the event fueled a campaign of repression that resulted in more than eight thousand arrests. In 1992, 279 al-Naḥdah members were tried before military tribunals; leaders in the government's custody were sentenced to life in prison.

It is unclear how much al-Nahḍah has been affected by the most recent and far-reaching efforts to stifle it. Its leadership has changed. In 1993 Rashid Ghannoushi was still formally recognized as the head of al-Nahḍah (although since 1989 he had been in self-imposed exile), but Mourou formally dissociated himself from the unauthorized party in 1991 following the attack on the RCD office. A new cadre of leaders emerged, and the government claimed to have uncovered a covert military wing. Meanwhile, *El fajr,* the al-Nahḍah publication that was to have illuminated its thought, has been silenced.

Concerted pressures in the early 1990s made al-Nahḍah less visible; in particular, many young women ceased to wear the symbolic *ḥijāb*. There has been evidence all the same that the Islamist movement continues to enjoy popular support—perhaps more than ever in the wake of disappointment with the Ben Ali government. A membership once described as young and chiefly comprised of students has now aged, without obvious attrition. Students, particularly those in religious and technical institutes, continue to supply recruits, but the Islamist message of social and political resistance and reform resonates in the humanities and social sciences as well. The movement has held particular appeal for sectors of society that have felt relatively disenfranchised by the modernist regime, and economic pressures in recent years have only increased those sentiments. Parents and others of an older generation are now commonly identified as sympathizers, and the movement is supported from abroad by a broad network of Tunisian students. It remains the most significant opposition group in contemporary Tunisia.

[*See also* Tunisia *and the biography of Ghannūshī.*]

BIBLIOGRAPHY

Centre National de Recherches Scientifiques. *Annuaire de l'Afrique du Nord, 1979*. Paris, 1981. Yearbook devoted to the special topic of Islam in the Maghrib, containing several articles on Tunisia.

Waltz, Susan. "Islamist Appeal in Tunisia." *Middle East Journal* 40 (Autumn 1986): 651–670.

Zartman, I. William, ed. *Tunisia: The Political Economy of Reform*. Boulder, 1991. Contains several insightful articles on Islam in Tunisia.

SUSAN WALTZ

ḤIZB AL-TAḤRĪR AL-ISLĀMĪ. Established in Jerusalem in 1953 by Taqī al-Dīn al-Nabhānī (1909–1977), an al-Azhar graduate and religious school teacher and judge from Ijzim in northern Palestine, and a group of colleagues who had separated from the Muslim Brotherhood, Ḥizb al-Taḥrīr al-Islāmī (the Islamic Liberation Party) declared itself to be a political party with Islam as its ideology and the revival of the Islamic nation—purged of the vestiges of colonialism and restored to an Islamic way of life—as its goal. The party sought to achieve this goal by creating a single Islamic state, erected on the ruins of existing regimes, which would implement Islam and export it throughout the world. Although the party never obtained official sanction, it enjoyed modest successes in Jordan and the West Bank until the suppression of the opposition in 1957. It indoctrinated recruits; disseminated its ideas through leaflets, lectures, and sermons; and contested parliamentary elections. The party early established branches in Syria, Lebanon, Kuwait, and Iraq. Although the ascendancy of Nasserism hindered its effort to gain popular support the early 1960s witnessed its growing confidence, which culminated in two attempts at a coup d'état in Amman in 1968 and 1969, each coordinated with simultaneous arrangements in Damascus and Baghdad. Other such plots emerged in Baghdad (1972), Cairo (1974), and Damascus (1976).

In recent years the party has construed the Islamic resurgence as evidence of society's reception of its ideas. Since the Gulf Crisis of 1990–1991 its optimism has grown, based on the beliefs that the insincerity of political movements and regimes in the region has been exposed and public opinion now appreciates the correctness of the party's understanding of Islam and its radical approach to change. Rigid adherence to its ideology makes it unwilling to cooperate with other Islamic groups, and its confrontational approach has brought it universal proscription. In spite of the isolation and marginalization consequent upon this, its members are currently active in Jordan, Syria, the Occupied Territories, Iraq, Lebanon, North Africa (especially Tunisia), Saudi Arabia, the United Arab Emirates, Kuwait, Sudan, Turkey, Pakistan, Malaysia, Indonesia, and parts of Europe, including Britain, France, Germany, Romania, and Yugoslavia. In the Muslim world it enjoys greater freedom in countries that it does not deem to possess the necessary economic, military, and human resources to support a viable new Islamic state, and therefore does not target directly, like Jordan and Kuwait.

Activities are coordinated and prioritized throughout the Arab-Islamic region, reflecting the party's well-organized, highly-disciplined, and overwhelmingly centralized structure. Membership is typical of modern mass parties, but the Ḥizb al-Taḥrīr exhibits totalitarian features, including a preoccupation with maintaining ideological homogeneity: to this end the leadership "adopts" ideological material, which becomes binding on members. Secondary school and university students and recent graduates constitute a significant proportion of new members. Conceptions of authority and leadership within the party derive from the Islamic tradition: executive power and authority are vested in a specific individual at each level of organization, but consultation (*shūrā*) also operates. In addition, the influence of quasi-fascist ideas is discernible.

Alongside its avowedly political nature, the party is distinguished by a consistent system of thought and a coherent political program. Central to the former is an attempt to construe Islam as an ideology superior to socialism and capitalism. This ideology comprises two parts: a rational doctrine that shapes Muslim thought and conduct and a system for ordering all aspects of Muslim life. The latter, which issues from the doctrine, is the *sharīʿah*. The party urges Muslims to practice *ijtihād* in its ongoing elaboration. It excludes all forms of consensus (*ijmāʿ*), except that of the Prophet's companions, as a source of jurisprudence and rejects the rational effective cause (*ʿillah*) as a basis for analogical deduction. It also rejects the principles of general interest (*al-maṣlaḥah al-mursalah*), applying discretion in deriving legal rules (*al-istiḥsān*) and in acquiring good and repelling evil (*jalb al-maṣāliḥ; darʿ al-mafāsid*). This stance effectively minimizes the role of reason in juridic elaboration and suspends mechanisms designed to serve the community's immediate interests and to take account of its changing circumstances.

The party considers the implementation of the *sharīʿah* as the lynchpin in the restoration of an Islamic way of life and the state as a *sine qua non* for achieving this aim. It upholds the classical model of the caliphate as the only authentic form of Islamic government, which it seeks to restore with its traditional accompanying institutions. To this end it has drafted a constitution detailing the political, economic, and social systems of the proposed state. This document vests executive and legislative powers in an elected caliph, in whom most functions of state are centralized. Citizens are encouraged to exercise their right to call the state to account through a political opposition based on the Islamic ideology and expressed through a system of party plurality. Although involvement in politics is construed as a collective religious duty (*farḍ al-kifāyah*), *shūrā* is not held to be a pillar of Islamic government. The party emphasizes the distinction between *shūrā* and democracy and holds that democracy is not compatible with Islam. It also denounces nationalism as a creation of unbelief.

The party's program evidences an attempt to employ the constructs of traditional Islamic discourse to legitimize adopting modes of political organization and mobilization characteristic of the emergent modern, secular political parties contemporary with it in the Arab East. The heart of this program is the endeavor to replace erroneous concepts, prevalent in Muslim societies due to both their decline and the legacies of colonialism, with the party ideology. The objective is to create an extensive fifth column that will support the revolutionary state, which is to be established through a coup d'état executed by the party and selected power groups that have been won over to its cause. It also aims to politicize the Islamic *ummah*, and to expose conspiracies hatched against it by the West. Its perceived role is confined to political and intellectual spheres: it expressly refuses to involve itself in social, religious, or educational projects.

The party's major publications include *Al-takattul al-ḥizbī* (The Party Formation), *Al-shakhsīyah al-Islāmīyah* (The Islamic Way of Life), *Niẓām al-Islām* (The Islamic Order), *Mafāhīm ḥizb al-taḥrīr* (Concepts of the Islamic Liberation Party), *Niẓām al-ḥukm fī al-Islām* (The System of Government in Islam), *Naẓarāt siyāsīyah li-Ḥizb al-Taḥrīr* (Political Reflections of the Islamic Liberation Party), and *Kayfa hudimat al-khilāfah* (How the Caliphate was Destroyed).

[*See also* Jordan.]

BIBLIOGRAPHY

Works on Ḥizb al-Taḥrīr al-Islāmī

Amīn, Ṣādiq. *Al-daʿwah al-Islāmīyah: Farīḍah Sharʿīyah wa Ḍarūrah Basharīyah.* N.p., 1982. Crude Muslim Brotherhood polemics against the party's platform and program. See pages 75–102.

Cohen, Amnon. *Political Parties in the West Bank under the Jordanian Regime, 1949–1967.* Rev. ed. Ithaca, N.Y., and London, 1982. Overview of the party in the West Bank, with greater emphasis on the period 1952–1957, based predominantly on reports of the Jordanian Security Service Archive (pp. 209–229). Provides little comment or analysis, and discussion of the party's ideology is limited. See, as well, Cohen's "Political Parties in the West Bank under the Hashemite Regime," in *Palestinian Arab Politics,* edited by Ma'oz Moshe, pp. 21–49 (Jerusalem, 1975).

Khairallah, Shereen. "The Islamic Liberation Party: Search for a Lost Ideal." In *Vision and Revision in Arab Society,* pp. 87–95. CEMAM Reports, vol. 2. Beirut, 1975. Incisive review, with citations, of *Naẓarāt siyāsīyah li-Ḥizb al-Taḥrīr* (n.p., 1972).

Samārah, Iḥsān ʿAbd al-Munʿim. *Mafhūm al-ʿadālah al-ijtimāʿīyah fī al-fikr al-Islāmī al-muʿāṣir.* Jerusalem, 1987. Apologetic treatment, including a biography of Taqī al-Dīn al-Nabhānī and a thorough discussion of aspects of the party's thought, concentrating on its rejection of the concept of social justice. See pages 140–163, 223–238.

Tawbah, Ghāzī al-. *Al-fikr al-Islāmī al-muʿāṣir: Dirāsah wa-taqwīm.* Beirut, 1969. Relatively sophisticated polemics against the party's ideology, with citations from a range of its publications. Misrepresentations of its concepts are not uncommon. See pages 285–311.

Works by Ḥizb al-Taḥrīr al-Islāmī

Ḥizb al-Taḥrīr. N.p., 1985. Comprehensive introduction to the party: includes a statement of its objectives and methods and a survey of concepts fundamental to its thought.

Mafāhīm siyāsīyah li-Ḥizb al-Taḥrīr. N.p., 1969. Detailed statement of the party's analysis of international politics.

Nabhānī, Taqī al-Dīn al-. *Niẓām al-ḥukm fī al-Islām.* Jerusalem, 1953. Detailed exposition of the caliphal system of government proposed by the party.

Nabhānī, Taqī al-Dīn al-. *Niẓām al-Islām.* Jerusalem, 1953. Contains the party's draft constitution for an islamic state (revised 1979).

Nabhānī, Taqī al-Dīn al-. *Al-shakhsīyah al-Islāmīyah.* Jerusalem, 1953. Volume 3 of this three-part work is an elaborate exposition of the party's views concerning the sources and mechanisms of jurisprudence.

Nabhānī, Taqī al-Dīn al-. *Al-takattul al-ḥizbī.* Jerusalem, 1953. Inspired discussion of the party's conception of revival and the method for engineering it. Includes a critique of the attempts of earlier and contemporary political movements in the Arab East.

SUHA TAJI-FAROUKI

ḤIZB-I ISLĀMĪ AFGHĀNISTĀN. Two political parties that from 1978 until 1992 fought against the Marxist government of Afghanistan share the name Ḥizb-i Islāmī Afghānistān. The better known and more influential of these parties is headed by Gulbuddin Hekmatyar and the other by Maulavi Yunus Khales. Both leaders are Pushtuns (Hekmatyar from northern Kunduz Province, and Khales from eastern Ningrahar Province), and their parties have their strongest bases of support in Pushtun regions of the country.

The origins of Ḥizb-i Islāmī can be traced to the efforts of a group of students at Kabul University who formed the Organization of Muslim Youth (Sāzmān-i Javānān-i Musulmān) in 1969. Initially an informal study group that was introduced to modern Islamic political ideology (particularly that of Sayyid Quṭb and the Ikhwān al-Muslimūn, (or Muslim Brotherhood) by professors who had studied in Egypt, the Muslim Youth began active political organizing and recruitment in response to the increasingly strident efforts of Marxist parties to expand their base within the student population during the early 1970s. The Muslim Youth was also concerned with the rapid secularization of Afghan society and the pro-Soviet direction of government policy, and its leaders railed against perceived corruption within the royal family and the traditional *ʿulamā'*. In its first years the Muslim Youth Organization was primarily involved in campus politics, but a series of violent confrontations between Muslim and Marxist students led to the first arrests of Muslim Youth leaders in 1972.

In response to the July 1973 coup d'état of Muḥammad Da'ūd, an avowed leftist, the Muslim Youth joined forces with other covert Muslim political parties to overthrow the new government. These efforts were unsuccessful, however, and led to further arrests and the flight of many of the top Muslim Youth leaders to Pakistan, where they continued their efforts to overthrow the Afghan government. In July 1975 guerrillas associated with the Organization of Muslim Youth initiated an operation intended to combine a military coup d'état in Kabul with rural insurrections in various provinces. The military coup never materialized, however, and the uprisings were unsuccessful, in large part because of the absence of popular support.

The failure of this plan was a major blow to the party; several hundred of its most enterprising members were captured and executed. It also created an enduring rift between the two principal leaders who survived the attack—Gulbuddin Hekmatyar, who advocated the planned uprisings but did not personally participate, and Burhānuddīn Rabbānī, a former professor at Kabul University, who opposed the plan as premature. From this time on, Hekmatyar's faction of the movement, which became known as Ḥizb-i Islāmī, and Rabbānī's group, known as Jamʿīyat-i Islāmī, have been engaged in often violent competition for leadership of the Islamic resistance against leftist domination in Afghanistan. Following the April Revolution of 1978, other Muslim parties also set up headquarters in Pakistan, and Ḥizb-i Islāmī itself split into two parties, one dominated by Hekmatyar and the other by Maulavi Yunus Khales. The latter has generally been more moderate in its ideology and tactics and more conciliatory in its relations with other parties.

In this milieu of competing factions, the claim of Hekmatyar's Ḥizb-i Islāmī party to authority was always somewhat uncertain; its principal leaders were students before the war, mostly in secular disciplines such as engineering, and consequently had no traditional religious authority or status to legitimate their claim to leadership. Hekmatyar's party has responded to this situation by emphasizing its early involvement in efforts to overthrow the government and the many student members it sacrificed to the cause during the 1970s, when the majority of traditional religious leaders remained apolitical. Because it was the first to declare *jihād*, Ḥizb-i Islāmī claimed the right to lead the Islamic movement against the Marxist government; in pursuit of that right, it has gained a reputation as the most authoritarian of the parties in terms of its organization and party discipline. It is also considered particularly ruthless in its suppression of dissent, and it has been the focus of criticism for its frequent conflicts with other parties and the attacks made by local Ḥizb-i Islāmī commanders against other fronts.

In ideological terms, Ḥizb-i Islāmī stands apart from other parties because of its combination of scriptural fundamentalism and revolutionary practice. While the party does not disavow the Ḥanafī school of jurisprudence that has long held sway in Afghanistan, it advocates adherence to the Qur'ān and *sunnah* as the principal foundations of law, over and above the Ḥanafī traditions that traditional *ʿulamā'* have long monopolized. Another ideological pillar of Ḥizb-i Islāmī concerns the role of the party itself. According to party doctrine, it is the only authentic Islamic party and the one vehicle through which a truly Islamic society can be realized in Afghanistan. As such, it is the obligation of every Muslim to join Ḥizb-i Islāmī and to summon others to the proper practice of the faith. Those who refuse to join Ḥizb-i Islāmī or who join other parties are suspect, as are those who join but do not exhibit absolute loyalty and obedience to the party leadership.

Hekmatyar's party tended to be somewhat isolated from other parties during the thirteen years of the resistance, but it was more successful than its rivals in gaining international backing from a variety of countries. Pakistan, Iran, and other Islamic states tendered financial, logistical, and military support to Ḥizb-i Islāmī. The party has also been the major beneficiary of American aid, despite the fact that Hekmatyar has been a frequent critic of the United States and has tended to back Iran and other radical Middle Eastern regimes against American policies and interests.

Following the collapse of the Soviet occupation of Afghanistan, Ḥizb-i Islāmī's foreign assistance declined, and the party has been increasingly isolated both domestically and internationally. This isolation culminated in May 1992 when an Islamically oriented coalition government was established from which Ḥizb-i Islāmī was initially excluded. Although overtures have been made between Ḥizb-i Islāmī and the other parties, it is uncertain whether it will ultimately be welcome by other Islamic leaders, given its radical ideology and history of intolerance toward other groups.

[*See also* Afghanistan *and the biography of Hekmatyar*.]

BIBLIOGRAPHY

Edwards, David B. "Summoning Muslims: Print, Politics, and Religious Ideology in Afghanistan." *Journal of Asian Studies* 52.3 (1993): 609–628.

Naby, Eden. "The Changing Role of Islam as a Unifying Force in Afghanistan." In *The State, Religion, and Ethnic Politics: Afghanistan, Iran, and Pakistan,* edited by Ali Banuazizi and Myron Weiner, pp. 124–154. Syracuse, N.Y., 1986.

Roy, Olivier. *Islam and Resistance in Afghanistan*. Cambridge, 1986.

Shahrani, M. Nazif, and Robert Canfield, eds. *Revolutions and Rebellions in Afghanistan: Anthropological Perspectives*. Berkeley, 1984.

DAVID B. EDWARDS

ḤIZBULLĀH. [*This entry comprises articles focusing on Iran and on Lebanon, the two countries where groups naming themselves as* Ḥizbullāh *have been active in the late decades of the twentieth century.*]

Ḥizbullāh in Iran

The Qur'ānic term *ḥizb Allāh* (mentioned in surahs 5 and 58) refers to the body of Muslim believers who are promised triumph over *ḥizb al-Shayṭān* (the Devil's party). Thirteen centuries later, the term was reemployed by Iranian Shīʿī faithful who described their amorphous political organization as "the Party of God" and claimed to emulate the teachings of Ayatollah Ruhollah al-Musavi Khomeini. The Ḥizbullāh philosophy was summed up nicely in its slogan: "Only one party, the Party of Allāh; only one leader, Ruhollah."

The lineage of Ḥizbullāh in Iran can be traced back to a few extreme right-wing organizations, such as the Fidā'īyān-i Islām, which were active in the 1940s and 1950s. Like their predecessors, Ḥizbullāh faithful have adhered to a politicized interpretation of Islam and have not shied away from using violent means to achieve their goals. They entered the Iranian political scene during the 1978–1979 revolutionary upheaval of Iran. Recruited mainly from the ranks of the urban poor, the *bāzārīs*, and the lumpenproletariat, the Ḥizbullāhis played an important role in organizing demonstrations and strikes that led to the downfall of the Pahlavi regime. Following the victory of the revolution, they served as the unofficial watchdogs and storm troopers of the clerically dominated Islamic Republican Party (established in 1979 and dissolved in 1987). Considering its amorphous nature and nonofficial status, there is no way one can correctly estimate Ḥizbullāh's numerical strength. However, the fact remains that along with such other (para)military-intelligence apparatuses as the Sipāh-i Pasdarān-i Inqilāb-i Islāmī (Revolutionary Guards), *komitehs* (revolutionary committees), and SAVAMA (the intelligence service), Ḥizbullāh played a crucial role in the consolidation of the new regime.

Often led by the firebrand Ḥujjāt al-Islām Hādī Ghaffārī, the Ḥizbullāhis were known to employ clubs, chains, knives, and guns to disrupt the rallies of opposition parties, beat their members, and ransack their offices. The Ḥizbullāhi ruffians, nicknamed by the opposition as "*chumaqdārs*" (club wielders), were instrumental in the undoing of President Abol-Hasan Bani Sadr, the closing of the universities, the enforcement of veiling, the suppression of the press, and cowing people into silence. In addition, the Ḥizbullāh provided an inexhaustible pool of faithful warriors who enlisted for the war with Iraq. The recruitment of many of these veterans by such organizations as the Basīj (youth volunteers), Jihād-i Sāzāndigī (Reconstruction Crusade), and Pasdarān has so far prevented the actual establishment of a formal party called Ḥizbullāh. Quite to the contrary, some Ḥizbullāhi squads have now been transformed into the private militias of powerful clerics and have even set on each other's benefactors.

The Iranian Ḥizbullāh is reported to have certain transnational links with like-minded groups in the region, in particular with its namesake in Lebanon. The Lebanese Ḥizbullāh was organized, trained, and financed by the Iranian Pasdarāns who were dispatched to Lebanon in 1982. The two groups share certain characteristics, such as a militant interpretation of Shīʿī doctrines, adoration for Ayatollah Khomeini, anti-Zionism, suspicion of Western governments, and propensity to use violence. Furthermore, some of the leading personalities of these two groups are linked through family ties or can boast of having studied with the same mentors at Najaf and Qom theological seminaries. However, while the Ḥizbullāh of Lebanon operates as a formal political party, the Iranian Ḥizbullāhis for the most part continue to operate as vigilante bands. Nonetheless, in both countries, they have proven themselves forces to be reckoned with.

[*See also* Fidā'īyān-i Islām; Iranian Revolution of 1979; Islamic Republican Party; Komiteh; Sipāh-i Pasdarān-i Inqilāb-i Islāmī; *and the biography of Khomeini.*]

BIBLIOGRAPHY

Akhavi, Shahrough. "Elite Factionalism in the Islamic Republic of Iran." *Middle East Journal* 41.2 (Spring 1987): 181–201. Excellent exposition of political infighting among Iran's postrevolutionary elites.

Bakhash, Shaul. *The Reign of the Ayatollahs: Iran and the Islamic Revolution*. New York, 1984. Comprehensive and insightful account of the Iranian Revolution and its aftermath.

Norton, Augustus Richard. "Lebanon: The Internal Conflict and the Iranian Connection." In *The Iranian Revolution: Its Global Impact*, edited by John L. Esposito, pp. 116–137. Miami, 1990. Informed account of Iranian attempts to influence Lebanese politics.

Shapira, Shimon. "The Origins of Hizballah." *Jerusalem Quarterly* 46 (Spring 1988): 115–130. Provides useful information on the background of some of Lebanese Ḥizbullāh's leading personalities and their ties to Iran.

MEHRZAD BOROUJERDI

Ḥizbullāh in Lebanon

A political and social movement that arose among Lebanon's Shīʿīs in response to the Islamic revolution in Iran, Ḥizbullāh means the "Party of God," after the Qur'ān (5.56): "Lo! the Party of God, they are the victorious." During the 1980s, Ḥizbullāh drew on Iranian support to become a major political force in Lebanon and the Middle East. It gained international renown, first for its attacks against the American, French, and Israeli forces deployed in parts of Lebanon, and later for its holding of Western hostages. Ḥizbullāh also emerged as the major rival of the established Amal movement for the loyalty of Lebanon's Shīʿīs. Ḥizbullāh's declared objective has been the transformation of Lebanon (and the region) into an Islamic state, a goal it has pursued by diversified means, ranging from acts of violence to participation in parliamentary elections.

Origins. The foundations of Ḥizbullāh were laid years before the Iranian Revolution of 1979 in the ties that bound the Shīʿī *ʿulamā'* (religious scholars) of Iran and Lebanon. Many of these *ʿulamā'* were schooled together in the Shīʿī theological academies in Iraq, especially in the shrine city of Najaf. During the late 1950s and 1960s, these academies became active in formulating an Islamic response to nationalism and secularism. Prominent *ʿulamā'* lectured and wrote on Islamic government, Islamic economics, and the ideal Islamic state. In Najaf, the Iraqi ayatollah Muḥammad Bāqir al-Ṣadr and the exiled Iranian ayatollah Ruhollah al-Musavi Khomeini both subjected the existing political order to an Islamic critique. Lebanese *ʿulamā'* and theological students overheard and joined in these debates.

Sayyid Muḥammad Ḥusayn Faḍlallāh, the future mentor of Ḥizbullāh, was an exemplary product of Najaf's mix of scholasticism and radicalism. Faḍlallāh was born and schooled in Najaf, where his father, a scholar from south Lebanon, had come to study. Faḍlallāh imbibed the ideas then current in Najaf and went to Lebanon in 1966, where he made his Beirut *ḥusaynīyah* (a Shīʿī congregation house) into a center of Islamic activism. Sayyid Mūsā al-Ṣadr dominated the Shīʿī scene at the time, and Faḍlallāh had a modest following. But in the 1970s, Faḍlallāh received an important reinforcement: Iraqi authorities expelled about a hundred Lebanese theology students as part of a crackdown on Shīʿī activism in the shrine cities. The expelled students became disciples of Faḍlallāh on their return to Lebanon and later formed the core of Ḥizbullāh. [*See* Najaf *and the biography of* Ṣadr.]

In Iran the early foundations of Ḥizbullāh were laid by members of the Islamic opposition who found refuge in war-torn Lebanon during the 1970s. The Palestine Liberation Organization (PLO) took this opposition under its wing and provided the Iranian dissidents with training and forged documents. Graduates of the Palestinian camps included Muḥammad Muntaẓirī, the son of a leading opposition cleric and future founder of the Liberation Movements Department of the Iranian Revolutionary Guards, and ʿAlī Akbar Muḥtashimī, future Iranian ambassador to Syria, who was to play a critical role in the creation of Ḥizbullāh. Both men arrived in Lebanon from Najaf, where they had studied under Khomeini, and both joined Khomeini in Paris in 1978.

After the Iranian Revolution of 1979, the Shīʿī traffic between Lebanon and Iran intensified. Faḍlallāh and his disciples became frequent visitors to Iran, while former Iranian dissidents who had spent time in Lebanon returned as emissaries of the Islamic revolution. Muḥammad Muntaẓirī made the first attempt, in 1979, to send six hundred Iranian volunteers to Lebanon, where they proposed to launch a *jihād* against Israel. However, the Lebanese government successfully appealed to Syria to block the entry of the volunteers, and most got no further than Damascus. Muntaẓirī, who accused "liberals" in Iran's government of failing to support his mission, died in a Tehran bombing in 1981.

The obstacles to an effective partnership between Lebanon's Shīʿīs and Iran lifted only in 1982, following the Israeli invasion of Lebanon and the deployment of American and French peacekeeping forces in Beirut. Syria, although defeated in battle, was determined to drive all other foreign forces out of Lebanon by encouraging popular resistance, especially among the Shīʿīs. Many Shīʿīs were receptive, believing that Israel and the West planned to restore Maronite privilege by force. When Iran offered to assist in mobilizing the Shīʿīs, Syria approved, permitting Iran to send about a thousand Revolutionary Guards to the Bekaa (Biqāʿ) Valley in eastern Lebanon. There they seized a Lebanese army barracks and turned it into their operational base.

Emboldened by the arrival of the Iranians, Faḍlallāh and a number of young *ʿulamāʾ* declared *jihād* against the Western and Israeli presence in Lebanon while pledging their allegiance to Khomeini. Similarly, a faction of the Amal militia led by a former schoolteacher, Ḥusayn al-Mūsawī, went over to the Revolutionary Guards, accusing the Amal movement of failing to resist Israel's invasion. Iran's ambassador to Damascus, ʿAlī Akbar Muḥtashimī (appointed in 1981), established a council to govern the new movement. The council included the Iranian ambassador, Lebanese *ʿulamāʾ*, and security strongmen responsible for secret operations and the movement's militia. Later, the council created the post of secretary general, held successively by Shaykh Ṣubḥī al-Ṭufaylī, Sayyid ʿAbbās al-Mūsawī, and Sayyid Ḥasan Naṣrallāh. Faḍlallāh declined all formal office, but his rhetorical genius and seniority assured his moral prestige in the movement.

The movement drew its support from two components of Shīʿī society. It especially appealed to some of the larger Shīʿī clans of the Bekaa Valley, for whom the war in Lebanon had brought prosperity fueled by the expansion of smuggling and hashish and opium cultivation. The leadership of the Amal movement, based on the Shīʿī professional and commercial classes, made insufficient room for this emerging counterelite of the Bekaa Valley. With the encouragement of the Iranian emissaries based in the valley, the clans flocked to Ḥizbullāh. Baʿlabakk, capital of the Bekaa Province, practically became an autonomous zone for Ḥizbullāh. Its buildings were plastered with posters of Khomeini and draped with Iranian flags.

The message of Ḥizbullāh also appealed to the Shīʿī refugees who had been forced by war into the dismal slums of southern Beirut. They included the Shīʿīs driven from their homes in the Phalangist assault on Palestinians in eastern Beirut (Nabʿa and Burj Ḥammūd) in 1976 and many more who fled the south following the Israeli invasions of 1978 and 1982. Faḍlallāh personified their grievance. His ancestral villages in the south (Bint Jubayl and ʿAynātā) had come under Israeli assault, then occupation; he lost his first pulpit in Nabʿa during the Phalangist siege of 1976. These Shīʿī refugees felt a strong sense of identification with the Palestinians and a deep resentment against Israel, the Phalangists, and the West. Many young Shīʿī refugees even joined Palestinian organizations during the 1970s, from which they acquired fighting experience. When Israel forced these organizations from Beirut in 1982, Shīʿī fighters who were left behind joined Ḥizbullāh, which promised to continue their struggle.

***Jihād* against the West and Israel.** Ḥizbullāh systematically formulated its doctrine in its "open letter" of 1985. "We are proceeding toward a battle with vice at its very roots," declared the letter, "and the first root of vice is America." The letter set four objectives for the movement: the termination of all American and French influence in Lebanon; Israel's complete departure from Lebanon "as a prelude to its final obliteration"; submission of the Lebanese Phalangists to "just rule" and trial for their "crimes"; and granting the people the right to choose their own system of government, "keeping in mind that we do not hide our commitment to the rule of Islam."

From the outset, Ḥizbullāh conducted its struggle on three discrete levels—open, semiclandestine, and clandestine. Faḍlallāh and the *ʿulamāʾ* openly preached the message of resistance to Islam's enemies and fealty to Khomeini in mosques and *ḥusaniyah*, which became the focal points for public rallies. The Revolutionary Guards trained the semiclandestine Islamic Resistance, a militia-like formation which attacked Israeli forces in south Lebanon. The Organization of the Islamic Jihad, the clandestine branch of the movement, operated against Western targets. It was reputedly led by ʿImād Mughnīyah, a shadowy Shīʿī figure from south Lebanon and a veteran of Palestinian service, who became the subject of much lore during the 1980s.

The violence of Islamic Jihad catapulted Ḥizbullāh to prominence. Assassinations of individual foreigners escalated into massive bombings, some of them done by "self-martyrs," which destroyed the U.S. embassy and its annex in two separate attacks in 1983 and 1984; the Beirut barracks of American and French peacekeeping troops in two attacks on the same morning in 1983; and command facilities of Israeli forces in the south in 1982 and 1983. Hundreds of foreigners died in these bombings, the most successful of which killed 241 U.S. marines in their barracks. As a result, the United States and France withdrew their forces from Lebanon; Israel, whose forces also came under attack by the Islamic Resistance, retreated to a narrow "security zone" in the south. In solidarity with Iran, Islamic Jihad also bombed the U.S. and French embassies in Kuwait in 1983, in an effort to compel Kuwait to abandon its support of Iraq in the Iran-Iraq War. Ḥizbullāh activists were also responsible for a spate of fatal bombings in Paris in 1986, meant to force France to abandon its policy of supplying Iraq with arms.

Ḥizbullāh also conducted operations to free members who had been imprisoned by governments in the Middle East and Europe. These operations included the hijacking of an American airliner in 1985, to secure the freedom of Lebanese Shīʿīs held by Israel, and two hijackings of Kuwaiti airliners in 1984 and 1988, to win freedom for Lebanese Shīʿīs held by Kuwait for the bombings there. The hijackers killed passengers in each instance to demonstrate their resolve. In addition, Islamic Jihad and other groups affiliated with Ḥizbullāh abducted dozens of foreigners in Lebanon, mostly American, French, British, and German citizens, for the same purpose. Some of these foreigners were traded for American arms needed by Iran in the Iran-Iraq War, but the motive for the wave of abductions remained the release of Ḥizbullāh's imprisoned fighters elsewhere. Only when the hostage holding became a political burden for Iran did it prevail on Ḥizbullāh to free the hostages. The last French hostages were freed in 1988; the last American and British hostages in 1991; and the last Germans in 1992.

Although the movement's *ʿulamāʾ* disavowed all direct knowledge of operations, and occasionally expressed reservations, they harvested the credit (and blame) for Ḥizbullāh's *jihād*. Their mosques filled to overflowing, and their statements and interviews resonated in the media. However, they themselves became the targets of assassination and abduction. Faḍlallāh narrowly missed death in a massive car bombing in 1985, which killed eighty persons; Israel abducted a local Ḥizbullāh cleric, Shaykh ʿAbd al-Karīm ʿUbayd, in 1988; and Israeli helicopter gunships killed Ḥizbullāh's secretary general, Sayyid ʿAbbās al-Mūsawī, and his family, in an attack on his motorcade in 1992.

Ḥizbullāh also found that its growing appeal among Lebanon's Shīʿīs made enemies within the existing Amal movement. As Ḥizbullāh gained momentum, it sought unimpeded access to the south, so it could promote the struggle against Israel. Amal regarded this as an encroachment on its last strongholds. Beginning in 1988, occasional skirmishes with Amal escalated into civil war. More than one thousand Shīʿī combatants and civilians died in this fighting, which was characterized by atrocities and assassinations. Ḥizbullāh usually enjoyed the upper hand in fighting, but Syrian intervention denied it the fruits of victory. The strife ended in late 1990 in an accord mediated by Syria and Iran.

Although Ḥizbullāh battled its adversaries, it also cooperated with Iranian aid agencies to fund a wide range of social and economic projects. These included a hospital and pharmacies in Beirut; small textile factories and sheltered workshops to employ families of members and "martyrs"; book allowances and scholarships for students; and street paving in Beirut and the digging of wells and reservoirs in rural areas. Ḥizbullāh sponsored a scout movement, summer camps, and a soccer league. The movement published a weekly newspaper and operated an independent radio station. These activities broadened the base of the movement and enhanced its ability to field fighters.

Resistance and Democracy. By the end of its first decade, Ḥizbullāh had fought and bought its way into the hearts of perhaps as many as half of Lebanon's Shīʿīs, but the objective of an Islamic Lebanon remained remote. On the basis of the 1989 Ṭāʾif Accord, Syria enforced an end to the civil war, based on a fairer confessional balance. Syria also disarmed the militias and launched a determined drive to build up the authority of a Syrian-backed government in Beirut. And in 1991, the governments of Syria and Lebanon sat down with Israel in direct talks to discuss territory, security, and a possible peace.

Ḥizbullāh's place in the new Syrian order remained uncertain. In Beirut and parts of the south, Ḥizbullāh surrendered its weapons and turned over positions to the reconstituted Lebanese army. In 1992, Ḥizbullāh and the Revolutionary Guards evacuated the Lebanese army barracks near Baʿlabakk, which had served as operational headquarters for ten years. Nevertheless, Ḥizbullāh's Islamic Resistance enjoyed an exemption from the general disarming of militias to permit it to continue a guerilla war of attrition against Israel's "security zone" in the south. The Islamic Resistance increased its operations, even in the midst of peace talks, and Syria pledged to disarm it only after a complete Israeli withdrawal from Lebanon.

Ḥizbullāh also opposed implementation of the Syrian-guaranteed Ṭāʾif Accord, which it denounced as an American plan. Ḥizbullāh denounced the first stage of implementation, establishing Muslim-Christian parity in government, for perpetuating confessionalism. Ḥizbullāh advocated a straightforward referendum on an Islamic state; in such a state, the Christians would be entitled to protection, not parity. However, Iran prevailed on Ḥizbullāh to participate in the 1992 parliamentary elections, the first held in twenty years, despite the fact that the elections still apportioned seats by confession. In the Bekaa Valley, Ḥizbullāh swept the Shīʿī vote, and the movement made a credible showing in the south, collecting a total of eight parliamentary seats—the largest single block in the fragmented parliament.

In parliament, Ḥizbullāh organized as an opposition to the Syrian-backed government. It denounced the government's negotiations with Israel and denied all interest in cabinet positions. In most respects, Ḥizbullāh still remained an extraparliamentary movement—a point emphasized by the deliberate obscurity of the movement's parliamentary candidates. Ḥizbullāh signaled that its actual leaders would remain in the mosques and in the fighting ranks of the Islamic Resistance. But the "Party of God" had moved one reluctant step toward becoming a true *ḥizb* (political party) of its followers. It remained to be seen whether Ḥizbullāh's votes would succeed, where its violence had failed, in creating an Islamic Lebanon.

[*See also* Amal; Hostages; Lebanon; Organization of the Islamic Jihād; Shīʿī Islam, *article on* Modern Shīʿī Thought; *and the biography of Faḍlallāh.*]

BIBLIOGRAPHY

Carré, Olivier. *L'utopie islamique dans l'Orient arabe.* Paris, 1991. Chapters 9 and 10 deal with the thought of Faḍlallāh.

Delafon, Gilles. *Beyrouth: Les soldats de l'Islam.* Paris, 1989. The best journalistic account to date, based in part upon Ḥizbullāh's own publications.

Kramer, Martin. *Hezbollah's Vision of the West.* Washington, D.C., 1989. Analysis of Ḥizbullāh's discourse on its adversaries, relying on the movement's own texts.

Kramer, Martin. "The Moral Logic of Hizballah." In *Origins of Terrorism: Psychologies, Ideologies, Theologies, States of Mind,* edited by Walter Reich, pp. 131–157. Cambridge, 1990. Considers the debate that occurred in Ḥizbullāh over "self-martyrdom" operations and the abduction of foreigners.

Kramer, Martin. "Redeeming Jerusalem: The Pan-Islamic Premise of Hizballah." In *The Iranian Revolution and the Muslim World,* edited by David Menashri, pp. 105–130. Boulder, 1990. Attitudes in Ḥizbullāh toward Iran and other Islamic movements.

Kramer, Martin. "Hizbullah: The Calculus of Jihad." In *Fundamentalisms and the State: Remaking Polities, Economies, and Militance,* edited by Martin E. Marty and R. Scott Appleby, pp. 539–556. Chicago, 1992. General overview of the movement, with extensive bibliographical notes.

Kramer, Martin. "Sacrifice and Fratricide in Shiite Lebanon." In *Violence and the Sacred in the Modern World,* edited by Mark Juergensmeyer, pp. 30–47. London, 1992. On the rivalry between Ḥizbullāh and Amal.

Mallat, Chibli. *Shīʿi Thought from the South of Lebanon.* Oxford, 1988. Early debate among Shīʿī *ʿulamāʾ* (including Faḍlallāh) which informed Ḥizbullāh's doctrine.

Piscatori, J. P. "The Shia of Lebanon and Hizbullah: The Party of God." In *Politics of the Future: The Role of Social Movements,* edited by Christie Jennett and Randal G. Stewart, pp. 292–317. Melbourne, 1989. Introduction to the movement, with an emphasis on its social base.

Rieck, Andreas. *Die Schiiten und der Kampf um den Libanon: Politische Chronik, 1958–1988.* Hamburg, 1989. Exhaustive chronicle of Shīʿī politics in Lebanon, including the emergence and development of Ḥizbullāh.

Shapira, Shimon. "The Origins of Hizballah." *Jerusalem Quarterly* 46 (Spring 1988): 115–130. Traces the origins of the movement through early initiatives and organizations.

U.S. Congress, House of Representatives, Select Committee to Investigate Covert Arms Transactions with Iran, and U.S. Senate, Select Committee on Secret Military Assistance to Iran and the Nicaraguan Opposition. *Report of the Congressional Committees Investigating the Iran-Contra Affair, with Supplemental, Minority, and Additional Views.* Washington, D.C., November 1987. Includes many American intelligence reports and assessments of Ḥizbullāh and Islamic *jihād.*

MARTIN KRAMER

HOLIDAYS. *See* Islamic Calendar.

HONOR. The notion of honor figures prominently in ensembles of ideas about respect and social status. As a comparative sociological concept, it denotes enhanced status and capacity for social relations. In more narrowly cultural terms, honor is a composite aspect of persons, social conduct, morality, and social metaphysics.

The grounds and expressions of honor are many and vary with what is important and problematic in personal interaction. Honor was first examined in tribal "codes" idealizing bravery, independence, generosity, self-control, and abilities to control the course of interactions with others. Common grounds and symbolic vehicles of honor in these milieus are ownership (in some sense of controlling the use) of land and other productive resources, the independence and generosity this facilitates along with family and kinship solidarities, the control of women's fertility, and personal characteristics of courage, wisdom, honesty, and self-possession. Although honor is sometimes represented as complementary to religion in tribal settings, piety is an essential part of honor in all its forms. For tribesmen, there is no honor apart from identity as a Muslim: the generous host, provident husband, and deferential wife and offspring are justified as God's pleasure.

Islamic piety looms larger as a source of honor for others. For descendants of the Prophet, Ṣūfī pirs and recognized "holy" families, honor may inhere primarily in religious identity. A composed demeanor, disinclination to conflict, and avoidance of degradation of others is the presumed style of religious people and sets a standard that others emulate.

Widespread distinctions between "face" or "point of honor" that can be manipulated in interaction, in contrast to honor as all that is sacred *(sharaf, ḥaram)*, have been productively united in two ways. One is by looking beyond talk about honor to the art of talking well and the way in which verbal performances demonstrate cultural mastery, particularly in poetic constructions. This more nuanced understanding of honor as expression has also opened up the realms of women's claims to honor and expressions of it through verbal performances.

Another new perspective has come with uncovering how concepts of honor and shame are related to metaphysical notions of persons and behavior as balances of socialized reason *(ʿaql)* and animal appetites *(nafs)*. Honor tips this balance in favor of reason-governed behavior, and shame toward behaviors denominated by emotion and appetites. These concepts are generalized from Islamic contexts as a sort of "folk" or ethnopsychology. For instance, hospitality (and material generosity generally) is ideally extended with humility and deference to show that egoism and ambition are subordinated to God's pleasure. The host and the parent become symbolic intermediaries or conduits in their realms, much like pirs and religious teachers in theirs, each with particular and situationally appropriate honor. Thus honor also takes on associations with the "greater" (personal) and "lesser" (communal) *jihād* or struggle for religion.

These concepts can link experiences without completely harmonizing them. Honor can come into conflict with religion when their symbolic expressions conflict, as for instance in the feud or in religious quietism. In this way, honor may be polarized with defining social relations in religious terms.

[*See also* Shame.]

BIBLIOGRAPHY

Abu-Lughod, Lila. *Veiled Sentiments: Honor and Poetry in a Bedouin Society*. Berkeley, 1986. Along with Grima (below), a seminal work on women's honor as verbal performance.

Caton, Steven. "The Poetic Construction of Self." *Anthropological Quarterly* 58 (1985): 141–151. Fundamental work on honor as verbal performance.

Grima, Benedicte. *The Performance of Emotion among Paxtun Women*. Austin, 1992.

Jamous, Raymond. *Honneur et baraka: Les structures sociales traditionnelles dans le Rif*. Cambridge, 1981. Along with Meeker (below), provides the best discussion of continuities between tribal and religious settings of honor.

Meeker, Michael E. *Literature and Violence in North Arabia*. Cambridge, 1978.

Péristiany, J. G., ed. *Honour and Shame: The Values of Mediterranean Society*. Chicago, 1966. See the essays by Pierre Bourdieu, "The Sentiment of Honour in Kabyle Society," and Ahmed Abou-Zeid, "Honour and Shame among the Bedouins of Egypt," both classic accounts of tribalist honor.

JON W. ANDERSON

HOSTAGES. Seizing, detaining, and threatening to injure a person in order to secure compliance with a condition or demand from a third party is the act of hostage taking. Before the advent of the modern regime of international law, belligerents often took hostages to secure compliance with requisitions, contributions, ransoms, bills, or treaties. The four 1949 Geneva Conventions and the 1977 Hague Protocols I and II prohibited the taking of hostages in international and internal armed conflicts. The 1979 United Nations International Convention against the Taking of Hostages imposed a duty to either prosecute or extradite hostage takers, but this convention has been ratified by only a few nations. Nevertheless, in contemporary times, hostage taking probably violates customary international law.

The Arabic term for hostages, *rahā'in,* means persons held as security. Like most medieval legal systems, classical Islamic law permitted the exchange of hostages to ensure compliance with a treaty. However, Islamic law considered such hostages inviolable and prohibited killing them even if the enemy violated the treaty or killed their Muslim hostages. On the outbreak of hostilities Muslim forces were commanded to safely return the hostages to their country. Furthermore, Islamic law prohibited Muslim forces from using enemy personnel or civilians as human shields in an armed conflict. Muslim jurists disagreed, however, on whether Muslim forces should attack if the enemy uses Muslim prisoners as shields.

There is some obscurity as to the distinction between prisoners of war and hostages. In classical Islamic law only *muqātilah* (combatants) could be prisoners of war. Muslim jurists disagreed on whether a prisoner of war could be ransomed, exchanged for Muslim prisoners, killed, or freed. Other than combatants, any non-Muslim who does not have *amān* (safe conduct) or who is a national of a territory without a peace treaty with Muslims could be placed into captivity. In the opinion of most jurists *amān* can be granted by any Muslim. Additionally, if the non-Muslim wrongly, but reasonably, believes that he or she enjoys safe conduct, then he or she cannot be made a captive. Under no circumstances could a captive be used to make demands on a third party, hence, no captive could be used as a hostage.

Classical Islamic law was developed over a long span of time, primarily from the eighth to twelfth centuries, in response to specific historical circumstances. Additionally, classical Islamic law is represented by a variety of Sunnī and Shīʿī schools of thought that often reached different conclusions on many issues. Consequently, Islamic law leaves a rich and diverse legacy to its modern adherents. From this complex legacy an argument for or against hostage taking can be constructed, since both positions are supported by certain historical practices.

Since independence, in the 1950s and 1960s, the governments of most Muslim states have ratified the Geneva Conventions and have observed the prohibition against the taking of hostages. Only a few Muslim states, however, have ratified the Hostages Convention. Hostage taking has continued to be an issue in the Middle East because of the fact that guerrilla groups or national liberation movements, particularly in the 1970s and 1980s, have used the taking of hostages as a means to secure compliance with their political demands. Typically, these groups have claimed that their captives are prisoners of war, but international law does not permit the endangering of the life of a captive in order to make demands on a third party.

In the 1980s the taking of hostages became a subject of debate among Shīʿī scholars when several pro-Iranian groups seized hostages in Lebanon. Some Shīʿī leaders, such as Ḥusayn al-Mūsawī, justified the taking of hostages in 1987 as a practical necessity. Interestingly, Ayatollah Ruhollah Khomeini (1902–1989) used the same logic in 1986 to defend the taking of hostages in Iran in 1979 and in Lebanon. Others, such as the Lebanese Shaykh Muḥammad Mahdī Shams al-Dīn, deputy chairman of the Higher Islamic Shīʿī Council, and Ayatollah Muḥammad Ḥusayn Faḍlallāh, a senior Lebanese Shīʿī cleric, have condemned hostage taking as un-Islamic and illegal. In 1992–1993 the Western hostages held in Lebanon were released, and the issue, for the time being, has fallen out of public discourse. Significantly, whether among proponents or opponents, serious discussions of the legality of hostage taking under Islamic law are very rare. Ultimately, hostage taking in the Middle East is motivated by political considerations and has little to do with any set of religious or legal injunctions.

[*See also* Diplomatic Immunity; International Law; International Relations and Diplomacy.]

BIBLIOGRAPHY

Antokol, Norman, and Mayer Nudell. *No One a Neutral: Political Hostage-Taking in the Modern World.* Medina, Ohio, 1990. Serves as an introductory source on the problem of hostage taking in the modern world.

Conrad, Gerhard. "Combatant and Prisoner of War in Classical Islamic Law: Concepts Formulated by Hanafi Jurists of the Twelfth Century." *Revue de Droit Penal Militaire et de Droit de la Guerre* 20 (1981): 271–305. Useful source on the treatment of prisoners of war in Islamic law.

Faḍlallāh, Muḥammad Ḥusayn. "Islam and Violence in Political Reality." *Middle East Insight* 4.4–5 (1986): 4–13. One of the few sources in English by a Shīʿī cleric explaining his view on the taking of hostages.

Hamidullah, Muhammad. *The Muslim Conduct of State.* 7th ed. Lahore, 1977. Makes several references to hostage taking in Islamic law.

Khadduri, Majid. *War and Peace in the Law of Islam.* Baltimore, 1955. Contains a small section on hostages.

Kramer, Martin. "The Moral Logic of Hizballah." In *Origins of Terrorism: Psychologies, Ideologies, Theologies, States of Mind,* edited by Walter Reich, pp. 131–157. Cambridge, 1990. Discusses the position of Faḍlallāh on the taking of hostages.

Kramer, Martin. "Hizbullah: The Calculus of Jihad." In *Fundamentalisms and the State: Remaking Polities, Economies, and Militance,* edited by Martin E. Marty and R. Scott Appleby, pp. 539–556. Chicago, 1993. Informative on the history of Ḥizbullāh's involvement with the taking of hostages.

Maḥmaṣānī, Ṣubḥī. "The Principles of International Law in the Light of Islamic Doctrine." *Recueil des Cours* 117 (1966): 201–328. Makes reference to the taking of hostages in Islamic law.

Ruwayha, Walid Amin. *Terrorism and Hostage-Taking in the Middle East.* 2d ed. Paris, 1990. One of the very few sources on point, but a very polemical work representing a particular point of view.

Schwartz, David Aaron. "International Terrorism and Islamic Law." *Columbia Journal of Transnational Law* 29 (Summer 1991): 629–652. Argues that hostage taking violates Islamic law.

Shaybānī, Muḥammad ibn al-Ḥasan. *The Islamic Law of Nations: Shaybānī's Siyar.* Translated by Majid Khadduri. Baltimore, 1966.

KHALED ABOU EL FADL and ASMA SAYEED

HOUSES. The dwellings that Muslims have constructed and occupied are as varied as the geographical and cultural landscapes in which they have lived. For building materials, until the last quarter of the twentieth century, they have relied on resources readily at hand. In many parts of Africa, Arabia, and Asia, the primary material used by sedentary peoples has been earth. In rocky regions, stone construction is widespread, as in Yemen, Mecca, Lebanon, and Palestine. Cut stone was the main material, often in combination with baked brick, used in the palace architecture of traditional elites in the Mamlūk, Ottoman, Ṣafavid, and Mughal empires. Wooden dwellings naturally have been most common in heavily forested regions such as Bosnia-Herzegovina, northern Iran, the Hindu Kush, Indonesia, and Malaysia. The marsh Arabs of southern Iraq have traditionally used reeds, while coral has been employed in Red Sea coastal communities. Nomadic peoples have manufactured their tents from woven grasses, branches, and the hair and skins of their flocks.

The courtyard house has been the vernacular architectural form most widely regarded as "Islamic," because of the facility with which it can be adapted to religiously sanctioned norms of privacy and gender segregation. It is also held to be well suited to arid climates and responsive to a traditional preference for patrilocal residence of extended families. Yet to posit this form as the archetypal Islamic house rests on faulty premises. It is true that various types of courtyard houses existed in the pre-Islamic settlements of Africa and the Near East; however, since the appearance of Islam, not only have non-Muslims continued to use this house form, but Muslims themselves have adopted other dwelling configurations. Among these are the tower houses of Yemen, the Hejaz, and the Maghrib, the *qāʿah*- and *maqʿad*-based residences of Cairo, and the *ṣuffah*-style houses in the Ottoman heartland.

These configurations, like the courtyard houses, contain central spaces—halls and reception areas—connected to smaller adjoining chambers. Each has proven amenable to housing extended families and adaptable to local climatic conditions. Moreover, each allows for varying degrees of interaction between public and private life. There is little evidence for a clear separation between public and private space in these configurations, nor has it been common for the houses to be physically divided into male and female quarters. Providing a harem—separate apartments for women—has been practiced more by landholding and urban elites than by Islamic peoples as a whole.

Relations between Islam and houses may best be considered in terms of the ways in which they are encoded in normative religious discourse, as well as the ways Muslims appropriate Islamic symbols and rules to construe meaning and order within the spheres of domestic life. The Qur'ān and *sunnah* contain domestic discourses, based on the Arabic house terms *dār* and *bayt*, that help symbolically to delineate the boundaries and relations between this world and the hereafter, God and humans, the prophet Muḥammad and his community, and belief and disbelief (for example, Qur'ān 13.20–24, 3.96–97, 16.80–83, 4.95–100, or 59.2–4). They express rules regarding domestic visitation, privacy, prayer, and hospitality (for example, Qur'ān 24.27–29, 35–37, 61; 33.53), which became incorporated into the legal canon, or which were assimilated in conformity—or opposition—to local customary practices.

Many Muslims have regarded their homes, or sections of them, as sacred areas where life-cycle rituals are observed and prayers are performed. To enhance domestic blessing, repel evil forces, and please guests, they embellish sitting rooms with verses of the Qur'ān, the names of God, and pictures of the Kaʿbah or the prophet Muḥammad's mosque in Medina. Shīʿī houses in Lebanon and Iran sometimes display invocations to the imams, pictures of respected mullahs, and mementos from shrine visits. In Egypt it has been customary for house and apartment facades to be decorated with murals in celebration of the performance of the *ḥajj*, thus symbolically linking a pilgrim's dwelling with Mecca, Medina, and paradise.

In most Muslim lands traditional domestic architecture, as well as customary ways of conceiving, organizing, and behaving in domestic space, has been profoundly affected by the forces of modernization during this century. Costly reinforced concrete, glass, steel, and baked brick are replacing indigenous building materials, while European and American architectural configurations and technologies displace native ones. Concomitantly, the forced settlement of nomads, voluntary rural migration to industrializing regions, increasing refugee populations, high population growth rates, and inefficient resource allocation by national governments have created severe housing shortages in many countries. They have also been agents in the growth of squatter settlements on the outskirts of cities such as Casablanca, Cairo, Istanbul, Tehran, Karachi, and Jakarta.

While government housing ministries and international relief agencies try to alleviate these problems, other private, national, and international organizations have arisen to promote the preservation of Islamic monuments and vernacular architectures or to conjoin the vernacular with the modern. In this context, precolonial Islamic juridical rulings concerning domestic privacy and gender segregation have been applied to the planning of several modern housing projects. At the same time, neglected areas of substandard "informal" housing have become centers of unrest and breeding grounds for radicalized Islamist groups, which recruit youthful members with promises of assistance in locating spouses and housing, and with visions of recovering the sanctified corporate solidarity of the past.

[*See also* Architecture.]

BIBLIOGRAPHY

Campo, Juan Eduardo. *The Other Sides of Paradise: Explorations into the Religious Meanings of Domestic Space in Islam*. Columbia, S.C., 1991. Groundbreaking historical inquiry into the domestic symbolism of the Qur'ān and *ḥadīth* collections, and how Islam is appropriated by Egyptian Muslims at home today.

Hakim, Besim S. *Arabic-Islamic Cities: Building and Planning Principles*. New York, 1986. An architect's inquiry into how Islamic principles are encoded in the design of Muslim dwellings and settlements, based on architectural field surveys in consultation with medieval legal texts. Limited to the North African region.

Hanna, Nelly. *Habiter au Caire: La maison moyenne et ses habitants, aux XVIIᵉ et XVIIIᵉ siècles*. Cairo, 1991. Brilliant study of the social, economic, and architectural history of urban middle-class housing in Arab Muslim lands on the eve of European colonization, based on Islamic court archives, architectural field surveys, and travel literature. Extensive bibliography.

Petherbridge, Guy T. "Vernacular Architecture: The House and Society." In *Architecture of the Islamic World: Its History and Social Meaning*, edited by George Michell, pp. 176–208. New York, 1978. Useful survey of different forms and functions of traditional houses in the Islamic world, although the premise that there is a distinctly "Islamic" house type is now widely disputed.

Safran, Linda, ed. *Housing: Process and Physical Form*. Philadelphia, 1980. Proceedings of the third Aga Khan Program conference on architectural transformations in the Islamic world (Jakarta, 1979). See also volumes in the Program's series, "Designing in Islamic Cultures," 1980–1984. These and other Program publications deal with the development of modern Islamic architectural design, as well as historical, sociological, and theoretical topics pertaining to the built environment in Muslim countries, from North Africa to Asia. Most publications contain valuable bibliographic information.

Université de Provence, Group de Recherches et d'Études sur le Proche-Orient. *L'habitat traditionnel dans les pays musulmans autour de la Mediterranée*. 3 vols. Cairo, 1988–1991. Valuable collection of articles by specialists on the precolonial domestic architecture of Muslim Mediterranean lands, supplemented by comparative studies of Arabian Peninsula and Ottoman Turkish housing. Includes detailed annotations, bibliographies, and glossaries.

JUAN EDUARDO CAMPO

ḤUDŪD. Classical Islamic law divides the punishment for crimes into two categories: *ḥudūd* (sg., *ḥadd;* lit., "limit" or "prohibitions") are mandatory punishments imposed for crimes against God, and *taʿzīr* ("deterrence") are punishments at the discretion of the *qāḍī* (judge). The traditional crimes for which *ḥudūd* punishments are imposed are those against morality (adultery, fornication, and false allegations of adultery), property (theft and highway robbery), and a residual group involving apostasy and drunkenness. These crimes must be contrasted with crimes that are the subject of a private claim, including murder, when it is possible for the victim and his family to opt for either retaliation or blood money.

The *ḥadd* punishments are severe. For instance, the first offense of theft, on the proof of two witnesses or a confession, results in amputation of the hand at the wrist, and the second, further amputations (Qur'ān, surah 5.42–43). For fornication, on the proof of four male witnesses or a confession, a married person is sentenced to stoning to death and others to one hundred lashes.

These punishments are traced to verses in the Qur'ān, although *sunnah* (prophetic example) and *ijmāʿ* (community consensus) have developed the details. For example, in relation to adultery and fornication, stoning as a punishment does not appear in the Qur'ānic verses (surah 24.2: "The whore and the whoremonger—scourge each of them with a hundred stripes"), but is based on *ḥadīth* (prophetic tradition).

The punishments, to an extent, are tempered by the strict rules of evidence. The evidence must be based on either a voluntary confession or the evidence of male eyewitnesses. Nonetheless, reports of *ḥudūd* penalties being imposed in Saudi Arabia, in particular, are fairly frequent. In February–March 1991 alone, five people had their right hands amputated for theft (*Amnesty International Report*, 1991).

With the notable exception of Saudi Arabia, however, *ḥudūd* punishments have fallen into disuse in the modern Muslim world, primarily because of Western notions of penology and sentencing. Increasing fundamentalist ideology, however, has brought about a call for the introduction of *ḥudūd* penalties. Thus, for example, Pakistan in 1979 and Sudan initially in 1983 both introduced laws that enable *ḥudūd* penalties to be imposed. In Sudan, the Penal Code (1983) s 318 states: "Whoever commits fornication shall be punished by death if he were married." A similar provision appears in article 5 of the Pakistan Offence of Zina (Enforcement of Hudood) Ordinance 1979.

In relation to theft, amputation is sanctioned under

Sudanese law when the stolen goods are above a certain value, they have been stolen surreptitiously, the thief has no real need, and the thief is not related to the owner. Article 5 of the equivalent ordinance in Pakistan (Offences against Property [Enforcement of Hudood] Ordinance 1979) states, "Whoever, being an adult, surreptitiously commits from any *hirz* [an arrangement made for the custody of property] theft of property of the value of the *nisab* [4.457 grams of gold] or more is said to commit theft liable to *ḥadd*."

Several justifications are offered for these penalties. It has been suggested that imposition of *ḥudūd* acts to reduce the crime rate by serving as an example to those who might turn to crime. It has also been argued that the sentences are retributive and even reformatory: society demands that those who transgress should be punished, and it is better to be punished harshly in this world and repent than to go to the next world unpunished and unrepentant. The danger, however, is that *ḥudūd* methods of punishment might be used by some for political purposes as a force for oppression.

[*See also* Criminal Law; Human Rights; Law, *article on* Legal Thought and Jurisprudence.]

BIBLIOGRAPHY

Bassiouni, M. Cherif, ed. *The Islamic Criminal Justice System*. New York, 1988. Helpful and systematic study of criminal law in Islam.

Heyd, Uriel. *Studies in Old Ottoman Criminal Law*. London, 1973. Describes the criminal justice system as it existed from the late fifteenth to the eighteenth centuries in the Ottoman Empire.

Lippman, Matthew, Séan McConville, and Mordechai Yerushalmi. *Islamic Criminal Law and Procedure*. New York, 1988. Introductory guide to the criminal law of Islam.

Mayer, A. "Libyan Legislation in Defense of Arab-Islamic Sexual Mores." *American Journal of Comparative Law* 20 (1980): 287–313. Stimulating article that discusses, in particular, the Libyan law on fornication.

Schacht, Joseph. *An Introduction to Islamic Law*. Oxford, 1964. Chapter 24 of this well-known work describes the penal system of Islam in detail.

Ṣafwat, Ṣafīyah. "Islamic Laws in the Sudan." In *Islamic Law*, edited by Aziz al-Azmeh, pp. 231–250. London, 1988. Useful description of the "islamization" of the Sudanese legal system, with a focus on penal law.

DAVID STEPHEN PEARL

ḤUJJATĪYAH. A conservative religio-political school of thought within Shiism, the Ḥujjatīyah was founded in the early 1950s. The Ḥujjatī founder, Shaykh Maḥmūd Ḥalabī, is rarely seen in public, and devotees of this tendency constitute the most conservative, ultratraditionalist clergy and laypersons. Originally founded as the Ḥujjatīyah Society in Mashhad, Iran, the group is known for having organized several anti-Bahā'ī campaigns.

Ḥujjatīyah derives from the word *ḥujjah,* meaning both proof and the presentation of proof. According to Marshall Hodgson, in Shiism, the term has had three meanings or applications. It has been used to refer to a person through whom the "inaccessible God becomes accessible" or to "a particular function within the process of revelation" (1960–, p. 544). The term has also been used to refer to "any figure in a religious hierarchy through whom an inaccessible higher figure became accessible to those below." In this connection, Shīʿī doctrine holds that the Imams are the proofs of Allāh.

During the reign of Muhammad Reza Shah Pahlavi (1941–1979), the shah frequently gave the clergy autonomy to mount missionary campaigns against the Bahā'īs, who are perceived by the religious hierarchy as heretics. Shaykh Ḥalabī emerged as a figure whose fiery anti-Bahā'ī sermons sent throngs of clergymen to various cities to lecture on the dangers of Bahā'ism. Characteristics of their missionary behavior include spreading the works of, or news about, those Bahā'īs who had repented their presumed sins.

These activities led to intimidation of Bahā'īs in the cities of Shiraz, Isfahan, Yazd, and Kashan. Moreover, Ḥujjatīyah supporters pressured the government to cut off work permits, licenses, documentations of property ownership, and so forth to the Bahā'īs. There is no evidence that Shaykh Ḥalabī met Ayatollah Ruhollah Khomeini (1902–1989) during these campaigns or that the grand ayatollahs in Qom supported Ḥalabī's actions. Whatever the situation, Ḥalabī had created a nationwide organization with a single objective: to seek out and eradicate all remnants of the Bahā'ī creed.

After the Iranian Revolution of 1979, the Ḥujjatīyah were accused by various fundamentalist clerics as oppositionists to the concept of *vilāyat-i faqīh* (rule of the jurisconsult), a constitutional power given to Khomeini. It was claimed that the Ḥujjatīyah took a passive stand on the return of the Hidden Imam (Mahdi) and hence are opposed to those who want to actively promote the necessary conditions for his return. In this fashion, Khomeini's revolutionary stand, as well as demands for unquestioned loyalty to the *faqīh,* as portrayed as anathema to Ḥujjatī ideology. Furthermore, the label of Ḥujjatīyah in the postrevolutionary factional struggle has been given to those who argue that the clergy must be less directly involved in the governing apparatus and who emphasize an islamization of all aspects of life. Also, those bazaari merchants who are keen to protect their trade from government taxes or other encroachments have been easily labeled Ḥujjatī.

In the summer of 1983, the Islamic regime mounted a public campaign against Ḥujjatīyah sympathizers. Khomeini alluded to the existence of *iqtishāsh* (commotion), "internal rift," and "the dangerous elements" that undermine the Islamic Revolution. He specifically alluded to the Ḥujjatīyah group when he said that some groups wanted "to force the return of the Hidden Imam," meaning, to oppose the *faqīh*.

After Khomeini's remarks, the two major dailies, *Kayhān* and *Iṭṭilāʿāt,* launched a series of attacks on the Ḥujjatīyah. *Kayhān* published extracts from a Ḥujjatī pamphlet in which the authors stated that they understood Khomeini's remarks to be directed at them and, having failed to gain an appointment with him, they consulted with Shaykh Ḥalabī. The pamphlet stated that because of the "current atmosphere," the Ḥujjatīyah could no longer continue its activities. They announced a suspension of the society. However, in conclusion, they directed an implicit criticism at Khomeini by stating, "Allāh and the Hidden Imam would appreciate what the movement [Ḥujjatīyah] had done for the Islamic cause." This gave the impression that Khomeini lacked this appreciation and therefore was out of line with God and the Hidden Imam.

Since the summer of 1983, the regime has practically ignored the existence of the Ḥujjatīyah. No one knows the whereabouts of Ḥalabī or the extent of support for his group in Iran today. On 29 August 1983, the chief revolutionary prosecutor, Ḥusayn Musavī Tabrīzī, was asked about his views on the Ḥujjatīyah Society and whether they were still continuing their activities. He replied, "They have said they have renounced their activities, they should get permission from the Ministry of Interior." Musavī Tabrīzī ignored the fact that the charter of the Ḥujjatīyah Society states specifically that it will not dissolve itself or end its activities until the appearance of the Hidden Imam.

BIBLIOGRAPHY

Gardet, Louis, and Marshall G. S. Hodgson. "Ḥudjdja." In *Encyclopaedia of Islam,* new ed., vol. 3, pp. 543–545. Leiden, 1960–.

Iṭṭilāʿāt (Tehran), 4, 6–9, 15 August 1983.

Kayhān (Tehran), 4, 9, 13, 15 August 1983.

Vali, ʿAbbas, and Sami Zubaida. "Factionalism and Political Discourse in the Islamic Republic of Iran: The Case of the Hujjatiyah." *Economy and Society* 14.2 (May 1985): 139–173. Discusses factionalism among clerical elites in Iran in the context of Khomeini's doctrine of *wilayāt al-faqīh* and the policies of the Islamic Republic.

BAHMAN BAKTIARI

ḤUKŪMAH. The modern Arabic term for "government," *ḥukūmah* (Tk., *hukûmet;* Pers., *ḥukūmat*) is commonly distinguished from *dawlah* ("state"). As in European usage, government is understood as the group of individuals who exercise the authority of the state. *Ḥukūmah* in this sense is a nineteenth-century neologism, adopted as Muslims became increasingly aware of and interested in European forms of government.

In classical Arabic usage, the term *ḥukūmah* had the broad sense of adjudication; along with other words derived from the root *ḥ-k-m,* it referred to the dispensation of justice, whether by an arbitrator, judge, or the ruler himself. Government in the narrow sense was referred to as *wilāyah* (from the primary meaning of closeness to something, hence administration or government), *sulṭān* (power), or *imārah* (from an Arabic root having to do with command). By the eleventh century, the word *ḥukūmah* had begun to take on a stronger political connotation and was used to refer to the function of *ḥākim* (provincial governor). Although the earlier judicial sense of the word was not lost, its special connection with governance became more pronounced in Ottoman times. By the late eighteenth century, it was used not only in the narrow sense of governorship, but with the more general meaning of administration, rule, and political authority. It was this general political sense of the term that allowed Turkish and Arabic writers in the nineteenth century to employ it in distinguishing between the various forms of government. For example, the encyclopedist Buṭrus al-Bustānī (1819–1883) refers to the democratic government (*ḥukūmah dīmuqrāṭiyah*) that Cromwell failed to establish in England; other examples include *ḥukūmah aristuqrāṭiyah, ḥukūmat fyudāl* (used to describe government in prerevolutionary France), *ḥukūmah muqayyadah* (limited, i.e., constitutional, government), and *ḥukūmat al-shaʿb bi-al-shaʿb* (republic, i.e., government of the people by the people).

This sort of usage does not require a conceptual break with the older meanings of the term. However, the formal distinction between government and state, attested in an Ottoman political treatise of the early nineteenth century and generally maintained in Turkish and Arabic ever since, is something quite new. In traditional Islamic juristic writings, the state does not itself exist as a corporate institution with legal personality; governmental institutions are shown to be legitimate because they are authorized by God and divine law, not by a state possessed of its own legal authority. (This does not mean that *sharīʿah* [the divine law] was systematically enforced or even carefully observed by most Muslim rulers; it simply means that Muslims legitimized their political institutions with reference to God rather than to a manmade state.) By contrast, the hardened distinction between state and government in the political discourse of the past century and a half reflects the process of political and legal secularization undergone by the Muslim world. It is consistent with the appearance of secular constitutions, law codes, and other features of Western-type territorial states.

The nature of government, and its relationship to Islam, is one of the central problems in modern Islamic thought. We owe the earliest theoretical exploration of the issue in a modern context to the Young Ottoman thinker Mehmet Namık Kemal (1840–1888). To a degree unequalled by his contemporaries, Namık Kemal attempted to blend elements of traditional Islamic and modern European political thought in considering the origins of government, the notions of popular sovereignty and majority rule, the idea of separation of powers, and the benefits of constitutional rule. Since then, the nature of government has been discussed by secularists, Muslim reformists, and neorevivalists, few of whom have so systematically integrated European political theory into their own work. [*See the biography of Kemal.*]

One of the chief contributors to this discussion on the secularist side was the Egyptian religious scholar ʿAlī ʿAbd al-Rāziq (1888–1966). His controversial treatise, *Al-Islām wa-uṣūl al-ḥukm* (Islam and the Fundamentals of Government), was written in the aftermath of the Turkish abolition of the caliphate in 1924. ʿAbd al-Rāziq's principal concern was to demonstrate, against those agitating for the reestablishment of the caliphate, that there is no such thing as an Islamic system of government. Islam properly understood mandates no particular form of government and no specific political institutions. The historical caliphate, according to ʿAbd al-Rāziq, has no basis in scripture or tradition. Its apparent religious legitimacy has always been based on a misreading of the Prophet's own mission (properly understood as purely spiritual), and a mistaken tendency from earlier times to associate religion and government and to ascribe religious significance to the community's political leader. By contrast, ʿAbd al-Rāziq wants to distinguish between the religious mission of the Prophet and his political activities and thereby cut the link between the political office of the caliph and Muḥammad's prophetic career. The caliphate has never been integral to Islam; it was invented for practical reasons, then given specious religious significance by the legal scholars. Muslims are free to construct any kind of government they choose, based on the customs and necessities of the time. [*See the biography of ʿAbd al-Rāziq.*]

Among the many objections lodged against ʿAbd al-Rāziq's treatise by traditionalist legal scholars was that it leaves Muslims without a law standing above the government. There can be no theoretical check on arbitrary rule without a touchstone of legitimacy beyond the government itself. This was also an issue which exercised a reformist contemporary of ʿAbd al-Rāziq, Muḥammad Rashīd Riḍā (1865–1935). Riḍā is sometimes credited with having originated the modern concept of the Islamic state. He does indeed use terms such as *al-dawlah* or *al-ḥukūmah al-islāmīyah* (Islamic state or government), *al-khilāfah al-islāmīyah* (Islamic caliphate), and *ḥukūmat al-khilāfah* (caliphal government). This is new terminology and reflects an attempt to establish the basis for Islamic rule within a twentieth-century political environment. Although his interest in the caliphate seems a throwback to earlier times, his understanding of the institution sets him quite apart from the classical tradition of political thought. Unlike the classical thinkers, Rashīd Riḍā appears to have seen the caliphate as a largely spiritual or pontifical institution. Through his law-making authority as *mujtahid* (chief religious scholar), the caliph can offer the various governments of the Muslim world divine legitimacy. The caliph keeps alive the process of *ishtirāʿ* (divine lawmaking) and thus guarantees that *ḥukūmah madanīyah* (civic government) continues to have an Islamic basis, as well as a flexible corpus of law. But he himself has no direct governmental responsibilities and serves mainly as the touchstone of legal authority for each local government. [*See the biography of Rashīd Riḍā.*]

Rashīd Riḍā's emphasis on the caliphate sets him apart from most neorevivalist thinkers of the late twentieth century, who are in other respects rightly considered his intellectual descendants. The only major thinker to speak of a caliphate was the founder of the Jamāʿat-i Islāmī in the Indian subcontinent, Abū al-Aʿlā Mawdūdī (1903–1979). However, Mawdūdī's use of the term caliph is nothing like Rashīd Riḍā's, nor does it mark a return to the classical conception. For Mawdūdī, the fact that sovereignty properly rests with God alone means that any temporal government with Islamic legitimacy must be called a caliphate: government is entrusted to men as God's vicegerents, or caliphs. But since all men can lay claim to this caliphal status (given the Qur'ānic usage of the term), the head of government is presented as operating with authority delegated most immediately from his fellow caliphs. By Mawdūdī's own evaluation, this system does not amount to popular sovereignty or democracy, both of which are secular Western concepts in which the authority underpinning government is human centered rather than divine. While reaffirming the old principle of *shūrā* (mutual consultation) in government, Mawdūdī does not insist on its identity with Western democracy, and in general does not see Islam as prescribing the particular institutions in which consultation takes place. He is in fact often vague on the specifics of government; he discusses in detail only the head of state and the *majlis-i shūrā* (legislature), largely ignoring subsidiary institutions as well as the judiciary. This avoidance of specifics (coupled with an insistence on the essentially political nature of Islam) is characteristic of much neorevivalist thought.

One thing that Mawdūdī does make clear is the activist and totalitarian nature of the state. The institutions of government must be employed in all their power to give God's sovereignty over people practical expression. No sphere of human activity is to be outside of this all-embracing, ideological state. There is no essential difference between state, government, and society: all are part of the larger Islamic order anchored in *sharīʿah*. As such, constitutional issues, such as the relationship between the executive, legislative, and judicial organs of government, are of little interest to Mawdūdī. [*See the biography of Mawdūdī.*]

This totalitarian emphasis is not echoed by the head of Sudan's Muslim Brotherhood, Ḥasan al-Turābī (b. 1932), perhaps the leading neorevivalist figure of the 1990s. It is not always easy to assess Turābī's ideas on government, since his thinking has evolved along with his changing political role in Sudan. In general, however, he seems to favor a limited, minimal role for Islamic government. Turābī's state is in theory noninterventionist; it leaves civil society alone as much as possible. He equates this approach explicitly with the Western liberal tradition, but finds ample precedent in Islamic history, both in the limited social role traditionally played by Muslim governments and in the practical separation that has almost always obtained between *sharīʿah* and government. Divine law has always existed apart from governmental institutions, and has ideally served as a constitutional check on them. For Turābī, the proper Islamic government must act in accordance with the law, but not as an agent of it. Government should not seek actively to shape society, but should allow an Islamic society to evolve naturally through the activities of individuals who live their lives in accordance with God's law. This autonomy of the individual is perfectly consistent with the values of *sharīʿah*, which focuses on the social relations of individuals rather than on the institutions constructed to regulate them. The fact that *sharīʿah* does not recognize the state as a repository of legal authority is proof that the true Islamic government is a limited one.

Much of Turābī's thinking is shaped, of course, by the particular circumstances of Sudan, even though it is often put in broad, theoretical language. Like other thinkers, he is not simply speculating about what true Islamic government should be, but is attempting to construct the theoretical basis for that government in response to specific political constraints. What Turābī says about limited and decentralized government, the status of non-Muslim minorities, and political parties (no legal bar, but factionalism would not arise in a truly Islamic society) is best seen in this light. At times he has equated the institutions of Islamic government with representative democracy; at other times he has stressed the differences between them. But one constant feature of his thought is a willingness to adopt political institutions from the West, as long as they are not specifically excluded by *sharīʿah* and can be put to appropriate use in the service of Islam. Just as the earliest Muslims adopted Roman and Persian institutions, Muslims in the twentieth century must be willing to look beyond their own borders for the best tools to organize public life. [*See the biography of Turābī.*]

The modern notion of Islamic government has faced its most visible test in postrevolutionary Iran, where the clerical leadership has had to go beyond general theorizing about religion and government and actually attempt to institutionalize an Islamic state. The theory of government that underpins the state, and that is embodied in the revised constitutions of 1979 and 1989, is known as *vilāyat-i faqīh* (Ar., *wilāyat al-faqīh;* the guardianship of the jurisconsult). It is this legal doctrine that lies at the heart of the claim that the *fuqahāʾ* (religious scholars) have a responsibility to exercise political leadership and that one *faqīh* (religious scholar) in particular must be recognized as the supreme authority in the country.

The credit for developing this doctrine into a powerful ideological tool is given to Ayatollah Ruhollah Khomeini (1902–1989). In a series of lectures delivered in Najaf in 1970 (generally known under the title *Islamic Government,* or *Ḥukūmat-i Islāmī*), Khomeini argued that Islam requires the establishment of political institutions which can give systematic, practical effect to *sharīʿah* and that the *fuqahāʾ* must play a leading role in the establishment and functioning of such a government. Khomeini is not at all specific about the institutional structure of this Islamic government, and is content merely to distinguish it both from a republic based on popular sovereignty and from a constitutional monarchy. Unlike these other forms of rule, the Islamic government recognizes the ultimate sovereignty of God and works to implement God's law in the world. Here, Khomeini's use of the term *ḥukūmah* is informed both by its modern sense (i.e., the official institutions of the state and the individuals who run them) and by the more traditional understandings of it as adjudication, and the process whereby authority is translated into effective power. This double meaning runs throughout the Najaf lectures; Khomeini puts it to especially good effect in playing on the ambiguity of the term *ḥākim,* which one famous Shīʿī tradition (the so-called *maqbūlah*) applies to the religious scholars: *ḥākim* can mean both judge and ruler, and it is the latter sense that has particular resonance to modern ears, accustomed to the political connotation of *ḥukūmah.* Whatever the *maqbūlah* tradition would have meant to Shīʿīs of earlier centuries, the political echoes are inescapable within Khomeini's text.

The revised Iranian Constitution of 1979 includes some elements typical of a nineteenth-century European liberal constitution and others linked to the Islamic ideology of the state. There is, on the one hand, an emphasis on the separation of powers between the executive, judiciary, and legislature (terms that Khomeini had in fact employed vaguely in his Najaf lectures with reference to the responsibilities of the clerics). This might have reflected the belief of some in the need to provide for a system of checks and balances in order to avoid future dictatorships like that of the shah. On the other hand, provisions were made for close clerical supervision of governmental activities, and the office of *faqīh* was institutionalized, with Khomeini its first occupant. The broad scope of authority granted the *faqīh* (anticipated in the Najaf lectures) was of course inconsistent with the notion of a balance of powers, but it helped to lock in clerical domination of the revolution. The move met with a small amount of opposition from religious scholars, some of whom remained unconvinced of *vilāyat-i faqīh*'s doctrinal legitimacy within the Shīʿī tradition. There might also have been a fear among some that too close a clerical involvement in the government could lead to a dangerous popular backlash if things should go wrong. This might explain why Khomeini himself was willing at first to accept a largely secular constitution with no special provisions for clerical control. [*See* Wilāyat al-Faqīh *and the biography of Khomeini.*]

The institutionalization of the *faqīh* has not resolved once and for all the tension between religion and government in Iran. Just before his death, Khomeini himself contradicted President Khamene'i's seemingly routine assertion that in an Islamic state, the executive and legislative branches of government are subordinate to the superior divine law. Khomeini insisted that the government is empowered to revoke, in the interests of the country as a whole, any *sharīʿah* agreements that it has concluded with the people. This is normally seen as part of an attack on the authority of the conservative Council of Guardians, the committee of clerics who examine the compatibility of parliamentary legislation with Islam. But the problem is a long-term one for Iran, and for any government with similar pretensions to legitimacy in Islamic terms. Whatever the utopian simplicity of Khomeini's *ḥukūmat-i islāmī,* the fact remains that the potential for conflict between the demands of government and the claims of God is not likely to disappear.

[*See also* Authority and Legitimation; Dawlah; Islamic State.]

BIBLIOGRAPHY

Ayalon, Ami. *Language and Change in the Arab Middle East.* Oxford, 1987.

Enayat, Hamid. *Modern Islamic Political Thought.* Austin, 1982.

Hourani, Albert. *Arabic Thought in the Liberal Age.* Cambridge, 1983.

Lewis, Bernard, et al. "Ḥukūma." In *Encyclopaedia of Islam,* new ed., vol. 3, pp. 551–568. Leiden, 1960–.

Lewis, Bernard. "Hukumet and Devlet," *Belletin,* 46 (1982): 415–421.

Lewis, Bernard. *The Political Language of Islam.* Chicago, 1988.

Mardin, Şerif. *The Genesis of Young Ottoman Thought.* Princeton, 1962.
Zubaida, Sami. *Islam, the People, and the State.* London, 1989.

KEITH LEWINSTEIN

HUMAN RIGHTS. The term "human rights," or *ḥuqūq al-insān* in Arabic, has only recently come into common use, as have the analogous terms *ḥuqūq-i insān* in Persian and *insan hukukları* in Turkish.

Early Reception. Concepts analogous to human rights have certain precursors in the Islamic heritage of philosophy and theology, but human rights lack precise equivalents in medieval *fiqh* (jurisprudence). In *fiqh* the category *ḥaqq al-ʿabd,* the right of the individual Muslim, was used to distinguish cases in which legal actions against a wrongdoer were left to the discretion of the injured party or parties from other cases belonging to the category of the right of God, *ḥaqq Allāh,* in which prosecution was mandatory and was to be undertaken by the government. One settled *fiqh* principle corresponding to a modern right was the right of the owners of property to seek legal relief against interference with their property.

Rather than constructing doctrines or proposing institutions designed to curb the powers of the ruler or to protect the individual from the ruler's oppression, Islamic legal thought long concentrated on defining the theoretical duties of believers, including rulers, vis-à-vis God. According to the prevailing perspective, rulers had the obligation to rule according to *sharīʿah* law; their subjects were to obey them unless ordered to do something constituting a sin. The development of institutions that could place real curbs on rulers' despotism or make them accountable to those they ruled was neglected; rebellion was commonly proposed as the remedy for tyranny.

To deal with the practical problems of protecting rights and freedoms, Muslim intellectuals and statesmen began to adopt the principles of European constitutionalism in the nineteenth century. In the latter half of the twentieth century, after the common acceptance of the principles of constitutionalism, the related question of the compatibility of international human-rights principles with Islamic doctrine was raised.

The strongest influences on Muslims' ideas came from French concepts and legal principles developed during the Enlightenment and the French Revolution. These included the first great statement of modern human rights, the 1789 Declaration des Droits de l'Homme et du Citoyen, and the 1791 French Constitution, as well as concepts of public liberties. In the areas of the Muslim world ruled by Britain, which lacked a written constitution expressly guaranteeing specified rights, the models were democratic freedoms as developed in the common law tradition and Britain's system of parliamentary government.

Many nineteenth-century officials, diplomats, and writers from Muslim countries played roles in disseminating European ideas of constitutionalism and public liberties. They included the Egyptian Shaykh Rifāʿah Rāfiʿ al-Ṭahṭāwī (1801–1871), an al-Azhar scholar who studied French legal and political institutions in Paris from 1826 to 1831. He prepared a report on concepts of political rights, the rule of law, liberty, equality, and the ideas of the Enlightenment, and translated the French constitution into Arabic; in 1839 his report was translated into Turkish. The Persian diplomat Mīrzā Malkom Khān (1833–1908), who was educated in Paris and had lived in Turkey, later becoming Persian ambassador to Great Britain, wrote extensively on European concepts of government, the rule of law, and liberty, claiming that these could be reconciled with Islam. In the Ottoman realm the literary figure Namık Kemal (1840–1888) was prominent in disseminating ideas of rights and freedoms and the notion of their compatibility with Islam. [*See the biographies of Malkom Khan and Kemal.*]

Constitutionalism and Rights. In the nineteenth century early clashes between inherited Islamic doctrines and modern norms regarding rights came on the question of the equality of Muslims and non-Muslims before the law. The issue was joined as European powers pressed for the elimination of the disabilities traditionally placed on non-Muslims.

A fundamental pact announced in Tunisia in 1857 under European pressure guaranteed equality for all before the law and in taxation as well as complete security for all inhabitants irrespective of religion, nationality, or race. Tunisia was the first Muslim country to promulgate a constitution, doing so in 1861 and affirming the rights established in the pact; however, the constitution was suspended by the French Protectorate (1881–1956). In Tunisia as in many other Muslim countries, the independence struggle against European domination accentuated people's consciousness of the importance of rights and democratic freedoms. After independence the 1956 Tunisian Constitution stated that the republican form of government was the best guarantee of "human rights."

The most important early reforms in the direction of realizing rights were undertaken in the Ottoman Empire, which had many non-Muslim subjects and which, owing to its military and economic vulnerability, was also exposed to pressures from European powers. The *hatt-ı şerif* of 1839, reinforced by the *hatt-ı hümayun* of 1856, was part of a series of modernizing reforms in the Tanzimat period that aimed to establish the security of life, honor, and property, fair and public trials, and equality before the law for all Ottoman subjects irrespective of religion. The principle of nondiscrimination based on language and race was added by the *hatt-ı hümayun*. In 1840 the new penal code affirmed the equality of all Ottoman subjects before the law. [*See* Tanzimat.]

By mid-century reformist pressures prompted the adoption of the 1876 Ottoman Constitution, which contained a section on *hukuk-i umumiye,* or public liberties, of Ottoman subjects, providing for equality regardless of religion, free exercise of religions other than Islam and freedom of worship, inviolability of personal freedom, and guarantees against arbitrary intrusions, extortion, arrest, or other unlawful violations of person, residence, or property. There were also provisions for freedom of the press, association, and education. This constitution was suspended in practice and not revived until after the Young Turk Revolution in 1908, a central goal of which was reviving the constitution and establishing the equality of all Ottoman citizens. The Young Turks' reforms expanded constitutional rights protections, prohibited arrests and searches except by established legal procedures, abolished special or extraordinary courts, and guaranteed press freedom. Turkey's second republic saw in 1961 the promulgation of a constitution that undertook in its preamble to ensure and guarantee "human rights and liberties" and made men and women equal (Article 12). In the area of free exercise of religion, conditions were imposed to safeguard the policy of secularism adopted by Mustafa Kemal Atatürk (1881–1938), the first president of the Turkish Republic. Article 2 of the 1982 Turkish Constitution proclaimed Turkey to be a law-state that respects human rights.

In Republican Turkey the energetic pursuit of Kemalist secularism, beginning in 1925, led to the repression of various Islamic groups, especially dervish orders. In Soviet Central Asia the atheistic policies of the Soviet Union curbed the religious freedoms of the Muslim population until the collapse of the Soviet state in 1991. Suppression of Islam and denials of religious freedom also occurred under the Marxist regimes that ruled Albania from 1945 to 1991 and Afghanistan from 1978 to 1992. Elsewhere in the twentieth century regimes with secular orientations often indulged in harsh persecutions of Islamic fundamentalists.

Popular agitation against the despotism of the Qājār shahs culminated in Persia's first constitution in 1906–1907. Persia's Shīʿī clerics were divided about the religious legitimacy of constitutionalism and its attendant rights provisions. The Supplementary Constitutional Law of 1907 included Islamic qualifications of two rights provisions: publications were said to be free except where heretical or harmful to Islam (Article 20); and the study and teaching of science, education, and art were to be free except as prohibited by religious law (Article 18). Moreover, ministers in the government were required to be Persian Muslims (Article 58). However, the country's inhabitants were to enjoy equal rights before the law (Article 8).

After the 1978–1979 Islamic Revolution in Iran, official spokesmen invoked Islam as the reason for the clerical regime's hostility to international human rights, which they often dismissed as products of an alien, Western cultural tradition; however, Iran did not repudiate its ratification of the International Covenant on Civil and Political Rights. The 1979 Iranian Constitution in Article 20 expressly provided that all citizens enjoyed human, political, economic, social, and cultural rights according to Islamic standards; Article 4 provided that Islamic principles prevailed over those in the constitution. Notwithstanding the reference in Article 20 to economic, social, and cultural rights, the concern seemed to be with using Islamic criteria to curb civil and political rights—many of the latter being expressly limited by Islamic criteria (see Articles 21, 24, 26, 27, 28, and 168). The limitations placed on human rights correlated with the policies of Iran's clerical leadership after 1979. The principle of equality and equal protection for women and religious minorities was breached in many ways. In the name of implementing Islamic criminal justice, the regime ignored principles of criminal procedure designed to protect the rights of the accused both before and during trial, as well as prohibitions of cruel and inhuman punishment. Religious minorities and individuals and groups opposed to clerical rule or the regime's religious ideology were excluded from the political process and were often subjected to harsh persecution.

Islamic and Western concepts were combined in the

Afghan Constitution produced between 1921 and 1924. For example, all inhabitants were to be equal before the government without distinction of religion and sect, and it was provided that all Afghans would be equal before the *sharīʿah* and the laws of the state. Nonetheless, Hindus and Jews (the only recognized non-Muslim communities) were required to pay the *jizyah*, the poll-tax traditionally imposed on *dhimmīs* (protected non-Muslims), and to wear distinctive emblems. [*See* Dhimmī; Jizyah.]

By the end of the twentieth century all Muslim countries had adopted constitutions containing some or all of the rights principles set forth in international human-rights law. The 1989 Algerian Constitution was noteworthy for its guarantee of equality before the law regardless of gender (Article 28), fundamental liberties and human rights (Article 31), and human-rights advocacy (Article 32). Like most Muslim countries, however, Algeria retained Islamic personal-status rules and constitutional provisions according Islam a privileged status, perpetuating the ambiguous relationship between religious and constitutional norms.

Fiqh survived longest as the official law of the land in Saudi Arabia. However, changes inaugurated in 1992 suggested that the country might be moving gradually toward a governmental system that would accord at least limited recognition to rights and constitutionalism—albeit subject to Islamic criteria. The principle that Islam entails limits on human rights was adopted in the Basic Law of Government promulgated by the Saudi Arabian regime in 1992; Article 26 provided that "the state protects human rights in accordance with the Islamic *sharīʿah*." What the *sharīʿah* limits on rights would entail was not defined. The basic law provided for many citizen entitlements in the area of social welfare, but only a few rights in the political or civil area were recognized. These included the provision that no one should be arrested, imprisoned, or have his actions restricted except as provided by law (Article 36); that homes should not be entered or searched save in cases specified by statutes (Article 37); that communications should not be confiscated, delayed, read, or listened to except in cases defined by statutes (Article 40); and that private property must be protected and could only be taken for the public interest and with fair compensation (Article 17).

Women's Rights. One of the areas where the clash between inherited Islamic principles and international human-rights norms was most acute was that of women's rights. Although conservatives propounded the notion that full equality for women violated Islamic precepts, feminists argued that it was patriarchal attitudes and inadequate study of the Islamic sources that led to the notion that Islam required keeping women in a subordinate position.

Already in the late nineteenth century liberal writers like the Egyptian Qasīm Amīn (1865–1908) had propounded the thesis that certain problems facing Middle Eastern societies—despotism, moral degeneration, and the degraded status of women—were not intrinsic to Islam but were the products of corrupting influences and social customs. While not advocating full equality for women, Amīn demanded that women's rights should be enhanced. He also linked the cause of women's freedom to the realization of freedom and rights for citizens in general. Feminists such as the Egyptian Hudā Shaʿrawī (1882–1947) became prominent advocates of women's rights and emancipation. One of the boldest attempts to reconcile Islam with full equality for women was offered by al-Ṭāhir al-Ḥaddād, a Tunisian graduate of al-Zaytunah, who in 1930 published *Imraʾatunā fi al-sharīʿah wa al-mujtamaʿ* (Our Woman in the *Sharīʿah* and Society), which propounded the idea that Islam had envisaged a progressive emancipation of women; he advocated the reform of Islamic laws to eliminate obstacles to male-female equality in the domestic as well as the public sphere. For the boldness of its thesis the book was condemned with particular vehemence by conservatives and its author denounced as a heretic.

Unequivocal support for full equality for women came from Kemal Atatürk, who in the wake of the Turkish war of independence proclaimed that women had the right to be equal; he subsequently took measures to remove the disabilities imposed by Turkish custom and Islamic law—without attempting to reconcile his reforms with Islamic precepts. In the Arab world, the most dramatic reform was embodied in the Tunisian Law of Personal Status of 1956 promulgated by President Habib Bourguiba. Presented as an Islamic law, the code undertook bold reforms improving women's status, such as abolishing polygamy and establishing equal rights for men and women in divorce.

Into the late twentieth century Muslim countries preserved laws that discriminated against women and denied them full civil and political rights, often in the face of constitutional provisions mandating the equality of all citizens. In general, laws afforded women considerable equality outside the family; it was in the area of personal status that discriminatory features taken from *fiqh* were retained. Saudi Arabia was notable for its reliance on Islam to justify its refusal to grant women rights and freedoms widely enjoyed elsewhere in the Muslim world.

Few Muslim countries ratified the 1979 Convention on the Elimination of All Forms of Discrimination Against Women, and those that chose to ratify did so subject to reservations regarding various central provisions. The reservations made by Bangladesh, Egypt, Libya, and Tunisia were specifically justified by their need to adhere to Islamic law. [*See also* Feminism; Women's Movements.]

Human Rights Movements. Independent, nongovernmental organizations founded for the defense of human rights have spearheaded campaigns to improve respect for human rights in Muslim countries. One of the earliest Muslim human-rights organizations was established by Moroccans in December 1933 in the Spanish-controlled enclave of Tetouan as an affiliate of a Spanish human-rights organization. A human-rights group with Islamic affiliations, the Iranian Committee for the Defense of Freedom and Human Rights, was formed with the participation of several religious figures; it aimed primarily at achieving democratization and the elimination of torture and *in camera* political trials. A central participant was Mehdi Bāzargān (b. 1907), a proponent of Islamic liberalism who went on to become Iran's first prime minister immediately after the Islamic Revolution. He and his associates later suffered persecution when their stance on human rights put them at odds with the clerical regime. Human-rights organizations in which educated professionals were prominent proliferated throughout the Muslim world in the 1980s in the face of daunting obstacles and dangers. One of the most important was the Arab Organization for Human Rights, which, like the overwhelming majority of independent human-rights organizations, espoused the human-rights standards set forth in international law. These organizations collaborated with international human-rights organizations.

Muslim States and International Human-rights Law. It was in the aftermath of World War II that the modern international formulations of human rights were produced, setting standards that became incorporated in public international law. Muslim countries were among the founding members of the United Nations, whose 1945 Charter called for respect for human rights and fundamental freedoms; all Muslim countries eventually joined the UN. Aspects of the Universal Declaration of Human Rights passed by the General Assembly in 1948 provoked criticism from representatives of Muslim countries, although in the end only Saudi Arabia failed to support its passage. Muslim nations differed greatly in their willingness to ratify the human-rights conventions subsequently drafted under UN auspices. Muslims sometimes charged that international rights norms had a Western or Judeo-Christian bias that precluded their acceptance in Muslim milieus. In terms of the compatibility of international rights norms and Islamic law, the alleged conflicts centered around civil and political rights; problems of the compatibility of Islam with economic, social, and cultural rights were rarely raised. The principles of freedom of religion—notably the right to convert from Islam to another faith—and the full equality of persons regardless of sex or religion seemed to pose particular problems.

The Charter of the Organization of the Islamic Conference (OIC), an international organization founded in 1973 to which all Muslim countries belong, indicated in its preamble that the members were "reaffirming their commitment to the UN Charter and fundamental human rights." In 1990, however, the OIC issued the Cairo Declaration on Human Rights in Islam, which diverged significantly from international human-rights standards; it was not made clear how this declaration was to be reconciled with the conflicting obligations undertaken by OIC members in ratifying international human-rights covenants or in their individual constitutional rights provisions, which in many cases corresponded to the international norms.

Like the many other self-proclaimed "Islamic" human-rights schemes that proliferated from the 1960s onward, the OIC declaration extensively borrowed terms and concepts from the International Bill of Human Rights, presenting a hybrid mixture of elements taken from Islamic and international law. The OIC Declaration asserted that "fundamental rights and universal freedoms in Islam are an integral part of the Islamic religion," but then proceeded to insert "Islamic" qualifications and conditions on the rights and freedoms guaranteed under international law—in conflict with international human-rights theory, which does not permit religious criteria to override rights. Representative provisions included the rule in Article 24 that all the rights and freedoms stipulated in the declaration were subject to the *sharīʿah,* without defining what limits this would entail.

There was no provision for equal rights for all persons

regardless of sex or religion. Instead, Article 1 stated that "all human beings are equal in terms of basic human dignity and basic obligations and responsibilities [not "rights"], without any discrimination on the grounds of race, color, language, sex, religious belief, political affiliation, social status or other considerations." Article 6 further provided that "woman is equal to man in human dignity" [not "rights"], but it imposed on the husband the responsibility for the support and welfare of the family. In contrast, Article 13 provided that men and women were entitled to fair wages "without discrimination." Article 5 provided that on the right to marry there should be "no restrictions stemming from race, color or nationality," but did not prohibit restrictions based on religion.

The provisions regarding religion did not aim at neutrality: Article 10 stated that Islam was the religion of unspoiled nature and prohibited "any form of compulsion on man or to exploit his poverty or ignorance in order to convert him to another religion or to atheism." Article 9 called for the state to ensure the means to acquire education "so as to enable man to be acquainted with the religion of Islam." The favored treatment of Islam carried over to freedom of speech, with Article 22(a) stating that expressing opinion freely was allowed "in such manner as would not be contrary to the principles of the *sharīʿah*." Article 22(c) barred the exploitation or misuse of information "in such a way as may violate sanctities and the dignity of Prophets, undermine moral and ethical values or disintegrate, corrupt or harm society or weaken its faith." Article 18 stipulated a right to privacy in the conduct of private affairs, in the home, in the family, and regarding property and relationships. Article 15 set forth "rights of ownership" to "property acquired in a legitimate way, barring expropriation except for the public interest and upon payment of immediate and fair compensation."

Noteworthy by their absence were provisions calling for the observance of democratic principles in political systems and guarantees of freedom of religion, freedom of association, freedom of the press, and equality and equal protection of the law. Although torture was prohibited in Article 20, there were no provisions explicitly endorsing international rights norms in the area of criminal procedure—only the vague assurance in Article 19 that the defendant would be entitled to "a fair trial in which he shall be given all the guarantees of defense." Since Article 25 stated that the *sharīʿah* "is the only source of reference or the explanation or clarification of any of the articles of this Declaration," the possibility was left open that a trial would be deemed "fair" as long as it was conducted in conformity with *sharīʿah* norms, which were historically underdeveloped in the area of criminal procedure. There was no principle of legality per se; the provision in Article 19 that there should be no crime or punishment except as provided for in the *sharīʿah* seemed to open the door to the application of *taʿzīr* (discretionary) penalties, as well as rules regarding *ḥadd* crimes. Article 2 prohibited taking away life except for a reason prescribed by the *sharīʿah*. Reflecting the third-world setting in which Muslim nations elaborate their positions on rights, Article 11 prohibited colonialism and stated that "peoples suffering from colonialism have the full right to freedom and self-determination." In sum, the OIC Declaration suggested that the official approach of Muslim countries to civil and political rights was distinguishable from that of non-Muslim countries by reason of their reliance on *sharīʿah* rules. [*See* Organization of the Islamic Conference.]

Governments and individuals throughout the Muslim world continue to take many positions on human rights that are by self-designation "Islamic." Given the variety of approaches and principles involved, it is evident that Muslim opinion remains divided on the relationship between international human-rights principles and the Islamic legal heritage, and on the compatibility of the two.

[*See also* International Law; Law, *article on* Modern Legal Reform; Modernism; *and* Women and Social Reform.]

BIBLIOGRAPHY

Blaustein, A. P., and G. H. Flanz, eds. *Constitutions of the Countries of the World*. Dobbs Ferry, N.Y., 1971–. Regularly updated collection, often with valuable historical essays, that includes constitutions from all Muslim countries.

Coulson, Noel J. "The State and the Individual in Islamic Law." *International and Comparative Law Quarterly* 6 (1957): 49–60. Examination of the relevant premodern jurisprudence.

Dwyer, Kevin. *Arab Voices: The Human Rights Debate in the Middle East*. Berkeley, 1991. Interviews and accounts of differing points of view.

Hairi, Abdul-Hadi. *Shīʿism and Constitutionalism in Iran*. Leiden, 1977. Scholarly examination of the early response of Iranian intellectuals and clerics to constitutionalism and related rights concepts.

Hourani, Albert. *Arabic Thought in the Liberal Age, 1798–1939*. London, 1962. Sensitive, thoughtful survey of early liberal currents in Arab thought.

Lewis, Bernard, et al. "Dustūr." In *Encyclopaedia of Islam*, new ed., vol. 2, pp. 638–677. Leiden, 1960–. Scholarly surveys of the history of constitutionalism in several Muslim countries.

Lewis, Bernard. *The Emergence of Modern Turkey*. 2d ed. London and New York, 1968. Classic history that examines the spread of modern political ideas in the late Ottoman Empire and early Turkish republic.

Mayer, Ann. *Islam and Human Rights: Tradition and Politics*. Boulder, 1991. Critical comparison of selected Islamic versions of civil and political rights with their international counterparts.

An-Naᶜim, Abdullahi Ahmed. *Toward an Islamic Reformation: Civil Liberties, Human Rights, and International Law*. Syracuse, N.Y., 1990. Original perspectives from a Sudanese specialist in public and international law.

Nashat, Guity, ed. *Women and Revolution in Iran*. Boulder, 1983. Essays written from a variety of perspectives on the status of women in postrevolutionary Iran.

Rosenthal, Franz. *The Muslim Concept of Freedom Prior to the Nineteenth Century*. Leiden, 1960. Learned exposition of relevant texts.

Relevant articles may be found in journals such as *Human Rights Quarterly* and *Index on Censorship*, and information is regularly compiled, analyzed, and published by human rights groups such as Amnesty International, the Lawyers Committee for Human Rights, Africa Watch, Asia Watch, and Middle East Watch.

ANN ELIZABETH MAYER

ḤURRĪYAH. *See* Democracy; Human Rights.

ḤUSAYN, ṬĀHĀ (1889–1971), Egyptian novelist, critic, and modernist reformer. His two Arabic nicknames summarize this famed writer's life. One, ᶜAmīd al-Adab al-ᶜArabī (dean of Arabic literature), signals his pivotal role as one of the towering figures of Arabic letters in the twentieth century. The other, Qāhir al-Ẓalām" (Conqueror of Darkness), alludes to his blindness, a handicap that gives his story a heroic cast.

Ṭāhā Ḥusayn was born in ᶜIzbat al-Kīlū, a small village in Upper Egypt, to a large family. At a young age he contracted ophthalmia, and the village barber's treatment caused the young boy to lose his sight. The handicap strengthened Ṭāhā's resolve. He broke barrier after barrier in his rise to a position of leadership in Egyptian society and letters.

Ṭāhā Ḥusayn's education began in the village *kuttāb* (Qur'ānic school). In 1902 he went to Cairo, pursuing his schooling at al-Azhar, the most prestigious place for traditional Muslim education. But secularism attracted him more than traditionalism, and he began studies at the newly founded university in Cairo, from which he received a doctorate in 1914. Like many other Arab intellectuals, he was drawn to Europe and studied in Montpellier and then Paris, where he received his second doctorate in 1919.

In France, Ṭāhā Ḥusayn met and married a Frenchwoman, Suzanne Ṭāhā Ḥusayn, who maintained the practice of her own religion, Catholicism. That, combined with much travel and residence abroad, meant that Ṭāhā participated in two civilizations; however, his impact was greatest on Egyptian society and contemporary Arab culture. In his roles as adviser to Egypt's Ministry of Education and then as minister from 1950 to 1952, he saw to the implementation of educational reforms that ensured the expansion of the state school system.

It is for his writings, however, that Ṭāhā Ḥusayn is best known in the Arab world today. Novels, short stories, historical and critical studies, and political articles sit side by side with his translations of Western classics into Arabic. He took the controversial critical position that the famous pre-Islamic odes were inauthentic; his criticism also includes impassioned writings on the blind ᶜAbbāsid poet Abū al-ᶜAlā' al-Maᶜarrī (d. 1058). In his cultural manifesto *The Future of Culture in Egypt* he predicates his positions on intimate connections between Egypt and the West. Of all his works, it is Ṭāhā Ḥusayn's autobiography *Al-ayyām* (The Days) that has earned him a position in world literature. The three-volume masterpiece was published over forty years, a period critical in the development of Arabic literature. Its third-person narrator exposes, among other things, the weaknesses of the traditional educational system.

More than a century after his birth, the figure of Ṭāhā Ḥusayn stills towers over the Arab cultural scene. As the Conqueror of Darkness, in a movie of the same title, he became familiar to millions of Arab cinema viewers. He stirred controversy during his lifetime with his ideas on pre-Islamic poetry and on Egypt and the West, and with his attitudes toward traditional learning. After his death he was treated in many quarters as a virtual secular saint. With the rise of the Islamists in the Middle East, the figure of Ṭāhā Ḥusayn has been drawn into the fray once again, this time as the object of attack by conservative religious thinkers. The arguments of his antisecular opponents would not surprise him. The question of the future of culture no longer applies only to Egypt, but to the whole of the Middle East and North Africa. Two decades after his death, Ṭāhā Ḥusayn has become a pawn in the cultural game in which he was such an active player.

[*See also* Arabic Literature, *overview article;* Egypt.]

BIBLIOGRAPHY

Cachia, Pierre. *Ṭāhā Ḥusayn.* London, 1956. Useful general study on the Egyptian modernist.

Ḥusayn, Ṭāhā. *Al-Ayyām.* Vol. 1. Cairo, 1971. Translated by E. H. Paxton as *An Egyptian Childhood.* Washington, D.C., 1982. *Al-Ayyām.* Vol. 2. Cairo, 1971. Translated by Hilary Wayment as *The Stream of Days.* London, 1948. *Al-Ayyām.* Vol. 3. Cairo, 1973. Translated by Kenneth Cragg as *A Passage to France.* Leiden, 1976. Classic of modern autobiography, and one of the most widely read and influential texts in the Middle East and North Africa.

Malti-Douglas, Fedwa. *Blindness and Autobiography: Al-Ayyām of Ṭāhā Ḥusayn.* Princeton, 1985. In-depth study of Ṭāhā Ḥusayn's autobiography that analyzes both its literary properties and its links to the Arabo-Islamic textual tradition.

ʿUṣfūr, Jābir. *Al-Marāyā al-Mutajāwirah: Dirāsah fī Naqd Ṭāhā Ḥusayn.* Cairo, 1983. Study of Ṭāhā Ḥusayn's critical and literary corpus by one of the Arab world's leading critics.

FEDWA MALTI-DOUGLAS

ḤUSAYNĪ, AL-ḤĀJJ AMĪN AL- (1895–1974), *muftī* of Jerusalem and a nationalist leader during the period of British rule over Palestine (1917–1948). Al-Ḥājj Amīn al-Ḥusaynī came from an aristocratic land-owning family that traced its lineage to the prophet Muḥammad. His grandfather, father, and half-brother served as *muftī*s of Jerusalem. Ḥusaynī studied briefly at al-Azhar University in Cairo (1912–1913) and, after serving in the Ottoman army, became an active Arab nationalist. From 1918 to 1920, he supported the unification of Palestine with Syria, as a step toward a Pan-Arab state, and protested the British Balfour Declaration (November 1917) that promised to establish a national home in Palestine for the Jewish people. He fled to Damascus after participating in violent anti-Zionist protests in Jerusalem in April 1920.

Ḥusaynī emerged as a powerful figure when the British not only pardoned him but appointed him *muftī* of Jerusalem (May 1921) and president of the Supreme Muslim Council (January 1922). He pledged to maintain order and the British hoped the move would pacify the Palestinian elite. As president, he gained control over the Muslim religious schools, courts, orphanages, mosques, and *awqāf* (sg., *waqf;* religious endowments) throughout the country.

Ḥusaynī's effort to maintain calm while pressing for substantive political concessions from the British became more difficult to sustain in the wake of the Wailing Wall crisis (1928–1929) and soaring Jewish immigration in the early 1930s. He headed a delegation to London (January 1930) that sought a national government with an Arab majority. He also organized the General Islamic Congress in Jerusalem (December 1931) to galvanize support in the Muslim world. The failure of these initiatives to alter the Palestinians' situation encouraged anti-British radicals to challenge Ḥusaynī's influence. They later criticized his efforts, as president of the Arab Higher Committee, to limit the scope of the general strike that began in April 1936.

Ḥusaynī only broke decisively with the British when the Peel Commission called for the territorial partition of Palestine in July 1937: the nationalist cause appeared lost and British support for the Zionist movement irresistible. At this point he escaped to Lebanon (October 1937) and became a bitter enemy of the British. He supported the violent Palestinian revolt against the British (1938–1939), encouraged anti-British political forces in Iraq (October 1939 to May 1941), and fled through Iran to Italy and Germany. Ḥusaynī tried to persuade Hitler to pledge support for Arab independence, and appealed over the radio for Arabs and Muslims to revolt against the Allies. At the end of the war, he escaped to France (May 1945) and then to Cairo (May 1946), where he resumed his political activities. Discredited by his support for Hitler and unable to prevent the establishment of Israel in 1948, he lived in exile in Egypt until 1959 and then in Beirut. Ḥusaynī's importance lies in his dual role as a religious and political leader. His religious stature enhanced his political leadership and he activated support for the Palestinian nationalist cause both inside Palestine and abroad.

[*See also* Arab-Israeli Conflict; Arab Nationalism; West Bank and Gaza.]

BIBLIOGRAPHY

Jbara, Taysir. *Palestinian Leader Hajj Amin al-Husayni, Mufti of Jerusalem.* Princeton, 1985. Generally laudatory biography based on Arab, British, and Israeli sources.

Johnson, Nels. *Islam and the Politics of Meaning in Palestinian Nationalism.* London and Boston, 1982. Extended essay on Islamic motifs in the Palestinian movement, including the role of al-Ḥājj Amīn al-Ḥusaynī.

Lesch, Ann Mosely. *Arab Politics in Palestine, 1917–1939: The Frustration of a Nationalist Movement.* Ithaca, N.Y., 1979. Concise overview of the radicalization of Palestinian politics during the British mandate, based on British, Arab, and Israeli sources.

Mattar, Philip. *The Mufti of Jerusalem: Al-Hajj Amin al-Husayni and the Palestinian National Movement.* New York, 1988. Careful account of Ḥusaynī's life, with emphasis on the shift in his role after 1936, when accommodation with the British proved impossible; based on British, Arab, Israeli, and American sources.

Porath, Yehoshofat. *The Emergence of the Palestinian-Arab National Movement, 1918–1929* and *The Palestinian Arab National Movement, 1929–1939*. London, 1974 and 1977. Detailed examinations of Palestinian politics, with appropriate attention to Ḥusaynī's role; based on Israeli and British sources.

ANN MOSELY LESCH

ḤUSAYN IBN ʿALĪ (626–680), the third Shīʿī imām, son of ʿAlī ibn Abī Ṭālib and grandson of the prophet Muḥammad. As Muḥammad had no male heirs, Ḥusayn and his elder brother Ḥasan are believed to have continued the Prophet's line through his daughter Fāṭimah and his cousin ʿAlī. Hagiographical tradition abounds with tales of love and affection of the Prophet for his two grandsons.

ʿAlī was assassinated in 661 after a short and turbulent caliphate and was succeeded by his elder son, Ḥasan. But Ḥasan soon abdicated as he realized the disunity and fickleness of his followers and the superiority of Muʿāwiyah's well-organized forces.

Ḥusayn reluctantly accepted his brother's compromise and refused to pay allegiance to Muʿāwiyah. However, during Muʿāwiyah's long reign (661–680), Ḥusayn honored his brother's agreement with the Umayyad caliph. Among the stipulations of this agreement was that after Muʿāwiyah's death his successor would be either chosen through *shūrā* (consultation) or that—according to Shīʿī reports—the caliphate would revert to one of the two sons of ʿAlī.

Ḥasan died in 671 and Muʿāwiyah appointed his own son Yazīd as his successor. Yazīd is reputed to have been a lewd character given to drinking and other illicit pleasures. Many, particularly in the Hejaz and Iraq, opposed Yazīd's appointment, and a small number of notables, including Ḥusayn, withheld their allegiance. Wishing to assert his authority and quell opposition at any cost, Yazīd in 680 ordered his governor in Medina to take everyone's oath of allegiance and execute anyone who refused.

Ḥusayn left Medina (Madīnah) secretly and sought protection in the sanctuary of Mecca (Makkah). There, he received numerous letters from the Shīʿah of Kufa inviting him to lead them in an insurrection against Yazīd. Ḥusayn sent his cousin Muslim ibn ʿAqīl to Kufa to investigate the situation. Muslim sent word that support for Ḥusayn was strong and that he should hasten to Kufa without delay.

Apprised of these developments, Yazīd dismissed the governor of Kufa and extended the authority of ʿUbayd Allāh ibn Ziyād, the governor of Basra, to include Kufa. Ibn Ziyād was a shrewd and ruthless politician. By means of threats and bribes he quickly contained the uprising and sent a small detachment to prevent Ḥusayn from reaching Kufa. He captured Muslim and had him executed with some of his close supporters.

Ḥusayn now set out for Iraq with his women and children and a small band of followers. Learning of Muslim's fate along the way, he released his relatives and followers from all obligations and advised them to go. Many did, and he was left with a small group of loyal supporters and family members. He was intercepted by a small detachment and diverted away from Kufa to a spot called Karbala on the banks of the Euphrates.

An army of about four thousand men was then assembled to confront Ḥusayn and his band of seventy-odd followers. The army was headed by ʿUmar ibn Saʿd ibn Abī Waqqāṣ, the son of a respected companion of the Prophet. Ibn Ziyād also made sure that some of Ḥusayn's Kufic supporters were conscripted.

Ḥusayn arrived at Karbala on the second of Muḥarram. After a week of fruitless negotiations between Ḥusayn and ʿUmar ibn Saʿd, Ibn Ziyād sent an alternative leader called Shamir ibn Dhī al-Jawshan with instructions to execute the reluctant ʿUmar ibn Saʿd should he refuse to carry out his orders. Ḥusayn, Ibn Ziyād ordered, should either surrender and be brought to him as a war-captive or be killed in battle. For some days, Ḥusayn and his followers were denied water from the Euphrates in order to force them to surrender.

On the morning of 10 Muḥarram AH 61/680 CE, the battle began. Greatly outnumbered, Ḥusayn and his followers were annihilated by the early afternoon. One by one, Ḥusayn witnessed his own children and other relatives fall. Even an infant whom he held in his arms was slain. Finally, after a brave fight, Ḥusayn himself fell. On orders from Ibn Ziyād, Ḥusayn's corpse was trampled by horses and his head and those of his followers were paraded in Kufa as a warning to others.

Few personalities in Muslim history have exerted as great and enduring an influence on Islamic thought and piety as Imam Ḥusayn. For Sunnī, and particularly Ṣūfī piety, Ḥusayn is the revered grandson of the Prophet and member of his household *(ahl al-bayt)*. Ḥusayn's shrine-mosque in Cairo is a living symbol of Sunnī devotion to the martyred imam.

Ḥusayn's revolt against Umayyad rule inspired not only religious Muslims, but also secular socialists. A powerful portrayal of Ḥusayn the revolutionary was made by the socialist Egyptian writer ʿAbd al-Raḥmān al-Sharqāwī in his two-part play, "Ḥusayn the Revolutionary" and "Ḥusayn the Martyr."

Although these ideas are also shared by many educated Shiʿis, Ḥusayn occupies a central place in Twelver Shīʿī faith and piety. Pilgrimage *(ziyārah),* actual or ritualistic, to his tomb is second in importance to the *ḥajj* pilgrimage. Moreover, the ʿĀshūrāʾ and other *taʿziyah* (passion play) celebrations have given the Shīʿī community an ethos of suffering and martyrdom distinguishing it sharply from the rest of the Muslim community.

The meaning and significance of the revolution, struggle, and martyrdom of Imam Ḥusayn continues to grow with changing times and political circumstances of Muslim society. He has become a symbol of political resistance for many Muslims, regardless of their ideological persuasion or walk of life. For Shīʿī Muslims Ḥusayn is also a symbol of eschatological hope, as the expected Mahdī (messiah) will finally avenge his blood and vindicate him and all those who have suffered wrong at the hands of tyrannical rulers.

Since the middle ages special mosque annexes appropriately called *ḥusaynīyahs* have served as centers for the memorial observances of the sufferings and martyrdom of Ḥusayn and his family and the social and political lessons that can be learned from this tragedy. It was in such centers in Beirut and south Lebanon that the first Shīʿī resistance movements were born. It was also in the Ḥusaynīyah-yi Irshād that the ideas of ʿAlī Sharīʿatī kindled the final spark of the Iran's Islamic Revolution. Indications are that the example of Ḥusayn will continue to inspire Muslim resistance and religious fervor for a long time to come.

[*See also* Ḥusaynīyah; Ithnā ʿAsharīyah; Karbala; Shīʿī Islam, *historical overview article;* Taʿziyah; *and the biography of ʿAlī ibn Abī Ṭālib.*]

BIBLIOGRAPHY

Ahmad, Fazl. *Husain: The Great Martyr.* Lahore, 1969. Useful source for a concise presentation of pious Shīʿī views of martyrdom.

Alsarat. *The Imam Ḥusayn.* Vol. 12. Edited by the Muhammadi Trust of Great Britain and Northern Ireland. London, 1986. Collection of papers presented at the Imam Ḥusayn Conference from a variety of Shīʿī and Sunnī scholars representing both traditional and modern views of Ḥusayn's personality and martyrdom.

Ayoub, Mahmoud M. *Redemptive Suffering in Islam: A Study of the Devotional Aspects of ʿĀshūrāʾ in Twelver Shīʿism.* The Hague, 1978. Offers a useful discussion of the development of the ʿĀshūrāʾ celebrations and their place in Shīʿī popular piety and culture.

Mufīd, Muḥammad ibn Muḥammad al-. *Kitāb al-Irshād: The Book of Guidance.* Translated by I. K. A. Howard. Elmhurst, N.Y., 1981. Classic work presenting a generally balanced account of Ḥusayn's life and martyrdom, by a respected tenth-century Shīʿī scholar. See part 2, chapter 2, "Imām al-Ḥusayn Ibn ʿAlī" (pp. 296–379).

Naqvī, ʿAlī Naqī. *The Martyrdom of Karbala.* Translated by S. Ali Akhtar. Karachi, 1984. Controversial and very important work representing the views of a noted Indian Shīʿī scholar.

Shams al-Dīn, Muḥammad Mahdī. *The Rising of Ḥusayn: Its Impact on the Consciousness of Muslim Society.* Translated by I. K. A. Howard. London, 1985. Stimulating study of the influence of Ḥusayn's revolution on the social and political consciousness of Muslim society, by a contemporary Lebanese Shīʿī scholar.

Ṭabarī, Muḥammad ibn Jarīr al-. *The History of al-Ṭabarī,* vol. 19, *The Caliphate of Yazīd b. Muʿāwiyah.* Translated by I. K. A. Howard. Albany, N.Y., 1990. The earliest account by an authoritative classical historian, based on the oldest sources.

Ṭāleqāni, Maḥmud, et al. *Jihād and Shahādat: Struggle and Martyrdom in Islam.* Houston, 1986. See especially chapters 5–8 in the book by ʿAlī Sharīʿatī.

MAHMOUD M. AYOUB

ḤUSAYN IBN ʿALĪ (c.1853–1931), *amīr* and *sharīf* of Mecca and leader of the Arab revolt against the Ottomans in World War I. Ḥusayn, of the ʿAwn branch of the Hashemite family, was appointed to the emirate by Sultan ʿAbdülhamid II in 1908. Ḥusayn and his son, ʿAbd Allāh (Abdullah), engineered the appointment, portraying the former as loyal to the sultan and opposed to the Committee for Union and Progress, which had proposed ʿAlī Ḥaydar of the Zayd branch of the Hashemites as its candidate.

Ḥusayn supported the Ottomans when he attacked ʿAbd al-ʿAzīz ibn ʿAbd al-Raḥmān Āl Saʿūd of Najd (1910) and the Idrīsī of ʿAṣīr (1911), but such operations dovetailed with his efforts to prevent those leaders from encroaching on tribes whose loyalty he claimed. However, attempts by the vali (Ar., *wālī;* Ottoman governor) to extend his control over the vilayet (Ar., *wilāyah;* Ottoman administrative district) of Hejaz (the district containing Mecca) and the threatened extension of the Hejaz railway from Medina to Mecca, moved Ḥusayn to seek help. In 1914, ʿAbd Allāh met Lord Kitchener in Cairo, asking for British support should the Ottomans attempt to remove Ḥusayn. Kitchener demurred, since the Ottomans had yet to enter World War I. Ḥusayn had coveted the emirate of Hejaz for himself and his progeny, but when the Ottomans entered the war in October, Britain sought Hashemite assistance by enticing Ḥusayn with promises of future glory. Kitchener cabled ʿAbd Allāh: "It may be that an Arab of true race will assume the Khalifate at Mecca or Medina, and so good may come by the help of God out of all the evil that is now occurring." These comments, although ambiguous, were heady words for Ḥusayn, and he must have swelled with expectation. In subsequent negotiations with Britain, London tried unsuccessfully to downplay the caliphal notion. Nevertheless, Britain let him believe that he would obtain large areas of Arab territory, including Syria, Palestine, and Iraq, to rule. It was on this basis, along with substantial financial assistance, that Ḥusayn loosed the Arab Revolt against the Ottoman Empire in June 1916.

Ḥusayn presented the revolt as more Islamic than Arab, and demonstrated this by the application of *sharīʿah* (the divine law) in Hejaz. But he contended that, although the revolt was inspired by Islam, the Arabs were best qualified to lead it.

Ḥusayn never received the support he hoped for from the Arab and Muslim world. Many Arabs later saw in him an accessory to British and French imperialism. Indian Muslims never forgave him for revolting against the caliph, and they castigated him for his abuse of pilgrims.

Ḥusayn's rule in Hejaz lasted until the fall of Mecca to Ibn Saʿūd in 1924, and it was plagued by financial problems exacerbated by the reduction and eventual suppression of his British subsidy. Ḥusayn's preoccupation with what he saw as British perfidy in Syria, Iraq, and Palestine, his inability to form the tribal confederacy necessary to confront Ibn Saʿūd, his cruel method of government, and his alienation of the Hejazi merchant class led to his downfall. Proclaiming himself caliph in March 1924 earned him only ridicule. As Ibn Saʿūd bore down on Hejaz, the British left Ḥusayn hanging. Neither of his sons, who ruled in Transjordan and Iraq, gave him shelter, and he died a broken man in Amman in 1931, after spending most of his exile in the distinctly non-Arab country of Cyprus.

[*See also* Arab Nationalism.]

BIBLIOGRAPHY

Baker, Randall. *King Husain and the Kingdom of Hejaz*. Cambridge and New York, 1979. The only published study to date of Ḥusayn, concentrating on his relations with the British.

Dawn, C. Ernest. *From Ottomanism to Arabism*. Urbana, Ill., 1973. Contains several excellent essays on the origins and ideology of the Arab revolt.

Kedourie, Elie. *In the Anglo-Arab Labyrinth: The McMahon-Husayn Correspondence and Its Interpretations*. London, 1976. The most thorough study of the Ḥusayn-McMahon negotiations and their historical and bureaucratic contexts.

Kostiner, Joseph. "The Hashemite 'Tribal Confederacy' of the Arab Revolt, 1916–1917." In *National and International Politics in the Middle East: Essays in Honour of Elie Kedourie*, edited by Edward Ingram, pp. 126–143. London, 1986. Excellent introduction to the sociopolitical context in Arabia during the Arab revolt.

Ochsenwald, William. *Religion, Society, and the State in Arabia: The Hijaz under Ottoman Rule, 1840–1908*. Columbus, Ohio, 1984. The best study to date of the Hejazi society, politics, and economy inherited by Ḥusayn from the Ottomans.

Joshua Teitelbaum

ḤUSAYNID DYNASTY. Ḥusayn ibn ʿAlī, founder of the Ḥusaynid dynasty (1705–1957), and his descendants ruled Tunisia during an era of increasing external pressures. Civil wars that provoked Algerian intervention plagued the early years of the dynasty and persuaded the Ḥusaynid beys, who were part of an Ottoman ruling elite only loosely integrated into Tunisian society, of the need to develop a broad base of support in the country. The beys began to integrate tribal warriors into their army and to elevate members of the urban bourgeoisie, especially the *ʿulamāʾ*, to positions of responsibility in the government.

A dramatic upturn in the economy owing to the revival of corsair activity during the Napoleonic Wars solidified the relationship between the beys and their subjects, but the absence of effective Ḥusaynid leadership following the death of Ḥamūdah Bey (r. 1782–1814) in 1814 left the country weak and vulnerable. A series of disastrous harvests and a widespread commercial slump in the following years gave European merchants an opportunity to insinuate themselves into the center of the Tunisian economy by lending money to Tunisians on the verge of financial ruin. The French occupation of Algeria in 1830 heightened the dangers of this European economic penetration by placing a major creditor on Tunisia's borders. An Ottoman effort to reassert direct control over Tripolitania in 1835 similarly jeopardized the bey's autonomy.

Determined to avert both French and Ottoman encroachment, Aḥmad Bey (r. 1837–1855) launched a campaign to strengthen the central government and make the country more self-sufficient, but the tax increases needed to implement these policies further undermined the economy. More important, Aḥmad's unchecked spending left his successors with no choice but to borrow money abroad. The highly unfavorable terms of these loans set off a spiral of indebtedness that placed Tunisia firmly in the grasp of its European creditors.

An intense competition between France and Great Britain for the economic and political domination of the country marked the quarter century between Aḥmad's death and the imposition of the French protectorate, with the Ḥusaynids trying in vain to maintain their autonomy. The eagerness of many Tunisian officials to enrich themselves by collaborating with foreign governments and business interests produced a debilitating atmosphere of graft and corruption. In the hope of appeasing the powers, the Ḥusaynids consented to demands for such "reforms" as the *ʿahd al-amān* and the constitution of 1861, but this agenda served primarily the Europeans' purposes and failed to promote either political or economic stability. When the European powers reached an agreement on the disposition of Tunisia at the Congress of Berlin (1878), a French occupation became inevitable.

The Bardo Treaty, signed after France invaded Tunisia in 1881, left Muḥammad al-Ṣādiq (r. 1859–1882) on the throne, but without real authority. For the next seventy-five years, the Ḥusaynids reigned but did not rule, their powers circumscribed by the protectorate bureaucracy. This long period of political impotence, the lack of interest in, or sympathy for, the nationalist movement on the part of the beys (with the possible exception of Munṣif [r. 1942–1943]), and the enormous popularity of the nationalist leader, Habib Bourguiba, all contributed to the ease with which al-Amīn Bey (r. 1943–1957) was deposed and the monarchy abolished in 1957.

[*See also* Tunisia.]

BIBLIOGRAPHY

Brown, L. Carl. *The Tunisia of Ahmad Bey, 1837–1855*. Princeton, 1974. This superb study of a modernizing ruler also contains valuable background information on Tunisian society in the middle of the Ḥusaynid era.

Chater, Khalifa. *Dépendance et mutations précoloniales: La Régence de Tunis de 1815 à 1857*. Tunis, 1984. Study in socioeconomic history illustrating the problems occasioned by the increase of European influence in Tunisia.

Cherif, Mohamed-Hédi. *Pouvoir et société dans la Tunisie de Husayn Bin Ali, 1705–1740*. 2 vols. Tunis, 1986. The best account of the rise and early years of the dynasty.

Valensi, Lucette. *Tunisian Peasants in the Eighteenth and Nineteenth Centuries*. Cambridge, 1985. Abridged translation of *Fellahs tunisiens: L'Économie rurale et la vie des campagnes aux 18ᵉ et 19ᵉ siècles*. Surveys economic, cultural, and social practices among both sedentary and nomadic peoples in rural Tunisia in the Ḥusaynid era.

KENNETH J. PERKINS

ḤUSAYNĪYAH. A special site where ritual ceremonies commemorating the life and martyrdom of Imam Ḥusayn are held, *ḥusaynīyah* can be a temporary tent set up especially for the Muḥarram mourning ceremonies or a permanent building that is also used for religious occasions throughout the year.

*Ḥusaynīyah*s are found in all Shīʿī communities throughout the world and are known as such in Iran, Iraq, and Lebanon. In Iran the terms *ḥusaynīyah* and *takīyah* are used interchangeably, with local custom determining the relative usage. Among the Shīʿī of Bahrain and Oman, such sites are called *ma'tam*, while among the Shīʿī of India the terms *imāmbārah*, *ʿāshūrkhānah*, *ʿazā-khānah* are used. Indian Shīʿī who were brought as indentured laborers to Trinidad also use the term *imāmbārah* (lit., "enclosure of the imam").

The apparent precedent for the *ḥusaynīyah* comes from tenth-century Baghdad, when a ruler of the Shīʿī Būyid dynasty (932–1055) ordered that tents be set up in public areas on the tenth of Muḥarram (ʿĀshūrā'), to allow mourners to commemorate the martyrdom of the third imam, Ḥusayn (d. 680). It was not until the Ṣafavid dynasty (1501–1722) established Shiism as the state religion of Iran in the sixteenth century, however, that these mourning ceremonies became fully integrated into popular religious practice. The most common sites for these early ceremonies were public areas, such as town squares or main crossroads, which were covered by a black cloth. Later, temporary *ḥusaynīyah*s were also set up in caravansaries, the courtyards of private houses, and mosques. By the eighteenth century, permanent *imāmbārah* structures were built in India, and only later in that same century do we find evidence for permanent *ḥusaynīyah*/*takīyah* buildings in Iran.

In Shīʿī Muslim cities, town and village *ḥusaynīyah*s are as common as mosques in popular religious practice, with the number of *ḥusaynīyah* in each community often quite large. Lucknow is said to have had about two thousand *imāmbārah*s in the early 1800s; Tehran in the late 1960s is reported to have had around 630 *ḥusaynīyah*/*takīyah*. Usually each neighborhood has its own *ḥusaynīyah* and minimally there is at least one *ḥusaynīyah* in each quarter of the city. Most often they have been built by wealthy individuals—village landlords, merchants, or, especially during the nineteenth-century Qājār dynasty in Iran, members of the nobility—who constructed them for reasons of personal piety and the desire for *savāb* (religious blessings) as well as social prestige. Many *ḥusaynīyahs* have been built as the result of a vow of repayment to God for curing illnesses or in gratitude for a successful commercial or other venture. The majority of *ḥusaynīyahs* are sustained by an annual revenue or rental income from *waqf* (endowed property), such as shops and warehouses in the bazaars. Sometimes guilds finance the construction and maintenance of *ḥusaynīyahs*, such as the Ḥusaynīyah-i ʿAṭṭār-hā (Grocers' *ḥusaynīyah*) or the Ḥusaynīyah-i Bazzāz-hā (Cloth-sellers' *ḥusaynīyah*) in Sabzavar, Iran.

Guild members and others in the community tend to be involved in a network of associations and confraternities *(hay'at-i maḥallah; hay'at-i ṣinfī; anjuman)* which sponsor religious gatherings at various *ḥusaynīyahs* in the community, especially during the month of Muḥarram. These individuals take responsibility for decorating the *ḥusaynīyahs* with black drapery and flags often embroidered with the name of the sponsoring group and words of lamentation for the martyred imam. On the day of ʿĀshūrā' women prepare food for distribution to those in attendance and the poor of the community. The word *takīyah* (also *tekke; tekkiye*), in fact, originally referred to a place where food and care was given to the poor and has associations with Ṣūfī brotherhoods and their lodging.

The central event of these intensely emotional gatherings are recitations *(rawẓah-khvānī)* of the tragic circumstances surrounding the martyrdom of Imam Ḥusayn along with the reading and chanting of *marāthī* (elegiac poetry) and, quite commonly, ecstatically induced rhythmic chest-beating. Often as well, especially in smaller towns and villages, the courtyard of the *ḥusaynīyah* is used for the performance of *taʿziyah* (passion plays). The *ḥusaynīyah* is also used as a starting and culminating point for ʿĀshūrā' *dastah* (mourning processions).

During the Pahlavi dynasty (1925–1979), the mourning processions often combined political and religious rhetoric, resulting in antigovernment demonstrations. Indeed, the symbolism of the martyrdom of Imam Ḥusayn has always had important political implications, signifying a struggle against oppression and injustice, of good against evil.

Although new *ḥusaynīyahs* are continually being built, a particular *ḥusaynīyah* was established in Tehran in 1965 which had profound implications for the future of the country and Islam in general. Ḥusaynīyah-i Irshād was founded by a wealthy philanthropist and built with funds collected from a heterogeneous segment of Iranian society—traditional bazaar tradesmen, merchants, intellectuals, and such professionals as doctors, lawyers, and engineers. It was a highly innovative and visionary religious center originally conceived to be a place where new methods could be developed for the teaching of Islam in order to reach the increasingly alienated educated youth of Iran. The building was air-conditioned and offered modern audiovisual techniques, such as closed-circuit television, film, and slide-shows, and for the very first time choirs were introduced into a Muslim place of worship (girl's choirs sang separately at the women's programs). Educated lay people (men *and* women) and young, enthusiastic members of the *ʿulamā'* (community of religious scholars) who understood the modern mentality offered new ideas through challenging lectures rather than repetitious, often obscurantist, sermons of staid theological assumptions. By the late 1960s and early 1970s, however, it was transformed through the thought-provoking lectures of ʿAlī Sharīʿatī into the major symbol of political dissent.

Women were encouraged to play significant roles and to participate fully in the upcoming struggle for social justice. The facilities of the religious center were set aside on certain days for the exclusive use of women who were inspired to model themselves after Fāṭimah, the wife of Imam ʿAlī, and Zaynab, Imam Ḥusayn's sister, who became a major voice of opposition to the Sunnī caliph Yazīd, her brother's mortal enemy. Through the enormously popular teachings at the Ḥusaynīyah-yi Irshād, a much wider segment of the Iranian population began to believe that it was perfectly acceptable to fight for an Islam that offered both national liberation as well as enlightenment. However, as a result of growing dissent and opposition, government troops forcefully closed Ḥusaynīyah-yi Irshād in 1973. It was too little, too late, for the seeds of the revolution had already been scattered widely by the Ḥusaynīyah-yi Irshād through its publications and tape recordings of Sharīʿatī's lectures. The Ḥusaynīyah-yi Irshād was reopened in 1979 after the Islamic Revolution but as a more conservative, subdued, and compliant institution.

[*See also* ʿĀshūrā'; Ḥusayn ibn ʿAlī; Imāmzādah; Khānqāh; Muḥarram; Rawẓah Khvānī; Taʿziyah; Zāwiyah.]

BIBLIOGRAPHY

Only one reasonably extensive article devoted solely to the *ḥusaynīyah* exists, published in Persian: Mahmoud Tavasoli, "Ḥusaynīyah-hā, takāyā, muṣallá-hā," in *Meʿmārī-ye Irān dawreh-ye Islāmī* (Iranian Architecture of the Islamic Period), edited by Mohammad Yousef Kiani (Tehran, 1987). However, this article is of somewhat limited use, since it deals exclusively with the architectural features of the *ḥusaynīyah*, rather than the socioreligious dimension. Scattered references to the *ḥusaynīyah* may be found in books and articles about other subjects. See the following sources:

Akhavi, Shahrough. *Religion and Politics in Contemporary Iran*. Albany, N.Y., 1980. Perhaps the first scholar to note the significance of Ḥusaynīyah-yi Irshād and its role in the Iranian Revolution of 1979.

Bonine, Michael. "Islam and Commerce: Waqf and the Bazaar of Yazd, Iran." *Erkunde* 41 (1987): 182–196.

Chelkowski, Peter. "Shiʿa Muslim Processional Performances." *Drama Review* 29.3 (Fall 1985): 18–30.

Cole, Juan R. I. *Roots of North Indian Shīʿism in Iran and Iraq: Religion and State in Awadh, 1722–1859*. Berkeley, 1988. Contains the best discussion of the socioreligious aspects of the *imāmbārah* (pp. 92–107).

Kheirabadi, Masoud. *Iranian Cities: Formation and Development*. Austin, 1991. Contains a very useful two-page discussion of the *ḥusaynīyah* and is, overall, an excellent book on urban Iran.

Peterson, Samuel R. "The Taʿziyeh and Related Arts." In *Taʿziyeh: Ritual and Drama in Iran*, edited by Peter Chelkowski, pp. 64–87. New York, 1979. Perhaps the best succinct overview of the *taqīyah/ḥusaynīyah*. Includes a brief discussion of the *taqīyah* as it relates to Sufism in Iran.

Sharārah, Waḍḍāḥ. *Transformations d'une manifestation religieuse dans un village du Liban-Sud (Ashura)*. Beirut, 1968. One of the few studies on Shīʿī religious practices in Lebanon, published by the Université Libanaise, Institut des Sciences Sociales, Centre de Recherches.

Sleiman, N. "Le célébration de la Ashura à Nabbatiye (Liban)." Thèse, Aix-en-Provence, 1974. Doctoral dissertation on Muḥarram ritual practices in Lebanon.

GUSTAV THAISS

ḤUṢRĪ, ABŪ KHALDŪN SĀṬIʿ AL- (1880–1968), leading ideologist and popularizer of Arab nationalism and Pan-Arabism. Born in 1880 in Sanʿa, Yemen, to Syrian Arab parents from Aleppo, young al-Ḥuṣrī moved often as his father filled Ottoman judicial posts in Yemen, Anatolia, and Libya. Since the family spoke Turkish at home, al-Ḥuṣrī learned Arabic late and spoke it with a heavy Turkish accent. Graduating in 1900 from the Mulkiye Mektebi (Civil Service College) in Istanbul, he spent eight years in the Balkan caldron of competing nationalisms, first as a schoolteacher and later as an Ottoman provincial official.

Although supporting the Committee of Union and Progress army officers who launched the Ottoman ("Young Turk") Revolution of 1908, he shied away from direct involvement in party politics throughout his life. His outspoken, even blunt manner often alienated his associates. Al-Ḥuṣrī moved to Istanbul after the revolution. He directed the Teacher Training College in Istanbul from 1909 to 1912, edited an Ottoman Turkish education journal, and won recognition as a leading educational reformer. Rejecting Islamism and Turkish and Arab nationalism, he remained a dedicated secular Ottomanist throughout World War I.

With the effective demise of the Ottoman Empire in 1918, al-Ḥuṣrī switched his allegiance to Arab nationalism and joined Fayṣal ibn Ḥusayn's regime in Damascus as director general, then minister, of education. Fleeing Syria's French conquerors in 1920, he moved to Iraq when the British made Fayṣal king there in 1921. For twenty years in Iraq—as director general of education, editor of an education magazine, head of the Teachers College, dean of the Law College, and director of antiquities—al-Ḥuṣrī promoted Arab nationalism at every opportunity. He was exiled when Britain overthrew Rashīd ʿAlī's nationalist regime in 1941 and moved to Syria, where he arabized the national education system (1944–1946) as the French mandate came to an end. The following decade he spent in Cairo as cultural adviser to the Arab League and first director of its Intitute of Higher Arab Studies. He retired at the age of seventy-seven in 1957 and died in Baghdad in 1968.

In both the Ottoman and Arab phases of his career al-Ḥuṣrī consistently worked for secular educational reform as a means of instilling patriotism in youth. Until 1919 he advocated secular Ottoman patriotism, with people of all religions, languages, and ethnic groups joining as equal citizens. He publicly clashed with Ziya Gökalp, the leading advocate of Turkish nationalism. But hothouse Ottoman nationalism proved too fragile to resist the centrifugal forces of other nationalisms. [*See the biography of Gökalp.*]

Al-Ḥuṣrī's belated conversion to Arab nationalism enabled him to admit the force of linguistic bonds, which he had earlier denied. Language and common history became the active ingredients of his theory of Arab nationalism. He believed that despite their fragmentation under Western colonial regimes, Arabic-speakers from Morocco to Iraq and from Syria to the Sudan constituted a single nation *(ummah)*.

Al-Ḥuṣrī so admired the fourteenth-century writer

Ibn Khaldūn—interpreting his concept of *ᶜaṣabīyah* (social solidarity) as a kind of national bond—that he named his son "Khaldūn," thereby adding "Abū (father of) Khaldūn" to his own name. Otherwise, most of the sources of al-Ḥuṣrī's thought were Western. He drew on the writings of French educators, scientific popularizers, and social thinkers, but after 1919 German romantic nationalists best suited his Arab nationalist purpose. French nationalists had taken their state for granted, whereas German nationalists had believed themselves to be an organic nation long before achieving a unified state in 1871. Above all, Fichte's *Addresses to the German Nation*, penned after the defeat of Prussia by Napoleon in 1806, seemed to al-Ḥuṣrī to speak to a similarly divided and occupied Arab nation. Like post-1806 German and post-1871 French educational reformers, he wanted the schools to emphasize patriotism, discipline, and self-sacrifice, not individual liberties.

Al-Ḥuṣrī's emphasis on language and history led him to refute writers who made religion, race, will (as argued by Renan), economic circumstances, or geography the key determinants of national identity. Unlike his Iraqi contemporary Sāmī Shawkat, al-Ḥuṣrī had no use for German racial theories. Roaming freely through modern history, he selected examples to prove his points.

Al-Ḥuṣrī denounced "regional" nationalisms centered on existing states—he was particularly keen to persuade Egyptians of their Arabism—and he considered Pan-Islamism an ineffective distraction. He took great pains to refute the westward-looking Egyptian nationalism of the liberal writer and reformer Ṭāhā Ḥusayn. [*See the biography of Ḥusayn.*]

Al-Ḥuṣrī opposed British, American, and other educators who advocated practical and vocational education and autonomy for foreign or minority schools. While in Iraq he made no concessions to the particular needs of the Kurdish minority in the north or the neglected Shīᶜī majority in the south. He resisted proposals to use the various Arabic vernaculars in writing, working instead for standardized curricula and textbooks throughout the Arab world.

Al-Ḥuṣrī's voluminous works were popular throughout the Arab world, leaving their mark on Baᶜthists and Nasserists, among others. Unable to imagine Arab unity without Egypt, he backed Nasser in 1961 when Syrian Baᶜthists and others took Syria out of the United Arab Republic. In 1979 the Iraqi Baᶜthist regime honored him with a commemorative postage stamp, but his determined secularism makes him unpopular with those for whom religion is an essential element of political identity.

[*See also* Arab Nationalism; Education, *article on* Educational Reform; *and* Iraq.]

BIBLIOGRAPHY

Cleveland, William L. *The Making of an Arab Nationalist: Ottomanism and Arabism in the Life and Thought of Satiᶜ al-Husri*. Princeton, 1971. Standard intellectual biography, with an annotated bibliography of al-Ḥuṣrī's works.

Hourani, Albert. *Arabic Thought in the Liberal Age, 1798–1939*. London, 1962. See pages 311–316.

Ḥuṣrī, Abū Khaldūn Sāṭiᶜ al-. *The Day of Maysalūn: A Page from the Modern History of the Arabs* (1947). Translated by Sidney Glazer. Washington, D.C., 1966. Describes al-Ḥuṣrī's failed attempt to mediate between Fayṣal's government in Damascus and the approaching French army in 1920.

Ḥuṣrī, Abū Khaldūn Sāṭiᶜ al-. *Mudhakkirātī fī al-ᶜIrāq, 1921–1941* (My Memoirs in Iraq, 1921–1941). 2 vols. Beirut, 1967–1968.

Kenny, L. M. "Satiᶜ al-Husri's View on Arab Nationalism." *Middle East Journal* 17 (1963): 231–256.

Simon, Reeva S. *Iraq between the Two World Wars: The Creation and Implementation of a Nationalist Ideology*. New York, 1986. Gives the context and content of al-Ḥuṣrī's educational program for Iraq.

Tibi, Bassam. *Arab Nationalism: A Critical Enquiry*. Translated and edited by Marion Farouk-Sluglett and Peter Sluglett. 2d ed. New York, 1990. About half the study is devoted to al-Ḥuṣrī, emphasizing his debt to the organic nationalism of the German romantics.

Donald Malcolm Reid

I

IBĀḌĪ DYNASTY. The moderate sect of Khārijī origin known as the Ibāḍīyah was introduced into Oman first through access to the many Omani tribes settling in Basra and by missionaries from the sect's headquarters in Basra early in the eighth century CE (first–second century AH). Some of the early Ibāḍī scholars and influential leaders were of Omani origin, including Jābir ibn Zayd al-Azdī (d. 711), the real founder of the sect. He was exiled to Oman by the governor of Basra. Three of the first four Ibāḍī organizational leaders had strong relations with Oman. The Ibāḍīyah has remained an important element in the history and political structure of Oman since that time, although it has declined greatly in other areas of its former influence. Over the past twelve centuries the Ibāḍī community of Oman has elected sixty-one imams who ruled over greater or lesser territories in the region, depending on the sect's political power at various times.

According to Ibāḍī doctrine, an imam must be elected with absolute ruling authority over the community; his authority is absolute as long as he abides by Ibāḍī principles and law, and he can be deposed if he has committed a great disobedience and has not repented. However, such conditions remain theoretical in general. There is a tradition of a "chief elector" which had its root deep in the development of Ibāḍīyah in Oman. Although there is no post in the Ibāḍī jurisprudence for the chief elector, the rules and acts considered correct are derived from the acts and judgments of the consecutive chief electors. Ibāḍī jurisprudence and literature hold in high esteem the *ʿulamāʾ* (learned men) in general, and the imam is expected to obey them and to abide by their rulings. However, when the time is considered convenient for electing an imam, it is the *ʿulamāʾ* who lead the tribal chiefs to prepare for such an election, and the leading figure of the *ʿulamāʾ* will act as the chief elector. This task begins by getting the main Ibāḍī scholars in the country to communicate with each other and to reach an agreement on a person who will be proper for the post. They prepare for the election and assure that the tribal chiefs will give their support to the elected imam. They continue, led by the chief elector, to check on the imam and to ensure that he abides by the Ibāḍī creed and rules of conduct.

Ibāḍī political power in Oman began with a seizure of power by the first publicly elected imam, al-Julandā ibn Masʿūd (r. c.749–751), who was slain in battle by an ʿAbbāsid force. The imamate was revived in 793 under Imām Muḥammad ibn ʿAffān. In 893 the ʿAbbāsid force reconquered Oman, after which the Ibāḍīyah continued to elect imams there and to exercise considerable authority. Imām Nāṣir ibn Murshid al-Yaʿrubī (r. c. 1624–1649) established an Ibāḍī dynasty in the course of his struggle against Portuguese colonial dominance. This dynasty was replaced by the present ruling family, whose first ruler was Imam Aḥmad ibn Saʿīd al-Būsaʿīdī (r. 1753/54–1783).

Ibāḍī revivalism in nineteenth-century Oman was characterized by disputes centered on the election of a *ẓuhūr* (public) imam, in which various rulers were accused of departing from true Ibāḍī principles (the only legitimate basis for deposing an imam). Thus the rise of Imām ʿAzzān ibn Qays (r. 1868–1871) was supported by the theologian Saʿīd ibn Khalfān al-Khalīlī (d. 1871), and that of Imām Rāshid al-Kharūṣī (r. 1913–1920) by the noted historian and theologian ʿAbd Allāh al-Sālimī (d. 1914).

[*See also* Ibāḍīyah; Oman.]

BIBLIOGRAPHY

Lewicki, Tadeusz. "Ibāḍiyya." In *Encyclopaedia of Islam*, new ed., vol. 3 pp. 648–660. Leiden, 1960–. Condensed version of the author's studies on the history and doctrine of Ibāḍīyah and the various communities of the sect.

Muʿammar, ʿAlī Yaḥyā. *Al-Ibāḍīyah fī mawkib al-tārīkh*. 3 vols. Cairo, 1384–1385/1964–1966. Study of the sect by a twentieth-century Ibāḍī. The first volume is devoted to the Ibāḍī creed and the second and third to the notables of the sect in Libya.

Sālimī, ʿAbd Allāh ibn Ḥumayyid al-. *Jawhar al-niẓām fī ʿilmay al-*

adyān wa-al-aḥkām. Cairo, 1381/1961. Long poem containing important references to Ibāḍī jurisprudence, written by a twentieth-century Omani scholar.

Sālimī, ʿAbd Allāh ibn Ḥumayyid al-. *Tuḥfat al-aʿyān bi-sīrat ahl ʿUmān*. 2 vols. Kuwait, 1394/1974. At the time of publication, this book was considered the most comprehensive coverage of Omani history by a native scholar.

Sālimī, Muḥammad ibn ʿAbd Allāh al-. *Nahḍat al-aʿyān bi-ḥurrīyat ahl ʿUmān*. Cairo, n.d. Local account of events in Oman in the first half of the twentieth century.

Ubaydli, Ahmad. "ʿAbdullāh al-Sālimi's Role in the Ibāḍī Revival, 1913–20." In *Proceedings of the 1988 International Conference on Middle Eastern Studies*, pp. 431–440. Leeds, 1988. Attempt to study Sālimī's role as a theorist for and chief supporter of Imām al-Kharūṣī in 1913.

Wilkinson, John C. *The Imamate Tradition of Oman*. Cambridge, 1987. Comprehensive study of the institute of the imamate in Oman and its development over the centuries, with particular reference to twentieth-century events.

AHMAD UBAYDLI

IBĀḌĪYAH. A moderate sect known as Ibāḍīyah (or Abāḍīyah), which finds its origin in the Khārijī division of Islam, originated late in the first century AH (seventh century CE), when a group of Muslims broke away from the Khārijīs. Prominent among them was ʿAbd Allāh ibn Ibāḍ, from whom the movement takes its name. A few decades later (c. 715 CE), under the impetus of its great scholar Abū ʿUbaydah Muslim ibn Abī Karīmah, the Ibāḍīyah conducted a process of training missionaries (*ḥamalat al-ʿilm*) and dispatched them to the peripheries of the Islamic world, particularly the Maghrib and Oman, with the goal of fomenting revolt and establishing a Pan-Islamic Ibāḍī state. In North Africa they gained support mainly among Berber groups and dominated large territories during the eighth and ninth centuries. The Ibāḍī state of Tahirt established by ʿAbd al-Raḥmān ibn Rustam, who seemed to have quite considerable support among Ibāḍīs as a legal iman, lasted from 776 to 909. The North African Ibāḍīyah persists today in a few locations, notably the Mzab, Jerba, and Jebel Nafusa.

The Ibāḍīyah took strongest root in Oman, where it has existed without interruption to the present and has exerted continuing influence on the state. The first publicly elected Ibāḍī imam there was al-Julandā ibn Masʿūd (r. c.749–751); the century from 793 to 893 may be described as the golden age of the Ibāḍī state in Oman, which ended with its defeat by the ʿAbbāsids. The seventeenth-century Imām Nāṣir ibn Murshid al-Yaʿrubī established an Ibāḍī dynasty during his struggle against the Portuguese; it was replaced by the present ruling family beginning with Imām Aḥmad ibn Saʿīd al-Būsaʿīdī (r. 1753–1783).

In contrast to more extreme Khārijī doctrine, the Ibāḍīyah accept coexistence with other Islamic sects. They observe a threefold hierarchy of believers: those who believe internally in the uniqueness of God (*lughatan wa sharʿan);* those who declare such a belief; and those who practice accordingly. Nonbelievers are divided into two differently treated categories: *kufr al-juhūd* (polytheists) and *kufr al-niʿmah* (non-Ibāḍī Muslims). Guided by their creed, Ibāḍīs adopt one of three modes of association with outsiders: association (*walāyah*), hostile avoidance (*barāʾah*) from them, or they may take a neutral stand (*wuqūf*) if it is difficult to reach a decision.

To face the unpredictable circumstances, Ibāḍīs developed their own political and organizational plans connected to the election of their imams. When the Ibāḍī community is suppressed by its enemies, it exists in a state of secrecy (*kitmān*) during which there may be no imam. The Ibāḍīyah is obligated to elect a public imam and to revolt against tyrant rule, by violence if necessary, when the following conditions occur: the Ibāḍīyah have become strong enough to overcome their enemies; there are among them at least forty free, adult, rational, physically sound men; and these men include at least six who are learned and pious, who will advise the imam. There are two levels of the Ibāḍī imamate, the *shirāʾ* imamate and the *difāʿ* imamate, that is, the defensive imamate. In the first case, the imam's authority is absolute and he can only be deposed by resignation or deposition, while in the second the imam's authority is time conditional (or linked with task fulfillment). Only one legal imam is elected in the country.

[*See also* Ibāḍī Dynasty; Khawārij; Oman.]

BIBLIOGRAPHY

Darjīnī, Aḥmad ibn Saʿīd al-. *Kitāb ṭabaqāt al-mashāyikh bi-al-Maghrib*. 2 vols. Edited by Ibrāhīm Ṭallāy. Constantine, Algeria, 1974. Contains information about notable Ibāḍī men who were influential in the early period of the sect.

Kindī, Aḥmad ibn ʿAbd Allāh al-. *Al-Muṣannaf*. 42 vols. Muscat, Oman, 1979–1983. Extensive study of Ibāḍī jurisprudence containing valuable raw material for further economic and social research.

Lewicki, Tadeusz. "The Ibádites in Arabia and Africa." *Cahiers d'Histoire Mondiale* 13.1 (1971): 51–130. Lewicki's well-known studies of the political history of the Ibāḍīs of North Africa are extended in this paper to cover the Ibāḍīs of Oman.

Sālimī, ʿAbd Allāh ibn Ḥumayyid al-. *Bahjat al-anwār: Sharḥ Anwār al-ʿuqūl fī al-tawḥīd.* 2 vols. Reprint, Muscat, Oman, 1981. Condensed traditional commentary of Ibāḍī jurisprudence written by a twentieth-century Omani scholar.

Ubaydli, Ahmad. "Early Islamic Oman and Early Ibāḍism in the Arabic Sources." Ph.D. diss., Cambridge University, 1993. Intended to introduce the large body of Ibāḍī material recently discovered or published in Oman, using classical Arabic sources along with this material to study the early history of the sect. See in particular chapters 1.B, 1.C, 1.D, and 2.

Wilkinson, John C. *Water and Tribal Settlement in South-East Arabia.* Oxford, 1977. Important study of the irrigation system and its influence on tribal settlement and Ibāḍīyah in Oman.

AHMAD UBAYDLI

IBLĪS. *See* Satan.

IBN ʿABD AL-WAHHĀB, MUḤAMMAD

(1703–1791), Saudi Arabian conservative theologian and reformer. Born in al-ʿUyaynah in Najd, Ibn ʿAbd al-Wahhāb belonged to a prestigious family of jurists, both theologians and *qāḍīs* (judges). Under the tutorship of his father, young Muḥammad studied Ḥanbalī jurisprudence and read classical works on *tafsīr* (exegesis), *ḥadīth* (tradition) and *tawḥīd* (monotheism). In his early twenties he began to denounce what he described as the polytheistic beliefs and practices of his society, rejecting its laxity and insisting on strict adherence to the *sharīʿah.*

His beliefs alienated him from the establishment *ʿulamāʾ* and led to the dismissal of his father from the position of *qāḍī.* Subsequently Ibn ʿAbd al-Wahhāb's family, including his father, had to leave al-ʿUyaynah to neighboring Huraymila in 1726. He himself remained in al-ʿUyaynah for a while, but after the *ʿulamāʾ* defamed his reputation and instigated the populace against him, he left al-ʿUyaynah and went to Hejaz.

In Hejaz, Ibn ʿAbd al-Wahhāb made his pilgrimage to Mecca and Medina, where he attended lectures on different branches of Islamic learning. Ibn Bishr reports in *ʿUnwan al-majd fī tārīkh Najd* (Riyadh, n.d., p. 6), that Muḥammad ibn ʿAbd al-Wahhāb studied under Shaykh ʿAbd Allāh ibn Ibrāhim ibn Sayf and Shaykh Ḥayāt al-Sindī, both of whom were admirers of the Ḥanbalī Ibn Taymīyah. Like Ibn Taymīyah, they opposed *taqlīd* (imitation), which was commonly accepted by the followers of the four Sunnī schools of jurisprudence. Both scholars felt the urgent need to reform the socioreligious situation of Muslims in Najd and elsewhere. Their teachings had a great impact on Ibn ʿAbd al-Wahhāb, who began to take a more aggressive attitude toward the establishment *ʿulamāʾ*.

Another important event in the intellectual evolution of Ibn ʿAbd al-Wahhāb was his visit to Basra. There he widened his study of *ḥadīth* and jurisprudence and came into contact with the Shīʿīs, who venerate ʿAlī's shrine in Najaf and the tomb of Ḥusayn in neighboring Karbala. Ibn ʿAbd al-Wahhāb's call to reform the Muslim world was rejected by the *ʿulamāʾ* of both Basra and Karbala, and he was ultimately forced to leave the area.

Ibn ʿAbd al-Wahhāb returned to Huraymila to rejoin his father and immediately began to criticize the innovations and polytheistic acts practiced by Najdīs and others. His criticism seems to have been so bitter that he met strong opposition from the *ʿulamāʾ* and even from his own father. During this period he composed his most famous work, *Kitāb al-tawḥīd* (Book of Monotheism), copies of which circulated quickly and widely in Najd. The year 1740 witnessed the death of his father and the consolidation of the Wahhābī movement. The death of his father allowed Ibn ʿAbd al-Wahhāb to adopt a more aggressive line, because he felt less constrained than before. He declared war on those who by word or act were violating the doctrine of monotheism.

In a relatively short time the influence of Ibn ʿAbd al-Wahhāb spread widely. The consolidation of his movement took place when the ruler of al-ʿUyaynah, ʿUthmān ibn Muʿammar, offered him protection. Ibn ʿAbd al-Wahhāb accepted the invitation to reside in al-ʿUyaynah because it allowed him to return to his birthplace, where his family enjoyed high social status, and provided the protection he needed to propagate his ideology. To cement his ties with the town's leader, Ibn ʿAbd al-Wahhāb married al-Jawharah, ʿUthmān's aunt.

The ruler of al-ʿUyaynah ordered his townsmen to observe the teachings of Ibn ʿAbd al-Wahhāb, who began to implement the principles of his call. Among his earliest acts was the destruction of the monument where Zayd ibn al-Khaṭṭāb was believed to be buried, as well as the tombs of other companions of the Prophet, all of whom were objects of veneration. He also revived the Islamic law of stoning an adulterous woman to death. Both incidents mark the establishment of a Wahhābī society in which the doctrines of *tawḥīd* were strictly observed; indeed, *tawḥīd* is considered the central theme in Wahhābī doctrine.

Ibn ʿAbd al-Wahhāb's activities and the protection he received from the leader of al-ʿUyaynah antagonized the

ʿulamāʾ of the region and led them to intensify their attacks on the Wahhābī movement, warning the rulers that Ibn ʿAbd al-Wahhāb was encouraging the common folk to revolt against established authority. Consequently, the ruler of al-ʿUyaynah terminated his support and asked the teacher to leave the town.

From al-ʿUyaynah, Ibn ʿAbd al-Wahhāb sought refuge in al-Dirʿīyah at the invitation of its ruler, Muḥammad ibn Saʿūd. For more than two years Ibn ʿAbd al-Wahhāb propagated his views and wrote letters to various rulers, scholars, and tribal leaders in Arabia. The response he elicited was as much a product of political and economic considerations as of religious dogma. Some leaders joined the new movement because they saw it as a means of gaining an ally against their local rivals. Others feared that their acceptance of the call would diminish their authority in favor of Ibn Saʿūd and oblige them to pay him at least part of the revenues they collected from their subjects.

By 1746 the time seemed ripe for Ibn Saʿūd and Ibn ʿAbd al-Wahhāb to declare *jihād* on those who opposed Wahhābī teachings. In 1773 the principality of Riyadh fell to them, marking a new period in the career of Ibn ʿAbd al-Wahhāb. He concentrated on teaching and worship until his death in 1791. His death, however, did not stop the expansion of the new state. Not only was the movement able to resist its opponents and gain territories in neighboring principalities, it was able within a relatively short period to spread to Mecca and Medina, which were captured in 1805 and 1806, respectively. A new order was established in the Arabian Peninsula, ushering in the period of the first Saudi state and establishing the Wahhābīyah as the religio-political driving force in the peninsula during the nineteenth and early twentieth centuries.

[*See also* Saudi Arabia; *and* Wahhābīyah.]

BIBLIOGRAPHY

Lebkicher, Roy, et al. *The Arabia of Ibn Saud*. New York, 1952.
Philby, H. St. John. *Arabian Highlands*. Ithaca, N.Y., 1952.
Schacht, Joseph, ed. *The Legacy of Islam*. 2d ed. Oxford, 1974.
Smith, Wilfred Cantwell. *Islam in Modern History*. Princeton, 1957.

AYMAN AL-YASSINI

IBN AL-ʿARABĪ, MUḤYĪ AL-DĪN (1165–1240),

influential Ṣūfī mystic and writer. Ibn ʿArabī is known as "the greatest shaykh" *(al-shaykh al-akbar)*. His thought and terminology have formed the foundation of most subsequent Ṣūfī intellectual discourse, and his voluminous literary output as famous for its abstruseness as for its content, has been the subject of numerous commentaries in many languages. His ideas, controversial even in his own time, continue to be an object of attack in the contemporary Muslim world.

Born in Murcia, Spain, into a prominent family that included a number of Ṣūfīs, Ibn ʿArabī spent his first thirty years in Spain before traveling east, where he spent the last forty years of his life and composed his major works. After traveling through North Africa and much of the Middle East, he finally settled in Damascus, where he is buried. Although he founded no Ṣūfī order, his ideas had a profound impact on Sufism throughout the Muslim world. He is credited with creating a systematic Ṣūfī philosophy, but his writings do not present this philosophy in a logical exposition. Rather, they reflect his mystical impulses and present ideas in an often unconnected fashion that some readers find self-contradictory. His interpretations of Qurʾānic verses and sayings of the Prophet utilize an associative word analysis that is unconventional and, to some Muslims, blasphemous. His most comprehensive work, *The Meccan Revelations*, is dauntingly long and dense. Ibn ʿArabī's ideas have been largely disseminated by his commentators, such as his disciple Ṣadr al-Dīn al-Qūnawī (1210–1274) and ʿAbd al-Karīm al-Jīlī (d. early fifteenth century); in the Arab world his ideas have been popularized by the widely read Ṣūfī writer ʿAbd al-Wahhāb al-Shaʿrānī (d. 1565).

The hallmark of Ibn ʿArabī's system is his doctrine of the "oneness of being." The only truly Real is God himself, who was, according to a saying of the Prophet, a hidden treasure desiring to be known. The Qurʾān says that the signs of God are contained in nature. Ibn ʿArabī takes this idea further by saying that God's names are manifested in the cosmos, which functions as a mirror in which God sees himself. While all of creation manifests the names of God, the perfect man, who is the only person to attain full humanity and is represented by a single person in every age, contains the totality of these names. The perfect man is therefore a microcosm and God's most perfect mirror. The individuals who are the perfect men are each exemplifications of an eternal spiritual essence called the "Muḥammadan reality," which is the articulating and mediating principle through which the creation comes into existence. God is the source of all love and beauty; our love for objects and people and our contemplation of beauty in other things are in fact a love for God and a witness of his beauty. Because the perfect man alone manifests the comprehensive divine name of God, he alone is able to worship God in reality. Ibn ʿArabī's famous poem—in which he affirms that he is capable of worshiping God in any form, whether through the tablets of the Torah, a temple of idols, or the Kaʿbah—has sometimes been interpreted as advocating religious tolerance, but it is better seen as a proclamation of his own high spiritual standing.

Ibn ʿArabī's philosophy has been criticized variously as pantheistic, as deifying Muḥammad, making all religions equal, creating an idol out of woman (because he affirms that man's contemplation of God in woman is the most perfect contemplation of the divine), and interpreting the Qur'ān in an unconventional and dangerous manner. His Sufism is widely regarded as extremist, and even in his own life some scholars in Egypt wanted him executed as a heretic. In Egypt today there are continuing attempts to ban his works. The banning of his works would not, however, put an end to his ideas, which continue to be disseminated in a simplified and popular form through the Ṣūfī orders.

[*See also* Sufism, *article on* Ṣūfī Thought and Practice.]

BIBLIOGRAPHY

Works by Ibn ʿArabī

The Bezels of Wisdom. Translated by R. W. J. Austin. New York, 1980. Ibn ʿArabī's most widely studied work, written near the end of his life, which sums up his philosophy most succinctly. In it each prophet represents a certain wisdom contained in the divine name he embodies.

Al-Futūḥāt al-Makkīyah (The Meccan Revelations). 4 vols. Beirut, n.d. His major work, which alone is more than most authors write in a lifetime. An edited version of this is being produced in Cairo by ʿUthmān Yaḥyā, who published the first volume in 1972.

Sufis of Andalusia: The Ruh al-quds *and* Al-Durrat al-fakhira. Translated by R. W. J. Austin. London, 1971. The lives of various Ṣūfīs of Spain, with many of whom Ibn ʿArabī had personal contact. Austin's introduction details the life of Ibn ʿArabī through quotations from Ibn ʿArabī's own writings, offering a fascinating insight into his mystical experiences.

The Tarjumán al-ashwáq: A Collection of Mystical Odes by Muḥyi'ddín ibn al-ʿArabí. Edited and translated by Reynold A. Nicholson. London, 1911. Poems inspired by a beautiful and spiritual Persian woman he met in Mecca. Ibn ʿArabī later wrote a commentary to show that they were not mere love poems, but had an underlying mystical meaning.

Works about Ibn ʿArabī

Chittick, William C. *The Sufi Path of Knowledge: Ibn al-ʿArabī's Metaphysics of Imagination.* Albany, N.Y., 1990. Thematically organized introduction to Ibn ʿArabī's thought that includes large portions translated from *Al-Futūḥāt al-Makkīyah.*

Chittick, William C. "Ibn ʿArabī and His School." In *Islamic Spirituality: Manifestations,* edited by Seyyed Hossein Nasr, pp. 49–79. New York, 1991. Possibly the best succinct introduction to Ibn ʿArabī's life, thought, and influence, by a well-informed scholar with a gift for clear exposition.

Corbin, Henry. *Creative Imagination in the Sufism of Ibn ʿArabi.* Translated by Ralph Manheim. Princeton, 1969. Important work by the famous French scholar of Islamic esotericism.

Homerin, Th. Emil. "Ibn Arabi in the People's Assembly: Religion, Press, and Politics in Sadat's Egypt." *Middle East Journal* 40.3 (1986): 462–477. Account of the enduring controversy over Ibn ʿArabī's ideas and its relevance in contemporary politics.

VALERIE J. HOFFMAN-LADD

IBN BĀDĪS, ʿABD AL-ḤAMĪD (1889–1940), Islamic reformer, national leader, and head of the Association of Algerian ʿUlamā'. ʿAbd al-Ḥamīd ibn Bādīs was born in Constantine, Algeria, to a prominent Berber family renowned for its scholarship, wealth, and influence. Ibn Bādīs received an Islamic education and in 1908 attended the famous Zaytūnah Mosque in Tunis. There, he was educated by scholars who had been influenced by the teachings of Jamāl al-Dīn al-Afghānī (d. 1897) and Muḥammad ʿAbduh (d. 1905) and introduced Ibn Bādīs to the reformist ideas of the Salafīyah movement. After obtaining the degree of *ʿālim* (scholar of religion), Ibn Bādīs returned in 1913 to Algeria and, until his death in 1940, devoted his entire career to teaching, reforming Islam, and defining the Arab and Islamic basis of Algerian nationalism.

The French colonial administration had closed down many centers of Arab and Islamic education, appropriated the financial institutions that backed them, restricted the teaching of Arabic and the Qur'ān, and spread French schooling and culture. It also encouraged missionary activities and supported the mystical Ṣūfī orders, which disseminated acquiescent attitudes among the Algerians. To quell the disorienting effects of French policies and the advocates of assimilation (*évolués*), Ibn Bādīs initiated a reform movement that sought to assert the national identity of Algeria, defend the cultural integrity of its people, and prepare them for eventual independence from France. In 1925, he founded a weekly paper, *Al-muntaqid* (The Critic), in which he disseminated Salafī ideas and attacked the "un-Islamic" practices of the Ṣūfī orders. *Al-muntaqid* was banned after eighteen issues, and Ibn Bādīs replaced it with *Al-shihāb* (The Meteor), in which he maintained a more moderate tone.

In 1931, Ibn Bādīs and other religious scholars formed the Association of Algerian ʿUlamāʾ, which he headed and which promoted the Arab and Islamic roots of the Algerian nation, the reform and revival of Islam, and criticism of the Ṣūfī orders and the assimilationists. The Association demanded religious freedom, restoration of the *ḥubūs* (religious endowment, *waqf*) properties, and recognition of Arabic as the national language. It opened hundreds of free schools and mosques to teach Arabic, Islam, and modern subjects, published its own papers to spread religious, cultural, and social reform, campaigned against the marabouts' (local venerated men) corrupt practices, and sent delegations to France and opened branches to involve Algerian residents there. In 1938, the Association issued a formal *fatwā* (legal opinion), which declared naturalized Algerians to be non-Muslims. Its activities disturbed the French administration, which tried to restrict the conduct of its members.

Ibn Bādīs perceived his mission as "not to produce books, but educated people." His thought is discernible in the numerous articles that he wrote and in his interpretation of the Qur'ān. He shared many viewpoints of the Salafīyah movement, blaming the deterioration of the Muslims on internal weakness, disunity, despotism, and the spread of non-Islamic practices.

Ibn Bādīs stressed education to purify Islam from popular accretions and improve the condition of the individual as a step toward reviving the entire society. He offered a modernist interpretation of the Qur'ān and emphasized reasoning and free will. His major contribution lies in linking reform and education with the promotion of an Algerian nationalism. He identified Islam, Arabism, and nationalism as the three components of the Algerian national character.

Ibn Bādīs and the Algerian ʿUlamāʾ laid the foundations for the national identity of the Algerian people. Throughout the Algerian war against France (1954–1962), the Association aligned with the Front de Libération Nationale (FLN), and was later represented in the provisional government of the Algerian Republic after independence.

[*See also* Algeria; Salafīyah.]

BIBLIOGRAPHY

Balāsī, Nabīl Aḥmad. *Al-ittijāh al-ʿArabī wa-al-Islāmī wa-dawruhu fī taḥrīr al-Jazāʾir* (The Arab and Islamic Trend and Its Role in Liberating Algeria). Cairo, 1990. Detailed study of the Arab and Islamic trend and its impact within the Algerian nationalist movement.

Jūrashī, Ṣalāḥ al-Dīn al-. *Tajribah fī al-iṣlāḥ: Ibn Bādīs* (A Case in Reform: Ibn Bādīs). Tunis, 1978. Overview of the role of Ibn Bādīs and the Association of Algerian ʿUlamāʾ in establishing a movement for reform and social change.

Qāsim, Maḥmūd. *Al-Imām ʿAbd al-Ḥamīd Ibn Bādīs, al-zaʿīm al-rūḥī li-ḥarb al-taḥrīr al-Jazāʾirīyah* (ʿAbd al-Ḥamīd Ibn Bādīs: The Spiritual Leader of the Algerian Liberation War). 2d ed. Cairo, 1979. Early and excellent study of Ibn Bādīs's life, reform ideas, and thought.

Rābiḥ, Turkī. *Al-Shaykh ʿAbd al-Ḥamīd Ibn Bādīs: Rāʾid al-iṣlāḥ wa-al-tarbīyah fī al-Jazāʾir* (ʿAbd al-Ḥamīd Ibn Bādīs: The Pioneer of Reform and Education in Algeria). 3d ed. Algiers, 1981. Comprehensive study of an important period in Algeria's modern history (1900–1940), with a special focus on Ibn Bādīs, social, cultural, economic, and political factors influencing his thought, and his contributions in providing the Arab and Islamic seeds for the Algerian nationalist movement.

ʿUthmān, Fatḥī. *ʿAbd al-Ḥamīd Ibn Bādīs: Rāʾid al-ḥarakah al-Islāmīyah fī al-Jazāʾir al-muʿāṣirah* (ʿAbd al-Ḥamīd Ibn Bādīs: The Pioneer of the Islamic Movement in Contemporary Algeria). Kuwait, 1987. Original comparison of Ibn Bādīs's thought and movement with that of Jamāl al-Dīn al-Afghānī, Muḥammad ʿAbduh, and Ḥasan al-Bannāʾ.

EMAD ELDIN SHAHIN

IBN IDRĪS, AḤMAD (1749/50-1837), Moroccan Ṣūfī and teacher and founder of the Idrīsīyah tradition. Despite his importance within nineteenth-century Islamic history, very little is known of the life of Ibn Idrīs, and contemporary accounts are sparse.

Ibn Idrīs was born near Larache in Morocco into a family of Idrīsī *sharīf*s. He studied for some thirty years at the Qarawyyīn mosque/school in Fez. Among his teachers there in the formal Islamic sciences was Muḥammad ibn Sūda (d. 1795), while his principal Ṣūfī master within the Shādhilīyah tradition was ʿAbd al-Wahhāb al-Tāzī (d. 1792). Ibn Idrīs left Morocco in 1798 and spent the next thirty years in and around Mecca and Medina, also making several extended visits to Luxor in Upper Egypt. He was in Mecca during its occupation by the Wahhābīs (1803–1813), only leaving for Upper Egypt when the town was conquered by the Egyptians. In 1828 he was forced by the hostility of the Meccan *ʿulamāʾ* to leave the Hejaz, although the exact circumstances are unclear. He moved to the Yemen and after a period of travel along the coast came to Asir, where he settled in Sabya at the invitation of the local ruler. He died and was buried at Sabya.

Ibn Idrīs's importance lay in his role as a Ṣūfī spiritual master *(murshid)* and teacher. Apart from prayers, litanies, a few sermons, and letters, he wrote little himself. His teachings are known mainly through the lecture notes and other writings of his principal students. The main compilation of his teachings is *Al-ʿiqd al-nafīs fī naẓm jawāhir al-tadrīs . . . Aḥmad ibn Idrīs* (Cairo, AH 1315/1896–97 CE, and many later editions).

Previous scholars have regarded Ibn Idrīs as a leading figure of the "neo-Ṣūfī" movement, described as a reformulation of the Islamic mystical tradition in the late eighteenth and early nineteenth centuries by such figures as Ibn Idrīs and Aḥmad al-Tijānī (d. 1815), the founder of the Tijānīyah *ṭarīqah*. [*See* Tijānīyah.] Some of the assumptions about the teachings of the neo-Ṣūfīs—that they rejected the teachings of Ibn al-ʿArabī (d. 1240), especially his doctrine of *waḥdat al-wujūd*, and opposed "popular" Ṣūfī practices like dancing and saint worship, or a revival of *ḥadīth* studies—are questionable, especially as applied to Ibn Idrīs. Nevertheless, neo-Sufism usefully describes the new orders inspired by figures like Ibn Idrīs that were to dominate much of Muslim Africa and elsewhere.

Doctrinally, Ibn Idrīs vehemently opposed the *madhhab*s and all forms of philosophy or reasoning; the pursuit of chains of transmission and the like was useless. The individual Muslim must rely on God alone to grant him an understanding of the Qur'ān and *sunnah:* "Knowledge is acquired by learning, namely from God; he who fears Him will know Him, and, contrarily, he who does not fear Him, will not know Him" (Ibn Idrīs, *Risālat al-radd ʿalā ahl al-ra'y*). Ibn Idrīs was as much opposed to *ijtihād* as he was to *taqlīd*. His teaching was antiauthoritarian, emphasizing the individual believer's duty to seek God, by whom he will be guided so long as he relies on *taqwā* ("godfearingness"). Although Ibn Idrīs's teaching may be regarded as "fundamentalist," his mystical apprehension of his religion marked him off sharply from those following the teachings of, for example, Ibn Taymīyah (d. 1328).

As a Ṣūfī Ibn Idrīs stood foursquare within the orthodox Ṣūfī tradition. The object of the mystical path was union with God. The assertion made by several scholars (H. A. R. Gibb and Fazlur Rahman among others) that he substituted a union with the spirit of the Prophet for the union with God seems without foundation. The mystic on the path may come to meet the Prophet, from whom he may receive direct revelation *(waḥy)*, the highest form of knowledge. Both his prayers and other aspects of his teachings show considerable traces of the influence of Ibn al-ʿArabī (d. 1240), a fact brought out by later commentators on his prayers. Although the *dhikr* of the later Idrīsīyah tradition is usually silent, Ibn Idrīs in *Kunūz al-jawāhir al-nūrānīyah fī qawāʿid al-ṭarīqah al-Shādhilīyah* describes a *dhikr* of movement.

Contrary to previous assertions, there is no evidence that Ibn Idrīs attempted to establish his own *ṭarīqah*. It was as a spiritual master that he exercised such extraordinary influence, establishing a tradition that was to spread to the Balkans and Istanbul, Syria, Cyrenaica and the central Sahara, Egypt, the Sudan, Somalia, and across to Indonesia and Malaysia. His principal students included Muḥammad ibn ʿAlī al-Sanūsī (1787–1859), founder of the Sanūsīyah; Muḥammad ʿUthmān al-Mīrghānī (1793–1852), founder of the Khatmīyah (from which derived the breakaway Ismāʿīlīyah in the Sudan); Ibrāhīm al-Rashīd (1813–1874), from whom stemmed the Rashīdīyah, Ṣāliḥiyah, and Dandarāwīyah orders; and Muḥammad al-Majdhūb (d. 1832). Also among his students were numerous lesser figures who established local schools, for example ʿAlī ʿAbd al-Ḥaqq al-Qūṣī (1788–1877), an Egyptian who settled at Asyut, founded a school, and wrote extensively on the *taqlīd/ijtihād* debate, and Aḥmad al-Dufārī, a Sudanese who taught Ibn Idrīs's prayers to Muḥammad Aḥmad ibn ʿAbd Allāh, the Sudanese Mahdi (d. 1885). A second generation of students spread Ibn Idrīs's teachings across the Indian Ocean to Southeast Asia, where his prayers were translated into Malay languages, as well as along the East African coast as far as Zanzibar. It was only some forty years after his death that a son, ʿAbd al-ʿĀl (d. 1878), worked to establish a formal Aḥmadīyah Idrīsīyah *ṭarīqah;* this has remained a local order in Upper Egypt and the northern Sudan. His descendants, the Adārisa, still live in Egypt and the Sudan, where the present head of the order is Sayyid Muḥammad al-Ḥasan al-Idrīsī.

[*See also* Idrīsīyah; Khatmīyah; Sanūsīyah.]

BIBLIOGRAPHY

Ibn Idrīs, Aḥmad. *The Letters of Aḥmad ibn Idrīs.* Edited by Einar Thomassen and Bernd Radtke. London and Evanston, Ill., 1993. Texts and translations of all the extant letters.

O'Fahey, R. S. *Enigmatic Saint: Aḥmad ibn Idrīs and the Idrīsī Tradition.* London and Evanston, Ill., 1990. First monograph devoted to Ibn Idrīs; contains an extensive bibliography.

O'Fahey, R. S., and Bernd Radtke. "Neo-Sufism Reconsidered." *Der Islam* 70 (1993): 52–87. Critical reexamination of neo-Sufism.

Voll, John O. "Two Biographies of Ahmad ibn Idris al-Fasi, 1760–

1837." *International Journal of African Historical Studies* 6 (1973): 633–646. Translations of two early hagiographies.

R. S. O'Fahey

IBN KHALDŪN, ʿABD AL-RAḤMĀN (1332–1406), influential thinker about Arab social structures and processes. Ibn Khaldūn was born in Tunis, at a time when North Africa, part of the Arab Muslim empire in decline, consisted of small states riddled by rivalries and plots. In this atmosphere, Ibn Khaldūn entered public life and held different positions including those of "the seal bearer," secretary of state, ambassador, and judge. In 1382, he went to Cairo where he taught and served as a judge until his death.

The continuous political instability and depressed intellectual life of the period did not prevent Ibn Khaldūn from pursuing his education. His major works are the *Autobiography* and the *Muqaddimah.* The first is a candid evaluation of his career; the second, still used by scholars, traces his thoughts on sedentary and desert populations, dynasties, the caliphate, and gainful occupations. In the *Muqaddimah* Ibn Khaldūn stated that he had established a new science, *ʿilm al-ʿumrān* (science of social organization), a science that he believed was entirely original. Several social thinkers considered the *Muqaddimah* a treatise in sociology and, accordingly, regarded him as the founder of sociology.

Ibn Khaldūn emphasized the necessity of observation and careful examination of information as the bases of reliable conclusions. The German scholar Heinrich Simon points out that "Ibn Khaldūn was the first to attempt to formulate social laws." (*Ibn Khalduns Wissenschaft von der Menschlichen Kultur,* Leipzig, 1959, p. 9). Ibn Khaldūn studied human society as *sui generis.* He also stressed the interdependence of the religious, political, economic, military, and cultural spheres of life and, hence, the need for effective social control of human activity.

ʿAṣabīyah (social solidarity) is the core of Ibn Khaldūn's thought concerning *badāwah* (nomadism-ruralism), *ḥaḍārah* (urbanism), and the rise and decline of the state. Founding a state is the goal of *ʿaṣabīyah,* especially of nomadic *ʿaṣabīyah.* The luxury and leisure of urban life tend to weaken this *ʿaṣabīyah;* if it is lost, significant disintegration starts to take place. Ibn Khaldūn's theory describes and analyzes the rise, development, maturity, decline, and fall of several states. In a sense, *ʿaṣabīyah,* as a unifying force, is analogous to the modern concept of nationalism. Like *ʿaṣabīyah,* nationalism is not a sense of identity alone; aspiration, loyalty, and devotion are also prerequisites for the preservation of the group.

Ibn Khaldūn's ideas are not void of shortcomings vis-à-vis present conditions, for example, he had emphasized the superiority of nomadic *ʿaṣabīyah,* but nomadic people today are unable to conquer urban areas. However, his theory is, to some extent, applicable to Arab society and Islamic culture as long as tribal traditions are strong. His observation that tyranny usually leads to *ta'alluh* (egotism) on the part of autocratic rulers is as conspicuous a phenomenon today as it was in his time. The significance of Ibn Khaldūn's ideas for understanding Arab society and Islamic thought and culture led A. al-Wardi (*Mantiq Ibn Khaldūn,* Cairo, 1962) to advocate the establishment of a "Khaldunian Sociology."

Some writers assert that Ibn Khaldūn must be studied against the background of medieval Islam; others emphasize that some of his ideas are astonishingly similar to those of Machiavelli, Vico, Comte, Durkheim, Tonnies, Gumplowicz, Spengler, Oppenheimer, and Wirth and should be analyzed accordingly. These approaches may be combined. Ibn Khaldūn must be studied in the light of his time; yet this method need not prevent one from selecting those aspects of his work that currently appear relevant and can be compared with "modern" and recent thought. This approach precludes exaggeration of Ibn Khaldūn's ideas and belittlement of modern writings.

[*See also* ʿAṣabīyah.]

BIBLIOGRAPHY

Baali, Fuad. *Social Institutions: Ibn Khaldun's Social Thought.* Lanham, N.Y., and London, 1992. Also *Society, State, and Urbanism: Ibn Khaldun's Sociological Thought.* Albany, N.Y., 1988. Detailed analysis of Ibn Khaldūn's ideas on social organizations and social life.

Issawi, Charles. *An Arab Philosophy of History: Selections from the Prolegomena of Ibn Khaldun of Tunis.* London, 1950. A must-read book for most readers for its excellent introduction and smooth translation.

Mahdi, Muhsin. *Ibn Khaldun's Philosophy of History.* Chicago, 1964. Thorough study of Ibn Khaldūn's contributions.

Rosenthal, Franz. Introduction to Ibn Khaldūn, *The Muqaddimah: An Introduction to History.* 3 vols. Translated by Franz Rosenthal. Princeton, 1957. Very useful analysis of Ibn Khaldūn's life and work (preceding this complete English version of *The Muqaddimah*).

Schmidt, Nathaniel. *Ibn Khaldun.* New York, 1930. One of the first brief studies on Ibn Khaldūn.

Fuad Baali

IBN TAYMĪYAH, TAQĪ AL-DĪN AḤMAD (1263–1328), a prominent, influential, and sometimes controversial thinker and political figure. Born in Harran to a family of Ḥanbalī scholars (including his paternal grandfather, uncle, and father), Ibn Taymīyah was himself a Ḥanbalī in many, though not all, juridical and theological matters, and a *Salafī* on a wider plane. He has had a strong influence on conservative Sunnī circles and, in the modern period, on both liberals and conservatives.

Ibn Taymīyah's life was a mix of intellectual activity, preaching, politics, and periodic persecutions and imprisonments. This was in the context of the great disruptions caused by the Mongol invasions. At the age of five in 1268, Ibn Taymīyah was taken with his family to Damascus, in flight from the Mongol threat. He was educated there in the traditional religious sciences and took over from his father as head of the *Sukkarīyah* mosque and professor of Ḥanbalī law in about 1282. Ibn Taymīyah taught and preached elsewhere in Damascus and in other cities. He incurred the wrath of some Shāfiʿī and other *ʿulamāʾ* (religious scholars) and theologians for some of his teachings on theology and law. He was persecuted and imprisoned in Syria and Egypt, for his *tashbīh* (anthropomorphism), his *ijtihād* (independent reason) and his idiosyncratic legal judgements (e.g., on *ṭalāq* [divorce]). Ibn Taymīyah was also active in anti-Mongol propaganda. His legal and theological definitions used in determining whether the Mongols (particularly Mongol rulers) were Muslims or *kāfirs* (nonbelievers) proved to be influential in some places. Ibn Qayyim al-Jawzīyah and Ibn Kathīr were Ibn Taymīyah's most important disciples, although in the modern period many have claimed to be spreading his word. Ibn Taymīyah wrote numerous works, most of which have now been published.

Ibn Taymīyah's main doctrine was, in Ḥanbalī fashion, based on the supremacy of Qur'ān and *sunnah* (received custom) and the *salaf* (early Muslims) as ultimate authorities. He applied an austere exegetical literalism to the sacred sources. Ibn Taymīyah condemned the popular practice of saint worship and condemned pilgrimages to the *ziyārat al-qubūr* (tombs of saints) as *bidʿah* ("innovation") and tantamount to worshiping something other than God. He rejected as alien and an innovation the methods and content of *ʿilm al-kalām* (discursive theology), *falsafah* (peripatetic philosophy), and metaphysical Sufism (though he did encourage pietistic Sufism). This conservatism was also, interestingly, the basis of Ibn Taymīyah's argument against blind obedience to *taqlīd* (established judgments). In his view, the *Salaf* had had to balance the sacred sources with their own *ijtihād* in order to understand and live according to God's law. Ibn Taymīyah thus employed an *ijtihād* which also incorporated *qiyās* (analogical reasoning). *Īmān* (a deep pietistic belief) was for Ibn Taymīyah the source and power of all religion as well as its epistemological foundation. Without it, he thought, doctrine could have no meaning or force. In Ibn Taymīyah's own life as a pietistic Ṣūfī he exemplified such belief. His treatise on *īmān (Kitāb al-īmān)* is one of the most profound and subtle treatments of the subject produced in medieval Islam.

A number of Ibn Taymīyah's ideas have a relevance to society and politics. His notion of the closeness between religion and state, his defining of the Mongols as *kāfirs*, in spite of their public Islamic discourse, and his general antipathy toward the *ahl al-kitāb* ("people of the book").

Ibn Taymīyah's significance for modern Islamic thought and culture is great. Particularly in conservative and Islamist circles his mark is deep. But some liberal trends have also invoked him, especially for his notion of *ijtihād* and his antipathy to *taqlīd*. Insofar as modern Islam has been profoundly preoccupied with issues of religion, state, and society, Ibn Taymīyah's influence is present, whether implicit or explicit. This is particulary true for the Arab world.

The Wahhābī movement and the Saudi state which emerged from it have been deeply affected by certain of Ibn Taymīyah's ideas. The Wahhābī emphasis on Qur'ān and *sunnah,* a literalistic exegesis, a distaste for speculative strains of theology and mysticism, a rejection of the visitation of tombs, and a conception of the *ummah* (community) in Medina as the model for an Islamic state, all reflect Ibn Taymīyah's outlook.

Many of the later Islamist thinkers and trends have depended deeply on Ibn Taymīyah for their general worldview, particularly in their conception of Islam and the *ummah* and the close connection between politics and religion. This is clear in the thought of Ḥasan al-Bannā' in Egypt, whose insistence on Islam as a synthesis of religion and state *(dīn wa dawlah)* and his practical religious tendencies owe much to the earlier thinker.

With the Egyptian Sayyid Quṭb, this tendency became pronounced. In his notion of *Jāhilīyah* (era of "ignorance") as the non-Islamic modern culture of moral and intellectual relativism and the absolute conflict between God's law and that culture, Quṭb exemplified Ibn Taymīyah's sharp distinction between Islam and non-Islam. Most particularly, Quṭb's persistent attack on Muslim rulers, regimes, and intelligentsia for allegedly ruling and teaching according to secular principles rather than Islamic teachings seems firmly based on Ibn Taymīyah's far-reaching pronouncement concerning the status of the Mongols. In this view, these moderns are like the Mongols in publicly espousing Islam but acting against it. They thereby confuse others whose belief is already weak. For this, the Muslim identity of such persons must be questioned. The more militant fundamentalist groups, particularly in the Arab world (and Iran), have explicitly argued for branding them *kāfirs*.

A prominent example of this principle of *takfīr* ("excommunication") can be seen in the widely disseminated tractate, *Al-farīḍah al-ghā'ibah (The Absent Precept)*, by Muḥammad ʿAbd al-Salām Faraj. Faraj, the intellectual voice of the group which engineered Anwar el-Sadat's assassination, cites Ibn Taymīyah's *fatwā* (ruling) on the Mongols as precedent in his *takfīr* of contemporary rulers and religious authorities. This book has been considered by the religious establishment in Egypt to be offensive, doctrinally wrong, and dangerous. Even years after Sadat's death, the *Majallat al-Azhar* (Journal of al-Azhar) in July 1993 published a special booklet criticizing Faraj's tractate point by point, in 112 pages of detailed critique. Concerning Ibn Taymīyah's *takfīr* of the Mongols as a universal precedent, the al-Azhar booklet argues that Ibn Taymīyah's *fatwā* was timebound, relevant only to that particular case, with no application to Egypt in the twentieth century: "Can there be any comparison between these people [the Mongols] who did to Muslims [the things] carried within the history books and [modern] Egypt, its rulers and its people? Can one really compare those with these? . . . These explanations . . . [which we have given] of the reasons for [Ibn Taymīyah's] *fatwā* show that Ibn Taymīyah took his position [solely] with regard to the contemporary situation of the Tartars. [Thus in his view] they were [*kāfirs*], non-Muslims, even though they spoke the language of Islam in an attempt to lead Muslims astray" (pp. 35–36).

With the polarization of modern Islamic political thought on these issues in the latter half of the twentieth century, Ibn Taymīyah's influence, through Sayyid Quṭb, the Islamic movements, and others, has become dominant on one side of the dispute.

BIBLIOGRAPHY

Ibn Qayyim al-Jawzīyah, Muḥammad ibn Abī Bakr. *Asmā' Mu'allafāt Ibn Taymīyah*. Damascus, 1953. Catalogue of Ibn Taymīyah's main works, written by a great disciple.

Laoust, Henri. *Essai sur les doctrines sociales et politiques de Takī-d-Dīn b. Taimīya*. Cairo, 1939. Standard book on Ibn Taymīyah's social and political thought.

Laoust, Henri. *La biographie d'Ibn Taimīya*. Damascus, 1943. The best biography of Ibn Taymīyah.

Makari, Victor E. *Ibn Taymiyyah's Ethics: The Social Factor*. Interesting and valuable discussion of Ibn Taymīyah's theory of social ethics.

Memon, Muhammad Umar. *Ibn Taymīya's Struggle against Popular Religion*. The Hague and Paris, 1976. Excellent account of Ibn Taymīyah's ideas on popular religious practices. The book also includes a valuable discussion of Ibn Taymīyah's refutation of Ibn ʿArabī's metaphysical Sufism.

RONALD L. NETTLER

IBRAHIM, ANWAR (b. 1947), Malaysian Muslim activist, thinker, and politician. Anwar was born at Cerok Tok Kun, Bukit Mertajam, Penang; both his parents were active in the United Malays National Organization (UMNO). He received a secular education and also, like most Malay children of the time, studied religion in the afternoon. While at the prestigious Malay College in Kuala Kangsar, Perak (1960–1966), Anwar became noted as an interscholastic debater and a school captain. He was also active in religious functions and read widely on Islam and society.

As a student of Malay studies at the University of Malaya (1967–1970), he presided over the two major student organizations, the Persatuan Kebangsaan Pelajar-pelajar Islam Malaysia (PKPIM, National Union of Malaysian Students) and Persatuan Bahasa Melayu Universiti Malaya (PBMUM, Malay Language Society of the University of Malaya). Following the communal riots of 1969, Anwar and Dr. Mahathir Mohamed formed an alliance against Premier Tunku Abdul Rahman and pushed for Malay educational and economic rights. However, antipoverty demonstrations in Baling, Kedah in 1974 set them politically apart for some time.

The establishment of Angkatan Belia Islam Malaysia (ABIM) in 1971 made Anwar the most influential young leader of Malaysia. While earnestly calling for the islamization of Malaysian life and an integrated form of development, he also argued for justice, including safeguards for the rights of the non-Muslim population.

Through ABIM Anwar had extensive contacts with most Malaysian leaders, Muslim intellectuals, and activists at home and abroad; however, neither UMNO nor its Malay Muslim opponent PAS (Partai Islam Se-Malaysia) was able to enlist Anwar, even though he shared some of the Islamic ideals of the PAS leadership. Meanwhile, Anwar concentrated on his school, Yayasan Anda, and on youth activities. His career was interrupted when he was detained for two years (1974–1976) without trial under the Internal Security Act following the Baling demonstrations. Nonetheless, on his release his popularity increased tremendously at home and abroad, so that the government could not simply ignore his stand on Islam and other issues. Hence joint programs on *daʿwah* (missionary activity) and related issues were held with the cooperation of various government religious agencies. In 1980 Anwar married Dr. Wan Azizah, a graduate of the Royal College of Surgeons in Dublin.

As a thinker, Anwar has consistently stressed justice, an integrated form of development, and excellence in education and economic production. He is influenced by such intellectuals as Syed Naguib al-Attas, Ismāʿīl al-Fārūqī, Yusuf al-Qardhawi, Ḥasan al-Turābī, Malik Bennabi, and Mohammad Natsir. He also shows familiarity with such varied writers as Ibn Khaldūn, al-Ghazālī, R. G. Collingwood, Malcolm X, Edward Said, and Francis Fukiyama.

Among his many activities, he has served as the leader of Malaysian Youth Council (1972), a member of United Nations Advisory Group on Youth (1973–1974), a representative of the World Assembly of Muslim Youth (WAMY) for Southeast Asia (1976–1982), and a cofounder of the International Institute of Islamic Thought (IIIT), Washington, D.C.; he is presently chancellor of the International Islamic University (IIU) at Kuala Lumpur. His 1982 entry into UMNO on Mahathir's invitation caused displeasure, especially among those who aspired to the party's top posts; nonetheless, with charisma and determination, he has risen to lead UMNO's youth wing and later to serve as one of its three vice presidents. Within the government, he rose rapidly to positions including deputy minister in the prime minister's department; minister of youth, culture, and sports; agricultural minister; and education minister; in 1993 he was minister of finance. His efforts led to the establishment of such institutions as the Islamic Bank, IIU, the Curriculum for Islamic Civilization, and other Islamically oriented programs. With his success as the new deputy president of UMNO in the November 1993 party elections, most observers consider it likely that he will be Malaysia's next prime minister.

[*See also* ABIM; Malaysia; United Malays National Organization.]

BIBLIOGRAPHY

Anwar Ibrahim. *Menangani Perubahan*. Kuala Lumpur, 1989.

Berita Harian, 22 October, 6 November 1993.

Borsuk, Richard. "Islamic Rising Cry." *Asiaweek* (August 1979).

Chandra Muzaffar. *Islamic Resurgence in Malaysia*. Petaling Jaya, 1987.

Morais, J. Victor. *Anwar Ibrahim: Resolute in Leadership*. Kuala Lumpur, 1983.

Risalah 6.6 (1980), 7.3 (1981), 8.1 (1982).

Sabda, S. "Anwar Ibrahim: Cita-cita Perjuangannya Lewat ABIM Sebelum Beliau Aktif Dalam Politik Lewat UMNO." *Al-Islam* (May 1982).

Yusof Harun. *UMNO Selepas Mahathir*. Kuala Lumpur, 1990.

FADHLULLAH JAMIL

ICONOGRAPHY. A discussion of the iconography of Islamic art must begin by defining the essential components or elements of this art and their application. Next, it is important to address the question of whether traditional iconography has changed in the modern Islamic world, or remained the same since the late seventh century (with the building of the Dome of the Rock in Jerusalem in 691). This will entail an investigation of both traditional Islamic iconography and its modern manifestations, dividing the art of each period into two main categories: surface decoration and structural form. The first category is comprised of calligraphy, geometric patterns, and the arabesque; the second includes the dome, *miḥrāb*, minaret, and arch.

Calligraphy. The art of calligraphy originated with the copying of the Qur'ān. When the Qur'ān was first completely edited, collated, and copied under the third caliph, ʿUthmān (r. 644–656), the need for a script worthy of divine revelation gave impetus to the development of Arabic calligraphy. Only the most artistically gifted, perfectly (hence arduously) trained, and spiritually pure calligrapher would be worthy of copying down the living word of God. Because of its association with the Qur'ān, calligraphy became the highest form of art in the Islamic world. Not only was Arabic calligraphy the mainspring of works of art on paper, but it was used extensively in inscriptions on architecture and virtually every medium of the decorative arts—ceramics, metalwork, woodwork, stone, ivory, glass, and textiles among them.

The most widely used early Qur'ānic script, which also adorned architecture and the decorative arts, was called Kufic, after the city of Kufa in Iraq. It is an angular script with extended horizontal and stately vertical letters, arranged on the page with clarity and harmony and lending itself to all sorts of decorative embellishments. After the thirteenth century, the use of Kufic became limited, but its design potential was never forgotten and it forms the basis of the work of a number of contemporary artists. (See figure 1.)

The many cursive scripts were first standardized in the tenth century and again in the thirteenth when the celebrated master Yāqūt laid down the rules for the most prevalent styles—Thuluth, Naskh, Muḥaqqaq, Rayḥānī, Riqʿah, and Tawqīʿ. The first three were used widely for copying the Qur'ān and for epigraphic programs, particularly Thuluth. Naskh became the model for Arabic print. Nastaʿlīq, an elegant, flowing style in which the letters slant downward to the left, was developed in Iran in the late fourteenth century. It was ideally suited for Persian poetry and was widely used in Turkey and India as well.

FIGURE 1. *Contemporary Calligraphy*. Silkscreened work "God, the Unique, the Noble, the Finder, the Loving," employing Kufic script, by Palestinian-born artist Kamal Boullata. The design is in shades of blue.

Calligraphic devices such as birds and animals formed by Arabic letters, as well as epigraphic designs repeated in mirror image, already popular in the sixteenth and seventeenth centuries, remained so during the nineteenth and even into the twentieth century. Some of the later works exhibit a tour de force quality not found before the nineteenth century, for example, an Indian prayer scroll with a text minutely written in the letters of a full-scale inscription, or a Persian prayer scroll on gazelle skin with text incorporated into figures of imams, or (a practice popular in Turkey) writing in gold on leaf skeletons.

Calligraphic designs and calligrams, in cursive scripts far more often than in rectilinear ones, frequently form the basis of the compositions of contemporary Muslim painters, who incorporate elements based on Arabic script into both abstract and realistic compositions. For example, there are two calligraphic paintings in the collection of the Metropolitan Museum of Art, New York, by the revered Indian painter Ṣādiqain and the highly regarded Pakistani painter Muḥammad Aslam Kamāl.

Islamic calligraphy, then, has both remained traditional and been incorporated into a contemporary idiom in a variety of ways. However, in the Muslim world, the practice of calligraphy has been and still is regarded, not only as the creation of a work of art, but as an act of grace.

Geometry. "Calligraphy is the geometry of the spirit." This Arabic proverb testifies to the relationship in Muslim culture between the two fundamental categories of Islamic iconography: the inherent unity, harmony, and immutability of geometric patterns reflects the attributes of God. Geometric patterns, based primarily on the circle, the triangle, the hexagon, and the square, ranging from the very simple to the infinitely complex, are found everywhere in the Islamic world, from the earliest periods to the present. Nowhere outside of Muslim societies have geometric patterns been used to such effect. Parallel to the impetus of the Qur'ān on the development of calligraphy, geometric designs were inspired by the desire to embellish the mosque, *miḥrāb*, minaret, and other religious edifices (later spreading to secular buildings), with a vocabulary suitable to Islam. Together with its epigraphic program, geometric (and arabesque) decorations provide another dimension of aesthetic and spiritual experience associated with a particular physical space or form.

In contemporary architecture in the geographically diverse lands of Muslim culture, the traditional vocabulary of the past is constantly being re-created for a present-day society. Take, as an unlikely example, the Arab World Institute (AWI), recently built in Paris by the French architect Jean Nouvel, inspired, as he claimed, by Arab architectural traditions. The southern facade of this daring and original building is made up of twenty-five thousand metal diaphragms—in their geometric shapes and function, reminiscent of traditional wooden *mashrabīyah* screens—with computer-controlled irises that regulate the flow of light to create varying geometric patterns on the interior floors.

Geometric patterns are also found on virtually all the decorative arts, again, as in architecture, often in combination with epigraphical and arabesque designs. It is frequently asked whether these decorative programs, when reinvented and reapplied by artists today, have lost either their creative spark or their spiritual content. Judging by their endurance to the present in highly diverse cultures, it is clear that, as with calligraphy, artists continue to find the form and content of traditional geometric designs relevant to their own production. Some artists credit this endurance to the process itself, in which the act of creating aesthetic unity through geometric patterning or calligraphic forms generates a sense of spiritual harmony and well being.

The Arabesque. An Islamic art form ideally suited for areas of all-over decoration, the arabesque has been incorporated into the artistic vocabulary of non-Islamic Western cultures, which have had the grace to endow it with a name that acknowledges its origins. The arabesque is formed by a split palmette leaf on a scrolling vine, with a stem growing inorganically out of the tip of the leaf to continue the pattern in aesthetically pleasing, unbroken rhythms. Paralleling the formal, angular patterns of geometry are the curvilinear dynamics of the arabesque, both modes expressing and reinforcing the all-embracing unity of the Islamic world vision. The arabesque reached pinnacles of delicacy, balance, and intricacy, as well as perfection of execution, particularly in highly sophisticated Muslim societies (such as al-Andalusian Spain, Timurid and Ṣafavid Iran, Ottoman Turkey, and Mughal and Deccani India), where the lyricism of its sometimes sensual internal cadences brings the arabesque closest, of all the visual arts, to poetry. Always an integral part of Islamic iconography, the arabesque has held its own, throughout history, with calligraphic and geometric design.

Structural Forms. Forms and structures, borrowed from neighboring cultures (the Byzantine and Sassanian empires) in the early years of Islamic expansion outside the borders of Saudi Arabia, developed specifically Islamic features as the need arose. Among those that in later periods have remained significant in Islamic iconographical terms are the dome, minaret, *miḥrāb*, and arch. The Dome of the Rock in Jerusalem is Islam's first great architectural achievement, built in 691 as a commemorative and victory monument. A single dome over a generally square or octagonal structure became widely used for tomb architecture, culminating in the Taj Mahal. The dome became a prominent feature of mosque architecture, used among other functions to emphasize the *miḥrāb*, the niche in the *qiblah* wall indicating the direction of prayer, facing Mecca, or to emphasize the entrance portal and the central axis to the *miḥrāb*. The most far-reaching exploitation of the dome occurred in the great Ottoman mosques, enabling the dramatic opening and lighting of interior space.

In contemporary mosque architecture, the dome has often been a dominating feature, employed with great verve and imagination, as in the Taubah Mosque in Karachi, Pakistan, the state mosque of Selangor in Malaysia, and the mosque of the Islamic Cultural Center in Rome (see figure 2). The dome's symbolism is multilayered. At its most basic level the dome represents the Heavens, hence the frequent use of sky-colored turquoise in its decoration. The dome and the minaret together, however, whatever the infinite variety of their shapes, symbolize the presence of Islam and serve as the focal point of the Muslim community. In early Islam, the faithful were called to prayer by the voice of the muezzin from the top of the minaret. While the minaret has no practical function today, it is so much a component of mosque iconography that it usually plays an integral part in the overall architectural scheme, for example, the 142-meter (455-foot) minarets of the Malaysian Selangor mosque mentioned above. Occasionally a minaret is a necessary but anomalous iconographic addendum, as in the classical Central Asian–style minaret of the Huaisheng mosque in China, built in a local style.

Iconographically the *miḥrāb* is an essential component of any Islamic religious building. From an art historical perspective, it is of immense importance as the focal

FIGURE 2. *Taubah Mosque, Karachi, Pakistan.* Recasting a dome, arches, and reflecting pools in a contemporary building.

point of the building (mosque, *madrasah,* shrine) to which the most innovative and creative decoration and advanced techniques were applied (for example, in the Great Mosque of Kairouan in Tunisia, the Great Mosque of Córdoba in Al-Andalus, and the *miḥrāb* of the Mongol Öljeitü in the Masjid-i Jāmiᶜ, Isfahan). However, in contemporary architecture, while the *miḥrāb* continues to be an essential iconographical and structural element, it tends to be understated, harmonizing with the overall architectural arrangement.

It may seem odd to think of an arch as a feature of Islamic iconography, but in fact it is such an integral part of most Islamic buildings as to be an identifying factor. The horseshoe arches of Islamic Spain and North Africa are dramatic examples. The early mosques were hypostyle halls with rows of arches resting on columns. The rhythmic repetition of forms provided a sense of community and unity. Arches, usually in combination with columns, but occasionally with piers, are found in almost all contemporary mosque architecture, used in facades, windows, doors, interior spaces, and, of course, *miḥrābs*.

All facets of Islamic iconography cannot be covered in this limited space, for example, the iconography of miniature painting, an enormous subject in itself. However, it should be clear that there is an identifiable Islamic iconography, apparent in Islamic decoration and in Islamic architectural forms. In spite of the tremendous historical, regional, and ethnic diversity within areas of Islamic dominance, there is still evident a cultural and aesthetic unity produced by a shared vision of the world. Arabic calligraphy, geometric patterns, the arabesque, the dome, minaret, *miḥrāb,* and arch, are all visual manifestations of the universal spirit of the Muslim community.

[*See also* Aesthetic Theory; Architecture; Calligraphy.]

BIBLIOGRAPHY

The general reader will find Barbara Brend's work, *Islamic Art* (Cambridge, Mass., 1991), a useful and well-illustrated survey. The Organization of the Islamic Conference (OIC) Research Center for Islamic History, Art, and Culture publishes a newsletter three times yearly in Istanbul, which features information about exhibitions and competitions of the works of contemporary calligraphers. For geometric design, consult Keith Critchlow, *Islamic Patterns* (New York, 1976).

For additional illustrations of some of the iconographical elements and aesthetic materials discussed here, please consult the following: *Aramco World* (September–October 1989): 24, for eighteenth- to nineteenth-century examples of calligraphic design in India; *Aramco World* (July–August 1990): 14–15, for another work by the contemporary Palestinian artist Kemal Boullata incorporating Kufic calligraphy; *Aramco World* (November–December 1991): 55, for the mosque at

Selangor; *Connaissance des Arts* (May 1992), for the mosque of the Islamic Cultural Center in Rome; *Aramco World* (November–December 1991): 50–51, 54, for the mosques at Sumatra and Sri Lanka; *Aramco World* (November–December 1989): 28–33, for a prayer hall designed by contemporary architect Abdel Wahid el-Wakil.

MARIE LUKENS SWIETOCHOWSKI

ʿĪD AL-AḌḤĀ. The Feast of the Sacrifice is celebrated throughout the Muslim world at the end of the period of the annual pilgrimage (*ḥajj*) to Mecca. One of the two most important annual festivals (the other is ʿĪd al-Fiṭr), ʿĪd al-Aḍḥā is also known as the Major Festival (ʿĪd al-Kabīr) and the Greater Bayram. It is celebrated according the lunar Islamic calendar, beginning on the tenth day of the twelfth month (Dhū al-Ḥijjah). On this day Muslims at Mina (near Mecca) and around the world sacrifice unblemished animals in commemoration of the ram substituted by God when Ibrāhīm (Abraham) was commanded to sacrifice his son Ismāʿīl (Ishmael) as a test of faith (Qur'ān 37.99–113; this account differs from that of Genesis, in which it is Isaac who was to be sacrificed). The day of the sacrifice is the first of three days of festive celebration known as *ayyām al-tashrīq*, after which most pilgrims take their leave of Mecca.

A *ḥadīth* attributed to the prophet Muḥammad by a companion says, "I heard the Prophet delivering a sermon, saying 'the first thing we begin with on this day of ours (the Feast) is to pray. Then we return to perform the sacrifice. Whoever does this has acted correctly according to our Sunna (practice).' " *Ḥadīth*s also indicate that it was the *sunnah* of the Prophet and his closest companions to deliver a sermon (*khuṭbah*) following the special Feast prayer, which customarily takes place in the early morning following the sunrise prayer.

In addition to the prescribed prayer and the blood sacrifice, the manuals of Islamic law (*fiqh*) recommend the following practices. Only males having reached the age of maturity, of sound mind, and able to afford an unblemished animal may perform the sacrifice; it is sufficient (*kifāyah*) for their families and the community as a whole that such qualified males make offering. The victim must be an unblemished animal, usually a sheep, but camels, goats, cows, and other animals considered clean according to Islamic law may be offered. For Muslims on the pilgrimage to Mecca the site of slaughter is at Mina, a few miles east of Mecca and one of the important stations of visitation during the *ḥajj*. The victim, no matter where the Feast is being celebrated, is faced in the direction (*qiblah*) of Mecca, and its throat (windpipe and jugular vein) is cut quickly. The act is accompanied by religious formulas, such as the *tasmiyah* or *basmalah* (*bi-ism Allāh*, "in the name of God"; see Qur'ān 6.121) and the *takbīr* (*Allāhu akbar*, "God is greatest"). Islamic law further recommends that only a portion, usually a third, of the slaughtered meat be cooked and eaten by the family of the one offering the sacrifice; the rest is to be given away to the poor and to other families.

Although the Feast of the Sacrifice commemorates the solemn occasion of God testing Ibrāhīm's faith, the annual celebration is festive and social. Aside from the morning visit to the mosque by males with their sons, families visit the graves of relatives to offer additional prayers. Receiving and visiting the extended family and friends of the family marks this three-day celebration. Frequently non-Muslim neighbors and friends offer their greetings and are invited to partake in the food and festivities. In current practice, following tradition, children are very much the focus of the Feast; gifts and sweets abound, and people wear their best clothing.

[*See also* Ḥajj; Sacrifice.]

BIBLIOGRAPHY

Denny, Frederick Mathewson. *An Introduction to Islam*. New York and London, 1985. Contains a useful discussion of Islamic festivals in the context of religious duties, including notes (see pp. 105–124).

Fakhouri, Hani. *Kafr el-Elow: An Egyptian Village in Transition*. New York, 1972. Describes contemporary local observance of the feast days (see pp. 84–85).

Mittwoch, Eugen. "Īd al-Aḍḥā." In *Encyclopaedia of Islam*, new ed., vol. 3, pp. 1007–1008. Leiden, 1960–.

Schimmel, Annemarie. "Islamic Religious Year." In *The Encyclopedia of Religion*, edited by Mircea Eliade, vol. 7, pp. 454–457. New York, 1987.

RICHARD C. MARTIN

ʿĪD AL-FIṬR. The Feast of Breaking the Fast is celebrated at the end of the month of fasting, Ramaḍān. Also known as the Minor Festival (ʿĪd al-Ṣaghīr) or the Lesser Bayram, ʿĪd al-Fiṭr is one of two canonical annual festivals celebrated universally throughout the Muslim world (the other is ʿĪd al-Aḍḥā). According to the lunar Muslim calendar, the festival begins on the first day of Shawwāl, the month following the Ramaḍān month of fasting, and lasts for three days.

Because it marks the end of the month of fasting, ʿĪd

al-Fiṭr—along with the Feast of the Sacrifice, ʿĪd al-Aḍḥā—is one time when fasting *(sawm)* is prohibited according to Islamic law manuals *(fiqh)*. Breaking the fast when required is as obligatory as keeping it during the days of Ramaḍān. Because the feast begins on the first of the month of Shawwāl, it is initiated by the sunset that follows the moment when religious leaders *(ʿulamāʾ)* first observe the crescent moon. The following day, the first day of Shawwāl, an additional communal prayer known as the prayer of the feast is celebrated following the sunrise. As in the case of the Feast of the Sacrifice, the prayer consists of two prostrations and is accompanied by a sermon *(khuṭbah)*, following the practice established by the prophet Muḥammad.

ʿĪd al-Fiṭr is oriented on the family and the community. All save their best attire for the occasion, and children receive gifts and sweets and much attention from adults. The three days are marked, especially in Muslim countries, by the closing of businesses and by invitations and visits from extended family, neighbors, and friends. In keeping with the general tone of good will, it is common for non-Muslim friends and neighbors to extend their greetings and to be invited to join in the celebrations.

Of special significance to this feast is the obligatory form of *zakāt* (alms) known as *zakāt al-fiṭr*. According to one *ḥadīth* recorded in the collection by al-Bukhārī, "the Prophet ordered the people to pay the *zakāt al-fiṭr* before going to the morning feast prayer." Another *ḥadīth* indicates that *ṣadaqat al-fiṭr* may be paid a day or two before the beginning of the feast. Remembering the poor and being generous with those less fortunate is characteristic of the special ethos of this three-day festival and of other religious occasions as well.

[*See also* ʿĪd al-Aḍḥā; Ramaḍān; Sawm; Zakāt.]

BIBLIOGRAPHY

Denny, Frederick Mathewson. *An Introduction to Islam*. New York and London, 1985. Contains a useful discussion of Islamic festivals in the context of religious duties, including notes (see pp. 105–124).

Fakhouri, Hani. *Kafr el-Elow: An Egyptian Village in Transition*. New York, 1972. Describes contemporary local observance of the feast days (see pp. 84–85).

Mittwoch, Eugen. "Īd al-Fiṭr." In *Encyclopaedia of Islam*, new ed., vol. 3, p. 1008. Leiden, 1960–.

Schimmel, Annemarie. "Islamic Religious Year." In *The Encyclopedia of Religion*, edited by Mircea Eliade, vol. 7, pp. 454–457. New York, 1987.

RICHARD C. MARTIN

IDENTITY. *See* Ethnicity.

IDEOLOGY AND ISLAM. In Islam, as in other world religious traditions, there is a historical trend toward objectification, making religion into an entity alongside other aspects of social and personal life. As a result, religious beliefs and practices, once central to a coherent vision of the world and often taken for granted, emerge as merely one facet of a person's life. As this trend intensifies, it becomes hard to separate religious doctrines from ideologies—a manner or content of thinking considered characteristic of an individual, class, or political party. Even as most Muslims claim that "Islam is one" and that it offers a blueprint for all aspects of life, Islam increasingly occupies a special place and time in the school curriculum, and states seek to guide what is said in mosques. Catechism-like pamphlets and essays, often in attractive, question-and-answer formats and popular language, offer believers quick, encapsulated formulations of belief and practice. Religious activists sometimes belittle Muslims unable to explain why they pray and fast, not always recognizing that the ability to formulate such credos is an indication of the compartmentalization of Islam.

Many recent writings on Islam, both scholarly works and religious tracts, illustrate how the notion of ideology in contemporary social and political contexts can substitute for that of Islam without loss of meaning where both terms mean little more than beliefs about the conduct of life or implicit understandings of the nature of the universe. In this respect, ideology inadvertently implies a system of illusory, consciously elaborated doctrines concerning the nature of the social, economic, or political world. Thus Islamists who hold that Islam should play a central role in the political arena argue that the religious principles elaborated in schools and government-controlled mosques in the conservative states of the Persian Gulf, Egypt, and elsewhere do not reflect genuine Islam but are principles propagated to secure the interests of a corrupt ruling class. During a June 1991 Friday sermon in Tehran, Ayatollah Muḥammad Yazdī, head of the Iranian judiciary, warned his listeners of the danger of an "American-style Islam—that is, one that says that the government has nothing to do with Islam—is far greater than that of weapons." Traditional Muslim conservatives argue in turn that Islamists have corrupted Islam by making religion a direct instrument of politics.

Carriers of modern religious traditions argue of course that they are not constructing new religious doctrines but are making them more accessible and easier to understand. But such organization implies a conscious systematization of doctrine and practice, so that large numbers of believers, not just specialist literati, can formulate such questions as: What is my religion? Why is it important to my life? How do my beliefs and practices guide my conduct? The ability of large numbers of Muslims to formulate such questions empowers them and creates new patterns of religious authority that is freed from reliance on a traditionally educated religious elite. Even as contemporary Muslims claim that they are only maintaining established traditions, the increasing objectification of these questions suggests an overall change in how religious belief and identity is expressed in the modern era.

Practical Ideologies and Islam. The term *ideology* often suggests consciously elaborated and maintained systems of belief, especially in the political domain, but it can also suggest implicit, shared notions of the social order so taken for granted that they are not codified or presented in an explicit manner. This second usage is called a *practical* ideology, which, in the case of Islam, means incompletely systematized but nonetheless pervasive notions of true Muslim practice. Paradoxically, it is those beliefs and practices that are firmly integrated with local understandings of Islam and everyday life—suggesting a unity of belief and social practice—that Muslim reformists and Islamists find most reprehensible.

Many North Africans, especially in Morocco, visit the shrines of marabouts or saints, often called *al-ṣāliḥūn* ("pious ones"), often leaving substantial gifts or sacrifices. They do not ordinarily articulate their beliefs, in part because many religious scholars and members of the educated elite disdain such practices or consider them un-Islamic. Many North Africans, however, regard such practices as an integral element of Islam and necessary to their well-being. Learned persons claim that the "pious ones" are mistaken by the ignorant as having a special relationship with God which enables them to act as intermediaries in securing collective or personal interests.

Nonetheless, there is often a dynamic tension between practical ideologies and formal declarations of belief and doctrine, which emphasize the equality of all persons before God, sustained by an educated and largely urban elite. In religion, as in notions of family, sexuality, gender, and honor, practical ideologies often are at odds with formal doctrines and constrain the extent to which formal doctrines are accepted as authoritative.

Women often play a leading role in such practices, as in visits to shrines in Afghanistan, Pakistan, and Turkey and in the *zār* cults of Sudan and East Africa. Educated outsiders see women as primarily responsible for these practices, not recognizing that women act on behalf of the household, extended family, or tribal group. Men's and women's activities must in fact be seen as complementary. Moreover, both North African maraboutic practices and *zār* cults can be seen as means of imagining alternative social and moral universes. Although not formally systematized, the practical ideologies implied by such practices point to a powerful set of beliefs and values closely tied to perceived social realities—more so than is the case for many explicit statements about the nature of Islamic belief and practice.

These practical ideologies form the backdrop against which successes and limitations of the Salafīyah (reformist) movements of the late nineteenth and early twentieth centuries can be understood. Salafīyah suggests a return to the Islamic practice of venerable forebears. In the Muslim world it is common for both modernists and conservatives to justify their ideological position by emphasizing that it is not innovative. Thus in the early twentieth century, most Algerian Muslims thought of maraboutism and belief in the "pious ones" as an integral element of Islamic practice, and most men belonged to *ṭarīqah*s (religious orders). The only alternative to marabouts was a clergy, subsidized by the French, that was officially authorized to conduct Friday prayers in the mosques.

The popular impact of the reformist movement accelerated after World War I, with the return of Algerians who had fought with the French and were unwilling to resume a subservient status. Despite linguistic and regional differences, Algerians from all parts of the country began to recognize their common situation. Distant problems became more familiar, and Algerians began to think actively in terms of a national community. "Young Algerian" began to be used as a conscious parallel to "Young Turk" for the Ottoman province of Anatolia. A small Algerian cadre of French-trained schoolteachers, doctors, journalists, and attorneys formed the vanguard of this movement, but their direct influence on other Algerians was limited by an inability to communicate effectively with the vast majority of Algerians. Because marabouts and the official clergy supported the

French against the Ottoman Empire (allied with the Germans) during the war, many Algerians became disillusioned with traditional religious leaders.

The career of ʿAbd al-Ḥamīd ibn Bādīs (1889–1940), a leading reformer from a family of urban notables in Constantine, suggests how the practical ideologies of religious beliefs shaped the expression and appeal of reformist doctrine. The elite status of Ibn Bādīs and other reformers meant that the French dealt circumspectly with them. They began to visit mosques throughout Algeria, emphasizing in their preachings the unity of Islam, charity, worship, and mutual assistance. Avoiding direct confrontation with marabouts, who were often strongly embedded in local political networks, they challenged maraboutic claims of communication with the Prophet, intercession, miraculous healing, and magic and sought to convince Algerians that these notions were not part of good Islamic doctrine [*See the biography of Ibn Bādīs.*]

Maraboutism was the backdrop against which reformist ideologies in Algeria were forged and elaborated, and these notions continue to play a role in popular thought. The formal ideologies of reformist doctrine offered interpretations of Islam that appealed primarily to a modern, educated elite. Consciously or not, urban values complemented the religious conceptions of the reformist movement and paved the way for rationalist understandings of Islam. Without intending to do so, the carriers of reformist Islam objectified Islam by formalizing it as a doctrine and practice set apart from other aspects of life.

Islam as Ideology: Precursor Movements. Muslim doctrines and practices are conditioned by the modern world, and distinctions among fundamentalists, traditionalists, modernists, and Islamists are misleading if they ignore the common ground of practical ideologies on which they all stand. No Muslim has remained unaffected by the normative and technological changes that have swept the world, and the spread and elaboration of all doctrines are conditioned by very real differences in education and social position. The Pan-Islamic movement that began in the 1880s was largely an elite phenomenon, elaborated in writings, speeches, and congresses of Muslims who emphasized the importance of Muslim political and communal unity and sought ways and means to achieve it. The movement bore structural parallels with the Pan-Hellenic and Pan-German movements that preceded it and thus can be seen as a reaction to European hegemony in the late nineteenth century. Pan-Islam first crystallized as an imperial ideology during the reign of the Ottoman sultan Abdülhamid II (r. 1876–1909), who supported it openly and through secret funding as a means of enhancing his role as head of an empire and leader of the Muslim community. Support for the movement declined with the rise of the nationalist Young Turk movement after 1908. [*See* Pan-Islam; Young Turks.]

A more successful and pervasive example of the objectification of Islamic belief and practice is Egypt's al-Ikhwān al-Muslimūn (Muslim Brotherhood), founded in 1927 or 1928. It grew rapidly, in part by offering an alternative that seemed more directly related to modern conditions than the religious authority and discourse of traditionally educated men of learning. Subsequent movements elsewhere followed the Egyptian model. Unlike competing religious organizations, members had to swear complete obedience to the movement, and there were punishments for negligent members. The Muslim Brotherhood became the first mass political movement built on the tenets of renewed unity and personal reform as a prelude to the realization of the Muslim community's full potential in the modern world. It did not exclude Western influences and institutions harnessed to the service of Islam.

Such ideological notions coincide in principle with the political goals of other states, and for that reason the Muslim Brotherhood has at times received tacit state support. Thus the Saudis sustained the Muslim Brotherhood in the 1950s and 1960s, in part as a counter to the Pan-Arabism of Egypt's Gamal Abdel Nasser and the secular Baʿth parties of Syria and Iraq. Jordan also tolerated the movement so long as it avoided direct criticism of the monarchy. Even Israel encouraged the movement in its occupied territories during the 1970s as an alternative to the Palestine Liberation Organization. [*See* Muslim Brotherhood, *overview article.*]

Radicalization of Islamic Ideology. The vigorous repression of Egypt's Muslim Brotherhood in the 1950s and 1960s and the destruction of its leadership laid the ground for more radical religious interpretations. They appealed to a younger generation of radicalized militants unwilling to compromise with state authorities. These militants sought an alternative to secular ideologies and political movements with a vocabulary and ideas that seemed alien to Islam. The prisons and prison camps of Nasser's Egypt became vivid metaphors for the moral bankruptcy of government and incubators for radical religious thought. *Jāhil* is a Qur'ānic term evoking the state of ignorance, violence, and self-interest that existed prior to the revelation of the Qur'ān, which, for radicals, hampers the full realization of Islamic community. Islamic militants and many other Muslims consider existing state organizations *jāhilī* ("barbaric"), because they do not govern in accordance with Islamic principles as they understand them.

A representative radical ideologue is Sayyid Quṭb (1906–1966). He was born in a village near Asyut in Upper Egypt and educated at a teacher's college. He taught and contributed to various newspapers, went to the United States for further training in education, and joined the Muslim Brotherhood on his return to Egypt in 1951. Like Ḥasan al-Bannā' (1906–1949), he could not claim the credentials of a traditional man of learning. From 1954 until his execution in 1966, he spent all but eight months (1964–1965) in prison.

Sayyid Quṭb's writings attracted a large audience among professionals, white-collar workers, and students. For many Muslims, his writings offer Islamic explanations for contemporary political and economic developments and for the perceived injustices of existing regimes. Prior to the 1950s, the Muslim Brotherhood never attacked the Egyptian or other Arab Muslim governments as un-Islamic. After Quṭb's death, radical elements of the Muslim Brotherhood regularly identified the rulers of Egypt and many other Arab states with the pharaohs of the Qur'ān. Vigorous attacks by government spokespersons only heightened the appeal of Quṭb's ideas. [*See the biography of Quṭb.*]

Ironically, his ideas engendered widespread debate and popular support only in the 1970s, when the *infitāḥ* (political liberalization) that accompanied the rule of Anwar el-Sadat (r. 1970–1981) allowed religious militants to add organizational muscle to radical ideas. One such group, known to its adherents as the Jamāʿat al-Muslimīn ("Society of Muslims") and to government prosecutors as Jamāʿat al-Takfīr wa al-Hijrah ("The Society of Repentance and Emigration"), assassinated Sadat in 1981. The group's name made the government uneasy, although it correctly indicated members' belief that those not adhering to its principles were infidels. They sought to separate from ordinary society by living together in so-called safe houses located in the lower-class, peripheral quarters of Cairo and elsewhere. [*See* Takfīr wa al-Hijrah, Jamāʿat al-.]

The appeal of such groups was heightened by a conjuncture of events: Sadat's bold visit to Jerusalem in 1977, a dismal economic situation, and political unrest in many Muslim states following the 1978–1979 Iranian Revolution. Such short-term factors are undoubtedly important, although other, long-term ones merit equal consideration. Foremost among these is the change in religious and political sensibilities engendered by the growth in mass higher education. The 1970s saw the coming of age of the first generation of postrevolutionary Egyptians to complete the entire mass educational cycle from the primary to the postsecondary level. Most participants in radical groups of the 1970s were in their twenties and thirties, the first beneficiaries of the revolution's commitment to mass education. One long-term effect of modern mass education was to inculcate the principle of individual authority based on books, pamphlets, and the word of popular thinkers, rather than reliance on the authority of traditionally trained religious scholars. The tactics of Sadat's assassins, who justified themselves by asserting the *jāhilī* nature of his rule, profoundly shocked most Egyptians, but the radicals' goal of stripping the state of claims to religious legitimacy found widespread support.

The ideas of many radical Islamists mirror the secular ideologies with which they compete. Morocco's ʿAbd al-Salām Yāsīn argues that there have been no Islamic governments since the time of the prophet Muḥammad and his first successors. Contemporary Muslim societies have been deislamized by imported ideologies and values, the cause of social and moral disorder, and Muslim peoples are subjected to injustice and repression by elites whose ideas and conduct derive more from the East and West than from Islam. Yet the content of Yāsīn's sermons and writings suggests that his principal audience is young, educated, and already familiar with the secular, imported ideologies against which he argues. His key terms, derived from Qur'ānic and Arabic phrases, are more evocative for his intended audience than the language and arguments of both the secular political parties and the traditionally educated religious scholars. In spite of claims to authenticity and uniqueness, contemporary Islamic ideologies, both conventional and radical, have much in common with their secular and non-Islamic counterparts and, like them, must be seen in the economic and political contexts in which their advocates and carriers operate.

The contemporary dilemma of Islamic ideologies and their adherents is exemplified by the Iranian constitution, which displays the coexistence of two contrasting notions of sovereignty. Some principles of the 1979 constitution affirm the traditional concept of the absolute sovereignty of Allāh, while others accommodate the contradictory idea of popular sovereignty in conceding the people's right to determine their own destiny, allowing for occasional referenda and a popularly elected assembly. As Islamic doctrine and practice become increasingly objectified and formalized, such contradictions inevitably develop, perhaps as an indication of the continued debate and reinvention of religious thought in the modern age.

[*See also* Fundamentalism; Modernism; Secularism.]

BIBLIOGRAPHY

Berque, Jacques. *French North Africa: The Maghreb between Two World Wars*. Translated by Jean Stewart. New York, 1967. Sensitive and colorful evocation of struggles among religious reformers, traditionalists, nationalists, and the French.

Donohue, John J., and John L. Esposito, eds. *Islam in Transition: Muslim Perspectives*. New York, 1982. Reader offering historical and contemporary examples of Muslim ideological thought.

Eickelman, Dale F. *Moroccan Islam: Tradition and Society in a Pilgrimage Center*. Austin, 1976. Chapter 6 explains the implicit ideology of maraboutism.

Eickelman, Dale F. "National Identity and Religious Discourse in Contemporary Oman." *International Journal of Islamic and Arabic Studies* 6.1 (1989): 1–20. Provides an example of the "objectification" of Islamic doctrine.

Hamidullah, Muhammad. *Introduction to Islam*. Exp. ed. Paris, 1959. A book intended as a handbook on Islam, responding to a demand to make doctrine accessible to nonspecialists.

Hefner, Robert W. "The Political Economy of Islamic Conversion in Modern East Java." In *Islam and the Political Economy of Meaning*, edited by William R. Roff, pp. 53–78. Berkeley, 1987. Explores the shift from local understandings of religion to Islamic reformist ones from the nineteenth century to the present.

Kepel, Gilles. *Muslim Extremism in Egypt: The Prophet and Pharaoh*. Translated by Jon Rothschild. Berkeley, 1986. First published in French in 1984, this book, with new material added for U.S. publication, remains the best introduction to Islamic radicalism in Egypt.

Mitchell, Richard P. *The Society of the Muslim Brothers*. London, 1969. Classic study of this group's ideology and organization.

Piscatori, J. P., ed. *Islam in the Political Process*. Cambridge, 1983. Remains the best collection of essays on ideology and religious politics in the Muslim world.

Piscatori, J. P. *Islam in a World of Nation-States*. Cambridge, 1986. Thoughtful essay on competing ideologies of Islam in international and transnational politics.

Rahman, Fazlur. *Islam and Modernity: Transformation of an Intellectual Tradition*. Chicago, 1982. Brilliant work by an Islamic modernist on the challenges of reform.

Smith, Wilfred Cantwell. *The Meaning and End of Religion*. New York, 1963. Discusses the compartmentalization of religious traditions in the modern world. Especially interesting for its discussion of Islam.

DALE F. EICKELMAN

IDRĪSID DYNASTY. This important early ruling family in North Africa owes its name to Mulay Idrīs ibn ʿAbd Allāh. In 788 CE Idrīs became involved in an anti-ʿAbbāsid revolt near Mecca and was forced into exile to escape the persecution of Hārūn al-Rashīd, the ʿAbbasīd caliph of Baghdad. Idrīs sought refuge in present-day Morocco, which some fifty years earlier had shaken caliphal rule. There he was welcomed by a recently converted Berber tribe, the Banū Awrabah. These Berbers were impressed with the idea of having a descendant of the Prophet to lead them and soon made Idrīs their chief. He rapidly united the Berber tribes of the area into a confederacy, and from this union emerged the first independent Islamic dynasty in Morocco.

Idrīs's rule was shortlived; he was poisoned in 791 by an agent of Hārūn al-Rashīd. Idrīs left no male heir at the time of his death, but he did leave behind a pregnant concubine, and it was her child, Idrīs II, who was to continue his father's work.

Idrīs II was the true founder of the modern Moroccan state. Although his father had subjugated and converted many tribes adhering to Christianity, Judaism, or indigenous religions, he still remained dependent on the Awrabah tribe. Idrīs II stressed the Islamic-Arab character of Morocco in an attempt to detach himself from the Awrabah, inviting Arab chiefs and warriors from Spain to his court. In 809 Idrīs II achieved what could be considered one of the most durable and important results of the dynasty—the refounding of the city of Fez. Originally founded in 789 by Idrīs I, Fez was still a Berber market town when Idrīs II decided to establish his authority independently from the Awrabah and make Fez his capital city. The arrival of several waves of immigrants, first from Córdoba and later from Tunisia, gave Fez a definitive Arab character.

Among his political achievements, Idrīs II managed to consolidate under his rule most of what is today northern Morocco. To stabilize the government he organized Morocco's first true *makhzan* (central government), an Arabic concept hitherto unknown to the Berber tribes of the region. In addition, the construction of the Qarawīyīn and Andalus mosques as well as the Qarawīyīn University, the oldest in the Muslim world, helped make Fez an important cultural and religious center.

Idrīs II was succeeded by his son Muḥammad II. While retaining the title of imam and rule over the capital, Muḥammad divided his father's kingdom among his brothers, demonstrating a departure from the political sagacity that had been evident in both his father and grandfather. This also effectively undermined centralized control held by the Idrīsids, as sections of the royal family and tribal groups engaged in a long struggle for power that characterized later Idrīsid rule. Although a strong centralized state was not established in the Idrīsid era, the political role of the *sharīf*s was confirmed and has remained a significant element in Moroccan politics ever since. The rise of the Fāṭimid dynasty in North Africa brought an end to Idrīsid pretensions, and the last successor to the throne was killed in 985. The Idrīsid legacy was a foundation for independent Moroccan monarchic rule and sharifian political power.

[*See also* Córdoba, Caliphate of; Fāṭimid Dynasty; Fez; *and* Morocco.]

BIBLIOGRAPHY

Abun-Nasr, Jamil M. *A History of the Maghrib in the Islamic Period.* Cambridge and New York, 1987. Includes an extensive bibliography.

Ibn Azzuz, Mohammad. *Historia de Marruecos hasta la dominación Almoravide.* Madrid, 1955. Excellent and detailed history of Morocco up to the Almoravid reign.

Julien, Charles-André. *History of North Africa: Tunisia, Algeria, Morocco, from the Arab Conquest to 1830.* Translated by John Petrie. London, 1970. Standard survey by a prominent French scholar with a helpful introduction to the dynasty's history and broader historical context.

A. Sofia Esteves and Michael K. Vaden

IDRĪSĪYAH. The thought and teachings of Aḥmad ibn Idrīs (1749/50–1837) gave rise to a spiritual tradition and various Ṣūfī orders. The term *Idrīsīyah* is used here in two senses: to refer to various Ṣūfī brotherhoods and schools established by his students, and to the *ṭarīqah* established by his descendants over a generation after Ibn Idrīs's death.

In its first sense, Idrīsīyah may be used to describe the geographically very widespread and multifaceted tradition derived from Aḥmad ibn Idrīs through his numerous students. By no means have all the branches of this tradition been fully charted. Within the Idrīsīyah tradition, one can distinguish a group of students, direct and indirect, including the Egyptians ʿAlī ʿAbd al-Ḥaqq al-Qūsī (1788–1877) and Muḥammad Nūr al-Dīn al-Ḥusaynī (1813–1887), who spread knowledge of Ibn Idrīs's prayers and litanies in Egypt and the Balkans. There were several such figures within the Ottoman Empire; similar figures elsewhere include the noted Sudanese teacher Muḥammad al-Majdhūb (d. 1832) from the Majādhīb holy clan. Most of these figures did not attempt to establish *ṭarīqah*s as such.

Aḥmad ibn Idrīs himself did not attempt to found any form of organized brotherhood. Although earlier writers have described a conflict over spiritual succession following the master's death, in reality his students seem each to have gone his own way. His senior students Muḥammad ibn ʿAlī al-Sanūsī and Muḥammad ʿUthmān al-Mīrghānī worked to establish their own orders, the Sanūsīyah and Khatmīyah, respectively. A Sudanese student, Ibrāhīm al-Rashīd al-Duwayḥī (1813–1874), seems to have been recognized at least by Ibn Idrīs's sons as their father's spiritual heir; he established a *ṭarīqah* called the Idrīsīyah, but later known as the Rashīdīyah. This order spread in the Hejaz, India, Somalia, and the Sudan.

After his death in Mecca, Ibrāhīm al-Rashīd's nephew al-Shaykh ibn Muḥammad al-Duwayḥī (c.1845–1919) took over the order, which became known as the Ṣāliḥīyah. The Ṣāliḥīyah spread widely in Somalia, where one of its most active proponents was the Somali leader Muḥammad ʿAbd Allāh Ḥasan (1864–1920), the so-called "Mad Mullah" who led Somali resistance to the British, Italians, and Ethiopians. From Somalia the Ṣāliḥīyah *ṭarīqah* spread along the East African coast as far as Zanzibar. Much less is known of the diffusion of the Idrīsiyah Ṣāliḥīyah (and later, the Dandarāwīyah) *ṭarīqah* to Malaysia, Thailand, and Indonesia from about the 1880s onward, presumably by pilgrims returning from the holy cities. There is now a considerable literature on this tradition in the various Malay languages, including translations of Ibn Idrīs's prayers (a detailed recent study in Malay is Hamdan Hassan's *Tarekat Ahmadiyah di Malaysia*, Kuala Lumpur, 1990).

An important and vigorous offshoot of the Ṣāliḥīyah was established by the Egyptian Muḥammad Aḥmad al-Dandarāwī (d. 1910/11) and his son, Abū al-ʿAbbās (d. 1953). The Dandarāwīyah spread in Egypt, where it has become one of the most active and influential brotherhoods, as well as in Syria, Somalia and East Africa, Europe, and Malaysia. Several scholars within the Dandarāwīyah tradition, including the Egyptian Muḥammad ibn Khalīl al-Hajrasī (d. 1910) and the Syrian Muḥammad Bahāʾ al-Dīn al-Bayṭār (d. 1910), wrote extensive commentaries on the prayers and litanies of Ibn Idrīs.

Ibn Idrīs's eldest son, known as Muḥammad al-Quṭb (1803/04–1889), lived his long life in seclusion in the Yemen. It was a younger son, ʿAbd al-ʿĀl (otherwise ʿAbd al-Mutaʿāl, 1830/31–1878), who worked actively to propagate his father's way in Egypt and the Sudan. Educated by al-Sanūsī, whom he accompanied to Cyrenaica, ʿAbd al-ʿĀl left the Sanūsīyah after al-Sanūsī's death in 1859. He settled first in Egypt at al-Zayniyya (Luxor) where his father had lived around 1813–1816; until today this has remained the center of the Idrīsīyah family and order in Egypt. He then traveled in the northern Sudan, where he married several times; he died and was buried in Dongola. It was ʿAbd al-ʿĀl's son Muḥammad al-Sharīf (1866/67–1937) and his son Mīrghānī al-Idrīsī (d. 1959) who consolidated the Idrīsīyah in both Upper Egypt and the Sudan (in the latter, the family's center is in Omdurman, where the present shaykh is Muḥammad al-Ḥasan al-Idrīsī).

In contrast to the Khatmīyah and Sanūsīyah, the Idrīsīyah of Egypt and the Sudan have never played a particularly overt political role. Membership has remained small and confined to particular tribes or regions; generally a "silent" *dhikr* is practiced, and no attempt has been made to "modernize" the order. (However, Michael Gilsenan, in *Saint and Sufi in Modern Egypt* [Oxford, 1973, pp. 171–173], describes a "noisy" Idrīsī *dhikr*.) In Egypt there is a small offshoot founded by Ṣāliḥ ibn Muḥammad al-Jaʿfarī (d. 1981), an al-Azhar *ʿālim* who published numerous works by or on Ibn Idrīs.

An exception to this political quietism was the career of Ibn Idrīs's great-grandson Muḥammad ibn ʿAlī al-Idrīsī (1876–1923); sometimes called "al-Yamanī," he was often referred to in contemporary European sources as "The Idrīsī." Born in Asir, he studied in Mecca, at al-Azhar in Cairo, and with the Sanūsīyah in Libya before spending a period with his Idrīsī relatives in Egypt and the Sudan. In 1905/06 he returned to Asir and in the following year led a successful revolt against the local Turkish administration. Between 1908 and 1932, the Idrīsī state of Asir was a factor of some importance in the politics of Arabia; al-Idrīsī negotiated with the Italians, the Young Turks, and the British, published a proclamation denouncing the Ottoman state and urging Arab independence, and built up a local army. After his death, the state rapidly declined and was peacefully absorbed into the Saudi state in 1932.

[*See also* Khatmīyah; Sanūsīyah; *and the biography of Ibn Idrīs*.]

BIBLIOGRAPHY

De Jong, Frederick. "Al-Duwayḥi, Ibrāhīm al-Rashīd." In *Encyclopaedia of Islam*, new ed., supplement, pp. 278–279. Leiden, 1960–.

Karrar, Ali Salih. *The Sufi Brotherhoods in the Sudan*. London and Evanston, Ill., 1992. Contains an extensive discussion of the brotherhoods of the Idrīsī tradition in the nineteenth-century Sudan.

Naguib al-Attas, Syed. *Some Aspects of Ṣūfism as Understood and Practised among the Malays*. Singapore, 1963. Contains some information on the Idrīsīyah in Malaysia.

O'Fahey, R. S. *Enigmatic Saint. Aḥmad ibn Idrīs and the Idrīsī Tradition*. London and Evanston, Ill., 1990. The first monograph devoted to Ibn Idrīs and his spiritual tradition; contains an extensive bibliography.

Reissner, Johannes. "Die Idrīsiden in ʿAsīr: Ein historischer Überblick." *Die Welt des Islams* 21 (1981): 164–192. History of the Idrīsī state in ʿAsīr.

R. S. O'Fahey

IIFSO. *See* International Islamic Federation of Student Organizations.

IʿJĀZ. *See* Qur'ān.

IJMĀʿ. *See* Consensus.

IJTIHĀD. In general usage, the Arabic word *ijtihād* denotes the utmost effort, physical or mental, expended in a particular activity. In its technical legal connotation, it denotes the thorough exertion of the jurist's mental faculty in finding a solution for a case of law. During the first century of the Hijrah (seventh century CE), when religious law was still being elaborated, and when the secular administrative and customary practices had not yet become integrated with the religious legal system, *ijtihād* was closely associated with *ra'y*, expedient and free reasoning in the sphere of law. *Ijtihād al-ra'y*, an expression that occurs frequently in this early period, thus stood, in one sense, in contrast to *ʿilm* or knowledge of the revealed texts and authoritative traditional practices and reasoning on the basis of these. In another sense, *ijtihād* stood alongside *ʿilm* in that it represented an intellectual quality that supplemented knowledge of the material sources of the law, whether revealed texts or prevalent administrative and customary practices. In this period complete islamization had not yet taken place, and so *ijtihād* linked with *ra'y* was still a legitimate activity; the term carried the connotation of exerting one's effort on behalf of the Muslim community and its interests (*al-ijtihād fī sabīl al-Muslimīn*).

In the second century (eighth century CE) *ijtihād* was gradually dissociated from *ra'y* as the latter increasingly fell under the category of objectionable practices. Indeed, a correlation exists between the gradual ousting of *ra'y* as a tool of free and discretionary reasoning and the growing perception that *ijtihād* represented a systematic method of interpreting and reasoning about the law on the basis of authoritative texts. Muḥammad ibn Idrīs al-Shāfiʿī (d. 821), the founder of the Shāfiʿī school of law, was the first to make a clean break from *ra'y* and to adopt *ijtihād* as a methodology synonymous with *qiyās*, an umbrella term encompassing a number of legal inferences.

In the eighth century *ijtihād* was also used in the sense of "technical estimate" or "fair judgment," particularly "an effort at setting the value of a thing," as in estimating due compensation or damages. This meaning of the term was to persist for centuries in the realm of substantive law.

With the elaboration of legal theory *(uṣūl al-fiqh)* toward the beginning of the tenth century, the meaning and scope of *ijtihād* finally became defined. *Ijtihād* now came to signify the utmost intellectual effort of the *mujtahid* (one qualified to practice *ijtihād*) to reach a solution or a rule *(ḥukm)* on a religious matter. Religious matters were deemed to be either rational or legal. The former constituted the bulk of theology, dealing with such issues as the creation or eternity of the world, the proofs for the existence of God, God's attributes, oneness, and so on. Since evidence pertaining to these matters was thought to be conclusive and not subject to contradiction, the results of *ijtihād* in theology could only be certain; here, there was no place for either probability or conjecture.

In legal matters, by contrast, *ijtihād* was restricted to the realm of probability. Wherever the authentic texts were unambiguous with regard to a certain matter, *ijtihād* had no role to play, since God had made his decree clear. The certainty of the knowledge that God had unambiguously stipulated his judgment on a particular matter was thought to preclude any human attempt at investigating the law concerning that matter. The duties to pray and to pay the alms-tax are two examples in point.

The province of *ijtihād* was further restricted to exclude those cases that had become subject to consensus *(ijmāʿ)*, since the sanctioning authority of this instrument was thought to render the judgments of such cases certain, irrevocable, and thus not subject to juristic interpretation. It therefore followed that *ijtihād* in legal matters must be confined to the gray areas of the law, where textual certainty was absent and where human reasoning on the basis of the texts might uncover the law as intended by God. This is why *ijtihād* is defined as the comprehensive exercise of the jurist's mental faculty in reaching a legal ruling that is inferential and thus probable *(ẓannī)*. [*See also* Consensus.]

The probability that is necessarily entailed by inferential reasoning clearly suggests that the outcome of *ijtihād* is fallible, and Sunnī legal theory admits this. Although *ijtihād* may result in rulings that do not correspond to the law as intended by God, it is deemed a duty incumbent on those who are qualified to perform it. The very practice of *ijtihād* is a religious duty, and a *mujtahid* who fails to fulfill it is thought to have sinned. To mistake the law as lodged in the mind of God, however, does not constitute a sin, because to demand that humans know with certainty what is concealed in the mind of God would amount to charging them with a responsibility far greater than they could assume. All aspects of life must be regulated by the *sharīʿah,* and therefore *ijtihād* must be commensurate with the obligation and need to attempt to discover the law; it is the attempt that is a religious duty—to be rewarded when made and punished when omitted—and not the success of that attempt. Accordingly, the great majority of scholars have espoused the doctrine that all attempts of *ijtihād* are rewarded by God, and those which have succeeded in uncovering the true law are doubly rewarded. This doctrine, however, seems to represent a justification of *ikhtilāf al-fuqahā'*, the institutionalized differences among jurists' doctrines.

Islamic legal theory has stipulated the requirements a jurist must fulfill in order to qualify as a *mujtahid*. Proficient knowledge of theology was deemed a necessary condition since it provides the proofs for the authority of the revealed texts that are the material sources of the law. To qualify as a *mujtahid* the jurist must also gain a comprehensive knowledge of legal theory *(uṣūl al-fiqh)*, which elaborates the interpretative principles of legal language (e.g., the imperative, ambiguous, metaphorical, general, and particular) and the methods of investigating the authenticity and transmission of texts, particularly prophetic traditions. *Uṣūl al-fiqh* also deals with the theory of abrogation, which includes a discussion as to what texts repeal others or are repealed by them. In addition, the jurist must have masterly knowledge of the conditions under which consensus may be reached, and he must know what parts of the law have become subject to such consensus. Finally, no *ijtihād* is possible without a sophisticated capability for legal reasoning or without thorough knowledge of the Arabic language, in which the material sources of the law are written.

The great majority of legal theoreticians hold that these qualifications are required of a jurist who wishes to embark on *ijtihād* in all spheres of the law. But those jurists who aim to practice *ijtihād* in a limited area of the law need not fulfill all the requirements, only those relative to the methodological principles and the textual materials that pertain to the case at hand.

By the beginning of the tenth century, the Sunnī legal schools (*madhhab*s) of Islam had reached a level of development where all essential questions on matters of positive law had been addressed. The detailed elaboration of the judicial system by this time represented a legal stability that was to continue until the premodern encounter with the West. This stability meant the continuity and persistence of the legal tradition, where society accepted the broad lines of the law as laid down by the early masters. It necessarily follows that adhering to the law elaborated in successive centuries would progressively restrict the scope of *ijtihād*.

This fact gave rise to the perception, prevalent among many Western scholars and modern Sunnī Muslims alike, that the so-called "gate of *ijtihād*" was closed at the beginning of the tenth century. Two elements further complicate this perception. It has often been suggested that the closure of the gate amounted to a complete ban on *ijtihād*, and that Muslim jurists themselves reached a consensus to that effect. This perception, though prevalent for nearly two centuries, has been shown by recent scholarship to be entirely without foundation. There exists no evidence of such a closure either in the tenth century or thereafter, and there certainly was no consensus on it. To the contrary, evidence shows that the practice of *ijtihād* continued throughout the centuries, although on a smaller scale than before because of the stability the legal system had attained.

The narrowing of the scope of creative legal reasoning after the eleventh century gave rise to various classifications in Sunnī legal literature, in which jurists were ranked according to their ability to practice *ijtihād*. One predominant classification credited the eponyms of the legal schools with the distinction of being absolute *mujtahid*s (*mujtahid muṭlaq*) who were capable of laying down a methodology of the law and of deriving from it the positive doctrines that were to dominate their respective schools. Next came the *mujtahid*s who operated within each school (*mujtahid muntasib* or *mujtahid fī al-madhhab*), who followed the methodology of their eponym but proffered new solutions for novel legal cases. The lowest rank belonged to the *muqallid*, the jurist-imitator who merely followed the rulings arrived at by the *mujtahid*s without understanding the processes by which these rulings were derived. Between the ranks of *mujtahid*s and *muqallid*s there were distinguished other levels of jurists who combined *ijtihād* with *taqlīd*. While it was universally acknowledged that the absolute *mujtahid* was a phenomenon of the past, incapable of repetition, Muslim scholars continued to maintain that all other levels were attainable. Indeed, countless jurists from the tenth century and to the early nineteenth century were considered to have attained the rank of *mujtahid* within their schools.

In Shīʿī Islam, discussions about "closing the gate of *ijtihād*" never arose, because non-Zaydī Shīʿīs in general, and the Twelvers in particular, deem *ijtihād* to be an ongoing process. It is noteworthy that the Shīʿīs, like the Sunnīs, accept the Qur'ān as the primary material source of law, although they rely on a different set of prophetic traditions. While the Sunnīs believe in consensus as the infallible source of truth after the age of the Prophet, the Twelvers take the pronouncements of the twelve infallible imams as a continuing source of truth. This source, expressed in the definite statements of the imams, increases the level of certainty in the law and as a consequence safeguards to a higher degree than in Sunnism the element of human intellection. Accordingly, Twelver Shiism acknowledges human reasoning and intellect as one of the legal sources that perfectly supplement the revealed texts.

Beginning in the seventeenth century, discourse on *ijtihād* as a binary opposite of *taqlīd* gained added significance in Sunnī Islam. No longer taken for granted, *ijtihād* and the need to practice it in the legal system became the focal point in the writings of eminent legists. Among the traditional reformers who argued the need to renew *ijtihād* were Shāh Walī Allāh al-Dihlawī (d. 1762), Ibn Muʿammar (d. 1810), Muḥammad ibn ʿAlī al-Shawkānī (d. 1832), and Muḥammad ibn ʿAlī al-Sanūsī (d. 1859). Their emphasis on the centrality of *ijtihād* amounted to a criticism of *taqlīd*, which they deemed a heretical religious innovation when practiced by learned jurists. *Taqlīd*, they maintained, is lawful only when applied on behalf of laymen who need the guidance of legal scholars in running their mundane and religious affairs. For the learned jurist, the ultimate authority lies not in the doctrines of past masters, but rather in the Qur'ān and the *sunnah,* which must be the jurist's sole frame of reference.

During the second half of the nineteenth century and the early decades of the twentieth, the reformist religious movement gained momentum against the backdrop of the massive introduction of European codes in place of the *sharīʿah.* The Salafī movement, which stressed the need to reinterpret Islamic teachings with direct reference to the Qur'ān and the *sunnah,* particularly called for abandoning *taqlīd* in favor of *ijtihād.* Wherever the textual sources offer explicit statements on matters of faith, worship, and personal status, there is no room for *ijtihād.* However, all other matters of a practical nature, affecting the affairs of the Muslim community and public life and policy, are subject to reinterpretation by means of *ijtihād.* Those who are capable of undertaking *ijtihād* are the legitimate holders of authority, the *ahl al-ḥall wa-al-ʿaqd* (or *ūlū al-amr*), who decide on behalf of Muslims and act in their best interests. But whereas traditional doctrines recognize the absolute authority of the *mujtahid* and his direct responsibility before God, modern reformists deem the *mujtahids'* authority to be derived from that of the community. Accordingly, if the *ijtihād* of *ahl al-ḥall wa-al-ʿaqd* failed to represent the will and wishes of the community, it would be considered invalid. At the same time, the validity of *ijtihād,* as expressing the will of the community, hinges on the premise that the outcome of *ijtihād* shall not contradict the spirit and letter of the revealed texts.

The theories of these reformists, however, remained without practical application, for the reformists lacked the power and the means to put their ideas into effect. It was the state apparatus and the political elite that dictated the actual legal reforms of the twentieth century. Here, both traditional and reformist theories of *ijtihād* were entirely ignored. Legal reform was carried out mainly through the introduction of novel administrative and procedural regulations, as well as through the implementation of an eclectic principle whereby new sets of laws were expediently gathered piecemeal from a variety of legal schools and jurists. In these reforms, *ijtihād* was resorted to infrequently, when neither administrative regulations nor eclecticism could serve. Perhaps the most prominent example of this form of *ijtihād* may be found in the Tunisian Law of Personal Status (1957), whereby polygyny was declared prohibited on the grounds that the Qur'ān allows a man to marry a second wife if he can treat both with complete impartiality. The Tunisian legislators stipulated that under modern conditions such impartiality is a practical impossibility; therefore, they argued, allowing polygynous marriage in the modern world would blatantly contravene the prescriptions of the Holy Book.

The *ijtihād* of modern reformers—if it can indeed be so called—remains without methodological and philosophical foundations. Like the reformers' other means of changing the law, their reinterpretation is still based on expediency, without due consideration of the intellectual integrity and systemic consistency of the law. They have set aside the traditional legal methodology, but they have not, at the same time, attempted to fashion a new methodology that can sustain the present and future need for legal change. Although such attempts have not yet been initiated in the Muslim world, there have been during the past decade or two a number of voices calling for a reformulation of *uṣūl al-fiqh* with a view toward fashioning a neo-*ijtihād* methodology.

[*See also* Ahl al-Ḥall wa-al-ʿAqd; Law, *article on* Legal Thought and Jurisprudence; Taqlīd; Uṣūl al-Fiqh.]

BIBLIOGRAPHY

Bravmann, M. M. *The Spiritual Background of Early Islam.* Leiden, 1972. Includes a detailed semantic analysis of the early meaning of *ijtihād;* see pages 188–194.

Coulson, Noel J. *A History of Islamic Law.* Edinburgh, 1989. Provides a succinct discussion of *ijtihād* in modern legal reform in the last two chapters.

Hallaq, Wael B. "Was the Gate of Ijtihad Closed?" *International Journal of Middle East Studies* 16 (1984): 3–41.

Hallaq, Wael B. "On the Origins of the Controversy about the Existence of Mujtahids and the Gate of Ijtihad." *Studia Islamica* 63 (1986): 129–141.

Schacht, Joseph. *The Origins of Muhammadan Jurisprudence.* Oxford, 1975. Still the definitive work on the development of *ijtihād* and related concepts in the early period.

Schacht, Joseph. *An Introduction to Islamic Law.* Oxford, 1979. Chapter 10 articulates traditional views on the closure of the gate of *ijtihād.*

Shāfiʿī, Muḥammad ibn Idrīs. *Al-Risāla.* Edited by Aḥmad Shākir. Cairo, 1892. English translation by Majid Khadduri, *Al-Imām Muḥammad ibn Idrīs al-Shāfiʿī's al-Risāla fī Uṣūl al-Fiqh.* 2d ed. Cambridge, 1987.

Shīrāzī, Abū Isḥāq Ibrāhīm. *Sharḥ al-Lumaʿ.* Edited by Abdel-Majid Turki. 2 vols. Beirut, 1988. Classical work on legal theory and *ijtihād.*

Weiss, Bernard G. "Interpretation in Islamic Law: The Theory of *Ijtihād.*" *American Journal of Comparative Law* 26 (Spring 1978): 199–212.

WAEL B. HALLAQ

ʿILM. The Arabic word *ʿilm* is commonly translated as both "learning" and "knowledge," for it refers both to the process of attaining knowledge and to the information that one gains by learning. As such, it is to be contrasted with *fiqh,* which refers not to the end product of learning but only to the process of understanding or deducing (see Rahman, 1979, p. 101, for a discussion of the difference).

Among Muslims, knowledge and the seeking of knowledge are of such importance that the latter is deemed to be an act of worship. The prophet Muḥammad is often quoted as saying, "Acquire knowledge from cradle to grave" and "seek knowledge everywhere, even in China." A. K. Brohi notes that from a Muslim perspective the best life is "the one that is devoted to the acquisition of knowledge, which may be regarded as a sacred religious duty imposed on every Muslim man and woman" (1988, p. 5). Consequently, those who attain greater knowledge are considered superior in rank and position to those having less knowledge (see Qur'ān, surahs 58.11 and 39.9).

It is significant that the first direct revelation to the illiterate prophet Muḥammad consisted of a command to *iqra'* (read or recite), that is, to gain or to pass on knowledge. In the opening verse of Surat al-ʿAlaq (96.1), he is told: "Read [or recite] in the name of thy Lord and cherisher . . . He who taught the use of the pen . . . who taught man that which he knew not." The command set forth in this verse obliges humans to seek knowledge through learning.

Nevertheless, the Qur'ān also emphasizes the limits to what humans can hope to know by their own efforts. This deficiency in, or limit to, human comprehension is indicated in many Qur'ānic verses and can be attributed either to God's desire to reveal only what he wishes to reveal or to an indication of human limitations (see, for example, surahs 17.85, "Of knowledge [*ʿilm*], only a little is communicated to you," and 27.65, "No one in the heavens or earth, God excepted, knows what is hidden.").

The idea then is that we must never lose sight of our limitations or become overly proud of what our learning allows us to achieve. As essential as scientific learning and human reasoning are—in the quest for awareness of what God ultimately knows more thoroughly—they are tools that always fall short of what is hidden.

Precisely because it is not clear why things are hidden, the question of whether we should have recourse to some other, nonrational method or exercise to attain such knowledge remains as much a subject of debate today as it was in the time of al-Ghazālī (AH 450–505/1058–1111 CE) and Ibn Rushd (Averroës, 520–595/1126–1198). And the rationalist might always urge that we must not be content with the mere acceptance of God's creation, that we must also reflect on it (see Qur'ān, surahs 7.185, "Have they not reflected upon the kingdoms of the heavens and the earth and what things God has created?" and 88.17, "Do they not reflect upon the camels, how they have been created, and upon the sky, how it has been raised up?").

BIBLIOGRAPHY

Brohi, A. K. "Islamization of Knowledge: A First Step to Integrate and Develop the Muslim Personality and Outlook." In *Islam: Source and Purpose of Knowledge,* pp. 5–12. Herndon, Va., 1988.

Rahman, Fazlur. *Islam.* 2d ed. Chicago and London, 1979.

CHARLES E. BUTTERWORTH and SANA ABED-KOTOB

IMAM. A title indicating leadership, governance, or rule, imam (Ar., *imām*) is used in a wide variety of contexts by both Sunnī and Shīʿī Muslims. The most common contemporary use of the word is to designate the leader of congregational prayers, this being justified by the etymological sense of *imām* as "one who stands in front." (In Iran, the leader of the Friday prayers held in large mosques or other appropriate spaces is called *imām-jumʿah*).

The word *imām* occurs in the Qur'ān as an attribute not only of prophets, such as Abraham (surah 2.124), but also of the revelation entrusted to Moses (surah 46.12), as well as serving as designation for the record of deeds with which man will be presented in the hereafter (surah 36.12). However, numerous traditions of the Prophet refer to the leader or ruler of the Muslim community as imam, and the term came to be recognized, by both Sunnīs and Shīʿīs, as meaning "the one exercising general leadership in both religious and political affairs" (Sharīf al-Jurjānī, *Kitāb al-taʿrīfāt,* Beirut, 1983, p. 35).

Gradually, however, the word came to acquire a special significance for Shīʿīs, for whom recognition of the legitimate leader of the Muslim community was an essential article of faith. The succession of twelve figures, identified by the majority of Shīʿīs as successors to the Prophet, were seen by them to possess not only the right to rule but also inerrancy and, therefore, supreme authority in all matters of jurisprudence and Qur'ānic exegesis. The last of the twelve was Muḥammad ibn Ḥasan al-ʿAskarī, who is believed, in 872, to have entered a state of occultation *(ghaybah)* from which he will ultimately reemerge. Precisely the anticipation of his parousia has enabled the Twelfth Imam to remain a focus of Shīʿī devotion, even while several of his functions have been exercised on his behalf by the jurists. More generally, awareness of the imams has been kept alive by the recitation of the supplicatory prayers that several of them composed and by pilgrimage *(ziyārah)* to their shrines at Najaf, Karbala, Kazimayn, and Samarra in Iraq and Mashhad in Iran, as well to countless tombs of their real or putative descendants *(imāmzādah)* scattered across Iran. [*See* Ziyārah; Imāmzādah.]

Modern times have not, in general, brought any change in Shīʿī conceptions concerning the Twelve Imams. However, the Iranian ideologue ʿAli Sharīʿatī (1933–1977) denounced what he regarded as an undue mythologization of them. This, he claimed, had resulted in their reduction to ritually invoked intermediaries between man and God or even in their transformation into angelic or supernatural beings, utterly removed from the plane of historical reality. He drew attention to the fact that *imām* is cognate with *ummah,* which he defined as a society "in which individuals come together in harmony with the intention of advancing and moving toward their common goal." Accordingly he reinterpreted the function of the imam, in radically modernistic fashion, as "a committed and revolutionary leadership, responsible for the movement and growth of society on the basis of its worldview and ideology, and for the realization of the divine destiny of man in the plan of creation" (*Islām-shināsī*, Tehran, n.d., vol. 1, pp. 97–98).

After the triumph of the Iranian Revolution of 1979, Ayatollah Ruhollah Khomeini (1902–1989), leader of the movement, was officially designated as imam (see, for example, preamble to the Constitution of the Islamic Republic of Iran). In view of the adulation that was widely accorded to Khomeini, it has sometimes been suggested that this use of the title made (or was intended to make) Khomeini the equal of the Twelve Imams in every respect. The designation of Khomeini as imam (first occurring in 1964 in a poem by Niʿmat Mirzāzādah) did not, however, attribute inerrancy to him; it was the consequence of the recognition that he was fulfilling a practical role of comprehensive leadership. The use of the title imam for the leader of a modern Shīʿī movement had, in any event, a precedent in the case of Imam Mūsā al-Ṣadr (disappeared in 1977), the founder of the Ḥarakat al-Amal in Lebanon. Adherents of the archconservative Ḥujjatīyah movement in Iran sought, nonetheless, to prevent all confusion by referring to Khomeini as *na'ib al-imām* ("deputy of the [Twelfth] Imam").

[*See also* Ghaybah; Mahdi; Shīʿī Islam, *historical overview article; and the biography of Khomeini.*]

BIBLIOGRAPHY

Āl Kāshif al-Ghiṭā', Muḥammad al-Ḥusayn. *The Origin of Shiʿite Islam and Its Principles*. Qom, 1982. See pages 48–55.

Mufīd, Muḥammad ibn Muḥammad al-. *Kitāb al-Irshād: The Book of Guidance*. Translated by I. K. A. Howard. Qom, 1981.

Muẓaffaz, Muḥammad Riḍā al-. *The Faith of Shiʿa Islam*. London, 1982. See pages 31–49.

Sachedina, A. A. *Islamic Messianism: The Idea of Mahdī in Twelver Shīʿism*. Albany, N.Y., 1981.

Ṭabāṭabā'ī, Muḥammad Ḥusayn. *Shiʿite Islam*. Albany, N.Y., 1977. See pages 173–222.

HAMID ALGAR

IMĀMAH. The meaning of *imāmah* ("religious-political leadership") of the Muslim community was the most practical question dominating Muslim minds following the Prophet's death in 632. Theological and juridical aspects of the imamate have engaged Muslim intellectual activity for many centuries and continue to do so as part of the community's accommodation to the realities of power. The major dispute concerning the imamate surrounded the question of investiture to exercise the Prophet's comprehensive authority *(wilāyah ʿāmmah)* as the temporal and spiritual leader of the *ummah* (community).

There were at least two main opinions on this matter. The view prevalent among the early Muslims headed by Abū Bakr and his associates regarded the imamate to be the right of the Meccan companions of the Prophet, belonging to the tribe of Quraysh. This was a reassertion of leadership that was in line with the tribal culture of seventh-century Hejaz. It was also an implicit rejection of the other major opinion that maintained that leadership was passed on through a special designation. This view was held by the Prophet's family *(ahl al-bayt)*, mainly the Hashemites, which regarded the imamate divinely invested in ʿAlī ibn Abī Ṭālib, the Prophet's cousin and son-in-law.

The dispute over the leadership, although arising immediately following the Prophet's death, did not find theoretical expression until the eruption of the civil strife connected with the caliphate of ʿUthmān. ʿUthmān's corrupt leadership raised the question about the qualification of the person holding the office and also the moral-religious obligation of the community when faced with a fait accompli in this regard. The murder of ʿUthmān assumed paradigmatic proportion in setting the precedent for dealing with unjust leadership. Although the debate over the rightness of the murder has continued to the present time, the majoritarian opinion, as it was subsequently formulated, upheld the legitimacy of ʿUthmān's leadership, making him one of the four "rightly guided" caliphs. This was the Sunnī conception of the imamate, which had the sole function of preserving the sense of the *ummah* under the historical caliphate against the counterclaims of the oppositional groups such as the Shīʿah and Khawārij. However, a distinction was made between those imams who fulfilled all the conditions of the imamate like the Rāshidūn, and hence, regarded as the "successors" of the Prophet, and those who fell short and were considered merely as kings. This distinction was necessary for the development of the juridical theory in which the *sunnah* (the prophetic paradigm), as the second most important source for religious prescriptions, included the actions and legal decisions of the Rāshidūn. Consequently, in the Sunnī juridical theory, the imamate of the Rāshidūn formed part of the prophetic precedent and was accorded an equally authoritative status for deriving the Muslim religious practice. The latter development is today being examined by some Sunnī intellectuals, both traditional as well as modern, who question the adequacy and relevance of those precedents in formulating practical rules for contemporary Muslims. (Several Egyptian scholars, including the Azharī Muḥammad al-Ghazālī, have undertaken critical assessment of these early prescriptive precedents and have challenged their authoritativeness merely on the basis of their being included as part of the Prophetic paradigm.)

The Khawārij, who had seceded from ʿAlī's camp during the Battle of Ṣiffīn (657), formulated their own version of the imamate, making it obligatory among believers to proclaim illegitimate and to depose the leader who had strayed from the right path. However, they too rejected the notion of imamate through special designation. They maintained that any believer with good standing in religion, whose character was beyond reproach, and who was proclaimed by the community as an imam was a legitimate leader, regardless of his being a non-Quraysh or even a non-Arab. Hence, they acknowledged ʿUthmān as legitimate only during the first six years of his imamate and ʿAlī until the Battle of Ṣiffīn. This general conception of political authority has survived among the Ibāḍīyah, the surviving moderate wing of the Khawārij, to the present day. [*See* Khawārij; Ibāḍīyah.]

The Shīʿīs, who included a spectrum of the radical to moderate subdivisions, such as the Ismāʿīlīyah, the Twelvers, and the Zaydīyah, shared their recognition of any member of the *ahl al-bayt* who claimed the imamate. The Zaydīyah differed with the Twelvers in some essential points. They did not regard the imamate to be limited in the particular line of ʿAlī's descendants through his son al-Ḥusayn, as the Twelvers had maintained. They acknowledged the imamate of any member of the *ahl al-bayt* who rose against the illegitimate rulers. They also rejected the Twelver tenet which had required the repudiation of the first three caliphs as illegitimate and the law handed down by them as vitiated. However, the Twelver rejection of the early caliphate and its role in the legal formulations of Islam came to prevail in the later Zaydism where the descendants of ʿAlī and Fāṭimah, regardless of whether they were imams or not, became the source for the Zaydī legal school. The Zaydī imamate shared the Shīʿī insistence that the imam's religious knowledge be connected with the aims of *sharīʿah* (divine law) and its application in human society, in addition to the imam having impeccable character.

The Twelver doctrine was firmly based on the rational need for an infallible leader and authoritative teacher to guide humanity to the prosperous life. The imam was regarded as *ḥujjah* (a competent authority) to execute the divine purposes by assuming the Prophet's comprehensive authority in both the temporal and the religious spheres of human activity. Consequently, disregarding and disobeying the rightfully appointed imam was equal to disobeying the Prophet. Although the imam was entitled to political authority, his imamate, contrary to the Zaydī requirement, was not dependent on it. Rather, the imam's role was seen as the infallible interpreter of the prophetic revelation. His existence, even under the requirement of *taqīyah* (prudential dissimulation), was regarded as necessary for the religious well-being of his followers. The circumstantial depoliticization of the imamate culminated in the concept of the "hidden" (*mastūr, ghayb*) imam, which was common among several Shīʿī subdivisions, including the Fāṭimid Ismāʿīlīyah. During the tenure of the hidden imams, the juridical and administrative functions of the imams were assumed by the prominent members of the Shīʿī community. They were proclaimed as the *nāʾib* ("deputy") or *dāʿī* ("guide") on behalf of the actual imams. The religious scholars (*mujtahid* and ayatollah) and guides functioning as imams have provided the community with tangible religious leadership that has survived among the Twelver Shīʿīs and the Ṭayyibī branch of Fāṭimid Ismāʿīlism. The only Shīʿī sect that still recognizes a manifest imam is the Nizārī branch of the Ismāʿīlīyah.

[*See also* Ahl al-Bayt; Ismāʿīlīyah; Ithnā ʿAsharīyah.]

BIBLIOGRAPHY

Madelung, Wilferd. "Imāma." In *Encyclopaedia of Islam*, new ed., vol. 3, pp. 1163–1169. Leiden, 1960–.

Madelung, Wilferd. "Ismāʿīliyya." In *Encyclopaedia of Islam*, new ed., vol. 4, pp. 198–206. Leiden, 1960–.

Nawbakhtī, Al-Ḥasan ibn Mūsā al-. *Firaq al-Shīʿah*. Istanbul, 1931.

Sachedina, A. A. *Islamic Messianism: The Idea of Mahdī in Twelver Shīʿism*. Albany, N.Y., 1981.

Sachedina, A. A. *The Just Ruler (al-Sulṭan al-ʿĀdil) in Shīʿite Islam*. New York, 1988.

ABDULAZIZ SACHEDINA

IMĀMĪ SHIISM. *See* Ithnā ʿAsharīyah.

IMĀMZĀDAH. Literally "offspring or descendent of an imam," *imāmzādah*, in Iran, is most commonly applied to a shrine-tomb of a descendent of the Shīʿī imams. *Imāmzādahs* are the centers of popular Shīʿī devotion and the objects of pilgrimages. Many of them are regarded as possessing miraculous and healing properties. The source of veneration of *imāmzādahs* in Iran is to be found in geopolitics. The *ziyārah* (pilgrimages to imams' tombs) constitutes a principal aspect of Shīʿī popular worship. However, only one of the Twelver Shīʿī imams, ʿAlī al-Riḍā, is buried in the vast territory of Iran. His shrine-tomb grew into a large shrine city called Mashhad ("sepulcher") in northeastern Iran. The other imams are buried in central and southern Iraq and in Medina.

The most important Shīʿī tombs, those of Imam ʿAlī at Najaf and Imam Ḥusayn at Karbala, are situated in present-day Iraq. Making a pilgrimage to those holy tombs was often physically, politically, and financially difficult for Iranian Shīʿīs. Hence, the basis for the veneration of the descendants of imams in Iran sprung from a practical necessity before becoming a part of popular piety. "These shrines (called *Imamzadas*) are to be found in large numbers in Iran, especially in the areas around Qumm [Qom], Tehran, Kashan, and Mazandaran, which have been Shiʿi from the earliest times, and, therefore, tended to be a refuge for ʿAlids, who were often being persecuted in other parts of the Muslim world" (Momen, 1985, p. 182). From the time that Shiism became the state religion of Iran (beginning in the sixteenth century), popular beliefs and rituals played a very important role in the spread of Shiism. Going on pilgrimages and paying homage to the descendants of the imams at their tombs has been one of the most popular activities of the Iranian Shīʿīs. They have been encouraged by the Shīʿī *ʿulamāʾ* (community of religious scholars) to participate in these pilgrimages in order to acquire merit and blessings. Shah ʿAbbās (1571–1629), the Ṣafavid king, however, encouraged the pilgrimages to *imāmzādahs* within the boundaries of Iran for economic reasons—it reduced the outflow of money from the country.

As the pilgrimages to the tombs of the imams and their descendants became increasingly elaborate activities, many guidebooks to such visitations were written. One of the most important manuals for Shīʿī pilgrims is *Tuḥfat al-zāʾirīn* (A Present for Pilgrims), written by one of the most powerful and influential members of the *ʿulamāʾ* of the late Ṣafavid period, Muḥammad Bāqir Majlisī (d. 1699). In this guidebook, Majlisī writes: "in all the cities there are many tombs attributed to *imāmzādahs* and other relations of the Imams. The graves of some of them, however, are not marked, and in the case of others, there is nothing in particular that is known of their lives. It is advisable to visit all of them whose tombs have been identified. Honour shown to them is equivalent to honouring the Imams" (Donaldson, 1933, p. 264).

The rituals connected with visitations to the tombs of *imāmzādahs* reflect the rituals of the pilgrimage to Mecca, the *ḥajj*. The most important part of the ritual is the recitation of the prayer of visitation, known as the Ziyārat-Nāmah. Each shrine has its own visitation prayer. As the *imāmzādah* shrines brought prestige and even economic benefits to a locality, some of the tombs of holy men who were not descendants of the imams fell under the rubric of *imāmzādah*. Many of the pilgrimages to *imāmzādahs* have been adapted into seasonal rituals and become embellished with colorful observances. *Imāmzādahs*, like mosques, traditionally have enjoyed the status of extraterritoriality in which *basṭ* (asylum) could be sought.

Among the most famous *imāmzādah* shrines of Iran is that of Shah ʿAbd al-ʿAẓīm in Ray on the outskirts of Tehran. During the late Qājār period (1796–1925), many famous men, including Jamāl al-Dīn al-Afghānī (1838–1897), fled to the Shah ʿAbd al-ʿAẓīm shrine seeking refuge. And during the Constitutional Revolution (1905–1911), many constitutionalists took refuge there. The first railway built in Iran was the five-mile stretch between the shrine of Shah ʿAbd-al-ʿAẓīm and the capital city of Tehran. This shrine was also the site of the assassination of Nāṣir al-Dīn Shāh Qājār in 1896. The mausoleum of Fāṭimah, venerated as Maʿṣūmah (The Innocent), in Qom should be the most famous *imāmzādah* in Iran, as Fāṭimah was the daughter of Imam Mūsā Kāẓim and the sister of Imam ʿAlī Riḍā. However, since only male descendents of the imams are accorded the title *imāmzādah,* the shrine of Fāṭimah, though visited daily by thousands, does not belong to this category.

People are drawn to the *imāmzādah*s in search of intercession. At the *imāmzādah* shrines people can unburden themselves of their personal problems and misfortunes. Women can pray for the conception of children and men for success in their professional endeavors. The upkeep of the *imāmzādah*s is paid by either *awqāf* (religious endowments; sg., *waqf*) or the donations of pilgrims.

Among the Shīʿīs of southern Iraq, the veneration of the descendants of the imams is of secondary importance, since the main imam tombs are situated in close proximity. The Shīʿīs of India, however, face even greater difficulty than the Iranians in visiting the tombs of the imams because of their great distance from them. In India, the visitation and veneration of the imams' tombs has been substituted by the building of replicas of these tombs, which are carried in processions during the month of Muḥarram. These replicas, known as *taʿziyah,* in reality bear little resemblance to the original tombs and have become the end product of an act of the artists' piety. Solid, artistic replicas of the imams' cenotaphs *(ẓarīḥ)* are housed in the *imāmbārah*s and *ʿashūrkhānah*s. The creation of these edifices by the Shīʿī communities of India solved the problem of local devotion and visitation. Together with the *dargāh*s, which contain what is believed to be the personal effects of the imams (such as *ʿalam* ["standard"] or a sword), *taʿziyah* have come to serve as the local centers of pilgrimage and devotion. The construction of the "local Karbalas," cemeteries where people and *taʿziyah*s are buried, further alleviated for the Indian Shīʿīs the need for pilgrimages to the actual tombs of the imams or their descendants.

[*See also* Imam; Karbala; Mashhad; Najaf; Qom; Shrines; Taʿziyah; *and* Ziyārah.]

BIBLIOGRAPHY

Ayoub, Mahmoud M. *Redemptive Suffering in Islam.* The Hague, 1978.

Donaldson, Dwight M. *The Shiʿite Religion.* London, 1933.

Lambton, Ann K. S. "Imāmzāda." In *Encyclopaedia of Islam,* new ed., vol. 3, pp. 1169–1170. Leiden, 1960–.

Majlisī, Muḥammad Bāqir. *Tuḥfat al-zāʾirīn.* Tehran, 1857.

Momen, Moojan. *An Introduction to Shiʿi Islam.* New Haven, 1985.

Nasr, Seyyed Hossein, Hamid Dabashi, and Seyyed Vali Reza Nasr, eds. *Shiʿism: Doctrines, Thought, and Spirituality.* Albany, N.Y., 1988.

Von Grunebaum, G. E. *Muhammadan Festivals.* New York, 1951.

PETER CHELKOWSKI

ĪMĀN. Literally "faith" or "belief," *īmān* is technically faith in the religion of Islam, the person with *īmān* being a *muʾmin.* The Arabic word connotes security: one who believes becomes secure against untruth and misguidance in this world and against punishment in the next. In surah 6.82, the Qurʾān throws light on this connotation through subtle wordplay: it is "those who have believed" *(alladhīna āmanū)* who shall enjoy "security" (*amn;* cf. surah 59.23, where God is described as *muʾmin,* "protector, guarantor of security")

Īmān, in the sense of "to become a believer," distinguishes a Muslim from a non-Muslim. As a summary statement, it represents belief in the following: the oneness of God, angels, prophets, revealed books, and the hereafter (see, e.g., surah 2.177). The phrase *īmān bi-al-ghayb,* usually translated "belief in the unseen," stands for belief in metaphysical realities that are inaccessible to the senses but are presumably affirmed by reason.

According to several Qurʾānic verses (e.g., surahs 6.111; 10.99, 100), if God had wished them to believe, all human beings would have believed. Such verses do not teach fatalism but the exact opposite, namely, that since God does not compel anyone to believe, therefore every individual is free to make his or her own choice. Surah 18.29 says: "And say: The truth is from your

Lord, so whoever wants to, let him believe; and whoever wants to, let him disbelieve." On the other hand we read in the Qur'ān that God hardens the hearts of those who have become thoroughly evil and so deserved the hardening of heart. Their hearts "stamped" by God, such people are rendered incapable of believing (surahs 2.88; 4.46, 155; 6.2; 10.33; 41.44; see also 10.88, where Moses prays to God to "seal up" the hearts of Pharaoh and his followers so that they may not believe until they see the promised punishment descending on them).

The Qur'ān establishes a close connection between faith and action, or *īmān* and *ʿamal:* true *īmān* manifests itself in right conduct, which, to be fruitful, must be grounded in right faith. The Qur'ān requires "those who have believed" to conduct themselves in certain ways. For example, the believers are commanded to obey God, the Prophet, and the authorities (4.59; 8.1, 20, 24; 33.36; 47.33), fulfill their commitments (5.1), speak the truth and say the right thing (33.70), perform the ritual prayer (4.103; 14.31), spend of their wealth in the way of God (2.254, 257), fight in the way of God (4.76) steadfastly (8.15, 45; 9.123), shun wine-drinking and gambling (5.90), refrain from making transactions involving interest (2.278; 3.130), and avoid treating condescendingly those they have done favors to (2.264). *Īmān* is also the basis of Islamic brotherhood, and the series of injunctions given, for example, in surah 49.9–12 are explicitly predicated on that premise. Surah 23 opens with the statement, "The believers have achieved success," and then explains who the believers are, giving details of a certain type of conduct. *Īmān* and *ʿamal* are thus inseparable, several verses explicitly stating that actions that are apparently good but lacking a basis in *īmān* will be nullified (4.124; 10.40; 16.97; 17.19; 20.75, 112; 21.94).

In view of this connection between *īmān* and *ʿamal* it might seem surprising that the question of the relationship of faith and works occasioned a serious debate in early Islamic history. According to one group, one guilty of a major sin ceases to be a Muslim. Since the militant Khawārij were not content to state their views but fought against all those who differed with them, they faced strong opposition from the majority of the Muslim population. On the doctrinal level, however, the anti-Khārijī polemic resulted in the formulation of a view that undermined the integral relationship between *ʿamal* and *īmān*. The Murji'ī reaction (the Murji'ah—from *irjā'*, "postponement"—put off the verdict on the grave sinner until the Last Day, leaving the matter in God's hands) stressed, or rather overstressed, the importance of *īmān,* in effect devaluing *ʿamal.*

The relationship between *īmān* and *islām* ("submission") is to be understood in similar terms. The prayer offered for a deceased person well illustrates the relationship: "Those of us whom you [God] would keep alive, keep them alive on *islām;* and those of us whom you would cause to die, cause them to die on *īmān.*" On this distinction *īmān* is the inner state of mind one should be in at the time of death—or at any given moment of one's life—whereas *islām* is activity and conduct through life as lived from one moment to another.

Another early debate was whether *īmān* remains static or registers an increase or decrease. Several Qur'ānic verses (e.g., 3.173; 8.2, 125; 48.4) say that the quality of *īmān* can change. Abū Ḥanīfah (d. 767), however, maintained that *īmān* remains the same, a view for which he was criticized. As a jurist, Abū Ḥanīfah was actually referring to the critical amount of faith that qualifies a person as a believer. In other words, he was speaking of legal *īmān* as opposed to the spiritual quality of *īmān,* which may increase or decrease.

In modern times the problem has become less of defining *īmān* in precise terms and more of vindicating *īmān*—especially in the sense of belief in realities that are beyond the perceptible world—in the face of a dominant secularist and scientific outlook. Can belief in the supernatural and the miraculous be sustained? Is there a rational explanation of faith or is talk of such an explanation a contradiction in terms? In brief, is there room or need for *īmān* at all today? Many Muslim scholars have produced works to safeguard the *īmān* of Muslims, especially of the Muslim youth. These works typically seek to assure Muslims that satisfactory responses to the present-day detractions of religion in general and of Islam in particular do exist and that there is no reason for Muslims to abandon their faith or entertain doubt about it.

BIBLIOGRAPHY

Ghazālī, Abū Ḥāmid al-. *Iḥyā' ʿulūm al-dīn.* 5 vols. Beirut, 1991. First quarter, Book 2, "Kitāb qawāʿid al-ʿaqā'id." Translated into English as *The Foundations of the Articles of Faith* by Nabih Amin Faris (Lahore, 1963).

Khaṭīb al-Tibrīzī, Muḥammad ibn ʿAbd Allāh al-. *Mishkāt al-maṣābīḥ.* Beirut, 1405/1985. Vol. 1, Book 1, "Kitāb al-īmān."

Shaltūt, Maḥmūd. *Al-Islām, ʿaqīdah wa-sharīʿah.* Beirut, 1403/1983.

Ṭanṭāwī, ʿAlī. *Taʿrīf ʿāmm bi-dīn al-islām.* Beirut, 1394/1974.

MUSTANSIR MIR

INDIA. The Muslim population of the Republic of India, which came into existence in 1947 as a successor state, along with Pakistan, to British India, consists of some 12 percent of the population as a whole; Indian Muslims thus number more than 100 million people and constitute one of the largest Muslim populations in the world, smaller only than Indonesia and roughly equal to the Muslim populations of Pakistan and Bangladesh. Muslims have always been spread unevenly throughout India. Today in the old Mughal heartland of the Gangetic plain they are no more than 15 percent of the population; in Kashmir they form a majority; and in Malabar in the southwest they are about one-quarter of the population. The areas of dense Muslim population in the northwest and northeast of British India, largely agricultural communities whose religious identification was linked to sedentarization during the period of Muslim rule, were assigned to Pakistan at the time of partition.

Muslims in India are characterized by diversity in economic and political status. Broadly speaking, they have been affected by India-wide forces like land reform, the Green Revolution, economic opportunities for merchants and artisans linked to industrialization and improved communications, and internal and external migration. Muslims have suffered particularly, however, from the loss of substantial numbers of the more prosperous and better educated to Pakistan, coupled with substantial resentment against them as a minority. Despite the success of some individuals and groups, and the visibility of such figures as Indian presidents Dr. Zakir Husain and Fakhruddin ʿAli Ahmad, Muslims on the whole have not done well since independence in such areas as literacy or government service. By the early 1990s the intensity of anti-Muslim behavior had increased, and influential Hindu nationalists spoke of revenge against Muslims for presumed historical misdeeds and called on Muslims to assimilate or leave.

Socially, the Muslims of India are divided by regional and linguistic affiliations such as Bengali, Deccani, Gujarati, Hindustani, Mappila, Oriyya, and Punjabi. Muslims typically marry within their region, and most prefer to marry within endogamous descent/status groups that are hierarchically ranked.

Most Indian Muslims are Sunnī and of these most are Ḥanafī, with some Shāfiʿī in the south (reflecting ocean trade connections to the Middle East). About 10 percent are Shīʿī—mostly Ithnā ʿAsharī. A small but significant Shīʿī community is the Ismāʿīlī, whose leader, the Aga Khan, made Bombay his home in the late nineteenth century; the core Ismāʿīlī population are traders based in that western area. Most Sunnī Muslims in the subcontinent have participated in the institutions of the Ṣūfī orders: the Chishtīyah, Suhrawardīyah, Qādirīyah, and Naqshbandīyah have been particularly strong in this area. The subcontinent has had great traditions, continuing to the present, of both scholarly and spiritual leadership. [*See* Ithnā ʿAsharīyah; Ismāʿīlīyah; Chishtīyah; Qādirīyah; *and* Naqshbandīyah.]

The variety of changes that have taken place among Muslims in the nineteenth and twentieth centuries, and the diversity of their cultural, religious, and political movements span the spectrum of patterns characteristic of Muslims worldwide. Several thinkers and leaders—among them Sayyid Aḥmad Khān (1817–1898), Mawlānā Abū al-Aʿlā Mawdūdī (1903–1979), the poet Muhammad Iqbal (c. 1877–1938), Mawlānā Muḥammad Ilyās (1885–1944), and Mawlānā Abulḥasan ʿAlī Nadvī (b. 1914)—have been influential beyond the subcontinent as well. Over all, Islam (like Hinduism in this context) has become the basis of horizontal or "census-based" community and a central focus of social identity: Islamic symbols have been debated and objectified as part of public life in ways that are characteristic of modern times and modern state structures in particular. A variety of movements have shared the goal of defining, or even standardizing, Islam, and they have largely focused their concern on the category, emergent in this period, of "Indian Muslim."

Eighteenth Century. This is increasingly recognized as a period of far-reaching changes in regionalization of power, of monetarization and long-distance trade, and of widening social networks of groups like traders, financial agents, and religious specialists. It was also a period of rich cultural change. These changes have been obscured by the emphasis on "decline," "decay," and "confusion," beloved of British and in turn of nationalist historians. That view stems from an understandable focus on Delhi and the decline of imperial power, made especially dramatic by attacks on this imperial city by the Persian Nādir Shāh in 1739 as well as by Afghan rulers, for whom North India was a familiar area, in mid-century.

Among those caught up in the crises of the Delhi court was Shāh Walī Allāh (1703–1762), whom virtually every Islamic movement in modern India has regarded as a forebear. Scion of a family of religious scholars patronized by the Delhi court, he was part of the scholarly circles based in the Hejaz that were concerned with setting a new standard of fidelity to *ḥadīth*. He himself linked the need for renewal to the political confusions of his day and expected religious reform to usher in worldly order as well. He urged scholars to draw freely from the four traditional legal schools instead of following blind imitation of one school. A spiritual leader in the Naqshbandī tradition, he was also known for his visions and piety.

Unlike leaders of later movements, Shāh Walī Allāh was not concerned with popular influence but rather with playing the traditional role of the *ʿulamāʾ* in offering guidance to princes. Faced with the decline of central authority and the disruptions of competitors for power in the new regional configurations that were emerging, he sought the power of Muslim princes like the Afghan Shāh Abdālī, who he believed could restore order. His disciples and sons, particularly Shāh ʿAbd al-ʿAzīz (1746–1824), continued his scholarly work on *ḥadīth*. Notable among the latter's contributions was a collection of advisory opinions (*fatwās*), one of the first of many collections produced by scholars throughout this period. These were to become an increasingly important method for disseminating religious guidance and particular styles of interpretation to ever larger numbers of Muslims, particularly with the utilization, from the 1820s on, of lithographic presses. Also notable were translations of the Qur'ān into Urdu prepared by members of this family. Such works contributed to the growing importance of Urdu, a regional language, among the courtly elite: Urdu incorporated vocabulary and utilized themes and genres from the cosmopolitan Persian it was rapidly replacing. [*See the biographies of Walī Allāh and ʿAbd al-ʿAzīz.*].

A second major North Indian family of *ʿulamāʾ* that emerged in this period were those associated with a center in Lucknow known as Farangī Maḥall. The Farangī Maḥallis pioneered a course of study known as the *dars-i niẓāmī* that became standard for training religious specialists. Like the Walī Allāhī family, the Farangī Maḥallis were both learned scholars and spiritual leaders in the Ṣūfī tradition. Among the new social formations emerging in the fluid world of the eighteenth and early nineteenth centuries was that of *ʿulamāʾ* whose ties to family and to scholarly centers increased in importance as court patronage declined.

Not only scholarly leadership but also Ṣūfī leadership changed in significant ways in this period. The Chishtī leadership in particular developed a parallel emphasis on new attention to scriptural sources. The Ṣūfī leadership also contributed to the newly significant regional configurations of the period through development of regional languages. Thus in both Punjab and Sind poets used the regional languages to express the themes of Persian mystical poetry; Shāh ʿAbdullaṭīf Bhiṭāʾī (1689–1752) and Bullhe Shāh (1680–1758) are particularly notable in this regard. Among the great poets of Urdu writing mystical love poetry in the Persian style were Mīr Taqī Mīr (1723–1810) and Khvājah Mīr Dard (1720–1785). [*See* Urdu Literature.]

Although the East India Company had established themselves in 1803 as overlords of the Mughal in Delhi as they moved north from their base in Bengal, the most significant Islamic movement of this period, led by Sayyid Aḥmad Barelwī (1780–1831) can be seen as an example of the regional state-building characteristic of the preceding century. A sometime soldier for the Nawwab of Tonk who had established a small kingdom southwest of Delhi, as well as a disciple and student of the Walī Allāhī family in Delhi, Sayyid Aḥmad sought to carve out a state where Muslim life could flourish. His was the first Islamic movement to utilize inexpensive publications to disseminate religious teachings, in this case intended to call Muslims to correct belief and practice and away from the corruptions of what were seen as false Sufism and Shiism that compromised the unity of God. Following tours throughout North India and a *ḥajj* undertaken in 1824, he launched a *jihād* in 1826 directed primarily against the Sikh kingdom of Ranjit Singh on the frontier; this movement collapsed as much from internal differences among the tribesmen as from Sikh resistance. Both Sayyid Aḥmad Barelwī and his associate Mawlānā Ismāʿīl were killed in 1831, and only embers of their movement remained. Their religious teachings and spiritual leadership, however, were disseminated across North India and into Bengal. [*See the biography of Barelwī.*]

In Bengal, at about the same time as Sayyid Aḥmad began his preaching, an independent reform movement also rose. It was known as the Farāʾiẕī because of its emphasis on religious obligations (*farẕ*). Led by Ḥājjī Sharīʿatullāh (1781–1840), who returned in 1821 from some twenty years in Mecca, the movement stressed reform of individual practice in a context of British power. After his death subsequent leadership, including his son known as Dudhu Miyāṉ, took up the cause of the Muslim peasantry against the Hindu landlords and resorted to military uprisings. These were suppressed in the 1830s with British help. The teachings of the movement, communicated in part by Bengali tracts, helped disseminate Islamic knowledge to ever larger numbers.

Nineteenth Century and Establishment of British Institutions. One of the most significant developments of the nineteenth century was the crystallization of the social category of *ashrāf,* the well born or privileged. This was typically marked by command of standard Urdu, embodiment of hierarchically correct behavior, and claims to descent from historically distinguished ancestors. Those claiming such descent took the titles of *sayyid,* a descendent of the Prophet; *shaykh,* a descendent of his companions; Mughal, a descendent of the Turco-Mongol ruling or military class; and Pathan, a descendent of the Afghan ruling or military class. *Ashrāf* families typically owned some land and might place some of their sons in government service; some might also be trained as religious specialists. By the end of the century the major cultural division of subcontinental society—that between the English-educated with their distinctive housing, habits, and skills, and all others—had begun to create a significant division within the elite.

The first major institution established for elite education in the Delhi area, however, contributed to the use of Urdu among the *ashrāf.* Delhi College, founded in 1825 and destroyed in the anti-British mutiny of 1857, introduced members of the Muslim elite to new patterns of institutional organization for education: a formal staff, a set curriculum, classrooms, examinations, and so forth. The presence of teachers and students associated with reformist circles meant that such educational patterns became known to the *ʿulamāʾ.*

Reprisals against Muslims after the Mutiny were particularly severe because they were regarded as the displaced rulers. The Mughal Empire came to a formal end, and with it an important symbol of Muslim political dominance; the last emperor was exiled, and the British crown claimed sovereignty in place of the East India Company. Some distinguished religious leaders moved to the Hejaz, maintaining their influence through correspondence, publications, and visits during the *ḥajj,* which was to become increasingly important with improving transportation. As part of the post-Mutiny settlement the British identified people they considered "natural leaders," among them princes and large landlords, and moved to secure their positions as a loyal and conservative force throughout the empire. Notable among the Muslim princes were the Shīʿī taluqdars of Oudh and the nawab of Rampur as well as the Sunnī nizam of Hyderabad. These aristocrats were an important source of patronage for Islamic learning, music, and Greco-Arabic medicine, which flourished in the Indian subcontinent (ultimately in a rationalized, modern form) as nowhere else. (That school of medicine, *Yūnānī ṭibb,* is today supported by the philanthropic Hamdard Foundation and to a limited extent by government agencies.) [*See* Medicine, *article on* Traditional Practice; *and* Hamdard Foundation.]

Central to the British idiom of rule was the notion that India was fundamentally divided into communities, above all the two great religious communities of "Hindu" and "Muslim." The emphasis on religion was in part a reflection of the British assumption that India represented an earlier stage of human culture, and that religion made a society "traditional" and not "modern." The framework set by that assumption helped created the reality. On the Muslim side, the leadership of Sayyid Aḥmad Khān, later knighted as Sir Sayyid, responded to the opportunity to argue that Muslims, far from being potentially disloyal, could be a base of support—well suited to cooperate in governing because of their former experience as the area's rulers and well able to relate to British culture on the basis of shared monotheism. In 1875 he founded the Mohammedan Anglo-Oriental College, later Aligarh Muslim University, modeled on Cambridge and Oxford and intended to produce English-educated gentlemen assimilated to British patterns. Sayyid Aḥmad Khān traced his intellectual heritage to the Walī Allāhī reformers. His overriding goal, however, was to show the fundamental harmony of Qurʾānic revelation and modern science, stripping away from Islam the elements contingent in particular times and places and maintaining only what was essential. He embraced *ijtihād* to replace historic interpretations.

Among those sharing his modernist position were Chirāgh ʿAlī (1844–1895), whose apologetic writing focused on *jihād* and Ottoman reforms; the poet Alṭaf Ḥusain Ḥālī (1837–1914), whose didactic poetry contributed to the idealization of past historic glory as a spur to change; the Shīʿī thinker Ameer Ali (1849–1928), whose best-known work was tellingly entitled *The Spirit of Islam;* the novelist Naẕīr Aḥmad (1830–1912), who wrote instructive Urdu novels for girls; and Shiblī Nuʿmānī (1857–1914), a distinguished essayist on Islamic topics, closely associated with the Nadvatul ʿUlamāʾ (an academy meant to produce reformed religious leaders), fluent in Arabic and linked to the Middle East, who would play a role in the councils of government. [*See the biographies of Aḥmad Khān, Chirāgh ʿAlī, and Ameer Ali.*]

Leaders of the *ʿulamāʾ* also responded to the changed situation that followed the Mutiny. In 1867 a group of *ʿulamāʾ* associated with Walī Allāhī reform and familiar with British institutions through Delhi College and government service founded the Dār al-ʿUlūm at Deoband. Deoband was intended to provide bureaucratically organized training in the traditional learning of the *ʿulamāʾ*. Students followed a six-year course, moving through a fixed syllabus, taking formal exams, and participating in a convocation. The school was particularly distinguished for its work in *ḥadīth* and by the end of the century had established a network of schools that has continued to grow to the present. Deoband also pioneered the use of widespread fundraising in an era when scholars could not depend on state patronage. The Deoband *ʿulamāʾ* sought to be apolitical and to devote themselves wholly to disseminating correct guidance through training teachers, prayer leaders, trustees of endowments, writers, and so on. Deoband, like Aligarh, helped make Urdu a lingua franca for Muslims throughout the subcontinent. [*See* Deobandīs; Aligarh.]

Rivals to the school's reformist style included the Ahl-i Ḥadīth, who favored direct use of sources instead of following the Ḥanafī or any other law school, and the "Barelwīs" (who would ultimately identify themselves simply as the Ahl-i Sunnat va Jamāʿat) associated with Mawlānā Aḥmad Riẓā Khān Barelwī (1856–1921); the latter were also Ḥanafī but were supportive of the customary practices associated, above all, with Ṣūfī shrines. [*See* Barelwīs.] All attempted to define Islam, made Islamic issues a subject of debate, and utilized the new technology of inexpensive publications for tracts and *fatwās*; all these activities contributed to a dissemination of Islamic teaching and a role for Islamic symbols as central to social identity. These *ʿulamāʾ* debated with one another, with the Aligarh reformers, and with Hindu groups like the Arya Samaj who were also attempting to eliminate present practice in favor of an ideal past as well as to reconvert non-Hindus to their presumably original Hinduism. The groups of *ʿulamāʾ* also debated with, and fiercely opposed, a movement that emerged at the end of the century under the leadership of Mirzā Ghulām Aḥmad (1839–1908) of the Punjab town of Qādiān. Claiming that he was the promised Mahdi of the Muslims, the Messiah of the Christians, and an avatar of Krishna, Mirzā Ghulām Aḥmad created a Ṣūfī-like, highly demarcated community whose members were notable for their mutual support, high educational level, and successful missionary work throughout the world. (In 1974 the Aḥmadīyah was declared non-Muslim by the National Assembly in Pakistan.) [*See* Aḥmadīyah.]

By the end of the century, at a national level stimulated by the foundation of the Indian National Congress in 1885, issues regarded as "Muslim" had entered into public discussion. Muslim leaders, following Sir Sayyid, argued that the proposed democratic elections were inappropriate in a society with a minority like themselves, the former rulers, who should be influential beyond their numbers. Issues of contention often revolved around what later would be called an "arithmetic" of communalism: the number of Muslims in schools, the number of Muslims in public employment, and so on. The three-part competition—Hindu, Muslim, and British "mediator"—also entailed issues like observation of holidays and adjudication of routes for religious processions. A major issue for Muslims at the end of the century was the status of Urdu as an official language, a status it enjoyed not only in the United Provinces but also in Bihar and Punjab. In 1900 Urdu, with its Persian heritage and Arabo-Persian script, was displaced as the sole indigenous official language for the United Provinces and made to share official status with Hindi, written in the Devanagari script associated with Sanskrit. The public symbols of Muslims—the Urdu language, processions, and mosques—were more the contribution of the politically active, many associated with Aligarh, than of the *ʿulamāʾ*.

Twentieth Century to Partition. Three issues were embraced in the early years of the twentieth century that focused a distinctively Muslim political agenda and intensified India-wide networks among a politicized Muslim elite. In 1905 the Government of India announced the division of the large state of Bengal into two new states, the eastern half emerging as a Muslim-majority area. The protests of Bengali nationalists, who saw this move as a way to narrow their base, produced a reaction defending the division and its opportunities for Muslims; indeed, the issue of creating Muslim-majority provinces was to be part of the arithmetic of communalism for the rest of British rule. In 1911 the British reunited the province and, as with the status of Urdu, the politicized Muslim elite felt that their assumed privileged position had been undermined.

A second issue of this decade was the announcement of the first of three occasions before independence of reforms to enhance Indian participation in the various councils of government. As a prelude to these reforms a delegation of Muslims, led by the *navvāb* of Dhaka and made up of other landed and aristocratic leaders, pressed the viceroy to acknowledge the particular place of Muslims. British rule operated in terms of various corporate groups and welcomed this initiative. The most important principle established in the Morley-Minto Reforms of 1909 was that not only would seats be reserved for Muslims, but separate electorates would also be established in which only Muslims could vote for Muslim representatives. The delegation took institutional shape as the All-India Muslim League. [*See* All-India Muslim League.]

The third issue was that of Pan-Islamic concerns regarding the political fate of Muslims beyond India, above all in the weakened Ottoman Empire and in what were seen as incursions on Muslim rule in the Balkans and in the holy places. Muslim concern had been evident as early as the Russo-Turkish war of 1878 and was stimulated by Jamāl al-Dīn al-Afghānī (1838–1897), who visited India several times. An organization to press for the defense of Muslim interests in the Hejaz (Anjuman-i Khuddām-i Kaʿbah) was formed in 1913, as was a medical mission to the Balkans. These concerns forged a persistant alliance between some of the *ʿulamāʾ* and the secularly educated leadership. An incident defending the washing place of a mosque in Kanpur in 1912, where the municipality planned to build a road, showed the extent of new networks as leaders from outside converged in a successful protest. By World War I there was a distinct Muslim intelligentsia linked not by a single organization but by a shared concern for certain public Muslim symbols and by an agenda of Muslim interests. They communicated through new media including the Urdu newspapers produced by intellectuals like Mawlānā Abū al-Kalām Āzād (1888–1958), who would become one of the most prominent Congress Muslims and India's first minister of education. [*See the biography of Āzād.*]

By the end of World War I the expectations of Indian political leaders had been raised by British promises, by a glimpse of European weakness, and by their own success during the war in forging platforms like the so-called Lucknow Pact between the Congress and the League. The British countered with continuation of wartime emergency legislation, and they announced very limited constitutional reform, not the hoped-for self-rule, in the Montagu Chelmsford Reforms of 1919. The Muslim leadership was particularly aggrieved at Britain's role in the dismemberment of the Ottoman Empire. In response the Khilāfat movement sought to defend the position of the Ottoman sultan as the caliph of all Muslims. The movement engaged a wide Muslim leadership, created a new level of mass support, and provided an occasion for Congress leadership—in particular Mohandas Gandhi with his new program of noncooperation—to embrace a Muslim issue. The movement was led jointly by the Aligarh-trained brothers Muḥammad ʿAlī and Shaukat ʿAlī, who adopted a religious style and dress, along with their spiritual guide Mawlānā ʿAbdulbārī (d. 1925/26), a saintly and scholarly man associated with Farangī Maḥall. The Khilāfat movement, while eliciting non-Muslim support, underlined and even reinforced the very differences (often articulated through religious symbols) between the League and the Congress. The cause of the caliphate proved a chimera when the Turks on their own initiative abolished the caliphate in 1924 under Atatürk's modernizing policy. At the height of Khilāfat-Congress cooperation a group associated with Aligarh, dismayed by the institution's political loyalty, broke off to form a new "national" Muslim university infused with Gandhian idealism, the Jamiʿah Millīyah Islāmīyah in Delhi. [*See* Khilāfat Movement.]

As plans for a further round of reforms continued, Muslim political leaders continued to focus on protecting Muslim interests, for example in the League's "Fourteen Points" of 1929. Some important issues were separate electorates and reserved seats, "weightage" in Muslim minority provinces, the number of provinces where Muslims dominated, and the degree of provincial power in relation to the center. In the Punjab and Bengal landlord parties emerged that expressed a powerful class rather than religious interest. The period witnessed an intensification of Muslim-Hindu friction at the popular level and competition that often manifested itself in communal riots. In this period three movements led by religious leaders took shape, all of them influential in the subcontinent to the present day.

The Jamʿīyatul ʿUlamāʾ-i Hind was founded in 1921 as an association of *ʿulamāʾ*, among them Mawlānā Ḥusain Aḥmad Madanī (1897–1959) and others from the seminary at Deoband. They turned from their long history of apoliticism to join with the Congress in their shared goal of expelling the British from India. Deobandī *ʿulamāʾ*, if not the school, had been caught up in politics over the previous decade, particularly in relation to Muslim interests abroad. The *ʿulamāʾ* had little interest in political negotiations as such: their primary concern was the end of British rule as a prelude (they hoped) to the opportunity for Muslims to order their community lives on Islamic terms and in so doing to draw non-Muslims to convert. They envisaged an independent India in which Muslims would control their own educational and jurisprudential lives. The Jamʿīyat (in an interesting parallel to traditionally educated Jewish leaders' position on the establishment of Israel) opposed partition. [*See* Jamʿīyatul ʿUlamāʾ-i Hind.]

The two other noteworthy religious movements of the period each extended the nature of religious leadership beyond that of the traditionally educated. The Tablīghī Jamāʿat was one of a number of movements in the 1920s that focused on *tablīgh,* a neologism conveying the enunciation or pronouncement of Islamic teaching with the goal of guidance or proselytization. Most proved ephemeral, but one—led by Mawlānā Muḥammad Ilyās, associated with the Deobandīs, and based in Delhi—flourished and is today one of the most influential Muslim movements in the subcontinent as well as in the diaspora. Ilyās's movement came into being in competition with Hindu movements trying to "reconvert" Muslims; however, it was radically apolitical and nonconfrontational, directed only at Muslims and providing gentle guidance in a nonjudgmental mode. His innovation was to engage everyone in similar teaching; the teachers thus teach themselves and assume a role that had heretofore been limited to the learned and spiritually connected. Although the movement always tried to enlist the learned *ʿulamāʾ,* it also insisted on the obligation of even the humblest Muslim to teach others. [*See* Tablīghī Jamāʿat.]

The Jamāʿat-i Islāmī, founded by Mawlana Abū al-Aʿlā Mawdūdī, widened the scope of religious leadership in yet another way, turning to people like Mawdūdī who were secularly educated but who had acquired Islamic authority without the traditional training of the *madrasah.* Convinced that Muslims needed to abandon the medieval interpretations of their faith and focus on Qurʾān and *ḥadīth,* Mawdūdī taught a scripturalist, non-Ṣūfī style of Islam, explicitly proposing Islam as a "system," "a complete way of life," in contrast to the decadent, materialist West that was epitomized above all by the unregulated lives of women. The Jamāʿat-i Islāmī was founded in 1941 as a highly selective core group who could bring society-wide change. Mawdūdī's vision of Islam, the party, and the state—explicitly anti-Western—replicated many characteristics of the capitalism and communism it opposed: the idea of a system, the cell-like organization explicitly copied from European fascism and communism, and even the elaboration of an essential female specificity based on European "science." Mawdūdī opposed partition but ultimately emigrated to Pakistan, where the party, although small, has been influential. His writings have been widely circulated outside India but are of marginal importance within. [*See* Jamāʿat-i Islāmī *and the biography of Mawdūdī.*]

By the time of elections following the third constitutional reform, the Government of India Act of 1935, the Muslim League found itself with little electoral appeal and with its concerns marginalized in the Congress-dominated provincial assemblies that took power in several states in 1937. At this point Mohammad Ali Jinnah, a Bombay lawyer who had been active in the Congress and had cooperated with it even after he joined the Muslim League, now determined to assert the League as a mass party and as the single voice of Muslims. His cause was helped by his expression of loyalty during World War II, when much of the Congress leadership were imprisoned for their unwillingness to participate in a war they had not been allowed to enter independently as well as for their participation in the "Quit India" movement of 1942. Jinnah was profoundly influenced by the great poet Muhammad Iqbal who drew on European philosophy and Islamic theology to celebrate Islamic history and the *ummah* but used nationalism as a context for the Islamic dynamism he enjoined. During the war the League persuaded Muslim leaders in Punjab and Bengal that a united, independent government with Congress at its center would not protect Muslim interests. At the conclusion of the war and following various constitutional proposals, a divided India gained independence on 15 August 1947. The "Muslim state" excluded the areas where most of the All-India leadership were based. [*See* Muslim League *and the biographies of Iqbal and Jinnah.*]

Although Hindu nationalist ideology by the 1990s vilified the League, and Jinnah in particular, as responsible for the "vivisection" of India, many hands were involved in that outcome. For decades religio-political movements had drawn ever sharper boundaries around communities. For decades too politicians had negotiated on the basis of community, to the point that some have argued that Jinnah used the ambiguous demand for a separate state (first articulated by the League in the Lahore Resolution of

1940) as a bargaining ploy, never expecting it to materialize. Many in the Congress, moreover, in the end welcomed the result: partition removed the claim for decentralized federalism that would, they thought, stand in the way of a socialist pattern of development. Similarly, it removed a powerful conservative force in the landlords of the League; finally, it was hoped in vain that partition would stabilize community relations.

In the horrific aftermath of partition, when as many as ten million people migrated and perhaps a million were killed, communal relations in the years until around the death of Nehru (1964) were marked by quiescence. India rejected separate electorates or reservation on religious grounds, and there emerged no single party or organization to speak for Muslim interests. At first Muslims largely supported the Congress party, who espoused secularism and wooed Muslim votes. Congress's decline, coupled with increased riots in the 1960s and fear for Muslim interests, led to new Muslim parties, including the Majlis-i Mushāvarāt (founded in Uttar Pradesh in 1964 but now dormant) and a revived Muslim League that has proven successful in Kerala. The former princely state of Kashmir, with its Muslim majority and a Hindu ruler who declared the state part of India, has been fought over in political councils and on the ground among India, Pakistan, and the Kashmiris themselves since 1947. By the late 1980s the central government could no longer control Kashmir, overtaken by a separatist movement, and the state has been under siege. [*See* Kashmir.]

Muslim interests have increasingly focused on protection of life and the complicity of local police and civil authority in anti-Muslim violence, particularly from the early 1980s. Culturally Urdu, once so important to Muslim *ashrāf* and even to community identity, has largely been eclipsed as a political symbol and a written form. The primary focus of Muslim leadership in cultural terms has been the preservation of a separate Muslim civil code, increasingly seen by Hindu nationalists as unacceptable in their goal of assimilating all Indians to a fundamentally Hindu culture (and contrary to the constitution's Directive Principle, Article 44, that calls for a common civil code, although no such code has yet been enacted). That issue came to a head over the case of an elderly Muslim woman, Shāh Bānū, who in 1985 sued for long-term maintenance from her estranged husband, despite the fact that such support is traditionally limited in Islamic law to a fixed period. The Supreme Court, following the Civil Procedure Code of 1973, ultimately required the husband to provide long-term maintenance. Some Muslims protested this modification of Muslim law on the part of the courts. Subsequently Prime Minister Rajiv Gandhi, seeking Muslim support (as he had done in ushering in the first ban on Salman Rushdie's *Satanic Verses*), pushed through parliament the Muslim Women (Protection of Rights on Divorce) Act of 1986, reasserting a separate Muslim code. This ruling intensified the backlash against Muslims.

Beginning in 1984, antagonism toward Muslims focused on the existence of a mosque built by a Muslim general of the Emperor Babur in the sixteenth century, commonly called the Bābarī Masjid and situated in the northern Indian town of Ayodhya. Hindu activists insisted that the mosque marked the birthplace of the god Rama and that Babur had destroyed a Hindu temple to build the mosque. The mosque was closed to Muslim worship after a statue of Rama was surreptitiously placed inside it in 1949, and Hindu *puja* ceremonies took place in close proximity. Led by the Vishva Hindu Parishad (World Hindu Organization or VHP) and often supported by the political party Bharata Janata Parishad (BJP), the conflict drew national attention. In response a Muslim organization, the All India Bābarī Masjid Action Committee, argued that there was no evidence for the birthplace or for a temple on that site and organized to defend the mosque. VHP-led mass actions—for example, All-India processions transporting bricks to rebuild the temple—led to far-reaching anti-Muslim violence. On 6 December 1992 activists succeeded in tearing down the entire stone mosque. This action was followed by many episodes of local violence in which the vast majority of victims were Muslim.

Although many decry this violence as a betrayal of Indian values and a distraction from pressing socioeconomic issues, for other Indians Muslims have become an essential element in defining what is seen as a moral response to an immoral and increasingly intrusive state structure. Muslims are imagined much as other minorities who have played similar roles in other countries: they are a vested interest with special privileges granted by a government whose very relation to them proves governmental immorality; they are disloyal to the Indian state, with connections to "foreign" interests in Pakistan, the Gulf, and elsewhere; and they refuse to assimilate to the values of Hindu morality. In short, Muslims for many Indians today stand for what is wrong in society—a role not of their choosing and not susceptible to refutation by reason.

Most Muslims in India are as rooted where they are as anyone else. They vary radically, particularly by region—a Muslim in Kashmir has very different prospects today from a Muslim in relatively prosperous and stable Kerala—by education, and by class. As a large minority, widely scattered and embedded in all segments of society, they will continue as a substantial presence in the nation.

BIBLIOGRAPHY

Ahmad, Aziz. *Islamic Modernism in India and Pakistan, 1857–1964*. London, 1967.

Ahmed, Rafiuddin. *The Bengal Muslims, 1871–1906*. Delhi, 1981.

Bayly, Susan. *Saints, Goddesses, and Kings: Muslims and Christians in South Indian Society, 1700–1900*. Cambridge, 1989.

Freitag, Sandria B. *Collective Action and Community: Public Arenas and the Emergence of Communalism in North India*. Berkeley, 1989.

Gilmartin, David. *Empire and Islam: Punjab and the Making of Pakistan*. Berkeley, 1988.

Hardy, Peter. *The Muslims of British India*. Cambridge, 1972.

Hasan, Mushir ul-. *Nationalism and Communal Politics in India, 1885–1930*. Delhi, 1979.

Lelyveld, David. *Aligarh's First Generation: Muslim Solidarity in British India*. Princeton, 1977.

Metcalf, Barbara D. *Islamic Revival in British India: Deoband, 1860–1900*. Princeton, 1982.

Metcalf, Barbara D., ed. and trans. *Perfecting Women: Maulana Ashraf ʿAli Thanawi's Bihishti Zewar*. Berkeley, 1991.

Minault, Gail. *The Khilafat Movement: Religious Symbolism and Political Mobilization in India*. New York, 1982.

Mujeeb, Mohammad. *The Indian Muslims*. London, 1967.

BARBARA D. METCALF

INDIAN OCEAN SOCIETIES. Apart from two major islands—Sri Lanka in the north and Madagascar in the south—the Indian Ocean otherwise has only very small islands and island groups, only one of which (Mauritius) has a population in excess of one million. The ocean has acted as a highway for Islam; for example, the great medieval Arab traveler and explorer Ibn Baṭṭūṭah visited both Sri Lanka and the Maldives during his fourteenth-century travels. Seven islands or island groups are considered here: the Comoros and the Maldives, whose peoples are nearly 100 percent Muslim; Madagascar, Sri Lanka, and Mauritius, with important Muslim minorities; and Reunion and the Seychelles.

Table 1 gives comparative 1992 figures for population and adherents of Islam for the seven islands. The Comoros and Maldives are closest in terms of size and background and in the fact that their populations are overwhelmingly Muslim, but even here there are some substantial differences. Comoros, which lies at the northern end of the Mozambique Channel between Madagascar and the African mainland, is a Federal Islamic Republic. Its people are an ethnic mixture; the majority come from Africa, but minority groups include Arabs, Indonesians, and Iranians, each contributing its own distinctive approach to Islam. When Europeans first visited the Comoros in the sixteenth century, the predominant influence was Arab.

TABLE 1. *Muslim Populations of Indian Ocean Islands*

COUNTRY	GENERAL POPULATION	MUSLIM POPULATION	PERCENT
Comoros	497,000	494,018	99.4
Madagascar	12,804,000	217,668	1.7
Maldives	230,000	230,000	100.0
Mauritius	1,081,000	139,449	12.9
Reunion	623,000	12,460	2.0
Seychelles	71,000	—	—
Sri Lanka	17,464,000	1,327,264	7.6

France took possession of the Comoros in 1843; in 1975 three of the four islands that make up the group declared their independence, while the fourth, Mayotte, remained linked to France. Ali Soilih was the leader of the coup that ousted President Ahmed Abdallah on 3 August 1975; in May 1977 his government passed a *loi fondamentale* under which Comoros became a "democratic, secular, socialist republic." The subsequent revolution of the left looked for its inspiration to a mixture of Islam and Maoism, which in fact were incompatible. Soilih, while insisting upon his adherence to Islam, made many attacks on traditional aspects of the country's life that were derived from Islam, and the resulting resentments led to his overthrow in a coup of May 1978. Later that year, on 1 October 1978, more than 99 percent of those voting approved a new constitution that made Comoros a Federal Islamic Republic. In its preamble the constitution claims that the will of the Comoran people is derived from the state religion, Islam, which is the inspiration for the regulation of government. The great majority of the people are Sunnī (Shāfiʿī) Muslims; the Comoran language is close to Swahili (in addition, some Arabic is spoken). The Shāfiʿī school predominates in eastern Africa where the majority of the Comoran people originated. There is a tiny Roman Catholic minority representing only 0.6 percent of the total population. The people of Mayotte, which has retained its links with France, are also predominantly Muslim.

The Maldives are a chain of coral islands lying some 370 miles southwest of India. Following Britain's seizure of Sri Lanka from the Dutch in 1796, the Maldives were also brought under British rule until they achieved independence in 1965. The British did not interfere with their religion, and the people remained overwhelmingly Muslim. Traders had visited the Maldives from earliest times, and the islands were converted to Islam in the twelfth century; according to legend, an itinerant Muslim holy man converted the people in 1153. Interestingly, Ibn Baṭṭūṭah, who visited the Maldives in the 1340s, remarked on the freedom enjoyed by women, a freedom that has remained a feature of Maldivian society ever since. Ismāʿīlī merchants from Bombay established themselves in Male in the nineteenth century and were expelled after 1960.

Today, as in the Comoros, Islam is the state religion of the Maldives, whose people are 100 percent Sunnī Muslims. Judges administer the law according to the tenets of the *sharīʿah* through a body appointed by the president, while traditional schools (*maktab*s) teach the Qur'ān. Under the constitution, within the provisions of Islam, freedom of "life movement," speech, and development are guaranteed as basic rights.

Muslims in Sri Lanka have traditionally been referred to as Moors: trade links with other Indian Ocean states led small groups of Moorish traders to settle in Sri Lanka beginning in the eighth century. Under the constitution of Sri Lanka freedom of worship is guaranteed, although Buddhism is given primacy and it is the duty of the state to protect and foster it. At the same time, any citizen is free to adopt the religion of his choice. The Muslim minority in Sri Lanka has managed to stay outside the ethnic confrontations that have troubled the country for the past decade and more. Sri Lanka's Muslim minority of 1.3 million is larger than the combined Muslim populations of all the other Indian Ocean societies under consideration here.

Islam reached Madagascar only during the later coastal settlements, and there are considerable Muslim communities in the northwest of the island. The main culture of Madagascar is Indonesian, though Arab and Islamic influences are to be found, for example, in the system of divination and the calendar. After the fourteenth century Muslim traders from East Africa probably established trading colonies in the north; during the sixteenth century the Portuguese raided the coast on a number of occasions in attempts to destroy its Muslim settlements.

Mauritius was not settled until the seventeenth century, following colonization by France. Its population is a mixture derived from France, Africa (Creoles and the descendants of slaves), India, and China. It is among the Indians that Islam is largely practiced: Indians now make up a majority of the population, and about one-third of them are Muslim. In Réunion the Muslims (2 per cent) are drawn from the Indian and Arab sections of the population. Islam has no influence in the Seychelles.

BIBLIOGRAPHY

Benedict, Burton. *Mauritius: Problems of a Plural Society*. London, 1965.

Bunge, Frederica M., ed. *Indian Ocean: Five Island Countries*. 2d ed. Washington, D.C., 1983.

Cohen, Robin, ed. *African Islands and Enclaves*. Beverly Hills, 1983.

Deschamps, Hubert, and Suzanne Vianes. *Les Malgaches du Sud-Est*. Paris, 1959.

Ibn Baṭṭūṭah. *Travels in Asia and Africa, 1325–1354* (1929). Translated and edited by H. A. R. Gibb. London, 1969.

Maloney, Clarence. *People of the Maldive Islands*. Bombay, 1980.

Prudhomme, Claude. *Histoire religieuse de la Réunion*. Paris, 1984.

GUY ARNOLD

INDONESIA. Approximately 85 to 90 percent of Indonesia's more than 180 million people are followers of Islam, the largest population of Muslims of any country in the world today. They are almost all Sunnīs and followers of the Shāfiʿī school. The remainder of the population are Christian, Hindu, animist, or followers of varying Confucian and Buddhist beliefs.

Historical Development. There is some dispute as to the exact dates of the arrival of Islam in the Indies. There were Arabs in the archipelago before the Hijrah, and Muslim merchants resided in East and Southeast Asia in the succeeding centuries. There is a general consensus that Islam became established within the local population of the Indies in the thirteenth century and expanded markedly in the fifteenth and sixteenth centuries. By the eighteenth century, the vast majority of the populations of Java and Sumatra had become Muslim. Islam appears to have been transported by Muslims from several countries. The initial sources of Islamic missionary activity apparently were Gujarat and Malabar in Western India, followed by Arabs, especially from the Hadhramaut. The people of the Indies were generally converted to Islam through peaceful means. It was first transmitted through traders who brought with them religious scholars and was further aided by elite conversions and political alliances. From the beginning, state and popular Islam continued to be imbued with a Hindu culture reframed within local traditions that had previously dominated the country. Rather than being obliterated by the new religion, Hindu and other non-Muslim elements became embedded in the character of traditional rule, poetry, dance, and music, and influenced how many converts, particularly on Java, approached Islamic thought and practice.

Early Islam was also greatly influenced by Ṣūfī views, and by the sixteenth century many of the archipelago's best-known Muslim scholars were from the Ṣūfī orders. In the years that followed, Ṣūfī orders such as the Qādirīyah and Naqshbandīyah attracted many Indonesians into their ranks, and branches were formed in many parts of the islands. Ṣūfī mysticism and its general tolerance of local traditions further abetted the growth of Islam in the islands. It also helped to frame the syncretic and eclectic nature of Indonesian Islam through the centuries. By the eighteenth century, more orthodox Hadhramaut Arab scholars began to make their views on Islam felt, and external influences on Indonesian Islam began to shift from its former center on the Indian subcontinent to the Middle East. In spite of this, mysticism has remained an important characteristic of Indonesian Islam.

Until the nineteenth century, contact with the rest of the Muslim world was relatively intermittent compared with the burgeoning interaction which was to follow. Muslim scholars from the Middle East and the Indian subcontinent continued to be the transmission channels for Islamic ideas, and a small but important group of Indonesians traveled to centers of Muslim learning in the Arab world. Arabs and Turks were also political and religious advisers in local sultanates. However, the number of Indonesians making the arduous journey of the *ḥajj* remained small.

The nineteenth and early twentieth centuries saw a significant increase in Indonesia's involvement with the rest of the Islamic world. The number of pilgrims to Mecca grew to the point where they were termed the "rice of the Hejaz," reaching 123,052 in 1926–1927. There was also a significant rise in the number of Indonesian scholars going to the Middle East for religious studies. During the mid-1920s there were some two hundred Southeast Asian students (mostly Indonesian) studying in Cairo, and, in spite of a decline in pilgrims during the Great Depression, during World War II there were reportedly more than two thousand residents of Saudi Arabia claiming Indies citizenship. Some of these individuals, the Jawa (as Southeast Asians were called by Arabs), became well-respected scholars in Mecca. Those who returned from Middle Eastern training became the backbone of religious education in the Indies, along with immigrants from Arab states who taught religion and Arabic in the *pesantren* and *madrasahs*. [*See also* Pesantren; Madrasah.]

This was also a period in which new religious ideas, and particularly modernism, made strong inroads into religious thinking in the Indies. The reformers were particularly critical of the syncretic, "non-Islamic" elements of Islam as it had developed in the archipelago and sought to eliminate these "un-Islamic" accretions. They also argued in support of *ijtihād* (independent judgment) and rejected *taqlīd* (adherence to tradition). Initially spread among Arab residents in Jakarta, modernism found a strong base in the Minangkabau area of West Sumatra. It was in Jogjakarta in East Java that the most important modernist organization, the Muhammadiyah, was founded in 1911. Its founder Ahmad Dahlan and other key members were trained in Cairo by followers of Muḥammad ʿAbduh. It became heavily involved in education and social change, although its focus varied according to area. In Sumatra it was more involved in purifying the faith, while on Java there was a greater tendency toward competing with Western challenges.

The postwar era has shown some of the greatest ferment within Islamic circles in Indonesia. Independence, an increasingly educated population, funds for religious development from the Middle East, and the ability to communicate ideas more easily across the Islamic world have brought Indonesia even more firmly into the intellectual and political core of Islam. The number of Indonesian students in the Middle East grew markedly from the hiatus of the Depression, wartime, and independence struggle. In 1987 there were 722 students in Cairo (585 in Al-Azhar University), and 904 in Saudi Arabia. Religious students from these institutions tended to assume lower-level religious educational and technical posts upon their return to Indonesia. Of considerable importance in influencing Islamic thinking in postwar Indonesia were those who did graduate work in North American, British, and Commonwealth universities.

Many of these individuals became the prime transmitters of contemporary revivalist thinking into the archipelago. Arab teachers have also remained important, particularly in language and literature. In 1980–1981 there were twenty-one Egyptian teachers at Indonesian universities.

Religious thought in postwar Indonesia can be characterized by a burgeoning indigenous literature on Islam and the large-scale importation and translation of works by Islamic writers from abroad. More traditional Indonesian religious writers such as Hamka, as well as those considered more current (e.g., Nurcholish Madjid and Abdurrahman Wahid), are now well-recognized interpreters of Islamic thought in the islands. There has also been an increase in the number of periodicals emphasizing Islamic issues, including *Panji Massyarakat, Dahwah, Kiblat,* and *Pesantren.* Among foreign Muslim writers, those most widely published in Indonesian have been ʿAlī Sharīʿatī, Sayyid Quṭb, Abu al-Aʿlā Mawdūdī, al-Ghazālī, Ḥasan al-Bannāʾ, and Muhammad Iqbal. There has also been some penetration of Shīʿī ideas. Part of this has been the result of romanticism among youth regarding the Iranian Islamic Revolution, but there has also been an intellectual interest in the more speculative and abstract elements of Shīʿī thought. A number of Shīʿī books and tracts have been translated into Indonesian and published in the islands. [*Each of the figures named above is the subject of an independent entry.*]

Character of Contemporary Indonesian Islam. While contemporary Indonesian Islam has been characterized as unified by its almost unanimous acceptance of its Sunnī roots, it has also been described as pluralistic in terms of belief and practice. At one level, Indonesian Muslims have been described as divided between those "nominal" Muslims who have been more deeply influenced by non-Muslim traditions and those more "orthodox" ones who follow a more universalistic pattern of belief and practice. The former, usually referred to as *abangan,* have been described as imbued with Hindu and animist elements reinforced by Sufism to create forms of rituals and mysticism peculiar to Indonesia and especially to Java. Within this culture, ritual feasts *(slametan),* spirit beliefs, traditional medical practices, and Hindu art and ceremonial forms intertwine with Muslim precepts. The latter group, termed *santri,* have perceived themselves as followers of a "purer" faith, adhering more rigidly to rituals such as prayer and fasting and less contaminated by animistic and mystical beliefs. The Indonesian government over the past several decades has been more closely attuned to the mystical interpretation of Islam, while many in the minority "orthodox" Muslim community have attacked what they perceive to be un-Islamic tendencies within the national political leadership.

However, this dichotomy is weakened both by the extent to which individuals within both groups may oscillate in belief and practice, and by the development in the postwar era of a more universalistic Islam. As late as 1960 the Ministry of Religion argued that only a small minority of Muslims in Indonesia practiced their faith in terms of prayer, *zakāt* (alms), and fasting. In some areas of Java, others reported that Hindu beliefs dominated the religious ways of nominal Muslims, and that elements of belief in spirits infused the faith of individuals in all religions throughout Indonesia. However, greater contact with the rest of the Muslim world and the teaching of Islam to Indonesia's growing school population have provided a stronger foundation for a more universalistic interpretation of the religion. The teaching of religion in the schools is now compulsory, and though often superficial, it does project a less parochial interpretation of Islam. Recent decades have seen major growth in the number of people attending Friday prayer and adhering more closely to other rituals, such as observing Ramaḍān. There has also been a greater interest in the *ḥajj,* more wearing of Islamic dress by women, and concern over *ḥalāl* products. This closer observance of Islamic practice has been particularly noticeable among educated youth, but it is also to be found in the villages.

Part of this change is the result of missionary *(dahwah;* Ar., *daʿwah)* activities by organizations seeking to "make Muslims better Muslims" or to "islamize Muslims." The postwar era has seen a proliferation of Muslim organizations, tracts, magazines, study groups, and lectures seeking to bring Indonesians a better understanding of Islam. An Indonesian Islamic Dahwah Council was formed in 1967, led by former Masjumi leader Mohammad Natsir, and there has been considerable recent cooperation among individual Muslims from disparate organizations such as the Muhammadiyah and Nahdatul Ulama. [*See also* Daʿwah.]

It would also be an oversimplification to divide Indonesian Islam sharply between modernists and traditionalists. There is general agreement that the principle of *sharīʿah* is the foundation for all Muslims and that Islam should regulate personal and state actions. A core issue that has divided the adherents of these two views has been somewhat resolved by a gradual closing of the gap on the question of *ijtihād*. While there has not been any significant official change in interpretation of the problem by traditional organizations such as Nahdatul Ulama, individual leaders have displayed greater flexibility. Even with this growing consensus among Indonesian Muslims, however, there still exist significant variations in belief and practice throughout the archipelago, not only in terms of adherence to the core of universal Islamic patterns, but also in the manner in which local cultural influences frame perception and maintenance of the religion.

Islam and Politics. Islam has played an important role in twentieth-century Indonesian politics. The first mass nationalist organization was Sarekat Islam, formed in 1912 and the dominant political organization of the colony for more than a decade. Given the great ethnic and linguistic diversity across the archipelago, Islam provided the one common thread for the vast majority of the population. It differentiated the Indonesians from their Christian masters and gave them a sense of identity with a universal cause. This seeking to be part of the wider community *(ummah)* was reflected in the large number of Indonesians making the *ḥajj* and the interest of many Indonesian nationalists in such international Islamic issues as the Caliphate question and the Pan-Islamic movement. Sarekat Islam also had an economic agenda that reinforced its religious platform. From the beginning it criticized un-Islamic (particularly Chinese) economic power in the islands and later attacked Dutch capitalism. For its part, the Dutch colonial administration tended to see Islam as a danger to domestic peace and order and expressed suspicion of returning pilgrims and students who had studied in foreign Muslim educational institutions. It was especially disturbed by what administrators saw as loyalties to authority outside the colony.

In the decades preceding World War II and during the Japanese occupation, Islam's role in domestic politics was weakened, first by the challenge of more secular nationalism and Dutch repression and later by Japanese suspicions of Muslim political loyalty. In the first instance, Sarekat Islam began to break up in the 1920s because of poor internal administration and competition from radical (especially communist) elements; it was ultimately overshadowed by more secular nationalist parties. Through these years Islamic political power was further fractured by religious differences among Muslims who formed competing parties. In 1926 Nahdatul Ulama was founded as a traditionalist counter to the reformist aspects of Sarekat Islam and to what its founders saw as an undermining of the power of the *ʿulamāʾ*. However, as in the postwar era when Islamic parties were again restricted, this vacuum gave rise to an increased role for nonpolitical groups like the Muhammadiyah; the 1930s have been described as the years of prominence for that organization. [*See also* Sarekat Islam.]

When Japan occupied the Indies during World War II, it assumed a somewhat ambivalent position regarding Islam. On one hand, it sought to foster public support by championing Islam against the Christian Dutch. Once in control, however, Japan's main focus was an attempt to direct Indonesian loyalties away from the Middle East and toward an East Asian community. The concept of the unity of Muslims did not fit the Japanese effort to emphasize the Greater East Asian Co-Prosperity Sphere. Leadership of the wartime nationalist movement tended to fall to secular forces, and Islam did not enter the independence years as a united political force.

The postwar era saw the rise of three political faces of Islam. At the party level, two major political organizations sought to dominate the Muslim majority in the new republic; both groups reflected the historic division among Muslims. Nahdatul Ulama supported more traditional non-modernist views, and Masjumi was formed as a modernist Islamic socialist party. They vied to lead Indonesians who were interested in a government based on Muslim values and expressed strong opposition to secular and particularly communist influences. Although it was believed that the majority of Indonesians supported the Muslim cause, in the country's first election in 1955 the Masjumi and Nahdatul Ulama each received approximately twenty percent of the national vote, and other Muslim parties obtained only a small percentage; the remainder went to primarily secular parties. The combined vote for all Muslim parties was 43.5 percent. The Masjumi became increasingly frustrated with its inability to influence the growing secularism of Indonesian politics, and in 1960 the party was outlawed for supporting dissident elements fighting the central government. This left the more traditional Nahdatul Ulama and small splinter parties to act as the legal voices of Islam at the national level. [*See also* Masjumi *and* Nahdatul Ulama.]

During this period Muslim political leaders were particularly concerned to establish Islam firmly within the

Indonesian constitutional framework. An original agreement among nationalist factions in 1945 would have obliged Muslims to practice *sharīʿah* law and would have required that the head of state be Muslim. However, a compromise altered the charter to reflect a more secular and pluralist view of the role of religion in the state. A new national ideology, the Pancasila (Five Principles), proclaimed as one of its five principles "belief in God" but did not describe this within a Muslim context, allowing Indonesians freely to choose their own religious expression. President Sukarno originally explained the concept as quite pluralist in nature:

> The principle of Belief in God! Not only should the Indonesian people believe in God, but every Indonesian should believe in his own God. The Christian should worship God according to the teachings of Jesus Christ, Moslems according to the teachings of the Prophet Mohammad, Buddhists should perform their religious ceremonies in accordance with the books they have. But let us all believe in God. The Indonesian State shall be a state where every person can worship his God as he likes. The whole of the people should worship God in a cultured way, that is, without religious egoism.

The 1945 constitution and provisional constitutions in 1949 and 1950 did not change this interpretation, and when President Sukarno reestablished the 1945 constitution in 1959 he gave strong support to the pluralist definition of the Pancasila. This issue of the place of Islam within the national ideology has remained a core source of Muslim dissatisfaction in the postwar era.

The third thread of Islam in the early years was characterized by the activities of radical Muslim military units such as Darul Islam, a Muslim militant group originally formed in West Java in 1948. In part, Darul Islam rationalized its war against the Indonesian Republic on the grounds that secularist forces had rejected Islam as the basis of the state. Through much of the 1950s the Darul Islam forces caused considerable destruction in West Java, and government units appeared incapable of controlling its activities as Darul Islam spread its influence into East Indonesia. During this period other Muslim groups in Sumatra and Sulawesi also prepared to employ force to defend Islam against what they saw as a secular regime in Jakarta. It was not until 1959 that negotiations largely brought an end to this period of conflict. However, the leader of Darul Islam was not captured and executed until 1962, and the Sulawesi rebellion did not collapse until 1965. [*See also* Darul Islam.]

Following an attempted coup in 1965 in which the Indonesian Communist Party became involved, some Muslim youth groups were particularly active in killing large numbers of communists (perhaps 400,000 or more died in the months after the failed coup). Communists were considered enemies of Islam both because of their perceived atheistic views and, to a lesser degree, because many landowners were members of religiously powerful families. These events led to the fall of the Sukarno regime; the military-dominated government of General, later President, Suharto has held power in Indonesia since then. It was initially hoped that the military would work closely with Muslim political organizations, and there was even a strong faction in the armed forces that sought to make Islam the unifying spiritual cement within the military. However, in the ensuing years important cleavages have developed between elements of the Muslim community and the Suharto regime. While the factors responsible for these differences are complex, they have centered upon three core issues: government efforts to establish secular bases for centrally important areas of interest to Muslims, such as education and marriage; attempts to emasculate Muslim political power; and the reimplementation of the Pancasila as the national ideology.

In the first instance, elements of the Muslim community were antagonized by such government efforts as the formulation of regulations that divorced the school calendar from Ramaḍān and discouraged Islamic dress for girls in public schools. The most incendiary issue arose over the marriage bill of 1973, when the Suharto regime attempted to give precedence to civil authority in cases of marriage and divorce. This policy was promulgated without consultation with Muslim leaders or organizations. Muslims were particularly affronted by requirements in the bill for civil permission for marriage, divorce, and polygamous marriage, and by the provision that religious differences were not to be an obstacle to marriage. This bill was considered by many Muslims to be a direct attack on Muslim law and religious authority, and the depth of opposition expressed led the government to withdraw the bill. Islamic codes still remain the foundation for family law in the country.

The second point of contention has been Suharto's efforts to contain the political power of Islam. After the 1965 coup, the outlawed Masjumi party was not allowed to reform in its original form, and in 1973 all Muslim parties were forced to unite into a single organization, the United Development Party (Partai Persatuan Pembangunan or PPP). In the 1970s the Muslim parties became the most noteworthy legal opposition to the government's party, Golkar. The majority of Golkar's membership reflects *abangan* religious views, but there have been elements within the party that have been critical of specific government policies such as the opening of schools during Ramaḍān. Although both the PPP and Golkar employed Islam as campaign tools—for example, having candidates participate publicly in Muslim rituals—in the ensuing years further attempts were made to emasculate the political power of Islam. Faced with the effective containment policies of the government, Muslim organizations were unable to launch successful political challenges to the central authorities in the 1970s and 1980s. The Jakarta government has sought to ensure that religion does not become the source of political ideology in contemporary Indonesia, a policy similar to that of the Dutch colonial regime. [*See also* Partai Persatuan Pembangunan.]

During the later 1970s and the 1980s, small radical elements in the Muslim community turned to violence to express their opposition to what they perceived to be an un-Islamic government; they demanded the formation of an Islamic state and the elimination of "yellow culture." An organization called Kommando Jihad was accused of conspiring to overthrow the government; another, the Islamic Youth Movement, allegedly attacked shopping centers in the name of Islam; and the Indonesian Islamic Revolution Board was charged with seeking Iranian support to eliminate Suharto's regime. There were isolated acts of airplane hijacking, arson, and store bombings, and the famous Buddhist monument the Borobudur was also bombed. There were largely unproven charges that seditious organizations were being aided by certain Middle Eastern governments, particularly Iran and Libya. Islamic religious spokesmen also released cassette recordings criticizing what they perceived as the corrupt and anti-Islamic activities of the Suharto administration. The government forcefully repressed these activities and used the incidents as further proof of the need to take religion out of politics.

This move to deemphasize Islam in politics reached its zenith with the demand by the Suharto government that all mass organizations affirm that the Pancasila was their only ideology. The government had previously emphasized the need proclaimed by Sukarno that all Indonesians should believe in God: to do otherwise would bring down suspicion of communist tendencies. Initially Muslim groups were strongly opposed to the state policy on ideology on the twin grounds that, first, the principle of "Belief in God" proclaimed in the Pancasila was at best agnosticism, and second, that the acceptance of that ideology as their sole foundation refuted their own religious bases. There was also fear that the Pancasila would become the official religion of Indonesia. After strong criticism from the Muhammadiyah, President Sukarno personally guaranteed that it would not become a religion. Under the Suharto regime those expressing public opposition to the Pancasila, as well as some Muslim religious leaders who attacked the government in the name of Islam, found themselves faced with long prison sentences. However, ultimately Nahdatul Ulama and other organs of the PPP capitulated and accepted the Pancasila as their sole ideological commitment. On its part, the government began to display greater willingness to meet Muslim requests in areas such as religious education.

This process has made it necessary for organizations such as Nahdatul Ulama to seek new directions. Given the weakening of Islam as a focal point of ideology, there have been questions as to the maintenance of their constituencies. Some have called for the formerly Muslim parties to withdraw totally from politics and concern themselves with development and education until conditions change in the Republic. There has been a major emphasis on Muslim alternatives to nationally directed development policies. At an organizational level at this time, however, Islam remains a relatively weak player in Indonesian national politics.

Finally, Muslim organizations have expressed increasing antagonism over what they see as the growing power of Christianity in the islands. There has been an almost threefold growth in the percentage of Christians in the population since the prewar years and a major increase since Suharto came to power. Rhetorical attacks have been made on Christians by a variety of Muslim organizations, including the Muhammadiyah, and there has been violence against Christians on Java and Sulawesi in particular. There have been accusations that the government is pro-Christian. Some Muslims also see this growth in conversions to Christianity as a result of the pluralism expressed in the Pancasila, although the government has argued that the Pancasila is a means of alleviating religious tensions.

Islam and Foreign Policy. Historically, Islam has not been a major factor in Indonesian foreign policy. The one period when it did play a positive role was during Indonesia's postwar effort to seek allies in its fight for independence from the Dutch. At that time it made major efforts to gain the support of Arab leaders, and the Arab League recommended that all its members recognize the new republic. It was in this period that Indonesia first initiated diplomatic relations with Arab states.

In the succeeding years the Indonesian government has tended to downplay Islam as a primary basis for foreign policy decisions, partially reflecting the more secular viewpoint of the country's leadership and partly the government's wish not to reinforce religious loyalties at home. Thus, although Indonesia criticized Israel's actions against the Palestinians and its Arab neighbors and the Soviet invasion of Afghanistan, it did so more in the name of Third World solidarity and not of Islam. Jakarta has also tended to be cautious about becoming involved in disputes among other Muslim countries, calling for peaceful solutions but not actively engaging in efforts to end these conflicts.

Although President Sukarno did support the Africa-Asia Islamic Conference in 1964 (in part to gain support for his confrontation with Malaysia), Indonesia did not formally participate in the Rabat and Jeddah meetings that formed the Organization of the Islamic Conference (OIC). It did not attend the meeting that promulgated the OIC Charter in 1972 and did not become a signatory to it. It was argued that by joining the organization Indonesia would have to accept the OIC's Islamic principles and declare itself an Islamic state. Since that time, Indonesia has worked more closely with the OIC and has become involved in a number of economically oriented Islamic international organizations. Indonesians in their private capacities have also been very active in many nongovernmental Islamic groups, such as the World Islamic League and World Assembly of Muslim Youth.

Islam and the Courts. During most of the period of Dutch rule from the end of the nineteenth century the colonial government followed the "Reception Theory." This view held that *adat* (Ar., *ʿādāt;* native customary) law was the legal framework within which the indigenous population was to be ruled, and that Islamic law was only to be enforced to the degree that it was accepted by *adat*. From 1882 to 1937, so-called Priestraad (Religious Court, later termed Penghulu Court) on Java and Madura had general jurisdiction over marriage, divorce, alms, and inheritance. In 1937 inheritance was officially taken from the religious courts, although they continued to rule on such issues.

During the Japanese occupation a Department of Religion (Syumubu) was established, and in 1946 the new Indonesian Republic formed a Ministry of Religion to govern all the nation's faiths. This ministry has not always been considered a friend of Islam by Muslim leaders and organizations, particularly after 1971 when it came under the control of less traditional ministers. While the ministry has directorates for other faiths, its main activities focus on Islam. It supervises religious education in both Muslim and state schools, the organization of the pilgrimage, Muslim foundations, Islamic marriage laws, and religious courts, and it supports Muslim places of worship.

Initially the new government maintained the former Dutch system of courts. In 1957 Penadilan Agama (Courts of Religious Justice) were formed for all the islands except the district of Banjarmasin on Kalimantan. The first-instance court is called the Mahkamah Syariah and the appeals court the Makkamah Syariah Propinsi. These courts cover marriage, divorce, child support, charity, and religious foundations. Inheritance is not included, and in certain regions *adat* law holds precedence. It is the general view of Muslim legal scholars that the "Reception Theory" is no longer valid and that Islamic law is equal to *adat* and Western law. All things considered, however, the religious courts in Indonesia have a quite restricted role. [*See also* Adat.]

Many Indonesian Muslims would like to see a greater infusion of Islamic principles into the juridical system, but there is no unanimity of agreement on how *sharīʿah* is to be implemented. Groups and individuals disagree as to whether to accept only the Shāfiʿī school of law, as well as on the role of *ijtihād*, the rights of non-Muslims, the place of *adat*, and the meaning of an "Islamic State."

[*See also* Islam, *article on* Islam in Southeast Asia and the Pacific; Muhammadiyah.]

BIBLIOGRAPHY

Alfian. *Muhammadiyah*. Yogyakarta, 1989.

Boland, B. J. *The Struggle of Islam in Modern Indonesia*. The Hague, 1971.

Geertz, Clifford. *The Religion of Java*. Glencoe, Ill., 1960.

Hooker, M. B., ed. *Islam in South-East Asia*. Leiden, 1988.

Kipp, Rita Smith, and Susan Rodgers, eds. *Indonesian Religion in Transition*. Tucson, 1987.

Noer, Deliar. *The Modernist Movement in Indonesia, 1900–1942*. London, 1973.

Snouck Hurgonje, Christiaan. *Selected Works*. Edited by G. H. Bousquet and Joseph Schacht. Leiden, 1957.

Taufik Abdullah and Sharon Siddique, eds. *Islam and Society in Southeast Asia*. Singapore, 1986.
von der Mehden, Fred R. *Religion and Nationalism in Southeast Asia*. Madison, Wis., 1963.
Woodward Mark R. *Islam in Java*. Tucson, 1989.

FRED R. VON DER MEHDEN

INDONESIAN LITERATURE. *See* Malay and Indonesian Literature.

INHERITANCE. The Islamic law of inheritance, *mīrāth*, constitutes the single most distinctive and complicated part of *sharīʿah* law. It is particularly closely tied to the text of revelation: the Qur'ān contains more extensive and specific rules on inheritance than on any other subject. For this reason, it is the part of *sharīʿah* law least affected by contemporary reforms, most Muslim countries having essayed only minor adjustments in the twentieth century. It is also one of the topics on which Sunnī and Shīʿī law most sharply diverge, as the two are based on incompatible premises.

The basic premise of Sunnī inheritance law is that the Qur'ānic verses on inheritance came to reform the existing system of inheritance in western Arabia, under which the *ʿasaba* (male relatives connected to the deceased through male ties) inherited. This necessitates reconciling the scheme of fixed portions allotted to the Qur'ānic sharers, the *dhaw al-farā'id*, with the claims of the *ʿasaba*, who are treated as residuary heirs. This is an extremely difficult task that has led to the development of rules of great complexity and many divergences between jurists.

In contrast, the Shīʿīs believe that the Qur'ānic scheme of inheritance was meant to supplant altogether the *ʿasaba*-based scheme. In application, the Shīʿī rules keep more of the inheritance within the nuclear family and often place the daughter(s) of the deceased in a more favorable position than under Sunnī law; in Sunnī law male agnates are more favored.

The Islamic law of inheritance introduced important changes in the pre-Islamic system. For the first time, women were allowed to inherit—although in almost all instances they were entitled to only one-half the share of a male inheriting in the same capacity. It also permitted inheritance to pass through the female line, although the situations in which uterine relations would actually be entitled to share in the inheritance were exceptional. In addition, the spouse relict was allowed to inherit, although shares were otherwise exclusively distributed to persons sharing a blood tie to the deceased.

Islamic law contemplates inheritance following a mandatory scheme of intestate succession, meaning that the power of the deceased to bequeath property by will (*waṣāyā*) is restricted; a testator may bequeath no more than one-third of the estate by will. In Sunnī law the testator may not use bequests to benefit persons already taking under the scheme of intestacy; in Shīʿī law, however, this is allowed. To avoid dissipation of the estate close to the time of death, a person during *maraḍ al-mawt* ("death sickness") may not dispose of property. *Maraḍ al-mawt* may last up to one year prior to death and is counted from the time when the condition that actually leads to the person's demise begins to take inexorable effect.

In the typical case, where there will be a number of heirs of the estate, Islamic inheritance law will lead to the fragmentation of property into small fractional shares that may be unusable. To avoid such fragmentation Muslims have resorted to various devices; one of these was constituting landed property as *waqf* and thereby excluding it from being passed on under the scheme of intestate succession.

[*See also* Property; Waqf.]

BIBLIOGRAPHY

Coulson, Noel J. *Succession in the Muslim Family*. Cambridge, 1971. Outstanding general study of Islamic inheritance law.
Layish, Aharon. "Mīrāth." In *Encyclopaedia of Islam*, new ed., vol. 7, pp. 107–113. Leiden, 1960–. Two scholarly essays on inheritance law.

ANN ELIZABETH MAYER

INNOVATION. *See* Bidʿah.

INSTITUTE OF MUSLIM MINORITY AFFAIRS. Incorporated in London in 1983, the Institute of Muslim Minority Affairs (IMMA) is an independent body with the objective of studying the conditions of life of Muslim minority communities wherever they reside. In order to fulfill its mandate the IMMA has invited and encouraged research and investigations on minority communities ranging from such large ones as those in India, the former Soviet Union, and China to small ones in the Pacific, such as the twenty-member-strong community on Tonga Island. Still, it cannot be claimed that all Muslim minority communities have been discovered and studied or that all aspects of existing minority communities have been examined and explored. With the constantly varying dimensions of the minority phenomenon and the ever-changing horizons and boundaries, the research must go on, albeit at an accelerated pace.

One of the most notable achievements of the IMMA has been the initiation of communication with other religious groups with regard to their principles and values in the treatment of Muslim minorities. It has been observed that even in societies where political constitutions included fair and liberal guidelines for the treatment of minorities and other disadvantaged groups, these provisions only implied legal and constitutional protection, whereas the attitudes of people in their daily life was actually conditioned by other factors. Legal and constitutional guarantees do not mean much when public sentiment remains hostile.

For these reasons, in 1985 the IMMA inaugurated a regular section in its periodical publication, the *JIMMA* (*Journal Institute of Muslim Minority Affairs*), under the heading of "Dialogue," and invited experts from different religious traditions to express their ideas and insights about the concept of human rights and minority rights in their respective traditions. In order to feed this section with regular, diverse, and quality input, the IMMA established a wide network of contacts with scholars and institutions in many countries where Muslim minority issues were pertinent and persistent, encouraging them to use the pages of the *JIMMA* for mutual understanding through sharing of views and exchange of grievances, and so forth.

Even though tangible achievements are difficult to measure, one indisputable advantage that has accrued from this initiative of the IMMA is the communication that has taken place between formerly contending religious groups. In the past the religious encounter has been characterized by hostility, accusations, and counteraccusations. There had been few occasions where Muslims and non-Muslims could engage in sober peaceful debate. What the IMMA did was to bring the two sides together on the same platform, not as gladiators but as dialoguers. The Dialogue section was open to all, Muslims and non-Muslims. Great effort is constantly exercised that the debate never descends to dissension or denunciation.

Reciprocally, besides having non-Muslims being able to express themselves in the *JIMMA*, the IMMA had access to non-Muslim religious forums, so that the Muslim point of view in regard to the rights and privileges of minorities in the Islamic tradition could be calmly and rationally presented on non-Muslim religious platforms. This has enabled non-Muslims to become familiar with Muslim positions and enabled Muslims to become acquainted with non-Muslim positions.

Although the IMMA has given effective expression to the problems faced by Muslim minorities in non-Muslim societies, it also recognizes that there are significant numbers of non-Muslims who live as minorities in Muslim societies. In 1985, therefore, efforts were made to take cognizance of how non-Muslim minorities were being treated in Muslim states. There followed spirited debate through articles and commentaries on the subject of *al-dhimmī* (protected non-Muslims) in Islam, and that process still continues. The IMMA has called for self-examination on the part of Muslim majority states. It has opened its forum for the use of non-Muslim minorities living in Muslim states to engage in a dialogue with their Muslim majorities, thus providing an opportunity for peaceful and perhaps productive exchange.

The point of view of non-Muslim minorities is being articulated perhaps for the first time in a cool debate. This exchange of ideas and opinion is likely to lead to growth of understanding and goodwill. Muslim majorities have been enabled to bypass the adversarial accusations and counteraccusations and through dialogue to get to know, and perhaps get more confidence in the intentions and sincerity of, the ideologically marginal components of their society.

Another major objective of the IMMA has been to internationalize the issue of Muslim minorities, that is, to get scholars, individuals, and organizations and official agencies to become aware of the nature of the Muslim minority problem, and to take interest in it, not necessarily as partisans, but as people of conscience with a quest for knowledge, justice, and fair play. However, it was first necessary to know where these people were and what these organizations were about.

Hence, soon after the IMMA was formed, it started collecting information about people around the world who were interested in minority issues, both Muslim and non-Muslim, from various sources—reference books, journals, magazines, personal contacts, and so forth. The IMMA was cognizant of the fact that many distinguished Muslim scholars (historians, political scientists, economists, sociologists, and other professionals) were widely dispersed not only in Muslim countries, but perhaps more so in Western countries. Most of them had no links outside their professional circles and generally none with Muslim national and international organizations. Because of this, their talent and expertise was lost to the Muslim *ummah* (community) and the Muslim organizations were constrained to operate from a limited human resource pool.

As a result of the IMMA's efforts a significant number of these Muslim professionals are now taking an active interest in minority studies. They make scholarly contributions to the *JIMMA* and readily attend seminars and conferences organized by the IMMA. For some of these scholars, this was the first time that they have appeared on a Muslim forum.

Currently, the IMMA has put together a list of ten thousand names of scholars from all over the world who are interested in minority affairs. This list is categorized and computerized. Perhaps no other organization has such a comprehensive human resource file.

The IMMA currently has in preparation another list of three thousand names which include Muslim national and international organizations, Muslim scholars currently in the field of minority affairs, and many non-Muslim national and international organizations as well as minority studies experts with whom IMMA has established direct and recurrent contact.

The third major objective of the IMMA related to the Muslim minorities in particular and the Muslim world in general can be termed a "home mission." On the one hand, the IMMA addressed itself directly to the Muslim minorities, urging them to focus inward and to try to analyze the nature of their predicament and understand it objectively and instead of waiting for outside support seek to solve their problems with the help of their own resources, ingenuity, and diplomatic skills. On the other hand, the IMMA addressed the Muslim *ummah* in Muslim majority countries at two levels: to persuade the intellectuals in these countries to study and define the Islamic concepts of social import, such as *ummah, daʿwah* (the call), and the concept of Muslim man; and to redefine the relationship between Muslims and non-Muslims in modern pluralistic societies where *dār al-ḥarb* (non-Muslim lands) and *dār al-Islām* (Muslim lands) have coalesced within the same political and social unit.

The interreligious encounter for Muslim minorities is a practical reality. They suffer in silence and isolation or resolve with guilt and integration. For the Muslim majorities it is but a distant and abstract challenge. Yet they could lead the way for discussion and the removal of the notion that Islam makes no distinction between situations where Muslims are dominant and situations where Muslims live as minorities with peoples of other faiths and philosophies. Perhaps then could the minorities living among non-Muslims participate with enthusiasm in the life of their societies, achieve economic and material consolidation, and thus escape the grinding poverty and backwardness which their self-imposed alienation has further aggravated, and at the same time maintain their Islamic identity.

The Institute of Muslim Minority Affairs declared through the pages of its journal its basic approach to the study of Muslim minority problems, both for the resolution of the minority crisis and the identification of the majority options, an approach that also guides the policy of its research and publications organs, the *JIMMA,* and the book series: "as we conceive it, the minority problem is not a one way street. Our responsibility does not end with making a statement. The statement is designed to elicit a response. . . . So that we not only speak, we also listen. Hopefully, this speaking and listening will be carried on in a spirit of compassion and tolerance. And we commit ourselves to making this possible." ("A Word about Ourselves," *Journal Institute of Muslim Minority Affairs* 5.1 [1983]: 5–6).

[*See also* Minorities, *article on* Muslim Minorities in non-Muslim Societies.]

BIBLIOGRAPHY

Abedin, Syed Z. "A Word about Ourselves." *Journal Institute of Muslim Minority Affairs* 13.1 (January 1992): 1–25. Written in the spirit of a "state of the union message," this article identifies problems faced by Muslim minorities and takes a long-term perspective, suggesting programs and policies for implementation.

SYED Z. ABEDIN and SALEHA M. ABEDIN

INTERCESSION. *See* Muḥammad; Sainthood.

INTEREST. The question of whether interest is a legitimate financial instrument has long been a source of controversy throughout the Islamic world. The origins of the controversy lie in Qur'ānic verses that prohibit *ribā,* the ancient Arabian practice whereby borrowers saw their debts double if they defaulted and redouble if they defaulted again. Over the centuries, many Muslims have inferred from these verses that any loan contract specifying a fixed return to the lender is immoral and illegal, regardless of the loan's purpose, its amount, or the prevailing institutional framework. And on this basis, they have condemned an array of common business practices as un-Islamic.

Anti-interest sentiment, however, has seldom translated into effective political action. At the start of the modern era the anti-interest movement was fragmented, disorganized, and lacking in forceful intellectual leadership. Under the circumstances, Muslim governments, firms, and individuals were openly charging and borrowing interest without encountering any serious opposition. The modern era's first powerful movement to abolish interest-laden business practices developed in India in the waning years of British rule. The movement's preeminent spokesman was Sayyid Abū al-Aʿlā Mawdūdī (1903–1979), a prolific writer who depicted interest as a tool of Western dominance and a source of Muslim decadence.

Since the mid-1960s, Mawdūdī's Pakistani and Indian followers have figured prominently among the contributors to a vast, and still growing, anti-interest literature within the field of Islamic economics. This literature offers numerous justifications for banning interest. The most prominent is that interest provides an "unearned gain" to the lender (who earns a return without exerting any effort), while imposing an "unfair obligation" on the borrower (who must repay the loan plus a finance charge even in the event of misfortune). Other justifications for the ban are that interest worsens the distribution of income by transferring wealth from poor to rich; that it promotes selfishness and weakens communal bonds; and that, by fostering idleness, it deprives society of the labor and enterprise of potentially productive people.

Muslims opposed to the anti-interest campaign argue that the purpose of banning *ribā* was simply to eliminate a specific source of exploitation, inequality, and communal tension. In this interpretation, *ribā* had to be prohibited because it was pushing large numbers of people into enslavement. The ban was never intended to apply to all forms of interest, as evidenced by the fact that prominent early Muslims distinguished between *ribā* and various other forms of interest. Another commonly expressed rationale for rejecting a total ban is that in modern economies interest-based financial contracts seldom create grave risks. Competitive pressures generally keep rates within bounds. Moreover, bankruptcy laws and social security programs protect borrowers against unanticipated contingencies.

The case against prohibiting all forms of interest was put forth boldly by Fazlur Rahman, a Pakistani professor of Islamic thought, in 1964. Rahman endured intense criticism for his position, which came to be dubbed "modernist." Over the years, a few other prominent Islamic thinkers and officials have embraced the modernist position. Most significantly, in 1989 Muḥammad Sayyid Ṭanṭāwī, *muftī* of Egypt, issued a *fatwā* (legal opinion) to the effect that "harmless" forms of interest, such as those payed by government bonds and ordinary savings accounts, do not violate the spirit of Islam. There have also appeared, mainly in Western publications, scholarly critiques of the anti-interest drive, including some written by Muslims residing in the West.

Within Islamic circles, however, mainstream intellectual opinion continues to hold that interest is an impediment to social justice. All the research institutes and economics departments that have been established to promote "Islamic economics" treat the abolition of interest as the sine qua non of veritable Islamic economic reform. Moreover, from the Far East to the Atlantic, political parties pursuing an Islamic agenda agree, at least officially, as to the urgent necessity of eradicating interest.

The rise of the modern anti-interest movement was not accompanied, at first, by any practical successes. Interest-based contracting remained common, with few opportunities—outside of informal local networks—for saving, investing, borrowing, or lending in an interest-free manner. The 1930s saw a few attempts to establish interest-free banks in India, but they all failed. The first successful bank operating on an interest-free manner was opened in 1963 in the Egyptian town of Mit Ghamr. Although modeled after West Germany's local savings institutions, this bank eventually claimed an Islamic identity, on the grounds that it payed no interest on deposits and charged no interest on loans, borrowing and lending strictly on the basis of profit-and-loss sharing. The first bank to assert an Islamic identity from the start opened in Dubai in 1975. The subsequent decade saw the spread of Islamic banking to more than fifty countries, including numerous predominantly non-Muslim countries. Many of these banks, like the schools and institutes that promote Islamic economics, were established largely through Saudi Arabian capital, although Saudi Arabia itself has remained closed to interest-free banking.

The greatest victories of the anti-interest movement have come in Iran and Pakistan, each of which has decreed interest illegal. Four years after the Islamic Revolution, Iran ordered its banks to purge interest from all their operations. For its part, Pakistan moved in 1979 to require its banks to abandon interest within five years, although the order's practical impact was deliberately muted by placing some common financial practices outside the Federal Shariat Court's jurisdiction. With the expiration of the exclusions in 1990, the court was quick to rule that Pakistani banks were continuing to engage in various un-Islamic practices. In 1992, it removed various critical exemptions.

Regardless of whether the practices declared illegal are in violation of Islamic teachings, it is true that Pakistan's Islamic banks have been paying and charging interest as a matter of course, albeit disguised as a "service charge" or "markup." Even the architects and executives of these banks admit, although generally only in private, that there is nothing inherently Islamic about their country's new financial system.

Outside of Iran and Pakistan, interest continues to be payed and charged relatively openly. And where Islamic banks exist, their operations rely almost exclusively on camouflaged interest. Alternatives to interest-based financing are emerging under the aegis not of Islamic banks, think-tanks, or regimes, but of secular organizations. Specifically, veritable profit-and-loss sharing is occurring in burgeoning stock markets that have been established outside the purview of Islamic economics.

[*See also* Banks and Banking; Economics, *article on* Economic Institutions.]

BIBLIOGRAPHY

Abdul Mannan, Muḥammad. *Islamic Economics: Theory and Practice.* Lahore, 1970. Widely available textbook that focuses on the urgency and feasibility of eradicating interest.

Ahmed, Ziauddin, et al., eds. *Money and Banking in Islam.* Jeddah, 1983. Essays on the mechanics of eliminating interest, including an influential 1980 report by Pakistan's Council of Islamic Ideology.

Chapra, Mohammad Umer. *Towards a Just Monetary System.* Leicester, 1985. The most forceful philosophical argument against interest.

Kuran, Timur. "The Economic System in Contemporary Islamic Thought: Interpretation and Assessment." *International Journal of Middle East Studies* 18 (May 1986): 135–164. Contains a critique of the anti-interest drive from an economic and sociological perspective.

Kuran, Timur. "The Economic Impact of Islamic Fundamentalism." In *Fundamentalisms and the State: Remaking Polities, Economies, and Militance,* edited by Martin E. Marty and R. Scott Appleby, pp. 302–341. Chicago, 1993. Contains an evaluation of practical attempts to eliminate interest.

Pryor, Frederic L. "The Islamic Economic System." *Journal of Comparative Economics* 9 (June 1985): 197–223. Critiques the anti-interest agenda, primarily from the vantage point of macroeconomics.

Qureshi, Anwar Iqbal. *Islam and the Theory of Interest.* 2d ed. Lahore, 1967. One of the first comprehensive arguments against interest.

Rahman, Fazlur. "Riba and Interest." *Islamic Studies* 3 (March 1964): 1–43.

Rodinson, Maxime. *Islam and Capitalism* (1966). New York, 1973. Best source on the history of the controversy over interest.

TIMUR KURAN

INTERFAITH DIALOGUE. *See* Muslim-Christian Dialogue; Muslim-Jewish Dialogue.

INTERNATIONAL ISLAMIC FEDERATION OF STUDENT ORGANIZATIONS. A worldwide organization of Muslim student associations, the International Islamic Federation of Student Organizations (IIFSO) received its initial impetus from the experience of Muslim students in North America. In 1963, the Muslim Students Association of the United States and Canada (MSA) was established on the campus of the University of Illinois at Champaign-Urbana. This was a new experiment in the history of Islamic student organizations, in the sense that the student constituency in the United States came from all parts of the Muslim and non-Muslim worlds. The Association provided a sense of identity to the foreign Muslim students and also gave them an opportunity to learn about Islam in a modern context. The free access to Islamic literature and to books and journalistic misrepresentations of Islam helped them to discover for themselves what the Islamic revival meant to Muslims and to those who insisted on misrepresenting it.

The American Islamic experience also created a greater global consciousness in these foreign Muslim students and provided the MSA with global links through its members and alumni. This experience was enriched further when the MSA began to attract Americans who embraced Islam. Representatives of the MSA participated in the conferences and conventions of other Muslim student organizations in different countries. In the course of these meetings, Muslim students who were becoming increasingly aware of the need to restructure Islamic thought and identity moved toward a common goal: the creation of an umbrella organization that could help in the organized promotion of concepts such as the unity of Islamic thought, the universality of the Islamic movement, and the consolidation of a mature Muslim leadership.

The plan to establish a world federation of Muslim student organizations, finally realized with the establishment of the IIFSO, was adopted at a convention held at Ibadan University, Nigeria, in July 1966; it was an all-African affair with representatives from Sudan, Nigeria, Sierra Leone, Gambia, Ghana, and Guinea. A preparatory committee was formed to mobilize ideas and resources for an international conference to be held in Sudan in December 1968.

Participation in the Sudan conference was more international; delegates of Muslim student organizations from Europe, North America, and Africa attended. The conference concluded with the adoption of an interim constitution. Three months later, in February 1969, a larger meeting was held in Mecca, during the *ḥajj*, at which delegates resolved to: reconsider the IIFSO constitution and make any appropriate amendments; make arrangements for convening the IIFSO General Constituent Assembly; and establish widespread contacts in order to introduce the IIFSO, its mission, and purpose, secure affiliation from a maximum number of student organizations, and ensure material support for the Constituent Assembly. The draft constitution was circulated among eminent Muslim thinkers who endorsed the idea and offered both support and useful suggestions.

The first inaugural conference of the IIFSO was held on 13–14 June 1969, at the Bilāl Mosque in Aachen, Germany. Since then, the organization has held international conferences in several countries. Each conference has had a profound effect on the local Islamic community. A second conference was held in Aachen in 1971; the third and fourth took place in Istanbul; the fifth in Kuala Lumpur; the sixth in Khartoum; and the seventh again in Malaysia in 1988. Regional conferences have been held in South and Southeast Asia, the Caribbean region and the Pacific region, North and South America, Europe, and Africa.

The roots of the IIFSO run deep in the experience of those members who were students in the West. Most of the secretaries general have been either past presidents or active members of the MSA. Their vision of an Islamic movement that integrates the best of the Muslim world and the West has helped impart a definite character to the IIFSO.

Approaches. The IIFSO's method is intellectual as well as practical. Combining scholarship with pragmatism, it has provided direction to various student movements and steered them toward constructive work aimed at rejuvenating Muslim thought. An important aspect of the IIFSO's work is the provision of continuing education to its membership; thus, it sponsors and supports training camps throughout the world. In order to provide a clear direction to this activity, Dr. Hisham Altalib, a former secretary general, has published a comprehensive *Training Guide for Islamic Workers*. The IIFSO has also played a major role in encouraging women to take an active role in the Islamic movement. It sent women delegates to the International Women's Conference at Nairobi, Kenya, in 1985, and its delegates played an active role in the founding of Muslim women's organizations in Pakistan.

In the Caribbean region, the IIFSO is a significant factor in the development of private enterprise through its program of providing loans and expertise to small businessmen. It has also organized Islamic work among Spanish-speaking people in North and South America. The details of such work were refined in two international conferences held by the IIFSO in Mexico (1987) and Columbia (1988). Finally, the IIFSO has been active in providing relief and reconstruction help in places struck by natural calamities.

The IIFSO's desire to create an independent financial base for itself has led to a new direction in Islamic publishing. Heretofore, most Islamic literature has been available only in its original language or in translation into the major traditional Muslim languages (Arabic, Farsi, Urdu). The IIFSO has made Islamic literature available in more than eighty languages. To date, it has published more than five hundred titles with ten million copies. The sale of these books has become a vital source of financing for the IIFSO's various activities. This experience has been duplicated by several other Islamic organizations within their own jurisdictions. Several Islamic organizations, including the World Assembly of Muslim Youth (WAMY), have relied heavily on IIFSO publications in building the libraries of Muslim youth organizations in different linguistic communities around the world.

This publishing venture has helped the IIFSO stay clear of fundraising activities and, at the same time, has given native speakers of many languages access to the works of several important Islamic thinkers. It is noteworthy that the IIFSO was among the pioneers that undertook translation of Islamic books, many written in

English in the United States, into languages of the former Soviet Union and into Cyrillic script.

Relations with International Islamic Organizations. The IIFSO maintains close ties with other international Islamic umbrella organizations. Its secretary general is an ex-officio member of the board of trustees of the World Assembly of Muslim Youth, a connection that provides a basis for mutual involvement and cooperation. Similarly, the IIFSO has close relations with the Muslim World League.

It was out of the IIFSO's experience of success that the WAMY was born. The WAMY was founded in 1972 in Riyadh, Saudi Arabia, at an international meeting of Islamic workers involved in youth activities and representatives of youth organizations. It was established to help youth organizations around the world implement their planned projects. It has been holding its international meetings about every three years and publishes a newsletter in Arabic and English, *Al-mustaqbil/The Future*. The headquarters of the WAMY is located in Riyadh and its regional offices are located in Jeddah (Saudi Arabia), Malaysia, Spain, Nigeria, and Kenya.

In keeping with its international outlook, the IIFSO has sought to maintain active communication not only with its various components and other Islamic organizations but also with international organizations. It has nongovernmental operation status with the United Nations. It participated in the World Youth Conference in Spain in 1985, in the Conference on Muslims for World Peace in 1987 in Baku, Azerbaijan, and in the International Conference on Youth Services in Chicago, sponsored by the United Nations in 1985. It took part in the U.N.'s Fifth Session of the High Level Committee on the Review of Technical Cooperation Among Developing Countries held in New York in May 1987, and an IIFSO representative attended the International Conference Against Drug Abuse in Vienna in 1987.

The IIFSO has participated in various national and international book fairs held in Cairo, Khartoum, Brussels, Washington, D.C., and several other American cities, Singapore, New Delhi, Riyadh, Abu Dhabi, Qatar, and Germany.

The IIFSO is active in promoting human rights throughout the world. It has lent its active support to human rights organizations focusing on problems in South Asia, North Africa, Eastern Europe, and the former Soviet Union. It took an early lead in the Peoples' Republic of China as soon as an opening for religious work seemed to appear. For several years, the IIFSO published *Al-akhbār* (The News) in Arabic and sometimes in English. A direct source of news about the Muslim world, it was an important source of information about the violation of the human rights of Muslim minorities.

[*See also* Youth Movements.]

BIBLIOGRAPHY

Altalib, Hisham. *Training Guide for Islamic Workers*. Herndon, Va., 1991.

The First 20 Years of IIFSO. Salīmīyah, Kuwait, 1989.

Toward a Global Islamic Brotherhood. Herndon, Va., 1987.

SAYYID MUHAMMAD SYEED

INTERNATIONAL ISLAMIC UNIVERSITY AT ISLAMABAD. In the wake of the islamization policy in Pakistan, a central institution for the coordination of this policy and for higher learning, the International Islamic University at Islamabad, was established. A Sharīʿah Faculty at Qa'id-i Aʿzam University was founded in 1979, but it could not meet the needs felt during islamization. In 1980, therefore, the Sharīʿah Faculty was upgraded into an Islamic University, functioning at first as a custodian of the Faiṣal mosque and mainly financed by the Saudi government. By moving into the cultural complex around the mosque, it became financially solvent. After the incorporation of several institutes and academies, the university acquired the status of a full-fledged International Islamic University (IIU) in 1985.

The IIU soon became a focal point for the dissemination of Islamic thought for Muslims in Pakistan, Central and Southeast Asia, and Muslim minority areas. Explicitly open to all classes and creeds, it aims to provide an intellectual base for and guidance in the process of islamization and the development of solutions to problems arising therefrom. It hopes to bring various existing Islamic identities into one common ideological platform for joint political and religious action and to eliminate the obstacles responsible for Muslims' schismatic differences.

This undertaking is, however, only possible with the moral and financial support of other Muslim countries and international organizations. Close academic collaboration with Egyptian, Saudi, and Malaysian governments and universities underlines the transnational character of the IIU. In 1990, cultural ties with the former Soviet Muslim Religious Board of Central Asia and

Kazakhstan were established as well. The composition of its leadership, teaching staff, and student body reflects this implicit "*ummah*-ization," which finds expression in international workshops and exchanges, scholarships, and a network of academic institutions. As an ideological body the university is formally exempt from state jurisdiction.

A conglomerate of different, already existing institutes, the IIU offers courses in Islamic law, *sharīʿah*, Islamic economics, *daʿwah*, *uṣūl al-dīn*, and Arabic. These institutes are as follows:

- The Faculty of Uṣūl al-Dīn (general Islamic studies)
- The Faculty of Sharīʿah, which conducts Sharīʿah courses at the national level for in-service judicial officers and public prosecutors, as well as for readers of the Friday sermons *(khuṭbah)*, leaders of prayers (*a'immah;* sg., *imām*), and teachers in religious schools *(mudarrisūn)*
- The Islamic Research Institute, in existence since 1960 and merged into the Islamic University in 1980. It is the research wing, and interprets the teachings of Islam within the context of the intellectual and scientific progress of the modern world
- The Institute for Social Studies, which soon became the International Institute of Islamic Economics. In its beginning stages, it is developing a body of Ph.D. graduates, with the help of the United States Agency for International Development, among others. It also organizes senior officers' training programs
- The Institute for Linguistics and Languages (Departments of Arabic and English). Arabic is taught in order to avoid the confusion and disunity in the Muslim world that arises from erroneous interpretations of the language of the Qur'ān; English is considered important for transnational communication
- The Institute of Daʿwah and Qirā'āt, now the Daʿwah Academy, which conducts Islamic leadership training camps for Muslims from Pakistan and other countries, (e.g., *a'immah,* community leaders, students, and army officers). It offers pre-university training to overseas candidates from Muslim minority countries and collaborates with the Regional Islamic Daʿwah Council for Southeast Asia and the Pacific, based in Malaysia. It also conducts correspondence courses, prepares area studies and literature for children, and has established translation and media sections.

As a federal corporation, the IIU is hierarchically structured, headed by the president of Pakistan, who appoints the rector and vice-chancellor. Administratively, the IIU is governed by a Board of Trustees consisting of Muslim scholars, technocrats, and educators primarily from Pakistan, but also from the Middle East, Southeast Asia, and international Islamic organizations. All academic matters are supervised by the respective Boards of Studies and the Academic Council, which in 1992 was chaired by an Egyptian.

In 1989–1990, the ten degree programs offered by the IIU, including economics, law, comparative religion, *uṣūl al-dīn,* Arabic, and the pre-university course at the Daʿwah Academy, were accredited and recognized by the University Grants Commission. The al-Azhar University has recognized the university's B.A. (Hons.) Uṣūl al-Dīn (Islamic Studies) only. [*See* Azhar, al-.]

Formally, the appointment of teachers is based on merit and commitment to Islam. Nearly half of the more than three hundred teachers and researchers originate in the Middle East, primarily Egypt. The majority of native teachers are not traditional scholars but possess Ph.Ds from foreign universities. They are paid from the university budget; overseas teachers are paid by the Egyptian government, the Rābiṭat al-ʿĀlam al-Islāmī (Muslim World League), Saudi universities, and from income accruing from endowments.

The composition of the student body is multinational as well. In 1991, out of more than a thousand students, approximately half were Pakistanis; the rest came from more than forty countries, chiefly from Muslim minority areas, Afghanistan, Southeast Asia (China, Indonesia, Thailand), Africa (Somalia, Kenya, Sudan), and the Middle East (Jordan, Turkey). Female students comprised about 7 percent of the total. Students are selected on merit and prior qualifications, which, in some cases, includes their traditional education. Places are reserved for foreigners, students belonging to deprived areas or low-income groups, and members of the armed forces. Self-sufficient students have better chances for admission; those with limited incomes are eligible for stipends. Residence is provided to all foreign students and to most Pakistanis for a nominal fee as is free medical care and transportation. More than half of the student body receives scholarships, approximately 60 percent of which are provided from abroad. A major portion of the stipends comes from the International Islamic Charitable Foundation (Kuwait), Zakat House Kuwait, and the International Scientific, Educational, Social and Cultural Organization. The majority of students are enrolled in law and *sharīʿah;* the next largest number study *uṣūl al-dīn*, Arabic, and economics. Female students are enrolled in LL.B (*sharīʿah* and law) and in *uṣūl al-dīn* only. If students do not complete their final examinations, they must repay all scholarship money received.

Since the IIU is considered an ideological production center, the conduct of its students and teachers is subject to rigorous supervision. They must follow accurately Islamic rituals, and participation in any political action or membership in any political party is strictly prohibited. Regular conduct reports are intended to guarantee the Islamic, apolitical and nonsectarian character of the institution. The introduction of required academic dress is in preparation as well. Thus, the university can be considered a custodian of the knowledge that produces ideologically sound Muslim leadership, in line with its universalizing *salafī* worldview.

In this context, the use of media is most important for the dissemination of Islamic learning, and several publication units publish contributions in different languages, for example, Urdu, Arabic, and English. A central library, comprised of the libraries of the different institutes and academies that have been incorporated, has a collection of more than 150,000 volumes as well as periodicals.

The IIU receives a regular grant from the government of Pakistan and also accepts donations from trusts and endowments; all capital held by any faculty or institute has been transferred to the university. Recently, the government allocated more than 700 acres of land for the university's permanent campus in Islamabad to meet growing demands.

[*See also* Universities.]

BIBLIOGRAPHY

No scholarly work on the IIU exists to date. All sources used for the article are, therefore, of an official nature:

Brohi, A. K. "Islamic University of Islamabad: Principles and Purposes." *Pakistan Studies* 1.2 (1982).

Government of Pakistan. *Islamic University, Islamabad: Annual Report, 1982–83*. Islamabad, 1984.

Government of Pakistan. *Islamic University, Islamabad: Vice Chancellor's Annual Report, 1982–83*. Islamabad, 1984.

Government of Pakistan. *Islamic University Calendar, 1985*. Vol. 1. Islamabad, 1985.

Government of Pakistan. *Islamic University Handbook, 1985–1986*. Islamabad, 1985.

Government of Pakistan. *International Islamic University Ordinance, 1985*. Islamabad, 1985.

Government of Pakistan. *Annual Report 1989/90 Session, International Islamic University*. Islamabad, 1991 (mimeo).

"The International Islamic University." *Pakistan Times*, Special Supplement, February 1992, pp. 6ff.

JAMAL MALIK

INTERNATIONAL ISLAMIC UNIVERSITY AT KUALA LUMPUR. Founded in 1983, the International Islamic University, Malaysia, seeks to permeate the teaching of all knowledge with Islamic values. The idea of establishing the International Islamic University (IIU) was first discussed on 12 January 1982 by the prime minister of Malaysia, Dr. Mahathir Mohamed at a meeting with the minister of education, the director general of education, and a few senior academicians. An amendment bill of the Universities and University Colleges Act of 1971 (Laws of Malaysia) was passed by Parliament, and given the Royal Assent in February 1983. This amendment allowed the International Islamic University, Malaysia, to be established outside the restrictions of the Rules and Regulations of the Universities and University Colleges Act of 1971 and to become international in nature with international cosponsorship and with ownership vested in a Board of Governors. The University is presently cosponsored by the Organization of the Islamic Conference and seven other Muslim countries in addition to Malaysia: Maldives, Bangladesh, Pakistan, Turkey, Libya, Saudi Arabia, and Egypt.

The university's objectives, among others, are:

> To re-establish, with Allāh's help, the primacy of Islam in all fields of knowledge consistent with the Islamic tradition of the pursuit of knowledge and truth, as reflected by those pioneering works of early Islamic scholars and thinkers that began with the teachings of our Holy Prophet Muḥammad (peace be upon him).
>
> To revive the ancient Islamic tradition of learning where knowledge was propagated and sought after in the spirit of submission to God (Tawḥīd).

Its philosophy of the integration of religious knowledge and worldly sciences, together with the vision of Islamization of human knowledge, were inspired by the recommendations of the first World Conference on Muslim Education held in Mecca in 1977.

As such, the university is not limited to Islamic theological studies but is a comprehensive professional institution of higher learning in which the teaching of all fields of knowledge is infused with Islamic values and the Islamic philosophy of knowledge. When it opened in 1983 with 153 students, it had two faculties, Laws and Economics, offering undergraduate degrees and two services centers, the Centre for Fundamental Knowledge and the Centre for Languages.

Dr. Abdul Rauf of Egypt served as rector for the first five years. In 1989 Dr. AbdulHamid A. AbuSulayman, former president of the International Institute of Islamic Thought in Washington, D.C., was appointed rector. With the support of the president of IIU, Anwar Ibrahim, who was then minister of education, he established a new faculty under the name of Islamic Revealed Knowledge and Human Sciences and departments covering Islamic studies, most of the social sciences, and the humanities. He also introduced the full credit-hour system in July 1990. Under this system, the class size has been kept small (averaging thirty-five students per class) to enable a more creative interaction between the instructor and students. Evaluation of the academic performance of students is based on regular tests and assignments, midterm examinations, and end-of-semester examinations. Students evaluate the academic staff at the end of each semester through the teacher efficiency rating system.

As of July 1992, the university offers a choice of undergraduate courses in law, business, accounting, economics, psychology, political science, history and civilization, philosophy, mass communications, English as a second language, Arabic as a second language, Islamic revealed knowledge and heritage, and sociology/anthropology. There are also masters and diploma courses available in various areas of Education as well as in English and Arabic as Second Languages. Masters' programs are offered in library and information science, economics, and revealed knowledge and heritage. The Faculty of Laws offers programs leading up to the Ph.D level. The university is expanding postgraduate courses to cover all disciplines available in its undergraduate program in order to develop the intellectual Islamic capacity of the students.

The next phase in the development of the university's undergraduate academic programs will see the establishment of the Faculty of Engineering, which will open in 1994, followed by one in architecture and one in the applied and basic sciences in 1995. The university also plans to establish a medical school, covering all the medical sciences including dentistry and nursing in Kuantan, Pahang, by 1998.

The original student body of 153 students grew to more than six thousand students in January 1992—3,071 undergraduate and 2,461 matriculation (pre-university) students. Postgraduate students now number 848 with 419 of this number enrolled in the Diploma of Education program. The university plans to increase gradually the number of international students to approximately 25 percent of the total student population. By July 1995, IIU will move to its permanent campus in Gombak, a suburb of Kuala Lumpur, which will have the capacity to accommodate a total of fourteen thousand students.

All professional courses are taught in English, but students are required to reach the level of advanced Arabic proficiency. Students taking the Sharīʿah, Arabic, and Revealed Knowledge courses must, of course, take them in Arabic, but their minor courses are offered in English.

The university has introduced a unique system of "double major": every student specializing in human and social science courses must take a minor concentration in a Revealed Knowledge discipline related to the major area of concentration. After receiving the first degree in the major discipline, it is possible for students to obtain another bachelor's degree in the minor area if they extend their studies another two semesters into a fifth year.

The staff of the university are committed to the goal of developing young men and women who are not only aware of contemporary problems and perceive the drawbacks of both the modern and the traditional approaches, but are also able to examine issues from Islamic perspectives founded on the principle of unity of revelation and reason, matter and spirit, the here and the hereafter.

[*See also* Education, *articles on* Educational Institutions *and* The Islamization of Knowledge; Universities.]

BIBLIOGRAPHY

International Islamic University. *University Handbook 1984/85*. Kuala Lumpur, 1984.

International Islamic University. *University Prospectus 1985/86*. Kuala Lumpur, 1985.

International Islamic University. *University Campus Master Plan Report*. Kuala Lumpur, 1991.

International Islamic University. *Undergraduate Prospectus 1993/94*. Kuala Lumpur, 1993.

Memorandum and Articles of Association of International Islamic University, Malaysia. Kuala Lumpur, 1983.

M. Kamal Hassan

INTERNATIONAL LAW. The expansion of Islam, territorial conquests, and the progressive formation of a Muslim empire that had its apogee between the eighth and ninth centuries led Muslim jurists to formulate a certain number of rules and standards that can be described as principles in the domain of international law. The primary sources of this law, and indeed of all *sharīʿah* (the divine law), are the Qur'ān and the *sunnah* (words and acts attributed to the Prophet). Secondary sources are essentially of two kinds: the consensus of the majority of the jurists *(ijmāʿ)* and analogy *(qiyās)*. The oldest Muslim code of law which refers to the *siyar*, or rules governing war and peace with non-Muslims, is probably the *Kitāb al-majmūʿ* of Zayd ibn ʿAlī (d. 738). Other jurists, such as Abū Yūsuf, al-Awzāʿī, Mālik ibn Anas, al-Wāqidī, and particularly al-Shāfiʿī, followed his example, devoting a portion of their works to questions relating to the law which today would be called international law. The great jurist Sarakhsī (d. 1090) wrote a lengthy commentary on those writings of al-Shāfiʿī that dealt with *siyar*.

At first, Muslim conquerors progressed very rapidly and undoubtedly believed that Islam would spread quickly throughout the entire world. Given this vision, the nature and form of eventual relationships with foreign powers were of little importance. However, from the ninth century onward, the conquerors' aim seemed increasingly unrealizable, and Islamic rulers were forced to accept the division of the world into two distinct realms: Islam and non-Islam. The acknowledgment of this division produced one of the founding principles of Islamic law. According to this vision, the world is divided into two territories: *dār al-Islām* ("realm of Islam"), where divine law governs, and *dār al-ḥarb* ("realm of war"), which temporarily evades the law of God, but which should be made to submit when the appropriate time comes.

Dār al-Islām is the ultimate Muslim realm, where the precepts of the true faith reign. In theory, *dār al-Islām* constitutes a group of unified territories, forming a single state, ruled by a single power and subject to the law of the one God. The substantial unity of *dār al-Islām* partakes as well of the universal and messianic character of the Islamic state. In fact, the legal concept of Islamic power rests on the direct continuation of religious belief and seeks the reunification of all men under the aegis of Islam. Thus, unlike modern international law, which recognizes the existence of a multitude of sovereign states, traditional Islamic law, like Roman law or the legal system of medieval Christendom, is based on the theory of the universal state.

The concept of *dār al-Islām* is linked to another notion fundamental to the Islamic vision, that of *ummah*, or the community of the faithful. According to Islam, it is religion that determines citizenship and not parentage or birthplace. According to this view, a Muslim who is in Islamic territory, even if far from his birthplace, can, if he is capable, fill any post, including political office. However, the idea of the *ummah* goes beyond the territory of Islam, in that there might be Muslim minorities who live outside of the *dār al-Islām*. Furthermore, non-Muslim religious communities can live in the heart of the Muslim world as protected minorities (*dhimmīs*) if they belong to the "people of the book" *(ahl al-kitāb)*, Jews, Christians, or members of other scriptural religions. *Dhimmīs* must pay a special tax *(jizyah)* and do not enjoy full civil rights. However, the government gives them protection and recognizes their right to govern themselves according to the conventions of their own community.

According to Muslim jurists, *dār al-Islām* and the rest of the world are in a state of war which will endure until Islam's eventual triumph over unbelief. This situation is justified by the existence in the Qur'ān of the notion of *jihād*, often incorrectly translated as "holy war." Literally, *jihād* means "effort," "endeavor," or "struggle," but in effect it implies the execution of an order from God enjoining Muslims to fight against the infidels in order to effect their conversion or their submission. However, *jihād* is not one of the five pillars of Islam. It is not a strict individual obligation, but a communal duty necessary to the defense and spread of Islam—hence the importance of the community's political/religious leaders in the call to *jihād*.

The Qur'ān repeatedly alludes to the duty to fight infidels, while also referring to the necessity for the war to be legally sanctioned and for its conduct to be lawful. Furthermore, many verses of the Qur'ān seem to characterize *jihād* as a defensive endeavor. However, there is a greater number of verses that urge armed struggle and make no distinction between offensive and defensive war. Be that as it may, the complex nature of the concept of *jihād* authorizes diverse interpretations. Thus, Muslim authors have offered varying and sometimes contradictory explications of it. Certain modernist and reformist nineteenth- and twentieth-century jurists have maintained that *jihād* should be understood in a spiritual rather than a military sense. Although this type of argument cannot be summarily dismissed, it must however be acknowledged that throughout history *jihād* has often signified the making of war. It must not be automatically concluded from this that Islam is a warlike religion. The concept of a just war is not unique to Islam, and in addition, Islamic law has elaborated rules helping to bring together Muslim countries with the non-Islamic world.

From the time when Muslims had to resign themselves to accepting the impossibility of the rapid realization of their ideal, that is, the foundation of a universal Islamic state, even if the state of war was maintained from a theoretical point of view, a new conceptual framework was necessary. With this aim in mind, some jurists recognized the existence of a third category of territories between *dār al-Islām* and *dār al-ḥarb: dār al-ʿahd* ("land of the covenant") or *dār al-ṣulḥ* ("land of truce"). In order not to clash with the fundamental principles of Islamic law, it was necessary to resort to a legal subterfuge (transformation of the non-Muslim state into a state that recognized Muslim suzerainty), while emphasizing the temporary aspect of the concept of *dar al-ʿahd.* From that point onward, various standards of peaceful relations were introduced, such as the principle of exchanging diplomatic missions. Until the end of the eighteenth century, Muslim sovereigns had not established permanent foreign embassies, but they often sent envoys on missions into neighboring countries and also received ambassadors from non-Muslim countries. In principle these delegations enjoyed diplomatic immunity, but there were occasions when one side or the other did not carefully respect this immunity.

The contacts between the Muslim world and the exterior world were also favored by the institution of *amān,* which is a safe-conduct guarantee granted to a non-Muslim by the government or even by an individual, authorizing travel in Muslim territory and yet exempting the traveler from restrictions imposed on *dhimmī*s. *Amān* can be extended to a group of people, and even to all citizens of a foreign country. In addition, Muslim sovereigns accepted rather quickly the signing of treaties with *dār al-ḥarb* countries, as well as the use of arbitration to resolve certain conflicts. The duration of treaties, however, was in principle limited. With arbitration, the cases submitted to this peaceful method of resolving disputes were more often technical than political.

The dualistic worldview, favored by Islam, and the hazards of history, were the bases for a certain number of rules of international law that until the mid-nineteenth century governed relations with the non-Muslim world. But this conceptualization assumes the unity of the Muslim world, whereas that world was divided into several parts. At the very time when the boundaries between Islam and non-Islam were established, differences in administrative and even legal practices between the various provinces were becoming more marked. Parallel to this development, and especially after the disappearance of the first Arab empire of the Umayyads (661–750), there were revolts and uprisings in surrounding regions. With the weakening of the ʿAbbāsid Empire (749–1258) and its progressive disintegration, autonomous principalities appeared. It was thus that independent dynasties trying to strengthen their authority and extend their territorial base emerged in all corners of the Muslim world. In the Mashriq (Arab East), the dismantling of the empire was followed by Turko-Mongolian invasions. Once islamized, the Turko-Mongolians in their turn founded new states. The end of the fifteenth century and the beginning of the sixteenth were marked by the formation of the Ottoman Empire, the Ṣafavid Empire in Persia, and the Mughal Empire in India. The founding of these new states, and above all the rivalries that grew up between them, introduced new elements of division in the heart of the Muslim world.

When all of these historical events are considered, it seems irrefutable that Islam was more distinguished by territorial pluralism over the course of centuries than by territorial unity, even if juridical fiction masked the reality of power relationships and of antagonisms between various political polities that shared the space of *dār al-Islām.* In reality, although only one single border was supposed to separate the Islamic world from the rest of the world, other demarcations developed which divided Muslim countries from one another. In practice, these administrative divisions, which were not meant to separate the faithful, effectively became boundaries between states. Thus, in the seventeenth century, Persians and Ottomans introduced the practice of drawing up treaties of precise delimitation of the borders between Muslim states. It was in this manner that the rules of Islamic international law, which originally had been applied to relations with non-Muslim states, were progressively extended, with some modifications, to the relations between Muslim states. However, official recognition of this extension was avoided by referring to the intrinsic unity of Islam and the Islamic world. With this aim in mind, each Muslim sovereign made a point to present himself more as a defender of Islam than as a prince holding sway over a clearly demarcated Muslim territory.

In the nineteenth century, *siyar* underwent internal transformations because of the fragmentation of the Muslim world, and changes in the practice of international law by Muslim states were added. These changes were the result of the intensification of relations with Europeans and the preeminence that Europe would henceforth take in international life. Two phenomena helped to introduce European notions of law into the Muslim milieu: colonial expansion, which either directly or indirectly affected most Muslim countries; and the increased involvement of some Muslim states, such as the Ottoman Empire, and to a lesser extent Persia, in the cooperative interplay of European nations. Concepts such as the state, national territory, sovereignty, borders, and the organization of international relations were from this time on seen in a new light. Later, decolonization and the recognition of the states' rights to their own natural resources contributed to the emergence in the Muslim world of fully independent states. These states wanted to be equal and thus similar to the other states of an international system born of the historical experience of the West and of the European tradition of international law.

The movement toward an international community founded on the concept of the plurality of states forced the Islamic theory of international law to undergo important transformations. Among these modifications the most significant are: the acceptance of the principle of peaceful relations and the renunciation of the principle of the state of war advocated by *jihād;* the acceptance of the idea of separation between religious doctrine and foreign affairs; and the explicit recognition of territorial sovereignty. Thus changes that began in the ninth century developed in the sixteenth within the Muslim world and intensified following the expansion of contacts with Europe, radically altered the very foundations of the Islamic concept of international law.

Although it can be said that at the end of the twentieth century the Islamic legal system and Western international law have moved closer together in an unprecedented fashion, one must not conclude that the classical concept of Islam has been totally lost in these matters. It is true that the idea of Islamic solidarity is largely a myth, yet it still endures in the minds of many Muslims. In fact, the traditional vision underlies certain actions of Muslim states and is at the root of certain contemporaneous doctrines. With regard to the desire for unity, for example, the creation of the Organization of the Islamic Conference in 1972, which brings together almost fifty Muslim countries, is obvious proof of a desire among Muslims for convergence. Admittedly, this entirely conventional intergovernmental structure has nothing in common with the creation of a great Islamic state, but it is, however, the only modern international organization created by specific reference to a religion.

Contemporary doctrines involve the fundamentalist discourse on international relations. The fundamentalists follow classical theory, on the one hand rejecting all modifications which that theory has undergone over time, and on the other hand infusing it with modern, anti-imperialist, Third World revolutionary jargon. They demand simultaneously the strengthening of the faith within the community, unity in that community, and the expansion of the boundaries of *dār al-Islām.* From their point of view, Islam has today, more than ever, a moral mission in the universal scheme, and not to accomplish that mission would constitute a renunciation of the very foundations of Islam.

Since the institution in 1979 of an Islamic republic in Iran, the revolutionary Islamists have for the first time had the opportunity to put into practice their ideas about international law. They have consistently challenged the standards which govern modern international relations, not hesitating to resort to unanimously condemned acts, such as taking hostage American diplomatic personnel, condemning a British novelist to death for blasphemy, and rejecting human rights as a secular concept of the Judeo-Christian tradition. However, they have rarely hesitated to use all of the resources of that same international law when it suited their interests. With time, noticing the counterproductivity of some of their decisions, the Islamists in power in Iran have tried to conform to the habits and customs of present-day international relations. Nevertheless, their ideological position remains fundamentally unchanged, and they still do not recognize any legal tradition other than the most conservative Islamic one.

[*See also* Dār al-Ḥarb; Dār al-Islām; Dār al-Ṣulḥ; Diplomatic Immunity; Diplomatic Missions; International Relations and Diplomacy; Jihād; *and* Law, *article on* Legal Thought and Jurisprudence.]

BIBLIOGRAPHY

Artz, Donna E. "The Application of International Human Rights Law in Islamic States." *Human Rights Quarterly* 12 (May 1990): 202–230.

Bahar, Sarvenaz. "Khomeinism, the Islamic Republic of Iran, and International Law: The Relevance of Islamic Political Ideology." *Harvard International Law Journal* 33.1 (Winter 1992): 145–190.

Djalili, Mohammad-Reza. *Diplomatie islamique: Stratégie internationale du khomeynisme*. Paris, 1989.

Khadduri, Majid. *War and Peace in the Law of Islam*. Baltimore, 1955. A classic work on the subject.

Lewis, Bernard. *The Political Language of Islam*. Chicago and London, 1988. A systematic study on the relationship of Islam and politics.

Maḥmaṣānī, Ṣubḥī. "The Principles of International Law in the Light of Islamic Doctrine." *Recueil de Cours* 117 (1966): 201–328.

Piscatori, J. P. *Islam in a World of Nation-States*. Cambridge, 1986. One of the best works on the territorial pluralism of Islam.

Rechid Ahmed. "L'Islam et le droit des gens." *Recueil des Cours* 62 (1937): 375–506. Although old, a still interesting text.

Reisman, M. H. A. "Islamic Fundamentalism and Its Impact on International Law and Politics." In *The Influence of Religion on the Development of International Law*, edited by Mark W. Janis, pp. 107–134. Dordrecht, 1991. A stimulating comparison of the views of several religions.

MOHAMMAD-REZA DJALILI
Translated from French by Elizabeth Keller

INTERNATIONAL RELATIONS AND DIPLOMACY. Muslim writers argue that the international and diplomatic realms are incorporated in the very comprehensiveness of Islam, and analogues to the concepts of international relations exist in Islamic history. The Prophet's compacts with the Medinans (623–624) as well as with the Jews and Christians of the Arabian Peninsula (e.g., in Najran and ʿAqabah) are presented as examples of treaties, and the despatch of envoys to the rulers of Abyssinia, Byzantium, Egypt, and Persia are regarded as evidence of early Islamic diplomatic practice. Despite the assumption that *jihād* against infidels or the unfaithful is an unremitting obligation, the Prophet's agreement with the Meccans in 628, the Ḥudaybīyah treaty, has become the prototype of a truce (though not lasting peace) between combatants. Following this precedent, the fifth Umayyad caliph, ʿAbd al-Malik (r. 685–705) concluded a truce with the Byzantine ruler and even paid tribute to him in the interest of securing one flank in order to turn against Muslim rebels on the other flank.

Since the time of Caliph Hārūn al-Rashīd (r. 786–809), the ʿAbbāsids routinely concluded treaties with foreigners for a number of reasons—in particular, in order to ransom their prisoners of war. They also regularly and lavishly received foreign envoys in Baghdad as representatives of fellow sovereigns. Around the year 800, for example, Caliph Hārūn received an ambassador from Charlemagne and sent one in return to Aix-la-Chapelle. Even during the Crusades, there were several formal treaties with Christian princes, such as the agreement in 1192 between Saladin (Ṣalāḥ al-Dīn, r. 1186–1193) and the English king Richard I, which facilitated Christian pilgrimage to the Holy Land.

The Politics of Conflict and Competition. Polemicists often disregard this early history and later events and conclude that Islam is preeminently concerned with the creation of a universal Muslim community and is intolerant of those who are not Muslims. The Qur'ān and the traditions of the Prophet (*ḥadīths*) have many references to the need and desirability of fighting the unbelievers, often to the bitter end. This is one dimension of the *jihād* which is especially emphasized in the case of polytheists: the Qur'ān urges the believers to fight them "wherever you find them" until they repent or are defeated (surah 9.5), and a *ḥadīth* records the Prophet as saying, "I am ordered to fight until they [the polytheists] say 'there is no God but Allah.' " *Ahl al-kitāb* ("People of the Book"), other monotheists such as Jews or Christians, are also to be fought until they pay a special tax and are "subdued" or "humbled" (9.29). Generally, the *ḥadīths* tell us that "whoever fights to make Allāh's Word superior fights in God's cause," and that even a single journey for this purpose is "better than the world and all that is in it."

This expansionist zeal accounts for the ʿAbbāsid elaboration of a bifurcated and conflict-ridden world—*dār al-Islām* (the Islamic realm of peace) and *dār al-ḥarb* (the non-Islamic realm of war). Moreover, within the realm of Islam, non-Muslims who pay *jizyah* (tax) in exchange for protection are to suffer certain disadvantages and are not to be treated equally with Muslim citizens. For example, they are not allowed to display their religious symbols openly or to carry arms—the former condition applied to non-Muslim Western military forces stationed in Saudi Arabia during the Persian Gulf crisis of 1990–1991. [*See* Dār al-Islām; Dār al-Ḥarb; Jizyah.]

Yet it would be facile to conclude that a built-in antipathy exists between the Muslim and non-Muslim worlds. One reason why such a conclusion is doubtful is that Islamic political theory is more complex than that outlined above. Rather, the scriptural sources also articulate a view that is at odds with the image of *jihād* as an instrument of Islamic militancy and expansionism. This alternative view is of a tolerant, nonviolent Islam that accommodates itself to the reality of political pluralism and non-Muslim centers of power. Indeed, there is to be no compulsion in religion (Qur'ān 2.256). It is important for Muslims to commit their wealth and very lives (61.11) to "strive" ceaselessly against falsehood, but combat constitutes the lesser form of "striving" (*jihād*, literally) and should be avoided if at all possible. Rather than relying on the sword, Muslims are to use their hearts, tongues, and hands for the good of their own souls (29.6) and to build the just society. Fighting is enjoined primarily for self-defense: "Fight in the cause of God those who fight you, but do not be aggressive, for God does not love aggressors" (2.190). Muslims may even, in certain circumstances, conclude a treaty with the enemy, which would take precedence over any obligations to fellow Muslims: "If they [Muslims] ask for help in the matter of religion, it is your duty to help them, except against a people with whom you have a treaty" (8.72).

The assumption of inherent conflict between the Muslim and non-Muslim worlds also ignores a variegated pattern of war and alliance, competition and cooperation, across the Islamic centuries. Although they may not have conceded that Western states were equal to them, Muslim states regularly entered into territorial agreements and concluded peace, as in an Ottoman treaty with Russia in 1739. In the sixteenth century, Muslim practice closed the earlier debates among Muslim jurists as to the length of a truce between Muslims and non-Muslims. Invoking the Ḥudaybīyah treaty, jurists of at least two legal schools argued that such agreements could last no more than ten years. But the treaty of 1535 between the Ottoman ruler Süleyman the Magnificent (r. 1520–1566) and Francis I of France endorsed the idea of "valid and sure peace" between them for their lifetimes, and from this point historical experience redefined the theoretical approach.

Compatibility of Islam and Nationalism. It is undeniably true that Islamic political theory places substantial emphasis on the idea of worldwide community. There is no distinction among the believers except in piety (Qur'ān 49.13), and the fraternity of the faith will inevitably extend to incorporate all peoples. Other bonds of loyalty, such as to tribe or race, must be replaced by common submission to the one God, and as the influential Indian/Pakistani writer Abū al-Aʿlā Mawdūdī (1903–1979) maintained, the Islamic community (*ummah*) can only be "universal and all-embracing, its sphere of activity . . . coextensive with the whole of human life" (*Political Theory of Islam*, Lahore, 1960, p. 26). Yet one can also point to indicators of an Islam that recognizes, implicitly and explicitly, ideological, political, and territorial divisions. One reading of the Qur'ān, for instance, seems to sanction such divisions. It says that God divided men into nations and tribes for a purpose—to come to "know each other" (49.13)—and the divisions of language and color "are signs for those who know" (30.22). At another point, the Qur'ān says, "If God had so willed, He would have made them one community" (42.8).

The texts of the various schools of law also accept territorial divisions to which the law must bend (such as when dividing the spoils of war), and medieval thinkers came to accept that there was pluralism within the Islamic realm as well as between it and the non-Islamic realm. Al-Ghazālī (1058–1111), for example, raised the possibility that caliphs owed their position to decisive, noncaliphal centers of power. Ibn Taymīyah (1263–1328) went further in stressing that because of Islam's essential religious unity, it need not have only one political regime, and Ibn Khaldūn (1333–1406) endorsed the idea of pluralism by arguing that the rise and decline of political units is natural and in accord with the divine plan.

Parallel to this intellectual adaptation is the flexibility that Muslim statesmen have displayed over the centuries. In addition to maintaining regular diplomatic relations with non-Muslims, Muslims have come to accept the reality of separate sources of power within the Islamic *ummah* itself. An early example is the dispute between ʿAlī (c.600–661), the Prophet's son-in-law and the fourth caliph, and Muʿāwiyah (c.602–680), the governor of Syria and later the first Umayyad caliph, over legitimate succession to the caliphate. The text of the arbitration between them is remarkable for the way it rendered the two equal, and territorially based, sovereigns.

Subsequent Islamic history confirms this tendency of the Muslim sovereign to concede that other, nominally subject, rulers possessed commensurate or superior power. The Sunnī Ottomans were unable to force the submission of the Persian Shīʿah, but in 1590, the two concluded a treaty whereby the Persians agreed to stop cursing the first three caliphs and to cede large amounts of territory to the Ottomans. It was a religious and territorial compromise that Shāh ʿAbbās (r. 1588–1629) felt that he had to make if he was to prevent the Uzbeks from moving into his empire from the east.

In the twentieth century, Muslim-Western relations and inter-Muslim relations came indisputably to be measured by the yardstick of territorial and national sovereignty. From the end of the eighteenth century onward, European colonialism had implanted itself, in turn fostering the growth of indigenous nationalisms. Local elites realized that they needed to rid themselves of imperial control, while simultaneously protecting their own prestige and power against rival claimants to postcolonial leadership. They recognized that, to achieve both goals, they had to play by the rules of the international game. Playing this game first involved securing recognition from the great powers, then enhancing the sense of national uniqueness in the greater society of nation-states.

In inter-Muslim relations, the norm roughly from the 1930s to today has been to acknowledge the spiritual and cultural unity of the faith while insisting on preserving the reality of territorial divisions. Most bilateral agreements and every multilateral one make clear that the form of association contracted must not be seen as a derogation or qualification of the individual sovereignties of the contracting parties. The Arab League Pact (1945), although "desirous of strengthening the close relations and numerous ties which link the Arab states" (Preamble), is committed to preserving the independence and sovereignty of its members (Article 2) and requires that "each member state shall respect the systems of government established in the other member states and regard them as the exclusive concerns of those states" (Article 8). The Charter of the Organization of the Islamic Conference (OIC, 1972) unambiguously affirms that the organization is based on the principles of "respect of the sovereignty, independence and territorial integrity of each member State" (Article 2b) and of "abstention from the threat or use of force against the territorial integrity, national unity or political independence of any member State" (Preamble).

Many Muslims, such as Mawdūdī, however, have rejected the institution of the nation-state as alien and destructive of pan-Islamic union. Ayatollah Ruhollah Khomeini (1902–1989) was the most notable recent exponent of this view, and Principle 11 of revolutionary Iran's constitution commits the government to promoting Islamic unity. Yet for all his wider aspirations, Khomeini implicitly accepted the legitimacy of the territorial state of Iran when it was under attack by the Iraqis during the Iran-Iraq War (1980–1988). In effect, Iran was validated as the vanguard of the Islamic Revolution. The demands of political and economic intercourse, the development of an intellectual and pragmatic consensus, even if unenthusiastically so, and the pervasive influence of modern, nationalized educational systems have combined to make nationalism and the nation-state a powerful presence on the modern Muslim landscape.

Transnationalism of Islam. Political Islam is clearly an international phenomenon, but as international politics has become more complex and is now more accurately described by the concept of world politics, so too Islam is more than simply international. This is demonstrated by the activities of the Muslim Brotherhood (al-Ikhwān al-Muslimūn), which, although rooted in individual countries, operates simultaneously in Egypt, Sudan, Syria, Jordan, the Palestinian territories, even South Asia, among other countries—and exhibits some degree of linkage among them. The Muslim Brotherhood is a nonstate actor, operating in the state environment and exercising an impact on the state system. [*See* Muslim Brotherhood.]

Nonstate actors are an increasingly prominent aspect of modern Islamic life, particularly in the field of *daʿwah* (the "call" to Islam). Such organizations as the Egyptian Muslim Brotherhood, but also the Palestinian Ḥamās (Ḥarakat al-Muqāwamah al-Islāmīyah, the Islamic Resistance Movement), are involved in providing a range of social welfare activities through such institutions as health clinics, schools, and housing cooperatives, which by their very efficiency and popularity provide a powerful challenge to the legitimacy of state institutions. Although their bases are securely located in their own national territories, there is no doubt that assistance in the training of activists, significant funding, and intellectual stimulation are derived from external sources.

Governments often seek to channel popular Muslim sentiments by sponsoring their own *daʿwah* organizations. The Islamic Propagation Office in Iran is concerned with various dimensions of the export of the Iranian revolutionary message, but like its counterpart in Libya, the Islamic Call Society (Jamʿīyat al-Daʿwah al-Islāmīyah), the degree of success can be overstated. The Saudi government, with its sponsorship of the Muslim World League (Rābiṭat al-ʿĀlam al-Islāmī), has been more successful in facilitating the spread of a nonrevolutionary but nonetheless assertive strain of Islamic activism. Through such journals as *Al-rābiṭah* (*The League;* English edition: *Journal of the Muslim World League*) and *Al-nahḍah* (*The Renaissance,* the journal of the allied Regional Islamic Daʿwah Council of Southeast Asia and the Pacific), transnational *daʿwah* groups provide a potent communications and information network. Such a network encourages the mobilization of Muslim opinion on broader, Pan-Islamic issues, such as the *jihād* against the Soviet authorities in Afghanistan, the plight of Muslim minorities in places such as the Philippines and Bulgaria, and the future of Muslim Bosnia in the former Yugoslavian federation. [*See* Islamic Call Society; Muslim World League; Regional Islamic Daʿwah Council of Southeast Asia and the Pacific.]

The Islamic transnational network was also instrumental in generating and sustaining the negative reaction to the publication in 1988 of Salman Rushdie's novel *The Satanic Verses,* which was widely regarded as blasphemous of the prophet Muḥammad. Britain and Iran broke off diplomatic relations over the affair and the European Community and the Organization of the Islamic Conference (OIC) put it near the top of their agendas. But in addition to these foreign policy results, the Rushdie affair generated more complicated politics.

One of the distinctive features of the Rushdie affair was the replication of Saudi-Iranian rivalry on British soil. The Union of Muslim Organizations and the Islamic Cultural Centre in London were instrumental in the early stages in bringing Muslim objections to the book to the attention of the government and public. Although these groups fall under Saudi patronage, the South Asian Jamāʿat-i Islāmī was also important in mobilizing the Islamic Foundation in Leicester to the cause. However, with the Ayatollah's *fatwā* (edict) against Rushdie in February 1989 amounting to a death sentence, the situation changed rapidly. The Saudis and their supporters in Britain appeared to become defensive, and Iranian-inspired groups, such as the Muslim Institute, grew vociferous in their attacks on Rushdie, the British government, and Saudi Arabia.

The vast majority of British Muslims were not as directly concerned with the Saudi-Iranian competition. But other rivalries were of consequence, mainly those between Barelwīs, who follow holy men (pirs) and are mystical in orientation but not entirely adverse to political activity, and Deobandīs, who tend toward scripturalism in spiritual matters and apoliticism in worldly matters. Deobandīs have been especially adept at disseminating their message of inner reform, owing largely to the Jamāʿat Tablīgh, a singularly devoted missionary movement with branches in many countries.

Partly because of the lack of full assimilation into British economic, social, and political life, and linguistic pluralism and ethnic rivalries (for example, among Mirpuris, Pathans, Bangladeshis, and Gujaratis), there is both a built-in competitiveness in British Muslim communities, reflected in identifiably sectarian mosques and schools, and a susceptibility to outside influences. These latter include pirs, Barelwī or Deobandī *ʿulamā',* the Jamāʿat Tablīgh, and Jamāʿat-i Islāmī from the Indian subcontinent. To a considerable extent, therefore, the politics of British Muslims, particularly during the Rushdie affair, has reflected the Pakistani or Indian politics of Islam. Correspondingly, the reactions of Muslim groups in Britain and their support for the *fatwā* had an impact on the factionalized politics of Iran. [*See* Barelwīs; Deobandīs; Tablīghī Jamāʿat; Jamāʿat-i Islāmī; Rushdie Affair.]

The ability of Muslims to live within national frontiers in the modern world and, at the same time, the presence of Islamic concerns in both domestic and foreign policy suggest that the vast majority of Muslims are seeking—for the foreseeable future—to create Muslim states, not to supplant the nation-state system itself. Pan-Islamic aspirations have not disappeared, certainly, and the ability of Muslim transnational organizations, ideologies, and communications to permeate national borders testifies that a greater degree of Muslim community is now apparent. One London-based Islamist has spoken of the need of British Muslims to "plug into the global grid of the power of Islam" (Kalim Siddiqui, speech on "Generating Power without Politics," 14 July 1990), and concretization of the *ummah* is indeed emerging in various ways. But as the simultaneous acceptance of territorial and political pluralism and the manifold differences of policy and conviction among Muslim states, nonstate actors, and movements indicated, Pan-Islamic political integration remains limited. International and transnational relations are thus likely to continue to evolve not only between the Muslim and non-Muslim worlds, but within the Islamic realm itself.

[*See also* Daʿwah, *article on* Institutionalization; Diplomatic Immunity; Diplomatic Missions; Human Rights; International Law; Nation; Organization of the Islamic Conference; Pan-Islam; Ummah.]

BIBLIOGRAPHY

AbūSulaymān, ʿAbdulḤamīd A. *The Islamic Theory of International Relations: New Directions for Islamic Methodology and Thought.*

Herndon, Va., 1987. Lucid analysis by modernist Muslim writer on the Islamic framework of diplomacy and interstate relations.

Abū Zahrah, Muḥammad. *Al-ʿalāqāt al-duwalīyah fī al-Islām* (International Relations in Islam). Cairo, 1964. Study of how Islamic norms have allowed Muslim states to engage in a fully functioning international practice.

al-Ahsan, Abdullah. *Ummah or Nation? Identity Crisis in Contemporary Muslim Society*. Leicester, 1992. Expert on the Organization of the Islamic Conference calls for the strengthening of Muslim identification with the *ummah* and the consequent enhancement of the OIC.

Dawisha, Adeed, ed. *Islam in Foreign Policy*. Cambridge, 1983. Valuable as a unique study of the roles that Islam plays in the foreign policy of several Muslim countries.

Djalili, Mohammad-Reza. *Diplomatie islamique: Stratégie internationale du khomeynisme*. Paris, 1989. Informed analysis of the international ideas and practice of the revolutionary regime in Iran.

Hamidullah, Muhammad. *Muslim Conduct of State*. 4th rev. ed. Lahore, 1961. One of the standard expositions on Islam's compatibility with the norms of the international system.

Hurewitz, J. C., ed. *The Middle East and North Africa in World Politics: A Documentary Record*. 2 vols. 2d ed. New Haven and London, 1975. Indispensable collection of treaties and other documents that present the record of Muslims' adaptation to prevailing international practice in their relations with both non-Muslims and fellow Muslims.

Iqbal, Afzal. *Diplomacy in Islam*. Lahore, 1977. Study of the Prophet's diplomatic practice.

Khadduri, Majid. *War and Peace in the Law of Islam*. Baltimore and London, 1955. Classic work on the theory of Islamic international law and international relations.

Landau, Jacob. *The Politics of Pan-Islam: Ideology and Organization*. Oxford and New York, 1990. The best study of how Pan-Islam emerged in the context of the transition from the imperial to the national age in the late nineteenth and early twentieth century.

Moinuddin, Hasan. *The Charter of the Islamic Conference: The Legal and Economic Framework*. Oxford, 1987. Detailed study of the structure of the OIC, placed in a larger discussion of Islamic ideas on international law and cooperation.

Proctor, J. Harris, ed. *Islam and International Relations*. London, 1965. An early examination of many of the enduring issues, such as nationalism and Pan-Islam, by eminent scholars.

Rajaee, Farhang. *Islamic Values and World View: Khomeyni on Man, the State and International Politics*. Lanham, Md., and London, 1983. Particularly insightful study of Khomeinist international thought written by a student of both Islamic political thought and international relations theory.

Saleem, Musa. *The Muslims and the New World Order*. London, 1993. Deals with a broad range of subjects, but last quarter of book directly deals with such matters as relations between rich and poor countries (including within the Islamic world) and such contemporary problems as Bosnia and Kashmir.

Schulze, Reinhard. *Islamischer Internationalismus im 20. Jahrundert: Untersuchungen zur Geschichte der Islamischen Weltliga*. Leiden, 1990. Excellent study of "international" Islam, particularly the activities of the Saudi-backed Muslim World League.

Siddiqui, Kalim. *Beyond the Muslim Nation-State*. London, 1980. Vigorous attack on the idea of Muslim national pluralism by a leading British Muslim who, more recently, has become the leading figure in "the Muslim Parliament" in Britain.

JAMES P. PISCATORI

INTIẒĀR. Until ʿAlī Sharīʿatī (d. 1977) introduced it in his presentation of Shiism, the term *intiẓār* (lit. "waiting"), had not been used as a specific concept in Islamic theology. In a general sense, every creed with an eschatological dimension inspires believers to *wait* for the end of time, the coming of the Savior, the resurrection of the dead, the final judgment. Since Shiism conveys a specific messianic notion of the end of time and stresses the Twelfth Imam's role of restoring justice and peace in this troubled world, it lays emphasis on the value of waiting. More than Sunnī Islam, Shiism is turned toward the future; it looks forward to the accomplishment of the work of salvation that the prophets and the imams initiated.

Accessory beliefs have developed the interest of Shīʿīs in the events to come at the end of time. Traditions ascribed to the imams themselves vividly depict the Twelfth Imam's return *(rajʿah)* to the earth before the final resurrection to avenge the house of the Prophet of all the prejudice and violence inflicted on it throughout the ages. This specific belief has been rejected in modern times by Sharīʿat Sangalajī (d. 1946), an Iranian theologian who has been anathematized by most of his colleagues. But ʿAbdol-Karim Ḥā'eri Yazdi (ʿAbd al-Karim Ḥā'iri Yazdi, d. 1937), the leading Shīʿī authority of his generation, issued a *fatwā* (formal legal opinion) to attenuate the importance of this doctrine. In fact, he allowed believers the possibility of denying it.

Sharīʿatī's point of view tends to be ideological rather than purely theological. According to him, Shiism has two faces. As a religious culture, it is mainly used to preserve the privileges of powerholders, and it deserves the name Ṣafavid Shiism (Tashayyuʿ-i Ṣafavī) after the Ṣafavid dynasty that took power in Iran in 1501 and established Shīʿī Islam as the state religion. The other face of Shiism is the pristine religion of the imam ʿAlī ibn Abī Ṭālib, called ʿAlid Shiism (Tashayyuʿ-i ʿAlavī), which primarily represents a struggle for justice. Thus Sharīʿatī's militant conception of Shiism rejects any passive acceptance of the present state of iniquity and oppression. As examples of this passivity, he noted the traditional rites of mourning for the Imams and the common attitude of Shīʿīs who take refuge from their adverse situation in a dream of future life after the Return of the Imam and thus, in fact, legitimate injustice. For Sharīʿatī, rejecting the old order of oppression and striving for the reestablishment of a just society are part of the Imams' legacy. "Waiting" means to say no to the status quo, concluded Sharīʿatī in a 1971 lecture called "Waiting: The Religion of Refusal." Very optimistic in his view on the future of humanity, he adopted a Marxist confidence in "historical determinism," but interpreted it in an Islamic way: the contradictions between classes and nations inevitably lead to the victory of those who have faith over those who are corrupted by their wealth and misuse of power. Thus a traditional Islamic passivity toward the future and compromise with iniquity is turned to an active participation in the new world of salvation.

[*See also* Imam; Mahdi; Messianism; *and the biography of Sharīʿatī.*]

BIBLIOGRAPHY

Sachedina, A. A. *Islamic Messianism: The Idea of the Mahdi in Twelver Shiʿism.* Albany, N.Y., 1981. Good summary of classical Shīʿī eschatology.

Sharīʿatī, ʿAlī. *Tashayyuʿ-i ʿAlavī va Tashayyuʿ-i Ṣafavī.* Collected Works, vol. 9. Tehran, 1359/1980.

Sharīʿatī, ʿAlī. *Ḥusayn vāris-i Ādam.* Collected Works, vol. 19. Tehran, 1360/1981. Contains the 1971 lecture, "Waiting: Religion of Refusal" ("Intiẓār: Maẕhab-i iʿtirāẓ").

YANN RICHARD

IQBAL, MUHAMMAD (1877–1938), Indo-Pakistani political and religious writer and poet. The poet-philosopher of Islam and Pakistan was born on 9 November 1877 at Sialkot, a border town of the Punjab. Iqbal's grandfather, Shaykh Muḥammad Rafīq, had left his ancestral village of Looehar in Kashmir not long after 1857, as part of a mass migration of Kashmiri Muslims fleeing brutal repression under the British-backed Hindu Dogra rulers installed in Kashmir in 1846. Although the family never returned to Kashmir, the memory of the land and its people was never erased from the mind of Iqbal, and he remained dedicated to the principle of self-determination for the people of Kashmir.

Life. Iqbal's father was born in Sialkot and worked as a tailor and embroiderer. His parents raised Iqbal in a profoundly Islamic environment. His older brother, ʿAṭāʾ Muhammad, married the daughter of a retired soldier who secured his son-in-law a position in the army, and after a few years he entered the engineering school at Rurki. He then rejoined the army as an engineer. ʿAṭāʾ Muhammad's success paved the way for Iqbal's progress later.

In Sialkot Iqbal finished high school and then joined the Scotch Mission College, subsequently named Murray College. He completed two years there and then went on to the Government College in Lahore, fifty miles away.

By this time Iqbal had acquired a good education in Urdu, Arabic, and Farsi under the guidance of Sayyid Mīr Ḥasan (1844–1929), who had been profoundly influenced by the Aligarh Movement of Sir Sayyid Aḥmad Khān (1817–1898). Under Sayyid Mīr Ḥasan's care, Iqbal's poetic genius blossomed early. He taught Iqbal the mechanics of classical Urdu and Persian poetry; Iqbal then found a master of Urdu poetry in Navāb Mīrzā Khān Dāgh (1831–1905), a fine poet who was poetic preceptor to Niẓām Mīr Maḥbūb ʿAlī Khān of Hyderabad. Iqbal was now on the road that was destined to bring him success and international fame; however, the year of his high school graduation laid the foundation of the personal unhappiness that was to mar much of his life. In 1892 his parents married him to Karam Bībī, the daughter of an affluent physician in the city of Gujerat. Two children were born to the couple, but soon differences began to develop and finally became intolerable. Iqbal married again and also had two children with his second wife; they were Dr. Justice Javid Iqbal and Munirah Banu.

At the Government College in Lahore Iqbal graduated *cum laude* and was also awarded a scholarship for further study toward a master's degree in philosophy. Two years later (1899) he won a gold medal for the unique distinction of being the only candidate to pass the final examination. By far the most pervasive influence on Iqbal's intellect at the Government College was that of Sir Thomas Arnold, an accomplished scholar of Islam and modern philosophy. In Arnold, Iqbal found a loving teacher who combined a profound knowledge of Western philosophy and a deep understanding of Islamic culture and Arabic literature and helped to instill this blending of East and West in Iqbal. Arnold also inspired in Iqbal the desire to pursue higher graduate studies in Europe.

In May 1899, a few months after Iqbal received the master's degree in philosophy, he was appointed the Macleod-Punjab Reader of Arabic at the University Oriental College of Lahore. From January 1901 to March

1904 Iqbal taught intermittently as assistant professor of English at Islamia College and at the Government College of Lahore.

In 1905 Iqbal went to Europe, where he studied in both Britain and Germany. In London he studied at Lincoln's Inn in order to qualify at the bar, and at Trinity College of Cambridge University, where he enrolled as a student of philosophy while simultaneously preparing to submit a doctoral dissertation in philosophy to Munich University. The German university exempted him from a mandatory stay of two terms on the campus before submitting his dissertation, "The Development of Metaphysics in Persia." After his successful defense of the dissertation, Iqbal was awarded a doctorate in philosophy on 4 November 1907. The dissertation, which was published the following year in London, was dedicated to Sir Thomas Arnold, his former teacher. In Cambridge, Iqbal came under the influence of the neo-Hegelians John McTaggart and James Ward. Two outstanding Orientalists at Cambridge, E. G. Brown and Reynold A. Nicholson, also became his mentors; the latter translated Iqbal's Persian masterpiece *Asrar-i Khudi* when it was first published at Lahore in 1915.

Iqbal was never at home in politics, but he was invariably drawn into it. In May 1908 he joined the British Committee of the All-India Muslim League. With one brief interruption Iqbal maintained his relationship with the All-India Muslim League throughout his life.

When Iqbal came back from Europe in 1908 after earning three degrees in Britain and Germany, he embarked simultaneously on three professional careers as an attorney, college professor, and poet. At length, however, the poet and philosopher won out at the expense of the professor and attorney, although he continued to be active to some degree as a political leader.

Iqbal was elected a member of the Punjab Legislative Assembly for a period of four years from 1926 to 1930 and soon emerged as the political thinker among the unionist politicians led by Sir Fazal-i Hussain. In 1930 the All-India Muslim League invited him to deliver a presidential address, which became a landmark in the Muslim national movement for the creation of Pakistan.

The opportunity for another journey to the West was provided by the second (1931) and third (1932) London Round Table Conferences, called by the British government to consult with Indian leaders on the problems of constitutional reforms for India. In February 1933 Iqbal was back in Lahore. Seven months later Muḥammad Nādir Shāh, the king of Afghanistan, invited him to visit Kabul along with Sayyid Sulaimān Nadvī and Sir Sayyid Ross Masood. The Afghan king wanted him to advise his government in the establishment of a new university and in utilizing the best of modern Western and traditional Islamic values in the reorganization of higher education; however, not much is known about the educational recommendations of Iqbal and his associates.

After his return from Afghanistan, Iqbal's health steadily deteriorated. His intellect remained sharp, however, and during this time he conceived many new projects, including proposed studies on Islamic jurisprudence and the study of the Qur'ān. During this period Iqbal also invited a younger Muslim scholar, Sayyid Abū al-Aʿlā Mawdūdī, to the Punjab, where he began to publish his well known journal, *Tarjumān al-Qur'ān.* Iqbal had hoped that Mawdūdī would become a modernist scholar who would update Islamic ideas. After 1947 Mawdūdī moved to Lahore and involved himself in the struggle for power in Pakistan.

By 1938 Iqbal's health had sharply declined, and he died on 20 April. He was buried to the left of the steps leading to the Badshahi Mosque in Lahore; construction of the present mausoleum on his grave was started in 1946, the marble being provided by the government of Afghanistan.

Religious and Political Thought. Iqbal's life was spent exclusively under British colonial rule, during which Muslims in the Indian subcontinent were profoundly influenced by the religious thought of Shāh Walī Allāh (1703–1762) and Sir Sayyid Aḥmad Khān (1817–1898). Shah Walī Allāh was the first Muslim thinker to realize that Muslims were encountering a modern age in which old religious assumptions and beliefs would be challenged. His monumental study *Ḥujjat Allāh al-bālighah* provided the intellectual foundations for updating Islam. Sir Sayyid, who lived through the life of the last Mughal emperor and then survived the unsuccessful war for independence in 1857, also profoundly influenced forty-one years of British rule when in 1858 the British East India Company was abolished and the British Crown assumed responsibility for the administration of the Indian empire.

After 1857 Sir Sayyid Aḥmad Khān's movement came to be known as the Aligarh Movement. It attempted to update Islam, popularize Western education, modernize Muslim culture, and encourage Muslims to cooperate with the British government in order to gain a fair share in the administration and political framework of India under British guidance. This intellectual legacy of Shah

Walī Allāh and Sir Sayyid Aḥmad Khān was inherited by Iqbal.

Iqbal's philosophical and political prose works are actually very few. Most notable among them are the following three works. *The Development of Metaphysics in Persia* (Cambridge, 1908) was originally a dissertation submitted to Munich University. *The Reconstruction of Religious Thought in Islam* (Lahore, 1930) was a collection of seven lectures delivered in December 1928 in Madras. Iqbal took three years to compose these lectures and considered them reflective of his mature philosophical and rational approach to Islam. He expected the younger generations to follow him in a responsible *ijtihād*, the interpretation of the Qur'ān and the *sunnah* and the formation of an entirely new opinion by applying analytical deduction. Iqbal had hoped to lay the groundwork for religion and science to discover mutual harmonies that would enable Muslims to learn modern sciences and use technology to improve their material existence. Finally, his *Presidential Address to the Annual Meeting of the All-India Muslim League, 1930* is a very extensive review of the interaction among the British, the All-India National Congress, and the All-India Muslim League, from the perspective of a Muslim thinker who was anxious about the political and cultural future of Muslims in the Indian subcontinent. Iqbal here expounded the concept of two nations in India. Subsequently this address came to be known as the conceptual basis for the state of Pakistan, although the name "Pakistan" is not used by Iqbal. On the contrary, Muslim nationalism is emphasized, giving shape and content to the national liberation movement of Muslims in India. Iqbal stressed the necessity of self-determination for the Muslims: "I'd like to see the Punjab, Northwest Frontier Province (NWFP), Sindh and Baluchistan, amalgamated into a single state. Self government within the British empire or without the British empire, and the formation of a consolidated Northwest Muslim Indian State appears to have to be the final destiny of the Muslims, at least of Northwest India."

Intellectually, however, Iqbal was not an enthusiastic supporter of nationalism, and especially nationalism among Muslims. He attempted to resolve this dilemma in a letter to Jawaharlal Nehru, his younger contemporary, writing:

> Nationalism in the sense of love of one's country and even readiness to die for its honor is a part of the Muslim faith; it comes into conflict with Islam only when it begins to play the role of a political concept and claims . . . that Islam should recede to the background of a mere private opinion and cease to be a living factor in the national life. Nationalism was an independent problem for Muslims only in those countries where they were in the minority. In countries with a Muslim majority, nationalism and Islam are practically identical, but in countries where Muslims are in the minority, their demands for self-determination as cultural unification is completely justified. ("Reply to Questions raised by Pandit Jawaharlal Nehru," in S. A. Vahid, ed., *Thoughts and Reflections of Iqbal*, Lahore, 1964.)

Iqbal composed his poetry in both Persian and Urdu. His six Persian works include *Asrār-i khūdī wa Rumūz-i bīkhūdī* (Secrets of the Self and Mysteries of Selflessness, 1915), *Payām-i Mashriq* (Message of the East, 1923), *Zabūr-i ʿAjam* (Scripture of the East, 1927), *Javīd-nāmah* (Book of Eternity, 1932), *Pas chih bāyad kard, ay aqvām-i sharq* (What Should Be Done, O Nations of the East, 1926), and *Armaghān-i Ḥijāz* (A Gift of the Hejaz, 1938). His Urdu works, which are primarily responsible for his popularity in Pakistan as well as in India, are *Bang-i darā* (Voice of the Caravan, 1924), *Bāl-i Jibrīl* (Gabriel's Ring, 1935), and *Ẓarb-i Kalīm* (The Rod of Moses, 1936). Poetry, like visual art, is susceptible to varied interpretations; consequently his admirers, relying primarily on his poetry, have variously attempted to prove him a Pakistani nationalist, a Muslim nationalist, a Muslim socialist, and even a secularist.

Before Iqbal Indian Muslim political thought was primarily concerned with their own community. For instance, to Sir Sayyid love was like a pyramid; at the top was the noblest form of love—love for the universe. This kind of love, however, "was unattainable." In the middle was love for those who "share human qualities with us." For Sir Sayyid, this was far too elusive a quality to be comprehended. He reasoned that at the bottom of the pyramid is placed the love of nation, "which I understand and I am capable of." Iqbal's intellectual evolution was the reverse of Sir Sayyid's. In his early works, Iqbal was absorbed in himself, agonizing over his personal disappointments. His emotional horizons then expanded to include India, particularly the Indian Muslims and the larger world of Islam. Then his love enveloped mankind, and at a still later stage it changed into a passionate involvement with the universe. Despite his commitment to the concept of a separate Muslim state, he remained a philosophical humanist, and humanism was truly his message.

Relations with Jinnah and Emergence of Pakistan. Iqbal remained a steady supporter of the founder of Pakistan, Mohammad Ali Jinnah. During 1936–1937 Iqbal wrote eight letters to Jinnah, emphasizing the partition of India into two states; however, during the 1920s when Jinnah was still groping for coexistence with the All-India National Congress, Iqbal opposed Jinnah's policies.

Reluctantly but steadily Iqbal had supported the establishment of a separate Muslim identity in the Indian subcontinent, while to the British and the Congress he often extended tactical cooperation. In the 1920s Jinnah was willing to compromise with the Congress by abolishing separate electorates for Muslims in the provincial legislatures. Jinnah had agreed with the President of the Congress on 20 March 1927 to accept the joint electorates under certain conditions. Muslim seats in the central legislature were to be no less than one-third of the total seats. This agreement came to be known as the Delhi Proposals. In May 1927 the Punjab Muslim League, under the leadership of Mian Muḥammad Shāfiʿ, Mian Faẕl-i Ḥusain, and Iqbal, denounced the Delhi Proposals. The Punjab's opposition seriously weakened Jinnah's bargaining position with the Congress, who nevertheless participated in the All Parties Conference from 12 February–15 March 1928, which produced the revisions of the Nehru Report. This granted Muslims only 25 percent of the legislative representation. The Congress adopted the Nehru Report and decided to initiate a policy of nonviolent noncooperation with the British if they did not accept it by 31 December 1929.

This reflected the Congress's determination to defy the British government for not including an Indian in the Simon Commission, which was established to make recommendations for future constitutional reforms in India. The appointment of the Simon Commission split the All-India Muslim League into two factions, one led by Jinnah and Kitchlew and the other by Mian Muḥammad Shāfiʿ and Iqbal. The Shāfiʿ League met in 1928 in Lahore, rejected the Delhi Proposals, and offered cooperation to the Simon Commission.

At Calcutta in 1928, the Jinnah League disavowed the Punjab Muslim League, adopting the Delhi Proposals and accepting the Nehru Report subject to four amendments; all four proposed amendments were rejected by the Congress. The Jinnah League was thus in a position of being repudiated by the Congress and simultaneously alienated from significant Muslim opinion. The split in the ranks of the Muslim League did not end until 1934, when Jinnah was finally elected president of the united Muslim League.

In the interim period, 1930–1934, Iqbal provided the ideological leadership articulating the Muslims' demand for a separate Muslim state. It is in light of this political split within the ranks of the League that Iqbal's presidential address of 1930 should be examined. The Allahabad address formulated the two-nation theory, which Jinnah finally accepted when he presided over the Muslim League's annual meeting in Lahore in 1940. He then demanded that India should be partitioned and that Muslim states should be created in the northwest and the east. Even though Iqbal was by no means a skillful politician, he nevertheless must be seen as a political mentor of Jinnah in regard to the creation of Pakistan.

[*See also* Aligarh; All-India Muslim League; India; Muslim League; Pakistan; *and the biographies of Aḥmad Khān, Jinnah, Mawdūdī, and Walī Allāh.*]

BIBLIOGRAPHY

Aziz Ahmad. *Studies in Islamic Culture in the Indian Environment*. Oxford and New York, 1964.

Beg, Abdulla Anwar. *The Poet of the East: The Life and Work of Dr. Sir Muhammad Iqbal*. Lahore, 1939.

Iqbal, Muhammad. *The Reconstruction of Religious Thought in Islam* (1930). Lahore, 1960.

Malik, Hafeez. *Iqbal: Poet-Philosopher of Pakistan*. New York, 1971.

Rushbrook, William L. F., ed. *Great Men of India*. Bombay, 1941.

Saiyidain, Khwaja Ghulam. *Iqbal's Educational Philosophy*. Lahore, 1945.

Schimmel, Annemarie. *Gabriel's Wing*. Leiden, 1963.

HAFEEZ MALIK

IRAN. Iranians have always called their country Iran (Land of the Aryans, or "noble people"), but outsiders long used the name Persia (Parsa; Gk., Persis), referring to Pars, now Fars, the southern part of the country. The name Persia remained in use until 1935, when the government in Tehran formally requested the world community to use the name Iran.

Iran has one of the world's oldest civilizations, dating back to about 2700 BCE, when the Elamites ruled over areas that include the present-day Khuzistan Province in southwest Iran and adjacent areas to the north and east. Indo-Europeans, migrating from the east, did not dominate the Iranian plateau until the Iron Age, about 1300 BCE. The Kingdom of the Medes, centered at Ecbatan (modern-day Hamadan), ruled the plateau and areas of the west and southwest from 728 to 559 BCE. During this time, other Indo-European peoples, such as the Scythians, crossed into the western plateau from the Caucasus Mountains. The Achaemenid (559–330 BCE), Parthian (247 BCE–226 CE), and Sassanian (224–651) dynasties secured their rule over areas of Iran, as well as regions of the Fertile Crescent, the Caucasus, Transoxonia, Afghanistan, and the Indian subcontinent. These dynasties left the indelible stamp of a recognizably Iranian civilization on the land.

The Arab invasion, beginning in 637, was a turning point in Iranian history. Zoroastrian beliefs, rooted in the idea of unceasing struggle between the forces of good and evil, were replaced by Islam, an austere, monotheistic religion. Although Iranians embraced Islam, they retained many of their native traditions. They also kept their language despite the fact that Arabic words pervaded it and the Arabic alphabet replaced the old script. For about a millennium, Iran became a territory of the caliphate and its successors, and Sunnism prevailed, except for local pockets of Shiism, as in the city of Qom (Qumm). During this period, Iranians contributed immeasurably to the development of literature, art, architecture, philosophy, mathematics, astronomy, medicine, and the Islamic sciences.

In 1501 a centralizing monarchy known as the Ṣafavid dynasty secured control over the plateau and its adjacent areas on behalf of Shīʿī Islam. Iran has since been the home of Ithnā ʿAsharī Shiism, although the short-lived Afshārid dynasty (1736–1747) tried to restore Sunnism. [*See* Ṣafavid Dynasty; Afshārid Dynasty.]

The Ṣafavid period witnessed the emergence of the Iranian *ʿulamāʾ* (community of religious scholars) as an important social force. Ṣafavid rule collapsed in 1722, later followed by the benevolent but brief Zand dynasty (1750–1779). The Zands were succeeded by the Qājār dynasty (1785/97–1925). The *ʿulamāʾ* increased their power significantly in the Qājār era. By the end of the nineteenth century, they had become key actors in the social movements and institutions of the country. [*See* Zand Dynasty.]

The Qājār dynasty, never matching the power of the Ṣafavids, was unable to withstand foreign military, economic, and political pressures or to overcome the ineptitude of its rulers. It was replaced by the Pahlavi dynasty, whose founder, Reza Shah and his son, Muhammad Reza, collectively ruled from 1925 to 1979. Their policies stressed modernization, westernization, and secular, integral Iranian nationalism. They resolved to uproot traditional practices and beliefs and to implant new ones from abroad. These policies led to the dynasty's overthrow and replacement by a clerical regime controlled by the *ʿulamāʾ* under the leadership of Ayatollah Ruhollah al-Musavi Khomeini (1902–1989; ruled 1979–1989). The Islamic Republic of Iran has undone many Pahlavi policies. Contrary to popular notions, however, it has retained many features of the state that it overthrew and has continued some of its predecessor's foreign policies.

Qājār Dynasty. The Qājār period was characterized by weak rulers, severe center-periphery problems, poor economic performance, and foreign domination. Iran lost territories to the Russians in 1804–1813 and 1825–1828. The British denied Iranian territorial ambitions in Afghanistan in the conflicts of 1836–1838 and 1856–1857. The Qājār shahs granted concessions and capitulatory rights to foreigners, allowing the British, Russians, French, Dutch, Swedes, Belgians, and Hungarians to dominate fields ranging from transport and banking to internal security. The most important concessions were the Reuters Concession of 1871 (mining, banking, and railroads), the Tobacco Regie of 1891, and the D'Arcy Concession of 1901 (oil). In 1891–1892 and in 1905–1909, largescale collective protests broke out in opposition to the shah's capitulations to foreign interests, as well as to his domestic policies and autocratic rule.

During the nineteenth century, the clergy became increasingly assertive. Explanations for this lie in certain doctrinal changes in Shīʿī Islam, as well as *ʿulamāʾ* reactions to historical events. As early as the medieval period, some clergymen, such as al-Muḥaqqiq al-Ḥillī (d. 1326), had claimed that the *ʿulamāʾ* collectively exercised *walaʾ al-imāmah* (guardianship) over the imamate of the Hidden Imam. In the late eighteenth and early nineteenth centuries a doctrinal dispute raged between those who maintained that the clergy were the deputies of the imam and those who believed that they were mere interpreters of the law with no special relationship to the Hidden Imam. The former group prevailed, signaling victory for the view that certain experts among the clergy (*mujtahids*) were entitled to exercise independent judgment *(ijtihād)* in determining the law in the absence of a clear textual rule in the Qurʾān or *sunnah*.

Controversy exists over whether the clergy, in their interventions against royal policies, were defending popular sovereignty, democratic ideas, the interests of the religious institution, or their own private ambitions. However, the consensus is that—whatever their private motives—many of the *ʿulamāʾ* did throw their moral authority behind challenges to foreign interference and the misrule of the shahs.

Some historians have held that the clergy harbored inherently antistate views on grounds that the doctrine of the imamate vests political rule exclusively in the imam, thus mandating opposition to secular rulers as usurpers. A more recent view is that Shiism has been apolitical ever since the sixth imam, Jaʿfar al-Ṣādiq (d. 765), suspended the political dimension of the imam's authority until some future unspecified date. This view holds that clergymen have not only not been doctrinally opposed to the state but in fact have supported it and called on it to protect Shiism and Shīʿī Muslims. Even Ayatollah Khomeini, who was later to abjure this position, argued in a work published in the early 1940s that the clergy had never opposed secular rulers in principle but merely asked the state to seek their counsel.

In 1891–1892 the clergy utilized the Shīʿī tax known as *khums* provided by believers, especially the bazaar merchants, to finance a collective protest against the Tobacco Regie. Later, most clergy demanded a constitution and a "house of justice" during the social movement known as the Constitutional Revolution of 1905 to 1909. Many *mujtahid*s at this time couched their admonitions to the Qājārs in the familiar terms of *ẓulm* (oppression of the justice of the Hidden Imam). The merchants were generally fed up with the influx of foreign goods and favorable terms extended to foreigners to sell their wares in Iran. Many had become declassed and others had been driven bankrupt by the competition of European entrepreneurs. Others also resented the shah's failure to repay their loans and hiring of a foreign financial expert to rationalize tax collection, suggesting further efforts to wrest money from them. At times, merchants took the initiative in challenging the state, while senior clergymen played a secondary role. [*See* Khums; Constitutional Revolution; Ẓulm.]

The constitutionalists, though victorious, still faced a problem that was to bedevil future constitutionalist movements, such as those of 1949–1953, 1960–1963, and 1978–1979: the relationship between revelation and positive law. Their opponents maintained that the promulgation of a fundamental law implied that *sharīʿah* (the holy law) had to be supplemented by manmade law, an idea they held as anathema. They additionally maintained that the creation of a Parliament suggested that sovereignty reposed in the nation, rather than Allāh, an intolerable *bidʿah* (heretical notion).

The Constitutionalists acknowledged these difficulties but stressed the urgency of upholding the principles of *ḥisbah,* the legal norm of holding an authority to account, and *al-nahy ʿan al-munkar* (prohibiting evil), both of which were ineluctable duties *(farḍ al-ʿayn/farḍ al-kifāyah)* of the Muslims as commanded by Allāh. Were Muslims to fail in such duties, they argued, the ruler's despotism could mortally endanger Islam itself. [*See* Qājār Dynasty.]

Pahlavi Dynasty. The Qājār period was known for the contrast between the shahs' claims to omnipotence and their actual weakness. By World War I, faced with external pressures and constant challenges to their authority by tribal chiefs, provincial governors, reforming bureaucrats, and obstreperous clergymen, the dynasty reached the brink of collapse. Iran narrowly escaped partition by Russia and Britain in 1907 and conversion into a British protectorate in 1919, in the latter case rescued by its parliament's refusal to back the prime minister's endorsement of the deal.

Under these circumstances, a military leader in the Russian Cossack Brigade, Reza Khan, seized power in 1921 and made himself Iran's strongman. In 1923, he installed himself as prime minister, and in 1925 he engineered the dissolution of the Qājār dynasty by the Constituent Assembly, followed in January 1926 by his formal elevation to the throne as Reza Shah Pahlavi. The dynasty's watchwords were Western-style modernization and centralization of authority. Reza Shah mounted successive military campaigns against the periphery, brutally suppressing the tribes, implanting a heavy-handed state bureaucracy, and forming a standing army loyal to him.

Reza Shah's reforms were modeled on those implemented by his neighbor and fellow ruler, Mustafa Kemal Atatürk in Turkey. Among them were wholesale legal changes involving the importation of European civil, criminal, and commercial law codes, and administrative centralization based on the French model. Most of the revenue from state monopolies (such as sugar and cement) were allocated to infrastructure development (especially roads and railroads) and to pay for his growing army. Unfortunately for him, private enterprise did not flourish, as financiers demurred from investing in new industries and instead directed their energies to speculation and real estate.

Reza Shah did try to secure more revenue from the British-owned and -operated Anglo-Iranian Oil Company (AIOC), but in the end, he contented himself in

1933 with a paltry 20 percent increase in revenues from annual profits. These added revenues were not invested in the economy, however, but were earmarked for the modernization of the shah's military forces.

Reza Shah's social reforms were more successful than his economic reforms, although advances were generally confined to the urban areas. The Qājārs had taken some halting steps toward establishing state schools, but Reza Shah's policies greatly accelerated their construction and the training of teachers to staff them. Admiring both the method and content of Western education, his government sponsored annual student missions to European universities to promote the study of law, economics, medicine, and engineering as an aid to the country's modernization. Tehran University, opened in 1934, was the first institution in what was to become a national university system. Significant gains were also made with the establishment of hospitals, clinics and laboratories, the testing of foods, and the inoculation of school children against debilitating diseases. Much less successful were the shah's efforts to abolish the veil, require the adoption of Western forms of dress, uproot the influence of the clergy in society, and streamline the operation of bureaucratic and business organizations. His policies did displace and declass the clergy, but this was only a temporary accomplishment.

The shah pointedly refused to allow any political liberalization or local autonomy. On the contrary, many who dared disagree with him, or even those whom he merely suspected, were either exiled, jailed, tortured, executed, or reported dead under suspicious circumstances. Perhaps the most famous individual to run afoul of Reza Shah's autocracy was Mohammed Mossadegh (Muḥammad Muṣaddiq), the future leader of the Iranian nationalist movement and prime minister from 1951 to 1953. Important clergymen, too, suffered from his tyranny. Moreover, the religious institution was not only deprived of most of its resources, but the original constitutional mandate in the 1906–1907 supplementary fundamental laws to create a committee of *mujtahid*s to ensure the conformity of parliamentary acts with Shīʿī law was never implemented.

In summary, Reza Shah tried to westernize the country through fiat. He gained the grudging respect of some, but his state was not securely rooted in any particular social class. The ease with which he was forced to abandon the throne underscores the narrow base of his rule.

Reza Shah, mindful of the weakness of the Qājārs in their submission to the great powers, was a nationalist who yearned to end foreign domination of Iran. As World War II approached, he permitted German agents to agitate against British interests in the south, especially in the oil fields. He followed this line not because he was sympathetic to Nazi ideology and conduct (although he undoubtedly admired what he perceived to be the Germans' "Prussian discipline") but for tactical reasons: to neutralize British influence. However, the German invasion of the Soviet Union in June 1941 sealed his fate. In September, British and Soviet troops invaded Iran and forced his abdication.

As with the first global war, World War II devastated Iran's economy. But politically this period witnessed liberalization. Political prisoners were released, the press grew freer, a more vital parliament emerged, and political parties arose. However, the landed aristocracy, a sodality left virtually intact by Reza Shah, retained its power and privileges. The new shah, Muhammad Reza Pahlavi, inexperienced and uncertain of himself, was a mere figurehead beholden to the British. Nonetheless, he succeeded in invigorating his ties with the army and, in 1949, oversaw the creation of a docile upper chamber (the Senate) in parliament that would support him against his critics, a move many regard to have been a virtual coup d'état.

Later in the same year a coalition was formed of nationalist groups known as the National Front, led by Mossadegh and ardently seeking the nationalization of the hated AIOC, a concession that symbolized British hegemony in Iran. As head of the oil commission in parliament, Mossadegh shepherded the nationalization bill to passage. At this point, the prime minister resigned, and public opinion compelled the reluctant shah to appoint Mossadegh as premier. The latter immediately moved to implement the nationalization decree and at once became involved in a bitter dispute with the British government, the AIOC's majority owner.

London, under American pressure, first tried negotiation, but it concomitantly embargoed Iranian terminals and threatened would-be purchasers with dire consequences. Mossadegh sought to overcome the embargo's effects by relying on nonoil exports, but these added only a fraction of the revenues needed to fund his programs. Meanwhile, his National Front coalition began to unravel, as leftists upbraided the prime minister for playing up to the Americans, while the clergy feared that he was falling under the sway of the communists. If Mossadegh had been able to secure revenues from other sources, he would likely have headed off catastrophe. The Truman Administration encouraged negotiation between Iran and Britain and generally distanced itself from London's hardline position. However, the Eisenhower Administration abandoned its predecessor's evenhandedness, believing that Moscow was controlling events in Iran. Furthermore, Eisenhower believed that an Iranian victory would set a precedent against Western oil interests, despite the fact that the precedent had already been set in the Mexican oil nationalizations of 1938. Eisenhower rejected Mossadegh's request for a loan and secretly planned with the British to overthrow him.

As the crisis unfolded, Mossadegh was also challenging the shah over authority to control the military. Mossadegh invoked the Constitution, whereas the shah cited his father's role in creating the army. With covert U.S. and British backing, a coup d'état was mounted against Mossadegh. Unfortunately for him, a key group within the National Front, led by Ayatollah Abol-Qāsem Kāshāni (Abū al-Qāsim Kāshānī; d. 1962), abandoned him and went over to the royalists. Kāshāni accused Mossadegh of being a dictator and condemned his request for extraordinary powers, his suspension of the 1952 elections in the countryside to prevent procourt landowners from winning any more seats, and his requirement that those opposed to him in the July 1953 referendum (on extending his extraordinary powers) must go to special precincts to vote no. Weakened by great-power pressures from without and internal crises from within, Mossadegh's government fell to the conspirators in August 1953. [*See the biography of Kāshāni.*]

This action earned the shah and the West the bitter hostility of many Iranians. Nothing seemed more symbolic of the shah's dependence on the British and Americans than their role in restoring him to his throne after his panic flight to Rome at the onset of the coup. Upon his reinstallation, the shah began to rule as an absolute autocrat. In the early 1960s, the Kennedy Administration urged him to implement reforms to gain popular support. He reluctantly agreed to do so only after it became clear to him that Iranian politicians in his own state bureaucracy, who were more responsive to the need for reforms than he, were gaining independent stature and popularity among the people.

The keystone of the shah's program was land reform, begun in the early 1960s and completed in the early 1970s. Scholars are divided as to the net impact of these reforms. Some believe that they merely served to replace the traditional aristocracy with the state in rural areas and were never intended to benefit the peasants. Others hold that a significant number of families obtained enough land to render them viable freeholders and thus to rescue themselves from destitution. Since the accuracy of these competing claims depends on the kinds of data one uses, it is not easy to make a conclusive assessment. It seems, however, that the great majority of landless peasants at the start of the reform (sometimes estimated to be half the population of rural Iran at that time) ended up still having no land.

During this period (1961–1963) professionals, intellectuals, elements of the bureaucracy, and the clergy and its supporters were engaged in collective protest. The secular opposition attacked the shah's violation of the Constitution in suspending parliament without calling for new elections. The clergy protested aspects of the monarch's reform program—the "White Revolution"—particularly women's suffrage and land reform. Some clergymen believed that any putatively meaningful reform the shah sponsored was a sham, because he would ensure its subversion to keep his power. Others, however, undoubtedly feared losing either their own lands or their administration of *waqf* (religious mortmain). Virtually all clerics maintained that enfranchising women would bring them into public arenas and endanger their modesty and virtue.

In March and June 1963 major clashes between students and the army broke out at Tehran University and the seminary in Qom, and Ayatollah Khomeini, then one of several *marjaʿ al-taqlīd*s, publicly and bitterly attacked the shah for unleashing his forces against the *ʿulamā'*, for his dependence on the United States, and for his commercial and intelligence cooperation with Israel. In October 1964, Khomeini openly accused the shah of restoring the hated capitulations by compelling his hand-picked parliament to pass, at Washington's request, an amendment to the Status of Forces Agreement with the United States. This amendment extended the protections of the 1961 Vienna Convention on Diplomatic Immunity to U.S. armed-forces personnel, their families, and any employees working for those families. The bill was so unpopular that even many pro-shah deputies could not vote for it, but enough deputies were rounded up to pass the measure by a narrow margin.

The regime, which had arrested Khomeini several times, reportedly was set to execute him this time but was stayed by the intervention of other *marjaʿ al-taqlīd*s. Instead, he was exiled, first going to Turkey, and then to Iraq, where he was to stay for about fourteen years. Although the regime survived the disturbances of 1961–1963, in retrospect they marked the beginning of the end of the Pahlavi dynasty.

Before its collapse, however, the monarchy appeared to be invulnerable. Economic growth in the 1960s and early 1970s was enviably high, reaching as high as 10 percent per year. The shah finally celebrated his rule by holding his coronation in 1967, investing his wife as empress and his son as crown prince. In 1971, scandalous amounts were spent on the so-called 2,500th anniversary of the Iranian monarchy. The shah apparently felt it necessary to match this pomp with commensurate military might, including the purchase of M1 tanks, spruance-class cruisers, hovercraft, and state of the art fighter planes. All of this cost enormous sums of money. On paper at least, Iran had become the most powerful regional actor.

The fragility of the system was its dependence on oil revenues. The huge increase in oil prices after the October 1973 Arab-Israeli War enabled the shah to purchase vast quantities of weapons but also so emboldened him that he discarded carefully crafted economic planning in favor of grandiose, showcase projects, such as nuclear reactors. The state's expenditures were so high that they fueled great rates of inflation and created major bottlenecks in the distribution system.

Meanwhile, a glut of oil worldwide led to a sudden decline in prices, caused a fiscal crisis, and forced the regime to borrow in the financial markets. The government alienated businesses by launching an antiprofiteering campaign and arresting merchants and businessmen. Inflation ate into workers' wages, although the regime repeatedly hiked wages to prevent collective action by labor. Compounding these difficulties were mounting attacks by guerrilla groups influenced by the writings and practice of Mao Zedong and Che Guevara. Although these attacks did not threaten the existence of the regime, they did contribute to the sense of its vulnerability. Increasingly, groups in society repudiated the cultural alienation spawned by the Pahlavis' westernization policies. The term *gharbzadagī* ("plagued by the West"), introduced by a well-known lay author from a prominent religious family, Jalāl Āl Aḥmad, became a particularly damaging charge that was used by the opposition to characterize these policies. It began to seem as though Iranians of all political hues were yearning for a reassertion of autochthonous values, which had so long been under official near-ridicule.

The shah's awareness that he was dying from cancer, coupled with mixed signals from Washington toward the regime, encouraged the ruler's liberal critics, especially the lawyers' syndicate, parliament, and the press. All these factors contributed to the collective protests of late 1977 to early 1979. But by themselves, they were insufficient to overthrow the shah.

From abroad, Ayatollah Khomeini continually berated the shah and his system for their dependence on the United States, ties to Israel, and domestic policies that he believed had impoverished the masses. At the same time, Khomeini's allies at home had established networks of mobilization and support for thousands of the urban poor population. Many of these had been driven into the cities from the countryside by land-reform policies that had failed to provide sufficient credit and other resources to the peasants to keep them on the land. Newly arrived migrants in these towns were absorbed not by the institutions of the Pahlavi state nor private enterprises but by the religious solidarity associations administered by the allies of Ayatollah Khomeini from neighborhood mosques.

When it came, the shah's overthrow was achieved not by the singleminded determination of any particular group in society but by the actions of a broad array of groups in response to a combination of factors. These included incompetent economic policies between 1973 and 1978, resentment over growing class disparities, the immobility of the state, policies that alienated industrialists and businesspeople, opportunities and willingness of key actors, especially the bazaar, to engage in largescale collective protest, inconsistent regime responses to such protest after January 1978, the organizational skills of the opposition, the willingness of the various groups in that opposition to unite behind the common objective of overthrowing the system, Khomeini's effectiveness as a leader of the opposition, and the shah's advancing cancer. [*For biographies of Reza Shah and Muhammad Reza Shah, see under Pahlavi.*]

Islamic Republic. The opposition's victory was secured with the return of Ayatollah Khomeini from exile in February 1979. The revolutionaries did not have a blueprint, but Khomeini had already revealed his general intentions in his book *The Mandate of the Jurist* (*Ḥukūmat-i Islāmī;* 1969–1970), which vindicated the clergy's right to rule and called for the implementation of Islamic law in all areas of life. He proceeded to appoint a provisional government, although effective power lay in his own hands and in that of the Revolutionary Council, which was made up mainly of his staunch supporters.

The provisional government was forced to resign in November 1979 when Prime Minister Mehdi Bāzargān was accused of plotting with the United States over the future role of the shah. Just weeks earlier, on 23 October, Washington, in a fateful decision, had agreed to permit the shah to enter the United States for medical care. Many Iranians rejected this explanation, feeling instead that the Americans were preparing to restore the shah to the throne the way they had done in 1953. In a defining moment of protest, students occupied the American embassy in Tehran on 4 November 1979 and held most of its diplomats hostage until Ronald Reagan was inaugurated as president in January 1981.

Although Khomeini had not ordered the storming and capture of the embassy, after the fact he realized that the hostages could be used for at least two purposes: to humiliate the United States, and to defeat the liberals in his own regime, people he saw as insufficiently committed to his policies. The key players in this power struggle were Prime Minister Bāzargān, President Abol-Hasan Bani Sadr, Ayatollah Muḥammad Ḥusayn Bihishtī (a powerful cleric who enjoyed Khomeini's total trust), and Bihishtī's numerous allies on the council. Bāzargān and Bani Sadr were accused of being pro-American liberals and were eventually removed from office. [*See the biography of Bāzargān.*]

The guerrilla groups, who had expected some reward for their role in the revolution, were the next targets of the regime. At first, the regime moved gradually against them through administrative measures designed to hamper their access to the media and encouraging street ruffians known as *ḥizbūllah* to attack their rallies and property. Later, blunter methods were used, including armed clashes, arrests, torture, and executions. In the middle of all this, Iraqi forces invaded Iran in September 1980, intending to overthrow Khomeini but instead unwittingly shoring up his support among Iranians. Ten months later, in a showdown with the regime, the main guerrilla group, Mujāhidīn-i Khalq, began to assassinate key clergymen in the government. Many of the top leaders, including Bihishtī, were killed, causing the regime to unleash a reign of terror, the bloodiest phase of which lasted for about a year and a half. [*See* Ḥizbullāh, article on Ḥizbullāh in Iran; Mujāhidīn, *article on* Mujāhidīn-i Khalq.]

In March 1979, a national plebiscite endorsed the restructuring of the political system from a monarchy to a theocratic republic. In December 1979, another referendum approved a new constitution that gave enormous powers to the *faqīh* (chief jurist; i.e., Khomeini). This aroused misgivings among certain senior clerics who opposed Khomeini's doctrine of *wilāyat al-faqīh* (guardianship of the jurisconsult) as usurping the prerogatives of the Hidden Imam and who believed that it could be invoked only during a temporary emergency when the normal institutions of the state had collapsed. [*See* Wilāyat al-Faqīh.] In January and March to May 1980, elections for the presidency and the parliament were held. By June 1981, Khomeini's supporters were in charge of all the crucial institutions of the state, including the judiciary, with its numerous revolutionary courts, both civilian and military. Using these powerful instruments, supplemented by Komitehs (revolutionary committees), the religious militia known as the Pasdaran (Sipāh-i Pasdarān-i Inqilāb-i Islāmī), quasi-governmental organizations known as *bunyād* ("foundations"), the Society of Combatant Clergymen, and a variety of so-called popular organizations, the government crushed its critics. Among these were eminent clergymen who had come to be distressed by all the bloodshed and violence. These senior clerics were threatened, placed under house arrest, and in one case tried for treason and "defrocked" (although there is no mechanism for defrocking clergymen in Islam). [*See* Komiteh; Sipāh-i Pasdarān-i Inqilāb-i Islāmī; Bunyād.]

Despite the triumph of the members of the central clerical tendency, who appropriated for themselves the name Maktabī (i.e., adhering to the true doctrinal line), cleavages continue to divide the ruling group. Although they are generally united on cultural issues, factionalism persists over economic matters. The key to these divisions is property ownership, nationalization of trade, and land reform. Despite all the efforts of Ayatollah Khomeini and his successors to pass final legislation on these matters, they remain unresolved. Bitter disputes have persisted among the officials of the state, the government, and other agencies over the proper role of the state in the economy. Recourse to scripture has not resolved these disputes, since the scriptures themselves are open to various interpretations.

Initially, few expected the rule of the clergy to endure, but as the years passed, the regime consolidated its power, marked by the regular holding of elections for the presidency and the parliament. The war with Iraq proved extremely costly to the government, but Ayatollah Khomeini and his supporters evidently saw its continued prosecution as necessary to maintain their hold on power, an advantage that outweighed the enormous costs. In order to retain the loyalty of its hardcore support, the urban poor and the petite bourgeoisie (small shopkeepers, artisans, smallscale merchants, the self-employed), the regime has favored them with ration cards and other services. It has also maintained a steady stream of criticism of Western *tahājum-i farhangī* ("cultural imperialism"), which resonates well with these constituencies, who believe that their very identities have been under attack by such things as Hollywood films, rock music, teenage dating, and even Western dress.

In July 1988, the government announced its acceptance of United Nations Security Council Resolution 598 of 1987, imposing a cease-fire in the Iran-Iraq War. Although the cease-fire was supposed to have been followed by exchange of prisoners of war, mutual withdrawal of troops behind existing international frontiers, and the initiation of an inquiry as to who was responsible for launching the war, none of these steps has yet been completed and some not even commenced. In June 1989, Ayatollah Khomeini died, and a month later, constitutional amendments were made to eliminate the post of prime minister. ʿAlī Akbar Hāshimī Rafsanjānī was elected president, while ʿAli Khamene'i was selected to replace Khomeini as *rahbar* (revolutionary leader).

However, since he was not even an ayatollah, the government had difficulty claiming that Khamene'i had the requisite stature to play the role of *faqīh*. Accordingly, arguments were advanced as to why the leader did not have to be a *marjaʿ al-taqlīd*, namely, that a *marjaʿ al-taqlīd* was likely to be a poor administrator, something the revolution could not afford. The press mounted a campaign to have Khamene'i recognized as a grand ayatollah *(āyat Allāh ʿuẓmā)*, but it soon dropped this and settled for the lesser appellation of ayatollah (which was still a promotion). In late 1993, the leader of the judicial branch of government, Ayatollah Muḥammad Yazdī, resumed the effort to have Khamene'i recognized as a *marjaʿ al-taqlīd* in the wake of the deaths of three grand ayatollahs—Abū al-Qāsim Khū'ī (Abol-Qāsem Kho'i), Shihāb al-Dīn Marʿashī Najafī, and Muḥammad Riẓā Gulpaygānī. It remains to be seen whether this effort will succeed, but if it does, it will set a precedent in view of the practice since the inception of *marjaʿīyat* in the nineteenth century of designating individuals as *marjaʿ al-taqlīd*s through popular acclamation. [*See the biography of Kho'i.*]

Iran remained officially neutral in the Gulf War of 1991, although it has refused to return Iraqi planes that had flown to Iran to escape destruction by coalition forces. Tehran has not, however, prevented smuggling over the Iran-Iraq frontiers, despite UN resolutions embargoing trade with Iraq. These frontiers, however, are notoriously immune to any attempt to stop all crossings along their entire length, no matter how much effort is exerted to this end.

The Islamic Republic's relations with most Arab states remain cool, and with Egypt in particular they are poor. The Egyptian and Algerian governments, as well as Washington, have accused Tehran of training radical Islamists from Sudan, Algeria, and Egypt in guerrilla warfare, with the purpose of overthrowing what the radicals consider un-Islamic governments and replacing them with Iranian style regimes.

In late 1993, tentative voices in the Parliament were raised calling for a restoration of ties with the United States. Even President Rafsanjānī, noting that much of the machinery and infrastructure of the economy, inherited from the monarchy, had been of American manufacture, called for limited economic ties with the United States. Meanwhile, trade relations with European countries seriously declined in 1992 and 1993 because of growing defaults on credits and loans on the part of the Islamic Republic. Thus Tehran's relations with the West overall remain troubled.

[*See also* Iranian Revolution of 1979; Shīʿī Islam; *and the biography of Khomeini.*]

BIBLIOGRAPHY

Abrahamian, Ervand. *Iran between Two Revolutions*. Princeton, 1982. Classic social history of nineteenth- and twentieth-century Iran.

Algar, Hamid. *Religion and State in Iran, 1785–1906*. Berkeley, 1969. Extended in-depth analysis of clergy-state relations under the Qājārs.

Arjomand, Said Amir. *The Shadow of God and the Hidden Imam*. Chicago and London, 1984. Detailed historical sociology of Shiism and the state from the perspective of Weberian sociology of religion.

Avery, Peter, et al., eds. *The Cambridge History of Iran*, vol. 7, *From Nadir Shah to the Islamic Republic*. Cambridge, 1991. Authoritative historical, cultural, and economic studies of nineteenth- and twentieth-century Iran.

Bakhash, Shaul. *The Reign of the Ayatollahs*. Rev. ed. New York, 1990. Political history of the early years of the Islamic Republic.

Bayat, Mangol. *Iran's First Revolution*. New York, 1991. Revisionist interpretation of the Constitutional Revolution, emphasizing the role of lower-ranking clergymen and nonreligious groups.

Bill, James A., and William Roger Louis, eds. *Musaddiq, Iranian Nationalism, and Oil*. Austin, 1988. Contains major research articles

on aspects of Iranian politics and economics during the early 1950s.
Chehabi, H. E. *Iranian Politics and Religious Modernism.* Ithaca, N.Y., 1990. Investigation of the rise of liberal Shīʿī thought in the late Pahlavi period, with a focus on the Liberation Movement of Iran.
Cottam, Richard W. *Nationalism in Iran.* Rev. ed. Pittsburgh, 1979. Examines the various strands of nationalist thought and practice in Iran under the Pahlavi shahs.
Dabashi, Hamid. *Theology of Discontent.* New York, 1993. Thorough investigation of the social thought of seven thinkers whose ideas were crucial to the Iranian Revolution of 1979.
Goodell, Grace. *The Elementary Forms of Political Life.* London and New York, 1986. Critique of the Pahlavi state's development policies under Muhammad Reza Shah.
Halliday, Fred. *Iran: Dictatorship and Development.* 2d ed. Baltimore, 1979. Examination of Iranian politics from the perspective of political economy and class structure, with a focus on the Pahlavi period.
Hooglund, Eric J. *Land and Revolution in Iran, 1960–1980.* Austin, 1982. Trenchant critique of the Shah's land reform policies.
Keddie, Nikki R. *Roots of Revolution.* New Haven, 1981. Overview of nineteenth- and twentieth-century Iranian history.
Lambton, Ann K. S. *Qajar Persia.* Austin, 1987. In-depth examination of nineteenth-century Iranian history.
Parsa, Misagh. *Social Origins of the Iranian Revolution.* New Brunswick, N.J., 1989. Detailed structural analysis of the Iranian Revolution of 1979, emphasizing particularly the role of the bazaar.
Zonis, Marvin. *Majestic Failure.* Chicago, 1991. A psychologically oriented analysis of Muhammad Reza Shah.

SHAHROUGH AKHAVI

IRANIAN REVOLUTION OF 1979. Like all great social upheavals, the Iranian Revolution of 1979 was many years in the making. Its effects will resound throughout history. In simple terms, the regime of Muhammad Reza Shah Pahlavi was overthrown by a coalition of opposition forces dominated by Shīʿī Muslim fundamentalists. The acknowledged leader of the revolution was Ayatollah Ruhollah Khomeini (1902–1989). The proximate causes of the revolution grew out of a complex interrelationship of social difficulties in Iranian society coupled with a breakdown in the personal health of the shah. However, in the minds of the people of the world the broad-based opposition between religious and secular forces was the central struggle of the revolution.

Although the specific events leading up to the ouster of Muhammad Reza Shah Pahlavi took place over a period of approximately one year before his departure from Iran on 16 January, 1979, the social conditions underlying the revolution spanned several centuries. An understanding of these social conditions is necessary to fully appreciate the course of events and their historical significance.

Early Religious-Secular Conflict. The Ithnā ʿAsharī (Twelver) branch of Shīʿī Islam had been the official state religion in Iran since the founding of the Ṣafavid dynasty in the sixteenth century. Shāh Ismāʿīl, founder of the dynasty, claimed that he was a direct descendant of the prophet Muḥammad through the Shīʿī line of leaders of the faith, called imams. Almost from the beginning of Ṣafavid rule, religious officials criticized the court for laxity in observance of Islam.

The shahs of the nineteenth-century Qājār dynasty found themselves in difficult military and economic conflict with European powers. They faced growing criticism by the clergy over territorial losses, foreign economic penetration, and incompetent government.

Since there was no constitution in Iran, the public had no direct voice in major public policy decisions. Nevertheless, religious leaders became alarmed at the marketing of Iranian patrimony and launched a series of public protests that forced the shahs to modify their activity. This protest was not limited to Iran. It spread to all Islamic lands owing largely to the efforts of the reformer Jamāl al-Dīn al-Afghānī (d. 1897), an Iranian who began to preach Islamic revival and resistance to European powers starting in the 1870s. In Iran, the public protest culminated in the Constitutional Revolution of 1905–1911, in which the Qājār monarch was forced to accept a constitution and a parliament. About twenty years later the dynasty collapsed. [*See* Qājār Dynasty *and the biography of Afghānī.*]

The rivalry between the new Pahlavi dynasty (1925–1979) and Khomeini had a long history. In 1921, Reza Khan, an army officer, emerged as a national leader in the tumultuous years following World War I. Ruhollah Khomeini was then entering theological studies in the shrine city of Qom south of Tehran. In 1926 Reza Khan formally crowned himself Reza Shah and established the Pahlavi dynasty. Khomeini was qualified as a mullah that same year.

Reza Shah ignored the new constitution and continued to rule by decree. Nevertheless, he launched a series of drastic reforms in Iranian life designed to modernize the nation. Reforms in dress, education, and law were far reaching. Many of the most drastic reforms were directed at the religious establishment. Religious institutions were placed under the control of the state, thus depriving the clergy of a major source of power and income. Many public protests, supported by the clergy against these reforms, were ruthlessly suppressed by the government.

In September 1941 Reza Shah was forced to abdicate by the Allied powers for his pro-German sentiments. He was succeeded by his young son, Muhammad Reza. At this time, Khomeini launched his first attack against the Pahlavi regime, denouncing their reforms with a tract entitled *Secrets Exposed*. Over the next thirty years Khomeini came to espouse the view that the mullahs should not just teach and advise; they should play an active role in governing the country to assure that religion would always serve as the basic guide to public life. In essence, the legitimate rule of the absent twelfth imam would be carried out by a *wilāyat al-faqīh* ("regency of the chief religious jurisprudent"), who would govern until his arrival on earth. This doctrine was controversial even among religious scholars. [*See* Wilāyat al-Faqīh.]

Khomeini continued to oppose the throne at every turn. In 1964 he was exiled by the shah for his public opposition to legislation that would exempt U.S. military personnel and their dependents from prosecution for any crime committed in Iran. He was already acclaimed as grand ayatollah at this time, a fact that prevented his outright execution. After seven months in Turkey, he settled in the Shīʿī holy city of Najaf, Iraq. From this location he continued to issue pronouncements against the Pahlavi regime to a growing group of supporters.

The National Front. Other secular oppositionists with claims to leadership also arose in the years following World War II. Chief among these was a coalition of parties known as the National Front, established in 1949 and led by Mohammad Mossadegh. No friend of the Pahlavis, Mossadegh had been a member of parliament at the time Reza Shah came to power in 1926 and had openly opposed ratifying him as shah. The National Front espoused many of the revolutionary ideals of the later Islamic reformers, such as limiting the powers of the shah and ending foreign domination. However, it did not advocate Islamic dominance of government.

The popularity of the National Front brought Mossadegh to power as prime minister in 1951. He came into conflict both with religious leaders and with the shah, who tried to oust him from office. The shah had underestimated his support, however, and was forced temporarily to flee. The United States and Great Britain, which had initiated the attempt to oust Mossadegh, largely because they feared communism in Iran, restored the shah to power two days later. This act established the United States as the chief foreign interventionist in Iranian affairs for all groups opposed to the monarchy.

Another important opposition group was the Mujāhidīn-i Khalq ("People's Warriors"), established in 1965 from other similar opposition groups. Their doctrine combined Islamic religious commitment with socialist doctrine. [*See* Mujāhidīn, *article on* Mujāhidīn-i Khalq.]

Prelude to Revolution. The United States continued active support of the shah. It anointed him as one of the protectors of Western interests in the Persian Gulf and sold Iran large supplies of advanced weaponry to support an increasingly powerful military sector. The shah, for his part, launched in 1963 a massive economic and social reform program known as the White Revolution that was designed to change every aspect of Iranian life. The program was predicated on fashionable Western economic models of the 1960s which promised economic "takeoff" if GNP growth could be sustained at 7 percent or better for a period of years. For Iran this growth was developed through a time-honored tradition: foreign investment in partnership with the throne and other economic elites.

In 1972 Britain withdrew its military from the Persian Gulf, and the United States began to arm Iran even more seriously. Then, in 1973 Iran and Saudi Arabia led the Organization of Petroleum Exporting Countries (OPEC) in a massive price increase in crude oil. This gave Iran far more income to fuel both its military and economic development.

Following the oil price increase of 1973, Iran's economy began to reel out of control. GNP growth continued unabated, but the profits were limited only to the top echelons of society. The shah finally achieved the elusive goal which had been pursued since the days of the Qājār shahs—financial independence from the population as a whole. In 1959 oil revenues contributed only 9.7 percent of Iran's total GNP. By 1974, the share had risen to 47 percent, and by some estimates the government was receiving fully 80 percent of its revenues from oil by 1978. Since those in power were not elected, these funds gave them almost unlimited license in the exercise of their power.

Consequently, the shah and his largely technocratic ministries turned the nation into a private economic laboratory. Real advances were made in education and in the development of roads and public utilities. Nevertheless, life became uncomfortable, as the population was poked and prodded in interminable experiments to decrease inflation, increase productivity, and improve social indicators. The traditional population was shocked by the sudden appearance of dress and public behavior that they deemed indecent. One noted social critic, ʿAlī Sharīʿatī (1933–1977), accused the regime of "Westoxication" *(gharbzadagī)* in the pursuit of Euro-American modernity at any social price. [*See the biography of Sharīʿatī.*]

By 1975 the increase in GNP topped 70 percent in real market prices, but inflation had begun to make itself felt at a rate exceeding 60 percent. In the next year the inflation rate topped the growth rate, causing negative real growth of about 2 percent. Agricultural production, lagging nearly 1 percent behind the birth rate (2.3 vs. 3.2 percent) went into real decline. For the first time in its history, Iran became a net importer of meat and grains. Ordinary Iranians, particularly those on fixed incomes, or on rigidly limited government salaries, were beginning to suffer. Housing costs were rising at yearly increments exceeding 100 percent. As a final blow, the new government of Jamshīd Amūzgār (August 1977) cut off the substantial subsidies to the clergy and religious institutions that had been instituted by the former prime minister, Amīr ʿAbbās Huvaydah. It is noteworthy that the shah in exile identified this act as the mistake that caused his downfall.

All of these acts alienated large sections of the traditional population. This gave the religious establishment its opening, and the revolutionary exhortations of Ayatollah Khomeini began to take hold throughout the population.

The Revolution. The beginning of the end for the shah began on 9 January 1978, when theology students in the city of Qom began a protest against a pseudonymous article published in the newspaper *Iṭṭilāʿāt* accusing Ayatollah Khomeini of licentious behavior and crimes against the state. The author was widely thought to have been Minister of Information Daryūsh Humāyūn. The demonstration met with violent confrontation by the police. Several students died. In accord with Islamic custom mourning ceremonies for the dead were held at forty-day intervals. Each of these mourning ceremonies turned into a public demonstration against the government, which was again confronted by the police or the military, resulting in more fatalities. Quite predictably the bulk of the protesters were young unemployed males in the large cities, and the protests were underwritten and financed from the traditional market, or bazaar.

Protests increased throughout the spring and summer. On 7 September 1978, the shah declared martial law and a ban on all demonstrations. Unfortunately, word of this decree had not spread. A demonstration at Jaleh Square in Tehran was confronted by the military, and a large number of defenseless people were shot. The government claimed that under a hundred people had died, but the religious establishment put the figure at over ten thousand. From this point onward, protests spread to every part of the nation. Even the state-controlled press began to report violence on a daily basis.

The shah seemed to have no definite strategy for dealing with the crisis. It was not generally known at the time that he was sick with lymphatic cancer. His illness was seen later as one cause of his irresoluteness in the face of these protests. Even so, he tried a number of tactics to diffuse the revolution. He changed prime ministers and arrested more than 130 former government leaders. Finally, he coerced Iraqi officials to expel Khomeini. The ayatollah eventually settled in a suburb of Paris, Neauphle-le-Château. He was better able to communicate with internal revolutionary forces from Paris by way of long-distance telephone than from Iraq.

Khomeini's central message was the same one that religious oppositionists had been preaching for a hundred years: the shah had conspired with foreign powers—primarily the United States—to once again exploit the Iranian people and undermine Islam. This message proved irresistable to the population as a whole. The revolution in its final months attracted broad-based participation, involving people from all economic classes and all regions of the country. Particularly crippling were strikes in Iran's oil industry, which brought exports to a near halt.

Eventually it became clear to the shah that he must leave Iran if stability were to be preserved. He attempted to appoint a number of individuals to become prime minister in a caretaker role, but all refused. Finally, Shahpour Bakhtiar (Shāpūr Bakhtiyār), a venerable National Front politician, accepted the job in order to allow the shah to leave. On 16 January 1979, the shah left Iran. The United States dispatched General Robert Huyser to Tehran to ensure the support of the Iranian military for the Bakhtiar government.

However, the Bakhtiar government was doomed from the start, as Khomeini appointed his own Provisional Revolutionary Government headed by another National Front politician, Mehdi Bāzargān. Bakhtiar never had any power. The real power during January and February of 1979 resided in roving *komitehs* (committees) of revolutionaries organized in mosques. These groups, in conjunction with veteran guerrilla fighters, such as the Mujāhidīn-i Khalq, ruled the streets of Tehran and other large cities. They engaged in periodic skirmishes with the military and other loyalist groups during this period. [*See* Komiteh; *and the biography of Bāzargān.*]

Khomeini returned to Iran on 1 February 1979. His return was greeted with extraordinary enthusiasm throughout the nation. On his return, sections of the military began to defect to the new Khomeini-led government. Tension between military groups climaxed on 9 February 1979, in a clash between air force cadets and technicians who had declared their loyalty to Khomeini and the shah's Imperial Guards. The cadets tried to take over the air force base at Doshan Tapah on the outskirts of Tehran and were opposed by the Imperial Guard. The cadets won the battle with the help of urban guerrillas in the area. This touched off a series of armed confrontations throughout the capital. On 11 February the Supreme Military Council announced that the military would no longer participate in the political crisis. All soldiers were ordered to their barracks. Bakhtiar went into hiding and eventually fled to Paris. The Khomeini-led government was officially in power. February 11 is now marked as the anniversary of the revolution.

The Aftermath of the Revolution. February to November 1979 was a transitional period in which the religious leaders fully established themselves in power in Iran. The Provisional Revolutionary Government established by Khomeini consisted largely of noncleric National Front leaders. These leaders envisioned the successor government as a secular democracy based on European models. However, hard-line religionists had a different vision. They favored an outright theocracy based on Islamic law.

On 30–31 March the Provisional Revolutionary Government held a national referendum on the form the new government would take. At Khomeini's insistence, the public was asked to vote yes or no on whether Iran should become an Islamic republic. Official tallies placed the yes vote at 98 percent.

The nation next decided on a constitution for the new government. In the summer of 1979 two drafts of a constitution were put forth, neither giving power to Khomeini or the clerical leaders. There was great debate between hard-line Islamists and secular nationalists. Eventually as a compromise an Assembly of Experts was elected to draft a third constitution. The assembly had heavy representation from religious hard-liners. This third draft invested ultimate power in a *faqīh* (chief jurisprudent) along with a five-person religious Council of Guardians. Great dissent over this document raged in Iran throughout the fall. The secular National Front leaders were chief in their opposition, fearing, as Bāzargān asserted, a new "dictatorship of the clergy."

Fate intervened in the ratification process to sway public opinion in favor of the hard-line religious leaders. The former shah, who was now deathly ill, had been traveling from nation to nation looking for a place to live. He appealed to the United States for medical treatment. Despite dire warnings from the U.S. embassy in Tehran of the dangerous consequences of admitting him to America, the Carter administration allowed him to fly to New York on 22 October 1979.

The reaction in Tehran was not long in coming. On 4 November a group of students took over the U.S. embassy and held all personnel hostage. The Americans remained captive for 444 days. The capture of the embassy touched off a huge anti-American reaction in Tehran that lasted for months. Officials of the Provisional Revolutionary Government, notably Bāzargān, were blamed for the decision to give refuge to the shah and were forced to resign. These events effectively blunted all secular nationalist opposition to the establishment of a theocratic government with Khomeini at its head. On 2–3 December 1979, the nation accepted the new constitution with a 99 percent approval vote.

In the ten years from the onset of the revolution until Khomeini's death on 3 June 1989, the new government groped toward stability. Despite continued infighting between political factions, internal political transitions were generally peaceful. A debilitating war with Iraq, begun in September 1980, was fought to a standstill by July 1988. The continued power of the *komiteh*s and their successors, the Sipāh-i Pasdarān-i Inqilāb-i Islāmī, were cause for public alarm. These groups continued to enforce a rough-and-ready Islamic morality along with keeping the peace. Those seen as offenders of Islamic codes of modesty and morality, as well as adherents of the former regime, were accosted on the streets and summarily presented before Islamic judges. Many were executed or imprisoned. Eventually the actions of these vigilante groups were curtailed, as they were redirected to fight the war with Iraq. The new government continued to be hostile toward the United States, but it improved relations with most other nations. [*See* Sipāh-i Pasdarān-i Inqilāb-i Islāmī.]

For people throughout the Islamic world, the Iranian

Revolution was a symbolically important event. It demonstrated that a Western-influenced secular regime could be overthrown by opposition forces organized under Islamic reformers. Since Islamic revivalists had been advocating just such a change since the late nineteenth century without success, the revolution gave new impetus to their struggle and triggered a rise in Islamic fundamentalist activities from Morocco to Southeast Asia.

It is safe to say that, although the dynamic tensions for opposition to the monarchy had long existed in Iran, no one could have predicted for certain that the final outcome of the revolution would be a theocratic government. For Muslims eager for reform and escape from Western domination, both in Iran and in other nations, the revolution was a deeply inspirational event. For secular nationalists and most of the Western world, the revolution continues to be disturbing. Throughout the entire period, however, the figure of Ayatollah Khomeini dominated the scene. He is correctly identified as the author of the revolution.

[*See also* Iran; Revolution; *and the biography of Khomeini. For biographies of Reza Shah and Muhammad Reza Shah, see under Pahlavi.*]

BIBLIOGRAPHY

Akhavi, Shahrough. *Religion and Politics in Contemporary Iran: Clergy-State Relations in the Pahlavi Period.* Albany, N.Y., 1980. Important work laying out the background leading to systematic clerical opposition to Pahlavi rule in Iran.

Arjomand, Said Amir. *The Turban for the Crown: The Islamic Revolution in Iran.* New York and Oxford, 1988. One of the most complete accounts of the events of the revolution from an acknowledged expert on Iranian contemporary history and politics.

Bakhash, Shaul. *The Reign of the Ayatollahs: Iran and the Islamic Revolution.* Rev. ed. New York, 1990. Account of the revolution by a seasoned journalist and historian, highly critical of the religious regime.

Bill, James A. *The Eagle and the Lion: The Tragedy of American-Iranian Relations.* New Haven, 1988. Account of relations between the United States and Iran during the Pahlavi era showing how the Iranian government systematically hid its internal political actions from U.S. officials.

Fischer, Michael M. J. *Iran: From Religious Dispute to Revolution.* Cambridge, Mass., 1984. Now-classic anthropological work showing how the revolution was constructed in Shīʿī religious symbolic terms by the militant clergy.

Huyser, Robert E. *Mission to Tehran.* New York, 1986. The final word by the American general thought to have engineered the Iranian military's capitulation to the Kohmeini-led revolutionary government.

Keddie, Nikki R. *Roots of Revolution: An Interpretive History of Modern Iran.* New Haven, 1981. See annotation to next item, below.

Keddie, Nikki R., ed. *Religion and Politics in Iran: Shi'ism from Quietism to Revolution.* New Haven, 1983. Two important works by a premier historian of Iran detailing centuries of confrontation between religious and secular officials.

Khomeini, Ruhollah. *Islam and Revolution: Writings and Declarations of Imam Khomeini.* Translated and annotated by Hamid Algar. Berkeley, 1981. Ayatollah Khomeini's philosophy of revolution and government in his own words.

Ramazani, Ruhollah K. *Revolutionary Iran: Challenge and Response in the Middle East.* Baltimore, 1986. Excellent account of government and international relations in postrevolutionary Iran.

Rubin, Barry. *Paved with Good Intentions: The American Experience in Iran.* New York, 1981. Masterful review of U.S. military and development efforts in the period leading up to the revolution.

Sick, Gary. *All Fall Down.* New York, 1985. The Iranian Revolution from the standpoint of a U.S. military analyst who saw it all.

Wright, Robin. *In the Name of God: The Khomeini Decade.* New York, 1989. A journalist's account of Khomeini's leadership in Iran replete with specific facts and dates.

Zonis, Marvin. *Majestic Failure: The Fall of the Shah.* Chicago, 1991. The author's account of the shah's failure to respond to the revolutionary challenge to his regime is based on his theory that the shah was unable to cope psychologically with a series of personal tragedies in the last years of his regime.

WILLIAM O. BEEMAN

IRAQ. As an Ottoman province, Iraq suffered in the eighteenth and nineteenth centuries from the waning of Istanbul's influence and from its geographical position at the center of four major historic confluences: in the south, the desert areas were prone to the raids of Najd tribes at a time when the Wahhābīyah movement was on the rise. To the north and east, Shīʿī Iran had proved for four centuries to be a major competitor to the Ottomans. The two Islamic powers shared their longest border in Iraq, and war between the Ottoman and Persian Empires was endemic. West and northwest, the Syrian desert and the conglomerate of the Levantine countries that formed Greater Syria constituted a millenarian rival which continued, for much of the twentieth century, the old antagonism between ʿAbbāsid Baghdad and Umayyad Damascus. North and northwest of Baghdad, Kurdish territory straddled the frontier with Turkey, the patron of Baghdad for the better part of four centuries.

This fourfold legacy continued its deep structural work through the domestic Iraqi historical prism since the constitution of Iraq in its present geographical form in 1920. The defeat of the Ottomans during World War I brought the country under British mandate until Iraq joined the League of Nations in 1932. Despite formal independence, British influence remained pervasive until the coup which destroyed the monarchy in the so-called Revolution of 1958.

The form taken by the legacy of regional neighbors can be sketched as follows. With Turkey, a constant problem of boundaries was increased by a dispute over the sovereignty of the city of Mosul and a recurring Kurdish problem. A similar Kurdish problem arose in the context of the relations with Iran, but the boundaries with Iran, which stretched over 1,200 miles, ranging from mountains peaking at 5,000 meters to the hot seas of the Persian Gulf, brought also a more delicate religious-confessional legacy which struck at the heart of Iraqi identity: Iranian Shīʿīs looked at the Iraqi holy cities of southern Iraq, Najaf and Karbala, as poles of continuity for their own cultural setup. Despite the absence of a formal census, the Arab Shīʿī population constitutes a clear majority in late twentieth-century Iraq (about 55 to 60 percent), against an Arab/Sunnī-dominated Baghdad (Arab Sunnīs are about 15 to 20 percent, Sunnī Kurds about 20 percent). In such a context, the Iranian neighborliness (Iran is 95 percent Shīʿī) often turned into an internal factor of disruption among Iraqis.

Greater Syria, whether in the form of its successors (Jordan and Syria), or as the link to the Arab world, dovetailed with Arab—as opposed to Kurdish—Iraq, and the flow of Syrian influences was particularly strong during the time of the first king of Iraq, Fayṣal I (r. 1921–1933). The son of Sharīf Ḥusayn of Mecca, Fayṣal was established as Iraqi monarch by the British after a brief reign of a few days as king of Syria in 1920. With him came a yearning for a united Arab Levant including Iraq, the Hejaz, Palestine, Syria, and Lebanon. This never materialized, but the seeds of a dominant Arab ideology at the center of the Iraqi state were sown. More significantly for the Iraqi domestic setup, Fayṣal I brought with him a cadre of army officials trained in Ottoman Turkey who were imbued with a sense of Arabism, and Iraq was involved throughout the century with the dreams and squabbles of the search for Arab unity in the Middle East, especially over the question of Palestine.

Finally, the desert nomadic legacy brought to Iraq a contrasted and tribal tradition in which cities did not represent the center of power, and in which boundaries meant little. The transboundary nomadic tradition is inherently irreconcilable with the pattern of a nation-state. In Iraq, tribal forces fused with international and regional alliances, which coincided with a weak or strong government in Baghdad, to undermine the solidity of arbitrary boundaries: a case in point is the issue of Kuwait, which benefited from the weakness of the Ottomans and the prying of imperial Britain to acquire a distinctiveness in the late nineteenth century which was eventually turned into a formal boundary in 1932, and in independence and sovereignty under British military protection in 1962. When the government in Baghdad became strong after its relative successes in the Iran-Iraq War (1980–1988), Kuwait was invaded and occupied for six months between August 1990 and February 1991. Iraq was brought back to the internationally recognized border only after the massive military effort undertaken in the second Gulf War. Since 1920, each of three successive Iraqi generations has experienced a serious international crisis over Kuwait.

Together, the contrasting and powerful neighbors mirrored a problem which haunts Iraq to date: the arduous cohesion of a nation-state. Iraq's internal constituencies share little common allegiance for a nation-state whose capital has seldom represented them politically. Iraqi ethnic and religious communities are prone to fall under regional and international influences which often lead to weakening their peaceful participation in the state.

The development of modern Iraq can be seen in the prism of its constituent groups, and the Iraqi scholar ʿAlī al-Wardī has identified several sociologically distinct areas, interacting over the past two centuries in a way he described as "the continuous war in Iraq": the mountainous areas, which include essentially Kurdish tribes and small Turkmen, Yezīdī, and Christian minorities; the Diyala area east of Baghdad, with agricultural dwellers; the area of the Jezira, north of Baghdad, between the Euphrates and the Tigris, where bedouin Sunnī tribes live; the desert area in the south and middle of Iraq, inhabited by tribes which espoused Shiism in the eighteenth and nineteenth centuries; the marsh areas with "old" dwellers who go back in their habits to the pre-Islamic era; and the cities, Basra, Baghdad, Mosul, Suleymaniyah, Kirkuk, Karbala, and Najaf.

The sociological setup and the various interests of these constitutencies explain how difficult the formation of the nation-state of Iraq has proved. Among these distinct groups, three poles continued to play a significant political role by the second half of the twentieth century: the Shīʿī south, the Kurdish north, and Baghdad.

The Shīʿī South. Tribes are important in the south of Iraq, but the Shīʿī factor has become dominant in the second half of the twentieth century in the wake of the rising importance of the cities against the countryside and the ensuing demographic shifts. The void resulting from the suppression of party politics was filled by the century-old structure of what is known as the *marjaʿīyah.*

The Shīʿī south is epitomized by Najaf and the *marjaʿīyah,* which is the conglomerate of religious leaders and their elaborate networks. Mostly assembled in periods of crisis, the *marjaʿīyah* has outgrown its original narrow religious mold to impress itself directly on the political sphere. The characteristics of the *marjaʿīyah* in the modern history of Iraq can be found at work in several major instances. In the first instance, the *marjaʿīyah* was the linchpin of the Arab revolt against the British in 1920, when the religious leaders of Najaf and Karbala, the two holy cities in the south of Iraq, took the lead in the uprising against Western occupation. Their defeat at the hands of the British meant the withdrawal of religious leaders from the sphere of politics until the Revolution of 1958. Beginning in 1958, the Shīʿī opposition directed from the *marjaʿīyah* in Najaf contributed in every major event in the country: opposition to the Communist threat in the early 1960s, focus of anti-Baʿthism from 1968 onward, and recurring uprisings culminating in the *intifāḍah* of March 1991.

As an educational institution, the *marjaʿīyah* was important for the intellectual renewal that took place in Najaf beginning in the 1940s. This effort started with the writings of Muḥammad al-Ḥusayn Āl Kāshif al-Ghiṭā' (d. 1954), but its most important innovative figure was Muḥammad Bāqir al-Ṣadr (1935–1980), who, under the benevolent protection of less-political older religious leaders, contributed to the firmer grounding in theory of the ideas of political Islam. However, the *marjaʿīyah* was torn after 1958 between a wing which was nonpolitical, whose main representative was Abol-Qāsem Kho'i (Abū al-Qāsim al-Khū'ī, d. 1992), and a political wing, which was encouraged by Muḥsin al-Ḥakīm (d. 1970) and spearheaded by Ṣadr after him. Until the revolt in the wake of the rout of the Iraqi army in the second Gulf War, these two tendencies were clearly distinct, but Kho'i played a more assertive role for the brief period of two weeks in March 1991 during which Najaf was freed from Baʿthist rule. [*See the biographies of Kho'i and Ḥakīm.*]

Another characteristic of the *marjaʿīyah* is its international character, as it also constitutes the center of what can be described as Shīʿī civil society. This structured sphere of interests and organized groups outside the reach of the state operates around a religious setting whose center is the schools of law in Najaf and Karbala and their *ʿulamā'* (scholars). The pilgrimage of Shīʿīs from the whole world to the city of Najaf, where the tomb of the first imam of the tradition is believed to be buried has transformed the south of Iraq into a center of learning for the whole Shīʿī world. Many of the ideas at work in the Persian Constitutional Revolution of 1905–1912 originated in Najaf. It is from Najaf also that the opposition to British rule was organized; and it is in Najaf that the Lebanese Shīʿī religious leaders were formed and where Khomeini remained over a period of fourteen years until coming to power in Iran in 1979.

Owing to its nature, however, the *marjaʿīyah* is traversed by a high degree of independently minded and financially self-supporting leaders. Their wealthy background has also, except for extreme cases, as under Baʿthist rule, encouraged forms of accommodation with the central government. This was patent under the monarchy, but the sectarian bent of the regimes of the two ʿĀrifs (1964–1968), and especially the narrow political basis of the Baʿth and a ruthless exercise of power have driven the *marjaʿīyah* into an open opposition. In turn, this has led to a rapprochement with the West, including the open espousal of democratic ideas against the theory of the late Ayatollah Ruhollah Khomeini's *wilāyat al-faqīh* and his anti-Western political worldview.

Kurdish Iraq. Unlike the south of Iraq, the Kurdish struggle is characterized by a breakaway secessionist tendency, which is derived from the scattering of the Kurdish people over four Middle Eastern states, and from the minoritarian position in terms of numbers which differentiates them from the equally disenfranchised Arab Shīʿīs. With the Kurds, the issue with the Arab Sunnīs in power is not "religious," but the pattern is strikingly similar. Practically, however, the rugged mountains of Iraqi Kurdistan, at least until military technology and air power caught up with that advantage in the 1970s, as well as the Kurdish territorial continuity in Iranian and Turkish Kurdistan, offered a major distinctive characteristic to the struggle with Baghdad. Another major difference in comparison with the Najaf-Baghdad opposition is rooted in the power setup in the Kurdish, as opposed to the Shīʿī, areas.

In Kurdish Iraq, party politics in the twentieth century was grafted onto Kurdish tribes along geographical patterns. Southern and southeastern Iraqi Kurdistan, where the dialect is Sōrānī, was dominated by the Barzinjī tribes under the leadership of Shaykh Maḥmūd, whose influence was continued with Jalāl Ṭālibānī and his Patriotic Union of Kurdistan. There is therefore a deep and traditional rivalry with the Kurdish Democratic party, the party of the Barzānī clan, which saw Masʿūd succeed his father Mullā Muṣṭafā (himself the brother of Aḥmad, the rival of Maḥmūd of Barzinjah in the south) after the latter's defeat in 1975 and his death in exile. The northern part of Kurdistan is more rugged and more "tribal," and the dialect, Kirmānjī, is also distinct.

The opposition of the Kurds as a whole to Baghdad has been characterized by a persistent struggle and several revolts, which were successively subdued by the British air force in the 1930s and the Iraqi army after the 1958 revolution. In March 1970, a constitutional agreement was reached between the Baʿth and the Kurdish leader Muṣṭafā al-Barzānī, but war resumed soon over the emptying of the agreement's terms by the central government and resulted in the rout of the Kurds in 1975. Low-level warfare continued until the notorious Anfāl genocidal campaign, which culminated in the use of poison gas in 1987 and emptied the Kurdish countryside of most of its inhabitants.

This secessionist drive, however, is tempered by a readiness to participate actively in Iraqi politics, for which the inclusion of various ministers in government at the end of the monarchy and into the early 1970s was one sign. These two opposite directions of Kurdish politics are a staple of twentieth-century Iraqi history: when, for the first time, the north of the country was protected from the rule of Baghdad under a "safe haven" (established April 1991), free elections were successfully carried out in May 1992 to create a Kurdish administration. Yet the Kurds are also actively involved, under the umbrella of the Iraqi National Congress, with other Arab Sunnī and Shīʿī oppositional groups vying for power in Baghdad.

Baghdad. It is in Baghdad that the history of Iraq is ultimately decided. The city, like many Third World metropolises, has grown enormously in the twentieth century, and it is estimated that a third of Iraq's 17 million people lives there. The legitimacy of the monarchy's (1921–1958) institutional buildup was eventually undermined by its dependence on Britain, which, especially after the discovery of oil in the 1920s, was keen to retain its control over the economic potential of the country. A series of coups starting in 1936 disrupted the slow but real progress toward a form of constitutional monarchy, and further uncertainty resulted from World War II and the rise of the Soviet Union as an international power in its aftermath. This, together with an uneven distribution of the growing wealth, meant that the pole of change increasingly became the Communist party, which grew in size and influence and came close to power when the coup of 1958 started a radical transformation of the Iraqi political scene.

This revolution heralded a stop to the slow opening up and diversification of the Iraqi political stage by bringing on the scene the more militant factions of Iraqi society into violent confrontations. Several coups and attempted coups followed, until the Baʿth, with a characteristically small membership of some three thousand individuals, took over in late July 1968. The benefits of oil production allowed the combination of ruthless power and financial assuaging to secure, within the Baʿth, a reinforcement of a "fittest to survive" mentality. By the end of the 1970s, the Baʿth strongman Saddam Hussein had succeeded in concentrating in his person all power in the Iraqi state. This developed into an adventurist foreign policy designed to cover up the poor domestic representation of the leadership and was repeated twice over a decade. In the first Gulf War, started on 22 September 1980, Iraq invaded Iran. On 2 August 1990, Iraq marched into Kuwait. In both instances, the end of the war saw Iraq back, in terms of territory, where it had started, but the Iraqi leadership had secured a political breathing space of some significance.

Despite the collapse resulting from the devastation and dead ends occasioned by the two Gulf Wars, the fragmentation of Iraqi oppositional politics remained. Northern and southern opposition were operating with little coordination. Signs of joint oppositional leadership appeared shortly before the second Gulf War, but it was only in June 1992 that several Iraqi groups came together in the Iraqi National Congress on a democratic and federalist program at a meeting in Vienna. This was achieved against significant opposition arising from regional powers. It is against the disunited domestic legacy and the fissiparous legacy of Iraq's neighbors, a combination which has seldom offered stability in Iraq's modern history, that the future of Iraq is being decided between the Baʿth and the Iraqi National Congress.

[*See also* Baʿth Parties; Karbala; Najaf; *and the biography of Ṣadr.*]

BIBLIOGRAPHY

The most significant scholarship on modern Iraq is by ʿAlī al-Wardī and Hanna Batatu. See al-Wardī, *Lamaḥāt ijtimāʿīyah min tārīkh al-ʿIrāq al-Ḥadīth,* 8 vols. (Baghdad, 1969–1972), which also covers the Ottoman period, and his shorter *Dirāsah fī Ṭabīʿat al-Mujtamaʿ al-ʿIrāqī* (Baghdad, 1966). For Batatu, see *The Old Social Classes and the Revolutionary Movements of Iraq* (Princeton, 1978). On Batatu's work, see Robert A. Fernea and William Roger Louis, eds., *The Iraqi Revolution of 1958: The Old Social Classes Revisited* (London, 1991).

For more general works on Iraq, consult ʿAbd al-Razzāq al-Ḥasanī, *Tārīkh al-Wizārāt al-ʿIrāqīyah,* 10 vols. (Sidon, Lebanon, 1953–1961), which contains a comprehensive chronicle of the Iraqi monarchy. Elie Kedourie's *The Chatham House Version and Other Middle-Eastern Essays,* 2d ed. (New York, 1984), features an excellent chapter on Iraq up to 1958. Three works by Majid Khadduri may be consulted for recent Iraqi politics: *Independent Iraq, 1932–1958: A Study in Iraqi Politics,* 2d ed. (London, 1960); *Republican Iraq: A Study in Iraqi Politics since the Revolution of 1958* (London, 1969); and *Socialist Iraq: A Study in Iraqi Politics since 1968* (Washington, D.C., 1978). Other useful works include Stephen Longrigg, *Iraq, 1900–1950: A Political, Social, and Economic History* (London, 1953); Phebe Marr, *The Modern History of Iraq* (Boulder, 1985); and Marion Farouk Sluglett and Peter Sluglett, *Iraq since 1958: From Revolution to Dictatorship,* 2d ed. (London, 1990).

Scholarship on Kurdish Iraq includes a comprehensive study by Ferhad Ibrahim, *Die Kurdische Nationalbewegung im Irak* (Berlin, 1983); Edmund Ghareeb, *The Kurdish Question in Iraq* (Syracuse, N.Y., 1981); and *The Kurds: A Contemporary Overview,* edited by Philip G. Kreyenbroek and Stefan Sperl (London, 1992). For southern Iraq, see Pierre-Jean Luizard, *La formation de l'Irak contemporain: Le rôle politique des Ulémas Chiites à la fin de la domination Ottomane et au moment de la construction de l'état irakien* (Paris, 1991); and Chibli Mallat, *The Renewal of Islamic Law: Muhammad Baqer as-Sadr, Najaf, and the Shiʿi International* (Cambridge, 1993).

Recent developments in Iraq are covered in Eberhard Kienle, *Baʿth v. Baʿth: The Conflict between Syria and Iraq, 1968–1989* (London, 1990); and Shahram Chubin and Charles Tripp, *Iran and Iraq at War* (Boulder, 1988). For the Gulf War, see Lawrence Freedman and Efraim Karsh, *The Gulf Conflict, 1990–1991: Diplomacy and War in the New World Order* (Princeton, 1993). On the struggle for democracy in Iraq, the reader may consult three articles by the author: "The Search for Law and Stability in Iraq," *Orient* 1 (1994); "Obstacles to Democratization in Iraq: A Reading of Post-Revolutionary Iraqi History through the Gulf War" and "Voices of Opposition: The International Committee for a Free Iraq," both in *Rules and Rights in the Middle East: Democracy, Law, and Society,* edited by Ellis Goldberg et al., pp. 224–247, 174–187 (Seattle, 1993).

CHIBLI MALLAT

ISHAKI, AYAZ (1878–1954), Tatar political activist and writer. Born on 23 February 1878 into the family of Gïylajetdin, the mullah of Yaushirmä village in Kazan guberniya, Ayaz (or Gayaz) Ishaki received a traditional education at the Chistay *madrasah* (1890–1893) and then at the Külbüe *madrasah* (1893–1898) of Kazan. In 1898 he entered the Kazan Teachers' School, from which he graduated in 1902, finding employment as a teacher of Russian at *madrasahs* in Kazan and Orenburg. In 1903 he returned to Yaushirmä to take up briefly the duties of village mullah.

As a student Ishaki became involved in the first Tatar literary-political circle organized by a group of Tatar youth in 1895. They published a mimeographed paper called *Tärakki* (Progress) and in 1901 organized the Shakirdlik party, which a year later changed its name to Hürriyet (Freedom) and adhered to purely political goals. At this time Ishaki also established links with the Russian socialist revolutionary circles of Kazan and acquired a taste for action, which may explain the brevity of his stay in Yaushirmä and his decision to return to Kazan.

Once back in Kazan, Ishaki became involved with radical circles; in 1905 he and Fuad Tuktar founded a secret Tatar political group called Tangchïlar revolving around two socialist papers advocating the overthrow of tsarism—*Tang* (Down) and *Tang yoldïzï* (Morning Star), both edited by Ishaki. In the fall of 1905 he and Tuktar organized the Socialist party Brek with its own journal, *Azat* (Free), succeeded by *Azat khalïq* (Free People).

In August 1905 Ishaki participated in the first Congress of the Muslims of the Russian empire, heading the group of twenty radical nationalists opposing the moderate views of the majority of delegates who advocated a political union of all Muslims. This disagreement grew even wider at the third congress (August 1906), where Ishaki argued that unity of religion and culture did not suffice to unite all Muslims into one political party as long as class differences endured.

By 1906 Ishaki had clashed not only with those Tatars who did not share his political radicalism but also with the Russian government. The newspaper *Tang yoldïzï* was banned in 1905, and Ishaki was arrested and sent to the Chistay jail. Upon release he launched the newspaper *Tavïsh* (The Voice), which continued the socialist revolutionary orientation of the previous two and prompted an immediate response from the government: Ishaki was arrested and jailed for six months and then sent to serve a three-year exile in Arkhangelsk. He escaped in 1908 and made his way to St. Petersburg, where he lived in hiding; however, the police caught up with Ishaki and deported him to Vologda, where he stayed until 1913.

Since Ishaki was not allowed to return to Kazan,

he chose St. Petersburg for launching his next projects—the publication between 1910 and 1913 of the newspapers *Il* (Country), *Süz* (The Word), and *Bezneng il* (Our Country). By this time Ishaki had mellowed politically, distancing himself from the radicalism of the socialists. He moved closer to the moderate platform of the Ittifak party, which had never regarded class differences as a hindrance to the unity of all Muslims. In 1915 Ishaki traveled to the Muslim regions of the Russian empire to promote the idea of unity and common action.

After the fall of the Romanov dynasty in February 1917, Ishaki helped organize the two congresses of Russian Muslims held during that year (May, Moscow; July, Kazan). On 22 July 1917, Ishaki was instrumental in having the national cultural autonomy of the Volga-Ural Muslims proclaimed by the Second Congress, which also elected a National Assembly (Milli Mäjlis), National Council (Milli Shura), and National Administration (Milli Idare). He became the head of the Foreign Affairs Committee of the Volga-Ural Muslims, but when the Red Army occupied the large cities of the Volga-Ural region in 1918, the National Administration was abrogated. Since the regional enemies of the Bolsheviks were also hostile to Ishakī, he and the National Administration moved to Kïzïlyar (Petropavlovsk) on the northern fringes of the Kazakh steppes, where he began to publish the newspaper *Mayak* (The Lighthouse).

In 1919 Ishaki left Russia (via Japan) to participate in the European Peace Conference as the representative of the Volga-Ural Muslims. This departure marks the beginning of his life as a political emigré, which took him to Warsaw, Paris, Berlin, Mukden, Ankara, and Istanbul. During this period he channeled his efforts toward keeping alive the "national memory" of the Volga-Ural Muslims and supporting their struggle to free their homeland. In Warsaw Ishaki was active in an organization called Promethée, aimed at achieving independence for the ethnic minorities of Russia. In Berlin in 1928, he launched the newspaper *Milli Yul* (National Path), which changed its name to *Yanga Milli Yul* (New National Path) in 1939.

Ishaki represented the Volga-Ural Muslims at the Muslim Congress held in Jerusalem in 1931 and continued to pursue the idea of Muslim and Turkic unity. Between 1934 and 1938 he traveled to Finland, the Arab countries, Manchuria, Korea, and Japan in order to create an organization of the Volga-Ural Muslim diaspora. When the national congress of the diaspora met in 1935 in Mukden, it elected Ishaki the president of its national council. To provide the diaspora with a voice, in November 1935 Ishaki started the newspaper *Milli bayrak* (The National Flag), which appeared until mid-1945; it was the only one of his journals to survive German suppression in World War II. After the war Ishaki moved to Turkey, where he lived until his death in Ankara on 22 July 1954.

Ishaki left a threefold legacy as a political activist driven by the idea of Turkic unity and national autonomy for the Volga-Ural Muslims, a journalist promoting that political credo, and a creative writer reflecting the ideals of enlightenment, justice, and economic and political advancement intimately associated with Jadīdism (Muslim reformism). [*See* Jadīdism.] His literary work includes close to fifty short stories, novellas, novels, plays, memoirs, and translations of historical essays, addressing a broad range of issues. In the fantastic novel *Iki yöz eldan song inkïyraz* (After Two Hundred Years—Extinction; Kazan, 1904), and the Story *Tägallemdä sägadät* (Happiness in Education; Kazan, 1899) he addressed the issues of reform and modernization of education as a condition of social progress; in the play *Zöleykha* (Moscow, 1918) the focus is on the tragedies brought about by Russian policies of forced conversion to Christianity of the Russian government. Other plays and stories address issues of social justice, women's lives, and the quest for education. The literary works that most clearly mirror Ishaki's political ideas are the play *Dulkïn echende* (In The Wave; Paris, 1920) and the novel *Öygä taba* (Homeward; Berlin, 1922), which are permeated by nationalist and Pan-Turkic ideas. [*See* Pan-Turanism.]

Ishaki's name was obliterated from histories of Tatar literature and culture published in the Soviet Union after 1926, and he was mentioned only to vilify him as a nationalist and enemy of the Soviet people. Not until 1988, in an article by I. Nurullin in the newspaper *Vechernyaya Kazan,* was the first step taken toward returning Ishaki to the peoples of his homeland. Since, newspapers and journals such as *Kazan utlarï* (Fires of Kazan), *Miras* (Heritage), and *Tatarstan* have carried many articles about him, also reprinting some of his works. In 1991 the Union of Writers of Tatarstan instituted a literary prize in honor of Ishaki; the first writer to receive it was Rabit Batulla, whose works embody Ishaki's ideals and hopes for the future of the Volga-Ural Muslims.

BIBLIOGRAPHY

Agay, H., A. S. Akış, and Tahir Çağatay, eds. *Muhammed Ayaz İshaki, Hayatı ve faaliyeti: 100. Doğum Yılı Dolayısıyla*. Ankara, 1979.

Nurullin, Ibrahim. "Vozvrashchenie Gayaza Ishaki." *Vechernyaya Kazan* 10.17 (1988).

Nurullin, Ibrahim. "Gayaz Iskhakïyga yogïntï." *Kazan Utlarï*, no. 2 (1993): 153–157.

Saadi, A. *Tatar ădăbiyatı tarikhı*. Kazan, 1926.

Sultan, S. "Ayaz Ishaki Idilli: A Biography." *Central Asian Survey*, no. 2 (1990): 133–143.

Validov, Dzhamaliutdin. *Ocherki istorii obrazovannosti i literatury Tatar*. Moscow and Petrograd, 1923.

AZADE-AYŞE RORLICH

IṢLĀḤ. The Arabic term for "reform," *iṣlāḥ* has come to denote the reform movement in the Islamic world in the last three centuries. In a modern Islamic context, the term primarily refers to the work and writings of Muḥammad ʿAbduh and his disciple, Rashīd Riḍā. The lexicographic and Qur'ānic origins of the word also imply meanings of "reconciliation" and, in the words of the master lexicographer Ibn Manẓūr in *Lisān al-ʿArab*, "the opposite of corruption." Variants of the word appeared in the Qur'ān to refer to striving a toward peace (surah 2.220) or to pious actions (surah 4.35).

Reform in an Islamic context should be distinguished from reformism within Christian churches. Islamic reformists did not—and do not—claim that Islam in itself needs any reform, but that various misunderstandings and misinterpretations have come to distort some of the original meanings of the texts, introducing some harmful practices. Islamic reformism is thus a movement aimed at returning Islam to its original message, with a theological emphasis on unity.

Although Islam (as a body of theological teachings and a system of devotional practices) has endured argumentation and debate about a variety of social, philosophical, and political issues on which there was an absence of *ijmāʿ* (consensus of the clerical elite), there have often been men (and sometimes women) who have attempted to influence or change the common understanding and practice of the religion. The thrust behind the current reform movement, which began in the last half of the nineteenth century, revolves around the need for fulfilling the ethical requirements of Islam. It developed in response to modern Western influences in Islamic societies.

Among religious thinkers, or thinkers concerned about the viability of Islamic thought and practice, the *iṣlāḥ* movement addresses modern problems by introducing modern answers that are drawn from the Qur'ān. The movement, which stresses the continuity of its message, approaches inevitably the realm of *ijtihād* (individual inquiry in legal matters). Muḥammad ʿAbduh and Muḥammad Rashīd Riḍā's major contributions to the movement were in the area of interpretations of religious texts. Strictly orthodox Muslims (such as the Wahhābīyah and mainstream Islamic scholars at al-Azhar University) downplayed any originality in their work and emphasized instead their dedication to the *sunnah* (the path set by the Prophet). To be sure, *iṣlāḥ* thinkers did not hesitate to criticize facets of religious beliefs and practices prevalent among Muslims in their times. In fact, Islamic reform stressed in its message the rejection of what it calls *bidʿah* (impermissible innovations). These innovations were dismissed, because they were seen as incompatible with the interests of the community and with the teachings of the Qur'ān and *ḥadīth*s.

Another staple of Islamic reformist thought, particularly as represented by ʿAbduh and his immediate disciples, lies in recognizing a prominent role for reason in the life of the believer. Equal emphasis was put on the reformation of educational systems, including traditional religious education as represented by the ultratraditional al-Azhar University, and the improvement of the status of women in society.

No consensus exists among Muslims on the true definition of reform in an Islamic context. Every religious movement claims the reformist title for itself, with reformism understood in the Qur'ānic notion of *salāḥ* (the general good) of the community. By some accounts, the ultraconservative Wahhābīyah movement is considered reformist, because it too aspired to purify religion from the harmful influences of innovations and to call for the return of the original simplicity of early Islam. This last element of the Wahhābīyah doctrine is shared by most Islamic thinkers, although they might disagree on the definition of the "simplicity" of early Islam.

[*See also* Bidʿah; Fundamentalism; Ijtihād; Revival and Renewal; *and* Wahhābīyah.]

BIBLIOGRAPHY

Esposito, John L. *Islam and Politics*. 3d ed. Syracuse, N.Y., 1991.

Hourani, Albert. *Arabic Thought in the Liberal Age, 1798–1939*. London, 1962.

Kerr, Malcolm H. *Islamic Reform: The Political and Legal Theories of Muḥammad ʿAbduh and Rashīd Riḍā*. Berkeley, 1966.

Levtzion, Nehemia, and John Obert Voll, eds. *Eighteenth-Century Renewal and Reform in Islam*. Syracuse, N.Y., 1987.
Merad, ʿAlī. *Le réformisme musulman en Algérie de 1925 à 1940*. Paris, 1967.
Voll, John Obert. *Islam, Continuity, and Change in the Modern World*. 2d ed. Syracuse, N.Y., 1994.

AsʿAD AbuKhalil

ISLAM. [*This entry consists of an overview of the origins and development of the classical Islamic tradition and eight historical surveys that trace the spread of Islam throughout the world:*

An Overview
Islam in the Middle East and North Africa
Islam in Sub-Saharan Africa
Islam in Central Asia and the Caucasus
Islam in China
Islam in South Asia
Islam in Southeast Asia and the Pacific
Islam in Europe
Islam in the Americas

For further discussions of classical Islam, see Sunnī Islam *and* Shīʿī Islam. *For further discussion of Muslim religious life in global perspective, see* Popular Religion.]

An Overview

Islam is the second largest of the world's religions. Muslim countries extend from North Africa to Southeast Asia, but the one billion members of the Islamic community stretch across the globe. Muslims constitute a majority in more than forty-eight countries and a significant minority in many others. Though the Arab world is often regarded as the heartland of Islam, the majority of Muslims are in fact to be found in Asia and Africa, homes to the largest Muslim communities: Indonesia, Bangladesh, Pakistan, India, Central Asia, and Nigeria. Islam has grown significantly in recent years in the West, where it is now the second largest religion in many parts of Europe and the third in the United States.

The term *islām* is derived from the Arabic root *s-l-m*, which means submission or peace. Muslims are those who surrender to God's will or law and as a result, Muslims believe, are at peace with themselves and with God. To embrace Islam is to become a member of a worldwide faith community *(ummah)*. Thus, believers have both an individual and corporate religious identity and responsibility or duty to obey and implement God's will in personal and social life.

Islam stands in a long line of Middle Eastern, prophetic religious traditions that share an uncompromising monotheism, belief in God's revelation, prophets, ethical responsibility, and accountability, and the Day of Judgment. Jews, Christians, and Muslims are children of Abraham (Ibrāhīm), although they belong to different branches of the same family. Jews and Christians are spiritual descendants of Abraham and his wife, Sarah, through their son Isaac, and Muslims trace their lineage back to Ismāʿīl, Abraham's first-born son by his Egyptian servant, Hagar. Islamic tradition teaches that Abraham, pressured by Sarah, who feared that Ismāʿīl as first born would overshadow her son, Isaac, took Hagar and Ismāʿīl to the vicinity of Mecca, where Ismāʿīl became the father of the Arabs in Northern Arabia.

Origins and Early Development. Arabia is the heartland of Islam where, in the seventh century CE, Muslims believe, the Qur'ān was revealed to Muḥammad, he preached God's message, and he established the first Islamic community. Pre-Islamic Arabian society, with its tribal, polytheistic ethos, provided the context for the rise of Islam. Tribal gods and goddesses served as protectors of individual tribes, were feared rather than loved, and were the objects of cultic rituals (sacrifice and pilgrimage). Mecca, the commercial and religious center of Arabia, possessed a central shrine, the Kaʿbah, a cube-shaped building that housed the 360 idols of tribal patron deities, the site of a great annual pilgrimage. Arabian polytheism also included belief in a supreme high god. Allāh ("the god") was the creator and sustainer of life, but remote from everyday concerns, and thus not the object of cult or ritual.

The value system or ethical code of Arabian society was not attributed to God, but was the product of a tribal tradition. The key virtue or basis for Arabia's code of honor, manliness *(murūwah)*, emphasized bravery and the preservation of tribal and family honor. Tribal justice was guaranteed not by God but by the threat of group vengeance or retaliation. Arabian fatalism denied meaning or accountability beyond this life—no resurrection of the body, divine judgment, eternal punishment or reward.

The monotheistic message of the Qur'ān and preaching of Muḥammad did not occur in a vacuum. Monotheism had been flourishing in Arab (Judaism and Christianity) and Iranian cultures (Zoroastrianism) for centuries preceding Muḥammad's ministry. Both Jewish and Christian Arab communities had also been present in Arabia itself before Muḥammad. Finally, in addition to biblical monotheism, a local or indigenous monotheistic presence existed among pre-Islamic Arab monotheists, called *ḥanīf*s. The Qur'ān (3.17) and Muslim tradition portray them as descendants of Abraham and his son Ismāʿīl. Muḥammad's travels as a caravan leader and his personal relationships brought him into contact with pre-Islamic forms of monotheism.

God, the Qur'ān, and the Prophet Muḥammad. At the center and foundation of Islam is Allāh, the God, whose name appears more than 2,500 times in the Qur'ān. In a polytheistic society, Muḥammad declared the sole existence of Allāh, the transcendent, all-powerful, and all-knowing Creator, Sustainer, Ordainer, and Judge of the universe. The absolute monotheism of Islam is preserved in the doctrine of the unity *(tawḥīd)* and sovereignty (*rabb*, ruler or lord) of God that dominates Islamic belief and practice. As God is one, God's rule and will or law are comprehensive, extending to all creatures and to all aspects of life. [*See* Tawḥīd.]

The Qur'ān underscores the awesome power and majesty of God and the Day of Judgment, but it also reveals a merciful and just judge. Its initial chapter and subsequent chapters begin with: "In the name of God, the Merciful and Compassionate". The Qur'ān declares that its author is the Most Merciful (36.5), in it is a Mercy (29.51) and its motivation is the Mercy of God (21.107). The lesson of God's mercy proclaimed by the Qur'ān has been institutionalized by the Muslim practice of beginning important matters, such as a letter, public speech, or book, with the phrase: "In the name of God, the Merciful and Compassionate." God's mercy exists in dialectical tension with his justice. Reward and punishment follow from individual ethical responsibility and accountability before an all-knowing and just judge. Thus, Islamic ethics follows from human beings' special status and responsibility on earth.

For Muslims, the Qur'ān is the Book of God *(kitāb al-Allāh)*. It is the eternal, uncreated, literal word of God *(kalām Allāh)*, sent down from heaven, revealed one final time to the prophet Muḥammad as a guidance for humankind (2.185). Islam teaches that God's revelation has occurred in several forms: in nature, history, and scripture. God revealed his will for humankind through a series of messengers (including Moses, Jesus, and Muḥammad): "Indeed, We sent forth among every nation a Messenger, saying: 'Serve your God, and shun false gods' " (16.36).

Although God had sent a revelation to Moses and Jesus, Muslims believe that the scriptures of the Jewish community (Torah) and of the Christian church (the Evangel or Gospel) are corrupted versions of the original revelation. The current texts of the Torah and the New Testament are regarded as a composite of human fabrications, nonbiblical beliefs that infiltrated the texts, and remnants of the original revelation. Thus, the Qur'ān does not abrogate or nullify, but rather corrects the versions of scripture preserved by the Jewish and Christian communities (5.19). From a Muslim viewpoint, Islam is not a new religion with a new scripture. Rather than being the youngest of the major monotheistic world religions, it is considered by Muslims to be the oldest religion. Islam represents the "original" as well as final revelation of the God of Abraham, Moses, Jesus, and Muḥammad.

History, Muslim belief, and legend portray Muḥammad (570–632) as a remarkable man and prophet. Although we know a good deal about Muḥammad's life after his "call" to be God's messenger, historical records tell us little about Muḥammad's early years prior to becoming a prophet. The Qur'ān has served as a major source for information regarding the life of the Prophet along with Prophetic traditions (sg., *ḥadīth;* reports about what Muḥammad said and did) and biographies that reveal Muḥammad's meaning and significance in early Islam. Muḥammad serves as both God's human instrument in bearing witness to and preaching his revelation and the model or ideal whom all believers are to emulate.

At the age of forty during the month of Ramaḍān (610), Muḥammad the caravan leader became Muḥammad the messenger of God. On "The Night of Power and Excellence," as Muslims call it, he received the first of many divine revelations which would continue over a period of twenty-two years (610–632). These messages were finally collected and written down in the Qur'ān (The Recitation), Islam's sacred scripture.

For the powerful and prosperous Meccan oligarchy, the monotheistic message of this would-be reformer, with its condemnation of the socioeconomic inequities of Meccan life, constituted a direct challenge not only to traditional polytheistic religion but also to the power and prestige of the establishment, threatening their economic, social, and political interests. The Prophet denounced false contracts, usury, the neglect and exploitation of orphans and widows. He defended the rights of the poor and the oppressed, asserting that the rich had an obligation to the poor and dispossessed. Muḥammad rejected polytheism, claimed prophetic authority and leadership, and insisted that all true believers belonged to a single universal community *(ummah)* that transcended tribal bonds.

Creation of the Islamic Community. After ten years of preaching, faced with limited success and mounting persecution, Muḥammad and two hundred of his followers emigrated in 622 to Medina. This migration, known as the Hijrah, marked a turning point in Muḥammad's fortunes and a new stage in the history of the Islamic movement. Islam took on political form with the establishment of an Islamic community/state at Medina. The significance of the Hijrah (and of community in Islam) is reflected in its adoption as the beginning of the Islamic calendar. Muḥammad became prophet-head of a religio-political community. He established his leadership in Medina, subdued Mecca, and consolidated Muslim rule over the remainder of Arabia through diplomatic and military means and conversion. [*See* Hijrah.]

Muḥammad's impact on Muslim life and history cannot be overestimated. The reformism of the first Islamic movement under the leadership of Muḥammad became the reference point and model for later Islamic renewal or revivalist movements. Moreover, his character and personality inspired uncommon confidence and commitment, so much so that the practice of the Prophet, his *sunnah* or example, became the norm for community life. Muslims observed, remembered, and recounted stories about what the Prophet said and did. These *ḥadīth*s were preserved and passed on in oral and written form. The corpus of tradition literature reveals the comprehensive scope of Muḥammad's example. Traditions of the Prophet provide guidance for personal hygiene, dress, eating, marriage, treatment of wives, diplomacy, and warfare. [*See* Ḥadīth.]

The reformist spirit of the Qur'ān and of the Prophet's message affected religious ritual as well as politics and society. A process of adaptation or islamization characterized much of early Islam's development. Although some pre-Islamic Arabian beliefs and institutions were rejected and others introduced, the more common method was to reformulate or adapt existing practices to Islamic norms and values. Rituals such as pilgrimage *(ḥajj)* and prayer *(ṣalāt)* were reformulated and reinterpreted. The Kaʿbah in Mecca remained the sacred center for annual pilgrimage. However, it was no longer a shrine associated with tribal idols, which were destroyed, but rather rededicated to Allāh, for whom, Muslims believe, Abraham and Ismāʿīl had originally built the Kaʿbah or House of God.

Muḥammad introduced a new moral order in which the origin and end of all actions was not self or tribal interest but God's will. Belief in the Day of Judgment and resurrection of the body added a dimension of human responsibility and accountability that had been absent in Arabian religion. Tribal vengeance and retaliation were subordinated to belief in a just and merciful creator and judge. A society based on tribal affiliation and manmade tribal law or custom was to be replaced by a religiously bonded community, governed by God's law.

The Qur'ān proclaimed that God "made you into nations and tribes" (49.13). As God had previously called the Jews and then Christians to a covenant relationship, the Qur'ān declared that Muslims now constituted the new community of believers who were to be an example to other nations (2.143) with a mission to create a moral social order: "You are the best community evolved for mankind, enjoining what is right and forbidding what is wrong" (3.110). This command has influenced Muslim practice throughout the centuries, providing a rationale for political and moral activism. Government regulations, Islamic laws, the activities of religious officials and police who monitor public morality or behavior have all been justified as expressions of this moral mission to command the good and prohibit evil. [*See* Ummah.]

The Paths of Islam: Law and Mysticism. Islam's message was formulated in the formative centuries of classical Islam, providing a way of life whose letter or duties were delineated by Islamic law and whose spirit was embodied in the emergence of Islamic mysticism or Sufism. Islam emphasizes practice more than belief. As a result, law rather than theology is the central religious discipline and locus for defining the path of Islam and preserving its way of life. Islamic law *(sharīʿah)*, and with it a system of Islamic courts and judges (*qāḍī*s), developed during the first Islamic centuries. Islamic law is a comprehensive law which combines a Muslim's duties to God and to society, incorporating regulations governing prayer and fasting as well as family, penal, and international law. The Straight Path of Muslim life is set forth in an idealized blueprint. The four sources of law came to be identified in Sunnī Islam as the Qur'ān, the example *(sunnah)* of the prophet Muḥammad, reason (rules derived from the Qur'ān and *sunnah* by analogy, *qiyās*) and community consensus (*ijmā*ʿ). Both Sunnī and Shīʿī Islam accept the Qur'ān and *sunnah* of the Prophet as authoritative textual sources, but the Shīʿīs have maintained their own collections of traditions that also include the *sunnah* of ʿAlī and the imams. In addition, the Shīʿīs reject analogy and consensus as legal sources, since they regard the imam as the supreme legal interpreter and authority. In his absence, qualified religious scholars serve as his agents or representatives, interpreters (*mujtahid*s) of the law. Their consensus guides the community and is binding during the interim between the seclusion of the imam and his final messianic return. [*See* Sunnah; Sharīʿah; Qāḍī; Consensus; *and* Law.]

While God, the Qur'ān, and the prophet Muḥammad unite all Muslims in their common belief, the Five Pillars of Islam provide a unity of practice in the midst of the community's rich diversity. The pillars are the common denominator, the five essential obligatory practices that all Muslims must follow: (1) the profession of faith; (2) worship or prayer; (3) almsgiving; (4) fasting; and (5) pilgrimage to Mecca.

1. *Profession of Faith.* A Muslim is one who proclaims (*shahādah,* witness or testimony), "There is no God but the God and Muḥammad is the messenger of God." This brief yet profound testimony marks a person's entry into the Islamic community. It affirms Islam's absolute monotheism and acceptance of Muḥammad as the messenger of God, the last and final prophet. [*See* Shahādah.]

2. *Worship or Prayer.* Five times each day Muslims throughout the world are called to worship (*ṣalāt,* worship or prayer) God. Facing the holy city of Mecca, Islam's spiritual homeland, Muslims recall the revelation of the Qur'ān and reinforce a sense of belonging to a single, worldwide community of believers. On Friday, the noon prayer is a congregational prayer which usually takes place in a mosque (*masjid,* place of prostration). Since there is no clergy or priesthood in Islam, any Muslim may lead (*imām,* leader) the prayer. [*See* Ṣalāt; Imam.]

3. *Almsgiving.* The third pillar of Islam is the *zakāt,* a religious tithe (or almsgiving) on accumulated wealth and assets, not simply income. Payment of the *zakāt* instills a sense of communal identity and responsibility, the duty to attend to the community's social welfare. [*See* Zakāt.]

4. *Fasting.* Once each year, Muslims fast during the month of Ramaḍān. From dawn to dusk, abstention from food, drink, and sex are required of all healthy Muslims. The primary emphasis is not so much on abstinence and self-mortification as such but rather on spiritual self-discipline, reflection, and the performance of good works. The month of Ramaḍān ends with a great celebration, Feast of the Breaking of the Fast, ʿĪd al-Fiṭr, one of the great religious holy days and holidays of the Muslim calendar. Family members come from near and far to feast and exchange gifts in a celebration that lasts for three days. [*See* Ṣawm; Ramaḍān; ʿĪd al-Fiṭr.]

5. *Pilgrimage.* Ramaḍān is followed by the beginning of the pilgrimage season. Every adult Muslim who is physically and financially able is expected to perform the pilgrimage (*ḥajj*) to Mecca at least once in his or her lifetime. In recent years, almost two million Muslims a year from every part of the globe make the physical journey to the spiritual center of Islam, where they again experience the unity, breadth, and diversity of the Islamic community. The pilgrimage ends with the celebration of Great Feast (ʿĪd al-Kabīr or ʿĪd al-Aḍḥā), the Feast of Sacrifice, which commemorates God's command to Abraham to sacrifice his son Ismāʿīl (Isaac in Jewish and Christian traditions). [*See* Ḥajj; ʿĪd al-Aḍḥa.]

Jihād, "to strive or struggle" in the way of God, is sometimes referred to as the "sixth pillar of Islam," although it has no such official status. In its most general meaning, *jihād* refers to the obligation incumbent on all Muslims, as individuals and as a community, to exert (*jihād*) themselves to realize God's will—to lead a virtuous life and to spread the Islamic community through preaching, education, and example. However, it also includes the struggle for or defense of Islam, holy war. Despite the fact that *jihād* is not supposed to include aggressive warfare, this has occurred, as exemplified by early extremists such as the Khawārij and contemporary *jihād* groups such as Egypt's Jamāʿat al-Jihād (which assassinated President Anwar Sadat in 1981). [*See* Jihād.]

The development of Islamic law was paralleled in the eighth and ninth centuries by another movement, Sufism or Islamic mysticism. If law is the exterior or outer path of Islam's duties and obligations, Sufism is the interior or inner path which emphasizes detachment from the distractions and deceptiveness of this world. It focuses more on an interior spiritual life of personal piety, morality, and devotional love of God. By the twelfth century what had been primarily circles of spiritual elites were transformed into a mass, popular movement. A vast network of orders or brotherhoods spread Sufism from the Atlantic to Southeast Asia, as its combination of the esoteric and the ecstatic offered a spirituality that won the hearts of educated and uneducated alike. Its attractiveness to the masses of Muslims and its strength as a missionary vehicle came from its spiritual vision and ritual practices as well as its more inclusive, accommodationist, and syncretist tendencies. As such, Sufism was experienced as a challenge to the law-centered, Islamic orthodoxy of the *ʿulamāʾ* (religions scholars), many of whom denounced its esoteric claims and accommodation of "foreign, un-Islamic" doctrines and practices. Ṣūfī orders became international in organization and scope, extending from North Africa across Central Asia to Southeast Asia. [*See* Sufism.]

The Muslim Community in History. The period of Muḥammad and the first four caliphs of Islam, the Four Rightly Guided Caliphs (632–661), is remembered by Sunnī Muslims as the best of times, the normative period to which the community has often returned for guidance and inspiration. During this time, the spread of Islam and conquest of Arabia were completed, and Islamic rule was extended throughout much of the Middle East and North Africa. In successive centuries, two great caliphates, the Umayyad (661–750) in Damascus and the ʿAbbāsid (749–1258) in Baghdad, oversaw the consolidation of Muslim power, the expansion of Islamic empire as a world political force, and the development and flourishing of Islamic civilization. [*See* Rightly Guided Caliphs; Umayyad Dynasty; ʿAbbāsid Dynasty.]

Muslim armies, fired by their new faith and lured by the spoils of war, overran the Eastern (Roman) Byzantine and the Sassanian (Persian) Empires. The purpose of the early wars or *jihāds* was not conversion but conquest, booty, and the spread of Islam's (God's) rule. As Islam spread to new territories, inhabitants were offered three choices: (1) conversion to Islam and full membership or citizenship; (2) "protection"—Jews and Christians, known as "People of the Book" (i.e., those who possessed a sacred book) in exchange for payment of a head or poll tax *(jizyah)* possessed a more limited form of citizenship as "protected people" *(dhimmī)*, by which they were allowed to practice their faith and be ruled in their private lives by their religious leaders and law; or (3) combat or the sword for those who resisted and rejected Muslim rule. Much of Islam's expansion throughout history was the result of the activities of merchants, traders, and mystics, as well as soldiers, who proved effective missionaries in carrying the message of Islam from Africa to Southeast Asia, from Timbuktu to Sumatra, and from Central Asia to Spain, Portugal, and southern Italy. [*See* Jizyah; Dhimmī.]

After the destruction of the ʿAbbāsid Empire by the Mongols in 1258, from the thirteenth to the eighteenth century the Islamic world consisted of a string of local states or sultanates. Among the most powerful sultanates or empires were the Ottoman (Turkey and much of the Arab world and Eastern Europe), the Ṣafavid in Persia, and the Mughal in the Indian subcontinent. [*See* Ottoman Empire; Ṣafavid Dynasty; Mughal Empire.]

Sectarianism: Sunnī and Shīʿī Islam. The issue of leadership after the death of Muḥammad led to a major split in the Muslim community and gave rise to its two major branches or divisions: the Sunnī, who today represent about 85 percent of the world's Muslims, and the Shīʿī, who constitute 15 percent. The Sunnī majority believe that Muḥammad died without designating a successor. Thus, the elders of the community selected or elected a caliph (*khalīfah* or successor of the prophet Muḥammad) to be political leader of the Islamic community-state or caliphate. The Shīʿī minority believe that Muḥammad did in fact designate the senior male of his family, his son-in-law and cousin, ʿAlī ibn Abī Ṭālib, to lead the community. The Shīʿīs, or partisans of ʿAlī, maintained that the leader (imam) of the Muslim community should be a descendant of the family of the Prophet. Thus, ʿAlī's followers believed that he, and not the first caliph Abū Bakr, should have succeeded the Prophet.

Shīʿī were among the early opposition to the Umayyad caliphs. The founder of the Umayyad dynasty, Muʿāwiyah, was a provincial governor who had challenged ʿAlī when he had "finally" succeeded Muḥammad and become the fourth caliph of Islam; subsequently he seized power at ʿAlī's death. Ḥusayn, the son of ʿAlī, led a small band of followers against the army of Yazīd, Muʿāwiyah's son and successor, in 680 in which he and his army were slaughtered at Karbala (in modern-day Iraq). The martyrdom of Ḥusayn and its ritual commemoration became a central religious paradigm for Shīʿī Islam and its history as a righteous and aggrieved minority community living under Sunnī Muslim rule. Thus the Shīʿī developed their own distinctive vision of leadership and history, centered on the martyred family of the Prophet and based on the belief that leadership of the Islamic community rightfully resided in the imamate, the religiopolitical leaders and descendents of ʿAlī or his sons Ḥusayn and Ḥasan. [*See* Karbala; *and the biographies of ʿAlī ibn Abī Ṭālib and Ḥusayn ibn ʿAlī.*]

The fundamental difference between Sunnī and Shīʿī Islam is their institutions for leadership, the imamate and the caliphate. For Shīʿī Islam the Imam is not just the political successor (caliph) of the prophet Muḥammad but the religiopolitical leader of the community. Though not a prophet, for Muḥammad is the last of the prophets, Shīʿī belief came to regard the Imam as religiously inspired, perfect and sinless. ʿAlī and his wife Fāṭimah, the daughter of Muḥammad, along with their children Ḥasan and Ḥusayn came to constitute a holy family in Shīʿī piety; their tombs are the objects of veneration and pilgrimage. Whereas Sunnī Islam came to place religious authority for interpreting Islam in the consensus *(ijmāʿ)* of the *ʿulamāʾ* who represented the collective judgment of the community, for Shīʿī Islam continued divine guidance could be found in the Imam, who is the final religious authority. Thus, the lives and traditions of ʿAlī and the other great Imams of Shiism, after the Qurʾān and the *sunnah* of the Prophet, are sources of guidance for Shīʿī Islam. Similarly, Sunnī and Shīʿī Islam developed differing concepts of the meaning of history. For Sunnī Muslims, early Islamic success, power, and wealth were the signs of God's guidance and reward for a faithful community as well as validation of Muslim belief and claims. For Shīʿī Muslims, history is the theater for the oppressed and disinherited minority community to restore God's rule on earth and the authority of the Imam over the entire community of believers. A righteous community was to persist in the struggle, as had ʿAlī against the Sunnī caliph Muʿāwiyah and Ḥusayn against Yazīd, to reestablish God's will, the righteous rule of the Imam. Realization of a just social order under the Imam was to become a messianic expectation for centuries as Shīʿī Muslims continued to struggle and live under Sunnī rule.

Historically, Shīʿī Islam split into two major branches in the eighth century, dependent on their recognition of either twelve or seven Imams or descendants of Muḥammad—the Ithnā ʿAsharī (Twelvers) and the Ismāʿīlīs (sometimes called the Seveners). The numerical designation of each was caused by the death or disappearance of their Imam and disruption of hereditary succession. The Twelvers believe that the twelfth Imam (Muḥammad al-Muntaẓir, or Muḥammad the Awaited One) disappeared in 874. His disappearance was theologically resolved by the belief that the imam had gone into hiding or occultation. Shīʿī were to await his return as the Mahdi (expected one) who would restore the Shīʿī community to its rightful place and usher in a reign of justice and peace. [*See* Ithnā ʿAsharīyah; Ismāʿīlīyah; Mahdi.]

Modern Islam. From the eighteenth to the twentieth centuries the Islamic world has witnessed a protracted period of upheaval and renewal. Muslims struggled with the failures of their societies, the impact of European colonialism, and subsequent superpower rivalry between the United States and the Soviet Union, and responded to the intellectual and moral challenges of a changing world. In the nineteenth century across much of the Muslim world, a series of revivalist movements rose up: the Wahhābī in Saudi Arabia, the Mahdists in Sudan, the Sanūsī in Libya, the Fulani in Nigeria, and the Padri in Indonesia. Though quite different in many respects, these shared a common concern about the decline of Muslim fortunes and a common conviction that the cure was a purification of their societies and way of life by a more faithful return to pristine Islam, to the teachings of the Qurʾān and the example of the Prophet. Many called for the suppression or reform of Sufism, rejected historical assimilation of foreign, un-Islamic "innovations" (beliefs and practices), and claimed the right to interpret *(ijtihād)* Islam. However, they did not seek to reinterpret or reformulate Islamic law and practice in light of contemporary needs, but rather to return to and restore the practice of the early Islamic community. These religiomoral movements created communities of like-minded believers, committed to the creation of Islamic societies. They were often transformed into political movements that established Islamic states, forerunners of modern states.

In the late nineteenth and early twentieth centuries, Islamic modernist movements responded to the intellectual and political challenge of Western hegemony. Wishing to bridge the gap between their Islamic heritage and modernity, between traditional religious and modern secular leaders, men such as Jamāl al-Dīn al-Afghānī and Muḥammad ʿAbduh in the Middle East and Sayyid Aḥmad Khān and Muhammad Iqbal in South Asia sought to rejuvenate and restore the pride, identity, and strength of a debilitated Islamic community. They advocated what was essentially a process of Islamic acculturation, emphasizing the compatibility of Islam with reason, science, and technology. All argued for Islamic reform, for the need to reinterpret Islam in light of the new questions and issues which were brought by modern life. Maintaining that Islam and modernity, revelation and reason, were compatible, they advocated religious, legal, educational, and social reforms to revitalize the Muslim community.

Islamic modernism inspired movements for reform and national independence but remained attractive primarily to an intellectual elite. It failed to produce a systematic reinterpretation of Islam or develop effective organizations to preserve, propagate, and implement its message. This limitation contributed to the emergence of Islamic organizations like the Muslim Brotherhood in Egypt and the Jamāʿat-i Islāmī (Islamic Society) in South Asia. The founders of the Muslim Brotherhood (Ḥasan al-Bannāʾ) and the Jamāʿat-i Islāmī (Abu al-Aʿlā Mawdūdī) criticized secular elites for simply emulating the West and Islamic modernist reformers for westernizing Islam. In particular, they condemned the tendency of most Muslim countries to adapt uncritically Western models of development and thus westernize Muslim societies. Instead they proclaimed the self-sufficiency of Islam as a response to the demands of modern life. Islam, they asserted, offers its own alternative path to capitalism and communism/socialism; it is a total, comprehensive way of life. The objective of these Islamic reformers was to establish effective organizations to implement an Islamic system of government and law through social and political action.

During the post–World War II era, most of the Muslim world regained its independence. Many of the newly emerging independent states, including Lebanon, Syria, Sudan, Jordan, Iraq, and Pakistan, were carved out by European colonial powers, who created states with artificial or arbitrarily drawn boundaries and even appointed their rulers. Thus, political legitimacy and national identity/unity compounded the problem of nation building and remained critical issues. Although Turkey chose a secular path and Saudi Arabia emerged as a self-declared Islamic state, the majority of Muslim nations, guided by Western-oriented elites, combined Western-inspired political, economic, legal, educational development with a minimal recognition of the role of Islam in public life. Because the West provided the models for modern development, the presupposition and expectation was that modernization and development would necessarily lead to progressive westernization and secularization. Iran's Islamic Revolution of 1979–1980 shattered this assumption and for many raised fears of the spread of "militant Islam," "Khomeineism," or "Islamic fundamentalism."

Islamic Revivalism or "Fundamentalism." Much of the reassertion of religion in politics and society has been subsumed under the term "Islamic fundamentalism." Although fundamentalism is a common designation, in the press and among many experts, it is used in a variety of ways. For a number of reasons, it tells us everything and yet, at the same time, tells us nothing. First, all those who call for a return to foundational beliefs or the fundamentals of a religion can be called fundamentalist. In a strict sense, this could include all practicing Muslims who accept the Qurʾān as the literal word of God and the *sunnah* of the prophet Muḥammad as a normative model for living. Second, understanding and perceptions of fundamentalism are heavily influenced by American Protestantism. *Webster's New Collegiate Dictionary*, for example, defines *fundamentalism* as "a movement in twentieth century Protestantism emphasizing the literally interpreted Bible as fundamental to Christian life and teaching."

For many liberal or mainline Christians, *fundamentalist* is a pejorative or derogatory term applied rather indiscriminately to all those who advocate a literalist biblical position and thus are regarded as static, retrogressive, and extremist. As a result, fundamentalism often has been regarded popularly as referring to those who are literalists and wish to return to and replicate the past. In fact, few individuals or organizations in the Middle East fit such a stereotype. Indeed, many fundamentalist leaders have had the best educations, enjoy responsible positions in society, and are adept at harnessing the latest technology to propagate their views and create viable modern institutions, such as schools, hospitals, and social-service agencies. Third, the term fundamentalism is often equated with political activism, extremism, fanaticism, terrorism, and anti-Americanism. While some Islamic activists or Islamists engage in radical religiopolitics, most work within the established order.

Perhaps the best way to appreciate the many faces and postures of fundamentalism is to consider the following. Fundamentalism is a term that has been applied to the governments of Libya, Saudi Arabia, Pakistan, and Iran. Yet the term fundamentalism reveals little about the nature of governments and of their Islamic character. Muʿammar al-Qadhdhāfī has claimed the right to interpret Islam, questioned the authenticity of the traditions of the prophet Muḥammad, silenced the religious establishment as well as the Muslim Brotherhood, and advocated a populist state of the masses. The rulers of Saudi Arabia, by contrast, have aligned themselves with the *ʿulamāʾ*, preached a more literalist brand of Islam, and used religion to legitimate a conservative monarchy. Qadhdhāfī's portrayal as an unpredictable, independent supporter of worldwide terrorism stands in sharp relief against the image of low-key, conservative, pro-American King Fahd. Similarly, the foreign policy of the clerically run Shīʿī state of Iran contrasted sharply with the military regime which implemented Pakistan's Islamic system *(niẓām-i Islām)* under General Zia ul-Haq (1977–1988). Iran under Ayatollah Khomeini was highly critical, even condemnatory of the West, often at odds with the international community, and regarded as a radical terrorist state, while Pakistan under the Islamically oriented Zia ul-Haq was a close ally of the United States, had relations with the West and the international community, and was generally regarded as moderate.

Islam reemerged as a potent global force in Muslim politics during the 1970s and 1980s. Contemporary Islamic revivalism embraced much of the Muslim world from Sudan to Indonesia. Governments in the Muslim world as well as opposition groups and political parties increasingly appealed to religion for legitimacy and to mobilize popular support. Islamic activists have held cabinet-level positions in Jordan, Sudan, Iran, Malaysia, and Pakistan. Islamic organizations have constituted the leading opposition parties/organizations in Egypt, Tunisia, Algeria, Morocco, the West Bank and Gaza, Malaysia, and Indonesia. Where permitted, they have participated in elections and served in parliament and in city government. Islam has been a significant ingredient in nationalist struggles and resistance movements in Afghanistan, the Muslim republics of Soviet Central Asia, in Kashmir, and in the communal politics of Lebanon, India, Thailand, China, and the Philippines.

Islamic activist (fundamentalist) organizations have run the spectrum from those who have participated within the system, such as the Muslim Brotherhoods in Egypt, Jordan, and Sudan, the Jamāʿat-i Islāmī in South Asia, Tunisia's Ḥizb al-Nahḍah (Renaissance Party), and Algeria's Islamic Salvation Front. At the same time, radical revolutionaries, such as Egypt's Society of Muslims (known more popularly as Takfīr wa-al-Hijrah, Excommunication and Flight), al-Jihād (Holy War), and the Jamāʿat al-Islāmīyah (Islamic Group), as well Lebanon's Ḥizbullāh (Party of God) and Islamic Jihād, have used violence and terrorism in their attempts to destabilize and overthrow prevailing political systems. [*See* Fundamentalism.]

Roots of the Resurgence. To speak of a contemporary Islamic revival can be deceptive if revivalism is equated with the conclusion that Islam had somehow disappeared or been absent from the Muslim world. It is more correct to view Islamic revivalism as a revitalization movement that has led to a higher profile of Islam in Muslim politics and society. Thus, what had previously seemed to be an increasingly marginalized force in Muslim public life reemerged in the 1970s, often dramatically, as a vibrant sociopolitical reality. Islam's resurgence in Muslim politics reflected a growing religious revivalism in both personal and public life that swept across much of the Muslim world and had a substantial impact on world politics.

The indices of an Islamic reawakening in personal life are: increased attention to religious observances (mosque attendance, prayer, fasting), proliferation of religious publications, audio- and videotapes, greater emphasis on Islamic dress and values, and the revitalization of Sufism. This broader-based renewal has also been accompanied by Islam's reassertion in public life: an increase in Islamically oriented or legitimated governments, organizations, laws, banks, social welfare services, and educational institutions. Both governments and opposition movements have turned to Islam to enhance their authority and to muster popular support. Governmental use of Islam has been illustrated by a cross section of leaders in the Middle East and Asia: Libya's Muʿammar Qadhdhāfī, Sudan's Jaʿfar al-Numayrī (Nimeiri), Egypt's Anwar Sadat, Iran's Ayatollah Khomeini, Pakistan's Zia ul-Haq, Bangladesh's Muhammad Ershad (Irshād), Malaysia's Mahathir Mohamed. Most rulers and governments, including more secular states, such as Turkey and Tunisia, aware of the potential strength of Islam, have shown increased sensitivity to and anxiety about Islamic issues and concerns. The Iranian Revolution of 1979 focused attention on "Islamic fundamentalism" and with it the spread and vitality of political Islam in other parts of the Muslim world. However, the contemporary revival has its origins and roots in the late 1960s and early 1970s when events in such disparate areas as Egypt and Libya as well as Pakistan and Malaysia contributed to experiences of crisis/failure as well as power/success that served as catalysts for a more visible reassertion of Islam in both public and private life.

Although political Islam has varied significantly from one country to another, there are recurrent themes: the belief that existing political, economic, and social systems had failed; a disenchantment with and at times rejection of the West; a quest for identity and greater authenticity; and the conviction that Islam provides a self-sufficient ideology for state and society, a valid alternative to secular nationalism, socialism, and capitalism.

The experience of failure triggered an identity crisis that led many to question the path and direction of political and social development and to turn inward for strength and guidance. The Western-oriented policies of governments and elites appeared to have failed. The soul searching and critique of the sociopolitical realities of the Arab and Muslim world, which followed the 1967 Israeli war and the crises in Pakistan, Malaysia, and Lebanon, extended to other Muslim areas, embraced a broad spectrum of society, and raised many questions about the direction and accomplishments of development. More often than not, despite the hopes and aspirations of independence, the mixed record of several decades existence was a challenge to the legitimacy and effectiveness of modern Muslim states. A crisis mentality fostered by specific events and the general impact and disruption of modernity spawned a growing disillusionment and sense of the failure of modern Muslim states.

Politically, modern secular nationalism was found wanting. Neither liberal nationalism nor Arab nationalism/socialism had fulfilled their promises. Muslim governments seemed less interested and less successful in establishing their political legitimacy and creating an ideology for national unity than in perpetuating autocratic rule. The Muslim world was still dominated by monarchs and military or ex-military rulers; political parties were banned or restricted, elections often rigged. Parliamentary systems of government and political parties existed at the sufferance of rulers, whose legitimacy, like their security, rested on a loyal military and secret police. Many were propped up by and dependent on foreign governments and multinational corporations.

Economically, both Western capitalism and Marxist socialism were judged incapable of effectively stemming the growing tide of poverty and illiteracy. Charges of corruption, concentration of and maldistribution of wealth found ready recipients as one looked at individual countries and the region. The disparity between rich and poor was striking in urban areas where the neighborhoods and new suburbs of the wealthy few stood in stark contrast to the deteriorating dwellings and sprawling shantytowns of the many. Socioculturally and psychologically, modernization was seen as a legacy of European colonialism perpetuated by Western-oriented elites who imposed and fostered the twin processes of westernization and secularization. As dependence on Western models of development was seen as the cause of political and military failures, so too, some Muslims charged, blind imitation of the West, an uncritical westernization of Muslim societies that some called the disease of "Westoxification," led to a cultural dependence that threatened the loss of Muslim identity. Secular, "valueless," social change was identified as the cause of sociomoral decline, a major contributor to the breakdown of the Muslim family, more permissive, promiscuous societies, and spiritual malaise. The psychological impact of modernity and, with it, rapid sociocultural change cannot be forgotten. Urban areas had undergone physical and institutional changes so that both the skylines and the infrastructure of cities were judged modern by their Western profile and facade. To be modern was to be Western in dress, language, ideas, education, behavior (from table manners to greetings), architecture, furnishings. Urban areas became the primary locations for work and living. Modern governments and companies as well as foreign advisers and investors focused their attentions and projects on urban areas so that the results of modernization only trickled down to rural areas.

Rapid urbanization led to the migration of many from outlying villages and towns. Their hopes and dreams for a better life were often replaced by the harsh realities of poverty in urban slums and shantytowns. Psychological as well as physical displacement occurred. Loss of village, town, and extended family ties and traditional values were accompanied by the shock and contrast of modern urban life and its westernized culture and mores. Many, swept along in a sea of alienation and marginalization, found an anchor or secure and safe ground for their lives in their religion. Islam offered a sense of identity, fraternity, and cultural values that offset the psychological dislocation and cultural threat of their new environment. Both the poor in their urban neighborhoods, which approximated traditional ghettos in the midst of modern cities, and those in the lower middle class, who were able to take advantage of the new educational and job opportunities of the city and thus experienced culture shock more profoundly and regularly, found a welcome sense of meaning and security in their religious faith and identity. Islamic organizations, their workers and message offered a more familiar alternative and answer which resonated with their experience, identified their problems, and offered a time honored solution.

Ideological Worldview. Contemporary revivalism is rooted in Islam's time-honored tradition of renewal (*tajdīd*) and reform (*iṣlāḥ*) embodied in Muḥammad's leadership of the first Islamic movement, seventeenth- and eighteenth-century revivalism, and Islamic modernist movements. At the heart of the revivalist worldview is the belief that the Muslim world is in a state of decline owing to Muslims' departure from the straight path of Islam. The cure is a return to Islam in personal and public life that will ensure the restoration of Islamic identity, values, and power. For Islamic political activists Islam is a total or comprehensive way of life, stipulated in the Qur'ān, God's revelation, mirrored in the example of Muḥammad and the nature of the first Muslim community-state, and embodied in the comprehensive nature of *sharī'ah*, God's revealed law. Islamic activists or Islamists believe that the renewal and revitalization of Muslim governments and societies require the restoration or reimplementation of Islamic law, the blueprint for an Islamically guided and socially just state and society. [*See* Iṣlāḥ; Revival and Renewal.]

Although the westernization and secularization of society are condemned, modernization as such is not. Science and technology are accepted, but the pace, direction, and extent of change are to be subordinated to Islamic belief and values in order to guard against excessive dependence on Western culture and values.

Radical movements go beyond these principles and often operate on the following assumptions:

1. Islam and the West are locked in an ongoing battle that began during the expansion of Islam, is heavily influenced by the legacy of the Crusades and European colonialism, and is the product today of a Judeo-Christian conspiracy. Radical extremists regard the Cold War's superpower rivalry and neocolonialism and the power of Zionism as the foreign sources of Muslim impotence and Western hegemony. The West (Britain, France, and especially the United States) is blamed for its support of un-Islamic or unjust regimes (Egypt, Iran, Lebanon) and biased support for Israel in the face of Palestinian displacement. Violence against these governments and their representatives as well as Western multinationals is regarded as a legitimate form of self-defense.

2. Islam is not simply an ideological alternative for Muslim societies but a theological and political imperative. Since it is God's command, implementation must be immediate, not gradual, and the obligation to do so is incumbent on all true Muslims. Therefore, those who hesitate, are apolitical, or resist—individuals and governments—are no longer to be regarded as Muslims. They are declared atheists or unbelievers, enemies of God, against whom all true Muslims must wage *jihād*.

From the Periphery to the Center: Mainstream Revivalism. While the exploitation of Islam by governments and by extremist organizations has reinforced the secular orientations of many Muslims and the cynicism of many in the West, a less well-known and yet potentially far-reaching social transformation has also occurred in the Muslim world. In the 1990s Islamic revivalism has ceased to be restricted to small, marginal organizations on the periphery of society but instead has become part of mainstream Muslim society, producing a new class of modern, educated, but Islamically oriented elites who work alongside, and at times in coalitions with, their secular counterparts. Revivalism continues to grow as a broadbased religio-social movement, functioning today in virtually every Muslim country and transnationally. It is a vibrant, multifaceted movement that will embody the major impact of Islamic revivalism for the foreseeable future. Its goal is the transformation of society through the Islamic formation of individuals at the grassroots level. Islamic organizations work in social services (hospitals, clinics, legal aid societies), in economic projects (Islamic banks, investment houses, insurance companies), in education (schools, child-care centers, youth camps), and in religious publishing and broadcasting. Their common programs are aimed at young and old alike.

Islamic ideology and movements are not solely a marginal phenomenon limited to small radical groups or organizations. They have become part and parcel of mainstream religion and society. The presence and appeal of a more pronounced Islamic orientation is to be found among the middle and lower classes, educated and uneducated, professionals and workers, young and old, men, women, and children. A new generation of modern, educated, but Islamically (rather than secularly) oriented leaders can be found in Egypt, Sudan, Tunisia, Jordan, Iran, Malaysia, Kuwait, Saudi Arabia, and Pakistan. Islamic activists have become part and parcel of the political process. They have participated in national and local elections; scored impressive victories in Algeria's municipal and parliamentary elections; emerged as the chief opposition parties or groups in Egypt, Tunisia, and Jordan; served in cabinet level positions in Sudan, Jordan, Pakistan, Iran, and Malaysia.

Both the implementation of Islam by governments

and the track record of Islamic movements have raised many questions about the use or manipulation of religion for political purposes as well as the nature and direction of Islamic reform. Two critical questions are: "Whose Islam?" and "What Islam?" While the *ʿulamāʾ* still assert their role as the primary interpreters of Islam, the guardians of Islamic law, both Muslim rulers and an educated lay Islamic leadership have threatened their domain. Libya's Muʿammar Qadhdhāfī has ignored and even denounced the *ʿulamāʾ*. The Saudi monarchy, while usually careful to cultivate strong ties with Saudi Arabia's religious establishment, has in the 1990s increasingly encountered opposition from more independent *ʿulamāʾ*. Pakistan's Zia ul-Haq, despite a sensitivity to *ʿulamāʾ* concerns, ultimately was the final arbiter of Pakistan's Islamic experiment. Only Shīʿī Iran has seen the *ʿulamāʾ* in power. Moreover, many Muslims increasingly call for greater political participation and democratization, more consensual (parliamentary or assembly) forms of government. The formation of Islamic governments or more Islamically oriented societies raises questions about the nature of the state and society and of its leadership. Who is to determine who shall define the Islamic character of the state and society—rulers (kings, military men, ex-military, the *ʿulamāʾ*, or the people through elected parliaments?

In the latter half of the twentieth century, the proliferation and growth of Islamic movements has witnessed the emergence of a lay Islamic elite leadership—modern, educated, Islamically oriented professionals who have been the founders and key leaders of Islamic movements and organizations. Their role as Islamic actors and their professional expertise have challenged the traditional monopoly of the *ʿulamāʾ* (the learned) as religious leaders and interpreters of Islam. Islam in theory knows no clergy and the right of personal interpretation (*ijtihād*) technically belongs to all qualified Muslims, but historically the *ʿulamāʾ* did constitute themselves as a professional class. The complex nature and the multiple disciplines necessary to address many modern political, economic, and social issues that are beyond the traditional areas of competence of most *ʿulamāʾ*, have led some to question of the need to broaden the definition of what constitutes a qualified scholar. Is there now a new *ʿulamāʾ*, a new class of *ʿulamāʾ*? Or should the *ʿulamāʾ* retain their authority as religious scholars based on their training in religion (knowledge of the Qurʾān, *sunnah, sharīʿah*) but now in complex decision making advise or be advised by "modern experts"?

"What Islam?" Does the reassertion of Islam in Muslim public life mean a process of restoration or reformation? Does the creation of more Islamically oriented societies require the wholesale reintroduction of classical Islamic law, developed in the early centuries of Islam, or will it require a substantial reformulation of Islam? At the heart of contemporary Islamic revivalism are a series of key issues that concern the nature and development of Islam. Whether it be issues of marriage and divorce, the nature of the state and political participation, or the status and role of women and minorities in society, the issue of change in Islam and the role of traditional concepts such as personal interpretation, community consensus, and consultation (*shūrā*) have become pivotal.

Some believe that the Islamic paradigm is fixed in classical Islamic law, but others distinguish between *sharīʿah and fiqh,* human understanding, interpretation, and application of *sharīʿah*. The latter would argue that Muslims must distinguish between those elements of Islamic law which are immutable and those that are the product of human interpretation and thus are capable of change and reform in light of new historical circumstances and social conditions. Similarly, although community consensus traditionally was reduced to the opinion or consensus of the *ʿulamāʾ* and consultation referred to the ruler's consultation with political and religious elites, today many, though certainly not all Muslims, transform or reconceptualize these concepts to support parliamentary systems of government and decision making.

However, the status of non-Muslims and the implications of political pluralism remain significant contemporary Islamic questions. The record of Islamic experiments in Pakistan, Iran, and Sudan raises serious questions about the rights of women and minorities under Islamically oriented governments. The extent to which the growth of Islamic revivalism has been accompanied in some countries by attempts to restrict women's rights, to separate women and men in public, to enforce veiling, and to restrict women's public roles in society strikes fear in some segments of Muslim society and challenges the credibility of those who call for islamization of state and society. The record of discrimination against the Bahāʾī in Iran and the Aḥmadī in Pakistan as "deviant" groups (heretical offshoots of Islam), against Christians in Sudan, and Arab Jews in Syria, as well as increased communal sectarian conflict between Muslims and Christians in Egypt and Nigeria, pose similar questions of religious pluralism and tolerance. Without a reinterpretation of classical Islamic law to safeguard the rights of non-Muslim minorities as "protected people," Islamic states today would have a weak pluralistic profile which would restrict the participation of minorities and limit their rights and opportunities.

Substantive religious/intellectual reform has lagged behind and thus not informed much of Islamic political and social activism. Islamic movements continue to be challenged to move beyond slogans and vague promises to concrete socioeconomic programs, to bridge the gap between traditional Islamic belief/institutions and the sociopolitical realities of the contemporary world. They are increasingly challenged to demonstrate their ability to be effective problem solvers, not just social critics, who can transform ideological commitment and slogans into concrete policies and programs that respond to national and local concerns in diverse sociopolitical contexts. They must do this in a manner that is pluralistic enough in scope to enjoy the support of a broad and diverse constituency, fellow activists, secularists, religious/ethnic minorities, and that broad-based majority of Muslims who, while wishing to be good Muslims, do not want to see the stability of their societies and their lives disrupted.

The history of the Islamic community has spanned more than fourteen centuries. As in the past Islam continues to be a vibrant and dynamic religious tradition, providing guidance for almost one-fifth of the world's population, continuing to grow and expand geographically, facing new problems and issues. There are often as many differences as similarities in Muslim interpretations of the nature of the state, Islamic law, the status of women and minorities as there are sharp differences regarding implementation of an Islamic order or system of government. For many Muslims, Islamic revivalism is a social rather than a political movement whose goal is a more Islamically minded and oriented society but not necessarily the creation of an Islamic state. For others, the establishment of an Islamic order requires the creation of an Islamic state. Thus, there is today, as in the past, a rich diversity of interpretations and applications of Islam. As with other religions and religious communities, Muslims continue to grapple with the role and relevance of Islam, and, in the process, demonstrate both the unity and diversity of Islam.

[*See also* Allāh; Muḥammad; Qur'ān; Shīʿī Islam; *and* Sunnī Islam. *In addition, see entries on the figures and organizations mentioned as well as entries on specific countries.*]

BIBLIOGRAPHY

Ayubi, Nazih. *Political Islam: Religion and Politics in the Arab World.* London and New York, 1991.

Esposito, John L., ed. *Islam in Asia: Religion, Politics, and Society.* New York and Oxford, 1987.

Esposito, John L. *Islam: The Straight Path.* Exp. ed. New York and Oxford, 1991.

Esposito, John L. *Islam and Politics.* 3d ed. Syracuse, N.Y., 1991.

Esposito, John L. *The Islamic Threat: Myth or Reality?* New York and Oxford, 1992.

Haddad, Yvonne Yazbeck, et al., eds. *The Contemporary Islamic Revival: A Critical Survey and Bibliography.* New York, 1991.

Piscatori, J. P., ed. *Islam in the Political Process.* Cambridge, 1983.

Voll, John Obert. "Renewal and Reform in Islamic History: *Tajdid* and *Islah.*" In *Voices of Resurgent Islam,* edited by John L. Esposito, pp. 32–47. New York and Oxford, 1983.

Voll, John Obert. *Islam, Continuity, and Change in the Modern World.* 2d ed. Syracuse, N.Y., 1994.

JOHN L. ESPOSITO

Islam in the Middle East and North Africa

Revelation in the Middle East comes in a variety of versions. Islam is one of them and, like Judaism and Christianity, it is constitutive of an entire civilization. Islamic civilization evolved according to its own dynamics, covering the periods of sacred foundation (634–750), scriptural formation (750–1050), classicism (1050–1800), and modern transformation (1800–present). The focus in this article is on the latter period in which, largely in response to the modern Western concept of rationality, Muslim thinkers sought and still seek to formulate the elements of an authentically rational Islam.

Revelation and Theology. The sacred story of Islam begins with Abraham's foundation of a shrine, the Kaʿbah, devoted to God *(Allāh)* the One, in Mecca. It includes accounts of peoples sliding back to paganism as well as biblical figures and Arab prophets calling them to return to God's law; the youth, prophetic calling, and community leadership of the prophet Muḥammad in Mecca and Medina; the rededication of the Kaʿbah to the God of Abraham; the unification of Arabia under Islam and the Arab-Islamic conquest of Syria, Iraq, Egypt, and Iran; the murder of Caliph ʿUthmān and the subsequent struggle for leadership between Caliph ʿAlī and governor Muʿāwiyah. The story concludes with the allegedly worldly rule of the Umayyad caliphs and the emergence of religious scholars liberating Islam from the caliphal embrace.

This sacred story is obviously built on empirical historical facts. At a minimum, the establishment of an

Arab caliphate in Syria, Iraq, and Egypt, the minting of caliphal coins with religious inscriptions (earliest extant specimens dating from 690/691), and the construction of the Dome of the Rock in Jerusalem with its Qur'ānic verses and anti-Christian pronouncements (690/691) are indubitable events. But, as in Judaism and Christianity, there is considerable disagreement over what else actually happened.

A growing number of contemporary scholars have come to the conclusion that the sacred story of Islamic origins should not be read as a secular history with the addition of a few religious flourishes. Scholars using the form-critical method have shown that the sacred story is inseparable from the community of religious scholars (*ʿulamā'*) that during the formative period (c.750–1050) was engaged in shaping the holy scripture (Qur'ān), extrascriptural tradition *(sunnah),* theology *(kalām),* and law *(sharīʿah)* of Islam in opposition to the older revelations of Christianity and Judaism. Our understanding of Islamic origins depends almost entirely on the scholars of the formative period, who wanted to present a sacred Islam that emerged fullblown in precaliphal times and in remote western Arabia during the early seventh century in order to provide the nascent Islam of their own time with its distinctive identity and to elevate it over the older revelations. Thus the sacred story of Islam is not the same as its history, which begins fully, in the empirical sense, only in the mid-eighth century. Two important characteristics of Islam date from the formative period.

First is the rejection of caesaropapism. In less than a century Arabs succeeded in creating a caliphal empire stretching from Iberia to northwestern India (c.712). This empire contained a hodgepodge of orthodox and heterodox Christian and Jewish groups, Zoroastrians, Buddhists, and various other populations. It was wracked by wars among the Arab ruling class (658–661, 683–692) and eventually by a revolution resulting in a change of caliphal dynasties from the Umayyads to the ʿAbbāsids (750) [*See* Caliph.]

Both dynasties sought to consolidate their power through caesaropapism, a policy of claiming divine sanction for the caliphate and imposing doctrinal unity on the empire. Religious scholars were engaged to devise the desired doctrines, although other scholars resented government control and offered alternative doctrines for the empire. In the course of the 900s a majority of the religious scholars managed to achieve independence from caliphal dictates; eventually, in 1063, it was a much chastened caliph who pronounced Sunnism, the scholars' anticaesaropapist version of Islam, as the official orthodox religion.

Although the religious scholars overcame caliphal control, they maintained the caliphal policy of fusing emergent Islam with the cultural and legal traditions of the empire's core countries, Syria and Iraq. They thereby succeeded in creating a religio-legal Islam that was largely independent from political regimes and their vicissitudes. Within this Islam the sacred story of a small and simple early Islamic community in Mecca and Medina, complete with divine law and communal institutions but without an empire, provided the inspirational core: Islam did not depend on imperial and dynastic political structures and was indeed better off without them. Contrary to widespread contemporary opinion, original Islam—that is, the scholarly Sunnism shaped in the period 750–1050—did not fuse religion and state. Although Sunnī scholars required their rulers to be good Muslims, they adamantly opposed caesaropapism.

The Shīʿī minority of Islamic civilization, the origins of which are rooted in the ruling class rifts of the seventh century, opposed Sunnism by upholding the notion of caesaropapism for the caliphs. However, the legitimate Shīʿī leaders (*imāms*) were not put to the test: these leaders, descended from the fourth caliph ʿAlī, were excluded from power, and their line died out altogether in 874. It was only with the Egyptian Fāṭimids (909–1171), who put forth a disputed claim to the line of ʿAlī, and the Iraqi Būyids (945–1055), that the Shīʿīs acquired a first experience with legislation.

A similar situation existed under the Ṣafavid shahs in Iran (1600–1722). Interestingly, however, from the end of the seventeenth century some Shīʿī scholars began to oppose the legislative independence (*ijtihād,* discussed below) of the shah. After the Afghan invasion and during the chaotic interregnum of the eighteenth century, religious scholars rediscovered the advantages of independence, which they managed to maintain under the subsequent Qājār dynasty (1796–1924). They succeeded in acquiring the right to collect a tax, the "share of the imam" *(khums);* they never deigned to regard the Qājārs as more than caretakers ruling in the name of the Mahdi (the rightly guided one or messiah) who would arrive at the end of time. Thus over the centuries Shīʿī scholars also came to reject caesaropapism, essentially restricting it to the eschatological figure of the Mahdi. In fact, bolstered by fiscal powers, their rejection became even more resolute than that of their Sunnī colleagues, who in the nineteenth century again lost their guardianship over religion to the modernizing state.

The second important characteristic is the emphasis on divine oneness *(tawḥīd)*. The famous "I am that I am" of *Exodus* 3.14 is perhaps the most succinct expression of this oneness but in its tautology it does not say anything about the relationship between oneness and Creation. Not surprisingly, the temptation to resort to further, metaphorical explanations has always remained strong, but if taken literally these explanations, borrowed from analogies with Creation, produce nonsense. Even the name "God" is a problematic metaphor because it implies the human characteristic of personality. Muslims were particularly sensitive about divine metaphors, coming, as they did, after the Jews and Christians. They accused the latter of falsification and polytheism in their scriptures and insisted on an uncompromising divine oneness.

One school of scholars during the formative period of 750–1050, the Muʿtazilah, drew a sharp line between God's eternal essence of oneness and his Qur'ānic attributes, such as knowledge *(ʿilm)*, power *(qudrah)* and will *(irādah)*, which they considered created. They did so as staunch partisans of divine oneness *(aṣḥāb al-tawḥīd)*, which did not admit of creation, but they were quickly mired in theological absurdities: what was God like before he created his own attributes? Why did he create them? Could he have created different ones? Therefore other scholars drew the conclusion—"without [questioning] how" *(bi-lā kayfa)*—that God was inexplicably one as well as being endowed with distinct qualities. These latter scholars eventually—through the theology of the Sunnī thinker Ashʿarī (d. 935)—carried the day, presumably because they were more honest than their opponents in admitting that formal logic did not permit the conceptualization of indivisible oneness without implying composition. The theology of divine oneness, "without questioning how," became a cornerstone of Islam, the new unitary revelation superseding all less rigorous ones. [*See* Tawḥīd.]

Mysticism and Brotherhoods. No orthodoxy is ever strong enough to enforce an absolute prohibition of questioning. Inevitably some Muslims challenged the formal logic that made divine oneness appear inexplicable. Today it is well recognized that the bivalent formal logic built on the rule of the excluded middle ("either/or, no intermediates") is a special case in the larger field of multivalent logic. During the classical period of Islam (1050–1800), when no formalism was yet available for multivalence, mysticism *(taṣawwuf)* instead assumed the informal role of making divine oneness comprehensible.

The Spaniard Muḥyī al-Dīn Ibn al-ʿArabī (d. 1240), who lived in Damascus, was perhaps the most articulate among the mystics of the classical period. The complex concept of "oneness of being" *(waḥdat al-wujūd)* is attributed to him by his disciple al-Qūnawī (d. 1273/74). In contemporary terms, it may be expressed as follows: one experiences God by stripping away all finite phenomena (sensations, concerns, memories, self) and slipping into a state of infinite latency or undifferentiated consciousness—an experience that, when named, is the actual infinite (oneness of being or God, in al-Qunawī's rendering). With this ingenious joining of a contemplative experiential state with the name of God, Ibn al-ʿArabī liberated the theological oneness of the formative period from its seeming inexplicability and provided a sophisticated vocabulary for pious Muslims to express both their experience and their understanding of God. [*See the biography of Ibn al-ʿArabī.*]

Religious scholars who prided themselves on mastery of the formal logic required for the practice of law found it difficult to accept Ibn al-ʿArabī's careful counterbalancing of experiential undifferentiated consciousness and complex metaphysical concepts. For example, Taqī al-Dīn Aḥmad Ibn Taymīyah of Damascus (d. 1328) virulently attacked the mystic for having allegedly preached pantheism by identifying the everyday experience of people and things with the omniscient and omnipotent God of scripture. Accordingly, he condemned saintly *(walī)* mystics whose tombs were visited by believers calling on their intercessory powers *(shafāʿāt)* or seeking divine blessings *(barakat)*. Ibn Taymīyah was careful, however, not to attack mysticism as such, since it was based on a piety that had legal standing. He censored what in his consideration went beyond piety, namely the alleged pantheism of oneness mysticism and saint worship. [*See the biography of Ibn Taymīyah.*]

Ibn Taymīyah remained a lonely critic. The period from the thirteenth to the eighteenth century witnessed an extraordinary outburst of mystical Islam in the form of brotherhoods (sg., *ṭarīqah*), which were unabashedly dedicated to oneness of being, saint cults, ecstatic rituals, and miracles, often without concern for Ibn al-ʿArabī's careful conceptual distinctions. It was this Islam that was carried in the renewed expansion of Islamic civilization—peaceful as well as military—into Central and Southeast Asia as well as Saharan Africa. In the original Islamic countries, where the highly literate

Islam of the legal scholars had failed to penetrate into the illiterate countryside, brotherhoods with their emphasis on mnemonics succeeded and successfully encompassed peasants and nomads. Eventually even the scholars, although sometimes scandalized by the dancing, swaying, handclapping, and shouting of the mystics, eventually deigned to join the more decorous brotherhoods. [*See* Sufism, *article on* Ṣūfī Orders.]

Ibn Taymīyah was also unsuccessful in another respect. As mentioned above, during the period 750–1050 religious scholars shaped the heterogeneous pre-Islamic legal heritage of the caliphal provinces into a unified body of rulings invested with Muḥammad's authority. By the twelfth century authoritative compendia (sg., *mukhtaṣar*) had appeared that "commanded the good and forbade the evil" (lit. *al-amr bi-al-maʿrūf wa-al-nahy ʿan al-munkar*); that is, they ostensibly ruled on everything, from the obligatory *(wājib)*, recommended *(mandūb)*, and permissible *(mubāḥ)* to the disapproved *(makrūh)* and forbidden *(ḥaram)*, making scholarly Islam a moral as well as a legal code.

With the growth of these compendia, the original accounts (*ḥadīths*) of Muḥammad's rulings receded into the background. Religious scholars became intolerant toward colleagues who resisted legal dependence *(taqlīd)* on compendia and, going back to Muḥammad's rulings, practiced independence *(ijtihād)* of judgment. A turning point was reached in the period 1400–1500: although Ibn Taymīyah continued to render independent decisions, the claim of, for example, the Egyptian Suyūṭī (d. 1505) to be the "leading independent scholar *(mujaddid)* of the tenth century [AH]" was met with strong opposition. The prestigious centers of legal Islam, especially Cairo and Mecca, demanded strict conformity with the compendia.

In practice, however, independent decisions continued to be promulgated, even if their authors eschewed the title of "independent scholar." For example, Ottoman religious scholars in the sixteenth century, such as Bali Efendi (a mystic of the Helveti [Ar., Khalwatī] brotherhood), ruled on the permissibility of cash trusts in addition to the existing real-estate endowments (sg., *waqf*). Similarly, the legal status of guns, coffee, tobacco, and hashish was debated. Legal dependence on compendia, although binding in theory, was attenuated in practice.

Outside the prestigious centers of law religious figures were less diffident about claiming the title of "independent scholar." For example, Aḥmad al-Sirhindī (d. 1624) in Mughal India, a mystic of the Naqshbandī brotherhood and an avid reader of the Prophet's rulings, claimed the title of "*mujaddid* of the second millennium." In addition, he replaced Ibn al-ʿArabī's concept of oneness of being with that of oneness of appearances *(waḥdat al-shuhūd)*: a mystic who attains the experience of undifferentiated consciousness should not call this experience "oneness of being" but rather "oneness of appearances," because God, "without questioning how," could neither be experienced nor comprehended. Sirhindī thus brought together independence from the law compendia and a theologically acceptable, albeit diminished mysticism. [*See the biography of Sirhindī.*]

In the later eighteenth and early nineteenth centuries, the new combination of legal independence and diminished mysticism attracted a number of religious figures who were able to make an impact in some of the more remote provinces of Islamic civilization. These figures acted in a situation of political decentralization from which the Mughal and Ottoman empires began to suffer after several centuries of territorial expansion and the beginning of European political and commercial encroachment. In India Shāh Walī Allāh (d. 1762) was the first to preach the new brand of Islam to local rulers. Two generations later Aḥmad Barelwī (d. 1831) provided the Pathans of the northwestern frontier with a new religious unity in their defense against neighboring Sikhs and Afghans. In Arabia Muḥammad ibn ʿAbd al-Wahhāb (d. 1787), a Najdī educated in mysticism as well as in Ibn Taymīyah's writings, inspired Muḥammad ibn Saʿūd (1746–1765) to embark on a campaign of destroying saints' tombs, renewing legal independence, and unifying Arabia under the nominal authority of the Ottoman sultan. [*See the biographies of Walī Allāh, Barelwī, and Ibn ʿAbd al-Wahhāb.*]

Reform and Revolution. The English colonial takeover in India (1784) and the French or English military invasions of Egypt, Yemen, and Algeria (1798–1830) shocked the surviving Muslim rulers into the realization that their only chance for preserving independence was a recentralization of power. The Ottoman and Moroccan sultans, Egyptian and Tunisian viceregents, and Iranian shahs struggled to adopt Western military technology in an attempt to reverse the decentralization process of the previous century and regain sovereignty. Administrative and legal reforms followed, and a small number of professionals emerged—the officers, diplomats, engineers, doctors, and journalists who were to become the vanguard of modernization in Islamic civilization.

In the past, civilizations of Europe and Asia had borrowed from each other without experiencing major cultural and social disruptions. Christians rediscovered Aristotle via Muslim philosophers in the twelfth century; Muslims adopted Western firearms technology in the fourteenth; and neither found themselves compelled to transform the foundations of their civilization because of these borrowings. In the Islamic countries of the nineteenth century, however, cultural and social disruptions proved to be unavoidable. After all, the West itself, in the course of its scientific-industrial revolution during the previous two centuries, had undergone the profound cultural transformation we call "modernity."

At the heart of this ascendant modernity in the West was the ideology of mechanism, according to which reality was atomic in structure and fully determined by the laws of motion. These laws were "rational," that is, they followed the rule of the excluded middle in formal logic. Since all atoms were equal to each other, the new principle of justice was equality, under which all traditional hierarchical institutions were viewed as "irrational" and had to be replaced by democratic structures. Religion, one of the traditional institutions, was required to be "rationalized" in order to escape the anathema of "irrationality." By the mid-nineteenth century the ideology of modernity had become dominant in England and was well on its way to conquering the Continent and the New World.

Among Muslims the first reaction to the pressures of Western modernity in the mid-nineteenth century was the discovery of rationality in an Islamic civilization that had somehow failed to produce modernity by itself. The most prominent representative of "Islamic rationalism" was the mystically educated Iranian Shīʿī Jamāl al-Dīn al-Afghānī (1838–1897), an indefatigable orator in the lecture halls, coffee houses, and salons of the Islamic world from India to Cairo and Istanbul. Central to his thought was the notion that reason (*ʿaql*) once reigned supreme in Islamic religion, philosophy, and science, but it was later disfigured by fanaticism (*taʿaṣṣub*) and tyranny (*istibdād*), thereby causing stagnation in Islam. Only through a return to the original thinkers, said Afghānī, would Muslims be able to modernize themselves on their own, without having to undergo the humiliation of European colonialism.

Afghānī never identified the fanatics and tyrants with any precision, although he blamed the authors of the twelfth-century legal compendia for their excessive conservatism. But since he also held up Muslims from Muḥammad to Mullā Ṣadrā (d. 1640) as paragons of rationality, as one would expect from an intellectual deeply steeped in mysticism, it is impossible to pinpoint the exact period in Islamic history when fanaticism and tyranny supposedly overpowered reason. Furthermore, by explicitly including mysticism in his definition of rationality, Afghānī remained within he mainstream of classical Islamic thought. Although he made the concept of rationality thematic, his interpretation remained fundamentally different from that of Western modernity. [*See the biography of Afghānī.*]

At the same time, in the Sunnī part of the Islamic world politicians carried the modernization of Islam much further. Their interest in the establishment of an efficient centralized administration functioning according to the principles of what Max Weber later called "goal-oriented rationality" naturally led them to clean up what appeared to them as the mumbo-jumbo of mysticism and to subject the leadership of the brotherhoods and shrines to state control. They thereby established the modern, "rational" equivalent of the former caliphal caesaropapism.

Egypt is a typical case. Here state administrators were appointed in 1812 to supervise all brotherhoods, as well as al-Azhar University, which had previously been autonomous. Subsequent regulations issued in 1881, 1895 and 1905 reduced the number of processions and pilgrimages. Customary practices such as self-flagellation or the eating of burning coals, glass, and serpents were abolished. Drumming, singing, twirling, and leaping during an ecstatic session (*ḥaḍrah*) were outlawed. The contemplative litanies (sg., *dhikr*) had to be purged of all words requiring panting. Strict administrative and financial controls were imposed on the brotherhoods. Thus, step by step, formerly autonomous religious institutions were rationalized and incorporated into the state, at least on paper.

In the early 1890s the direct and indirect disciples of Afghānī, loosely grouped in a movement devoted to a "return to the ancestors (*salaf*)," joined government efforts at religious reform. The most prominent figure in this movement (the Salafīyah), was Muḥammad ʿAbduh (1849–1905), an Egyptian educated in mysticism, theology, and law, who was a member of the administrative council of al-Azhar and the grand *muftī* for the religious courts, both since 1882 under the protectorate authority of Great Britain. [*See* Salafīyah.]

In 1905 ʿAbduh published his *Essay on Oneness* (*Risālat al-tawḥīd*), a restatement of al-Ashʿarī's theology of "without questioning how." With this explicit return to the formative period he inaugurated the modern reformist program of rationalizing Islam. God, according to ʿAbduh, revealed himself through the angel Gabriel to Muḥammad, an upright but not saintly human being, and called him to lead a corrupt society back to the path of righteousness. The Prophet succeeded through the rational persuasiveness of his message; no miracles were necessary. Even though ʿAbduh as a former mystic was willing to admit the existence of "knowers" *(ʿurafāʾ)* of God, he left no doubt that mysticism and sainthood had no place in rational Islam. That Ashʿarī's "without questioning how" nevertheless constitutes an ultimate residue of irrationality according to the either/or logic of modernity is passed over in silence. [*See the biography of ʿAbduh.*]

The efforts at rationalizing mysticism by the centralizing governments and at creating a rational Islam by reformist intellectuals did not produce immediate results in the general population. It is true that the Republic of Turkey, which succeeded the Ottoman Empire in 1921, outlawed the brotherhoods; moreover, in many countries modern education was expanded during the interwar period. But the great mass of the population remained ensconced in its traditional rural employments until well after World War II. The peasants saw no reasons voluntarily to desert their local brotherhoods or the saints who continued to heal them of afflictions, end droughts, and bless fields and women with fertility. Even when some rurals began to migrate to towns and cities in the 1920s as a result of administrative urbanization and early industrial ventures, most joined urban brotherhoods.

Nevertheless, during the interwar period reformed Islam began to attract a few converts in urban areas, mostly from the ranks of modern-educated midlevel employees in the administration or services. These converts were organized in a number of private educational, social action, and welfare organizations founded by a new generation of Salafīyah intellectuals who were impatient with ʿAbduh's reform from within and wished to return to the anticaesaropapist tradition of Sunnī Islam. Characteristically, whereas Afghānī and ʿAbduh were still steeped in the mystical tradition, the new generation represented a transitional group no longer fully at home in it.

Among these intellectuals was the Egyptian Ḥasan al-Bannāʾ (1906–1949), founder in 1928 of the Society of Muslim Brothers (Ikhwān al-Muslimūn), who had roots in the Ḥasāfīyah brotherhood. The Algerian ʿAbd al-Ḥamīd Ibn Bādīs (1889–1940), founder of the Association of Religious Scholars ((Jamʿīyat al-ʿUlamāʾ) in 1931, was familiar with mysticism only as an academic subject during his studies at Zaytūnah University in Tunis. However, Abū al-Aʿlā Mawdūdī (1903–1979), founder of the Indian (later Pakistani) Islamic Association (Jamāʿat-i Islāmī) in 1941, was a failed university student before becoming a journalist and self-taught Islamic reformer. Sayyid Quṭb (1906–1966) was a modern-educated schoolteacher who had spent time as a postgraduate in the United States before he assumed, in 1951, the directorship of propaganda *(daʿwah)* in the Egyptian Muslim Brotherhood. Whatever their backgrounds, these activists considered themselves as modern, practical, goal-oriented Muslims in contrast to what they regarded the irrational Islam of mysticism. [*See also* Muslim Brotherhood; Zaytūnah; *and the biographies of the figures mentioned in this paragraph.*]

When colonialism ended in the Islamic world after World War II (beginning with Pakistan in 1947 and culminating with Algeria in 1962), the new governments were no more willing than the older ones to accept autonomous religious and legal establishments. Islam in its reformed version became the official or privileged religion (except in Lebanon and a number of sub-Saharan African and East Asian countries) and as such was taught in the systems of compulsory primary education. Ambitious state industrialization plans were adopted, and a massive urbanization process was set into motion; together with compulsory education, these became potent forces of religious change.

This change became manifest in the 1970s when the first postcolonial generation of Muslims with a modern education graduated from primary school. These young urban Muslims were completely divorced from the heritage of the brotherhoods, which now, for the first time in more than five hundred years, were reduced to marginal status in society. To be sure, mysticism is still today a force in Morocco, Turkey, Egypt, and Sudan below the middle-class levels of society, but Islamic reform has become socially and culturally dominant.

Without mysticism the contemporary adherents of reformed Islam, or Islamists as they are generally called, are caught in two intellectual dilemmas. First, even though during the European Enlightenment (1650–1800) modernity began with demands for a rational religion, once religion was rationalized with the help of the bivalent formal logic of either/or, this logic could easily be turned against religion altogether. Either everything, including God, is explicable, or it is not—and if not, why should something inexplicable be believed in? Islamists inevitably find themselves on the defensive against secular modernists who push this logic to its full agnostic consequences.

Second, since Islamists can no longer fall back on mysticism and are unwilling to accept multivalent logic with its broader definition of rationality, theirs is a rather narrow world. They share this world with the secular modernists, who are similarly narrow. Both are correct in concluding that organized mysticism in its traditional sense of brotherhoods and saintliness is now beyond resurrection. In fact, it is even difficult to imagine how the spiritual mysticism of Ibn al-ʿArabī or Mullā Ṣadrā, with its classical metaphysical vocabulary, can be revived. Nevertheless, without the adoption of some form of multivalence the Islamists will not be able to accommodate all faithful Muslims.

For the time being, the freshness of the Islamist phenomenon still obscures its intellectual dilemmas. The Islamic Revolution of Iran in 1979, although itself the result of a decade of preparation, is less than half a generation old. Its leader Ruhollah Khomeini (1902–1989) was extraordinarily inspiring in confronting the "either" of secular modernity with an attractive religious "or" building on existing anti-imperialist resentments. The West (especially the United States), according to Khomeini, has become the contemporary embodiment of Satan by creating the "oppressed" (*mustaḍʿafūn*, Qur'ān 4.75, 98) of the Third World. Since Satan exists, so must God, whether he is incomprehensible or not; hence it is only a return to divine law (the *sharīʿah*) that will restore dignity and justice to the oppressed. [*See* Mustaḍʿafūn *and the biography of Khomeini.*]

In the Iranian revolutionary constitution divine law is under the protection of the regime of the leading legal scholar (*velāyet-i faqīh;* Ar., *wilāyat al-faqīh*), who is assisted by the counsel (*shūrā*) of the lesser scholars in an elective assembly (*majlis*). Together they interpret the law and issue rulings of absolute (*muṭlaq*) binding power so that opposition to these rulings equals apostasy. This elevation of a single scholar to the position of supreme legal authority is quite unprecedented in Shīʿī Islam, where in the absence of the Mahdi leadership is supposed to be exercised by the shah and the collective of religious scholars. This power of the leading scholar is mitigated, of course, by the institution of parliament. [*See* Wilāyat al-Faqīh; Majlis.]

Khomeini resembled the early reformers in another respect: he was fully educated in the unadulturated "oneness of being" tradition descending from Ibn al-ʿArabī to Mullā Ṣadrā. As a young religious scholar in Qom during the 1920s, he composed several commentaries on mysticism that earned him the hostility and later jealousy of his reform-minded colleagues. Although practical constitutional concerns dominated Khomeini's thinking in the 1980s, he nevertheless remained faithful to his mystical antecedents, as is exemplified by the reissue of his commentaries in 1982–1986 and by his curious letter to Mikhail Gorbachev in January 1989 extolling the superiority of Ibn al-ʿArabī's spirituality over Marxist materialism. This stern man, unpredictably pragmatic as well as otherworldly, dared his less knowledgeable contemporaries to challenge him on a field of Islam the definition of which he reserved to himself— reformist mutterings about the alleged irrationality of his mystical convictions notwithstanding.

Even though Khomeini personally succeeded with a revolution al-Afghānī only dreamed of, his achievements will be fuel for scholarly debate for years to come. His own broadly inclusive Islam of the classical period was no longer alive for the majority of Iranians, and the revolution certainly was unable to resuscitate it. The revolutionary epigones of Khomeini in both the Shīʿī and Sunnī parts of the Islamic world face the much less exalted task of convincing Muslims of the superiority of a religious over a secular modernity. Meanwhile, the nonrevolutionary majority of Muslims range themselves somewhere in the undefined middle, intuitively aware that rationality transcends facile either/ors.

[*Each country of the Middle East and North Africa is the subject of an independent entry.*]

BIBLIOGRAPHY

General Surveys

A good concise overview of the evolution of Islam is Andrew Rippin, *Muslims: Their Religious Beliefs and Practices*, vol. 1, *The Formative Period*, and vol. 2, *The Contemporary Period* (London, 1990–1993). Formative and classical Islam are discussed from the perspective of mysticism in Henry Corbin, *History of Islamic Philosophy* (London, 1993; French original, 1964). Ernest Gellner, *Postmodernism, Reason, and Religion* (London, 1992), addresses the dilemmas of "rational" Islam in modernity from a comparative vantage point. A well-informed, detailed overview of the contemporary currents in Islam is Reinhard Schulze, *Islamischer Internationalismus im 20. Jahrhundert* (Leiden, 1990). Reformed Islam in its historical evolution is discussed by John Obert Voll, *Islam: Continuity and Change in the Modern World* (Boulder, 1982), and in its social setting (in the Arab Middle East) by

Michael Gilsenan, *Recognizing Islam: Religion and Society in the Modern Arab World* (New York, 1982).

Revelation and Theology

Volume 1 of Rippin (above) contains an evaluation of the form-critical method (first applied by John Wansbrough) and its results in the study of the sacred story of Islam (e.g., Michael Cook, Patricia Crone, Yehuda D. Nevo). The most up-to-date and complete discussion of al-Ashʿarī's theology is Daniel Gimaret, *La doctrine d'al-Ashʿari* (Paris, 1990).

Mysticism

Ibn al-ʿArabī's complex thought is expertly considered by William C. Chittick, *The Sufi Path of Knowledge: Ibn al-ʿArabi's Metaphysics of Imagination* (Albany, N.Y., 1989). Ibn Taymīyah has yet to find his critical intellectual biographer; his attitude toward mysticism is accessible through *Ibn Taimīya's Struggle against Popular Religion*, translated by Muhammad Umar Memon (The Hague, 1983). On Islamic law in the classical period, see Wael B. Hallaq, "Was the Gate of Ijtihad Closed?" and "On the Authoritativeness of Sunni Consensus," *International Journal of Middle East Studies* 16.1 (1984): 3–41, 18.4 (1986): 427–454. The controversy over the beginnings of reformed Islam (did it begin in some Islamic provinces during the eighteenth century?) is examined in Nehemia Levtzion and John Obert Voll, eds., *Eighteenth-Century Renewal and Reform in Islam* (Syracuse, N.Y., 1987), and R. S. O'Fahey, *Enigmatic Saint: Ahmad Ibn Idris and the Idrisi Tradition* (Evanston, Ill., 1990).

Reform and Revolution

The standard biography of al-Afghānī is Nikki R. Keddie, *Sayyid Jamāl al-Dīn "al-Afghānī": A Political Biography* (Berkeley, 1968). On the reform of Islam by the Egyptian state, see F. de Jong, *Turuq and Turuq-Linked Institutions in Nineteenth-Century Egypt* (Leiden, 1978). Muḥammad ʿAbduh's *Risālat al-tawḥīd* is available in English under the title *The Theology of Unity*, translated by Ishaq Musaʿad and Kenneth Cragg (New York, 1980). His standard intellectual biography is by Charles C. Adams, *Islam and Modernism in Egypt* (New York, 1968). The interwar and early post–World War II reform movements are covered by Richard P. Mitchell, *The Society of the Muslim Brothers* (London, 1969); Ali Merad, *Le réformisme musulman en Algérie de 1925 à 1940: Essai d'histoire religieuse et sociale* (Paris, 1967); Sheila McDonough, *Muslim Ethics and Modernity: A Comparison of the Ethical Thought of Sayyid Ahmad Khan and Mawlana Mawdudi* (Waterloo, Ont., 1984); and Ahmad S. Moussalli, *Radical Islamic Fundamentalism: The Ideological and Political Discourse of Sayyid Quṭb* (Beirut, 1992). The most detailed study on Iranian Islamic revolutionism is by Hamid Dabashi, *Theology of Discontent: The Ideological Foundations of the Islamic Revolution in Iran* (New York, 1993). Khomeini's mysticism has been studied by Alexander Knysh, "*Irfan* Revisited: Khomeini and the Legacy of Islamic Mystical Philosophy," *Middle East Journal* 46 (1992): 631–653. The literature on contemporary (including revolutionary) Islam is immense. A few books stand out: John L. Esposito, *Islam and Politics*, 3d ed. (Syracuse, N.Y., 1991); Gilles Kepel, *Muslim Extremism in Egypt: The Prophet and Pharaoh*, translated by John Rothschild (Berkeley, 1985); and Emmanuel Sivan, *Radical Islam: Medieval Theology and Modern Politics* (New Haven, 1990).

PETER VON SIVERS

Islam in Sub-Saharan Africa

The history of Islam in Africa is almost as old as the history of the religion itself. Islam may have arrived in Ethiopia even before the beginning of the Islamic calendar era, when a few believers, persecuted in Mecca, crossed the Red Sea and went to the Ḥabash of Abyssinia in search of asylum. Ethiopians celebrate this event to the present day.

Islam's earliest African convert may have been Bilāl (Bilāl ibn Rabāḥ), the slave who was freed as a result of the Prophet's intervention. Bilāl became the first muezzin in Islamic history and a favorite companion of the prophet Muḥammad.

Cultural Diffusion: Religion and Language. With the Arab conquest of North Africa in the seventh and eighth centuries CE, two processes were set in motion that have remained of relevance for Africa as a whole ever since—the processes of islamization and arabization. Islamization was the gradual transmission of the Islamic religion as more and more conquered peoples embraced the faith. Arabization was the transmission of the Arabic language. Arabization in North Africa took much longer than islamization, but when North Africans became native speakers of Arabic, it was only a matter of time before they came to identify themselves as indeed Arabs. It was not just their language, it was their very identity.

Up the Nile Valley, the twin processes of islamization and arabization continued. Increasing numbers of northern Sudanese were not only converted to Islam, but increasingly saw themselves as part of the Arab world. The Arabic language became their mother tongue, long after Islam had become their faith.

The establishment of British control in the Sudan (1898–1955) slowed down the processes of islamization and arabization farther south; southern Sudan was effectively insulated from the arabized north on British orders. Christianization was encouraged in the south, but islamization was essentially banned. The foundations of a religious apartheid system were being laid under British control.

This ethnoreligious compartmentalization had devastating consequences after Sudan's independence in 1955. The first Sudanese civil war between north and south lasted from 1955 until 1972 and was widely perceived as a war between the Arabo-Muslim north and the Christian and animist south. The second Sudanese civil war broke out in 1983, partly in protest against

President Jaʿfar Nimeiri's decision to make Islam the state religion and the *sharīʿah* the law of the land. The southern military leader, Colonel John Garang, continued to rebel against the north despite the overthrow of Nimeiri and the succession of other regimes in Khartoum. Islam was further consolidated politically under the government of General ʿUmar Ḥasan Aḥmad al-Bashīr.

Despite the war, the Arabic language continued to spread in southern Sudan. Indeed, this was probably the only part of sub-Saharan Africa where arabization proceeded faster than islamization. Elsewhere, it was the religion rather than the language that was making the greatest inroads into African life.

In southern Africa, and especially in South Africa, Islam arrived as a victim. The importation of Muslim Malay slaves into South Africa in the eighteenth century created a distinct context for the religion in subsequent generations. While Islam in northern Africa was brought directly by the Arabs, Islam in southern Africa was partly a legacy of Southeast and South Asians. In North Africa Muslim majorities lived with deepening westernization; in southern Africa, Muslim minorities later experienced even more rapid westernization. For North Africa this westernization had come mainly through the region's proximity to Europe and colonization; for southern Africa it occurred mainly through the massive white settlement locally, despite the region's remoteness from Europe. Finally, in southern Africa there was islamization without any significant arabization.

East and West Africa also present contrasting models of islamization. Basil Davidson has argued that Islam in sub-Saharan Africa owed "nothing to Arab conquest but much to Berber influence." The trans-Saharan trade went back to pre-Phoenician times and had resulted in the settlement of Berber communities in parts of West Africa. But later, "Islam could more effectively bind all these communities together," whether in Sudanic Africa, the connecting oases, or North Africa (*Africa in History*, New York, 1991, p. 134).

Davidson does concede that there were two major Moroccan military invasions, the destructive Almoravid raids of the eleventh century and the Moroccan invasion of Songhay in 1591. But these incursions from the north did not help Islam in West Africa and, according to Davidson, might even have undermined it. Of more lasting significance was the quiet spread of Islam as a result of Berber settlements, trans-Saharan trade, and the broader historical intercourse between the Berber peoples and their Southern neighbors. It was not the sword of the Arab but rather the socializing of the Berber that laid the foundations of Islam in West Africa.

By contrast, in East Africa the Arab factor has been pronounced in the arrival and expansion of Islam from the earliest days into the twentieth century. Major religious leaders were overwhelmingly people who claimed Arab descent, if not indeed descent from the prophet Muḥammad himself. One adverse consequence of this Arab leadership was that it prolonged the image of Islam as a "foreign" religion. Another was that Arab leadership inhibited the emergence of dynamic indigenous African Muslim leaders, in contrast to the towering role of local African leaders in West African Muslim affairs. This may be why Islam in West Africa continued to expand numerically and geographically even under the dominion of Christian imperialist powers, while its spread in present-day Tanzania, Kenya, and Uganda was arrested because the foundations of the religion in the hinterland had not yet been adequately africanized.

In earlier centuries Islam in both West Africa and East Africa had been a major spur in state formation. In West Africa these included the imperial states of Kanem-Bornu (thirteenth to nineteenth centuries), Mali (thirteenth to fifteenth centuries), and Songhay (fourteenth to sixteenth centuries). In East Africa Swahili city-states such as Kilwa, Pate, and Mombasa lasted until they were disabled by the Portuguese following Vasco da Gama's circumnavigation of the Cape of Good Hope in 1492. Zanzibar under the Omani Sultanate later fell under British "protection." The British departed in 1963; in January 1964 a revolution by indigenous Africans (themselves mainly Muslims) overthrew the Arab sultanate.

Islam was also a major force in the history of urbanization. In ancient Mali and Songhay the social tensions were sometimes between the islamized towns and the far less islamized countryside. Monarchs sometimes played the forces of the countryside against the towns; a good example is Sunnī ʿAlī, ruler of Songhay, in the late fifteenth century.

Agents of Islamic Expansion. Underlying the whole sage of religion and society are the five modes by which Islam has spread in Africa. The most spectacular mode is expansion by conquest. This mainly affected Arab North Africa, which was islamized initially by the sword. Sub-Saharan examples of islamization by conquest are few, but some did take place, as in the case of the Almoravids' devastating incursions into West Africa from 1052 to 1076. Ibn Khaldūn confirms that the conquerors did force Africans to become Muslims, but this harmed the image of Islam rather than helping it. Such invasions are therefore not useful in explaining the spread of Islam: people were subsequently converted despite the memory of the Almoravids.

The second agency for the expansion of Islam was Muslim migration and settlement in non-Muslim areas. Arabs from Yemen and Oman, settling in East Africa, were among the founders of the Swahili civilization in what is today Tanzania and Kenya. The rapid islamization and arabization of North Africa was achieved not only through conquest but also through migration and settlement. Doctrinally, this mode of transmission of the Message goes back to the great *hijrah* itself, the prophet Muḥammad's own mid-career migration from Mecca to Medina. Migration may sometimes be of victims rather than victors. This is true of the Malay slaves and laborers imported into South Africa, who have kept the flame of Islam burning in South Africa for three hundred years.

The third agency for the spread of Islam was trade, in particular the trans-Saharan trade. The camels that crossed the great desert carried varied commodities in each direction, but perhaps the greatest commodity of all was cultural diffusion—the spread of Islam from North Africa to West Africa especially. Today countries like Guinea, modern Mali, Senegal, and Niger are overwhelmingly Muslim. Arab and Swahili traders in eastern, Central, and southern Africa also played a part in carrying the torch of Islam to parts of what are today Uganda, Zaire, Malawi, and Mozambique.

The fourth agency for the spread of Islam was purposeful missionary work *(da'wah).* In earlier centuries this was carried on by traveling imams, healers, and teachers. Muslim healers acquired such a reputation that to the present day many of their African patients are non-Muslims, including Christians. Their healing techniques have employed verses of the Qur'ān, including the popular prescription of writing out the verse in washable ink on a slate, then washing it into a bowl and having the patient "drink the sacred verse."

In more recent times Islamic missionary work has included written materials for use in *madrasah*s and schools. Books or pamphlets have been written in African languages to explain the religion not only to students but also to non-Muslims. Pamphlets in the Swahili language have poured forth from Zanzibar, the Kenyan coast, and the coast of Tanzania. In the twentieth century the Qur'ān was translated into K̄iswah̄ili, first by the controversial Aḥmadīyah movement and later by Sunnī scholars. Some Muslims believed that translations of the Qur'ān were a sinful imitation of the holy book, but the chief Muslim jurists of East Africa have given *fatwā*s contradicting that doctrine; they have argued that if it is not sinful to translate the Qur'ān orally in a sermon in a mosque, it is not sinful to translate it in writing.

In parts of Africa, the most active missionary group for Islam has been the Aḥmadīyah movement, founded by the nineteenth-century Indian religious militant Mirzā Ghulām Aḥmad. The movement is widely regarded as heretical by African Muslims and has had a hard time gaining legitimacy in countries such as Nigeria. The main issue is that members of the Aḥmadīyah do not regard the prophet Muḥammad as the last of the prophets; they only acknowledge him as the greatest. Mirzā Ghulām Aḥmad was, to his followers, a prophet in his own right, though not as great as Muḥammad. In Nigeria in the twentieth century the Aḥmadīyah have sometimes been denied the privilege of foreign exchange to enable them to make the pilgrimage to Mecca because they were not recognized as Muslims; the Saudi authorities also wanted the Aḥmadīyah to be controlled at its source. Nonetheless, the movement continues to be one of the most active missionary forces in Africa. [*See* Aḥmadīyah.]

Sunnī and Shī'ī missionary work entered a new stage in the second half of the twentieth century with the arrival of oil wealth in Saudi Arabia, Iran, Libya, and other parts of the Muslim world. It became possible for the cause of Islam in Africa to command considerable financial resources. Schools and mosques could be built, clinics were subsidized, and scholarships to study abroad offered. On the whole, this wealth was used not so much to attract new converts as to support the welfare of those who were already Muslims, but there were incentives for new conversions as well. Sunnī Islam is still by far the main beneficiary of such conversions, for even Shī'ī Iran has sometimes been ready to subsidize Sunnī missionary work in Africa in a spirit of Muslim unity. The Ismā'īlī movement under the leadership of the Aga Khan (more Shī'ī than Sunnī) sometimes explicitly committed its missionaries to the propagation of Sunnī Islam rather than of its own denomination. The fifth and last agency in Africa's historical experience has been periodic revivalist movements. These may take the form of an internal, morally purifying *jihād,* or they may occur under the leadership of a self-proclaimed Mahdi. Among the most spectacular of these revivalist movements were those that unleashed the *jihād* led by Usuman dan Fodio in what is today Nigeria. Inspired in part by a glorified vision of the ʿAbbāsid dynasty centuries earlier, the nineteenth-century Mahdist movement partook of both revivalism and conquest. Its long-term consequence was the relative unification of much of Hausaland, formerly a loose and contentious federation, under a single sovereign. Usuman's son, Muhammad Bello, became the first *amīr al-Muʾminīn* (commander of the faithful) in the region, and Islam expanded under his control. [*See the biography of Dan Fodio.*]

Also notable was the movement in eastern Sudan led by Muḥammad Aḥmad ibn ʿAbd Allāh. This Muslim reformation started in 1881 in the wake of many years of Turco-Egyptian rule, compounded by British manipulation. Unlike Dan Fodio's *jihād,* that of Muḥammad Aḥmad was also a struggle for national independence; religious revivalism intertwined with political nationalism. Muḥammad Aḥmad declared himself the Mahdi, appointed by God to reunite the Muslim *ummah.* His vision extended well beyond the Sudan; in a sense, he wanted to fuse Pan-Islamism with Pan-Africanism and Pan-Arabism. His dream was too big for his base, and too vulnerable to the new European imperialism, and his movement was finally defeated, but his religious and political legacy lives on in the political configuration of the Sudan. [*See* Mahdi; Mahdīyah.]

In Africa since independence two issues have been central to religious speculation—Islamic expansion and Islamic revivalism. Expansion involves the spread of religion and the number of new converts; revivalism calls for a rebirth of faith among those who are already Muslims. Expansion is a matter of geography and populations, while revivalism is a matter of history and nostalgia. The spread of Islam in postcolonial Africa is basically a peaceful process of persuasion and consent, but its revival is often an angry process of rediscovered fundamentalism.

In sub-Saharan Africa the central issue concerning Islam is not the revivalism that has created such strife in North Africa, but rather the speed of Islamic expansion. It is not often realized that there are more Muslims in Nigeria alone than in any Arab country, including Egypt. Muslims in Ethiopia constitute nearly half of the population. Islam in South Africa is three centuries old; the four most populous countries in Africa—Nigeria, Egypt, Ethiopia, and Zaire—account for well over 120 million Muslims. Nearly half the population of the continent is now Muslim.

Eclecticism and Missionary Competition. Of the three principal religious traditions of Africa—indigenous, Islamic, and Christian—perhaps the most tolerant is the indigenous tradition. Precisely because the two latter faiths are universalist in aspiration, seeking to convert the whole of humanity, they are inherently competitive; Christianity and Islam have often been in competition for the soul of the African continent, and this rivalry has sometimes resulted in conflict.

Indigenous African religions, by contrast, are basically communal rather than universalist. Like Hinduism and modern Judaism—and unlike Christianity and Islam—indigenous African traditions have not sought to convert humanity. Thus they do not compete with one another. The Yoruba do not seek to convert the Igbo to Yoruba religion, nor vice versa; nor do either the Yoruba or the Igbo compete for the souls of the Hausa. Over the centuries Africans have waged many kinds of wars among themselves, but before the universalist creeds arrived hardly ever religious ones.

In contemporary Africa, indigenous tolerance has often mitigated the competitiveness of Christianity and Islam. An example is Senegal, which is more than 80 percent Muslim. Its Christian founder-president, Léopold Sédar Senghor, presided over postcolonial Senegal for two decades in political partnership with the Muslim leaders of the country, the marabouts. His designated successor was Abdou Diouf, a Muslim married to a Roman Catholic, and several of Diouf's ministers are Christian. Senegalese religious tolerance has also continued in other spheres. What in other Islamic countries might be regarded as provocative has been tolerated in Senegal. A Christian festival such as a First Communion, accompanied by feasting, merrymaking, and singing, may be publicly held in Dakar in the middle of the Islamic fast of Ramaḍān, and the Christian merrymakers left undisturbed (Susan MacDonald, "Senegal: Islam on the March," *West Africa* 3494 [6 August 1984] p. 1570).

Predominantly Muslim countries south of the Sahara have in general been above average in religious tolerance. The capacity to accommodate other faiths may be part of the historical Islamic tradition in multireligious empires, but far more tolerant have been indigenous African traditions. In Black Africa this indigenous tolerance has often moderated the competitive propensities of Christianity and Islam.

The former president of Uganda, Milton Obote (a Protestant), used to boast that his extended family in Lango consisted of Muslims, Catholics, and Protestants "at peace with each other." Obote's successor, Idi Amin Dada (a Muslim), had a similarly multireligious extended family and once declared that he planned to have at least one of his sons trained for the Christian priesthood. However, Amin's general record was not one of tolerance. Eventually, he found political refuge in Saudi Arabia as a guest of the custodians of the Islamic holy cities of Mecca and Medina.

Tanzania's population has a Muslim plurality, but Roman Catholic Julius K. Nyerere dominated the nation as president from 1961 to 1985 with no challenge to his religious credentials. His successor as president, Ali Hassan Mwinyi, is Muslim; Nyerere remained head of the ruling party, Chama cha Mapinduzi. A truly ecumenical Tanzania was forged—a Muslim head of state was accompanied by a Christian head of the ruling party. Once again the competitiveness of Christianity and Islam was moderated by the more tolerant tendencies of indigenous African culture. (However, Muslim Tanzanians accepted Christian leadership more graciously than Christian Tanzanians have accepted Muslim leadership.)

The nearest that Islam has come to providing a secretary-general of the United Nations was when Salim Ahmed Salim of Tanzania was a candidate. Later Salim became secretary-general of the Organization of African Unity. The most important Muslim in the history of United Nations Educational, Scientific and Cultural Organization (UNESCO) was Ahmadou-Mahtar M'Bow of Senegal, who served as director-general from 1974 to 1987. He was both the highest-ranking African and the highest-ranking Muslim in the United Nations system. M'Bow became a controversial figure; the United States, the United Kingdom, and Singapore withdrew from UNESCO partly in protest against his leadership. However, his regime brought UNESCO much closer to Third World concerns than it had ever been. In both Salim's and M'Bow's cases, African and Muslim aspirations for leadership in the United Nations were obstructed by the United States in the face of broadly based African support.

Nonetheless, there are situations in Africa when even indigenous culture fails to ameliorate religious divisions between Christians and Muslims. This is true of the north/south divide in Sudan, with an overwhelmingly Muslim and arabized north and a Christian-led black southern region; the religious differences have reinforced other historical, cultural, and ethnic divisions.

Similar ethnoreligious cleavages in postcolonial Africa have manifested themselves from time to time in Ethiopia, Chad, and Nigeria. When the Christian/Islamic divide coincides with ethnic frontiers, the competitiveness of Christianity and Islam overwhelms the natural ecumenism of indigenous Africa.

In his book *Consciencism* Kwame Nkrumah, Ghana's founder-president, traced the genesis of the contemporary African heritage to these three forces—indigenous traditions, Islam, and what Nkrumah called the "Euro-Christian impact." It was the synthesis of these three forces that Nkrumah called "Consciencism." These three forces are sometimes mutually supportive, sometimes antagonistic, and sometimes independent, parallel lines in a nation's history. One must distinguish between Western religious impact on a country like Nigeria (in the form of Christianity) and Western secular impact, which ranges from capitalism to the English language. Let us take the religious domain first.

What is the balance between Muslims, Christians and followers of African traditional religions? The situation in Nigeria provides an important case study. The hardest figure to estimate is the third, partly because African traditional religion can be combined with either Christianity or Islam. Millions of Nigerians follow both indigenous religions and Christianity; further millions of Nigerians are both traditionalist and Muslims. Beyond this, many Nigerian intellectuals empathize with Kwame Nkrumah's affirmation, "I am a Marxist-Leninist and a non-denominational Christian and I see no contradiction in that." Postcolonial Muslim countries such as Guinea, Algeria, Iraq, and Somalia have produced hybrid Muslim-Marxists; some would describe the Nigerian scholar Bala Usman as such. But can one be both a Muslim and Christian? Here lies the rigid line of mutual exclusivity. Although Christianity and Islam are much closer to each other than either is to Marxism or African traditional religion, in reality the two Semitic religions tend to be mutually exclusive.

There are occasions when African Muslims are tempted to say "The best way of being a Christian is to be a Muslim." This is because Jesus is a major figure in Islam. Muslims recognize the virgin birth of Jesus and accept many of the miracles he performed; they accept the bodily ascent of Jesus to heaven on the completion of his earthly career. But although theoretically Islam does encompass a version of Christianity, in reality no

Muslim is likely to describe himself as a Christian, or vice versa. What does combine easily with other creeds are African traditional religions.

Imperative of Expansionism. Because of the syncretism discussed above, it is difficult to quantify the followers of the indigenous tradition in Africa's religious experience. With regard to the number of Christians and Muslims in postcolonial Nigeria, the most reliable percentages recognized by the outside world were based on the 1963 census, which gave 47 percent of Nigerians as Muslim and 35 percent as Christian. Since 1963 the balance may have changed. We have no current and reliable figures for Nigeria, but on the basis of experience elsewhere in Africa, the end of colonial rule slowed the spread of Christianity without necessarily slowing that of Islam.

On the whole, colonial rule was favorable to Christian expansion, so its end was bound to be costly to Christianity, at least in the short run. The factors that slowed the spread of Christianity after Nigerian independence included the postcolonial decline of the prestige of Western civilization in Africa, the decline of the influence of Christian missionaries, and the shift in Christian missionary focus from commitment to salvation in the hereafter to commitment to service in the here and now. In addition, the postcolonial prosperity of oil-rich Arab countries has given Islam resources for missionary work in Africa that are unprecedented in modern Islamic history. Islam is beginning to be economically competitive with Christianity in the rivalry for the soul of Africa.

Although in the competition between Islam and Christianity in Nigeria Islam may be winning, in the competition between Islam and secular westernization, Islam is probably losing for the time being. The greatest threat to Islam is not the Passion on the Cross but the ecstasy of Western materialism; it is not the message of Jesus but the gospel of modernity; it is not the church with a European face but capitalism in Western robes. As young Nigerian Muslims are mesmerized by disco music and the nightclub, their faith is endangered more than by a Christian preacher. Western materialism is a greater threat to African Islam than is Western Christianity.

The strongest and most resilient indigenous culture in West Africa may well be Yoruba culture; it is certainly the most persistent of the three major heritages of Nigeria. Igbo society has been all too ready to be westernized; Hausa society has been all too ready to be islamized. Yoruba culture, however, has absorbed both westernization and Islam and still insisted on the supremacy of the indigenous. Christianized Yoruba are usually Yoruba first and Christians second; islamized Yoruba are usually Yoruba first and Muslims second. No system of values in Nigeria has shown greater indigenous resilience than the Yoruba.

The best illustration in Nigeria of Islam triumphant is among the Hausa-Fulani, and of westernization triumphant, among the Igbo. But the best illustration in Nigeria of the triple heritage at work—with the indigenous as the first among equals—is the Yoruba experience. Yorubaland is capable of producing distinguished westernized scientists with startling tribal facial scarifications, or remarkable commodities for traditional medicine and sorcery sold alongside both the Qur'ān and the Christian Bible in the streets of Ibadan. On the other hand, if Nigeria consisted of only these three major groups, the Islamic factor would predominate more clearly. The alliance between Hausa-Fulani Islam and Yoruba Islam would have overwhelmed any alliance between Igbo Christianity and Yoruba Christianity in the postcolonial era. However, among the smaller minority peoples of Nigeria the balance tilts in favor of Christianity and indigenous religions. The small ethnic groups were once the least alienated of all the groups, but they were also among the most exposed to Christian missionaries. The minorities exhibit some of the purest forms of Africanity and some of the most westernized.

The three forms of power in Nigeria have been economic and educational power, held for a while by Ibo and Yoruba; political power, held for a while by northerners under Hausa-Fulani leadership; and military power, held subtly and sometimes unknowingly by minority groups. The first to recognize their own power were the Igbo and Yoruba. Well before independence, the Igbo and Yoruba saw that they stood a chance of inheriting Nigeria because of their economic skills and Western educational qualifications. The Hausa-Fulani were slower in recognizing the political power of their own numerical superiority. On the eve of independence the Muslim north was so nervous about southern power that there was a strong separatist sentiment among the Hausa-Fulani. It was not the Igbo who were first tempted by secession, but the Muslim north. Nnamdi Azikiwe and Chief Obafemi Awolowo began to worry that Nigeria was going to be another India, partitioned along religious lines. These Nigerian leaders, and even Kwame Nkrumah in Ghana, began to condemn what they called "Pakistanism."

This meant that southerners in Nigeria were very self-confident, while northerners were insecure and nervous about independence. However, within a few years the North became increasingly self-confident, while the south was frustrated and insecure.

Some writers have attributed this reversal of fortune to the brilliant regional leadership of Ahmadu Bello, the Sardauna of Sokoto. The former editor of *West Africa* magazine, David Williams once put it in the following terms:

> When the Sardauna of Sokoto entered party politics in 1951 . . . the leading politicians of Nigeria's then northern region were convinced that their own region . . . was threatened by political and even economic domination by the two Southern regions.
>
> When he was assassinated in 1966 the politicians in the Southern regions were denouncing political domination by 'the north.' It was the towering personality and political skill of the Sardauna . . . which produced this reversal. (*Financial Times*, 24 February 1986)

Before long separatist sentiment became a characteristic of the south rather than the north—"Pakistanism" in reverse. Southern separatism took its most tragic form in Biafra's bid to secede. The latest version of southern separatism is captured in the debate about confederation, a looser form of Nigerian union. The ghost of "Pakistanism" has been changing shape. The south is still self-confident and strong economically and educationally, but it has become insecure politically.

The last groups to discover their power are the minorities of Nigeria, the smaller ethnic groups. This self-discovery began during the civil war under General Yakubu Gowon's administration and gathered momentum during the 1970s. But self-discovery can sometimes result in precipitate acts of self-assertion; this is one possible interpretation of the "Dimka affair" and the events that resulted in the assassination of President Murtala Muhammed in 1976. The minorities had been a sleeping giant without realizing it. The new awakening has had brief moments of danger, but the power is becoming domesticated.

Islam and Foreign Policy. The triple heritage affects foreign policy as well as domestic politics. Among African regions, the best illustration of the triple heritage is West Africa. Here the three forces of indigenous Africanity, Islamic culture and the Western impact are truly balanced as can be seen in the Nigerian experience.

Nigeria's policy toward the Middle East and the Arab-Israeli conflict has certainly been affected by its triple heritage within Nigeria. Some Nigerian Christians tend to support Israel, sometimes forgetting that there are more Christians among Palestinians than among Israelis. Again, it is ironic that Nigerians who favor a secular state at home support Israeli interests, when it has been Palestinians who demand a secular state encompassing Christians, Muslims and Jews. Israel, on the other hand, is not a secular state. Nonetheless, many Nigerian Christians give special support to Israel, and much of the explanation lies in the tensions of the triple heritage—especially the latent stresses in relationships between Nigerian Muslims and Nigerian Christians. Muslim attitudes to Israel are probably inherent in their being Muslim, but Christian attitudes to Israel are a reflection of the domestic politics of Nigeria.

Two issues arose when Nigeria applied for and was admitted to full membership of the Organization of the Islamic Conference (OIC). One issue concerned the method by which admission was sought and then announced. The other issue concerned the legitimacy of Nigeria's membership in itself. The method of application and announcement was a matter of style; what was a matter of substance was whether or not Nigeria's membership was legitimate or defensible. There was first the question of short-term defensibility. Did former president Ibrahim Babangida's effort to have a more regionally representative Armed Forces Ruling Council and other powerful institutions go too far for Muslim Nigerians? Had the balance in the governing bodies tilted in favor of Christians? If so, there could have been a short-term advantage in compensating Nigerian Muslims with a foreign policy bonus like membership in the OIC. In the long term, however, some question whether a secular state such as Nigeria can afford to be a member of a religious organization like the OIC. [*See* Organization of the Islamic Conference.]

Christian Strategies in Nigeria. Aspects of Christian culture have been incorporated into Nigeria's national lifestyle almost unnoticed. The Christian sabbath Sunday and its eve Saturday are days of rest nationally, but the Muslim sabbath, Friday, is not. The national calendar of Nigeria is the Euro-Christian Gregorian calendar; the timetable for the nation's business is never worked out on the basis of the Islamic calendar. Nigeria's Independence Day falls on a different day according to the Islamic calendar than according to the Christian, but it is always celebrated according to the latter. The criminal law of Nigeria, and much of the civil law, are based partly on Euro-Christian concepts of justice.

A final form of cultural domination lies in the preference of English over Hausa as the official language of Nigeria. Theoretically, upon independence the country could have either chosen the indigenous language with the biggest number of speakers, Hausa, or the language of the departing imperial power, English. Or Nigeria could have adopted both Hausa (the numerically preponderant) and English (the politically convenient) as national languages. Countries that have sought compromises of this kind include Tanzania and Kenya (Swahili and English), and Algeria, Tunisia, and Morocco (French and Arabic).

For understandable political reasons, independent Nigeria preferred the functionally convenient English language to the numerically preponderant Hausa language. The Hausa language is saturated with Islamic imagery, expressions, and concepts; English has been deeply influenced by Christian civilization. From a religious point of view, the adoption of English as a national language has had consequences vastly different from what would have ensued upon the adoption of Hausa. Hausa would have introduced non-Muslim Nigerians to wider Islamic perspectives, but English has instead introduced non-Christian Nigerians to Euro-Christian literature and idiomatic Christian-influenced usage.

Islam between Revivalism and Expansion. Islamic revivalism in postcolonial Africa has had contradictory causes. Sometimes it has arisen out of economic disadvantage and desperation, almost echoing Karl Marx's portrayal of religion as "the sigh of the oppressed creature and the soul of soulless conditions." At its most dramatic in postcolonial Africa, Islamic revivalism has emerged out of famine and drought, as if the physical barrenness of the soil has given rise to spiritual fertility. Susan MacDonald notes, in discussing Senegal and the Sahel, that "Persistent drought and the spreading desert have caused poverty, misery and hardship. This diversity has created a favourable terrain for increased religious fervour" (*op cit.*, p. 1568).

Islamic revivalism in Muslim Ethiopia and Somalia was at one time a consequence of drought and famine. While in the 1960s and 1970s Somali poets sang about the ravages of "amputation" (lamenting the political fragmentation of the Somali nation and dreaming of reunification), poets and writers of the 1980s like Nuruddin Farah have lamented the agonies of hunger and deprivation, as well as the curse of domestic tyranny. Problems of political and economic refugees have merged. By the 1990s, the poets lamented anarchy and banditry in Somalia.

In Sudan Islamic revivalism has also drawn sustenance from social and economic deprivation. Nimeiri's declaration of the *sharīʿah* was partly in response to new hardships in the country in the 1980s and to the regime's need for new allies among orthodox Muslims. The Bashīr regime subsequently took the crusade of islamization even further.

On the other hand, Islamic reformers in search of new interpretations were more vulnerable to fundamentalists than ever. The most dramatic martyrdom of an Islamic reformer in Sudan was the execution of Maḥmūd Muḥammad Ṭāhā in 1985. His modernist Islamic ideas got him into trouble with the more orthodox *ʿulamāʾ*. He was accused of apostasy under Islamic law and subsequently executed. But while revivalism in the Horn of Africa and the Sahel was in part the product of hardship and desperation, revivalism in Libya arose with new wealth and confidence. In this respect, revivalism in Libya had something in common with fundamentalism in Iran. Both were the outcome of a convergence of oil wealth and the threat of Western hegemony.

Underlying the outward confidence of both forms of Islamic revivalism, however, is the constant threat of Western cultural hegemony. The fear of Western imperialism is a constant inspiration behind Islamic fundamentalism. The ayatollahs in Iran were radicalized by American imperialism; Qadhdhāfī was radicalized by the threats of Western imperialism and Zionism. Economic deprivation, economic wealth, and the threat of cultural disruption from the West have all played their part in sustaining the new wave of Islamic revivalism.

As for the geographical expansion of Islam, it is more modest in East Africa than in West. The reasons are both colonial and postcolonial. European colonization of West Africa earlier in the century never really arrested the spread of Islam, although it did considerably aid the spread of Christianity. Both introduced religions expanded at the expense of indigenous beliefs, but drew few converts from each other.

By contrast, Islam in East Africa was seriously harmed by the advent of European colonial rule. During the European colonial period Islam in East Africa continued to be Arab-led, whereas the leadership of Islam in West Africa had already been deeply indigenized. In East Africa it appeared as if Arab and European missionary efforts were two rival foreign forces. However, even the nineteenth century *jihāds* in West Africa were entirely indigenous African phenomena. This degree of africanization in West Africa sustained that region's Islam against the counterforce of European colonization.

Second, Islam in East Africa was hurt by the image of the Arab slave trade, especially when that image was exploited by Euro-Christian propaganda during Western colonization. Colonial schools in East Africa dramatized the Arab role in the slave trade and underplayed the Western, trans-Atlantic slave trade. East Africans emerging from colonial and missionary schools learned far more about the Arab slave trade, and far less about the trans-Atlantic flow, than did young colonial West Africans. Islam in East Africa therefore suffered more from anti-Arabism that did Islam in the western part of the continent.

After independence Muslims in West Africa were strong enough numerically and politically to take up the reins of power in countries like Mali, Guinea, and Niger. In Nigeria under civilian rule Muslims were also triumphant from 1960 to 1966 and, to some extent, from 1979 to 1983. In Senegal a Roman Catholic rose to the presidency with Muslim support; in Cameroon a Muslim, Ahmadou Ahidjo, did the same. And in Gabon a Christian ruler, Omar Bongo, converted to Islam.

In East Africa, Somalia and Sudan had Muslim majorities which inherited postcolonial power. But in Uganda it took the military coup of Idi Amin Dada to put Muslims in supreme power from 1971 until 1979; succeeding regimes in Uganda have politically marginalized Islam to levels below those it enjoyed before the rise of Idi Amin.

Tanganyika under the Catholic Nyerere united with Zanzibar under the Muslim Abeid Karume in 1964. From that year until 1985, the country had a Christian president and a Muslim vice-president. Since then both the president and the vice-president have been Muslims.

In Zaire, Rwanda and Burundi, and in Southern Africa generally, the chances of a Muslim head of state in the foreseeable future appear remote. (Malawi's Bakili Muluzi's electoral victory and ascendance to the presidency in May 1994 is an interesting exception, however.) Kenya's Muslim population is estimated at about six million, a quarter of the total, but with disproportionately small political influence. The spread of Islam in Kenya may have been helped by two factors—the missionary activism of the Aḥmadīyah movement and the new financial aid given to Muslim institutions by the Muslim members of the Organization of Petroleum Exporting Countries (OPEC). But while the support of Libya and Iran to African movements may have helped the cause of Islamic revivalism among those already converted, the radicalism of Iran and Libya has sometimes caused political anxiety in countries like Kenya and even Zaire, and has slowed Islam's expansion into new ethnic and geographical areas.

Islam in African Art. In architecture and in verbal arts, the impact of Islam on sub-Saharan Africa has been that of a stimulus, opening up new horizons of creativity. In sculpture and the performing arts, Islam has often been an inhibition rather than a stimulus. In painting the impact of Islam has been mixed—stimulating in some respects, repressive in others.

In West Africa one of the most important milestones in the islamization of architecture came after the legendary pilgrimage to Mecca of Mansa Musa, emperor of ancient Mali (r. 1312–1337). His legend emphasizes how he traveled in golden splendor through Cairo to the holy cities of Islam; but more fundamental for the future of West Africa was Mansa Musa's decision to bring back an architect (al-Sāḥil) from Arabia. New mosques rose with impressive minarets and domes in Timbuktu. Mansa Musa also presided over the use of a revolutionary new building material, brick instead of *pisé* or pounded clay. The architectural civilization of Muslim West Africa was changed forever. Timbuktu became a major center of learning, and the new mosques were at once places of worship and centers of scholarship.

The architectural changes affected private homes also, many of them now built with a flat roof and a central dome. Subsequent influences from the Maghrib helped to stimulate local African innovations, culminating in subsequent centuries in such splendid creations as the Mouride mosque in Touba, Senegal.

In East Africa the Muslim stimulus in architecture came from the Arabian Peninsula and the Gulf, contributing to the rise of Islamic city-states on the East Africa coast such as Kilwa, Mombasa, Sofala, and Pate. The deserted ancient city of Gedi on today's Kenya coast preserves much of the Afro-Islamic character in its ruins.

While Islam was a creative stimulus in African architecture, it may have been a stumbling block for African sculpture, the performing arts, and painting. It is to this inhibiting tendency of Islam that we should briefly turn.

Islam is in a problematic relationship with African sculpture than with African architecture. One reason is Islam's uncompromising monotheism and concomitant wariness of idolatry. Yet African sculpture sometimes depicts deities or offers protection against magic. The tension between Islam and the African art of masks and figurines can be traced back to idolatry in pre-Islamic Mecca.

Pre-Islamic Arabs had worshipped idols in the very places where Muslims now circumambulate the Kaʿbah in Mecca. According to Islamic tradition, the prophet Muḥammad himself destroyed some of those idols with his own hands. In order to discourage the return of idolatry, arts such as sculpture and painting became circumscribed in terms of what they could represent; in time, according to some schools of Islam, to paint an animal was regarded as an attempt to imitate God. Thus the depiction of living organisms became increasingly taboo. Mosques were decorated with verses of the Qur'ān rather than with creatures from nature; the culture of letters was sacralized. Islam was a stimulus to creative calligraphy, but a block to portraiture.

Islam's uncompromising stance on this subject has often militated against African masks and bronze figures. The rich tradition which produced the bronzework of ancient Benin and Ile-Ife, and much later inspired such European artists as Picasso, was threatened quite early by this school of Islam. Of course, some African Muslims did mix the culture: syncretism is part of Africa's religious history. But in general, Islam's distrust of representational and organic art remained in continuing tension with this form of African art.

There has also been conflict between Islam and African dance. Islam distrusts African dance for two principal reasons—the dance's apparent proximity to idolatry and to sexuality.

In later centuries even African governments that were not Muslim also tended to avoid celebrating indigenous gods. Today almost all African countries celebrate some Christian festivals. African countries that are Muslim celebrate festivals like ʿĪd al-Fiṭr, ʿĪd al-Ḥajj, and sometimes the Prophet's birthday. Some countries, such as Nigeria, celebrate all of those, Christian and Muslim, and a few secular ones. What no African country has really celebrated nationally in the twentieth century are the indigenous religious traditions.

Fear of neglect of African indigenous ritual is not peculiar to Islam as a tradition: African governments themselves fall short. But Islam and missionary Christianity have also distrusted African dance for reasons unconnected with idolatry: for its presumed sexuality, and perhaps because certain dances are performed by women. In the case of Christian missionaries the distrust of the dance sometimes resulted in banning it in missionary schools, and their dislike of African patterns of dress sometimes led to special innovations to satisfy the rules of Christian modesty in dress. Islamic rules of dress have often been even more severe for women.

On the issue of African languages and literature, Islam has played a more stimulating role, though sometimes dialectically. On the one hand, Islam appears to be linguistically intolerant: liturgy has to be in Arabic, and the muezzin calls the believers to prayer in Arabic. On the other hand, Islam and the Arabic language have created whole new indigenous creoles in Africa, or have profoundly enriched indigenous tongues. Such Afro-Islamic languages include Kiswahili and Hausa, arguably the two most successful indigenous tongues of the continent. In the verbal arts of Africa, Islam has been a great creative stimulus.

It may fairly be asked whether indigenous African traditions of poetry have been enriched by interactions with other traditions, including Islam. In regard to the range of subject matter treated by poets, Islam has sometimes been an inhibiting factor; Islamic values made certain topics sinful. On the other hand, in terms of depth of meaning and sophistication of the craft of versification, Islam has probably been immensely enriching.

While the art of African fiction in indigenous languages has been greatly influenced by contact with the West, African poetry in indigenous languages has been more enriched by contact with Islam. African languages with the most complex poetic forms are probably disproportionately within civilizations that have been in contact with Islam. The most remarkable preoccupation with poetry is probably found in Somali culture. Despite their political troubles, the Somalis developed an exceptional culture of oral and even extemporaneous poetry. Their greatest modern national hero, Muhammad Abdilleh Hassan (Muḥammad ʿAbd Allāh Ḥasan), was both a savior of his nation and a hero of his language.

As for the art form of song, in a way an even older aesthetic, is there a tense relationship with Islam? It probably depends on the themes of the songs. There may be certain themes in African culture that appear immodest by Islamic criteria, even if not by Islamic criteria of beauty. But song is of course a major part of Islamic as well as of African culture.

As for more recent trends in painting, there have been Muslim artists who have broken out of the confines of doctrine and painted people, sculpted animals, or drawn living forests. These artists have seen themselves not as imitators of God but as sparks of the Almighty. Human genius at its best is but a spark of the First Cause. Painter Ali Darwish of Zanzibar sometimes immersed himself in both living forests and dazzling calligraphy. Ibrahim Noor Shariff painted galloping horses in a "fourth dimension." To him Islam was always a stimulus, and human genius was a spark from the radiance of God. Such aesthetic reformers may be the wave of the future for Muslim artists in Africa.

[*See also* African Languages and Literatures; *and entries on specific countries.*]

BIBLIOGRAPHY

Abu-Lughod, Ibrahim. "The Islamic Factor in African Politics." *Orbis* 8 (1964): 425–444. Early reminder of the significance of Islam in modern and contemporary Africa, written before the political importance of Islam received much attention.

Cruise O'Brien, Donal B. "Islam and Power in Black Africa." In *Islam and Power,* edited by Alexander S. Cudsi and Ali E. Hillal Dessouki, pp. 158–168. Baltimore, 1981. Helpful discussion giving some emphasis to the role of Ṣūfī orders.

Davidson, Basil. *The Story of Africa.* London, 1984. Chapter 8, "The Impact of Islam," places the expansion of Islam in the broader context of African history.

General History of Africa. Vol. 6, *Africa in the Nineteenth Century until the 1880s.* Edited by J. F. Ade Ajayi. Berkeley, 1989. Vol. 7, *Africa under Colonial Domination, 1880–1935.* Edited by A. Adu Boahen. Berkeley, 1985. Researched and published as part of a major project by UNESCO under the leadership of Amadou-Mahtar M'Bow. The coverage of movements provides interpretations that go beyond the stereotypes of imperial scholarship.

Levtzion, Nehemia. "Islam: Islam in Sub-Saharan Africa." In *The Encyclopedia of Religion,* vol. 7, pp. 344–357. Broad survey with emphasis on the medieval period.

Lewis, I. M., ed. *Islam in Tropical Africa.* 2d ed. Bloomington, 1980. Contains an extended historical introduction and a number of important interpretive case studies.

Mazrui, Ali A. "African Islam and Competitive Religion: Between Revivalism and Expansion." *Third World Quarterly* 10. 2 (April 1988): 499–518. Important contemporary interpretation of the different developments within African Islam.

Mazrui, Ali A., and Toby Kleban Levine, eds. *The Africans: A Reader.* New York, 1986. Collection of readings, prepared for use along with the excellent television series, "The African: A Triple Heritage," that provides an excellent source for understanding the "triple heritage" interpretation of African realities.

Nyang, Sulayman S. *Islam, Christianity, and African Identity.* Brattleboro, Vt., 1984. Helpful introduction to some important issues.

Trimingham, J. Spencer. *The Influence of Islam upon Africa.* 2d ed. London, 1980. Broad survey by one of the most influential scholars on the subject. Provides useful information despite the Christian missionary viewpoint.

ALI A. MAZRUI

Islam in Central Asia and the Caucasus

Islam came to Central Asia and the Caucasus not long after its birth in the seventh century. The Arab conquest spanned roughly the period 600–800 CE, with further penetration via traders until 1200. The Mongol empire threatened Islam in the thirteenth century, but the faith withstood this and expanded as Russian conquests dominated the region in the sixteenth through nineteenth centuries. The Bolshevik Revolution and the subsequent antireligious campaign slated Islam for extinction; it again persisted and was freed to develop anew when the Soviet Union collapsed in 1991.

Islam in the different regions of Central Asia even today displays characteristics traceable to the agents and means of its original diffusion. For example, Islam in Central Asia and the Caucasus, imposed during the Arab conquest, tends to be conservative and traditionalist. By contrast, Islam in the middle Volga region, especially among the Kazan Tatars, is modernist and liberal, reflecting its purveyance by merchants and diplomats. In the North Caucasus, which received Islam largely through the efforts of Ṣūfī brotherhoods (*ṭarīqahs*), it is radically conservative and occasionally militant.

History. In the middle of the seventh century CE conquering Arabs imposed Islam on eastern Transcaucasia. Azerbaijan fell in 639, and Daghestan first in 642. Despite opposition from Georgian Christians and Jewish Khazars in the region, islamization continued rapidly, so that by the eighth century the majority of the population was already Muslim. In the impenetrable mountains of Daghestan islamization took until the twelfth century, when resisting Christians and Jews for the most part disappeared. Central Asia at this time was divided among Buddhists, Manicheans, and Nestorian Christians. Arab conquest of the region south of the Syr Darya was complete by 716, and by the middle of the tenth century Islam was virtually the only religion in this territory.

A peaceful period of Islamic expansion into Central Asia and the Caucasus followed the violent Arab conquests. From 800 to 1200 Islam came with merchants along the famous fur and silk trade routes. The first ran from north to south along the Volga and the second from west to east from the Black Sea to China. The Bulgar Kingdom of the Middle Volga, presentday Tatarstan, received Islam as early as the ninth century from traders and Arab diplomats. Already by the middle of the tenth century, the world-famous fur trade that originated there was mostly a Muslim activity. In the eleventh and twelfth centuries Islam spread into the Urals through the territory of present-day Bashkortostan. As Muslim merchants moved north from the Syr Darya to the steppes of Kazakhstan and the mountains of Kirghizia (modern Kyrgyzstan) and finally to Eastern Turkestan (presentday Chinese Xinjiang), Islam took root, although somewhat more slowly among the nomads, whose islamization took until the eighteenth century.

The thirteenth century was a particularly dark one for Islam in Central Asia because of the Mongol invasion. At the beginning, Mongol rule had a strong anti-Islamic character, as many Mongol leaders were Buddhists and Nestorian Christians. Islam survived largely through the efforts of the Ṣūfī brotherhoods, which proselytized extensively among the masses. Eventually important Mongol rulers of the Golden Horde and the Chagatai Khanate would become Muslims themselves. By the middle of the sixteenth century, Crimea, the southern Russian steppes north of the Black and Caspian seas, the Kazakh steppes, and western Siberia had joined the Islamic world. Islam was brought to the North Caucasus in the fifteenth and sixteenth centuries by the Nogai Horde, the Crimean Khanate, and the Ottoman Turks.

By the middle of the fourteenth century, the centralized Muscovite state began to throw off its Tatar yoke and push back the remnants of the Golden Horde. In the process, important Muslim territories were brought into the expanding Russian empire: Kazan (1552), Astrakhan (1556), and western Siberia (1598). By 1700, the Russians had reached the North Caucasus. Russian occupiers expelled Muslims from all the important cities and from the best land along the rivers. Under Ivan the Terrible and the first Romanovs, Muslims were treated as Russian subjects and denied the rights given to Christians. The Muslim aristocracy (especially in the Caucasus) was coopted and encouraged to convert to Christianity. In some regions Muslim religious leaders were expelled to the countryside and mosques destroyed. Sometimes Muslims were subjected to forcible conversion.

Still, Islam advanced, especially under Catherine the Great, who considered Islam a better civilizing influence on Asia than Christianity. Catherine guaranteed Muslims important rights—particularly regarding religious practice—sponsored the building of mosques, and created Islamic institutions with broad authority over the Muslim population of the Russian empire. Ironically, under her reign the first Naqshbandī Ṣūfī missionaries arrived in the North Caucasus, where they laid the foundations for the most militant resistance to Russian expansion in that region.

Ṣūfī brotherhoods have been an important element of Islamic civilization in the Russian Empire from the earliest days. At the time of Russian conquest four brotherhoods were active in Central Asia—the Naqshbandīyah, Yasawīyah, Qādirīyah, and Kubrawīyah. The Naqshbandīyah was founded in Bukhara in the fourteenth century and is in most respects the most prestigious *ṭarīqah* in the region. Most of the greatest Turkestani poets were members of the Naqshbandīyah, including ʿAlī Shīr Navāʾī, ʿAbd al-Raḥmān Jāmī, Mahtūm Qulī, and Ẓalīlī. The Yasawīyah brotherhood was founded in the twelfth century in the northern part of Mavarannahr. It played an important role in the islamization of the nomadic tribes, then became inactive. It emerged again in the twentieth century under Russian and Soviet rule, and one of its offshoots, the *ṭarīqah* of the "Hairy Ishans," became one of the most radical in Central Asia. The Qādirīyah brotherhood was founded in the twelfth century in Baghdad and was introduced to Central Asia in the Middle Ages. The Kubrawīyah was founded in the twelfth century in Khorezm (Khwārazm), and it played an important role in the islamization of the Golden Horde's nomadic tribes. Today it has little influence in Central Asia.

The Naqshbandīyah and the Qādirīyah also penetrated the North Caucasus, where their influence has been central. While Ṣūfī activity in Central Asia has been generally less militant and radical, the brotherhoods in the North Caucasus provided active leadership in the struggle against Russian domination. The Qādirīyah in particular has given birth to several militant Ṣūfī organizations that forcibly opposed Russian rule until the disintegration of the Soviet Union, treating the struggle as a *jihād*. [*See also* Sufism, *article on* Ṣūfī Orders; Naqshbandīyah; Qādirīyah.]

Russian conquest of Central Asia and the Caucasus continued throughout the nineteenth century; by 1900 it was complete. With the exception of the protectorates of Khiva and Bukhara, Central Asia was ruled by the Russian governor general of Turkestan from Tashkent. Russian policy toward the vast Muslim population of the empire returned to one of religious and cultural assimilation, although with more subtle techniques. These techniques became known as the "Il'minski system" after the Kazan missionary who espoused them.

Islam nevertheless continued to expand in the Russian empire at least until the Bolshevik Revolution of 1917 and even until the Soviet antireligious crackdown of

1928 and beyond. Lenin and most Bolsheviks were unremittingly hostile to all religions, including Islam, but their precarious political position, their need for political and military allies—especially among non-Russians—and their desire to bring the Russian Empire fully under Soviet control led them alternately to tolerate religion and to repress it.

Under Soviet rule, Islam faced seven distinct policy periods. The first was the period of the "cavalry raids," which lasted from 1917 to 1919. This period marked a general offensive by local Bolsheviks against all religious institutions, including Islam. The second period, 1919–1928, is that of Muslim National Communism, the creation of a number of innovative Muslims, especially the Kazan Tatar Mir Said Sultangaliev, who had joined the Bolshevik movement to pursue largely nationalist goals. Sultangaliev and others synthesized nationalism, socialism, and Islam into a doctrine that gave priority to the distinctly national and Islamic concerns of Russia's Muslims. In this paradigm Islam was the chief bulwark against russification. Despite the Muslim National Communists, or perhaps because of them, Communist Party authorities worked assiduously to reduce the power of Muslim clerics by outlawing *waqf*s (the basis of clerical economic power), suppressing the *sharīʿah* and *ʿādāt* courts, and eliminating the *mektep*s and *medresseh*s (Ar., *maktab, madrasah*).

The third period, a frontal assault by Soviet authorities on Islam, lasted from 1928 to 1941. In 1912 there were 26,279 registered mosques in the Russian empire. Communist authorities now closed or destroyed thousands of these, and Muslim clerics were shot and imprisoned. In the fourth period, during World War II, Soviet authorities relaxed this policy to attract full cooperation with the Russian war effort against Germany. Nonetheless, thousands of Muslims defected to the Germans and actively fought against Russia. The fifth period, a time of relaxed official pressure on Islam, occurred in the immediate postwar period. In the sixth distinct period, Nikita Khrushchev launched a new antireligious campaign in 1959. Over the next five years Soviet authorities closed the majority of working mosques. In 1958 there were approximately 1,500; by 1968 the number had dropped to fewer than 500.

In the final period following Khrushchev's ouster, the Soviet leadership abandoned the open offensive against Islam as counterproductive. Beginning in the 1940s, some Soviet strategists had begun advocating the use of Islam as a diplomatic weapon in the struggle with the West. To this end, the Soviet leadership created special Islamic organizations in the USSR that played an important role in Moscow's efforts to woo the Islamic third world and served as diplomatic links to important Islamic countries, especially in the Arab world, with whom Moscow had no official diplomatic relations. This policy continued throughout the Brezhnev years until the Iranian revolution, which gave the Soviets unprecedented opportunities to cultivate an anti-American policy among Muslim countries; the subsequent Soviet invasion of Afghanistan, however, caused the Soviet pro-Islamic policy abroad to suffer a serious, albeit temporary, setback.

With the rise of Mikhail Gorbachev and his policy of *glasnost'*, religious expression among all groups in the USSR burst into the open and could no longer be constrained. In Central Asia in particular, the Islamic spillover effect of the war in Afghanistan became evident in Uzbekistan and Tajikistan by the mid-1980s. By August 1991 at the time of the coup against Gorbachev, unofficial Islamic organizations had come into the open in most of the Muslim regions of the USSR and in some cases were openly competing for political power. With Gorbachev's eclipse and the official demise of the Soviet Union as a unitary state, Islam again emerged in full bloom. As of the beginning of 1993, thousands of mosques and hundreds of new Islamic schools were being opened in all post-Soviet Muslim states as well as in Muslim territories still part of the Russian Federation; the leaders of these new states, even those who came up through the ranks of the Communist Party, espouse Islam as the national religious creed, both from sincere belief and from political necessity; and ties between the new Muslim states and the Islamic world abroad have been established, including fully accredited embassies and membership in exclusively Islamic economic associations.

Organization and Practice. Most Muslims of Central Asia and the Caucasus belong to the Sunnī creed and to the Ḥanafī school (*mazhab*). In Daghestan, the Shāfiʿī school prevails (the Nogais are an exception). The Jaʿfarī rite of Shiism, adhered to in most of Iran, is also practiced by about 70 percent of Azeris, the Ironis of Central Asia, the Tats of Daghestan and Azerbaijan, and an undetermined number of citydwellers. These Azeris numbered approximately 6.8 million in 1989; the other groups probably number no more than 250,000 collectively. The Ismāʿīlīs of the Nizārī rite, or followers of the Aga Khan, include the Pamirian peoples (Mountain Tajiks, Vakhis, Yazgulams, Ishakashimis, Shugnans and Bartangs), who probably number no more than 160,000 today. Finally there are the Bahā'īs, mostly descendants of émigrés from Iran and mostly citydwellers in Azerbaijan, Turkmenistan, and Russia (Astrakhan); they probably number no more than 60,000. Soviet statisticians often listed the Yezidis ("devil worshipers") among Muslims of the empire, but this is in error; their religion is a syncretist creed of Manichean origin. [*See* Ismāʿīlīyah; Bahā'īs.]

Demographics. According to the Soviet census of 1989, forty-one traditionally Muslim groups exist in the new states of the former empire (see Table 1). Whatever its shortcomings, the Soviet 1989 census is the best practical source on the Muslim population of the post-Soviet states. The borders of the former USSR were political borders, not ethnic ones, and many of the groups represented here also live in states adjoining the former Soviet Union. Azeris in Iran, for example, may number as many as 20 million, and many representatives of nationalities related to the Caucasian peoples live in Turkey. A conservative estimate would place approximately 12 to 13 million people of Central Asian nationalities outside the borders of the former Soviet Union. Even these figures are in dispute: the Uighur and Kazakh scholars of Chinese Xinjiang, for instance, dispute the official Chinese census figure for their populations as being as much as 50 percent too low.

The majority of the Muslims of Central Asia and the Caucasus are Turkic peoples and speak Turkic languages. The major exception is the Tajiks, who are ethnically and linguistically Indo-Iranian. The smaller Muslim nationalities of the North Caucasus belong to a variety of Turkic, Iranian and Caucasian linguistic groups. There is thus an almost unbroken Turkic continuum from Chinese Central Asia to Turkey.

Present Practice. The Soviet attitude toward Islam was self-contradictory. On one hand, within the USSR Soviet authorities repressed Islam and subjected Muslims to an unremitting process of antireligious sovietization in hopes that Islamic consciousness could eventually be eliminated altogether. On the other hand, Russian strategists viewed Islam in the Soviet Union as a useful instrument for pursuing specific strategic interests in the larger Islamic world, and to this end they created a variety of "official" Islamic institutions in Soviet Muslim territories to serve as conduits for Soviet propaganda. Many Western scholars were thus seduced into concluding that Soviet social engineering was successful, and that Islam was little more than folklore among Soviet Muslims, dead as a religion and dying as a culture. Many foreign Muslims concluded just the opposite—that Islam in the USSR was thriving and free—although these notions were usually dispelled during personal visits. The judgment of both groups was seriously in error.

TABLE 1. *Population of Muslim Groups in Former Soviet States*

GROUP	POPULATION	GROUP	POPULATION	GROUP	POPULATION
Uzbeks	16,686,240	*(Daghestan, cont'd.)*		Kurds	152,952
Kazakhs	8,137,878	Rutuls	20,672	Adygei	124,491
Azerbaijanis	6,791,106	Tsakhurs	20,055	Balkars	88,771
Tatars	6,645,588	Aguls	19,936	Dungans	69,686
Tajiks	4,216,693	Baskhirs	1,449,462	Cherkess	52,356
Turkmen	2,718,297	Chechens	958,309	Iranians	40,510
Kirghiz	2,530,998	Ossetians	597,802[a]	Abazi	33,801
Peoples of Daghestan	2,072,071	Karakalpaks	423,436	Tats	30,817
Avars	604,202	Kabardians	394,651	Baluchis	29,091
Lezgins	466,833	Crimean Tatars	268,739	Talysh	21,914
Dargins	365,797	Uighur	262,199	Arabs	11,599
Kumyks	282,178	Gypsies	261,956[b]	Afghans	8,951
Laks	118,386	Ingush	237,577	Albanians	4,085
Tabasarans	98,448	Turks	207,369		
Nogai	75,564	Karachai	156,140		

[a]Probably 50 percent of Ossetians are Christian. [b]Central Asian and Caucasian Gypsies are Muslim.
Source: Ann Sheehy, *Report on the USSR*, 19 Jan. 1990.

There is now no doubt that Islamic consciousness on Soviet territories—both religious and cultural—could not be expunged by subtle or brutal methods. Although religious observance among Muslims of the former USSR is imperfect owing to their isolation from the larger Islamic world for nearly eight decades, their sense of belonging to that world is strong and growing. Popular Islamic consciousness is clearly on the rise. In several new countries (e.g., Tajikistan and Azerbaijan) substantial political groups have called for the establishment of "Islamic republics." In all cases, the leaders of the new countries routinely pay obeisance to the Islamic component of their own political power. Thus the debate over Islam's survival is over; the debate over its future in Central Asia and the Caucasus is just beginning, as the extent of its potential political, cultural, and religious power among peoples so long deprived of their Islamic heritage is just now becoming known.

[*See also* Azerbaijan; Bukhara Khanate; Central Asian Literatures; Crimea Khanate; Kazakhstan; Kazan Khanate; Khiva Khanate; Khoqand Khanate; Kyrgyzstan; Tajikistan; Turkmenistan; Uzbekistan.]

BIBLIOGRAPHY

A great deal of Western scholarship on the Islamic peoples of the former Soviet Union has been produced in recent years. Unfortunately, much of it is characterized by erroneous judgments on Islam's persistence in these lands. The following are among the better sources available in English.

Allworth, Edward. *The Modern Uzbeks, from the Fourteenth Century to the Present*. Stanford, Calif., 1990. History of the largest Muslim nationality of Central Asia.

Altstadt, Audrey L. *The Azerbaijani Turks: Power and Identity under Soviet Rule*. Stanford, Calif., 1992. Comprehensive modern history of the most populous Muslim region of the Caucasus.

Baddeley, John F. *The Russian Conquest of the Caucasus*. London, 1908. *The Rugged Flanks of the Caucasus*. 2 vols. London, 1940. These two works contain more information on the history and customs of the Muslim peoples of the Caucasus than any other source in English.

Bennigsen, Alexandre, and Chantal Lemercier-Quelquejay. *Islam in the Soviet Union*. London, 1967. Classic work on the subject. Includes a good history of the origins, development, and treatment of Islam in the Russian empire and an excellent bibliography.

Bennigsen, Alexandre, and S. Enders Wimbush. *Muslims of the Soviet Empire: A Guide*. London and Bloomington, 1985. Comprehensive reference work on demographic, linguistic, social, and religious information. Includes an extensive bibliography of sources in many languages.

Bennigsen, Alexandre, and S. Enders Wimbush. *Mystics and Commissars: Sufism in the Soviet Union*. London, Berkeley, and Los Angeles, 1985. Complete treatment of the origins and practice of Sufism in the USSR and its successor states.

Broxup, Marie, ed. *The North Caucasus Barrier: The Russian Advance towards the Muslim World*. London, 1992. Breaks new ground in this little-known area. Deals with both nineteenth- and twentieth-century developments.

Carrère d'Encausse, Hélène. *Islam and the Russian Empire: Reform and Revolution in Central Asia*. Berkeley, 1988. Study of the nationalist awakening among Central Asian Muslims in the late nineteenth and early twentieth centuries.

Central Asian Survey. London, 1982–. Quarterly journal, published by the Society for Central Asian Studies in London, the only one of its kind devoted exclusively to Central Asia and the Caucasus.

Fierman, William, ed. *Soviet Central Asia: The Failed Transformation*. Boulder, 1991.

Hayit, Baymirza. *Islam and Turkestan under Russian Rule*. Istanbul, 1987. Summation of a lifetime of scholarship by an Uzbek scholar who defected to the West during World War II.

Henze, Paul B. "Fire and Sword in the Caucasus: The Nineteenth-Century Resistance of the North Caucasian Mountaineers." *Central Asian Survey* 2.1 (1983): 5–44. Concise history and analysis of Muslim resistance to Russian encroachment in the North Caucasus by one of the West's leading specialists.

Henze, Paul B. "Turkestan Rising." *Wilson Quarterly* 16.3 (Summer 1992): 48–58. The best current analysis of Central Asian political dynamics since the disintegration of the USSR.

Poliakov, Sergeĭ. *Everyday Islam: Religion and Tradition in Rural Central Asia*. Armonk, N.Y., 1992. Study based on many years of fieldwork in Central Asia by a Soviet ethnographer who deplores the persistence of Islamic values, but provides a vivid and detailed description of Islam in Central Asian society.

RFE-RL Weekly Report. Newsletter published by the RFE-RL Research Institute, a division of Radio Free Europe–Radio Liberty in Munich, containing up-to-date analyses of developments among the Muslims of the post-Soviet states. The work of Ann Sheehy (on Central Asia and Islam generally) and Elizabeth Fuller (on the Caucasus) are particularly noteworthy.

Rorlich, Azade-Ayşe. *The Volga Tatars: A Profile in National Resilience*. Stanford, Calif., 1986. Comprehensive work on the most numerous Muslim nationality still within the Russian Federation.

Rywkin, Michael. *Moscow's Muslim Challenge: Soviet Central Asia*. Armonk, N.Y., and London, 1982. Excellent summary and analysis of the Soviet treatment of Islam in Central Asia and the Muslim response.

S. Enders Wimbush

Islam in China

Islam in China has been propagated over the past thirteen hundred years primarily among the people now known as "Hui," but many of the issues confronting them are also relevant to the Turkic and Indo-European Muslims on China's Inner Asian frontier. "Hui teaching" *(Hui jiao)* was the term once used in Chinese for Islam in general; it probably derives from an early Chinese rendering of the term for the modern Uighur people. According to the reasonably accurate 1990 national census of China, the total Muslim population is 17.6 million, including Hui (8,602,978), Uighur (7,214,431), Kazakh (1,111,718), Dongxiang (373,872), Kyrgyz (141,549), Salar (87,697); Tajik (33,538), Uzbek (14,502), Bonan (12,212), and Tatar (4,873). The Hui speak mainly Sino-Tibetan languages; Turkic-language speakers include the Uighur, Kazakh, Kyrgyz, Uzbek, and Tatar; combined Turkic-Mongolian speakers include the Dongxiang, Salar, and Bonan, concentrated in Gansu's mountainous Hexi corridor; and the Tajik speak a variety of Indo-Persian dialects. It is important to note, however, that the Chinese census registered people by nationality, not religious affiliation, so the actual number of Muslims is still unknown.

Although the Hui have been labeled as the "Chinese-speaking Muslims" or "Chinese Muslims," this is misleading, because by law all Muslims living in China are "Chinese" by citizenship, and many Hui speak only their local non-Chinese dialects; they include the Tibetan, Mongolian, Thai, and Hainan Muslims, who are also classified by the state as Hui. Yet most Hui are closer to the Han Chinese than the other Muslim nationalities in terms of demographic proximity and cultural accommodation, adapting many of their Islamic practices to Han ways of life, which became the source for many of the criticisms by later Muslim reformers. In the past this was not such a problem for the Turkish and Indo-European Muslim groups, who were traditionally more isolated from the Han and whose identities were not so threatened, though this has begun to change in the past forty years. As a result of state-sponsored nationality identification campaigns over the past thirty years, these groups have begun to think of themselves more as ethnic nationalities than just as "Muslims." The Hui are unique among the fifty-five identified minority nationalities in China in that they are the only nationality for whom religion is the only unifying category of identity, even though many members of the Hui nationality may not practice Islam.

As the result of a succession of Islamic reform movements that swept across China over the past six centuries, one finds among the Muslims in China today a wide spectrum of Islamic belief. Archaeological discoveries of large collections of Islamic artifacts and epigraphy on the southeast coast suggest that the earliest Muslim communities in China were descended from Arab, Persian, Central Asian, and Mongolian Muslim merchants, militia, and officials who settled first along China's southeast coast in the seventh to tenth centuries; there followed larger migrations to the north from Central Asia under the Mongol Yuan dynasty in the thirteenth and fourteenth centuries, gradually intermarrying with the local Chinese populations and raising their children as Muslims. Practicing Sunnī, Ḥānafī Islam and residing in independent small communities clustered around a central mosque, these relatively isolated Islamic village and urban communities interacted via trading networks and recognition of membership in the wider Islamic *ummah*. Each was headed by an *ahong* (from Persian *ākhūnd*) who was invited to teach on a more or less temporary basis.

Sufism began to make a substantial impact in China proper in the late seventeenth century, arriving mainly along the Central Asian trade routes with saintly shaykhs, both Chinese and foreign, who brought new teachings from the pilgrimage cities. These charismatic teachers and tradesmen established widespread networks and brotherhood associations, most prominently the Naqshbandīyah, Qādarīyah, and Kubrāwīyah. The hierarchical organization of these Ṣūfī networks helped to mobilize large numbers of Hui during economic and political crises in the seventeenth to nineteenth centuries, assisting widespread Muslim-led rebellions and resistance movements against late Ming and Qing imperial rule in Yunnan, Shaanxi, Gansu, and Xinjiang. The 1912 Nationalist revolution allowed further autonomy in regions of Muslim concentration in the northwest, and wide areas came under virtual control by Muslim warlords, leading to frequent intra-Muslim and Muslim-Han conflicts until the eventual communist victory led to the reassertion of central control. In the late nineteenth and early twentieth centuries, Wahhābī-inspired reform movements known as the Yihewani (from Arabic *ikhwan*) rose to popularity under Nationalist and warlord sponsorship; they were noted for their critical stance toward traditionalist Islam as too acculturated to Chinese practices, and Sufism as too attached to saint and tomb veneration.

Many Muslims supported the earliest communist call for equity, autonomy, freedom of religion, and recognized nationality status, and were active in the early establishment of the People's Republic, but they became disenchanted by growing critiques of religious practice during several radical periods in the PRC beginning in 1957. During the Cultural Revolution (1966–1976), Muslims became the focus for both antireligious and antiethnic nationalist critiques, leading to widespread persecutions, mosque-closings, and at least one massacre of one thousand Hui following a 1975 uprising in Yunnan province. Since Deng Xiaoping's post-1978 reforms, Muslims have sought to take advantage of liberalized economic and religious policies while keeping a watchful eye on the ever-swinging pendulum of Chinese radical politics. There are now more mosques open in China than there were before 1949, and Muslims travel freely on the *ḥajj* to Mecca, as well as engaging in cross-border trade with coreligionists in Central Asia, in the Middle East, and increasingly in Southeast Asia.

Increasing Muslim political activism on a national scale and rapid state response indicates the growing importance Beijing places on Muslim-related issues. In 1986 Uighurs in Xinjiang marched through the streets of Urumqi protesting a wide range of issues, including the environmental degradation of the Zungharian plain, nuclear testing in the Taklamakan, increased Han immigration to Xinjiang, and ethnic insults at Xinjiang University. Muslims throughout China protested the publication of the Chinese book *Sexual Customs* in May 1989, and of a children's book in October 1993 that portrayed Muslims—particularly their restriction against pork, which Mao once called "China's greatest national treasure"—in derogatory fashion. In each case the government quickly responded, meeting most of the Muslim demands, condemning the publications, arresting the authors, and closing down the printing houses.

Islamic factional struggles continue to divide China's Muslims internally, especially as increased travel to the Middle East prompts criticism of Muslim practice at home and exposes China's Muslims to new, often politically radical Islamic ideals. In February 1994 four Naqshbandī Ṣūfī leaders were sentenced to long-term imprisonment for their support of internal factional disputes in southern Ningxia Region, which led to at least sixty deaths on both sides and required intervention by the People's Liberation Army. Throughout the summer and fall of 1993 bombs exploded in several towns in Xinjiang, indicating the growing demands of organizations pressing for an independent Turkestan. Beijing has responded with increased military presence, particularly in Kashgar and Urumqi, as well as diplomatic efforts in the Central Asian states and Turkey to discourage foreign support for separatist movements. At the same time cross-border trade between Xinjiang and Central Asia has grown tremendously, especially with the reopening in 1991 of the Eurasian Railroad linking Urumqi and Alma Ata with markets in China and eastern Europe. Overland travel between Xinjiang and Pakistan, Tajikistan, Kyrgyzstan, and Kazakhstan has also increased dramatically with the relaxation of travel restrictions based on Deng Xiaoping's prioritization of trade over security interests in the area. The government's policy of seeking to buy support through stimulating the local economy seems to be working in 1994, as income levels in Xinjiang are often far higher than those across the border; however, increased Han migration to participate in the region's lucrative oil and mining industries continues to exacerbate ethnic tension. Muslim areas in northern and central China continue to be left behind as China's rapid economic growth expands unevenly, enriching the southern coastal areas far more than the interior.

While further restricting Islamic freedoms in the border regions, at the same time the state has become more keenly aware of the importance foreign Muslim governments place on China's treatment of its Muslim minorities as a factor in China's lucrative trade and military agreements. The establishment of full diplomatic ties with Saudi Arabia in 1991 and increasing military and technical trade with Middle Eastern Muslim states enhances the economic and political salience of China's treatment of its Muslim minority. The increased transnationalism of China's Muslims will be an important factor in their ethnic expression as well as in their accommodation to Chinese culture and state authority.

BIBLIOGRAPHY

Bai Shouyi, ed. *Huimin Qiyi* (Hui Rebellions), 4 vols. Shanghai, 1953.

Broomhall, Marshall. *Islam in China: A Neglected Problem.* New York, 1910.

Chen Dasheng, ed. *Islamic Inscriptions in Quanzhou.* Translated by Chen Enming. Yinchuan and Quanzhou, 1984.

Forbes, Andrew D. W. *Warlords and Muslims in Chinese Central Asia.* Cambridge, 1986.

Gladney, Dru C. *Muslim Chinese: Ethnic Nationalism in the People's Republic.* Cambridge, Mass., 1991.

Israeli, Raphael. With the assistance of Lyn Gorman. *Islam in China: A Critical Bibliography.* Westport, Conn., 1994.

Leslie, Donald Daniel. *Islam in Traditional China: A Short History to 1800.* Canberra, 1986.

Lipman, Jonathan N. *The Border World of Gansu, 1895–1935.* Ph.D. diss., Stanford University, Stanford, 1981.

Ma Tong. *Zhongguo Yisilan Jiaopai yu Menhuan Zhidu Shilue* (A history of Muslim factions and the Menhuan system in China). Yinchuan, 1983.

Pillsbury, Barbara. *Cohesion and Cleavage in a Chinese Muslim Minority.* Ph.D. diss., Columbia University, New York, 1973.

Dru C. Gladney

Islam in South Asia

The experience of Islam in South Asia is at once vast and varied. It encompasses nearly 300 million residents of the subcontinent who either define themselves as Muslim or are so defined by others. These 300 million Muslims belong to myriad groups whose members speak different languages, live in separate spheres, and confront disparate social and economic circumstances. These groups differ from one another in almost every sense except in their identity as Muslims.

Moreover, South Asian Islamic culture is not limited to Muslims. Hindus attend festivals for Muslim saints and holy men, engage in poetic contests, and enjoy the music of a centuries-old Muslim culture. At the same time, Islam persists as a multivalent release valve, especially for marginal groups. It functions as a site of symbolic protest, an avenue of social mobility, and even an alternative religious identity; this was the case with the untouchables of South India, one group of whom converted to Islam en masse in recent decades (Abdul Malik Mujahid, *Conversion to Islam: Untouchables' Strategy for Protest in India,* Chambersburg, Pa., 1989).

Islam in South Asia is an experience for women as much as for men. Despite the absence of women's names from almost all accounts, one should not assume a bias against women. Rather, the deficit of female voices reflects the kind of narrative writing that prevailed in Asia, as in Europe, until the mid-twentieth century; the experience of South Asian Muslim women is no less dynamic for its concealment, and they have both thought and acted in distinctive ways worthy of sustained inquiry. The modern disciplines of sociology and anthropology have begun to discover the world of women, which is also the world of children, in South Asian Islam. (See, for instance, Patricia Jeffery, *Frogs in a Well,* London, 1979), and Hannah Papanek and Gail Minault, eds., *Separate Worlds: Studies of Purdah in South Asia,* Columbia, Mo., 1983.)

The more common approach to South Asian Islam is not to accent experience but to restate history—to fix and narrate dates, events, persons, and themes as if they alone provide access to the character of Islam in the subcontinent. To restrict the account to historical markings, however, is to ignore the human variety that does not admit of a single or even a composite historical narrative. Muslims of Kerala, Sri Lanka, or Kashmir each have their story. Unless it accounts for these peripheral branches, the single trunk narrative, however sensitively constructed and skillfully deployed, risks being reductive rather than representative. One must thus take account of several cultural-political core areas here in order to grasp the spectra of contemporary experience and historical formation that characterize South Asian Islam. The greatest danger, as Peter Mayer has pointed out, is "to project the specific conditions of North Indian, Urdu-speaking Muslims over the whole subcontinent" ("Tombs and Dark Houses," *Journal of Asian Studies* 40.3 [1981]: 486).

Kerala. Life in the South Indian coastal state of Kerala is above all reflected in the Mappila community, as the majority Muslim residents of Kerala are known. Their life is shaped by the cultural tradition of the South Arabian seacoast and is dependent on its trade. Arab traders had come to Kerala even before the advent of Islam. The indigenous language, Malayalam, is venerated in its own right, but in religious instruction it is combined with Arabic. There is a vast corpus of Arabic-Malayalam religious writings, narrative poetry, and songs, including song-stories that celebrate the lives of Ṣūfī saints such as Shaykh ʿAbd al-Qādir Jīlānī and Shaykh Aḥmad Rifāʿī, eponymous founders of important brotherhoods. These songs are sung mostly by men; other song-stories are memorized and sung by women, for example the romantic ballads and battle songs popular at annual feast celebrations.

Connection to an Arab past is also evident in the distinctive status accorded Mappilas of Arab descent who through marriage can trace their paternal line to the family of the prophet Muḥammad. In Kerala, however, patrilineal descent shares prestige with a matrilineal system common to the Nayar caste influential in the history of North Kerala. Under this system descent is traced through female relatives, with the eldest sister enjoying preeminence, and property is controlled through a joint rather than nuclear family system. Moreover, religious architecture does not follow the expected pattern of domes and minarets; instead, like Kerala Hindu temples, Mappila mosques are marked by peaked roofs. During the past decade, however, the influx of Gulf petrodollars has funded an explosion of new mosque-building on familiar Middle Eastern architectural lines.

R. E. Miller has suggested that Mappila Muslims are as closely connected to Arabian Islam as they are isolated from Indo-Persian Islam, and indeed that the Gulf connection "has affected the Mappilas more profoundly than any other Indian Muslims" ("Mappila," *Encyclopaedia of Islam,* new ed., 1960–, vol. 5, p. 459). However, the relationship remains partial and restrained by numerous factors, most of which are historically based. One is the allegiance of Mappilas to the Shāfiʿī school of law, which diverges somewhat from the Ḥanbalī *madhhab* of Saudi Arabia. Another is the prominence accorded *tangals*, a Malayalam term for saintly individuals—not only practicing spiritual directors but also those related to families of illustrious saints. Still another is lack of consensus about the norms and practices of Sunnī Islam. Almost all Mappilas are Sunnī Muslims, but they do not interpret orthodox Islam with one mind. Some are traditional religious specialists who prefer a strict *madrasah* education without the inclusion of modern subjects or professions; others strive to be both traditionalists and modernists; still others are committed, outspoken reformers. A very few are secularists, content to retain only the cultural markings of Kerala Islam and eschewing institutional Islam. All these subgroups are united by their common commitment to Islam as the decisive emblem of cultural pride, but they differ on programs for its assertion and maintenance.

Other historical factors haved shaped the Mappilas. Numbering almost 7.5 million by the early 1990s, they extend their influence across South India. While they enjoy a sympathetic and symbolic relationship to the Arabian Peninsula, they also relate to other parts of the subcontinent, especially to the adjacent areas of Tamil Nadu and Sri Lanka. Mappilas had prospered through trade during the centuries before 1498, but when the Portuguese explorer Vasco da Gama arrived in Calicut, the lucrative Arab trade was cut off, and new alliances were sought. They were disappointed by the Dutch, then by the British, and finally by the French. The latter seemed to offer some hope during the last part of the eighteenth century, when Muslim rulers from nearby Mysore state briefly controlled Kerala, but by 1792 the British had resumed their rule that was to persist until 1947.

The economic status of Mappilas has declined relative to the rest of the Kerala since the serial occupation by European colonial powers. Insofar as Muslims tended to be more urban than the population as a whole, they reacted sharply to the loss of administrative posts, commercial links, and educational options. Their grievances were expressed in numerous sporadic revolts throughout the period of British ascendancy, culminating in the Mappila Rebellion of 1921, a watershed in Kerala Muslim history. It focused on the formation of an independent state, Moplastan, in southern Kerala, and was also fueled by the attempt of Mappila leaders to make common cause with North Indian Muslims on behalf of the beleaguered Ottoman caliph. Their efforts proved fruitless: they antagonized not only the British but also Hindus of Kerala who had initially been sympathetic to their cause. Repeatedly repressed, the Kerala Muslim community by the mid-1920s had sunk to its nadir, after which it began to recover and to reassert itself.

Sri Lanka. The experience of Sri Lankan Muslims relates closely to that of their Kerala coreligionists. The majority community is usually designated by the name given by the detested Portuguese, "Moors"; the other smaller subcommunities of Muslims in Sri Lanka are also frequently glossed as Moors. The Moors, like the Mappilas, are Sunnī Muslims subscribing to the Shāfiʿī school of law; they, too, have been shaped by the location of their home straddling major trade routes in the Indian Ocean. A disproportionately urban population—40 percent are citydwellers in a country that is only 20 percent urbanized—they trace their ancestry through both migration and conversion on a patrilineal model going back to the seventh century CE and the time of the prophet Muḥammad. They are a small community, numbering perhaps 1.2 million of the total population of 15 million Sri Lankans. The majority of Sinhalas are Theravada Buddhists, with a minority of Tamil Hindus in one section of the island. It is with the Tamils that the Moors share their closest linguistic affinity, even though their political preferences are strongly Sinhala. Most Moors regard Tamil as their mother tongue, and the great song-poems they recite on popular and religious feast days are written in Arabic Tamil; the Arabic Tamil literary corpus of the Moors is regarded as a significant subset of the Arabic Tamil literature of South India.

The Moors thus share more with the Mappilas, despite linguistic and cultural differences, than either group does with the large North Indian Muslim community. Historical events make the separation of South Indian Muslims from their North Indian coreligionists even sharper. Like the Mappilas, the Moors were devastated by a Portuguese invasion in 1505. Portuguese control of Sri Lanka was even greater than their intervention in Kerala, for they succeeded in cutting off Sri Lankans from the mainland. The Moors ceased to have relations with Tamil Muslims, at the same time that the Portuguese curtailed and in time closed down the *madrasahs*. The succeeding Dutch colonialists pursued an explicitly commercial agenda, showing little interest in direct religious confrontation but not encouraging the restoration of institutions destroyed by the Portuguese. Their benign neglect of Islam was shared by their successors, the British.

For more than three centuries the Moors were forced to develop in isolation from other subcontinent Muslims; when they did experience a revival, it came not from Delhi or Mecca but via Kerala and Tamil Nadu, in the nineteenth century. It was brought by Ṣūfī orders that had been introduced into Kerala in the eighteenth century and then spread to Sri Lanka during the nineteenth. Chief among them was the Qādirīyah, but there were also notable adherents to other orders, such as the Shādhilīyah, the Chishtīyah and the Naqshbandīyah.

To commercial and social ties was added the common bond of Tamil Arabic. The first translator of the Qur'ān into Tamil Arabic was a nineteenth-century Sri Lankan scholar, Shaikh Muṣṭafā. Another Sri Lankan provided the first Tamil Arabic version of the famed Ḥanafī legal compendium, the *Hidāyah* of Marghīnānī (d. 1197). The late nineteenth century also saw the establishment there of the first traditional Arabic *madrasah* since 1505.

There are three features of special note about the nineteenth century. First, it saw the diffusion of Islamic learning and observance on a new scale, with the introduction of more frequent and rapid travel to other parts of the Muslim world, the spread of journalism and print media, and the advocacy of Pan-Islamic causes, such as support for the Ottoman caliph/sultan in Istanbul. Second, there was a revival of multiple expressions of Islamic piety; some were linked to renewed stress on original Arabic sources—Qur'ān, *ḥadīth* and *fiqh*—but others extended to speculative, popular forms of piety deriving from Sufism. The latter development flies in the face of standard interpretations of Islamic movements during the colonial period, which tend to stress either accommodation to Western influence, as in the case of Muḥammad ʿAbduh and Sayyid Aḥmad Khān, or antagonism against Western influence, as in the case of the Wahhābīs or neo-Wahhābīs. Both developments were thought to undercut Sufism in general and the major brotherhoods in particular; yet throughout South Asia, and not just in the cultural-political core area of Kerala–Tamil Nadu–Sri Lanka, one finds Ṣūfī orders and a Ṣūfī worldview integrally linked to the Islamic movements and prominent personalities of this period.

Finally, the revival of Islam was related to a dynamic expression of scriptural norms and a renewed interest in ritual activities among other religious communities in South Asia, including Theravada Buddhist activists in Sri Lanka, Shaiva reformers in Tamil Nadu, and Advaita modernists in Bengal. It was a crucial time for rethinking the categories of foreign rule, and Muslims shared with other religious communities, largely in urban centers, the concern to resist external pressures to conform. The Muslim heroes from Sri Lanka in this period, like their coreligionists, chose to restate their own norms and advocate their own values. Foremost among them were Siddi Lebbe, founder of the newspaper *Muslim nesan* and other educational institutions in Kandy; his successor, I. L. M. Abdul Azeez, who, in addition to journalistic and community activities, wrote the first comprehensive history of Sri Lankan Muslims (*Ethnology of the Moors of Ceylon,* 1907); and perhaps the most skillful minority politician in the subcontinent, A. R. A. Razik, who assured both Muslim support of the nationalist movement and the inclusion of Muslim officials in the governments that have ruled Sri Lanka since 1947.

North India. The experience of North Indian Muslims is charted above all by a set of cultural and linguistic shifts unknown in the South Indian core area. Islam was introduced there not by sea but by land, through Central Asia, and more by military conquest and forced migration than by trade and commerce. It embodies Turkish and Persian rather than Arabic ethnic/linguistic features. Lumping North India and South India as South Asian Islam is already a shorthand, simplifying and also distorting a complex historical process. The communities did not really meet until the late colonial and early modern period. Their delayed interaction is charged with significance; before addressing that interaction, we must first examine the northern historical prologue that is at variance with the pattern in Kerala and Sri Lanka.

Apart from early Arab conquests in the region of Sind, it was Turco-Afghan groups displaced by rival groups in Central Asia who became the vanguard of the emergence of Muslim polities in the subcontinent. The expansion of Turco-Afghan military might and political power was gradual rather than sudden. There was no single pitched battle but rather a series of small-scale skirmishes, not unlike those that took place simultaneously among regional Indian rulers. The Muslim advance occurred in several stages over long intervals. It was not until the mid-ninth century that the Ṣaffārids came to control most of present-day Afghanistan. More than a century later the Ghaznavids controlled much of the Indus River region; at the end of the twelfth century the Ghurids finally conquered Delhi and established a pattern of Muslim rule that continued through the Mughal period up to the fateful Battle of Plassey in 1757. There the British prevailed and, as a result, they extended military and then political control over most of India until 1947.

The Turco-Afghan ruling elites were Muslim but not Arab. They maintained and developed Persian as the preferred language, not only in the court and bureaucracy but also in the culture at large. Persian poetry marked off the elites from the non-elites, binding North Indian Muslims to other urban elites of the *ʿajam,* as the non-Arabic-speaking Muslim segment of Asia was known. The Delhi sultans organized themselves—whether in court life, army protocol, or administrative practices—along lines that dated back to the last pre-Muslim dynasty of Iran, the Sassanians. They also based their legitimacy as rulers on Persian notions of semidivine kingship: though not quite God's emissary, the sultan could reckon himself as God's shadow on earth and expect of his subjects a commensurate and abject obedience. Such a notion of divine authority was alien to Islam, but it did not compete openly with the notion of central authority that pertained elsewhere until the mid-thirteenth century. The Delhi sultans continued to acknowledge the caliph in Baghdad as the nominal leader of the *ummah* or Muslim community. They did not become, like the Umayyad caliphs of Andalusia, rival claimants to rule over the *ummah.*

Within South Asia the new rulers established powerful institutions that bore the impress of Islam. The capital city was to be adorned as the chief center of Muslim ritual observance. Because the sultan was expected to acknowledge the force of the *sharīʿah,* even though that law might conflict with other dynastic or local laws, he also had to endow institutions crucial to Muslim collective identity—mosques (of which one must be a central mosque or *jāmiʿ masjid*), *madrasah*s or religious schools, and hospitals. While the ruler could expend funds from the central treasury, private individuals preferred to create charitable trusts *(awqāf;* sg., *waqf)* in order to establish and perpetuate such institutions.

None of these developments, however, accounts for the rapid growth of the Muslim population in North India from the twelfth century through the twentieth. Even when the Delhi sultans were pious, observing scrupulously the spirit as well as the letter of Muslim ritual requirements, they were not committed to extend the Muslim population base or to deepen the Islamic character of the Muslims under their rule. The latter task was left to the *ʿulamāʾ*, but the former task was not deemed important. It is difficult to attribute to the ruling elite the rapid growth of Islam in North India, from less than half a million in 1200, to 15 million in 1600 and more than 60 million by 1900 (roughly calculated on the basis of K. S. Lal, *Growth of Muslim Population in Medieval India,* Delhi, 1973, the standard albeit flawed work on this subject). Even though some of the elite patronized the arts, especially poetry, and others endowed *madrasah*s, mosques, and other charities, none was explicitly concerned to expand the base of Muslim society. Why then did so many persons become Muslim?

It is first necessary to establish how many did become Muslims, and that is far from simple. During the Mughal period records of population by religion were not kept; that practice was introduced by the British, as an element of the decadal census figures beginning in the latter part of the nineteenth century. The total population of India was around 284 million in 1901, of whom more than 25 percent or approximately 63 million were Muslim (Lal, p. 156). By 1991 the total population for all of South Asia approached 950 million, while the number of Muslims in the three nation-states of India, Pakistan, and Bangladesh was not less than 275 million.

It is difficult to explain these figures without recourse to speculation, and of all the speculative explanations the one that seems the most plausible focuses on the activities of another subset of elites that worked parallel with the official apparatus of Turco-Afghan rule but not in tandem with it. These were the *ṭarīqah*s or Ṣūfī brotherhoods. They date back to the time of the earliest military conquests. Middle Eastern or Central Asian in origin, they were elites; nearly all their members had privileged birth, religious training, and geographic mobility that set them apart from most of their generation. Yet their ethos was elastic rather than elitist.

The impact of the *ṭarīqah*s is probably related to the fact that their great shaykhs followed a pattern of jurisdiction known as *vilayet.* Each *vilayet* demarcated a region or subregion of spiritual authority that then became the responsibility of a major shaykh or his successors to rule. The rule was to confer blessing or benefit on those who came to *khanqah*s, listened to shaykhs, sang at musical assemblies, and observed loyalty to the way. It also made these figures authorities parallel to ruling elites. If the kingdoms depended on arms for expansion, the Ṣūfīs depended on good will.

Domination and extraction were the hallmarks of the ruling groups, collaboration and inclusion the strategy of the brotherhoods. In terms of the expansion of a Muslim population base in North India, the latter seem the more likely candidates for success, though the actual process remains unclear.

What is clear is that by the end of Sultanate period and the beginning of the Mughal period in the sixteenth century, India had become a major node within the larger Muslim world. Muslim military expansion had provided the structure of dominance that continued through the Mughal period; Islamic India also provided a haven of retreat and opportunity for migrants from elsewhere in the Muslim world. From the medieval to the modern period the numbers of Muslims grew both by conversion and by immigration until they became a majority community in parts of northwestern and northeastern India, and a significant minority community in other parts of the subcontinent. The Mughal dynasty, by dominating North India, inspired a continuous cultural definition and renewal for the late medieval and early modern Muslim world. These transient heirs of Timur commanded the allegiance of the most populous, and arguably also the most powerful and wealthy, state within *dār al-Islām*.

Neither the power nor the prestige of Mughal India, however, could forestall its decline and eventual collapse. The last great Mughal was Awrangzīb. During his nearly fifty-year reign indigenous groups such as Sikhs in the Punjab, Jats in Central India, and Marathas in the Deccan challenged and often defeated Mughal military forces. His heirs suffered an even worse fate: in 1739 an Iranian-Afghan raider, Nādir Shāh, was able to plunder Delhi and take away the famed Peacock Throne.

There were, however, forces for reform that thrived even in the shadow of crisis, and the eighteenth century saw the ascent of such brilliant religious figures as Shāh Walī Allāh (d. 1763) and his successors Khvājah Mīr Dard and Mīrzā Maẓhar Jān-i Jānān. All of them lived and worked in the region of Delhi forging a legacy for future generations of North Indian Muslims.

Also surviving into the 18th century were remnants of Shīʿī polities that had flourished throughout South Asia in different periods, appearing as alternative regional kingdoms in the Deccan, Kashmir, Awadh, and Bijapur. Despite the pattern of Sunnī domination, in both the South Indian core area and most of the North Indian region one must note the distinctive characteristics of Shīʿī community life; for two recent approaches, see Juan R. I. Cole, *Roots of North Indian Shi'ism in Iran and Iraq: Religion and State in Awadh, 1722–1859* (Berkeley, 1988), and Vernon J. Schubel, *Religious Performance in Contemporary Islam: Shi'i Devotional Rituals in South Asia* (Columbia, S.C., 1993).

British Colonial Period. The most profound change for the Muslims of North India came not through the decline of the Mughals, the attrition of indigenous groups, or the persistence of Shīʿī polities, but rather through the advent of the British. From the fifteenth century onward, commercial expansionism emanating from northwestern Europe and claiming long-distance maritime routes gradually affected all of Africa and Asia. The rise of capitalist states in one part of the world transformed the entire network of international trade. Until the end of the eighteenth century this unprecedented expansion provided some space for urban Muslim traders and religious figures, who were able to use the routes of intensified international commerce to visit other parts of the Muslim world and to further support for Islam as the locus of religious and community identity. But by the nineteenth century a new international culture challenged the older Islamic framework. Overwhelming European domination of economic and political arteries reinforced the alleged superiority of a scientific, capitalist culture. The British who ruled India could not only claim control of public space, they could also allege that the basis of that control was a superior way of life.

This transformation of political authority and cultural outlook affected all religious communities, but it pitted Muslims against Hindus in a new relationship as minority versus majority. Muslims had always been a minority, but they had never been singled out or deprived of access for that reason. Hindus had always been a majority, but they had never assumed privilege or calculated a collective strategy on the basis of numerical strength. In the eyes of the British, Islam and Hinduism represented two distinct and bounded cultures. Although their mutual interaction and influence was at times acknowledged, it was more usual to perpetuate their differences as historically determined and irreversible. If objective knowledge could demonstrate that Hindus and Muslims were antagonistic, it was argued, then administrative control was needed to mediate that antagonism and ensure peace in the public domain. Census definitions of identity, beginning in the late nineteenth century, made religious categories binding. Recruitment into the Indian army and the application of personal and family law also presupposed and reinforced religiously based identity. To the extent that those defined as Muslims or Hindus (or Sikhs, Parsees and others) accepted these strictures and tried to operate within them, they began to compete publicly, both for regional opportunities and for influence within the emerging national movement. A new generation of religious reformers emerged; they all fought British control, but they also opposed other indigenous groups who similarly articulated a scriptural basis for Muslim or Hindu identity.

Such an appeal to scriptural authority had been previously unknown. During the Mughal period conflict was widespread, bitter, and destructive, but it was waged on a cluster of interests: religion intermingled with land, language, and race as expedient claims for struggle. Nineteenth-century British Christian missionaries singled out native religion as an object of contempt. For North Indian Muslims the twin bases of their religious identity were put at risk: the prophethood of Muḥammad and the sanctity of the Qur'ān. Christians ridiculed the former as pretension and the latter as a testament of forgeries. What resulted were polemical exchanges, but also multiple efforts by Muslim elites to reclaim Islam as an authentic banner of public loyalty. One school of thought suggested accommodation to European values along with the retention of the kernel of Islamic faith. "Travel lightly but travel as Muslims" became the slogan of Muslim modernists, best typified by the Aligarh reformer and educator Sir Sayyid Aḥmad Khān. Another response was to reject all association with Europe and to retreat into a textualist bunker, counterattacking both European and Hindu influences. This became the strategy of the Deoband *madrasah* and other *ʿulamā'*-directed reform movements in North India. Still another reaction was to crystallize Islam into a new millenarian creed articulated by a charismatic leader, as did the Aḥmadīyah under the direction of Ghulām Aḥmad of Qādiān in northwestern India. There was also a groundswell of localized Islam-based mass movements, such as that of Mawlānā Ilyās, a Ṣābirī Chishtī popularist, who founded the Pan-Indian and now international reform movement known as Jamāʿat-i Tablīgh. [*See* Aḥmadīyah; Tablīghī Jamāʿat.]

The most significant reaction, however, was that of the Khilāfat (or Caliphate) movement, which affected the entire subcontinent. It was felt by Muslim elites in North India and also by emerging elites in Kerala. It is impossible to discuss twentieth-century South Asian history without accenting the hope engendered by the Khilāfat movement. It countered the prevailing trend, favored by the British Raj, of politicizing Muslims into units of religiously based representation, sequestering them from Hindus as separate electorates while adjudicating their grievances under an independent legal system. Because the Ottoman sultan remained the titular leader of the world's Muslims through World War I, the turmoil that took place in Turkey during the 1920s had repercussions throughout South Asia. In the name of a global Muslim community, others who were discomforted by national politics took up with zeal the cause of the Ottoman caliph. For a brief moment the Khilāfat Committee and the noncooperation movement headed by Mohandas K. Gandhi cooperated, but the depth of suspicion was too great. When two of the leaders of the movement, Shaukat and Muḥammad ʿAlī, were tried on charges of sedition in 1921, it was Muslims from Kerala who protested most loudly. The Khilāfat trial fueled the Mappila Revolt in Kerala, turning Muslims against the British but also against Hindus. Efforts to retain Hindu-Muslim cooperation through the Congress Party failed. [*See* Khilāfat Movement.]

The Khilāfat movement also failed, at least in its avowed intent. The Ottoman Caliphate was abolished by Kemal Atatürk in 1928; the Mappila Revolt was put down with gruesome efficiency; and the National Muslim Party came into being as a direct response to the Nehru Report of 1928, which allotted Muslims only 26 percent of the seats in a future all-India independent parliament, instead of the 33 percent they sought.

Subsequent events reflected and at the same time intensified the deeprooted conflict over community representation. Consensus was never attainable, as Farzana Shaikh has made clear (*Community and Consensus in Islam,* Cambridge and New York, 1989), because the struggle over who represented the community ensured internal debate as well as external confrontation. Muslims were divided among themselves: opposed to British colonial rule, they were also fearful of Hindu dominance in a "secular" post-independence polity. In 1930 Muhammad Iqbal, the poet-philosopher, proposed the idea of a separate Muslim state within the Indian federation. Later the acronym Pakistan was coined, and despite arguments over what territory would become Pakistan, in 1947 the British withdrew from the subcontinent, leaving as their legacy two independent and hostile polities. Pakistan was divided not only from India but also within itself. It consisted of two wings, a western Urdu-speaking minority and an eastern Bengali-speaking majority. It was a mismatch destined to fail, and in 1971, with assistance from India, the former East Pakistan led the only successful secessionist movement since World War II, from which Bangladesh emerged as the third major nation-state in the subcontinent.

In the meantime, a truncated but still vital Muslim minority community continued to claim India as homeland and to participate, though not with one voice, in the events of its post-independence public life and cultural struggle. The grim events of the 1980s, including the shrill claims, counterclaims, and bloodshed over a Hindu-Muslim site of worship in North India, suggest that the seeds of religious conflict planted a century earlier under British rule continue to bear bitter fruit. Although it is possible for Muslims, Hindus, and Sikhs to plan for common goals, too often leaders using religious shibboleths will undermine and so preclude long-term commitment to an identity that places homeland over religion. Yet neither fascism nor fundamentalism is the most likely future ideology for the Republic of India. To secure Bharat as the domain of all divinities and devotees remains the hope of secular India; it is also the goal shared by silent majorities among Muslims, Hindus, and Sikhs.

[*See also* Afghanistan; Bangladesh; India; Kashmir; Mughal Empire; Pakistan; Popular Religion, *article on* Popular Religion in South Asia; *and* Sufism, *article on* Ṣūfī Orders.]

BIBLIOGRAPHY

At present there is a vast and numbingly circular literature on Islam in South Asia. It is characterized by sweeping narratives, mostly focused on dynastic histories into which economic, social, cultural, and religious history is spliced. It is also rigidly diachronic: the unspoken assumption is that all history must be teleological, that we begin at the beginning (with Muslim raids, conquests, and empire-building) and then move through the centuries toward some putative end. In the case of South Asian Islam, it is always a grim end, since the advent of the West and the bitterness of the colonial/postcolonial eras confirm the prejudgment that Islam is in political decline and, with few exceptions, reduced to a hopeless, private sphere of personal piety.

For a representative sample of this view, see Peter Hardy, "Islam in South Asia," together with its several bibliographic entries, originally published in *The Encyclopedia of Religion,* vol. 7, pp. 390–404 (New York, 1987), and reprinted in *The Religious Traditions of Asia,* edited by Joseph Kitagawa, pp. 143–164 (New York and London, 1989).

Several nonstandard sources have been given in the text above, and a comprehensive (though not exhaustive) bibliographical compilation of more than three thousand English-language entries is now available. See Mohammed Haroon, *Muslims of India: Their Literature on Education, History, Politics, Religion, Socio-Economic, and Communal Problems* (Delhi, 1991).

Additionally one must call attention to the antigovernmental, universalist view of Ṣūfī masters and their legacy, best set forth in Khaliq Ahmad Nizami's overview essay, "Hind. V. Islam," in *Encyclopaedia of Islam,* new ed., vol. 4, pp. 428–438 (Leiden, 1960–). This essay epitomizes the life work of the most productive scholar of South Asian Islam. Its multiple insights into the traditions that molded the community of North Indian Muslims may be usefully supplemented by consulting any of Nizami's more than forty books and countless articles, in both Urdu and English. See Mohammad Ahmad, comp., *The Literary Contribution of K. A. Nizami* (Delhi, n.d.). The publisher of this volume, Idarah-i Adabiyat-i Delhi, intends to bring out all of Professor Nizami's works in alternative English and Urdu volumes by the end of the 1990s.

Also of interest for a different approach to South Asian Islam are the several monographs in the New Cambridge History of India, a series edited by Gordon Johnson (Cambridge and New York, 1987–), relating Islam and Muslims to the larger political trends of the subcontinent during the past five hundred years. Divided into four topical segments—"The Mughals and Their Contemporaries," "Indian States and the Transition to Colonialism," "The Indian Empire and the Beginnings of Modern Society," and "The Evolution of Contemporary South Asia"—these thirty monographs will encourage a revisionist view of both Mughal and post-Mughal history.

Finally, the Oxford Centre of Islamic Studies has announced its intention to publish an atlas of Muslim social and intellectual history under the editorship of the Centre's director, Farhan Nizami. The first volume will be devoted to South Asia, integrating rural with urban patterns of development, while also accounting for the emergence of distinctive mystical orders and scholarly institutions that shaped all phases of South Asian Muslim society. Together with the relevant monographs in the New Cambridge History of India, the Oxford atlas will set a new standard for future research into the largest community of Muslims in the modern world.

BRUCE B. LAWRENCE

Islam in Southeast Asia and the Pacific

Islam is the religion of about 220 million people in Southeast Asia who live in a "Muslim archipelago" extending from southern Thailand, through Malaysia, Singapore, and Indonesia, and north to the southern Philippines. There are in addition isolated pockets of Muslims in Burma (Myanmar), northern and southern Thailand, and Cambodia; however, the major Islamic presence is in the "archipelago," and the language of Islam there is Malay or one of its variants. This last fact has two important consequences for the understanding of Islam in the region: the consequences of geography and indigenous settlement patterns, and the crucial importance of language.

The typical settlements of the archipelago from prehistory to the recent past have been riverine or on estuaries. Trade has always been important. Beginning in the late twelfth century, the Arab-controlled trade of the Mediterranean, Central Asia, and the Indian subcontinent reached the islands of the archipelago. The Arab traders represented both a source of wealth and a window on the glamorous civilizations of West Asia. The impact of Islamic philosophy and the accounts of the great Muslim kingdoms of West and Central Asia (and later India) offered the indigenous rulers both a justification and a model for rule. The processes of physical transmission and intellectual acceptance are of course complicated, but the important point is that Islam was successful in the archipelago, despite preexisting Hinduism and Buddhism, because it was initially accepted and later imposed by rulers (rajas, later sultans) on the populations. This process took considerable time, and indeed, one may argue, it is not yet over.

In regard to language, Malay or one of its variants has always been the language of Islam in the archipelago. Arab speakers and readers have always been present in some areas, and at some times in considerable numbers. Islam was, however, transmitted in Malay, the language of all classes. Islam thus came early to be associated with the state *(ke-rajaan)* and with the Malay language; this relationship has persisted into the present.

Early Literature. The literature of Islam in Malay from the sixteenth to nineteenth century comprises a chronicle of royalty, an explanation of the world, various dogmas of faith, simple guides for life, and a theory and justification of power and its forms and expressions. Malay forms include *sejarah* (chronicle), *hikayat* (history), and translations in the fields of theology, the history of Islam, the life of the Prophet and his Companions, and apocryphal tales of individuals and kings in the Arabic and Persian worlds. This has been a rich heritage for the intellectual culture of Southeast Asian Islam. Yet it was far more than mere heritage, received, held, and copied; it was not static, as some nineteenth-century European scholarship supposed. Instead, from the seventeenth century onward there was a positive flowering of Malay scholarship on Islam in all its forms.

On the more general side, there exist various genres that explain the nature of religion and introduce the reader to the necessary Arabic history and ritual. In this group are popular tales about the Prophets and other persons mentioned in the Qur'ān. There are a number of named texts (e.g., *Hikayat Anbiya, Hikayat Yusuf*), all taken from Arabic sources; together they may be said to form a historical hagiography given in popular terms, with contents that are by no means theologically sophisticated. A closely related class concentrates on the prophet Muḥammad himself, his life, the miracles attributed to him, and the deeds of his companions. Major texts include *Hikayat Nur Muhammad* and *Hikayat Nabi Bercukur*. These works are all without named authors; no scholastic doctrine is stated, although there is considerable emphasis on didactic elements.

On the scholastic side, there is a group of works in theology, dating from the seventeenth century, which represents a burst of indigenous creativity unequaled in later Southeast Asian Islamic thought. Doctrine is discussed within the threefold classification of knowledge *(al-kalām, al-fiqh, al-taṣawwuf)*. In addition, there were extensive translations and reworkings of established Arabic texts, ranging from commentaries on the Qur'ān and *ḥadīth* to works on Sufism and the varieties of rituals *(dhikr, duʿā', rawātib)*.

Four outstanding contributions to Islamic writing were produced in the seventeenth century in the Sultanate of Aceh, in both Malay and Arabic. The author Hamzah Fansuri was famous for his *shāʿir* (a genre of poetry) but most famous for his mystical writings. In his *Sharab al-ashikin* he discusses the four stages of the mystical path—the law, the path of renunciation, self-knowledge, and gnosis. His other famous work is the *Asrar al-arifin*, an exposition of the nature of God. Both works are still studied and remain highly influential in Southeast Asia today. An important commentary on Hamzah was written by the second of the great seventeenth-century authors, Shams al-Din. Only one of his works has survived complete, an orthodox *Mirat al-mumin*. His main interest was the doctrine of the unity of existence; he saw man as a mere appearance of the absoluteness of God. In his words, "Man is but a puppet in God's shadow play." As with Hamzah, self-knowledge is the first step toward perfect knowledge. The arguments of both scholars have been discussed in detail, but the striking feature is that intellectual Islam in the Malay world was, in its origins, speculative and mystic.

Naturally there was a reaction, and this is found in the work of al-Raniri, who was not just a translator from Arabic but also a great systematizer. His *Bustan al-salatin* is a compendium of Islamic knowledge for his time. He was also a polemist, and his attacks on unorthodoxy, especially Hamzah (which he compared with the nihilism of the Vedantas), are still read today. At the close of the seventeenth century there seems to have been a return to "practical" mystic practices in the writings of Abd al-Rauf, who published a translation of al-Baydawi on the Qur'ān as well as textbooks on *dhikr* and *rawatib*.

The archipelago seems to have a fondness for the mystical and speculative side of Islam, with a desire to find the outer permissible limits of doctrine. Given the very strong pre-Islamic cultures of the area, this is perhaps not surprising. The adoption or adaptation of such a universal theology, with its political implications, always involves tensions, and often inconsistency. Thus, in the late nineteenth century in Patani (now in southern Thailand), Shaykh Daud Patani worked as a brilliant translator from Arabic but was essentially a medieval man; in contrast was Shaykh Mohammed Zain, somewhat younger, whose *fatwās* disclose a determined effort to adapt—and if necessary to change—the world of Islam in his place and time. Neither can be classed simply as "orthodox" or "heretical"; they are both entirely within the Islamic tradition of Southeast Asia, in which intellectualism and royal power were clearly differentiated from social reality. [*See also* Malay and Indonesian Literature.]

Ethnography. The Muslim world of Southeast Asia is complex in its languages and cultures. Further, the translation of the Qur'ānic injunction into daily life has been a complex and often inconsistent process, and it remains so today. There has been no single explanation of what constitutes acceptable Islamic practice for all of Southeast Asia. Instead, there are many culturally devised variations within the Islamic spectrum. Three structural features appear especially important.

First, there is a reasonable diversity of actual religious practices. These range from highly orthodox practices with emphasis on scripture and scholarship to various forms of "modernism" in which dogma is reinterpreted to cope with contemporary conditions. Notable in the latter respect is the fact that the nation-states of the area are avowedly secular. Secularism as such has become identified as the main problem for Islam. Paradoxically, this has resulted in a greater degree of tolerance for diversity of religious practice rather than the opposite. Pressure for conformity, in fact, seems to come from the state or from government-sponsored religious publications. The growing number and variety of millennial movements, especially since the 1960s, is part of this rich diversity.

Second, Islam is, like Judaism and Christianity, a religion of revelation. Its meaning is thus to be sought by each person in reading the holy words of God. Alternatively, understanding can be sought in recognized texts of interpretation and in commentaries. The essential scholarship of Islam is in Arabic and was for the most part written before the close of the twelfth century. This is part of the Muslim heritage in Southeast Asia; it describes Islam, and it is how one "knows" Islam. At the same time, the facts of life in the region are by no means easily assimilable in such terms. For example, local marriage practices, systems of land tenure, contracts of sale and purchase, adoptions and family relationships, punishment for crimes, and explanations of social and political ideas all operate under quite different principles from the ideals and revealed prescriptions of Islam. From the purist's point of view, the difference is often seen in terms of a conflict between *adat* and Islam.

Adat (Ar., *ʿādāt*) means "custom" and usages in the widest senses, as well as in legal prescription; there is no doubt that serious differences, practical as well as intellectual, did and still do exist between it and Islamic law. It is common, however, to find a wide degree of relativity for each term. A tendency toward compromise, syncretism, and local sophistry was the norm rather than the exception. As with religious practices themselves, the ethnography of Islam shows that formal doctrine is but one element in the social manifestation of theology. This is unsurprising, since the same situation can be found in any Muslim society.

A third important referent is the fact that the terms "Islam" and "Muslim" have always been used as an idiom for conceptualizing an identity and so legitimizing a status. What is a "Muslim," and what does it mean to be one? In the European colonial period, especially in the late nineteenth century, these were important questions. For example, a whole range of rights, duties, and privileges depended upon holding Muslim status; these same rights were devised to "heretical Muhammadans." The legal system of the Netherlands East Indies was even posited on the view that it was local custom (*adat*, not *sharīʿah*) that should form the basis of laws for the indigenous peoples. [*See* Adat.]

Finally, it is to be noted that in the postindependence period, Islam has become institutionalized in governmental ministries and offices of religious affairs. There is in effect a developing sociology of Islamic institutions, especially in Malaysia, Singapore, Borneo, and Indonesia.

Islam and the State. The Islamic response to the realities of dominion in Southeast Asia is complex because state histories are complex. Even the definition of "state" itself is debatable, and it has certainly changed over time.

The premodern state. The sultanates of the Malayan peninsula, Sumatra, Java, and the southern Philippines and Borneo cannot really be described as "Islamic" states. Thus, for example, while *sharīʿah* was important in written texts, it did not solely determine either administration or personal law or finance; rather, it was a part of a system in which pre-Islamic practices continued. The respective balances between *sharīʿah* and other elements of course varied from place to place. Comparing the *Sejarah Melayu* with the roughly contemporaneous *Adat Aceh* illuminates the varying emphases on religion and its place in the indigenous state systems.

There is, however, no question of the legacy of rule and theories of government bequeathed to Southeast Asia by the medieval Islamic tradition. The ruler (sultan) is himself *khalīfah* (caliph) or *al-insān al-kāmil.* He draws an important justification for his position from these attributes and, in turn, is a focus of power for the officers of religion in his state. He might trace his genealogy back to Rum (Constantinople) through Persia, or back to Adam through Sulayman—an almost physical transferance of power from the heartlands of Islam to its outer dominions. The legacy is not just the code of *sharīʿah* and commentary, but also ideas of rule and sovereignty and of perfection in the ruler.

There were of course reactions against this, most notably from the various Muslim reform movements, such as Wahhābīyah; however, the reaction was itself expressed in terms of Islamic philosophy. The important point is that in the period up to establishment of firm European control, there was a Muslim theory of state in the archipelago, as well as a vibrant, sometimes violent argument about the theological and practical nature of this state.

The European colonial state, 1800–1940. In this period of a century and a half, the Muslim policies of the Malayan peninsula and of Sumatra and Java became subordinated to the British and the Dutch, respectively. Their subordination was military and economic but—more important in the long term—intellectual as well. Formerly at least the ethos of the sultanates, and in most cases much more than that, Islam became much reduced in status.

The state came to be defined in European terms. While the precise nature of the constitutional and political theories differed, there was no doubt that the Muslim archipelago was dependent territory and that ultimate sovereignty lay in Europe. Within this scheme, whether British, French or Dutch, there was simply no room for Islam as the basis of a theory of state. There was of course resistance, sometimes armed, but essentially religion had to give way to European secular formalism. The consequences of this persist; by the mid-nineteenth century Islam had become irrelevant to the definition of the state.

There was a second fundamental redefinition in the colonial period. The formal status of Islam declined to that of a mere religion, and only one among others. Regulation made Islam a private, personal religion and a personal law (not even the latter in the Netherlands East Indies). The state was secular, and religion was totally divorced from it. The only exception was in British Malaya, where the sultans were theoretically heads of religion in their states, but this concession was so heavily regulated as to render it nugatory.

Islam was in fact reduced from an essential of the state, its basic foundation, to mere individual belief. As though this were not enough, the religion itself became subject to government fiat at a very basic level. The respective colonial bureaucracies so regulated many of the fundamental institutions of Islam that even today it is impossible, or very difficult, to see Islam except in the terms imposed then. For example, "Islamic law" is not the *sharīʿah;* it is certain selected principles expressed in European form and administered in European-style courts. Similarly, licensing restraints (which still exist) were placed on *zakāt,* the building of mosques, the publication of literature, and the teaching of Islam. In short, the religion had become just one of the matters that clerks in ministries were charged to regulate.

Modern states. The reference to "modern states" is primarily to Malaysia and Indonesia, the heartlands of Southeast Asian Islam. The relatively small Muslim population of Myanmar (Burma) comprises two groups. The first includes the descendants of Indian immigrants (1880–1940), most of whom either left during World War II or in the 1960s; some, mostly from the economically depressed classes, remained. This class also includes the "Zerbadi," the offspring of Indian Muslim males and Burmese females. There are no data on the numbers or situation of these people, but they have been consistent targets of Burmese racial chauvinism, so it is possible that they no longer survive as a discrete group. Second, the Rohingha of the Arakan are Muslim in religion but Arakanese in all else. They have been and are now subject to considerable aggression on the part of the Burmese army.

In Malaysia and Indonesia, two factors have determined the position of Islam in the postwar period. First, the newly independent states are modeled on the European secular tradition. They have constitutions, bureaucracies, national economic and social policies, and, to varying degrees, political pluralism. Political ideology ranges from variants of parliamentary democracy to versions of presidential and corporate rule. Essentially, however, the state is defined in terms of rational secularism.

Second, and contrasted with this, in the new states Islam for the first time gained a legitimate political voice. It was no longer a proscribed vehicle of protest and anticolonial agitation. Islam and Islamic activists in both the Netherlands East Indies and in British Malaya, especially in the former, had a long and proud history of resistance to the European *imperium*. But with the legitimization of at least some political pluralism with independence, the focus has changed: Islamic parties have entered the new political process as contributors rather than as resisters. This has not happened in Thailand or the Philippines, where Muslim minorities still resist the central governments, occasionally violently, in the name of Islam.

In Malaysia and Singapore, however, the Islamic political parties very quickly found themselves in a rather serious dilemma. How could the democratic political process within a secular state and their participation in it be reconciled with classical theories of *ummah* and the functions of *imām*, *qāḍī* and *ʿulamāʾ*? Theoretically the dilemma is irreconcilable, because an Islamic government, once established, has no mechanism by which it can be replaced. A further complication in both states has been that Islam was very heavily organized in the prewar period, and such important functions as the teaching of religion, the collection of *zakāt* and *fitrah* (charity/tax), the *ḥajj*, and judicial administration had become fully controlled by the state bureaucracy. This process continued after independence with the establishment of ministries of religion and departments of religious affairs. The public existence of Islam, whether in politics or in other sectors, had become accommodated within the institutions of the nation-state. This again is the dilemma of contemporary Islam: its participation in the politics and institutions of the secular state is combined with varying degrees of nonacceptance of the principles on which such states are based.

The history of Islamic politics in Southeast Asia is the history of "varying degrees of nonacceptance." As already mentioned, the Muslims of southern Thailand have in the past resorted to violence (the Patani Liberation Front), as have the Moro of the southern Philippines (the Moro National Liberation Front); resistance in both areas continues. [*See* Patani United Liberation Organization; Moro National Liberation Front.]

In Indonesia (90 percent Muslim) the history of Islamic political parties has been complex and characterized by the formation of large overarching groups, followed by their splitting into various specific interest and ideological groups. The interesting point about these regroupings and the shifting alliances that went with them is that they were not based on differences of doctrine. One cannot explain the sometimes bewildering political changes in such terms as "traditionalism" or "modernism." Instead, differences arose over competition for the political posts available to Muslim representatives in alliance with secular parties. The detailed history is unedifying, probably because the Muslim parties have never held power or even the balance of power; yet the experience has not been without profit for Muslims. The Islamic perspective is politically important and has been recognized in the fields of family law and in parts of the education system, but no further. To some extent, Islam still remains an ideology of resistance in Indonesia, albeit in a more sophisticated form than before World War II. More recently, under the New Order government, Islamic political movements have been subsumed under a general "United Political Party" that emphasizes Pancasila as the national ideology.

In Malaysia, about half the population is Muslim, and Islam is recognized in the constitution as the official religion of the country. The rulers (sultans) of the various states in Malaysia are guardians of Islam in their own states. Each state has a Department of Religious Affairs, and there is also a National Council for Religious Affairs. Muslim political representation is divided into two unequal parts. On one hand is UMNO (United Malay National Organization), an ethnic Malay secular and nationalist party that has been dominant since independence. It accommodates Islam to a reasonable degree, but not to the extent of allowing religion to determine policy in any sphere. On the other hand, there has been a succession of "Islamic" parties concentrated almost entirely in the east coast and in the northwest, the rural heartlands of Islam. The latest party is the PAS (Partai Islam Se-Malaysia), whose program is avowedly Islamic, but at a fairly primitive level—women should not be allowed to work at night, and thieves should have their hands cut off. Although the Islamic parties have controlled states in the Malaysian Federation, they, like the Indonesian parties, have never come close to forming a national government. [*See* United Malay National Organization; Partai Islam Se-Malaysia.]

In summary, the history of Islam in Southeast Asia falls into three parts. Initially (fifteenth to eighteenth century) it was an ideology of rule in the Malay-speaking lands and the inspiration for an extensive and complex literature. Second, in the period of high colonialism it became subordinated to European forms of government, heavily bureaucratized, and politically suppressed. In literature, there was little except repetition until the inspiration of the West Asian reform movement reached Southeast Asia in the late nineteenth century. Even here, however, most of the Islamic revival was derivative of West Asian models. Finally, with independence came real political accommodation between Islam and the state in the areas of Muslim majority, Malaysia and Indonesia. Islam as a truly alternative way of life is not seriously espoused by any political party; that remains the aim only of various fringe groups ("fundamentalists"). There is currently little in the way of original literary work; instead there is a vast array of rather naive short books and pamphlets of an almost entirely admonitory and didactic nature.

On the other hand, and on a more positive note, both Malaysia and Indonesia have established "Islamic Banks." These operate on a variety of Muslim contracts which eschew interest *(ribā);* instead profits stem from various sharing and commission arrangements. The central banks of Malaysia and Indonesia exercise supervisory control. [*See* Banks and Banking.]

Islam in the Pacific. Islam is not a historical religion in the Pacific basin. Its presence in this region is the result of postwar immigration. The majority of immigrants are from Turkey, the Levant, Egypt, and to a lesser extent the Muslim Balkans. There is also a small representation from the Indian subcontinent and Indonesia.

The main areas of Muslim population are in Australia and New Zealand but there are increasing numbers in Japan, Korea, the Solomon Islands, Vanuatu, Western Samoa, and Papua New Guinea. In these last six states Muslim missionary work has been carried out with some vigor since the 1970s. A small but steady stream of local converts is now appearing. In the more developed states such as Japan and Korea they are supported with quite elaborate administrative structures including various sorts of councils and advisory bodies. There is even an "Islamic Company" in Japan.

The main centers, however, remain Australia and New Zealand. Until fairly recently Islam has had a low profile in both countries but international politics and missionary activity have greatly raised its public profile. In addition, internal disputes within the Muslim communities are now often reported in news media. Community organizations are often invited by governments (especially in Australia and New Zealand) to offer the Muslim position on such subjects as women, the family, and the custody of children.

There have been occasional difficulties with the host communities (for example, objections over locating mosques in suburban areas) but they are all of a relatively minor nature. There are also signs that conversion is proceeding among the native populations. There is little in the way of any serious political problem facing Islam or the Muslims.

[*See also* Australia and New Zealand; Brunei; Cambodia; Indonesia; Malaysia; Myanmar; Philippines; Singapore; Thailand; *and* Regional Islamic Daʿwah Council of Southeast Asia and the Pacific.]

BIBLIOGRAPHY

Benda, Harry J. *The Crescent and the Rising Sun.* The Hague, 1958. Islam and the Japanese occupation in Indonesia, 1942–1945.

Boland, B. J. *The Struggle of Islam in Modern Indonesia.* The Hague, 1971.

Boland, B. J., and I. Farjon. *Islam in Indonesia: A Bibliographical Survey, 1600–1942.* Dordrecht, 1983.

Gowing, Peter G., and Robert D. McAmis, eds. *The Muslim Filipinos.* Manila, 1974.

Hooker, M. B., ed. *Islam in Southeast Asia.* Leiden, 1983. Contains papers on history, sociology, philosophy, literature, law, and politics, plus an extensive bibliography.

Hooker, M. B. *Islamic Law in South-East Asia.* Kuala Lumpur, 1984. Contains chapters on Islamic legal history, Burma, Singapore, Malaysia, Brunei, the Philippines, and Indonesia. The only general survey for the area, but now somewhat dated.

Hooker, M. B., ed. *The Laws of South-East Asia.* 2 vols. Singapore, 1986–1988. Volume 1 contains an article on Muslim texts (pp. 347–434) and an extensive bibliography (pp. 539–554).

Majul, Cesar Adib. *Muslims in the Philippines.* Quezon City, 1973.

Al-nahdah (Journal of the Regional Islamic Daʿwah Council of Southeast Asia and the Pacific). A quarterly with useful information on contemporary Islamic affairs in the area.

Ner, Marcel. "Les Musulmans de l'Indochine française." *Bulletin de l'École Française d'Extrême Orient* 41 (1941): 151–200. The only general account, focused mainly on the Cham of Cambodia.

Taufik Abdullah and Sharon Siddique, eds. *Islam and Society in Southeast Asia*. Singapore, 1986. Valuable collection of papers on all aspects of Islam in the region.

Yegar, Moshe. *The Muslims of Burma*. Wiesbaden, 1972. Good account of the history of the mainly immigrant Indian Muslim community in Burma.

M. B. Hooker

Islam in Europe

The historical antagonism between the western and eastern parts of Europe is reflected, to this very day, in their diverging social, political, and religious traditions. This division has also put its mark on the historical vicissitudes of Islam in the European world. Growth and blossoming in one part of Europe were often concomitant to downfall and destruction in the other. During the late Middle Ages, Western Christian powers were reconquering the last Muslim territories in Spain and the Mediterranean. During the sixteenth and the early seventeenth centuries, they extirpated the last vestiges of Islam from the West. Meanwhile, the Turks were preparing for the conquest of Constantinople (1453) and for expansion into areas of southeastern Europe, the modern Balkan states. However, when the dismantling of the Ottoman Empire, the dominance of communist rule, and the contemporary revival of nationalism caused the suppression of southeast European Islam and destroyed much of its ancient heritage and infrastructure, western Europe opened its doors to a stream of Muslim migrants and refugees. Significant Muslim communities are now present in all countries of western Europe.

Phases and Groups in the History of European Islam. The premodern history of Islam in western Europe consists of two parts. First, from the eighth century until the end of the fifteenth century there were territories under Muslim rule, where Islam acquired a majority position. Apart from Muslim Spain, this was the case during various periods in some islands in the Mediterranean and small enclaves in southern France and southern Italy. Second, there is the history of Islam as a minority religion in western Europe starting around the ninth century, when Christian rulers, especially in the Iberian Peninsula, decided to abandon their practice of executing Muslim captives and started selling and using them as slaves. From the end of the eleventh century the social phenomenon of Muslim slaves in Christian territories increased in importance, especially in the Iberian Peninsula, Italy, southern France, Sicily, and the Balearic islands. Theirs was a history of rapid christianization and assimilation under the combined pressure of society and church.

For some Christian kingdoms of the Iberian Peninsula, the period from the twelfth to the sixteenth century formed an exception to this pattern. When large territories of Muslim Spain were reconquered by Christian kings, religious freedom and protection were granted to local Muslim communities, notwithstanding the ongoing protests by the Catholic church. But after the fall of Granada (1492), these communities were baptized by force, and finally, at the beginning of the seventeenth century, with the stigma of being labeled "incurable heretics," they were expelled, mainly to North Africa. However, this did not end the social phenomenon of Muslim slaves. Their presence in European countries around the Mediterranean is documented, without interruption, until the nineteenth century. Only the period of the Enlightenment, followed by the French Revolution, the proclamation of religious freedom as a universal human right and the abolishment of slavery, created the essential conditions for the modern era in western European Islam.

In the late twentieth century, there are about 18 million Muslims in Europe, with approximately 9 million each in western and southeastern Europe. In addition, small communities of a few thousand Muslims live in Poland and Finland. The Muslims of Poland are the descendants of Tatar and Crimean immigrants who arrived respectively in the fourteenth and fifteenth and the seventeenth and eighteenth centuries. The Muslim community in Finland consists of people of Turko-Tatar origin from the Idel Ural and Volga regions who mainly arrived after the Communist Revolution of 1917.

Large numbers of Muslims of European origin are mainly found among the populations of the Balkan states. They are the descendants of various groups who converted to Islam during Ottoman rule, as well as Muslim groups of non-European origin, especially Turks. In view of their longstanding history, many of these groups consist of all social levels, including religious, intellectual, artistic, and commercial elites. In western Europe, however, Islam shows much less social diversity. In essence, it is still the religion of migrants, with a high percentage of unskilled laborers, small merchants, and white-collar people of the lower strata. It lacks a sufficiently trained religious and intellectual leadership. Another important factor determining their sociojuridical position is the fact that numbers of them have not yet obtained the nationality of the western European state in which they live. It seems likely that the process of naturalization will take a few more decades to be fully completed.

Autochthonous converts to Islam can be found in all western European countries, but their number is very limited indeed. Prominent among them are women married to Muslims, who actually play a pioneering role in the foundation of organizations of Muslim women, attracting members from all Muslim ethnic groups. Male converts are much fewer in number, yet play an important role in processes of negotiation and intercultural communication between Muslim groups, on the one hand, and western European governments and societies, on the other. Some of them enjoy fame as scholars and writers, both in the West and the Muslim world. Examples are the Austrian journalist Leopold Weiss (Muhammad Asad), who converted before World War II, and the French philosopher Roger Garaudy. The only region in Europe with numbers of male converts of some significance is Andalusia in Spain, where, under the influence of a specific form of regionalism, conversion to Islam could be experienced as the rediscovery of an identity that had been suppressed during many ages. (Some African-Americans in the United States similarly claim that their return to Islam is a reversion to their earlier religion.)

Muslim migrants in western Europe can be divided into three distinct categories. The first of these consists of inhabitants who came from former colonies. Among them one finds groups who cooperated closely with the European colonial armies and preferred to leave their countries at the time of decolonization. Examples are the former Algerian and Moluccan soldiers and their families in France and the Netherlands. Others in this category are people who had settled as migrants in former colonies, where they had created their own communities as ethnic minorities. Their settling in Europe was the result of a second migration, mainly for socioeconomic and political reasons. Among them are many skilled laborers, merchants, and white-collar people. Examples are the Hindustanis from East Africa and Suriname in the United Kingdom and the Netherlands.

The second category of Muslim migrants consists mainly of unskilled laborers and their families. They have come from countries around the Mediterranean, from the Indo-Pakistani subcontinent, as well as from other Muslim countries in the Near and Far East. In France and the United Kingdom, this migration process had an early start, before World War II, but in other countries it was mainly confined to the period between the late 1960s and 1970s. Especially from the late 1970s onward, the process of family reunion—the basis for the institutionalization of a religious infrastructure—had begun.

In some countries groups of a specific ethnic or geographic origin form the majority among the Muslim inhabitants. This is the case for migrants from the Maghrib and West Africa in France, Spain, Italy, and Belgium; for Turks in Germany and the Netherlands; and for Muslims from the Indo-Pakistani subcontinent in the United Kingdom. In comparison with the societies in which they live, upward social mobility among the second and third generations of these groups has remained very limited. Percentages of unemployment among them are significantly higher than among the autochthonous groups.

The current stream of Muslim migrants consists of political refugees from various Muslim countries. There is an important percentage among them that has gone through various forms of (nonreligious) higher education, including universities. Many of these have a secular outlook, and they have, so far, not provided the existing Muslim communities with a specifically religious leadership. They do play important roles, however, in cultural and sociopolitical activities of a more general nature. Depending on the existing government policies, concentrations of refugees from specific countries can be found in certain states. Important Iranian communities, for instance, are found in Italy and Sweden.

Religious Infrastructure. Contrary to the established religious infrastructure of the Muslims in Southeastern Europe, the contemporary history of Islam in Western Europe shows many examples of local communities moving from the initial stage of meeting in a prayer hall toward the more advanced stage of establishing a mosque and appointing an imam. In the early days, loose groups of worshipers often rented accommodations on a temporary basis. Later, more permanent solutions were found. In the initial stage, non-Muslims nationals, especially church members, played a prominent role in the initiatives of religious institutionalization. In the second stage, initiatives were mainly taken by informal leaders of the communities concerned. Finally, one observes the establishment of mosques by groups affiliated with an Islamic organization at a national or international level.

Generally speaking, mosques have been founded in western Europe on a monoethnic and a monodenominational basis. With rare exceptions, multiethnic and multidenominational places of worship are to be found in smaller towns or villages with no more than one mosque or prayer hall. In towns with two mosques or prayer halls one usually finds a division of the Muslims along ethnic lines. In larger communities a further division according to confessional denominations within a single ethnic group becomes a possibility. This can generally be observed in towns with three or more mosques.

Parallel to the preceding developments runs an increase in the functional aspects of these local religious institutions. At the very beginning, the function of this form of institutionalization of Islam was to take care of the need for religious services. Quite logically, the foundation of these places of worship, where scattered Muslims would join in prayer, implied the creation of social spaces and networks on the basis of a common religious identity. To these religious and social functions the task to cater for elementary religious education of the communities' children was added, especially within the context of official family reunion schedules. In many cases the initial religious instruction provided by the communities was given by qualified volunteers. However, the best way to provide for these needs was to appoint an imam who, apart from his tasks during the daily religious services, could function as a teacher to the children as well. The mosques have become the most important centers of Islamic education in western Europe, where an estimated 15 percent of all children with a Muslim background regularly receive religious instruction. A similar role was played by the mosques in southeastern Europe (with the exception of Greece), where during the communist period no room was left for state-recognized elementary Islamic schools.

The increase in community life stimulated by the mosques enhanced their central role. In the countries of origin many culturally defined institutions used to exist separately from the mosques. These institutions, however, did not exist in the host countries. Endowing the mosques in western Europe with some of the functions of this absent infrastructure was a constructive solution, because in doing so one was granting further material support to the maintenance of the mosques, and therefore of Muslim community life itself. This resulted in all kinds of activities in the fields of education, sports, and recreation, among others, and providing an alternative for youngsters to behavioral patterns rejected by Islam.

As a result, mosque buildings in western Europe were to be used for various kinds of religiously colored feasts and ceremonies not usually celebrated in or around mosque buildings in the Muslim world itself, such as wedding parties, circumcisions, and mourning ceremonies. In addition to this, attached to many mosques there are shops owned by the Muslim organization that sell religious objects (including books) and products from the countries of origin and that add to the social and financial basis of the community life centered around the mosque.

Most mosques are presided over by a board of governors. The members of the board usually take care of the financial interests of the mosque and its maintenance. Unless special arrangements have been made with the government of the country of origin, the imam of the mosque is appointed by the board. The board's tasks are both external and internal. Those of the imam, however, are mainly internal, and they are specifically connected to the knowledge and application of the values of Islamic religion. Members of the board should be able to manage the mosque and to communicate and negotiate with the surrounding non-Muslim society. For these purposes fluency in the host country language and knowledge and understanding of its laws and social customs are required.

The imams, on the other hand, can hardly be expected to have the just-mentioned communicative bicultural abilities. Many of them—in the absence of a sufficient number of men in western Europe who are qualified for the post—have been recruited comparatively recently in the countries of origin. Also, the mainly internal and traditional coloring of their most important tasks runs counter to such characteristics. Entrusted with the daily prayer services in the mosque, the religious counseling of the individual members of their community, the elementary religious education of the community's children, as well as with the performing of ceremonial tasks at various important occasions in the lives of individuals and families, the imams can be said to be the main custodians of the cultural, and especially the religious, values of the countries of origin.

In the absence of the social infrastructure of the countries of origin (family, acquaintances, etc.), the function of the imam of a mosque community has increased considerably in western Europe. The pastoral tasks of spiritual counseling and social care, including the visiting of community members in hospitals and prisons, are cases in point. There are many essential similarities between the tasks of an imam in western Europe and his Christian or Jewish colleagues, the pastor and the rabbi. As a logical outcome, governments and courts also tend to identify the imams as Muslim clerics to be dealt with in the same way as the Christian and Jewish clergy. Countries where Islam has been officially recognized by the state, such as Belgium and Spain, have legalized this view explicitly. In other countries, the same viewpoint is expressed implicitly, in jurisprudence and government policies. In the Netherlands, the juridical equalization of pastors, rabbis, imams, Hindu priests, and humanistic spiritual counselors was settled by an official verdict of the Supreme Court.

In all countries of western Europe Muslim communities become increasingly aware of the need to create their own educational centers for the training of imams. This process is stimulated by public discussions and government policies attaching much value to the founding of such provisions within western Europe itself. Apart from the strictly theological requirements, new educational challenges are posed by the unprecedented posts for imams which are being created in western European armies, hospitals, and prisons—on a par with the state-appointed ministers, pastors, and rabbis already working in those institutions. Obviously, this new category of imams indeed would need forms of additional training enabling them to cope with a whole series of nontraditional tasks. The creation of Islamic theological seminaries no doubt would form a step of great historical momentum in the history of western European Islam. However, several obstacles stand in the way of their realization. Most prominent among these is the heterogeneity and division of the Islamic organizations that hampers the successful coordination of various small-scale initiatives that already exist in various countries. The religious infrastructure of Islam in southeastern Europe for example, is already in place; in Bosnia-Herzegovina, imams and religious scholars can be trained in several *madrasah*s and in a theological faculty in Sarajevo.

At national and international levels, a great variety of Islamic organizations are in competition with each other to obtain influence over the local mosque-communities. Among the first attempts, during the 1970s, to create umbrella structures for local mosques were organizations representing confessional streams that are in opposition to the official doctrines of Islam promoted by governments in their countries of origin. These initiatives were counteracted by the activities of the non-European governments concerned, who started to build up their own networks of mosque-communities among their citizens in western European countries. A clear example of this pattern is found among Turkish Islamic organizations.

As a reaction to the mushrooming of independent and oppositional religious movements, such as the Süleymanlıs, Millî Görüş, and Nursis, the Presidium of Religious Affairs of the Turkish government (usually referred to as the Diyanet) developed a policy to stimulate the foundation of a religious infrastructure for the Turkish Muslims in western Europe under its direct supervision. This policy was to include the foundation of mosques and the appointment of imams and religious teachers trained in one of the official Turkish colleges or faculties. These imams, who have the status of civil servants of the Turkish government, are working in western Europe on a temporary basis. The policy included also the appointment of religious attachés with the status of *muftī*s to the Turkish embassies concerned. Mosque-communities attached to the organizations of the Diyanet have to comply with the transfer of the management of their mosque buildings to specially created foundations in each country, which are subjected to the direct supervision of the presidium itself.

Similar organizational divisions, the result of the transplanted competition between oppositional religio-political groups on the one hand, and the governments in their countries of origin on the other, can also be observed among Muslims of other origins, such as those from Morocco. Other governments, such as that of Tunisia, tend to abstain from a policy of direct interference in the religious life of their (former) subjects in western Europe. In fact, western Europe has become a haven for the free organization of Islamic oppositional movements. The writings of the Moroccan oppositional leader ʿAbd al-Salām Yāsīn, for example, forbidden in Morocco itself, are circulating among all Moroccan communities in western Europe.

In addition, international organizations, such as the Muslim World League, backed up by governments of Muslim states, have succeeded in establishing Islamic Centers in various western European capitals, including Brussels, Madrid, and Rome. These centers aim at controlling Islamic religious life in the respective western European states, and they are usually governed by diplomatic representatives of Muslim countries, under the predominant influence of Saudi Arabia. They add to the complexities of rivalry and conflict that continue to characterize the relations between the Islamic umbrella organizations at national levels.

Religion and State. In the present time, all European states claim to be democratic and to respect the fundamental principle of religious freedom, notwithstanding all the differences in the relations between religion and state, enshrined in their respective constitutions and applied in their actual policies. This principle applies to all citizens and inhabitants, including Muslims, both individually and in the form of their religious organizations. The constitutional principle of religious freedom is surrounded by various kinds of legal limits that are molding Islam, after the pattern to be observed in Europe's churches and synagogues, into the shape of religious institutions which mainly focus on certain areas of social life. These areas comprise the preaching of faith and morals, the practicing of rituals and festivals, the organizing of religious education and learning, and the strengthening of various kinds of religiously based community life. In all other areas of social life, the public order and the monopoly of the states prevail. With the exception of Greece, where Islamic family law has been respected (to various degrees) since the Treaty of Lausanne of 1923 and where the Greek Orthodox church still plays a dominant role, at present no European state knows a system of legal pluralism based on the religious denomination of the individual citizens.

This does not mean, of course, that the principles of Islamic family law have no value for Muslims in European countries. On the contrary, just like the adherents of other religions, Muslims are free to abide by them, voluntarily and with due respect to the existing juridical order. They may even create their own religious courts to which they may subject, out of their free choice, internal disputes concerning all kinds of matters affected by *sharīʿah,* including matters concerning marriage, divorce, and inheritance. The creation of such informal *sharīʿah* courts, which can be compared with the Jewish institution of the rabbinical courts, is on its way in several countries of western Europe. However, no public validity is attached to their decisions.

Interpretations of the principle of religious freedom, though shared by all, differ from one state to another. These differences are closely related to the complex political and cultural histories of each state. The slaughtering of animals according to Islamic (and Jewish) religious prescriptions, for instance, is allowed in many states (under specific conditions prescribed by law), but forbidden in some, including Switzerland and Sweden. Disputes concerning the wearing of head-scarves by Muslim girls in public schools have, again, been differently concluded. In some countries, such as the Netherlands, this expression of Islamic religious behavior is respected, but in others, for example, Belgium and France, the decision about its permissibility was delegated to the governors of the individual schools. During the Rushdie Affair, existing laws on blasphemy appeared only to apply to established religions in the United Kingdom, but they were applicable to Islam also in the Netherlands. Attitudes toward the right to celebrate religious holidays still differ widely, though the existing jurisprudence in various countries tends to recognize the right of employees to take one or more unpaid days off for this purpose, provided that the employer was informed in advance and that no serious damage was thereby caused to the interests of the enterprise. A verdict of the European Commission on Human Rights stipulated that a Muslim employee with full employment should have the right to attend Friday services if he informs his employer at the moment of his employment that the observance of this religious duty could be in conflict with his duties as an employee. Research shows many variations within the actual policies of government authorities toward this problem also depends on the practical possibilities in each labor sector involved.

An important aspect of the relations between religion and state is the predominant attitude in each country toward the social value of religion. This differs not only between the states, but also within each state, and even from one period to another and among the various political parties. Some states officially ascribe great importance to religion in maintaining the norms and values of society at large. If certain legally prescribed conditions are fulfilled by religious organizations, these states are willing to cooperate with them and even to subsidize, again to varying degrees, their religious and sociocultural activities. Other states tend to underline the private nature of religion, the secular character of their society, and, consequently, are reluctant in financing religious organizations. They may, nevertheless, allow forms of indirect subsidies to religions, for instance, by making donations to them tax deductible, a practice existing in many European states.

These differences are also related to Europe's divergent constitutional traditions regarding the relations between religion and state. With the exception of Vatican City, these traditions can be broadly classified according to the two models of union and separation.

The model of union involves some direct juridical relations between religion and state. This model can be subdivided into three types. First, some states practice the official recognition of religious communities. This implies that they take into account officially the existence of these religious communities in order to create relations between them and society at large (examples of this type are Spain, Belgium, and Germany). The second type is that of the existence of an official state religion with constitutionally guaranteed respect for religious freedom and the right of nondiscrimination of all other religions. This is the case, for instance, in Denmark, Sweden, and the United Kingdom. The third type is that of the officially sanctioned preferential treatment of one religious community over all the others. This can be found in Greece, for instance, and is usually qualified as with the term "confessionalism."

In addition, there is also the model of separation between religion and state, which underlines the neutrality of the state, the equality of all religions and philosophies of life, and, to varying degrees, the secular character of all public spaces of society. This model is found, for instance, in France and the Netherlands. However, in its application, these countries show many significant differences. For instance, on the basis of the well-known Dutch "pillarization system," which grants the right to all religious communities in the Netherlands, also at local levels, to develop with state subsidies all kinds of religiously colored institutions in the educational and sociocultural spheres, about thirty Islamic primary schools have been founded. This example illustrates the restricted significance of the various constitutional theories for a correct assessment of the real possibilities available to religious groups in each state. An adequate treatment of the complexities and variants involved in these models and types by far surpasses the scope of this article. Only some details will be provided of the realities that can be involved in this kind of recognition of Islam.

Spain's constitution expresses the state's readiness to cooperate with the churches and the religious confessions insofar as is necessary to make the right of its citizens to enjoy religious liberty "real and active." In order to obtain the recognition which is necessary to reach an agreement to cooperate, parties involved have to prove, on the basis of inscription in the official Register of Religious Entities, at least the existence of a certain number of believers. Apart from the established arrangements with the Roman Catholic church, Protestant, Jewish, and Islamic confessions have in fact been awarded this statute, and official agreements between the state and these confessions were signed in 1992.

The Comisión Islámica de España (CIE) was recognized as the official representative of the Muslims of Spain. It was chosen by the two federations inscribed in the official Register of Religious Entities, to which other federations or communities can be added in the future. The agreement has settled a long list of relevant subjects, like the statutes of mosques and prayerhalls, of Islamic cemeteries, of the Islamic rules concerning inhumation, graves, and funerary rites, and of the imams and other religious leaders. It also regulated the religious rights of Muslim soldiers and Muslim personnel of the army and of Muslim prisoners and patients in hospitals. Muslim parents and their children were guaranteed the right to receive Islamic religious education in schools at primary and secondary levels. The Islamic Committee of Spain, as well as the communities pertaining to it, may establish and manage teaching centers of primary and secondary levels, as well as universities and centers of Islamic formation, in accordance with the general legislation regarding these matters. The agreement also grants a number of tax privileges to the CIE and the attached communities. It defines the rights of Muslim students and employees to celebrate religious holidays, to heed to the prescriptions of Ramaḍān, and to attend weekly Friday services. Finally, it stipulates that the CIE will be the sole authority in Spain to assign the mark "*ḥalāl*" to food products in order to designate that they have been prepared in accordance with the religious law of Islam. The dietary rules of Islam will be respected in prisons, army dependencies, hospitals, and schools for those Muslims who request this. This holds true also for the timetable of Ramaḍān.

The government of Spain has assumed an active role in the constitution of a representative organ on behalf of the Muslims in Spain. In Belgium, where the state recognized Islam officially in 1974, this has, however, not been the case. In order to effectuate the financial aid that the Belgian state in principle is ready to convey to a great variety of Islamic religious activities (including the salaries of imams, the expenses of mosques, the foundation of Islamic schools, the religious education in public schools, etc.), committees with corporate capacity have to be established by law. These committees are in charge of the properties used for the cults and function at the same time as intermediaries with the national government. They have to be elected at provincial levels, in accordance with legally prescribed rules. The organization of the elections was put into the hands of the

Islamic Cultural Center in Brussels (financed by the Muslim World League) with which the Belgians had been dealing on a temporary basis as the sole representative of the Muslims of its state since the official recognition of Islam. However, the elections that took place were not recognized, with the result that many potential measures that could considerably have improved the religious infrastructure of Belgian Islam were not taken at all. Nevertheless, teachers of Islamic religious education have been appointed in many Belgian public schools at the recommendation of the center in Brussels or the "Provisional Council of Wise Persons for the Organization of the Islamic Cult in Belgium," created, again on a temporary basis, in 1990.

From a general point of view, one must conclude that Muslims have not made full use of the opportunities offered to them by the widely divergent legal systems of the European states. Their discord and lack of qualified leadership are certainly important factors to explain this. However, of equal importance is the outspokenly negative attitude of large sectors of European societies toward the ethnic minorities living among them and the adherents of the religion of Islam in particular. Extremist political movements with bluntly racist ideologies have appeared on the European scene over the past few years and have been able to attract significant percentages of voters in local and national elections. Their influence is clearly reflected in the changing attitudes of some of the established political parties. Acts of violence against the life and property of Muslims and other minority groups have become the sad reality. Hardly any mosque or prayer hall is now opened without accompanying protests by non-Muslims. And a politician defending the constitutional rights of minority groups runs the risk of losing the favor of many voters. The dramatic events in southeastern Europe have created fears about the survival of freedom, democracy, and equality in regard to Europe's Islam.

[*See also* Albania; Balkan States; France; Germany; Great Britain; *and* Popular Religion, *article on* Popular Religion in Europe and the Americas.]

BIBLIOGRAPHY

Western Europe

Arkoun, Mohammed, Rémy Leveau, and B. El-Jisr, eds. *L'Islam et les musulmans dans le monde*. Volume 1, *L'Europe occidentale*. Beyrouth, 1993. Special emphasis on France and western Europe in general; separate chapters on Italy, Spain, United Kingdom, Belgium, Germany, Netherlands, Denmark, Sweden, and Norway.

Koningsveld, P. S. van. *Islamitische slaven en gevangenen in West-Europa tijdens de late Meddeleeuwen*. Leiden, 1994. Inaugural lecture in the Chair of the Religious History of Islam in Western Europe, delivered at Leiden University on 4 February 1994. An English version, entitled "Muslim Slaves and Captives in Western Europe during the Late Middle Ages," will appear in a future issue of the journal *Islam and Christian-Muslim Relations*.

Nielsen, Jørgen N. "Migrant Muslims in Western Europe." Portion of entry "Muslimūn" in *Encyclopaedia of Islam*, new ed., vol. 7, pp. 699–702. Leiden, 1960–.

Nielsen, Jørgen N. *Muslims in Western Europe*. Edinburgh, 1992. Contains general analysis of family, law and culture, and Muslim organizations. Separate chapters are on France, West Germany, United Kingdom, the Netherlands and Belgium, Scandinavia, and southern Europe.

Shadid, W. A. R., and P. S. van Koningsveld. *Religious Freedom and the Position of Islam in Western Europe: Opportunities and Obstacles in the Acquisition of Equal Rights*. Kampen, Neth., 1994. Contains an extensive bibliography of studies on Islam in all countries of the European Community published from 1987 through 1993.

Southeastern and Northern Europe

Kettani, M. A. "Islam in Post-Ottoman Balkans." *Journal of Muslim Minority Affairs* 9 (1988): 381–403. Review essay of Popovic 1986 (see below), with important additional data.

Popovic, Alexandre. "The Old Established Muslim Communities of Eastern Europe." Portion of entry "Muslimūn" in *Encyclopaedia of Islam*, new ed., vol. 7, pp. 695–699. Leiden, 1960–. Also treats the Muslim communities in Finland and Poland.

Popovic, Alexandre. *L'Islam balkanique: Les musulmans du sud-est européen dans la période post-ottomane*. Berlin, 1986. Encyclopedic survey of the history and sociology of Islam in the Balkan states.

P. S. van Koningsveld

Islam in the Americas

Persons of Islamic background were among the explorers, traders, and settlers who visited the New World from the time of Columbus. A considerable number of Moriscos (Spanish Muslims who concealed their faith after 1492) migrated to both Portuguese and Spanish America, but their increasing numbers threatened the Christian rulers, who had them exterminated by the Inquisition.

African Muslim slaves from Senegal, Gambia, the southern Sahara, and the upper Niger came to the Americas between the mid-1500s and the mid-nineteenth century. Estimates of the proportion of Muslims within the total numbers of African slaves brought to the Western Hemisphere range from 14 to 20 percent.

After abolition in the Caribbean, the British in Guyana transported between 1835 and 1917 large numbers of Indians as indentured servants. Most were Hindus, but a sizable minority (16 percent) were Muslims, who comprise more than 10 percent of the nation's population today. In Trinidad and Tobago there is also a longstanding Muslim minority of about 6 percent. Suriname, long a Dutch colony, has few African Muslims left, but its Muslim population is 23 percent owing to the large numbers of Indian and Javanese Muslims who were imported for labor in the nineteenth and early twentieth centuries. Although many African slaves came from Islamic backgrounds, the conditions of slavery made it impossible for large numbers of them to sustain their religious beliefs, practices, and institutions. But there are records of very remarkable individual African Muslim slaves (see Allan D. Austin, *African Muslims in Antebellum America: A Sourcebook,* New York, 1984). Indian and other Muslim immigrants, however, were not slaves and thus were able to maintain their spiritual, cultural, and social institutions sufficiently well to preserve an Islamic identity.

Muslim Immigration to North America. Significant numbers of free Muslims did not start arriving in the Americas until the late 1800s, when Arabs from greater Syria, especially, began to arrive. Most of these people were poor, working-class males who made their living by peddling and menial jobs. They tended to assimilate into American society and often took American spouses, if a Muslim wife—whether from back home or among the immigrant community—was not available. They found it difficult to sustain a Muslim identity, but there was some activity in mosque and community building, for example, in Cedar Rapids, Iowa, and Edmonton, Alberta, where strong and growing Muslim communities flourish today. This first "wave" (I follow here Yvonne Y. Haddad's periodization in her pamphlet *A Century of Islam in America,* Washington, D.C., 1986) of immigration continued until World War I, after which a second wave continued through the 1930s, ending with World War II.

A third wave of Muslim immigration after World War II included many people from the elites of Middle Eastern and South Asian countries seeking education and professional advancement. Although many returned to their home countries, a large number remained. The members of this third wave have tended to maintain their Islamic identity while assimilating into North American life at a moderate rate. Sometimes more observant and strict Muslims refer to these people as "ʿEed [ʿĪd] Muslims," because of their supposed habit of attending the mosque only during the two canonical religious festivals each year, ʿĪd al-Aḍḥā and ʿĪd al-Fiṭr. But these people extended the establishment of Islamic centers and mosques, as well as larger-scale Muslim associations, such as the Federation of Islamic Associations, a somewhat loose organization of mosques in the United States, whose Canadian affiliate is the Council of Muslim Communities of Canada (CMCC). Another active organization that encourages the building of new mosques and cooperation among Islamic congregations is the Council of Masajid ("mosques") of the United States, Inc. Still another is the Muslim Students Association of U.S.A. and Canada (MSA), which was organized by international Muslim students studying in North America in 1963. The MSA evolved into and is connected with the Islamic Society of North America (ISNA), currently the largest Muslim "umbrella" organization, with several affiliated associations pursuing a variety of Islam-related interests. [*See* Federation of Islamic Associations *and* Islamic Society of North America.]

A fourth wave of Muslim immigration to North America began in the mid-1960s and continues today. It was made possible by changes in U.S. immigration laws, which opened the doors to people from many parts of the world whose talents and occupational capabilities filled acknowledged needs. Large numbers of immigrants from the Middle East, Asia, and beyond migrated to America to take up permanent residence with citizenship. Among these were considerable numbers of Muslims, particularly from the Arab world, Turkey, Iran, Afghanistan, Pakistan, India, and Bangladesh. Today the majority of Muslims in North America are immigrants, with Arabs more numerous in the United States and Pakistanis second, whereas the proportions are reversed in Canada.

The most recent wave of Muslim immigrants is also generally the most motivated to sustain and hand down a strong Islamic identity and establish permanent institutional and community structures to that end. There is much less interest in assimilating into North American life among the more recently arrived Muslims. The worldwide Islamic revival, including its "fundamentalist" aspects, in its North American circles has among its highest goals the establishment of an Islamic environment on that continent. It intends to do that by means of *daʿwah* (missions), Islamic schools, publications, building new mosques and centers, becoming involved in politics, public relations, and developing Islamic financial institutions, such as interest-free banking.

Muslims who are either immigrants or the descendants of immigrants live in all the metropolitan regions of North America, but in the United States there are particularly large communities in Boston, New York, the Detroit-Toledo corridor, Chicago, Houston, and Los Angeles/Orange County, whereas in Canada there is a large Muslim community in Toronto, with sizable ones also in Montreal, Windsor, Winnipeg, Edmonton, Calgary, and Vancouver.

Muslim African Americans. The second largest North American Muslim community is the Muslim African Americans in the United States. Three major reasons for conversion to Islam by many African Americans are: the consciousness among many of a lost Islamic heritage dating back to the time of slavery, the related proliferation of new, quasi-Islamic religious movements among African Americans in the twentieth century, and the strong trend of conversion to Islam by African Americans in correctional facilities.

The fact of Muslim slaves in the Americas has been mentioned above. In 1913 the Moorish Science movement was established in Newark, New Jersey, by Timothy Drew (1886–1929), who came to be known among his followers as Noble Drew Ali. He taught that black Americans would discover their true identity only through an educative process centered in his text called *The Holy Koran*. Noble Drew Ali considered black Americans to be "Asiatics," or "Moors," but not "Negroes." Islam was seen as the true religion of Asiatics, whereas Christianity was a religion for the whites. The movement borrowed some aspects of Islam but followed its own course, gradually splitting up into a few small circles today.

The next quasi-Islamic movement to arise in the United States was the Nation of Islam. It was founded in Detroit in 1930 by a foreign national of uncertain origin named W. D. Fard (with variants), who called for education, a common ritual, and strong community defense, all regulated by a strict ethic. One of Fard's principle followers, the black American Elijah Poole (1897–1975), carried on the movement in 1934 after Fard's mysterious disappearance. There was little Islamic about the movement except its name. For example, the doctrine came to regard Fard as Allāh incarnate and Elijah Muhammad (i.e., Poole) as his prophet. White people were regarded as devils who had robbed the blacks of their preeminent place in the order of things. [*See* Nation of Islam *and the biography of Elijah Muhammad.*]

The Nation of Islam attracted many African Americans, who were inspired and helped by its message of hard work, abstinence, strong family values, and commitment to improving the general lot of black people. The Nation of Islam came to have organizations—in the form of mosques—throughout the urban United States. One of Elijah Muhammad's most outstanding associates was Malcolm X (1925–1965), who was converted in prison and changed his name from Little to protest the humiliation of having been christened with a white, "slave" name. Malcolm X, who made the pilgrimage to Mecca and converted to normative Islam, was assassinated in 1965 by members of the Nation of Islam. Since then his image has grown as one of America's most powerful visionaries for empowerment of black people. [*See the biography of Malcolm X.*] His embracing of mainstream Sunnī Islam has been a major factor in the increasing identification of Muslim African Americans with the world Islamic community. The beginnings of this occurred in 1975 when, on the death of Elijah Muhammad, his son and designated heir to leadership, Wallace Deen Muhammad, announced that the Nation of Islam would henceforth leave behind much of his father's teaching and move in the direction of normative Islam. Although this successor movement had a number of names, it now prefers to call itself simply "Muslim" and has effectively liquidated its organizational infrastructure, except for the leader's (whose name became Warith Deen Muhammad) preaching and teaching mission in Chicago and the weekly newspaper *Muslim Journal*, which covers news of interest to all Muslims.

Not all Nation of Islam followers agreed with the dramatic change brought about by Warith Deen Muhammad. One longtime associate, the former Louis X, has continued the Nation of Islam's struggle to lift up and empower poor black people and strengthen them with the effective message of Elijah Muhammad. Minister Louis Farrakhan, as this leader came to be known, is a charismatic preacher who alarms much of white America with his provocative discourses. There are some aspects of Islam in the continuing Nation of Islam, but orthodox Muslims in America reject it as an authentic Islamic movement. One widely distributed pamphlet refers to it as "Farrakhanism," a distinct religion, protected under the First Amendment, but not Islamic.

The conversion of large numbers of African Americans to Islam in prison started in the days of the Nation of Islam. Malcolm X remains a beacon of hope for those who have been brought as low as prison. Nation of Islam chaplains have been very effective in preaching to and helping inmates, and their record of successful litigation in American courts for prisoners' religious rights (e.g., Friday noon prayers and a pork-free Islamic diet) has improved the general lot of incarcerated persons.

Inmates declare Islam as their religion for a variety of reasons, including physical protection, but many come to lead exemplary lives both inside prison and after release. In some corrections systems, such as New York State and New York City, Muslim African American inmates make up a major proportion of the prison and jail populations. Although many incarcerated Muslims become model inmates, many also get caught up in a cycle of recidivism and reincarceration. This is a great challenge to the entire Muslim community that is only beginning to be addressed.

There is a considerable cultural, occupational, educational, and economic gap between most Muslim immigrants and most Muslim African Americans. Racism also plays a part in the separation of the two communities. But Muslim "chaplains," as prison imams are often called by administrations, increasingly recognize that the support system and caring community of fellow Muslims that a Muslim inmate benefits from in prison is usually not available to poor urban blacks on release. Rather, the former, chronic conditions of life on the street in the American underclass often win out. Halfway houses and other measures are being called for, but resources and the will to innovate in this often discouraging and sometimes dangerous Islamic social work are scarce.

Challenges to Muslims in the Americas. In the Americas, the numbers, diversity, organizational development, and Islamic identity of Muslims are strongest in North America, but substantial Muslim communities exist throughout the hemisphere. In addition to the small but well-established communities in the Caribbean basin, there are other Latin American immigrant communities, composed mostly of people from Arab countries, in Mexico, Brazil, Argentina, Colombia, and Venezuela. The Muslim populations of Argentina and Brazil, for example, are each at least twice the Muslim population of Canada (estimated at 200,000 in 1992).

In North America, and especially the United States, with its Muslim population of perhaps 4 million or more (no precise census has been conducted yet), the worldwide Islamic *ummah* is gathered in a kind of microcosmic form in a single (if complex) American social and political order. The great variety of Muslims there includes numerous Shīʿīs of different types, although the vast majority are Sunnī, reflecting the ratio worldwide. Muslims in North America are urgently concerned about building Islamic unity even as they acknowledge ethnic, racial, and cultural divisions and tensions.

Muslim congregations in North America range from narrowly ethnic enclaves (e.g., Turkish, Syrian, and Pakistani) to richly diverse communities. Most congregations try to have imams who are well trained in Arabic and to practice *fiqh* (jurisprudence) and the classical religious sciences. Thus they tend to import imams from Middle Eastern or South Asian Islamic countries. There are sometimes difficulties when imams fail to perceive the nature of North American society and the problems Muslims have coping with it. Often members of a local congregation want an imam who can provide counseling and other services similar to what Jews and Christians expect from their rabbis and ministers (see Waugh, 1982). But this problem is increasingly recognized, and initiatives to train foreign as well as native imams have begun.

The long-established Islamic Center of Greater Toledo, Ohio, has a membership of about six hundred families drawn from more than thirty national and ethnic backgrounds. Most of the members are Sunnīs, but Shīʿīs are included, too. The center has a large Friday mosque, extensive educational and activity wings, a bookstore, clinic, mortuary, cemetery, recreation field, and extensive kitchen/dining facilities. Similar large centers exist in major urban areas, such as Los Angeles, San Diego, Houston, Toronto, and central New Jersey. In Houston, several mosques have banded together in a cooperative association with a central coordinating staff and a model for developing noncompetitive Islamic organizations and services in different quadrants of the metropolitan area. Although this octopuslike comity arrangement is not without problems, it might serve as a prototype for other urban regions with large, dispersed Muslim populations. In Oakland, California, there is a large Sunnī mosque with an affiliated, full-time Islamic school that was originally a Nation of Islam congregation. Now, although it consists mostly of Muslim African Americans, it also numbers Arab Americans and other immigrants among its members.

Large Islamic Associations. The Islamic Society of North America, introduced above, represents the type of large-scale coordinating effort that many Muslims consider essential to the long-term well-being of the *ummah* (community) in North America. The ISNA, which has a headquarters campus near Indianapolis, Indiana, has both individual and institutional memberships, publishes a glossy magazine, *Islamic Horizons,* and holds an annual meeting each Labor Day weekend attended by around five thousand people in recent years. ISNA is essentially a Sunnī organization, but it attracts the support of Muslims from many different ethnic and national backgrounds, including African Americans. ISNA strongly emphasizes Muslim family values, *daʿwah,* Islamic education, youth activities, political activism, Islamic publishing, cooperative and continuing relations with Muslim groups and countries overseas, helping in the development of new mosques and centers, and so forth. ISNA also shares with other Islamic groups an urgent concern for developing a *fiqh* that is both true to the mainstream Islamic tradition and responsibly adaptive to new circumstances and problems found by Muslims living as minorities in the West.

Although large organizations such as ISNA offer the advantages of a wide communication network, educational research and development, publications, an image of Muslims seeking unity, and certain economies of scale, many Muslims prefer to pursue their Islamic goals at the local level. Large congregations in effect compete with ISNA by sponsoring their own public outreach and *daʿwah* initiatives. The Islamic Society of Southern California, for example, sponsors an Islamic Education Service that has a television network and distributes sound and video cassettes of sermons, speeches, conferences, and panel discussions on a variety of contemporary topics including human sexuality, AIDS, relations with Christians and Jews, and spirituality. It publishes *The Minaret,* a sophisticated magazine with a national readership.

There is a feeling among many Muslims in North America that, although large-scale coordination of Islamic activities is desirable, the right means for this has not yet been devised. In 1992 the first North America–wide Islamic Coordinating Conference was held, in Indianapolis. It brought together the widest range of representatives of Muslim organizations in a spirit of mutual consultation and seeking a vision for the future. But the assembled participants proceeded cautiously, aware that the processes of Muslim unity and cooperation in North America are as diversely complex as the constituencies that represent the *ummah* there.

[*See also* Brazil; Canada; Suriname; Trinidad and Tobago; *and* United States of America.]

BIBLIOGRAPHY

Haddad, Yvonne Yazbeck, ed. *The Muslims of America.* New York and Oxford, 1991. Informative essays on organizations, Islamic thought, Muslims in prison, political activity, *daʿwah,* women, and other topics.

Haddad, Yvonne Yazbeck, and Adair T. Lummis. *Islamic Values in the United States: A Comparative Study.* New York and Oxford, 1987. Well-documented study based on interviews and questionnaires.

Husaini, Zohra. *Muslims in the Canadian Mosaic: Socio-Cultural and Economic Links with Their Countries of Origin.* Edmonton, Alberta, 1990. Good demographic and sociocultural data, with particular emphasis on Alberta.

Kettani, M. Ali. *Muslim Minorities in the World Today.* London and New York, 1986. Muslims in the Americas are covered, with statistics, on pages 191–213.

El-Kholy, Abdo A. *The Arab Moslems in the United States: Religion and Assimilation.* New Haven, 1966. Careful empirical study that, though dated, still has considerable historical value.

Lee, Martha F. *The Nation of Islam: An American Millenarian Movement.* Lewiston, N.Y., 1988. Carries the story beyond Lincoln (below) into the period of Minister Louis Farrakhan.

Lincoln, C. Eric. *The Black Muslims in America* (1961). 3d ed. Grand Rapids, 1993. The most thorough study of the Nation of Islam, by a distinguished African-American sociologist.

Marsh, Clifton. *From Black Muslims to Muslims: The Transition from Separatism to Islam, 1930–1980.* Metuchen, N.J., and London, 1984. Useful information on the Moorish Science Temple and the ways in which Wallace (Warith) Deen Muhammad diverged from his father's doctrine. Contains a list of African American *masjids* (mosques).

Melton, John Gordon, ed. *The Encyclopedia of American Religions.* 3d ed. Detroit, 1989. Contains an annotated listing of Islamic organizations in the United States, with addresses (pp. 825–842).

Waugh, Earle H. "The Imam in the New World: Models and Modifications." In *Transitions and Transformations in the History of Religions,* edited by Frank E. Reynolds and Theodore M. Ludwig, pp. 124–149. Leiden, 1980.

Waugh, Earle H., Baha Abu-Laban, and Regula B. Qureshi, eds. *The Muslim Community in North America.* Edmonton, Alberta, 1983. Very useful source of information on such topics as survival strategies, socioreligious behavior of Muslims, Islamic studies, Pakistani Muslims in Canada, and Minister Louis Farrakhan.

Waugh, Earle H., Sharon McIrvin Abu-Laban, and Regula B. Qureshi, eds. *Muslim Families in North America.* Edmonton, Alberta, 1991. Sequel to the above, with excellent essays on religion, ethnicity, family life, sex/gender, women, mate selection, divorce, immigrant groups, and other topics.

Williams, Raymond Brady. *Religions of Immigrants from India and Pakistan: New Threads in the American Tapestry.* Cambridge and New York, 1988. Contains reliable and informative treatment of South Asian Muslims in the United States.

FREDERICK MATHEWSON DENNY

ISLAMIC CALENDAR. The traditional Islamic (or Hijrah) calendar consists of twelve lunar months, each of which lasts from one first sighting of the crescent moon to the next. The twelve months of the Islamic calendar in order are Muḥarram, Ṣfar, Rabīʿ al-Awwal, Rabīʿ al-Thānī, Jumādā al-Ūlā, Jumādā al-Ākhirah, Rajab, Shaʿbān, Ramaḍān, Shawwāl, Dhū al-Qaʿdah, and Dhū al-Ḥijjah. Because of the lunar nature of the calendar, each month lasts approximately 29 or 30 days. Thus the Islamic calendar, which is approximately 354 days long, shifts in relation to the 365-day solar year, with each month beginning ten or eleven days earlier each year. Furthermore, because the sighting of the moon may vary with longitude and latitude, the Muslim calendar also may vary from region to region. Because of this shifting nature of the Hijrah calendar, various solar calendars have also been used in the Muslim world. The solar year has advantages for administrative organization, in particular for the collection of agricultural taxes. The Hijrah calendar, however, is exclusively used for setting the months of the Islamic calendar and the associated important fasts and festivals of the Islamic ritual year.

The Islamic calendar maintains a seven-day week that runs concurrently with the Gregorian or universal solar calendar. As in the Jewish calendar, the days run from sunset to sunset rather than sunrise to sunrise. Friday (al-Jumuʿah) is significant in Islam as the day of *jumuʿah* or congregational prayers. Often businesses are closed on Friday afternoons so that men can attend congregational prayers at a mosque. Thursday is also important as a day of fasting for many Muslims. Shīʿī Muslims in India and Pakistan often attend religious assemblies *(majlis)* that are regularly held on Thursday evenings.

"Year One" of the Islamic calendar begins with the establishment of the first Muslim polity in Medina, following the migration or Hijrah of the prophet Muḥammad and his followers from the city of Mecca in 622 CE. This year is thus designated as AH 1 (After Hijrah). Because of the lack of concordance in length between the Muslim and universal solar calendars, it is not possible simply to add 622 to the Hijrah date to establish the common era (CE) date. The formula for converting these dates is as follows: the Hijrah date equals the Gregorian date minus 622 plus the total of the Gregorian date minus 622 divided by 32. Even this formula is somewhat inaccurate, and it is thus better to consult a conversion table.

By orienting itself around the formative historical event of the Hijrah, which corresponds with the establishment of the first Islamic polity—rather than from the birth of Muḥammad or, as one might expect, from the first revelation of the Qur'ān—the Islamic calendar manifests the centrality of the *ummah* or community as a principle in Islam. It also expresses the importance of historical events in Islam—what the historian Marshall Hodgson has called "kerygmatic piety"—a piety that seeks to locate ultimacy in terms of irrevocable, datable, and nonrepeatable events. Kerygmatic piety is expressed in the days of the Islamic religious calendar that commemorate events that occurred during the formative period of Islamic history, such as the celebration of the birthday of the prophet Muḥammad and the commemoration of the martyrdom of his grandson Ḥusayn ibn ʿĀlī. The Islamic calendar also designates as sacred certain days and months that, in contrast, are linked to no particular historical events. These dates correspond to the category of piety that Marshall Hodgson has called "paradigm tracing," where ultimacy is sought in enduring and recurrent cosmic patterns. Such dates follow a cyclical and repeatable pattern and are the opportunities for regularly established religious observances and festivals. Daily and weekly prayers follow this pattern. Similarly, the Islamic calendar reflects this type of piety in the yearly observance of Ramaḍān, the month of fasting, and the festival of ʿĪd al-Fiṭr that celebrates the final breaking of this fast, as well as in Dhū al-Ḥijjah, the month of the pilgrimage to Mecca, and its festival of ʿĪd al-Aḍḥa (or ʿĪd al-Qurbān), which commemorates the willingness of Abraham to offer his son Ismāʿīl (Ishmael) as a sacrifice. These "paradigm-tracing" festival months and days are shared by Sunnī and Shīʿī alike and are commemorated by both communities in similar ways with a few minor deviations. In fact, for most Sunnī Muslims these two ʿĪds are the two major public religious observances of the Islamic ritual year.

The month-long fast of Ramaḍān takes place during the eighth month of the lunar year. During this period Muslims abstain from food, drink, smoking, and sexual contact from dawn until dusk. In some parts of the Islamic world the beginning of the fast is announced by groups of men who go from door to door through the streets of neighborhoods before the morning call to prayer, waking people so that they can prepare for the onset of the fast. The fast is broken each day around the time of the evening prayer with a small meal, often shared by family and friends. One activity recommended to pious persons is the recitation of the entire Qur'ān over the course of the month; to facilitate this the Qur'ān is divided into thirty equal sections called *guzʿ* or *paras*. Sometimes Shīʿī Muslims gather to hear discussions on religious topics during this period, particularly on the anniversary of ʿAlī's martyrdom on 21 Ramaḍān, which is also a time for public processions. The first revelation of the Qur'ān on Laylat al-Qadr (the Night of Power) is commemorated by Sunnīs on the 27th and by Shiʿis on the 19th, 21st, and 23rd. On this night, it is customary for pious Muslims to stay awake all night engaged in devotions. Many Muslims enter into a period of religious seclusion for ten days at the end of the month in connection with this date.

The fast of Ramaḍān concludes with the celebration of ʿĪd al-Fiṭr on the first day of the month of Shawwāl. Following the breaking of the fast Muslims gather together in the courtyards of large mosques, called *ʿīdgāh*s, to perform the morning prayers. The poor gather outside the mosque, as this is also a time when people distribute alms. In the afternoon families visit friends and relatives and distribute ʿĪd presents. On this day it is customary to dress in one's finest clothes and to distribute sweets, and also to pay one's servants and employees a bonus (*ʿīdī*). In general it is a festive day: not only has the disciplined and demanding fast come to an end, but those who have completed the fast believe that their sins are forgiven and thus feel assured of their admission to paradise.

The *ḥajj*, or pilgrimage to Mecca, takes place in the month of Dhū al-Ḥijjah, when millions of pilgrims go to Mecca and Medina to participate in the rites of the *ḥajj*. During the *ḥajj*, on the tenth day of Dhū al-Ḥijjah, ʿĪd al-Qurbān, also called ʿĪd al-Aḍḥā, is celebrated in the valley of Mina near Mecca where, in commemoration of the slaughtering of the lamb that God miraculously substituted for Abraham's son Ismāʿīl, pilgrims purchase and ritually slaughter an animal. Throughout the Muslim world it is customary for a family to similarly purchase an animal—a sheep, goat, or cow—and raise it for slaughter on 10 Dhū al-Ḥijjah. In cities and towns huge livestock markets spring up to provide families with these animals; on the actual day of the ʿĪd, the animals are ritually slaughtered. Portions of the meat are distributed to the poor, and the rest is eaten in celebratory meals with friends and family.

The kerygmatic dimension of Islamic piety can be found in the numerous days that commemorate specific events in Islamic history. These include the birth and death anniversaries of important individuals and dates connected with important events in the first generation of Islam. The Twelver Shīʿīs celebrate many more of these days than do Sunnī Muslims. Not only do the Shīʿīs commemorate the birth and death anniversaries of the Prophet, his daughter Fāṭimah, and the twelve imams, they also observe other important events, such as Muḥammad's recognition of his son-in-law ʿAlī as his successor (*mawlā*) at the pool of Ghadir Khumm during his last pilgrimage; the meeting between Muḥammad and his family and the Christians from Najaran at Mubahila; and most importantly, the month of Muḥarram—specifically ʿĀshūrā, the tenth of Muḥarram—which, although clearly important to both Sunnī and Shīʿī Muslims, has special significance for Shīʿīs.

This Shīʿī emphasis on historical events is linked to their understanding of personal allegiance as a central element of their piety. Allegiance to Muḥammad is seen as a necessary corollary to allegiance and obedience to God. For Shīʿīs this extends to allegiance and obedience to Muḥammad's legitimate successors, the imams. The importance of allegiance to these individuals has resulted in rituals for the remembrance and evocation of the narratives of the lives of the Prophet and his family. Of all these events, the most significant is the martyrdom of the Prophet's grandson, Imam Ḥusayn ibn ʿĀlī, on the tenth of Muḥarram in 642 CE. The month of Muḥarram is a time of daily ceremonies of public and private mourning, culminating on the tenth of Muḥarram (ʿĀshūrā') in huge public assemblies and processions. During Muḥarram an atmosphere of deep mourning is established in Shīʿī neighborhoods. Shīʿī Muslims don black clothing and attend lamentation assemblies (*majlis*) where the events of Karbala are evoked and tearfully remembered. Processions are held in which replicas of coffins (*tābūt*) and tombs (*taʿziyah*) are carried through neighborhoods as focuses of devotion. Some people physically mourn the death of the imam with breast-beating and self-flagellation. It should be noted that Sunnī Muslims also remember and honor the sacrifice of Ḥusayn, but there is less intensity and mourning, since devotion to the family of the Prophet is not as central to Sunnī piety as it is to Shīʿī.

There are also joyful celebrations in the Shīʿī ritual calendar. On the birthday of the Twelfth Imam, people write letters and place them in streams and rivers in the belief that the imam will receive these messages. In fact, the birthday anniversaries of all the imams are celebrated. On these occasions the assembly halls (called *imāmbārah*s in South Asia and *ḥusaynīyah*s by Persian speakers) are often brightly decorated with colored lights. [*See* Ḥusaynīyah.]

The Shīʿīs are not alone in the remembrance of historic events. For example, in modern times the celebration of the Mawlid al-Nabī or birthday of the prophet Muḥammad, which originated in the Fāṭimid period, has become increasingly popular among Sunnīs. In Pakistan and India large public processions on 12 Rabīʿ al-Awwal celebrate the Prophet's birth.

Another important element in the Muslim religious calendar is the celebration of the death anniversaries of Ṣūfī saints. In places as far-flung as Pakistan, Turkey, and Egypt, the tombs of the *awliyāʾ* (saints) are sites of frequent *ziyārahs* (pilgrimages) throughout the year and also of important celebrations known as *mawlid* or *ʿurs*. (*ʿUrs* is an Arabic word for "wedding" and signifies the spiritual wedding of the saint with his true beloved, God.) In South Asia large fairs are held in connection with these celebrations; their striking mix of sober piety and joyful celebration is often surprising to visitors who do not share the worldview of the participants. Merchants and professional performers—acrobats, motorcycle daredevils, and others—travel from tomb to tomb in order to participate in the highly profitable events surrounding the celebration of various *ʿurs*. [*See* Ziyārah; Mawlid.]

The Islamic calendar has important implications for Muslims in the modern world. Modernity has fundamentally altered the way people in the industrial world think of time. Work and leisure are now measured and defined as the periods in which people are either engaged or not engaged in industrial labor. The Islamic calendar was established in a preindustrial world where notions of work and leisure were more fluid and in tune with the natural progression of the seasons. The hegemony of the solar calendar has emerged concurrently with the hegemony of European industrial society, which has led some Muslim countries to modify their organization of time. Some governments have experimented with setting weekends on Saturday and Sunday, largely for economic reasons.

Modernity has also had implications for the Ramaḍān fast. Since the month of Ramaḍān moves from year to year, the fast sometimes takes place in the winter—when days are short and the weather is cool—and sometimes in the summer when the fast is particularly difficult. The requirements of labor in the modern industrial world make the fast a difficult ordeal for many Muslims who must work in great heat for long hours. Furthermore, fasting Muslims in urban environments often must travel long distances across cities, negotiating dense traffic in late afternoon heat while experiencing hunger and thirst. Tourism is also affected by the fast; for example, in Pakistan the *iḥtirām-i Ramaḍān* ordinances bring tourism to an effective halt by closing restaurants and beverage stands for Muslims and non-Muslims alike. Despite these added difficulties, large numbers of Muslims remain committed to the fast out of a deep sense of piety and a fervent desire to obey the commands of God.

The heterogeneity of modern Muslim communities in urban environments is also affected by the Islamic religious calendar and its festivals. Ordinarily, the distinguishing characteristics between Sunnī and Shīʿī, and to some extent even Muslims and non-Muslims, are invisible in daily life. However, during Muḥarram and other occasions of public performance, these normally invisible differences are brought to the surface, sometimes resulting in hostile confrontations.

For Muslims living outside the Muslim world, arranging for religious observances is made more difficult by the pressures of the solar calendar that determines the rhythm of the economy. In places where Muslims are a minority, public Muslim ritual performances may inflame the passions of non-Muslims who either do not understand or do not accept Muslim practices. For example, animal-rights activists in Europe have objected to the animal sacrifice of ʿĪd al-Aḍḥa. Similarly, in India Hindus have long objected to animal sacrifice, particularly of cows. On the other hand, Islamic performances—such as the yearly Muḥarram processions held by North American Shīʿī Muslims—provide an opportunity for Muslims to share their faith with others and to present themselves and their religion to their neighbors.

[*See also* ʿĀshūrāʾ; Ḥajj; ʿĪd al-Aḍḥā; ʿĪd al-Fiṭr; Muḥarram; Ramaḍān.]

BIBLIOGRAPHY

Bacharach, Jere L. *A Near East Studies Handbook*. Seattle, 1976.

Freeman-Grenville, G. S. P. *The Muslim and Christian Calendars*. London, 1963.

Hodgson, Marshall G. S. *The Venture of Islam*, Vol. 1. Chicago, 1974. Hodgson provides an excellent discussion of the Islamic calendar in his introduction to this masterful history, as well as a presentation on the useful categories of kerygmatic and paradigm-tracing piety.

Jaʿfar Sharīf. *Islam in India, or, The Qānūn-i Islām* (1927). Translated by G. A. Herklots. New rev. ed. London, 1975. Provides a detailed description of Islamic practice in nineteenth-century India.

Schimmel, Annemarie, "Islamic Religious Year." In *The Encyclopedia of Religion*, vol. 7, pp. 454–457. New York, 1987. A great improvement on previous expositions of the Islamic calendar in that it stresses its religious and devotional component.

Schubel, Vernon. *Religious Performance in Contemporary Islam: Shiʿi Devotional Rituals in South Asia*. Columbia, S.C., 1993. My own work provides a detailed discussion of the Muḥarram performances of Muslims in Karachi.

Turner, Victor. *From Ritual to Theater*. New York, 1982. Contains Turner's interesting discussion of the relationship between work and leisure in the modern world.

Von Grunebaum, G. E. *Muhammadan Festivals*. New York, 1951. Still useful general survey of Muslim festivals.

VERNON JAMES SCHUBEL

ISLAMIC CALL SOCIETY. Founded in Libya in 1972, the Islamic Call Society is entrusted with the task of missionary activity. The Revolutionary Command Council (RCC), under the leadership of Muʿammar al-Qadhdhāfī (who on 1 September 1969 overthrew Libyan King Idrīs al-Sanūsī), has from the beginning designated the revolution as an Islamic revolution. Among the concrete measures taken to emphasize the Islamic character of the revolution, besides the prohibition of alcohol and the Latin alphabet, and the appointment of a Supreme Committee on Revision of Positive Law (28 September 1971), were institutional interventions that strengthened the position of Islam in the state and simultaneously placed it under the RCC control. These latter measures included the reorganization of religious institutions and the system of religious education, as well as the scope of the Islamic mission, whose meaning, goals, and structure were the focus of the First Conference on the Islamic Mission in Tripoli (December 1970). Through a conference resolution the RCC first entrusted the task of the Islamic mission to a Corporation for the Islamic Call, from which the Islamic Call Society (ICS) emerged. In order to implement some of the tasks set forth in the ICS statute, primarily the preparing of preachers and missionaries, the Faculty of the Islamic Call, subservient to the ICS, was created. Instruction in this faculty began in the academic year 1974–1975. Four years of study leads to the Islamic Mission License; further study may lead to a Ph.D. in Islamic Call. The students, numbering three hundred in 1980–1981, come primarily from Asia and Africa.

The ICS is directed by three organs: the Administrative Council, with at least five members, which plans and oversees all ICS activities and chooses a general secretary from among its ranks; the general secretary, who serves as the official external representative of the ICS (Shaykh Maḥmūd Ṣubḥī held this position from 1972 to 1978; since then, it has been the former education minister Dr. Muḥammad Aḥmad al-Sharīf); and the General Assembly, which meets annually and evaluates the work of the Administrative Council. The number of members on the ICS is unknown. The main financial sources for the highly endowed ICS budget are state subsidies, primarily from the so-called Jihād Fund (created by law in 1972). The general budget for Libya does not provide for the ICS, which is exempt from all taxes and duties, is subject to no restrictions on capital transfers, and has the right to work with any organization if this furthers the spread of Islam. The ICS, though an independent juristic entity with its main office in Tripoli, retains the right to found branch offices in other countries. One of the largest of these, in Paola, Malta, has been associated since early 1990 with the newly founded Islamic World Studies Center and the journal *The Future of the Islamic World*.

The Second Conference for Islamic Mission in Tripoli (14–19 August 1982), called by Qadhdhāfī, produced a new institutional arm of the ICS when its four hundred participants created a World Council of Islamic Call (WCIC). Since its founding, Dr. Muḥammad al-Sharīf has acted as secretary *ex officio* of the thirty-six-member WCIC, which meets annually and is elected by the Conference for the Islamic Mission, which meets once every four years (third conference, 1986; fourth conference, 1990). The WCIC is concerned not only with the international dimension of the impact of the ICS's role as a point of contact with the Islamic communities it supports worldwide, but also propagates Qadhdhāfī's version of Islam as an instrument of Libyan foreign policy.

Since the early 1980s, the organization of Muslims by the ICS (or World Islamic Call Society [WICS], as it has been known since 1982) into so-called regional councils (which have long existed in the Caribbean, West Africa, Central and East Africa, and South Asia) is part of an attempt to tie Muslims to Libya and to counter the activities especially of the Saudi Muslim World League with a putatively progressive version of Islam. In addition to sending missionaries and medical relief caravans and granting financial aid, the ICS has begun publishing books and brochures. It does so partly for purely missionary purposes (the brochures include *How to Be a Muslim, How to Pray, Rules that Govern Fasting*), and partly to blend a political and religious message (the books include *Islam: The Religion of Unity, The Cultural Invasion: The Weapons of the Zionists and the Modern*

Crusaders). These are supplemented by three periodicals: the weekly newspaper *Al-daʿwah al-Islāmīyah,* published from 1980 to 1992 (with English and French sections); the monthly *Risālat al-jihād,* appearing regularly from 1982 to 1992, and occasionally distributed in English and French editions; and the scientific yearly journal *Majallat kulliyat al-daʿwah al-Islāmīyah,* published since 1984–1985 by the Faculty of the Islamic Call. Despite immense expenditures, successful proselytization in Asia, Africa, and Latin American remains numerically limited; in Libya in 1987 some voices within the basic popular conference (especially in the spring of 1992) expressed displeasure and criticism of the ICS's inefficiency, indeed to the point of discussing its dissolution.

The central tenets of the religious revolution, propagated by Qadhdhāfī in May 1975, include the removal from power of the tradition religious scholars, the rejection of *sunnah* and *ḥadīth,* the sole reliance upon the Qur'ān accompanied by the simultaneous elevated valuation of *ijtihād* and rejection of the four legal schools. Since the revolution, the ICS has propagated this interpretation of Islam abroad. According to Article 2 of the 1972 law concerning the establishment of the ICS, the main task of the ICS is the dissemination of the official Libyan or Qadhdhāfian interpretation of Islam "all over the world by all available peaceful means." The word "peaceful" was struck from the 1980 revision of the law in reaction to the controversy with Saudi Arabia, which provoked Qadhdhāfī's call for a *jihād* for the liberation of the holy sites of Mecca and Medina and charges of heresy against Qadhdhāfī from the Saudi *ʿulamā'*. The 1972 law cites, among other things, the following goals: the implementation of the Islamic Call Conference's resolution of 1970; the spread of the Arabic language; the clarification of Islamic laws to make them conform to correct doctrine; the organization of courses of studies to prepare devout and cultured men of faith from the different Muslim nations (a task given to the Faculty of the Islamic Call in 1974); the preparation of propagators of Islam (a task also given to the Faculty of the Islamic Call in 1974); the reform of Muslim countries' administrative, educational, informational, and social systems so that they are in conformity with Islamic principles and their policies and proposals stem from Islam.

The orientation of the ICS to foreign countries means that it carries out only limited internal activities. Religious instruction of Libyans is the task of the Qur'ān schools and mosques; the construction of mosques is undertaken by other state organs. However, the ICS does organize Qur'ānic recitation contests and is responsible for the production of a new edition of the Qur'ān. The most important domestic activity of the ICS was proselytizing among the many non-Muslim employees (there were 439 conversions in 1980–1988) and financial support to foreign Muslims in need.

[*See also* Daʿwah; Libya.]

BIBLIOGRAPHY

Ayoub, Mahmoud M. *Islam and the Third Universal Theory: The Religious Thought of Muʿammar al-Qadhdhafi.* New York and London, 1987. A somewhat apologetic introduction to the Qadhdhafian interpretation of Islam.

Mattes, Hanspeter. *Die innere und äussere islamische Mission Libyens.* Munich, 1986. Detailed study of the activity of the Islamic Call Society, with an emphasis on Africa. Includes numerous documents, most in English and French.

The World Call Society from the Second to the Third Congress: Report on Activities and Programs between 1/9/1982 and 1/9/1986. Tripoli, 1987. Report on the activity of the Islamic Call Society, documenting the variety of its work.

HANSPETER MATTES

Translated from German by Stephen R. Ingle

ISLAMIC CHAMBER OF COMMERCE. An organ of the Organization of the Islamic Conference (OIC), the Islamic Chamber of Commerce (ICC) is composed of federations, unions, and national chambers of commerce in forty-six countries, all members of the OIC. The ICC is comprised of a general assembly, an executive committee, a general secretariat, a president, and six vice presidencies representing the zonal distribution of the membership, with offices in Pakistan, Morocco, Senegal, Syria, Bangladesh, and Kuwait. The ICC is funded by contributions from member countries according to a formula based on per capita incomes. Proposed in 1976 at the meetings of the OIC in Istanbul, Turkey, the ICC was formally established in 1977, with headquarters to be in Karachi, Pakistan. The ICC serves to promote trade, industry, and agriculture throughout the Islamic world; preferential terms of trade for members; cooperation between Islamic nations in finance, banking, insurance, and communications; arbitration of industrial and commercial disputes; fairs and joint showrooms, exhibits, seminars, lectures, and publicity campaigns; and the eventual establishment of an Islamic economic community.

The activities of the ICC to date can be grouped in

four categories: (1) building the physical and human infrastructures necessary for its operations, such as the headquarters in Karachi and a viable staff; (2) establishment of an institutional framework for the promotion of trade and commerce, such as fairs, exhibits, and the exchange of trade missions; (3) creation of committees and task forces to formulate designs and models and raise funds for joint industrial and manufacturing ventures in member countries; and (4) creation of the necessary organs to protect members against outsiders, such as the promotion and monitoring of the economic boycott against Israel and support of the Palestinian people and the Arab countries. The ICC thus only indirectly involves itself in business and commerce by disseminating information and facilitating contact among countries and trade organizations. An important organ of the ICC is its *Information Bulletin*, published quarterly in English and French to advertise fairs and exhibits; disseminate summaries of the proceedings of the general assembly and other official meetings; provide data on exports and imports of Islamic countries and Islamic companies (although the identity of the latter is not clearly defined); present occasional feature articles about member countries, the OIC, and the Islamic Development Fund; and publicize proposals for and news of joint ventures.

The ICC's activities extend beyond its member countries. It occupies a consultative status with the Economic and Social Council of the United Nations and the United Nations Industry and Development Organization. It cooperates with the United Nations Council on Trade and Development and the General Agreement on Tariffs and Trade, and it works more directly with institutions in the Islamic countries, both governmental and nongovernmental. Its contact with private institutions and businesses is particularly important, since one of the major obstacles facing the ICC has been the difficulty of persuading the private sector in member countries to cooperate with the public sector. Apparently the private sector is adequately served by national and local chambers of commerce and believes that any assistance or cooperation with the public sector could be confining and limiting to business activities. Furthermore, business enterprises in member countries are little prepared to identify with a confessional doctrine, such as Islam or Christianity, and the ICC is identified is an organ of the OIC. Ironically, most OIC members consider themselves secular and not bound by any religious or confessional policy restrictions. Turkey, Lebanon, Syria, Nigeria, Indonesia, Tunisia, Iraq, and Algeria, for example, are members of both the OIC and the ICC, but all of them consider themselves secular states and willingly conduct most of their economic transactions with non-Islamic countries. Their own chambers of commerce are guided by business and national interests, not by religion. Where it applies, *sharīʿah* (the divine law) relates only to personal status, while trade and commerce relations are extended to all countries, with the possible exception of Israel. Another complication is that the ICC encourages preferential treatment for contractors from member countries, which is not always consistent with the basics of private business, economic efficiency, and profit making. Still another restrictive factor is the implicit political orientation of the ICC. Its strong stand against Israel, overt support of the Palestinian Intifāḍah, and intent to prematurely promote an Islamic economic community might have limited its achievement.

Most of the accomplishments of the ICC to date have centered around meetings of its organs, the creation of committees and production of reports, and the construction of its headquarters. A few other tangible results include the establishment of a tomato-paste-processing joint venture in Cameroon, an oil storage and distribution venture in Mali, and the Tidekelt salt project in Niger; in the meantime the ICC has received more than seventy proposals for joint ventures. The limiting political character of the ICC is also indicated by the fact that it was created by foreign ministers of the OIC, funded by OIC governments, and is only indirectly influenced by business people. It is ironic, however, that in spite of its identification as Islamic, the ICC has no clear Islamic rules or regulations, economic principles, or philosophies and doctrines governing trade and commerce of the member countries. The ICC apparently takes member-country commitment to Islamic principles for granted, which obviously is not so.

To a certain extent, the functions of the ICC overlap with those of the national and local chambers of commerce, and more so with the international chambers in the member countries. The most obvious difference between the ICC and these other chambers is that the ICC is an organ of the OIC and plays a major political role among the members and in the international community. Except for the ICC's objective of persuading the private sector to cooperate with the public sector, it would have been just as appropriate to call it simply the political-economy committee of OIC. Indeed, such a description would be fully representative of its economic functions, political orientation, and heritage as an organ of the OIC.

[*See also* Organization of the Islamic Conference.]

BIBLIOGRAPHY

In addition to the following specific items, I have depended heavily on correspondence with and documents received from the national chambers of Algeria, Turkey, Oman, Qatar, Bahrain, Kuwait, and from the International Chamber of Malaysia, as well as from the National US-Arab Chamber and the US-Arab Chamber (Pacific), Inc. I am grateful to all of them for their kind responses to my inquiries.

Aḥsan, ʿAbdullāh al-. *OIC: The Organization of the Islamic Conference.* Herndon, Va., 1988.

Islamic Chamber of Commerce and Industry. *International Bulletin,* series 1981–1991. Particularly important for the summary of proceedings of the General Assembly.

Islamic Chamber of Commerce and Industry. *Tasks and Achievements.* Karachi, n.d.

ELIAS H. TUMA

ISLAMIC CULTURAL CENTERS. In 1973 the Süleymanlı movement began to found Islamic Cultural Centers (İslam Kültür Merkezleri Birliği) in Germany and other countries to organize labor migrants from Turkey and meet their religious needs. With 313 communities and about 18,000 members, the Association of Islamic Cultural Centers became one of the largest associations of Turkish workers in Germany. In 1980, there were also fifteen Islamic Cultural Centers in the Netherlands, nine in Austria, six in Switzerland, two in Denmark, and one each in Sweden, Belgium, and France. The influence of these other nongovernmental Muslim organizations has decreased, however, since the Turkish Islamic Union of the Office for Religion (Diyanet İşleri Türk-İslam Birliği) started to organize Turkish Muslim communities in Germany and other European countries in the 1980s.

The Süleymanlı movement, today with around 300,000 members in Turkey, originated with Süleyman Hilmi Tunahan (1888–1959). A member of the Naqshbandī, a Ṣūfī order, Tunahan founded a tradition-oriented, fundamentalist movement for the revival of Islam. It presses for Qur'ān courses and for a reestablishment of the *sharīʿah* and caliphate in Turkey. Like the Naqshbandīs, the Süleymanlıs are Sunnīs and tend to the Ḥanafī dogma and the orthodox theology of Maḥmūd al-Māturīdī al-Samarkandī (d. 944). The Süleymanlıs believe that they can find enlightenment only through the mediation of Tunahan by the ritual of *rābiṭah* (mystical union). The dogma is clandestine, known totally only by the shaykh himself and revealed partially to believers. The Süleymanlı movement was forbidden from time to time in Turkey because of its anti-laicist tendencies. It is alleged to have developed a camouflage ideology, which encourages followers to infiltrate other groups and, for tactical reasons, to express views they do not really hold.

The Islamic Cultural Centers are organized strictly hierarchically as an association of communities subordinated to the Islamic Cultural Center in Cologne, Germany. Two basic structures are to be distinguished: the inner circle formed by the members of the Süleymanlı movement and the outer circle by the members of the Association of Islamic Cultural Centers. In 1980 the Islamic Cultural Centers were accused, particularly by the German Trade Unions (DGB), of advocating Islamic fundamentalist and ultraright positions in their Turkish language papers while stressing in their German publications their desire for integration, cooperation with the state authorities, and recognition of the constitution of the Federal Republic. Since the end of the 1980s, some authors point out that the Islamic Cultural Centers are well accepted by other Muslim organizations, that the Islamic lessons they offer to the outer circle enjoy a good reputation, and that political concepts are propagated especially within the inner circle. In 1979 the Islamic Cultural Center in Cologne made an application for recognition as a "public law body," but the application was refused.

[*See also* Germany.]

BIBLIOGRAPHY

Gerholm, Thomas, and Yngve Georg Lithman, eds. *The New Islamic Presence in Western Europe.* London and New York, 1988. Collection of essays on the institutionalization of Islam in various countries and on the changes in the religious experience through migration.

Özcan, Ertekin. *Türkische Immigrantenorganisationen in der Bundesrepublik Deutschland.* Berlin, 1989. Insightful study of political organizations and political orientations among Turkish immigrants in Germany.

HANNS THOMĂ-VENSKE

ISLAMIC DEVELOPMENT BANK. The Islamic Development Bank is a unique aid institution, as all its funding is on an interest-free basis using financing techniques which are permissible under *sharīʿah*. It is a development assistance agency rather than a charity or a commercial bank, but, given that overheads are not fully covered, there is an element of subsidy in much of its funding. The paid-up capital in early 1993 of over two billion Islamic dinars was provided entirely by the governments of the Muslim states. An Islamic dinar, the unit of account, is equivalent to an International Monetary Fund Special Drawing Right, which was worth approximately U.S. $1.45.

Saudi Arabia subscribed over a quarter of the initial capital, and the bank is based in Jeddah, the kingdom's main commercial center. The other major Arab oil-exporting states—Libya, Kuwait, and the United Arab Emirates—have substantial shareholdings and collectively enjoy majority voting rights, although decisions are not usually taken in this way. There are forty-five states which participate in the bank, all with either predominantly Muslim populations or substantial Muslim minorities, such as Uganda. Pakistan, Indonesia, and Malaysia are the largest non-Arab subscribers, but Turkey has been much involved with the bank, and even Iran has joined in spite of its political differences with several Arab states.

Following agreement by the member states of the Organization of the Islamic Conference, the Islamic Development Bank started operating in 1975. Much of its initial funding was trade related and short term in nature. As a result of the quadrupling of oil prices in 1974, many Muslim countries had difficulty in financing their oil imports and were in severe balance-of-payments difficulty. The oil-price boom may have helped the Muslim members of the Organization of Petroleum Exporting Countries (OPEC), but it created problems for the more-populous Muslim states. One obvious solution was for the Islamic Development Bank to provide bridging finance, which would help both petroleum importers and oil exporters.

Using the principle of *murābaḥah* (resale with specification of gain), the bank purchased the oil or petroleum products on behalf of the importing country, which repaid at a markup, usually within eighteen months. The markup was well below commercial rates of interest and in line with the terms of concessionary finance from such institutions as the World Bank. As the repayments were denominated in Islamic dinars, this imposed an additional local currency burden on countries whose exchange rate was depreciating. This was less of a problem in the 1970s, when most deficit countries had strict exchange controls, but with economic liberalization and market-determined exchange rates, the costs of hard-currency repayment have risen.

The attraction of *murābaḥah* trade finance is that the credit is revolving, and the bank can get its money back. As the bank is not a deposit-taking institution, and cannot borrow conventionally in international financial markets, its resources are limited to the paid-up capital which its members are prepared to contribute. If disbursed funding is not repaid and becomes bad debt, the bank will soon run out of resources to finance new initiatives.

The Islamic Development Bank has therefore been very cautious about long-term equity participation through *mushārakah* (profit-and-loss "partnership"), and there has been little *muḍārabah* (silent or limited) partnership finance in which one partner provides finance and another entrepreneurial or management skills. The problem is how to disinvest, especially in the poorer Islamic countries which lack stock markets. Equity participation has mainly been in government institutions, such as national development banks, or quoted companies, such as Jordan Cement.

Long-term interest-free loans have been provided for projects with a significant socioeconomic impact, usually involving infrastructural work, such as roads or irrigation schemes. Funding has also been disbursed for hospitals, schools, and other social projects. These advances are for periods of up to thirty years, with a service fee to cover administrative expenses. Over $750 million has been lended in this way, often in cofinancing involving other agencies, such as the World Bank or the various Persian Gulf Arab development funds.

Since the mid-1980s the Islamic Development Bank has concentrated much of its funding through installment sales and leasing *(ijārah)*. Both methods of financing are permissible under *sharī'ah* law. By 1990 over $600 million had been advanced for the leasing of equipment in sixty separate deals, and a similar amount had been offered for installment sale. Usually these arrangements cover a five-year period, although the bank is very flexible over the terms it is prepared to negotiate.

The bank has made considerable efforts to support the poorest Muslim countries, such as Bangladesh, Mali, and Niger, but finance is only one of many development constraints which these states face. The identification of projects with any potential in such countries is far from easy, and the local government officials are either unable or unwilling to produce well-conceived applications for assistance. The Islamic Development

Bank, like other international agencies, has moved into the area of technical assistance in project design and implementation. Often such work is tendered out to specialized consultants, and the bank follows a highly professional approach to such matters, seeking independent external advice if necessary. It has adhered closely to its articles of association and not succumbed to political pressures.

In recent years the bank has taken tentative steps to harness new capital, develop internationally acceptable Islamic financial instruments, and build a closer relationship with the Islamic commercial banks. It has the potential to serve as a central bank for these commercial institutions. The Islamic banks portfolio was launched in 1987 in order to attract funds from the Islamic commercial banks and provide them with a safe yet profitable liquid instrument which they could hold. Over $65 million was subscribed, the money being used to finance Islamic trade on a *murābaḥah* markup basis with the profits shared according to *muḍārabah*.

In 1986 agreement was reached to establish a Unit Investment Fund, and after three years of study and consultation with *sharīʿah* lawyers the fund became operational. The Islamic Development Bank, acting as *muḍārib* (manager) for the funds provided by Islamic commercial banks, invests both in Islamic countries and international equity markets. Shares can be purchased in London, New York, and Tokyo, but the investment must be in companies whose activities are acceptable to Muslims (*ḥalāl*). Electronics and communications companies are acceptable, for example. A brewery or other company engaged in the manufacture or sale of alcohol is clearly not.

Further initiatives are being planned. The Islamic Development Bank has examined the feasibility of an export-credit insurance scheme to encourage trade between Muslim countries and the creation of a multilateral Islamic clearing union. Growing interest exists in the republics of the former Soviet Union with majority Muslim populations. Some of these are expected to become shareholders of the bank, making them eligible for Islamic financial assistance. The Islamic Development Bank has become a well-established institution which is respected in international banking circles. Much has been achieved, and its role is likely to grow in the years ahead, both in terms of geographical coverage and in the range of Islamic financing facilities provided.

[*See also* Banks and Banking; Economics, *article on* Economic Institutions.]

BIBLIOGRAPHY

Iqbal, Munawar. *Distributive Justice and Need Fulfillment in an Islamic Economy*. Leicester, 1988. A Muslim view of poverty and development problems.

Meenai, S. J. *The Islamic Development Bank: A Study of Islamic Cooperation*. London, 1990. Comprehensive, if somewhat uncritical, account of the Bank's first decade.

Wilson, Rodney. *Banking and Finance in the Arab Middle East*. London, 1983. The Islamic Development Bank is examined in chapter four and compared with Arab development agencies in chapter seven.

Wilson, Rodney. "The Islamic Development Bank's Role as an Aid Agency for Moslem Countries." *Journal of International Development* 1.4 (October 1989): 444–466. Quantifies the Bank's activities.

Uzair, Mohammad. "Central Banking Operations in an Interest-Free Banking System." In *Monetary and Fiscal Economics of Islam*, edited by Mohammad Ariff. Jeddah, 1982, pp. 211–236. Relevant for the wider role that the Bank is seeking to play in relation to Islamic commercial banks.

RODNEY WILSON

ISLAMIC FOUNDATION. Established in 1973, the aims of the Islamic Foundation are to encourage research into the implementation of Islam in the modern world, to project the image of Islam in Britain and Europe, and to meet the educational needs of Muslims, especially young people. To implement these objectives, the foundation works with young people and publishes research, especially in economics and about issues of Islam in the modern world, Christian-Muslim relations, and Muslim Central Asia.

The foundation came into being primarily at the initiative of a Pakistani Muslim economist, Professor Khurshid Ahmad, who was a leading figure in the Jamāʿat-i Islāmī of Pakistan. Ahmad was the foundation's first director, serving until he returned to Pakistan to become minister of planning soon after President Muhammad Zia ul-Haq came to power. He was succeeded by Khuram Murad, another leading member of the Jamāʿat-i Islāmī. Both men have since become deputy amirs of the organization. The current director is Dr. Manazir Aḥsan, who is not a member of the Jamāʿat. The foundation is registered as an educational institution under the British law governing organizations with charitable purposes.

Initially housed in a small office in Leicester, United Kingdom, the foundation moved into an eighteenth-century mansion in 1976. At the end of the 1980s it bought a small conference center from the regional health service, some ten miles north of Leicester. This

Markfield Daʿwah Centre now houses the foundation and hosts courses and conferences.

The foundation traditionally has relied for its funding on gifts from wealthy individuals around the Muslim world, with some particularly large donations coming from Saudi Arabia; such a donation allowed it to establish the Markfield Centre. More recently, the flow of such donations has abated, and the foundation has resorted to more intensive fundraising methods.

In its early years, the foundation was involved in establishing about twenty mosques and community centers. It owns the buildings of the Sparkbrook Islamic Centre in Birmingham, although it has handed over the running of its programs to the United Kingdom Islamic Mission. The foundation was the first Muslim organization in Britain to establish cooperative relations with higher education institutions, working with the then Leicester Polytechnic on multicultural education and with the University of Leicester on Islamic economics. Ahmad played a leading role in the establishment of the Centre for the Study of Islam and Christian-Muslim Relations at Selly Oak Colleges, Birmingham.

During the 1980s the foundation increasingly concentrated its efforts on publishing; today most members of its permanent staff are working in this area. Regular bulletins on Muslim Central Asia and on Christian-Muslim relations have been published, and a series of books for Muslim children continues to appear. The Foundation has published a range of books on Islamic subjects, including theoretical works and those relating to various particular regional situations. Islamic economics has been a particular area of concentration, and, currently, a multivolume English translation of Abū al-Aʿlā Mawdūdī's large Qur'ānic commentary is being published (1990–).

The foundation has taken the lead in encouraging Muslim youth organizations, and it has a close relationship with the National Association of Muslim Youth. The wider Muslim community perceives it as being an expression of the Jamāʿat-i Islāmī, although the links to the Pakistani movement are personal rather than organic. While large parts of the Muslim community thus have an ambivalent view of the foundation (when it is not one of outright rejection), outside the community the foundation has established itself as a major representative of Islamic interests and expression, especially in educational circles.

[*See also* Great Britain.]

BIBLIOGRAPHY

Islamic Foundation. *The Islamic Foundation: Objectives, Activities, Projects*. Markfield, England, n.d.

Nielsen, Jørgen S. *Muslims in Western Europe*. Edinburgh, 1992. See pages 43–51, 134–136.

JØRGEN S. NIELSEN

ISLAMIC RENAISSANCE PARTY. Surfacing in the Soviet Union during the summer of 1990, the Islamic Renaissance/Revival Party (IRP, or Hizb-i Nahzat-i Islami) developed as opportunities for religious expression expanded under the policy of *glasnost* (openness) introduced by Mikhail Gorbachev. Just as the Soviet Tatars persuaded Stalin in 1942 to allow the formal Islamic hierarchy to function, so too the formation of the IRP began under Tatar Islamic leadership. The movement for Islamic revival represents the convergence of two streams in Soviet Islam—one official and represented by the four official directorates (at Ufa, Makhachkala, Tashkent, and Baku), and the other unofficial and underground. As the Soviet Union disintegrated, the support system for the maintenance of the official and restricted structure of Islam, marked by a limited number of functioning mosques, trained clergy, and seminaries (*madrasahs*), also began to diminish. This shifting situation allowed the emergence of young, educated, outspoken clerics who were less subservient to the directives of the Communist Party, and it removed the fear of persecution that had kept influential religious leaders underground. While some clerics were removed as a result of popular protest (for example, Muftī Ziauddin Babakhanov), others achieved wide influence (Muftī Tajuddin and Qazi Akbar Turajonzoda among them). During the period between 1990 and 1991 when the political situation in all parts of the former Soviet Union was fluid, the divisions between official and unofficial Islam became blurred, only to separate again in those parts of Central Asia where Islamic political activity unsuccessfully challenged the political dominance of the reemerging elites of the old order. The surfacing of unofficial Islam and the organized activities of the IRP have resulted in a transformation of Islam in Russia and in Central Asia into a more confident, moralistic, and potentially powerful force.

Organization. The IRP was established on the broad pattern of the Communist Party in that it was an all USSR party initially, with individual parties in each of the republics; parties were formed in Russia, Kazakhstan, Ukraine, Azerbaijan, Uzbekistan, Kyrgyzstan, Turkmenistan, and Tajikistan, and possibly also in Moldavia and Georgia. Where forced to remain an underground organization, the IRP was organized into cells. It declared itself an all-Union religio-political organization of Muslims. Its three fundamental goals are spiritual revival, economic freedom, and the political and legal awakening of Muslims with the aim of activating in everyday life the basics of the Qur'ān and the *sunnah.* Three methods to achieve these goals are outlined in the party bylaws: "to spread Islam by all the communications means available among all people; active participation by Muslims in the economic, political and spiritual life of the country; living, on a daily basis, by every member of the IRP a life according to the precepts of Islam."

By the summer of 1991, one year after its official formation, the party functioned openly throughout the Soviet Union, although it was formally banned in some republics, including Uzbekistan and Tajikistan. The existence of the IRP, even under the ban, exerted influence on the religious establishments of these two republics perhaps more than elsewhere. In Uzbekistan, the Office of the Muftī promoted Islamic precepts through all media, especially with regard to moral family life, proscription of alcohol, and Qur'ānic education. Moreover, the influence of the IRP could be seen in the extensive programs for the education of women in proper Muslim decorum and dress, conducted through the official Islamic establishment. In Tajikistan the IRP played a pivotal role in the opposition movement (1992) and in the subsequent civil war that has spilled over into Afghanistan.

Membership in the IRP is open to Muslim men and women fifteen years and older, regardless of ethnic background. Republic parties were urged to avoid ethnic exclusiveness and to concentrate on the Muslim *ummah.* Members must live according to Islamic precepts, support the program of the IRP, and be recommended for membership by two current members. Any member who joins another party would be excluded from membership, a provision that was intended specifically to exclude Communist Party members.

The members of the IRP are mainly small-town and village youth who have received advanced education in cities but whose formative years were spent in unobtrusively religious surroundings. Because the IRP agenda is specifically attuned to the concerns of youth and professionals as well as to the propagation of Islamic principles, the party attracts students. It takes a conciliatory stance vis-à-vis the religious establishment, although its political agenda keeps some clerics aloof from the party. However, the existence of the party allows for a more visible advocacy of Islamic customs such as observation of fasts, modest female attire, and national celebration of religious occasions.

Agenda. The thirty-two-point agenda of the IRP is marked by a call for active Islamic practice in all sectors of society, especially cultural, social, and economic. To this end it stresses moral interpersonal actions, the defense of Islam against the grafting on to it of any "ignorant contemporary" (i.e., non-Islamic) doctrine, and the resolution of disputes through the Qur'ān and *sunnah.* In addition, the agenda supports the promotion of sports and health programs, provision of welfare for the needy, private ownership of property, and support of ecological activity to restore human-caused damage to nature. The last acknowledges the degradation of the Aral Sea, which affects most of the Muslims of the former Soviet Union. The establishment of an Islamic society is the ultimate goal of the IRP; however, it remains unclear whether this means the formation of an Islamic government, as the IRP has yet to gain sufficient political power to put its agenda into action.

Activity in Tajikistan. The IRP officially formed in Tajikistan on 26 October 1991, although it had become active long before, especially at universities, polytechnics, and pedagogical institutions, and among skilled workers at factories and state farms. Its semiclandestine newspaper, *Najot* (Salvation), appeared sporadically during the spring of 1991. During the national elections in November 1991 the IRP did not endorse any of the eight candidates; its membership appeared split between the two leading candidates, although the youth tended to favor the candidate standing in opposition to the Communist Party slate. After the election the IRP gained legal status in Tajikistan for a period until, after the political turmoil of civil war, it was banned again on 21 June 1993 together with all other active parties in the country. Perhaps because its past was unblemished by Communist Party association (a problem for leaders of the other parties), the IRP was widely regarded as able to muster popular support from the outlying regions as well as in the capital, Dushanbe. For this reason it held a place of importance in the coalition that formed in opposition to Rahman Nabiev in late 1991 and throughout 1992. Additionally, Akbar Turajonzoda, the *qazi* (Ar., *qāḍī*) of Tajikistan, a vigorous man in his late thirties—though appointed by the official directorate in Tashkent—was regarded as a progressive activist by much of the IRP membership. The IRP became part of the coalition, to which Turajonzoda lent his active support.

Months of opposition activity and the division of Tajikistan into armed camps along lines of regional allegiance erupted into a civil war that forced many among the opposition to flee into Afghanistan. Many of these opposition figures were stripped of immunity as legislative deputies and indicted in absentia on criminal charges for "terrorism," a tactic specifically prohibited by the IRP.

Relations with Outside Countries. The IRP looks south to the rest of the Islamic world for models and for moral support. Some members regard Ayatollah Ruhollah Khomeini as a courageous if not model Muslim, particularly for inviting Mikhail Gorbachev to accept Islam or risk destruction. Others regard the Afghan *mujāhidīn,* including the controversial Gulbuddin Hekmatyar, as praiseworthy Muslims. Within their own historical background, Tajik IRP members prefer to think of themselves as following in the path carved by the Jadīdists or reformists of the early twentieth century. They share with the Jadīdists both anti-imperialism (against the West and Russia) and progressive ideas for the betterment of society. Because most Jadīdists perished at the hands of the Communists, they may be models for the idealists of the IRP. However, unlike the IRP, Jadīdism in general did not regard any religion, even Islam, as the route to sociopolitical development. The IRP has as its ultimate goal stepping into the modern world through the morals and concepts of Islam.

[*See also* Islam, *article on* Islam in Central Asia and the Caucasus; Jadīdism; *and* Tajikistan.]

BIBLIOGRAPHY

Gretsky, Sergei. "Qadi Akbar Turajonzoda." *Central Asia Monitor* 1 (1994): 16–24. Extensive article by an employee of the *qazi* of Tajikistan about the role of the Islamic opposition after 1990.

Malashenko, Alexie V. "Islam versus Communism: The Experience of Coexistence." In *Russia's Muslim Frontiers: New Directions in Cross-Cultural Analysis,* edited by Dale F. Eickeleman, pp. 63–78. Bloomington, 1993. A presentation of the role of the IRP in Central Asia by a leading member of the (Soviet) Russian Oriental Institute of the Academy of Sciences who gives the Moscow perspective.

EDEN NABY

ISLAMIC REPUBLICAN PARTY. Founded in February 1979, shortly after the fall of the Iranian monarchy, the Islamic Republican Party (IRP) had the approval of Ayatollah Ruhollah Khomeini (1902–1989), and its key founding members were among his top clerical loyalists. Foremost among them were Muḥammad Bihishtī, ʿAbd al-Karīm Mūsavī Ardabīlī, ʿAli Khamene'i, ʿAlī Akbar Hāshimī Rafsanjānī, and Muḥammad Javād Bāhunar. All were also members of the Revolutionary Council. Bihishtī was the secretary general of the IRP and the Revolutionary Council concurrently. The close connection between the two bodies was acknowledged by Rafsanjānī during the first party congress in 1983. The Revolutionary Council, however, had been disbanded in July 1980.

The IRP was not a regular political party. It neither institutionalized a party structure nor encouraged increased membership. Formal membership was never emphasized and did not seem important. From the start, the party served as a mobilizer of some of the traditional and reactionary forces of Iranian society. It formed a united front through a loose coalition of various Islamic groups and organizations, clerics, and nonclerical elements that endorsed Khomeini's version of an Islamic government. A multitude of persons and groups whose interests ran counter to the religious moderates, secularists, liberals, and leftists was utilized by the IRP to undermine these voices. The divided character of the non-IRP groups, their ideological, organizational, and personal conflicts, as well as their inexperience in the intricacies of governance, helped contribute to the IRP success.

Under the shrewd leadership of Bihishtī, the IRP moved swiftly toward monopolizing state power. It became a focal point for unleashing Islamic forces on grassroots organizations and independent groups, and it organized Islamic associations inside the workplace to counter the independent workers' councils. On university and college campuses, Islamic student groups were encouraged to take matters into their own hands. The IRP organized rallies and demonstrations against other groups, advocated purges of government institutions and the overhaul of the state bureaucracy, pushed for the execution of the officials of the previous regime, and ordered the confiscation of their properties and the takeover of some sectors of the Iranian economy. The IRP also played an important role in the takeover of the American Embassy in Tehran in November 1979.

These activities did not always occur under the rubric

of the IRP or the person of Ayatollah Khomeini. The presence of autonomous and semiautonomous groups and individuals in the party facilitated a chain of action with the sole purpose of eliminating those perceived as the enemies of the revolution and guaranteeing governance for the Khomeini loyalists. For example, although Sipāh-i Pasdarān-i Inqilāb-i Islāmī (the Revolutionary Guards) and the Ḥizbullāh (the Party of God) adherents were not part of the IRP, they served as its agents. [*See* Sipāh-i Pasdarān-i Inqilāb-i Islāmī; *and* Ḥizbullāh, *article on* Ḥizbullāh in Iran.] Also, not all pro-Khomeini clerics and groups were supportive of the IRP or of Bihishtī. The most prominent among these nonsupporters were members of the religiously conservative Jamʿīyah-yi Mudarrisīn-i Qom (Theological Teachers' Association of Qom). The teachers' group was sharply critical of the idea of a political party, but since such groups could not dominate the political scene or singlehandedly eliminate the liberal or left factions, it sided with the IRP. Other groups, such as the Jamʿīyah-yi Rūḥānīyat-i Mubāriz (Association of the Combatant Clerics) never directly joined the IRP but formed a temporary coalition in order to gain a foothold in the 1980 parliamentary elections.

A majority of the elected candidates to the Majlis-i Khabarīgān (Assembly of Experts), a crucial body charged with drafting a new constitution, came from the IRP coalition. Ayatollah Bihishtī became vice chair of the Assembly of Experts and ran most of its public and private meetings. The Revolutionary Council and the IRP vigorously campaigned for the approval of the constitution in the December 1979 referendum.

Abol-Hasan Bani Sadr's election in January 1980 as the first president of postrevolutionary Iran was a significant setback for the IRP. The party had pressed for the postponement of the presidential elections until the last day. Bani Sadr's close connection to Khomeini, his popularity among the anti-IRP groups, and the top clerics' general ambivalence about the IRP's capability to govern joined to bring about the IRP defeat in January 1980. Yet in February, Bihishtī, maintaining all his previous positions, became the head of the Supreme Court.

Thereafter, the IRP put all of its efforts into gaining a majority in the first parliamentary elections after the revolution, to be held in March 1980. Several developments are of political significance. In mid-February 1980, the Revolutionary Council decided to change the election law. An absolute majority was required in order to win the first round of balloting, failing which the top two candidates had to participate in a runoff election. With the exception of the IRP, most groups and organizations opposed the two rounds of balloting, arguing that it worked to the disadvantage of small parties. The IRP then moved to form a grand coalition of diverse Islamic groups. It also used its connections and clout to change the boundaries of various constituencies to the IRP's advantage. Obstruction of the campaigns of other political parties was systematic. Many small-party candidates were disqualified and demonstrations were disallowed; Friday prayer sermons and religious broadcasts on television and radio were used as campaign forums. On the day of the elections, fraud and irregularities were rampant. The result was an impressive success for the IRP and the independent Islamic elements. About half of those elected in the first round in March and more than half in the second round of elections in May were part of the IRP coalition. Rafsanjānī was elected speaker of the Majlis (parliament) on 20 July 1980.

IRP control of the parliament presented an added challenge to Bani Sadr. The IRP and the president clashed over many issues, including the choice of a prime minister and cabinet heads. Muḥammad ʿAlī Rajā'ī, a Majlis deputy from Tehran and an IRP member, was imposed as prime minister on the president, touching off a constitutional crisis and immobilizing state functions. Ignoring the chain of command, Rajā'i regularly opposed Bani Sadr. These confrontations came to symbolize anticlerical versus clerical rule. Petitions were signed and demonstrations were held asking for the dissolution of the IRP. Grand Ayatollahs ʿAbd Allāh Shīrāzī and Ḥasan Ṭabāṭabā'ī Qummī declared their support for the president. Ayatollah Khomeini interceded, asking all sides to cease their quarrels, but to no avail. The IRP's propaganda and mobilization of street mobs and parliamentary deputies eventually resulted in Bani Sadr's removal by Khomeini on 22 June 1981 and a major crackdown against all anticlerical groups. The Temporary Council of the Presidency was established to oversee the change. Its three members were Bihishtī, Rajā'ī, and Rafsanjānī.

On 28 June, 1981, the IRP headquarters in Tehran was destroyed in a major bomb blast. Seventy-four people were killed, including Bihishtī, Majlis deputies, high-ranking government officials, and other party members. Although the government blamed the organization known as the Mujāhidīn-i Khalq, no one claimed responsibility for the blast. This fueled rumors that interclerical rivalry and anti-Bihishtī sentiments were responsible for the bombing. [*See* Mujāhidīn, *article on* Mujāhidīn-i Khalq.]

Muḥammad Javād Bāhunar, the minister of education, became secretary-general of the party; in July elections Rajā'ī was elected president (confirmed by Khomeini on 2 August 1981), and he chose Bāhunar as his prime minister. Mūsavī Ardabīlī replaced Bihishtī as the head of the Supreme Court. On 30 August 1981, both Bāhunar and Rajā'ī were killed in another bomb blast in the premier's office. Again, with impressive speed, the regime moved to fill the gap. Khamene'i became secretary-general of the IRP and, in October, was elected the third president of the Islamic Republic of Iran. He held both positions concurrently until the dissolution of the IRP in 1987.

The goals of the IRP were not spelled out until its first and last party congress in May 1983. Many observers believe that the congress was convened in order to regroup the party and save it from internal fracture. Prior to this date, the IRP had not issued any document on its general ideological outlook. The congress revealed that the goal of the party was to bring together and coordinate dispersed Islamic forces in order to prevent them from neutralizing each other. Difficulties and sharp ideological divisions in the party were acknowledged, yet party members were urged to cooperate with nonparty persons and groups, because they were a valuable asset to the Islamic regime. No statements were made on possible plans to increase membership. Reports indicated that around a thousand members and several nonparty political dignitaries were invited as guests and observers. For the first time, a general plan of action was approved and members were voted on for two councils: the Central Council of the party and the Council of Jurisdiction. The latter's task was to mitigate infighting and to remove factional disputes. Its five members were Khamene'i, Rafsanjānī, Muḥammad-Mahdī Rabbānī Amlishī, ʿAbbās-Vaʿẓ Ṭabarsī, and Muḥammad ʿAlī Muvaḥḥidī Kirmānī.

The precise ideological orientation of the IRP is more difficult to describe. It was a goal-oriented party whose task, the institutionalization of an Islamic state, had already been accomplished. It is clear, however, that the fall of Bani Sadr and the death of Bihishtī prompted a resurfacing of personal and ideological conflicts among Islamic forces. Bihishtī's death, in particular, marked the beginning of the end for the IRP. His sagacious and farsighted managerial skill and his ability to bring together diverse and hostile forces under the party umbrella were lost forever. The nature of the intraelite conflict remains obscure owing to its fluid nature, secrecy, and personalism. Personal rivalries were often disguised as ideological disagreements, and individuals shifted their positions and allegiances from one group or issue to another. Adding to the confusion is that certain groups and individual clergy already independent from the IRP still worked with the party on issues of mutual interest. This was acceptable to the party, which did not attempt to coerce any entity into joining the organization; there was no particular reward or punishment for membership. These independent centers of power were both a source of attraction and emulation by inner-party circles.

Observers of elite factionalism have identified various tendencies within the IRP. Although a concise categorization is an impossible task, some conflicting ideological tendencies are identifiable. In 1983, on the eve of the formation of the Assembly of Experts to decide on a successor to Khomeini, a number of ideological clashes resurfaced. The naming of Husein Ali Montazeri (Ḥusayn ʿAlī Muntaẓirī) as the successor to Khomeini prompted a public display of political and personal rifts. Two prominent camps were referred to as the Maktabī and the Ḥujjatīyah groups. Each embraced several minigroups with clerical adherents from the IRP. The two groups seem to have differed on the type of leadership that they wanted in the post-Khomeini era (individual cleric versus collective leadership), the nature of social and economic reform (strong centralized government versus less government monopoly), the extent of clerical involvement in politics (more active versus a less-visible role), and several other issues. In the summer of 1983, the Ḥujjatīyah group was attacked in the media and accused of being antirevolutionary and in doubt of Khomeini's leadership. Then, public references to the Ḥujjatīyah suddenly ceased, prompting rumors that the group had suspended its activities. Rarely was there any mention of even the Maktabīs after this incident. Public displays seemed to have turned private again.

It is not certain which clerical elite belonged to which faction. Both Khamene'i and Rafsanjānī were rumored to belong to either group. Bihishtī, Bāhunar, and Muḥammad Riẓā Mahdavī-Kānī were identified with the Ḥujjatīyah. Prime Minister Mīr Ḥusayn Mūsavī, Mūsavī Ardabīlī, Muḥammad Mūsavī Khū'īnīha (the leader of the Students of the Imam's Line—the group that took over the American embassy in November 1979), and ʿAlī Mashkīnī (chair of the Assembly of Experts) were rumored to be Maktabīs.

Throughout 1984, 1985, and 1986, elite factionalism in the party's top leadership intensified. Khamene'i and Rafsanjānī were rumored to be heading opposing factions of the party. In public, however, they acknowledged the presence of factionalism but exhibited comradery toward each other. Some observers believe that the nature of the conflict was in terms of left versus right; the leftists were understood to be more militant on foreign policy and favored a state monopoly of principal economic assets; and the rightists were believed to be dominated by the rich bazaaris and to favor less central control and the toning down of antiimperialist rhetoric. The two factions were unable to reach an agreement or to compromise.

Another dimension of this conflict is the dubious role played by small associations, individual cliques, and sympathizers. The followers of one faction who worked in semiautonomous institutions and government offices and ministries could easily undermine any coherent action by the opposite side. Smaller groups were splitting into several subfactions.

In an environment of much less diversity and of clerical domination, war with Iraq, popular discontent, and elite factionalism, the second parliamentary elections were held in 1984. Voters were told that they had options other than the Islamic Republican Party and the clerics. The IRP list of candidates appeared along with other groups and associations' lists. Almost two-thirds of the candidates appeared on most lists, yet beneath the surface, there was fierce competition between the two dominant party factions. The election resulted in the IRP being the only political party and holding a little less than half of the parliamentary seats.

In October 1985, Khamene'i became president for a second term. Factionalism remained and rivalries were exposed in the presidential campaign, as well as in the nomination of Prime Minister Mūsavī. A significant feature of this presidential election was the way in which groups and individuals were trying to disassociate themselves from the party. For instance, Sayyid Maḥmūd Kāshānī, who was an IRP member, ran against Khamene'i, claiming that he was not a member of the party. Meanwhile, both Khomeini and Montazeri made repeated appeals to various factions to stop their infighting.

Public exposure of the secret negotiations with the United States and the Reagan administration in the Iran-Contra affair further worsened the inner-party struggle. A major meeting of the party elite failed to bring about a peaceful resolution. The Central Council of the IRP discussed the viability of different options, including maintaining the party, dissolving it, or dividing it into several parties. Arguments raised at the inception of the IRP were raised again with more vigor. Ḥizbullāh, for example, unhappy with the title of "party" for anyone but the Party of God, now raised its objections again to the idea of continuing the IRP. Worsening conflict penetrated provincial and city levels, hindering party activity. In many parts of the country, party headquarters were either closed or operated part-time.

It is unclear which faction originally recommended the end of the IRP. It was rumored that the right wing favored the continuation of the party. Officially, however, Khamene'i and Rafsanjānī, in a letter to Khomeini, explained that under the circumstances there was no need for a political party and that the two opposing camps might hurt national unity. By order of Ayatollah Khomeini, on 2 June 1987, the Islamic Republican Party was officially dissolved.

[*See also* Iran; Iranian Revolution of 1979; *and the biography of Khomeini.*]

BIBLIOGRAPHY

Scholarship devoted exclusively to the Islamic Republican Party is scarce. Information for the above article was obtained from primary sources and the following works:

Akhavi, Shahrough. "Elite Factionalism in the Islamic Republic of Iran." *Middle East Journal* 41 (Spring 1987): 181–201. Outstanding analysis of the nature of intra-elite conflict and its impact on public policy.

Bakhash, Shaul. *The Reign of the Ayatollahs.* New York, 1984. Insightful account of developments leading to the clerical takeover of the state apparatus.

Bayat, Assef. "Labor and Democracy in Post-Revolutionary Iran." In *Post-Revolutionary Iran,* edited by Hooshang Amirahmadi and Manoucher Parvin, pp. 41–55. Boulder and London, 1988. Excellent analysis of the relationship between the independent workers' councils and Islamic forces, including the Islamic Republican Party.

Menashri, David. *Iran: A Decade of War and Revolution.* New York and London, 1990. Extremely useful interpretive survey of developments in Iran based on more than a dozen newspapers and periodicals and an array of reports from news agencies, radio stations, and monitoring services.

Schahgaldian, Nikola B. *The Clerical Establishment in Iran.* Santa Monica, Calif., 1989. Useful analysis of the evolution of Shīʿī clerical rule, including various Islamic associations and groups.

Eliz Sanasarian

ISLAMIC SALVATION FRONT. During the 1970s Algeria pursued an ambitious oil- and natural gas-based program of national industrialization that was initially quite successful in providing the urban population with education, jobs, and income. But with the oil price decline of the mid-1980s the program ran into a structural impasse, coinciding with the ascent of a new, postindependence generation to adulthood. For some Algerians the passing of the torch called for an epochal, systemic shift: instead of merely introducing a change in industrial policy, the entire underlying idea of catching up with the industrialized West had to be altered. Nationalism was dismissed as a rank imitation of the West; Islamism, with its emphasis on ancestral *(salafī)* morality and particularly on female modesty *(tawāḍuʿ)*, was offered as the truly alternative, indigenous path toward the establishment of an industrial urban society.

Catching up has been a difficult if not also humiliating process for any eventually successful country, European or non-European, since the Industrial Revolution. Not surprisingly, new generations have sometimes attempted to opt out of the competitive pressure and find alternative ways to industrialization that would also restore their self-respect. Islamism in North Africa and the Middle East is the most recent manifestation of the wider search for an indigenous alternative, sharing many of its attractions as well as its shortcomings.

Political opposition, Islamism included, was still illegal in the mid-1980s. But when popular riots against increases in staple food prices occurred in October 1988, the regime, still too proud of its economic achievements to contemplate fundamental economic reform, incautiously agreed to permit political pluralism; other regimes in the region were more careful, beginning with economic liberalization in order to maintain their control over the political process.

The Islamic Salvation Front (generally known as the FIS, Front Islamique du Salut [Ar., Jabhat al-Inqādh al-Islāmī]) registered as a party in March 1989 and rapidly developed into the main Islamist opposition party. Membership dues, contributions from the small business sector, and Saudi subsidies (acknowledged in March 1991) enabled the party to run an intense campaign for the communal elections of June 1990, and the FIS promptly captured 850 of 1,541 municipalities. In Algiers, Oran, and Constantine it scored 70 percent of the vote; even in cities of fewer than 10,000 inhabitants it ran no worse than the National Liberation Front (FLN). Everywhere in urbanized Algeria—except for non-Arab Kabylia and non-Sunnī Mzab—the party won the support of the mass of young men and women who had at least a primary education but were unable to benefit from state employment.

The party was led by an executive committee composed of the three founding members ʿAbbāsī Madanī (president), ʿAlī Bel Ḥajj (vice president), and al-Hāshimī Saḥnūnī plus Zubdah Ben ʿAzzūz (editor of the party newspaper *Al-munqidh*). They were all self-taught popular preachers except for Madanī, a former FLN fighter and a deputy in the Algiers regional assembly; Madanī also held a Ph.D. from the University of London and was a professor of education at the University of Algiers. The executive committee presided over a female executive committee and an advisory council *(majlis al-shūrā)* of thirty-five or forty members, appointed all members to regional and local party functions, and drafted all decisions taken in the municipal councils, such as the orders for the closing of liquor stores and female veiling. The party eschewed democratic structures; Bel Ḥajj and Saḥnūnī in particular made no secret of their distaste for democracy and the national constitution.

Central in the FIS ideology is the notion of a hierarchically structured, organic totality, the messianic society *(al-mujtamaʿ al-risālī)* in which religion and politics form a harmonious whole. The religious scholar *(ʿālim)* alone is permitted to interpret religion and law and provides political leadership; the Islamist *(islāmī)* as the propagandist of righteousness *(salāḥ)* inspires the ordinary Muslim; and the husband protects his wife, producer of men. Equality, as expressed in coeducation, gender mixing at the workplace, and universal national citizenship rights, are pernicious evils through which a still actively crusading West seeks to destroy Muslim authenticity *(turāth)* and to maintain its world dominance. In much of the FIS literature the positive message is overwhelmed by strident militancy, more indicative of defensiveness than of self-confidence.

The government could not retreat from its promise of national elections in June 1991 but tried its best to reduce FIS influence through the gerrymandering of election districts. The FIS responded with increasingly violent demonstrations and strikes that eventually caused the government to cancel the elections, declare a state of emergency, and arrest some fifty top and two thousand middle-level officials. However, when the other, mostly non-Islamist parties raised a chorus of protest, the elections were rescheduled. In the first round in December the FIS once more emerged as the overwhelming winner. With its leaders still in prison, the party gained 193 out of a total of 430 seats outright and was poised to win a large majority of the rest in the runoff scheduled for January 1992.

The runoff never took place. On 11 January 1992, the National Liberation Army (ALN) staged a coup d'état and forced President Chedli Benjedid, the engineer of political pluralization and ironically himself a former colonel, to step down. In the subsequent months the FIS was banned; at least seven thousand more members were put into detention camps in the Sahara; and nearly half the FIS-dominated municipal councils were dissolved. Remnants of the FIS went underground and began a campaign of attacks on soldiers and bombings of public facilities. The new president, Mohammed Boudiaf, an original leader of the FLN who had been invited from his exile in Morocco to give the coup a mantle of respectability, was assassinated on 29 June 1992, although FIS involvement has yet to be proven. The army struck back with force, but the government found it difficult to regain the initiative: with limited credentials at home or abroad and political reform on ice, the overdue economic reforms will not be easily accomplished.

[*See also* Algeria *and the biography of* Madanī.]

BIBLIOGRAPHY

The most detailed discussion of Islamism in Algeria is Ahmed Rouadjia's *Les frères et la mosquée: Enquête sur le mouvement islamiste en Algérie* (Paris, 1990). Two important articles are Robert Mortimer's "Islam and Multiparty Politics in Algeria" (*Middle East Journal* 45.3 [1991]: 575–593) and Arun Kapil's "Les partis islamistes en Algérie: Éléments de présentation" (*Maghreb-Machrek* 133 [July–September 1991]: 103–111). The main text containing the ideology of the FIS is ʿAbbāsī Madanī's *Mushkilāt tarbawīyah fī al-bilād al-Islāmīyah*. (Educational Problems in Islamic Countries; Algiers, 1986).

PETER VON SIVERS

ISLAMIC SOCIETY OF NORTH AMERICA. Formed in 1982, the Islamic Society of North America (ISNA) is an umbrella organization for several Muslim professional groups that have grown out of the Muslim Student Association (MSA), including the Association of Muslim Social Scientists, the Association of Muslim Scientists and Engineers, and the Islamic Medical Association. Various Muslim communities and mosques have also affiliated themselves with the ISNA. These locally based affiliate organizations vary in size, membership, ethnic composition, and styles of leadership. But, regardless of these variations, each of these Islamic centers and mosques are perceived by local Muslims as mirror images of the national organization, the ISNA.

The ISNA is headquarted in Plainfield, Indiana, where its general secretariat operates out of a mosque *cum* office complex built with funds donated by the United Arab Emirates. The building was designed by a Muslim architect, and it sits on Indiana farmland that is on the verge of urban transformation. The headquarters consists of a general secretariat run by a secretary general who is directly accountable to the elected president of the ISNA. The staff at the headquarters work under directors, who supervise the following units: Islamic Teaching Center; Islamic Schools Department; Membership and Field Services Department; Convention and Audiovisual Department; and Publications Department.

The constitution of the ISNA recognizes two policy-making bodies, namely, the Majlis Ash-Shura (Consultative Council) and the Executive Council. The first body consists of twenty-four members: seven of these members are elected by the ISNA's general body; five are elected by the presidents of the ISNA's chapters and affiliates; and six are ex-officios, including the presidents of the constituent organizations. In addition, the Majlis Ash-Shura includes the president of the ISNA, the ISNA vice presidents for the United States and for Canada, the chairman of the North American Trust Fund (the publishing arm of the ISNA), the chairman of the Communities Islamic Trust Fund, and the presidents of the following national organizations affiliated with the ISNA: the Muslim Arab Youth Association, the Muslim Youth of North America, the Council of Islamic Schools of North America, the Muslim Chamber of Commerce and Industry, and the Malaysian Islamic Study Group.

The society has a membership and support base of about four hundred thousand Muslims. Its leadership is drawn predominantly from the Muslim immigrant communities, although the number of native-born American Muslims serving in the organization is growing. Its members are kept informed of national and international affairs through its organ, *The Islamic Horizons*, edited by an American-born Muslim of Pakistani origin, Kamran Memon. Since its inception, the ISNA has held an annual meeting every summer. Muslim leaders from overseas are invited to address the gathering.

BIBLIOGRAPHY

Haddad, Yvonne Y. *The Muslims of America*. New York and Oxford, 1991.

Islamic Society of North America. *1990 Annual Report*. Plainfield, Ind., 1991.
Islamic Society of North America. *ISNA Companion*. Plainfield, Ind., 1991.

SULAYMAN S. NYANG

ISLAMIC STATE. Although the original Islamic sources (the Qur'ān and the *ḥadīth*s) have very little to say on matters of government and the state, the first issue to confront the Muslim community immediately after the death of its formative leader, the prophet Muḥammad, in 632 CE was in fact the problem of government and of how to select a successor, *khalīfah* (caliph), to the Prophet. From the start, therefore, Muslims had to innovate and to improvise with regard to the form and nature of government. The first disagreements that emerged within the Muslim community (which led to the eventual division of Islam into Sunnīs, Khawārij, Shīʿīs, and other sects) were undeniably concerned with politics. But theorizing about politics was very much delayed, and most works of Islamic political literature seem to have emerged when the political realities that they addressed were on the decline.

Historical Islamic States. Islam is indeed a religion of collective morals, but it contains little that is specifically political—that is, the original Islamic sources rarely convey much on how to form states, run governments, and manage organizations. If the rulers of the historical Islamic states were also spiritual leaders of their communities, this was not because Islam required the imam (religious leader) to be also a political ruler, but because—on the contrary—Islam had spread in regions where the modes of production tended to be control based and where the state had always played a crucial economic and social role. The "monopoly" of a certain religion had always been one of the state's usual instruments for ensuring ideological hegemony, and the historical Islamic state was heir to this tradition.

The main piece of political literature inherited from the Muḥammadan period is *al-ṣaḥīfah*, the document often known as the Constitution of Medina, the text of which is attributed mostly to the Hijrah episode of 622 to 624. This constitution speaks of the believers as forming one *ummah* (community), which also includes the Jews of Medina. Although composed of tribes, each of which is responsible for the conduct of its members, the *ummah* as a whole is to act collectively in enforcing social order and security and in confronting enemies in times of war and peace.

Given the limited nature of political stipulations in the Qur'ān and the *ḥadīth*s, Muslims have had to borrow and to improvise in developing their political systems. These systems, however, have been inspired by *sharīʿah* (Islamic law) as represented in the Qur'ān and the *sunnah;* by Arabian tribal traditions; and by the political heritage of the lands Muslims conquered, especially Persian and Byzantine traditions. The influence of the first source was more noticeable during the era of the first four Rāshidūn (rightly guided) caliphs (632–661), the second during the Umayyad dynasty (661–750), and the third during the ʿAbbāsid (749–1258) and Ottoman (1281–1922) dynasties.

Muslims had indeed been state builders, in the practical sense, in such fields as military expansion, government arrangements, and administrative techniques—in this respect they probably preceded Europeans. But these were not really states in the modern sense of the term: they were externally imperial systems, and internally dynastic systems, akin to many other ancient and medieval systems that are normally distinguished from the modern state. Since the state is a Western concept, representing a European phenomenon that developed between the sixteenth and twentieth centuries in relation to various factors including the Renaissance and the growth of capitalism and individualism, it is natural not to find such a concept in Islamic thought prior to the modern era. However, Islamic political thought did have much to say about the body-politic and, of course, about rulers and governments: this, when examined and reconstructed, can give us an understanding of what is the closest thing to the concept of the state in traditional Islamic thinking. If the concept of the state in Europe cannot be understood in isolation from the concepts of individualism, liberty, and law, the Islamic concept of the body-politic cannot be understood in isolation from the concepts of *jamāʿa* or *ummah* (the group or the community), *ʿadl* or *ʿadālah* (justice or fairness), and *qiyādah* or *imāmah* (leadership). Basically, the category of politics in traditional Islamic thought is a classification of types of statesmanship, not types of state; it pertains to the problem of government and especially to the conduct of the ruler, not to the polity as a social reality or to the state as a generic category or legal abstraction.

Islamic political theory took shape subsequent to the historical development that it addressed, and indeed most major political concepts did not develop except during periods when the political institutions about which they were theorizing were in decline. Thus, for example, the caliphate theory goes back to the period of the deterioration of the caliphate as an institution during the ʿAbbāsid dynasty, the appearance of more than one caliph in several Muslim cities (i.e., the division of the Islamic *ummah*), and the growth of opposition movements of Shīʿīs, Khawārij, Muʿtazilīs, Ikhwān al-Ṣafā', and others, against the Sunnī ruler in Baghdad. Indeed, the caliphate theory was mainly a Sunnī refutation of the arguments put forward by the escalating opposition movements (including the Shīʿah), and it represented a quest for the ideal, not a positive description of what was actually there. It was only with the process of *tadwīn* (inscription and registration) in the middle of the ninth century that writings on the caliphate emerged, first among the Shīʿīs, then by way of reaction among the Sunnīs, but most particularly after Muḥammad ibn Idrīs al-Shāfiʿī, (d. 820), a founder of one of the four legal schools, had specified the methodological rules of Sunnī thought and had enumerated the sanctioned sources of *sharīʿah:* the Qur'ān, the *sunnah*, *ijmāʿ* (consensus of the learned), and *qīyās* (reasoning by analogy).

Juridical Theory of the State. A brief examination of the main propositions of the juristic theory of the caliphate is helpful here, starting with the issue of legitimacy. Initially, Abū Bakr and ʿUmar, the first two rightly guided caliphs, had emphasized the aspect of legitimacy by resorting as much as possible to the nomadic-inspired tripartite principle of *shūrā* (inner consultation), *ʿaqd* (ruler-ruled contract), and *bayʿah* (oath of allegiance). This method was used in the appointment of their successor, ʿUthmān. Gradually, however, *shūrā* was overlooked, then *ʿaqd* and *bayʿah* were also dropped with the establishment by the Umayyads of a hereditary, semiaristocratic monarchy. During the ʿAbbāsid era, the contradiction between the legitimacy of government and the unity of the *ummah* came to the fore. Aḥmad ibn Ḥanbal (d. 855), founder of the Ḥanbalī school of law, established a precedent by opting for unity of the community over legitimacy of government in case the two were irreconcilable.

From then on, the emphasis in the juridical theory was on the authority of the caliph as a political symbol and the unity of the *jamāʿa* as a human base. The classical writings of Abū al-Ḥasan al-Māwardī (d. 1058) and Abū Yaʿlā al-Farrā' (d. 1066) are illustrative of such an emphasis. Later on, when the authority of the leader and the unity of the community ceased to be intact and absolute, the emphasis, as in the work of Taqī al-Dīn Ibn Taymīyah (d. 1328), was to shift to *sharīʿah* as a basis for ideological unity, since political and human unity were no longer obtainable. From the twelfth century onward, the main realistic source of legitimacy for the regional dynasties might have become the defending of Muslim lands militarily against invaders, whether Crusaders, Mongols, or Latins. This might have given the regional sultanic dynasties a new type of legitimacy for as long as they could confront the foreign enemy and keep it at bay.

Writings on the caliphate by such jurists as al-Māwardī, al-Farrā', and ʿAlī Ibn Ḥazm (d. 1064) are concerned mainly with the caliph—his qualifications and traits. Rights are classified mainly into those of the imam and those of the *ummah*. There is hardly any trace of rights of the individual. Even Ibn Taymīyah, who subtitles one of his major works *Fī ḥuqūq al-rāʿī wa-al-raʿīyah* (On the Rights of the Ruler and the Subjects), speaks only of civil individual rights over one's life and possessions and does not mention public or political rights of any sort. The subject of individual rights and the related subject of liberty receive very little attention from the jurists. This has indeed been the case until well into the nineteenth century: the Arabic concept of liberty has usually implied authenticity and lack of bondage and has had hardly any political connotation. When explaining the French notion of political freedom (*ḥurrīyah*) to his nineteenth-century readers, the al-Azhar scholar Rifāʿah Rāfiʿ al-Ṭahṭāwī (1801–1873) was obliged to liken it to the Arabo-Islamic concept of *al-ʿadl wa-al-inṣāf* (justice and equity).

The Shīʿī jurists were in a somewhat different position, since many Shīʿīs had to take office under Sunnī rulers. The Shīʿīs held that all government in the absence of the imam was usurped, and so they were not concerned to legitimize the authority of government in either its central or delegated levels. Their concern was to justify dealings between their following and the government and to allow some degree of participation by Shīʿīs in public affairs. Unlike the Sunnīs, Shīʿī jurists did not strive to impart legitimacy to government in favor of stability; rather, by having recourse to *taqīyah* (concealment of belief in adverse conditions), they were able to cooperate for specific purposes with the holders of power while refusing to accept any responsibility for the existence of an unjust government—this was, in other words, a de facto recognition and compliance rather than legitimization. The Sunnīs therefore ended up legitimizing government power, and the Shīʿīs evaded the issue—but in both cases, the end result was popular acquiescence and political quietism. Because the Shīʿīs were not politically dominant for much of the time and because they adopted the concept that all government in the absence of the imam was usurpatory, their jurists had much more leeway in the condoning or condemning of specific rulers.

In the Sunnī tradition, however, which merged spiritual *imāmah* with political leadership *(imārah; mulk)* in the institution of the caliphate, it was less easy to incite disobedience against the usurping or unjust ruler and remain firmly within the tradition. To resist government one had to resort either to open militancy or to spiritualistic disdain. In the first case, the group was subjected to unrelenting war from the state; in the second case, the individual was often subjected to a tortuous ordeal. The Sunnī juridical theory of the Islamic state was obsessed with an attempt at rescuing the community from its unhappy destiny by overemphasizing its presumed religious character. It pictured a utopian ideal of how things should be in a sort of pious polity *(madīnah fāḍilah)* far more than it described how things were in reality. The theory of the Islamic state was in fact little more than elaborate *fiqh* (jurisprudence) presented as though it were pure *sharīʿah*. But as this fiction was elaborated on and repeated over time, in volume after volume, it came to represent to subsequent generations not simply an ideal that should be aspired to, but a reality that is believed to have existed—history is read into the *fiqh* (which was prescribed by the jurists) and is then taken to be a description of what things were like in reality. Hence the continued political potential (and even power) of that *fiqh*-cum-*sharīʿah*, especially among the contemporary militant movements.

Political authority was understood within this jurisprudence as the instrument through which the application of the main tenets of the divine message is overseen. Sovereignty is not therefore for the ruler or for the clergy, but for the Word of God as embodied in *sharīʿah*. The ideal Islamic state is therefore not an autocracy or a theocracy, but rather a nomocracy. The state is perceived merely as a vehicle for achieving security and order in ways conducive to Muslims attending to their religious duties, which are to enjoin good and to prevent evil ("Al-amr bi al-maʿrūf wa-al-nahy ʿan al-munkar"). Legislation is not really a function of the state, for the (divine) law precedes the state and is not one of its products. The legal process is confined to deducing detailed rules and *aḥkām* (judgments) from the broader tenets of *sharīʿah*. A certain element of equilibrium and balance is presumed among three powers: the caliph as guardian of the community and the faith; the *ʿulamāʾ* (religious scholars) involved in the function of rendering *iftāʾ* (religio-legal advice); and the judges who settle disputes according to *qaḍāʾ* (religious laws).

The social functions of the state are the subject of very little attention. The concept of *tadbīr* (administration; management; possibly economy) is sometimes invoked, and the caliph is likened to a shepherd attending to his flock, but this is less typical of the juridical writings. The concept of *siyāsah* (politics) itself was originally used in the sense of dealing with livestock; its usage with regard to humans implies having to persuade or coerce the presumably less wise and capable. The leader in such a case must possess a certain clout (*shawkah;* lit., "goad") in order to secure obedience. The main function of the state in juridical Islamic writings is really ideological: the state is an expression of a militant cultural mission that is religious in character and universalist in orientation. The state has no cultural autonomy from the society; it has an emphasized moral content which does not recognize any separation between private and public ethics and which accepts no physical or ethnic boundaries—its civilizational target is the entire universe.

Although external conquests slowed in the ʿAbbāsid period, the universalist ideal came nearer to realization by an opening up to the non-Arab communities through a process of internal islamization. The state became less ethnically derived and more abstract and autonomous through the creation of a regular army and differentiated administrative and financial institutions, while maintaining a cosmopolitan but broadly Islamic character. Gradually, an Islamic political theory would be elaborated, premised on the principle of obedience to the ruler and the necessity of avoiding civil strife. This theory would gradually owe less and less to the nomadic egalitarian ethos and would become increasingly "orientalized." From Iranian culture in particular the concept was borrowed of a whole cosmology in which everything is arranged in a certain order, governed by a universal principle of hierarchy: a hierarchy of things, of "organs," of individuals and groups. Everyone has a proper station and rank in a stable and happy order, with the caliph/king standing at the top of the social pyramid. His authority is made to sound almost divine (he is now the successor of God—not of Muḥammad—on earth), and opposition to him, bringing strife to the Islamic community, is made to sound tantamount to downright blasphemy. And so it continued until the end of the eighteenth century.

Modern Intellectual Contributions. It is possible to say that up to the beginning of the nineteenth century Muslims thought of politics in terms of the *ummah* (a term originally connoting any ethnic or religious community but eventually becoming nearly synonymous with the universal Islamic community) and of a caliphate or a sultanate (i.e., government or rule of a more religious or a more political character, respectively). A concept of the state that might link the community and the government was not to develop until later on. The term *dawlah* (used today to connote "state" in the European sense) existed in the Qur'ān and was indeed used by medieval Muslim authors. However, in its verbal form, the word originally meant "to turn, rotate, or alternate." In the ʿAbbāsid and subsequent periods, it was often used to describe fortunes, vicissitudes, or ups and downs (e.g., *dālat dawlatuhu;* "his days have passed"). Gradually the word came to mean "dynasty," and then, very recently, "state." Al-Ṭahṭāwī paved the way for a territorial, rather than a purely communal, concept of the polity when he emphasized the idea of *waṭan* (or fatherland, as expressed in the French, German, and Russian words *patrie, Vaterland,* and *rodina*). Nonetheless he could not break away completely from the (religious) *ummah* concept, nor did he call for a national state in the secular European sense. According to Bernard Lewis (1988), the first time that the term *dawlah* (Tk., *devlet*) appears in its modern meaning of "state," as distinct from "dynasty" and "government," is in a Turkish memorandum of about 1837. [*See also* Dawlah.]

Islamic thinkers, however, were in no hurry to espouse this new concept of the state. Jamāl al-Dīn al-Afghānī (1839–1897) and Muḥammad ʿAbduh (1849–1905) still spoke in terms of the Islamic *ummah* and its "tight bond" *(al-ʿurwah al-wuthqā)* and of the Islamic ruler and his good conduct. ʿAbd al-Raḥmān al-Kawākibī (1854–1902) went a step further by talking about the Islamic league *(al-jāmiʿah al-Islāmīyah)* as a religious bond. He used the term *ummah* not in an exclusively religious but sometimes in an ethnic sense and the term *waṭan* when he spoke of what united Muslim with non-Muslim Arabs. He also distinguished between the politics and administration of religion *(al-dīn)* and the politics and administration of the "kingdom" *(al-mulk),* saying that in the history of Islam the two had only united during the Rāshidūn era and that of Caliph ʿUmar ibn ʿAbd al-ʿAzīz (r. 717–720).

The modern concept of the Islamic state emerged as a reaction and response to the demise of the last caliphate in Turkey in 1924. Muḥammad Rashīd Riḍā (1865–1935) started the move in that direction when, as a protest against the Turkish decision after World War I to turn the caliphate into a purely spiritual authority, he published his *Caliphate or Grand Imamate,* in which he argued that the caliphate had always been, and should continue to be, a combination of spiritual and temporal authority. He called for an Arab *khilāfat ḍarūrah* ("caliphate of necessity or urgency") and maintained that this would give the Arab Muslims and the Arab non-Muslims a state of their own.

The well-known dictum about Islam being a religion and a state ("al-Islām dīn wa dawlah") owes its origins to the alarmed reaction in Muslim circles to the final abolition of the caliphate at a time when most Muslim communities were suffering from territorial division under the impact of European colonialism. In 1925, the al-Azhar shaykh ʿAlī ʿAbd al-Rāziq (1888–1966) published his most controversial book *Islam and the Fundamentals of Government* in which he argued that Islam was a "message not a government: a religion not a State." Although there had been earlier indications of this idea (such as in the writings of the Syrian ʿAbd al-Ḥamīd al-Zahrāwī [1871–1916]) the unambiguous, hard-hitting style of ʿAbd al-Rāziq's book was unprecedented and provoked a vigorous reaction and an extremely heated debate.

ʿAbd al-Razzāq al-Sanhūrī (1895–1971) (the distinguished jurist who later codified Egyptian, Iraqi, and other Arab civil laws in a modernized form combining *sharīʿah* and European principles) could hardly ignore the controversy over the abolition. In his book *Le Califat* (Paris, 1926) he called for a new caliphate to preside over a general assembly composed of delegations from all Muslim countries and communities. Although al-Sanhūrī was almost a secularist (or only a cultural Islamist), the contemporary writer Muḥammad Saʿīd al-ʿAshmāwī credits him with having coined the phrase "al-Islām dīn wa dawlah" in an article published in 1929.

The intellectual evolution of the concept of "al-Islām

dīn wa dawlah" took another step forward about a decade later. The Indian-Pakistani writer Abū al-Aʿlā Mawdūdī (1903–1979) was a major contributor to its promotion. Indian Muslims had indeed reacted most vociferously to the demise of the Ottoman caliphate by, among other things, forming the Khilāfat movement. Partly the product of a siege mentality, most of Mawdūdī's political ideas were developed in India in the turbulent period between 1937 and 1941. But whereas many saw the emergence of Pakistan as grounds for optimism, what Mawdūdī wanted was not a Muslim state but an Islamic state, an ideological state run only by true believers on the basis of the Qur'ān and *sunnah*. Consequently, Mawdūdī directed much of his writing against nationalism and against democracy, because he believed that either or both would result in a non-Muslim government. A particular idea that would be widely echoed was his Khawārij-inspired concept that *al-ḥākimīyah* (total absolute sovereignty) should be for God alone, not for law and not for the people. Also influential was his emphasis on the Khawārij–Ibn Taymīyah concept that what makes a Muslim is not simply acceptance of the credo (Al-Shahādatayn) that there is no god but God and that Muḥammad is his prophet, but rather active involvement in enforcing the Islamic moral order on the legislative, political, and economic affairs of the society.

Ḥasan al-Bannā' (1906–1949), founder of the Muslim Brotherhood in Egypt in 1928, appeared to arrive at similar if less-sweeping conclusions about a decade after the movement's formation. From a moralistic and social emphasis, al-Bannā' began to move in a political direction and to speak in his *Tracts* (Cairo, n.d.) of "an Islamic nationalism that is far superior to any local nationalism." In line with the Islamic distaste for *aḥzāb* ("parties"), connoting division not unity, he denied that the Muslim Brotherhood was a political party, but he admitted that "politics on the foundation of Islam is at the heart of our idea." To him Islam was everything: "a belief and a form of worship, a fatherland and a nationality, *a religion and a state*, spirituality and action, a book and a sword" (italics added). Such a formulation becomes even more extreme with his fellow Muslim Brother ʿAbd al-Qādir ʿAwdah (d. 1954), according to whom Islam is also "a religion and a state." The two are so blended that they cannot be distinguished: "the State in Islam has become the religion, and religion in Islam has become the State." And "just as religion is [the first] part of Islam, so is government the second part—indeed it is the more important part."

Sayyid Quṭb (1906–1966), another member of the Muslim Brotherhood, has been a most influential figure for contemporary political Islamists. Arrested with other Muslim Brotherhood leaders following a major confrontation with Egyptian president Gamal Abdel Nasser in 1954 and sentenced to hard labor, he produced much of his politically relevant literature in the harsh conditions of imprisonment. The key concept in this discourse (especially as it appears in *Signposts on the Road* [1964]) is undoubtedly that of Jāhilīyah, total pagan ignorance. Inspired partly by Ibn Taymīyah but particularly by Mawdūdī, Quṭb gave this concept a universal validity to cover all contemporary societies, including Muslim ones. To counter this sad state, the concept of *ḥākimīyah* must be adopted in order to "revolt fully against human rulership in all its shapes and forms . . . destroy the kingdom of man to establish the kingdom of God on earth . . . and cancel human laws to establish the supremacy of Divine law alone." To achieve this goal, the *jamāʿa* (an organic, dynamic community inspired by the early companions of the Prophet) should be reformed in isolation from all polluting influences and according to a purely Islamic method and culture *(minhāj Islāmī)* that is purged of any non-Islamic influences, such as those of patriotism and nationalism. Through *jihād* (struggle) and not through mere teaching and preaching, such a group will be able to establish the kingdom of God on earth. It is only after establishing such a new Islamic order, and not before, that one should worry about the detailed laws and systems of its government. Such radical ideas have since guided several of the militant Islamic groups in the Arab world; groups that have set themselves the task of confronting the existing secularist states, which they find both alien in their spirit and ineffectual in their performance.

The one theory on the Islamic state that was to have the most direct impact on actual government was, perhaps ironically, that of Ayatollah Ruhollah Khomeini of Iran (1902–1989). Khomeini's most daring contribution to the modern debate on the Islamic state was his idea that the essence of such a state was not so much its compliance with religious laws as it was the special quality of its leadership. Muslims do not necessarily have to wait indefinitely for the return of the Hidden Imam (as in conventional Shīʿī teaching) in order to have a pious government: an Islamic state can be established here and now, provided that its leadership should come under *wilāyat al-faqīh* ("guardianship of the jurisconsult"). The "obligatoriness" of Islamic government, and more particularly the requirement that the jurisconsult should become the guardian of such a government, was not based directly on the religious texts but was deduced from the "logic of Islam" as understood by Khomeini [*see* Wilāyat al-Faqīh]. The important point to observe is that by shifting the emphasis from *sharīʿah* to the jurisconsult, any act of rulership that the latter might deem appropriate could then be defined as being Islamic. This was indeed the case during the years of Khomeini's leadership of the Iranian Revolution (1979–1989) and was particularly evident in his proclamations of December 1987/January 1988, in which he maintained that government has primacy in Islam over devotional matters, such as prayers, fasting, and pilgrimage. The Islamic government can thus break any contract or stop any activity based on *sharīʿah* whenever this is considered to be in the interest *(maṣlaḥah)* of the country and Islam. [*All of the major figures discussed in the preceding paragraphs are the subjects of independent entries.*]

Contemporary Islamic States. Further evidence for the thesis that the form of the state and the nature of government cannot be deduced directly and unambiguously from the Qur'ān and the *ḥadīths* is provided by the fact that the few contemporary polities that call themselves, or are taken to be, Islamic states are very different from each other in their most important political aspects. Such countries might be similar in terms of applying so-called Islamic penalties *(ḥudūd)* or of trying to avoid the receiving or giving of banking interest (taken to be forbidden usury [*ribā*]), yet they are very different from each other with regard to their political forms and constitutional arrangements. Nor do they usually have mutual recognition of each other as being Islamic states.

Saudi Arabia is taken to be the earliest contemporary Islamic state, dating at least to the early 1930s. It is a monarchy (a form considered un- or even anti-Islamic by many), although the king has recently dropped the title of "his royal majesty" and replaced it with the more Islamic one of *khādim al-ḥaramayn* ("servant of the two sanctuaries") of Mecca and Medina. Saudi Arabia owes its origins to tribal conquests and alliances, and it continues to rely on tribal solidarity for maintaining the cohesion of the regime. It does not have a constitution (the Qur'ān being its fundamental law), nor does it have a parliament or political parties, although it has a modern-looking cabinet and bureaucracy. It is socially conservative, although in terms of employment and services it functions in many ways as a welfare state. What gives the state its Islamic character is mainly the role of its *ʿulamā'*, who, following a strict Ḥanbalī/Wahhābī tradition, exercise an unmistakable influence through issuing *fatwā* (counsel) on social and political matters, controlling *sharīʿah* courts, and directing the morals police.

Although different in most respects, Morocco has sometimes been likened to Saudi Arabia in being an Islamic monarchy. The ʿAlawī tribal dynasty has been ruling Morocco since the seventeenth century, and part of its royal legitimacy is supposed to derive from its Sharīfian (related to the prophet Muḥammad) lineage. The state is constitutional with a certain measure of pluralism represented by the political parties and other associations. The constitution is unambiguous, however, about describing Morocco as an Islamic state and in describing the king as the Commander of the Believers and the Protector of the Religion *(Amīr al-mu'minīn . . . ḥāmī ḥima al-dīn)*.

Islamic Iran, by contrast, is a republic with a constitution, a president, a Parliament, and political parties, as well as the cabinet, bureaucracy, and courts; none of these institutions is particularly Islamic. The current state owes its existence to a multiclass popular revolution within which the religious wing, led by the Shīʿī *ʿulamā'*, was able to assume the upper hand. Islam played a mobilizational role and Khomeini's discourse made it possible to combine social conservatism with political radicalism and to construct a basically étatist economy in postrevolutionary Iran. The distinct features of such a regime have been the supreme role of the jurisconsult as "Leader of the Islamic Republic," the high representation of clerics in the parliament (Majlis) and the key part they perform in the Council of Guardians and Assembly of Experts, and the important role played by the Islamic Republican party (until its dissolution in 1987) and by the Islamic Revolutionary Guards.

Yet another variety of regime claiming to construct an Islamic state has its origins in a military coup d'état. Pakistan under Zia ul-Haq (r. 1977–1988) is one such example. Initiating the process in 1980, an Islamic legal code, to be applied through *sharīʿah* courts, was issued by decree, but this was resented by the Shīʿīs and scorned by the women's movement. Tightly controlled elections were held without functioning political parties. Interest-free banking was declared but faced serious difficulties, and commissions were formed for the islamization of the economy and of education. Such moves were halted by Zia's death in a plane crash in 1988, but the islamization trend has continued its momentum. The government of Nawaz Sharif was brought to power in 1990 with a coalition including the Jamāʿat-i Islāmī, Jamʿīyatul ʿUlamā'-i Islām, and Jamʿīyatul ʿUlamā'-i Pākistān. The political mobilization of the masses by the Islamic parties during the Gulf crisis of 1990–1991 and the formation of a United Sharīʿah Front prompted Sharif to introduce his own *sharīʿah* bill for islamizing the state, which was duly given the vote of approval by the National Assembly. The process of islamizing the state initiated under military rule was therefore continued by a government brought to power by elections.

Sudan is another country where the establishment of an Islamic state was attempted by a military regime, in this case with the process being resumed later by another military regime. Jaʿfar Nimeiri's regime (1969–1985) started with distinct socialist and Arabist leanings but was tempted, with the escalation in its economic and political problems, to adopt an increasingly Islamist orientation, in alliance with the Sudanese Muslim Brotherhood led by Ḥasan al-Turābī. In 1983–1984 the application of *sharīʿah* laws was announced, combined with sweeping powers for Nimeiri himself stipulated in the emergency law of 1984. Courts were hurriedly formed, summarily handing down severe punishments, including limb amputations. The escalating socioeconomic crisis and the growing resistance in the non-Muslim South, combined with Nimeiri's eccentric arbitrariness, resulted in a popular uprising that ousted him in 1985. But the Islamic movement had utilized its period in government with Nimeiri to consolidate its organization and to spread its influence within the country's institutions, including the army. This enabled the movement to win in various syndicate and political elections. When Lieutenant-General ʿUmar al-Bashīr installed another military regime in 1989, it was markedly influenced by the National Islamic Front.

It should be clear from these cases that although so-called Islamic states may adopt similar practices with regard to moral and social issues (pertaining to the family, gender, dress, drink, and so forth) there is hardly any similarity in the political features of such states or even in their socioeconomic orientations.

A heated controversy over the issue of the Islamic state has naturally accompanied the political revival of Islam, especially since the 1970s. A mainstream position recognizes that Islam is a religion pertaining to devotional as well as to social matters *(dīn wa dunyā)*, that it is indeed concerned with the collective enforcement of public morals. Such people also acknowledge the actual unity between religious authority and political authority in many stages of development of the historical Islamic state, but they regard this unity as a historical reality and not a doctrinal requirement. They would indeed admit that the doctrine and the jurisprudence have far less to say about politics in the technical sense than they have to say about many other moral and social matters, and that Muslims need therefore to improvise and innovate with regard to the forms and systems of state and government according to the requirements of time and place.

The political Islamists argue, on the contrary, that there is a distinct Islamic model of the state and government whose immediate application is mandatory. Their main textual evidence is the verses in Ṣūrat al-Mā'idah condemning those who do not "judge" according to what God has revealed (e.g., surah 5.44: "Wa-man lam yaḥkum bimā anzala Allāhu fa-ula'ika hum al-kāfirūn"). The most crucial word here is *yaḥkumu*. This expresses the related notions of "judgment" and "wisdom," and in the verb form it means "to judge" or "adjudicate." The use of the term *ḥukūmah* to mean "government" is much more recent, apparently not predating the nineteenth century. The Islamists would like nonetheless to impute the modern meaning of government to this Qur'ānic term. However, when asked to enumerate the political features of such an Islamic state or government, they either evade the question by maintaining that an Islamic order will have to be created first and then its political features will become clear by themselves; or else they will refer to matters of moral conduct and collective penalties *(ḥudūd)* with regard to things like the relations between the sexes, or the manner of dressing, or with drinking alcohol, and so forth, but not to political aspects as such (the formation of states, the selection of governments, the making of decisions, the representation of interests, etc.). The emergence of various so-called Islamic states in the contemporary period that have very different political origins, features, and orientations has not lent credence to the Islamists' thesis that the concept of the Islamic state is unambiguously enshrined in the religious text itself. But the heated controversy goes on and carries with it very important political implications.

[*See also* Authority and Legitimation; Caliph; Ḥukūmah; Imāmah; Monarchy.]

BIBLIOGRAPHY

ʿAbd al-Salām, Aḥmad. *Muṣṭalaḥ al-siyāsah ʿinda al-ʿArab* (The Term "Politics" among the Arabs). Tunis, 1985. Useful historical study of some political concepts in Arabic, including the state.

ʿAshmāwī, Muḥammad Saʿīd al-. *Al-Islam al-sīyāsī* (Political Islam). Cairo, 1987. The best contemporary refutation of the dictum *dīn wa dawlah.*

Ayubi, Nazih N. *Political Islam: Religion and Politics in the Arab World.* London and New York, 1991. Study of the intellectual sources, social origins, and political attitudes of the Islamists, who contend that Islam has a theory of politics and the state, the implementation of which is mandatory.

Ayubi, Nazih N. *Al-ʿArab wa-mushkilat al-dawlah* (The Arabs and the Problem of the State). London, 1992. Study of the ways Arab writers have conceptualized the state.

Donohue, John J., and John L. Esposito, eds. *Islam in Transition: Muslim Perspectives.* New York, 1982. Good, balanced selection of excerpts by Muslim and Islamic authors.

Enayat, Hamid. *Modern Islamic Political Thought.* Austin, 1982. Good introduction to Sunnī and Shīʿī political ideas in the modern period.

Esposito, John L., ed. *Voices of Resurgent Islam.* New York and Oxford, 1983. Useful mix of analytic and polemical articles on Islamic identity and Islamic resurgence.

Halliday, Fred, and Hamza Alavi, eds. *State and Ideology in the Middle East and Pakistan.* London, 1988. Good selection, including excellent pieces by Halliday, Alavi, and Batatu.

Ibn Taymīyah, Taqī al-Dīn Aḥmad. *Al-siyāsah al-sharʿīyah.* Beirut, 1983. Major classic by a medieval jurist with great influence on modern political Islamists.

ʿImārah, Muḥammad. *Al-Islām wa-al-sulṭah al-dīnīyah* (Islam and Religious Authority). Cairo, 1970. Balanced treatment of the relationship between religion and state in Islam.

Jābirī, Muḥammad ʿĀbid al-. *Al-ʿaql al-siyāsī al-ʿArabī* (The Arab Political Mind). Beirut, 1990. Interesting study of Islamic political thought and how it has been influenced by tribal and religious factors and by the "modes of production."

Kerr, Malcolm H. *Islamic Reform: The Political and Legal Theories of Muḥammad ʿAbduh and Rashīd Riḍā.* Berkeley, 1966. Subtle treatment of the ideas of two influential Islamic thinkers.

Khomeini, Ruhollah. *Al-ḥukūmah al-Islāmīyah.* Cairo, 1979. Arabic translation of *Vilāyat-i faqīh;* English translations also available. Main statement of the novel theory of "guardianship of the jurisconsult."

Lambton, Ann K. S. *State and Government in Medieval Islam.* Oxford, 1981. Solid introduction to the political theory of the Islamic jurists.

Laroui, Abdallah. *Mafhūm al-dawlah* (Concept of the State). Casablanca, 1981. One of the best discussions by an Arab writer on the state.

Lewis, Bernard. *The Political Language of Islam.* Chicago and London, 1988. Useful, technically competent monograph.

Mawdūdī, Sayyid Abū al-Aʿlā. *Al-ḥukūmah al-Islāmīyah* (Islamic Government). Jeddah, 1984. Influential statement of the "Islamic state" position. English translations also available.

Naṣṣār, Nāṣīf. *Taṣawwurāt al-ummah al-muʿāṣirah* (Perceptions of the Contemporary Nation in Modern Arabic Thought). Kuwait, 1986. Valuable, comprehensive survey of Arabic writing on community, nation, and state.

Quṭb, Sayyid. *Maʿālim fī al-ṭarīq* (Signposts on the Road). New ed. Damascus and Qom, 1985. Main statement on the "alterity" of the contemporary social and political order and the necessity of a complete Islamic reversal.

Sayyid, Riḍwān al-. *Al-ummah wa-al-jamāʿah wa al-sulṭah* (Community, Group, and Authority). Beirut, 1984. Good discussion of some major political concepts in Islamic history.

NAZIH N. AYUBI

ISLAMIC STUDIES. [*This entry comprises two articles. The first presents a history of the study of Islam from its origins to the present, emphasizing scholarship in the West; the second provides a critical analysis of methods developed in Western academies to study Islam as a religion, a civilization, and a culture.*]

History of the Field

Islamic studies arose in the ninth century in Iraq, when the religious sciences of Islam began to take their present shape and to develop within competing schools to form a literary tradition in Middle Arabic. Rather than treating the study of Islam within Islamic civilization, however, the focus of this discussion is Islam as a subject matter in the West.

Theological Beginnings. Even before the rise of Islam in the seventh century CE, the Arabs were known to the ancient Israelites, the Greeks, and later to the church fathers. Arabic names appear in the Bible; for example, an Arab named Geshem is mentioned in *Nehemiah* (6.6) among local tribal leaders who opposed the return of the Israelites to power in Palestine after the Exile. Arab names also appear in the Talmud. The historian Herodotus of the fifth century BCE knew of and wrote about the Arabs. After the rise of Greek Hellenistic hegemony in the Middle East in the fourth century BCE, it was Arab kingdoms such as the Nabateans with their capital at Petra in the northeast Sinai peninsula that provided continuing Arab contact with traders, travelers, and soldiers from the Seleucid and later the Roman Empire. In the early centuries of the common era, some Arab tribes converted to Christianity and served as vassal kingdoms to the Byzantine and Sassanian empires, thus providing cultural links between Eastern Christendom and some Arab peoples.

The European view of Islam throughout the Middle Ages was derived from biblical and theological constructs. Mythology, theology, and missionary evangelism provided the main modes of formulating what the church knew about Muslims as well as its reasons for developing an official discourse on Islam. Mythologically, Muslims were conceived as peoples (Arabs, Saracens) descended from Abraham through his concubine Hagar and their son Ishmael (Ar., Ismāʿīl, see *Genesis* 16.1–16). Indeed, some sources refer to the early Muslim Arabs as "Hagarenes." Scholars have speculated on the common Arabic root for Hagar/Hagarenes *(Hājar)* and the fundamental Islamic notion of religious emigration *(hijrah/muhājirūn)*. In the *Genesis* legend, supplemented by passages in the Apocrypha and Talmud, Hagar and Ishmael are turned out of Abraham's home at Sarah's insistence and under God's direction are taken by Abraham to the wilderness of Beer-sheba, whence they later emigrate to Paran (Sinai). In the *Genesis* account, God says to Abraham: "Do not be distressed over the boy or your slave; whatever Sarah tells you, do as she says, for it is through Isaac that offspring shall be continued for you. I shall make a nation of him, too, for he is your seed" (*Genesis* 21.12–14).

Religious Polemics, 800–1100. Judeo-Christian myth and legend could account, then, for the appearance of non-Jewish, non-Christian Arab monotheists in the seventh century. It was through theological polemics, however, that the boundaries that separated Jews, Christians, and Muslims were worked out in the eighth to eleventh century. Theological disputations *(munāẓarāt)* often took place in public or in the audience of a caliph or other high official, conducted by spokespersons *(mutakallimūn)* for the various confessional communities. The Nestorian, Monophysite, and Orthodox Christians (as well as Samaritan, Karaite, and Rabbanite Jews) had little contact with the Holy Roman Empire and Western Christendom in the early Middle Ages. Regarded as "protected" *(dhimmī)* confessional communities, Eastern Christians and Jews participated in the social rituals of public discourse and disputation with Muslims (and with each other); this required some knowledge of Muslim doctrine, if only for the purpose of refuting it. [*See* Dhimmī.]

European Christians and Jews, by contrast, had to construct their own understanding of Islam, again as a theological enterprise. Lacking the symbiotic experience among scriptuary religions living under Islamic hegemony in the East, the Roman church experienced Islam more as an alien "other," a non-Christian enemy to be converted and/or defeated. Whereas Eastern Christian communities could not mount successful missionary and military campaigns against the their Muslim rulers, Western Christendom lay outside of the territory of Islamic rule *(dār al-Islām)*. The Islamic conquests that began under the Rāshidūn ("Rightly Guided") caliphs in the seventh century were stopped in Europe at Poitiers, France in 712 by Charles Martel. Sicily was ruled by the Muslim Aghlabid dynasty from the ninth to the middle of the eleventh century, when it was reconquered by the Normans.

For the next four centuries until the beginning of the Crusades, Europeans lived in virtual ignorance of the religion and people thriving nearby in Spain. Like the Germanic tribes, Slavs, Magyars, and the heretical movements such as the Manichaeans, Islam was seen as one of several enemies threatening Christendom. It was not until the time of the Crusades, beginning in the eleventh century, that the name Muḥammad was known among Europeans, and then in a very pejorative way. Until the eleventh century the Bible provided for Western, as it did for Eastern, Christendom the exegetical means for identifying the Saracens as the Ishmaelites—descendants of Abraham through Hagar. This was the conclusion drawn by the Venerable Bede (672–735) in his *Ecclesiastical History of the English People* and in his biblical commentaries. Before Bede and Isidore of Seville, Christian exegesis had seen Isaac as the precursor of Christ and the Jews as the descendants of Ishmael. Now Islam replaced Judaism in the Christian world view as the alien Ishmaelites.

Crusades and Cluniac Scholarship, 1100–1500. The study of Islam for missionary purposes began in the twelfth century in the time of Peter the Venerable (c.1094–1156), Abbot of Cluny in France. This was the period of the beginning of the Crusades as well as the great reforms of monasticism, which was until then the main institution of Christian learning. Indeed, both the Crusades and the scholarly pursuits of monks—translating the Qur'ān and other Muslim texts—served as offensive measures against Islamic civilization, which formed the southern and eastern boundaries of Western Christendom. In 1142 Peter, then abbot of Cluny, undertook a journey to Spain ostensibly to visit Cluniac monasteries. Nonetheless, on the occasion of his journey he determined to undertake a wide-ranging project, involving several translators and scholars, to begin a serious systematic study of Islam. By the time Peter the

Venerable had commissioned translations and interpretations of Arabic Islamic texts, many salacious accounts of Muḥammad had long been in circulation, presenting the Prophet as a god of the Muslims, an impostor, a licentious womanizer, an apostate Christian (in one version even a fallen cardinal), a magician, and so on. The "Cluniac corpus," as the results of Peter the Venerable's efforts came to be known, was the beginning of a Western canon of scholarship on Islam. Peter commissioned renowned translators like Robert of Ketton to translate such texts as the Qur'ān, the *ḥadīth,* the biography of Muḥammad *(sīrah)* and other Arabic texts, particularly polemical texts written against Muslims.

In letters to leaders of the First Crusade, Peter made it clear that the mission of the church was his principal concern and that Christianity could and should triumph over Islam. Nonetheless, like a few other scholars, he was critical of the blatantly false accounts by Christian authors of Muḥammad and the Qur'ān, and he was also critical of military campaigns and slaughter, even of infidels, in the name of Christianity. Peter the Venerable's attempts to provide Europeans with authentic accounts of Islamic texts and doctrines was not well received by the church at a time when Western Christendom was attempting to drive Islam out of the Holy Land. The irony of leveling a critique against the Islamic use of war to spread the faith precisely at the time when Christians were marching across Europe in the first of several Crusades to retake the Holy Land from Muslims was not lost on a few Christian scholars like Peter the Venerable.

One of the most influential translations of an apologetic text was that of the "Apology of al-Kindī," a contrived disputation between a Muslim and a Christian set in the days of the caliph al-Ma'mūn (r. 813–833). Modern scholarship has not been able to reach consensus on when the text was actually composed; estimates range from the ninth to the eleventh centuries. The translator of this famous text was Peter of Toledo, a Jew who converted to Christianity and who contributed, along with other Jewish translators from Hebrew and Arabic into Latin, to the compilation of the Cluniac corpus. Al-Kindī's "Apology" gained circulation and popularity among Christian scholars in the Middle Ages because it provided a model of argumentation against Islam. These attacks focused in particular on the Qur'ān, the prophethood of Muḥammad, and the spreading of the faith by conquest *(jihād).* These three themes formed the main topics of Christian scholarship on Islam in the Middle Ages.

In this sociopolitical environment another kind of translation activity proved to be of much more genuine scholarly interest in Christian Europe. By the late twelfth century a collection of the works of the Muslim peripatetic Avicenna (Ibn Sīna, d. 1037) appeared and circulated in Europe. As more and more philosophical and scientific works were translated from Arabic to Latin, European scholars of the late Middle Ages came to view the contemporary Muslim world as a civilization of savants and philosophers, in sharp contrast to the popular pejorative views of Muḥammad and of Islamic religious practice. Another way in which the Islamic world commanded the respect of Europeans in the Middle Ages came from the Crusades themselves. The military and diplomatic successes of the Ayyūbid sultan Saladin (Ṣalāḥ al-Dīn, 1138–1193) turned into legends that circulated in Europe. Even the religious comportment of Muslims, observed by many European Christians to be simple and pious in the practice of their religion, earned Islamic religion a certain respect among some Christian clerics and scholars. [*See* Philosophy.]

Reformation, 1500–1650. As Europe entered the period of profound religious, political, and intellectual change in the sixteenth-century Reformation, the knowledge and study of Islam were also affected. In the fourteenth and fifteenth centuries eastern Europe had replaced Spain and Palestine as the main front between Western Roman Christendom and Islam. At the battle of Kosovo in 1389 the Ottomans took control of the western Balkans, driving a non-Christian wedge between Western and Eastern Christendom. By 1453 the Ottomans had taken Constantinople and had pushed back the borders of Serbia to the Danube. By 1500 the Turks exercised rule over Greece, Bosnia, Herzegovina, and Albania. Many Orthodox Christians in these conquered territories were absorbed into the Ottoman military and administration, creating a religious pluralism dominated by Islam that was at once symbiotic and contentious. The Orthodox churches, following longstanding practice in Islamic lands, were protected by Islamic law, and the Ottomans put the hierarchy in charge of the church's local affairs in the Balkans. Such measures in turn earned support for Ottoman rule from the church.

Western Christendom had a different relationship to the Ottomans. From their base in the Balkans the Ottomans were able to contend militarily with Europe for two centuries. In 1529 and again in 1683 Ottoman armies laid siege to Vienna, both times unsuccessfully, but with the clear warning that an Islamic empire was again a threat to western Europe. The Ottoman challenge did not go unnoticed by Christian clergy and scholars in Europe. With Sulaymān the Magnificent at the gates of Vienna, two humanist scholars, Bibliander (Theodor Buchmann) and Oporinus (Johann Herbst), ran afoul of the Basel city council in 1542 for clandestinely publishing a new edition of the Qur'ān. The matter was resolved in favor of publishing the Qur'ān by no less a figure than Martin Luther. The Reformer said in a letter to the Basel city council that no greater discredit to Islam could be presented to Christians than to make available to them Muslim scripture and other texts in Latin and vernacular languages. The Bibliander edition of 1543 carried introductory essays by Martin Luther and Philip Melanchthon. The view that a rational reading of Muslim texts would evoke self-evident indictments against the Muslim faith did not contribute to a disinterested European tradition of scholarship in Islam. The Reformed impetus to translate religious texts, Christian and Muslim, into vernacular languages, however, was of far-reaching significance.

Reformers like Melanchthon viewed the Turkish "Saracens," along with the Church of Rome, as the Antichrist of the Apocalypse; Bibliander saw Muḥammad as the head and Islam as the body of the Antichrist. Protestant comparisons between Rome and Islam indicated a tendency, found already in Catholicism in the Middle Ages, to see Islam as a heresy—as Christianity gone astray, rather than as a distinct religion in its own right. The threat posed by the fall of Hungary at the back door of western Europe was interpreted not in the favor of Islam but rather in the manner of the Hebrew prophets, as God's scourge for moral and religious laxness. It should be noted that the Reformers produced little new actual scholarship on Islam. In the sixteenth century published editions of the Qur'ān and other Muslim texts in Europe leaned heavily on the Cluniac corpus of four centuries earlier.

Discovery and Enlightenment, 1650–1900. New and original European scholarship on Islam was to develop in the late sixteenth and seventeenth centuries for several reasons. First were the new political realities of Ottoman aggression. The Ottoman threat to Europe did not diminish until the eighteenth century, when the Ottoman Empire fell into decline and the balance of power shifted in Europe's favor. Another factor that helped to raise European consciousness about the world of Islam was the increase of navigation and the accompanying expansion of trade beyond the Mediterranean. The expansion of markets and of military interests was a prelude to colonial ventures and imperial ambitions. Europe entered into treaties and alliances with Muslim states—for example, the French and Ottomans against the Hapsburgs. Europe sent envoys to the Ottoman court and elsewhere in the Muslim world, although reciprocal diplomacy was not as forthcoming from Muslim rulers during this period. In sum, the Protestant/Catholic separation within Western Christendom redirected much of the polemic to doctrinal disputes within Western Christendom, and anti-Muslim polemic waned somewhat. On the other side, European interest in Islamic lands went beyond the polemical interests of the church to include state interest in the potential for trade, politics, and military ambitions. European reasons for studying Islam were no longer confined to theological disputes about the Qur'ān, the Prophet and early Muslim conquests.

At the broadest level, religion was conceived differently during the Enlightenment in Europe. The recognition that other peoples had religions that were not simply heresies or aberrations of Christianity was an important aspect of the new concept of religion. The new theory of "religions" of humankind called for new methods for the study of Islam and other religions that went beyond theological polemic but did not replace it. Late in the sixteenth century the study of Arabic was introduced at the Collège de France, and by 1635, it was taught at Leiden in the Netherlands and at Cambridge and Oxford in England. It fell to the early Arabists to construct grammars and dictionaries of the classical Arabic language—work that has long since been superseded but that was essential to later progress and exemplary in its own time. The work of these university Arabists was the first broad and serious European scholarship on the Arabic textual tradition since the Cluniac corpus in the twelfth century.

An important result of the changing conception of religion during the Enlightenment was a new concern with the life and mission of the prophet Muḥammad. By the late eighteenth century some scholars saw in Muḥammad a preacher of a religion that was more natural and rational than Christianity. Others saw in him homiletical grist for the ongoing mill of Christian reform—Muḥammad the man of sexual and political extremes, some argued, was an example divinely provided in history to help Christianity avoid such mistakes. This latter interpretation of Islam serving divine purposes as a lesson for Christians was a modern variant of the view that had prevailed from the eighth century onward, that Islam had been sent as an apocalyptic scourge to punish Christians for aberrations of faith and practice. The late eighteenth-century variant, however, reflects the growing importance of the study of history. The portion of Islamic history that interested Enlightenment scholars most was still the life of Muḥammad and the military and political intrigues of the Rāshidūn and the Conquests.

Interest in the life of Muḥammad and other aspects of Islamic history was not confined to specialists. In *The Decline and Fall of the Roman Empire*, Edmund Gibbon (1737–1794) devoted a chapter to the life of the Prophet and the early stages of Islamic history. Gibbon paid little heed to the scurrilous medieval Christian biographies of the Prophet, relying instead on more recent European scholarship and accounts by travelers. He presented Muḥammad as a man of spiritual genius who, in the solitude of his Meccan retreats, conceived an admirably pure form of monotheism; however, with the emigration from Mecca to Medina came success and military power. The latter point is reminiscent of the ancient Christian charge that Islam all too readily spread its faith by the sword, yet Gibbon's assessment of Muḥammad was on the whole positive. The distinction between Muḥammad in Mecca and Muḥammad in Medina was to become a familiar theme in later European scholarship. So, too, was the attempt to credit Muḥammad for his spiritual and leadership qualities without going so far as to acknowledge him as a true prophet.

The eighteenth century ended with a European project to study Islam that was more thorough than any such attempt since the compilation of the Cluniac corpus. In 1798 Napoleon invaded Egypt with a military force, accompanied by a large team of scholars assigned to study and document the language, culture, and religion of the Egyptian people. The transparent link between scholarly means and political ends was to replace—some would say supplement—the evangelistic ends of Islamic studies in Europe.

Nineteenth Century. The remoteness of the Middle East and other parts of the Islamic world began to disappear in the nineteenth century. Steamships, railroads, and telegraph made travel and communication to, from, and within the Islamic world much easier. With this came increased opportunity for European scholars, missionaries, entrepreneurs, and travelers to encounter contemporary Islamic societies—an ingredient that had been largely absent from Islamic studies. Opportunities to discuss Islam with Muslims still often took the form of disputations between Christian and Muslim clerics and leaders, but the terms of these polemics had changed, reflecting new ideas about religion and the evolution of scholarly inquiry into the "human sciences."

One important development in nineteenth- and early twentieth-century Islamic studies was historicism, the idea that events like the rise of a new religion can be explained as being historically dependent on previous events. One implication of historicism is the denial of absolute originality to the historical phenomena under explanation. Another implication and result of historicism is the view that only Orientalists, Arabists who specialize in Islamic texts, have the scholarly skills to study Islam. Islamic history, religion, science, art, and other topics became the almost exclusive scholarly domain of Orientalists rather than of historians or specialists in religion, science, and art.

The prophet Muḥammad and the rise of Islam continued to be a chief preoccupation of Western scholars, joined increasingly in the 1800s by Jewish scholars as well as more secular thinkers. Characteristic of historicist scholarship on Islam was Abraham Geiger, *Was hat Mohammed aus dem Judentum aufgenommen?* (1833). The counterthesis of Christian historicist scholarship on Islam—that Islam was based on the model of Christianity—was epitomized a century later in Karl Ahrens, *Muhammad als Religionsstifter* (1935). Although historicism has fallen out of favor among most twentieth-century historians of Islam, the charge of historicism is still frequently made against those who discuss the rise of Islam against the background of pre-Islamic Arabia and the Middle East.

Quite a different approach was that of William Muir, who reflected in his four-volume *Life of Mohamet* (1858) the growth of evangelicalism in Protestant Christianity, with the expressed missionary claim that salvation is not attainable for Muslims because they do not accept Christ as their savior. Muir regarded Muḥammad and the religion he founded as dangerous to evangelical Christianity because Islam had borrowed so many ideas and locutions from Christianity as to be confused with some form of Christianity or a preparation for it. Muir rejected the ultimate consanguinity of Christianity and Islam, and he emphasized Gibbon's point that the worst of Muḥammad's qualities came in the later Meccan period with the accumulation of power over his enemies.

Expressing a different nineteenth-century conception of religion, the idea that religion is endemic to human nature, was Thomas Carlyle. For Carlyle, as for many Western scholars since the nineteenth century, a religion's authenticity must be judged in relation to its own intellectual and cultural environment. In his widely influential lecture on Muḥammad titled "The Hero as Prophet" (published in 1841), Carlyle argued that Muḥammad was an authentic prophet on his own terms, although he was less charitable in his analysis of the Qur'ān and Muslim response to Qur'ānic recitation.

The idea that human beings are religious by their very nature *(homo religiosus)* was to have a profound effect on religious studies and hence on the study of Islam. Throughout the latter half of the nineteenth century and the first half of the twentieth, various attempts were made to construct a science of the study of religion *(Religionswissenschaft)*. Characteristic of *Religionswissenschaft* was the dependence on philology as the chief method of understanding another, particularly an ancient civilization. Friedrich Max Müller (1823–1900) held that "he who knows one, knows none," meaning that one does not really understand religion if he knows and acknowledges only his own. That Islam could and should be studied as a religion in its own right was made possible by the academic science of philology. Müller supervised the *Sacred Books of the East* series in the 1870s, some fifty volumes of texts and translations of Asian scriptures into English. Volumes 6 and 9 contained E. H. Palmer's translation of the Qur'ān. By placing an edition of the Qur'ān in a textual series on Asian religions, Orientalism was linked with efforts at many European universities to found a scientific method of studying religions.

Orientalism and the Twentieth Century. The study of Islam as a separate discipline, like so many disciplines of the modern university, also emerged in the nineteenth century. The discipline was called Orientalism. Classical humanism with its interest in recovering the richness of past human achievement through the textual record, along with the lingering spirit of the Enlightenment, deeply influenced Orientalism. Nineteenth-century philology was moreover imbued with the worldview of Romanticism and its search for what is noble in the past and in the exotic "other."

Arabic manuscript work was undertaken mainly by scholars who were broadly erudite in biblical and classical philology. Medieval Islam left one of the richest legacies of written works in manuscript form among the major world civilizations. Thousands of manuscripts in collections throughout the Middle East, Europe, and North America have yet to be edited critically and studied seriously. The task of recovering the ancient literary tradition of Islam by producing scholarly editions of ancient texts surviving in manuscript form was an important achievement of nineteenth-century Orientalists. The training of scholars in the Muslim world as well as in Europe and North America to carry on this important work has generally regressed during the latter half of the twentieth century. As in biblical criticism and historical work on the origins and early periods of Judaism and Christianity, Orientalists had set about to reconstruct a critical account of the origins and rise of Islam. Nineteenth-century historians tended to see their objective the recovery and reconstruction of an accurate picture of the past, which the German historiographer von Ranke was to call history *wie es eigentlich gewesen*—as it actually was.

Some historians of Islamic studies have noted that Western Orientalists and orthodox Muslim scholars have tended to share a common trait of conservatism in their approaches to historiography. Orientalism has by and large accepted the traditional account of Muḥammad's life, the articulation of the Qur'ān in Mecca and Medina, and the early formation of the Muslim community. While disputes about the age, exact provenance, and authenticity of many of the sayings (*ḥadīths*) attributed to Muḥammad have been disputed between Orientalists and modern Muslim scholars, radical source criticism of the Qur'ān and other early Islamic texts has been attempted by virtually no Muslim scholars and by very few Westerners.

Despite the shared conservatism of historiography between Orientalists and traditional Muslim scholars, a great deal of criticism has been leveled at Orientalism in the twentieth century, particularly during the last twenty-five years. The most trenchant articulation of this criticism is *Orientalism* (1979) by the Arab-American literary critic Edward Said. One of the most important criticisms against Orientalism has been that it served European imperial designs on much of the Muslim world: from Napoleon's invasion of Egypt until the rise of independent Muslim states, Orientalism was charged with being the willing handmaiden of European economic and political ambitions. Another factor has been the wider trend in postmodern scholarship to deconstruct the sciences and disciplines that were born of the Enlightenment. As a result, by the end of the twentieth century, many Western scholars have preferred to exchange the academic departmental label "Oriental Studies" for less eurocentric labels, such as "Islamic Studies."

Another twentieth-century configuration of scholarship in the United States since World War II has been area studies. Funded by the U.S. government at select graduate institutions, the purpose of these area studies centers was to train Americans in the languages and cultures of non-American societies. Islamic studies have been carried on mainly in Middle Eastern area studies centers, but also in South Asian and Southeast Asian centers.

Some have argued that Orientalism is a frame of mind, a form of scholarly discourse about a reality, the Muslim orient, that has been under construction in the Western consciousness since the days of European colonialism. Orientalism set about the hard task, however, of reading and interpreting Islamic texts. It was at once political and romantic. The texts that held the most interest for Orientalists were the religious and cultural texts of Islam. It follows that the fall from scholarly grace of Orientalism has been associated with a decrease in competent linguistic scholarship on religious and other cultural texts by Western scholars. Area studies, by contrast, has been more focused on the study of Islamic societies in modern times, especially public policy issues, political science, social science, economics and development, and social anthropology. The study of Islamic languages and literatures has been seen more as a means to other ends, not as a humanistic ends in itself.

A different view of Islamic studies has been voiced by some scholars in light of the critiques and failures of Orientalism and area studies. Advocates of this view argue that research on Islam and the production of knowledge about it is the province of disciplines, not of centers organized and financed by special interests in government and organized religion. In this view, the quality of what we know about Islamic history should be judged by academic historians and not just by Arabists; the cultural geography of Muslim peoples should be done by scholars who are geographers, the history of Islamic science by historians of science, and so on. At the end of the twentieth century, this view seems to call for the domestication of Islamic studies within the framework of the modern university, rather than isolating it as a special subject that does not quite fit into conventional departments and disciplines. Nonetheless, the modern university is constantly evolving its construction of scholarly knowledge, governed by discipline. The current trend toward studying Islam comparatively in world history, epitomized by Marshall Hodgson's *The Venture of Islam* (3 volumes, 1974), may herald the direction Islamic studies will take in the twenty-first century. The increased participation of Muslim scholars and cooperative work between Muslim and non-Muslim scholars are also important aspects of current trends in Islamic studies.

[*See also* Orientalism.]

BIBLIOGRAPHY

Binder, Leonard, ed. *The Study of the Middle East: Research and Scholarship in the Humanities and the Social Sciences*. New York, 1976. Collection of substantial essays on the study of Middle Eastern societies and cultures, by distinguished representatives of the disciplines that contribute to area studies. Of particular interest are the editor's introductory essay and the chapter by C. Adams on the study of the Islamic religious tradition.

Hourani, Albert. *Islam in European Thought*. Cambridge and New York, 1991. Collection of articles and reviews (most previously published) about European and American conceptions of Islam and Islamic studies.

Daniel, Norman. *Islam and the West: The Making of an Image*. Edinburgh, 1960. Still important comparative study of Christian and Islamic intellectual encounters in Europe in the Middle Ages.

Ismael, Tareq Y., ed. *Middle East Studies: International Perspectives on the State of the Art*. New York, 1990. Essays by scholars around the world, including Asia, on the state of Islamic studies in their respective countries.

Kritzeck, James. *Peter the Venerable and Islam*. Princeton, 1964. Thorough assessment of the Cluniac corpus of writing and scholarship on Islam.

Otterspeer, Willem, ed. *Leiden Oriental Connections, 1850–1940*. Leiden, 1989. Informative essays on Dutch scholarship on Islam, including various assessments of the effect of Dutch colonialism on Islamic studies.

Rodinson, Maxime. "A Critical Survey of Modern Studies on Muhammad." In *Studies on Islam*, translated and edited by Merlin L. Swartz, pp. 23–85. New York and Oxford, 1981. Critical assessment of Western biographical studies of the prophet Muḥammad since the nineteenth century.

Rodinson, Maxime. *Europe and the Mystique of Islam*. Translated by Roger Veinus. Seattle and London, 1987. Excellent brief history of Islamic studies in Europe, with a concluding essay on proposed future directions.

Said, Edward W. *Orientalism*. New York, 1978. Polemical critique of Orientalism and its effect on European and American conceptions of Islam.

Southern, Richard W. *Western Views of Islam in the Middle Ages*. Cambridge, Mass., 1962. Interpretive essays on how Islam was viewed by Europeans in the Middle Ages.

Richard C. Martin

Methodologies

The term "Islamic studies," currently used in scientific and professional journals, academic departments, and institutions, encompasses a vast field of research with Islam as its common bond. References to Islam, whether in the sense of culture, civilization, or religious tradition, have become even more frequent since the appearance of a plethora of literature in European languages treating the notion of political ("fundamentalist") Islam. The literature speaks of Islamic banks, Islamic economics, Islamic political order, Islamic democracy, Islamic human rights, and so on. A cursory glance at catalogs of published works in the past three decades reveals countless titles containing the word "Islam" and its corresponding adjective "Islamic," indicating the subject matter of what has become part of "Islamic studies" in academia.

This interest in the phenomenon of "political Islam" is not entirely recent. Since the nineteenth century, Islamic studies, also called Near Eastern studies, have been a component of a broader academic field known as Oriental studies. The period from 1821 to 1850 saw the creation of the Royal Asiatic Society in England, the Société Asiatique in France, the Deutsche Morgenländische Gesellschaft in Germany, and the American Oriental Society in the United States, all of which served a practical purpose from the perspective of the colonial powers. On the one hand, these societies conducted ethnographic research and were therefore a source of information for the colonizers; on the other, they studied cultural and scholarly texts written by Eastern thinkers. This led to the publication by E. M. Quatremere of Ibn Khaldūn's *Muqaddimah* and, subsequently, to its first translation into French by Baron de Slane. The histories of al-Tabārī and al-Masʿūdī and several other Arabic texts were also edited and translated for publication. The predominance of philological and historical approaches, particularly in German circles, is evident in Theodore Nöldeke's study on the history of the Qur'ān, Ignácz Goldziher's work on the prophetic tradition (*ḥadīth*), or D. S. Margoliouth's study of Muslim historiography.

Traditional Orientalist Islamic scholarship had defined Islam as a corpus of beliefs and abstract norms that determine the various spheres that characterize a culture. *A History of Islamic Societies* (1988) by Ira M. Lapidus and several works by Bernard Lewis—notably *The Islamic World* (1989) and *The Political Language of Islam* (1988)—have been widely translated into all the European languages, thereby promulgating a certain vision and usage of the term "Islam." One need only contemplate the titles chosen by Gustave von Grunebaun—*Modern Islam, Medieval Islam,* and *Classical Islam*—to engage in academic discourse on Islamic civilization and culture. The latter two works reflect the creation of a "scientific" discipline wholeheartedly accepted by Orientalist scholars of Islam: a study of Islam based on Muslim law, Islamic political systems (caliphal states, imams, sultanates, emirates, and so on), and so-called "Islamic" architecture and art (which in fact reflect either a certain continuity with earlier pre-Islamic styles or a foreign, non-Islamic influence, as demonstrated by Oleg Grabar's works on the subject).

The fact is that in this treatment of Islam, Orientalist scholarship has exercised little or no intellectual caution in overgeneralization of the data concerning Islam. Such generalizations seem particularly unwarranted given that most monographs focus on a single culture or a single aspect, text, era, or author. The term "Islamic philosophy" used by several historians (Henry Corbin, Majid Fakhry) has not elicited the kind of theoretical debate provoked by its counterpart "Christian philosophy," a notion rejected by Emile Bréhier in the 1930s when E. Gilson attempted to introduce it. The aforementioned titles related to Islam have no equivalents bearing the words "Christianity" or the adjective "Christian."

The academic discourse on "Islamic studies" has still to proffer explanation as to how so many diverse fields, theories, cultural spheres, disciplines, and concepts came to be associated with a single word, "Islam," and why the discussion remains so one-dimensional where Islam is concerned. In contrast, the study of Western society is characterized by careful scrutiny, attention to precise detail, meticulous distinctions, and theory-building. Indeed, the study of Western cultures continues to develop along such lines and to move in a different direction altogether from the unfortunate approach adopted in the area of "Islam" and the so-called "Arab world."

The standard explanation that has emerged in the recent debates about this monolithic approach based on philological studies consists of reciting dogma or sacred Islamic texts. The discipline of Islamic studies faithfully and objectively reflects the myriad and sometimes confusing perspectives, levels, and views of reality expressed in the fundamental Islamic texts, including the scripture and prophetic tradition.

Where Islam as a religious tradition is concerned, however, the philological method has a drawback that continues to be either minimized or denied by its advocates among the Orientalists. In fact, philology rejects all legends, mythologies, and apocryphal materials in favor of authentic, verifiable facts, duly dated and easily situated in real space. Even after anthropologists had established the value of myths as a rich source of historical-psychological information, Orientalists continued to view and write history in a linear, factual way along strictly chronological lines, dividing historical periods according to successive political dynasties. Numerous ethnologists conduct fieldwork in Islamic countries, yet scholars of Islamic studies have so far neglected to engage in dialogue with them.

Louis Massignon's brilliant dissertation on al-Ḥallāj, the Muslim mystic, in many respects heralded the methodological and epistemological changes that gradually began to occur in the 1960s. Along with Goldziher, Massignon contributed to the recognition of Islam as a well-established religion based on sacred texts and, therefore, comparable to the two other monotheistic religions. Unfortunately, their work did not succeed in preventing widespread confusion concerning the definition of the word "Islam" used to refer to the religion, culture, society, political systems, and their intellectual production.

A further case in point is provided by the ways in which Orientalist scholarship ignores the reality of the Muslim community by confining itself to the written texts and the comparison of Islamic civilization and political culture with that of Christendom. It regards Islam as an object of study, a topic of scientific discourse, making no attempt to participate in the living Islamic tradition. Hence, in the study of Islamic law, Orientalism treats its historical development as an explanation for the "facts" of Islam. However, law is more fruitfully understood as a practice than as a fact. Law is an endeavor engaged in by fellow humans, not by aliens. Understanding a practice requires participation, if only the virtual participation of the sympathetic intellectual who suspends judgment and listens to another's argument. To understand Islamic law, one must be given some sense of what it means to think like a Muslim who is engaged in implementing the *sharīʿah*. The Orientalist tradition is unwilling to do this; it rests secure in its own explanatory apparatus. This security often leads to substantive errors, often owing to the Orientalists' refusal to recognize the presence of cultural elements that are underrated by their own political schema. Religion figures surprisingly seldom, and usually as a mask for power politics, in the accounts of Islamic law offered by Orientalists. The adoption of a rigorously external view of law creates a false sense of precision, as seen, for example, in the works of Joseph Schacht.

Chapter 9 of the Qur'ān, for instance, lays the groundwork for city legislature, the social class system, and the rights of the individual vis-à-vis the state as well as the Muslim community. Muslims constitute a dominant, elite "citizenship." These norms and classification systems were subsequently standardized and became part of the Islamic legal tradition: the social and political realms were divided into the spheres of "Islam" and "war" (*dār al-islām* and *dār al-ḥarb*). Unlike Christian Europe where the religious and political spheres became distinct domains, in the Islamic world the interdependency of the two was never severed. There is evidence today of a strong resurgence and dissemination of those early generalizations and misconceptions about the "Arab world." This amounts to denying the very essence of Islam by continually comparing its features to those that characterize Christian and European history, not only in theory but also in practice.

The implicit and explicit tenets underlying the notion of "Islamic studies" that follows will discuss the cognitive dimension of the social sciences, and, insofar as possible, analyze the extent to which scholars of Islamic studies have—or have not—relied on such an approach. Furthermore, it will make a case for certain methodological approaches that are considered to be inseparable from epistemological theories that would make it possible to integrate Islam and Muslim cultures into a global critical theory of knowledge and values.

A recently published monumental study by Josef Van Ess, *Theologie und Gesellschaft im 2. und 3. Jahrhundert Hidschra: Eine Geschichte des religiösen Denkens im frühen Islam* (Berlin, 1991–1992; volumes published to date), dispels many misconceptions that have proliferated regarding philological and historical methodology pursued by Orientalist scholarship, when contrasted with that used in the social sciences, particularly since the introduction of linguistics and semiotics. Van Ess's work represents the finest example of the German philological tradition associated with a historical approach. He has greatly enriched our investigations of historical sociology. The very title of his work reveals this clearly: theology is not treated abstractly or prescriptively in isolation but rather is historicized and sociologized; that is, it is placed in its historical context and studied over the course of two critical centuries. Moreover, theology is considered in its sociological context, insofar as the author seeks to enumerate the distinctive traits of the schools that proliferated during the second/eighth and third/ninth centuries (AH/CE) in Syria, Iraq, Iran, the Hejaz, southern Arabia, and Egypt. Van Ess's approach differs from previous methods, which focused on a description of each sect's tenets or an abstract list of sects, such as that found in Henri Laoust's *Les schismes dans l'islam* (2d ed., Paris, 1977).

Van Ess demonstrates with unparalleled scholarship that the westernization (or, to use his term, the "standardization") of Islamic thought and the appearance of organized religious institutions date back only to the founding of Baghdad and the creation of the ʿAbbāsid state. This historic fact has important methodological implications for the study of Islamic thought and the redefining of the loosely used term "Islam."

The philological approach taken by Van Ess remains vital to our ongoing examination of the overwhelming amount of "Islamic" resources available to us. Numerous texts have yet to appear in critical editions or to be read using methods drawn from philology and the social sciences jointly. In that respect, the Orientalists have already provided us with a valuable model for the critical study of ancient texts and the application of historical reading—a linear, narrative, descriptive reading of the texts rather than a deconstructionist approach. Until the 1950s, Orientalist scholars could only imitate their counterparts studying Western societies and cultures. Philological criticism and a historical approach to Christian texts during the nineteenth century were extended to the Qur'ān, the *ḥadīth,* and the books of *fiqh* by researchers including Theodor Nöldeke, Ignácz Goldziher and Joseph Schacht. But, whereas in Europe theologians adopted a historical approach in order to revitalize Christian theology (as did Rudolph Bultmann, Karl Barth, Paul Tillich, Jacques Maritain, or Marie-Dominique Chenu, Orientalists continued to rely on the damaging conclusions of philological critics where Islam was concerned. The latter limited themselves to denouncing conservative Muslims who refused to follow the lead of their Christian counterparts. Consequently, the field of "Islamic studies" was left in ruins, deserted on the one hand by Islamic researchers unable to make sense of foreign religious beliefs, and on the other by Muslims who, after 1945, adopted the ideology of the wars of liberation from colonial rule and the subsequent struggle to forge a national identity.

The present state of Islamic studies, then, suffers from the limitations of Western scientific reasoning when applied to foreign cultures or concepts outside the realm of Christian Europe and secular Western civilization. So-called scientific reason has been, first and foremost, hegemonic in nature; it has always imposed its classifications, categories, definitions, distinctions, concepts, and theories on others without fear of denunciation or refutation, except perhaps on polemical or ideological grounds. This has been possible because, to this day, the Muslim world that has been the object of all this "scientific" research has yet to come up with its own conceptual view of its history, culture, and religion—one that would challenge the hegemonic perspective and force it to acknowledge an alternative interpretation. A French scholar writing on Goethe, Kant, Cervantes, or Dante consults German, Spanish, and Italian scholarly works in an effort to be thorough; when it comes to Islamic authors, texts or cultures, however, previous research published in Arabic, Persian, or Turkish is considered negligible, with some exceptions. To make matters worse, scholars of Islamic studies constitute a closed group; they read and critique one another's work without incurring the risk of being judged by researchers in other disciplines whose techniques they should be using to analyze Islam. In other words, the key factor in a successful multidisciplinary approach is the researcher's educational background as well as his/her willingness and efforts to seek the opinions of colleagues known for their innovative perspectives.

The above remarks obviously do not apply to research in linguistics, literary studies, archeology, or economic and social history, since these domains do not necessarily condition, or are only indirectly affected by, religion. This brings us to a crucial issue rarely addressed by Islamic scholars: the epistemological status and cognitive aims of the social sciences applied to the study of Islam as a religion.

Status of the Social Sciences. Introduced a number of years ago in France, the term "science of man and society" carries global, all-encompassing connotations: it underscores the crucial notion that humanity is both the object and agent of scientific investigation. The fields of political science, economics, and law have over time become somewhat autonomous and independent from more obviously subjective domains, such as psychology, intellectual history, literature and the arts, philosophy, and theology. Indeed, because of their subjective nature, the philosophy and anthropology of law, the philosophical and psychological ramifications of production and trade, and the role of the sacred, symbolic, mythical and religious in political affairs have been viewed as speculative and have become fragmented to the point of being intellectually mutilated and mutilating.

Several recent books have clearly shown a relationship between the development of the social sciences and political science as fields and the increased, urgent demands of industrial nations. Logical reasoning based on empirical, operational, and productive knowledge—economically speaking—has acquired a status and dominance comparable to theological-legal reason in the Middle Ages or to Enlightenment reason with its indisputable ties to classical, philosophical reason.

This change with regard to the aims of knowledge has forced thinkers to adopt ways of looking at the world, articulating their ideas and dealing with political and economic realities that have resulted in a new form of intellectual approach that renders all talk and defense of the concepts of truth, law, and worth insignificant and lacking in credibility. Such an intellectual approach generalized through scholarship and teaching generated a hegemonic rise of reason interiorized by scholars as well as average people on the receiving end of such information. As long as Marxism and liberalism succeeded in convincing us that the ultimate stakes in their ideological struggle involved individuals' rights to seek the truth freely and to create laws based on "universal" values, we could accept placing practical concerns ahead of critical thinking. Since the downfall of Marxism, political and social scientists have proven unable to fill the void left by fifty years of illusions and ideological fever. Political economics, which reigned supreme for so long, can barely handle the contradictions and conflicts that characterized the period from 1960 to 1970, when so-called "underdeveloped" countries attempted to forge ahead by destroying their agricultural industries and traditional solidarities in order to embrace the industrialization they saw as the key to their salvation.

Modern-day political experts who speak of the "threat" to "Western values" posed by Muslim "religious fanatics" only occasionally mention in passing the "economic mistakes" made by "scientific experts." Their analyses never call into question the underlying hegemonic way of thinking that continues to set priorities based on scientific reasoning and to promote research methods, agendas, and programs grounded in the social sciences.

The single party nation-states that monopolize power in developing countries have reinforced this hegemonic reason at all levels of function while at the same time imposing a nationalistic ideology that exalts national identities and denounces Western "imperialism" or "neocolonialism." Thus they perpetuate political, economic, and social conditions studied by researchers but far removed from the real problems affecting their countries. As a result, Islam, which is claimed by the believers to be a model "superior" to the one imposed by the West for acting in history, has become a "collective fantasia" (*fantasm* in French), unrealistic and preoccupied with a romanticized past. This "collective fantasia" has replaced Islam in its religious, traditional meaning and function. It is the new historical force generated through struggles for liberation and national emancipation since the nineteenth century. As a new historical force, it has to be considered, analyzed, and interpreted by means of tools and methodologies of social psychology and cultural anthropology, and no longer through the vocabulary of traditional historiography and the language of Muslim orthodoxy. Neither Western Islamicists and political scientists nor Muslim scholars and intellectuals have made this shift from the ideological framework related to Islam to the problematics provided and required by social scientists.

In contemporary Muslim societies ethnology and anthropology are still rejected on the grounds that they continue to depend on colonial strategies. This is, of course, in itself a pure ideological posture imposed by the single party nation-states. In fact, ethnology, anthropology, and sociology as well as philosophy are seen as dangerous sciences because they may reactivate local identities that would be obstructive to the political will to bring about national unification. These fields are strictly controlled in order to limit their subversive effects on religious orthodoxy and, by extension on the state's legitimacy. Consequently, critical study of the religious phenomenon as a whole is excluded in contemporary Muslim societies and the fundamental tendencies inherent in each religious tradition had the possibility to develop and to relegate any scientific approach to Islam out of the approaches required by the new methodologies, increasingly elaborated especially in cultural anthropology, linguistics, semiotics, and critiques of discourse.

By contrast, apologetic historiography, which reinforces nationalist dreams, glorifies past grandeurs in epic style *(al-turāth),* and emphasizes Islam's "universal" values, has produced a plethora of widely disseminated literature. Some researchers have resisted this trend, but they are few in number and their work has not been substantial enough to counteract the destructive effects of the state's official ideology or the widespread and irresistible lure of fundamentalism.

It is necessary to analyze thoroughly this contrast between the current status and goals of the social sciences in the West and their precarious position and timid initiatives in Islamic contexts, where they are carefully watched. Such an analysis would enable us to realize the extent to which Islam, as a religion, as a tradition of thought, system of beliefs and nonbeliefs, and source of hope for millions of faithful followers has been the object of individual and collective *imaginaire* (this concept in French social sciences has taken an expanding import in the last fifty years), ideological manipulations, and descriptivist accounts by outside observers. The Islamic world has not benefited intellectually or spiritually from the kind of debates over theological and philosophical issues, controversies concerning laws and their interpretation, rich mystical experiences, and historical studies that have characterized past eras. Islam has been intellectually and spiritually disinherited ever since the Ṣafavid and Ottoman dynasties reduced the *ʿulamāʾ* to the status of servile guardians of an orthodoxy divorced from the *disputatio (munāẓarah)* among the different schools of thought.

Changes in the past thirty years have had even more dramatic effects than those engendered by bringing the religion under the state control since the classical age under the Umayyads and even more under the Ṣafavids and the Ottomans. Whereas areas of ignorance continue to spread in the so-called politically "liberated" nations, the science of "man and society" in the West pursues its task of arbitrary division of the world and fragmentation of the reality, disseminating and imposing postures of mind, models of knowledge, ways of acting and creating strategies of domination, types of articulation of meanings and so on which have led ultimately to the "We/Us" mentality aptly described by James Clifford as the "mankind of Western social science." This "We" exercises total intellectual and scientific sovereignty over all other cultures and countries by means of market economy "laws," universally accepted and adopted by all political regimes, along with their implicit philosophies, and rarely contested.

This far-reaching and unprecedented phenomenon has affected more lives and has had more widespread and serious consequences for the philosophical and juridical status of the human person as well as for the orientation of human destiny than did colonialism during most of the nineteenth century through 1960. Postcolonial countries can no longer express resentment or level moral accusations against the former colonial powers; their own elite classes have amply demonstrated their own moral and political weaknesses vis-à-vis their fellow citizens whom they claimed to have liberated from servitude by casting out the foreign dominators. Those intellectuals who persist in denouncing Western neocolonialism while neglecting to examine critically the past and recent history of their respective countries display an irresponsible attitude and ignore the irrefutable lessons of modern science and progress, which extend beyond the history of the West's domination of oppressed societies.

If moral protest is no longer an appropriate reaction, neither is Orientalist criticism—even less so. The fact remains that hegemonic reason, which reigns supreme thanks to the triumph of modern technology and the reinforcement of its "legitimacy" by means of market economy laws that supersede the social sciences, must be made to reconcile its claims for reaching universality with the humiliations inflicted on the human conditions and degradation visible wherever long-oppressed minorities strive to acquire their legitimate, inalienable rights to freedom and dignity.

Islamic studies as currently carried out in the West remains the victim of hegemonic reason. While rectifying the excesses of colonial rule, hegemonic reason continues to place "Islam" in an epistemological framework inherited from the Enlightenment—this despite the fact that the latter has been declared obsolete by all the creators, thinkers, and innovators of the postmodern condition. All of the recent literature on supposed Islamic fundamentalist, radical, or integrist groups only serves to reinforce the narrow epistemological confines imposed on Islam and the Muslim world since the nineteenth century.

In what follows we will examine the ways in which an intellectual, scientific approach based on recent developments in the cognitive sciences may be applied to the study of Islam and the Muslim world.

A Global Theory of Knowledge. By this phrase I mean a critical knowledge, continuously reconsidered in light of not only the new information provided in each discipline, but also the changing postures of reason facing its own procedures, postulates, and statements. This situation is well illustrated by the objections addressed by postmodernists to the reason of enlightenments. It is a fact that a majority of scholars in Islamic studies do not pay enough attention to these shifts in the postures of reason. Needless to say, this kind of epistemological issue represents what I call the *unthinkable* and the *unthought* for contemporary Islamic thought. That is why all social scientists and political scientists who just transfer into European languages the various discourses articulated by Muslims in the present context of their societies, contribute themselves to consolidating and spreading the *unthinkable* and the *unthought* in the scientific discourse of Islam beyond Muslim discourse itself.

Let us consider, for example, the following vocabulary currently used by scientists dealing with religions: faith, belief, sacredness, rites, myth, narration, symbol, parable, metaphor, time, profane, secular (*laïc* in French), spiritual, spirituality, divine, God, gods, revelation, interpretation, imagination, imaginary, marvelous, nature, culture, orthodoxy, heterodoxy, sects, truth, violence, and so on. Each one of these words has been worked out in several contexts by historians, sociologists, anthropologists, ethnographers, psychologists, psychoanalysts, and others. How are they used in the "scientific" literature on Islam in its classical and contemporary periods? How far, how often, are they applied as crossdisciplinary concepts to deconstruct—make explicit the implicit postulates—of all types, all levels of Muslim discourses? Ernest Gellner has done this when he deals with reason in European context (cf. his recent work *Reason and Culture: New Perspectives on the Past*, Oxford, 1992); when he writes on Muslim society (see his book *Muslim Society*, Cambridge, 1981), however, he just uses uncriticized, unelaborated old categories.

In my two books *Lectures du Coran* (2d ed., Tunis, 1991) and *Critique de la raison islamique* (Paris, 1984), I have listed a number of issues that should receive priority in a strategic program aiming at a new critical, deconstructive articulation of a scientific discourse on Islam and "Muslim" societies (inasmuch as one can speak of "Muslim" societies). Some of these issues are as follows:

1. The Qur'ānic phenomenon and the historical experience of Medina
2. Jāhilīyah, *ʿilm,* and *islām* as anthropological paradigms
3. The generations of *ṣaḥābah* and *tabiʿūn* (the companions of the Prophet and the succeeding generations) as symbolic figures of mythical memory
4. Living tradition, ethnographic traditions, and traditionalization as an ideological strategy
5. Authority, power, and the search for legitimacy
6. Violence, sacredness, and truth in religious discourses and collective practice
7. Oblivion, elimination, and repression as dimensions of cultural and intellectual history
8. Orthodoxy as an ideological process
9. From the societies of the *Book-book* to the secularized societies
10. The concept of hegemonic reason

Many other examples may be given of yet unexplored topics and fields in Islamic studies. In each subject mentioned above, it is easy to perceive the necessity to use historical approaches, sociological inquiries (sociology of the failure of Ibn Rushd, Ibn Khaldūn, Ibn Ḥazm, and others in intellectual history), anthropological problematics, linguistic analysis, and so forth.

This multidisciplinary elaboration of a comprehensive, analytical, critical presentation of Islam and societies influenced by Islamic principles is not imposed only by a speculative, theoretical discussion; it is much more required by the actual forces at work in the history of every society. This means that "Muslim" societies should no longer be approached and cloaked by our ethnographic view. Ethnography insists on *local* particularities to single out each ethno-cultural group or community from all others; anthropology, on the contrary, considers *global* structures and mechanisms, universal forces such as violence, sacredness, sacrifice, authority, power, time and narration, historicity, and so on to reach encompassing explanations. This distinction is not strictly respected with the same lucidity displayed, for example, in the works of Clifford Geertz.

All these observations may be systematized in the following diagram:

(1)	State	↔	Writing	↔	Learned Culture	↔	Orthodoxy
	↕		↕		↕		↕
(2)	Segmentary Societies	↔	Orality	↔	Popular/Populist Culture	↔	Heterodoxies

To comment fully on this diagram would require an entire book, but some illustrations can be found in my work *Rethinking Islam* (Bloomington, Ind., 1994). I shall add here a few brief remarks.

Traditional historiography has imposed in all known societies a narration starting from an origin, developing a linear evolution until the present time of each historian. This vision is related to a centralizing political power (the state, more or less complex according to the period considered); the social group able to *write* and to read produces a learned culture, structures a type of knowledge with established, controlled, reproduced rules, norms and principles that become the orthodox way to write, to think, to believe, to behave. The arrows horizontally linking the four forces operating in a dialectic interaction express the historical evolution, the sociological mechanisms at work in the leading, dominating level of society; this is the level currently described and studied by historians using *written* documents that speak on the social aspects more or less dependent on the state (some can be opposed to it), but separated, indifferent, and more often *hostile* to all the social agents belonging to the second level. In this second level there are also four forces linked horizontally by the same dialectic interaction, but opposed vertically to the forces of the upper level. The lower level is studied by ethnographers who are obliged to live with tribes, clans, peasants, and bedouins, to learn the local dialects, to collect oral memories, and so forth.

The conceptualization, the description, the knowledge concerning the lower level are decided, fixed, articulated, and evaluated with selections, eliminations, fragmentations, marginalizations, and minimizations by those who write, read, and teach orthodox norms on the upper level. How do we speak of or interpret the so-called *popular* or, as termed in the last thirty years in Third World societies, *populist* culture? Who uses the words magic, superstitions, paganism, polytheism, heterodoxies, sects to refer to *wrong* beliefs, underdeveloped cultures, anarchy, rebellion (*bilād al-siba* versus *bilād al-makhzan* in Morocco in the nineteenth century, for example) as opposed to political order, logocentrist writing, reason, high culture, civilization, and so forth. (Jack Goody has written the well-known book *The Domestication of the Savage Mind*, Cambridge, 1977, translated into French with the more suggestive title *La raison graphique*, Paris, 1979; he has also recently published *The Interface between the Written and the Oral*, Cambridge, 1987. I point exactly to this anthropological opposition when I work out the concept of the societies of the Book-book.) We see clearly here how our modern scholarship reflects, perpetuates, and supports very old, deep, universal divisions that are political and ideological divisions hidden with cultural, intellectual, and ethical vocabulary.

In European societies these oppositions have evolved since the eighteenth century (and even the sixteenth century in some respects) toward a generalization of the upper forces and mechanisms to the global social space; illiteracy is almost eradicated; democracy, the rule of law, and human rights are guaranteed to each citizen; but the anthropological tensions have been at work during centuries and are still at work in many respects today. In Third World societies—including, of course, all "Muslim" societies—the tensions shown by the diagram are more devastating than ever since the emergence of the phenomenon of the single-party nation-state. The political will to eradicate illiteracy in a short time has been so brutal and inspired by ideological goals that oral culture lost its centuries-old social, psychological, and ethical functions. Populist culture is the result of this destructive policy imposed by nationalist "elites" to deliver "masses" of peasants, highlanders, and bedouins from their "ignorance."

The above investigative framework is particularly useful in that it incorporates and links political and social history, intellectual and cultural history, religious history, and, of course, languages, including the various forms used by different social groups. Removed from a strictly theological perspective, religion is studied in its historical, sociological, and anthropological context, thereby setting the stage for a theory of religion as a sociohistoric, universal phenomenon. In this perspective, Islam is but one example among others that can be studied via the social sciences as part of a global theory of knowledge. Such an approach contrasts starkly with the view promulgated by Islamologists and political scientists who have focused instead on its irrefutable specificity as a hieratic force, a kind of monster that has survived for centuries and controlled the fate of nations that have embraced Islam. Rather than focusing exclusively on "Islam," the above framework enables us to analyze the forces that drive the protagonists at all levels of society: social classes and groups, the elite versus the less privileged, as well as intragroup conflicts that arise in both the social and political domains.

At the same time, the scholar is freed from the narrow ideological bonds inherent in opting either to examine society globally on the basis of literature produced and edited by an elite group (arrow 1) or to limit one's research to an exhaustive study of a specific ethnocultural group isolated from the larger sociohistorical process (ethnographic monographs, included in arrow 2). Unfortunately, historical/anthropological studies that attempt to address the weaknesses and dangers inherent in either of these two approaches (particularly when the two are totally distinct) are all too rare.

The study of Islam as a purely religious phenomenon results in major gaps and neglected areas, which are all the more unforgivable for being nonexistent in the study of Christianity and Judaism. Indeed, it seems inconceivable that Islam should be relegated to a separate historical, doctrinal, and sociological status in relation to Christianity and Judaism, given the close links among them. Whether one examines the deeply rooted continuities or the contrasts between Islam, Christianity, and Judaism, a semiological and anthropological perspective would allow us to test the theoretical validity of two constructs that underlie the study of religions.

The first is the mimetic rivalry and competition for the exploitation and control of an original symbolic capital that appeals to diverse sociocultural groups. This occurred in the Near East from ancient Iran to ancient Egypt, where the notions of monotheism, revelation, prophetism, immortality, the heavenly book (as Geo Widengren called it), light and darkness, and good and evil gradually came to constitute a single mindset and way of conceptualizing true knowledge and ultimate truth. At the same time, they provided a set of tools for constructing belief systems which were used by competing forces to justify their power and guarantee support.

Second, this analytical and theoretical framework, the concept of a *new cultural code departure,* will enable us to explain the emergence and social construction of differentiated systems of beliefs and how beliefs called Judaism, Christianity, and Islam fragmented themselves through history into "sects" or derived religions. And yet, when one considers the founding of a religion from a historical or anthropological viewpoint, it is apparent that the same constructs merely have different cultural and semiological representations; the outwardly diverse ideologies and mythologies disguise the fact that the underlying symbolic systems stem from the same creative process, especially in the context of large empires. The acts of building a mosque on the site of an ancient temple, of designating Friday as a day for collective prayer, of facing Mecca rather than Jerusalem, of fasting for an entire month as opposed to a few days, of changing the mythical figures of Isaac, Ishmael, Abraham, Moses and Jesus, of discussing God's existence, of redefining the revelations are all forms of encoding—ritual, cultural, ethical, judicial, and political levels of human existence to transform each religion into the unique "true religion" (*dīn al-ḥaqq* as the Qur'ān says and Hegel will say in a pure philosophical context).

The ill-defined Muslim opposition that views the application of social sciences to the interpretation of religions as reductionist should not stop scientific research on Islam, in the same way that the study of Christianity proceeded in spite of Christian theologians' objections and refusal to accept the conclusions of researchers. For that matter, the very act of rejection should itself be studied from a sociological, historical, and psychological viewpoint: the ways in which this refusal is manifested, the underlying concepts, and the personal and collective motives behind it. Only then will we comprehend that open or closed postures of the mind are the result of behaviors and representations imposed by social agents; this means that Islam, as all other religions, is not the determinant factor, but is itself shaped, transformed, and obliged to fulfill functions corresponding to the needs of social agents.

Islam continues to be excluded from the fields of sociology, social psychology, discourse analysis, and cultural anthropology; since Ibn Rushd, Islam has been ignored by philosophers in their discussions on truth and its theory and practice. How does philosophy affect religious interpretations and discourses? Conversely, how can a cognitively based study of religion stimulate philosophical inquiry? Any Muslim scholar daring to venture down this path succeeds only in earning the condescension of "serious" fellow scholars or in becoming totally isolated by refusing to accept the predominant orthodox view of Islam to which the majority subscribe. By contrast, even the most minor text written by fundamentalist militants becomes the basis for a doctoral thesis or a highly successful book.

The preceding observations have shown that Islamic studies have a long way to go before they are fully integrated into the Western tradition of academic and cultural research. Meanwhile, they continue to be restricted to Asian Studies, Middle Eastern Studies, or Near Eastern Studies departments where a handful of aspiring or recognized experts jealously guard their territory, refusing to collaborate on a wider academic level with other departments for fear that their ideas might be scrutinized and judged by true social scientists. Islamic studies should be recognized as a field integrated within departments of history, sociology, psychology, linguistics, philosophy, anthropology and religion, for Islam and Islamic thought are an integral part of Mediterranean cultural history, politics and economics, and, by extension, Europe and modern Western civilization, including North America. Orientalist scholars serving on university faculties have perpetuated an ideological perspective dating back to the nineteenth century, and in some respects even to the Middle Ages (particularly where the history of religions and theology are concerned). This has been done in order to protect individual privileges that are gradually diminishing. These views are in no way reflective of the polemical unjustified criticism of "Orientalism."

It is pertinent to state that universities and researchers in the West insist on viewing Islamic studies in the same intellectual and scientific light as "postmodern" theories of knowledge. The reason appears to be that there is a structural link between the growth of social sciences and the needs of democratic, industrialized nations. From a political and economic standpoint, Islamic countries neither favor nor encourage a scholarly/empirical approach to Islamic studies because of the inherently fundamentalist nature of the political system. It remains to be seen whether research on Islam will be limited to narratives and descriptive studies, or whether it will adapt to the demands imposed on it by intellectual modernity in spite of the fundamentalist opposition based precisely on the fact that this type of modernity is for them *unthinkable*. Such demands already exist but are neither encouraged nor satisfied because of the strict official ideology supported by the collective *imaginaire* that narrowly defines intellectual and scientific pursuits.

Yet another reason why it is crucial to alter the existing intellectual perspective on Islam and Islamic cultures is that Orientalist writings on Islam continue to reflect philosophical principles taken exclusively from the reason of Enlightenment, despite the fact that these tenets have been deemed outdated by social scientists since the 1960s. It seems that contemporary Western philosophy and civilization only acknowledge two ways of looking at and thinking about the world: the effects of the "postmodern condition" on the one hand, and on the other, the use of criteria, definitions, and values inherited from the Enlightenment tradition to analyze all other cultures and societies. It is time to put an end to this state of affairs, reminiscent of the establishment by France in Algeria of one electoral system for French citizens and another for Algerian "natives."

Methodological and epistemological issues are directly, albeit not always visibly, tied to the world's great ideologies. Social psychology has revealed that all knowledge is linked to a policy of refusal or integration of new knowledge that, in the former case, undermines and, in the latter, reinforces or confirms existing ideological views. Several verses of chapter 9 of the Qur'ān (5–29) explicitly state what Muslims should reject or integrate. Equivalent Christian and Jewish sacred texts have fulfilled a similar function since the Middle Ages. With the advent of the Age of Reason, universal values were proclaimed, reinforced by Kant's transcendental reason and Hegel's philosophical spirit, all leading to the supremacy of liberal socialism and, for seventy years, communism. Since the downfall of communism with its aberrant tenets, history has ceased in the sense that there is no single logic or worldview in a position to contradict, rival or supersede liberal philosophy.

Very few fellow Islamologists intend to incorporate the scientific method evident in their writings on Islam and the Muslim world into a larger philosophical and autobiographical framework. Under such circumstances, it seems reasonable to conclude that Islamic studies will most likely remain the domain of erudite scholars, experts, essayists, narrators, journalists, hurried observers, political scientists, and academics more concerned with their careers than with improving and enhancing our knowledge—unless, of course, a group of particularly gifted and fortunate researchers and thinkers succeeds in changing the rules of the academic game and in breaking the pious molds used to reproduce existing knowledge and current intellectual theories.

[*See also* Historiography; Orientalism; *and* Social Sciences.]

BIBLIOGRAPHY

Arkoun, Mohammed. *L'état du Maghreb*. Paris, 1991.

Clifford, James. *The Predicament of Culture: Twentieth-Century Ethnography, Literature, and Art*. Cambridge, Mass., 1988.

Guillaume, Marc, ed. *L'état des sciences sociales en France*. Paris, 1986.

Lyotard, Jean-François. *The Postmodern Condition: A Report on Knowledge*. Translated by Geoff Bennington and Brian Massumi. Minneapolis, 1984.

Wagner, Peter, et al., eds. *Social Sciences and Modern States: National Experiences and Theoretical Crossroads*. Cambridge, 1991.

Mohammed Arkoun

ISLAMIC TENDENCY MOVEMENT. *See* Ḥizb al-Nahḍah.

ISMĀʿĪLĪYAH. The Shīʿī movement called the Ismāʿīlīyah, with a number of widely differing subsects, deeply influenced Islamic intellectual life in the tenth through thirteenth centuries. It is quite separate from the majority sect of Shīʿī Muslims, the Twelvers or Imāmīs.

The origins and early history of the Ismāʿīlīyah are obscure. Following the death in 765 CE of the sixth Shīʿī imam, Jaʿfar al-Ṣādiq, some of his followers insisted that his son Ismāʿīl, whom Jaʿfar had named his successor but who had already died, was nevertheless the seventh imam. Hence, Ismāʿīlīs are often known as "Seveners."

Central to Ismāʿīlī doctrine from the beginning has been the distinction between exoteric aspects of religion, which are said to change from prophet to prophet, and esoteric aspects that remain constant behind transient symbols. Early Ismāʿīlī esotericism involved both cosmological myths (of a noticeably gnostic character) and a cyclical view of sacred history that recognized seven eras, each inaugurated by a prophet. In the tenth century, however, the original myth was displaced by Neoplatonic ideas of an incomprehensible and severely transcendent God who, having created "Intellect" *ex nihilo,* allowed the remainder of the universe—other intellects, soul, the celestial spheres, and the four elements of the ordinary world—to come into existence by emanation from that first created being.

Nothing is known about the Ismāʿīliyah from its origin until after the mid-ninth century, when the Ismāʿīlīs emerged as a secret revolutionary movement operating in Iraq, Persia, Yemen, and the Indian subcontinent. The activities of the Ismāʿīlī missionary organization, the *daʿwah,* seem to have been directed from a central headquarters, located first near the Persian Gulf and later in Syria. During this early phase, the leaders of the Ismāʿīliyah apparently claimed to be acting on behalf of the absent imam Muḥammad, son of Ismāʿīl, whose imminent return as world ruler they proclaimed. Converts were required to take an oath of initiation, which included an obligation of secrecy.

In 899 ʿUbayd Allāh al-Mahdī, a new leader in Syria, announced that he himself was the imam, the latest in a continuous line of imams since the days of Ismāʿīl. This innovation split the movement. By and large, the Ismāʿīlīs of Iraq, Bahrain, and western Persia refused to accept ʿUbayd Allāh's claim. Among the eastern Ismāʿīlīyah, the faction known as the Qarmatians (Qarāmiṭah), still anticipating the return of a hidden imam, concentrated on eastern Arabia and Bahrain, where they had some success, and briefly even held Mecca.

To the west, ʿUbayd Allāh and his heirs succeeded in establishing an important state, first in North Africa (909) and afterward in Egypt (from 969), where they founded the city of Cairo. The complex history of this Fāṭimid dynasty extended over approximately two centuries. [*See* Fāṭimid Dynasty.]

Toward the end of the rule of al-Ḥākim (996–1021), certain members of the *daʿwah* proclaimed his divinity. The official *daʿwah* organization fought the new heresy vigorously, but the attitude of the caliph himself is difficult to determine. In the years following al-Ḥākim's death, the Fāṭimid government eliminated his adherents from Egypt; however, they established themselves in the mountains of Syria-Palestine, where, moving theologically beyond the boundaries of Ismāʿīlism and even of Islam, they became the Druze movement. [*See* Druze.]

In 1094 Nizār, eldest son and designated successor of the caliph al-Mustanṣir, was deposed in a coup d'état and put in prison, where he eventually died. He was replaced by al-Mustaʿlī, the younger son. The Ismāʿīlī organization in Egypt accepted al-Mustaʿlī, but the eastern Ismāʿīlīs remained loyal to Nizār. One of these was a *dāʿī* or missionary known as Ḥasan-i Ṣabbāḥ, founder of a group that eventually came to be widely known as "the Assassins"—part of their program can be inferred from their name—who had established his base of command in the mountain fortress of Alamut. Ḥasan now came forward as the de facto leader of a new Ismāʿīlī sect, the Nizārīs, although he did not assume the title of imam.

Al-ʿĀmir, the son of al-Mustaʿlī, was assassinated in 1130. After considerable turmoil he was succeeded by his cousin al-Ḥāfiẓ. Another schism was born when many Ismāʿīlīs continued to support the rights of al-ʿĀmir's infant son al-Ṭayyib; the baby, however, had disappeared, and nothing further is known about him.

In 1171 the famous Saladin conquered Egypt and ended the Fāṭimid dynasty. With the fall of their state, Ismāʿīlīs essentially disappeared from Egypt, where they had remained an elite and had never managed to win over the general population. Some took refuge in Yemen.

Meanwhile the Assassins underwent major upheavals in the east. For a time their leaders appear to have claimed the imamate on the basis of alleged descent from Nizār. At one point, the lords of Alamut even repudiated Islamic law (*sharīʿah*). This all came to an end in 1256 when the Assassin stronghold fell to the Mongols and the last grand master was executed.

The Ismāʿīlīyah survived in scattered communities of Persia, Central Asia, Yemen, and Syria. It was in India, however, that the movement found its greatest success in the post-Fāṭimid period. Nizārī missionaries established a community there that has come to be known as the Khojas. Their imam is known as the Aga Khan. His departure from Persia and his permanent settlement in Bombay in the mid-nineteenth century effectively mark the beginning of the modern period in the history of the Nizārī Ismāʿīlīyah. Adherents of the movement have prospered, by and large, and have developed a reputation for progressivism throughout the Islamic world and beyond. Successive modern Aga Khans have been active in international and Indian subcontinental politics and reforms, as well as in educational and humanitarian work. Mustaʿlīs too came to the subcontinent and founded the sect of the Bohrās, who are closer to Sunnī Islam than are their Nizārī counterparts.

Today, Ismāʿīlīs of both schools are chiefly located in India, although notable communities also exist in Yemen, Syria, Central Asia, Iran, and through relatively recent migration in East Africa, where they have formed an important element in the commercial life of the region. Sizable populations of Ismāʿīlī expatriates are to be found in Europe and North America, with the largest single concentration located in London. The total number of Ismāʿīlīs is probably in the vicinity of two million.

[*See also* Aga Khan; Bohrās; Khojas; *and* Shīʿī Islam, *historical overview article.*]

BIBLIOGRAPHY

Daftary, Farhad. *The Ismāʿīlīs: Their History and Doctrines*. Cambridge, 1990. Very useful one-volume survey of the subject, to modern times.

Hodgson, Marshall G. S. *The Order of Assassins: The Struggle of the Early Nizârî Ismâʿîlîs against the Islamic World*. The Hague, 1955.

Ivanov, Vladimir A. *The Alleged Founder of Ismailism*. Bombay, 1946.

Lewis, Bernard. *The Origins of Ismāʿīlism: A Study of the Historical Background of the Fāṭimid Caliphate*. Cambridge, 1940. Important but somewhat idiosyncratic approach.

Lewis, Bernard. *The Assassins: A Radical Sect in Islam*. London, 1967.

Nasr, Seyyed Hossein, ed. *Ismāʿīlī Contributions to Islamic Culture*. Tehran, 1977. Interesting anthology of essays.

Poonawala, Ismail K. *Biobibliography of Ismāʿīlī Literature*. Malibu, Calif., 1977. Massive annotated catalogue of literature and writers from earliest times to the modern period.

Stern, S. M. *Studies in Early Ismāʿīlism*. Jerusalem and Leiden, 1983. Collection of papers, some of them classics, on early Ismāʿīlism.

DANIEL C. PETERSON

ISRAEL. In 1992 the Arab minority in Israel numbered approximately 914,000, or 18.5 percent of the total Israeli population (the figures include the Arab residents of East Jerusalem, estimated at 146,000, but not of the West Bank and the Gaza Strip). Seventy-seven percent of the Arab minority (704,000) were Muslim, while the rest were Christian (14 percent or 128,000) and Druze (9 percent or 82,000).

The 1948 Arab-Israeli War created a structural vacuum in the life of the Muslim community in Israel. Organized Islam virtually disappeared. Almost every member of the Muslim religious establishment of Mandatory Palestine fled. The Muslims in the newly established State of Israel were left without religious court judges, prayer leaders, and other functionaries necessary to sustain the religious life of the community. The Supreme Muslim Council ceased to exist, having been superseded by the Jordanian religious authorities.

Israel was faced with the challenging task of reestablishing the Muslim religious apparatus and applying the *sharīʿah* in the new Jewish state. Muslim religious affairs, including the administration of *awqāf* (sg., *waqf;* religious endowments), devolved to the Israeli authorities, primarily to the Muslim Department of the Ministry of Religious Affairs.

The *sharīʿah* court system was gradually reconstructed, but it took years to restore the situation to normal, mainly because there were few people qualified to assume religious appointments. By necessity, underqualified men were occasionally engaged. In May 1961 the Knesset (parliament) ratified the Qāḍīs Law, which stipulated that the *qāḍīs* be selected by a committee with a Muslim majority, appointed by the president of Israel, and dispense justice in accordance with Israeli laws. In 1993 there were seven *qāḍīs* in seven *sharīʿah* courts of first instance and one appeals court located in Jerusalem. In 1992 the courts reviewed 4,952 cases, 40 percent of which dealt with divorce and alimony.

The Muslim religious courts in Israel were granted exclusive and extensive jurisdiction in matters of personal status and *waqf*. The Knesset, however, restricted the jurisdiction of the *sharīʿah* courts in certain areas with the intention of thoroughly reforming the legal status of women.

As Aharon Layish has shown ("Muslim Religious Jurisdiction in Israel," *Asian and African Studies* 2 [1966]: 50–79), Israeli legislation in matters of personal status proceeded along two different lines. With regard to marriage and divorce, the Knesset imposed several restrictions: it prohibited the marriage of girls under seventeen, outlawed polygamy, and forbade divorcing a woman against her will. The secular legislation did not supersede religious law in these matters, but it was enforced by penal sanctions.

The other line entailed the supersession of Muslim religious law; for example, the Knesset's legislation regarding natural guardianship of the mother was alone binding. With the 1965 Succession Law, the exclusive jurisdiction of the *sharīʿah* courts in matters of succession and wills was abolished, and the power to deal with these matters was transferred to the state district courts.

After 1948 Muslim *waqf* properties whose administrators or beneficiaries were absentees were entrusted to a special custodian. Consecrated Muslim sites and their secular appurtenances were administered by the Muslim Department of the Ministry of Religious Affairs, which served as an agent of the Custodian of Absentees' Property. The law was amended in 1965 to allow the release of *waqf khayrī* property to several Muslim trustee committees.

Since the late 1970s the Muslim community in Israel has been undergoing a process of Islamic revivalism. The resurgence derives from a combination of local conditions particular to the Arab minority in Israel as well as more general causes.

Renewed contacts with the Palestinians of the West Bank and Gaza after the 1967 war strengthened the religious component in Israeli Muslims' collective identity. It gave them renewed access to the holy places of Jerusalem and Hebron and exposed them to the activities of the Muslim High Council in Jerusalem, reconstituted after 1967. It was through the intervention of the council that in 1978 Israeli Arabs were permitted to perform the *ḥajj;* until then holders of Israeli passports had been barred from doing so. The council also helped young Israeli Arabs study at Islamic colleges in the occupied territories.

The resurgence of Islam must also be seen against the background of the Arab sector's socioeconomic crisis. The intensive process of modernization that the Arabs in Israel experienced weakened their conservative family value system and clan structure. This partial disintegration of old social frameworks created a void and a sense of confusion, causing more Arabs to turn to Islam for moral guidance.

Since the early 1970s the Arab sector in Israel has become increasingly aware of and distressed by its socioeconomic situation relative to that of the Jews. The sizable gap between the Arab and Jewish populations in such fields as education, health services, housing, and industrialization has become increasingly acute. The gaps developed partly through governmental neglect and partly through the government's inability to meet the growing needs occasioned by the Arabs' rapid population growth. The ultimate outcome was a deepening sense of Arab bitterness, frustration, alienation, and dissent.

As the discrepancies between Jews and Arabs widened and the secular Arab political bodies failed to improve matters, the Arab community became increasingly eager for some external force to step in and remedy the imbalance. As elsewhere in the Muslim world, the Islamist movement filled the void, providing practical solutions to the deteriorating local conditions.

Ayatollah Ruhollah Khomeini's rise to power in Iran led to the formation of the first clandestine group of Islamic militants in Israel. Set up within a year of the Iranian revolution, it called itself Usrat al-Jihād (the Jihad Family) and was organized as a paramilitary unit. The group's objective was to wage *jihād* against Israel, undermine the basis of Jewish-Zionist existence, and cause the state to collapse from within. Usrat al-Jihād carried out a number of acts of sabotage, including arson; it also took action against secular or permissive trends among Israeli Muslims. However, soon after their first sabotage operations in 1981, all seventy members of the organization were arrested and sentenced to prison terms ranging from one to fifteen years. The arrest and trial dampened Muslim militancy in Israel.

In the mid-1980s the Islamic activist Shaykh ʿAbd Allāh Nimr Darwīsh moved to center stage. A resident of Kufr Qasim, Darwīsh was a graduate of the Nablus *sharīʿah* college. In 1979 he joined Usrat al-Jihād; he was arrested and convicted in 1981 and released in 1983. When Darwīsh resumed his politico-religious career, he gave Islamic activism in Israel a new nonmilitant direction. Darwīsh focused on the community, trying to win the hearts of the local Muslims by means of religious education and community work. Islamic associations were soon founded in a number of Arab localities. The Islamic Movement, as it came to be known, succeeded in changing the face of Arab village society. Mosque attendance increased steadily; the number of mosques in Israel grew from 60 in 1967 to 240 in 1993.

The movement has been especially successful in mobilizing the inhabitants for active, Islamically oriented work in their communities. Muslim volunteers built internal roads in Arab villages, put up sex-segregated bus-stop shelters, opened kindergartens, libraries and clinics, and established drug-rehabilitation centers. Considerable efforts were directed to the promotion of sports. Indeed, the Islamic movement found solutions to many of the daily hardships that resulted from the authorities' failure to meet the Arab sector's needs. "If the state is not ready to help us, we shall help ourselves," declared Shaykh Darwīsh, in what came to be the movement's central motto.

This approach proved to be a prescription for success. In the 1989 municipal elections Islamic representatives competed in fourteen localities and won nearly 30 percent of the total seats. In five villages and townships Islamic candidates won the mayoralty. In Umm al-Fahm, the second largest Arab town in Israel, Islamic candidates under the leadership of Shaykh Rā'id Ṣalāḥ secured a majority in the town council as well as the mayor's office. In the 1993 municipal elections the movement increased its power. The number of representatives grew from 51 to 59 and the Islamic trend won representation in sixteen localities (compared to fourteen in 1989). All incumbent mayors and heads of local councils representing the movement (except one) were reelected.

The religious views of the Islamic movement appear to have been influenced by various sources. One is the traditional orthodox Sunnī approach taught in Arab schools and Islamic colleges in the West Bank. A second is the ideas of nineteenth- and twentieth-century Islamic reformists and modernists. The third, and perhaps most important, is the doctrine of the Muslim Brotherhood, which helped shape the social and political perceptions of the Israeli Islamic movement to a large extent.

From its inception the local Islamic movement has been torn between three contradictory foci of loyalty or solidarity—Islam, Israel, and Palestine. The Islamic movement's program genuinely reflected the problematic interrelationship among Islamic revivalism, the declared secular character of Palestinian nationalism, and the need to act within the boundaries of Israeli law. This gave rise to the confusion and the often ambiguous language on sensitive issues such as the components of identity, the Palestine Liberation Organization, the solution of the Palestinian problem, the idea of a Palestinian Islamic state, the Islamic movements in the territories (Ḥamās, Islamic Jihād), the *intifāḍah,* and the Palestinian/Islamic armed struggle.

The complexities facing the revivalists can best be exemplified by their treatment of the issue of national identity. The four orbits of identity often mentioned by the Islamic movement in Israel are Islam, Arabism, humanism, and Palestinian nationalism. Some local Islamic leaders refrain from mentioning Israel at all; others, wary of provoking a harsh reaction on the part of the Israeli authorities for implicitly denying Israel's existence, do mention the state, but only with reference to the technicality of citizenship. Leaders of the movement have been put under house arrest, and the movement's press has been temporarily closed in reaction to what was described as publication of inflammatory material.

Similarly complex is the question of a Palestinian Islamic state. Unlike their counterparts in the territories—who do not hesitate to call for a state from "the River to the Sea," that is, from the Jordan to the Mediterranean—the Israeli Islamists are reserved. Some, like Shaykh Darwīsh, make a clear distinction between their support of the idea that genuine Islamic states should be established in the region and their rejection of the idea that an Islamic state should replace Israel. Others fully endorse the views of Ḥamās that the land of Palestine is an Islamic endowment *(waqf),* which the *sharī'ah* rules that Muslims must liberate. They do not, of course, expound pursuing this goal, for this would compel the Israeli authorities to take action against them.

The Islamic movement's continued success in Israel depends on the skill of its balancing act: its relentless promotion of the Islamization of Israeli Muslims in their personal conduct and community life on the one hand, and on the other its keeping political action and propaganda at a level compatible with their unique situation of a Muslim-Arab minority living in a Jewish state.

[*See also* Arab-Israeli Conflict; Ḥamās; Jihād Organizations; Palestine Liberation Organization; *and* West Bank and Gaza.]

BIBLIOGRAPHY

Israeli, Raphael. *Muslim Fundamentalism in Israel*. London, 1993.
Layish, Aharon. "The Muslim Waqf in Israel." *Asian and African Studies* 2 (1966): 41–47.
Layish, Aharon. *Women and Islamic Law in a Non-Muslim State*. New York, 1975.
Mayer, Thomas. *Hitʿorerut ha-Muslemin be-Yisra'el*. Givʿat-Ḥavivah, 1988.
Rekhess, Elie. "Resurgent Islam in Israel." *Asian and African Studies* 27 (1993).

ELIE REKHESS

ISTIQLĀL. The leading Moroccan nationalist party in the period 1943–1962, the Istiqlāl (Ḥizb al-Istiqlāl, "Independence party") was founded in December 1943 by Aḥmad Balafrej and a group of younger Moroccan nationalists drawn from the urban bourgeoisie of Fez, Rabat, Tangier, and Tetouan. Together with King Muḥammad V, Istiqlāl played a major role in bringing about the end of the French and Spanish protectorates in March 1956.

From the outset, the movement drew both on currents of Islamic reformism (Salafīyah) and political organization and on the emerging younger generation of French-educated elites. Salafīyah-influenced young leaders, such as Muḥammad ʿAllāl al-Fāsī, joined forces with more secular individuals, such as Aḥmad Balafrej and Makkī Nāṣirī. Politically, Istiqlāl was the successor of the Kutlah al-ʿAmal al-Waṭanī (National Action Bloc), which had been established in 1932. The Kutlah was an elite-based nationalist organization that drew its supporters chiefly from the urban bourgeoisie of northern Moroccan cities. Many of the leaders of the Kutlah, among them Muḥammad Haṣan al-Wazzanī, Aḥmad Balafrej, Makkī al-Nāṣirī, and ʿAllāl al-Fāsī, later went on to play important roles in the nationalist movement in the 1940s. In 1934, the group issued a Plan of Reforms that criticized the French protectorate government and demanded far-reaching reforms. A major weakness of the Kutlah and other early nationalist groups is that they were primarily based among the elites and not mass based. By 1937, when French authorities banned it and jailed or exiled most of the leadership, members numbered only around 6,500.

After 1946, an alliance with the Moroccan king, Muḥammad V, permitted Istiqlāl to extend its influence rapidly among peasants and workers. In the ensuing years, the Istiqlāl party successfully developed into a mass-based nationalist organization, playing a particularly crucial role in the independence movement in the period following the French deposition and exile of Muḥammad V in August 1953. However, its lack of support in the countryside and the emergence of guerrilla groups outside its control marked the limits of its effectiveness. The return of Muḥammad V from exile in November 1955, and the subsequent independence of Morocco in March 1956, inaugurated a new phase in the party's political role.

Following Moroccan independence, Istiqlāl became the largest political party in the Moroccan *majlis* (national assembly). Divergent interests and personal rivalries gradually undermined its alliance with the crown, however. When Muḥammad V encouraged the emergence of political parties favoring his policies, Istiqlāl gradually moved into opposition. At the same time, younger and more militant elements in the Istiqlāl party led by Mehdi Ben Barka (al-Mahdī Ibn Barakah) split off and formed a new party, the National Union of Popular Forces (UNFP). Following the death of Muḥammad V in February 1961, Crown Prince Ḥasan ascended to the throne. The adoption of a Moroccan constitution in 1962 transformed the political arena. Since 1956, periods of representative government have alternated with periods of direct rule by the crown. Throughout, the king has continued successfully to pose as political arbiter. Istiqlāl was an important participant in several Moroccan governments. By the 1990s, no longer the dynamic force it once was, Istiqlāl has declined in political influence, although it continues to have a constituency among urban voters.

[*See also* Morocco *and the biography of* Fāsī.]

BIBLIOGRAPHY

Abun-Nasr, Jamil M. "The Salafiyya Movement in Morocco: The Religious Bases of the Moroccan Nationalist Movement." In *Social Change: The Colonial Situation*, edited by Immanuel Wallerstein, pp. 489–502. New York, 1966.
Ashford, Douglas E. *Political Change in Morocco*. Princeton, 1961.
Bernand, Stephane. *The Franco-Moroccan Conflict, 1943–1956*. New Haven, 1968.
Fāsī, ʿAllāl al-. *Al-Ḥarakāt al-istiqlālīyah fi al-Maghrib al-ʿArabī*. Cairo, 1948. Translated by Hazem Zaki Nuseibeh as *Independence Movements of Arab North Africa*. Washington, D.C., 1954.
Halstead, John B. *Rebirth of a Nation: The Origins and Rise of Moroccan Nationalism, 1912–1944*. Cambridge, 1967.
Rezette, Robert. *Les partis politiques marocaines*. Paris, 1955.

EDMUND BURKE, III

ITHNĀ ʿASHARĪYAH. The followers of the twelve imams regarded as the rightful successors of the Prophet, the Ithnā ʿAsharīyah, or Twelvers, constitute the major subdivision within Shīʿī Islam. The Ithnā ʿAsharīyah are also known as Imāmīyah because of their main tenet regarding the necessity of the imam for the establishment of the ideal Muslim community under divine revelation. The term Shīʿah is generally applied to the Twelvers, despite the fact that there are other factions, such as the Ismāʿīlīyah and Zaydīyah, that are also included within Shīʿī Islam.

Historical Development. The Ithnā ʿAsharīyah trace their history to the investiture, in Ghadīr Khumm (modern-day Juḥfah), of ʿAlī ibn Abī Ṭālib, the first imam, with *wilāyah* (discretionary authority) by Muḥammad after the Prophet's Farewell Pilgrimage. Following Muḥammad's death in 632, the leadership of the nascent community was assumed by the Prophet's leading companion, Abū Bakr, but a group of Muslims refused to accept him as caliph. This group constituted the nucleus of the early Shīʿah ("partisans"). They believed that ʿAlī was Muḥammad's rightful successor and that those who usurped his right were sinners. This belief marked the genesis of the Shīʿī concept of imamate. Although ʿAlī did not assume political authority until after the third caliph, ʿUthmān, was murdered in 656, he was regarded by the Shīʿah as the imam, that is, a person qualified to assume temporal and spiritual authority. Following ʿAlī's murder in 660, the imamate continued with Ḥasan (d. 669) and Ḥusayn (d. 680), the sons of ʿAlī and his wife Fāṭimah Muḥammad's daughter. [*See* Wilāyah *and the biography of* ʿ*Alī.*]

The second most significant event during the formative period of the Ithnā ʿAsharīyah was the murder of the third imam, Ḥusayn, on the plains Karbala, Iraq, in 680. The Karbala episode provided the Shīʿah with the ethos that led to the distinct Shīʿī belief system, which is constructed around the notion of divinely designated ideal leadership, and the pathos that set the tone of the Ithnā ʿAsharī religious praxis for posterity. From the Ithnā ʿAsharī perspective, Karbala became the paradigm for defiance against the unjust authority that culminated in martyrdom (*shahādah* in the sense of sacrificial death in the path of God). It also marked a shift in the subsequent role of the Shīʿī imam from politically activist upholder of just authority to politically quietist successor of Ḥusayn. The imamate was identified more in terms of the imam's religious-legal knowledge of Islamic revelation than his activist posture as the redresser of the wrongs committed against the *ahl al-bayt* (the Prophet's family). [*See* Karbala; Ahl-al Bayt; *and the biography of Ḥusayn ibn ʿAlī.*]

ʿAlī Zayn al-ʿĀbidīn (d. 714), Muḥammad al-Bāqir (d. 733), and Jaʿfar al-Ṣādiq (d. 765), the fourth, fifth, and sixth imams, inaugurated the era of devotional, theological, and juridical formulations of the Ithnā ʿAsharīyah. Whereas for the Muslim community in general the second half of the eighth century was a period of political and social unrest, for the Shīʿah it was the critical phase of self-definition in the face of competing and politically supported religious expression. The replacement of the Umayyads by the ʿAbbāsids in 748 and the political turmoil that ruled in the central lands of the caliphate afforded these imams necessary time to shape the future direction of the Ithnā ʿAsharīyah. Through the spiritual and intellectual leadership of al-Bāqir and al-Ṣādiq, the Shīʿah developed distinctly Shīʿī Qur'ānic exegesis, through well-documented Prophetic *ḥadīths* (reports), including ones related by the imams, and a highly sophisticated juridical tradition, which subsequently earned them a distinct recognition in the larger community as the followers of the Jaʿfarī *madhhab* (rite).

The succeeding imamate of al-Ṣādiq's descendants, from Mūsā al-Kāẓim (d. 799), the seventh imam, to Muḥammad al-Mahdī (disappeared in 874 to return as the Mahdi, "divinely guided" leader of the *ummah* [community], at the End of Time), the twelfth and last imam, was the most difficult period for the Ithnā ʿAsharīyah. The imams lived either incarcerated or under surveillance for suspected activities against the caliphate. The Shīʿah were faced with unrelenting ʿAbbāsid atrocities and had little or no access to their imams. Under those conditions, the imams appointed their *nuwwāb* (personal deputies), who conveyed their teachings and collected religious dues, such as the *khums* (originally a fifth of the spoils of war) and *zakāt* (alms), from their followers. This deputyship gradually evolved into the influential religious institution among the Shīʿīs that culminated in the *wilāyah* (comprehensive guardianship) of the qualified *mujtahid* (or *faqīh;* jurist-theologian) under the Qājār and post-Qājār jurists.

During al-Kāẓim's imamate, the concept of an imam in *ghaybah* (occultation), who continued to direct his community's affairs through his trusted associates, found theological and legal expression in the *ḥadīths* attributed to the imams al-Bāqir and al-Ṣādiq. [*See* Ghaybah.] The requirement of *taqīyah* (prudential concealment of one's true belief) as a strategy of survival in the midst of the hostile majoritarian Sunnīs also became more pronounced among the Shīʿīs at this time.

The occultation of the twelfth imam is divided into two forms: the Short (or Lesser) Occultation and the Complete (or Greater) Occultation. During the Short Occultation (874–941), the last imam appointed some of his prominent followers as his "special deputies" to carry on the function of the imamate in religious and social affairs. During the Complete Occultation (941–), the learned jurists among the Shīʿīs were believed to have been appointed by the twelfth imam as his "general deputies" to guide believers pending his return.

The period of the general deputies has been dominated by two concerns: first, stabilization of the theological imamate of the twelve imams; and second, consolidation of the juridical and functional imamate of the leading Shīʿī scholars who, being de facto leaders of the Shīʿah, were solely responsible for directing their social and religious life. Whereas the former concern provided the Twelver community with its distinctive creedal identity based on the doctrine of divine justice and infallible leadership of the imams, the latter was instrumental in providing authoritative religious praxis and hierarchical intellectual and spiritual organization to ensure the continuity of the minority community spirit living at times under hostile Sunnī power.

The establishment of the Būyid dynasty (932–1055) and its patronage of Shiism, despite its support for the continuation of the Sunnī caliphate as symbolic of the unity of the majority of the Muslims, created favorable political and social conditions for the Shīʿīs. It was intellectually the most productive period of the Ithnā ʿAsharīyah. Prominent scholars representing the rationalist trend of the Baghdad theologians wrote major works vindicating the imamate of the Hidden Imam. Baghdad was also the point of convergence for the two important centers of Shīʿī *ḥadīth,* Kufa and Qom. Qom remained an important center for other cities of Shīʿī learning in Khurasan.

Al-Kulaynī (d. 941) and Ibn Bābūyah (d. 991), the renowned Imamite traditionists, produced multivolume *ḥadīth* works that included everything that was needed in formulating the Imamite creed and praxis. Some of the most detailed and systematic treatment of Imamite jurisprudence was undertaken by Shaykh al-Mufīd (d. 1023) and his prominent disciples, such as al-Sharīf al-Murtaḍā (d. 1045) and Shaykh al-Ṭāʾifah al-Ṭūsī (d. 1067). Unlike Shīʿī theology, which never conceded extending the imamate to other than the infallible successors of the Prophet, Shīʿī jurisprudence essentially reflected the conclusion of Sunnī jurists regarding the rationalization of existing political authority, which was deemed indispensable for safeguarding and widening the application of normative *sharīʿah.*

In view of the prolonged occultation of the imam, jurists developed a profile of a just Shīʿī authority other than the infallible imam that would manage community affairs. A number of Shīʿī dynasties followed the Būyids, although the first Shīʿī state in Iran was not established until the sixteenth century under the Ṣafavids. Shīʿī jurists had no difficulty in validating the temporal authority of the Ṣafavids. As experts in *sharīʿah,* they justified their own authority as the legally sanctioned *walī* (guardians) of the community, thereby making themselves responsible for carrying out the obligation of enjoining the good and forbidding the evil. The full implications of such investiture became plain with the establishment of the Qājār dynasty in the late eighteenth century. The role of the Shīʿī religious leadership received fuller elaboration during the nineteenth and early twentieth centuries, until it reached its logical conclusion under Ayatollah Ruhollah Khomeini (1902–1989) in 1980 in the constitutionalization of the *wilāyat al-faqīh* ("guardianship of the jurist") in the modern nation-state of Iran. [*See* Wilāyat al-Faqīh.]

With its rational theology founded on the notion of divine justice and the ideal civil-moral authority of the imam, Shiism during the Ṣafavid and Qājār periods provided the impetus for a renewed interest in Neoplatonist philosophy, more specifically, the Illuminationist theosophy of Suhrawardī. Among the prominent figures whose elaboration of the Avicennian philosophy led them to formulate their own metaphysics were Mīr Dāmād (d. 1631) and Mullā Ṣadrā (Ṣadr al-Dīn Shīrāzi, d. 1640). In jurisprudence, the old tension between the uncritical upholders of the authority of traditions, known as the Akhbārī, and the supporters of rationalist methodology, the Uṣūlī, flared up during the later part of the Ṣafavid period and into the Qājār era. The controversy resulted in the resounding victory of the Uṣūlī jurists under the leadership of Vaḥīd Bihbahānī (d. 1793) and his disciples. The notion of centralized leadership of the most qualified *mujtahid,* the *marjaʿ al-taqlīd,* whose authority was institutionalized by the Uṣūlī deduction regarding the necessity of formally pledging obedience to a *taqlīd* (expert) in matters of *sharīʿah,* was also legalized during this period. [*See* Akhbārīyah; Uṣūlīyah; Marjaʿ al-Taqlīd.]

The Qājār and post-Qājār eras coincided with the introduction of modernization, including a modern system of administration, education, and modern values. Although introduced gradually and haphazardly, modernization of traditional Shīʿī society created tensions in the community and undermined the effectiveness of traditional religious leadership. The Shīʿīs exerted enormous pressure on their *marjaʿ al-taqlīd* to resolve the tensions caused by the changed expectations of modern living. Not many *mujtahid*s were willing to undertake methodological revision and rethinking in order to provide legal-religious justifications for making Islam a relevant system for modern times. Nor did many regard it permissible for a *mujtahid* to assume political authority to implement *sharīʿah* norms in a modern society. However, Ayatollahs Khomeini and Muḥammad Bāqir al-Ṣadr (d. 1980) of Iraq regarded it appropriate for a qualified *mujtahid* to assume political power in his role as the executor of the affairs of the Shīʿīs in a modern nation-state. Khomeini offered his own nuanced interpretation of Shīʿī religious leadership in both theory and practice.

Religious Beliefs and Practices. Unlike the Sunnī Five Pillars of Islam, which include both the *shahādah* (fundamental belief) and religious practice, Twelver Shiism adheres to the *uṣūl al-dīn* (principles of religion) and *furūʿ al-dīn* (derivatives of religion). The *uṣūl* expounds the five tenets of the Shīʿī belief system: (1) *tawḥīd* (affirmation of the unity of God); (2) *ʿadl* (justice of God); (3) *nubūwah* (necessity of prophecy); (4) *imāmah* (necessity of imamate); and (5) *maʿād* (Day of Judgment). In the principles of *tawḥīd, nubūwah,* and *maʿād,* identified as *uṣūl al-islām* (essential for being a Muslim), the Shīʿīs in general share a common ground with the Sunnīs, although there are differences on points of details. The principles of *ʿadl* and *imāmah* are peculiarly Shīʿī in that they are regarded as *uṣūl al-īmān* (essential to the faith). Shīʿī belief in God's justice is similar to that of the Muʿtazilah, who taught that God is infinitely removed from every evil act and from being remiss in doing what is good for humanity. Divine justice also means that God provides humanity with the knowledge of good and evil and creates reason to guide a person to such knowledge. However, there is no guarantee that reason would always seek out the most beneficial way to perfection. Hence, God sends revealed messages through prophets as a complementary source to reason to remind humanity of its *fiṭrah* (innate disposition) inclined toward perfection. The principle of *imāmah* is regarded as part of the divinely appointed office of the prophecy to continue the Prophet's mission of establishing the ideal community on earth. [*See* Tawḥīd; Justice, *article on* Concepts of Justice; *and* Imāmah.]

The imamate, like the prophecy, is protected from sin and is regarded as a divinely designated office. Through the imamate, survival of religion is guaranteed, hence the Shīʿī belief that "the earth cannot be set aright except by the Imam." This means that there is an imam in every age, either manifest or concealed, who has the knowledge of the lawful and unlawful in Islam and who calls people to the way of God. There are times when the community can be without a manifest imam; this happens when God is enraged at the people for endangering the imam's life. Thus, the twelfth imam went into occultation in 874 and will continue to live in this state for as long as God deems necessary; eventually, God will command him to reappear and take control of the world in order to restore justice and equity. During the occultation, the imam has deputies, in the person of the *marjaʿ al-taqlīd,* who can act on God's behalf and guide the Shīʿīs in their religious and social matters.

As for *furūʿ*, in addition to the four pillars recognized by Sunnī Islam (*ṣalāt* [ritual worship], fasting of Ramaḍān, *zakāt,* and the *ḥajj*), the Shīʿīs add a number of juridically sanctioned acts. Shīʿīs are required to pay the *khums* on all gainful acquisition (wages, inheritance, treasure, wealth acquired through diving, and so on) after deducting all expenses connected with support of one's family, including education, marriage, assistance to the underprivileged, and so forth. *Khums* donations are divided into two equal portions: one portion is distributed among the needy, the orphaned, and wayfarers among the Prophet's descendants (the Hashemites); and another portion belongs to the imam, who uses it for all benevolent purposes in the community. During the absence of the twelfth imam, his share is administered by the *mujtahid.* This share has become the single most important source of financial independence of the Shīʿī religious class, which has used these donations to expand its influence over the community by supporting the establishment of religious institutions, including mosques and schools, and by providing religious personnel to represent its views and opinions in the community. Indirectly, such independence has increased the prestige of the religious class trustworthy protectors of the Shīʿīs against perceived oppression and tyranny of government officials. [*See* Khums.]

Jihād, "enjoining the good and forbidding the evil," "befriending (*tawallā*) those who befriend the Prophet and his descendants," and "disassociating *(tabarra'a)* from those who hate them" are also listed in the Shīʿī *furūʿ* alongside the other pillars. However, in the absence of the twelfth imam, only a defensive form of *jihād* is permitted in Shīʿī law, and "enjoining" and "forbidding" by use of force is limited to the legitimate Shīʿī authority, including the deputized jurist. [*See* Jihād.]

The obligation of *tawallā* ("befriending") has led to two important religious practices unique to the Shīʿīs: first, the *ziyārah* (visitations) to the *mashhad* (mausoleums) of the imams and their descendants; and second, *majālis* (devotional gatherings) to mourn the martyrdom of Imam Ḥusayn on ʿĀshūrā', the tenth day of Muḥarram, in Karbala. Both these practices have provided the Shīʿī minority with a renewed sense of loyalty to the Prophet's family. The shrine cities of Karbala, Najaf, Mashhad, and Qom have functioned as the religious centers for the ordinary Shīʿīs and learning centers for their *mujtahid*s, who continue to teach in the holy sanctuaries. The Muḥarram commemoration has fostered among the Shīʿīs an identity consonant with their vision of history in which the godly people suffer at the hands of the oppressors until God commands the Mahdi to restore justice and equity on earth. The Iranian Revolution of 1979 not only utilized the religious symbols of Karbala to overthrow the shah's regime; it also used its most powerful message—challenging the tyranny of the time—by mobilizing support of the Shīʿī populace in the first ten days of Muḥarram (December 1978). Similar demands for the end of tyranny were heard in the neighboring Persian Gulf states, including Bahrain and Saudi Arabia, with large Shīʿī minorities, during the Muḥarram celebrations of 1978 and 1979. Thus, Muḥarram devotional gatherings held in special buildings for that purpose and known as *ḥusaynīyah* have served as important indicators of political and social awareness among Shīʿīs. The *ḥusaynīyah* have also provided influential Shīʿī preachers with a platform to educate masses in religious observances and to prepare them to pledge their loyalty to the *marjaʿ*, whose stance on religious and political matters they represent among the Shīʿīs. [*See* Ziyārah; Mashhad; Ḥusaynīyah.]

[*See also* Shīʿī Islam.]

BIBLIOGRAPHY

Ayoub, Mahmoud M. *Redemptive Suffering in Islam: A Study of the Devotional Aspects of ʿĀshūrā' in Twelver Shīʿism.* The Hague, 1978.

Jafri, S. H. M. *Origins and Early Development of Shiʿa Islam.* London, 1979.

Momen, Moojan. *An Introduction to Shiʿi Islam: The History and Doctrines of Twelver Shiʿism.* New Haven, 1985.

Sachedina, A. A. *Islamic Messianism: The Idea of the Mahdī in Twelver Shīʿism.* Albany, N.Y., 1981.

Sachedina, A. A. *The Just Ruler (al-Sulṭan al-ʿĀdil) in Shīʿite Islam: The Comprehensive Authority of the Jurist in Imamite Jurisprudence.* New York, 1988.

Sachedina, A. A. "Activist Shiʿism in Iran, Iraq, and Lebanon." In *Fundamentalisms Observed,* edited by Martin E. Marty and R. Scott Appleby, pp. 403–456. Chicago, 1991.

ABDULAZIZ SACHEDINA

İTTİHAD-İ MUHAMMADİ CEMİYETİ. A political and religious organization was founded around the newspaper *Volkan* (Volcano) in February 1909 by Hafiz Derviş Vahdeti, a Naqshbandī from Cyprus. Named İttihad-i Muhammadi Cemiyeti (Muhammadan Union), it is known for its role in the insurrection of April 1909 in Istanbul that aimed to destroy the Committee of Union and Progress (CUP).

Conservative forces in the Ottoman Empire had been alarmed by the winds of change that blew through the capital after the restoration of the 1876 constitution in July 1908. The press flourished with the end of censorship, workers went on strike, and smart middle-class women left the home to take their place in public life alongside men. The world of the conservatives was shaken, and they blamed the constitution. They objected to the sultan-caliph's loss of power and to the weakened role of *sharīʿah* in daily life. Initially, this opposition took religious form.

The first manifestation of religious reaction was the "Blind Ali Incident" of 7 October 1908. A certain Hoca Ali Efendi led a large crowd to Yildiz Palace and asked Sultan Abdülhamid to abolish the constitution and restore the *sharīʿah,* even though it was still recognized. This demonstration proved ineffective; it was spontaneous and disorganized and lacked the support of the liberal-conservative faction within the Young Turk movement.

During the first nine months of revolutionary activity, the real struggle for power was between the radical Unionists and the moderate liberals. The liberals were sure that they would win the December elections, but the elections were won by the CUP, though the liberals controlled the government. Only after the CUP had voted out the cabinet of Kamil Pasha on 13 February 1909 did the opposition come out into the open. It took religious form, even though the liberals were as commited to reform as the CUP; the liberals were willing to use Islam to destroy their rivals.

The first issue of *Volkan* appeared on February 16. It was the voice of İttihad-i Muhammadi and called for Islamic unity as the basis of the Ottoman state. The İttihad's doctrines and program were clerical and opposed to the reforms envisaged by the constitutional regime. Its own goals were described as nonpolitical, limited to reforming public morality in keeping with the principles of the *sharīʿah*.

Volkan used its columns to attack the CUP and Freemasons, as well as the constitutional regime, which it denounced as the "regime of devils." The religious prejudices of its readers were exploited fully with attacks on "modern" women and non-Muslims. The paper was distributed free, leading to rumors that it was financed by the Palace or the British Embassy. The İttihad's propaganda made great headway, and on 6 April the Şeyhülislam (Ar., Shaykh al-Islām) was forced to defend his government's policies against *Volkan*'s accusations that these policies violated the *sharīʿah*. Feelings against the CUP rose dramatically following the murder of an opposition journalist on 7 April and his funeral the next day. Meanwhile, Islamist propaganda had reached the troops of the Istanbul garrison through itinerant theological students; on 10 April the troops were forbidden to have contact with such men. In this atmosphere of tension, the garrison mutinied on the night of 12/13 April and almost succeeded in destroying the CUP. But the mutiny was crushed, the İttihad was proscribed, and some of its leaders, including Derviş Vahdeti, were hanged. Thereafter, the İttihad-i Muhammadi and the events of 1909 have come to symbolize religious reaction in Turkish political life.

[*See also* Young Turks *and the biography of Abdülhamid II.*]

BIBLIOGRAPHY

Ahmad, Feroz. *The Young Turks*. Oxford, 1969. Useful for the history of the period 1906–1914.

Fahri, David. " "The Şeriat as a Political Slogan, or, The 'Incident of the 31st Mart.' " *Middle Eastern Studies* 7 (1971): 275–316. Critical evaluation of the religious factor in the insurrection.

McCullagh, Francis. *The Fall of Abd-ül-Hamid*. London, 1910. Gripping eyewitness account of the insurrection and the activities of the *Volkan* group.

Feroz Ahmad

İTTİHAD VE TERAKKİ CEMİYETİ. *See* Young Turks.

J

JABHAT AL-INQĀDH AL-ISLĀMĪ. *See* Islamic Salvation Front.

JADĪDISM. The nineteenth- and early twentieth-century movement called Jadīdism developed among Russian Muslim intellectuals in response to colonial hegemony and the modern age. The name is a contraction of the phrase *uṣūl al-jadīd* ("new method"), proposed in the 1880s to describe the phonetic method of language instruction introduced into *mektebs* (Ar., *maktab;* elementary school) first in Crimea and the Caucasus and later in other areas of Russian Muslim settlement. Initially applied to education, Jadīdism always had a larger agenda: to reform many aspects of Islamic society so as to raise the quality of life of Muslims, to improve their economic and technical competitiveness, and restore something of the power, wealth, and dignity gradually lost over previous decades and centuries.

The extraordinary transmutation of Western society and culture between the fifteenth and mid-eighteenth centuries, with which Russia was linked closely if not directly, posed unremitting challenges to the Muslim communities drawn under Russian control. They found themselves unable to change sufficiently so as to sustain the parity that had characterized intercivilizational relations since ancient times. Beginning in areas having the longest and most extensive contact with Russian culture, such as the Volga region, Crimea, and the Caucasus, such concerns generated calls from the intellectual and political elite for revitalizing society. The waning and apparent incompetence of indigenous political authority, the generally stultifying conservatism of intellectual life, and the limitations of traditional economic resources and techniques—as well as the Russian intrusion into the local sociocultural fabric—inspired reformist impulses. These responses took a variety of forms; the most pronounced initially were first a resurgence of Ṣūfī brotherhoods stressing the inner awakening and moral reformation of the individual, and second, an intellectual reassessment by segments of the learned (*ʿulamāʾ*) of the accepted traditions underpinning Islamic civilization. By the turn of the nineteenth century both phenomena were contributing to a growing interest in renewal *(tajdīd)* as the means for returning Islamic life to its presumed vital forms—a renewal that promised a better future by authenticating and implementing the fundamental tradition established in the seventh century when Muḥammad lived to guide the faithful.

As the nineteenth century unfolded, calls for change resonated in various Russian Islamic communities. As failures mounted, as the West's challenge (through Russia) struck deeper and deeper, and as circumstances shaping colonial relations within the empire generated more opportunities for Muslims, these backward-looking modalities of reform seemed increasingly inadequate. For all its political and technical impact, the West's most significant influence came from its effect on Muslim minds—on the way knowledge was viewed, categorized, appreciated, and pursued. One consequence was a revolutionary intellectual transformation that led more and more Muslims to accept, however reluctantly, not only new ways of looking at the past and present but also an alien modality of change rooted in an idea of progress. In the process a cadre of russianized Muslims emerged whose worldview reflected the effects of expanding contact with Russian culture and the modern way of life it represented. These included Abbas Kuli Aga Bakikhanov (1794–1848), Mirza Fetali Akhundov (1812–1878), Chokan Valikhanov (1835–1865), and Mirza Kazem-Bek (1802–1870), all of whom participated actively and fully in Russian life, holding various military, government, or academic positions; to this list should be added Shihabeddin Merjani (1818–1889), Abdülkayyum Nasiri (1825–1902), Hasan Bey Zerdabi (1837–1907), Alimjan Barudi (1857–1921), Rizaeddin Fakhreddin (1859–1936), Ismail Bey Gasprinskii (1851–1914), Münevver Kari (1880–1933), Mahmud Hoja Behbudî (1874–1919), and Abdurrâuf Fıtrat (1886–1938). All strove to ameliorate matters by consciously adapting aspects of modern culture to a base of Islamic identity. To be sure, these "new Muslims" were themselves a rather diverse group in terms of ethnic, social, and intellectual background, extent of commitment to secularization, and interest in syncretic solutions to intercultural contacts, but through their accumulated activities and writings all contributed in some measure to the emergence of the modernist discourse that became known as Jadīdism.

Despite the diversity that characterized Jadīdism, it possessed a central message and focus that recognized the nineteenth century as fundamentally different from every other and accepted the need for basic changes in how life was viewed and practiced. Not all the wisdom and experience of the Islamic past had been rendered irrelevant, but the painful consequences of not sharing in the West's engagement with technology revealed that more was needed for Muslims than could be found in any single culture. If the long-term goal of reacquiring wealth, power, and dignity were to be attainable, the immediate agenda had to focus on developing instruments for appropriate change and on more effective mobilization of material and human resources. At its most basic level, the strategy for implementing the Jadīdist message included the following points: (1) redefining and reading new lessons from history as well as adopting the analytical methodology (including critical use of sources) that had been evolving in Western historiography; (2) refocusing Islam as a cultural force, so that while continuing to regulate human behavior it would cease to be the exclusive object of experience; (3) redefining education and restructuring both its curricula and physical arrangements so as to expand the experience for children and raise its effectiveness; (4) empowering women and moving them from marginal to more central status in society in such a way that many traditional restrictions on them, such as veiling and inequitable practices associated with polygamy and divorce, would be cleared away and women's public role would be expanded; and (5) strengthening material productivity so as to reverse economic stagnation and the consequent inability to compete with the technically more advanced and aggressive powers of the Christian West and the "pagan" East (especially Japan).

Jadīdism never fully supplanted more traditional modes of thought and action, but from the second half of the nineteenth century to at least 1917 its influence spread ever more widely and deeply among new generations of Muslims, even beyond Russia's borders. With the passage of time efforts were made to institutionalize the movement: a political faction (Ittifak-i Müslümin) was established in 1906 to speak for Muslims in governing circles by convening empire-wide congresses to debate goals and aspirations; and professional organizations were created with an eye toward unifying thought, word, and deed in the service of a common purpose. The press for unity, however, diminished rather quickly in the early twentieth century as regional differences among Russian Muslims sparked counterarguments and actions emphasizing parochial and ethnic identities. As a force for change, the spirit of Jadīdism retained its vitality and leading role, but it fragmented geographically in the last decade of the tsarist system, rendering it unable to put up more than a token defense shortly thereafter against the more extreme challenge posed by Bolshevism.

[*See also the biographies of Fakhreddin and Gasprinskii.*]

BIBLIOGRAPHY

Abdullin, Yahya I. G. *Tatarskaia prosvetitel'skaia mysl'*. Kazan, 1976.

Akhmedov, Enver M. *Filosofiia azerbaĭdzhanskogo prosveshcheniia*. Baku, 1983.

Allworth, Edward. *The Modern Uzbeks*. Stanford, Calif., 1990.

Arsharuni, A. M., and Kh. Z. Gabidullin. *Ocherki panislamizma i pantiurkizma v Rossii* (1934). London, 1990.

Bennigsen, Alexandre, and Chantal Lemercier-Quelquejay. *La presse et le mouvement national chez les musulmans de Russie avant 1920*. Paris, 1964.

Lazzerini, Edward J. "Ethnicity and the Uses of History: The Case of the Volga Tatars and Jadidism." *Central Asian Survey* 1.1 (November 1982): 61–69.

Rorlich, Azade-Ayşe. *The Volga Tatars: A Profile in National Resilience*. Stanford, Calif., 1986.

Validov, Dzhamaliutdin. *Ocherk istorii obrazovannosti i literatury tatar* (1923). Oxford, 1986.

Zenkowsky, Serge A. *Pan-Turkism and Islam in Russia*. Cambridge, Mass., 1960.

EDWARD J. LAZZERINI

JAʿFARĪ. *See* Law, *article on* Legal Thought and Jurisprudence.

JĀHILĪYAH. In classical usage, the term *Jāhilīyah* refers to the period of time and the condition of society in Arabia before the advent of Islam. Often translated as "the age of ignorance," Jāhilīyah connotes a time of paganism before men and women recognized the oneness of God or knew God's sacred law.

In modern usage, Jāhilīyah has come to refer to what is deemed as the un-Islamic state of affairs in the contemporary Muslim world. The concept of "modern Jāhilīyah," which is at the heart of the twentieth-century Islamic revival, was first formulated by the Indian scholar Sayyid Abū al-Aʿlā Mawdūdī in 1939. For Mawdūdī, modernity was "the new barbarity," incorporating values, lifestyles, political theories, and systems of government that were, in his view, fundamentally incompatible with Islam. Mawdūdī's ideas became known in the Arab world through his meetings with Ḥasan al-Bannā' and Sayyid Quṭb as well as through the translation of his most important works from Urdu into Arabic in the early 1950s. They attained wide popularity through the work of his student, Abulḥasan ʿAlī Nadvī, whose 1950 work "What Did the World Lose due to the Decline or Islam?" expounded on Mawdūdī's theory of "modern Jāhilīyah," which held Muslims accountable for the sorry state they were in because they were implementing alien, un-Islamic institutions in their countries.

In Egypt, the modern Jāhilīyah theory began to be developed in the late 1940s by Sayyid Quṭb, a university-educated literary critic who became active in the Muslim Brotherhood after returning from a visit to the United States in 1950. In 1953, influenced by the work of Nadvī and Mawdūdī and his own dislike of the United States, Quṭb wrote a treatise, *Fi ẓilāl al-Qur'ān* (In the Shadow of the Qur'ān), in which he first explained his concept of modern Jāhilīyah. For Quṭb, Jāhilīyah is a state signified by the domination of man over man rather than the submission of man to God. Jāhilīyah, he believes, denotes any government system based on manmade values and institutions, such as democracy, monarchy, or dictatorship. Jāhilīyah is also, in his view, materialism, communism, or any other philosophical system in which there is no place for God.

For Quṭb, as well as for Mawdūdī and Nadvī, a total rejection of Western values was needed to combat the new Jāhilīyah. The Indian theorists had directed their concerns primarily against the external challenges of modernity from Western colonial powers; Quṭb, however, focused on the challenges coming from within Egypt, especially from the secularist military regime of Gamal Abdel Nasser. This new Jāhilīyah was not something outside the Islamic world to be kept at bay; the most dangerous Jāhilīyah has already come from the West and is festering within Muslim society. In *Maʿālim fī al-ṭarīq* (Signposts on the Road, 1964) he wrote that Muslim society is infected with a "cultural poisoning" coming from the West. Western manners and morals, art, literature, and laws permeate Islamic society. Furthermore, much of what is considered Islamic culture has actually been derived from the West.

In the face of the new Jāhilīyah, humankind is confronted with a moral choice—to observe God's laws in their entirety, or to observe laws made by humans. The choice is absolute, according to Quṭb: either Islam or Jāhilīyah. For Quṭb, emulating the West is the Jāhilī option: conditions in Europe and America, he says, are parallel with those in Arabia before Islam, in that humans are under the domination of humans rather than of God. As a result the West has become the locus of unbridled individualism and moral depravity.

The solution to the modern Jāhilīyah, in Quṭb's view, is that society must change. True Muslims must embrace *jihād* as a religious duty and wage it against forces of repression and injustice within the Muslim community. It is a duty to be carried out against westernizers and against other Muslims who foster modernity, so that the values of the *sharīʿah* can rise to the surface and alone guide the actions of Muslim believers.

In cleansing Muslim society of the West, Quṭb does not reject science and technology, which are acceptable and even desirable as long as they do not conflict with religious law. In the ideal society domination *(ḥakimīyah)* belongs to God alone, whose guidance would establish the kingdom of God on earth. Quṭb, however, would not have approved of passing the reins of power to men of religion. Rather, the goal in eradicating the new Jāhilīyah was that the *sharīʿah* should reign as an all-embracing way of life.

Quṭb was executed in 1966, but his ideas have been translated into action by several Islamist groups that take them quite literally. For these groups, including Takfīr, Hijrah, and al-Jihād al-Islāmī, the Muslim world is in a state of apostasy of which it is unconscious. This is derived from Western media and the promotion of Western lifestyles by authoritarian regimes committed to the modern Jāhilīyah. For true Muslims who find themselves surrounded by apostasy, *jihād* is both a defensive reaction and a moral imperative. *Jihād*, however, takes different forms. Some groups, such as the Muslim Brotherhood in Egypt and the pre-1992 Islamic Salvation Front in Algeria, sought to combat the new Jāhilīyah by working within the existing system, by standing for election, and by creating social reform through charitable, religious, and educational organizations. For radical fundamentalist groups, *jihād* against the modern Jāhilīyah has become a justification for militant action against secular regimes throughout the Arab world.

[*See also* Fundamentalism *and the biographies of Mawdūdī and Quṭb.*]

BIBLIOGRAPHY

Esposito, John L. *Islam and Politics*. 2d ed., rev. Syracuse, N.Y., 1987.

Haddad, Yvonne Yazbeck. "Sayyid Qutb, Ideologue of Islamic Revival." In *Voices of Resurgent Islam*, edited by John L. Esposito, pp. 67–98. New York and Oxford, 1983.

Mawdūdī, Sayyid Abū al-Aᶜlā. *The Islamic Way of Life*. Translated and edited by Khurshid Ahmad and Khurram Murad. Leicester, 1986.

Quṭb, Sayyid. *Milestones*. Beirut, 1978.

Sivan, Emmanuel. *Radical Islam: Medieval Theology and Modern Politics*. New Haven, 1985.

ELEANOR ABDELLA DOUMATO

JAMĀᶜAT AL-ISLĀMĪYAH, AL-. A broad range of Islamic organizations in Egypt use the name al-Jamāᶜat al-Islāmīyah (Islamic Groups). These groups operate primarily through independent mosques and student unions on university campuses and appeal primarily to Egyptian youths. There does not appear to be any single leadership uniting the various groups; rather, they represent the general trend in Egyptian society toward Islamic resurgence. However, since the mid-1980s an increasing number of clashes have occurred in Upper Egypt between government forces and more politically militant groups acting under the banner of al-Jamāᶜat al-Islāmīyah. The self-proclaimed leader of these groups is Shaykh Omar Abdel Rahman (Umar ᶜAbd al-Raḥmān), a blind preacher from al-Fayyum who lived in exile in the United States in the early 1990s.

The use of the term al-Jamāᶜat al-Islāmīyah originated in the early 1970s under the new government of President Anwar Sadat. Sadat released members of al-Ikhwān al-Muslimūn (the Muslim Brotherhood) who had been imprisoned under President Gamal Abdel Nasser and officially permitted new Islamic organizations to form under the umbrella of al-Jamāᶜat al-Islāmīyah. This move to reconstruct the conservative religious sectors of society was an early sign of Sadat's intention to shift Egypt's political course. Through the 1970s, as Sadat developed his plans to restructure the Egyptian political economy, these Islamic groups served as an important counterbalance to the old Nasserist constituency and other groups further to the left. While the regime reduced government programs and encouraged general privatization, the number of private *(ahlī)* mosques in the country doubled in one decade from twenty thousand to forty thousand.

These private mosques and the many Islamic organizations associated with them began to play an important role in large urban areas, including Cairo, Alexandria, Port Said, and Suez in Lower Egypt, and Asyut, al-Fayyum, and al-Minya in Upper Egypt. Continued rural migration to these cities, combined with the government's restructuring policy, exacerbated social and economic tensions and led to a growing sense of urban alienation. While the government reduced its social welfare programs, the activities of al-Jamāᶜat al-Islāmīyah provided a social safety net at private mosques, with centers for food and clothing distribution as well as for the study of the Qur'ān. These mosques also had new independent sources of funding in the form of private remittances from members' relatives who migrated to work in the Arab Gulf countries during the oil-boom years. An additional factor affecting the growth of the movement was the expansion of the country's university system, especially in Upper Egypt where new campuses were founded in the 1970s in al-Minya, al-Fayyum, Sohag, Qina, and Aswan. Students at these schools and the older university in Asyut organized unions and fraternities under the name of al-Jamāᶜat al-Islāmīyah.

By the late 1970s, as Sadat faced growing opposition at home for signing the Camp David peace treaty with Israel, there were a number of independent religious leaders associated with al-Jamāᶜat al-Islāmīyah who became very popular for their outspoken criticism of the Sadat regime. Prominent among these were Shaykh Aḥmad al-Maḥallawī at Qā'id Ibrāhīm Mosque in Alexandria and Shaykh Ḥāfiẓ Salāmah of al-Shuhadā' Mosque in Suez and al-Nūr Mosque in Cairo. Just before his assassination in 1981, Sadat made public attacks on both Shaykh Mahallawī and Shaykh Salāmah. Shaykh Omar Abdel Rahman was also critical of the regime and was later charged with having links to the Jihād group that carried out Sadat's assassination, but was not found guilty. In the government crackdown on public opposition both before and after Sadat's assassination, each of these religious leaders experienced state censorship and imprisonment.

It is difficult to generalize about the ideology, practices, and aims of the various al-Jamāʿat al-Islāmīyah organizations. In general, they advocate stronger Islamic rule and oppose non-Islamic practices in Egyptian society. They call for the adoption of *sharīʿah,* the Islamic legal code, as the official law of the state, and they oppose attempts by the government to control and supervise the work of mosques and religious groups through the shaykh of al-Azhar and the Ministry of Awqāf. More than other al-Jamāʿat leaders, Shaykh Omar Abdel Rahman has denounced the official religious institutions of the state and has even been critical of entry by moderates in the Ikhwān into electoral party politics. After the Iranian revolution he identified closely with its Islamic government and urged his followers to confront the Egyptian government directly for its non-Islamic practices.

The Egyptian government and official media have attempted to link Shaykh Omar with the clandestine and subversive Jihād group, but he has always denied the connection. The main difference between his activities and those of Jihād is that he openly sought to mobilize popular resistance to the government through his public preaching and the organizing of large conferences in cities along the Nile river. By the summer of 1988 there were an increasing number of clashes in al-Fayyum, al-Minya, and other cities in Asyut province between the local police and his followers as they left mosques after the Friday sermons. Cities and universities throughout the area experienced increasing repression by the state as the government closed mosques, disrupted student union elections, and banned all activities under the name al-Jamāʿat al-Islāmīyah. As tensions rose there were reports of house-to-house police searches, mass arrests in the thousands, and an increasing number of killings in many cities of Upper Egypt. In 1988 and 1989 Shaykh Omar was arrested and detained on at least two occasions. During his imprisonment, his followers staged large protests that led to further confrontations with the police; there were also demonstrations of support reported in the Cairo suburbs of Imbabah and ʿAyn Shāms, indicating his broad following and the shared identity of al-Jamāʿat organizations around Egypt. As the clashes between the government and al-Jamāʿat continued, Shaykh Omar left the country, reportedly first to Afghanistan and Pakistan and then to the United States.

Following Shaykh Omar's exile the level of conflict between al-Jamāʿat followers and the government increased, with military troops, armored cars, and helicopters deployed to several cities. The nature of the confrontation also assumed three new forms. First, the political assassinations of People's Assembly speaker Rifʿat al-Maḥjūb in October 1990 and of liberal author Faraj Fawdah in June 1992, were blamed on al-Jamāʿat and said to have been ordered by Shaykh Omar. Attacks on prominent officials continued, such as the attempted assassination of Prime Minister ʿĀṭif Ṣidqī, in November 1993. Second, in 1991 violent sectarian clashes between Muslims and Christians erupted in several cities of Upper Egypt, notably Dayrut; the government claimed these were instigated by members of al-Jamāʿat, but they mainly resulted from old social rivalries. Third, by late 1992 extremist elements in al-Jamāʿat claimed responsibility for at least two attacks on foreign tourists visiting pharaonic monuments in Upper Egypt. The government claimed the al-Jamāʿat were pursuing a new strategy to disrupt the tourist trade and thus damage the national economy. These attacks on foreign tourists continued into 1993.

In the summer of 1992 the government passed a strict new antiterrorism law limiting al-Jamāʿat's activities, and in the fall it announced that all mosques and prayer leaders would be put under state control. In August 1992 the government claimed to have arrested twenty-five leaders of al-Jamāʿat, including two foreign citizens—a Sudanese and Jordanian—at an organizational meeting in Alexandria. The government has always maintained that al-Jamāʿat is foreign-inspired, primarily by Iranians and Sudanese, and it now claimed to have exposed this international connection. Despite these arrests, however, al-Jamāʿat will probably remain a significant factor in Egyptian society; it has wide appeal among the youth and university students and seems to have established popular roots in several parts of the country. It is also unlikely that the Egyptian government will be able to establish state control over the thousands of independent mosques that have served as the base of the movement. Many Egyptian political analysts see the government's conflict with al-Jamāʿat continuing and perhaps intensifying, and indeed from June 1993 the government has shed an earlier hesitation to carry out the execution of Islamists convicted in military tribunals. It is unlikely, however, that al-Jamāʿat will be able to seize power from the present ruling elite in Egypt, not only because the elite is shielded by a powerful security apparatus and the army, backed by the "silent majority" of the middle classes and intelligentsia, but also because al-Jamāʿat ultimately lacks the organizational strength and cohesion necessary to assume popular leadership.

[*See also* Egypt; Fundamentalism; Muslim Brotherhood, *article on* Muslim Brotherhood in Egypt; Organization of the Islamic Jihād; *and the biography of Abdel Rahman.*]

BIBLIOGRAPHY

Ansari, Hamied. "The Islamic Militants in Egyptian Politics." *International Journal of Middle East Studies* 16 (1984): 123–144.

Ayubi, Nazih N. "The Politics of Militant Islamic Movements in the Middle East." *Journal of International Affairs* 36 (Fall 1982–Winter 1983): 271–283.

Foreign Broadcast Information Service. *Daily Reports: Near East and South Asia.* New Canaan, Conn., 1980–1992. Summary of Arab newspapers and radio broadcasts.

Ibrahim, Saad Eddin. "Anatomy of Egypt's Militant Islamic Groups: Methodological Note and Preliminary Findings." *International Journal of Middle East Studies* 12 (1980): 423–453.

Kupferschmidt, Uri M. "Reformist and Militant Islam in Urban and Rural Egypt." *Middle Eastern Studies* 23 (October 1987): 403–418.

McDermott, Anthony. "Mubarak's Egypt: The Challenge of the Militant Tendency." *The World Today* 42.10 (October 1986).

Sayyid Aḥmad, Muḥammad. "Egypt: The Islamic Issue." *Foreign Policy,* no. 69 (Winter 1987–1988): 22–39.

Sonbol, Amira El Azhary. "Egypt." In *The Politics of Islamic Revivalism: Diversity and Unity,* edited by Shireen Hunter, pp. 23–38. Bloomington, 1988.

IBRAHIM IBRAHIM

JAMĀʿAT-I ISLĀMĪ. An Islamic revivalist party in Pakistan, Jamāʿat-i Islāmī (the Islamic Organization/Party) is one of the oldest Islamic movements and has been influential in the development of Islamic revivalism across the Muslim world in general and Pakistan in particular. It was founded in Lahore on 26 August 1941, mainly through the efforts of Mawlānā Sayyid Abu al-Aʿlā Mawdūdī (d. 1979), an Islamic thinker and activist who had dedicated his life to the revival of Islam in India. Mawdūdī had been involved since 1938 with the struggle to reverse the decline of the Muslim community. He had opposed accommodating the Congress Party, believing that Hindu rule behind the veneer of secular nationalism would spell the end of Islam in India. He had been equally if not more vehemently opposed to the Muslim League, which he believed to be a secularist entity, completely ill-equipped to respond to the imperatives before the Muslim community. The Jamāʿat was in large measure created to rival the Muslim League for the leadership of the Pakistan movement, especially after the Lahore Resolution of 1940 that committed the League to creating a separate Muslim state.

Mawdūdī's call for the creation of a new Muslim organization that would better address the predicament facing Muslims was supported by a number of young *ʿulamāʾ* who joined him in Lahore to form the new organization. The most notable of these were Mawlānās Sayyid Abulḥasan ʿAlī Nadvī of Nadvatul-ʿUlamāʾ and Muḥammad Manẓūr Nuʿmānī, a Deobandī. Mawdūdī was elected by the founding body of seventy-five members as the Jamāʿat's first *amir* (president), a title he held until 1972. The party's constitution was also ratified in that opening session. Soon after its creation, the party established its headquarters in Pathankut, a hamlet in East Punjab. The seclusion of Pathankut permitted the Jamāʿat to consolidate and to create a community *(ummah),* which had been a principal objective behind its creation. Between 1941 and 1947, the Jamāʿat spread its message across India through its widely distributed literature, rallies, conventions, and public sessions.

Structure and Ideology. The Jamaʿat has closely followed the teachings of Mawdūdī, which emphasize the exoteric dimensions of faith, disparage traditional Islam, rationalize faith, and predicate eschatology and salvation on social action. The Jamāʿat views Islam as a holistic ideology analogous to Western ideologies such as Marxism. It promises a utopian order to be constructed in the temporal realm; and it encourages Muslims to embark upon an Islamic revolution, shaping society and politics in accordance with the precepts of the faith as interpreted by Mawdūdī.

According to the Jamāʿat's founding constitution, revised and amended since 1941, the party consists of members *(arkan,* sg. *rukn)* and a periphery of sympathizers (*muttafiq*s and *hamdard*s), all of whom provide it with a cadre of workers *(kārkun).* Members alone, however, may hold office in the party. In 1947 the Jamāʿat had 385 members; in 1989 this figure stood at 5,723, and the party also boasted 305,792 official affiliates. The Jamāʿat is guided by the *amir* in consultation with the Shūrā (consultative assembly). The internal affairs of the party are supervised by the office of the *qayyim* (secretary-general). In later years, this structure was reproduced at all levels of the party from the nation to village, creating an all-encompassing pyramidal structure of authority. Since the 1960s the party has also developed a women's wing, as well as semi-autonomous organizations such as publication houses and unions—especially a student union, Islāmī Jamʿīyat-i Ṭulabā (Islamic Society of Students)—to extend the purview of its activities [*see* Youth Movements].

The Jamāʿat's structure from inception has been that of an *ummah,* a virtuous Muslim community. Its creation both signaled the "rebirth" of Islam and provided Indian Muslims with an organizational model in their drive to assert their political rights and cultural demands. Party discipline has always been rigorous, and members are expected to reform all aspects of their lives to conform to standards set by the party. Emphasis therefore rests on quality rather than numbers. The Jamāʿat has not been a mass party, but a community which aims at absorbing society as a whole. It has sought to do this by compelling society to change in accordance with its teachings. In political terms, the Jamāʿat's organizational model has performed the function of a vanguard party in the struggle for Islamic revolution.

History and Politics. Following the partition of India, the Jamāʿat divided into three separate units for India, Jammu and Kashmir, and Pakistan. Mawdūdī, along with the bulk of the original party leaders and members, left India for Pakistan and established the headquarters of the Jamāʿat-i Islāmī of Pakistan in Lahore. Soon afterward the party abandoned the relative isolationism of its Pathankut days and became fully immersed in Pakistani politics. Its political vision continued to be guided by Mawdūdī's religious exegesis.

Pakistani politics meanwhile proved receptive to the Jamāʿat, and the party soon found a niche in the political arena that expanded over time. Pakistan's particularly arduous experiences with nation-building and consolidation of the state in the subsequent years, the deep-seated cleavages in its polity, the uneasy coexistence between democracy and military rule, and civil war and secession by the majority of its population made the emotional power of Islam increasingly more appealing and its promise of unity ever more poignant.

The Jamāʿat's political agenda was premised on a program of training a vanguard "Islamic elite," who would oversee the revival of Islam on a national level and would mobilize the masses using religious symbols and ideals. The party organized a tightly knit network of activists and sympathizers who not only propagated Mawdūdī's views but also enabled the party to project power in the political arena. Mawdūdī and the Jamāʿat quickly closed ranks with the *ʿulamā'* and other self-styled religious movements in pressing the newly formed state for an Islamic constitution. The party's ideas and policy positions featured prominently in the ongoing debates between the government and the religious alliance from 1947 to 1956, most notably in the Objectives Resolution of 1949. Jamāʿat's activism in these years culminated in an open confrontation with the government over the role of religion in politics.

No sooner had the state declared its independence than the Jamāʿat forbade the citizenry to take an oath of allegiance to the state unless it became Islamic. The government was troubled by the Jamāʿat's challenge to its legitimacy, especially when such challenges involved foreign relations. In 1948, while observing a cease-fire with India, Pakistan had resumed support for insurgency in Kashmir, which was largely spearheaded by armed paramilitary units dispatched from Pakistan. The fighters had harped on the theme of *jihād* to justify their uprising and to gather new recruits and material support for their cause. Mawdūdī, challenging the legitimacy of the declaration of a *jihād* in Kashmir, argued that vigilante groups could not declare *jihād,* nor could the government surreptitiously support a *jihād* when observing a cease-fire. *Jihād* had to be properly declared by a central government to justify a legitimate and ongoing war. Mawdūdī thus asserted that the government should either formally go to war with India over Kashmir, or abide by the terms of the cease-fire to which it had agreed. India understandably found Mawdūdī's opinion of considerable political value, which led Pakistani authorities to accuse the Jamāʿat of pro-Indian sympathies and anti-Pakistan activities. Several Jamāʿat leaders, including Mawdūdī, were incarcerated, and the party was declared a seditious entity on par with communist organizations.

Mawdūdī's arguments not only placed the government on the defensive by questioning the wisdom of its policy of cessation of conflict with India over Kashmir, but also revealed its susceptibility to criticism from the religious quarter. The entire episode moreover confirmed the Jamāʿat's place in the ongoing sociopolitical and constitutional debates in Pakistan, and increased the government's sensitivity to religious activism. The government, however, was unable to dismantle the Jamāʿat or to extirpate Islam from the political arena. Even while in prison, Mawdūdī continued his activities and successfully mobilized the *ʿulamā'* and various other religious groups to press the Constituent Assembly to move Pakistan toward islamization.

Following Mawdūdī's release from prison in 1950, the Jamāʿat's activities were further intensified, producing a formidable religious alliance that effectively anchored national constitutional debates in Islam. In 1951 the Jamāʿat became directly active in politics by taking part in the Punjab elections. It was, however, the anti-Aḥmadīyah agitations in Punjab in 1953–1954 that catapulted the Jamāʿat to the forefront of Pakistani politics.

In 1953, agitators organized and led by the *ʿulamāʾ* and religious activists demanded the dismissal of Zafaru'llah Khan, Pakistan's Aḥmadī foreign minister, and the relegation of the Aḥmadīyah to the status of a non-Muslim minority. These measures, the agitators argued, would serve as litmus tests for the government's commitment to Islam. Although the agitations were led by the *ʿulamāʾ* and religious groups such as the Anjuman-i Aḥrār, the Jamāʿat's role proved critical in providing convincing justification for them, especially in the form of a book, *Qadiyani mas'alah* (The Aḥmadīyah Question). In fact, the government viewed the Jamāʿat's support for the agitations as more alarming and invidious than the provocative activities of the Aḥrār. As a result, once the government clamped down on the agitations, Mawdūdī and a number of prominent Jamāʿat leaders were apprehended and put on trial. Mawdūdī was convicted of sedition and sentenced to death. That sentence was later commuted and was eventually reversed by the country's supreme court. [*See also* Aḥmadīyah.]

By pitting the Jamāʿat against the state over a popular cause, the anti-Aḥmadīyah issue enhanced the party's political standing. Moreover, the agitations placed Islam more squarely at the center of the constitutional debates regarding the nature of the Pakistani state, all to the Jamāʿat's advantage. As a result, it used its growing power to exert renewed pressure on the government, this time regarding the issue of the constitution of 1956.

Since 1947 the Jamāʿat and its allies had successfully anchored constitutional debates in a concern for the Islamicity of the state. In the aftermath of the anti-Aḥmadīyah disturbances, and with the religiously inclined Chaudhri Muhammad ʿAli as prime minister, the Constitutional Assembly began to accommodate the religious activists to an increasing extent. Consequently, with the promulgation of the constitution of 1956, the Jamāʿat and its allies among the *ʿulamāʾ* claimed victory and accepted the new constitution as an Islamic one.

This paved the way for the Jamāʿat to become more directly involved in politics. In 1957, despite opposition within the party, Mawdūdī directed the Jamāʿat to recognize the legitimacy of the state by declaring that it would participate in the national elections of 1958 as a full-fledged party. The constitutional victory was, however, short lived, for the armed forces of Pakistan under the command of General Muhammad Ayub Khan (d. 1969), with a modernizing agenda that disparaged the encroachment of religion into politics, took over power in 1958.

Over the following decade the political establishment became dominated by an authoritarian and bureaucratic elite who actively promoted religious modernism as a way of retarding the drive for the islamization of the country. Advocates of religious revival and an Islamic state were increasingly pressed into retreat. The Jamāʿat's offices were closed down, its leaders were excoriated in government-sponsored publications, and its activities, networks, and operations were restricted. Mawdūdi himself was imprisoned twice during Ayub Khan's rule.

Unable to advocate freely the cause of Islam in the political arena, the Jamāʿat became more concerned with the removal of Ayub Khan and the restoration of a political climate that would be conducive to religio-political activism. The party's experiences with Ayub Khan's government forced it to look for new allies outside the circle of religious revivalists. Consequently, the Jamāʿat joined the alliance of political parties that advocated restoration of democracy and an end to Ayub Khan's hegemony in Pakistan, going so far as to support the candidacy of Fatimah Jinnah in the presidential elections of 1965. The Ayub era politicized the Jamāʿat further, transforming it into a consummate political party.

The result of this transformation was clear in the Jamāʿat's policies in the post-Ayub period. In 1970 it participated in national elections with the aim of capturing power. Those hopes were dashed when the party won only four seats in the National Assembly and four seats in various provincial assemblies. In 1971 the Jamāʿat responded to the advent of civil war in East Pakistan by mobilizing its resources in support of the central government and by joining the attempt to prevent East Pakistan from seceding as Bangladesh.

The secession of East Pakistan and the rise of Zulfiqar ʿAli Bhutto (d. 1979) to power in 1971 intensified the Jamāʿat's political activism. The socialist content of the Pakistan Peoples' Party's political program was particularly instrumental in prompting the Jamāʿat into action. Viewing Bhutto's populism as a direct challenge to the

Islamic basis of Pakistan and to its own place in the country's political order, the party directly confronted the government on numerous political issues, notably during the movement against recognition of Bangladesh in 1972–1974 and the anti-Aḥmadīyah disturbances of 1974.

Throughout the Bhutto years the Jamāʿat spearheaded a political movement that consciously appealed to religious sentiments in order to weaken the Bhutto regime. While the opposition to Ayub had brought religious groups into an alliance for democracy, opposition to Bhutto took shape under the banner of religion. The Jamāʿat's religio-political program proved instrumental in giving shape to this alliance—the Niẓām-i Muṣṭafā (Order of the Prophet) movement—and in managing its nationwide agitations. The struggle against Bhutto greatly bolstered the Jamāʿat's popular standing. In the elections of 1977, widely believed to have been rigged to favor Bhutto, the Jamāʿat won nine of the thirty-six seats won by the opposition. During the subsequent antigovernment protests the party's popularity soared further. It was the Jamāʿat and the movement it led that eventually undermined the Bhutto government and in 1977 provoked a military coup d'état.

The cause of the Islamic opposition, now enjoying wide popularity, could not be ignored by the martial-law administration of General Muhammad Zia ul-Haq (d. 1988), who in his search for legitimacy was quick to appease the Niẓām-i Muṣṭafā movement. Zia's eleven-year rule from 1977 to 1988 was therefore a period of unprecedented success and political influence for the Jamāʿat. During the Zia period the Jamāʿat, once a dissident party outside the pale of mainstream politics, became a political and ideological force at the helm of power. Jamāʿat leaders occupied important government offices, including cabinet posts, and the party's views were reflected in government programs. The party played a direct role in the islamization of the country, as well as in articulating state policy, especially concerning the Afghan *jihād* and the position of the federal state on provincialist and ethnic demands.

The rise in the fortunes of the Jamāʿat during the Zia period, however, turned out to be a pyrrhic victory; for despite its influence at the top, the party failed to expand its social base, nor was it able to exercise political influence outside the channels provided by the government. As a result, in the national elections of 1985 it won only ten seats in the National Assembly and thirteen in the provincial assemblies. Unable to utilize its newly found prominence to advance its own political position or to distinguish its programs from those of the government, the Jamāʿat became an instrument of government policy-making and was, therefore, effectively coopted by the regime.

The Jamāʿat's experience with the Zia regime not only dealt a blow to the party's morale and prestige, but also rendered it politically vulnerable. As Zia gradually fell out of favor with the masses, so did the Jamāʿat witness a turn in its political fortunes. The party's predicament manifested itself in its modest showings in Pakistan's national elections of 1988, 1990, and 1993. In the first two it participated as part of the Islāmī Jumhūrī Ittiḥād (IJI or Islamic Democratic Alliance), a coalition of Islamic and right-of-center parties that emerged following Zia's death to challenge the Pakistan Peoples' Party. In the elections of 1988 the Jamāʿat won eight seats in the national assembly and thirteen in the provincial assemblies; in the elections of 1990, the Jamāʿat's tally of seats stood at eight and twenty, respectively. In the 1993 elections the Jamāʿat contested alone, winning only three seats to the national assembly and six to provincial assemblies.

Yet, despite its limited electoral showings, by the end of the Zia period it was apparent that the Jamāʿat had become a powerful political force with significant social and cultural influence, derived mainly from its organizational structure and ability to manipulate the religious factor in Pakistan's political balance. While unable to increase its political prowess in the Pakistani parliament, the Jamāʿat remains an important political party capable of influencing the course of politics through the use of its organizational muscle. The Jamāʿat's political stature is reflected in the power which it has wielded in the IJI between 1988 and 1993.

Continuity and Change in Party Structure. During its five decades of existence the Jamāʿat has gone through a number of purges and reorganizations as well as periods of uncertainty and redirection—none more significant than the transition from one leader to another. The Jamāʿat has been led by three *amir*s and has passed through two succession periods: from Sayyid Abu al-Aʿlā Mawdūdī (1941–1972) to Miyān Ṭufail Muḥammad (1972–1987), and then to Qāẓī Ḥusain Aḥmad (since 1987); each such period has engendered a reorientation of the party.

Of equal importance are changes in the social base of the Jamāʿat. The party has at one point or another been associated with various constituencies or ethnic groups, notably the urban middle classes, the petit-bourgeoisie, the Muhajirs (those who performed *hijrah* or migrated from India to Pakistan in 1947), the Punjabis, and more recently the Pathans. In its concern for the islamization of the state, the party has eschewed populist politics and sought to establish a base among the intelligentsia. Although it has failed to inculcate support among any one social class or to gain a large following, it relies on the power of discipline and organization rather than the power of numbers.

The party has, however, compensated for its restricted social base by developing ties with students, Pakistan's future politicians, bureaucrats, and intellectual leaders. It is its success with students that best explains the Jamāʿat's incremental rise in importance in the bureaucracy and the civil service. This strategy also manifests Mawdūdī's doctrine of islamizing the state from within and above: revolution through education and conversion rather than by coercion.

[*See also* Pakistan *and the biography of Mawdūdī.*]

BIBLIOGRAPHY

Abbott, Freeland. "The Jamaʿat-i-Islami of Pakistan." *Middle East Journal* 11.1 (Winter 1957): 37–51. Good account of the Jamāʿat's activities up to 1957.

Adams, Charles J. "The Ideology of Mawlana Mawdudi." In *South Asian Politics and Religion,* edited by Donald E. Smith, pp. 371–397. Princeton, 1966. A standard work on Mawdūdī's ideology.

Adams, Charles J. "Mawdudi and the Islamic State." In *Voices of Resurgent Islam,* edited by John L. Esposito, pp. 99–133. New York, 1983. Overview of the Jamāʿat's ideology.

Aḥmad, ʿAbdul-Ghafūr. *Phir Mārshal Lā Ā-Giyā* (Then Came the Martial Law). Lahore, 1988. Good account of the Jamāʿat's politics during the Zia years.

Aḥmad, Isrār. *Taḥrīk-i Jamāʿat-i Islāmī: Ek Taḥqīqī Muṭālaʿah* (The Movement of Jamāʿat-i Islāmī: A Critical Study). Lahore, 1966. Critical history of the Jamāʿat by a former member.

Ahmad, Mumtaz. "Islamic Fundamentalism in South Asia: The Jamaat-i-Islami and the Tablighi Jamaat." In *Fundamentalisms Observed,* edited by Martin E. Marty and R. Scott Appleby, pp. 457–530. Chicago, 1991. Good history of the Jamāʿat.

Bahadur, Kalim. *The Jamaʿat-i Islami of Pakistan.* New Delhi, 1977. Useful account of Jamāʿat's politics through the 1970s.

Binder, Leonard. *Religion and Politics in Pakistan.* Berkeley, 1961. Excellent account of the Jamāʿat's politics in the 1947–1956 period.

Dastūr-i Jamāʿat-i Islāmī, Pākistān (Constitution of Jamāʿat-i Islāmī of Pakistan). Lahore, 1989. The Jamāʿat's constitution, which governs the party's operation.

Hasan, Masudul. *Sayyid Abul Aʿala Maududi and His Thought.* 2 vols. Lahore, 1984. Detailed history of the Jamāʿat.

Ijtimāʿ Se Ijtimāʿ Tak, 1963–1974: Rūdād-i Jamāʿat-i Islāmī, Pākistān (From Convention to Convention, 1963–1974: Proceedings of the Jamāʿat-i Islāmī of Pakistan). Lahore, 1989. Official report on the Jamāʿat's activities in the 1963–1974 period.

Ijtimāʿ Se Ijtimāʿ Tak, 1974–1983: Rūdād-i Jamāʿat-i Islāmī, Pākistān (From Convention to Convention, 1974–1983: Proceedings of the Jamāʿat-i Islāmī of Pakistan). Lahore, 1989. Official report on the Jamāʿat's activities in the 1974–1983 period.

Ilāhī, Chaudhrī Raḥmat. *Pākistān Meṇ Jamāʿat-i Islāmī Kā Kirdār* (The Jamāʿat-i Islāmī's Activities in Pakistan). Lahore, 1990. Official account of the Jamāʿat's history.

Kennedy, Charles H. "Islamization and Legal Reform in Pakistan, 1979–89." *Pacific Affairs* 63.1 (Spring 1990): 62–77. Provides insights into the Jamāʿat's politics during the Zia period.

Munīr, Muḥammad. *From Jinnah to Zia.* Lahore, 1979. Critical examination of the role of Islamic parties in Pakistan's history.

Nasr, Seyyed Vali Reza. "Islamic Opposition to the Islamic State: The Jamāʿat-i Islāmī, 1977–1988." *International Journal of Middle East Studies* 24.4 (November 1992): 261–283. Account of the Jamāʿat's politics during the Zia period.

Nasr, Seyyed Vali Reza. "Students, Islam, and Politics: Islāmī Jamiʿat-i Ṭalaba in Pakistan." *Middle East Journal* 46.1 (Winter 1992): 59–76. Examination of the history and politics of the Jamāʿat's student wing.

Rūdād-i Jamāʿat-i Islāmī (Proceedings of the Jamāʿat-i Islāmī). 7 vols. Lahore, 1938–1991. Official historical chronicle of the Jamāʿat.

Shahpuri, Abad. *Tārīkh-i Jamāʿat-i Islāmī* (History of the Jamāʿat-i Islāmī). Lahore, 1989. Official history of the Jamāʿat's early years.

SEYYED VALI REZA NASR

JAMĀʿAT TABLĪGH. *See* Tablīghī Jamāʿat.

JĀMIʿAH AL-SAYFĪYAH, AL-. This Arabic academy in Surat, India, is the principal institution for the religious education and training of the Dā'ūdī Bohrā Ismāʿīlīs. The academy was established in 1814 by the forty-third *dāʿī muṭlaq,* (head of the Dā'ūdī Bohrās), Sayyidnā ʿAbd ʿAlī Sayf al-Dīn (1798–1817). The institution was then known as al-Dars al-Sayfī ("Sayfī learning assembly") in which the *dāʿīs* and their learned disciples conducted sessions in the mosque or courtyard (*īwān*) of the academy, disseminating authoritative knowledge on Fāṭimid Ismāʿīlī thought. Even then, the academy had promoted a system of education that remains its hallmark to this day. That is to view all knowledge, religious or otherwise, as essentially part of a broader Islamic knowledge and to require contemporary subjects to be taught harmoniously with Islamic lore. Sectarians regard this to be a Fāṭimid practice and thus part of their heritage.

During the leadership of the fifty-first *dāʿī* Ṭāhir Sayf al-Dīn (1915–1965), the academy was given its present name, and changes were introduced to make the traditional religious knowledge accessible to contemporary believers. Without changing the content, core subjects were taught using modern educational methods. Contemporary subjects were reinstituted and taught in English, whereas Arabic remained the foundation of traditional learning. Arabic and an arabicized form of the Indian language Gujarati serve as the media for religious discourse within the academy. A building program was also initiated which simultaneously improved facilities and introduced Fāṭimid architecture into the campus. The present *dāᶜī*, Sayyidnā Muḥammad Burhānuddīn, has continued his predecessor's work and completed the modernization and building program. Modern facilities such as a language laboratory for the teaching of Qur'ānic sciences have been provided, and the architecture now reflects the Fāṭimid origins of the academy. A new branch of the academy was also built by him in Karachi, Pakistan, in 1983. These improvements were implemented by the academy's eminent rector, Yūsuf Najm al-Dīn (d. 1987), to whom the academy's current academic and administrative policies may be attributed.

Al-Jāmiᶜah al-Sayfīyah houses some of the rarest Islamic and Ismāᶜīlī manuscripts of the Fāṭimid and Yemenite periods. These priceless manuscripts are zealously preserved by the academy; recently attempts have been made to publish edited versions of some of them.

One of the distinctive features of the academy is its system of examination, which tests the qualifications of advanced students in a public gathering of academics, community leaders, and general members presided over by the *dāᶜī*. The system helps to confirm the credentials of future religious guides in the presence of the community and its leader and also helps to assess the method of instruction.

The academy is essentially a residential campus, with boarding and lodging provided free to both male and female students by the *dāᶜī*. It was one of the world's first theological institutes to enroll female students. Islamic mores requiring separation of men and women in living quarters and in classes are observed strictly.

The academic program at the Jāmiᶜah lasts eleven years and is divided into three stages. The first four years, which the students begin at the age of twelve, are spent in foundational studies designed to equalize the preparation of students from differing educational backgrounds. The subjects taught include Arabic poetry and prose, jurisprudence, Islamic history, Islamic religious practice, English, humanities, social sciences, and natural sciences. Arabic is taught by usage rather than by formal instruction. The student is required to memorize a great deal of Arabic poetry, a practice that has made the Bohrā community poetry rich. The student is also evaluated for religious practice and piety. A diploma, *mubtaghī al-ᶜilm* ("seeker of knowledge"), is awarded on successful completion of this stage. Over the next five years the same subjects are developed further, but in addition, psychology, philosophy, and subjects peculiar to Fāṭimid Ismāᶜīlī Ṭayyibī Shiism are taught. At the end of this stage the degree of *al-faqīh al-mutqan* ("perfect jurist") is awarded. The last two years are reserved for graduate work, in which the student specializes in specific subjects such as Arabic literature, Islamic jurisprudence, and Islamic history. The graduate of this stage is awarded the degree of *al-faqīh al-jayyid* ("accomplished jurist"). This degree is recognized as equivalent to a Master of Arts by Karachi University.

While in training, students are given the opportunity to obtain practical experience by being sent to different towns to lead local communities during Ramaḍān and Muḥarram. About forty students complete the full eleven-year course each year, out of an annual intake of about a hundred in both branches of the academy. Most graduates are appointed as religious guides to serve the community wherever they are dispatched by the *dāᶜī*, although some choose independent careers.

[*See also* Bohrās; Ismāᶜīlīyah.]

BIBLIOGRAPHY

Background information on the Saifee Foundation and a statement of its future development is contained in *Foundation* 1 (June 1960): 57–60, and 5 (March 1965): 56–68, 76–80. Detailed information on the academy's teaching philosophy, curriculum, and course contents is contained in its publication, *Malāmiḥuhā wa-manāhijuhā* (Bombay, 1979). General information on the academy's beginnings and its pedagogy may be found in *A Novel Experiment in Islamic and Arabic Studies* (Bombay, 1991), as well as the academy's *Prospectus* (Surat, 1984), Y. Najmuddin's *Inauguration of New Jamea Masjid and Academy Building* (Surat, 1961), and A. R. Kazi's *The Architecture of al-Jamea-tus-Saifiyah Karachi* (Karachi, 1983). For comparisons with other Islamic colleges, the reader may consult F. R. C. Bagley, "The Azhar and Shīᶜism," *Muslim World* 50 (April 1960): 122–129, and Fāḍil Jamāli, "The Theological Colleges of Najaf," *Muslim World* 50 (January 1960): 15–22.

MUSTAFA ABDULHUSSEIN

JAMᶜĪYAT AL-SHUBBĀN AL-MUSLIMĪN. A Pan-Islamic Egyptian political association founded in 1927 in Cairo, the Jamᶜīyat al-Shubbān al-Muslimīn was apparently modeled in part on the YMCA and is often referred to as the Young Men's Muslim Association, the Y.M.M.A. It was created in the midst of the social and political turmoil of Egypt following the nationalist revolution of 1919 and was one of a large number of societies and associations, of a variety of political stripes, formed in Egypt in that period. No doubt the most important of these groups was the Muslim Brotherhood (al-Ikhwān al-Muslimūn) under the leadership of Ḥasan al-Bannā'. Al-Bannā' played an active role in the creation of the Y.M.M.A. and is said to have related the group's founding to an increasing dissatisfaction among younger Egyptian activists seeking a central role for Islamic ideals in political and social life with a perceived unwillingness of the religious hierarchy of al-Azhar to address contemporary issues (Mitchell, 1969, p. 5). Despite his support for the Y.M.M.A, al-Bannā' never devoted his full attention to the group. Al-Bannā's assassination in 1949 took place outside the headquarters of the Y.M.M.A.

Among those involved in the creation of the Y.M.M.A. and in the formulation of its initial policies and activities were ʿAbd al-Ḥamīd Bey Saʿīd, at the time a leading nationalist and member of the Egyptian parliament; Muḥībb al-Dīn al-Khaṭīb, a bookseller and editor of *Majallat al-fatḥ*, a weekly publication promoting Islamic views that is often associated with the Salafīyah movement; and Yaḥyā Aḥmad al-Dardīrī, who served as editor and a frequent contributor to the official publication of the Y.M.M.A. Al-Dardīrī also published a history of the organization entitled *Al-ṭarīq* (The Way). Like the Muslim Brotherhood, the Y.M.M.A. set out rather quickly to establish branches in other areas of the Middle East, chiefly in Palestine, Syria, and Iraq. Branches were established in Jerusalem, Acre, Haifa, and Jaffa by the end of 1928 and in Baghdad and Basra by 1929.

The group was established initially as a social, cultural, and religious organization seeking to appeal directly to Egypt's youth. Its headquarters was the center of literary and educational gatherings, and its members were encouraged to set a moral example for their peers. Perhaps inevitably the leaders of the Y.M.M.A. joined in the many political debates of their day. In writings and lectures, al-Dardīrī and other spokesmen for the group addressed grievances related to the presence of a large non-Muslim population in Egypt and its influence on Islamic life; they attacked Jewish immigration into Palestine and the activities of Zionist organizations; and they criticized French colonization of Algeria and Morocco.

[*See also* Muslim Brotherhood, *article on* Muslim Brotherhood in Egypt; *and the biography of Bannā'*.]

BIBLIOGRAPHY

Gibb, H. A. R. *Whither Islam?* London, 1932.

Harris, Christina. *Nationalism and Revolution in Egypt.* The Hague, 1964.

Heyworth-Dunne, James. *Religious and Political Trends in Modern Egypt.* Washington, D.C., 1950.

Ḥusaynī, Isḥāq Mūsā al-. *The Moslem Brethren.* Translated by John F. Brown et al. Beirut, 1956.

Mitchell, Richard P. *The Society of the Muslim Brothers.* London, 1969.

MATTHEW S. GORDON

JAMʿĪYATUL ʿULAMĀ'-I HIND. An organization of Muslim religious scholars of India, the Jamʿīyatul ʿUlamā'-i Hind (Association of the ʿUlamā' of India) was established in November 1919, when numerous *ʿulamā'* from all parts of India came to participate in the Khilāfat Movement conference in New Delhi [*see* Khilāfat Movement]. The organization came into being when Indians of all religious affiliations were united in the anti-British struggle. Mohandas Gandhi embraced the cause of the Ottoman caliphate, and most Muslim leaders participated in the noncooperation movement with the Indian National Congress. The Jamʿīyatul ʿUlamā'-i Hind maintained its pro-Congress attitude throughout the struggle for independence and stood at the head of those Indian Muslims who supported the idea of a united India and opposed the Pakistan movement. (Some of its members, however, seceded in 1946 and established the Jamʿīyatul ʿUlamā'-i Islām, which supported Pakistan [*see* Jamʿīyatul ʿUlamā'-i Islām].) Many of the members were associated with the Dār al-ʿUlūm of Deoband. Since its establishment in 1919, the association has held annual conferences in which the *ʿulamā'* have expressed their views on the central issues of the day.

The main contribution of the Jamʿīyatul ʿUlamā'-i Hind to Indo-Muslim thought is the theory of "composite nationalism" *(muttaḥida qawmīyat)*. This theory, which was elaborated in speeches and writings of the Jamʿīya leadership and particularly in the works of its longtime president Ḥusain Aḥmad Madanī (1879–1957), served as an alternative to the "two nations theory" *(do qawmī naẓarīyat)* of the Muslim League, which formed the ideological basis of the Pakistan movement. According to the theory of "composite nationalism," nations can be created by various factors, such as religion, race, homeland, language, or color. In this analysis, a "nation" *(qawm)* is not an exclusive category: a person can belong simultaneously to several "nations" created by different characteristics. In modern times, the most important nation-building factor has been the homeland; the Muslims of India therefore belong to the same nation as other Indians, and India constitutes a nation despite its religious diversity. Nevertheless, according to the religious criterion, Muslims continue to belong to the Muslim *qawm*.

The Jamᶜīyatul ᶜUlamā'-i Hind thus accepted the idea of territorial nationalism. This is a novel idea in Islamic thought, and the *ᶜulamā'* devoted considerable intellectual effort to provide it with Islamic legitimacy. The classical Islamic precedent repeatedly used for this purpose is the Covenant of Medina *(ᶜahd al-ummah)*, the document that the Prophet is said to have issued in order to regulate the relationship between the Emigrants *(muhājirūn)*, the Helpers *(anṣār)*, and the Jews in Medina after the Hijrah. One of its sections states that "the Jews of ᶜAwf are one community with the believers; the Jews have their religion and the Muslims theirs." The *ᶜulamā'* concluded from this passage that the Prophet himself agreed to the inclusion of non-Muslims in the same nation with Muslims. The history of Mughal India is also seen as vindicating the composite nationalism theory. The Mughal period knew no communalism *(firqah vārīyat, firqah parastī)*; all Indians were treated equally by the rulers. Although the Muslims who established the Mughal empire came from outside India, once they settled there they became an inextricable part of Indian nationhood *(hindustānī qawmīyat)*. Communalism emerged in India only as a result of British policies.

The practical political conclusion from this interpretation of Muslim and Indo-Muslim history was the demand that Muslims cooperate with the Indian National Congress in order to expel the British from India and to achieve independence for the country. The *ᶜulamā'* envisaged that in an independent and united India, achieved with Muslim cooperation, the Muslims would have significant influence, their family law and religious institutions would be maintained, and governments with a Muslim majority would be established in several provinces. On the basis of these expectations, they appealed to Muslims not to join the Muslim League, even declaring membership in it a sin. The *ᶜulamā'* were convinced that the Western-educated element so prominent in the League's leadership would never be able or willing to establish an Islamic state compatible with the traditional religious ideal of the *ᶜulamā'*. They also maintained that the establishment of Pakistan would not solve the communal problem because many millions of Muslims would remain in the Indian part of the subcontinent and would live in an atmosphere of hate generated by the partition. On the other hand, the establishment of a strong and unified India, in which the Muslims would be an influential and significant minority, would benefit not only the Muslims of the subcontinent but also the Muslims of the rest of the world.

The views of the Jamᶜīya did not prevail during the struggle for independence, and in 1947 the subcontinent was partitioned between India and Pakistan. In independent India the Jamᶜīya acquired increased importance in the new political structure. In contradistinction to the Muslim League and other organizations that supported the creation of Pakistan, the Jamᶜīya possessed impeccable credentials of opposition to partition and was a natural candidate to represent Indian Muslims. Shortly after independence, the *ᶜulamā'* called upon Indian Muslims to declare their unswerving loyalty to India. Several of the ideas adopted by the *ᶜulamā'* after partition were rather bold from the vantage point of traditional Islam. They accepted the idea of a secular state, which they conceived as neutral in matters of religion. They gave qualified support to the idea of a composite Indian culture. They severed all ties with Jamᶜīya branches in the territories now incorporated in Pakistan, even though this was a country established in the name of Islam and inhabited mostly by Muslims. They supported Indian policies even on issues that were sensitive from the Muslim point of view, such as Kashmir and Hyderabad.

The Jamᶜīyatul ᶜUlamā'-i Hind is a rare, and possibly unique, case of an association of traditional Muslim religious scholars who have willingly bestowed legitimacy upon the policies of a non-Muslim and professedly secular government, born out of conflict with the generally acknowledged leadership of their own community.

[*See also* All-India Muslim League; India; Pakistan.]

BIBLIOGRAPHY

Ahmad, Aziz. *Islamic Modernism in India and Pakistan, 1857–1964*. London and New York, 1967, pp. 186–194.

Faruqi, Zia-ul-Hasan. *The Deoband School and the Demand for Pakistan*. Bombay, 1963.

Friedmann, Yohanan. "The Attitude of the *Jamᶜiyyat al-ᶜulamā'-i*

Hind to the Indian National Movement and to the Establishment of Pakistan." *Asian and African Studies* 7 (1971): 157–180.
Friedmann, Yohanan, "The *Jamᶜiyyat al-ᶜulamā'-i Hind* in the Wake of Partition." *Asian and African Studies* 11 (1976): 181–211.
Hardy, Peter. *Partners in Freedom—and True Muslims: The Political Thought of Some Muslim Scholars in British India, 1912–1947*. Lund, 1971.
Mushir-ul-Haq. *Islam in Secular India*. Simla, 1972. Important for the postindependence period.
Qureshi, Ishtiaq Husain. *Ulema in Politics: A Study Relating to the Activities of the Ulema in the South-Asian Subcontinent from 1556 to 1947*. New Delhi, 1985. Criticism of the activities of the Jamᶜīyatul ᶜUlamā'-i Hind from a Pakistani vantage point.

YOHANAN FRIEDMANN

JAMᶜĪYATUL ᶜULAMĀ'-I ISLĀM. The origins of the Jamᶜīyatul ᶜUlamā'-i Islām (JUI, Society of Muslim ᶜUlamā') can be traced to the Deoband movement in prepartition India and to the *ᶜulamā'* who consitituted the Jamᶜīyatul ᶜUlamā-i Hind (Society of Indian ᶜUlamā'). Such *ᶜulamā'* have been typically characterized as "Indian nationalists," because during the latter days of British India they were unalterably opposed to British imperialism, supported the aims and policies of the Indian National Congress, and opposed the Muslim League's struggle for an independent Pakistan. Consequently, following the partition of the subcontinent in 1947 and the creation of Pakistan, the political significance of the JUI was limited, and its leadership was held suspect by successive Pakistani regimes that condemned the JUI's role in the independence struggle as anti-Pakistan. Indeed, until the late 1960s the JUI remained almost wholly a religious organization with little if any political significance.

This situation changed during the so-called "Disturbances" of 1968–1969 that led ultimately to the resignation of General Muhammad Ayub Khan and to the holding of general elections in 1970. During the ferment of 1969 the JUI split into two factions—a Karachi-based faction under the leadership of Maulānā Ihtishāmul Ḥaqq Thānvī (later named Jamᶜīyatul ᶜUlamā'-i Pākistān, Thānvī Group), and a larger and far more politically active faction led by Maulānā Muftī Maḥmūd and Maulānā Ghaus̱ Hazārvī and based in North-West Frontier Province (NWFP). The latter faction (the Muftī-Hazārvī Group, hereafter JUI) actively participated in the 1970 general elections as a populist-oriented party, appealing to activist Islamic sentiment. The JUI's program called for the establishment of an Islamic constitution in accordance with the recommendations of the Board of ᶜUlamā' as presented to the Basic Principles Committee of 1954, which had called for the adoption of the *sharīᶜah* as the basis of Pakistan's consitutional structure. The JUI also called for the end of "capitalist exploitation" and for the establishment of a program of Islamic social welfare including free education, health care, and the introduction of minimum-wage legislation.

The combination of such populist rhetoric, the prestige of the *ᶜulamā'*, and the JUI's effective control of relevant mosques led to success at the polls. In the 1970 general election the JUI swept the electoral districts of southern NWFP and entered into a coalition with the National Awami Party (NAP) to form provincial governments in NWFP and Baluchistan. The subsequent naming of Maulānā Muftī Maḥmūd as chief minister of the NWFP (1971–1973) marked the first and only time in Pakistan's history that an Islam-based party has headed a provincial government.

During Muftī Maḥmūd's short-lived tenure his government managed to introduce three laws designed to promote Islam in the province. The first established prohibition of alcohol; the second introduced an Islamic law of pre-emption (i.e., regarding inheritance of land); and the third mandated the enforced observance of the Ramaḍān fast. These laws have remained on the books in NWFP and have significantly influenced the course of the islamization process in Pakistan during the 1980s and 1990s. The JUI-NAP government of NWFP resigned in early 1973 in protest over Zulfiqar ᶜAli Bhutto's perceived persecution of NAP leaders. In the 1977 general elections the JUI allied itself with the anti-Bhutto coalition, the Pakistan National Alliance. Subsequently the party cooperated, at times reluctantly, with the regime of Zia ul-Haq (1977–1988), and it tacitly supported the IJM (Islamic Democratic Alliance) government of Nawaz Sharif (1990–1992). The JUI maintains a small but loyal and enthusiastic following in the southern region of NWFP and the Pathan-majority areas of Baluchistan. In the 1988 and 1990 general elections it gained seven and six seats respectively in the National Assembly.

During the past decade, under the leadership of Maulānā Faẕlur Raḥmān, son of the late Muftī Maḥmūd, the JUI has become increasingly associated with Islamic orthodoxy. In their religious views JUI members are often criticized by their opponents as "uncompromisingly rigid," insisting on the strict enforcement of the *sharīᶜah* as interpreted by the four schools of Islamic jurisprudence. In addition, it is often charged that the JUI is anti-Shīᶜī. The JUI did support Iraq during the Iran-Iraq war, but it joined the TNFJ (Taḥrīk-i Nifāẕ-i Fiqh-i Jaᶜfarīyah, the most prominent Pakistani Shīᶜī group) in its condemnation of the United States' role in the Gulf War. Also, JUI *ᶜulamā'* are often characterized as opposed to innovation in matters Islamic and as favoring a strict social and moral code, especially with respect to gender relations. Indeed, JUI *ᶜulamā'* often draw the ire of Pakistan's feminist organizations.

Politically, the JUI has been at the forefront of the attempt to implement far-reaching Islamic reforms. This is evidenced by the formulation and introduction in 1985, by the JUI Senators Maulānā Samīᶜul Ḥaqq and Qāẕī ᶜAbdullaṭīf, of the so-called "Shariat Bill." The JUI version of this bill proposed that the *sharīʿāh* wholly replace Pakistan's secular constitution. *ᶜUlamā'* associated with the JUI have also been very active in proposing petitions before the Federal Shariat Court calling for significant changes in Pakistan's social and moral practices to bring them more into keeping with Islamic norms. Generally, JUI members were displeased with what they viewed as the slow pace of Islamic reform under President Zia, and they have been even less pleased with successor regimes.

The 1993 general election proved disappointing to the JUI. The party contested the election under the banner of the newly created Islāmī Jumhūrī Maḥāẕ (Islamic Democratic Association, IJM) and entered into an "electoral arrangement" with the Pakistan People's Party. However, even after intensive electoral campaigning, the IJM was only able to gain 2.3 percent of the popular vote and four seats. Despite such electoral disappointment, the JUI remains a potent social and political force in the NWFP and Baluchistan. Indeed, the party has deepened its populist image and style. But more important, it has maintained its control over the largest number of mosques and *madrasah*s in Pakistan, and therefore has the strongest base among the *madrasah* student body in the state.

[*See also* Pakistan.]

BIBLIOGRAPHY

Ahmad, Mumtaz. "The Politics of War: Islamic Fundamentalisms in Pakistan." In *Islamic Fundamentalisms and the Gulf Crisis*, edited by J. P. Piscatori, pp. 155–185. Chicago, 1991.

Kennedy, Charles H. "Repugnancy to Islam—Who Decides? Islam and Legal Reform in Pakistan." *International and Comparative Law Quarterly* 41 (1992): 769–787.

CHARLES H. KENNEDY

JAMᶜĪYATUL ᶜULAMĀ'-I PĀKISTĀN. The party of Pakistan's Barelwī *ᶜulamā'*, the Jamᶜīyatul ᶜUlamā'-i Pākistān was formed in Karachi in 1948 at the behest of Mawlānās ᶜAbdulḥamīd Badā'unī, Sayyid Muḥammad Aḥmad Qādirī, and ᶜAllāmah Aḥmad Saᶜīd Kāẓimī. After the Jamᶜīyatul ᶜUlamā'-i Islām, it has been the largest *ᶜulamā'* party of Pakistan. The Jamᶜīyat follows the Barelwī school of Islamic thought, also known as the *ahl-i sunnat wa jamāᶜat* ("people of the custom and community"), a term that reflects their claim to represent the true faith. The Barelwīs trace their origin to the teachings of Aḥmad Riẕā Khān Barelwī (1856–1921), a scion of a notable *ᶜulamā'* family of Bareilly, Uttar Pradesh, who had strong ties to the Qādirīyah Ṣūfī order. The Barelwīs, unlike other *ᶜulamā'* groups of the period or the Islamic movements that surfaced later, were not interested in promoting a puritanical interpretation of orthodoxy. Instead, they emerged to counter the impact of the Deobandī and Ahl-i Ḥadīth traditions, both of which had sought to cleanse Islamic practices of cultural accretions and Sufism. The Barelwīs adhered to the Ḥanafī school of law but aimed to preserve the place of Sufism and the popular customs associated with it in the life and thought of Indian Muslims. The Barelwīs also accord the *ᶜulamā'* and Ṣūfī pirs a central role as community leaders, vested with authority to intercede with God on behalf of the faithful.

By the turn of the century the Barelwī school had developed a strong following in northern India, relating popular Ṣūfī practices to an orthodox reading of Islam. In Punjab too, where the Qādirīyah order has traditionally wielded much power, the Barelwīs found a base, especially after the founding of the Dārul Ḥizb-i Aḥnāf (Congregation of the Ḥanafī Parties) in Lahore in the 1920s. They had little influence in the other four provinces that after 1947 became Pakistan—East Bengal, Sind, and the predominantly Deobandī North-West Frontier and Baluchistan. Throughout the struggle for partition, the Barelwīs supported the Muslim League and were especially effective in bolstering the League's position in Punjab. In 1946 this support was formalized when Barelwī *ᶜulamā'* from across India congregated in Benares to endorse Pakistan openly and to provide it with religious legitimacy.

Given this background, many Barelwīs migrated to Pakistan in 1947, establishing a base in Sind among the refugee (*muhajir*) community. With a following in rural Punjab and urban Sind, Barelwīs emerged as an important national force on the religious scene, second only to the Deobandīs. The rivalry between the two for power and prominence, and the Barelwīs' desire to defend their flock from challenges by the Deobandīs, soon led to the creation of a Barelwī *ᶜulamā'* party.

The Pakistani Deobandīs had broken away from the pro-Congress Deobandī Party, Jamᶜīyatul ᶜUlamā'-i Hind, to support the Muslim League and the demand for partition. In 1945 they had formed the Jamᶜīyatul ᶜUlamā'-i Islām, whose contribution to the creation of the country was quickly rewarded with government patronage. The Barelwīs viewed the privileged status of Jamᶜīyatul ᶜUlamā'-i Islām with envy and concern, especially as Islam came to dominate national political discourse. Against this background in 1948, the Barelwī *ᶜulamā'* formed the Jamᶜīyatul ᶜUlamā'-i Pākistān. The Jamᶜīyat was initially an *ᶜulamā'* forum designed to voice the interests of Barelwīs; it had no plans for direct political activity. Between 1947 and 1958, the Jamᶜīyat actively participated in the debates among various Islamic parties and the government over the nature of the state of Pakistan and the necessity of an Islamic constitution for the country. Beyond this, it did not envisage a role for itself in national politics.

By the late 1960s, however, the Jamᶜīyat had become fully embroiled in politics under the force of three factors. The first was the increasing prominence of the Jamᶜīyatul ᶜUlamā'-i Islām and other Islamic parties such as the Jamāᶜat-i Islāmi in the religious and political arenas from 1958 onward. Recall that the Barelwīs had emerged in the first place to check the growth of puritanical interpretations of orthodoxy; thus it was not unexpected that the Jamᶜīyat would mobilize its resources to offset the influence of Jamᶜīyatul ᶜUlamā'-i Islām and the Jamāᶜat-i Islāmī. The Jamᶜīyat challenged the Jamāᶜat-i Islāmī in forty-two constituencies in the national elections of 1970, defeating their opponents in several contests and dividing the religious vote in others to the advantage of secular parties. The rivalry between the two also stemmed from the fact that both had courted the Muhajir community of Sind since 1947.

Second, the Jamᶜīyat was made aware of the power and potential of Islam in the political arena by revivalist groups in general, and the Jamāᶜat-i Islāmī in particular. The Jamᶜīyat was not immune to the attraction of political power; moreover, it did not wish to leave the growing religious vote to be dominated by revivalist parties or the Jamᶜīyatul ᶜUlamā'-i Islām. The decision to participate in the national elections of 1970, the first for the Jamᶜīyat, was taken after the Jamāᶜat-i Islāmī flaunted the electoral potential of Islamic symbolisms by introducing its campaign with the Yaum-i Shaukat-i Islām (Day of Islam's Glory), which was held throughout Pakistan in May 1970.

Third, the Jamᶜīyat became interested in politics in response to the challenge of the secularist regime (1958–1969) of Field Marshal Muhammad Ayub Khan to the place of Islam in Pakistani society. The Ayub regime sought to roll back the gains made by religious parties during the preceding decade, proposed a modernist view of Islam with the aim of depoliticizing the Islamic parties, and finally sought to extend the power of the state into the domain of the *ᶜulamā'*. The Jamᶜīyat was opposed to Ayub's modernist agenda but was especially perturbed by the government's appropriation of religious endowments and takeover of the management of religious shrines; both actions affected Barelwīs and their allies in the Ṣūfī establishment directly. The Jamᶜīyat was also opposed to the government's attempts to seize control of its mosques. In response to Ayub Khan's policies, the Jamᶜīyat became more directly involved in politics in the 1960s to protect the Barelwīs' interests. By the mid-1960s, under the leadership of Mawlānā Shāh Aḥmad Nūrānī, the Jamᶜīyat became a vociferous actor in the political arena; it now included lay members and leaders and addressed issues of national concern. In 1970, for instance, it launched a strong campaign to counter Bengali nationalism in East Pakistan (now Bangladesh).

Following the secession of Bangladesh and the rise of the populist Zulfiqar ᶜAli Bhutto to power, the Jamᶜīyat, along with other Islamic parties, became even more actively involved in politics. The secularist and left-of-center politics of the Bhutto government allowed the Islamic parties to assume the leadership of the opposition. The Jamᶜīyat coordinated its activities closely with those of other Islamic parties in the antigovernment Niẓām-i Muṣṭafā (Order of the Prophet) movement, which undermined the Bhutto regime. In fact, Nūrānī was chosen by the movement to succeed Bhutto as prime minister. Later the Jamᶜīyat also lent support to the military regime of General Muhammad Zia ul-Haq, who took over the reins of power in 1977.

True to its founding ideals, the Jamᶜīyat was also the first Islamic party to distance itself from the Zia regime and its puritanical view of Islam. The party was not, however, able to escape the impact of the increasingly strict adherence to orthodoxy that swept across Pakistan in the 1980s. By the end of that decade, elements within the Jamʿīyat had moved close to the doctrinal positions of Jamʿīyatul ʿUlamā'-i Islām and the Jamāʿat-i Islāmī. More significantly, the party suffered as a consequence of its direct involvement in politics. Clashes over policy decisions since 1969 divided the Jamʿīyat into factions. One faction led by Nūrānī decided to stay away from the Islāmī Jumhūrī Ittiḥād (IJI or Islamic Democratic Alliance), which was formed by the pro-Zia parties to challenge Benazir Bhutto's Pakistan Peoples' Party, and instead allied itself with an offshoot of Jamʿīyatul ʿUlamā'-i Islām to form the Islamic Democratic Front. The other faction under the leadership of Mawlānā ʿAbdussattār Niyāzī decided to remain with IJI.

Since 1986, the Jamʿīyat, like other Islamic parties, has lost much of its support because of the proliferation of self-styled Sunnī parties throughout Pakistan, and because of the meteoric rise of the ethnic party Muhajir Qaumi Mahaz (MQM or Muhajir National Movement) in the urban centers of Sind. In the 1970 elections the party received 8.2 percent of the popular vote and won seven seats in the National Assembly, but in the 1990 elections its share of the vote had fallen to 1.47 percent, winning only four seats. Despite this setback, the party continues to operate as an important force on the religious scene and wields significant power in the political arena from its stronghold in rural Punjab. The party's student wing, Anjuman-i Ṭulabā-i Islām (Association of Islamic Students), established in the 1980s, now controls numerous campuses in Punjab.

[*See also* Barelwīs; Deobandīs; Jamāʿat-i Islāmī; Jamʿīyatul ʿUlamā'-i Islām; Pakistan; Qādirīyah.]

BIBLIOGRAPHY

Abbott, Freeland. *Islam and Pakistan*. Ithaca, N.Y., 1968. Good summary of interactions between various Islamic groups in Pakistan.

Afzal, Rafique. *Political Parties in Pakistan, 1947–1958*. Islamabad, 1976. Concise account of party politics in Pakistan in the 1947–1958 period.

Aḥmad, ʿAbdul-Ghafūr. *Phir Mārshal Lā Ā-Giyā* (Then Came the Martial Law). Lahore, 1988. Good account of the politics of the Islamic parties in the 1970s.

Ahmad, Mumtaz. "Islam and the State: The Case of Pakistan." In *The Religious Challenge to the State*, edited by Matthew Moen and Lowell Gustafson, pp. 239–267. Philadelphia, 1992. Good account of the issues before Islamic parties during the Ayub, Bhutto, and Zia regimes.

Binder, Leonard. *Religion and Politics in Pakistan*. Berkeley, 1961. The standard work on religion and politics in Pakistan in the 1947–1956 period.

Ewing, Katherine. "The Politics of Sufism: Redefining the Saints of Pakistan." *Journal of Asian Studies* 42.2 (February 1983): 251–268. Authoritative outline of the changing political issues surrounding Sufism in Pakistan.

Gilmartin, David. *Empire and Islam: Punjab and the Making of Pakistan*. Berkeley, 1988. Contains a good account of the activities of the Barelwīs in the Punjab between the two world wars.

Metcalf, Barbara D. *Islamic Revival in British India: Deoband, 1860–1900*. Princeton, 1982. Contains an excellent sketch of the Barelwī tradition.

SEYYED VALI REZA NASR

JANISSARIES. In the late fourteenth century the government of the Ottoman Empire established an elite slave infantry known as "new troops" or Janissaries (Turkish, *yeniçeri*), differentiating them from the traditional levies of free Muslim warriors. Interpreting freely the ancient rules of Islamic warfare, by which a portion of enslaved prisoners taken in battle went to the ruler, the Ottoman government continued the enslaving process in peacetime. It instituted a quadrennial collection (*devşirme*) that selected approximately 20 percent of the young boys from conquered regions, particularly (but not limited to) the Christian Balkans.

All *devşirme* boys entered a complicated educational system in which each took a Muslim identity, learned Turkish, and practiced the arts of war and leadership. After being thoroughly examined, the most promising entered the palace school and eventually became the slave rulers of the empire. The majority, however, graduated as Janissaries, placed into companies of daily-wage, uniformed infantry—archers and later musketmen and artillerymen. The sultan personally appointed their commander, the agha, whose power ranked with the highest of imperial advisers; their spiritual needs were met by the dervish order of the Bektāshīs.

Thus the will of the sultan, through the power of the Janissaries, extended to all the empire, helping to control the free landholding Muslim warriors. The sultan could depend on Janissary loyalty: not only did the slave realize he must obey or be executed without trial, but that obedience also gave him enormous personal power and tax-exempt status. Janissaries gained great influence because they were responsible for enforcing the sultan's law in the provinces and keeping peace between Muslims and non-Muslims. After the time of Sultan

Mehmed II (d. 1481), they grew powerful enough to play the role of kingmakers in any sultan's quest for the throne.

By the mid-seventeenth century, when Ottoman political expansion ceased and the central government weakened, police control of outlying regions increasingly fell into the hands of Janissary constabularies. Janissaries began to participate in local politics, joining with guilds, working with influential local *ulema,* and entering business. After about 1640 the enslavement of Christian boys ceased, and the Janissaries replenished their ranks with their sons and with free Muslims who bought their way into the privileged status. As their numbers grew, their demands for pay (often in arrears because of the weakening economy) led them to revolt, even against the sultans. They often determined regional public policy as well as holding extraordinary influence in Istanbul. By 1700 few sultans could muster the courage to contradict them, and in 1789 the reformer Selim III fell to their violence.

In 1826 Sultan Mahmud II, relying both on the power of his newly formed military force and on public contempt for Janissary tyranny, slaughtered most of the Janissaries at a muster in Istanbul and drove from power those remaining in the provinces. Historians often cite this "Auspicious Incident," as it is known by the Turks, as essential to the beginning of Ottoman modernization.

[*See also* Military Forces; Ottoman Empire.]

BIBLIOGRAPHY

Gibb, H. A. R., and Harold Bowen. "The Janissaries." In *Islamic Society and the West,* vol. 1, pp. 56–66. London, 1950. Some details of Janissary organization within the general system of "The Ruling Institution." See also Appendix A, "The Janissaries."

Huart, Claude. "Janissaries." In *First Encyclopaedia of Islam, 1913–1936,* vol. 4, pp. 572–574. Leiden, 1987. Standard, if dated, survey.

Itzkowitz, Norman. *Ottoman Empire and Islamic Tradition.* New York, 1972. Extremely useful, easily understood outline of the Ottoman ruling system and the Janissaries' role.

Shaw, Stanford J. "The Ruling Class." In *The History of the Ottoman Empire and Modern Turkey,* vol. 1, *Empire of the Gazis: The Rise and Decline of the Ottoman Empire, 1280–1808.* Cambridge, London, and New York, 1976. The essentials of the Janissary organization in the context of the imperial Ottoman story. See especially pages 113–117, 122–125.

Uzunçarşılı, İsmail Hakkı. *Osman Devleti teşkilâtından kapukulu Ocakları,* vol. 1. Istanbul, 1943. In Turkish, the most comprehensive monographic study yet available.

WILLIAM J. GRISWOLD

JAYSH. *See* Military Forces.

JERUSALEM. One of Islam's three holiest cities, Jerusalem was originally an old Canaanite settlement where David, king of Israel, built his capital and his son Solomon, the Temple. Generally called simply "the Holy" *(al-Quds)* by the Muslims, Jerusalem is not mentioned by name in the Qur'ān, but the Muslim tradition unanimously sees a reference to it in the allusion in surah 17.1 where Muḥammad was borne by night from Mecca to "the distant shrine" *(al-masjid al-aqṣā).* Muslim armies took Jerusalem without resistance in 635 CE and immediately set to refurbishing its chief holy place, the neglected Temple mount of the "noble sanctuary" *(al-ḥaram al-sharīf).* They first built at its southern end their congregational mosque (al-Aqṣā), and, by 692, had completed at its center the splendid shrine called the "Dome of the Rock," revered both as the terminus of the Night Journey and the biblical site of Abraham's sacrifice and Solomon's Temple.

Excavations of extensive buildings south of the Ḥaram suggest that the Umayyads may have had ambitious political plans for Jerusalem, which they apparently aborted when Damascus became the new capital of the "Abode of Islam." The city's history was generally uneventful until the Crusades, and Christians and Jews (Jerusalem was filled with Christians and Christian holy places and the Jews had been permitted by the Muslims to return to the city for the first time since their ban by the Romans in 135 CE) may have outnumbered the Muslims. The Egyptian ruler al-Ḥākim bi-amr Allāh had the Christians' Holy Sepulcher Church burned down in 1009, one of the events that provoked the Europeans' invasion of Palestine and their occupation of Jerusalem in 1099. The Latin Christian interregnum in Jerusalem lasted a scant century before Ṣalāḥ al-Dīn (Saladin) drove them out in 1187, long enough, however, for the Crusaders to convert the Dome of the Rock into a church and al-Aqṣā into the headquarters of the Knights Templars.

Under Ṣalāḥ al-Dīn, the Muslim holy places were restored to their original use, and it was he, aided by popular preachers, who raised Muslim appreciation of what was, after Mecca and Medina, the third holiest city in Islam. The Frankish Crusade appears to have taken the Muslims by surprise, but, thereafter, they were well aware of European intentions toward Jerusalem. In the centuries after the Crusades, the level of hostility between the Muslims and the indigenous Christian population, and particularly the European pilgrims who continued to visit the city (and whose accounts graphically document life there) rose appreciably. Ṣalāḥ al-Dīn also wished to make Jerusalem a safely Sunnī city; the Shīʿīs were regarded as far more subversive enemies than the Christians. His goal was realized under the Mamlūks, his family's successors in Egypt and Palestine. From their accession in 1250 they invested heavily in Jerusalem; many of the Sunnī law schools (*madrasahs*) and convents (*khānaqāhs*) they constructed around the northern and western margins of the Ḥaram still retain some of their expensive elegance, though they are now empty of the students and Ṣūfīs who used to inhabit them.

The Ottomans, who inherited the city in 1517 from the Mamlūks, continued their predecessors' generous support of the holy city. The walls that still set off the "Old City" today were built by the Ottomans, somewhat uselessly, perhaps, since the greatest threat to the city came from abroad, not in the form of armed warriors. The might of the Ottomans was tested and broken in the Balkans during the seventeenth to nineteenth century; consequently, their control of their own affairs in their own dominions was progressively eroded. Even before the Crusades, the Christians of Jerusalem, the Latins, Greeks, and Armenians, had learned the benefit of invoking the protection of the more powerful of their coreligionists; somewhat later, the European powers learned what benefits might accrue to them from manipulating those invocations.

The disintegration of Ottoman sovereignty was nowhere more evident than in Palestine and Jerusalem in the nineteenth century. The city began to fill up with European consulates, European missionaries, and, finally, European archaeological missions, many of them instruments of national policy and all of them far beyond the reach of the Ottoman authorities in what was by then an exceedingly poor city. Even the Jews, always the least considerable and most wretched of Jerusalem's medieval population, discovered that they too had powerful friends and benefactors in Europe. With the aid of those benefactors, the Montefiores and Rothschilds chief among them, the lot of the Jews of Jerusalem improved, and their numbers began to spiral upward. By 1900 there were 35,000 (Muslims and Christians each 10,000) out of a total population of 55,000.

Turkey joined Germany in its unsuccessful war against the Allies in 1914; in December 1917 Jerusalem fell, without harm, to General Edmund Allenby and a British Expeditionary Army. It rested under the uneasy control of British governors during the entire Mandate period (1922–1948). When the British withdrew in 1948, the Jordanians hastened to occupy the Old City, despite the United Nations' recommendations for internationalization. It remained a part of Jordan until the 1967 war, when the Israelis took it after fierce fighting. The whole city has since been integrated into the State of Israel, and declared its capital, though in June 1967 the Israeli minister of defense, Moshe Dayan, acknowledged the entire Ḥaram al-Sharīf to be the possession of the Muslims. The policy has remained in force to this day.

BIBLIOGRAPHY

Ben-Arieh, Yehoshua. *Jerusalem in the Nineteenth Century: The Old City*. New York, 1984. Charts in detail the rapid and radical changes to Jerusalem in the nineteenth century.

Benvenisti, Meron. *Jerusalem: The Torn City*. Jerusalem, 1976. Generally balanced account of the fate of Jerusalem, its Muslim population, and its Muslim holy places, after 1967.

Burgoyne, Michael. *The Architecture of Islamic Jerusalem*. Jerusalem, 1976. Inventory of the chief Islamic monuments of the city.

Busse, Heribert. "The Sanctity of Jerusalem in Islam." *Judaism* 17 (1968): 441–468.

Goitein, S. D. "al-Ḳuds: Part A. History." In *Encyclopaedia of Islam*, new ed., vol. 5, pp. 322–339. Leiden, 1960–. Succinct yet detailed account of the history of Muslim Jerusalem.

Grabar, Oleg. "al-Ḳuds: Part B. The Monuments." In *Encyclopaedia of Islam*, new ed., vol. 5, pp. 339–344. Leiden, 1960–. The best brief survey of the monuments of Muslim Jerusalem.

Peters, F. E. *Jerusalem: The Holy City in the Eyes of Chroniclers, Visitors, Pilgrims, and Prophets from the Days of Abraham to the Beginning of Modern Times*. Princeton, 1985. Broad collection of sources on the city, its visitors, and their impressions, from the earliest days to the 1830s.

Peters, F. E. *Jerusalem and Mecca: The Typology of the Holy City in the Near East*. New York, 1987. Comparative study of two of Islam's holiest cities.

Peters, F. E. *The Distant Shrine: The Islamic Centuries in Jerusalem*. New York, 1993. Shaping of the city of Jerusalem from the seventh to the nineteenth century.

Silberman, Neil Asher. *Digging for God and Country: Exploration, Archeology, and the Secret Struggle for the Holy Land, 1799–1917*. New York, 1982. Informative and entertaining account of the archaeological "invasion" of Jerusalem in the nineteenth century.

Tibawi, A. L. *Jerusalem: Its Place in Islamic and Arabic History*. Beirut, 1969. Muslim's account of the importance of Jerusalem.

F. E. PETERS

JIHĀD. Carrying the basic connotation of an endeavor toward a praiseworthy aim, the word *jihād* bears many shades of meaning in the Islamic context. It may express a struggle against one's evil inclinations or an exertion for the sake of Islam and the *ummah,* for example, trying to convert unbelievers or working for the moral betterment of Islamic society ("*jihād* of the tongue" and "*jihād* of the pen"). In the books on Islamic law, the word means an armed struggle against the unbelievers, which is also a common meaning in the Qur'ān. Sometimes the "*jihād* of the sword" is called "the smaller *jihād,*" in opposition to the peaceful forms named "the greater *jihād.*" Today often used without any religious connotation, its meaning is more or less equivalent to the English word *crusade* ("a crusade against drugs"). If used in a religious context, the adjective "Islamic" or "holy" is currently added to it *(al-jihād al-Islāmī* or *al-jihād al-muqaddas).*

Origin. The concept of *jihād* goes back to the wars fought by the Prophet Muḥammad and their written reflection in the Qur'ān. It is clear that the concept was influenced by the ideas on war among the pre-Islamic northern Arabic tribes. Among these, war was the normal state, unless two or more tribes had concluded a truce. War between tribes was regarded as lawful and if the war was fought as a defense against aggression, the fighting had an additional justification. Ideas of chivalry forbade warriors to kill noncombatants like children, women, and old people. These rules were incorporated into the doctrine of *jihād* as fixed in the latter half of the second century AH.

The Qur'ān frequently mentions *jihād* and fighting *(qitāl)* against the unbelievers. Surah 22.40 ("Leave is given to those who fight because they were wronged—surely God is able to help them—who were expelled from their habitations without right, except that they say 'Our Lord is God.' "), revealed not long after the Hijrah, is traditionally considered to be the first verse dealing with the fighting of the unbelievers. Many verses exhort the believers to take part in the fighting "with their goods and lives" *(bi-amwālihim wa-anfusihim),* promise reward to those who are killed in the *jihād* (3.157–158, 169–172), and threaten those who do not fight with severe punishments in the hereafter (9.81–82, 48.16). Other verses deal with practical matters such as exemption from military service (9.91, 48.17), fighting during the holy months (2.217) and in the holy territory of Mecca (2.191), the fate of prisoners of war (47.4), safe conduct (9.6), and truce (8.61).

It is not clear whether the Qur'ān allows fighting the unbelievers only as a defense against aggression or under all circumstances. In support of the first view a number of verses can be quoted that expressly justify fighting on the strength of aggression or perfidy on the part of the unbelievers: "And fight in the way of God with those who fight you, but aggress not: God loves not the aggressors" (2.190) and "But if they break their oaths after their covenant and thrust at your religion, then fight the leaders of unbelief" (9.13). In those verses that seem to order the Muslims to fight the unbelievers unconditionally, the general condition that fighting is only allowed in defense could be said to be understood: "Then, when the sacred months are drawn away, slay the idolaters wherever you find them, and take them, and confine them, and lie in wait for them at every place of ambush" (9.5) and "Fight those who believe not in God and the Last Day and do not forbid what God and His Messenger have forbidden—such men as practice not the religion of truth, being of those who have been given the Book—until they pay the tribute out of hand and have been humbled" (9.29). Classical Qur'ān interpretation, however, did not go into this direction. It regarded the Sword Verses, with the unconditional command to fight the unbelievers, as having abrogated all previous verses concerning the intercourse with non-Muslims. This idea is no doubt connected with the pre-Islamic concept that war between tribes was allowed, unless there existed a truce between them, the Islamic *ummah* taking the place of a tribe.

During the second half of the eighth century, the first comprehensive treatise on the law of *jihād* was written by ʿAbd al-Raḥmān al-Awzāʿī (d. 774) and Muḥammad al-Shaybānī (d. 804). The legal doctrine of *jihād* was the result of debates and discussions that had been going on since the Prophet's death and through which the doctrine had been developed. This period in which the doctrine of *jihād* was gradually formulated coincided with the period of the great Muslim conquests, in which the conquerors were exposed to the cultures of the conquered peoples. The doctrine of *jihād* may have been influenced somewhat by the culture of the Byzantine Empire, where the idea of religious war and related notions were very much alive. It is, however, very difficult to identify these influences. If there are similarities, they are not necessarily the result of borrowing but may be due to parallel developments.

Classical Doctrine. The doctrine of *jihād* as written in the works on Islamic law developed out of the Qur'ānic prescriptions and the example of the Prophet and the first caliphs, as laid down in the *ḥadīth.* The crux of the doctrine is the existence of one single Islamic state, ruling the entire *ummah.* It is the duty of the *um-*

mah to expand the territory of this state in order to bring as many people as possible under its rule. The ultimate aim is to bring the whole earth under the sway of Islam and to extirpate unbelief: "Fight them until there is no persecution [or "seduction"] and the religion is God's entirely" (2.192 and 8.39). Expansionist *jihād* is a collective duty *(farḍ al-kifāyah),* which is fulfilled if a sufficient number of people take part in it. If this is not the case, the whole *ummah* is sinning. Expansionist *jihād* presupposes the presence of a legitimate caliph to organize the struggle. After the conquests had come to an end, the legal specialists specified that the caliph had to raid enemy territory at least once a year in order to keep the idea of *jihād* alive.

Sometimes *jihād* becomes an individual duty as when the caliph appoints certain persons to participate in a raiding expedition or when someone takes an oath to fight the unbelievers. Moreover, *jihād* becomes obligatory for all free men capable of fighting in a certain region if this region is attacked by the enemy; in this case, *jihād* is defensive.

Sunnī and Shīʿī theories of *jihād* are very similar. However, there is one crucial difference. The Twelver Shīʿīs hold that *jihād* can only be waged under the leadership of the rightful imam. After the Occultation of the last one in 873, theoretically no lawful *jihād* can be fought. This is true for expansionist *jihād*. However, as defense against attacks remains obligatory and the *ʿulamāʾ* are often regarded as the representatives of the Hidden Imam, several wars between Iran and Russia in the nineteenth century have been called *jihād*.

War against unbelievers may not be mounted without summoning them to Islam or submission before the attack. A *ḥadīth* lays down the precise contents of the summons:

> Whenever the Prophet appointed a commander to an army or an expedition, he would say: ". . . When you meet your heathen enemies, summon them to three things. Accept whatsoever they agree to and refrain then from fighting them. Summon them to become Muslims. If they agree, accept their conversion. In that case summon them to move from their territory to the Abode of the Emigrants [i.e., Medina]. If they refuse that, let them know that then they are like the Muslim bedouins and that they share only in the booty, when they fight together with the [other] Muslims. If they refuse conversion, the ask them to pay poll-tax *(jizya)*.. If they agree, accept their submission. But if they refuse, then ask God for assistance and fight them. . . ."
>
> (*Ṣaḥīḥ* Muslim)

This *hadīth* also neatly sums up the aims of fighting unbelievers: conversion or submission. In the latter case, the enemies are entitled to keep their religion and practice it, against payment of a poll-tax *(jizyah)* (see surah 9.29, quoted above). Although the Qur'ān limits this option to the People of the Book, that is, Christians and Jews, it was in practice extended to other religions, such as the Zoroastrians (Majūs).

Whenever the caliph deems it in the interest of the *ummah,* he may conclude a truce with the enemy, just as the Prophet did with the Meccans at al-Ḥudaybīyah. According to some schools of law, a truce must be concluded for a specified period of time, no longer than ten years. Others hold that this is not necessary, if the caliph stipulates that he may resume war whenever he wishes to do so. The underlying idea is that the notion of *jihād* must not fall into oblivion.

The books on law contain many practical rules concerning warfare, such as exemptions from the obligation to fight, the protection of the lives of noncombatants, lawful methods of warfare, treatment of prisoners of war, safe-conduct to enemy persons, and the division of the spoils.

Function. The most important function of the doctrine of *jihād* is that it mobilizes and motivates Muslims to take part in wars against unbelievers, as it is considered to be the fulfillment of a religious duty. This motivation is strongly fed by the idea that those who are killed on the battlefield, called martyrs (*shāhids*), will go directly to Paradise. When wars were fought against unbelievers, religious texts would circulate, replete with Qur'ānic verses and *hadīths* extolling the merits of fighting a *jihād* and vividly describing the reward waiting in the hereafter for those slain during the fighting.

Another function was to enhance the legitimation of a ruler. After the year 750, the political unity of the *ummah* was lost, never to be restored. Several rulers would govern different regions of the Muslim world. One of the ways to acquire greater legitimacy was to wage *jihād* against unbelievers, which is one of the main tasks of the lawful caliph.

A final function of the *jihād* doctrine was that it provided a set of rules governing the relationship with the unbelieving enemies and behavior during actual warfare. *Muftīs* could invoke this set of rules and issue *fatwās* showing that a ruler's foreign policy was in conformity with the rules of Islamic law. These rules could be molded to fit the circumstance. A case in point is when, after the collapse of Islamic political unity, two Muslim states would be at war with one another. In such situations *muftīs* would usually find cause to label the enemies either as rebels or as heretics, thus justifying the struggle against them.

During Islamic history, but especially in the eighteenth and nineteenth centuries, radical movements striving for a purification of Islam and the establishment of a purely Islamic society proclaimed *jihād* against their opponents, both Muslims and non-Muslims. To justify the struggle against their Muslim adversaries, they would brand them as unbelievers for their neglect in adhering to and enforcing the strict rules of Islam.

Changing Modern Interpretations. The colonial experience affected the outlook of some Muslim intellectuals on *jihād*. Some would argue that in view of the military superiority of the colonizer, *jihād* was not obligatory anymore on the strength of surah 2.195 (". . . and cast not yourselves by your own hands into destruction, . . ."). Others, however, elaborated new interpretations of the doctrine of *jihād*.

The first one to do so was the Indian Muslim thinker Sayyid Aḥmad Khān (1817–1898). After the Mutiny of 1857 the British, arguing that the Muslims wanted to restore Moghul rule and that the doctrine of *jihād* made them fight the British, began favoring the Hindus in the army and in government service. Sayyid Aḥmad Khān wanted to show that Islam did not forbid cooperation with the British colonial government; in this he was motivated by his desire to safeguard employment for the young Muslims from the middle and higher classes. In order to demonstrate that the Indian Muslims were not obliged to fight the British and could be loyal subjects, he gave a new interpretation of the *jihād* doctrine. On the basis of a new reading of the Qur'ān, he asserted that *jihād* was obligatory for Muslims only in the case of "positive oppression or obstruction in the exercise of their faith . . . impair[ing] the foundation of some of the pillars of Islam." Since the British, in his opinion, did not interfere with the practice of Islam, *jihād* against them was not allowed. [*See the biography of Aḥmad Khān.*]

Middle Eastern Muslim reformers like Muḥammad ʿAbduh (1849–1905) and Muḥammad Rashīd Riḍā (1865–1935) did not go as far as Sayyid Aḥmad Khān. On the strength of those Qur'ānic verses that make fighting against the unbelievers conditional upon their aggression or perfidy, they argue that peaceful coexistence is the normal state between Islamic and non-Islamic territories and that *jihād* is only allowed as defensive warfare. This view, however, left the way open to proclaim *jihād* against colonial oppression, as the colonial enterprise was clearly an attack on the territory of Islam. A recent development in this line of thinking is the presentation of the *jihād* doctrine as a form of Muslim international law and the equation of *jihād* with the concept of *bellum justum*. Those who have elaborated this theory proudly point out that Muḥammad al-Shaybānī (d. 804) had formulated a doctrine of international public law more than eight centuries before Hugo Grotius. [*See the biographies of ʿAbduh and Rashīd Riḍā.*]

Contemporary thinking about *jihād*, however, offers a wider spectrum of views. Apart from the conservatives, who adhere to the interpretation given in the classical books on Islamic law, there are the ideologues of the radical Islamic opposition, who call for *jihād* as a means to spread their brand of Islam. Some of these radical groups call for the use of violence in order to defeat the established governments. They are faced, however, with a serious doctrinal problem as they preach an armed revolution against Muslim rulers; Islamic law allows revolt only in very rare circumstances. One of these is when a ruler abandons his belief; as the apostate deserves capital punishment, fighting against him is allowed. Throughout Islamic history, governments and opposition movements have declared their Muslim adversaries to be heretics or unbelievers (*takfīr*, declaring someone to be a *kāfir*, unbeliever) in order to justify their struggle against them. It is this line of reasoning that is used by contemporary radical Islamic groups to give legitimacy to their use of arms against rulers who are to all appearances Muslims. In modern times these views were first propagated by fundamentalists like Sayyid Quṭb (d. 1966) and Abū al-Aʿlā Mawdūdī (1903–1979). [*See the biographies of Quṭb and Mawdūdī.*]

The most eloquent and elaborate statement of this view can be found in a pamphlet published by the ideologue of the Jihad Organization, whose members assassinated President Anwar Sadat of Egypt in 1981. The pamphlet is called *Al-farīḍah al-ghā'ibah* (The Absent Duty), referring to the duty to wage *jihād*, which, according to the author, ʿAbd al-Salām Faraj, is not fulfilled anymore. The author borrows his arguments from two *fatwās* issued by the fundamentalist author Ibn Taymīyah (1263–1328), when his opinion was sought regarding the legitimacy of Mongol rule in the Middle East. The prop of Ibn Taymīyah's reasoning is the fact that the Mongol rulers apply their own law instead of the *sharīʿah*. This, in his opinion, is sufficient cause to regard them as unbelievers, even if they pronounce the profession of faith. Further, if this argument is not accepted, they still have forfeited their right to demand the obedience of their Muslim subjects, and they may be fought.

Faraj argues that the situation Ibn Taymīyah describes is similar to the Egyptian situation, as Egyptian law, with the exception of family law and the law of succession, is based on codes of Western inspiration. Observing that, in spite of the vocal demands of the Islamic groups, the government has always refused to introduce the *sharīʿah,* the author concludes that such a government cannot be regarded as Islamic and that it is an individual duty of each Muslim to rise in armed rebellion against this heathen regime in order to replace it with an Islamic one.

BIBLIOGRAPHY

Arberry, A. J., trans. *The Koran Interpreted.* New York, 1955. All Qur'ānic quotations herein follow this standard English translation.

Bakker, Johan de. "Slaves, Arms, and Holy War: Moroccan Policy vis-à-vis the Dutch Republic during the Establishment of the ʿAlawī Dynasty, 1660–1727." Ph.D. diss., University of Amsterdam, 1991. Examines the function of *jihād* doctrine in Morocco's foreign relations, especially with the Dutch Republic, and its role in enhancing the ʿAlawid dynasty's legitimacy.

Ghunaimi, Mohammad Talaat al-. *The Muslim Conception of International Law and the Western Approach.* The Hague, 1968. Attempt to present the doctrine of *jihād* as a form of Islamic international law.

Hamidullah, Muhammmad. *Muslim Conduct of State.* 6th rev. ed. Lahore, 1973. Survey of classical *jihād* doctrine based on an extensive reading of classical sources, but somewhat marred by the author's apologetic approach.

Jansen, J. J. G. *The Neglected Duty: The Creed of Sadat's Assassins and Islamic Resurgence in the Middle East.* New York and London, 1986. Analysis and translation of *Al-farīḍah al-ghā'ibah.* The translation, especially of the abundant quotations of the classical works on Islamic law and the *ḥadīth,* is not always reliable.

Kelsay, John, and James T. Johnson, eds. *Just War and Jihad: Historical and Theoretical Perspectives on War and Peace in Western and Islamic Traditions.* New York, 1991.

Khadduri, Majid. *War and Peace in the Law of Islam.* Baltimore, 1955. Reliable survey of the classical doctrine of *jihād.*

Krüger, Hilmar. *Fetwa und Siyar: Zur internationalrechtlichen Gutachtenpraxis der osmanischen Şeyh ül-Islām vom 17. bis 19. Jahrhundert unter besonderen Berücksichtigung des "Behcet ül-Fetāvā".* Wiesbaden, 1968. Examines the role of *jihād* doctrine in Ottoman foreign relations from the seventeenth to nineteenth centuries.

Kruse, Hans. *Islamische Völkerrechtslehre.* Bochum, 1979. Deals especially with treaties between Islamic and other states according to classical Ḥanafī law.

Noth, Albrecht. *Heiliger Krieg und heiliger Kampf in Islam und Christentum.* Bonn, 1966. Comparison of *jihād* with similar notions in Christianity against the historical background of the Crusades.

Peters, Rudolph. *Jihad in Medieval and Modern Islam.* Leiden, 1977. Translation of the chapter on *jihād* from Averroes' (d. 1198) legal compendium, *Bidāyat al-mujtahid,* and of a modernist treatise on *jihād* written by Maḥmūd Shaltūt (d. 1963).

Peters, Rudolph. *Islam and Colonialism: The Doctrine of Jihad in Modern History.* The Hague, 1979. Deals with *jihād* as a means of mobilization in anticolonial struggles and with new interpretations of *jihād* doctrine.

Peters, Rudolph. "The Political Relevance of the Jihad Doctrine in Sadat's Egypt." In *National and International Politics in the Middle East: Essays in Honour of Elie Kedourie,* edited by Edward Ingram, pp. 252–273. London, 1986.

Shaybānī, Muḥammad ibn al-Ḥasan.. *The Islamic Law of Nations: Shaybānī's Siyar.* Translated and introduced by Majid Khadduri. Baltimore, 1966. Translation of one of the earliest works on *jihād.*

Sivan, Emmanuel. *L'Islam et la Croisade: Idéologie et propagande dans les réactions musulmanes aux Croisades.* Paris, 1968.

RUDOLPH PETERS

JIHĀD ORGANIZATIONS. The number of *jihād* organizations has been increasing in the Arab world, and indeed in much of the Islamic world. This fact does not say as much about Islam, as is often assumed in the West, as it says about desperate attempts to exploit Islam politically. The word *jihād* is often translated in the Western press as "holy war," although the original Islamic concept, on the basis of a well-known *ḥadīth,* does not have an exclusive military connotation. *Jihād* is Arabic simply means "struggle," and it came to denote in Islamic history and classical jurisprudence the struggle on behalf of the cause of Islam. In classical and modern times, Islamic governments, or more accurately governments that base their legitimacy on Islamic rationalization, have used the word to describe all combat efforts of their armies.

In the turbulent politics of the Arab world, the radical opposition groups are now fighting their own governments with the same weapons that have been used against them. Just as Arab governments have exploited Islam for purely political purposes, radical opposition groups that espouse Islam as an ideology now use the term to attribute their violent deeds to Islamic requirements. While many groups in the Middle East have used the phrase "Islamic Jihād" as the name for their organizations, it is important to note that those organizations are not necessarily in coordination with one another. There is very little, if any, coordination between those groups, and each should be analyzed within the context of the particular country in which it exists. There is no central *jihād* structure that conspiratorially creates and manipulates those groups in question.

Lebanon. The Lebanese-based Organization of the Islamic Jihād is probably the most notorious *jihād* group in the world, because it has claimed responsibility for the bombing of American interests in Lebanon (such as the embassy and the marines' barracks). Islamic Jihād also claimed responsibility for kidnapping Western hostages in Lebanon. Nevertheless, there is no such organization in Lebanon. The name was used by Ḥizbullāh (the Party of God) in Lebanon to maintain a degree of deniability for fear of retaliation by Western military forces. The Party of God also used other names, including the Organization of the Oppressed on Earth and the Revolutionary Justice Organization, in the course of their anti-Western and anti-Israel attacks. Some press reports linked Islamic Jihād to the security branch of the Party of God and to ʿImād Mughnīyah and ʿAbd al-Hādī Ḥammādī personally. But it is impossible to ascertain the truth of such reports in the absence of verifiable documentation, and party members and leaders have been consistently secretive about Islamic Jihād. [*See* Organization of the Islamic Jihād; Ḥizbullāh, *article on* Ḥizbullāh in Lebanon.]

Palestine. As in other Muslim nations, there is more than one organization using the word *jihād* in its name among Palestinians. The first Palestinian organization to use the word *jihād* was the Usrat al-Jihād (Family of Jihad), which was founded in 1948 by ʿAbd Allāh ʿIzz Darwīsh. The second organization is the Detachment of the Islamic Jihād, which claimed responsibility for the killing of Israeli soldiers in October 1986. This organization was believed to be tied to the faction within Fatah that was under the control of the late Palestine Liberation Organization leader Abū Jihād. The basis of support for this organization was in the West Bank.

The main *jihād* organization among the Palestinians is the Islamic Jihād Movement, the existence of which was revealed to the public in 1987. It emerged in Gaza and engaged in violent attacks in the course of the Palestinian uprising. Unlike *jihād* organizations in Egypt, the Islamic Jihād Movement seems to be less fixated on issues of theology and more insistent on the need for the eviction of Israeli occupation from Arab lands. It believes in the efficacy of armed struggle and has shown no reluctance to use violence against its enemies.

The Islamic Jihād Movement cannot be understood in a vacuum; it should be seen within the context of the contemporary transformation of the various cells of the Muslim Brotherhood in the 1960s and especially following the humiliating Arab defeat in 1967. The writings of the Syrian Islamic fundamentalist thinker Saʿīd Ḥawwā served as the ideological inspiration of the movement. Leaders of the movement claim that it had emerged from the milieu of Palestinian Islamic fundamentalist activists of the 1970s. Most of the members who initiated contacts with one another regarding the need for a new Islamic Palestinian party were formerly active members of the establishment Muslim Brotherhood. The Islamic Jihād Movement represents an offshoot of the mainstream Islamic fundamentalist movement by dissatisfied members who resented the political and military passivity of the Muslim Brotherhood.

The Islamic Jihād Movement refuses to consider its birth as an original act; rather, it is perceived as a continuation of a long line of Palestinian activists and martyrs who combined their anti-Zionist stances with a political ideology based on their interpretations of Islam. The name of ʿIzz al-Dīn al-Qassām (the Syrian Islamic activist who died fighting for the Palestinians in 1935) is frequently invoked in this regard. The spiritual leader of the movement, ʿAbd al-ʿAzīz ʿAwdah, often expresses his firm belief in the efficacy of military combat against Israel. For the movement, the struggle against Israel does not revolve around the question of the rightful ownership of the land, but over the religiopolitical duty of Muslims to fend off religious enemies. Like other Islamic fundamentalist groups, the movement underlines the religious significance of Palestine from the standpoint of Islamic history.

The political thought of the movement also carries some nationalistic elements. It is hard for any Palestinian movement to go very far in political mobilization without reflecting the nationalistic sentiments of the Palestinian people. Thus, for ʿAwdah, it is not the Palestinian cause that is in the service of Islam, but Islam is to be used in the service of the Palestinian cause. In other words, the Palestinian movement is understood and analyzed from both secular and religious points of view. On the question of the two-state solution, the movement rejects any compromise of the goal of liberating all of Palestinian lands.

It is a mistake to treat the Jihād movement as an organization with an original ideology. In fact, its political thought and practice is indistinguishable from other militant Islamic fundamentalist groups in the Middle East. Moreover, the Palestinian Jihād organization comprises within its ranks some former members from the Fatah movement. And it reflects the mood of disillusionment that prevailed among the Palestinians in the late 1970s. The Islamic fundamentalist groups among the Palestinians promote themselves as the credible alternatives to the secularist and nationalist agendas that are considered bankrupt by most Palestinians.

In recent times, the Islamic Jihād Movement failed to become the major political force that the Ḥamās organization has became. It also suffers from a reputation of blind allegiance to the Iranian regime. Information about the nature of financial, military, and political ties between the Palestinian Jihād movement and the Iranian regime are not easily verifiable.

Egypt. Much confusion surrounds the study of Jihād organizations in Egypt because there have been several groups using the name in their activities. Islamic fundamentalists from the ranks of the Muslim Brotherhood have been using the label of Jihād since 1958. Originally, the notion of Jihād simply referred to the attempt by some groups to use Islam to rationalize their violent activities. The organizational development of Jihād groups is the product of more recent times. The Jihād organization in Egypt can be traced back to 1979 when the engineer Muḥammad ʿAbd al-Salām Faraj founded the Islamic Jihād Community. There were groups at the time that characterized their activities as Jihād activities but they did not choose the name Jihād for their organizations. Faraj's organization came about as a result of the merger of three militant Islamic fundamentalist groups: Faraj's group; Karam Zuhdī's group; and the Jordanian Salīm al-Raḥḥāl's group. The unity of the three groups was firmly established in 1981 when the leadership was centralized in a joint *shūrā* (council) headed by the prince *(amīr)* of the organization, Faraj himself.

The council was divided into three committees: one dealt with propaganda and jurisprudent inculcation, the second dealt with economic and fund-raising issues, and the third dealt with preparation and military affairs. The political platform of the organization was presented in the booklet *Al-farīḍah al-ghā'ibah* (The Missing Obligation), which was written by Faraj and which inspired, according to court records, the assassins of Sadat in 1981. The religiopolitical thought of Faraj was not original; he merely repeated the claims by Sayyid Quṭb and others that certain Muslims (including rulers who use Islam for political legitimacy) could be declared *kāfirun* (infidel). The practice of *takfīr* (declaring the unbelief of other Muslims) is, of course, not new. It was practiced by the Khawārij in the first century of Islam. What is distinctive about Faraj is his ability to produce an accessible pamphlet that could articulate the opposition of Islamic fundamentalists to thc rulc of Sadat on religious grounds. The inspiration for Faraj, and for other contemporary fundamentalists, was found in the writings of Ibn Taymīyah, who in the fourteenth century urged and led the Muslim resistance to the Mongol invasion of Damascus despite the Islamic faith of the invaders. The ability of a Muslim to question the authenticity of the Islamic profession of another Muslim is the strongest political weapon in the hands of contemporary fundamentalists, because it belittles the Islamic claims of modern Islamic governments.

Faraj and other members of militant Islamic fundamentalist groups in Egypt believed that Muslims should not live under any laws except those that are derived from the Qur'ān. The divine source of rulership constitutes a major element in the thought of modern Islamic fundamentalist groups. But the groups refuse any application of Islamic laws if it does not conform to their specific interpretations of *sharīʿah* (the divine law). The goal of the establishment of an Islamic republic founded on the principles of *sharīʿah,* and only on the principles of *sharīʿah,* becomes a religious obligation that all Muslims are required to work for. No means are to be excluded in the struggle for the new Islamic order and for "restoration of the caliphate," and violence occupies a central part of the strategy of the Jihād organization, as is illustrated in the booklet by Faraj. The rulers of Egypt cannot be removed without the employment of violent means *(jihād* in the lexicon of Faraj), because they are supported by the enemies of Islam. The Islamic credentials of the government in Egypt and of the establishment religious institutions (like al-Azhar) are totally discredited, because their interpretations are seen in the thinking of the Jihād group as tantamount to unbelief.

The Jihād group never enjoyed an ideological or organizational coherence; it always served as a vehicle for a loose association of individuals and factions. Shaykh Omar Abdel Rahman (ʿUmar ʿAbd al-Raḥmān), for example, who now serves as the leader of the Islamic Community (al-Jamāʿah al-ʿIslāmīyah), was identified with one of the factions of the group. He is also responsible for the promotion of the notion of "restoration of the caliphate" in the literature of the group, especially in the mouthpiece of the group Kalimat Ḥagg, which was circulated on college campuses.

The confusion over the exact role of the Jihād group in Egypt arose from the splits that afflicted the group in the mid-1980s. There are still reports in the Arabic and

Western press that claim that Abdel Rahman, for example, is the leader of the Jihād organization. In reality, the brief unity between the various factions that formed the Jihād organization did not last very long. The various leaders and members of the group engaged in lively and arduous debates and deliberations in jail after their arrest in the wake of the assassination of President Anwar el-Sadat in 1981. In the course of the debates, it became clear the Abdel Rahman saw himself as the overall leader of the Jihād group, and he was attracting followers from among the political prisoners. Others, headed by ʿAbbūd al-Zumar, strongly disagreed with Abdel Rahman and objected to the imamate (leadership of the Islamic community here) of the blind man. Zumar and his followers argued that Abdel Rahman could play a leading role in the group but could not assume the ultimate leadership position. Sometime in 1984 (in jail) the two groups parted ways, and each developed an independent organizational existence. Zumar became the overall head of the Jihād organization, which now was different from the old one because of the defection of other factions, while Abdel Rahman became the head of what is known as al-Jamāʿah al-ʿIslāmīyah (The Islamic Community). [*See* Jamāʿat al-Islāmīyah, al-; *and the biography of Abdel Rahman.*]

Much of the violent activities in Egypt in the past several years are often mistakenly attributed to the Jihād organization, while in reality the Islamic Community is responsible for most of the acts. The Islamic Community continues to have a number of leaders and followers active in the countryside, while the leadership and membership of the Jihād remains in jail serving long sentences. Zumar, who is serving a forty-year sentence for his involvement in the assassination of Sadat, continues to exercise leadership responsibilities from behind bars, and he sometimes succeeds in smuggling interviews and speeches to the outside world. He strictly rejects the principle of party politics and is very suspicious of coordination with other parties and groups.

In 1993, it was revealed that the organization Ṭalāʾiʿ al-Fatḥ (Vanguards of Conquest) was now part of the Jihād organization; at that time efforts were underway to rejuvenate the Jihād organization by inviting a variety of small militant Islamic fundamentalist groups to join the Zumar-led Jihād group. It appeared that Ayman al-Ẓawāhirī, who resides in Pakistan and is the deputy commander of the Jihād organization, was concentrating on the need for expanding the power base of his organization.

BIBLIOGRAPHY

Aḥmad, Rifʿat Sayyid. *Al-ḥarakāt al-Islāmīyah fī Miṣr wa-Īrān* (The Islamic Movements in Egypt and Iran). Cairo, 1989.

Aḥmad, Rifʿat Sayyid. *Tanẓīmāt al-ghaḍab al-Islāmī* (Organizations of Islamic Anger). Cairo, 1989.

Esposito, John L. *Islam and Politics*. Rev. ed., Syracuse, 1991.

Muṣṭafā, Ḥālah. "Al-jihād al-Islāmī fī al-arḍ al-muḥtallah" (The Islamic Jihad in the Occupied Territories). *Qaḍāyā Fikrīyah* (April 1988).

Muṣṭafā, Ḥālah. "Al-tayyār al-Islāmī fī al-arḍ al-muḥtallah" (The Islamic Current in the Occupied Territories). *Al-mustaqbal al-ʿArabī* 11.113 (July 1988).

Sārah, Fāyiz. "Al-ḥarakah al-Islāmīyah fī Filasṭīn: Waḥdat al-īdiyūlūjīyah wa-inqisāmāt al-siyāsah" (The Islamic Movement in Palestine: The Unity of Ideology and the Divisions of Politics). *Al-mustaqbal al-ʿArabī* 12.124 (June 1989).

Sivan, Emanuel. *Radical Islam*. New Haven, 1990.

Wardānī, Ṣalāḥ al-. *Al-ḥarakah al-Islāmīyah fī Miṣr: Wāqiʿ al-Thamānīnāt* (The Islamic Movement in Egypt: The Reality of the 1980s). Cairo, 1990.

Wright, Robin. *Sacred Rage: The Wrath of Militant Islam*. New York, 1985.

AsʿAD AbuKhalil

JINNAH, MOHAMMAD ALI (1876–1948), Quaid-i-Azam ("Great Leader") and first governor-general of Pakistan. Born in Karachi, the eldest child of well-to-do Khojas, young Jinnah was sent to London in 1893 and apprenticed to a British managing agency. He was bored by business, however, and turned to the study of law at Lincoln's Inn and also aspired to acting. Jinnah helped the "grand old man" of India's National Congress, Parsi Dadabhai Naoroji, win a seat in the House of Commons, and with Dadabhai's support joined the Indian National Congress in 1906. By then a successful Bombay barrister, Jinnah also joined the Muslim League in 1913 and was instrumental in drafting the jointly adopted Congress-League Lucknow Pact of 1916. As the brightest ambassador of Hindu-Muslim unity, Jinnah seemed destined to lead a united Indian dominion after World War I, but Mohandas K. Gandhi returned from South Africa to revolutionize the Congress Party and become its postwar leader. Jinnah tried his best to dissuade Congress from following Gandhi's "dangerous" and "radical" lead, but he failed in 1919 and withdrew.

Jinnah then focused on his legal practice and served as an independent Muslim member, elected from Bombay, on the Viceroy's legislative council in Calcutta and New Delhi. In 1930 he sailed back to London to attend the first Round Table Conference on Indian Constitutional Reforms, just when Allamah Muhammad Iqbal (1877–1938) was presiding over the Muslim League in Allahabad. The latter called for "a consolidated North-West Indian Muslim state" for the first time from any League platform, a decade prior to the Lahore "Pakistan Resolution." Jinnah and Sir Shah Nawaz Bhutto managed in London to win separate provincial status for their home province of Sind, which in 1935 became the only Muslim-majority province of British India (Eastern Bengal and Assam having been reunited with West Bengal in 1910). Liaquat Ali Khan (1896–1951) lured Jinnah back from London to become permanent president of the Muslim League. But Congress won most of the provincial contests in 1937 and refused to admit any League leaders to its provincial cabinets. Outraged by Congress arrogance, Jinnah now appealed to India's Muslim masses, transforming himself at his League's Lucknow session of 1937 into their Quaid-i-Azam. By March 1940, when the League met in Lahore, Jinnah insisted that British India's Muslims were no longer a "minority," but a "nation." The Lahore Resolution's demand for a separate, single Pakistan became his sole platform and a goal to which he devoted the rest of his life and fast-failing energies. He survived long enough to preside over his new nation's birth in mid-August 1947, but expired of lung cancer before he could bring to fruition his fondest dream of firmly establishing in Pakistan a secular and democratic polity free of corruption and internal conflicts.

[*See also* All-India Muslim League; Pakistan; *and the biography of Iqbal.*]

BIBLIOGRAPHY

Hasan, Khalid Shamsul, ed. *Quaid-i-Azam's Unrealised Dream*. Karachi, 1991.

Mujahid, Sharif. *Quaid-i-Azam Jinnah: Studies in Interpretation*. Karachi, 1981.

Pirzada, Syed Sharifuddin, ed. *The Collected Works of Quaid-e-Azam Mohammad Ali Jinnah* (1906–1921). Vol. 1. Karachi, 1984.

Saiyid, Matlubul Hasan. *Mohammad Ali Jinnah (A Political Study)*. Lahore, 1945.

Wolpert, Stanley A. *Jinnah of Pakistan*. New York, 1984. Standard biography of Jinnah.

STANLEY WOLPERT

JIZYAH. A word meaning recompense, compensation, or requital, as in the Qur'ān: "Fight those who believe not in Allāh, nor the Last Day, nor hold that forbidden which has been forbidden by Allāh and His Messenger, nor acknowledge the Religion of Truth—from those who have been given the Book—until they pay the *jizyah* by hand and are subdued" (9.29). In Islamic history *jizyah* has most commonly referred to a head tax, levied on non-Muslim *dhimmīs* (protected monotheists under a contract of obligation) as a form of tribute and an exemption from military service.

Little guidance about the nature of *jizyah* is found in the canonical *ḥadīth* collections, other than exempting converts from paying the tax after they have embraced Islam. This lack of textual guidance has led to considerable confusion in regard to its definition and regulation. In the early caliphal period *jizyah* was often confused with *kharāj*, a tax on land that was paid in kind. In the ʿAbbāsid era (749–1258), *jizyah* was formally defined as a head tax, specific to the *dhimmīs*, and was paid in specie.

According to the Ḥanafī jurist Abū Yūsuf (d. 808) *qāḍī* (chief judge) for the ʿAbbāsid caliph Hārūn al-Rashīd, *jizyah* was a form of tribute that exempted the person who paid it from military service. Consequently, it was not required from those incapable of fighting. Abū Yūsuf also conceived of *jizyah* as a graduated head tax, in which the poor paid less than the rich, and the elderly, women, children, the sick, and the penniless were exempted. For the jurist and law-school founder al-Shāfiʿī (d. 820), *jizyah* was a tributary and protection tax that was required of all *dhimmīs*, regardless of status. However, if a Muslim ruler failed his non-Muslim subjects by not providing them with adequate security, he was obliged to return the money. This was actually done for Christians by the Egyptian *amīr* Ṣalāḥ al-Dīn al-Ayyūbī ("Saladin," d. 1193), when he was compelled to withdraw his army from Syria.

Sometimes, the requirements for *jizyah* could be interpreted severely. In *Tafsīr al-kashshāf*, the Muʿtazilah exegete al-Zamakhsharī (d. 1144) assumes that the intent of the Qur'ānic commandment was to highlight the subordinate status of the *dhimmī* in Muslim society. Therefore, the *jizyah* should be exacted as a form of humiliation. The non-Muslim should come to pay the tax walking, not riding. When he pays, he is made to stand, while the tax collector sits. The collector should seize him by the scruff of the neck, shake him, and say, "Pay the *jizyah*!" cuffing him on the back of the head once the tax has been paid. A similarly hard line is taken by the modern commentator and political activist Sayyid Quṭb (d. 1966) in his widely read commentary,

Fī ẓilāl al-Qur'ān. This prominent ideologist of the Muslim Brotherhood is defiantly triumphalist, claiming that *jizyah* amounts to a punishment for polytheism (especially for Christians) and is required before peaceful relations can be established between Muslims and the "people of the book." Seeing *sharīʿah* (the divine law) as a sort of positive law, Quṭb intimates that *jizyah* is a recompense or protection, not from military service or external enemies, but from *jihād*. If it is not paid as part of a peace agreement, the Islamic state owes no obligation to non-Muslims, whether at home or abroad.

A more liberal stance is taken by the contemporary Muslim writer Abdul Rahman Doi, who prefers to cite the Qur'ānic verse, "There is no compulsion in religion" (surah 2.256). For Doi, *jizyah* is an obligatory tax paid by non-Muslims in return for being exempted from the *zakāt* (alms tax). Therefore, the amount paid ought to be proportional to the *zakāt* itself. Furthermore, the Muslim is obliged to treat the *dhimmī* honorably and with respect. Doi stresses that in the present day, when protecting the state requires vast sums of money, the *jizyah* is mainly symbolic and can be waived at any time. To prove his point he cites a historical account from the *Ṭabaqāt* of Ibn Saʿd (d. 844), in which the prophet Muḥammad says on the death of his son Ibrāhīm, who was born to Maria, a Coptic concubine: "If my son Ibrāhīm had lived, I would have exempted every Copt from the *jizyah*." The difference of opinion between Doi and Quṭb illustrates the fact that there is no more of a consensus about *jizyah* today than there was in the past.

[*See also* Dhimmī; Taxation.]

BIBLIOGRAPHY

Doi, Abdul Rahman I. *Non-Muslims under Sharīʿah (Islamic Law)*. Lahore, 1981. Somewhat idealistic, but still the best treatment of the subject in English. The perspective is middle of the road and reflects the ideology of Pakistan's Jamāʿat-i Islāmī.

Lewis, Bernard. *The Jews of Islam*. Princeton, 1984. Despite the fact that Lewis judges the past according to modern values, chapter 1 (pp. 3–66) is a good introduction to medieval Muslim attitudes toward the Peoples of the Book.

Quṭb, Sayyid, *Fī ẓilāl al-Qur'ān*. Cairo and Beirut, 1981. Although most of this commentary on the Qur'ān has not been translated into English, it remains one of the most influential works of its genre published in the twentieth century. See pages 1220–1250.

VINCENT J. CORNELL

JORDAN. The modern state of Jordan first emerged in 1921 as the Emirate of Transjordan. Until the end of World War I this area had been part of greater Syria under Ottoman rule. After the defeat of the Ottoman Empire in 1918 the Allied Powers divided the Middle East into spheres of influence, with Transjordan and Palestine under British mandate and trusteeship. In 1946 Transjordan achieved independence to become the Hashemite Kingdom of Jordan, with Prince Abdullah ibn al-Hussein its first monarch (1921–1951).

In 1948 the United Nations partitioned Palestine, and the Arab-Israeli War began. The portion of Palestine under Arab control at the end of the war merged with Jordan. After King Abdullah's assassination in 1951 his son, King Talal ibn Abdullah, ruled for nearly a year and then abdicated in favor of his son, King Hussein ibn Talal, who has remained in power since then.

In 1967 Israeli forces occupied the West Bank of Jordan. Following sustained occupation, in July 1988 Jordan formally severed legal and administrative ties with the West Bank, and in 1989 ordered a parliamentary election involving only residents of the East Bank.

Jordan occupies nearly 57,354 square miles, more than two-thirds of it semiarid. Nearly 93 percent of the land under cultivation depends on annual rainfall, and only 8.6 percent receives more than the 7.8 annual inches required for cultivation. Because agriculture's contribution to the national economy fluctuates with rainfall, Jordan relies on food imports to meet its basic needs.

Continuous population growth has steadily increased this dependence and aggravated the budget deficit. In 1921 Jordan's population was estimated between 200,000 and 400,000 (a rough estimate because of the mobility of the bedouin segment). By September 1991 it had increased to an estimated 3.5 million, an annual increase rate of 3.4 percent. Rapid population growth in Jordan during the second half of the twentieth century is in part the result of political upheavals in the Middle East. Palestinian refugees settled on the East Bank of Jordan in two waves, first after the partition of Palestine in 1948 and later after the 1967 Israeli occupation of the West Bank. A third influx occurred with the return from Kuwait of more than 300,000 Palestinians and Jordanians during the 1990–1991 Gulf War.

Islam is the dominant religion in Jordan, and 95 percent of the population are Sunnī Muslim. Another 1 percent of the population consists of Druze and Bahā'īs; Christians comprise the remaining 4 percent. Before the twentieth century most residents of Jordan were farmers and small merchants residing in villages and towns.

Around the turn of the century, groups such as the Shishans, Circassians, and Armenians came from the Baltic States and the Caucasus to escape political and religious turmoil, maintaining their languages and other ethnic traits. During the same period, individuals or families from neighboring Arab countries such as Syria, Lebanon, Palestine, Iraq, and Egypt arrived in increasing numbers.

Political parties began to emerge in Jordan after its creation as a modern state in 1921. During the 1920s and 1930s a few national secular political parties called for independence from Britain but failed because of British influence on the government and a lack of political awareness among the native population. During the late 1940s and early 1950s, however, modern secular and religio-political ideologies entered Jordan from neighboring Arab countries. Jordanian students who had attended higher academic institutions in Egypt, Syria, and Lebanon were influenced by these active and organized movements and led them in Jordan. Political awareness was spurred by the continuing threats of Western colonialism. The creation of Israel in 1948 and the subsequent military and political humiliations of Arab forces radicalized the political atmosphere.

Two basic types of organized Islamic religious movements exist in Jordan. The first focuses on political goals, and the second on religious revival. Among the first, some parties have legal status, but others do not. For example, the Muslim Brotherhood, registered as a socioreligious philanthropic organization, organizes and functions freely because it has openly declared support of the king and Hashemite family rule. By contrast, the Islamic Liberation Party (Ḥizb al-Taḥrīr al-Islāmī), the Islamic Holy War Party (Jamāʿat al-Jihād al-Islāmī), Ḥamās, Muḥammad's Army (Jaysh Muḥammad), and the Muslim Youth movement (Ḥarakāt Shabāb al-Nafīr al-Islāmī) have no legal status. These parties, with the exception of Ḥamās, have called for the overthrow of ruling Arab regimes and their replacement by Islamic governments. The second type of organized religious Islamic movements, which focus only on religious objectives, includes Ṣūfī orders, the Jamāʿat al-Tablīgh and Jamāʿat al-Sulūfīyah.

The most active and dominant Islamic political party is the Muslim Brotherhood, which originated in Egypt and spread into Palestine in 1946 and thence into Jordan. One major factor that contributed to the Muslim Brotherhood's credibility and visibility was its participation in the Arab-Israeli War of 1948. Its open support of King Abdullah also helped. The king backed the movement because he shared its Islamic beliefs and values. Royal favor has continued with King Hussein. This harmonious relationship was confirmed when both the regime and the party became targets of criticism and attacks by various Arab regimes and secular Pan-Arab movements, especially in the 1950s and late 1960s. The Muslim Brotherhood reacted by attacking all secular political parties as the "enemy of God." In 1954 an assassination attempt on the late Egyptian president Gamal Abdel Nasser was attributed to followers of the party in Egypt. When many of the leadership were arrested and jailed, some took refuge in Jordan, including the son-in-law of the movement's founder Ḥasan al-Bannā', Saʿīd Ramaḍān, who has maintained an active role.

In 1957 the Jordanian government imposed martial law, and secular political parties were not permitted to function. As a result, for nearly three decades the Muslim Brotherhood was able to build support at all societal levels without much competition. In 1989 martial law was lifted and political freedom granted to all parties, but the Muslim Brotherhood had consolidated its position, especially after 1967.

The impact of the 1967 Arab-Israeli War and Israeli occupation of Arab territories fueled the political comeback of various Islamic movements in Jordan. The Muslim Brotherhood's slogan was "Islam is the solution," and its members criticized the government but not the king. They pressed for reforms based on the *sharīʿah* and Islamic values to stamp out corruption and eliminate Western influence. The party carried that message to all societal levels with its five-point agenda: (1) to develop a national educational program and curriculum based on and shaped by Islamic teaching and values and compatible with modern times; (2) to develop the Islamic world economically and to ensure a just distribution of wealth; (3) to establish unity among different Islamic governments and coordinate policy and functions to maintain strong links among all Muslims; (4) to establish a social policy encouraging economic charities in order to eradicate poverty, ignorance, and diseases; and (5) to develop and promote Islam as a base for a universal civilization (al-Kīlānī, 1990, p. 58).

The Muslim Brotherhood's reform agenda was put to the test when King Hussein asked Maẓhar Badrān, a leading figure in the movement, to form a cabinet in January 1991. Five Muslim Brotherhood members headed important cabinet ministries, including education, social services, and justice. Among the important reforms introduced by the newly appointed minister of Education, Abdullah al-ʿAqaliya, were segregation by gender in the workplace and in schools, revisions of textbooks, appointments of Muslim Brotherhood members to key positions in the ministry and, in some cases, replacement of women in strategic positions by men.

Over the past four decades the Muslim Brotherhood in Jordan has built and operated nearly two hundred private Islamic elementary and secondary schools, as well as Qur'ānic teaching centers, funded entirely by private donations. Independent of government support, it has also launched a program to open hospitals and health care clinics nationwide to provide services based on the individual's ability to pay. Through its control of a broad range of organizations and institutions that provide services to the public, the Muslim Brotherhood is transmitting its religio-political message and widening its support among the masses.

The Muslim Brotherhood in Jordan has more political power than its counterparts in many other Arab countries. This was reflected in the national parliamentary election of 1989, which gave the Islamists around 40 percent of the seats in the lower house. The leadership of the Muslim Brotherhood in Jordan are highly educated, many holding doctorates from American universities. Furthermore, many of the leaders come from prominent families with tribal backgrounds where patronage plays an important role. The traditional tribal segment of the Jordanian population still dominates the social and political structure of the society.

The parliamentary elections of November 1993 demonstrated the continuing strength of the Muslim Brotherhood, which remained the largest single organized bloc. However, it did not win as many seats as in 1989, reflecting both more restrictive election laws and changes in public views as a result of experiences with Islamists in positions of responsibility. The Muslim Brotherhood has been registered since the 1950s as a religious charitable organization. In response to the election law of 1993, the Muslim Brotherhood, in cooperation with other independent Islamist individuals and political groups, created a political party under the name "Islamic National Action Front." The new Islamic Action Front was licensed in February 1993. This strategy allowed the Muslim Brotherhood to remain politically influential but not directly involved in partisan politics.

Another Islamic movement with a political agenda, the Islamic Liberation Party (Ḥizb al-Taḥrīr al-Islāmī), has not been legalized. Its founder, Shaykh Taqī al-Dīn al-Nabhānī, was born in Palestine in 1910. Educated at al-Azhar during the 1940s, al-Nabhānī studied the forces that led to the disintegration of the Islamic empire at the beginning of the twelfth century and the collapse of the Ottoman Empire at the end of World War I. He identified the key forces as Western influence and domination, and the separation of church and state in the Islamic world (Ubaydat, 1989, p. 245). While pursuing his studies he joined the Muslim Brotherhood, but he withdrew in 1952 to establish the Islamic Liberation Party. After the partition of Palestine in 1948, al-Nabhānī submitted an official request to the Jordanian government to operate legally within the political system, but this was denied. Continual pressure by the government, harsh treatment, and imprisonment forced many party leaders to leave Jordan. Al-Nabhānī fled to Syria in 1953 and then to Lebanon, where he lived until his death in 1974.

Ideologically the Islamic Liberation Party maintains that Islam is not only a religion, but that it defines and includes every other aspect of life. With this view the party urges Muslims to replace current governments with an Islamic caliphate, by force if necessary. The Islamic Liberation Party's ideology rejects all participation in social, economic, or religious charitable activities because they distract from the main objective—the creation of the Islamic state.

Because the leadership thought that its ideology would appeal to the masses and be accepted rapidly, it sought to expedite its objectives by wresting authority from the hands of corrupt regimes. This led to several unsuccessful attempts to take over regimes: in Jordan in 1969, in Egypt in 1973, and in Iraq in 1973, as well as in Tunisia, Algeria, and Sudan.

Ḥamās, another secretly organized Islamic religio-political movement, developed in the occupied West Bank and Gaza Strip. This organization played an important role in the *intifāḍah* that began in 1988. It has publicly declared no other political interest than the liberation of Palestine from its Israeli occupiers, nor has it conducted any political activities on the East Bank of Jordan.

Other nonlegal religio-political Islamic groups, less popular than the Islamic Liberation Party, include the Islamic Holy War Party, Muḥammad's Army, and the Islamic Youth Organization. During the past few years these groups were involved, according to the government, in more than one attempt to overthrow the regime in Jordan, and some of their members were arrested. Two prominent members of parliament, elected in 1989, were detained for alleged connections with banned Islamic organizations and were accused of being financially supported by the Islamic regime in Iran. Convicted by a military court on 29 September 1992, they were given twenty-year jail sentences. A few days later, despite his public support of the court decision, King Hussein pardoned several hundred prison inmates including both men, who resumed their seats in parliament. One of them, Layth Shubaylat, has since denied the government accusation and any link to banned Islamic movements. He contends that he was framed by the Jordanian government because he was chairing a parliamentary judicial committee charged with investigating the misuse of public funds and corruption. The committee's inquiries revealed that high government officials, including previous prime ministers, were involved in unlawful activities (personal interview with Shubaylat, 18 July 1993). Another factor in the case may have been the Islamic National Front's opposition to Jordanian government participation in the Palestinian peace negotiations that began in Madrid in 1991.

The organized religious Islamic groups that have no political agenda include the Ṣūfī orders and the groups Jamāʿat al-Tablīgh and Jamaʿat al-Sulūfīyah. The orders, which spread into Jordan from various neighboring countries during the past four or five decades, emphasize individual spiritual and religious conduct and relationship to God the creator. All Ṣūfī orders disregard materialistic values, which they believe corrupt people. They call for a return to the straight path of God and religious conduct. Ṣūfī orders that practice in Jordan include the Shādhilīyah al-Yashrūṭīyah, Kīlānīyah, Qādirīyah, Rifāʿīyah, Naqshbandīyah, Burhānīyah, Taymīyah, and Qulūṭīyah. They recruit from all socioeconomic strata in both urban and rural communities. Members gather on a regular basis to recite religious songs and verses from the Qur'ān; a major effect of their activities is heightened awareness of Islam.

The Jamāʿat al-Tablīgh (or Tablīghī Jamāʿat), which began in India, emphasizes spreading God's word and Islam. Members are required to devote an hour a day or one full day a month to preaching God's word. The Jamāʿat al-Sulūfīyah calls for a return to the Qur'ān and *sunnah* as well as the practices of the early centuries of Islam. Despite consensus on general objectives, its followers disagree on the means of attaining them. This disagreement has led to much ideological fragmentation of thought in the movement.

Political Islam in Jordan bears certain similarities to its counterparts in neighboring Islamic countries. The political and religious ideologies of the various Islamic movements have been influenced and shaped by Islamic thought and philosophy. All share the same objective: the replacement of the present ruling regime by an Islamic government based on the Qur'ān and the *sharīʿah*. The rise, spread, and success of political Islam as reflected in the Muslim Brotherhood in Jordan is attributed to the same forces that influenced political Islam in other countries in the Middle East.

External as well as internal political, economic, and sociological forces have fed this process. The negative image of Islam in Western societies began with the Crusades and continued with European colonialism in the Middle East between the eighteenth and twentieth centuries. This negative image, perpetuated by Orientalists, novelists, journalists, and recently the mass media, was seldom balanced by an account of the positive values of Islam and its contribution to Western civilization. More recently the failure of the West to differentiate between Islam and political Islam has led to the perception that Islam itself is a threat to Western values and national interest. Western governments fail to understand that political Islam includes both moderate and radical groups. Islamic protest movements reject Western ways of life and interference in the internal affairs of Arab Islamic society, but this interference is usually conducted through the vehicle of local authoritarian and corrupt regimes. The hostile Western attitude toward Muslims has stimulated a similar attitude among members of various Islamic movements toward the Western world and further contributed to the rise of political Islam.

On the Jordanian national scene, internal political and sociological forces played an important role in the spread and growth of political Islam. First, the continuing Palestinian-Israeli struggle and the failure of Arab governments to stop further Israeli territorial expansion, particularly after the 1967 war, increased the influence of political Islam in the region at the expense of various Pan-Arab national movements. Second, the economic, political, and sociological impacts of the oil boom of the 1970s and 1980s were both negative and positive. It widened the gap between the rich and poor and changed the pattern of consumption by the rich, whose way of life was viewed with envy and hostility by the unemployed and the poor. Islamic movements have capitalized on the economic situation and championed the cause of the poor by referring to the unjust distribution of wealth. The oil boom also directed a flow of financial contributions by individuals and governments to various Islamic movements in the region. Third, government corruption, the misuse of public funds, and the inability of the regime to create jobs for the unemployed, especially college graduates, provided fertile ground for Islamic movements to recruit members. Furthermore, broad grassroots support is found among Palestinians in refugee camps in Jordan.

The success or failure of political Islam in Jordan will depend on three factors: changes in Western attitudes toward Islam; a just and peaceful settlement of the Palestinian-Israeli problem; and political, economic, and social reforms in Jordan.

[*See also* Ḥamās; Ḥizb al-Taḥrīr al-Islāmī; Jihād Organizations; Muslim Brotherhood, *article on* Muslim Brotherhood in Jordan; *and* Tablīghī Jamāʿat.]

BIBLIOGRAPHY

Antoun, Richard. *Muslim Preacher in the Modern World: A Jordanian Case Study in Comparative Perspective*. Princeton, 1989.

Government of Jordan, Ministry of Information. *Facts about Jordan* (Sheet no. 1–9). Amman, September 1991.

Kīlānī, Mūsā Zayd al-. *Al-ḥarakāt al-Islāmīyah fī al-Urdun*. Amman, 1990.

Māḍī, Munīb, and Sulaymān Mūsā. *Tārīkh al-Urdun fī al-qarn al-ʿishrīn*. Amman, 1959.

Muḥāfaẓah, ʿAlī. *Tārīkh al-Urdun al-muʿāṣir*. Amman, 1973.

Saʿdānī, ʿIṣām al-. "Al-ḥarakah al-waṭanīyah al-Urdunīyah, 1921–1946." Ph.D. diss., St. Joseph University, Beirut, 1991.

Satloff, Robert B. *They Cannot Stop Our Tongues: Islamic Activism in Jordan*. Washington, D.C., 1986.

ʿUbaydāt, Maḥmūd Sālim. *Athar al-jamāʿāt al-Islāmīyah al-maydānī khilālā al-qarn al-ʿishrīn*. Amman, 1989.

HANI FAKHOURI

JUDAISM AND ISLAM. From Islam's inception, it has had a varied and profound relationship with Judaism. In scripture and thought, in society and politics, in culture and intellectual life, the two religious civilizations have exemplified their relations. In modern times, these relations have reflected major historical dislocations. This article selectively surveys the history and range of contacts between Islam and Judaism, while emphasizing the modern period.

Islam's formation, seen mainly through internal sources, revealed a prominent "Judaic dimension." Some of the content of Islam's revelations and the tradition emerging from this, as well as the actual relations between Muslims and Jews in Medina, constituted the beginning of the Muslim-Jewish encounter.

Muḥammad's revelations evinced ideas and stories, enjoined practices, and established institutions which had Judaic resonances and forms, including a profile of the Jews themselves. Notions of monotheism, revelation, prophecy, scripture, the next world, and God's relationship with his creatures are, among others, central here. Institutions such as ritual worship and its directional orientation (*ṣalāt, qiblah*) and fasting (*ṣawm*) seem to have had quasi-Judaic forms in Mecca before their later islamization in Medina. Prophet figures, such as Joseph (surah 12), Noah (surah, 7.59ff; 10.72ff.), Solomon (and the Queen of Sheba) (surah 27.15ff.), and Moses (surah 28.3ff.), to name but a few, though often somewhat different from their Judaic and biblical counterparts, prove in their very Qur'ānic presence the hovering influence of that model.

Although there was a Judaic and biblical presence in Muḥammad's revelations, it did not always represent canonical Judaism and the Bible, as much earlier Western scholarship presumed. It is likely that a mélange of ancient Near Eastern traditions, which, though in part Judaic, represent a synthesis of many related cultural strands (including, obviously, the Christian), was reflected in early Islam. These cultural interactions are highly complex and are amenable to many interpretations.

One main Qur'ānic conception of the Jews does have a Torah and biblical form close to a canonical Jewish depiction, but it also deviates from that biblical form in a way which indicates the early Islamic self-definition in regard to the (Jewish) other: the Jews (Banū Isrā'īl, or "Israelites") in covenant with God, repeatedly violating the covenant and Torah, opposing the prophets and thereby incurring divine wrath. This coincides with the original biblical conception. The Bible also foresaw ultimate redemption of the Jewish people (Deuteronomy 30.1ff.). The Qur'ān omits Jewish redemption with an implicit supercessionist view of Islam in regard to Judaism (Qur'ān 2.83ff.).

The Qur'ānic and other early Islamic portrayals of the Jews also reflect the situation in contemporary Medina. A complex relationship between the Prophet and the Jewish tribes there (al-Yahūd, or "the Jews") is revealed in (sometimes oblique) references to Jewish machinations against Muslims and alliances with the Munāfiqūn ("Hypocrites"; opponents of Muḥammad). This gave substance to the Qur'ān's more abstract depictions of the historical Banū Isrā'īl rebellion against prophecy. Reported Jewish rejection of Muḥammad's teachings in Medina seemed a living example of the ancient problem.

Contrary to—perhaps in dialectical tension with—this rather polemical (and political) portrayal is a Qur'ānic respect for the Jews and Judaism. This is shown in the notion of the *ahl al-kitāb* ("people of the book"), which, while referring also to Christians (and Sabians) seems often to incorporate the Jews as its main example. The "book," so revered as an ideal type, is here firmly attached to the Jews and their tradition. This is in spite of the Qur'ānic claim of the corruption of the Jewish book and other wrongdoing of the *ahl al-kitāb*.

In the field, relations between Islam and Judaism worsened, culminating in a series of Muslim campaigns against the Jewish tribes and a final Muslim victory. These campaigns were interwoven with the long series of Muslim campaigns against the Meccans, in a sort of "point-counterpoint" fashion. Thus the early battle dramas of Badr (624), Uḥud (625), the Ditch (627), and al-Ḥudaybīyah (628) had an alter ego in the Muslim trials with the Jewish tribes of Banū Qaynuqāʿ, Banū Naḍīr, and Banū Qurayẓah.

The resolution came with the Muslim defeat of the Jews of Khaybar (628), among whom were the Banū Naḍīr expelled by the Muslims from Medina. Here a clear conception of the practical relationship between Islam and Judaism emerged. This meant the Jews would live as a protected minority, paying, in return, a special tax. A model for later arrangements was thus established. The full institution of *dhimmah* (protection), covering Jews, Christians, and other scriptuaries, gradually evolved in accordance with Muḥammad's revelations and events on the ground. Derived from the later so-called Pact of ʿUmar (in various seventh- and eighth-century rescensions), this institution governed the traditional Islamic-Jewish relationship throughout the medieval era, until its dissolution in the modern period.

The foundation of Islamic-Jewish relations established during Islam's formative period remained in place and gave direction to subsequent developments. The span between 632 (Muḥammad's death) and the beginning of Islam's modern period (late eighteenth century) saw an extension and development of this foundation. The great Jewish communities of Babylonia, Palestine, Egypt, and the Levant came under Islamic sway (seventh century), as did smaller and less venerable ones. Living administratively as "protected peoples" (*dhimmīs*), the Jews then interacted with Muslims in various ways.

The cultural and intellectual interchange was profound. In theology, exegesis, philosophy, law, mysticism, and poetry, Jews and Muslims contributed to and learned from one another. The Judaic component in Islam, for example, was augmented by works of Jewish and quasi-Jewish prophetic stories (*Qiṣaṣ al-Anbiyā'* and *Isrā'īlīyāt*), which, while sometimes proscribed by Islam for theological reasons, still achieved a massive presence in Islamic texts, particularly in the *tafsīr* (exegetical) tradition and in popular folklore and Sufism. The Islamic philosophical tradition, on the other hand, aided the Jews in establishing their own philosophical learning. Maimonides' debt to Muslim philosphers and theologians, for example, was very great. And the existence of the Muslim al-Tabrīzī's (thirteenth century) commentary on a portion of Maimonides' *Guide to the Perplexed* is a sign of great interest in the other direction. Maimonides' son, Abraham, was a proponent of a so-called Jewish Sufism, which utilized the framework and technical terminology of the Islamic mystical tradition. Examples in these areas can be multiplied many times.

The classical Islamic depictions of Judaism and the Jews found in the Qur'ān and other early sources were later augmented and elaborated by Muslim scholars working in various disciplines. Their discussion sometimes reflected the more polemical as well as the positive side of the classical portrayal, and severe and straightforward vilification of the Jews was not typical. The Muslim intellectuals, rather, either commented on the sources in a neutral manner or generally elaborated on the earlier depictions in such a way as to make of the Jews a kind of "warning model" to Muslims of a people who had strayed and been chastised by God. Such discussions were usually detached, abstract, and not applied to the actual Jewish communities living within the Islamic fold. This was an important difference between the medieval and certain twentieth-century Islamic interpretations of the early sources on the Jews.

The life of Jewish communities in the Muslim world throughout this long period was governed by the elaborate laws of *dhimmah*. Itself derived from traditional hierarchical conceptions of Islamic spiritual finality and superiority to the other faiths, the *dhimmah* idea and practice mainly imposed practical regulations and restrictions as a way of implementing these notions of difference. Thus were the Jews (and other *ahl al-kitāb*) subject to certain legal, economic, occupational, dress, and other restrictions. Although this created a legal status and feeling of inferiority for the Jews in Muslim countries, they could often be autonomous in their internal communal life while also interacting with the majority culture. Harsh treatment, although certainly not unknown, was also not the rule but the exception. In later centuries, the situation of Jews (and other minorities) deteriorated generally, but this occurred unevenly in different times and places. These developments reflected a difficult period of relative political and economic decline in parts of the Islamic world. The dawn of the modern era witnessed an exacerbation of the general Islamic situation and a radical change in the Jewish position.

The late eighteenth century is usually held to be the beginning of the modern history of the Islamic Middle East. After a long period of growing Western economic and political involvement in the area, Napoleon's entrance (1798) and brief stay with his army in Egypt presaged an era of great Western influence and domination. The general changes wrought by this situation profoundly affected the life of the *dhimmīs* in general and the Jews in particular. The institution of *dhimmah* eventually virtually disappeared and, with a few pockets of exception, the great ancient Jewish communities of the Islamic Middle East and North Africa went with it. Islamic-Jewish relations in the Middle East then took a form very different from anything previously known. The chronology of this period of change is from the nineteenth century onward.

In the nineteenth century, until World War I, the Western powers, France and Britain in particular, consolidated their presence in the Middle East. One prominent feature of this presence in some regions was a Western policy of equal rights for minorities, a direct challenge to the institution of *dhimmah*. Some indigenous Muslim powers responded to this in legislation, if not always in its implementation. Thus the Ottomans, in a two-stage legislation in 1839 and 1856, in principle provided a framework for a total equalization of *dhimmīs* and Muslims. In spite of the less than total acceptance and application of these laws throughout the realm, they did reflect real changes being effected in other ways by the powers. *Dhimmīs* were being liberated according to new Western ideas. By the end of World War I, this had to a great extent been completed.

The period between the two world wars saw a continuation of the Western powers' presence in the Islamic Middle East. This encouraged stronger nationalist sentiment among indigenous peoples. The Jews, by no means uniformly Zionist, did in places respond positively to that movement, as their Muslim (and Christian) neighbors promoted their own new nationalist ideologies. The period 1929 to 1939 saw an exacerbation of Muslim-Jewish tensions in various places in response to the worsening conflict in Palestine. The World War II period witnessed a continuation of the troubles in the midst of the complex politics of that time.

In the postwar period, the tensions of previous years rose to new heights, with the intensification of the Palestine problem. Anti-Jewish disturbances occurred, for example, in November 1945 in several Arab countries, with greater or lesser severity. With the UN partition resolution of 29 November 1947, the situation became more acute, and in subsequent months more disturbances took place. Within twenty years the vast majority of the Jews in Arab countries had left, going mainly to Israel and, to a lesser extent, Europe and North America. North Africa, Turkey, and Iran were less affected, but gradually they too saw a diminution of their Jewish population. With Middle Eastern Jewry now concentrated in Israel, Islamic-Jewish relations in the Middle East (and elsewhere) were subsequently to be colored by the politics of the Arab-Israel dispute. Aside from the natural tensions which ensued here, a very prominent and original aspect of the new relations was an innovative Islamic thought concerning Judaism and Zionism.

Though derived from the traditional ideas concerning the Jews and Judaism, the new thought also represented a sharp departure from that foundation. The differences can be found in the existential import of the new thought as well as in certain new conceptions and formulations. Like much of modern Islamic thought, this genre too is a direct response to some aspect of Islam's situation in the world. Unlike the majority of premodern Islamic discussions of the Jews, which have a more historical conception of Judaism and an academic way of discussing it, here the subject was given a practical and emotional significance which it had not had for centuries, if ever. At the same time, Judaism was given an essential nature—derived from sacred sources but removed from history—which might help to explain the new historical development. Old myths became new realities, giving rise to new concepts.

The beginning of this thought might be located in its earliest form in certain Islamic Arabic publications of the late 1930s. Prominent here was the Egyptian journal

Al-fatḥ. Loosely linked with more populist Islamic trends rather than with the official *ʿulamāʾ* (community of religious scholars), *Al-fatḥ* published many articles and editorials on the intensifying Palestine problem. This was a still early and fluid stage of that problem's development, before the creation of Israel and the Jewish exodus from Muslim countries. There was as yet no clear doctrinal line or framework story; there was, rather, a continuous commentary, from an Islamic perspective, on the developing situation. Three points, however, were clearly made and reiterated: (1) fear of a gradual judaization *(tahwīd)* of Palestine and a displacement of indigenous peoples; (2) concern over the security of Islamic sacred sites; and (3) most plaintively, an appeal to the Jews of Arab and Muslim lands not to abjure the centuries-old symbiosis of Muslims and Jews, Islam and Judaism, in favor of the new "un-Jewish" Zionism. Zionism was held to be as bad for the well-being of the Jews themselves as it was for its Muslim and Arab opponents.

Subsequent to Israeli statehood, a framework story emerged which informed almost all the wide variety of new intellectual trends: the new Jewish phenomenon of national movement and nation-state was held to be a recapitulation of the rebellious behavior of the ancient Israelites and the Jews of Muḥammad's time. The traditional stories here became interpretative models through which contemporary problems were given meaning. Tales of Muḥammad's trials with the alleged machinations of Medinan Jews, for example, were abstracted and read into modern Israel's national character. Or, sometimes, modern Israel was little mentioned but present by implication. Either way, past and present were mixed so as to create an eternal present. The time-bound traditional presentation of Jewish stories was here effaced; and an ahistoricity ensued which rendered stories universal in their applicability to historical events.

Examples of this approach abound in the voluminous new (Arabic) Islamic literature on Judaism as seen through the prism of modern events. From al-Azhar and other *ʿulamāʾ* to Islamist fundamentalists to Muslim intellectuals writing from an Islamic perspective, many minds have attempted to wrestle with this aspect of Islam's situation in this way. The large, two-volume proceedings of the 1968 al-Azhar Conference (Cairo, 1970) provide one interesting example of this line of thought. Written as responses of Muslim religious scholars to the shocking Israeli victory in June 1967, the papers in these volumes seek guidance in the early sources in confronting this modern catastrophe. The fundamentalist Muslim Brotherhood's publications, *Al-daʿwah* and *Al-iʿtiṣām,* in the late 1970s elaborated on and applied this reasoning to President Anwar el-Sadat's visit to Jerusalem. In a proliferation of articles, these magazines argued not only that Sadat's initiative was wrong in an Islamic sense, but that, if a peace agreement ensued, the Israeli Jews would cause offense to Islam in Egypt and would attempt to subvert the foundations of faith as their ancestors had done in Medina of the Prophet. Consonant with the new possibility of official Israeli Jewish presence in Egypt, and expressing a particular fundamentalist concern with internal Islamic moral values, the emphasis is on Jewish Israel as a cultural challenge *within* Muslim Egypt. This special angle in Sunnī revivalist and fundamentalist circles can be traced back at least as far as the Egyptian Sayyid Quṭb (d. 1966), whose long essay "Our Struggle with the Jews" (early 1950s) was seminal. On the other hand, with President Sadat's visit to Jerusalem and the subsequent Camp David Agreements, certain Islamic circles (particularly in al-Azhar) proclaimed support for a peaceful settlement, based on their own interpretations of Qur'ānic verses. Noticeable here were a more pragmatic view and an absence of the common modern framework story of the Jews. Also, as might have been expected, Palestinian Islamic circles produced their own brands of thought on these issues, partaking of the larger themes created elsewhere, while providing a local Palestinian Islamic nationalist flavor. Especially striking here are the publications of Ḥamās, the Palestinian fundamentalist movement.

Jewish responses to their new situation in regard to Islam were not equal, quantitatively or qualitatively, to those of Islam. But they do exist, mostly unstudied, and deserving of serious research.

The Islamic attempts ideologically to confront the collapse and disappearance of the institution of *dhimmah,* the emigration of the Jewish communities from the Islamic Near East, and their reconstitution in Israel, considered illegitimate in some quarters, constitute part of a more general Islamic search for early exemplars which would provide a gloss on Islam's modern situation. Of necessity, this approach usually could not include the great medieval models of Islamic-Jewish cultural and intellectual interaction, even when calling for a return to the practices and ethos of that era. In removing this interaction by dismantling the legal, social, and political structures which supported it, history has altered Islamic-Jewish relations in an unprecedented way.

[*See also* Arab-Israeli Conflict; Dhimmī; Muslim-Jewish Dialogue; *and* People of the Book.]

BIBLIOGRAPHY

Ashtor, Eliyahu. *The Jews in Moslem Spain.* 2 vols. Jerusalem, 1960–1966 (Hebrew); Philadelphia, 1973–1979 (English). The basic work on the subject.

Chouraqui, André N. *Between East and West: A History of the Jews of North Africa.* Translated by Michael M. Bernet. Philadelphia, 1968. Good survey written for a general audience.

Fischel, Walter J. *Jews in the Economic and Political Life of Mediaeval Islam* (1937). London, 1968. Standard general work.

Goitein, S. D. *A Mediterranean Society: The Jewish Communities of the Arab World as Portrayed in the Documents of the Cairo Geniza,* vol. 2, *The Community.* Berkeley and Los Angeles, 1971. One of four superb volumes, particularly accessible to the general reader.

Landau, Jacob. *Jews in Nineteenth-Century Egypt.* New York and London, 1969. Standard general work.

Laskier, Michael. *The Alliance Israélite Universelle and the Jewish Communities of Morocco, 1862–1962.* Albany, N.Y., 1983. Standard general work.

Lewis, Bernard. *The Jews of Islam.* Princeton, 1984. Standard work on the history of Jews in the Muslim world from Islam's beginnings to the latter half of the twentieth century. Particularly good on intellectual and cultural aspects.

Maimonides, Moses. *Guide of the Perplexed.* Translated by Shlomo Pines. Chicago, 1963. The standard translation of this classic work. The translator's introduction and notes give much information about Islamic influence on Maimonides.

Nettler, Ronald L., ed. *Studies in Muslim Jewish Relations.* Vol. 1. Reading, U.K., 1993. The first volume in a projected series of annual volumes. Contains a variety of articles on the subject.

Newby, Gordon D. "Tafsir Israiliyat: The Development of Qur'an Commentary in Early Islam in its Relationships to Judaeo-Christian Traditions of Scriptural Commentaries." *Journal of the American Academy of Religion* 47 (1979): 685–697. Excellent study of this aspect of Islamic-Jewish cultural interchange.

Nissim, Rejwan. *The Jews of Iraq: Three Thousand Years of History and Culture.* London, 1985. Good survey for the general reader.

Peters, F. E. *The Children of Abraham: Judaism, Christianity, Islam.* Princeton, 1982. Excellent study of the beliefs and other features held in common by the three religions. Special emphasis is given to the ancient Near Eastern background.

Stillman, Norman A. *The Jews of Arab Lands: A History and Source Book.* Philadelphia, 1979. Introductory survey of Jewish history in Arab lands and a much longer section of translated representative texts concerning various aspects of history. Covers the period from Islam's beginnings to the third quarter of the nineteenth century.

Stillman, Norman A. *The Jews of Arab Lands in Modern Times.* Philadelphia, 1991. Following the same format as the earlier volume (survey essay and translated sources), this book covers the period from the late nineteenth century to the late 1960s.

Tritton, A. S. *The Caliphs and Their Non-Muslim Subjects: A Critical Study of the Covenant of ʿUmar.* London, 1970. Still the standard work on the subject. A very good overview, though somewhat dated in some of its details.

Ronald L. Nettler

JUDGE. *See* Qāḍī.

JUMBLATT, KAMAL (Kamāl Junblāṭ, 1917–1977), Lebanese politician, traditional Druze chieftain, leader and ideologue of the Left. Born in the mountain village of al-Mukhtārah, Jumblatt attended the Lazarist school of ʿAyntūrah and received his university education at the Sorbonne. He later studied law at the Jesuit Saint Joseph University in Beirut.

Elected to parliament for the first time in 1943 at the age of twenty-six, Jumblatt entered politics following the death of his brother-in-law, Hikmat Jumblatt, and assumed the three-century-old leadership of one of the two clans of the Druze community in Mount Lebanon, the other being the Arslānī clan. (Kamal's father, Fuad Jumblatt, was assassinated in 1921 in unclear circumstances.) At odds with an entire generation of notables, Jumblatt's career deeply marked Lebanese politics. In 1949, he launched the Progressive Socialist Party. With its predominantly Druze power base, the party grew to become a loose coalition of deputies from different sectarian groups, mostly from Jumblatt's electoral district in the Shouf (Shūf).

In 1952, Jumblatt, along with a number of influential politicians, including Camille Chamoun (Shamʿūn), played a central role in the opposition campaign against President Bechara al-Khoury (Bishārah al-Khūrī), thus forcing his resignation. Jumblatt's first political setback was his defeat in the 1957 parliamentary elections, believed to have been influenced by President Chamoun, who was Jumblatt's Maronite rival in the Shouf. For Jumblatt, this one-time electoral defeat was an intolerable challenge to his historical leadership of the Druze community. A year later, in 1958, Jumblatt was a leading instigator of the short-lived armed rebellion against Chamoun.

Prior to the 1958 crisis, Jumblatt had distanced himself from Arab nationalism, but by the late 1950s he began to draw closer to Arab nationalist politics. Under the regime of General Fouad Chehab (Fuʿad Shihāb), who was elected president after the 1958 crisis, Jumblatt held several cabinet posts. Jumblatt held seven cabinet posts, the first in 1946–1947 and the last in 1969–1970.

But he never declared a truce with the political system, the governments he backed, or even the cabinets of which he was a member.

Beginning in the late 1960s, Jumblatt opted for unprecedented maximalism, as evidenced by his support for Palestinian militarism in Lebanon and a radical leftist platform. Jumblatt was instrumental in the prolongation of the six-month ministerial crisis in 1969, which ended only after the signing of the 1969 Cairo Agreement between the Lebanese government and the Palestine Liberation Organization (PLO). In his capacity as minister of the interior in the cabinet formed after the 1969 crisis, Jumblatt legalized a number of radical and antisystem parties.

The high point of Jumblatt's career came in the first half of the 1970s. In 1972, Jumblatt was the recipient of the Soviet Lenin Medal for Peace. A year later, he became secretary-general of a leftist, pro-PLO, Pan-Arab organization, the Arab Front for the Support of the Palestinian Revolution.

Jumblatt's actual power peaked just before the outbreak of war in 1975–1976, when Jumblatt's protégé, and nominee for the premiership, Rashīd al-Ṣulḥ, formed the last prewar cabinet. Jumblatt's growing influence on the eve of the war was due not only to his leadership of the Left and his close alliance with the PLO, but also to his ability to mobilize Lebanon's Pan-Arab "street," particularly in Beirut. This ability to inspire Arab nationalist protest undercut the power base of traditional Sunnī leaders, thus upsetting the Maronite-Sunnī confessional political balance, which had been in operation since independence in 1943.

In the 1975–1976 war, Jumblatt initially sought a political settlement. In August 1975, the Jumblatt-led leftist coalition, known as the Lebanese National Movement, proposed an Interim Program for Democratic Reform calling for sweeping changes. In October 1975, a National Dialogue Committee was formed to discuss reform proposals and ways to end the war, but no agreement was forthcoming.

The stalemate was broken with the announcement by President Suleiman Frangiyeh (Sulaymān Franjīyah) on 14 February 1976 of a Syrian-sponsored proposal known as the Constitutional Document. The proposal called for a more equitable confessional representation in government, but it reaffirmed the allocation of the top three government posts to Lebanon's three largest communities (Maronite, Sunnī, and Shīʿī). The proposal greatly displeased Jumblatt, and his differences with Damascus, the main architect of the Constitutional Document, turned into open hostility.

By March 1976, when Jumblatt was publicly calling for a "military solution," fighting spread to new areas, notably Mount Lebanon, where Palestinian forces launched large-scale offensives against Christian forces. In the fall of 1976 fighting escalated between Palestinian forces, backed by Jumblatt and the Left, and the Syrian army, backed by Christian and Muslim leaders. Hostilities ended when Syrian troops overran Palestinian strongholds and advanced toward Beirut. Jumblatt, the main loser in the war, retreated to his home village, where he was assassinated on 16 March 1977.

At the age of twenty-nine, Jumblatt's son, Walīd, succeeded his father as the leader of both the Jumblatti Druze clan and Lebanon's Left. Walīd also became the heir to his father's controversial politics, in which, ironically, he had played not even a minor role.

[*See also* Druze; Lebanon.]

BIBLIOGRAPHY

Works by Kamal Jumblatt

Lubnān fī wāqiʿihi wa-murtajāh. 2d ed. Beirut, 1957. Revealing lecture delivered on 10 December 1956 at the Cénacle Libanais in which Jumblatt outlines his reading of Lebanese and Arab politics prior to the 1958 crisis and his embrace of Arab nationalism.

I Speak for Lebanon. Translated by Michael Pallis. London, 1982. Jumblatt's critical reading of Lebanon's confessional politics and his account of the internal and external dimensions of the 1975–1976 war, written after defeat. Published posthumously.

Aḥādīth ʿan al-ḥurrīyah. 2d ed. Beirut, 1987. Collection of writings by Jumblatt.

Ḥaqīqat al-thawrah al-Lubnānīyah. 2d ed. Beirut, 1987. Jumblatt's account of the 1958 crisis.

Lubnān wa-Ḥarb al-Taswīyah. 2d ed. Beirut, 1987. Collection of Jumblatt's writings on the 1975–1976 war.

Rubʿ qarn min al-niḍāl. 2d ed. Beirut, 1987. Detailed account of Jumblatt's political activities, with emphasis on the Progressive Socialist party.

Works on Kamal Jumblatt

Abu Izzedin, Nejla M. *The Druzes: A New Study of Their History, Faith, and Society.* Leiden, 1984. General work on the Druze.

Betts, Robert B. *The Druze.* New Haven, 1988. Brief overview of the origins, social structure, and modern history of the Druze in Lebanon, Syria, and Israel.

El-Khazen, Farid. "Kamal Jumblatt, the Uncrowned Druze Prince of the Left." *Middle Eastern Studies* 24 (April 1988): 178–205. Thorough assessment of Jumblatt's chameleon politics, particularly his role in the 1975–1976 war.

Khalīl, Khalīl Aḥmad. *Kamal Junblāṭ: Thawrat al-amīr al-ḥadīth.* Beirut, 1984. Overview of Jumblatt's political career and thought written by a party member.

Shtai, Fāris. *Al-Ḥizb al-Taqadumi al-Ishtirāki wa Dawruhu fi al-Siyāsah al-Lubnāniyah*. 3 vols. Beirut, 1989. Comprehensive work on the Progressive Socialist Party and its role in Lebanese politics.

Suleiman, Michael. *Political Parties in Lebanon*. Ithaca, N.Y., 1967. The best study in English on prewar political parties in Lebanon, including the Progressive Socialist party.

FARID EL-KHAZEN

JUMHŪRĪYAH. *See* Republic.

JUSTICE. [*This entry comprises two articles. The first discusses concepts of justice that inform Islamic political discourse and that, more broadly, suffuse the Islamic worldview; the second focuses on the notion of social justice in modern Islamic thought as developed in the writings of Sayyid Quṭb and others.*]

Concepts of Justice

It has been argued that if the Christian worldview is predominantly cast in terms of love, then the Islamic one is suffused by a discourse of justice. As one commentator has put it, "neither in the Qur'ān nor in the Traditions are there measures to indicate what are the constituent elements of justice or how justice can be realized on Earth" (Khadduri, 1984, pp. 10–11). However, the ideas of paying one's moral and fiscal debts and of tempering retribution with mercy are features that characterize both God and the just person. For an individual to be *ʿadl* (just) is, as the term implies, to be balanced, to engage in acts that are framed by an awareness, born of the pursuit of reason over passion, of the harm that may be done to the ties that bind individuals to one another and all believers into a single community. The Qur'ān (6.152) thus enjoins one to "be just, even if it should be to a near kinsman" and demonstrates practical application when, for example, it recommends that contracts be written down in order to avoid subsequent doubt. It is, therefore, possible to see in the Qur'ān and Muḥammad's own actions an implicit theory of justice that informs later interpretations and applications.

Central to the prophetic conception of justice are three features: relationships among men and toward God are reciprocal in nature, and justice exists where this reciprocity guides all interaction; justice is both a process and a result of equating otherwise dissimilar entities; and because relationships are highly contextual, justice is to be grasped through its multifarious enactments rather than as a single abstract principle.

Just individuals are those to whom power appropriately devolves, because they have regulated their ties with others according to balanced, reciprocal obligations. These reciprocal obligations reduce social chaos and facilitate ever-greater networks of indebtedness among those who develop their God-given reason to understand the divine word and the mundane world alike. Justice as the process of equating implies that reason and experience must be used to calculate similarities, a process that shows itself in *qiyās* (analogic reasoning), no less than in attending to the differences between men and women, Muslims and non-Muslims, and assigning each category to its respective domain. The contextual quality of justice shows itself in the quest for an understanding of the spheres within which each person or historical moment exists and the ways in which fundamental qualities and kaleidoscopic changes must be scrutinized and balanced.

The elements of Islamic justice were the source of contention among moral and political theorists from the outset of Islam. During his lifetime the Prophet governed in direct accord with divine precept. After his death disagreement centered on which line possessed the capacity to rule justly and which procedures for rule should hold sway. For Sunnīs political justice lay in acknowledging legitimate authority through *ijmāʿ* (community consensus); for the Shīʿī it lay in the strict perpetuation of the line of legitimate succession. For the Sunnī the ruler's legitimacy was in theory hedged by the need for *shūrā* (consultation). The Sunnī Umayyad dynasty, however, combined the doctrine of an elected caliph with the idea that the responsible believer is the one who does not fail to obey the legitimate successor to the Prophet. Others, known collectively as Qādirīyah, believed that each man is responsible for his own acts and that political justice lies not in compulsory obedience but in holding even the caliph responsible for his unjust acts.

Notwithstanding its claims for continuity, the model of the caliphate failed to provide specific guidance for a theory of the just sovereign. During the brief period in the eighth century when the ʿAbbāsid dynasty favored them, the Muʿtazilah argued that divine justice is beyond human grasp but that human reason can best approximate divine justice through the exercise of reason and free will. Indeed, they argued, it is by such acts that one gains unity with that inner sense of justice toward which all men are naturally directed. Although the Muʿtazilī emphasis on reason and unity brought them into conflict with more powerful opponents, the terms of the debate were set: to the legalists (including the later systematizer al-Shāfiʿī [767–820]) men choose to do justice or injustice through their adherence to the law; to al-Ashʿarī (d. 935 or 936) men could do justice but could not create its very terms; to al-Ṭaḥāwī (d. 933) and al-Bāqillānī (d. 1012) the very uses to which God's created justice are put are themselves creative acts. By contrast, the Shīʿī theorists of the Būyid and Fāṭimid dynasties of the tenth and eleventh centuries argued that, in the absence of an infallibly sinless imam, men may even defend themselves through *taqīyah* (dissimulation) against an unjust caliph—a practice that Sunnīs regarded as little more than personal convenience. To both of these positions Ṣūfī theorists, such as Ibn al-ʿArabī (1165–1240), countered that justice can be made manifest in this world not by creative acts of reason but only by engagement in ecstatic devotion.

As Islam spread into new territories and as contact with classical Western thought increased, Islamic thinkers had to consider the practical applications of justice in law and politics. The Virtuous City of al-Fārābī (c. 878–c. 950) was to be characterized by the division and protection of all good things among the people; the Just City of Ibn Sīnā , (980–1037) was constituted by a social contract among administrators, artisans, and guardians, the welfare of all being secured by a common fund of resources. As the demands of actual administration increased, specific content for these propositions developed. The concept of *maṣlaḥah* (public interest), as elaborated by al-Ghazālī (1058–1111) and al-Tawfī (d. 1316), received legal force by calculating social consequence against individual interest; procedural justice lay in the qualities of the judge's character, in the use of a council of adviser/assessors, in the use of advisory opinions by outside scholars, and in the increasing use of elaborate procedures for ascertaining the credibility of witnesses. The traditional absence of appellate structures reduced dependence on any fallible judge, although the accepted legitimacy of different schools of Islamic law and resident experts allowed local custom to inform the practice of daily justice.

Because justice was seen to pervade all domains of life, Islamic thinkers sought to unify political, legal, and social justice. In the face of Mongol invaders and Western crusaders, Ibn Taymīyah (1263–1328) sought to stem the decline of Islam by urging that despotic rulers must give way to a politicized *sharīʿah* (the divine law) in which, for example, precedence would be given to family unity over emotion-laden repudiation, and just wars would be limited to defensive actions. From his initial emphasis on society as a fluctuating balance of religion and *ʿaṣabīyah* (social solidarity), Ibn Khaldūn (1332–1406), observing the decadence of fourteenth-century Egypt, increasingly stressed procedural regularities and *taʿzīr* (discretionary penalties) as a check on political injustice. Although he and others believed men were inherently unjust, their more secular political approach to issues of justice had to wait until later ages to achieve a more activist orientation.

The intrusion of Western colonialists, particularly in the nineteenth century, prompted two major strands of thought on the question of justice. Modernists sought to include institutions modeled after those of the West into their political systems, although traditionalists found Western approaches inconsistent with Islam. Jamāl al-Dīn al-Afghānī (1838–1897) believed that the injustices of Muslim despots could be rectified by renewing the principle of consultation in the form of elective assemblies and by the political unity of all Muslims against Western powers. Like his predecessors he combined moral renewal through revitalized virtues with a political program that would insure fuller community participation. But when al-Afghānī's proposals failed to move Muslim tyrants or the populace at large, some, like his student Muḥammad ʿAbduh (1849–1905), looked to Western procedural standards, which they did not regard as incompatible with Islam, for guidance. As a judge and grand *muftī*, ʿAbduh issued *fatwā*s allowing, for example, the use of interest through postal bank accounts. He often spoke in terms of revelation and natural law as well as in terms of the compatibility of revelation with evolution and social reformation, but his equivocation and his deep concern with the moral transformation of society signaled precisely the dilemma faced by many of his era who were drawn to both Western and indigenous forms of injustice.

Many of the conflicts between modernists and traditionalists centered on the adoption of new legal codes. The very idea of a code was largely a Western one, but the process of codification forced many Muslims to consider which propositions they regarded as essential to Islam and which as dispensable accretions. Moreover, the process of adopting codes offered the opportunity for establishing a system for legal changes. Of central importance was the formulation of the Mecelle (Ar., Majallah; Civil Code), which was applied throughout Ottoman territories in the 1870s. Together with the short-lived Ottoman constitution of 1876, it marked the trend that culminated in Turkey's unilateral disestablishment of Islam and its wholesale adoption of European codes. By contrast French colonial territories adopted French commercial and criminal law, but these countries retained relatively intact their Islamic family law practices until they achieved national independence. [*See* Mecelle.]

Owing largely to the efforts in the late 1940s of the Egyptian jurist ʿAbd al-Razzāq al-Sanhūrī (1895–1971), civil codes were drawn up for Egypt, Iraq, and Kuwait, with other countries drawing on elements of his work. In each instance the codes left it to *sharīʿah* principles to fill in where the code was silent. In fact, more often than not Western substantive law filled in the whole of the civil law, and the sense of distinctive Islamic principles—of fault and liability, of intentionality in contracts or unconscionable agreements—was largely replaced by non-Muslim concepts.

By contrast, the strain between Western Islamic standards of justice has been most significantly tested in family law. Following independence in 1956, Tunisia took the more extreme position, formally abolishing polygamy and requiring all divorces to be pronounced by the judge. At the other extreme, Pakistan and the Gulf States continued highly traditional forms of Muslim family law, largely unaffected by outside forces. In between lay a vast array of compromises: from Morocco, where the code remains very close to Mālikī principles but places increased discretion in the hands of the *qāḍī* (judge), to Malaysia, where *ʿādāt* (local custom) grants wives a share of all marital assets at the time of divorce. [*See* Family Law.]

The struggles over appropriate laws of personal status have profoundly affected views of the nature of Islamic justice: as women became more educated and occupied a greater role in the economy, justice was conceived by many as requiring greater equalization, though not full equality, of men and women. At the same time the very forces that led to such liberalization contributed to the backlash against it: fundamentalists, from Ayatollah Ruhollah Khomeini in Iran to the Muslim Brothers in Egypt, find the relations of men and women one of the domains where Western influence has distorted justice by rendering an imbalance among what they see as natural differences.

Similarly, in the criminal law the precepts of divine revelation have been read to imply *ḥudūd* (invariant punishments) for listed offenses and *taʿzīr* (discretionary punishments) for a broader range of infractions. Some of these penalties, though rarely applied, conflict with international human rights conventions, while others bespeak localized standards of justice—as when, for example, a learned man may be held to a higher standard of behavior than an unlettered one, because his acts are thought to have greater consequences for society. Recent attempts by the ministers of justice of Islamic nations to compose a uniform penal law has yielded a document none is likely to adopt, because each nation adheres to quite different standards of punishment. The very process of drawing up such a document reveals both the commonalities and the discrepancies wrought by different histories and attitudes. [*See* Criminal Law; Ḥudūd.]

Issues of social justice have also taken very different paths. Although the language of distributive justice is broadly shared, neither modernists nor traditionalists have succeeded in capturing its terms for any universally accepted program. The combination of Islam and socialism in Algeria and Libya, for example, has resulted in the greater use of the central government for the redistribution of resources; moderate states, such as Indonesia and Jordan, have used public funds to reconstruct the educational system and provide greater security against disaster. But again, what is seen to be just depends far more on the political and economic circumstances of each country than uniformly adopted beliefs about Islamic justice. In this respect the intellectual history of the concept of justice replicates much of earlier history, for it is the local amalgam, proffered as distinctly Islamic, that both unites and separates Muslim nations.

One common concern is the nature of economic justice, exemplified by the permissibility of charging interest. *Ribā*, which is usually translated as "usury" but more accurately refers to any form of unjust enrichment, was historically avoided by various legal fictions. The rise of Islamic banking, however, has resulted in practices that are commensurate with modern economic institutions but are felt to conform to the prohibition on interest. This development is particularly important, because it is rare for Islamic conceptions of justice to be embraced in specific institutional enactments. [*See* Banks and Banking; Interest.]

As fundamentalist regimes have taken power in Iran,

Sudan, and several Malaysian states—and as their influence expands in Pakistan, Algeria, and Jordan—the equation of *sharīʿah* with justice has been no more fully consummated than at other times in Muslim history. Although formally preeminent, Islamic law is not, in fact, given unalloyed application in any of the Islamic republics. Moreover, justice—in the sense of receiving a fair share of the wealth of the state—has led to an emphasis on delivery of actual services rather than the imposition of formal law alone. Thus the terms of justice have been put into play once again, and the quest for new equivalences, contexts, and forms of reciprocal obligation have become embroiled in bureaucratic and party structures.

If justice is central to the way that Muslims think of themselves, it must also be noted that *jawr* (injustice) plays no less a role. Injustice is often felt rather than articulated, and Muslims tend to believe, like Montaigne, that institutions, far from eradicating injustice, often provide a forum for its elaboration. Justice, for most Muslims, can only be expected where face-to-face constraints allow reciprocity to work, whereas the state is seen as unreciprocity incarnate. Where international actions or local corruption lead to a felt sense of imbalance, the personal offense that is taken is profound. Justice, to Muslims, is not, as Adam Smith had it for the West, the least of the virtues, because it is one that merely entails the avoidance of harm. Rather, justice is the most essential, if indeterminate, of virtues for Muslims, because it keeps open the quest for equivalence, a quest seen as central to both human nature and revealed orderliness in the world of reason and passion.

[*See also* Law, *article on* Legal Thought and Jurisprudence.]

BIBLIOGRAPHY

Abdul Mannan, Muḥammad. *Islamic Economics: Theory and Practice*. London, 1986. Thorough analysis of the implementation of banking, trade, planning, and labor relations in accordance with revitalized Islamic concepts.

Antoun, Richard. *Muslim Preacher in the Modern World*. Princeton, 1989. Case study of a Jordanian preacher whose sermons exemplify popular justice.

Ewing, Katherine, ed. *Sharīʿat and Ambiguity in South Asian Islam*. Berkeley, 1988. Collection of essays showing the relation of various Muslim law codes to local customs and historical situations.

Iqbal, Munawar, ed. *Distributive Justice and Need Fulfillment in an Islamic Economy*. Islamabad, 1986. Essays by Muslim scholars on landownership and poverty law that could be practiced in accordance with Islamic precepts.

Kassem, Hammond. "The Idea of Justice in Islamic Philosophy." *Diogenes* 79 (1972): 81–108.

Kerr, Malcolm H. *Islamic Reform: The Political and Legal Theories of Muḥammad ʿAbduh and Rashīd Riḍā*. Berkeley, 1966. Excellent analysis of the idealist tradition in Islamic jurisprudence as represented by two leading thinkers of the late nineteenth and early twentieth centuries.

Khadduri, Majid. *The Islamic Conception of Justice*. Baltimore, 1984. The most comprehensive study of texts on Islamic justice, covering classical as well as modern writers.

Mahmood, Tahir. *Family Law Reform in the Muslim World*. Bombay, 1972. Carefully selected and translated excerpts from codes promulgated in almost every modern Muslim nation.

Mammeri, Mouloud. *The Sleep of the Just*. Translated by Len Ortzen. Boston, 1956. Algerian novel demonstrating the conflicted sense of identity and justice surrounding the life of an Arab living under colonialism.

Rosen, Lawrence. *The Anthropology of Justice: Law as Culture in Islamic Society*. Cambridge, 1989. Study of a modern Islamic court in Morocco and its implementation of justice in the light of current social and cultural norms.

Yamānī, Aḥmad Zakī. *Islamic Law and Islamic Issues*. Jeddah, 1968. Insightful study of Islamic law as practiced in a traditional Islamic context by a scholar best known as Saudi Arabia's former oil minister.

LAWRENCE ROSEN

Social Justice

The Nahḍah (renaissance; rebirth), which began in the latter part of the nineteenth century; is a vast intellectual, cultural, religious, and political movement that sought to translate the main principles of Western progress into an Arab and Muslim environment, and as a result, it stood against the degeneration of Islam while attempting to rescue the achievements of classical Islamic civilization from centuries of decline and oblivion.

The main representatives of the Nahḍah movement in the Arab world, such as Jamāl al-Dīn al-Afghānī, Rifāʿah Rāfiʿ al-Ṭahṭāwī, Muḥammad Al-Ṣaffār, Muḥammad ʿAbduh, Qāsim Amīn, and others, discussed the need of their societies to overcome decadence and stagnation and find answers to the increasing Western challenge, in both its technical and intellectual aspects. One such challenge was the necessity of attaining a new Muslim social and political order that would put an end to poverty and helplessness in Muslim societies. In many ways, one must see the issue of social justice in nineteenth century Muslim thought as a product of two interchangeable factors: prevailing backward social and economic conditions that did not attract the serious attention of the traditional *ʿulamāʾ* class, and Western domination that neglected to ameliorate the social conditions of the dominated people as a whole. Nahḍah thinkers criticized these two factors. For instance, al-Afghānī's critique of the Indian (Muslim) *ʿulamā'* summarizes the position of the Nahḍah thinkers on the social question in the Muslim world at the time:

> Why do you not raise your eyes from those defective books and why do you not cast your glance on this wide world? . . . Yet you spend no thought on this question of great importance, incumbent on every intelligent man, which is: What is the cause of poverty, indigence, helplessness, and distress of the Muslims, and is there a cure for this important phenomenon and great misfortune or not? (Nikki R. Keddie, *An Islamic Response to Imperialism: Political and Religious Writings of Sayyid Jamal ad-Din al-Afghani*, Berkeley, 1983, p. 64.)

Social justice was closely bound with a host of religious, political, and educational issues and questions facing the Arab and Muslim world of the nineteenth century. Nevertheless, because of the existing political conditions, that is, the hegemony of colonialism, the Nahḍah movement "did not manage to formulate a coherent and efficacious program of social transformations, as would have been necessary to resist the imperialist aggression" (Samir Amin, *The Arab World: Nationalism and Class Struggle*, London, 1983, p. 33). The failure of the Nahḍah movement in attaining its immediate social and political goals, as a result of the formidable challenge of colonialism, placed the issue of social justice at the forefront of Muslim debate in the twentieth century.

In twentieth-century Islamic thought, the issue of social justice became more sharply defined, especially with the influx of a large number of peasants from the countryside to the urban areas of the Muslim world. This migration created social and demographic tensions that, to a large extent, gave religion, that is, Islam, a definite ideological and political role in society (see Joel Beinin, "Islamic Response to the Capitalist Penetration of the Middle East," in *The Islamic Impulse*, edited by Barbara F. Stowasser, Washington, D.C., 1987, pp. 87–105). The foundation by Ḥasan al-Bannā' of the Muslim Brotherhood in Egypt in 1928, and its spread to the rest of the Arab world soon after, was a reflection of an endemic social crisis in Egyptian and Arab societies. The Muslim Brotherhood has always thought of itself as an organizational and religious response to the plight of the poor and downtrodden in society.

In order to analyze the position of Islamic resurgence on the issue of social justice, one must distinguish between three broad phases of resurgence: resurgence as a reaction to imperialism and colonialism; resurgence as a reaction to the emerging nation-state, especially in the 1950s and 1960s; and resurgence as a reaction to the contemporary situation. This last phase is exemplified by the lack of political unity in the Arab world; the rise of the Persian Gulf states and petrodollar diplomacy as two major political and economic factors in the area; and increasing social gaps in a number of Arab countries, mainly in Egypt, Sudan, Lebanon, and Algeria (see John L. Esposito, *The Islamic Threat: Myth or Reality*, New York, 1992, especially chaps. 3, 4, and 5).

In the first stage, Islamic resurgence reacted to issues of social justice in the context of imperialism. This warrants us to consider resurgence as a modern phenomenon that uses Islamic concepts and motifs in order to respond to a formidable modern situation. As "a psychosocial phenomenon taking form under European domination and in direct reaction to it" (Hisham Sharabi, *Neopatriarchy: A Theory of Distorted Change in Arab Society*, New York, 1988, p. 64), the Islamic resurgence produced a number of outstanding thinkers, such as Ḥasan al-Bannā', Muḥammad al-Ghazālī, ʿAbd al-Qādir ʿAwdah, and Sayyid Quṭb, who carried the banner of social justice both in writings and through activism.

Ḥasan al-Bannā' used the mosque as a medium to spread his social and economic message. His perception of the mosque as a dynamic domain for the propagation of Islam and the preparation of an active Muslim group developed in the social context of the early days of the Muslim Brotherhood. At the time, the Muslim Brotherhood attracted the poor and the uneducated, "The first Muslim Brethren were humble Egyptians: the lowliest workers, the poor peasants, impoverished students—the undernourished and the underprivileged of all classes" (Christina Harris, *Nationalism and Revolution in Egypt: The Role of the Muslim Brotherhood*, The Hague, 1964, p. 157). Therefore, the mosque, as a sacred place, and as a place that gives emotional comfort and security to the poor, was the ideal medium for the preaching and transmission of the Muslim Brotherhood's ideas. Al-Bannā', according to a contemporary theorist, was aware of the total dependency of the Third World in general, and the Muslim world in particular, on the West. He understood that "Islam, far from being a philosophical doctrine or cultural trend, was a social movement aiming at social improvement in all aspects of life. In other words, it was necessary [in al-Bannā's view] to formulate an Islamic ideology, i.e., a holistic Islamic theory capable of putting forth a cure for prevailing social conditions" (ʿAbd Allāh al-Nafīsī, *Al-Ikhwān al-Muslimūn, al-tajribah wa-al-khaṭa': Awrāq fī al-naqd al-dhātī* [The Muslim Brothers, Trial and Error: Readings in Self-Criticism], Cairo, 1989, p. 12).

This phase of Muslim reaction also witnessed a major controversy around issues of religion and social justice between the Islamist camp, represented by Muḥammad al-Ghazālī, and the liberal camp, represented by Khālid Muḥammad Khālid. This controversy, to be sure, was reminiscent of two previous cases in Egyptian intellectual life represented by two liberal thinkers, Ṭāhā Ḥusayn and ʿAlī ʿAbd al-Rāziq (see Leonard Binder, *Islamic Liberalism: A Critique of Development Ideologies*, Chicago, 1988). In *From Here We Start*, Khālid maintains that one major reason behind the deteriorating social and economic conditions in Egypt at the time (late 1940s), besides Western hegemony, was the existence of a Muslim priesthood "pregnant with pernicious doctrines and deadly principles" (translated by Ismāʿīl R. al-Fārūqī, Washington, D.C., 1953, p. 32). According to Khālid, the sole aim of this class has been to exploit people's spirituality and devotion to religion, while maintaining its social prestige. It also:

> commingled its interests with religious doctrine itself, thereby completing the desecration of religion. . . . Later on, the priesthood, with consistency and with perseverance, went about envenoming everything with its deadly poison, consecrating economic and social reactionism and preaching eloquently the virtues and excellence of poverty, ignorance and disease (*Ibid.*, p. 32).

In Khālid's view, then, the type of truth represented by the priestly class is "a form of mental and religious terrorism" (I borrow this statement from Pauline M. Rosenau, *Post-Modernism and the Social Sciences: Insights, Inroads, and Intrusions*, Princeton, 1992, p. 78).

As a liberal thinker who believes that social justice can be only achieved in the context of state-religion separation, Khālid also criticizes the Muslim Brotherhood's doctrine of religion-society and religion-state compatibility. He notes that any "priestly class," ancient or modern, *ʿulamā'*-oriented or Muslim Brotherhood-oriented, is the embodiment of social injustice and exploitation of the poor. This class, "the fastest runner after booty, wealth, and pride," (Khālid, *op. cit.*, p. 33) promotes superstitions instead of rationalism and poverty instead of wealth. Khālid draws the conclusion that any meddling of religion in the affairs of society is apt to "annihilate the personality of the nation, to drag the whole people down into an abyss of servility and subjection, and to breed an instinct of following" (*Ibid.*, p. 36). [*See the biography of Khālid.*]

Muḥammad al-Ghazālī, a leading Muslim Brotherhood thinker, also held the view that some of the *ʿulamā'* he knew acted just like parasites sucking the blood of the poor (Muḥammad al-Ghazālī, *Al-Islām al-muftarā ʿalayhi bayna al-Shuyūʿīyīn wa-al-ra'smālīyīn*, Cairo, 1952, p. 27). However, he bases his critique of these *ʿulamā'* on different conceptual principles than does Khālid. He argues that a new generation of Muslims must come into being, mainly because:

> The men who now lead the defense of Islam are, without exception, bringing shame to themselves and their cause. . . . The service of God and Mammon cannot be combined; nor can the duty of *jihad* be compatible with the pursuit of pleasure and comfort. It requires a really deranged mind to bring these opposites together in any system of human life. Such must be the minds of those Azharites who grow fat while Islam grows thin, and repose in comfort while [Muslims] suffer in anguish. These deceivers have devised devilish means for escaping the genuine duties of Islam. They are more crafty and sly than those *hashish* smugglers who escape justice and the police. On one hand, we have a group of men satisfied merely with the performance of personal worship. When they are asked to take care of the public, or observe the social duties of Islam, they answer despondently, 'politics is not our business.' . . . On the other hand, we have a group that fights sectarianism and worship of the dead, yet its members profess to belong to Muhammad bin Abd al-Wahab. They silently worship the living and sheepishly submit to the tyrants and despots of their "Wahabi" [Saudia Arabia] land. . . . We have seen many leaders of al-Azhar who did not leave their office chairs until their pockets bulged with riches, though they claimed to be the "spiritual continuation" of the legacy of Muhammad ʿAbduh and Jamal al-Din. (*Our Beginning in Wisdom*, translated by Ismāʿīl R. al-Fārūqī, Washington, D.C., 1953, pp. 69–70.)

Muḥammad al-Ghazālī paved the way in his 1940s writings, especially in *Al-Islām wa-al-awḍā' al-iqtiṣādīyah* (Islam and Our Economic Conditions, Cairo, 1942), *Al-Islām wa-al-istibdād al-siyāsī* (Islam and Political Dictatorship, Cairo, n.d.), and *Al-istiʿmār: Aḥqād wa-atmā'* (Imperialism: Hatred and Greed, Cairo, n.d.), to the emergence of Sayyid Quṭb (1906–1966), whose thought on social justice reflects the transitional phase in Egypt's life from colonialism to national independence in the 1950s. [*See the biography of Ghazālī.*]

In 1948, Sayyid Quṭb wrote a major work that has shaped the thought of many Islamists on social and economic issues (see Sayyid Quṭb, *Social Justice in Islam*, translated by John Hardie, Washington, D.C., 1953). One must view Quṭb's *Social Justice in Islam* as a critical comment on the social, economic, cultural, and educational conditions and policies of the Egpytian state in the interwar period. In this book, Quṭb lays down the theoretical framework of proper conduct in social, legal, and political affairs. Nothwitstanding his normative analysis and his idealistic solutions, Quṭb's main goal is to dissect the socioeconomic and political problems in the light of what he perceives as "genuine Islam." In a sense, he takes it for granted that there is a widespread malaise in Egyptian society, and he offers the "true" Islamic solution to remedy this situation. Quṭb's arguments reflect the thoughts of a complex man in transition, as well as a complex situation in flux. Furthermore, Quṭb's arguments underlie the foundations of many theoretical arguments in the Muslim Brotherhood movement and its different offshoots in the 1960s and 1970s. No doubt it is a major work with a significant influence on a generation of Arab and Muslim intelligentsia in the post–World War II period.

Quṭb points out that the past independence of Islam as a socioreligious and political system stands in sharp contrast to its present manifestations. In other words, he argues that the current secular state's monopoly over religion must be dismantled. One way of doing that is to attack the privileges of the religious hierarchy that, to his mind, was always linked with the state. Quṭb contends that the *ʿulamāʾ*, as the established Muslim clergy, have robbed the poor of their social prestige and economic growth. Islamic history has known *ʿulamāʾ* who have exploited religion for their worldly benefits and have kept the workers and lower classes drugged by means of religion (*Ibid.*, p. 16).

Quṭb's argument is that the Islamic notion of social justice is all embracing; it takes account of the material as well as the spiritual dimensions of man's well-being. Quṭb enumerates the following principles as the foundations of the Islamic theory of social justice: absolute freedom of conscience; complete equality of all men; and the permanent mutual responsibility of society. The individual is the supreme example of social justice. The individual, according to Quṭb, has to place his trust in Divine and not human authority. To him, divine authority in indivisible. Therefore, man has nothing to fear is this life; he should not allow anxiety to run his life; neither should he be sacred of transient matters in life. Yet, in spite of all this encouragement, Quṭb draws our attention to an important aspect in man's life: the material need for food and shelter. He says that "the empty belly cannot appreciate high-sounding phrases. Or else he is compelled to ask for charity, and all his self-esteem leaves him lost, forever" (*Ibid.*, p. 19). Therefore, the main conclusion Quṭb reaches is that social justice cannot prevail in a society if the material foundations of society are not sound and if the minority exploits the majority. One way then of insuring the material well-being of the members of society is through mutual responsibility. The individual must care about the community, which should, in turn, be responsible for feeding the poor and destitute members. That is why, maintains Quṭb, Islam has instituted the *zakāt* as an individual as well as a social responsibility in order to combat poverty.

Although Islam, according to Quṭb, respects the individual's property, justice is not always concerned to serve the interests of the individual. The individual is in a way a steward of property on behalf of society. And therefore, property in the widest sense is a right which can belong only to society, which in turn receives it as a trust from God who is the only true owner of anything. Thus, although the individual has the right to possess property, the community's interest is supreme. Communal property is a distinguishing mark of Islam, and therefore communal wealth "cannot be restricted to individuals, a wealth of which the Messenger enumerated three aspects, water, herbage, and fire" (*Ibid.*, p. 109). One honest way of gaining money is through work. Therefore, Islam, according to Quṭb, is against monopoly, usury, corruption, wastefulness, and dishonest commercial practices. Above all Islam stands against luxury-loving people. Luxury is both an individual as well as a social disease.

In his search for a historical foundation of what he calls "the true spirit of Islam," Quṭb finds that Abū Dharr, a companion of the Prophet, was the true embodiment of this spirit. Abū Dharr was unpopular with the corrupt rulers, and any person emulating his example at present will find the same treatment from "the present-day exponents of exploitation." According to Quṭb, Abū Dharr stood against the system of preferential treatment instituted by the third caliph, Uthmān, and he was for a complete system of justice like the one instituted by ʿAlī. When Muʿāwiyah came to power, he used public money for bribes and gifts, buying the allegiance of others. Also the Umayyad rulers, in his view, did not distinguish between their private funds and public money.

In short, social and political corruption is an old story. Quṭb traces it all the way down to the early Islamic state. The deviation from the Islamic ideal begins early on. Quṭb, in a sense, considers present history to be the culmination of all that complexity beginning with early Islam. Present Muslim history is unfaithful to its origins. The pious have always been the steadfast few, from Abū Dharr in the first century of Islam to Quṭb in the present century. Is most Muslim history, then, just a story of deviation from and betrayal of the ideal? What about the creative tension throughout Islamic history?

Social Justice in Islam by Sayyid Quṭb contains the theoretical principles and foundations of the Muslim Brotherhood's social thought. Quṭb's line of analysis, although grounded in idealistic solutions, dispels the notion of social and human harmony in Egyptian society. It is a society torn apart between feudalists and exploiters, including the professional men of religion, on the one hand, and foreign imperialists, on the other. A radical criticism of this state of affairs, therefore, necessitates the criticism of two parallel, but equally hegemonic mentalities and forces, one indigenous and the other foreign.

In the postindependence phase of the history of the Arab world, social justice was expressed in a variety of ways: Islam and socialism; Islam and nationalism; Islam and the emergence of the Persian Gulf states, and Islam and *al-takāful al-ijtimāʿī* (social solidarity) (see Sami A. Hanna, "*Al-takaful al-Ijtimaʿi* and Islamic Socialism," *The Muslim World* 59.3–4. [July–October 1969]: 275–286). For example, according to the Syrian Muṣṭafā al-Sibāʿī, writing in the late 1950s, Islam and socialism are compatible, and Islamic socialism as an actual movement after independence rests on five main principles: the right to live; the right to liberty; the right to knowledge; the right to dignity, and the right to property (al-Sibāʿī, "Islamic Socialism," in *Political and Social Thought in the Contemporary Middle East*, edited by Kemal Karpat, New York, 1968, pp. 123–24). On the other hand, Maḥmūd Shaltūt, a former rector of al-Azhar University under the rule of Nasser, believes social justice could be achieved in the context of the secular nation-state: "Whoever holds authority in the Muslim community and influences its interests must therefore take steps to see to it that the nation draws the greatest profit possible from agriculture, commerce, and industry by coordinating the three sectors of activity" (Shaltūt, "Socialism and Islam," in *Ibid.*, p. 131). [*See the biographies of Sibāʿī and Shaltūt.*]

Also, this phase witnessed the active participation of a number of Arab Shīʿī thinkers in formulating social issues based on their vision of social justice. One must mention two important thinkers in this regard: Muḥammad Bāqir al-Ṣadr of Iraq and Muḥammad Ḥusayn Faḍlallāh of Lebanon. Al-Ṣadr wrote a major work entitled *Iqtiṣādunā* (Our Economics) in which he proposes that the conceptual roots of both capitalism and socialism are incompatible with Islam and that Islam provides a unique economic system that, if applied correctly, could meet the demands of the modern age. Likewise, Faḍlallāh identifies with the downtrodden, especially in Lebanese society, and he, following in the footsteps of liberation theology, links the issue of social justice with the empowerment of the poor and the weak. In his *Al-Islām wa-manṭiq al-qūwah,* Faḍlallāh argues that in order to achieve social justice in society, the poor must rise against their oppressive conditions. [*See the biographies of Ṣadr and Faḍlāllah.*]

Social justice has proven to be a pivotal issue in modern Islamic thought, at least in the Arab world. Any increase in social and economic gaps in Arab society is not likely to push the issue to the side.

[*See also* Modernism.]

BIBLIOGRAPHY

Abu-Rabiʿ, Ibrahim, ed. *Islamic Resurgence: Challenges, Directions and Future Perspectives.* Tampa, 1994.

ʿAwdah, ʿAbd al-Qādir. *Islam Between Ignorant Followers and Incapable Scholars.* Riyadh, 1991.

Aziz, T. M., "The Role of Muhammad Baqir al-Sadr in Shi'i Political Activism in Iraq from 1958 to 1980." *International Journal of Middle East Studies* 25.2 (May 1993): 207–222.

ʿAẓm, Ṣādiq Jalāl al-. *Naqd al-fikr al-dīnī* (Criticism of Religious Thinking). Beirut, 1969.

Bennabi, Malek. *Islam in History and Society.* Islamabad, 1988.

Carré, Olivier. *Mystique et politique: lectur revolutionnaire du Coran par Sayyid Qutb, frère musulman radical.* Paris, 1984.

Donohue, John J., and John L. Esposito, eds., *Islam in Transition: Muslim Perspectives.* New York, 1982.

Ennaifer, Hamida. "La pensée sociale dans les écrits musulmans modernes" *IBLA: Revue de L'Institut des Belles Lettres Arabes* 50.2 (1987): 223–253.

Faḍlallāh, Muḥammad Ḥusayn. *Al-Islām wa manṭiq al-qūwah* (Islam and the Logic of Power). Beirut, 1987.

Freire, Paul. *Pedagogy of the Oppressed.* New York, 1988.

Hanna, Sami A. "Islam, Socialism, and National Trials." *The Muslim World,* 58.4 (October 1968): 284–294.

Hanna, Sami A., and George M. Gardner, *Arab Socialism: A Documentary Survey*. Leiden, 1969.

Hourani, Albert. *Arabic Thought in the Liberal Age, 1798–1939*. Cambridge, 1983.

Karpat, Kemal H. *Political and Social Thought in the Contemporary Middle East*. New York, 1968.

Mallat, Chibli. *The Renewal of Islamic Law: Muhammad Baqer As-Sadr, Najaf and the Shi'i International*. Cambridge, 1993.

Ṣaffār, Muḥammad al-. *Disorienting Encounters, Travels of a Moroccan Scholar in France in 1845–1846: The Voyage of Muhammad As-Saffar*. Translated and edited by Susan Gilson Miller. Berkeley, 1992.

Sharīʿatī, ʿAlī. *On the Sociology of Islam*. Berkeley, 1979.

Zebiri, Kate. *Mahmud Shaltut and Islamic Modernism*. Oxford, 1994.

Ibrahim M. Abu-Rabiʿ

K

KABYLIA. The rugged mountainous area known as the Kabylia lies to the east of Algiers, adjacent to the Mediterranean littoral. Endowed with meager resources, it is one of North Africa's most densely populated regions; densities range from 70 to more than 250 inhabitants per square kilometer. Its traditional economy depended upon arboriculture, supplemented by grain production and small-scale livestock breeding; vast forests of oak and cork provided additional sustenance. These resources would hardly have sufficed had not the Kabyles historically migrated as laborers to Algeria's cities and, in this century, increasingly to France.

A unique geographic and ecological zone, the Kabylia has long constituted a cultural unit apart from the rest of Algeria. Here ancient Berber culture, with its own language, customary laws, social organization, and traditions, has been preserved. While the Kabyles are all Sunnī Muslims, Arabic has only imperfectly penetrated their mountain strongholds; Berber languages are still spoken in some places. Under the Ottoman Turks (c. 1525–1830), the Kabyles maintained their own political, religious, and administrative institutions. The village constituted a sort of municipal republic under a quasidemocratic council of notables (the *jamāʿah*). Intrepid warriors and fiercely independent, the Kabyles were among the last conquered by France in bitter campaigns waged between 1847 and 1857. During Amīr ʿAbd al-Qādir's *jihād* (1832–1847), he appointed a caliph to the Kabylia; yet its inhabitants characteristically declined to recognize the *amīr* as sultan. The Kabyles were the major participants in the great Muqranī insurrection of 1871, the last rebellion of this scale until the 1945 Sétif uprising, a prelude to the liberation movement.

Several sociopolitical developments under the colonial regime placed the Kabyles in the vanguard of the national liberation struggle. Through a deliberate policy of divide and rule, the French provided modern secular education to the region, which claimed more gallicized schools than elsewhere. Concurrently, Kabyle emigration to the cities commenced just before World War I. In Paris the Kabyles played a predominant role in the Étoile Nord-Africaine (North African Star), a militant nationalist party established in 1926 under Messali Hadj (Messali al-Ḥajj). [*See the biography of Messali al-Ḥajj.*] After the brutal suppression of the Sétif uprising, a small group of largely Kabyle activists under Belkasem Krim took to the *maquis* to oppose colonial rule. When the nationalist insurrection erupted on 1 November 1954, this group formed the nucleus for the FLN (National Liberation Front).

Recently the region has evinced a movement of Berber (Kabyle) cultural irredentism, a reaction to the program of arabization and centralization launched in the late 1960s under President Houari Boumédienne. Resistance coalesced in the early 1980s into the Kabyle Cultural Movement, culminating in student strikes and demonstrations at the university in Tizi Ouzou, Kabylia's provincial capital. The short-lived experiment in democratization beginning in 1989 spawned several Berber parties. The Rally for Culture and Democracy, under Saʿid Saadi, is the successor to the semiclandestine Cultural Movement party, created during the so-called Berber Spring of 1980. In addition, the Kabylia produced a latter-day version of the Socialist Forces Front (FFS), whose current leader, Hocine Aït Ahmad, was among the FLN's founders. Both parties' platforms advocate minority rights, a secular state, and a pluralistic society. In the December 1991 elections the FFS placed second after the FIS (Islamic Salvation Front; Jabhat al-Inqādh al-Islāmī) and ahead of the FLN, Algeria's single dominant party since 1962. While some votes cast for the Kabyle parties may have represented votes against both the discredited FLN and the Islamic party, the FFS's success may indicate that the Kabyles will again play a leading role in Algerian political life.

[*See also* Algeria; Islamic Salvation Front.]

BIBLIOGRAPHY

Ageron, Charles-Robert. *Modern Algeria: A History from 1830 to the Present*. Translated from the French and edited by Michael Brett. London, 1991. The most succinct statement of modern Algerian history available, by the premier French historian of colonial Algeria.

Bourdieu, Pierre. *The Algerians*. Translated from the French by Alan C. M. Ross. Boston, 1962. This work by France's leading sociologist and expert on the Kabylia contains a chapter devoted to Kabyle society.

Quandt, William. "The Berbers in the Algerian Political Elite." In *Arabs and Berbers: From Tribe to Nation in North Africa*, edited by Ernest Gellner and Charles Micaud, pp. 285–303. Lexington, Mass., 1972.

Roberts, Hugh. *Algerian Socialism and the Kabyle Question*. Norwich, 1981. Concentrating mainly on the postcolonial period, this study contains valuable background information on the Kabyles and the Kabylia in terms of economy, society, and politics.

JULIA CLANCY-SMITH

KALĀM. *See* Theology.

KĀMIL, MUṢṬAFĀ (1874–1908), Egyptian nationalist. The name of the *zaʿīm* Muṣṭafā Kāmil is borne by several major city streets and squares in Egypt. A lawyer by education, he was a passionate orator who fought unrelentingly for Egyptian independence from the British rule that lasted from 1882 to 1952. Kāmil and other nationalists were radicalized by the autocracy of British rule under Lord Cromer, and by events at Dinishwai village in 1906 where a military tribunal passed death, prison, and flogging sentences on peasants who attacked British officers hunting pigeons in their village. In the process a village woman was shot dead, and a British officer who went for help on foot suffered a sunstroke from which he later died.

Kāmil's obsession with independence was equaled by his dismay by his countrymen's weakness and acquiescence to British rule. Therefore his actions took two directions—calling for social and educational reforms and working for the creation of a national university, while at the same time undertaking political agitation within and outside Egypt. He was the first to organize massive demonstrations mobilizing students. He founded the National Party and its newspaper *Al-liwā'*, which presented a radical nationalist and Islamic voice in opposition both to Aḥmad Luṭfī al-Sayyid's *Al-jarīdah* and its liberal constitutional ideas and to Shaykh ʿAlī Yūsuf's *Al-mu'ayyad* and conservative Islamism. His publication of the English *Standard* and the French *L'étendard* to deliver the *Liwā*'s message to Egypt's foreign community indicated the importance he attributed to foreigners in deciding Egypt's destiny.

On the international stage, together with Khedive ʿAbbās II, Kāmil formed a secret society whose purpose was to intrigue against the British. Financed by the society, he traveled to Paris in 1895 to present Egypt's case to the European public, particularly in France, where he drew attention to French interests in supporting Egypt's cause. There he introduced himself to Juliet Adam, editor of *La nouvelle revue*, who was to have great influence on him and his career. Through her Kāmil met important public personalities, political figures, and members of the press. She arranged for him to give public lectures and helped him publish his ideas in French journals. His success in propagandizing Egypt's cause did not bring about the hoped for results, and Kāmil realized the naïveté of his idealism when he saw Britain and France agree after Fashoda and sign the Entente Cordiale in 1904. Breaking off with ʿAbbās II, Kāmil allied himself with Ottoman Sultan Abdülhamid and began to work toward a closer relationship with Germany. This was the context of his turn toward Pan-Islamist principles, his support of an Islamic caliphate, and ultimately his support of the Sultan's right to Taba against the British who were defending Egypt's rights to it. There was much conjecture regarding Kāmil's stand on the Taba issue, but Kāmil's words "if I were not an Egyptian I would have wished to be an Egyptian" continue to symbolize Egyptian patriotism. His funeral, following a sudden unexplained death, was the first of the demonstrations of mass public grief for which Egypt would later become famous.

[*See also* Egypt.]

BIBLIOGRAPHY

Kāmil, Muṣṭafā. *Lettres égyptiennes françaises addressées à Mme Juliette Adam, 1895–1908/Rasā'il Miṣrīyah Faransīyah*. Cairo, 1909.

Kāmil, Muṣṭafā. *Awrāq Muṣṭafā Kāmil: Al-Murāsalāt*. Cairo, 1982.

Rāfʿī, ʿAbd al-Raḥmān al-. *Muṣṭafā Kāmil*. Cairo, 1982.

AMIRA EL AZHARY SONBOL

KARBALA. One of the holiest places of Shīʿī pilgrimage in Iraq, some 60 miles (95 km) southwest of Baghdad, Karbala (Karbalā') derives its fame from the fact that Ḥusayn ibn ʿAlī, the grandson of the prophet Muḥammad and the third Shīʿī imam, was killed there, along with his supporters, in the district of Ninawah on ʿĀshūrāʾ, the tenth day of Muḥarram AH 61/680 CE. The name *Karbalāʾ* probably comes from the Aramaic name *Karbela*. However, Shīʿī pious literature suggests that the word is made up of two parts: *karb* (sorrow) and *balāʾ* (calamity), joined by a conjunction *wa* (and). Many famous dirges lamenting the martyrdom of Ḥusayn mention *karb wa balāʾ* as his *mashhad* (shrine). Karbala attained great importance in Shīʿī piety as early as 63/682, when Ḥusayn's family, having been released from an Umayyad prison in Damascus, decided to perform the *ziyārah* ("visitation" for pilgrimage) to the *mashhad* before returning to Medina. By 65/684–685, when Sulaymān ibn Ṣurad, the prominent Shīʿī leader from Kufa, and his followers visited the burial site as penitents (to purge themselves of the feeling of shame as a consequence of their failure to help Ḥusayn on ʿĀshūrāʾ), the practice of visitation had been religiously legitimized through several traditions related on the authority of the imams Muḥammad al-Bāqir and Jaʿfar al-Ṣādiq, encouraging Shīʿīs to undertake the hardship of the journey to Karbala. Some traditions went as far as to compare the virtue of visitation to Karbala with the performance of *ḥajj*.

By 236/850–851 the practice had become so widespread that al-Mutawakkil, the ʿAbbāsid caliph, destroyed the tomb and prohibited visits to Karbala under heavy penalties. Apparently, the Sunnī ʿAbbāsids were concerned about the growing sanctity and piety connected with the martyr's shrine, which generated radical activism among the downtrodden Shīʿīs. There were also messianic traditions about Karbala being the cornerstone of the Mahdi's eschatological revolution in the Final Days. Moreover, this revolution would, as predicted in these apocalyptic traditions, take place on the day of ʿĀshūrāʾ to redress the wrongs committed against the imams and their adherents. Consequently, both the visitation to Karbala and the annual mourning for Ḥusayn were treated by the Sunnī authorities with suspicion. This suspicion continues to dominate the Sunnī "puritanism" of the Wahhābīyah, who regard both these practices as Shīʿī *bidʿah* (innovation meaning "sinful deviation" from the *sunnah*) and who raided and destroyed the shrines at Karbala and Najaf in 1216/1801.

Besides Ḥusayn, Karbala also enshrines the tomb of al-ʿAbbās ibn ʿAlī, Ḥusayn's half brother, whose shrine is famous for the miraculous powers attributed to it in curing the sick. Both these shrines are richly endowed, and lavish gifts have been given by different Muslim rulers, especially the Shīʿī dynasties of Iran.

The shrines, greatly adorned with magnificent and costly ornamentation, have become the center of the spiritual and commercial lives of the inhabitants of Karbala, whose number has steadily grown to more than a hundred thousand. During ʿĀshūrāʾ celebrations the number swells to twice as many. Half of this population is Persian, and there is a large number of Indian and Pakistani Shīʿīs in residence. Many aged pilgrims have sojourned in Karbala, waiting to die there to secure entrance to Paradise, because Karbala is believed to be one of the gates of the Garden promised to the righteous in the Qurʾān.

Karbala is a particularly rich city, with religious endowments all over the Shīʿī world to support the shrines and the pilgrims visiting them. By virtue of their sanctity, until recently these shrines were a place of refuge for those who feared reprisal from the tyrannical rulers of Iran and Iraq.

Of all the holy sanctuaries in the Shīʿī world, Karbala has served a unique place in Shīʿī piety with its message of salvation and spiritual power through sacrifice. This essential religious truth has inspired thousands of Shīʿīs. Karbala has functioned as a paradigm expressed through diverse cultural forms mirrored in ritual and personal piety throughout the world. It shapes the trajectory of history and has a certain historical resiliency. Large collective remembrances, such as the ʿĀshūrāʾ commemoration every year, place the story of Karbala in the wider context of the human suffering and human emancipation from all kinds of exploitation in changing sociopolitical and religious circumstances. Shīʿī leaders have appropriated and codified the Karbala paradigm in ways that serve their own interests. They have given eloquent expression to Ḥusayn's confidence in the moral authority of his cause, while appealing to collective Shīʿī discontent, whether living under Sunnī or other, often tyrannical authority. The result is that the political dimension of the Karbala paradigm is well developed in the Shīʿī collective memory. In recent times, Karbala has served as a metaphor for the Iranian Revolution of 1979 under Ayatollah Ruhollah Khomeini (1902–1989).

[*See also* ʿĀshūrāʾ; Mashhad; Shrine; Ziyārah; *and the biography of Ḥusayn ibn ʿAlī*.]

BIBLIOGRAPHY

Algar, Hamid. *Religion and State in Iran, 1785–1906: The Role of the Ulama in the Qajar Period*. Berkeley, 1969. Discusses Karbala in the politics of Muslim powers.

Ayoub, Mahmoud M. *Redemptive Suffering in Islam: A Study of the Devotional Aspects of ʿĀshūrāʾ in Twelver Shīʿism*. The Hague, 1978. Covers Karbala in Shīʿī piety.

Honigmann, Ernest. "Karbalāʾ." In *Encyclopaedia of Islam*, new ed., vol. 4, pp. 637–639. Leiden, 1960–.

ABDULAZIZ SACHEDINA

KĀSHĀNI, ABOL-QĀSEM (1882–1962), more fully, Ayatollah Ḥājj Sayyid Abū al-Qāsim Kāshānī, Iranian religious and political leader during the national movement in the 1950s. Born in Tehran, Kāshāni made a pilgrimage to Mecca at the age of fifteen and settled in Najaf, Iraq, to pursue his education. He studied under Ayatollahs Khurāsānī, Khalīlī Tihrānī, and Kamarah'ī and became a *mujtahid* at twenty-five. His political activity began against British rule in Iraq when his father was killed in an uprising in April 1916. Sentenced to death in absentia, he escaped to Iran around February 1921.

Between 1921 and 1941, Kāshāni initially enjoyed Reza Shah Pahlavi's support and was elected to the Constituent Assembly, which approved the establishment of the Pahlavi dynasty in 1925. However, he soon lost the shah's friendship, abstained from politics, and confined himself to teaching.

Toward the end of Reza Shah's reign, Kāshāni became involved in pro-German activities. In January 1942, Kāshāni, General Fazlullah Zahedi (Faẕl Allāh Zāhidī), and several army officers and politicians founded the Nahẕat-i Millīyūn-i Īrān (Movement of Iranian Nationalists). The group was soon discovered, its members were arrested, and Kāshāni was sent into exile.

After World War II, Kāshāni, in cooperation with the grand *muftī* of Jerusalem, al-Ḥājj Amīn al-Ḥusaynī, and the Iraqi military officer, Rashīd ʿAlī al-Kīlānī, opposed the establishment of Israel, mobilized volunteers to aid Palestine, and collected funds for Palestinians. At home in Iran, Kāshāni opposed nearly all governments after 1945 either on policy or personal grounds. Prime Ministers ʿAbd al-Ḥusayn Hazhīr and Hossein ʿAli Razmara were both assassinated by the Fidā'īyān-i Islām—presumably with Kāshāni's blessing.

On 4 February 1949, after an attempt on the shah's life, Kāshāni was exiled to Lebanon. In June 1950, he returned from exile and was elected to the Majlis ("parliament") from Tehran.

Kāshāni's power and popularity increased enormously during the movement to nationalize the Iranian oil industry. In the Majlis and outside, his followers began to mobilize support for the National Front under Mohammad Mossadegh's leadership. On 30 April 1951 Mossadegh was appointed prime minister.

Kāshāni's relations with Mossadegh had three phases: April 1951–20 July 1952 marked the strengthening of their friendship and cooperation; the 20 July 1952 uprising saw Kāshāni working actively to remove Qavvām al-Salṭanah and bring Mossadegh back to the premiership; October 1952 until the coup d'état of 19 August 1953, when differences emerged between them, Kāshāni finally broke with Mossadegh and turned to General Zahedi and the Pahlavi court. The main reasons for the break were: Kāshāni's expectation of more power and control over the cabinet; Mossadegh's desire to keep the clergy out of the governmental process; Mossadegh's inability to settle the Anglo-Iranian oil dispute; and the clergy's fear of the growth of communism.

The coup d'état of 19 August 1953 that overthrew Mossadegh's government also ended Kāshāni's political career. General Zahedi, the new prime minister, offered Kāshāni a seat in the senate. Kāshāni rejected the offer and pressured Zahedi to implement the oil nationalization law. Zahedi ignored the ayatollah, who then declared Zahedi a dictator; Kāshāni's continued activities against Zahedi's government resulted in his arrest and imprisonment in July 1956 on charges of cooperation with the Fidā'īyān-i Islām in Razmara's assassination in 1951. However, Kāshāni's old age and the mediation of Ayatollahs Moḥammad Ḥosayn Borujerdi (Muḥammad Ḥusayn Burūjirdī) and Abū al-Faẕl Zanjānī saved his life. In 1958 his son, Muṣṭafā, was mysteriously poisoned. This tragic event and disillusionment with politics caused Kāshāni to leave politics. He died on 14 March 1962.

Kāshāni was a nationalist, a Constitutionalist, anti-British, anticolonialist, anticommunist, Pan-Islamist, and a pragmatist. He was combative, loved power, and lacked modesty but did not seek worldly and material possessions. Indeed, he died a poor man. He advocated the unity of the spiritual and the temporal spheres, seeing the separation of religion and politics as a colonial plot. However, he never sought direct rule by the clergy.

Kāshāni welcomed technological modernization and adoption of certain aspects of Western institutions. He advocated political reform in Iran but did not desire structural change in its political system. He strongly believed in legality and saw a role for both secular and religious law in public life.

Kāshāni's major contribution to the status of the Iranian *ʿulamā'* was his revival of their traditional leadership role as spokesmen of popular discontent. The clerical opposition toward the government after 1963, and the developments that led to the 1979 revolution, were considerably influenced by Kāshāni's ideas and activities. Although his views differed greatly from his clerical successors regarding Iranian nationalism, the place of *sharīʿah* in society, and attitudes toward the West, many of his ideas were elaborated by Ayatollah Khomeini and formed the foundations of his government. The messianic mission for the *ʿulamā'* that Kāshāni so often emphasized was expanded by Khomeini and formulated in the doctrine of *vilayat-i faqih (wilāyat al-faqīh).* Finally, Kāshāni's most important legacy was his dream of a nonaligned political bloc of all Muslim states, which found resonance in Khomeini's "neither East nor West" policy.

[*See also* Fidā'īyān-i Islām; Iran.]

BIBLIOGRAPHY

Akhavi, Shahrough. "The Role of the Clergy in Iranian Politics, 1949–1954." In *Musaddiq, Iranian Nationalism, and Oil,* edited by James Bill and Roger Louis. London, 1988.

Āyat, Ḥasan. *Darshā'ī as Tārīkh-i Siyāsī-i Īrān.* Tehran, 1984.

Faghfoory, Mohammad H. "The Role of the Ulama in Twentieth-Century Iran with Particular Reference to Ayatullah Haj Sayyid Abulqasim Kashani." Ph.D. diss., University of Wisconsin–Madison, 1978.

Gurūhī az Havādārān-i Nahẕat-i Islāmī-i Īrān dar Urūpā. *Rūḥānīyat va Asrār-i Fāsh Nashudah az Nahẕat-i Millī Shudan-i Ṣanʿat-i Naft dar Īrān.* Qom, 1358/1979.

Kāshānī, Maḥmūd. *Qiyām-i Millat-i Musulmān-i Īrān.* Tehran, 1359/1980.

Richard, Yann. "Ayatullah Kashani: Precursor of the Islamic Republic?" In *Religion and Politics in Iran: Shʿism from Quietism to Revolution,* edited by Nikki R. Keddie, pp. 101–124. New Haven and London, 1983.

MOHAMMAD H. FAGHFOORY

KASHMIR. The state of Jammu and Kashmir has been a disputed territory between India and Pakistan since the partition of the subcontinent in 1947. Situated in the extreme northwest corner of the South Asian subcontinent, it was one of the largest and most populous princely states of British India, sharing borders with India, Pakistan, Afghanistan, and China. The undivided state of Kashmir had an area of 84,471 square miles and comprised five distinct regions: the Vale of Kashmir, Jammu, Ladakh and Baltistan, Poonch, and Gilgit. The Kashmiri people are a mixture of different ethnic groups—Aryan, Mongol, Turkish, and Afghan. According to the 1941 census, its total population was 4,021,616; of these 77 percent were Muslims, 20 percent were Hindus, and 3 percent were Sikhs and other minorities. According to the 1981 Indian census, the total population of Indian-controlled Kashmir was 5,987,389; it consisted of 64.2 percent Muslims, 32.25 percent Hindus, 2.23 percent Sikhs, and the remainder Buddhists, Christians, and Jains. The population of the Pakistani part of Kashmir, according to the 1981 Pakistani census, was 1,983,465; 99.8 percent of the population was Muslim, while the rest consisted of Aḥmadīs, Christians, and Hindus.

The early history of Kashmir was dominated by clashes between Buddhism and Brahmanism, as rulers belonging to one or the other religion persecuted their adversaries. Islam entered Kashmir in the fourteenth century. Rinchan, a Buddhist ruler of Kashmir, embraced Islam in 1320 at the hands of Sayyid Bilāl Shāh (also known as Bulbul Shāh), a widely travelled Musavī Sayyid from Turkistan. Islam consolidated its hold during Shāh Mir's reign (1339–1344). The spread of Islam among the masses, however, was primarily due to "a long continued missionary movement inaugurated by and carried out mainly by *faqirs* or friars or dervishes and *ʿulamā'* or theologians" (Sūfī, 1949, pp. 80–82). A large number of Muslim *ʿulamā'* came from Central Asia to Kashmir to preach Islam. Sayyid Bilāl Shāh, Sayyid Jalāluddīn of Bukhara, Sayyid Tajuddīn and his brother Sayyid Ḥusayn Sīmānī, Sayyid ʿAlī Hamadānī and his son Mir Muḥammad Hamadānī, and Shaykh Nūruddīn are some of the well-known *ʿulamā'* who played a significant role in spreading Islam.

The contribution of Sayyid ʿAlī Hamadānī, popularly known as Shah-yi Hamadān, stands out above the rest. He was born at Hamadan (Iran) in 1314 CE. The rise of Timur in Central Asia forced him to leave for Kashmir. He belonged to the Kubrawī order of Ṣūfīs, a branch of the Suhrawardīyah. He paid three visits to Kashmir in 1372, 1379, and 1383 along with seven hundred followers and was successful in converting thousands of Kashmiris to Islam. His son Sayyid Muḥammad Hamadānī continued in the footsteps of his father in vigorously propagating Islam and influenced the Muslim ruler Sikander (1389–1413) to enforce the *sharīʿah* and to establish the office of the Shaykh al-Islām. Hindu historians have blamed Sikander for the persecution of Hindus and destruction of their temples. By the end of the fifteenth century, a majority of the inhabitants of Kashmir had embraced Islam. The Muslim rule in Kashmir lasted for five centuries from 1320 to 1819, including the periods of the independent sultans (1320–1586), the Mughals (1586–1753), and the Pathans (1753–1819).

In 1819 Kashmir was conquered by Ranjit Singh, the Sikh ruler of Punjab, who ruled it until 1846. In the wake of the first Anglo-Sikh war the British sold Kashmir to Gulab Singh for 7,500,000 rupees under the Treaty of Amritsar, signed on 15 March 1846. He founded the Dogra dynasty that ruled Kashmir until 1947. Despite being the majority of the population, the Muslims were heavily oppressed during the Sikh and Dogra rule. Heavy taxation, forced work without wages (*begar*), laws discriminatory against Muslims, rural indebtedness, and widespread illiteracy were the common characteristics of the Sikh and Dogra rule. The state interfered in every aspect of Muslims' lives; many mosques were in the possession of the state; the slaughter of cow was an offense punishable by death; and the murder of a Muslim was considered a crime of a lesser degree than the murder of a Hindu.

Two popular Islamic institutions—the Mir Waiz, the hereditary office belonging to Jāmiʿah Mosque of Srinagar (of the Ḥanafī school), and the Shāfiʿī institution of Shāh Hamadān at Khānqāh-i Muʿallā—played a useful initial role in highlighting the socioeconomic grievances of the Muslims; however, with the rise of the educated middle class, a political consciousness began to emerge among the Muslims of Kashmir. In 1922, the Young Men's Muslim Association was formed in Jammu by Choudhry Ghulam Abbas, and a Reading Room Party was established by Shaikh Abdullah in 1930 to address the situation of the Muslims. A mass resistance movement was triggered in 1931 when a state functionary forbade the imam to deliver the khuṭbah (sermon) before the Friday prayer. A fiery speech was delivered by one ʿAbdulqadīr against the Maharaja's un-Islamic injunctions. On 13 July 1931, twenty-two Kashmiri Muslims were martyred when the police opened fire on the mob protesting against the arrest of ʿAbdulqadīr. On 14 October 1932, the All Jammu and Muslim Conference was formed under the leadership of Shaikh Abdullah. This organization became the principal vehicle for mobilizing the Muslim masses against the Maharaja's oppressive rule. The Mir Waiz, Muḥammad Yūsuf Shāh, initially gave enthusiastic support to Shaikh Abdullah but later distanced himself and became actively hostile to him.

Soon the political situation in Kashmir came under the influence of politics in the subcontinent, where the All-India National Congress was promoting the "one nation theory" that India, despite its communal divisions, was one nation; the Muslim League answered with the "two nation theory" that there existed two major nations in the subcontinent, Hindus and Muslims, that differed from each other in all respects. A split occurred among the Kashmiri Muslims as well when Shaikh Abdullah grew closer to the secularist-nationalist view of Indian National Congress and renamed the Muslim Conference the National Conference. Choudhry Ghulam Abbas revived the Muslim Conference in October 1941; it became closely identified with the Muslim nationalist view of the Muslim League and passed a resolution in favor of joining Kashmir with Pakistan. [*See* All-India Muslim League.]

On the eve of the partition there were three main political forces in Kashmir: The National Conference, the Muslim Conference, and the Dogra dynasty. The National Conference led by Shaikh Abdullah wanted to join India; the Muslim Conference led by Choudhry Ghulam Abbas was in favor of joining Pakistan; and the Dogra Maharaja Hari Singh apparently wanted to remain independent, because he knew that accession to India or Pakistan would eventually mean the loss of his throne and the replacement of his autocracy by some form of democratic government. The Maharaja offered a standstill agreement to both India and Pakistan in order to maintain communication and supplies. Pakistan entered into agreement, but India did not. In that emotionally charged atmosphere, there began a planned mass murder of Kashmiri Muslims in Jammu and Poonch with the active connivance of Maharaja Hari Singh, and this led to an estrangement of relations between Pakistan and Kashmir. The Maharaja's government charged Pakistan with aiding the rebels and establishing an economic blockade to force accession. Pakistan saw a plan by the Hindu ruler to exterminate the Muslim majority. The Pakistanis were further alarmed by the frequent contacts of the Indian leaders with Maharaja and the speedy construction of the road linking India to Kashmir. Further developments were the replacement of Prime Minister Pandit Kak (who had signed the standstill agreement with Pakistan), by Mehr Chand (who openly sided with India) and the sudden release from jail of Shaikh Abdullah, whose policy was decidedly anti-Pakistan. All these events convinced the Pakistanis of the Maharaja's long-term plan to accede to India. The scale of the mass murder of Muslims can be assessed from the fact that two hundred thousand Muslims were massacred by the Maharaja's forces in Jammu alone. At this point hundreds of Pathan tribesmen from the North-West Frontier province of Pakistan entered Kashmir to help their Muslim coreligionists. The Maharaja quickly decided to accede to India on 22 October 1948. India accepted the accession provisionally, subject to a referendum held under international auspices to ascertain the wishes of the people of Kashmir. India dispatched its own troops to Kashmir and also complained to the United Nations, charging Pakistan with aggression against the territory that had legally become part of India. Pakistan challenged the legality of the accession on the grounds that the Maharaja had already fled from the scene and was no longer in authority to sign the instrument of accession. Over the years, several mediation efforts by the UN, bilateral Indo-Pakistani negotiations, and the two India-Pakistan wars over Kashmir (1947 and 1965) failed to resolve the dispute. India now continues to hold the greater part of Kashmir, while Pakistan maintains its control over a smaller part known as "Azad Kashmir."

India continued to maintain a facade of legitimacy through Shaikh Abdullah's National Conference in the post-partition era. Faced by the prospects of public unrest and international attention on Kashmir, the Indian government sought to rely on Shaikh Abdullah's popularity among the Kashmiri masses. On 11 August 1952 Shaikh Abdullah announced an agreement between himself and Jawaharlal Nehru that granted the state of Jammu and Kashmir special privileges within the Indian Union. It was vested in the Constituent Assembly to determine the scope and extent of the state's accession to India. This was the first of the three attempts by the Nehru family to agree with the Shaikh Abdullah family on the controversial status of Kashmir; the other two were Shaikh Abdullah's accord with Indira Gandhi (February 1975) and Shaikh Abdullah's son Farooq Abdullah's agreement with Rajiv Gandhi (November 1986). Shaikh Abdullah and his son used the unsettled issue of the accession of the state to improve their bargaining position with Delhi. However, Shaikh Abdullah's government was dismissed by India in 1953, and he was put behind bars for a long time. Puppet governments installed by India compromised on the issue of accession, legalizing it through the state assembly according to Indian government's wishes. With the death of Shaikh Abdullah in 1982 a major contextual change occurred in Kashmiri politics as the Indian government lacked a popular public figure with whom it could negotiate.

A powerful mass resistance against Indian rule has emerged since 1987, with the Islamic movement playing the leading role. The origins of the current mass uprising in Kashmir can better be understood in the context of the Indian state's policies (1947–1987) in the political, economic, and cultural spheres. Politically, despite Indian promises at the highest level to the Kashmiri people and the UN, the Indian government never allowed the Kashmiris to exercise their right of self-determination. The view of the Indian government has been that the Kashmiri people have expressed through the successive state assembly elections their desire to remain with India. However, the UN, in response to Pakistan's complaint, made it clear that the state elections under the Indian control cannot be considered a substitute for a plebiscite held under UN auspices. After 1953, India went back on its promise of holding a plebiscite under UN auspices and declared Kashmir to be an integral part of India. The results of most of the state elections held since the partition have been characterized as manipulated or completely rigged by observers. The issue of self-determination has never died down.

Absence of genuine political participation created a deep-rooted alienation among the masses. Economically, Kashmir continued to remain a hinterland with little infrastructural development and a subsidy economy dependent on the center. Expansion of educational facilities continued to increase the number of unemployed graduates, whose joblessness exacerbated their dissatisfaction with the political process. In the cultural sphere, growing emphasis on secularism generated a backlash contributing to the popularity of Islamic political parties, especially the Jamāʿat-i Islāmī (established in 1953) and the Islāmī Jamīʿat-i Ṭulabā, its allied student body. Islam remained the most powerful stimulus despite the secular outlook of successive governments. [*See* Jamāʿat-i Islāmī.] This was evident from the several crises faced by the state that led to severe breakdowns of law and order: the Hazratbal riots in 1963–1964, the mass agitation of July 1965, the riots of May 1973, and continuing mass resistance since 1987.

The current phase of mass resistance against Indian

rule began in 1987 when an alliance of several Islamic parties, the Muslim United Front (MUF), was expected to win convincingly but ended with a mere four seats, allegedly because of massive rigging in the state elections. The state elections of 1987 were the catalyst for a new phase of armed struggle against Indian rule. The Indian government alleges that the Kashmiri struggle has been instigated and supported by Pakistan, while Pakistan maintains that the Kashmiri resistance is entirely indigenous in character and that Pakistan supports the movement only morally. The movement has been remarkably successful in mobilizing widespread support among the Muslim population over the past five years. Several offers of political dialogue made by the Indian government have been turned down by the freedom-fighters, who declared that they were not willing to talk within the framework of the Indian union; according to them, talk is possible only after the implementation of the UN resolutions on the Kashmir dispute.

The Kashmiri resistance is divided into two major factions. The Jammu and Kashmir Liberation Front (JKLF), established in 1965 under the leadership of Maqbool But and currently headed by Amānullāh Khān, wants an independent Kashmir based on secular nationalism; the Ḥizbul Mujāhidīn, founded in 1989 and headed by Ghulām Mohammad Saffi, is committed to *jihād* and seeks the accession of Kashmir to Pakistan. The Ḥizbul Mujāhidīn is more powerful than the JKLF and enjoys widespread grassroots support. The Indian government has responded with massive repression of the Kashmiri people, employing security forces of more than four hundred thousand men. According to the most conservative estimates, since 1987 the Indian security forces have killed more than twenty thousand Kashmiris, engaged in widespread molestation of women, burnt down houses, and brutally tortured able-bodied youths, leading to thousands of deaths in custody. These harrowing atrocities have been documented in detail by Indian human rights groups as well as such international groups as Amnesty, Asia Watch, and Physicians for Human Rights (see *Kashmir under Siege: Human Rights in India, An Asia Watch Report,* Washington, D.C., 1991; *Kashmir 1991: Physicians for Human Rights,* London, 1991; and Amnesty International's 1993 Report, reproduced in the daily newspaper *Dawn,* Karachi, 10 April 1993). Despite this massive repression, the Kashmiri peoples' struggle continues unabated and shows little signs of weakness.

[*See also* India; Pakistan.]

BIBLIOGRAPHY

Bamzai, P. N. K. *A History of Kashmir.* New Delhi, 1973. Useful but somewhat biased account of the political, economic, and social history of Kashmir.

Bazaz, P. N. *The History of Struggle for Freedom in Kashmir.* Reprint, Islamabad, 1976. Personalized but insightful account of the contemporary history of Kashmir.

Brecher, Michael. *The Struggle for Kashmir.* Toronto, 1953. Excellent study of the origins of the Kashmir dispute during the partition of the Subcontinent.

Gupta, Sisir. *Kashmir: A Study in India-Pakistan Relations.* Bombay, 1967. Relatively sophisticated Indian perspective on the Kashmir dispute.

Korbel, Josef. *Danger in Kashmir.* Princeton, 1954. Excellent account of UN involvement in the Kashmir dispute.

Lakhanpal, Puran L., ed. *Essential Documents and Notes on the Kashmir Dispute.* Delhi, 1965. Useful collection of important documents on Kashmir.

Lamb, Alastair. *The Kashmir Problem.* New York, 1966. Fairly unbiased and brief account of the Kashmir dispute.

Lamb, Alastair. *Kashmir: A Disputed Legacy, 1946–1990.* Hertfordshire, 1991. The best account of the Kashmir dispute, up to date and authoritative.

Parmu, R. K. *A History of Muslim Rule in Kashmir, 1320–1819.* New Delhi, 1969. Contains an excellent account of the spread of Islam in Kashmir.

Saraf, Muhammad Yusuf. *Kashmiris Fight for Freedom.* 2 vols. Lahore, 1977. Detailed and in-depth study of the modern history of Kashmir, including personal recollections.

Sūfī, Ghulām Muhyi'd Dīn. *Kashmir.* 2 vols. Lahore, 1949. Comprehensive and monumental history of Kashmir from the earliest times.

Suharwardy, Abdul Haq. *Tragedy in Kashmir.* Lahore, 1983. Good account of the origin and evolution of the Kashmir dispute from a Pakistani perspective.

Thomas, Raju G. C. *Perspectives on Kashmir.* Boulder, 1992. Combines Indian, Pakistani, and Kashmiri perspectives on the Kashmir dispute.

TAHIR AMIN

KASRAVI, AḤMAD (1890–1946), major historian of modern Iran, political thinker, iconoclastic secularist, and founder of an ideological school named the Āzādigān (Freedom) Society.

Kasravi was born into a traditional middle-class family in Tabriz and raised for the clerical profession. But in his late youth he broke with Islam in general and the Shīʿī *ʿulamā'* in particular. This breach was prompted in part by the local clergy's opposition to the Constitutional Revolution (1905–1909) and in part by the failure of the traditional sciences to calculate the movement of the stars, particularly the 1911 arrival of Halley's comet. This led Kasravi to study Western astronomy, which in turn led him to explore rational-scientific thought, especially that of the French Enlightenment.

Leaving the clerical profession, Kasravi served as a civil judge until 1929, when he was dismissed for ruling in favor of small landlords expropriated by Reza Shah. He also taught for a while in Tehran University, until he was removed for openly criticizing Ḥāfiẓ, Saʿdī, Khayyām, and other mystic Persian poets. He criticized them for using esoteric language and for advocating fatalism, wine drinking, and homosexuality.

From 1932 until his assassination in 1946, Kasravi single-mindedly devoted himself to developing a civic ideology stressing the importance of social solidarity and national integration. He termed this ideology Pākdīn (Clean Religion). He argued that Iran's backwardness was not so much owed to foreign intervention and despotic governments—although both, he admitted, played a role—but to individual egoism overriding social altruism and factionalism dividing the nation along sectarian lines. He ennumerated these factional cleavages as tribalism, regionalism, linguistic communalism, and religious sectarianism—especially the Bahā'ī faith, Sufism, Shaykhīyah, and most serious of all, Shiism. He also argued that the recent introduction of Marxism into Iran was further dividing the country along class lines.

He hammered away at these themes in over fifty pamphlets as well as in his journals *Paymān* (The Promise) and *Parcham* (The Flag). Even his monumental history of modern Iran—*Tārīkh-i mashrūṭah-yi Īrān* (The History of the Iranian Constitutional Movement) and *Tārīkh-i hījdah ṣalāḥ-yi Āẕarbayjān* (Eighteen-Year History of Azerbaijan)—was written to stress the importance of national integration and social solidarity. As he admitted, he had undertaken the work to show that Azerbaijan was an integral part of Iran, that the reform movement had been damaged by social conflicts, and that the 1905 revolution had been shipwrecked on the dangerous rocks of factionalism ("Again Concerning Azerbaijan," *Parcham*, 6 December 1942).

Kasravi directed his sharpest attacks at Shiism. He denounced it for having begun as a dynastic power struggle; for imposing itself on Iran during the Ṣafavid era (1501–1722) through sheer terror; for falsifying history by inventing the Twelfth Imam (Mahdi) and claiming that he had gone into occultation *(ghaybah);* for undermining the legitimacy of the state by questioning its authority to levy taxes and impose military conscription; for encouraging mendacity through the practice of *taqīyah* (dissimulation); for implicity opposing democracy and popular soverignty by claiming that true soveignty lay with the Hidden Imam and his deputies, the *mujtahids;* and for insisting that the faithful should blindly follow their clerical leaders. He also denounced Shiism for perpetuating such "medieval superstitions" as that the imams predated the universe; that the dead imams resided in their tombs, listened to pilgrims, interceded on their behalf with God, and even cured incurable diseases—something even the Prophet had never claimed. He further noted that the Shīʿīs had taken their concept of the Mahdi from Christianity and Zoroastrianism. [*See* Mahdi; Ghaybah; Taqīyah.]

Not surprisingly, Kasravi aroused the wrath of the *ʿulamā'*. Ayatollah Ruhollah Khomeini, in his very first political work, *Kashf al-asrār* (Secrets Unveiled; 1943), defended the traditional Shīʿī doctrines against Kasravi. Other clerical leaders declared him an "apostate" and claimed that the Āzādigān Society, in its periodic book-burning sessions, was incinerating not only Ṣūfī poetry but also the Holy Qur'ān. In March 1946, Kasravi was assassinated by a member of the fundamentalist Fidā'īyān-i Islām. Years later, Khomeini described Kasravi as an "excellent historian" who had later gone "crazy," claiming to be a prophet sent to establish a new religion (*Kayhān,* 19 July 1980). Khomeini always featured prominently Kasravi's *History of the Iranian Constitutional Movement* in his study.

[*See also* Iran.]

BIBLIOGRAPHY

Abrahamian, Ervand. "Kasravi: The Integrative Nationalist of Iran." *Middle East Studies* 9 (October 1973): 271–295.

Jazayery, Mohammad Ali. "Ahmad Kasravi and the Controversy over Persian Poetry" (Parts 1 and 2). *International Journal of Middle East Studies* 4 (April 1973): 190–203, and 13 (August 1981): 311–327.

Kasravī, Aḥmad. *On Islam and Shiʿism.* Translated by Mohammad R. Ghanoonparvar. Costa Mesa, Calif., 1990. Contains a good outline of Kasravī's thought by Mohammad Ali Jazayery.

ERVAND ABRAHAMIAN

KAWĀKIBĪ, ʿABD AL-RAḤMĀN AL- (1854–1902), Islamic revivalist and advocate of an Arab caliphate. Al-Kawākibī was born to a prominent family in Aleppo, Syria, and was educated thoroughly in religion, Ottoman administrative law, Arabic, Turkish, and Farsi. He began his career in journalism and the law and from 1879 to 1896 held several senior public posts.

After suffering from the intrigues of Ottoman officials, in 1898 al-Kawākibī fled to Egypt where he remained until his death in 1902.

Al-Kawākibī is best known for his two books *Umm al-qurā* (The Mother of the Villages), one of the names of Mecca, and *Ṭabā'iʿ Al-istibdād* (The Attributes of Tyranny). He published them in Cairo under the pen names of al-Sayyid al-Furātī and Traveller K, respectively, to avoid the harassment of the Ottoman authorities. Published in 1899, *Umm al-qurā* is an account of the proceedings of a fictitious secret congress (The Congress of Islamic Revival) in Mecca attended by twenty-two Muslim delegates from Arab, Muslim, European, and Asian countries. The participants' purpose was to discuss the causes of the decline of the Muslim peoples and design a reform program for their recovery.

Al-Kawākibī attributed this decline to religious, political, and moral factors. Influenced by the reform ideas of Jamāl al-Dīn al-Afghānī and Muḥammad ʿAbduh, he advocated a return to the original purity of Islam, which had been distorted by alien concepts and currents such as mysticism, fatalism, sectarian divisions, and imitation. These distortions had led to ignorance among the Muslims and their submission to stagnant theologians and despotic rulers who suppressed freedoms, promoted false religion, and corrupted the moral, social, educational, and financial systems of the Muslim nation.

Al-Kawākibī proposed the formation of a society, with branches throughout the Muslim world, to educate Muslims and promote in them the aspiration for progress. Holding non-Arabs, namely the Turks, accountable for the degeneration of Islam, he called for an Arab caliphate, which would exercise religious and cultural leadership, not temporal authority, and become the basis for the revival of Islam and an Islamic federation. He stipulated that the caliph be from the tribe of Quraysh, have limited powers, and be subject to election every three years and accountable to an elected council. He viewed the true Islamic state as one based on political freedoms and government accountability.

Alluding to the autocratic rule of the Ottomans, *Ṭabā'iʿ al-istibdād* is an outright attack on tyranny. Al-Kawākibī discussed the nature of despotism and its devastating effects on society as a whole. A despotic state conducts the affairs of its citizens without fear of accountability or punishment, suppresses their rights, and prevents their education and enlightenment. Its purpose is to keep the people acquiescent and inactive; consequently, it destroys their moral, religious, and national bonds. Al-Kawākibī advocated education and gradualism as the means to uproot tyranny.

Al-Kawākibī contributed greatly to the evolution of Arab nationalist thought. Unlike the proponents of Pan-Islam at the time, he drew a clear distinction between the Arab and non-Arab Muslims, exalted the former on the basis of their language, descent, and moral attributes, and explicitly called for an Arab state. His fictional congress in *Umm al-qurā* inspired many reformers who later adopted the idea and put it into practice. Thus, he gave an organizational form and a political content to the cause of reform and to the Arabs' aspiration for independence from the Ottomans. Al-Kawākibī was far from being a secularist; in his endorsement of an Arab spiritual leadership and a restricted caliphate, however, he separated the temporal and spiritual, a division that represented a break from classical Islamic thought.

[*See also* Arab Nationalism; Caliphate.]

BIBLIOGRAPHY

Amīn, Aḥmad. *Zuʿamā' al-iṣlāḥ fī al-ʿaṣr al-ḥadīth* (Reform Leaders in the Modern Time). Cairo, 1979. Chapter on al-Kawākibī is a thorough study of his two books.

ʿAqqād, ʿAbbās M. al-. *ʿAbd al-Raḥmān al-Kawākibī: Al-Raḥḥālah Kāf* (ʿAbd al-Raḥmān al-Kawākibī: Traveler K). Beirut, 1969. Excellent analysis of al-Kawākibī's background, thought, and contributions.

Haim, Sylvia G., "Alfieri and al-Kawakibi." *Oriente Moderno* 34 (1954): 321–334. Haim suggests that al-Kawākibī's ideas on despotism were influenced by the Italian poet Vittorio Alfieri (1749–1803).

Haim, Sylvia G. "Blunt and al-Kawakibi." *Oriente Moderno* 35 (1955): 132–143. Haim unconvincingly claims that al-Kawākibī's call for an Arab caliphate was inspired by the English poet Wilfred S. Blunt (1840–1922).

Haim, Sylvia G., ed. *Arab Nationalism: An Anthology*. Berkeley and Los Angeles, 1976. Haim's introductory chapter, "Writers on Arab Nationalism," is a comprehensive overview of the evolution of the ideology of Arab nationalism.

Husry, Khaldun S. *Three Reformers: A Study in Modern Arab Political Thought*. Beirut, 1966. Chapter on al-Kawākibī is a thorough and insightful study of his life and thought. Husry attempts to refute Haim's thesis.

Kawākibī, ʿAbd al-Raḥmān al-. *Al-aʿmāl al-kāmilah li-ʿAbd al-Raḥmān al-Kawākibī* (The Complete Works of ʿAbd al-Raḥmān al-Kawākibī). Edited by Muḥammad ʿImārah. Cairo, 1970. Al-Kawākibī's works are prefaced by a detailed study of his life and thought.

Kramer, Martin. *Islam Assembled: The Advent of the Muslim Congresses*. New York, 1986. Section dealing with al-Kawākibī (pp. 30–35) is a significant study of his contribution to the idea of an Arab caliphate and Muslim congresses.

EMAD ELDIN SHAHIN

KAZAKHSTAN. Sunnī Islam of the Ḥanafī school was introduced to the territory of what is now Kazakhstan in the late eighteenth century on the order of Catherine the Great, with the intention of civilizing and pacifying the pastoral nomads with whom her expanding empire was coming into increasing conflict. Her missionaries of choice were Tatars from Kazan, who began to spread the faith among the northern and western Kazakhs; in the south, missionaries from the Khoqand Khanate voluntarily took the opportunity to begin proselytizing on behalf of a much more conservative brand of Islam than that brought by the Tatars.

The nomadic Kazakh lifestyle made proper religious training difficult, however, and the Russians soon had second thoughts about the wisdom of permitting the spread of Islam, and so the Kazakhs were only superficially converted. Travelers' accounts from the 1820s and 1830s indicate that there were few clergy and that the Kazakhs had little knowledge of dogma. By the middle of the century Islam was making inroads among the Kazakh aristocracy, and by the 1860s there were Qur'ānic schools in some Kazakh cities. By the end of the nineteenth century Islam was solidly established among the Kazakhs; in 1900 there were sixty-one mosques in the town of Ak-mola, and by 1910 five hundred people a year were requesting Russian visas in order to go to Mecca on the *ḥajj*.

By this period Islam was sufficiently well established among the Kazakhs to be a part of their identity. Traditional Kazakh society was shattered, however, from the time of the general Central Asian Uprising of 1916, to the end of the Civil War in 1922, and then during the Soviet collectivization drive of 1929–1934. In those eighteen years 3.3 million Kazakhs died and another 1.3 million were driven into exile, reducing the population to about one-third of what it had been in 1916. Prominent among the victims were the clergy, who from the late 1920s until World War II were imprisoned or killed during the Soviet authorities' aggressive antireligious campaigns, which also closed *madrasah*s, *mekteps* (Ar., *maktabs*), and mosques throughout Central Asia.

In 1943 the antireligious pressure was eased somewhat as part of Stalin's effort to ensure that the Soviet people would fight against the Nazis. An official Ecclesiastical Administration of Central Asia and Kazakhstan (SADUM) was established to give an appearance of religious independence for Muslims, whose practice in fact remained severely restricted.

Soviet antireligious pressure all but eliminated doctrinal Islam, but it had virtually no impact on rural practices in Kazakhstan or elsewhere, which remained a mixture of Islamic and pre-Islamic cultural rituals. By 1989, when Soviet authorities finally relaxed their opposition to religion, virtually all Kazakhs identified as Muslims as part of their ethnic and linguistic heritage, and many retained vestiges of Islamic practice within families or communities, at least for life transitions such as birth, marriage, and death. Very few Kazakhs, however, had any religious training or knowledge of Arabic, and almost none had access to Qur'āns or other liturgical material.

Since relatively unhindered religious practice has become possible, Islam has enjoyed a resurgence of attention in Kazakhstan. Particularly since independence (declared 16 December 1991) there has been considerable religious activity, with many mosques and religious schools opening and new buildings begun, some financed by Saudis, Turks, Egyptians, and others, and some by contributions from local believers. Kazakhstan's president, Nursultan Nazarbayev, created a state basis for Islam in Kazakhstan in 1990, when he removed his republic (then still part of the USSR) from under the authority of Tashkent-based SADUM to create a separate Kazakh muftiate. The republic's constitution, adopted in January 1993, specifically guarantees freedom of religious worship, and programs have been initiated to send young Kazakhs to Turkey for training, both secular and religious.

Despite these supportive attitudes, in modern Kazakhstan the potential spread of Islam has a serious political dimension of which the current leadership is acutely aware. Kazakhstan is an arbitrary geographic creation of the Stalinist period in which 40 percent of the population (of about 17 million) is ethnic Russian, heavily concentrated in the industrial north and west of the nation. The allegiance of this possibly irredentist population to the Kazakh-dominated state is fragile at best and would disappear entirely if Kazakhstan seemed about to become more Islamic.

In order to preserve this fragile detente the state constitution not only forbids adoption of a state religion but also bars the creation of political parties that seek to impose any "ideology"—including religion—on the state. Unlike those of other Central Asian states, Kazakhstan's constitution makes no mention of an Islamic dimension to the nation's past or identity. President Nazarbayev, a Kazakh and thus a Muslim by heritage, is obviously aware of the potential for investment and aid represented by the Muslim countries of the Middle East, and he has visited Iran and Turkey. However, Nazarbayev prefers to cast Kazakhstan as a bridge between Muslim East and Christian West and has therefore initially accepted only observer status in the Economic Cooperation Organization, the other members of which are Pakistan, Iran, Turkey, and the other Central Asian states. Unlike his fellow presidents in Uzbekistan and Turkmenistan, Nazarbayev has not made the *ḥajj* and has not permitted any of the Muslim holy days to become state holidays. The government has refused to allow the most Islamic of the Kazakh nationalist parties, Azat, to be legally registered. Further, it has actively prosecuted a group of activists who tried to force the removal of Kazakhstan's first official *muftī*, Ratbek Haji Nysanbaev, accusing him of financial irregularities, religious mispractice, and collaboration with the Soviet and later Kazakh state security apparatus.

Opposition to the centrist policies of the Nazarbayev government and hostility to the huge Russian presence has stimulated nationalism among the 40 percent of Kazakhstan's population who are ethnic Kazakhs—but only for some does that national identity include a companion interest in doctrinal Islam. The 25 to 40 percent of the Kazakh population (estimates vary) who are urbanized and sovietized, or even russified, tend to find Islam as alien and as threatening as do the Russians. President Nazarbayev typifies many of the present Kazakh elite when he stresses his own atheism and his belief in the necessity of creating a secular Kazakhstan.

[*See also* Islam, *article on* Islam in Central Asia and the Caucasus.]

BIBLIOGRAPHY

Akiner, Shirin. *Islamic Peoples of the Soviet Union*. Rev. ed. London, 1990.

Allworth, Edward, ed. *Central Asia: A Century of Russian Rule*. New York, 1967.

Barthold, V. V. *Four Studies on the History of Central Asia*. Translated by Vladimir Minorsky and Tatiana Minorsky. Leiden, 1956–.

Bennigsen, Alexandre, and Chantal Lemercier-Quelquejay. *Islam in the Soviet Union*. New York, 1967.

Bennigsen, Alexandre, and S. Enders Wimbush. *Muslims of the Soviet Empire: A Guide*. Bloomington, 1986.

Demko, George J. *The Russian Colonization of Kazakhstan, 1896–1916*. Bloomington, 1969.

Krader, Lawrence. *Peoples of Central Asia*. Bloomington, 1963.

Olcott, Martha Brill. *The Kazakhs*. Stanford, Calif., 1987.

Rywkin, Michael. *Moscow's Muslim Challenge*. Rev. ed. Armonk, N.Y., 1990.

Zenkowsky, Serge A. *Pan-Turkism and Islam in Russia*. Cambridge, Mass., 1960.

MARTHA BRILL OLCOTT

KAZAN KHANATE. A Chinggisid successor state to the so-called "Golden Horde", the patrimony granted to Chinggis Khan's oldest son Jochi in the early thirteenth century CE, the Kazan Khanate was centered on the city of Kazan, located in present-day Tatarstan on the eastern bank of the Volga River north of its confluence with the Kama. This territory had once formed a part of Volga Bulgaria, the first Muslim state in eastern Europe (already converted to Islam by the time of Ibn Faḍlān's visit in 922; it later formed a part of the territories of the Golden Horde. Islam became the state religion of the Golden Horde in the first half of the fourteenth century, and the Kazan Khanate continued its tradition of a Muslim Turkic high culture and literature (forming the basis of the Kazan Tatar culture that emerged in this period), although less survives from the Kazan Khanate than from its contemporary sister states.

The foundation of the Kazan Khanate (1438 or 1445 are traditional dates) followed Uluğ Muhammed's flight north from the Crimea, where he had ruled previously. One of Uluğ Muhammed's sons, Mahmud (r. 1446–1466), succeeded his father as khan. Another son, Kasim, founded the Kasimov Khanate, which was a client state in the service of Muscovy. As early as 1468 Muscovy attempted to interfere in the dynamic relationship between the khan (the sovereign descended from Chinggis Khan) and the four *karaçı* beys (the leaders of the four main tribes, the Şirin, Barın, Arğin, and Kıpçak) to support Kasim's bid to assume leadership of the khanate. It was not until 1487, with the installation of the Muscovite client Muhammed Emin as khan for a second reign, that the balance tipped in favor of Muscovy. The four main tribal leaders, who traditionally controlled succession and other affairs of state, became dissatisfied with this arrangement and in 1496 sought an alternative ruler in the person of Mamuk of the Şibanid line. This proved disastrous for the local tribal leadership, and they had to agree in 1497 that a new Muscovite client, ʿAbdüllatif, younger brother of Muhammed Emin, would become the new khan. The arrest of ʿAbdüllatif and the reinstallation of Muhammed Emin by Muscovy in 1502 is evidence of Muscovite control over affairs in the khanate during this period. Muhammed Emin's unexpected break with Muscovy during 1505–

1507, however, apparently allowed the khanate to reassert its independence.

With the death of Muhammed Emin in 1518 and the end of the line of Uluğ Muhammed, the Crimean Khanate became more actively involved in the affairs of the Kazan Khanate. Sahib Giray, brother of the Crimean khan, helped the local tribal leadership depose the young Muscovite client Şah ʿAli (r. 1518–1521). Sahib Giray was then installed as khan against Muscovite wishes and was later succeeded by his nephew Sefa Giray (r. 1525–1532). Kazan served as an important mercantile center, but as relations with Muscovy worsened during this period, the latter began to remove commercial activities from Kazan to competing centers under its own control in order to deprive the khanate of revenue. Under pressure from Muscovy, Sefa Giray was later replaced by Can ʿAli, brother of Şah ʿAli, but was reinstated a few years later (r. 1536–1546). In the meantime, the former khan Sahib Giray had become a powerful ally of Kazan as the new Crimean khan. While relations between the khans of the two states were very close, the local leadership of the Kazan Khanate complained that many revenues were being assigned to Crimeans. Sefa Giray was temporarily deposed by the tribal leadership in favor of Şah ʿAli, only to be reinstated soon afterward. During his final reign (1546–1549), Sefa Giray undertook a purge of the local nobility, favoring closer ties with Muscovy. Following Sefa Giray's death, his wife Süyün Bike acted as regent for his young son Ötemiş Giray (r. 1549–1551). Muscovy's ongoing eastward expansion finally reached the khanate and in 1551 forced the local leadership to accept Şah ʿAli as khan for a third time under harsh terms. The Kazan Khanate was finally conquered on 2 October 1552. Much of the population was then resettled, and Orthodox Christian settlers were introduced into the territory. Over the following centuries numerous campaigns would be undertaken to convert and assimilate the local Muslim Turkic population.

[*See also* Crimea Khanate.]

BIBLIOGRAPHY

Keenan, E. L. "Muscovy and Kazan: Some Introductory Remarks on the Patterns of Steppe Diplomacy." *Slavic Review* 26 (1967): 548–558. Offers important insights into the role of the tribal aristocracy in relations between Muscovy and the Kazan Khanate.

Khudiakov, Mikhail. *Ocherki po istorii Kazanskogo khanstva* (1923). Reprint, Moscow, 1991. Standard treatment.

Pelenski, Jaroslaw. *Russia and Kazan: Conquest and Imperial Ideology, 1438–1560s*. The Hague and Paris, 1974. The most authoritative work in English on the Kazan Khanate, including a revised chronology and detailed study of Russian sources.

Rorlich, Azade-Ayşe, *The Volga Tatars: A Profile in National Resilience*. Stanford, Calif., 1986. Useful survey down to the twentieth century; contains a chapter on the history of the Kazan Khanate, including cultural information.

Smith, R. E. F. *Peasant Farming in Muscovy*. Cambridge, 1977. Includes an excellent chapter on agricultural conditions in the territory of the former Kazan Khanate a half-century following the conquest.

Uli Schamiloglu

KEMAL, MUSTAFA. *See* Atatürk, Mustafa Kemal.

KEMAL, MEHMET NAMIK (1840–1888), Ottoman Turkish poet, prose writer, and libertarian theoretician. Namık Kemal was born in 1840 in the small town of Tekirdağ, but his life was shaped by more exalted influences, including his family's tradition of state service, immersing him in Ottoman culture at an early age. His own career in the Ottoman bureaucracy brought him into contact with Western culture, especially through the medium of works in French. He was born in the year after the proclamation of the Tanzimat rescript of 1839, which inaugurated an era of Western-inspired political, social, and economic reform in the Ottoman Empire. The Tanzimat also promoted a new diplomatic policy built on concerns for the stability of the Ottoman state felt by officials who were architects of the reform movement, among them the Minister of Foreign Affairs and Grand Vizier Mustafa Reşid Paşa and his successors Âli and Fuad Paşa. Through their control of reform, this new westernizing political elite established control over the formation of all state policy. Namık Kemal was primarily involved in formal criticism that these policies had relegated the sultan to the background, but the substance of his criticism was an attempt to show that government by an elite was illegitimate according to both Islamic and Western principles.

Namık Kemal received his education from private tutors and assumed a position in the bureaucracy in 1859. Between 1861 and 1867 he was employed in the Translation Bureau of the Ottoman Porte. Kemal also took over the editing of *Tasvir-i efkâr*, a newspaper that had initiated sociopolitical commentary about the empire. Its former editor Şinasi Efendi fled Turkey in 1865, and Kemal's stance became more clearly political. Kemal was also among the founders of a conspiratorial antigovernment group organized in Istanbul with the aim of bringing modern constitutional and parliamentary institutions into the empire.

In 1867 the government became uneasy with Kemal's criticism in *Tasvir* of its conduct of foreign affairs that urged a more forceful defense of Ottoman interests against the European powers. Kemal was appointed assistant governor for the province of Erzurum. Instead of accepting the appointment he left Turkey for Paris and London with his friend Ziya Bey (later Paşa) and began the publication of a newspaper, the *Hürriyet*. *Hürriyet* continued the tradition set by *Tasvir,* outspokenly criticizing the Ottoman government for its lack of direction and its autocratic policies. The ideas he proclaimed were known in the West as those of the Jeune Turquie; the group, however, referred to itself as the New (or Young) Ottoman Society. Its members had been helped to flee Turkey and to establish the newspaper by an Ottoman Egyptian, Prince Mustafa Fazıl Paşa, who had independently warned the sultan of the necessity for democratic reforms.

Dissension soon arose among the editors and Kemal returned to Istanbul in 1870. His writings thereafter appeared in *Ibret,* another newspaper with a political slant, but one much more focused on questions of culture and Ottoman identity. Shortly after his return he was appointed to an administrative post in Gelibolu (1872) in order to deflect the criticism that his natural journalistic ability made so effective. He returned to Istanbul shortly thereafter to resume his publishing activities and was once more exiled to Cyprus in 1876. He returned under amnesty but was again exiled to Mytilene, purportedly for the disturbance created by his play *The Fatherland or Silistre*. He died in 1888 while serving as an administrator in Mytilene.

Kemal's political ideas are a mixture of traditional Islamic concepts and the libertarian theories common in Europe of his time, reflecting the influence both of the eighteenth century Philosophes and also of France's evolution toward a "liberal empire" in the 1860s. The association of prodemocratic Ottoman Turkish intellectuals, the Young Ottoman Society, however, was a heterogeneous group. Another of its leaders was Ziya Paşa, a somewhat older bureaucrat and poet who generally shared Kemal's political opinions and also his theories concerning language. The latter stated that the Turkish used by the cultural and political elite had to be shorn of its flowery embellishments derived from Arabic and Persian roots, which were little used by most people. The new approach of Kemal and Ziya was aimed primarily at communicating with the "man in the street," but it also implies pursuit of a cultural identity more clearly Turkish than Arabic. Ziya Paşa's poetry and political ideas were much more conservative that Kemal's, although he was a constitutionalist; his verse also showed the influence of more traditional models. Other members of the Young Ottomans such as the autodidact Ali Suavi also constructed divergent theories for their own times.

It is through his impassioned patriotic poetry that Namık Kemal is best remembered by the current generation of Turks. Part of this was due to an image created in modern times. The Turkish Republic (established 1923) made a somewhat biased use of Namık Kemal, highlighting those aspects of his thought that focused on the defense of the fatherland. In fact, this use of patriotism was more in tune with the Turkish nation-state that emerged after World War I than with the multiethnic Ottoman Empire. The Turkish Republic completely ignored in its praise Kemal's concern that ideas of constitutionalism should be harmonized with Islam.

[*See also* Tanzimat; Young Ottomans; *and the biography of Suavi.*]

BIBLIOGRAPHY

Kemal, Namık. *Küliyat-i Kemal: Makalat, Siyasiye ve edebiye*. Edited by Ali Ekrem. [Bulayir] Istanbul, 1910.

Kemal, Namık. *Namık Kemal'in mektupları*. 3 vols. Edited by Fevziye Abdullah Tansel. Ankara, 1967–1973.

Mardin, Şerif. *The Genesis of Young Ottoman Thought*. Princeton, 1962.

Şerif Mardin

KEMALISM. The ideas and principles of Mustafa Kemal Atatürk, the founder and first president of the Turkish Republic, are termed Kemalism; Kemalism constitutes the official ideology of the state, and endured publicly unchallenged until the 1980s. Kemalism proper is symbolized in the six points enumerated in the Republican People's Party (Cumhuriyet Halk Partisi, or CHP) Statutes of 1935; these were incorporated in the constitution of 1937, which remained in effect until 1961, then only to be reformulated with slight modifications. These six principles are republicanism, statism (in economic policy), populism, laicism, nationalism, and reformism. Together they represent a kind of Jacobinism, defined by Atatürk himself as a method of utilizing political despotism in order to break down the social despotism prevalent among the traditionally minded Turkish-Muslim population, for which he blamed foremost the bigotry of the men of religion (*ulema;* Ar., *ʿulamāʾ*).

Populism did not imply democracy in either its liberal or socialist sense, but rather a solidaristic opposition to status privileges and monarchy inspired by the French Revolution of 1789. Nationalism circumscribed Kemalist populism; its reference to the Rousseauist concept of general will evaded the head-counting requirement of democracy. Atatürk himself was to be the embodiment of the national will; hence whatever he decreed—as he was careful to adhere to formalism, this was always an act of legislation or a cabinet decision—was regarded as in accordance with the people's wishes (or rather, what they should wish).

The principle of laicism, and in particular the manner of its application, diminished the enormous popular prestige Atatürk had acquired as a victorious general in the war of independence. In fact, in wartime Islamic solidarity had been stressed to an unprecedented degree, also helping to secure the collaboration of non-Turkish Muslim elements. Therefore, steps taken toward full secularization (abolition of the caliphate, removal of the article in the constitution making Islam the official religion of the state, and almost all the modernizing reforms that departed from Islamic practice) created far-reaching repercussions. The failure to replace religious social bonds with a generally accepted civic ideology led to cleavage between the ruling westernized elite and the ruled traditional masses. Although the official formulation was content to separate the worldly from the divine and to oppose the exploitation of religion for political purposes, in reality Kemalist laicism became an instrument for control and supervision of Islam by the state.

Atatürk was not an outright atheist but a deist who believed in a rational theology, denying the absolute truth of revealed religions. For tactical reasons, at the beginning of his political career he recognized Islam as the latest and most perfect of all religions; this declaration, however, equated Islam with the natural religion he fancied.

Kemalism (or Atatürkism, in more recent terminology) arose after his death as an indirect criticism of his successor. It was used by the CHP to oppose the Demokrat Parti's concessions to believers, for example, lifting the ban on calls to prayer in Arabic. In all three military coups that marred democratic development in Turkey from 1960 on, Atatürkism was used as a pretext.

All Turkish political parties in the aftermath of 1960 paid lip service to Kemalism/Atatürkism, defining it, however, according to their own tastes. The junta of 1980 hailed it as the sole true path, obligatory for everyone. The constitution of 1982, still in effect in 1993, refers in its preamble to nationalism, the conception of the "immortal leader and unequalled hero, the founder of the republic," and to his guiding principles.

[See also Cumhuriyet Halk Partisi; Turkey; *and the biography of Atatürk.*]

BIBLIOGRAPHY

Though there is an immense literature on Kemalism, Western authors in general assume a paternalistic (good-enough-for-the-East) attitude of appraisal. Most of the indigenous books on Mustafa Kemal Atatürk are sheer hagiography; there is, however, a novel current in Turkey evaluating his ideology more critically. See, for instance, Levent Köker, *Modernleşme, Kemalizm ve Demokrasi* (Istanbul, 1990), and Taha Parla, *The Social and Political Thought of Ziya Gökalp* (Leiden, 1985). The latter author has also begun a series of books aimed at a critical rereading of the "Official Sources of Political Culture in Turkey."

METE TUNÇAY

KHALAFALLĀH, MUḤAMMAD AḤMAD (b. 1916), contemporary Islamic modernist thinker. Born in Sharqīyah Province in Lower Egypt, he attended traditional Islamic schools, a government school, and then Dār al-ʿUlūm, followed by the Faculty of Arts at the Egyptian (later Cairo) University, from which he graduated in 1939. He completed his M.A. in 1942 with a thesis on "Al-jadal fī al-Qurʾān" (Polemic in the Qurʾān), later published as *Muḥammad wa-al-quwā al-muḍāddah* (Muḥammad and the Forces of Opposition), and then joined the university faculty as a tutor. In 1947 he presented a doctoral dissertation on the Qurʾān to the Faculty of Arts which stirred up considerable controversy and was not sustained, so he resigned from his university position in 1948. This dissertation was published after revision in 1951 under the title *Al-fann al-qiṣaṣī fī al-Qurʾān al-karīm* (The Art of Narrative in the Qurʾān) and has been reprinted several times since. He gained his doctorate in 1954 with a thesis on Abū al-Faraj al-Iṣbahānī. He worked for many years in the Ministry of Culture, becoming undersecretary for planning in this ministry. Since retirement he has been active in the Egyptian Committee for Asian-African Solidarity and has been vice president of the National Progressive Unionist (Tajammuᶜ) party. He is chief editor of the magazine *Al-yaqẓah al-ᶜArabīyah* (Arab Awakening), has written many articles on the Qur'ān and Islam for popular periodicals, such as *Rūz al-yusūf,* and has written a large number of books, including works on modern reformers such as ᶜAbd Allāh Nadīm and ᶜAbd al-Raḥman al-Kawākibī and works on Islamic topics, such as *Al-Qur'ān wa-mushkilāt ḥayātinā al-muᶜāsirah* (The Qur'ān and Our Contemporary Problems), *Al-Qur'ān wa-al-dawlah* (The Qur'ān and the State), and *Al-Islām wa-al-ᶜurūbah* (Islam and Arabism).

Khalafallāh's doctoral dissertation on Qur'ānic narrative caused controversy, because he argued that the Qur'ānic narratives concerning previous prophets and other past events do not aim at providing precise historical information but are literary and artistic stories designed to sway the hearts of their hearers. Hence, one is free to reject the accounts as strict history, if led to do so on rational grounds. Although the work was published, it has been the subject of rebuttals. Khalafallāh's experience, reminiscent of that of Ṭāhā Ḥusayn (1889–1971) earlier, shows the limits of tolerance on this sensitive issue.

In his writings on political and social matters, Khalafallāh calls for a very broad interpretation of the Qur'ān and argues that Arab socialism is consistent with Islam. Fixed prohibitions and commands can be established only by a very clear text of the Qur'ān, and in social matters *maṣlaḥah* (the welfare of Muslims) generally takes precedence over *naṣṣ* (text). He has been prominent among those opposed to the kind of link between religion and state demanded by the Muslim Brotherhood. In his writings he has sought to show a continuity between his thinking and that of earlier modernists, such as Muḥammad ᶜAbduh, as well as more classical writers.

BIBLIOGRAPHY

Haddad, Yvonne Y. *Contemporary Islam and the Challenge of History.* Albany, N.Y., 1982. Chapter 4 provides a brief but good treatment of Khalafallāh's views on the Qur'ānic narratives and the controversy surrounding them. Jomier and Wielandt (below) provide longer treatments.

Jomier, Jacques. "Quelques positions actuelles de l'exégèse coranique en Egypte révélées par une polémique récente, 1947–1951." *Mélanges de l'Institut Dominicain d'Études Orientales du Caire* 1 (1954): 39–72.

Khalafallāh, Muḥammad Aḥmad. "The Constitution for the Return to Islamic Legislation." In *Islamic Law and Change in Arab Society,* pp. 79–81. CEMAM Reports, vol. 4. Beirut, 1978.

Wielandt, Rotraud. *Offenbarung und Geschichte im Denken moderner Muslime.* Wiesbaden, 1971. See chapter 6.

WILLIAM E. SHEPARD

KHĀLID, KHĀLID MUḤAMMAD (b. 1920), Egyptian writer and essayist. Born in Sharqiyyah Province, he graduated from al-Azhar in 1947 with an ᶜĀlimīyah degree from the Faculty of Sharīᶜah and then gained a teaching certificate, also from al-Azhar. He worked as an Arabic language teacher and then in the Cultural Bureau (Idārat al-Thaqāfah) of the Ministry of Education and with the Writers' Committee (Hay'at al-Kuttāb) connected to the Ministry of Culture. He later became a supervisor in the Department for the Publication of the Heritage (Al-Ishrāf ᶜala Idārat Taḥqīq al-Turāth). He has written more than thirty books, as well as political and religious articles in newspapers and magazines, such as *Al-sharq al-awsaṭ* (London), *Al-muslimūn, Al-muṣawwar, Al-ahrām,* and *Al-wafd.*

His first book, *Min hunā nabda'* (From Here We Begin, 1950), was confiscated because of objections from al-Azhar and then released by order of the Cairo district court. In this book he mounted a forceful attack on "priesthood," clearly having al-Azhar or at least its conservative elements in view, and called for separation of religion and state, using arguments reminiscent of those made in the 1920s by ᶜAlī ᶜAbd al-Rāziq. He also called for a moderate and democratic socialism, effective birth control, and furtherance of the rights of women. He expressed similar views in other passionately written books in the 1950s and early 1960s, such as *Muwāṭinūn . . . la raᶜāyā* (Citizens . . . not Subjects, c. 1951), which was also confiscated for a time, *Maᶜan, ᶜalā al-ṭarīq . . . Muḥammad wa-al-Masīḥ* (Together on the Road—Muḥammad and Christ, 1958), in which he presented both prophets as standing for the same values of humanity, life, love, and peace, *Al-dīmugrāṭīyah abadan* (Democracy Forever, 1953), and many others. Some of the suggestions in these books were enacted into law by the post-1952 government, although he did not favor Nasser's one-party system.

Beginning in the early 1960s, Khālid turned his attention to more specifically Islamic topics, including several books on Muḥammad and other early Islamic heroes. In *Al-dawlah fī al-Islām* (The State in Islam, 1981), he revised the secularist position of his first book, describing it as "exaggerated," and he argued that, although Islam does not prescribe the sort of "religious government" attacked there, it does have a civil as well as a religious mission and does call for the state to apply Islamic principles. He maintained that an Islamic state aims at liberty and opposes despotism and that the divine command of *shūrā* (consultation) today takes the form of parliamentary democracy.

In the development of his thinking, Khālid Muḥammad Khālid appears to illustrate the shift of much Egyptian and Muslim thinking over the same time period, from the strong emphasis on social justice and reform, or even revolution, of the 1950s to the greater concern for Islamic authenticity in the 1980s. He has come closer to the position of his friend, Muḥammad al-Ghazālī (b. 1917). who criticized his first work from an Islamic point of view.

BIBLIOGRAPHY

Abdel-Malek, Anouar, ed. *Contemporary Arab Political Thought*. Translated by Michael Pallis. London, 1983. Includes translation of a few passages of Khālid Muḥammad Khālid's work. See pages 116–119.

Branca, Paolo. "Riformismo e identità islamica nel pensiero di Khalid Muhammad Khalid." *Islàm: Storia e Civiltà* 5 (1986): 85–95. Useful recent account.

Cragg, Kenneth. *Counsels in Contemporary Islam*. Edinburgh, 1965. See pages 100–102.

Ghazālī, Muḥammad al-. *Our Beginning in Wisdom (Min hunā naʿlam)*. Translated by Ismāʿīl R. al-Fārūqī. Washington, D.C., 1951; reprint, New York, 1975. Written as a rebuttal to *From Here We Start* by a friend of Khālid Muḥammad Khālid.

Khālid, Khālid Muḥammad. *From Here We Start (Min hunā nabdaʾ)*. 3d ed. Translated by Ismāʿīl R. al-Fārūqī. Washington, D.C., 1953. Translation of Khālid Muḥammad Khālid's first book. Includes an account of the efforts to ban it and the court decision favoring it.

Tafāhum, ʿAbd al-. "A Cairo Debate on Islam and Some Christian Implications." *Muslim World* 44 (1954): 236–252. Discusses Khālid Muḥammad Khālid along with Muḥammad al-Ghazālī and Sayyid Quṭb.

WILLIAM E. SHEPARD

KHALWATĪYAH. This Ṣūfī *ṭarīqah* derives its name from *khalwah*, periodic retreat, which is an important feature in most branches of the Khalwatīyah. It is significant that the order derives its name from an institution rather than from an eponym, because the *ṭarīqah* does not trace its origin to one founder. Originating in Central Asia, the Khalwatīyah entered the Ottoman Empire in the fifteenth century. Within a century it had become the most widespread Ṣūfī order in the empire, although it experienced periods of stagnation, regression, and revival.

As a *sharīʿah*-oriented *ṭarīqah*, the Khalwatīyah stressed the combination of knowledge (*ʿilm*) and practice (*ʿamal*). It also required the tying of the heart (*rabṭ al-qalb*) of a disciple (*murīd*) to that of his master (*shaykh* or *pīr*) so that the relationship between the two should be stronger than that between a father and his son. Other features, in addition to the *khalwah* are silence (*ṣamt*), vigil (*saḥar*), participation in the *dhikr* (the chanting of God's names), and the communal recital of *wird al-sattār*, composed by Yaḥyā al-Shirwānī in the fifteenth century, which is the center of the Khalwatī ritual.

The revival of the Khalwatīyah was initiated by Muṣṭafā ibn Kamāl al-Dīn al-Bakrī (1688–1748), a native of Syria who lived most of his life in Jerusalem. But it was in Egypt that the Khalwatīyah experienced a radical change through al-Bakrī's disciple Muḥammad ibn Sālim al-Ḥifnī (1689–1768). In the middle of the eighteenth century the Khalwatīyah rose from a marginal group to become the dominant order in Egypt. In the words of al-Jabartī, it was "the best of the Ṣūfī orders (*khayr al-ṭuruq*)." For eighty years (1757–1838) all but one of those who held the office of shaykh of al-Azhar were Khalwatīs.

Three elements in al-Bakrī's teaching probably contributed to the resurgence of the Khalwatīyah: the demand for an exclusive affiliation to the *ṭarīqah*, and stricter discipline in the performance of the litanies; a larger scope for the participation of common people in the rituals of the *ṭarīqah;* and adherence to the *sharīʿah*. Inspired by al-Bakrī, al-Ḥifnī made the Khalwatīyah in Egypt into a cohesive, *sharīʿah*-oriented order that accommodated leading scholars but also reached out to the common people.

Scholars from the Maghrib, mainly pilgrims on their way to Mecca, visited Cairo in the eighteenth century in growing numbers, where they were deeply influenced by al-Ḥifnī and by the Khalwatī shaykhs who succeeded him, like Maḥmūd al-Kurdī (1715–1780) and Aḥmad al-Dardīr (1715–1786). Subsequently two new orders developed in the Maghrib as offshoots of the Khalwatīyah. Muḥammad ibn ʿAbd al-Raḥmān al-Azharī (1713–1793), who had been initiated to the Khalwatīyah by al-Ḥifnī, spread the Khalwatīyah in Algeria, where the new branch became known after him as the Raḥmānīyah. It was al-Azharī who initiated Sīdī Aḥmad al-Tijānī to the Khalwatīyah. Al-Tijānī learned additional secrets from Maḥmūd al-Kurdī in Cairo and from Muḥammad ibn ʿAbd al-Karīm al-Sammān in Medina. The latter had been initiated by Muṣṭafā al-Bakrī during one of his pilgrimages. [*See* Tijānīyah.]

Two of al-Sammān's disciples spread a *ṭarīqah* called al-Sammānīyah to Sumatra and to the Sudan. One was ʿAbd al-Ṣamad al-Palimbānī (c.1703–1788), who spent most of his working life in Arabia and initiated students from Sumatra into the Sammānīyah. The Sammānīyah was introduced into the Sudan by Aḥmad al-Tayyib ibn al-Bashīr (d. 1823), who had been initiated by al-Sammān in Medina. The Sammānīyah, organized on a wider geographical and societal scale with a central hierarchical authority, expanded in the Sudan at the expense of the two older *ṭarīqahs*, the Qādirīyah and the Shādhilīyah, which had been adapted to the local parochial pattern of holy families. [*See* Qādirīyah; Shādhilīyah.]

In the nineteenth century these three extensions of the Khalwatīyah gave rise to militant movements in different parts of Africa. The Rahmāniyah led the revolt against the French in Algeria in 1871; al-Ḥājj ʿUmar al-Fūtī initiated a *jihād* of the Tijānīyah in West Africa; and the Mahdī of the Sudan, Muḥammad Aḥmad, had been a member of the Sammāniyah for ten years (1861–1871).

In Egypt the activities of the Khalwatīyah, together with other Ṣūfī orders, were regulated and brought under close government supervision by a decree of Muḥammad ʿAlī in 1812. Almost a century and a half later, another authoritarian government, that of Gamal Abdel Nasser, further reduced the influence and economic resources of the Ṣūfī orders. In a list of Ṣūfī orders in Egypt prepared in 1964, ten branches of the Khalwatīyah were recorded, although most of them were inactive. In 1988 Gideon Weigert visited the *zawāyā* of two branches of the Khalwatīyah in Cairo, the Demīrdāshīyah and the Shabrāwīyah, which were physically in a state of neglect and ruin, and spiritually without a shaykh.

In Turkey, the Ṣūfī orders were declared illegal in 1925 as a part of the Kemalist reform programs. However, the orders continued in clandestine form and began to reemerge in public life by the late 1950s. The Khalwatīyah was a part of this process but did not assume a highly visible role in the Islamic resurgence of the late twentieth century. In the Balkans, some Khalwatīyah centers continued to be active, especially in Albania, where the order survived in the official atheism of the Communist era.

BIBLIOGRAPHY

Bannert, E. "La Khalwatiyya en Egypte, quelques aspects de la vie d'une confrérie." *MIDEO* 8 (1964–1966): 1–74.

Jong, F. de. *Ṭuruq and Ṭuruq-Linked Institutions in Nineteenth-Century Egypt*. Leiden, 1978.

Kissling, Hans Joachim. "Aus der Geschichte des Chalwetijje Ordens." *Zeitschrift der Deutschen Morgenländische Gesellschaft* 102 (1953): 233–289.

Martin, B. G. "A Short History of the Khalwati Order of Dervishes." In *Scholars, Saints, and Sufis*, edited by Nikki R. Keddie, pp. 275–305. Berkeley, 1972.

Weigert, Gideon. "The Khalwatiya in Egypt in the Eighteenth Century: A Nucleus for Islamic Revival." *Bulletin of the Israel Academic Centre, Cairo* 19 (1994).

NEHEMIA LEVTZION and GIDEON WEIGERT

KHAN. As a title, khan has traditionally designated leaders of tribally organized nomads from Central Asia to Northern India, Iran, Anatolia/Turkey, and Southern Russia. The title became widely spread following Chinggis Khan's Mongol unification in the thirteenth century. *Khān* was not used in the Arabic-speaking world, except in the Persian Gulf region. It is commonly found in Il-khānid and post-Il-khānid sources in Persian, where its plural form is *khavānīn*, an Arabic broken-plural pattern, rather than *khānān*, which would be in accordance with most Persian human plurals. In colloquial Persian, however, khan with the suffix *-hā* is heard.

The etymology of khan (leader) is obscure and probably Turkic; however, there is also the possibility of an etymological link with Korean and ultimately with Chinese (or possibly proto-Mongolian and then Chinese), but a link with Persian is generally rejected. Khan, among the Avars in the context of the Byzantine Empire, like that of Mongol usage, is linked with the titles *khāqān* (Persian); *hākān* (Turkish); and *qaɣan* or *khaghan* (Mongolian), which are used to designate a holder of an office higher than khan, such as a great khan or emperor. In addition, *khāqān* was used in Arabic as early as the seventh century to designate a rank such as emperor. The thirteenth-century *Secret History of the Mongols* makes the distinction between rulers of nomadic confederations *(khans)* and the emperor of China *(khāqān)*. Ögedei (r. 1229–1241), son and successor to Chinggis Khan (d. 1227), was first titled khan and then *khāqān* (great khan or emperor), which became the form for successors in the Chinggisid lineage. Furthermore, the Mongols called Beijing "Khānbalīq"—Turkish for "City of the Khan"—after they moved there from Karakorum. Khan consequently signifies a title, an office, a form of address, membership in the ruling

Mongol lineage and Mongol successor states and thus an attribute of rulership.

Similar usage of khan, and even *khāqān* in terms of universal lordship, was followed by the Ottomans and the Ṣafavids, Afshārs, and Qājārs of Iran and by nomads tribally organized in Central Asia and Iran, even Persian-speaking ones, such as the Bakhtiyārī. Khan followed the Ottoman sultan's name in his *tughrā* (imperial monogram) on official documents, and Ottoman sultans often styled themselves as "khāqān al-barrayn wa-al-baḥrayn" ("ruler of the two lands and the two seas"). For rulers in all of these dynasties, the use of *khan* identified them with a tribally organized nomadic past and the Mongol tradition of rule and constituted an element in their legitimacy.

Khan was also used as an administrative title and then as an honorific and form of address. In Ṣafavid Iran, khan designated a governor of lesser rank than the *beylerbeyī* (governor-general) but higher than sultan, and in Mughal India its use was limited to nobles and courtiers. In eighteenth-century Iran, khan was a rank that could be bestowed by the shah on administrators and military and tribal leaders. In the case of Karīm Khān Zand (r. 1758–1779), founder of the Zand dynasty who never assumed the title of shah, khan even stood in place of shah. In the Bakhtiyārī confederation, khan gradually displaced the Turkish term *āqā* (elder, leader) as a general male honorific in the nineteenth century, and its use was no longer restricted to the ruling Bakhtiyārī lineage. Ḥusayn Qulī Khān (d. 1882), the first Bakhtiyārī Il-khānī, or confederation leader, appropriated *khāqān* as his title in a stone-carved inscription (c.1880).

In the twentieth century, *khan* as an honorific and form of address fell from general use except for tribal leaders, and after the Iranian Revolution of 1979 and the formation of the Islamic Republic of Iran, its use even in the tribal context, with the implications of hierarchy and subordination, was discouraged. In Pakistan, however, khan has survived as a surname. Khan continues today as part of the title for the Ismāʿīlī spiritual leader, the Aga Khan, not unlike *khāqān*, universal lordship, in meaning.

[*See also* Aga Khan.]

BIBLIOGRAPHY

Cleaves, Francis Woodman, trans. *The Secret History of the Mongols.* Cambridge, Mass., 1982–.

Garthwaite, Gene R. *Khans and Shahs.* Cambridge, 1983.

Krader, Lawrence. "Qan-Qaγan and the Beginnings of Mongol Kingship." *Central Asiatic Journal* 1 (1955): 17–35.

Sinor, Denis. "Qapqan." *Journal of the Royal Asiatic Society* (1954): 174–184.

GENE R. GARTHWAITE

KHĀNQĀH. The institution of a residential teaching center for Ṣūfīs seems to have emerged in Iran with the formalization of Ṣūfī activity in the late tenth or eleventh century. Support for these religious institutions by the ruling elites gradually broadened and led to significant patronage in building *khānqāh*s and endowing stipends for the Ṣūfīs living there. *Khānqāh*s developed ritual functions in later periods, serving as centers for devotions such as listening to poetry or music and the performance of the *dhikr* and *samāʿ* ceremonies of specific Ṣūfī orders. Some Ṣūfī leaders were buried in their *khānqāh*s, thus making them into popular pilgrimage sites. The residential function of the *khānqāh* does not seem to be essential, and the name indicates the function performed by a space rather than any inherent physical structure, since the same buildings could shift their usage, for example by becoming schools.

The term is of Persian origin and probably derives from words meaning "a place of residence" *(khāna-gāh)* for Ṣūfīs, although many other etymologies have been suggested (Mīrā, 1990, pp. 55–64). Some scholars see a precedent for the *khānqāh* in Buddhist and Manichean activities in Iran. This institution has numerous regional manifestations and has undergone a number of transformations in the premodern and modern periods, primarily owing to the changing nature of institutional Sufism and its role in society.

Several other terms have a similar connotation. *Zāwiyah,* based on Arabic *zawā,* "to bring together, gather, contract, conceal," also conveys the idea of withdrawing into a corner, or going into seclusion (Behrens-Abouseif, 1985, p. 116). *Ribāṭ* is an Arabic term that originally indicated a fortress or outpost for the defense of the faith, associated in Ṣūfī contexts with centers for Ṣūfī striving *(jihād)* against the lower self *(nafs).* While some sources used the above three terms as equivalents, Fernandes (1988, p. 18) argues on the basis of Mamlūk endowment documents *(waqfīyah*s) that each had a distinct function. In Mamlūk Egypt *ribāṭ*s served as refuges for Ṣūfīs as well as for the needy and homeless of both sexes. *Tekke* (Turkish) or *takīyah* (Arabic and Persian) is the term used for the Ṣūfī institution of the dervish lodge in Turkey and other parts of the Ottoman Empire. It is said to be derived from the Arabic root *w-k-'*, which conveys the idea of a chamber in which one rests while being fed.

South Asia. In the predominantly South Asian Chishtī order an institution for Ṣūfī activity was called *jamāʿat khāna* and was centered on the residence of the *shaykh*. Sections of these Ṣūfī complexes were named according to their particular functions—*samāʿ maḥall* (room for audition) or *langar khāna* (room for the preparation and distribution of food). Today they function predominantly as shrines to deceased saints where pilgrims can receive blessings or cures and make vows.

In contemporary Pakistan the function of providing instruction to novices through contact with a living master and association with other spiritual aspirants has faded, and the buildings are in many cases converted to residential schools offering a standard *madrasah* curriculum. The students are young and seem to be there primarily for charity-based education rather than for individual spiritual guidance. One may speculate that this has to do with the decreasing charisma of the Ṣūfī teachers and the social pressures for young people to pursue education that is somewhat more economically productive than being a full-time disciple.

Turkey. An article by Klaus Kreiser suggests that classical Ṣūfī *tekke*s in Turkey were generic, with no particular *ṭarīqah* affiliation. *Tekke*s often converted their function back and forth to being *madrasah*s, relocated, or switched *ṭarīqah* affiliation depending on the fortunes of the associated *shaykh* (1992, p. 51). Kreiser found that in 1870 in Istanbul there were 1,826 registered *tekke* residents drawn from various orders, the majority being Naqshbandīs. Many of the centers were very small (three or fewer permanent residents) (p. 52). However, the fact that few persons actually might have lived permanently in a *khānqāh* does not imply that the *shaykh* had only a small following: hundreds of disciples might attend Friday prayers or devotional practices at the center. Although the Turkish republic closed the *tekke*s in 1925, Ṣūfī activities continued in less public ways and are currently undergoing some revival in Turkey.

Egypt. In Cairo "the spread of Sufism during the fourteenth century and its integration into popular religious life led to a gradual abandonment of the *khānqāh*'s role as a place for seclusion and retreat. At the same time, mosques and madrasah(s) were opening their doors to Ṣūfī practices" (Behrens-Abouseif, 1985, p. 81). In the Egyptian context *zāwiyah*s as opposed to *khānqāh*s were characterized as being more open and associated with the popularization of Sufism rather than its elite-supported, formally organized and sanctioned forms. *Khānqāh*s in Cairo were often linked with non-Egyptian Ṣūfīs who took up residence there and received official patronage. *Zāwiyah*s seem generally to have been built at the bequest of particular patrons, and some became *waqf*s on the death of the patron. From the thirteenth to the fifteenth century in Egypt the term *zāwiyah* referred to a structure built for the *shaykh* of a particular order to serve as a residence for him and a meetingplace for his disciples. When the *shaykh* was buried there after his death, the *zāwiyah* would become a shrine. After this period in Egypt institutional Sufism and the *khānqāh* declined; but since popular Sufism flourished, the functions and architectural importance of the *zāwiyah* increased.

In the late Mamlūk period the separate designation *khānqāh* disappeared as part of a general decline in institutionalized Sufism. The designation *zāwiyah* grew in importance, and buildings called *zāwiyah*s, *tekkiyya*s and *ribāṭ*s were built by patrons in Ottoman Cairo.

Today in popular Egyptian Sufism, the ritual or performative aspects of Ṣūfī devotions are often performed in mosques. *Zāwiyah*s may be founded by individual *shaykh*s and persist in functioning as hospitality centers for those who travel the circuit of shrine celebrations (*mawlids*). [*See* Mawlid.]

North and East Africa. In regions of Africa as diverse as Libya, the Sudan, and Somalia, *khānqāh*-like institutions called *zāwiyah*s or *jamāʿat* emerged in the nineteenth century. R. S. O'Fahey (1990) suggests that these Ṣūfī communities established in Africa were a novelty for this part of the Islamic world, arising out of the contemporary movement of reformist Sufism. Noteworthy in this context were the effects of these Ṣūfī institutions in forging loyalties that tended to transcend tribal and social boundaries. For example, in southern Somali society *jamāʿat*s are bases for Ṣūfī mediators (*wadaad*s) of local clan rivalries. The *wadaad*s usually gather around charismatic *shaykh*s in this region and form self-sufficient agricultural enclaves. In Libya, Sanūsī *zāwiyah*s were an effective form of organization in resisting European encroachment.

Iran. The role of Sufism and Ṣūfī shrine complexes increased in prominence in fourteenth-century Mongol Iran. At this time Ṣūfī ritual became institutionalized, and relations of Ṣūfīs with the political authorities were important. This link between the state and Sufism can explain some of the vicissitudes of the Ṣūfī orders and their institutions in the Ṣafavid and Qājār periods. The Qājār period basically saw an increase in the establishment of Niʿmatullāhī *khānqāh*s when this order was patronized by the state as a balance to the power of the *ʿulamāʾ*. During recent decades some Persian orders, in particular the Niʿmatullāhī, have established *khānqāhs* in a number of cities in America, Europe, and other parts of the world.

[*See also* Niʿmatullāhīyah; Sufism; Zāwiyah.]

BIBLIOGRAPHY

Behrens-Abouseif, Doris. "Change in Function and Form of Mamluk Religious Institutions." *Annales Islamologiques* 21 (1985): 73–93. An art historian's perspective.

Ernst, Carl W. *Eternal Garden: Mysticism, History, and Politics at a South Asian Sufi Center*. Albany, N.Y., 1992.

Fernandes, Leonor E. "The Zāwiya in Cairo." *Annales Islamologiques* 18 (1982): 116–121, plus illustrations.

Fernandes, Leonor E. *The Evolution of a Sufi Institution in Mamluk Egypt: The Khanqah*. Berlin, 1988.

Kiyānī, Muḥsin. *Tārīkh-i Khānqāh dar Īrān*. Tehran, 1369/1990. Primarily a textual study of the Khānqāh during the classical period of Iranian Sufism.

Kreiser, Klaus. "The Dervish Living." In *The Dervish Lodge: Architecture, Art, and Sufism in Ottoman Turkey*, edited by Raymond Lifchez, pp. 49–56. Berkeley, 1992.

Lifchez, Raymond, ed. *The Dervish Lodge: Architecture, Art, and Sufism in Ottoman Turkey*. Berkeley, 1992. Important collection of articles.

O'Fahey, R. S. *Enigmatic Saint: Ahmad ibn Idris and the Idrisi Tradition*. Evanston, Ill., 1990. Considers African developments in the nineteenth century.

Popovic, Alexandre, and Gilles Veinstein, eds. *Les ordres mystiques dans l'Islam*. Paris, 1986. Offers a number of up-to-date articles on regional and contemporary manifestations of Sufism.

Marcia K. Hermansen

KHARĀJ.

KHARĀJ. A tax system designed for agrarian land owned by non-Muslims, *kharāj* is distinct from the tax system for agrarian land owned by Muslims. The Islamic state is allowed to charge *kharāj* (which is actually a rental) even for uncultivated land. In Islamic fiscal administration, the meaning of the word *kharāj*, if used without qualification, is land tax; it is imposed on landed properties owned by the conquered people, who were left on them in return for an annual tax. The *kharāj* was first introduced after the Battle of Khaibar when the Prophet allowed the Jews of Khaibar to return to their lands on condition that they paid half of their produce as *kharāj*. Although the only taxes recognized by the Qur'ān are *zakāt* (alms) and *jizyah* (the first of which is imposed on Muslims and the second on non-Muslims), the legislation of *kharāj* is based on the legal principle of discretionary interests (*al maṣāliḥ al mursalah*), which falls within the framework of the *uṣūl al-fiqh* (four foundations of Islamic jurisprudence), and it is generally agreed that Muslims have an unconditional right to *kharāj*. In this regard, the Ḥanbalī jurists Ibn ʿAqīl and Ibn Taymīyah state that the *kharāj* should be understood as a specific act (*sui generis*) and akin to a contract, based on the consideration of the general interests of the people and their faith.

Since *kharāj* is imposed on land that had remained in the possession of its original owners, who were initially non-Muslims, *kharāj* was sometimes called "*jizyah* on land" and likewise *jizyah* (poll tax) was sometimes called "*kharāj* on heads." Legally, the *kharāj* is a cost paid to the government for protection and safety of the land. The *kharāj* parallels the *ʿushr* (tithe), which is a similar tax taken from a Muslim and constitutes the *zakāt* on crops. The *kharāj* land is defined either as land conquered by Muslims, or land that was abandoned by inhabitants who fled, or land whose inhabitants undertook to pay a tribute to Muslims and retain ownership of the land. The lands of the regions that fall under the category of *kharāj* land are arable lands, pasture and hunting grounds, and plantations. Houses and places of business were regarded by most jurists as being exempt from *kharāj*. Payment for *kharāj* is assessed in several ways, including on the basis of acreage, percentage of the actual harvest, amount of the crop, and a fixed amount irrespective of any factors. It is commonly agreed that one full year should pass after the time of collection before the *kharāj* can be taken again. *Kharāj* belongs to the community as a whole and not to a particular group and should be expended according to the prevailing view on the common interests of the Muslim community.

[*See also* Jizyah; Land Tenure; Property; Taxation; Zakāt.]

BIBLIOGRAPHY

Abū Yūsuf. *Kitāb al-kharāj*. Cairo, 1352/1933.

Ṭabāṭabāʾī, Ḥusayn Mudarrisī. *Kharāj in Islamic Law*. London, 1983.

Yaḥyā ibn Ādam. *Kitāb al-kharāj*. Translated by Aharon Ben Shemesh. Leiden, 1967.

Abdul Rahman I. Doi

KHĀRIJITES. *See* Khawārij.

KHATMĪYAH. The Ṣūfī order *(tarīqah)* known as the Khatmīyah was introduced into the Sudan in 1817 by its founder Muḥammad ʿUthmān al-Mīrghānī. The founder's family, the Mirghanī, is thought to have come to Mecca from Central Asia and claimed descent from the prophet Muḥammad. The founder was educated in Mecca as a pupil of the reformist teacher Aḥmad ibn Idrīs al-Fāsī (1760–1837) and was initiated into the Qādirīyah, Shādhilīyah, Naqshbandīyah, Junaydīyah, and Mīrghānīyah Ṣūfī orders. He asserted that the Khatmīyah was the "seal" *(khatm)* of all Ṣūfī orders, whose secret *(sirr)* became the prerogative of the Mirghanī family. Al-Ḥasan (1819–1869), the founder's son, whose mother was Sudanese, was responsible for the spread of the order in the Sudan and for the founding of the Khatmīyah town in Kasala province, which became an important seat of the order. The Khatmīyah spread its influence among the river communities of northern Sudan and the nomadic and settled peoples of eastern Sudan. Some followers are also found in Eritrea, Egypt, and western Sudan.

The Khatmīyah prescribes devotion and quiet contemplation of *al-nūr al-Muḥammadīyah* (the light of the prophet Muḥammad), as well as the performance of a twice-weekly ritual in which the *mawlid,* the poetic biography of the prophet Muḥammad written by Muḥammad ʿUthmān, is recited. The *mawlid* is performed on various secular and religious occasions to give spiritual rejuvenation and reaffirm belief. Recitation of litanies *(awrād)* written by the founder and some of his descendants is also recommended. The Khatmīyah Youth organization brings young men into the order, but its influence has declined with the spread of secular education. Urban dwellers maintain affiliation, and educated members are especially active politically. Allegiance to the Khatmīyah cuts across tribal and geographic boundaries, bringing together its followers through a loosely organized religio-political structure.

Under Turco-Egyptian rule (1820/21–1885) the Khatmīyah assumed the role of intermediary between its followers and the authorities. During the establishment of the Mahdist state (1885–1898), the Khatmīyah refused to join the Mahdists, and the order's head went to Egypt. With the collapse of the Mahdist state in 1898, the Khatmīyah regained its prominence during the Anglo-Egyptian condominium (1898–1956). Its religious status remained unchanged, and it joined other political forces—including those of its rival, the Mahdīyah (commonly known as the Anṣār)—in the years before Sudan's independence. Recognizing the cultural and religious diversity of Sudan, it saw the necessity for such political dialogue.

ʿAlī al-Mīrghānī (1878–1968), the great-grandson of the founder, played an important role in the nationalist movement for independence. Under his leadership the Khatmīyah's political wing, the People's Democratic Party, was formed in 1958; he later agreed to its merger in 1967 with the National Unionist Party, and the combined forces came to be known as the Democratic Unionist Party. ʿAlī's son Muḥammad ʿUthmān (b. 1936), the head of the order in the early 1990s, took a more direct political role, and his brother Aḥmad (b. 1941) accepted the chairmanship of the Council of State in 1986. This overt political activity aroused some criticism.

Since independence the Khatmīyah has played an important role in government, either in coalition, sometimes with the Anṣār, or in opposition. Successive military regimes (1958–1964, 1969–1985, and since 1989) have tried to weaken its political influence, but with limited success. The failure of military rule and the one-party system strengthened the position of the Khatmīyah. Muḥammad ʿUthmān was praised for concluding an agreement with the leadership of the Sudan People's Liberation Army in Addis Ababa in 1988 in an attempt to resolve the civil war in southern Sudan; however, this came too late to prevent a military coup in 1989. Criticism and factionalism within the Democratic Unionist Party has emerged within the last two decades, but the Khatmīyah leadership continues its dual political and religious role—a position it assumed during the Turco-Egyptian regime.

[*See also* Anṣār; Mahdīyah; Sudan.]

BIBLIOGRAPHY

Al-Shahi, Ahmed. *Themes from Northern Sudan.* London, 1986. Includes articles on the Khatmīyah in the Sudan from an anthropological perspective.

Trimingham, J. Spencer. *Islam in the Sudan.* 2d impr. London, 1965. Very useful history, particularly of the Ṣūfī orders.

Voll, John O. *A History of the Khatmiyyah Tariqah in the Sudan.* 2 vols. Ann Arbor, 1978. Excellent detailed study of the history and religious background of the Khatmīyah.

Warburg, Gabriel. *Islam, Nationalism, and Communism in a Traditional Society: The Case of the Sudan.* London, 1978. Useful study of sectarian and secular politics in the Sudan.

Willis, C. A. "Religious Confraternities of the Sudan." *Sudan Notes and Records* 4.4 (1921): 175–194. Early enquiry into the history of Ṣūfī orders.

Woodward, Peter. *Sudan, 1898–1989: The Unstable State*. London, 1990. Analysis of politics in the Sudan; includes the role of various religious groups.

AHMED AL-SHAHI

KHAṬṬĀBĪ, MUḤAMMAD IBN ʿABD AL-KARĪM AL-. *See* Abd el-Krim.

KHAWĀRIJ. The third major sectarian grouping in Islam, neither Sunnīs nor Shīʿīs, came into existence as a consequence of "the great *fitnah*" between 656 and 661 CE and became known as the Khawārij ("exiters," plural of Kharījī). When the caliph ʿAlī agreed to submit his quarrel with Muʿāwiyah to arbitration at the battle of Ṣiffīn, a group of his followers, mostly from the tribe of Tamīm, accused him of rejecting the word of the Qur'ān, surah 49.9, "If two parties of the faithful fight each other, then conciliate them. Yet if one is rebellious to the other, then fight the insolent one until it returns to God's command." ʿUthmān, they held, had deserved to die for his faults; ʿAlī was the legitimate caliph; and Muʿāwiyah was a rebellious aggressor who was not entitled to arbitration. By agreeing to it, ʿAlī had committed the grave sin of rejecting God's *ayyahs* ("signs"; verses of the Qur'ān) and had excluded himself from the true community of the faithful. He should, they held, have obeyed the Qur'ān, surah 8.39–40: "Fight them until there is no *fitnah* (temptation), and religion is wholly unto God." God had given his *ḥukm*, or ruling, and there could be no other. *Lā ḥukma illā lillāh* (no ruling but for God), became their watchword.

The dissenters left ʿAlī's camp and gathered at Ḥarūrā' on the Nahrwan Canal, earning the name Ḥarūrīs. They were persuaded by ʿAlī to return to Kufa, but when the attempted arbitration failed, they left the city with many sympathizers. It was at this point that they were labeled *Khawārij*, or exiters. From Nahrwan they agitated and raided ʿAlī's territories. When attempts at conciliation failed, he was forced to fight them on 7 July 658. This bloodshed caused them to swear vengeance, and on a Friday late in January 661 ʿAlī was murdered at the mosque in Kufa by Ibn Muljam al-Murādī, seeking retribution for "the slain of Nahrwan."

From the first, Khawārij insisted that all Muslims must be treated equally, regardless of tribe or race ("there is no *nasab* [inherited honor] in Islam"). "Even a black slave" might be the first in the community. They were always successful in recruiting non-Arabs for their cause, although many early Khawārij came from the bedouins, as well as from South Arabian tribesmen opposed to the hegemony of the northern Arabs and to their ban on agriculture by Arabs. They also took very seriously—at a time when few did—the obligations of Muslims toward *dhimmīs*, or protected non-Muslims.

Basra soon became the intellectual center of the Khawārij, who also had adherents in South Arabia and upper Mesopotamia. Arab armies carried the doctrine to North Africa, where it soon became the dominant form of Islam among the Berbers. The Khawārij are noted for steadfastness and unwillingness to compromise. Heresiographers mention more than twenty sects, each of which tended to elect its own imam and to regard itself as the one true Muslim community.

Khārijism's basic tenets affirmed that a Muslim who commits a major sin *(kabīrah)* is an apostate from Islam and outside the protection of its laws. If the imam sinned or lost his rectitude *(ʿadālah)*, he might be deposed. Non-Khārijī Muslims were deemed either polytheists or infidels, but people of the scriptures who sought Khārijī protection were to be treated generously. The Qur'ān was created, and human beings have free will.

Particularly well-known sects of Khawārij were the Azāriqah, the Ṣufrīyah, and the Ibāḍīyah; the first were probably named after Nāfiʿ ibn al-Azraq, the son of a Greek ex-slave. The Azāriqah excluded from Islam all Muslims who would not make common cause with them, and they practiced *istiʿrāḍ*, the review of the beliefs of their opponents. Those who failed to pass were to be put to death, including women and children, since the children of polytheists were to be damned with their parents. They left the other Khawārij of Basra in 684 to conduct a fearful war in southern Iraq and Iran; in the end, all seem to have found the martyrdom they sought.

The Ṣufrīyah also believed that non-Khārijī Muslims were polytheists, but that it was permissible to dwell in truce with them as long as they did not attack. After failure to establish a firm base in the East during the third *fitnah* at the end of the Umayyad period, they concentrated on North Africa and established an imamate around 770 at Sijilmāsah in southern Morocco, where they were active traders, like other Khawārij.

The Ibāḍīyah, the only sect to survive to modern

times, has held that non-Khārijī Muslims are only infidels, not polytheists. They produced some of the earliest *mutakallimun* (theologians) in Islam and were willing to live peaceably with other Muslims who did not harass them. From their Basra headquarters they sent out teams of teachers to spread their doctrine and, where possible, set up imams in the provinces. Like the Zaydī Shīʿīs and many Muʿtazilīs, with whom they were in close contact, they admitted the possibility of more than one imam at a time, if true believers were widely separated. Under the Rustamī imams of Persian origin who ruled at Tāhart in central Algeria from about 760 to 909, they had a great following among Berber tribes from Tripolitania to Morocco and were recognized as far away as Oman. Ibāḍīs admit four possible positions: manifestation (of the imamate), defense (where a war leader is recognized), *shirā'* or vending (this world for Paradise, in a struggle that must end in martyrdom), and *kitmān* or concealment (when no imam is possible and a council of shaykhs makes religious decisions)—all equally appropriate at their times. At present there is no imam; the time for one will come.

The majority of Muslims and the ruling family in the Sultanate of Oman are Ibāḍīs, and they are also found in the oases of the Mzāb and Wargla in Algeria, on the island of Jerba off Tunisia, in Jabal Nafūsa and Zuwāghah in Libya, and in Zanzibar and some towns of the East African coast. Today they may not number many more than one million. In this period of *kitmān,* Ibāḍīs dislike being called Khawārij; they emphasize their sympathy with other Muslims (with whom they will pray and cooperate socially and politically, though rarely intermarry), and they prefer to be called Sunnīs, never Shīʿīs.

[*See also* Ibāḍīyah.]

BIBLIOGRAPHY

Baghdādī, ʿAbd al-Qāhir al-. *Al-Farq bayna al-Firaq.* Translated by Kate C. Seelye as *Moslem Schisms and Sects* (1920). Reprint, New York, 1966.

Levi della Vida, G. "Khāridjites." In *Encyclopaedia of Islam,* new ed., vol. 4, pp. 1074–1077. Leiden, 1960–.

Lewicki, T. "Ibāḍiyya." In *Encyclopaedia of Islam,* new ed., vol. 3, pp. 648–660. Leiden, 1960–.

Muqaddimat al-Tawḥīd. Muscat, n.d. An extensive Ibāḍī statement of doctrine, with commentaries, dating perhaps to the tenth century CE. This creed has been translated with other Ibāḍī materials in John Alden Williams, *The Word of Islam,* chap. 6 (Austin, 1993), and is still highly regarded by Ibāḍī scholars today.

Rubinacci, R. "Azārika." In *Encyclopaedia of Islam,* new ed., vol. 1, pp. 810–811. Leiden, 1960–.

Shahrastānī. "Kitāb al-Milal wa'l Niḥal (The Khārijites and the Murji'ites)." *Abr-Nahrain* 10 (1970–1971): 49–75. Like Baghdādī, this Sunnī author gives a hostile but useful description.

Vaglieri, L. Veccia. "Ḥarūrā'." In *Encyclopaedia of Islam,* new ed., vol. 3, pp. 235–236. Leiden, 1960–.

JOHN ALDEN WILLIAMS

KHEDIVE. *See* Muhammad ʿAlī Dynasty.

KHILĀFAH. *See* Caliph; Vicegerent.

KHILĀFAT MOVEMENT. An agitation on the part of some Indian Muslims, allied with the Indian nationalist movement, during the years 1919 to 1924, the Khilāfat Movement's purpose was to influence the British government to preserve the spiritual and temporal authority of the Ottoman sultan as caliph of Islam. Integral with this was the Muslims' desire to influence the treaty-making process following World War I in such a way as to restore the prewar boundaries of the Ottoman empire. The British government treated the Indian Khilāfat delegation of 1920, headed by Muḥammad ʿAlī, as quixotic Pan-Islamists, and did not change its policy toward Turkey. The Indian Muslims' attempt to influence the provisions of the Treaty of Sèvres failed; the European powers went ahead with their territorial adjustments, including the institution of mandates over formerly Ottoman Arab territories.

The significance of the Khilāfat movement, however, lies less in its supposed Pan-Islamism and its attempt to influence British imperial policy in the Middle East than in its impact on the Indian nationalist movement. The leaders of the Khilāfat movement forged the first political alliance among Western-educated Indian Muslims and *ʿulamā'* over the issue of the *khilāfah* (caliphate). This leadership included the brothers Muḥammad ʿAlī and Shaukat ʿAlī, who were products of Aligarh College; their spiritual guide Mawlānā ʿAbdulbari of Firangi Mahal in Lucknow; the Calcutta journalist and Islamic scholar Abū al-Kalām Azād; and the leading Deobandī *ʿālim* (scholar) Mawlānā Maḥmūdulḥasan. These publicist-politicians and *ʿulamā'* viewed the European attack on the authority of the caliph as an attack on Islam, and thus as a threat to the religious freedom of Muslims under British rule. [*See also the biography of Azād.*]

The Khilāfat issue crystallized anti-British sentiments

among Indian Muslims that had been increasing since the Tripolitan and Balkan wars of 1911–1912, followed in 1914 by the British declaration of war against the Ottomans. Further, the violence that had followed the British demolition of a portion of a mosque in the Indian city of Kanpur in 1913, and the subsequent agitation that resulted in its restoration, had demonstrated the effectiveness of religious issues in political mobilization. The Khilāfat leaders, most of whom had been imprisoned during the war, were already nationalists. Upon their release in 1919, the religious issue of the Khilāfat provided a means to achieve Pan-Indian Muslim political solidarity in the anti-British cause, as well as a vehicle of communication between the leaders and their potential mass following.

The Khilāfat movement also benefited from Hindu-Muslim cooperation in the nationalist cause that had grown during the war, beginning with the Lucknow Pact of 1916, when the Indian National Congress and the Muslim League agreed on proposals for postwar governmental reforms, and culminating in the protest against the Rowlatt anti-sedition bills in 1919. The Congress, now led by Mohandas K. Gandhi, had called for peaceful demonstrations against the Rowlatt bills, but violence broke out in several places. In the Punjab on 13 April 1919, soldiers fired on a peaceful meeting in Amritsar, killing 379 and injuring many more. The Amritsar massacre, together with the Khilāfat issue, provided the stimulus for the Muslim-Congress alliance in the Noncooperation movement of 1919–1922. Gandhi espoused the Khilāfat cause, seeing in it an opportunity to rally Muslim support for the Congress. The ʿAlī brothers and their allies in turn provided the Noncooperation movement with some of its most enthusiastic troops.

The combined Khilāfat-Noncooperation movement was the first India-wide agitation against British rule. It saw an unprecedented degree of Hindu-Muslim cooperation, and it established Gandhi and his technique of nonviolent protest (*satyāgraha*) at the center of the Indian nationalist movement. Students boycotted schools, lawyers boycotted the courts, voters boycotted elections, and Indians began to spin, weave, and wear homespun cloth as a protest against British economic domination. Mass mobilization using religious symbols was remarkably successful, and the British Indian government was shaken.

In late 1921 the government moved to suppress the movement. The ʿAlī brothers were arrested for incitement to violence, tried in Karachi, and imprisoned. The Noncooperation movement was suspended by Gandhi early in 1922 following a riot in the village of Chauri Chaura in which the local police force was incinerated inside their station by a mob. Gandhi was arrested, tried, and imprisoned soon thereafter. The Turks dealt the final blow by abolishing the Ottoman sultanate in 1922 and the caliphate in 1924.

The aftermath of the Khilāfat movement saw a rising incidence of interreligious violence. The Mappila rebellion of 1921, in which the Muslim peasantry of Malabar rose against their Hindu landlords, increased Hindu-Muslim suspicions, even though the Khilāfat leadership denounced the Mapillas for resorting to violence. During the period 1922–1924, Hindu-Muslim relations further deteriorated, with riots often fomented by communal organizations. Among these organizations were the Hindu Mahāsabha, an exclusively Hindu political party, and Shuddhī and Sangathan, groups dedicated to "purification" and "solidarity" among Hindus. Tanẓīm and Tablīgh, groups devoted to solidarity among Muslims and the propagation of the faith, responded aggressively. Thus the Khilāfat movement, launched amid Hindu-Muslim amity and cooperation, ironically resulted in an aggravation of communal differences. Muslims, aroused to anti-British political activity by the use of religious symbols, found that religious issues separated them from their fellow Indians. The Indian National Congress under Gandhi's leadership found that many of their national symbols were alienating to Muslims. It was a dilemma that ultimately had no solution.

BIBLIOGRAPHY

Bamford, P. C. *Histories of the Non-Cooperation and Khilafat Movements* (1925). Reprint, Delhi, 1974. Government intelligence report issued shortly after the collapse of the movement.

Brown, Judith M. *Gandhi's Rise to Power: Indian Politics, 1919–1922.* Cambridge, 1972. Perceptive study of Gandhi's early career in India.

Hardy, Peter. *The Muslims of British India*. Cambridge, 1972. The best short intellectual history of Muslims in nineteenth- and twentieth-century India.

Hasan, Mushir ul-, ed. *Communal and Pan-Islamic Trends in Colonial India*. Rev. ed. New Delhi, 1985. Useful collection of articles.

Hasan, Mushir ul-. *Nationalism and Communal Politics in India*. Rev. ed. New Delhi, 1991. Balanced study of the relationship between Muslims and the Congress in the period 1916–1929.

Minault, Gail. *The Khilafat Movement: Religious Symbolism and Political Mobilization in India*. New York, 1982. Standard work on the Khilāfat movement.

Nanda, B. R. *Gandhi, Pan-Islamism, Imperialism, and Nationalism in*

India. Delhi, 1989. Study of the Khilāfat movement from the Congress point of view.

Robinson, Francis. *Separatism among Indian Muslims: The Politics of the United Provinces' Muslims, 1860–1923*. Cambridge, 1974. Important study of the early development of Muslim politics in India through the Khilāfat movement, with emphasis on British sources and viewpoints.

GAIL MINAULT

KHIVA KHANATE. The Khanate of Khiva was formed in the early sixteenth century when Ilbars, a chieftain of Uzbek descent, succeeded in uniting a number of the local fiefdoms *(beylik)* on the lower reaches of the Amu Darya, in the territory of ancient Khwarem. By the early seventeenth century the khanate had become an important regional power. During the reigns of Abū al-Ghāzī (1643–1663) and Muḥammad Anūshah (1663–1674) it continued to extend its sway westward toward the Caspian, northward to the river Emba, southward into Khorasan, and eastward into Bukharan lands.

Inevitably this brought it into conflict with neighboring states such as the Emirate of Bukhara and Iran, as well as the nomadic Turkmen tribes. For the next two centuries the region was wracked by struggles between these rival powers. In the early eighteenth century the incumbent of the Khivan throne, Khān Shāh Niyāz, sent ambassadors to Peter the Great to explore the possibility of Khiva being taken under Russian protection. However, this did not prevent the Khivans from annihilating the Russian expedition to the eastern shores of the Caspian led by A. Bekovich-Cherkassky in 1717. In 1740 Khiva was conquered by Nādir Shāh of Iran and regained its independence only after his death in 1747.

The remainder of the eighteenth century was marked by internal strife and fragmentation. Power passed into the hands of the tribal chiefs, and central authority was restored only under Inaq Iltüzer (r. 1804–1806) the first ruler of the Qungrat dynasty that was to remain in power until the dissolution of the khanate in 1920. He was succeeded by Muḥammad Raḥīm Khān (1806–1825), an astute and able sovereign. During his reign the Khiva Khanate reached the widest limits of its territorial expansion, acquiring control over some of the Karakalpak lands. Relations with neighboring states were improved and a number of important domestic reforms undertaken, most notably in the fields of taxation and administration. This brought greater stability, which in turn facilitated economic development. Much of this was based on the export of agricultural produce to Russia (cotton, hides, wool, and dried fruits), but the trade in slaves captured during raids on the surrounding lands was also extremely lucrative. The next half-century was a time of considerable prosperity, dramatically reflected in the splendid, richly-decorated buildings erected during this period. Literature written in the Chagatai language also flourished, in particular the genre of historical chronicles.

Russia had long had designs on Central Asia. A number of military expeditions were dispatched to the region during the eighteenth and nineteenth centuries, but none met with success (that led by General Perovsky against Khiva in 1839 was especially catastrophic). By 1870, however, Russian forces had all but encircled Khivan territory. The final assault on the khanate under the command of General Kaufman was launched in June 1873; the Khivans sued for peace shortly afterward, and in August of that year Khān Saʿīd Muḥammad Raḥīm II signed the treaty whereby the Khanate formally became a Russian protectorate. It was allowed to maintain a degree of internal autonomy (although the khan had to agree to abolish the slave trade "for all eternity"), but its foreign relations were henceforth to be conducted by the Russians; furthermore, Russian merchants were to be accorded special tax privileges. The Khivans undertook to pay a heavy indemnity (2.2 million rubles, spread over a twenty-year period) toward the cost of the war. The lands on the right bank of the Amu Darya were ceded to Russia and were thus no longer even nominally under Khivan control.

The final years of the Khanate were plagued by factional infighting, particularly between the Turkmen and the Uzbek groups. In 1918 Khān Isfandiyār (r. 1910–1918) was assassinated at the instigation of the Turkmen leader Junayd Khān. He was succeeded by the last Khivan khan, Saʿīd ʿAbd Allāh (1918–1920), who was little more than a puppet ruler. In April 1920 a communist-led coup overthrew the remnants of the former administration and proclaimed the creation of the Khorezm People's Soviet Republic (PSR) on the territory of the Khivan Khanate. The Khorezm PSR survived until 1924, when it was incorporated into the newly formed Turkmen and Uzbek Soviet Socialist Republics.

BIBLIOGRAPHY

Becker, Seymour. *Russia's Central Asian Protectorates: Bukhara and Khiva, 1865–1925*. Cambridge, Mass., 1967.

Skrine, Francis Henry, and E. Denison Ross. *The Heart of Asia: A History of Russian Turkestan and the Central Asian Khanates from the Earliest Times*. London, 1899. See especially pages 238ff.

SHIRIN AKINER

KHO'I, ABOL-QĀSEM (1899–1992), widely followed Shīʿī *mujtahid* (interpreter of Islamic law). Abol-Qāsem Kho'i (or Abū al-Qāsim Khū'ī) was born in the city of Kho'i, province of Azerbaijan, Iran. At the age of thirteen, he entered religious training in Najaf, Iraq, studying with Shaykh Fatḥ Allāh al-Aṣfahānī (al-Sharīʿah) and Shaykh Muḥammad Ḥusayn Nā'īnī, among others. Kho'i remained in Najaf's *ḥawza* (theological center), rising to become a teacher of jurisprudence and theology, writer, and spiritual leader of millions of Shīʿī Muslims in Iraq, Pakistan, India, and elsewhere.

With the death of Ayatollah Muḥsin al-Ḥakīm in 1970, Kho'i became the most widely followed Shīʿī *mujtahid*. He maintained contact with his followers worldwide through a well-organized network of representatives, using the religious tithes conveyed to him to provide stipends to seminary students and to establish Islamic schools in Iraq, Iran (Qom), Thailand, Bangladesh, India, Pakistan, and Lebanon. He founded a publishing house in Karachi and mosques with cultural centers in Bombay, London, New York City, and elsewhere.

Among Kho'i's many well-known books are *Al-bayān fi tafsīr al-Qur'ān* (Exegesis in Qur'ānic Commentary); *Al-masā'il al-muntakhabah* (Selected [Religious] Questions); and *Minhāj al-ṣāliḥīn* (The Path of the Righteous), a two-volume work on religious practices and law. In his theology, Kho'i was traditional and scholarly; in his personal life, austere. He opposed all political activity by high-ranking religionaries and advanced two doctrinal objections to Ayatollah Ruhollah Khomeini's advocacy of *wilāyat al-faqīh* (guardianship of the jurist): (1) the authority of Shīʿī jurists cannot be extended by humans to the political sphere; and (2) the authority of Shīʿī jurists during the absence of the Twelfth Imam cannot be restricted to one jurist or a few. For this he was subjected to severe criticism from Khomeini's followers.

In the area of women's rights, Ayatollah Kho'i funded religious schools for girls but took the position that women could not be religious guides for others. He issued *fatwās* (religious decrees) allowing unrelated men and women to attend religious and social functions together.

Kho'i was the only ayatollah in Iraq after the Iraqi government expelled Ayatollah Khomeini in 1978 and executed Ayatollah Muḥammad Bāqir al-Ṣadr in 1980. He applied for an exit visa but was refused. His funds were confiscated; his students were arrested and tortured; and he himself was placed under a virtual house arrest that continued until his death twelve years later. Despite pressure from the Iraqi government to endorse its war effort against Iran, he held to his refusal to take any political positions. After Iraq's invasion of Kuwait in 1990, he issued a *fatwā* forbidding Shīʿīs to purchase goods brought from Kuwait, on the grounds that the goods were stolen. In March 1991, after the failed Shīʿī uprising against Iraqi president Saddam Hussein, Kho'i was detained in police custody and the *ḥawza* was closed by the government.

Ayatollah Kho'i's students number in the thousands and include the previously mentioned Ayatollah al-Ṣadr (Iraq); Sayyid Mahdī Shams al-Dīn, acting chairman of the Supreme Assembly of Lebanese Shīʿī Muslims; Imam Mūsā al-Ṣadr (Lebanon); Sayyid Muḥammad Ḥusayn Faḍlallāh (Lebanon), and Ayatollah Ardabīlī, former chief justice of Iran.

[*See also* Al-Khoei Benevolent Foundation *and the biographies of Faḍlallāh, Ḥakīm, Nā'īnī, and Ṣadr.*]

BIBLIOGRAPHY

Al-Khoei Benevolent Foundation. "Concepts and Projects." Fourteen-page historical account of the Al-Khoei Benevolent Foundation.

Momen, Moojan. *An Introduction to Shīʿi Islam*. New Haven and London, 1985. Excellent depiction of Shiism and its prominent leaders.

Muslim Group of the U.S. and Canada, Washington D.C. Chapter. "Al-Khu'i." Washington, D.C., 1992. Five-page obituary addressing Ayatollah Kho'i's contributions and his trials under Iraq's Baʿthist regime.

JOYCE N. WILEY

KHOJAS. The Indian term *khoja* is derived from the Persian *khvājah* ("master, teacher, respected, well-to-do-person"), which was the title given by the Persian Ismāʿīlī missionary Pīr Ṣadruddīn to his Hindu Indian converts to Islam in the fourteenth century. The definitive history of the Khoja community remains to be written: the community experienced factionalism in its early period, so much written in subsequent decades suffered from subjective (at times, hostile and prejudicial) analysis of its genesis and the later conflicts over questions of both leadership and doctrine. Some Khoja histories reveal the sentiments and emotions that led to dissension and ultimate division on the matter of how Shiism and the leadership of the Persian Ismāʿīlī missionaries was to be construed by the Khojas.

The Hindu converts to Islam in the fourteenth century belonged to the Kshatriya caste (which provided the soldiers assigned to protect boundaries) and at the time of their conversion followed the Shakti Marg path of Hinduism. Some, however, believe that the Khojas came from the Vaishya caste of traders. On the basis of the professions followed by its members, Hindu society was further divided into different communities. The Khojas, according to their historians, formed the Lohana community, having descended from the mythic Indian king Rama's son, Lav. As such, they were known as *thakkar,* from an Indian title, *thakor* ("lord, master"); this word is close in meaning to the Persian word *khvājah* applied by Pīr Ṣadruddīn to these newly converted Hindus.

Between Hinduism and Sunnī Islam. The Khoja community retained the caste system inherited from their Hindu ancestors for a long time because they had to continue to live openly as Hindus, but this caste identity has no relationship to Islam. There is nothing in the basic characteristic of being a Khoja that competes for loyalty with that of a Shīʿī Muslim in this community. A Khoja is a Khoja only by birth; even if a Khoja changes his religious affiliation from Shiism to Sunnism, he still remains a Khoja. This caste identity explains much about the early conversion of the Lohana Hindus to Ismāʿīlī Islam and about why certain religious practices resembling those of Hindus were retained among them for more than four centuries.

From the beginning of their conversion to Shiism the Khojas were persecuted by the Sunnī Muslim rulers of Gujarat. Consequently, many Khojas were advised to live a *taqīyah*-oriented life; in order to deflect the hostile attitude of the Sunnī majority, they pretended to be Sunnīs or members of some other tolerated minority, such as the Twelver Shīʿī community. In the course of time, there appeared three varieties of Khojas organized under three different *jamāʿat*s: the Sunnī Khojas, who are very few; the Twelver Khojas; and the majority who are the Nizārī Ismāʿīlī Khojas, followers of the Aga Khan.

The Nizārī and Twelver Split. The major split into Nizārī and Twelver Khojas occurred in the first half of the nineteenth century. This period has been described as the beginning of "Khoja awakening" which bore fruits in the second half of this century. By that time Bombay had become the point of convergence for many Khojas who had migrated from Kutch and Kathiavar to take advantage of its commercial growth. In 1829, the rich merchant Ḥabīb Ibrāhīm, also known as "Barbhaya" because of his twelve brothers, refused to pay the religious dues known as *dassondh* ("tithe, a tenth") to the administrators of the *jamāʿatkhanah* (prayer-hall and meetingplace for the Nizārī Khojas). The *dassondh* was imposed by the Nizārī Imam and accordingly was regarded by Ḥabīb Ibrāhīm and some fifty families who followed his lead as lacking proper Islamic justification. Moreover, the dissenting group, because of its long contact with Sunnī mullahs, was inclined toward the Sunnī school of thought in its religious practices. In 1830 all these families were expelled from the *jamāʿatkhanah;* although the representative of the Ismāʿīlī Imam, Ḥasan ʿAlī Shāh Maḥallatī (the first Persian Nizārī leader to have been granted the title Aga Khan by the Qājār monarch), who was in Iran at this time, contemplated filing a civil case against the group, the timing was felt to be improper.

The period between 1845 and 1861 was marked by socioreligious turmoil in the Khoja community. In 1850 four members of Ḥabīb Ibrāhīm's group were killed by the followers of the Aga Khan in the Mahim *jamāʿatkhanah,* and nineteen followers of the Aga Khan were subsequently arrested. Four of these persons were sentenced to death by the Bombay High Court. Following these events, and with a view toward establishing his religious authority in India, on 20 October 1861 the Aga Khan circulated a general announcement declaring the Khojas to be Shīʿīs; hence, their marriage and funeral rites were to be performed in accordance with Shīʿī practice. Moreover, he required his followers to put their signatures under this announcement, declaring their Shīʿī affiliation and unquestioning loyalty to him. The document was kept in Bhindi Bazaar in the house of Aga Khan's son, where some seventeen hundred Khojas (the majority) signed it. However, Ḥabīb Ibrāhīm and his group refused to do so. Copies of the document were sent to Gujarat and Kathiavar and also to Zanzibar and East Africa to collect signatures of supporters of the Aga Khan.

After this incident the Ḥabīb Ibrāhīm group attempted through court procedures to have all the Khoja property held by the Aga Khan placed under an independent trust that would ensure its proper use for the religious benefit of all Sunnī Khojas, excluding the Nizārī Khojas. There were also other demands meant to reform community conventions that were deemed unjust and disposed toward the protection of the Aga Khan's ultimate rights over everything owned by the Khoja community. Of greater alarm to the Aga Khan and his followers was a plan to sever the Khoja community's relationship to the Aga Khan through a suit filed in Bombay High Court.

The end result of this conflict was the permanent excommunication of the Ḥabīb Ibrāhīm group in September 1862. By 1864 the Aga Khan had ordered the Sunnī mullahs to stop conducting religious services for his followers and had installed Shīʿī mullahs to lead the regular prayers in accordance with the Twelver Shīʿi rite. The court case against the Aga Khan was lost, and the supporters of Ḥabīb Ibrāhīm separated from the main group of the Khojas, establishing a separate Sunnī mosque and graveyard. When the Twelver Khoja *jamāʿat* was formed following further friction in the Khoja community on issues related to Islamic authenticity, many Sunnī Khojas joined this group and began to intermarry with them.

Religious Awakening and Affiliation. From the time of their conversion to Islam until the 1860s, the influence of Sunnī mullahs led the Khojas to favor the Sunnī school. The beginning of the "Khoja awakening" in the first half of the nineteenth century ushered in the revival of the community's religious identity as a consequence of increased religious knowledge. With the exception of the Ḥabīb Ibrāhīm group, the Khoja community, following the public announcement circulated by the Aga Khan in 1861, had asserted their Shīʿī identity.

However, religious practices among the Khojas until that time were not fully islamized or formalized. Pīr Dādū, in the mid-sixteenth century, had traveled to Iran and had obtained from Ismāʿīlī religious leaders prayer manuals that were used by the Khojas. Following this period knowledge about Shiism based on Persian works began to take roots among the Khojas. Religious books were written in the Sindhi language, based on the Persian *jangnāmah,* describing the martyrdom of Imam Ḥusayn in Karbala. These *jangnāmah* were recited at the commemorative gatherings to mourn the tragedy of Karbala in every *jamāʿatkhanah,* following the festival of ʿĪd al-Āḍḥā, through the month of Muḥarram until the fortieth *(chihlum)* of the martyrs of Karbala. These gatherings primarily functioned as religious schools for the Khojas, and Shiism became firmly established among them.

Nonetheless, an 1847 court case established the fact that prior to this period the Khojas had little knowledge about their Shīʿī affiliation, not understanding the differences between the Shīʿī and Sunnī schools. Thus, when Aga Khan in 1861 required the Khojas to declare their Shiism, the community had no hesitation in doing so. The Shīʿī mullahs had prepared the community for this declaration of allegiance; more importantly, the Aga Khan and his son ʿAlī Shāh regularly led the community in prayers and commemorative gatherings. These and other Iranian religious practices were based on Twelver Shiism, which consequently formed the basis of the Islamic religious practices that gradually took root among the Khojas under Aga Khans.

In 1862 a Twelver mullah, Qādir Ḥusayn, opened a *madrasah* in the Khoja quarter of Bombay. In this religious school, not only did the Khoja children learn to recite the Qur'ān, their parents also joined them to receive instruction about Twelver Shīʿī religious practices. After a few years Qādir Ḥusayn returned to Karbala; in response to a request by a leading Twelver Khoja, Ḥājjī Devjī Jamāl, to the Shīʿī *mujtahid* in Iraq, the mullah was sent again to Bombay in 1872 to teach Shiism.

The presence of Mullah Qādir Ḥusayn in Bombay and his ceaseless efforts in educating the Khojas made community members aware of the syncretic Nizārī Khoja religious rituals, which had continued to employ the Sindhi Hindu vernacular without requiring strict adherence to the *sharīʿah.* Ironically, the Persian Ismāʿīlī leadership of the Aga Khans was an important factor in this awareness of Twelver Shiism among the Khojas. The Nizārī leaders had introduced Twelver religious practices in the *jamāʿatkhanah*s to combat Sunnī influences and to assert their absolute authority among their Khoja followers. In addition, the presence of other Shīʿīs from the Northern Province of India and their continuous moral support of the Khojas resulted in the spread of the Twelver Shiism.

Nevertheless, the Twelver Khojas were still part of the larger Khoja community under the leadership of the Aga Khan. On realizing this influence of Twelver Shiism among their followers, the Nizārī leaders started to impose restrictions on Twelver Shīʿī practices. Under the Aga Khan III the Nizārī Khoja community asserted its separate identity, dissociating itself from Twelver religious practices, including their basic ceremonial laws connected with fundamental teachings of Islam and the practice of commemorative gatherings to mourn Imam Ḥusayn. The dissenting Khojas, although afraid of being ostracized from the *jamāʿatkhanah,* still dared to meet with Mullah Qādir Ḥusayn and swore that if any one of their group was outcast, every other member would join that person. The news of this resolution reached the Ismāʿīlī leaders. However, the number of Mullah Qādir Ḥusayn's followers was small, and they thought that the group could be talked into abandoning its move toward Twelver Shiism. Two prominent persons who provided moral as well as financial support for the new group were Ḥājjī Devjī Jamāl and Ḥājjī Khalfān Ratansī.

When Ḥājjī Ratansī's daughter died, the Nizārī Khoja community required that he abandon the Twelver faith as a precondition for attending his daughter's funeral. Ḥājjī Ratansī refused, and his daughter had to be buried in the Iranian cemetery. What helped the "smaller *jamāʿat*" of the Khoja (as it came to be known) was the support of many non-Khoja Twelver Shīʿīs in Bombay. The success of the Twelver Khojas in Bombay in forming their own group spread throughout the Khoja world; everywhere new *jamāʿat*s were formed, and the movement of spreading Twelver teachings was symbolized by the construction of proper Islamic mosques instead of the *jamaʿatkhanah,* as well as the performance of the regular *ṣalāt* practiced by all other Muslims regardless of their sectarian affiliation.

In this movement the disciples of Mullah Qādir Ḥusayn played a major role. Mullah ʿAbdullāh Ṣāliḥ Sachedīna went to Zanzibar, where his lectures had enormous influence in the Twelver Khoja community. Another prominent student of Mullah Qādir Ḥusayn, Ḥājjī Najī, began to preach the Twelver faith and launched a monthly journal, *Rāhi najāt,* during these critical days.

Nizārī and Twelver Khojas Today. The Nizārī Khojas, under the long and progressive leadership of the Aga Khan III (d. 1957), consolidated their Nizārī identity and became thoroughly modernized through education and socioeconomic reforms that made the community self-sufficient. The unquestioning devotion of the Nizārī Khojas to the Aga Khan, in addition to the restructured hierarchical communal organization with the Aga Khan as the supreme authority, facilitated the implementation of religious, social, and economic reforms. The policy of sociocultural assimilation of the Nizārī Khojas—who live as minorities in many parts of the world—through an elaborate administrative system of councils has continued under the Aga Khan IV.

The Twelver Khojas in many ways share the administrative and organizational structures of their Nizārī brothers. In religious matters they accept the authority of the *mujtahid*s in Iran and Iraq, to whom they are bound doctrinally in the absence of the Twelfth Hidden Imam. However, a conservative spirit dominates their outlook on questions of sociocultural integration. Calls for reforms within the community are regarded as a threat to long-established traditions of Indo-Muslim origin. Since the religious leadership in Iran and Iraq has little understanding of Khoja culture, it has not been able to provide the necessary directives to move the Twelver Khoja community toward Islamic solutions to the problems of sociocultural assimilation in a rapidly changing social and political climate, nor has the community recognized a single leadership within itself to provide such solutions.

Today the Khoja followers of the Aga Khan have formally abandoned their "khojaism" with its elements of Hinduism in favor of a more universal Shīʿī Ismāʿīlī *ṭarīqah* (a remnant of the Persian Ṣūfī connections of the Persian Ismāʿīlī missionaries). Similar efforts toward shedding the Hindu past can be observed among the Twelver Khojas—who, ironically, in their worldwide organizations adhere to their "khojaism." The inconsistency of clinging to a title that implies privilege claimed on the basis of birth while maintaining commitment to universal Islamic brotherhood has been the main reason for its abandonment in the recent decades of globalization of the Khoja community.

[*See also* Aga Khan; Ismāʿīlīyah.]

BIBLIOGRAPHY

Three basic histories on which I have depended to draw the material are: Sachedina Nanjiani, *Khoja Vratant* (Ahmedabad, 1892); Adalji Dhanji Kaba, *Khoja Qawm ni tavarikh: The History of the Khojas* (Amreli, 1330/1912); and Jaffer Rahimtoola, *History of Khojas* (1905). Most of these works were compiled during the second part of the nineteenth century, the period of "Khoja awakening." Accordingly, we have remarkably objective reports on the events that led to the division in the Khoja community at this time. In fact, A. D. Kaba reports episodes in which he himself was an eye witness. In addition, see the following works:

Daftary, Farhad. *The Ismaʿilis: Their History and Doctrines.* Cambridge, 1990.

Ivanow, Wladimir. "Khodja." In *The Shorter Encyclopaedia of Islam,* p. 256. Leiden, 1953.

Madelung, Wilferd. "Isma'iliyya." In *Encyclopaedia of Islam*, new ed., vol. 4, p. 201. Leiden, 1960–.

ABDULAZIZ SACHEDINA

KHOMEINI, RUHOLLAH AL-MUSAVI (1902–1989), Iranian Shīʿī cleric and leader of the Islamic Revolution. Born into a longstanding clerical family on 24 September 1902 in Khomein, a small village in central Iran, Ruhollah al-Musavi Khomeini was the youngest of six children. His father, Muṣṭafā, who had studied theology in Isfahan and Najaf, was murdered seven months after Khomeini's birth.

As a child, Khomeini studied Arabic, Persian poetry, and calligraphy at a government school and a *maktab* (elementary religious school). When he was sixteen, his mother and aunt, both of whom had been strong influences on him, died. At seventeen, he left Khomein to study in a *madrasah* (Islamic school) in Arak under Shaykh ʿAbd al-Karīm Ḥā'irī Yazdī (1859–1936) and later followed him to Qom. There, he completed the three steps of religious education, and by the early 1930s he had become a *mujtahid*. At twenty-seven, he married Batūl Saqafī. [*See* Qom *and the biography of Ḥā'irī Yazdī.*]

In the 1930s, Khomeini, as a very confident teacher with a growing circle of students, began to expound on ethics in response to Reza Shah Pahlavi's modernization and secularization of Iran. Khomeini gave public lectures which brought him to the attention of the authorities for the first time. And when Reza Shah was forced to abdicate in 1941, Khomeini saw it as the thin end of the wedge of a Western ideological and cultural offensive. To counteract this influence, Khomeini advocated a united clerical establishment. [*See the biography of Pahlavi.*]

His first political statement appeared in a visitors' book in a mosque at Yazd in 1944. It began with the Qur'ānic verse, "Say, I do admonish you on one point: that you do not stand up for God, in pairs or singly." The significant point in the lines which followed was his emphasis on rising up in the name of God.

By the end of the 1940s Khomeini's interest in the political field, which he considered just as much part of Islam as philosophy and theology, increased. In the early 1950s, he was to witness the rise of the nationalist Mohammad Mossadegh and his rapid fall brought about by the United States and Britain. In 1962, when the chief Iranian theologian, Ayatollah Moḥammad Ḥosayn Borujerdi, died, the burden of fusing religion and politics fell to Khomeini, whose aim was more to islamize politics rather than to politicize Islam. [*See the biography of Borujerdi.*]

The shah's secularization policies of the early 1960s gave Khomeini his first excuse to oppose the ruler. He accused the government of aping the West and eroding Islam, and he showed great ability in mobilizing his network of opposition. *Bāzārīs* were one group which increasingly turned to Khomeini, as they felt their livelihood was threatened by the shah's attempt to shift power to the burgeoning commercial and industrial bourgeoisie. Khomeini helped the merchants to establish an alliance of Islamic missions. Some of Khomeini's trusted students, such as Murtaẓā Muṭahharī and Muḥammad Ḥusayn Bihishtī, acted as this alliance's supervisory body, whose core members were later to create the Islamic Republican Party (IRP) after the Iranian Revolution of 1979. [*See* Islamic Republican Party *and the biography of Muṭahharī.*]

During the mourning ceremonies in the month of Muḥarram in 1963, Khomeini took the opportunity to utilize the Shīʿī zeal for tragedy and martyrdom by comparing the shah's regime with that of the hated Caliph Yazīd, who had killed Imam ʿAlī's son, Ḥusayn. On the day of ʿĀshūrā', Khomeini delivered a forceful sermon railing against the shah, Israel, and the United States, ending with a warning to the shah to heed his actions. The result was a wave of antishah marches in Tehran that day and the next, which prompted the shah to have Khomeini arrested and removed to Tehran.

Such was Khomeini's stature in the country after his imprisonment and house arrest in Tehran that the government seemed anxious to appease him, for it understood only too well that he was now the undisputed leader of disparate factions within Iranian society. In a series of statements, he turned his attention away from Islamic rituals to the social, political, and cultural aspect of Islam. His speech on the issue of granting extraterritorial rights to the United States led to his arrest again in October 1964. Thereupon, Khomeini was sent into exile in Turkey from where he went to Najaf. In Najaf, Khomeini set about emphasizing to the clergy that they had a responsibility to introduce Islamic laws, rules, and codes to the educated youth, and indeed it was with left-wing, anti-shah Iranian student organizations abroad that Khomeini now started to develop a strong relationship. His written statements and audiotapes were widely distributed and proved to be a most effective weapon in the buildup to the revolution. Likewise, the preachings of ʿAlī Sharīʿatī, Murtaẓā Muṭahharī, and Maḥmud Ṭāleqāni brought intellectuals into the Khomeini camp [*See* Najaf *and the biographies of Sharīʿatī and Ṭāleqāni.*]

Khomeini returned to Tehran in February 1979 as the imam—a title used in the Arab Shīʿī world for a religious leader. He had come to serve the clergy and Iranian society, which had been transformed by revolution. Khomeini's main objectives for the future were twofold: to control those forces unleashed by the revolution and to consolidate his regime. Mehdi Bāzargān, who had successfully attracted many young people to religion in the 1960s and 1970s, was appointed prime minister of an interim government, with the task of preparing Iran for the transition from a monarchy to an Islamic republic, which was approved by referendum in March 1979. The IRP was set up by a group of Khomeini's disciples, which included ʿAlī Akbar Hāshimī Rafsanjānī, Muḥammad Javād Bāhūnār, ʿAbd al-Karīm Ardabīlī, ʿAli Khamene'i and Bihishtī. Khomeini, then aged seventy-seven, withdrew to Qom.

Bāzargān felt his wings clipped by Khomeini supporters within government departments, the revolutionary committees, radio, and television. Together with some leading clergy, such as Ayatollahs Muḥammad Kāẓim Sharīʿatmadārī and Ḥasan Qummī, liberals, lawyers, and minority leaders, he was critical of the IRP and the revolutionary courts. Two days after the seizure of the U.S. embassy by a group of students, Bāzargān resigned. Affairs were left in the hands of the Revolutionary Council, under Bihishtī. Khomeini, however, always had the last word. [*See the biography of Bāzargān.*]

Shortly after the hostage taking, a newly formed rival party called the MPIRP, which had the support of Sharīʿatmadārī, tried to seize power in Tabriz. It failed but demonstrated that even among the *ʿulamā'* there was a diversity of ideas on government. However, Khomeini was not prepared to compromise with anyone over his vision of the Islamic Republic. In November 1979 the Assembly of Experts drafted the Islamic constitution, which mandated three branches of government (executive, legislative, and judicial), presided over by a jurisprudent).

The following month the constitution was ratified in a national referendum, followed by the election of Abol-Hasan Bani Sadr as president in January 1980. The son of an ayatollah, Bani Sadr, a self-styled Islamic economics expert, political writer, and long-winded speaker, was an admirer of Mossadeq and not a believer in clerical supremacy. Also, he was no match for the leader of the IRP, Bihishtī. The former student of Khomeini, Bihishtī was instrumental in the political transition of power from the shah to Khomeini, highly instrumental in controlling the machinery of revolutionary terror, and the formulator of the constitution.

The eight-year war with Iraq was a great testing time for Khomeini and one which he withstood. Coming as it did soon after the revolution, it led to food rationing, shortages, and other economic troubles. To extreme dissatisfaction, Khomeini told the nation that revolution was not about material well being and went on to pursue the war regardless of the burden it imposed on the country. In fact, he used the war to undermine various institutions to sustain the regime.

As with Bāzargān's prime ministry, Bani Sadr's presidency was neither smooth nor long. He immediately set about resolving the hostage issue, seeing the students in the U.S. embassy as potential rivals. But in the long run he succeeded in antagonizing Iran's radical and anti-Western forces and Khomeini himself. He filled the presidential office and other organizations with Western-trained technocrats who had little sympathy for "reactionary" or "incompetent" religious leaders. Even his supporters in the Majlis (parliament) ultimately went to the IRP side, as they found Bani Sadr's tactics abrasive, ill timed, and provocative. Further confrontation took place when Muḥammad ʿAlī Rajā'ī was appointed prime minister by the Majlis on Khomeini's recommendation. In the conduct of the war, too, Bani Sadr clashed with Khomeini.

Events in summer 1981 were potentially perilous for Khomeini. Amid all the differences between the religious establishment and Bani Sadr, who had recently gained the support of the Mujāhidīn-i Khalq, Khomeini dismissed Bani Sadr and replaced him with Rajā'ī. The Mujāhidīn took the streets and Bani Sadr called for a mass uprising. On 28 June a bomb in the IRP headquarters killed Bihishtī and more than seventy others, followed by another bomb on 30 August, killing the president of five weeks, Rajā'ī, and his prime minister, Bāhūnār. Khomeini appealed to the nation in a broadcast to spy on the neighbors and hunt out the opposition, the counterrevolutionaries, which the nation obligingly did, heralding a period of indiscriminate imprisonment, torture, and killing.

Khomeini, victorious again, this time decided to exclude all who did not agree with political Islam and *vilāyat-i faqih* [*see* Wilāyat al-Faqīh]. Thus the upper religious class came to take over the government of the country, more serving Islam through Iran than serving Iran through Islam. In October 1981 Ḥujjat al-Islām ʿAli Khamenei became the third president of Iran, with Mir Ḥusayn Mūsavī, a member of the central council of the IRP, as prime minister. Rafsanjānī took over the Majlis and Ardabīlī the judiciary. So Khomeini could now relax with the knowledge that his former disciples were in charge of the country. "We [i.e., the clergy] are here to stay", he told his critics.

In a speech in summer 1982, Khomeini said "our aim is to rid Iraq of its tyrannical rulers and move to liberate Jerusalem." But internal shortages and external pressure in response to Iran's intransigent policies put Khomeini on the defensive. He defied all those who continually pleaded with him to agree to end the war. Opposition to continuation of the war after the liberation of Khurramshahr, which had fallen to the enemy early on, grew inside the country.

Khomeini pursued the war regardless of the burden it imposed on the country. He was growing bolder in focusing on Islamic internationalism. His 1987 message entitled "The Charter of the Islamic Revolution," which he sent to Iranian officials in Saudi Arabia, began with the Qur'ānic verse: "And he who goes forth from his house, a migrant to God and his Apostle, should he die his reward becomes due and sure with God" (Surah 4.100).

By early 1988, Khomeini's promise that the final offensive would bring military victory had become palpably unattainable. In April 1988, Iran lost the dearly won Faw peninsula. Meanwhile the "War of the Cities" reached its peak with Iraq firing long-range missiles at Iranian cities. After each Iraqi missile, a new wave of resentment came to the surface over the inability of the regime to protect its citizens. Donations for the war were drying up. Volunteers were scarce. Soldiers were deserting from the war front. Diplomatic pressures were mounting, and Iranians increasingly felt the effects of the tightening of the international black market loophole.

Khomeini's defensive tone was evident in his opening speech to the Majlis read out by his son Aḥmad on 28 May 1988. The *faqīh* was feeling adversity both internally and internationally. The last straw for him came on 3 July 1988 when an American warship shot down an Iran Air Airbus, killing 290 on board, the ship's crew claiming that it had mistaken the plane for an attacking jet fighter. He finally realized that his revolution was in serious trouble. Faced with the choice between the continuation of the revolutionary struggle or the survival of the republic, he chose the latter. In the biannual meeting of the Assembly of Experts on 16 July the frail ayatollah's willingness to seek a diplomatic solution to the war was first discussed, and on 18 July Iran unconditionally accepted United Nations Security Council resolution 598. Two days later Khomeini issued a statement declaring that he had accepted the truce in the interest of the revolution and the Islamic system. It was, said the old man, more bitter for him than a poisoned chalice.

Having suppressed or driven underground all organized opposition, Khomeini had had time to look at the question of succession. He firmly told the Assembly of Experts to choose the next leader. It took the assembly more than two years to reach a decision. In November 1985 it was announced that the assembly had appointed Ayatollah Ḥusayn ʿAlī Muntazirī to succeed Khomeini.

Muntazirī acted as a loyal opposition leader, often protesting against human rights abuses, corruption, and red tape. But on foreign policy he was more in tune with the radicals, especially in their anti-Americanism. When the radicals tried to turn Muntazirī's office into a power center from which to seize control of the leadership after Khomeini's death, Rafsanjānī, Ayatollah ʿAlī Mishkini, and Aḥmad Khomeini responded with alarm and caused a souring of relations between Khomeini and Muntazirī.

Muntazirī was blunt: "Unfortunately," he said, ". . . I agree with the new generation of the revolution that there is a great distance between what we promised and what we have achieved . . . if government means to compromise our values and principles, we had better not have government." For Khomeini, who valued ideology only if it could be translated into power and for whom the road to holiness was only through action, abjuring governmental control could only be a worst-case scenario. Muntazirī's stand highlighted Khomeini's increasingly defensive posture since he had accepted the ceasefire.

What tipped the balance was Khomeini's *fatwā* (edict) in February 1989 against Salman Rushdie following the publication of that author's *The Satanic Verses*, sentencing him to death for what many Muslims saw as an attack against the integrity of the prophet Muḥammad. He called on all intrepid Muslims to execute both Rushdie and his publishers. He said "whoever is killed on this path would be regarded as a martyr." By issuing this *fatwā* Khomeini was putting himself forward as leader of entire Islamic world and became the putative spokesman for Muslims everywhere. [*See also* Fatwā, *article on* Modern Usage; *and* Rushdie Affair.] In March 1989 Khomeini removed Muntazirī from office and set up a body to review the constitution.

Khomeini died on 3 June 1989. His funeral was again the occasion of tumultuous scenes as everyone wished to say a last farewell to "the most divine personality in the history of Islam after the Prophet and the Imams," in the words of the joint statement issued by Rafsanjānī, Khamene'i, Ardabīlī, and Mūsavī. Khomeini did not bring about the just and virtuous society he had promised but stated in his will that "he was proud to be trying to implement the rules of the holy Qur'ān and the traditions of the Prophet." Khamene'i was then selected as the next leader of the Islamic Republic of Iran—a smooth transition of power to conclude the long life of Khomeini, who had engineered one of the most significant revolutions of the twentieth century.

[*See also* Ayatollah; Iran; *and* Iranian Revolution of 1979.]

BIBLIOGRAPHY

Akhavi, Shahrough. *Religion and Politics in Contemporary Iran*. Albany, N.Y. 1980. Excellent guide to clerical politics in recent decades.

Algar, Hamid. *Religion and State in Iran, 1785–1906: The Role of the Ulama in the Qajar Period*. Berkeley, 1969.

Bakhash, Shaul. *The Reign of the Ayatollahs: Iran and the Islamic Revolution*. London, 1985.

Bāzargān, Mehdi. *Inqilāb-i Īrān dar dū ḥarakat* (Iranian Revolution in Two Acts). Tehran, 1363/1984.

Khomeini, Ruhollah. *Kashf al-asrār*. Amman, 1987. Arabic translation of Khomeini's first political work, originally published in Persian in 1941; a useful source on his early worldview.

Khomeini, Ruhollah. *Islam and Revolution: Writings and Declarations*. Translated by Hamid Algar. Berkeley, 1981. A most useful collection of Khomeini's theoretical work on Islamic government.

Khomeini, Ruhollah. *Taḥrīr al-wasīlah*. Beirut, 1987. Khomeini's major work on Shiʿi law, written in exile in Turkey, which reflects some of his views on government.

Moin, Baqer. *Khomeini: Sign of God*. London, 1994. A major biography of Khomeini.

Rajaee, Farhang. *Islamic Values and World View*. Washington, 1983. Excellent book on the thought of Ayatollah Khomeini.

Rūḥānī, Ḥamīd. *Bar'rasī va taḥlīlī az nahẓat-i Imām Khumaynī* (Analytical Study of Imam Khomeini's Movement). 3 vols. Tehran, 1981–1993. Very useful source book on Khomeini written by one of his students.

BAQER MOIN

KHOQAND KHANATE. This Central Asian state of the eighteenth and nineteenth centuries took its name from its capital, the city of Khoqand (locally pronounced Kukon or Kokan, and in Russian and Western literature rendered Kokand) in the central part of the Ferghana valley. During the post-Mongol period, before the eighteenth century, Ferghana had been only a province of the khanates, whose centers were elsewhere, mostly in Transoxania. With the political and economic decline of the Khanate of Bukhara by the end of the seventeenth century and its disintegration into a number of independent Uzbek tribal chiefdoms, several such chiefdoms emerged in Ferghana, but most of the region was dominated first by Naqshbandī *shaykh*s (*khoja*s) from the village of Chadak in the northern part of the valley. The leaders (*biy*s) of the Uzbek Ming tribe, which had its *yurt* (tribal territory) in the central part of Ferghana, gradually gained strength. One such leader, Shāhrukh Biy, eliminated the Chadak *khoja*s in 1709–1710; his son ʿAbd al-Karīm Biy founded the city of Khoqand in 1740. During most of the eighteenth century the Ming chiefdom was only one of four competing principalities in Ferghana. During the rule of Nārbūta Biy (c.1770–1798) most of Ferghana was united under the Mings, and his son ʿĀlim (1798–1810) was proclaimed *khan,* thus founding a new reigning dynasty in Central Asia that had a status equal to those of Bukhara and Khiva. A genealogical legend was created according to which the Ming dynasty traced its origin back to the Timurids and the Chingisids.

In the first half of the nineteenth century the Ming khans embarked on a policy of vigorous expansion beyond the Ferghana valley. ʿĀlim Khan conquered Khojand (1805) and Tashkent (1809); his son and successor ʿUmar Khan captured the city of Turkestan (1816) and expanded the possessions of Khoqand in the southern parts of the Kazakh steppes. Muḥammad ʿAlī ("Madali") Khan (1823–1842) annexed vast areas in the Zheti Su (Semirech'e) and central Tian Shan and subdued Kirghiz tribes in this region; his troops invaded Kashgar twice (1826 and 1830), but without lasting result. During the first decades of the nineteenth century the khanate also experienced fast economic growth owing to the influx of population from Transoxania, the expansion of irrigation systems undertaken by the government, and especially the rapidly growing trade with Russia via Tashkent. In cultural life this period was marked by intensive building activity in the cities of the Ferghana valley and by the flourishing of literature and poetry, in both Persian and Turkic, especially under ʿUmar Khan, who was a poet himself.

In the early 1840s, however, the khanate entered a period of almost uninterrupted political turmoil—civil wars and rebellions, caused by sharp conflicts between the major ethnic groups of its heterogeneous population (sedentary Uzbeks, Sarts, and Tajiks, and nomadic Kipchaks, Kirghiz, and Kazakhs), coupled with frequent wars with the neighboring Khanate of Bukhara. The authority of the central government weakened considerably, and the khanate was unable to offer effective resistance to Russia, which began its military advance into the territory of the khanate in 1853. In 1865 the Russians captured Tashkent and in 1866 Khojand. By 1868 the territory of the khanate was reduced to the Ferghana valley, and it had to sign a commercial convention with Russia that established a de facto Russian protectorate. In 1875 a popular uprising began against the oppressive rule of Khudāyār Khan and had to be put down by Russian troops. The khanate was abolished in 1876, and its territory was annexed to the Russian Governorate-General of Turkestan.

[*See also* Bukhara Khanate; Khiva Khanate.]

BIBLIOGRAPHY

Barthold, Wilhelm. "Khoḳand." In *Encyclopaedia of Islam*, vol. 2, pp. 963–965. Leiden, 1913–.

Bregel, Yuri. *Bibliography of Islamic Central Asia*. Vol. 1. Bloomington, 1994. Works cited are almost all Russian; see pages 85–91 for pertinent citations.

Nalivkin, Vladimir Petrovich. *Histoire du khanat de Khokand*. Paris, 1889. Originally published in Russian as *Kratkaia istoriia Kokandskogo khanstva*. Kazan, 1886. The only existing general history of the khanate, but inadequate (no references to the sources) and outdated.

Nettleton, Susanna. "Ruler, Patron, Poet: Umar Khan and the Blossoming of the Khanate of Qoqan, 1800–1820." *International Journal of Turkish Studies* 2.2 (1981–1982): 127–140.

Saguchi, Tōro. "The Eastern Trade of the Khoqand Khanate." *Memoirs of the Research Department of the Toyo Bunko* (Tokyo) 24 (1965): 47–114.

Yuri Bregel

KHŪʾĪ, ABŪ AL-QĀSIM. *See* Kho'i, Abol-Qāsem.

KHUMS. The *khums* ("fifth") as a tax developed in very early Islam and was based on the principle that one-fifth of war booty taken by Muslims belonged to the prophet Muḥammad. It was used for the benefit of the holy family as well as some categories of the indigent. Later on, it was interpreted as an Islamic tax on profits of various sorts beyond expenditures. In Sunnī Islam this tax was less important than in the Shīʿī branch; for instance, Hanafīs could give the *khums*, but it was used primarily for succoring the poor and was not donated to the descendants of the Prophet, called Sayyid or *sharīf*.

In Shiism, which maintained the right of the family of the Prophet to continue to receive many of the perquisites associated with his office, *khums* was seen as a tax owed by the Muslim community for the support of sayyids. With the occultation of the Twelfth Imam in AH 260/873–874 CE and the end of the line of visible direct descendants of the Prophet exercising spiritual authority from God, the question arose in medieval Shiism of whether believers should continue to pay the *khums*, and if so, to whom. The conservative, literalist Akhbārī school of jurisprudence tended to see the obligation to pay the *khums* as having lapsed in the absence of the imam, although some Akhbārīs advocated setting aside the amount due and burying it in expectation of the Judgment Day.

The later Uṣūlī school of jurisprudence, which grew influential beginning in the thirteenth century CE, advocated that the *khums* as a tax be revived and divided into two. One portion should go to the support of indigent sayyids. The other should benefit the Uṣūlī jurisprudents or *mujtahid*s, who determined the law for the community based on their individual reasoning. Most *mujtahids* were themselves sayyids. Uṣūlīs believed in the consensus of juridical tradition as a source of law and said that the consensus in Shiism was that the *khums* should be paid on war booty, on mined precious metals after costs, on hidden treasure that was found, on pearls and other valuables found in the sea, on profits from handicrafts, trade, and farming, on lawful money any time it became tainted with ill-gotten wealth from any source, and on the proceeds of land sales by Shīʿīs to Jews, Christians, and Zoroastrians. The *khums* was to be paid to an upright *mujtahid*, who accepted half of it as the share of the imam *(sahm-i Imām)* and who distributed the other half to the poor, orphans, and wayfarers among the sayyids (no other Shīʿīs were eligible for charity from this tax).

Nikki Keddie and others have argued that the payment of *khums* by artisans and merchants in the bazaar gave Shīʿī clergymen in Iran a source of income that contributed to their independence from the state. It might also be argued that the *mujtahids*' control of charity monies gave them substantial patronage to distribute and allowed them to build networks of support among the poor. Such payments and donations from the bazaar to radical clergymen helped fuel the Iranian Revolution of 1979. [*See* Bazaar.]

BIBLIOGRAPHY

Calder, Norman. "Khums in Imāmī Shīʿī Jurisprudence from the Tenth to the Sixteenth Century A.D." *Bulletin of the School of Oriental and African Studies* 45 (1982): 39–47.

Keddie, Nikki R. "The Roots of the Ulama's Power in Modern Iran." In *Scholars, Saints, and Sufis,* edited by Nikki R. Keddie, pp. 211–219. Berkeley, 1972.

Sachedina, A. A. "Al-Khums: The Fifth in the Imāmī Shīʿī Legal System." *Journal of Near East Studies* 39 (1980): 276–289.

JUAN R. I. COLE

KHUṬBAH. An address called a *khuṭbah* is delivered by a *khaṭīb* (orator), usually in a *masjid* (mosque), during the Friday service, celebration of religious festivals, or on other occasions. According to Bernard Lewis (*The Arabs in History,* London, 1966, p. 135), among the pre-Islamic Arabs the *khatib* is often mentioned along with the *shāʿir,* or poet; both had prominent positions in the Arab tribes. In flawless language they extolled the glories of their own tribe while exposing the weaknesses of their adversaries.

According to S. D. Goitein (*Studies in Islamic History and Institutions,* Leiden, 1966), before the Prophet migrated to Medina the Muslim community did not hold Friday services in Mecca. As the Muslim community grew larger in Medina, it became necessary to designate a time when all the members could congregate in the mosque so that the Prophet could meet with them regularly. Thus prayer on Friday at noon was made obligatory for every free adult male Muslim. The Prophet, and eventually his successors—the caliphs and provincial governors—became imams or leaders of the collective worship, which took place in the chief mosque of the city. Some sort of address was made at the gathering, which was identified as a political community. The significance of the mosque gathering was embodied in the *minbar* (pulpit), an elevated structure from which the *khuṭbah* is delivered, following the precedent of Muḥammad. The *minbar* gradually became a kind of throne used on official occasions by state dignitaries. In his inauguration ceremony the caliph would ascend the *minbar,* receiving the homage of the community, and deliver a *khuṭbah.* In the provinces the governors stood in the same relation to the central mosque as did the caliph in the capital: they too made their formal entry into office by ascending the *minbar* and delivering a *khuṭbah.*

There also developed a custom that the enemies of the ruler and his party be cursed from the *minbar.* Along with this tradition there emerged the practice of bestowing a blessing on the ruler in whose name the Friday *khuṭbah* was delivered. The *khuṭbah* was also used for defending policies, stirring public emotion, or disseminating propaganda.

During the ʿAbbāsid period (750–1258 CE) the expansion of the Islamic domain and the preoccupation of the caliphs with ceremonials and traditions of the Persian monarchy prevented officials from delivering the *khuṭbah* personally. Instead, a man learned in religious matters was appointed to the position of *khatib.*

From an early period there also emerged, besides the official preacher or *khatib,* another type of orator who reminded the congregation of their religious duties with stories. The term used for these preachers was *qāṣṣ* (storyteller). As discussed by Johannes Pedersen ("The Criticism of Islamic Preacher," in *Die Welt des Islam* 2 [1953]: 215–231), the difference between the *khatib* and the *qāṣṣ* was that the former was the representative of the head of the Muslim community. His speech was bound to special forms and, early in Islam, had a political character. Along with this differentiation, there developed a distinct separation between the *khaṭīb* and the *qāṣṣ* owing to the informal interpretations of the Qur'ān and the traditions by the latter. C. E. Bosworth reports (*The Medieval Islamic Underworld,* Leiden, 1976, pp. 27–28) that the lower fringe of this profession gradually merged with the underworld and some popular preachers were also suspected of playing the role of political agents. Some of the more established and better-known of these preachers were very influential, and their followers were prepared to defend them against any authority.

Furthermore, after Muḥammad, people without institutional support, had entirely on their own given themselves over to the study of religion. Gradually scholars in each locality grouped themselves into exclusive bodies, each adhering to a common method and a common body of law under the name of a great teacher. These scholars studied, commented on religious matters, and became involved in legal and community affairs as judges, administrators, and teachers. Thus they gained social and religious leadership of the masses, who turned to them rather than to the caliphs for religious instruction and moral guidance.

With the expansion of Islam, the appearance of imperial caliphal administration, the emergence of the popular preachers, and the development of independent religious authorities, the mosque became less an instrument of polity and more a place for religious practice. The *khuṭbah,* which in earlier days was pronounced by the sovereign himself or his governors and generals and dealt with political, military, and other state affairs, became less important. It gradually became more of a religious service or sermon with the dwindling of the political function of the mosque.

Nonetheless, the political character of the mosque never entirely disappeared. Utterance of prayers for the ruler during the *khuṭbah* remained one of the recognized tokens of sovereignty in Islam; its omission was a signal of revolt. The political character of the mosque had also been retained in another sense. In the case of a major crisis or community dissatisfaction, members flocked to the mosque to discuss the problem or seek remedy. Throughout the history of Islam the mosque has been the center of numerous uprisings, revolts, and social movements, often led from the *minbar.* In this respect, the role of the *minbar* in the nineteenth and twentieth centuries is especially notable during periods of unrest precipitated by Western incursion into Islamic territory.

Colonization of Muslim lands and the increasing political and commercial influence of the Christian West shocked Muslim leaders. In response they were divided into three groups: the traditionalists believed that Islam would eventually be triumphant; the modernists sought salvation through uncritical imitation of the West; and the moderates thought that a freer use of human reason in reinterpreting traditional Islamic ideas would remedy the situation. Some moderate users of the *minbar* in the nineteenth and twentieth centuries tried to introduce borrowed ideas and institutions to Muslims via a reinterpretation of traditional Islamic teachings. Although some intellectuals have been reluctant to admit this novel function of the *khuṭbah* and *minbar* as agents of social change, some devout Muslim social scientists of today openly recommend it.

The experience of colonialism motivated widespread use of the *minbar* in anti-colonial movements. Shāh ʿAbd al-ʿAzīz (1746–1824), a well-known religious leader, issued a *fatwā* declaring all land under British occupation to be *dar al-ḥarb* or the territory of the enemies of Islam. Through his preaching from the *minbar*s of two chief mosques in Delhi, he maintained contact with the masses and disseminated his anticolonial views. [*See the biography of ʿAbd al-ʿAzīz.*]

In 1890 Nāṣir al-Dīn Shāh of Iran granted a concession to a British subject for the control and sale of tobacco. The indigenous tobacco growers and merchants opposed the idea and sought assistance from the religious leaders, who were also unhappy about the influence of the Christians in the country. When the shah persisted, a *fatwā* proclaimed from the *minbar* banning the use of tobacco was unanimously accepted throughout the country. The shah was forced to cancel the concession in 1891. Fourteen years later the conflict between a group of religious leaders and the state was an important factor in the development of the constitutional movement in Iran. The alliance between the reformists and these religious leaders helped develop a truly national movement in which the *minbar* played a significant role.

Philip Hitti (*History of the Arabs,* London, 1958, p. 267), emphasized that the chief or congregational mosque has always been more than a building for devotion. He further noted that "in recent years the principal outbreaks against European authority in Syria and Egypt have had their inception in the Friday mosque meetings." Although Hitti does not directly discuss the role of the *minbar* in these meetings, the following cases leave no doubt about the involvement of the *minbar* in the struggle against colonialism.

In "The Origins of Arab Nationalism in Algeria," (*Islamic Culture* 46 [1972]: 285–292), Dennis Walker writes that the French colonial authorities in Algeria were so disturbed by the unrest generated by religious leaders at every point of their contact with the masses that these leaders were barred from the country's mosques, which the colonial authorities had always tightly controlled. The Prefect of Algiers, in a 1933 circular that has remained famous to this day, refused the reformist religious leaders entry to the mosque on the ground that they were rousing the people.

In 1912 Morocco became a protectorate of France. As reported by Asghar Fathi ("The Social and Political Functions of the Mosque in the Muslim Community," *Islamic Culture* 58 [1984]: 189–199), most of the religious leaders believed in resistance to France and the defense of Islam. Some advocated the adoption of new practices, including changes in the archaic format of the Friday *khuṭbah* in the mosque for more effective communication of political ideas. The fact that the Arabic press was under the control of French authorities made this reform more urgent. The fusion of state and religion in early Islam and the role of the ruler as both temporal and spiritual leader was also revived. Muḥammad V (1927–1961) claimed descent from the Prophet, and as spiritual leader of the people led the prayer of the assembly on Fridays and pronounced *khuṭbah*s in the mosque. The French authorities, who were aware of the anti-French character of the mosque assemblies, opposed this practice and sought ways to prevent the ruler from entering the mosque. They often restricted public access to the mosques in times of unrest; sometimes the army occupied the mosques or drove out the assembly forcibly.

In Shīʿī Iran the split between the state and the religious leaders had turned the latter into a natural opposition party, but in the Sunnī Ottoman Empire the sultan was considered both the caliph (successor to the Prophet) and the head of state. The tradition of state intervention in religious affairs has continued up to the present in Egypt, once part of the Ottoman Empire. According to Asghar Fathi ("Communication and Tradition in Revolution: The Role of the Islamic Pulpit," *Journal of Communication* 29 [1979]: 102–106), after World War I some religious leaders in Egypt began to criticize the dull and outdated *khuṭbah*s that ignored contemporary problems. As a result of this movement the Friday *khuṭbah* was revitalized and restored as a channel of political communication, as it had been in early Islam.

After abolishing the monarchy in 1952, the new regime in Egypt recognized that Islam remained the widest and most effective basis for consensus both within Egypt and among Arabs more generally. Therefore, in 1968 it proclaimed that the mosque, state, and community would be closely associated under government guidance. In practice this meant not only that opposition parties such as the Muslim Brotherhood were barred from the mosque, but also that the content of the Friday *khuṭbah* was under strict control. Egyptian preachers were directed by the state to amalgamate socialism, nationalism, and industrial development with the tenets of Islam. The new regime had already revived the symbolic fusion of state and religion in Islam. For example, during the invasion of Egypt by England, France, and Israel in 1956, Gamal Abdel Nasser as president of the republic performed the Friday prayer of the assembly in al-Azhar Mosque in Cairo on 2 and 9 November; he then ascended the *minbar* and delivered orations similar to other fiery speeches he gave during this national crisis.

King Muḥammad of Morocco and President Nasser of Egypt used the *khuṭbah* to promote modernist policies in the garb of "true Islamic traditions"; by contrast, Abdur Rauf, a Pakistani social scientist, has openly recommended the Friday *khuṭbah* as an instrument for social change and for transforming traditional lifestyles ("A Mosque-Centered Rural Development Plan," *Islamic Education* 6 [1973]: 26–36). Rauf has suggested that a mass movement for the development of rural life in Pakistan could be extensively and effectively implemented through the Friday *khuṭbah,* which should be made more simple in language and more relevant to the daily problems of the rural population. He argues that the problems of apathy, ignorance, ill health, and low productivity can be effectively solved with the help of communication via the *minbar,* backed by such measures as a well-planned training program for mosque leaders and promotion of the attendance of women and children at the Friday prayers. Unlike the Moroccan and Egyptian governments' use of the mosque, in the Pakistani case the religious assembly in the mosque is not confined to political communication. Rauf implies that with creative planning and imaginative use, the Friday *khuṭbah* could compete with the cinema, radio, television, and novels, which some believe promote harmful alien cultural values and deviant standards of behavior.

The cases discussed above point to the revival of the political and social functions of the *khuṭbah* and other orations from the *minbar*. In the case of Iran, because of the split between the state and the religious leaders, the *minbar* had increasingly become a rallying point against the government since the turn of the century. In the cases of Morocco and Egypt, with the revival of the fusion of state and religion the governments have consistently used the *khuṭbah* to their own advantage. For instance, in Egypt recently the mosque has become an arm of the government and not infrequently has been used as an instrument for the legitimization of government programs. The attention of Muslim intellectuals to indigenous institutions such as the *khuṭbah* as means of establishing rural community development programs, and the *minbar* as a medium of public communication combating the allegedly harmful effects of modern mass media, is exemplified by the Pakistani case.

Thus during the nineteenth and twentieth centuries the *khuṭbah* and the *minbar* have increasingly become a medium of political communication through which users try to promote various causes. At the same time some Muslim intellectuals, as cultural brokers, also hope that by these means they can maintain an accommodation between the traditional way of life in their communities and the influence of an ever-shrinking world.

[*See also* Mosque, *articles on* Historical Development *and* The Mosque in Politics.]

BIBLIOGRAPHY

Antoun, Richard. *Muslim Preacher in the Modern World: A Jordanian Case Study in Comparative Perspective*. Princeton, 1989. Anthropological study of the relationship between a rural community and its preacher who, through his Friday *khuṭbahs*, functions as a mediator between the forces of change and indigenous ways.

Borthwick, Bruce M. "The Islamic Sermon as a Channel of Political Communication." *Middle East Journal* 21.3 (1967): 299–313. Based on the author's 1965 doctoral thesis, this article deals with the renewal of the political function of the *khuṭbah* in Syria, Jordan, and Egypt.

Fathi, Asghar. "Preachers as Substitutes for Mass Media: The Case of Iran, 1905–1909." In *Towards a Modern Iran*, edited by Elie Kedourie and Sylvia G. Haim, pp. 169–184. London, 1980. Demonstrates the important role played by the pulpit in disseminating opposing views during the Iranian Constitutional Revolution.

Fathi, Asghar. "The Islamic Pulpit as a Medium of Political Communication." *Journal for the Scientific Study of Religion* 20.2 (1981): 163–172. Compares the Islamic pulpit with the modern media of public communication from a sociological perspective.

Ibn al-Jawzī, Abū al-Faraj ʿAbd al-Raḥmān ibn ʿAlī. *Kitāb al-Quṣṣāṣ wa-al-Mudhakkirīn*. Translated and edited by Merlin L. Swartz. Beirut, 1971. Study of the *khuṭbah* and *khaṭīb* in the late ʿAbbāsid period, including their political use. The translated book also contains what would today be called a code of ethics for Muslim preachers.

Pedersen, Johannes. "Khaṭīb." In *Encyclopaedia of Islam*, vol. 4, pp. 1109–1111. Leiden, 1960–.

Pedersen, Johannes, et al. "Minbar." In *Encyclopaedia of Islam*, vol. 7, pp. 73–80. Leiden, 1960–.

Pellat, Charles. "Ḳāṣṣ." In *Encyclopaedia of Islam*, vol. 4, pp. 733–735. Leiden, 1960–.

Samb, A. "Masdjid." In *Encyclopaedia of Islam*, vol. 6, pp. 644–707. Leiden, 1960–.

Wensinck, A. J. "Khuṭba." In *Encyclopaedia of Islam*, vol. 5, pp. 74–75. Leiden, 1960–.

ASGHAR FATHI

KING FAISAL FOUNDATION. A philanthropic organization established in 1976 by the eight sons of King Fayṣal ibn ʿAbd al-ʿAzīz Āl Saʿūd (1906–1975), who play a major role in the civic and cultural life of Saudi Arabia, the King Faisal Foundation is intended to promote within Saudi Arabia and abroad all charitable endeavors that the late king strove to accomplish, namely, helping fellow Muslims, expanding Islamic *daʿwah* (missionary activity), and fostering solidarity among Muslim states. The foundation is comprised of three distinct entities: The King Faisal Center for Research and Islamic Studies, the King Faisal International Prize, and the King Faisal Foundation General Secretariat. The director general of the foundation is Prince Khālid al-Fayṣal, emir of ʿAsīr Province, and most of the high-ranking posts of the foundation, particularly in the finance and investment section, are held by Saudis. In 1991, the research center's library held some 63,000 books and 2,000 periodicals in sixteen languages as well as 10,300 manuscripts. The children's library attached to the center provides a reading space for eighty children, and it holds 15,000 children's books and serials in Arabic, English, and French. The computer search services of the center provide college students and researchers, free of charge, with full bibliographies on any topic related to the Arab world and Islam.

The King Faisal International Prize, valued at 350,000 Saudi riyals (approximately US$93,000), is awarded annually to outstanding international figures whose contributions are universally recognized in five major fields: service to Islam, Islamic studies, Arabic literature, medicine, and science. Since the inception of the prize in 1979, an average of six scholars per year, from twenty-six countries, have won this award.

In financing philanthropic projects in Islamic states, the foundation oversees a multitude of programs directed to nongovernmental institutions, particularly schools, orphanages, and hospitals. This aid is independent of any assistance programs provided to these countries by the Saudi Government. The only requirement is that such bodies must conform to the *sunnah* (authentic teachings) of the Prophet and be run on sound business principles.

The foundation also encourages young students and scholars from the Muslim world to pursue medical and engineering studies in advanced industrial countries. Open to both men and women, most scholarships have gone to Muslim students from countries other than Saudi Arabia. In 1991, forty students received full scholarships; another twenty-two had already graduated and returned to their home countries.

Structurally, the foundation's secretariat is divided into two main divisions: the investment section and the programs and research section. A steering committee coordinates the work of the two divisions. The foundation's assets amounted to $332 million in 1991. Its holdings include a large shopping mall in Riyadh, one residential building, two high-rise office buildings, a five-star international hotel, a supermarket, and a modern boarding school. The foundation is also developing two more shopping centers in the southern Saudi cities of Abha and Khamīs Mushayt. In addition, the investment section actively deals in shares, stocks, and bonds, and it holds partnerships in some business and touristic ventures in eastern Saudi Arabia. Earnings from these investments in the past fourteen years were directed toward financing some ninety-nine projects in twenty-seven countries. In 1991, total earnings amounted to $18 million, half of which was spent on programs and projects and one-fourth on administration; the remaining quarter was kept as a reserve and for the upkeep and maintenance of existing facilities.

[*See also* Daʿwah, *article on* Institutionalization; Saudi Arabia.]

BIBLIOGRAPHY

The foundation publishes a multitude of pamphlets, a newsletter, and an annual report, mostly in Arabic. It also publishes a monthly Arabic cultural journal, *Al-fayṣal,* with a circulation of twenty-two thousand. The foundation commemorated its tenth anniversary by the publication of two books in Arabic reviewing its accomplishments. Few articles about the foundation's work are available in English.

SALEH ABDUL-REHMAN AL-MANIʿ

KIRGHIZIA. *See* Kyrgyzstan.

KISAKÜREK, NECIP FAZIL (1905–1983), Turkish poet, playwright, and essayist. One of the most striking figures of modern Turkish literature, Necip Fazıl combined in his life concerns for literary style and political ideology. Today he is remembered primarily for the second, but in fact his poetry, prose, journalism, and theater bring together experimentation with form and concerns about the cultural identity of the modern Turk.

Necip Fazıl was born in Istanbul in 1905 of a family with ancient roots in the town of Maraş in southeastern Turkey. The early death of his father and the somewhat retiring role of his mother in the family strengthened the influence on him of his grandparents, who had strong, idiosyncratic personalities. From his grandfather he acquired a knowledge of Ottoman culture and history; from his grandmother he absorbed her attempts to join the stream of Western culture and to imitate Western manners, shaped by her immersion in French novels. These sources instilled in the boy a curiosity about the West that eventually led to his reasonably wide knowledge of European culture. It also generated a suspicion of the suitability of western European values and of westernization in general as a model for Turkish modernization. This concern increased as he aged and grew into the primary focus of his later years.

He irregularly attended a number of the schools that during the nineteenth century had replaced the traditional *madrasah* (seminary) with programs copied from western European schools. After a five-year stint he dropped out of the Naval Cadet School in Istanbul. While registered at the Faculty of Philosophy of Istanbul University, he won a government scholarship for study abroad in 1921. As a student in Paris he refined his knowledge of French literature and culture but never received a university degree. He pursued a bohemian lifestyle, some traces of which remained for the rest of his life.

Upon his return he worked in various banks and taught at the Conservatory of Arts in Ankara, at the Academy of Fine Arts in Istanbul, and at Robert College, an American missionary school with strict academic standards. His poetic pieces and short stories appeared in such Istanbul literary magazines as *Yeni Mecmua, Millî Mecmua, Anadolu, Hayat,* and *Varlık* in the 1920s. His earliest pieces show a pervasive pessimism and often highlight motifs of boredom, despair, or death combined with a search for identity.

His versification was in the modern Turkish "syllabic" style, in which he showed an originality that brought him to the attention of the literary establishment. His poems show the influence of French symbolism promoted by his predecessor Ahmet Haşim but also have aspects reminiscent of the worldview of Ottoman Sufism. Orhan Okay has described such cultural mixture and use of themes from Western sources as characteristic of Turkish writers who lived through the transformation of the Ottoman Empire. With the establishment of the Turkish Republic (1923) the change of values from Islamic to secular, at work since the nineteenth century, was greatly accelerated. For Necip Fazıl the transformation brought up the problem of achieving a degree of authenticity amid the clash of two cultures, a dilemma prominent in his plays of the 1930s, such as *Tohum* (The Seed) and especially *Bir adam yaratmak* (To Create a Man).

To resolve these matters Necip Fazıl adopted a philosophy that placed the East and Islam at the foundation of his outlook on life. In his autobiography *Ove ben* (He and Myself) he ascribed this change to the influence of a shaykh of the Naqshbandī order, Abdulhakim Arvasi, whose path he followed thereafter. Although ideologically committed to Islam, Necip Fazıl never abandoned a frankly Western way of life, nor did he succeed in erasing the bohemianism of his early days, which brought him repeatedly to the gambling table.

His adoption by the younger generation of Turkish conservatives at a time when Turkish nationalism was giving way to the stronger influence of Islam may be attributed to the theme of a revival of the East first broached in his periodical *The Great East* (1943–1978), where he presented a critique of the emptiness of the basic social and humanistic philosophy of republican Turkey. Although frequently interrupted for long periods, the journal and the themes found in its columns, which reappeared in a number of collected essays, make up a compendium that younger conservative Turks use for ideological guidance.

BIBLIOGRAPHY

Kısakürek, Necip Fazıl. *O ve Ben*. 3d ed. Istanbul, 1978.
Mavera (Ankara) Special number on Kısakürek (July–August 1983).
Okay, M. Orhan. *Necip Fazıl Kısakürek*. Ankara, 1987.

ŞERIF MARDIN

KISHK, ʿABD AL-ḤAMĪD (b. 1933), more fully, Shaykh ʿAbd al-Ḥamīd ʿAbd al-ʿAzīz Muḥammad Kishk, immensely popular Egyptian preacher, known to many of his followers as Shaykh ʿAbd al-Ḥamīd. Born in 1933 in Shubrākhīt, a village not far from Damanhūr, Kishk went to school in Alexandria and became blind at the age of twelve. Graduating from the *uṣūl al-dīn* (dogmatics) faculty of al-Azhar, he worked for some time in the service of the Egyptian *awqāf* (religious endowment) ministry as a mosque preacher and imam. From 5 May 1964 until 28 August 1981, he was an independent preacher in the ʿAyn al-Ḥayāh Mosque in Miṣr wa-'l-Sudān Street in the Cairene quarter known as Ḥadā'iq al-Qubbah. This mosque is also known as the Masjid al-Malik. It was from here that his fame and popularity spread.

Under the regime of President Gamal Abdel Nasser (1952–1970), Kishk came into conflict with the authorities over several questions. For instance, he refused to give a *fatwā* that approved of the death sentence imposed by the regime on Sayyid Quṭb in 1966; and he avoided answering the question of Arab socialism's compatibility with Islam. By such attitudes he identified himself as a dissident, and he consequently spent time in prison.

Under the regime of Anwar el-Sadat (1970–1981), Kishk's sermons became immensely popular. In these, he continued to criticize sharply any behavior that he regarded as a deviation from the norms of Islam. However, the regime was a little more tolerant of such criticisms, since it needed the support of the Islamic movement in the struggle against "communism and atheism." Nevertheless, Shaykh Kishk, unlike Islamists such as Shaykh al-Shaʿrāwī, did not appear on state-run television or publish in the official printed media.

In spite of the official media boycott, Kishk's sermons were widely distributed on cassette tapes, as were, in the same period, those by the Iranian leader Ayatollah Khomeini, who came to power in 1979. Hence, the Western media have sometimes called Kishk an Egyptian Khomeini. It is now more obvious than it was in the 1980s that the resemblance between the two men is superficial at best. Whereas Khomeini founded a revolutionary movement that came to power in Iran and survived the death of its founder by years, Kishk's political views (as far as they can be found in his books) resemble a form of anarchism. He writes, for instance, with great nostalgia about the days when there were no policemen to stop people and ask for their driver's licenses, or frontier guards to ask for passports and entry or exit visas: those were the days when the Muslims conquered the world, so Kishk wants his audience to remember.

Anarchism, obviously, is too strong and too Western a word to describe the traditional dislike for rulers and government officials in the Middle East and elsewhere. This common attitude is perhaps best put into words by Saʿd Zaghlūl (1857–1927; prime minister of Egypt from January to November 1924), who once remarked that Egypt's citizens tend to look at their rulers in the same way a bird looks at the hunter.

The emphasis in Kishk's preaching falls on personal and private piety, not on something as transitory as worldly power. The shaykh is occupied with the end of the world, the miracles of the Ṣūfī saints, the metaphysics of the soul, eschatology, and death. Nevertheless, in a politically tense atmosphere the statements he makes about this world may easily be understood as veiled demands for the introduction of a theocracy, especially by those who are in favor, or in fear, of an Islamic theocracy. There can, however, be little doubt that many in the shaykh's audiences, in the traditions of the Islamic quietist Ṣūfī movements, are only superficially, or not at all, interested in political (Islamic) utopias.

"The believer's creed must be compressed into: loving God," Kishk once wrote (Kishk, 1978–, vol. 13, p. 159). It is not plausible, although admittedly possible, that such an emphasis on love, also known from Islamic mysticism, accompanies political ambitions, revolutionary schemes, and participation in the struggle for worldly power. Yet Kishk's social criticisms may be thought to imply political consequences. In a sermon on 12 December 1980, he attacked not only Jews, Christians, lax Muslims, and a former rector of al-Azhar University, but also a soccer captain and a businessman who was reported to have presented his wife with an expensive coat. Since the shaykh was intermittently sent to jail, one has to assume that those in power were concerned about the force of such sweeping criticisms.

In the first days of September 1981, on the eve of the assassination of Sadat, which took place on 6 October, Kishk was again thrown into prison. He shared this fate with 1,526 others of all political persuasions who were put under "precautionary arrest." In anticipation of the publication of a complete official list of detainees, the first page of *Al-ahrām* on September 4 noted the imprisonment of Kishk along with a small number of prominent Egyptians. In spite of controls on the media, the shaykh's fame had clearly spread.

On 24–25 January 1982, Kishk was released from detention. In February, the Egyptian semiofficial weekly devoted to religious affairs, *Al-liwā' al-islāmī*, contained minor contributions by Kishk—an indication that a compromise with the regime of Hosni Mubarak had been reached. His books and cassette tapes were to be freely available (they still were in 1993), but his life as a public preacher was over—for the time being at least. His mosque in Cairo has since been transformed into a public health center.

Kishk's uniqueness is closely connected to the way in which he chants his sermons. His voice expresses nostalgia for the Kingdom of Heaven in a way that moves many members of his audiences.

[*See also* Egypt.]

BIBLIOGRAPHY

Jansen, Johannes J. G. "The Voice of Sheikh Kishk." In *The Challenge of the Middle East*, edited by Ibrahim A. El-Sheikh et al., pp. 57–67. Amsterdam, 1982. Discusses the teachings of Shaykh Kishk.

Jansen, Johannes J. G. *The Neglected Duty: The Creed of Sadat's Assassins and Islamic Resurgence in the Middle East.* New York and London, 1986. Discusses the teachings of Shaykh Kishk and his reaction to the assassination of Sadat. Contains quotations from his sermons and his booklets (pp. 91–120).

Kepel, Gilles. *The Prophet and Pharaoh.* London, 1985. Contains translated excerpts of Shaykh Kishk's sermon for 10 April 1981 (pp. 172–190).

Kishk, ʿAbd al-Ḥamīd. *Maktabat al-Shaykh Kishk.* Cairo, [1978–]. More than thirty-two small volumes, most of them reprinted several times. The first volume, *Ṭarīq al-najāḥ*, was written, or rather dictated, before 1973.

Kishk, ʿAbd al-Ḥamīd. *Qiṣṣat ayyāmī: Mudhakkirāt al-Shaykh Kishk.* Cairo, n.d. [1986]. Autobiography.

Kishk, ʿAbd al-Ḥamīd. *Al-khuṭab al-minbarīyah.* Cairo, 1987–. Literal texts of the shaykh's sermons. Thirteen volumes had appeared by 1992. Date of delivery is given for some sermons; not arranged chronologically.

Kishk, ʿAbd al-Ḥamīd. *Fatāwā al-Shaykh Kishk: Humūn al-Muslim al-muʿāṣir.* Cairo, n.d. [1988?]. Ten volumes had appeared by 1992. Contains answers (*fatāwā*) to questions by concerned Muslims.

JOHANNES J. G. JANSEN

KOMITEH. Revolutionary committees active in the Iranian Revolution of 1979, the Komitehs arose in the fall of 1978 when students and young people formed neighborhood defense units against government-backed clubwielders who attacked protesters and set fire to shops, stores, and schools. Initially, the Komitehs were comprised of individuals with differing political ideologies and were not directed by any central authority. Two processes brought them under the control of the fundamentalist clergy, who employed them as a coercive organ. First, many members who had supported a democratic revolutionary outcome voluntarily left these organizations in the face of increasing authoritarianism. Second, in the summer of 1979, the clergy initiated an ideological purge of the Komitehs, dismissing forty thousand who did not meet with their ideological approval. The purified Komiteh members were largely drawn from the lower middle class, urban poor, and recent rural migrants.

With the collapse of the monarchy in February 1979, the Komitehs mobilized offensively to arrest and punish officials of the shah's regime. Many Komiteh members had armed themselves with weapons confiscated during attacks on army barracks in the last two days of the revolutionary conflicts in February. During the first six months of the Islamic Republic, the Komitehs arrested a large number of officials and executed more than 220 police and army officers, SAVAK (secret police officials), and politicians linked to the monarchy. Over the next five years, they imprisoned numerous nonpolitical Bahā'īs, executing more than 200.

Liberal and nationalist political leaders who remained in the government, such as Prime Minister Mehdi Bāzargān and President Abol-Hasan Bani Sadr, repeatedly complained about the arbitrary nature of Komiteh activities. There were even some large-scale demonstrations in Tehran against the repressive measures taken by the Komitehs. In response to growing criticism, Ayatollah Ruhollah Khomeini stated in late February 1979 that as soon as the government was in complete control of the cities, the Komitehs should relinquish their power and avoid involvement in government affairs. In mid-April, however, Khomeini, recognizing the threat posed by mounting social and ideological cleavages, modified his stand, declaring that the Komitehs needed purging, not dissolution. He stated that as long as corrupt individuals existed, there was a need for the Komitehs.

As the revolutionary coalition broke down and new conflicts emerged within the Islamic Republic, the Komitehs directed their attention against those who opposed fundamentalist rule. The Komitehs were significant in the dissolution of Workers' Councils that sprang up in factories, the closure of colleges and universities throughout the country beginning in 1980, the repression of liberals aligned with President Bani Sadr in 1981, and the armed struggle against the socialist Islamic group, the Mujāhidīn-i Khalq, during the early 1980s. In addition, the Komitehs were instrumental in the arrest and execution of more than seven thousand leftist, Kurdish, and Türkmen opponents of the regime between 1981 and 1984.

By 1984, with the repression of the opposition virtually complete, the Komitehs moved out of the local mosques, where most of them had been headquartered. Their tasks were redefined and directed toward controlling smuggling and drug trafficking, and enforcing the use of the veil by women. In 1991, they were incorporated into the regular police force and ceased to exist as an independent entity.

[*See also* Iranian Revolution of 1979.]

BIBLIOGRAPHY

Abrahamian, Ervand. *Iran between Two Revolutions*. Princeton, 1982. Excellent history and analysis of the rise and demise of the Pahlavi dynasty and the creation of the Islamic Republic.

Amnesty International. *Law and Human Rights in the Islamic Republic of Iran*. London, 1980. Discusses the formation and functions of revolutionary organizations and issues of human rights in the early months of the Islamic Republic.

Bakhash, Shaul. *The Reign of the Ayatollahs: Iran and the Islamic Revolution*, New York, 1984. Insightful narrative of the post-1979 conflict and the establishment of the theocratic state.

Parsa, Misagh. *Social Origins of the Iranian Revolution*. New Brunswick, N.J., and London, 1989. Analyzes the nature of the state, economy, social conflicts, and collective action by various social groups between 1951 and 1981, with special emphasis on the 1977–1979 conflicts.

MISAGH PARSA

KUFR. A key concept in Islamic tradition is denoted by the Arabic term *Kufr,* "disbelief." It derives from the root *k-f-r,* whose basic sense is "to cover," "to conceal," or by extension "to ignore" or "to fail to acknowledge," "to reject," hence "to be thankless," "to disbelieve." In a religious context the latter meanings are more relevant, especially in relationship to the signs and benefits that God has extended to human beings. *Kāfir* (pl., *kuffār* or *kāfirūn*), an active participial form, signifies one who does or exercises *kufr,* while *kafūr* and *kaffār* both refer to one who goes to extremes in *kufr. Takfīr,* an infinitive or verbal noun, indicates the action of judging or pronouncing someone to be a *kāfir. Kaffārah* refers to expiation for wrongdoing, hence atonement. All these words occur frequently in Islamic religious texts, beginning with the Qur'ānic revelations.

Qur'ānic Concepts. The very high frequency at which words derived from *k-f-r* in the sense of unbelief (482 forms) occur in the Qur'ān testifies to the importance of the concept of *kufr.* In the structure of Qur'ānic thought it typifies all things that are unacceptable and offensive to God. It is, in fact, one of the pivotal ideas of the Qur'ān; around it clusters a group of concepts signifying negative qualities, all of which help to define the precise nature of *kufr. Kufr* is, as it were, the negative pole of Qur'anic thought, diametrically opposed to *īmām* or faith.

In its most fundamental sense in the Qur'ān *kufr* means "ingratitude," the willful refusal to acknowledge or appreciate the many benefits that God has bestowed on humans. At many places (e.g., 26.18–19) the context compels this meaning because no other would yield sense. More important from a religious perspective are those verses that set *kufr* against *shukr* (thankfulness) as its antonym (e.g., 16.112–114, 2.52). Gratitude toward God is incumbent upon all humans for the divine benevolence and mercy offered them. Not only the bounties of nature and other material things but even the very existence of the race are owed to God. After enumerating the favors of God, the Qur'ān says in Surah 16.83, "They recognize the favors of God, and yet they deny them, for most men are *kāfirūn.*" God has the strong expectation that people should be grateful for his blessings: "Be thankful to Me, and be not ungrateful" (*takfurūna,* a verbal form; 2.152).

The appropriate response to God's beneficence is joyful gratitude and submission to the divine will, not harsh and unheeding rejection. *Kufr* is precisely this refusal and the haughtiness or presumptuous arrogance it implies. It is at once the antithesis of thankfulness toward God and of the humility the true Muslim should bear toward God. All who are guilty of *kufr* are deserving of eternal punishment in Hell.

The concept of *kufr* also has a related but somewhat different dimension in the Qur'ān, that of unbelief, a meaning that dominated in later Islamic thought and continues as the primary sense of the term today. Among God's blessings are signs given to men, scriptures and revelations sent in previous times through prophets, and evidences of his mercy in the order of nature. These signs were powerfully renewed with the appearance of Muḥammad and the revelations collected in the Qur'ān. Despite their unequalled value, the signs were not accepted by many as being truly from God; instead Muḥammad's opponents mocked his claims, impugned his sincerity, and attributed his declarations to his own invention. By rejecting the prophetic message they offered an affront to its divine originator. Thus *kufr* also meant refusal to give credence to the prophetic mission and refusal to perform the religious duties the Prophet's teachings demanded. The harshest and most offensive expression of disbelief was the accusation against Muḥammad (and implicitly against God) that he was lying, and consequently those who "give the lie" (*takdhīb*) to God and his Prophet are the objects of special opprobrium.

One group in particular whom the Qur'ān reproaches for their *kufr* is the people of the book (Jews and Christians) (9.30–31), to whom revelations had come before and who should have been the first to embrace Muḥammad's message: "Oh, People of the Book, why do you disbelieve (*takfurūna*) in the signs of God when you yourselves bear witness to them? Oh, People of the Book, why do you confound the truth with falsehood and knowingly conceal the truth?" (3.70–71). These stubborn unbelievers had not only themselves gone astray, but they endeavored also to lead the believers after them and were, therefore, a threat to the community (5.149). Christians especially are singled out for their acceptance of the Trinity: "They surely disbelieve (*kafara,* verbal form) who say: 'God is the third of Three.' Nay, there is no God save one God. If they do not desist from saying so, a painful doom will befall those of them who disbelieve" (5.73). Jesus himself is made to testify to the unity of God; and the Qur'ān, in addition to denying his divine sonship (10.68) indicates that he was but a messenger like others before him, a man who subsisted on earthly sustenance (5.72, 75).

The great fault of the Christians is the same as that of the polytheists: they ascribe associates to God and thus are guilty of the capital sin of *shirk*. In the Qur'ān God alone is held to be worthy of worship and without comparison. He does not have offspring, nor does he have partners, neither the *jinn* (5.100), the angels, the pagan deities, nor any other. To worship these beings or ascribe power to them is to disbelieve in the uniqueness of God, and that is *shirk*. *Shirk* is *kufr* of the most heinous kind.

The aspect of prophetic teachings that evoked the greatest scorn in Muḥammad's contemporaries was the doctrine of the resurrection, which the pagan Arabs considered absurd: " 'What! after we have become dust? Shall we then be created afresh?' These are they who disbelieve in their Lord. . . . And these are they who shall be the fellows of the Fire, therein to dwell forever" (3.5). This skepticism is one of the most characteristic manifestations of *kufr,* according to the Qur'ān.

There are further concepts inseparable from the idea of *kufr* and to some degree synonymous with it. Verses 44, 45, and 47 of surah 5 afford an excellent example:

Whoso judges not by what God has sent down: such are *kāfirūn*.

Whoso judges not by what God has sent down: such are *ẓālimūn* (wrongdoers).

Whoso judges not by what God has sent down; such are *fāsiqūn* (those who persist in extreme *kufr*).

From the above it appears that the concepts of *kufr*, *ẓulm*, and *fisq* overlap if they are not simply equivalent. Elsewhere in the Qur'ān a similar relation obtains between *kufr* and concepts such as immorality, transgression of the limits set by God, excessive behavior, rebellion against God, attachment to worldly life, and hypocrisy. As indicated above, *kufr* is the polar idea around which these many negative qualities cluster and to which they are ultimately reducible.

Traditional Interpretations. The concept of *kufr* also figures prominently in the great collections of *ḥadīth* which with the Qur'ān serve as the fundamental authority in Islamic tradition. Here the punishments to be endured by the *kāfirīn* in Hell are set out in vivid detail. There is also much interest in the relationship of the believers to the *kāfirīn*, a matter that was taken up also by the schools of law. A major issue arose from the Qur'ān's characterization of unbelievers as unclean (9.28) and their prohibition from visiting the sacred shrine in Makkah (Mecca). Although the people of the book are called *kuffār* in the Qur'ān, some later thinkers made a distinction between them and the polytheists (*mushrikīn*, those who commit *shirk*), who were unbelievers in the strictest sense. In fact, in return for payment of special taxes a high degree of tolerance has been extended to the people of the book, who for much of Muslim history have been guaranteed protection and allowed to practice their own religions, to follow their own laws within their own communities, and to hold important positions in government and society. In some parts of the Muslim world, for example India, similar tolerance has also been extended to polytheists. The range of Muslim attitudes extends from quite lenient to very strict, depending on the school of thought and the perspective of a particular thinker.

There was also a question of the relationship of Muslims to *kuffār* living outside Muslim-controlled territory. In this connection there arose the distinction between the *dār al-Islām* (abode of Islam) and the *dār al-ḥarb* (abode of war). Their relationship was assumed normally to be hostile, as it was the duty of a Muslim ruler to subject the *kuffār* to the control of the Muslim *ummah*. In consequence the *ḥadīth* and the schools of law have much to say on the matter of *jihād*, the rules that should govern it, and the consequences for anyone taken prisoner.

In the development of *kalām* or scholastic theology, discussions of *kufr* have a place in the controversies concerning the effects of sin upon the religious and legal status of a Muslim. Has a Muslim who commits a grave sin become a *kāfir?* Does failure to perform the prayers or other ritual duties render a person no longer a Muslim? Has such a one cut himself off from the *ummah* and all its rights and privileges? In this context and in many others the notion of the *kāfir* bears the sense of "outsider," one who is excluded or has excluded himself from the righteous community. Such questions had social and political as well as religious implications, especially in the early period. As parties contended for power, the debates over *īmān* and *islām* (faith and works), big and little sins, and other questions were eventually thrashed out. Again the opinions ranged from the very lenient—represented by the Murji'ah, who would leave the decision about who is a Muslim to God since only God can know the heart—to the severe, represented by the Khawārij, for whom the unrepentant sinner was an apostate (*murtadd*, a particularly heinous type of *kāfir*) and therefore deserving of death. Much of the evidence for the contending views is found in *ḥadīth* included in the Ṣaḥīḥ collections.

According to ḥadīth, it is unacceptable for one Muslim to declare another a *kāfir*. Nevertheless, *takfīr* (the declaration of a judgment of *kufr*) by Muslims against their coreligionists has been and continues to be a regular feature of Islamic history. The concept has been a formidable weapon against those of opposing views, even when the opponents have been pious, well-intentioned Muslims. It was used, for example, to justify the murderous excesses of the Khawārij and the Qarāmiṭah. The destructive impact of *takfīr* was such that al-Ghazālī felt compelled to pen a rational and balanced definition of *kufr* to moderate its effects. [*See* Takfīr.]

In the treatises that deal with *kufr* there exists a number of classifications of unbelief. The modern Indian figure Abū al-Aʿlā Mawdūdī, for example, in his commentary on the Qur'ān, indicates that *kufr* may be of four kinds: the general state of being without faith, the denial of faith, ingratitude towards God, or failure to carry out those duties required by faith in God. The lawyers and theologians of later times, he charges, have simplified the term and lost its multidimensionality. Thomas Hughes in his *Dictionary of Islam* cites five classes of *kāfirīn* from a classical source: those who do not believe in the First Cause; those who do not believe in the unity of God, such as people who accept two eternal principles like light and darkness; those who believe in the unity of God but do not believe in a revelation;

those who are idolaters; and those who believe in God and in revelation but do not accept that Muḥammad's mission was for all mankind, such as Christians and Jews (p. 260). In its definition of *kufr* the dictionary *Lisān al-ʿArab* describes the following types of unbelief: neither recognizing nor acknowledging God; recognizing God but not acknowledging Him with words, that is, remaining an unbeliever in spite of knowing better; recognizing God and acknowledging Him but obdurately refusing to submit; and outwardly acknowledging though not recognizing God at heart, thus being a hypocrite. (*Encyclopedia of Islam,* new ed., Leiden, 1960–, vol. 4, p. 408).

Premodern and Modern Interpretations. In the immediately premodern and modern periods of Islamic history *kufr* has taken on a new significance in the thought of reform and revivalist movements. These movements have seen the conditions prevailing among Muslims, including their religious beliefs and practices, to be so far removed from true Islam as to constitute *kufr,* or *shirk,* or *jāhilīyah* (the situation before the advent of Islam)—concepts effectively equivalent, though some thinkers prefer one or another.

For the reformers of the premodern period, the community's lapse into *kufr* or *shirk* was seen most readily in the practice of popular religion, especially the veneration of saints associated with the Ṣūfī orders. Sufism dominated the religious life of the majority of Muslims in the premodern period, but in the eyes of the reformers many of its expressions were no more than forms of idolatry and innovation from which Islam urgently required to be purged. Some reforming movements adopted reformed modes of Sufism, but others sought to eliminate its influence completely.

The best-known premodern movement is that of the Wahhābīs. They looked upon themselves as the only upholders of *tawḥīd* (the unity of God), considering all other Muslims to be *mushrikīn.* According to them *shirk* took many forms: the attribution to prophets, saints, astrologers and soothsayers of knowledge of the unseen world which only God possesses and can grant; the attribution of power to any being except God, including the power of intercession; reverence given in any way to any created thing, even to the tomb of the Prophet; such superstitious customs as belief in omens and in auspicious and inauspicious days; and swearing by the names of the Prophet, ʿAlī, the Shīʿī imams, or the saints. Thus the Wahhābīs acted even to destroy the cemetery where many of the Prophet's most notable companions were buried on the ground that it was a center of idolatry. The Wahhābīs were by no means alone; the same concerns were reflected in the teachings of Shāh Ismāʿīl Shahīd and Sayyid Aḥmad Barelwī (Barēlī), leaders of the Mujāhidīn movement on the northwest frontier of India in the early nineteenth century, and among similar movements elsewhere. [*See* Tawḥīd; Wahhābīyah; *and the biography of Barelwī.*]

In more recent times the notion of *jāhilīyah* featured in the voluminous writings of Abū al-Aʿlā Mawdūdī. His central concern was the massive influence of the western world, which seduced Muslim peoples into adopting ideas, institutions, and values from outside the Islamic tradition. The community had thereby destroyed the basis of its strength and had actually become part of the anti-Islamic *jāhilī* system. All people face one basic choice: either to follow the jāhilī system of life or the Islamic system—that is, to live in accord with God's will or contrary to it. The purpose of the Islamic movement that Mawdūdī founded was to do away with *jāhilīyah* and replace it with a government, social structure, and way of life based on the Qur'ān, the *sunnah,* and the life of the early community. To this end he insisted that Muslims must enter the political arena, seize power, and establish an Islamic polity. These ideas, which are among the defining concepts of Islamic fundamentalism, were highly influential in the thinking of Sayyid Quṭb, the ideologist of the Muslim Brotherhood, who was executed in 1966 for his call to overthrow the Egyptian *"jāhilī"* government. [*See the biographies of Mawdūdī and Quṭb.*]

The same ideas found radical expression in the manifesto of the group responsible for the assassination of Anwar el-Sadat: the manifesto is entitled *The Neglected Duty,* referring to *jihād* or the religious obligation to take up arms for the propagation of Islam. Basing itself on the Qur'ānic verse that says: "Whoso judges not (or rules not) by what God has sent down is a *kāfir,*" the manifesto condemns all governments in the Muslim world as *kāfir* governments, and no *kāfir* has the right to rule. It is the solemn, inescapable duty of true Muslims to fight against them by any means, including assassination and open warfare. Essentially the same ideas are held by other groups in the radical wing of Islamic fundamentalism, for instance the Shabāb Muḥammad of Egypt.

BIBLIOGRAPHY

The best source for concise and authoritative information on any aspect of Islam is the *Encyclopaedia of Islam* in both its old and new editions (Leiden, 1913–1936, 1960–), along with the *Shorter Encyclopaedia of Islam* (Leiden, 1953). In addition to the article on *kāfir*, those on *shirk, dhimmī, djihād, dār al-Islām, dār al-ḥarb,* and others are relevant to this subject. Each article is followed by a bibliography. *The Structure of the Ethical Terms in the Koran* by Toshihiko Izutsu (Tokyo, 1959) and its revised edition, entitled *Ethico-Religious Concepts in the Qur'an* (Montreal, 1966), offer a detailed, in-depth analysis of *kufr* in relation to other key Qur'ānic ideas, using a method of semantic analysis. It is the most thorough study of the concept in a European language. Another book by Toshihiko Izutsu, *The Concept of Belief in Islamic Theology* (Tokyo, 1965), also deals *in extenso* with the concept of *kufr,* but goes on to consider the opposing concept of *īmān* in equal detail. The work is especially important for its analysis of the understanding of *kufr* among the early Muslim sects. W. Montgomery Watt's *The Formative Period of Islamic Thought* (Edinburgh, 1973) is the mature summation of many years of work devoted to the early development of the Muslim community. It traces the controversy about the status of a Muslim sinner and indicates the positions on the matter of the sectarian groups involved. Also of great value for theological developments in the early period is the classic study by Louis Gardet and Georges C. Anawati, *Introduction à la théologie musulmane* (Paris, 1948), which remains the best account of the historical development of theological thought among the Muslims, in spite of its age. John L. Esposito, in his *Islam and Politics* (Syracuse, N.Y., 1984), presents a readable and clear analysis of Islamic movements in the premodern and modern periods. *Islam, Continuity, and Change in the Modern World,* by John Obert Voll, sets modern developments into a broad historical framework, while also giving information on particular movements and thinkers. J. J. G. Jansen has translated the manifesto of Sadat's assassins under the title *The Neglected Duty* (New York, 1986). In addition to his own analysis of the document, Jansen sets out the reaction to it of other religious groups in Egypt, providing information that is seldom available to those who do not read Arabic.

Charles J. Adams

KUNTĪ, AL-. *See* Bakkā'ī al-Kuntī, Aḥmad al-.

KUWAIT. *See* Gulf States.

KYRGYZSTAN. The Central Asian republic of Kyrgyzstan, formerly known as Kirghizia, stretches from the Pamirs to the Tian Shan. Its geographical features include the Pobeda Peak, Issyk Kul, the Naryn, Chu, and Talas Rivers, and the Ferghana Valley. Historically, the Kyrgyz, an ancient Turkic people, were a major power along the Yenisei River, where they had developed a "runic" script and established an elaborate civilization. After the Mongol onslaught, they moved west and became mountain-dwelling pastoral nomads in the grasslands of the Tian Shan. During the eighteenth century, influenced by Muslim traders and Sunnī Uzbeks, they accepted Islam. Their past is celebrated in the great Kyrgyz epic, the *Manas*.

Kyrgyzstan was incorporated into the Russian Empire in 1876. Thereafter, Russian peasants routinely displaced the Kyrgyz and confiscated their grazing lands. In 1916, pressured by shortages at the front, Tsar Nicholas II drafted Kyrgyz youth into the army. The decision set off revolts throughout Muslim Central Asia, resulting in the death of many Kyrgyz; many more fled to eastern Turkistan.

In the 1920s the Basmachi movement, which advocated national independence and the return of the *waqf* (religious endowment) lands was crushed, and the Kyrgyz were forced to abandon their nomadic lifestyle. In the 1930s the Jadīdist movement, which sought Turkish unity and modernization of Islam, met with a similar end. In both cases, the Muslim intellectuals who had advocated the reforms were liquidated. After 1937 all the manifestations of the Kyrgyz past celebrated in the *Manas* were dissolved in efforts toward collectivization and industrialization. Mosques and *madrasahs* masqueraded as museums and opera houses, while programs of sovietization and russification dominated Kyrgyz education. The Arabic script gave way to Latin and then to Cyrillic. Eventually Russian became the state language. The *sharīʿah* and the *ʿādāt* legal codes were replaced by the Soviet civil code, and prayers, death rituals, pilgrimages, and circumcisions were outlawed. Even Islamic marriages, including the traditional practice of *kalym* (bride price) and *ichkari* (confinement of women to their quarters), were forbidden.

Today Kyrgyzstan has a population of 4,590,000 (55 percent Muslim), made up of Kyrgyz, Russians, Uzbeks, Ukrainians, and Germans; the highest birthrate occurs among the Kyrgyz. The republic has established a democratic government and is instituting a market economy. Through privatization, the state-held enterprises are being divided among small concerns in the public sector. Agriculture, livestock raising, mining, and manufacturing are also being privatized. While this process might inspire unrest elsewhere, the political stability stemming from the curtailment of communist power in Kyrgystan may help it succeed. The recent referendum, empowering President Asghar Akayev to implement extensive reforms, is proof that the Kyrgyz are determined to effect change in their republic. This, of course, is not a new phenomenon; intellectuals like Chingiz Aitmatov have advocated political, cultural, and economic reforms since the late 1960s.

Islam in Central Asia must be understood within a north-south geographic orientation. In Kazakhstan the influence of Islam is slight; Alma-Ata, the republic's capital, has only one mosque located in the bazaar district, and the population is virtually unaware of its existence. Conversely, in Tajikistan, a southern republic, Muslim groups actively rehabilitate mosques, open *madrasahs*, and teach the Qur'ān. However, since the November 1992 civil war and the introduction of anti-Wahhabi measures resulting in a factional bloodbath, the general goodwill for Islam has noticeably diminished. Furthermore, Tajikistan's gradual domination by Russia—Tajikistan is now in the ruble zone; is heavily in debt to Russian; lacks skilled cadres, raw material, and parts for its factories; and the 201st Russian division defends its southern border—has led to the sociopolitical and economic unification of three of Tajikistan's Turkic neighbors: Kazakhstan, Kyrgyzstan, and Uzbekistan. While all those states pay lip service to Islam, on their way to Pan-Turkism, they control their Muslim groups very firmly. This is particularly true of Uzbekistan.

Islam in Kyrgyzstan is influenced both by the Kazakh conservativism reflected in the speeches of Imam Ratbek Nisanbayev, and by Tajik extremism. In the capital Bishkek, in the north, Islam is taking its first steps, while in Osh, on the edge of the Ferghana, many young people are finding their salvation in Islam. They perform the rituals and attend the mosque. The urban faithful, however, are only a fraction of the main body of Kyrgyz devotees of the rural south, where Imam Abdulmajid Qari and the chief Islamic judge of the republic, Abdulrahman Kimsenbayev, expend most of their energies. As a result of their efforts, today Kyrgyzstan has more than two hundred mosques whereas in 1985 it had only forty. By the end of 1992, Bishkek alone was scheduled to add six more mosques to its existing four. Kyrgyzstan also has two *madrasahs*, the Bishkek Islamic Seminary and the Qara Qul Seminary. The Islamic Republic of Iran, Turkey, and Saudi Arabia provide funds for many Islamic activities in Kyrgyzstan, including the organization of pilgrimages to Mecca, the acquisition of books for instruction in Islam, and the building of mosques and *madrasahs*.

[*See also* Basmachis; Islam, *article on* Islam in Central Asia and the Caucasus; Jadīdism.]

BIBLIOGRAPHY

Allworth, Edward, ed. *Soviet Nationality Problems*. New York and Boston, 1971.

Allworth, Edward, ed. *Central Asia: One Hundred and Twenty Years of Russian Rule*. Durham, N.C., and London, 1989. Gives an overall view of the social, cultural, and economic dynamics of the republics.

Bennigsen, Alexandre, and Marie Broxup. *The Islamic Threat to the Soviet State*. New York, 1983. History of Russian and Soviet interactions with the Muslims of Central Asia from the Mongol invasion to the present.

Bennigsen, Alexandre, and S. Enders Wimbush. *Muslims of the Soviet Empire: A Guide*. Bloomington, 1986. Provides vital information for all the republics, especially about their Muslim peoples.

Fierman, William, ed. *Soviet Central Asia: The Failed Transformation*. Boulder, 1991.

Hatto, A. T., ed. *The Memorial Feast for Kokotoy-Khan: A Kirgiz Epic Poem*. London, 1977. The best portrayal of Kyrgyz nomadic lifestyle before sovietization.

Massell, Gregory. *The Surrogate Proletariat: Moslem Women and Revolutionary Strategies in Soviet Central Asia, 1919–1929*. Excellent study of the role of women in the integration of Muslim Central Asia into the Soviet system.

Olcott, Martha. "Central Asia: The Reformers Challenge a Traditional Society." In *The Nationalities Factor: Soviet Politics and Society*, edited by Lubomyr Hajda and Mark Beissinger, pp. 253–280. Boulder, 1990. Comprehensive overview of social, political, and cultural issues in Central Asian republics in recent years.

Rywkin, Michael. *Moscow's Muslim Challenge: Soviet Central Asia*. New York, 1982. Examines the effectiveness of Moscow's policies for the Central Asian republics.

Shahrani, M. Nazif. *The Kirghiz and Wakhi of Afghanistan: Adaptation to Closed Frontiers*. Seattle and London, 1979. Good study of the struggle of the displaced Kyrgyz and the odds of their survival in a changing world.

IRAJ BASHIRI

L

LABOR PARTY OF EGYPT. The only legal Islamist party in Egypt, and from 1987 the leading opposition party, the Labor Party was founded as the Socialist Labor Party in December 1978. It was represented in the Egyptian parliament, the People's Assembly, from 1979 until 1990. In the 1987 elections, the last in which the opposition took part, the Labor Party became the leading opposition party with 17 percent of the vote and 56 out of 448 representatives. Only 22 of these representatives, however, were party members; the majority were Muslim Brothers; the brothers, denied recognition as a political party, had joined an Islamic alliance with the Labor Party and the small Liberal Party. The parliamentary elections of 1990 were boycotted by the opposition; however, in the local elections in 1992 the Labor–Muslim Brothers alliance emerged even more clearly than before as the dominant opposition force. The Party's twice-weekly newspaper, *Al-shaʿb* (The People), has increased its circulation from 45,000 in late 1985 to 250,000 in early 1994, making it the largest opposition paper.

Origin. Ibrāhīm Shukrī, the president of the Labor Party from its inception, was a member of the last parliament before the 1952 revolution. He was the only representative of the Socialist Party, the name taken by the Young Egypt movement from 1949. This movement, founded in 1933, was strongly nationalist and anti-British. Its form of Egyptian nationalism fused quite different ideological strands: it emphasized the pharaonic heritage but at the same time took pride in Egypt's Arabism, advocating exclusive use of the Arabic language in all fields of life. It advocated Islamic morals as the basis for a sound social life and national strength and demanded the application of the *sharīʿah*. Its program of social reform included radical land reform, expanded and cheap education, and an extensive program of state-led industrialization.

The early Labor Party membership was dominated by former Young Egypt members and sympathizers. ʿĀdil Ḥusayn, at present the undisputed ideologue of the party, considers its line today to be a continuation of the ideas of Aḥmad Ḥusayn, the charismatic founder and leader of Young Egypt. Kinship also binds the party to the Young Egypt tradition: ʿĀdil Ḥusayn is Aḥmad Ḥusayn's younger brother; Muḥammad Ḥilmī Murād, vice president of the Labor Party, is a brother-in-law of the Ḥusayn brothers; and Majdī Ḥusayn, editor of the party newspaper since 1993, is the son of Aḥmad Ḥusayn.

Ideology. The Labor Party was initially basically a radical nationalist party. At the party's fifth congress in March 1989, however, a clearcut Islamist platform was voted in, and the positions of leadership were filled exclusively with Islamists. This provoked a major split, and many leading members, including half the parliamentary group, refused to accept the results of the conference.

A former communist, ʿĀdil Ḥusayn, general secretary of the party since 1993, refers to his ideas as "enlightened Islamism." He favors applying the *sharīʿah,* but he emphasizes that it must be a *sharīʿah* for the twenty-first century. There are some clear rulings in the Qurʾān and *sunnah,* but wide scope is left for human reason to interpret the law in keeping with changing times and circumstances.

The Labor Party's immediate political goal is putting an end to the present one-party rule and the emergency laws that severely limit freedom of political activity. The fight against corruption at high levels is also high on the agenda and has earned the party much popular sympathy. The party links its stand for democracy to Islam: because Islam recognizes no priesthood with a monopoly on interpreting the scriptures, the existence of different interpretations is legitimate, and this may crystallize into different political programs and parties. However, this freedom must be regulated by respect for the Islamic framework of the state, and for what Ḥusayn calls the state's "grand strategy for development." This strategy should aim at building a strong independent Egypt that satisfies the material and spiritual needs of its inhabitants. Local production should be boosted in order to secure independence, and this will involve strict regulation of imports. Private capital must accept working within the limits of such a strategy.

The party is very critical of the economic open-door policy initiated under President Anwar Sadat, which it sees as undermining the basis for independent development and as carrying with it a redistribution of wealth from the poor to the rich. The Labor Party strongly opposes the present IMF-sponsored reforms—cutting food subsidies, reducing remaining import barriers, and letting foreign capital buy into a privatized public sector. The West, primarily the United States with its local ally Israel, is seen as the main enemy of Egyptian and Arab development. The party sharply criticized the U.S.-led coalition that fought Iraq during the Gulf War.

The discourse of the Labor Party on economic reform highlights an important difference in its general approach to politics when compared with its alliance partner, the Muslim Brothers. The writings of the Brothers on economic issues tend to proceed from traditional Islamic precepts like the canonical tax (*zakāt*) or prohibition of interest (*ribā*), which they discuss in the abstract. In contrast, the Labor Party proceeds from concrete analyses of Egypt's development problems. Islam is not seen so much as offering readymade solutions but rather as a moral force to unite the population in enduring the effort and hardships of independent development, as well as offering broad principles of social justice and harmony. In this sense the Labor Party can be seen as a modernist wing within the broader Islamist movement.

Achieving unity with the Egyptian Copts on an Islamic platform is a stated goal; in fact, in the 1987 elections the Labor Party–Muslim Brothers alliance was the only party to have a Copt topping a slate. The party states that the Copts should have equal rights, including political rights, "at all levels," although it is not clear whether this actually means that a Copt would be acceptable as president or as minister for education.

The electoral alliance with the Muslim Brothers and the opening of the pages of *Al-shaʿb* to the Islamist movement at large express a central concern of the Labor Party: the establishment of the broadest possible unity both within and beyond the Islamist movement vis-à-vis the government. In particular, the party tries to bridge the traditional gap between the Muslim Brothers and the Nasserist tendencies within the opposition.

[*See also* Egypt.]

BIBLIOGRAPHY

Burgat, François, and William Dowell. *The Islamic Movement in North Africa*. Austin, 1993. Excellent analysis of the growth of Islamism, containing a presentation of the intellectual development of the Labor Party ideologue, ʿĀdil Ḥusayn.

Jankowski, James P. *Egypt's Young Rebels*. Stanford, Calif., 1975. Main source for the history of the Young Egypt movement.

Singer, Hanaa Fikri. *The Socialist Labor Party: A Case Study of a Contemporary Egyptian Opposition Party*. Cairo, 1993. Gives a brief outline of the party's history, with special emphasis on the struggle over the "islamization" of the party.

Springborg, Robert. *Mubarak's Egypt: Fragmentation of the Political Order*. Boulder, 1989. Gives a well-informed account of the emergence of the present party system in Egypt.

BJØRN OLAV UTVIK

LAND TENURE. Throughout the nineteenth and twentieth centuries land tenure in the Islamic world was heavily affected by political factors, although this was hardly new. The three main influences on land tenure are the rules and choices imposed by political elites, Islamic law, and customary provisions, including pre-Islamic systems and adaptations to specific environments. Land tenure itself can be seen as including formal rules of ownership, rules guiding access to land for nonowners, and the distribution of landholdings according to these rules.

Major trends and changes in the last two hundred years include the liberalization of land tenure in the nineteenth century to allow for individual property in land, and the wave of land reforms that followed the Egyptian land reform of 1952. Land tenure in the Middle East is now moving toward more private land ownership and the dismantling of the systems set up under government land reform.

Islamic Land Law. In many traditional Islamic systems it was considered that the state (or the ruler), as the representative of the Islamic community, was the ultimate owner of the land. This right was predicated on conquest. While the state or the ruler held absolute ownership (*raqabah*), the actual farmers held usufruct rights (*taṣarruf*). One of the consequences of this form of land ownership was that it allowed actual practices of access to land to be governed by non-Islamic rules, since property rights were not involved. Only a small part of the agricultural land in the Islamic world was owned as "freehold" (*milk*), in the sense that the owner had rights against the state. And in legal theory only *milk* land could be transformed into *waqf* (endowed) land, although the actual history and distribution of *waqf* land suggests there was considerable flexibility in practice. Both usufruct rights and freehold rights could be established by bringing land into cultivation; this "living" land was then contrasted to "dead" or unused land. Under this system agricultural land was rarely held in freehold tenure: less than 1 percent in Iraq at the time of the 1958 revolution, although in practice the difference between freehold and usufructuary tenure was small (Batatu, 1978, p. 53).

Traditional Patterns and Ecological Adaptations. Many traditional practices governing access to land were based on use by a community rather than by an individual. This practice was often covered by the fiction of state ownership of the land; the land involved could also have been established as a *waqf,* or it could also be an undivided inheritance. One much-cited example is *mushāʿ* tenure in the grain-growing interior of the fertile crescent (Syria, Palestine, and Jordan). Rights to land were vested in the village community, which would then periodically redistribute those rights to its members. Villagers thus held provisional use rights in the land and were generally only motivated to plant annual crops rather than to invest in land that might soon be allocated to another. *Mushāʿ* tenure generally disappeared during the early twentieth century.

Periodic redistribution among shareholding villagers was also common in Iran, where shares were often calculated on the basis of the number of draft animals each villager held. Among the Pathans of the Swat valley in Pakistan not only was the land redistributed every decade, but entire villages would move to new lands; this system was halted around 1930 by the local ruler (Fredrik Barth, *Political Leadership among Swat Pathans,* London, 1959). A system of redistribution was also practiced along the Nile in Upper Egypt and the Sudan before modern times, where it reflected the recession cultivation system; this is also reported from the Senegal and Niger valleys in Islamic West Africa, where redistribution was combined with nonexhaustive rights.

The land tenure situation was particularly complex in oases and river valleys where irrigation was needed. Here it was necessary to ensure that the land received the water it required. Although water rights usually matched land rights, sometimes water rights were held independently of land rights. In the Egyptian Fayyum, landholders are entitled to the entire flow of water in a canal during a certain period of time for each unit of land, while in parts of Iran, the local magnates owned the water source separately from the land. Currently in Egypt farmers may take water freely from the government canals, which are themselves on a rotation system, but there will be pressure to change this system as demand for the limited Nile waters increases. Elsewhere in the Islamic world irrigation may be from wells, from government projects, or from traditional systems around springs and oases.

The intensity of cultivation in the oases also gave rise to intricate elaborations of land tenure laws, such as the thousand-year leases that were a feature of the oases around ʿUnayzah in Saudi Arabia (Altorki and Cole, 1989, pp. 34–38). In new irrigation projects such as the Ghab in Syria, the initial strong state control based on a "rational" system of land and water distribution is undermined by the many private arrangements that farmers make.

Ownership was not the only form of access to land. In the premodern Islamic world sharecropping was common but has since generally given way to rentals. Sharecropping allowed for decentralization of farming decisions to the household level. The balance of power between owner and sharecropper varied but was usually in favor of the owner. The sharecropper's share tended to be higher in irrigated areas producing for an urban market, or where he brought additional capital such as draft animals to the partnership. In modern times conditions of rental have often been fixed by the state, as in Egypt. A current trend, with ancient antecedents, is for merchants to finance the farming of certain crops, often fruits and vegetables, by offering advance payment to the farmers.

Islamic land tenure rules reflect agricultural land better than pasture land. Thus in those substantial parts of the Islamic world where pastoralism was a key economic activity, other forms of rights emerged, involving both collective rights and nonexhaustive rights. Certain pastoral groups had the accepted right to use certain resources in a land area, while other groups might have the right to use other resources, or to use the same resources at a different season. These collective rights to pastureland emerged in desert, semidesert, and mountain areas.

Early Modern Political Changes. The growth of individual property in land (in the form now present) can be traced back to the land laws of the mid-nineteenth century. In the Ottoman Empire a land law was passed in 1858 that required, among other things, the registration of land in the name of an individual. The application of this law in Palestine from 1867 to 1873 led to the registration of much land in the names of urban, absentee landlords, many of whom eventually sold the land to Jewish settlers, thus clearing the way for the Zionist establishment in Palestine. The same law, whose application in Iraq was begun by the Ottomans after 1869 but not completed until the land law of 1932 under the British mandate, effectively gave the major tribal shaykhs de facto ownership rights, with their fellow tribesmen as tenants. The application of the 1858 law in Anatolia does not seem to have been so disruptive, and much of Anatolia entered the modern era dominated by smallholders.

A series of Egyptian laws between 1847 and 1858 helped establish the right to private land ownership in Egyptian agricultural land, although it has been pointed out that the effect of the laws themselves may have been exaggerated (Cuno, 1992). In Algeria a series of French laws between 1856 and 1873 had the same effect, although a large part of the motivation was to break up the collective ownership patterns of the Algerian tribes and make land available for European purchasers. By the end of the colonial period in 1962 roughly one-quarter of the farmland was in colonial hands, and it was by and large the best land. Shortly after the French protectorate was established in Tunisia, a law in 1885 also required land registration according to the Australian Torrens system. This also had the effect of allowing much land to be acquired by colonialists, who controlled about 20 percent of the farmland by the 1950s.

Samir Amin (1978) argues that this evolution created a class of large and often absentee landholders, an agrarian bourgeoisie. For Amin this was the first adaptation of the Arab world to the expansion of world capitalism. It happens that in North Africa the landholders were mostly colonial, while in the Arab East they were more likely to be indigenous; however, the economic structure was comparable. These large landholders were also responsible for introducing mechanization, for switching over from sharecropping to wage labor as a means for organizing cultivation of the land, and for establishing links with a banking system for credit rather than individual moneylenders. They also fostered changes in the irrigation system where that was appropriate. The end result was a highly unequal pattern of distribution of rights over land.

Socialism and Land Reform. Land reform began in Egypt in 1952, where it was the first substantial act of the revolutionary government. It was largely motivated by the desire to dispossess the old ruling class. It did not respond to a grassroots social movement; in Egypt as elsewhere, land reform was the outcome of deliberations of urban intellectuals and politicians. In Egypt the first wave of agrarian reform divided the estates among small farmers, often their former workers, who were then organized into agrarian reform cooperatives. The second wave, after 1961, continued this process but was more notable for consolidating the relationship between owners and renters and for requiring all farmers to join a village credit cooperative. "By 1970, an area of 817,538 feddans, or slightly less than 13 percent of the total cultivated land of Egypt during that year, had been distributed to 341,982 families comprising some 1.7 million persons, or about 9 percent of the rural population" (Raḍwān, 1977, p. 16; a feddan is approximately .42 hectare). Perhaps a third of the farmland was initially affected by the regulations on rentals, and all land was brought under the supervision of the cooperatives after 1961. Whether this reform was too great or too small a change has been hotly argued in Egypt; certainly it did little directly for the landless, but it did make the distribution of landholding more equitable. The reforms (land tenure rules, cooperatives, subsidies on inputs, and marketing quotas) had the effect of making the government into the partner of each farmer and structured Egyptian agriculture for about forty years after the 1952 reform.

Agrarian reforms of various types, often modeled on the Egyptian experience, were enacted in Iraq, Syria, Tunisia, Algeria, Iran, Pakistan, and elsewhere. In Algeria, the one-quarter of the land that had been held by colonial farmers largely passed into the "self-management" sector after independence in 1962. Workers on the estates took on the responsibility for managing them as they were, within the framework of a government bureaucracy. Later, with the agrarian reform law of 1971, the larger Algerian-owned farms were organized into cooperatives, covering 22 percent of the land. The remaining private land (53 percent) was marginal, but it employed 90 percent of the workers, contrasted to 3 percent in the socialist sector and 7 percent in the agrarian-reform sector. Thus the relative privilege of the best land persisted. Tunisia underwent a parallel evolution. In the late 1980s and early 1990s, Algeria passed a number of laws that have the general effect of restoring to individuals the right to own land and to dispose of it fully. The immediate result was to foster rivalry between individuals of various categories for the rights to the land newly made available. There has been a shift from rights based on work to rights based on property ownership.

In Iran, the "white revolution" of the shah undercut the traditional ownership and use pattern for land and tended to establish individual private property (agrarian reform of 1962). Traditional large landowners and village use patterns were displaced in favor of agribusiness, particularly in newly irrigated areas. After the overthrow of the shah in 1978 a renewed debate over land tenure broke out between those who wanted to use the power of the state to guarantee that the poor would have access to the land, and those who argued that Islam necessarily guaranteed an untrammeled right to private property. It appears that the latter point of view carried the day. With political conflict at the national level, the situation on the ground remains unsettled.

Liberalization. Recent changes in Egypt have modified the strong pattern of government involvement in agriculture. The system of enforced crop rotation, subsidized inputs, and marketing quotas has been dismantled, and the village cooperative has lost much of its role. The agrarian reform cooperatives survive a little better. A 1992 land law restricted the rights of tenants in favor of owners, thus changing the status of the roughly one-quarter of the land that was under tenancy. This law is supposed to be fully implemented by 1997. During the parliamentary debate around this law it was argued that this change would bring rights in land more into accord with Islamic law: the point in question was whether giving a renter a permanent right to rent land and pass that right on by inheritance was an infringement on the Islamic law of contract, which was held to withhold legitimacy from such unchangeable contracts. But it was also argued that some owners of land were being deprived of their legitimate income from that land. The interests of renters were not taken into consideration. The liberalization was also thought to be the result of pressure from international financial organizations.

Various factors have entered into the debates about land law. In the name of equity some argued that land tenure systems should permit maximum access to the land by farmers and farm workers. Others argued that the inviolability of private property is grounded in Islamic law, and that accumulation is no sin. At all times rulers and the state have used donations of land to win followers. Little thought has been given to devising a land tenure system that will foster development, and less to allowing some voice to the small farmers. Meanwhile the population grows, especially in the rural areas. The relative uncertainty of land ownership is likely to continue into the near future, and this will shape the development patterns of the Islamic countries.

[*See also* Agriculture; Economics; Property.]

BIBLIOGRAPHY

Abdel-Khalek, Gouda, and Robert Tignor, eds. *The Political Economy of Income Distribution in Egypt*. New York, 1982. Collection of papers, many by Egyptian economists and several dealing with the role of land tenure in income distribution (see, in particular, the papers by Dessouki, Korayem, Ibrahim, Mohie-Eldin, and Zaytoun).

Altorki, Soraya, and Donald P. Cole. *Arabian Oasis City: The Transformation of ʿUnayzah*. Austin, 1989. Team of anthropologists analyzes the present and recent history of a town in Saudi Arabia.

Amin, Samir. *The Arab Nation*. Translated by Michael Pallis. London, 1978. Leading Marxist economist interprets the history of the Arab world.

Batatu, Hanna. *The Old Social Classes and the Revolutionary Movements of Iraq*. Princeton, 1978. Thoroughly documented account of social change in Iraq in the twentieth century, with many specific references to land tenure and land distribution.

Chaulet, Claudine. "Agriculture et nourriture dans les réformes algériennes: Un espace pour les paysans?" *Revue Tiers Monde* 32 (1991): 741–770. Provides a wide-ranging summary of the agrarian situation in Algeria at the beginning of the 1990s.

Cuno, Kenneth M. *The Pasha's Peasants: Land, Society, and Economy in Lower Egypt, 1740–1858*. Cambridge, 1992. Gives many details on land tenure and society in early modern Egypt, linking cases and law.

Hooglund, Eric J. *Land and Revolution in Iran, 1960–1980*. Austin, 1982. Argues that one of the sources of the Iranian Revolution was the disruption of the land tenure and land use pattern under the Shah.

Hopkins, Nicholas S. *Agrarian Transformation in Egypt*. Boulder, 1987. Analysis of land tenure, land use patterns, and irrigation in an upper Egyptian village.

Lambton, Ann K. S. *Landlord and Peasant in Persia: A Study of Land Tenure and Land Revenue Administration*. London, 1953. Account of Iran in the 1940s, with historical background.

Lambton, Ann K. S. *The Persian Land Reform, 1962–1966*. London, 1969. Measured account by a leading expert, covering the early phases and social background of the land reform in Iran.

Marei, Sayed. *Agrarian Reform in Egypt*. Cairo, 1957. Statement by the man responsible for the land reform program in Egypt; a useful source both for its attitudes and its figures.

Mehanna, Sohair, et al. *Irrigation and Society in Rural Egypt*. Cairo, 1984. Account of irrigation in Fayyūm, Minūfīyah, and Minyā governorates, stressing the diversity of local practices.

Metral, Françoise. "State and Peasants in Syria: A Local View of a Government Irrigation Project." *Peasant Studies* 11.2 (1984): 69–90. Account of how land tenure and irrigation in the Ghab project were transformed by resettled peasants.

Meyer, Ann Elizabeth, ed. *Property, Social Structure, and Law in the Modern Middle East.* Albany, N.Y., 1985. Collection of papers, including some on irrigation and land law; note papers by Attia, Leveau, and Hammoudi.

Raḍwān, Samīr M. *Agrarian Reform and Rural Poverty: Egypt, 1952–1975.* Geneva, 1977. Probably the best summary of the effects of agrarian reform in Egypt.

Saab, Gabriel S. *The Egyptian Agrarian Reform, 1952–1962.* London, 1967. Thorough study, but one that best reflects the first phase of agrarian reform, of which the author was not a warm supporter.

Valensi, Lucette. *Tunisian Peasants in the Eighteenth and Nineteenth Centuries.* Cambridge, 1985. Excellent account of early modern Tunisia, with considerable information on landholding practices.

Warriner, Doreen. *Land Reform and Development in the Middle East: A Study of Egypt, Syria, and Iraq.* 2d ed. London, 1962. The author was the major authority on this topic in the Arab world, based on extensive experience in several countries from the 1940s to the 1960s.

NICHOLAS S. HOPKINS

LAW. [*To treat the interaction between Islamic law and religion, this entry comprises four articles:*

Legal Thought and Jurisprudence
Sunnī Schools of Law
Shīʿī Schools of Law
Modern Legal Reform

The first surveys the historical development of religious law in Islam; the second and third trace the rise of schools of law in the Sunnī and Shīʿī traditions; and the last presents an analysis of legal reform in the Muslim world in the nineteenth and twentieth centuries. For discussion of more specific fields of Islamic law, see Criminal Law; Family Law; Public Law. *See also* International Law.]

Legal Thought and Jurisprudence

The idea of divine law in Islam is traditionally expressed by two words, *fiqh* and *sharīʿah. Fiqh* originally meant understanding in a broad sense. The specialist usage, meaning understanding of the law, emerged at about the same time as the first juristic literature, in the late eighth and early ninth centuries. All efforts to elaborate details of the law, to state specific norms, to justify them by reference to revelation, to debate them, or to write books or treatises on the law are examples of *fiqh.* The word connotes human and specifically scholarly activity. By contrast, *sharīʿah* refers to God's law in its quality as divine. Loosely used, it can indicate Islam, God's religion. It refers to God's law as it is with him or with his Prophet, or as it is contained (potentially) within the corpus of revelation. Practitioners of *fiqh* (the *fuqahā'*; sg., *faqīh*) try to discover and give expression to the *sharīʿah.* For Muslims, the *sharīʿah* evokes loyalty and is a focus of faith; *fiqh* evokes at best respect for juristic scholarship and for a literary tradition—and, among some modern thinkers, distaste for dry-as-dust legalism. The word *sharīʿah* is sometimes used in place of *fiqh,* in which case its positive connotations will be transferred to the scholarly tradition; it has also been applied to actual bureaucratic systems thought to conform adequately to the norms expressed in theoretical writings—always a matter of perception. Western designation of the Muslim juristic tradition as "Islamic law" has led to the emergence, perhaps in the late nineteenth century, of the calque realized in Arabic as *al-qānūn al-Islāmī,* and now part of the vocabulary in all Muslim countries. This phrase, though applied to the tradition as a whole, carries many of the connotations of "legal system" in a Western sense, related to the bureaucratic structures of a nation-state. Such ideas have now permeated much Muslim thinking about the law.

Juristic Schools and Hermeneutical Traditions. The traditional processes of juristic understanding depend on a theological construct that is presented as history. It states that the words and actions of the prophet Muḥammad (his *sunnah*), being an embodiment of the divine command and an expression of God's law (*sharīʿah*), were preserved by the companions of the Prophet and their followers in the form of discrete anecdotes (*ḥadīth*). These were transmitted from generation to generation, inspiring first discussion and then systematic juristic thinking (*fiqh*). Beginning in about the mid-eighth century, a number of masters made distinctive contributions to the discipline that stimulated the emergence of separate traditions or schools. The most important masters for the Sunnīs are Abū Ḥanīfah (d. about 767), Mālik ibn Anas (d. 795), Muḥammad ibn Idrīs al-Shāfiʿī (d. 820), and Aḥmad ibn Ḥanbal (d. 855), associated respectively with the Ḥanafī, Mālikī, Shāfiʿī, and Ḥanbalī schools. The four Sunnī schools acknowledged one another and gave more or less qualified recognition to a number of other short-lived schools that emerged within Sunnism; the most important was probably the Ẓāhirī (Literalist) school, whose major exponent was ʿAlī ibn Ḥazm (d. 1064).

Of sectarian groups, only the Ithnā ʿAsharī (or Imāmī) Shīʿīs generated a continuous and creative juristic tradition that matched the Sunnī traditions. They looked back to the sixth imam, Jaʿfar al-Ṣādiq (d. 756), as a founding figure. The Zaydīs, Khārijīs, and Ismāʿīlīs all produced minor traditions.

Development of the law within the schools can be seen to depend on two major hermeneutical principles. The first, the synchronic principle, required that any formulation of the law, at any time, must be justifiable by reference to revelation. The second, the diachronic principle, was equally important, though frequently overlooked by observers and possibly underestimated by some practitioners. It required that participants in a school tradition, whether Sunnī or Shīʿī, preserve loyalty to the tradition by taking into account the interpretative achievement of older masters; the law had to be justifiable by reference to the continuity and established identity of the school. Muslim jurists were not, as individuals, in solitary and direct confrontation with revelation: they found their way back to the meaning of revelation through tradition. This principle was a source of strength and flexibility, for the tradition held the accumulated experience of the community and gave it a sophisticated literary form. It was nonetheless sometimes attacked. Within Sunnism, the Ẓāhirīs objected to precisely this feature of juristic thought and advocated instead a return to a literal reading of the sources. The same mood, if not the same extreme, is expressed in the Salafī (Primitivist—the word *salaf* refers to the earliest generations of Islam) orientation associated with Ibn Taymīyah (d. 1328), and perhaps in the Akhbārī movement within Imāmī Shiism. All these movements evince distrust of the complexity and indeterminacy expressed in the ongoing dominant traditions.

Revelation in the classical period meant the canonical collections of *ḥadīth* (the Shīʿīs and the Sunnīs had different collections) and the Qur'ān. These two were equal *qua* authority, although the Qur'ān was superior in its nature and origins (word of God, miracle). The *ḥadīth* collections, by virtue of their size alone, dominated the hermeneutical process, but the relationship between Qur'ān and *ḥadīth* was difficult to express. Some jurists accepted that the *sunnah* might "abrogate" the Qur'ān; others preferred to say that the *sunnah* "passed judgement" on the Qur'ān, or that it "clarified" and "explained." There were variant views within schools. Whatever the preferred wording, none would disagree with the statement attributed to the Syrian jurist Awzāʿī (d. 774) that the Book is in greater need of the *sunnah* than the *sunnah* is of the Book. The vitality, complexity, and exuberance of *fiqh* literature—and many of the fundamental norms of the law—are unthinkable except in relation to the large body of revelation constituted by *ḥadīth*.

Western Scholarship on Islamic Law. Modern historians have not generally accepted the traditional account of the origins of Islamic law. They have produced an important alternative account, associated with the names of the three scholars Ignácz Goldziher (1888–1890), Joseph Schacht (1950), and John Wansbrough (1977). Goldziher demonstrated that historical and theological *ḥadīth* could not be accepted as reflecting the lifetime of the Prophet, but must be the product of dispute within the community throughout the first and second centuries after the Hijrah. Schacht extended this insight to include juristic *ḥadīth*, perceived by him as not a cause but a product of juristic debate in Muslim communities. Wansbrough has argued that the Qur'ān too is not a product of the Prophet's lifetime but a liturgical reflection of two hundred years of community worship and sectarian debate. For this tradition of scholarship, revelation is not an event but a process; its creative agent is not the Prophet but the community (or communities); and its geographical locus is not the Hejaz but the Muslim cities of North Africa, Syria, and Iraq.

With specific regard to the juristic traditions, Schacht argued that these began as local traditions in Medina, Basra, Kufa, and other cities, reflecting local practice at a greater or lesser distance. Even if the local traditions were claimed to be prophetic in origin (which is likely), the idea that legal norms must be related directly to prophetic *ḥadīth* emerged only gradually, as a result of polemical debate among different communities or segments of community. The real architect of the classical hermeneutical system, according to Schacht, was Shāfiʿī. In works attributed to him are found the first systematic arguments that defend norms by reference to *ḥadīth* or derive norms directly from them. His *Risālah* contains the first general account of the methodology of relating law to revealed texts. Many western scholars and Muslims have reacted to Schacht's theories with dismay and have tried to reassert the core of truth that (it is claimed) must lie behind the traditional accounts of the origins of Islam and of Islamic law.

Modern scholarship has made little progress in describing the characteristics of Islamic law in the classical period or in providing a sensible and justified periodization. From the tenth century to the nineteenth, the formal structures of juristic literature, and many specific statements, imply that the *sharīʿah* is a set of static and unchanging norms. This is an illusion deliberately contrived to stress diachronic continuity and synchronic harmony with revelation. The literature in fact admits (to a degree) the reality of development, for example, in ubiquitous reference to the moderns and the ancients *(al-muta'akhkhirūn, al-mutaqaddimūn)*. Western scholars have not found it easy to describe or assess this development. Failing to find a terminology that will uncover the purpose or acknowledge the degrees of openness and creativity that characterize hermeneutical traditions of this kind, they have perpetrated a number of errors. At the most general level, they have described nearly all of the tradition in terms such as decline, decay, failure, or ankylosis. More specifically, Schacht, in an uncharacteristically muddled set of arguments, asserted that the "closing of the door of *ijtihād*," meaning an end to independent reasoning in the law, began about 900. He may have intended something sensible, but the pernicious results of these comments have haunted academic descriptions of Islamic law ever since; recent studies suggest improvement.

Juristic Literature. The literature of *fiqh* is of two kinds, *furūʿ al-fiqh* (branches) and *uṣūl al-fiqh* (roots). It is sometimes said that works of the latter type explore the four sources (or roots) of the law, namely Qur'ān, *sunnah*, consensus *(ijmāʿ)*, and analogical reason *(qiyās)*. [*See* Consensus; Uṣūl al-Fiqh.] This is an indigenous but inadequate description. Such works do contain a definition of revelation, which may be extended to include the words and actions of the companions, but their main purpose is to describe the intellectual structures that can be brought to bear on revelation for the purposes of interpretation. These begin with linguistic and rhetorical sciences, usually dealt with under simple antithetical headings: general and particular, command and prohibition, obscure and clear, truth and metaphor. With regard to *ḥadīth* alone, the epistemological categories of multiple and single transmission (*tawātur* and *āḥād*, with only the former giving certain knowledge) are discussed. The workings of abrogation *(naskh)*, the application, ramifications, and limitations of analogical argument, and the value and limits of consensus, are all discussed, along with a variable body of other materials. The whole set of interpretative structures is brought together in the idea of *ijtihād*. As a juristic term, this means the exertion of the utmost possible effort to discover, on the basis of revelation interpreted in the light of all the rules, the ruling on a particular juristic question. The theory of *ijtihād* in its several forms concedes that there will be variant views on all but the fundamental structures of the law. By acknowledging dispute, it preempts its capacity to divide. It justifies the authority of the *fuqahā'*, who alone have the right to give rulings, which must be obeyed by the masses. Finally, it controls and justifies intellectual play and so permits the remarkable florescence of juristic literature that characterizes all Islamic societies down to the nineteenth century (and in some areas beyond it).

In spite of many differences of detail, the broad structures and all the major topics of *uṣūl* works are the same for Sunnīs and Shīʿīs. Initially resistant to the idea of *ijtihād*, the Shīʿī tradition embraced it in the works of ʿAllāmah al-Ḥillī (d. 1325), and, in spite of internal disputes, they have made it a central part of their juristic thinking. The Shīʿīs also lay considerable theoretical stress on the independent capacity of the intellect to make moral and ethical judgements, but this scarcely affected the overall structure of their works. [*See the biography of Ḥillī.*]

The literature of *furūʿ* consists fundamentally of norms that regulate (or appear to regulate) all areas of community ritual and public social life. They are usually divided into *ʿibādāt* (rituals) and *muʿāmalāt* (social relations). More sophisticated divisions have been attempted, but the preferred approach of the *fuqahā'* was atomistic, topic by topic. Only the superior significance of ritual was consistently marked by placing it at the beginning of a work. The topics of ritual are purity, prayer, alms *(zakāt)*, pilgrimage, fasting, and sometimes *jihād*. The remaining topics occurred in no stable order and included at least the following: marriage, divorce, and inheritance; rules of buying, selling, lending, hire, gift, testamentary bequest, agency, deposit, and so on; crimes, torts, penalties, and compensations for injury; judicial practice and procedure; rules relating to slaves, land ownership and holding, contractual partnerships, slaughter of animals for food, oaths and their effects, and more. The list was capable of considerable conceptual refinement, but it was finite and more or less closed. Its major technical terminology was static. Real developments in social life following the formation of the tradition might be caught in the network of the law through exploration and refinement of concepts, but much was not; moreover, little was lost from the tradition, even when it became irrelevant to real life. Thus the terminology and the reality of governmental administration scarcely entered works of *fiqh*, even when it was more or less recognized by the *fuqahā'* as a realization of *sharīʿah* (as under the Ottomans). Conversely, the fossilized terminology for the assessment of *zakāt* on camels was a part of *fiqh*, even if camels were not a part of social life.

It is usual to state that works of *furū*ᶜ classify acts according to five headings: mandatory, recommended, permitted, abhorred, and prohibited. In fact, classificatory terminology goes considerably beyond this, and the full message of the *fuqahā'* is more complex than is implied by this classification. There are two major types of *furū*ᶜ literature, *mukhtaṣar*s (concise epitomes of the law) and *mabsūṭ*s (expansive compendia, characterized by proliferation of cases, intricate conceptual subdivision, recording of variant views from within the tradition or from other traditions, and generous provision of justificatory arguments for all recorded positions). The size of the great *mabsūṭ*s marks the exploratory intentions of their authors—writers who, whether for strict practical ends or from mere intellectual exuberance, drew out endlessly the possibilities of a past that was never abandoned: there were no new beginnings in the tradition of *fiqh*. The point was reflected in literary form: commentary, gloss, supercommentary, multiple citation of authority—the signs not of a static tradition but of a hermeneutically engaged one.

The genre of *mukhtaṣar*s was necessarily less exploratory. Works of this type were marked by organizational neatness, precise clarity of exposition, and sometimes by a conceptual and syntactic dexterity that charms and dazzles as well as teaches. The *Mukhtaṣar* of the Mālikī scholar Khalīl ibn Isḥāq (d. 1374) was described admiringly as "woven on a magician's loom." Aesthetic skills and intellectual exuberance were both a part of the task of the *fuqahā'*, and clearly relevant to the expression as well as to the understanding of God's law.

The Shīᶜī tradition was not substantially different from the Sunnī in literary form or in presentational technique. The differences in detail among the four Sunnī schools are of roughly the same order as those between them and the Shīᶜī tradition. There is, however, one systematic difference that warrants comment. Wherever the rules of the *sharīᶜah* required a governor as executive agent, the Sunnī tradition recognized the actual ruler as having this right, at least potentially. The Shīᶜī tradition initially perceived these functions as having lapsed during the absence of the hidden imam. Over time, however, they interpreted the acknowledged judicial authority of the *fuqahā'* as extending, again potentially, to all the executive functions otherwise reserved for the imam. One result was that the Shīᶜī *fuqahā'* became the managers of *sharᶜī* taxes (*zakāt* and *khums*) and so acquired financial independence; this, coupled with their potential claim to political authority, led (especially in the nineteenth and twentieth centuries) to a remarkable increase in their authority and power.

Social Influences and Legal Institutions. The structures of the law of course had practical influence. Most broadly, they influenced education. From the tenth century onward, the dominant form of publicly accessible education in all Islamic lands began with training in the Qur'ān and *sunnah* and ended with training in *fiqh*. This discipline provided the basic conceptual structures through which Muslims thought about society and God's relationship to society and demands of it. The basic rules were a part of their moral life, the constituent principles of all normative thought. The training in systematic thought and controlled argument served the purposes of the merchant classes and governing bureaucracies and ensured a homogeneous educated class across vast geographical areas.

The basic rules of the law both lived in the imaginations of Muslims and structured their activities. All Muslims knew, for example, that it was their duty to pray five times a day, that Muslims did not drink wine or take interest, that married persons who indulged in fornication were subject to death by stoning. In historical Muslim societies, of course, not all Muslims prayed five times a day; ways were found to secure access to wine and to interest; and fornication did not necessarily lead to the prescribed penalties. The interpreters of the law were both idealists and facilitators. Thus the principle that fornication by married persons merited the death penalty was constantly restated (a sign of abhorrence), but the option of putting that penalty into effect was removed; the rules of evidence and procedure were carefully written so as to prevent the penalty from taking place. This is particularly noticeable in the Ḥanafī tradition, which has the longest history of practical experience and close alliance with government. (It is less obvious in the Shīᶜī tradition, which for many centuries did not aspire to partnership in government.) The prohibition on interest perhaps signaled a distaste for exploitation. In practice, however, some forms of interest were required for normal economic activity; this was acknowledged by the *fuqahā'*, who worked out legal devices (*ḥīlah*s) to facilitate practice or simply affirmed that there were fair rates of interest (Ottoman Ḥanafī jurists in the sixteenth century usually cite 15 percent).

The point of contact, or the judgment of relevance,

between theory and practice is not predictable. Different areas of the law generated different kinds of theory/practice relationships, few of which have been given serious consideration by modern scholars. Criminal law in the *sharīʿah* is limited to only a few specified crimes. Exploration of these within *fiqh* is extensive but almost never refers to the reality of practical administration, though the *fuqahā'* were not unaware of the governmental systems, often based on local practice, that actually existed. Some principles of international law are articulated under the topic *jihād,* but the *fuqahā'* explored the tradition and not the needs or the desires of contemporary governors. No Sunnī *faqīh,* for example, denied the right of every individual Muslim to issue a valid and binding contract of safe-conduct *(amān)* to individuals from non-Islamic territory, yet no governing institution could ever have tolerated such practice. [*See* Diplomatic Immunity.]

The only areas of the law that were, in premodern times, systematically transformed into administrative structures were those related to the office of judge *(qāḍī).* His competence traditionally covered many aspects of family law (marriage, divorce, inheritance, testamentary bequest), the administration of charitable endowments *(waqf)* and the property of orphans, declaratory judgments on the significance and validity of contracts, and civil disputes. In order to make this administrative system work, there had to be compromises with theory. In the Sunnī system, the governor (just or unjust) was accorded the absolute right to appoint judges and to define their spheres of competence; he also had the right in areas of juristic dispute to declare the rules that would be put into effect. Various types of judicial hierarchy emerged to ensure predictability and order in judicial decisions. Numerous subordinate officials and deputy judges derived their authority from appointment by the *qāḍī.* (In spite of the *de jure* illegitimacy of Shīʿī rulers, the practical situation was not very different under Shīʿī governments.)

Many aspects of civil and criminal law could not be dealt with under the norms of the *sharīʿah,* and some of the norms of the *sharīʿah* could not be rendered practically effective. (If the laws of evidence were preemptively stringent in the case of fornication, they were probably too easy in the case of wine-drinking; few *qāḍī*s could listen to unlimited complaints against neighbors who drank wine.) Careful definition of spheres of judicial competence was one way of dealing with these problems. But already by early ʿAbbāsid times, a system of courts was required in addition to the *qāḍī*s' courts, which would take a more expedient and flexible approach to *sharʿī* rules and might in some areas go beyond them. These were initially called *maẓālim* ("injustices") courts, though the nomenclature varied through time. They were administered directly by the governing bureaucracy, usually with the help and advice of trained jurists. They dealt with complaints against government officials and administered an extended criminal law that was only loosely related to *sharīʿah.* Petty crimes were often dealt with by local police and market inspectors in accordance with local custom, again loosely linked to *sharīʿah.*

Probably the most significant theoretical exploration of the law in relation to judicial practice, in the classical period, is contained in the *Kitāb adab al-qāḍī* of the Shāfiʿī jurist al-Māwardī (d. 1058), one of a long tradition of monographs on judicial authority. The most effective and complex practical exploitation of the *qāḍī*'s office took place in the Ottoman Empire. Here the integration of the *qāḍī*'s office into a bureaucratic structure was accompanied by a considerable expansion of the practical and administrative duties of the judge, causing the separate *maẓālim*-type structures to disappear.

The second major institutional office that emerged to serve the structures of *fiqh* was that of *muftī.* Originally, a *muftī* was any qualified *mujtahid* who was capable of providing reasoned responses (*fatwā*s) to the questions of those not educated in the law. Informal *muftī*s never disappeared, but, in the Sunnī community, governmental structures often signaled official preference for some *muftī*s over others. In the Ottoman period, officially appointed *muftī*s became fully integrated into the structures of government. The rulings of a *muftī* could be issued on request to individuals, to *qāḍī*s, and to agents of government, and could have broadly legitimizing effect (e.g., in respect to government policies) or, if translated into government edicts, strict practical effect (e.g., in relation to judicial practice).

The great Ottoman jurist-administrator and grand *muftī* of Istanbul, Abū Saʿūd (d. 1574), may be taken as representative of those jurists whose achievement in the law was thoroughly practical. He brought the real tax-collecting activities of the empire (in practice varied and based on regional traditions) under the formal, technical terminology of *fiqh.* This was in part a control on arbitrary taxation, but it also provided a reasonable degree of legitimacy and authority to the working system of the day. For Abū Saʿūd, the Ottoman system was a broad realization of the *sharīʿah,* and his aim was to ensure that it was a practical, efficient, and more or less just system. This required the recognition of governmental decrees (*gānūns*), the promulgation of administrative rules that were not reflected in traditional *fiqh* (though they were felt not to contravene *sharīʿah*), and decisive rulings on matters of dispute. In a *fatwā,* Abū Saʿūd declared that there can be no decree of the sultan ordering something that is illegal according to the *sharīʿah,* thereby committing jurists to a considerable hermeneutical task or to formal, discursive opposition. He declared that marriage without a *qāḍī*'s knowledge was invalid, subsequent to the issue of a sultanic decree to that effect—thereby serving the interests of orderly administration, even though the *sharīʿah* does not require any form of registration for a valid marriage. He also gave rulings in favor of the cash-*waqf* (pious foundations in the form of cash). Governmental decrees confirmed the latter ruling, but in the tradition of Ḥanafī *fiqh,* the legitimacy of cash-*waqf*s remained a matter of dispute.

In the Shīʿī world, though low-ranking jurists might serve the government, the highest-ranking jurists preserved their independence. Consolidation of theory and improvements in communication led in the nineteenth century to a strengthening of their position and the emergence of a new titulature (notably *marjaʿ al-taqlīd*) reflecting their increasing status. They had great capacity for political gestures, usually marking their dissociation from government, but, significantly, no opportunity for the mundane, bureaucratic, participatory legitimizing activities of Sunnī *fuqahā'*. [*See also* Marjaʿ al-Taqlīd.]

Modern Developments. The nineteenth century brought changes, and in many areas a gradual end, to the indigenous traditions of *fiqh.* New ideas from the West, a defensive analysis of Islam, and not least the emergence of secular educational systems that excluded traditional juristic studies, all helped to precipitate new approaches to the law. Muslim administrators and Muslim reformists alike began to feel that the *sharīʿah* ought to be practical and to resemble Western codes. The earliest sign of movement in this direction came with the enactment of the Mecelle in 1876 by the Ottoman authorities. This was a Ḥanafī codification of some parts of the *sharīʿah,* designed for practical purposes. It remains partially effective in some former Ottoman territories (e.g., Iraq and Israel). [*See* Mecelle.] The Egyptian reformer Muḥammad ʿAbduh (d. 1905) advocated a new, creative approach to *ijtihād*: a disregard of school traditions as such, and an eclectic approach to the tradition as a whole (an approach known as *talfīq,* "patchwork"). His aim was to define and embody in administrative and institutional forms specific rules that would serve the needs of independent Muslim communities. The Shīʿī tradition showed its ability to accommodate modern law-making techniques when a majority of high-ranking jurists rallied to the cause of the constitution in Iran in 1906.

With the withdrawal of imperialist and mandate authorities from the Middle East and elsewhere, modern Muslim nations have for the most part provided themselves with practical, eclectic law codes that draw on ideas from both the Muslim tradition and the West. It is in the traditional practical areas of marriage, divorce, and inheritance that the influence of the *sharīʿah* has been strongest. Some countries (e.g., Tunisia) have achieved notably progressive codes of personal status while still asserting a very creative interpretative link between the code and the tradition of *fiqh.* The greatest theoretician of the idea that the *sharīʿah* could be a source for practical and effective codification was probably the Egyptian jurist ʿAbd al-Razzāq al-Sanhūrī, who played a part in drafting new civil codes for more than one Arab country. The magnitude of the achievement of modern Muslim states in creating and implementing their new legal structures is rarely appreciated outside legal circles, but it is an achievement of immense importance and complexity, and not one that is unduly at odds with the practical history of the *sharīʿah.*

If codification is one aspect of the heritage of nineteenth-century reform, another, more complex, is Islamic fundamentalism. This term is used in many ways, not always carefully. In the history of religious doctrine it can describe those movements that deny the authority of tradition and overleap the accumulated historical and intellectual experience of the community to return to the sources, the early generations, the fundamentals. In this sense, it is possible to recognize in the history of Islam a recurring fundamentalist tendency, which can be associated with, for example, the Ẓāhirīs (Literalists) and the Salafīs (Primitivists). The word *fundamentalist* is also used to describe groups that espouse radical or activist political views. It is not accidental that many of these groups, from the Wahhābīs of the eighteenth century to the Muslim Brothers of the twentieth, have also been fundamentalist in a strictly doctrinal sense. They are explicitly Salafī, and they look back to the great Salafī theoretician Ibn Taymīyah as symbol and hero. Here too Muḥammad ʿAbduh bears a measure of responsibility for initiating a tradition of distaste for the Muslim intellectual traditions (as well as for the mystical experience of the Ṣūfīs). Sayyid Quṭb, the ideologue of the Muslim Brothers executed in Egypt in 1966, was in this respect an intellectual descendant of ʿAbduh. For him, in the end, all of Islamic history after the early generations was only a continuation of the Jāhilīyah, the Age of Ignorance, and the works of the *fuqahā'* were something like a betrayal of the existential task they should have executed. In his work of Qur'ānic exegesis, *Fi ẓilāl al-Qur'ān,* he frequently made the point: "The *sharīʿah* has been revealed in order to be implemented, not to be known, to be studied, and to be changed into culture in books and treatises" (Beirut, 1971, vol. 1, p. 746). This reverses the priorities and denies the achievement of an ancient juristic tradition of thought and literature; and it promotes the word *sharīʿah* as if it designated a blueprint for the Islamic state. In this form, *sharīʿah* could be part of a call to political action, and it was subject to the usual constraints of political expediency. This has sometimes taken the form of promoting fragments of the law as symbols of islamization. For example, in Sudan in 1983, President Nimeiri enacted the Islamic canonical penalties for fornication, wine-drinking, and other offenses. Politically insensitive at best, these moves (reenacted and extended later by an Islamic government) were also a trivialization of the tradition of *fiqh.*

The Islamic Revolution in Iran (1978–1979) is sometimes described as a fundamentalist movement, but it is not so in the strictly doctrinal sense. The theory that underlay the Ayatollah Khomeini's propaganda and provided him legitimacy in his own eyes and in those of his followers was central to the tradition of juristic thought in Shīʿī Islam. Khomeini built on the tradition; he did not abandon or cheapen it. And the tradition was not in the end incompatible with substantial continuity in the constitutional and legal structures of Iran, as well as in its political institutions.

Islamic law has been throughout the history of Islamic culture the prime focus of intellectual effort. It is a correspondingly complex affair, a structure in which several traditions of juristic thought and many types of social reality have had to be discovered to be in some kind of justificatory harmony with one another and with the texts of revelation. Its rewards as an object of study are evident. For the Muslim community, the assimilation of its messages to the needs of the current generation is, now as in the past, both an intellectual and an imaginative challenge, as well as a generally acknowledged a religious duty.

[*See also* Faqīh; Ḥadīth; Ijtihād; Qāḍī; Salafīyah; Waqf.]

BIBLIOGRAPHY

Anderson, J. N. D. *Law Reform in the Muslim World.* London, 1976.
Goldziher, Ignácz. *Muhammedanische Studien.* 2 vols. Halle, 1888–1890. London, 1967.
Heyd, Uriel. *Studies in Old Ottoman Criminal Law.* Edited by V. L. Ménage. Oxford, 1973.
Liebesny, Herbert J. *The Law of the Near and Middle East: Readings, Cases, and Materials.* Albany, N.Y., 1975.
Schacht, Joseph. *The Origins of Muhammadan Jurisprudence.* Oxford, 1950.
Schacht, Joseph. *An Introduction to Islamic Law.* Oxford, 1964.
Wansbrough, John. *Quranic Studies.* Oxford, 1977.

NORMAN CALDER

Sunnī Schools of Law

The beginnings of the schools of law in Islam go back to the late Umayyad period, or about the beginning of the second Islamic century, when Islamic legal thought started to develop out of the administrative and popular practice as shaped by the religious and ethical precepts of the Qur'ān and the *ḥadīth.* The role of the Qur'ān at this very early stage can be taken for granted, but the role of *ḥadīth,* or traditions of the Prophet, has been subject to dispute among scholars; some maintain that they became efficacious only after Muḥammad ibn Idrīs al-Shāfiʿī (d. 820) insisted that they be. In the main centers of the early Islamic world, local scholars and private jurists developed their doctrines based on combinations of local practice, the Qur'ān, and their knowledge of the traditions, using varying degrees of analogical reasoning in the interpretation and application of the holy texts. This geographical variation thus gave rise to varying doctrines. Shāfiʿī says, "Every capital of the Muslims is a seat of learning whose people follow the opinion of one of their countrymen in most of his teachings." He goes on to mention the local authorities of the people of Mecca, Basra, Kufa, and Syria; elsewhere he speaks of the Iraqis and the Medinese. They all followed their own doctrines based on what Joseph Schacht calls their "living traditions" and the free exercise of personal opinion, in the absence of strict rules for deriving legal norms like those elaborated by Shāfiʿī. At this stage the adage had not yet arisen that the true home of the *sun-*

nah (the model behavior of the Prophet) was Medina.

Comparatively little is known about the doctrines of the Meccans, the Basrans, and the Syrians, although we possess some documentation of the famous representative of the latter, ʿAbd al-Raḥmān al-Awzāʿī (d. 773), particularly about the laws of warfare. Of the Medinese and the Kufan doctrines we know more, possibly because they later developed into the Mālikī and the Ḥanafī schools, respectively, which have continued to this day. Shāfiʿī, the founder of the school that carries his name, considered himself a member of the Medinese school, but he was uncompromising in taking the Medinese and other early law schools to task for not making the traditions of the Prophet supersede their customary practices. He insisted that nothing could override the practice of the Prophet even if that were attested by only a single tradition. His insistence was to have a lasting influence on the legal theory of all schools that accorded traditions a place second only to the Qur'ān in formulating rules, and that identified *sunnah,* previously understood as the model practice of the community, with the traditions of the Prophet. The Medinese until that time appear to have authenticated only those traditions agreed upon by the people of Medina, and to have allowed sound reason and analogy to supersede traditions. The Iraqis, who were accused by their opponents of caring little for traditions, seem actually to have been more knowledgeable about the traditions than were the Medinese, whose attitude toward traditions they shared. Still, some Iraqis, particularly Muḥammad ibn al-Ḥasan al-Shaybānī (d. 804), seemed to anticipate Shāfiʿī in insisting on the decisive role of traditions.

This article will treat the development of the various Sunni schools, four of which are extant and three extinct. It will discuss their main doctrines, their major figures, their major books, and their provenance and present locations. Although the legal theories as developed by the various jurists may be regarded as more closely related to the topic of *uṣūl al-fiqh* ("roots of jurisprudence"; the bases through which practical legal rules are derived), some reference will be made to them here as well. [*See* Uṣūl al-Fiqh.]

Ḥanafī School. One of the geographical centers of legal thought was Kufa in Iraq. The servant and companion of the Prophet, ʿAbd Allāh ibn Masʿūd (d. 653), had been sent there by the caliph ʿUmar as a teacher and jurist. His students and theirs in turn achieved prominence as jurists; notable among them were ʿAlqamah al-Nakhaʿī, Masrūq al-Hamadānī, al-Qāḍī Shurayḥ, Ibrāhīm al-Nakhaʿī, ʿĀmir al-Shaʿbī, and Ḥammād ibn Abī Sulaymān (d. 738), the teacher of Abū Ḥanīfah, the eponym of the school.

Abū Ḥanīfah (699–767) is the agnomen of Nuʿmān ibn Thābit, of Persian extraction and a native of Kufa. He first studied scholastics and then concentrated on the jurisprudence of the Kufa school while gaining his living as a textile merchant. His training in scholastics coupled with his experience as a merchant imparted to him the unusual ability to use reason and logic in the application of rules to the practical questions of life, and to broaden those rules by the use of analogy *(qiyās)* and preference *(istiḥsān).* His liberal use of opinion in the formulation of analogy and preference caused his school to be dubbed the People of Opinion, as distinguished from the People of Traditions who depend on traditions in the formulation of rules—even though his school was not less knowledgeable about traditions. He was reported to have said, "This knowledge of ours is opinion; it is the best we have been able to achieve. He who is able to arrive at different conclusions is entitled to his opinion as we are entitled to our own."

On the whole, the legal doctrines of Abū Ḥanīfah evidence a liberality and a respect for personal freedom that are not that pronounced among other jurists. He was the first to formulate contract rules concerning contracts, which reflect his attachment to the principle of freedom of contract as exemplified in the contracts of *salam* and *murābaḥah.* The first allows the immediate payment of the price of goods for future delivery, although the contract of sale stipulates the immediate exchange of an object and its price; the second allows a merchant to sell to another what the former had bought at the original price plus a stipulated profit, provided that usury is not involved. In the field of personal law, he allows a free girl who had reached her majority to marry without the intercession of a marriage guardian, although later Ḥanafī doctrine restricted that right to a woman who had previously been married. Also contrary to all other jurists, including the dominant opinion in his own school, he would not interdict the spendthrift, contending that a person who has reached majority is independent and can do as he wishes with his property.

The legal thought of Abū Ḥanīfah was transmitted by his students, four of whom achieved fame—Abū Yūsuf, Ẓufar ibn al-Hudhayl, Muḥammad ibn al-Ḥasan al-Shaybānī, and al-Ḥasan ibn Ziyād. In particular, Abū Yūsuf and Muḥammad were able to spread the influence of the school through their writings and their high positions in the ʿAbbāsid state; they were often referred to as al-Ṣāḥibān (the Two Companions). Abū Yūsuf, whose name was Yaʿqūb ibn Ibrāhīm al-Anṣārī (731–798), was appointed a judge in Baghdad and later became the first *qāḍī al-quḍāt,* or chief justice, with authority to appoint judges in the empire. On various occasions he differed with the opinions of his master, basing his decisions on traditions that may not have been available earlier. His book *Kitāb al-kharāj* is in the form of a treatise he prepared for Caliph Hārūn al-Rashīd on taxation and the fiscal problems of the state.

To Muḥammad ibn al-Ḥasan al-Shaybānī (749–804) goes the credit for writing down the legal thought of the Ḥanafī school. He was trained in the jurisprudence of the Iraqi school as well as in that of Medina, for he traveled to Medina and studied under the scholar Mālik ibn Anas, a version of whose book *Al-muwaṭṭa'* was transmitted by him. Caliph al-Rashīd appointed him *qāḍī* of Raqqah and later removed him, but he accompanied the caliph to Khurasan and died at Rayy. The books he compiled contain many of the detailed rules he extracted, particularly on the laws of inheritance, as well as the doctrine of his school. Often the dominant opinion of the school reflected his opinion on a disputed topic. His books have been classified into two categories: Ẓāhir al-Riwāyah, whose transmission from him has been authenticated, and al-Nawādir, books transmitted by less reliable authorities. The first category consists of the six books *Al-mabsūt, Al-jāmiʿ al-kabīr, Al-jāmiʿ al-ṣaghīr, Al-siyar al-kabīr, Al-siyar al-ṣaghīr,* and *Al-ziyādāt.* These books were collected in one volume known as *Al-kāfī* by Abū al-Faḍl Al-marwazī, better known as al-Ḥākim al-Shahīd (d. 955). This collection was later annotated in a thirty-volume work, *Al-mabsūt,* by the distinguished scholar Muḥammad ibn Aḥmad al-Sarakhsī (d. 1090). This work was the basis of the Ottoman civil code of 1869, the *Mecelle* (Ar., *Majallah*), part of the legal reforms of the Tanzimat period. [*See* Mecelle.] The second category, al-Nawādir, consists of *Amālī Muḥammad* or *Al-kaysānīyāt* reported by Shuʿayb al-Kaysānī, *Al-raqqīyāt* (cases submitted to al-Shaybānī while he was a judge in Raqqah), *Al-makhārij fī al-hiyal* on legal fictions and devices, and five other lesser-known collections.

Famous scholars of the next generation or two include Hilāl al-Ra'y (d. 859); Aḥmad ibn ʿAmr al-Khaṣṣāf (d. 874), author of *Al-ḥiyal* on legal fictions and devices, *Al-waqf* on religious foundations, and *Adab al-qāḍī* on procedure and evidence (commented on by Abū Bakr Aḥmad ibn ʿAlī al-Jaṣṣāṣ (d. 980), author of *Aḥkām al-Qur'ān;* and Abū Jaʿfar al-Ṭaḥāwī (d. 933), author of *Al-jāmiʿ al-kabīr fī al-shurūṭ* on legal formularies. Still later generations produced Abū al-Ḥasan al-Karkhī (d. 951); al-Sarakhsī, mentioned earlier; ʿAlī ibn Muḥammad al-Bazdawī (d. 1089), author of *Al-uṣūl* on jurisprudence; Abū Bakr al-Kāsānī (d. 1191), author of *Badā'iʿ al-ṣanā'iʿ fī tartīb al-sharā'iʿ;* and Burhān al-Dīn ʿAlī al-Marghīnānī (d. 1196), author of the famous and authoritative *Al-hidāyah,* which has been the subject of many commentaries.

There followed a period of stagnation and imitation of earlier jurists in which existing works were abridged and annotated. An abridgement that received wide recognition was *Al-mukhtaṣar* by Aḥmad ibn Muḥammad al-Qudūrī (d. 1036). Also compiled were some *fatwās,* works presenting actual or theoretical questions and answers. Chief among these were *Al-fatāwā al-khānīyah* by Qāḍīkhān Ḥasan ibn Manṣūr (d. 1195), *Al-fatāwā al-khayrīyah* by Khayr al-Dīn al-Ramlī (d. 1670), *Al-fatāwā al-Hindīyah*—compiled in India by order of the Mughal emperor Awrangzīb ʿĀlamgīr (d. 1707) and consisting of extracts from the authoritative works of the school—and *Al-fatāwā al-mahdīyah* by the Egyptian *mufti* Muḥammad al-ʿAbbāsī al-Mahdī (d. 1897). In addition, a number of later Ḥanafī works achieved prominence in the Ottoman Empire, chief among which were *Multaqā al-abḥur* by Ibrāhīm al-Ḥalabī (d. 1549) and *Radd al-muḥtār* by Muḥammad Amīn ibn ʿĀbidīn (d. 1836).

The Ḥanafī is the most widespread school in Islamic countries. The fact that it was the dominant school during the ʿAbbāsid Caliphate, owing to the efforts of Abū Yūsuf and other early Ḥanafīs, gave it an advantage over the others. Moreover, it was the official school of the Ottoman Empire with its farflung dominions, and in 1869 its doctrines were enshrined in the *Mecelle,* or civil code, to be applied in the newly created secular *(niẓāmīyah)* courts, Ḥanafī law continued to be applied to Muslim personal-status matters. It is still the official school for issuing *fatwā*s and for application to the personal-status matters of Sunnī Muslims in the successor states of the Ottoman Empire, including Egypt, Syria, Lebanon, Iraq, Jordan, and Israel-Palestine. In Turkey, which is officially secular, Ḥanafī law governs religious observances. It continues to be the dominant school for application to personal-status matters and/or for religious observances among the Muslims of the Balkans, the Caucasus, Afghanistan, Pakistan, India, the

Central Asian republics, and China. It is estimated that its adherents constitute more than one-third of the world's Muslims.

Mālikī School. This school developed in the Arabian peninsula, the original abode of Islam. It was originally referred to as the School of Hejaz or the School of Medina, and its doctrines are often attributed to such early Muslims as ʿUmar ibn al-Khaṭṭāb, ʿAbd Allāh ibn ʿUmar, Zayd ibn Thābit, ʿAbbās (the Prophet's uncle), and ʿĀ'ishah (the Prophet's wife). Of the early jurists of the school who achieved fame, mention may be made of Saʿīd ibn al-Musayyab, ʿUrwah ibn al-Zubayr, and Abū Bakr ibn ʿAbd al-Raḥmān. A later generation of jurists and traditionists were the teachers of Mālik, the eponym of the school. These included Rabīʿah ibn ʿAbd al-Raḥmān (d. c.748–753), known as Rabīʿah al-Ra'y or Rabīʿah of Opinion (or of Good Judgment, as suggested by Amīn al-Khawlī); Nāfiʿ (d. 735 or 737), the freedman of Ibn ʿUmar; Ibn Shihāb al-Zuhrī (d. c.740–742); Ibn Hurmuz (d. 765); and Jaʿfar al-Ṣādiq (d. 765), the revered Shīʿī imam and eponym of the Jaʿfarī Shīʿī school of law.

Mālik ibn Anas al-Aṣbaḥī, of Yemenite descent, was born in Medina in 713 and lived there until his death in 795, having left it only to perform the pilgrimage at Mecca. He thus epitomized the learning of the people of Medina. In his book *Al-muwaṭṭa'*, a collection of traditions from the Prophet, companions, and followers arranged according to the subjects of jurisprudence, he often would confirm a legal point by saying, "And this is the rule with us", or "And this the rule agreed upon by consensus here." It was said that *Al-muwaṭṭa'* was transmitted in several versions, but only two have reached us: the version transmitted by the Ḥanafī al-Shaybānī, mentioned earlier, and the version transmitted by Yaḥyā al-Laythī (d. 848) and commented upon by al-Zarqānī, al-Suyūṭī, and others. Fragments of a third version transmitted by the Tunisian ʿAlī ibn Ziyād (d. c.800) have also survived.

Mālik was undoubtedly tradition-bound in his legal doctrines. He would often emphasize that he would not deviate from what he had received from his teachers or from the consensus of the scholars of Medina. Sometimes, however, he utilized a form of thinking similar to analogy, which has prompted Abū Zahrah to assert that Mālik used *ra'y* (personal opinion) as well as *qiyās* (analogy) in arriving at a rule. Actually, he himself said, "As for those matters that I did not receive from [my predecessors] I exercised my reasoning and reflection *(ijtahadtu wa-naẓartu)* according to the course of those I have met . . . so that I would not deviate from the course of the people of Medina and their opinions *(ārā'ihim)*. If I did not hear anything specifically about a matter I attributed the opinion *(ra'y)* to me." Amīn al-Khūlī explains that the word *ra'y* at that time did not bear its later technical meaning of opinion vis-à-vis analogy, but meant rather "understanding" and "good judgment." He also considers the attribution by some authors of the technical concepts of preference *(istiḥsān)* and public interest *(maṣāliḥ mursalah)* to Mālik as rather anachronistic, because the science of *uṣūl al-fiqh* was still in its infancy at that time.

In the field of law proper, the Mālikī school, compared to the Ḥanafī school, evidences some conservative attitudes, particularly with regard to women. Perhaps this reflects the conservative milieu of Medina at the time of Mālik. A woman can only be married with the consent and participation of her marriage guardian; in Ḥanafī law a guardian is necessary only for a virgin below the age of puberty, and she can repudiate the marriage upon attaining puberty. Also in Mālikī law, the father or paternal grandfather has the right to give in marriage his virgin daughter or granddaughter without her consent and even, within some limits, against her wishes; in Ḥanafī law such susceptibility to compulsion *(jabr)* terminates at puberty.

Mālik's students included Muḥammad ibn al-Ḥasan al-Shaybānī, mentioned above, and Muḥammad ibn Idrīs al-Shāfiʿī, the founder of the school that carries his name. His followers included Yaḥyā al-Laythī, mentioned earlier as a transmitter of Mālik's *Al-muwaṭṭa;* the Tunisian Asad ibn al-Furāt (d. 828); and ʿAbd al-Salām al-Tanūkhī, known as Saḥnūn from Kairouan (d. 854). Andalusian jurists who gained fame included Abū al-Walīd al-Bājī (d. 1081), Ibn Rushd (d. 1126), Ibn Rushd the grandson (d. 1198), and Muḥammad ibn ʿAbd Allāh ibn al-ʿArabī (d. 1148). Later generations of jurists included Abū al-Qāsim ibn Juzayy (d. 1340), author of *Al-qawānīn al-fiqhīyah fī talkhīṣ madhhab al-Mālikīyah;* Sīdī Khalīl (d. 1365), author of the authoritative *Al-mukhtaṣar;* and Muḥammad ibn ʿAbd Allāh al-Khirshī (d. 1690), a rector of al-Azhar and author of a commentary on Khalīl's work. The major reference work for this school nowadays is *Al-mudawwanah,* compiled by Asad ibn al-Furāt and later edited and arranged by Saḥnūn under the title of *Al-Mudawwanah al-kubrā.* A concise work on law that has received some attention from Orientalists is *Al-risālah* by Ibn Abī Zayd al-

Qayrawānī (d. 996). Mālikī jurists who attained fame in specific fields include the Egyptian Shihāb al-Dīn al-Qarāfī (d. 1285) and the Andalusian Abū Isḥāq al-Shāṭibī (d. 1388) in questions of jurisprudence, Ibn Farḥūn (d. 1396) in legal procedure, and Aḥmad al-Wansharīsī (d. 1508) and Muḥammad Aḥmad ʿUlaysh (d. 1882) in *fatāwā* works.

Since the birthplace of the Mālikī school was Medina, it was natural that the school should spread in the Hejaz. Because of the contacts that the scholars of North Africa and Andalusia established with the scholars of Medina during the yearly pilgrimage, the Mālikī school spread to those parts and displaced the Ẓāhirī school in Andalusia where the latter, now extinct, had held sway. It continues to be the predominant school among the people of Morocco, Algeria, Tunisia, and Libya. It has also spread to upper Egypt and the Sudan as well as to Bahrain, the Emirates, and Kuwait. A number of other countries also have some Mālikī adherents.

Shāfiʿī School. This school was not so much the product of a geographical area as it was the result of a synthesis conducted by a single jurist who was thoroughly familiar with the doctrines of the two other schools. That jurist was Muḥammad ibn Idrīs ibn al-ʿAbbās ibn ʿUthmān ibn Shāfiʿ (hence the *nisbah* or attribution Shāfiʿī), a companion of the Prophet and a descendant of al-Muṭṭalib, brother of the Prophet's ancestor Hāshim. Thus he was closely enough related to the Prophet to qualify for a stipend from the fifth of the spoils of war assigned to kinsmen, among others. Shāfiʿī was born in Gaza, Palestine, in 767 and died in Egypt in 820. When he was two years old his father died, so his mother took him to Mecca to be among his kin and to preserve his noble heritage. After memorizing the Qur'ān and studying *ḥadīth,* he was sent to the desert where he accompanied the Hudhayl tribe, which was famous for its eloquent speech and poetic tradition. Later he traveled to Medina to study *fiqh* under Mālik, whose reputation had spread far and wide. When Mālik died, Shāfiʿī worked with the governor of Yemen and later was taken to Iraq on the orders of Caliph al-Rashīd to answer charges that he was an ʿAlīd sympathizer. His eloquent defense, added to a word in his favor from the Qāḍī Muḥammad ibn al-Ḥasan al-Shaybānī, saved his life. He then applied himself to the study of Iraqi *fiqh* under al-Shaybānī and read the latter's books. This opportunity to combine the knowledge of Iraqi *fiqh* with that of the Hejaz, added to the experience gained in his extensive travels, placed Shāfiʿī in a good position to formulate the theoretical bases for law in his famous *Al-risālah. Al-risālah* was written in Baghdad during a second visit to that city and refined when the author moved to Egypt in 814–815.

In the field of law Shāfiʿī continued to regard himself as a member of the school of Medina even though he had adopted the essential thesis of the traditionists that the traditions were superior in the formulation of laws to the customary doctrines of the earlier schools. Through vigorous polemics he tried to convert the adherents of the other schools to his doctrine, but they were not willing to abandon their own doctrines, although they accepted his legal theory, which is traditionist by inspiration. Those legal specialists of both schools who accepted Shāfiʿī's thesis completely became his followers, and thus a new school arose with a doctrine formulated by an individual founder. The doctrine was first formulated in Iraq, but when Shāfiʿī moved to Egypt he retracted some of his earlier pronouncements; the resulting doctrine has come to be known as the Egyptian, or new, version of the school.

Shāfiʿī authored or dictated to his pupil al-Rabī ibn Sulaymān (d. 884) the book known as *Al-umm,* a truly seminal work that defines not only the doctrine of Shāfiʿī but also many of the differences among the other schools. The seven-volume work deals with the various topics of law including transactions, religious observances, penal matters, and matters of personal status. It also includes such topics as the differences between ʿAlī and Ibn Masʿūd, the disagreement between Shāfiʿī and Mālik, the refutation by al-Shaybānī of some doctrines of Medina, the dispute between Abū Yūsuf and Ibn Abī Laylā, and the reply of Abū Yūsuf to the work on *siyar,* or the law of war and peace, by al-Awzāʿī. *Al-umm* above all treats Shāfiʿī's favorite topic, an attack on those who do not accept the entire body of traditions in the formulation of rules, and the invalidation of preference *(istiḥsān)* as a source of law. On the page margins of volume seven of *Al-umm* as printed in Cairo (1968) is another work by Shāfiʿī entitled *Ikhtilāf al-ḥadīth,* also reported by al-Rabī.

Certain students of Shāfiʿī in Iraq founded their own schools; these were Aḥmad ibn Ḥanbal, Dāwūd al-Ẓāhirī, Abū Thawr al-Baghdādī, and Abū Jaʿfar ibn Jarīr al-Ṭabarī. All but the school of Ibn Ḥanbal have become extinct. In Egypt Shāfiʿī's students included Abū Yaʿqūb al-Buwayṭī (d. 845), Ismāʿīl al-Muzanī (d. 877), the author of *Al-mukhtaṣar* on Shāfiʿī jurisprudence, and al-Rabī.

Some famous jurists who later propagated the Shāfiʿī school included Abū Isḥāq Ibrāhīm ibn ʿAlī al-Shīrāzī (d. 1083), the author of *Al-muhadhdhab* and the scholar for whom the vizier Niẓām al-Mulk built the Niẓāmīyah school in Baghdad; the philosopher and jurist Abū Ḥāmid al-Ghazālī (d. 1111), who authored *Al-mustaṣfā* and *Al-wajīz* in jurisprudence and law; ʿIzz al-Dīn ibn ʿAbd al-Salām (d. 1261), the author of *Qawāʿid al-aḥkām fī maṣāliḥ al-anām,* a magnificent treatment of detailed principles and maxims of jurisprudence; Muḥyī al-Dīn al-Nawawī (d. 1277), the author of the famous *Minhāj al-ṭālibīn;* Taqī al-Dīn al-Subkī (d. 1355), the author of *Fatāwā al-Subkī;* and the encyclopedic author Jalāl al-Dīn al-Suyūṭī (d. 1505), who wrote *Al-ashbāh wa-al-naẓā'ir* on Shāfiʿī law.

Since Egypt was the home of the new school of Shāfiʿī, it was natural that it would strike deep roots there. It was the official school during the Ayyūbid dynasty (1169–1252) and occupied a prime position during the Mamlūk regime that followed. Only when the Ottomans occupied Egypt in 1517 did the Ḥanafī school displace it. Today, although the Ḥanafī school is officially enforced by the courts in matters of personal status, many Egyptians, particularly in the rural areas, follow the Shāfiʿī school in their religious observances. So do the great majority of Muslims in Palestine and Jordan, many adherents in Syria, Lebanon, Iraq, the Hejaz, Pakistan, India, and Indonesia, and the Sunnī inhabitants of Iran and Yemen.

Ḥanbalī School. This is also a personal school in that it represented in the main the legal opinions, sayings, and *fatwā*s of a single person, Aḥmad ibn Ḥanbal. Ibn Ḥanbal was born in Baghdad in 780 and died there in 855. He traveled widely to Syria, the Hejaz, and Yemen as well as to Kufa and Basra in Iraq in pursuit of the traditions collected in his monumental work *Musnad al-Imām Aḥmad* in six volumes containing more than forty thousand items. This, added to the fact that he never authored a work on *fiqh* at a time when many others were writing on the subject, made many Muslim biographers consider him a traditionist rather than a jurist. His students, however, collected his legal opinions and *fatwā*s, and the result was a body of juristic principles and laws worthy of being designated a school.

The attachment of this school to traditions is reflected in its departure from the other schools concerning the sources of law. According to Ibn Qayyim al-Jawzīyah (d. 1350), a late Ḥanbalī jurist, the sources are five: the texts of the Qur'ān and *sunnah;* the *fatwā*s of the companions when not contradicted by the former sources; the sayings of single companions when in conformity with the Qur'ān and *sunnah;* traditions that have a weak chain of transmission or lack a name of a transmitter in the chain; and finally, reasoning by analogy when absolutely necessary.

Ibn Ḥanbal became famous in Islamic history for his rigorous attachment to his faith and his principled stand against the doctrine of the createdness of the Qur'ān during the Inquisition in Baghdad, even though he was beaten and imprisoned. This tenacious attachment to principle was later reflected in two followers who rejuvenated his school—Ibn Qayyim, mentioned above, and his teacher Taqī al-Dīn ibn Taymīyah (d. 1327), both of whom were imprisoned in the citadel of Damascus. It was also apparent in the career of Muḥammad ibn ʿAbd al-Wahhāb (d. 1792), the famous Ḥanbalī reformer of Nejd.

Followers of this school include Muwaffaq al-Dīn ibn Qudāmah (d. 1223), the author of the monumental twelve-volume *Al-mughnī* as well as *Al-ʿumdah;* Taqī al-Dīn ibn Taymīyah, author of the famous *Fatāwā* and *Al-siyāsah al-sharʿīyah;* and Ibn Qayyim al-Jawzīyah, author of *Iʿlām al-muwaqqiʿīn* and other works. The rejuvenated school, which had not enjoyed many followers before Ibn Taymīyah, was further strengthened in the eighteenth century by Ibn ʿAbd al-Wahhāb and his reform movement in Arabia, which aimed at taking Islam back to its simple and pristine beginnings, depending on the Qur'ān and the *sunnah* instead of later scholars. The success of the Wahhābiyan and the return of the Saudi family to power early this century established the Ḥanbalī school as the official school of Saudi Arabia. It is also the official school of Qatar and has many adherents in Palestine, Syria, Iraq, and elsewhere. [*See* Wahhābīyah; Saudi Arabia; *and the biographies of Ibn Taymīyah and Ibn ʿAbd al-Wahhāb.*]

Extinct Sunnī Schools. The most important of these were the schools of al-Awzāʿī, al-Ẓāhirī, and al-Ṭabarī. ʿAbd al-Raḥmān al-Awzāʿī was born in Lebanon and died there in 773, his tomb being just south of Beirut. His school flourished in Syria and Spain for some time but was overwhelmed by the Shāfiʿī and the Mālikī schools in those two regions, respectively. What is known about it is derived from the writings of the other schools, particularly on the laws of war and peace, since we possess no independent works on its jurisprudence. Apparently it depended on traditions for its doctrines.

Abū Sulaymān Dā'ūd al-Ẓāhirī (d. 883), a student of

Shāfiʿī, founded his own school on the apparent and literal (*ẓāhir*) meanings of the Qur'ān and the *sunnah*, rejecting many of the other sources accepted by the other schools. The school flourished in Spain but died out by the fourteenth century. One of its most celebrated adherents was Ibn Ḥazm (d. 1064), author of *Al-iḥkām fī uṣūl al-aḥkām* on jurisprudence and *Al-muḥallā* on *fiqh*.

The historian and exegete Abū Jaʿfar Muḥammad ibn Jarīr al-Ṭabarī (d. 922) was also a jurist who developed his own school, which lasted until the twelfth century. Among his books on jurisprudence was *Ikhtilāf al-fuqahā'*, a comparative study of the various schools of law.

Two developments this century have the potential to affect the structure of law schools in the Islamic world. One was the call for a new *ijtihād* that would disregard, or at least not follow completely, the established schools. The motivating spirit for this call has been the progressive teachings of prominent Islamic leaders such as Shaykh Muḥammad ʿAbduh (d. 1905) in Egypt and Sir Sayyid Aḥmad Khān (d. 1898) and the Aligarh movement in India. Although the call was strong, the end results were very modest. [*See* Aligarh *and the biographies of ʿAbduh and Aḥmad Khān.*] A proponent of this course of reform, the prominent Egyptian judge Muḥammad Saʿīd al-ʿAshmāwī, has recently been the target for attacks by conservative elements. In Syria this call for a new *ijtihād* has been vehemently attacked in several articles by prominent rectors of mosques and *muftīs* in a book edited by Aḥmad al-Bayānūnī of Abū Dharr Mosque in Aleppo. The prospects for this call in the present era of fundamentalist thinking are, therefore, not very promising, although the exercise of new *ijtihād* has resulted in the decree of monogamy in Tunisia.

The other development, which has proven to be more successful, is crossing the boundaries of the various schools in an effort to find juristic opinions that support reform in many aspects of the law of personal status as it is applied in most Islamic countries. This process is called *takhayyur*, or choosing a juristic opinion, and was applied successfully in several reforms of the law. For instance, the Ottoman Law of Family Rights of 1917 derived several of its provisions from the dominant doctrines of Sunnī schools other than the Ḥanafī, which was the official school. Later reforms in Egypt and the Sudan went even further by accepting any opinion of a jurist from one of the Sunnī schools, or even a Shīʿī opinion, without announcing its provenance. An example of the latter is the Egyptian Law of Testamentary Dispositions of 1946, which allowed a bequest to an heir within the "bequeathable third" without the consent of the other heirs, although the Sunnī position has always been that there can be no bequest to an heir. Reformers even resorted to *talfīq*, or combining parts of the doctrines of different schools or jurists, into a new doctrine. Because the four orthodox Sunnī schools are considered authentic and acceptable by all Sunnīs provided one is adhered to consistently by an individual, a sentiment has arisen among modern Muslims that it is perfectly acceptable to effect reform by drawing on the provisions of all four.

BIBLIOGRAPHY

Abū Zarah, Muḥammad. *Ibn Ḥanbal*. Cairo, n.d. Account of the life and jurisprudence of the founder of the Ḥanbalī school.

Abū Zarah, Muḥammad. *Muḥaḍarāt fī tārīkh al-madhāhib al-fiqhīyah*. Cairo, n.d. Comprehensive history of law schools in Islam.

Abū Zarah, Muḥammad. *Al-Shāfiʿī*. Cairo, n.d. Account of the life and jurisprudence of the founder of the Shāfiʿī school.

Anderson, J. N. D. *Law Reform in the Muslim World*. London, 1976. Comprehensive treatment of the philosophy and methods of reform, and the actual achievements of reform, in various fields of law.

Bayānūnī, Aḥmad ʿIzz al-Dīn al-. *Al-Ijtihād wa-al-Mujtahidūn*. Aleppo, 1968.

Coulson, Noel J. *A History of Islamic Law*. Edinburgh, 1964. Highly readable survey of the genesis of Islamic law, doctrine and practice in the medieval period, and Islamic law in the modern world.

Al-fatāwā al-ʿālamgīrīyah. Translated by Neil B. E. Baillie as *A Digest of Moohummudan Law* (1865). Reprint, Lahore, 1957. This is the work ordered by Sultan Awrangzib and based on the most famous Ḥanafī texts. It is also called *Al-fatāwā al-hindīyah*.

Fyzee, Asaf A. A. *Outlines of Muhammadan Law*. Oxford, 1949. Comparatively modern treatment of the application of Islamic law in the Indian Subcontinent.

Khūlī, Amīn al-. *Mālik: Tarjamah Muḥarrarah*. 3 vols. Cairo, n.d.

Marghīnānī, ʿAlī ibn Abī Bakr al-. *Al-Hidāyah*. Translated by Charles Hamilton as *The Hedaya* (1791). Reprint, Lahore, 1957. Convenient source for Ḥanafī law.

Nuʿmān ibn Muḥammad, Abū Ḥanīfah. *Daʿā'im al-Islām*. Edited by Asaf A. A. Fyzee. Bombay, 1974. Major Ismāʿīlī work on jurisprudence and law.

Schacht, Joseph. *The Origins of Muhammadan Jurisprudence*. Oxford, 1950. Pioneering work on the early development of schools of law and doctrine.

Schacht, Joseph. *An Introduction to Islamic Law*. Oxford, 1964. Concise treatment of the historical development of schools and doctrine, and a systematic presentation of legal topics.

Shakʿah, Muṣṭafā al-. *Al-a'immah al-arbaʿah*. Cairo, 1979. Account of the life, work, and jurisprudence of the founders of the four orthodox schools of law.

Vesey-FitzGerald, Seymour Gonne. *Muhammadan Law: An Abridgement*. Oxford and London, 1931. An old classic about the actual application of Islamic law in the Indian Subcontinent and East Africa. Outlines the doctrines of the various schools.

FARHAT J. ZIADEH

Shīʿī Schools of Law

Shiism maintained a strong eschatological and legalist tradition through its central doctrine regarding continued divine guidance available through the living imam, whether manifest or concealed. Muslim eschatology taught that the Mahdi among the descendants of the Prophet would come as the ultimate ideal ruler to establish the ideal public order. The Shīʿīs identified the Mahdi as their imam, and he also served as the authoritative precedent in extrapolating the terms of the Islamic revelation in order to formulate fresh legal decisions. Since the Shīʿīs also believed that the imam like the Prophet was infallible, the imam's guidance was treated as the living tradition, enjoying the same unequivocal status as that reserved by the Sunnīs for the Qur'ān and the *sunnah* (received custom).

Besides the Qur'ān and the *sunnah* as sources for deriving religious praxis, Shīʿī legal theorists regarded human reason as an equally decisive basis for determining the scope of divine purposes for humanity.

Shīʿī legal thought was closely related to its rational theology in which reason, as a discoverer of a legal injunction, was prior to both sources of Islamic revelation, the Qur'ān and the *sunnah.* Reason guides a person to ethical knowledge, and it asserts that good and evil are rational categories. However, reason needs a more categorical verdict on the religious injunctions, which can be derived only from the absolute religious authority of the Prophet and his legitimate successors, the imams. In practice the role of reason is confined to establishing the correlation between the requirements of *al-sharʿ* (the revelation) by extracting the general rules from the Qur'ān and the *sunnah* and inferring the ruling in particular cases through *al-ʿaql* (reason). Consequently, besides the Qur'ān and the *sunnah,* the Shīʿīs included reason as a valid source for the judicial decision that was essentially deduced from the revelation. As for the *ijmāʿ* (consensus), which in Sunnī jurisprudence occupies a decisive status as a a source of legal prescriptions, the Shīʿī jurists admitted it as evident only if it included the infallible imam's opinion, sometimes transmitted by his associates who had participated with him in reaching a consensus. Otherwise consensus lacked authoritativeness for deducing law. The authority of the imam's utterances was so central to the decision-making process in jurisprudence that even when *ijtihād* (independent reasoning) was admitted as a valid intellectual process in deducing judicial decisions, it was reasoning based on revelation and not on the intellect that was regarded as valid.

The major Shīʿī legal school with an uninterrupted tradition of jurisprudence is the Jaʿfarī *madhhab.* The school derives its name from Abū Jaʿfar Muḥammad al-Bāqir and Jaʿfar al-Ṣādiq (eighth century), the fifth and sixth imams, whose disciples are among the earliest *fuqahā'* (jurists) of the Shīʿah. Members of the Jaʿfarī school (also known as the followers of *al-madhhab al-khāmis* ["fifth school"], after its accreditation by Maḥmūd Shaltūt, the rector of al-Azhar in Cairo, along with the four Sunnī schools in 1959) are Twelver Shīʿīs—believers in the line of twelve imams, of whom the last one is in occultation and is awaited as the messianic imam, or Mahdi. The other minor Shīʿī schools of law, such as the Zaydī and the Mustaʿlī Fāṭimid Ismāʿīlīyah, although sharing the centrality of the Shīʿī belief in the imam's position as the absolute legal precedent, have maintained close affinity with the Sunnīs in matters of law. A number of Zaydī jurists, including Muḥammad ibn Ibrāhīm ibn al-Wazīr (d. 1436), Muḥammad ibn Ismāʿīl al-Ṣanʿānī (d. 1768), and Muḥammad ibn ʿAlī al-Shawkānī (d. 1839), have argued that their form of jurisprudence, which shares features with Twelver *fiqh,* constitutes a fifth school of jurisprudence alongside the four Sunnī schools. The Mustaʿlī school, resembling in many respects the Twelver praxis, is closer to Sunnism and has retained its symbiotic relation with the Mālikī school as formulated by the Fāṭimid judge Nuʿmān ibn Muḥammad al-Tamīmī (d. 974), originally a Mālikī himself.

Medina and Kufa were the centers of Shīʿī learning under the early Shīʿi imams. Rulings of the imams were circulating in the form of *ḥadīth* reports among the close associates of the imams and were systematically compiled in the tenth century under appropriate juridical rubrics which were established by such Sunnī compilers as al-Bukhārī and Muslim. The four major compilations of the transmitted material needed to guide the social-political and religious life of the Shīʿīs are: Muḥammad ibn Yaʿqūb al-Kulaynī's *Kitāb al-kāfī;* Muḥammad ibn ʿAlī ibn Bābawayh's *Man lā yaḥḍuruhu al-faqīh;* and Muḥammad ibn al-Ḥasan al-Ṭūsī's *Tahdhīb al-aḥkām* and *Al-istibṣār.*

These four books are held with same esteem among Shīʿīs as the six famous Sunnī compilations among the Sunnīs. However, the most widely used work in the Shīʿī tradition is *Wasā'il al-Shīʿah* by al-Ḥurr al-ʿĀmilī (d. 1699), which compiles traditions dealing with all legal topics from the above four books and other Shīʿī sources. After the transmitted traditions were epitomized and systematized, they were subjected to the strict discipline of the *uṣūl al-fiqh* (principles of jurisprudence), which lays down the rules for deriving legal norms. This period of testing was the most productive period of Shīʿī jurisprudence, headed by leading Shīʿīs in eleventh-century Baghdad. The element of the Shīʿī jurisprudence that favored reasoning based on the textual evidence provided by the Qur'ān and the Shīʿī traditions was firmly incorporated into legal theory. Both the method of deducing legal norms and the procedure of reasoning were laid down in the *uṣūl* works. The profound training of Shīʿī jurists in Muʿtazilī rational theology, and their own exposition of Shīʿī theology on the basis of those rational principles, inseparably joined Shīʿī jurisprudence to the two fundamental doctrines of Shiism: Justice of God and the imamate.

Ongoing theological debate on the priority of reason over revelation had far-reaching implications for Shīʿī law in view of the absence of the infallible imam through his prolonged concealment. In theory, only the Hidden Imam could ascertain that the interpretation of revelation was categorical. With the development of a legal theory that critically examined the documentation used as evidence for rulings, the authority of the *akhbar* (traditions) could not be maintained without question. Some Shīʿī jurists, however, were inclined to accept the authority of the traditions uncritically and tended to be rigid in their juridical rulings. In the seventeenth century Akhbārī jurists, who were staunchly opposed to the Uṣūlī methodology based on assigning human reason a substantive-normative role in deriving new decisions, emerged. Toward the end of the seventeenth century the Akhbārī thesis was defeated, and Uṣūlī methodology, with *ijtihād* as its recognized intellectual process, became the benchmark of Shīʿi jurisprudence. Shaykh Murtaḍā al-Anṣārī (d. 1864) is regarded as the "seal" of the *mujtahids* for applying the principles of legal theory in deducing laws. Leading Shīʿī jurists, such as Ayatollah Ruhollah al-Musavi Khomeini (1902–1989), who are also regarded as the *marājiʿ al-taqlīd* (supreme legal authorities) by their followers, were heirs to the Uṣūlī methodology of al-Anṣārī. Rapid sociopolitical development in the context of modern intellectual currents in the Islamic world, in the years following World War II, brought about significant change in the general education of Shīʿī jurists; they began to address some of the problems faced by a modern Shīʿah in managing public life. Additionally, the creation of the Iranian Islamic Republic marks a new era in Shīʿī jurisprudence. The convergence of the moral-legal and political authority in a modern nation-state under a Shīʿī *mujtahid* has, for the first time, forced Shīʿī jurists to provide authoritative guidance to the Shīʿah in the modern world.

[*See also* Akhbārīyah; Ismāʿīlīyah; Ithnā ʿAsharīyah; Marjaʿ al-Taqlīd; Shīʿī Islam; *and* Uṣūlīyah.]

BIBLIOGRAPHY

Sachedina, A. A. *The Just Ruler* (al-Sulṭan al-ʿĀdil) *in Shīʿite Islam: The Comprehensive Authority of the Jurist in Imamite Jurisprudence.* New York, 1988.

Ṭabāṭabāʾī, Hossein Modarressi. *An Introduction to Shīʿi Law: A Bibliographical Study*. London, 1984.

ABDULAZIZ SACHEDINA

Modern Legal Reform

Reforms affecting Islamic law in the nineteenth and twentieth centuries were more far-reaching than any undertaken previously. The impetus for reform came both from within the Islamic tradition, as specialists in Islamic law sought to reform laws in the face of changing attitudes and social needs, and from without, as political leaders imposed changes designed to eliminate archaic features that impeded governmental modernization programs. Although many reforms occurred during periods of European occupation or colonial rule, some of the earliest were undertaken under indigenous leadership, as in the Ottoman Empire and its semi-autonomous province Egypt, before the British occupation of 1882. Reforms proceeded at the levels both of theory and positive law. At the level of theory, outmoded doctrines were challenged or discarded and changes in methodologies were proposed. Reforms were made in positive law as states expanded the role of legislation to encompass areas formerly covered by juristic formulations of Islamic law. Legal reforms originating in the Middle East often radiated eastward and southward, whereas reforms originating elsewhere had relatively few repercussions in the Middle East.

The course of legal reform was linked to the problematic relationship of the Muslim world with the West. The Islamic law of nations was ill-adapted to the realities of this relationship; it was of necessity discarded. The encounter with European legal models led to extensive borrowings of both their substantive and systemic features and the reworking of Islamic doctrines. Although blends of Islamic and common law traditions emerged in some areas like the Indian subcontinent, Islamic law was for the most part assimilated into the civil law tradition of continental Europe, where laws were set forth in codified form. With the devising of Islamic codes, which offered uniform, systematic statements of Islamic law on various topics, states were able to dictate what would officially constitute Islamic law and to impose one version of it on their territories. Insofar as Islamic law survived as positive law, it was in variants circumscribed by national frontiers and in formulations that inevitably reflected the interplay of local political forces. Once the backlash against westernization made itself felt in the 1970s, states began enacting laws that selectively revived elements of Islamic law and tradition—without, however, abandoning the systemic features that had come in with westernization.

In the Ottoman Empire the process of creating new institutions began in the Tanzimat period with the Council of Judicial Ordinances in 1839, the 1847 establishment of mixed civil and criminal courts staffed by both European and Ottoman judges and utilizing elements of European procedure and evidence, and the promulgation in 1850 of a new commercial code to be applied by commercial tribunals. The latter were merged with the mixed courts in 1860; in the same era new European-style codes were enacted—a land code and a third version of a penal code in 1858, a new commercial code in 1861, and a maritime code in 1863. Commercial procedure and penal procedure codes were also enacted in this period. In 1868 a Council of State modeled after the French Conseil d'État and a Divan of Judicial Ordinances were created, the latter headed by Ahmet Cevdet Pasha (1822–1895), who later became minister of justice. In that capacity he instituted new courses for judges and established the secular Niẓāmī courts. This pattern of enacting new codified laws and establishing parallel Western-style courts, including special courts for Europeans, was emulated subsequently in other countries. The expertise of scholars trained exclusively in the traditional Islamic academies of higher learning became less relevant for the actual operation of legal systems as legal education was reconstituted along European lines and the jurisdiction of religious courts was restricted or eliminated. Tensions developed between the *ʿulamāʾ* and legal professionals trained along Western lines as the latter gained ascendancy in the newly-established Western-style legal institutions. The cultural gulf separating the two classes of legal specialists grew and impeded communication; only rarely did individuals combine full competence in both Western and Islamic systems. [*See* Tanzimat.]

The pace and extent of nineteenth-century reform varied with the subject involved. European models of public law were widely emulated at an early stage. Islamic criminal law, which was weakly developed and contained principles sharply at variance with modern norms, tended to be replaced by Western penal codes. Reforms in Islamic procedural rules, which were archaic and cumbersome, were neglected, the preference being simply for abandoning the old rules and adopting European ones. Similarly, European commercial codes were commonly adopted in lieu of reforming Islamic law affecting commerce.

The first major attempts to codify Islamic rules were undertaken in the late nineteenth century. The most influential Islamic code was the Ottoman Code of Obligations, the *Mecelle* (*Majallah*) compiled in 1869–1876. Its rules concerned contracts, property, torts, and some procedural rules; they were preceded by ninety-eight general maxims distilled from *sharīʿah* law. The *Mecelle* incorporated rules taken from a variety of Ḥanafī jurists; regardless of whether they were idiosyncratic or minority views, these rules were selected according to what best furthered social welfare. The *Mecelle* stayed in force in some former Ottoman territories after the fall of the empire. [*See* Mecelle.]

The 1917 Ottoman Law of Family Rights embodied an innovative eclecticism, selecting rules not only from the four main Sunnī schools but also from opinions of isolated jurists from minority and ancient schools of law, with the goal of making a code that was Islamic in derivation but also suited to the needs of contemporary society. Its impact was reduced by its abrogation in 1919 and the secularizing reforms adopted in Turkey in the 1920s, although it did remain in force in Jordan, Lebanon, Palestine, and Syria.

In 1923 the Treaty of Lausanne finally ended the regime of capitulations under which Ottoman Turkey had for centuries accorded subjects of Western powers exemptions from the jurisdiction of the local courts. The potential for further Islamic reforms in Republican Turkey was eliminated by the decision of its first president, Mustafa Kemal (1881–1938), later Kemal Atatürk, to adopt European codified laws across the board in 1926. A direct challenge to the popular notion that Islam had a political vocation came in Turkey with the 1924 abolition of the Ottoman caliphate, the 1928 elimination of the clause making Islam the state religion, and the 1937 declaration that Turkey was a secular state. A major controversy was generated in Egypt and elsewhere by the 1925 book, *Al-Islām wa-uṣūl al-ḥukm* (Islam and the Principles of Government), by the al-Azhar scholar and judge, ʿAlī ʿAbd al-Rāziq (1888–1966); this justified Turkey's abolition of the caliphate and argued that Islam did not mandate any particular form of government—positions strongly opposed by conservatives.

With the disintegration of the Ottoman Empire and the abolition of the caliphate in the twentieth century, the nation-state emerged in practice as the only viable form of political organization. The political divisions of the state system proved difficult to reconcile with Islamic ideals of a unified *ummah,* and doctrinal disputes about the compatibility of the nation-state with Islamic law continued through the end of the century. Some national constitutions tried to reconcile the ideal of a supernational Islamic community with provisions affirming national sovereignty by asserting their commitment to promote Islamic unity or solidarity. The 1972 Charter of the Organization of the Islamic Conference, the international organization to which all Muslim countries belong, offered the compromise of affirming that the OIC aimed to promote Islamic solidarity among OIC members, which in turn were obligated to respect the sovereignty, independence, and territorial integrity of all other member states. By joining the United Nations system, Muslim countries in practice indicated their acceptance of a world order based on nation-states. [*See* Nation; Organization of the Islamic Conference.]

At the end of the twentieth century Atatürk's secularizing reforms remained the boldest undertaken in this area. In almost all other Muslim countries, the constitutions enacted after they achieved independence provided that Islam was the state religion—the idea of a state religion being borrowed from the West. Even Saudi Arabia, which only belatedly promulgated a basic law in 1992, adopted the concept of a state religion, providing in article 1 that the kingdom was an Arab Islamic state, enjoying full sovereignty, and that its religion was Islam. The 1973 Syrian constitution was unusual in failing to provide that Islam was the religion of the state. In practice, in all Muslim countries the majority sect of Islam enjoyed the favored status of an established religion. Constitutions commonly required that the head of state should be Muslim and that Islamic law should be either a source or the sole source of legislation. Opinions differed as to whether it was permissible to provide for popular sovereignty, or whether a constitution of a Muslim country should provide for the sovereignty of God. Constitutional rights provisions did not necessarily indicate the degree to which discriminatory features of Islamic law remained in force; constitutions might proclaim that all citizens were equal even though the rules of personal status relegated women to a subordinate status and non-Muslims encountered various forms of *de jure* discrimination.

Indian Subcontinent. The subcontinent was cut off from developments in the Middle East by being incorporated into the British Empire and thereby made part of the common-law world with its judge-made case law. Under British rule, the subcontinent adapted to a system of judicial precedent supplemented by statutes. The result was Anglo-Muhammadan law, in which English became the language of the law and the overall method and philosophy were of British inspiration. In this system, judges brought from Britain and British policies of justice, equity, and good conscience determined the scope and application of Islamic doctrine. The influence of Anglo-Muhammadan law extended to other British-ruled countries such as Burma, Singapore, and the Malay States. The hierarchy of courts established by the British enabled the appellate courts to exercise a unifying influence on Islamic law, and the impact was largely conservative, the British judges showing a reluctance to challenge doctrines established by great Islamic jurists. British legislative initiatives on the subcontinent included the Caste Disabilities Removal Act of 1850, abolishing the civil disabilities that Islamic law imposed for apostasy. The Muslim Personal Law (Shariat) Act of 1937 provided that the official version of Islamic law as embodied in statutes and case law should supersede conflicting custom. [*See* Anglo-Muhammadan Law.]

The influence of the reformist thought of Shāh Walī Allāh (1703–1762) of Delhi was potent. A famous disciple of his, Sayyid Aḥmad Khān (1817–1898), rejected the authority of any *ijmāʿ*, or juristic consensus, advocating that legal rules be freely chosen from the doctrines of the four orthodox Sunnī schools. As many Muslims of the subcontinent were inclined to do subsequently, he discounted the *ḥadīth*s as a source of law, expressing doubts about their reliability and claiming that all those repugnant to reason or to the dignity of prophethood should be discarded. On various controversial issues, Sayyid Aḥmad Khān took positions that tended to harmonize Islamic rules with contemporary norms, arguing for example that Islam condemned slavery, that *jihād* was meant to be defensive in nature, and that simple interest charges were allowable. [*See the biographies of Walī Allāh and Aḥmad Khān.*]

Another influential reformist thinker was Muhammad Iqbal (1875–1938), who downgraded the significance of the juristic treatises and maintained that contemporary Muslims must be free to undertake *ijtihād*, independent reasoning from the sources. Iqbal maintained that the Qur'ān had to be understood in the light of contemporary needs and that the *ḥadīth*s should be used with caution. In a significant break with traditional conceptions of *ijmāʿ*, Iqbal maintained that *ijmāʿ* could be exercised by the legislative assemblies of Muslim states. [*See the biography of Iqbal.*]

After the independence of India and Pakistan, case law and statutes reformed personal status law. In the Pakistani decision *Balqis Fatima v. Najm-ul-Ikram Qureshi* (1959 PLD Lah 566) the wife was given an absolute right to divorce in return for making an appropriate payment to the husband, a ruling that involved reinterpreting the traditional institution of *khulʿ* and borrowing the Mālikī rule that a judge might dissolve a marriage on the grounds of discord, or *shiqāq*, between the spouses. In Pakistan the Family Laws Ordinance of 1961 undertook reforms to curb polygamy by requiring that the husband first obtain permission from his wife and an arbitration council before taking a second wife, and that to obtain a divorce the husband should notify his wife and an arbitration council, which was to try to effect a reconciliation. The wife's right to a divorce was ensured by requiring that all marriages use a standard marriage contract, which delegated to the wife the husband's right to divorce. The Indian case *Itwari v. Asghari* (1960 AIR All 684) ruled that in the conditions of contemporary India, a husband's taking a second wife constituted such an insult to the first that, barring unusual circumstances, it would be inequitable to oblige the first wife to continue to live with the polygamous husband.

Algeria. France made Algeria its colony in 1830, and the powerful French influence on Algerian law warrants separately classifying *le droit musulman algérien*, which was shaped by French legal categories and concepts of equity and natural law. The establishment of a French-style hierarchy of courts exerted a unifying control on judicial decisions within Algeria. Over the course of French colonization Islamic law on most subjects fell into desuetude, the area of personal status being an exception. Whether Islamic law should be codified along French lines was debated, and in 1916 the draft code known as the Code Morand presented a modernized version of Islamic principles selected on the basis of what would advance equity, morality, and economic interests, and conform to the state of social development. This draft code, which covered matters such as personal status, real property, and evidence, exerted considerable influence on Algerian jurisprudence even though it was never enacted into law.

Egypt. Among Arab countries, Egypt was the fulcrum of Islamic reform from the late nineteenth century onward. It was also one of the countries where Muslims were first exposed to French law and French legal education, Egyptian students having been sent to study law in France as early as 1828. Egyptians assumed a leading role in efforts to synthesize the French and Islamic traditions.

The most powerful single influence on liberal reformist thought in Islam was the work of the Egyptian *ʿalīm* Muḥammad ʿAbduh (1849–1905), who was educated at al-Azhar and was associated with the Egyptian nationalist cause. His international eminence as an Islamic reformer was enhanced by the stature he attained on becoming grand *muftī* of Egypt in 1899, in which capacity he rendered many *fatwās*. ʿAbduh's liberal ideas and his commentary on the Qur'ān, *Tafsīr al-manār*, were disseminated by his disciple Muḥammad Rashīd Riḍā (1865–1935). Ibn Taymīyah (1263–1328) was one of his intellectual precursors, particularly insofar as ʿAbduh held that only the Islamic rules related to matters of worship were inflexible, whereas rules covering the everyday lives of Muslims could be adjusted as circumstances warranted in accordance with the criterion of social welfare. There were also precedents for his ideas in the work of Muḥammad ibn ʿAbd al-Wahhāb (1703–1787), who advocated stripping Islam of its later accretions and restoring it to its original purity, an approach that justified disregarding solutions offered by medieval jurists and returning to the Qur'ān and *sunnah* to make fresh interpretations. ʿAbduh also resorted to *takhayyur*, being prepared to devise legal solutions to problems based on a comparative evaluation and selection of rules taken from the doctrines of various schools of law. In his rationalism ʿAbduh also owed an intellectual debt to the long-suppressed Muʿtazilah. In practice he favored interpretative techniques that would produce rules that promoted the welfare of society. An example of his approach could be seen in his critique of polygamy, which rested on reading the Qur'ānic verses 4.3 and 4.129 together. The permission of polygamy in surah 4.3 was accompanied by an injunction to those who feared being inequitable to marry only one woman, traditionally understood as being addressed to men's consciences. ʿAbduh treated this as a legal precondition for a valid second marriage, and—given the remark in 4.129, "You will not be able to treat your wives equitably"—he concluded that polygamy should be ruled out except in the case of the exceptional man who was able to treat his wives equitably. ʿAbduh took into account his own observations that in practice husbands had proved unable to treat their wives justly. Although ʿAbduh's influence on reformist thought was far-reaching, his actual impact on the reform of Egyptian law was limited, for by his day the process of adopting French law was already far advanced in Egypt, and the jurisdiction of *sharīʿah* courts had been reduced. [*See the biographies of the figures mentioned above.*]

Muḥammad Qadrī (1821–1888) became an expert in the comparative study of Islamic and French law, and during his tenure as minister of justice (1879–1892) he oversaw the promulgation of a number of new codes. He also produced highly regarded codified versions of Ḥanafī law. ʿAbd al-Rāzzaq al-Sanhūrī (1895–1971), a scholar who combined expertise in both Western and Islamic law, was one of the most influential figures in modern Arab legal history. Possessing a doctorate in law and political science from Lyon and a doctorate from the Institut des Hautes Études Internationales, he later became dean of the faculty of law at Cairo University and president of the Egyptian Conseil d'État. He wrote on a variety of legal topics, including the caliphate; he published a treatise on the latter in French in 1926, providing a program for reestablishing it and at the same time converting it into a modern organization along lines of the contemporary League of Nations. He published studies in 1936 and 1938 on the codification of civil law and proposed that the successful revival of the Islamic legal heritage would require that it be restudied in the light of principles of modern comparative law. Civil codes devised by Sanhūrī were adopted by Egypt in 1949 and subsequently by most Arab countries. They synthesized Islamic doctrines within a matrix of codified laws inspired by a variety of models, including European law and existing Arab and Turkish codes, and actual court jurisprudence. They permitted reference to Islamic law and custom in default of applicable code provisions. With the adoption of this code, Egypt was able to enact a law abandoning its separate system of mixed courts, which beginning in 1874 had assumed jurisdiction over civil and commercial cases between Egyptians and foreigners, between foreigners of different nationalities, or where a foreign interest was involved. [*See the biography of Sanhūrī.*]

Egypt's national courts, organized in 1884, functioned alongside the mixed courts. Personal-status matters remained relegated to *sharīʿah* courts. The government undertook the regulation of the organization of the *sharīʿah* courts and the qualifications of their judges, setting up a new school for their training in 1907. Meanwhile, various *millah* courts survived, serving the different non-Muslim religious communities as the forums for resolving their personal-status disputes; these were outside state regulation. Only in 1955 did Egypt unify its court system, placing all cases under the jurisdiction of the national courts. However, in personal-status cases, the applicable law remained indicated by the parties' religious affiliations.

Personal-Status Reforms. In the twentieth century reform efforts focused on personal-status matters, which remained governed by Islamic law. Most governments enacted codified versions of Islamic family law, some of which dramatically deviated from the doctrines of the established schools of law. To minimize objections from conservatives, reforms were often taken indirectly via procedural expedients. For example, new laws commonly imposed requirements that in order to be legally valid marriages had to be registered, and that the spouses had to be of certain minimum ages, thereby deterring child marriages and forced marriages. To discourage polygamy and the husband's use of discretionary divorce, governments required that marriages and divorces comply with certain bureaucratic formalities and conditions.

The most radical reforms of Islamic family law were taken by Tunisia in 1956, which abolished polygamy and gave men and women equal rights in divorce. This law, in theory based on Islamic principles, was applicable to all citizens of Tunisia. In 1958 adoption was legalized. In recognition of the financial hardships often faced by divorced women under Islamic law, an amendment was enacted in 1981 providing that a divorced wife could be given either a payment or an allowance to maintain her in the same standard she had enjoyed when married.

The Iranian Family Protection Act of 1967 was almost as far-reaching as its Tunisian counterpart. It placed strict conditions on polygamy, requiring that a husband persuade a court that he was able financially and otherwise to treat more than one wife justly. The husband and the wife were accorded the same ability to obtain a divorce from a court, which first had to seek to reconcile the two. Part of the law's text was deemed to be inserted in all marriage contracts, with the result that the husband's right of divorce would be in all cases delegated to the wife. Courts were also assigned a central role in deciding matters of child custody and post-divorce maintenance. The Islamic Revolution of 1979 heralded a reversal in the previous policy of enhancing women's rights; it was followed by laws imposing disabilities on women in the name of adhering to Islamic principles.

In Egypt, a reforming personal-status law was promulgated by decree by President Anwar Sadat in 1979. Among other things, it eliminated a husband's right to compel his disobedient wife to return to the marital home, required that a husband would have to register a *ṭalāq* divorce and inform the wife he was divorcing her, provided that a husband's taking of a second wife constituted grounds for divorce as of right by the first wife, and enhanced the wife's rights in matters of maintenance, child custody, and post-divorce division of property. Even such modest reforms provoked a strong counterreaction on the part of conservatives, and in 1985 Egypt's High Constitutional Court ruled that the manner of its promulgation had been unconstitutional, to the great disappointment of Egypt's growing feminist movement. After the nullification of the 1979 law, in an attempt to placate both sides, a compromise law that diluted the 1979 reforms was enacted by the People's Assembly.

The conservative shift in legal trends was evinced by Algeria's decision in 1984, after long debates, to enact a family law that resurrected most institutions of Mālikī law, except for forced marriage. The law relegated women to the status of wards of male marriage guardians, accorded the husband the right to divorce at will while requiring the wife to establish grounds, and reaffirmed the husband's right to have up to four wives.

The aspect of Islamic personal status least susceptible to reform was inheritance law, where one saw only occasional modest reforms—such as measures designed to augment the portion going to the widow and to enable orphaned grandchildren to inherit. The boldest reform measure attempted by an Arab government came in Iraq, the population of which was divided between the Sunnī and Shīʿī sects, where a 1959 law adopted German inheritance law. A 1963 law canceled this change, adopting an original reform scheme, whereby elements of the dissimilar Sunnī and Shīʿī inheritance rules were combined. The order of priorities by class established under Shīʿī law was to be followed in all cases, but the schemes for distributing shares within a class could follow either Sunnī or Shīʿī law. [*See* Family Law; Marriage and Divorce; Polygyny.]

Developments in Asia. In Indonesia, the Malay States, the Philippines, the Straits Settlements, and Singapore, local customary or *adat* law was a powerful force. Muslims disputed whether Islam should be understood in terms of the local culture or whether Middle Eastern versions of Islamic law should be treated as authoritative; similar disputes arose in Bangladesh after it separated from Pakistan. Singapore's Administration of Muslim Law Act of 1966 allowed Malay custom to modify the application of Islamic law. In the colonial era Britain had tended to respect Malay *adat* law. After independence in 1957, the States of Peninsular Malaysia moved in the direction of Islamic legalism via legislation and setting up religious courts and agencies. Councils were established that could issue *fatwās*, following Shāfiʿī doctrine except where it was not in the public interest, in which case they could choose rules from other schools. However, the (secular) High Court remained the ultimate authority in legal disputes. Islamization measures carried out in the 1980s included placing Islamic judges and courts on a par with the civil judiciary, promoting the ideas of Islamic economics, and reinforcing the Malaysian version of Islamic morality with penal sanctions.

Despite the existence of a large Muslim minority, in the Philippines Islamic law had tended to be only erratically applied. In 1977 a Code of Muslim Personal Laws was enacted, which restated general principles of Shāfiʿī law and set up new *sharīʿah* courts to apply it. The code allowed liberal grounds of divorce for the wife, but it retained the Islamic rule that adoption could not confer legitimacy, a rule which went against the local *adat* law.

Notwithstanding their official allegiance to the Shāfiʿī school, Indonesian Muslims tended to follow *adat* law and to be unfamiliar with *fiqh*. In Indonesia under Dutch rule, Islamic law was subordinated to *adat* law and the religious courts accorded an inferior position. The Regulation on Mixed Marriages of 1898 abandoned a fundamental rule of Islamic law by allowing Muslim women to marry non-Muslim men. Generally, however, the Dutch showed little interest in changing Islamic substantive law, being more concerned with regulating the courts and the procedural or bureaucratic aspects of the legal system. After Indonesia achieved independence in 1949, rulings by religious courts generally depended on secular courts for their execution and enforcement; secular courts could review the rulings on procedural, evidentiary, and policy grounds. Subsequent legislation indicated that religious courts had jurisdiction over personal status cases only to the extent that local customary law indicated that they were to be resolved according to the *sharīʿah*. In their approach to cases, Indonesian courts tended more to focus on the practicalities of dispute resolution rather than strictly following Shāfiʿī doctrine. When liberal reforms of Islamic personal-status law were proposed in the early 1970s, they were strongly opposed by conservatives. The family law enactment eventually passed as the Marriage Law of 1974 was stripped of the bolder reforms that had earlier been proposed; these had included the legalization of adoption, allowing free intermarriage between faiths, and requiring that a husband obtain permission from a secular court to marry more than one wife or to obtain a divorce. Because of the gap between Indonesian and Middle Eastern culture, there was advocacy of establishing a separate Indonesian national *madhhab* (legal school). [*See* Adat.]

Islamization Programs. Beginning in the 1970s and continuing into the 1980s, initiatives were launched to reinstate Islamic law in Libya, Iran, Pakistan, and the Sudan, and revivalist groups who had long called for the repeal of Western laws in other countries demanded similar islamization measures. These programs resulted in selective retrieval of elements of *sharīʿah* law that were then integrated in legal systems that remained profoundly influenced by the previous westernizing reforms.

The most important islamization program was undertaken in Iran. There the victory of clerical forces in the 1979 Islamic revolution heralded a halt to the process of liberal reform, and the inauguration of policies of entrenching clerical power over political and legal matters, resulting the dismantling of Iran's westernized judiciary and legal profession. According to article 4 of the constitution, all laws were based on Islamic principles, which were to prevail over not only the laws but even over the constitution. Laws were to be enacted by elected members of the parliament, and their conformity with Islam was to be ensured by having them vetted by six clerical members of the Council of Guardians. Important proposed legislation was blocked by rulings that violations of Islamic principles were involved. In 1989 several constitutional amendments were adopted, including one providing for a new council to try to mediate conflicts between the parliament and the Council of Guardians regarding the compatibility of legislation with Islamic criteria. The rights and freedoms of women and minorities were reduced by new policies and legislation, and Islamic criminal laws were enacted and enforced with zeal. With the adoption of the 1979 constitution, Iran became the first contemporary Muslim country where the structure of government itself was altered to conform to a theory that the state should be headed by an Islamic jurist, following the ideas of Ayatollah Ruhollah Khomeini about *vilāyat-i faqīh* (Ar., *wilāyat al-faqīh*), or government by the jurist. Article 167 of the Iranian Constitution called for courts to make decisions based on codified laws, only in default of which were they to consult Islamic sources or *fatwā*s. [*See* Wilāyat al-Faqīh.]

Pakistan struggled since its founding to resolve the role that Islam should play in its government and constitution. In the 1973 constitution, Article 227 provided that all laws should be brought into conformity with the Qur'ān and *sunnah* and that no law should be enacted that was repugnant to their "injunctions." The Islamic Ideology Council played a major role in the islamization campaign that commenced in 1979 and led to the replacement of many existing laws by rules taken from Sunnī *fiqh*. The most striking changes came with the revival of Islamic criminal law, the enactment of a law converting the *zakāt* (charitable tithe) into a tax payable to the state, laws designed to eliminate interest from many bank deposits and investments, and the replacement of judges with secular training by persons with Islamic legal education. In 1991 an Enforcement of Sharīʿah Act was announced that aimed to make Islamic law the supreme law in the country, overriding both previous laws and the constitution. Because of the turbulence that characterized the political scene in the wake of the death of President Zia ul-Haq (d. 1988), it was unclear to what extent the islamization campaign would be pursued.

In Sudan there was a brief experiment in 1983–1985 with an idiosyncratic islamization campaign conducted by the military dictatorship, a campaign in which the implementation of *ḥudūd* penalties figured prominently. After a brief interlude of democracy, islamization was pursued in a more sustained and systematic way under a new military dictatorship, which seized power in 1989 and was allied with a Sudanese faction of the Ikhwān or National Islamic Front. Distracting the government from its goal of making Sudan into a model Islamic state was the conflict resulting from determined resistance of African Sudanese in the south, mostly animists or Christians, who opposed both islamization and the arabization policy that accompanied it. The civil war that had broken out over islamization in 1983 continued unabated into the 1990s.

In Egypt in the 1970s and 1980s, proposals for measures to islamize laws were put forward that would have, among other things, reinstated Islamic criminal law, banned interest charges, and imposed a strict version of Islamic morality according to which women were to be segregated from men in public transport and university education and excluded from certain professions. Egypt's Coptic community objected to some of the islamization proposals—such as the one that would have made apostasy from Islam a capital offense—and confessional tensions rose in consequence. Although most proposals came to nothing, a law prohibiting alcohol was passed and came into force in 1976—but with exceptions that vitiated its impact. Meanwhile, drafts of various new codified versions of Islamic law were prepared under governmental auspices, but after their presentation to the People's Assembly in 1982, none of the draft codes were ultimately enacted into law. As a concession to the sentiment favoring islamization, the second article in Egypt's constitution was altered in 1980 to make the *sharī^cah* "the principal source" of legislation, rather than "a principal source" as it had been in the previous wording. An attempt in 1985 to obtain a ruling from the High Constitutional Court that a civil code provision calling for interest to be charged when a loan repayment was delayed should be voided as being contrary to the reworded article 2 was rejected, the court ruling that the article had no retroactive effect on existing legislation that was in conflict with the *sharīʿah.* In Egypt the calls for making the state and its laws more Islamic were countered by proponents of the idea that the unity of religion and state under modern conditions was deleterious to both, among them Muḥammad Saʿīd al-ʿAshmāwī and Faraj Fawdah (d. 1992).

Powerful fundamentalist movements, appealing to popular sentiment and favoring the application of the *sharīʿah* and the reinstatement of Islamic law, were vigorously repressed in many countries, where governments with basically secular outlooks saw in them a threat to their hold on power. In Algeria in 1991 a fundamentalist party almost came to power by democratic processes, but it was forestalled from actually taking over the government by military intervention in early 1992.

Recent Trends. Especially from the 1960s onward, the implications of the Islamic sources were developed in areas where Islamic law had not previously been elaborated or where earlier doctrines were deemed inadequate, such as matters of public law. As Muslims produced theories that eluded traditional categories, the barriers formerly dividing the doctrines of schools of law and Shīʿīs and Sunnīs became more permeable. A new literature was produced by Muslims with a variety of educational backgrounds and outlooks, many of whom were oriented more toward ideology than jurisprudence. A major concern was rethinking the application of Islamic precepts to public-law issues such as government, penal law, and macroeconomic principles. In the area of macroeconomics, the traditional prohibition of *ribā* (interest or usury) was reinterpreted as a principle that required the elimination of interest charges. Among those writing on this subject were Sayyid Abū al-Aʿlā Mawdūdī (1903–1979), a Pakistani fundamentalist ideologue, and Muḥammad Bāqir al-Ṣadr (1931–1980), an Iraqi Shīʿī cleric. However, whereas proponents of Islamic economics concurred that Islamic banks needed to be established in which interest would be prohibited, they disagreed sharply on other economic issues, such as whether Islam allowed for a free market or required the adoption of socialist policies, as evinced by the controversies in Iran after the Islamic revolution over issues like land reform and state control of trade. Proponents of islamization advocated establishing "Islamic" states, that is, states constituted according to Islamic criteria, although there was no consensus as to what this model entailed. One of the influential writers on the role of Islam in the state was the Sudanese Ḥasan al-Turābī, a Western-educated law professor who went on to a career as an ideologue of Islamic revival and a leading force in Sudanese politics. In these circumstances, theoretical debates went on about the degree to which Islam was compatible with the post–World War II system of international law and the degree to which an Islamic system could incorporate democratic principles. [*See* Banks and Banking; Interest; *and the biographies of the figures mentioned above.*]

Meanwhile, international organizations like the Organization of the Islamic Conference sponsored initiatives that had the potential to encourage greater uniformity in approaches to Islamic law. For example, the OIC issued a statement of Islamic human rights principles in 1990. [*See* Human Rights.] Controversies were engendered about women's rights in Islam, in which fundamentalists and other supporters of *sharīʿah* rules as they had stood in the past were pitted against increasingly outspoken Muslim feminists. Muslims' growing familiarity with feminist ideas and international human rights principles meant that laws affecting women, including those of Islamic provenance, were increasingly evaluated in terms of their conformity with the modern norm of male-female equality. Fatima Mernissi, a Moroccan, became one of the most vigorous advocates of the proposition that male attitudes rather than authentic Islamic teachings stood in the way of women's equality. [*See* Feminism; *and the biography of Mernissi.*]

Mohammed Arkoun, an Algerian Islamologist teaching in France, produced provocative and original analyses of the state of Islamic thought and proposals for updating methodologies and enhancing interdisciplinary and comparative dimensions of the study of Islam. Although not specifically directed to the problems of legal reform, the implications of Arkoun's work for the science of interpretation of the Islamic sources are potentially great. [*See the biography of Arkoun.*]

BIBLIOGRAPHY

Adams, Charles C. *Islam and Modernism in Egypt: A Study of the Modern Reform Movement Inaugurated by Muhammad ʿAbduh.* London, 1933. Excellent study of ʿAbduh's life and impact on Islamic reform.

Ahmad, Aziz. *Islamic Modernism in India and Pakistan, 1857–1964.* London, 1967. Valuable general study.

Anderson, J. N. D. *Law Reform in the Muslim World.* London, 1976. Concise overview of contemporary legislative reforms.

Arkoun, Mohammed. *Pour une critique de la raison islamique.* Paris, 1984. Collection of essays offering original and critical perspectives on the Islamic heritage, by a distinguished Muslim intellectual.

Borrmans, Maurice. *Statut personnel et famille au Maghreb de 1940 à nos jours.* Paris, 1977. Outstanding in-depth study of law reform affecting personal status in North Africa.

Enayat, Hamid. *Modern Islamic Political Thought.* Austin, 1982. Survey of trends in Sunnī and Shīʿī thought.

Esposito, John L. *Women and Muslim Family Law.* Syracuse, N.Y., 1982.

Ghunaymī, Muḥammad Ṭalʿat al-. *The Muslim Conception of International Law and the Western Approach.* The Hague, 1969. Useful survey comparing Islamic and Western approaches to international law.

Hooker, M. B. *Islamic Law in South-East Asia.* Singapore, 1984. Surveys of recent developments involving Islamic law in the region.

Kerr, Malcolm H. *Islamic Reform: The Political and Legal Theories of Muḥammad ʿAbduh and Rashīd Riḍā.* Berkeley, 1966. Scholarly examination of the ideas of two central figures in Islamic reformist thought.

Kuran, Timur. "The Economic Impact of Islamic Fundamentalism." In *Fundamentalisms and the State: Remaking Polities, Economies, and Militance,* edited by Martin E. Marty and R. Scott Appleby, pp. 302–341. Chicago, 1993. Examination of Islamic economics and review of recent experiments in applying its tenets.

Lewis, Bernard. *The Emergence of Modern Turkey.* 2d ed. London and New York, 1968. Fine history of the late Ottoman period and the early republic, exploring reformist influences and trends.

Mayer, Ann Elizabeth. "The Fundamentalist Impact on Law, Politics, and Constitutions in Iran, Pakistan, and the Sudan." In *Fundamentalisms and the State: Remaking Polities, Economies, and Militance,* edited by Martin E. Marty and R. Scott Appleby, pp. 110–151. Chicago, 1993. Assessment of the legal changes wrought by fundamentalist programs in three countries.

Peters, Rudolph. *Islam and Colonialism: The Doctrine of Jihad in Modern History.* The Hague, 1979. Thoughtful examination of how the doctrine of *jihād* has evolved.

Sanhūrī, ʿAbd al-Razzāq al-. *Le califat, son évolution vers une société des nations orientale.* Paris, 1926. Treatise by an eminent Arab jurist on how the principles of the caliphate can apply in contemporary political circumstances.

Ziadeh, Farhat. *Lawyers, the Rule of Law, and Liberalism in Modern Egypt.* Stanford, Calif., 1968. Excellent historical survey of the development of modern legal institutions and the legal profession in Egypt.

ANN ELIZABETH MAYER

LEBANON. In Lebanon's remarkably diverse society eighteen separate sects or confessional groups are recognized within the political system. In addition to a variety of Christian sects, which account for about 40 percent of the country's population, five Muslim sects are found in the country: Sunnīs, Shīʿīs, Druze, ʿAlawīs, and Ismāʿīlīs. As of 1992 the first four enjoyed political representation in parliament; the Ismāʿīlīs, commonly referred to as "Seveners," number only a few hundred and play no significant role in Lebanese politics. Personal status law, which governs key domains of social life such as marriage, divorce, birth and death, remains the preserve of religious officials.

The individual's political identity in modern Lebanon is largely determined along sectarian lines. Even the 1989 Ṭā'if Accord, which set the framework for ending the civil war that had raged since 1975, preserved the distribution of the major political offices among the major confessional groups. Thus the presidency remained the sole domain of the Maronite Christians, the office of prime minister continued to be a Sunnī Muslim privilege, and the speaker of the parliament was to be Shīʿī Muslim. The relative power of these offices changed somewhat, but the underlying principle of confessional distribution of political office and privilege was sustained. Thus religion continues to be a prime factor in defining Lebanese politics and society. In a very real sense, all Lebanese have a hyphenated identity; while religiosity may decline from one period to another, secularism has been only a weak force in public life.

Sunnī Muslims. In the Arab world, as in the *ummah,* Sunnī Islam accounts for nearly 90 percent of all Muslims, but in Lebanon the Sunnīs represent only about one-fifth of the population. Nonetheless, until the 1980s the Sunnīs were unquestionably the dominant Lebanese Muslim sect. Concentrated for the most part in the coastal cities—Tripoli, Saida, and especially Beirut—the Sunnī Muslims held the privilege of speaking for Islam in Lebanon. Favored over four hundred years of Ottoman rule, Sunnī Muslim leaders were senior partners in the founding of the modern republic. In fact, the unwritten National Pact *(mīthāq al-waṭanī)* of 1943, which defined the terms of confessional power-sharing in the independent state, was an agreement between the leading Sunnī of the day, Riyāḍ al-Ṣulḥ, and his counterpart from the Maronite community, Bishārah al-Khūrī. Al-Sulh and al-Khūrī became Lebanon's first prime minister and president, respectively.

Unlike the Christian and Muslim sects that sought refuge in the hinterlands and mountains of Lebanon, the Sunnī Muslims were at home in the Arab world. In 1920 France, enjoying a League of Nations mandate over Lebanon, created Greater Lebanon (Le Grand Liban) in order to establish a viable state under Maronite domination. The Sunnīs mounted resistance to the decision, preferring to be part of a greater Syria. The creation of Lebanon in 1943 was a compromise between the Sunnīs' preference for the independent state's Arab identity and the Maronites' preference for sustaining links with the West and France in particular.

Sunnī prominence was reflected not only in the allocation of the position of prime minister but also with respect to religious leadership. As part of its Ottoman heritage, the *muftī* of the republic is a state employee, and the office is naturally filled by a senior Sunnī cleric, usually one trained at al-Azhar, the venerable Islamic university in Cairo. "Azhar Lubnān," as the *sharīʿah* college in Beirut is known popularly, is of much lower status, and its graduates seldom enjoy great upward mobility. The Lebanese Sunnīs generally follow the Shāfiʿī school of law *(madhhab),* although some Sunnīs in the north follow the Mālikī school.

The *muftī* of the republic is nominally the senior authority in interpreting Islamic law, but he effectively shares his authority. Lebanon is divided into provinces (the North, Mount Lebanon, Beirut, the South and Nabaṭīyah, and the Biqāʿ [Bekaa]), and in each province there is a *sharīʿah* court headed by a *muftī*. In Beirut the *muftī* of the republic heads the provincial court, but the other provincial courts exercise a fair amount of autonomy. The Supreme Islamic Council, which until 1969 nominally represented all Lebanese Muslims, is chaired by the *muftī* of the republic and is charged with representing Muslim interests in the nation.

There is a system of public schools in Lebanon, but many Lebanese attend private, confessionally organized schools where the quality of education usually surpasses that of the public schools. Among the Sunnīs, the Maqassid Foundation (Jamʿīyat al-Maqāṣid Khayrīyah al-Islāmīyah, established 1878) oversees a number of schools, as well as a hospital in Beirut and a complex of other social-welfare institutions like orphanages. For many years the head of Maqassid was Sa'ib Salām, the prominent Sunnī political boss or *zaʿīm* who served several Lebanese governments.

Although senior Sunnī clerics often enjoy a broad public reputation, few of them have exercised significant political power. In Sunnī Islam, in contrast to the Shīʿī pattern, the cleric is not indispensable to the practice of the faith, and most Sunnī clerics remain dependent on the support of lay benefactors as well as the salaries provided by the state.

During the civil war only a relative handful of Sunnī *ʿulamāʾ* were actively engaged in organizing paramilitary forces. In Tripoli, Shaykh Saʿīd Shaʿbān founded the Islamic Unity Movement (Ḥarakāt al-Tawḥīd al-Islāmīyah). Shaʿbān, known for his militant views, maintained especially close ties with the Islamic Republic of Iran, and among the Sunnī *ʿulamāʾ* he is arguably Iran's closest ally in Lebanon. The Rally of Muslim Clergymen (Tajammuʿ al-ʿUlamāʾ al-Muslimīn) led by Shaykh Māhir Ḥammūd, a Sunnī, and Shaykh Zuhayr Kanj, a Shīʿī, is committed to Muslim unity and argues that Sunnī-Shīʿī differences are merely juridical. Like Tawḥīd, the Rally is closely aligned with the Iranian-supported Party of God (Ḥizbullāh); both emerged in 1982 following the Israeli invasion of Lebanon. Also noteworthy, though led by laypeople, is the older Islamic Group (al-Jamāʿah al-Islāmīyah) that grew out of the Muslim Brotherhood (Ikhwān al-Muslimūn). The brotherhood has enjoyed a notable following among

Lebanon's Sunnīs but has generally maintained a low public profile.

Shīʿī Muslims. In contrast to the urban-dwelling Sunnī Muslims, the Shīʿīs lived for centuries on the periphery of Lebanon. Until the twentieth century they were concentrated in the south and in the northern Bekaa Valley, where most of them lived in deep poverty. Tribal organization prevailed in the Bekaa; in the south, the heartland of Shiism in Lebanon, the Shīʿīs comprised a large peasantry engaged in agricultural labor and subsistence farming in the hills and valleys of Jabal ʿĀmil (the region east of Tyre and Saida and centered on the city of Nabaṭīyah). The region is an important historic center for Shīʿī scholarship and remains the heartland of Shiism in Lebanon.

In the census of 1932, the last official census conducted in Lebanon, the Shīʿīs were counted as the third-largest group in Lebanon and accordingly were allocated the position of speaker of the national assembly or parliament in the National Pact of 1943. Despite their numbers, the Shīʿīs as a whole were decidedly subordinate to the Sunnīs, who enjoyed generally higher social and economic status, reflecting their superior access to public services—including education, health, and sanitation—as well as centuries of preferential treatment under Ottoman rule. Only in the twentieth century did a significant number of Shīʿī Muslims begin migrating from the hinterland to Beirut and to overseas locales—particularly West Africa, where an emerging Shīʿī bourgeoisie won a financial foothold in the middle class.

The Shīʿī counterpart to the Sunnīs' Maqassid Foundation is the ʿĀmilīyah Foundation (Jamʿīyat al-Khayrīyah al-Islāmīyah), created in 1923. It finances a range of welfare activities and religious events, especially ecumenical commemorations of the martyrdom of Imam Ḥusayn, whose death in Karbala in 680 CE is the marking event in Shīʿī history. The foundation's most far-reaching program has been to support a number of schools, especially in village settings where only Qur'ānic schools *(kuttāb)* existed previously, as well as an important high school in Beirut.

While the Shīʿī middle class grew in size and ambition, the population share of the Shīʿīs swelled as well. Over time, and certainly by the early 1980s, they comprised the largest single confessional group in Lebanon. Thus the underlying demographic logic for the dominance of the Sunnī Muslims, not to mention the Maronites, came to be challenged.

As the forces of modernity were propelling the Shīʿīs into a potentially dominant political position in Lebanon, the Shīʿī clergy was not left behind. The Shīʿī *ʿulamā',* in contrast to their Sunnī counterparts, are integral to the practice of the faith. The Lebanese Shīʿīs, except for the small community of Ismāʿīlīs, are commonly referred to as Twelvers or Ithnā ʿAsharī, a reference to the central role in their dogma of the Hidden Imam. In his absence the authoritative interpretation of religious law devolves to the Shīʿī clergy, the *mujtahid*s (those qualified to interpret the *sharīʿah*). The believer, doctrinally incapable of autonomously interpreting the faith, must follow a qualified cleric in the Jaʿfarī school of Islamic law. The senior religious judge is the Jaʿfarī Muftī al-Mumtāz, presently ʿAbd al-Amīr Qablān. Shaykh Qablān emerged as an assertive but moderate voice for Shīʿī rights, especially in the 1980s and 1990s.

In the latter half of the twentieth century Najaf in Iraq became the locus for the reformulation of Shiism as an ideology of political activism and protest. Among the Lebanese leaders who were trained there are Mūsā al-Ṣadr, founder of the leading Shīʿī populist movement in Lebanon; Muḥammad Mahdī Shams al-Dīn, who heads the Supreme Shīʿī Council; and Muḥammad Ḥusayn Faḍlallāh, the militant ideologue who has given definition to the Party of God or Ḥizbullāh.

In 1967 the Lebanese parliament voted to create a Supreme Shīʿī Council (al-Majlis al-Shīʿī al-Aʿlā). The council began activity in 1969 under the presidency of Mūsā al-Ṣadr. Its founding marked the autonomy of the Shīʿī community in Lebanon, no longer subsumed by the Islamic Council and the *muftī* of the republic. In 1974 al-Ṣadr created the Movement of the Deprived (Ḥarakat al-Maḥrūmīn), a dynamic force in Lebanese politics and the forerunner of Amal, the populist Shīʿī movement.

Druze. The Druze people, offshoots of Ismāʿīlī Shiism, trace the beginnings of their sect to Fāṭimid Egypt. After the mysterious eleventh-century disappearance of al-Ḥākim, the Fāṭimid ruler whom the Druze believe to be divine, they found refuge in what is today Israel, Syria, and Lebanon. The largest single concentration is in Lebanon, where approximately 200,000 Druze comprise about 7 percent of the population. They have long been associated with the history and governance of Mount Lebanon, and there are important concentrations of Druze in southern Lebanon, particularly in Rashaiya and Hasbaiya (site of the al-Baiyada monastic retreat).

Druze practitioners are dividers into two categories—the *juhhāl* (the ignorant) and the *ʿuqqāl* (the mature or wise). Upon reaching middle age a Druze of either gender may opt to join the *ʿuqqāl* and thereby be admitted to the study of the *Messages of Wisdom,* through which the *tawḥīd* (highest fulfillment of religious knowledge) is disclosed. The Druze do not proselytize, and membership is restricted to those born into the faith. Thus, even in a region in which endogamy is the rule, the Druze have been unusually successful in sustaining their communal identity.

Traditionally the Druze have been split between two factions, the Jumblatt (Junblāṭ) and the Yazbak, although they have exhibited remarkable unity in times of tribulation. In fact, the Druze are unique in having sustained their solidarity throughout the fifteen years of civil war that wracked Lebanon from 1975 to 1990.

The highest legal authority among the Druze is the Mashyākat al-ʿAql. In the 1950s and 1960s two men shared this position, one representing the Jumblattis and the other the Yazbakis. The Shaykh al-ʿAql heads a High Council that brings together distinguished men of religion with secular notables. The High Council is the counterpart to the Sunnī Islamic Council and the Shīʿī Supreme Council, and like those institutions it supervises the dispensation of justice and charity, the overseeing of religious trusts, and the operation of schools.

The Mashyākat al-ʿAql plays an important role in linking the Druze community to the state, but the moral consensus of the Druze is sustained by the *ajāwīd,* the religious specialists, who number about 1,500 or almost one per one hundred people. Each Druze village maintains a *majlis* that meets weekly on Thursday evenings. The *majlis* combines elements of a prayer meeting and a town meeting and is the forum where local issues are discussed. Major issues that confront the Druze as a whole are dealt with at a *khilwa,* a meeting of *ajāwīd*s. The Druze distinguish between shaykhs of religion *(shuyukh al-dīn)* and shaykhs of the highway *(shuyūkh al-ṭarīq)* who wield coercive power; when the community is at risk, the shaykhs of religion predominate. Thus Druze *ajāwīd*s have not played any significant role in organizing political or paramilitary organizations.

ʿAlawīs. The ruling minority in Syria, the ʿAlawīs are numerically insignificant in Lebanon, where by the late 1980s they numbered about twenty thousand. However, with the growing influence of Syria on Lebanon, particularly after the Gulf War of 1990–1991, the ʿAlawīs have risen in importance. In the 1992 parliamentary elections the ʿAlawī community was allocated two seats out of 128 (the parliamentary seats are now divided evenly between Muslims and Christians), marking the first time they enjoyed formal political representation in Lebanon.

The ʿAlawīs revere ʿAlī as the last manifestation of divinity, and for this reason—coupled with their observance of a number of Christian and Persian holidays and their use of sacramental wine in religious ceremonies—they are viewed as apostates by some Muslims. It is noteworthy, though, that the respected Shīʿī leader Mūsā al-Ṣadr recognized the ʿAlawīs as a Shīʿī sect, thereby enhancing their legitimacy.

Like the Druze, the ʿAlawīs divide society into two broad sectors, one centered on religion and the other on power and coercion. Thus they distinguish between emirs and imams—men of power and men of religion. Men of power who evince religious purity may, however, combine the two roles. Hafez al-Assad, the Syrian president and himself an ʿAlawī, approximates this coalescence of roles, and he is the dominant political figure for the Lebanese ʿAlawī community, which has benefited from his protection and leadership.

Conclusion. Islam in Lebanon is not an easy subject for generalization. If there is a theme that crosscuts the major Islamic sects, it is the rejection of secularization *(ʿilmānīyah)* in favor of preserving the sacred character of public life. Yet Lebanon's confessional political system is widely condemned for its corruption, inequity, and instability. The challenge for Muslims in Lebanon is to preserve their identity as believers while improving a political system that is still badly in need of reform. Moreover, there is no denying the internal tensions that the rise of an assertive Shīʿī community has provoked in Sunnī quarters, and even more among the Druze.

Radical Islamic voices from both the Shīʿī and Sunnī communities have called for the replacement of the present regime with a government informed by the *sharīʿah,* but some of the more thoughtful thinkers in these groups have long recognized that Lebanon's diversity, including its large Christian minority, makes this infeasible. Moreover, there is no consensus even among Muslim activists about the form of an Islamist government in Lebanon. A striking feature of the 1990s is the inchoate willingness of many of these groups to change the system from within. Thus Ḥizbullāh, notorious for its role in terrorist acts like the kidnapping of innocent foreigners, participated quite successfully in the 1992 elections. Although Lebanon is not a precise microcosm of the Arab world or the Middle East, it is still a fascinating experiment in managing cultural and religious diversity. The pragmatic adaptation that many Lebanese Muslims now demonstrate might well be an instructive example for other societies.

[*See also* ʿAlawīyah; Amal; Druze; Ḥarakāt al-Tawḥīd al-Islāmī; Ḥizbullāh, *article on* Ḥizbullāh in Lebanon; Zaʿīm; *and the biographies of Fadlāllah and Sadr.*]

BIBLIOGRAPHY

Bar, Luc-Henri de. *Les communautés confessionnelles du Liban*. Paris, 1983. Indispensable guide to all of Lebanon's significant confessions.

Cobban, Helena. *The Making of Modern Lebanon*. London, 1985. Good introduction.

Collelo, Thomas, ed. *Lebanon: A Country Study*. 3d ed. Washington, D.C., 1989. Useful primer.

Collings, Deidre, ed. *Peace for Lebanon? From War to Reconstruction*. Boulder, 1994. Important collection of articles by leading scholars and participants in Lebanese politics.

Deeb, Marius K. *Militant Islamic Movements in Lebanon: Origins, Social Basis, and Ideology*. Washington, D.C., November 1986. Handy overview of some of the Sunnī and Shīʿī organizations that emerged in Lebanon over the course of the early 1980s.

Khalaf, Samir. *Lebanon's Predicament*. New York, 1987. Fine collection of studies analyzing the creation of social organizations in Lebanon, among other themes.

Khuri, Fuad I. *Imams and Emirs: State, Religion, and Sects in Islam*. London, 1990. Thoughtful examination of the doctrines and social organization of a number of Middle Eastern Muslim and Christian sects, by a Lebanese social anthropologist.

Makarem, Sami N. *The Druze Faith*. Delmar, N.Y., 1974. One of the few reliable treatments available in English.

Mallat, Chibli. *Shiʿi Thought from the South of Lebanon*. Oxford, 1988. Incisive introduction to Shīʿī political thought.

Norton, Augustus Richard. *Amal and the Shiʿa: A Struggle for the Soul of Lebanon*. Austin, 1987. Close look at the emergence of the Shīʿī Muslims in Lebanese politics.

Saadeh, Safia Antoun. *The Social Structure of Lebanon: Democracy or Servitude?* Beirut, 1993. Provocative exploration of Lebanese politics in the post–civil war period.

Smock, David R., and Audrey C. Smock. *The Politics of Pluralism: A Comparative Study of Lebanon and Ghana*. New York, 1975. Dated but still useful analysis of how Lebanese politics "work."

AUGUSTUS RICHARD NORTON